Concepts of Physics

②

CONCEPTS OF PHYSICS

[VOLUME 2]

H C VERMA, PhD
Retired Professor
Department of Physics
IIT, Kanpur

Bharati Bhawan
PUBLISHERS & DISTRIBUTORS

Published by
BHARATI BHAWAN (Publishers & Distributors)
www.bharatibhawan.in email: editorial@bbpd.in

4271/3 Ansari Road, Daryaganj, NEW DELHI 110 002, Phone: 23286557
A-61 B/2 Sector 63, NOIDA 201 307, Phone: 4757400
Thakurbari Road, PATNA 800 003, Phone: 2670325
10 Raja Subodh Mallick Square, KOLKATA 700 013, Phone: 22250651
No. 98 Sirsi Circle, Mysore Road, BENGALURU 560 018, Phone: 26740560

First edition 1993
Revised print 2017
Second reprint of 2020

Concepts of Physics 2
Printed at Manipal Technologies Limited, Manipal

Dedicated to
Indian Philosophy & Way of Life
of which
my parents were
an integral part

FOREWORD

A few years ago I had an occasion to go through the book *Calculus* by L V Terasov. It unravels intricacies of the subject through a dialogue between Teacher and Student. I thoroughly enjoyed reading it. For me this seemed to be one of the few books which teach a difficult subject through inquisition, and using programmed concept for learning. After that book, Dr Harish Chandra Verma's book on physics, *CONCEPTS OF PHYSICS* is another such attempt, even though it is not directly in the dialogue form. I have thoroughly appreciated it. It is clear that Dr Verma has spent considerable time in formulating the structure of the book, besides its contents. I think he has been successful in this attempt. Dr Verma's book has been divided into two parts because of the size of the total manuscript. There have been several books on this subject, each one having its own flavour. However, the present book is a totally different attempt to teach physics, and I am sure it will be extremely useful to the undergraduate students. The exposition of each concept is extremely lucid. In carefully formatted chapters, besides problems and short questions, a number of objective questions have also been included. This book can certainly be extremely useful not only as a textbook, but also for preparation of various competitive examinations.

Those who have followed Dr Verma's scientific work always enjoyed the outstanding contributions he has made in various research areas. He was an outstanding student of Physics Department of IIT Kanpur during his academic career. An extremely methodical, sincere person as a student, he has devoted himself to the task of educating young minds and inculcating scientific temper amongst them. The present venture in the form of these two volumes is another attempt in that direction. I am sure that young minds who would like to *learn physics in an appropriate manner* will find these volumes extremely useful.

I must heartily congratulate Dr Harish Chandra Verma for the magnificent job he has done.

Y R Waghmare
Professor of Physics
IIT Kanpur.

PREFACE

Why a new book ?

Excellent books exist on physics at an introductory college level so why a new one ? Why so many books exist at the same level, in the first place, and why each of them is highly appreciated ? It is because each of these books has the privilege of having an author or authors who have *experienced* physics and have their own method of communicating with the students. During my years as a physics teacher, I have developed a somewhat different methodology of presenting physics to the students. *Concepts of Physics* is a translation of this methodology into a textbook.

Prerequisites

The book presents a calculus-based physics course which makes free use of algebra, trigonometry and co-ordinate geometry. The level of the latter three topics is quite simple and high school mathematics is sufficient. Calculus is generally done at the introductory college level and I have assumed that the student is enrolled in a concurrent first calculus course. The relevant portions of calculus have been discussed in Chapter 2 so that the student may start using it from the beginning.

Almost no knowledge of physics is a prerequisite. I have attempted to start each topic from the zero level. A receptive mind is all that is needed to use this book.

Basic philosophy of the book

The motto underlying the book is *physics is enjoyable.*

Being a description of the nature around us, physics is our best friend from the day of our existence. I have extensively used this aspect of physics to introduce the physical principles starting with common day occurrences and examples. The subject then appears to be friendly and enjoyable. I have taken care that numerical values of different quantities used in problems correspond to real situations to further strengthen this approach.

Teaching and training

The basic aim of physics teaching has been to let the student know and understand the principles and equations of physics and their applications in real life.

However, to be able to use these principles and equations correctly in a given physical situation, one needs further training. A large number of *questions and solved and unsolved problems* are given for this purpose. Each question or problem has a specific purpose. It may be there to bring out a subtle point which might have passed unnoticed while doing the text portion. It may be a further elaboration of a concept developed in the text. It may be there to make the student react when several concepts introduced in different chapters combine and show up as a physical situation and so on. Such tools have been used to develop a culture: *analyse the situation, make a strategy to invoke correct principles and work it out.*

Conventions

I have tried to use symbols, names, etc., which are popular nowadays. SI units have been consistently used throughout the book. SI prefixes such as *micro, milli, mega,* etc., are used whenever they make the presentation more readable. Thus, 20 μF is preferred over 20×10^{-6} F. Co-ordinate sign convention is used in geometrical optics. Special emphasis has been given to dimensions of physical quantities. Numerical values of physical quantities have been mentioned with the units even in equations to maintain dimensional consistency.

I have tried my best to keep errors out of this book. I shall be grateful to the readers who point out any errors and/or make other constructive suggestions.

H C Verma

ACKNOWLEDGEMENTS

The work on this book started in 1984. Since then, a large number of teachers, students and physics lovers have made valuable suggestions which I have incorporated in this work. It is not possible for me to acknowledge all of them individually. I take this opportunity to express my gratitude to them. However, to Dr S B Mathur, who took great pains in going through the entire manuscript and made valuable comments, I am specially indebted. I am also beholden to my colleagues Dr A Yadav, Dr Deb Mukherjee, Mr M M R Akhtar, Dr Arjun Prasad, Dr S K Sinha and others who gave me valuable advice and were good enough to find time for fruitful discussions. To Dr T K Dutta of B E College, Sibpur I am grateful for having taken time to go through portions of the book and making valuable comments.

I thank my student Mr Shailendra Kumar who helped me in checking the answers. I am grateful to Dr B C Rai, Mr Sunil Khijwania & Mr Tejaswi Khijwania for helping me in the preparation of rough sketches for the book.

Finally, I thank the members of my family for their support and encouragement.

H C Verma

TO THE STUDENTS

Here is a brief discussion on the organisation of the book which will help you in using the book most effectively. The book contains 47 chapters divided in two volumes. Though I strongly believe in the underlying unity of physics, a broad division may be made in the book as follows:

Chapters 1–14: Mechanics
15–17: Waves including wave optics
18–22: Optics
23–28: Heat and thermodynamics
29–40: Electric and magnetic phenomena
41–47: Modern physics

Each chapter contains a description of the physical principles related to that chapter. It is well supported by mathematical derivations of equations, descriptions of laboratory experiments, historical background, etc. There are "in-text" solved examples. These examples explain the equation just derived or the concept just discussed. These will help you in fixing the ideas firmly in your mind. Your teachers may use these in-text examples in the classroom to encourage students to participate in discussions.

After the theory section, there is a section on *Worked Out Examples.* These numerical examples correspond to various thinking levels and often use several concepts introduced in that chapter or even in previous chapters. You should read the statement of a problem and try to solve it yourself. In case of difficulty, look at the solution given in the book. Even if you solve the problem successfully, you should look into the solution to compare it with your method of solution. You might have thought of a better method, but knowing more than one method is always beneficial.

Then comes the part which tests your understanding as well as develops it further. *Questions for Short Answer* generally touch very minute points of your understanding. It is not necessary that you answer these questions in a single sitting. They have great potential to initiate very fruitful dicussions. So, freely discuss these questions with your friends and see if they agree with your answer. Answers to these questions are not given for the simple reason that the answers could have cut down the span of such discussions and that would have sharply reduced the utility of these questions.

There are two sections on multiple-choice questions, namely OBJECTIVE I and OBJECTIVE II. There are four options following each of these questions. Only one option is correct for OBJECTIVE I questions. Any number of options, zero to four, may be correct for OBJECTIVE II questions. Answers to all these questions are provided.

Finally, a set of numerical problems are given for your practice. Answers to these problems are also provided. The problems are generally arranged according to the sequence of the concepts developed in the chapter but they are not grouped under section-headings. I don't want to bias your ideas beforehand by telling you that this problem belongs to that section and hence use that particular equation. You should yourself look into the problem and decide which equations or which methods should be used to solve it. Many of the problems use several concepts developed in different sections of the chapter. Many of them even use the concepts from the previous chapters. Hence, you have to plan out the strategy after understanding the problem.

Remember, no problem is difficult. Once you understand the theory, each problem will become easy. So, don't jump to exercise problems before you have gone through the theory, the worked-out problems and the objectives. Once you feel confident in theory, do the exercise problems. The exercise problems are so arranged that they gradually require more thinking.

I hope you will enjoy *Concepts of Physics.*

H C Verma

Table of Contents

□

CHAPTER 23

HEAT AND TEMPERATURE

23.1 HOT AND COLD BODIES

When we rub our hands for some time, they become warm. When a block slides on a rough surface, it becomes warm. Press against a rapidly spinning wheel. The wheel slows down and becomes warm. While going on a bicycle, touch the road with your shoe. The bicycle slows down and the shoe becomes warm. When two vehicles collide with each other during an accident, they become very hot. When an aeroplane crashes, it becomes so hot that it catches fire.

In each of these examples, mechanical energy is lost and the bodies in question become hot. Where does the mechanical energy vanish? It goes into the internal energy of the bodies. We conclude that the cold bodies absorb energy to become hot. In other words, a hot body has more internal energy than an otherwise identical cold body.

When a hot body is kept in contact with a cold body, the cold body warms up and the hot body cools down. The internal energy of the hot body decreases and the internal energy of the cold body increases. Thus, energy is transferred from the hot body to the cold body when they are placed in contact. Notice that no mechanical work is done during this transfer of energy (neglect any change in volume of the body). This is because there are no displacements involved. This is different from the case when we lift a ball vertically and the energy of the ball–earth system increases or when a compressed spring relaxes and a block attached to its end speeds up. In the case of lifting the ball, we do some work on the ball and the energy is increased by that amount. In the case of spring–block example, the spring does some work and the kinetic energy of the block increases.

The transfer of energy from a hot body to a cold body is a nonmechanical process. The energy that is transferred from one body to the other, without any mechanical work involved, is called *heat.*

23.2 ZEROTH LAW OF THERMODYNAMICS

Two bodies are said to be in *thermal equilibrium* if no transfer of heat takes place when they are placed in contact. We can now state the Zeroth law of thermodynamics as follows:

If two bodies A and B are in thermal equilibrium and A and C are also in thermal equilibrium then B and C are also in thermal equilibrium.

It is a matter of observation and experience that is described in the Zeroth law. It should not be taken as obvious. For example, if two persons A and B know each other and A and C know each other, it is not necessary that B and C know each other.

The Zeroth law allows us to introduce the concept of temperature to measure the hotness or coldness of a body. All bodies in thermal equilibrium are assigned equal temperature. A hotter body is assigned higher temperature than a colder body. Thus, the temperatures of two bodies decide the direction of heat-flow when the two bodies are put in contact. Heat flows from the body at higher temperature to the body at lower temperature.

23.3 DEFINING SCALE OF TEMPERATURE: MERCURY AND RESISTANCE THERMOMETERS

We are now in a position to say whether two given bodies are at the same temperature or not. If they are not at the same temperature, we also know which is at higher temperature and which is at lower temperature. Our next task is to define a scale of temperature so that we can give numerical value to the temperature of a body. To do this, we can choose a substance and look for a measurable property of the substance which monotonically changes with temperature. The temperature can then be defined as a chosen function of this property. As an example, take a mass of mercury in a glass bulb terminating in a long capillary. The length of the mercury column in the capillary changes with temperature. Each length corresponds to a particular temperature of the mercury. How can we assign a numerical value corresponding to an observed length of the mercury column ?

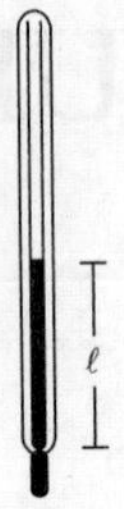

Figure 23.1

The earlier method was to choose two fixed points of temperature which can be easily reproduced in laboratory. The temperature of melting ice at 1 atm (called ice point) and the temperature of boiling water at 1 atm (called steam point) are often chosen as the fixed points. We arbitrarily assign a temperature t_1 to the ice point and t_2 to the steam point. Suppose the length of the mercury column is l_1 when the bulb is kept in melting ice and it is l_2 when the bulb is kept in boiling water. Thus, a length l_1 of mercury column means that the temperature of the bulb is t_1 and a length l_2 of the column means that the temperature is t_2. The temperature corresponding to any length l may be defined by assuming a linear relation between l and t,

$$t = al + b. \qquad \dots (23.1)$$

A change of one degree in temperature will mean a change of $\frac{l_2 - l_1}{t_2 - t_1}$ in the length of mercury column. Thus, we can graduate the length of the capillary directly in degrees.

The centigrade system assumes ice point at 0°C and the steam point at 100°C. If the length of the mercury column between its values for 0°C and 100°C is divided equally in 100 parts, each part will correspond to a change of 1°C.

Let l_0 and l_{100} denote the lengths of the mercury column at 0°C and 100°C respectively. From equation (23.1),

$$0 = al_0 + b$$

$$\text{and } 100 = al_{100} + b$$

$$\text{giving } b = -\,al_0$$

$$\text{and } a = \frac{100}{l_{100} - l_0}\cdot$$

Putting in equation (23.1), the temperature corresponding to a length l is given by

$$t = \frac{l - l_0}{l_{100} - l_0} \times 100 \text{ degree.} \qquad \dots (23.2)$$

To measure the temperature of a body, the bulb containing mercury is kept in contact with the body and sufficient time is allowed so that the mercury comes to thermal equilibrium with the body. The temperature of the body is then the same as that of the mercury. The length of the column then gives the temperature according to equation (23.2).

Another popular system known as Fahrenheit system assumes 32°F for the ice point and 212°F for the steam point. A change of 1°F means $\frac{1}{180}$ of the interval between the steam point and the ice point. The average temperature of a normal human body is around 98°F. The conversion formula from centigrade to Fahrenheit scale is

$$F = 32 + \frac{9}{5}C.$$

The expansion of mercury is just one thermometric property that can be used to define a temperature scale and prepare thermometers. There may be many others. Electric resistance of a metal wire increases monotonically with temperature and may be used to define a temperature scale. If R_0 and R_{100} denote the resistances of a metal wire at ice point and steam point respectively, we can define temperature t corresponding to the resistance R_t as

$$t = \frac{R_t - R_0}{R_{100} - R_0} \times 100 \text{ degree.} \qquad \dots (23.3)$$

The temperatures of the ice point and the steam point are chosen to be 0°C and 100°C as in centigrade scale. A platinum wire is often used to construct a thermometer based on this scale. Such a thermometer is called platinum resistance thermometer and the temperature scale is called the *platinum scale.*

Platinum Resistance Thermometer

The platinum resistance thermometer works on the principle of *Wheatstone bridge* used to measure a resistance. In a Wheatstone bridge, four resistances P, Q, R and X are joined in a loop as shown in figure (23.2a). A galvanometer and a battery are also joined as shown. If

$$\frac{P}{Q} = \frac{R}{X},$$

there is no deflection in the galvanometer and the bridge is called balanced. If the condition is not fulfilled, there is a deflection.

Figure (23.2b) represents the arrangement for a platinum resistance thermometer. A thin platinum wire is coiled on a mica base and placed in a glass tube. Two connecting wires YY going through the

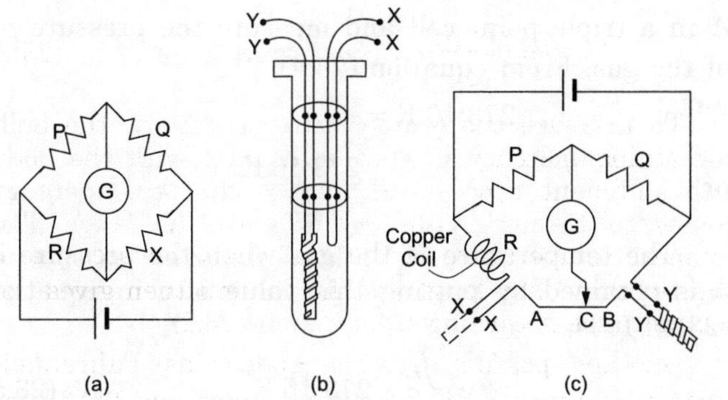

Figure 23.2

ebonite lid of the tube are connected to the platinum coil. A similar copper wire XX, called compensating wire, also goes into the tube as shown in the figure. A Wheatstone bridge is arranged as shown in figure (23.2c). Two equal resistances P and Q are connected in two arms of the bridge. A copper coil having resistance roughly equal to that of the platinum coil is connected in the third arm through the compensating wire XX. The platinum coil is inserted in the fourth arm of the bridge by connecting the points Y,Y in that arm. The end C of the wire connected to the galvanometer can slide on a uniform wire AB of length l. The end A of this wire is connected to the wire XX and the end B is connected to the wire YY. Thus, the copper coil, the compensating wire and the wire AC are in the third arm and the platinum coil, the connecting wire YY and the wire CB are in the fourth arm of the bridge. The test tube containing the platinum coil is immersed in the bath of which we want to measure the temperature. The end C is slid on AB till the deflection in the galvanometer becomes zero. Let $AC = x$.

Suppose the resistance of the copper coil connected in the third arm is R, that of the compensating wire is R_c and that of the wire AB is r. The resistance of the connecting wire YY is the same as R_c and that of the platinum coil is R_t. The resistance of the wire $AC = \frac{r}{l}x$ and that of the wire $CB = \frac{r}{l}(l-x)$. The net resistance in the third arm is $R + R_c + \frac{r}{l}x$ and that in the fourth arm is $R_t + R_c + \frac{r}{l}(l-x)$. For no deflection in the galvanometer,

$$\frac{P}{Q} = \frac{R + R_c + \frac{r}{l}x}{R_t + R_c + \frac{r}{l}(l-x)}.$$

As $P = Q$, we get

$$R_t + \frac{r}{l}(l-x) = R + \frac{r}{l}x$$

or, $$R_t = (R-r) + \frac{2r}{l}x.$$

If x_0, x_{100} and x_t are the values of x at the ice point, steam point and the temperature t respectively,

$$R_{100} = (R-r) + \frac{2r}{l}x_{100}$$

$$R_0 = (R-r) + \frac{2r}{l}x_0$$

and $$R_t = (R-r) + \frac{2r}{l}x_t.$$

This gives

$$t = \frac{R_t - R_0}{R_{100} - R_0} \times 100 = \frac{x_t - x_0}{x_{100} - x_0} \times 100.$$

Absolute Scale and Ideal Gas Scale

Equation (23.3) tells us that the change in resistance ΔR when the temperature increases by one degree ($\Delta t = 1°$) is

$$\Delta R = \frac{R_{100} - R_0}{100}$$

and is the same for all temperatures. This means that the resistance increases uniformly as the temperature increases. Note that this conclusion follows from the particular definition (23.3) of temperature and is not the property of platinum or the other metal used to form the resistance. Similarly, it follows that the expansion of mercury is uniform on the mercury scale defined by (23.2). If we measure the change in resistance of a platinum wire against the temperature measured on mercury scale, we shall find that the resistance varies slowly at lower temperatures and slightly more rapidly at higher temperatures. Similarly, if the expansion of mercury is measured against the temperature defined on platinum scale (23.3), we shall find that mercury does not expand at uniform rate as the temperature varies.

Thus, the two scales of temperature do not agree with each other. They are forced to agree at ice point and steam point but for other physical states the readings of the two thermometers will be different. In general, the scale depends on the properties of the thermometric substance used to define the scale.

It is possible to define an absolute scale of temperature which does not depend on the thermometric substance and its properties. We now define the ideal gas temperature scale which happens to be identical to the absolute temperature scale.

23.4 CONSTANT VOLUME GAS THERMOMETER

A gas enclosed in a container has a definite volume and a definite pressure in any given state. If the volume is kept constant, the pressure of a gas increases monotonically with increasing temperature. This property of a gas may be used to construct a thermometer. Figure (23.3) shows a schematic diagram of a constant volume gas thermometer.

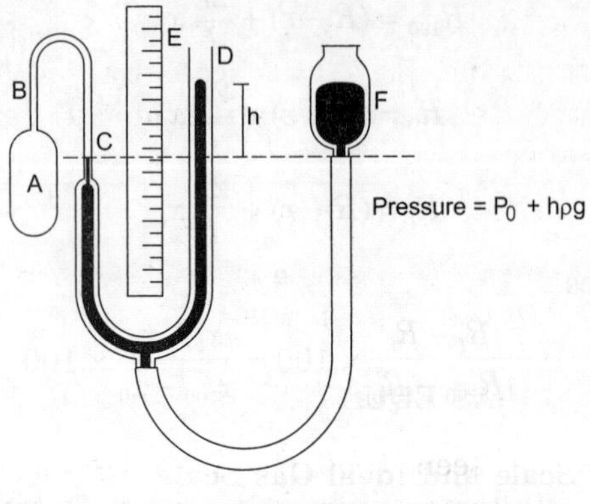

Figure 23.3

A mass of gas is enclosed in a bulb *A* connected to a capillary *BC*. The capillary is connected to the manometer *CD* which contains mercury. The other end of the manometer is open to atmosphere. A vertical metre scale *E* is fixed in such a way that the height of the mercury column in the tube *D* can easily be measured. The mercury in the manometer is connected to the mercury reservoir *F* through a rubber tube.

The capillary *BC* has a fixed mark at *C*. By raising or lowering the reservoir *F*, the mercury level in the left part of the manometer is maintained at *C*. This ensures that the volume of the gas enclosed in the bulb *A* (and the capillary *BC*) remains constant. The pressure of the gas is equal to the atmospheric pressure plus the pressure due to the difference of the mercury columns in the manometer. Thus, $p = p_0 + h\rho g$, where p_0 = atmospheric pressure, h = difference of mercury levels in the manometer tube, ρ = density of mercury and g = acceleration due to gravity.

If the temperature of the bulb is increased and its volume is kept constant by adjusting the height of the reservoir *F*, the pressure of the gas $p = p_0 + h\rho g$ increases. Thus, a temperature scale may be defined by choosing some suitable function of this pressure. Let us assume that the temperature is proportional to the pressure, i.e.,

$$T = cp \, , \qquad \text{... (23.4)}$$

where c is some constant.

In addition, the temperature of triple point of water is assigned a value 273·16 K. (Triple point is a state in which ice, water and water vapour can stay together in equilibrium.) The unit is called a kelvin and is denoted by the symbol K. To get the value of the constant c in equation (23.4), we can put the bulb *A* in a triple point cell and measure the pressure p_{tr} of the gas. From equation (23.4),

$$273{\cdot}16 \text{ K} = cp_{tr}$$

or,
$$c = \frac{273{\cdot}16 \text{ K}}{p_{tr}} .$$

The temperature of the gas when the pressure is p is obtained by putting this value of c in equation (23.4). It is

$$T = \frac{p}{p_{tr}} \times 273{\cdot}16 \text{ K}. \qquad \text{... (23.5)}$$

To use the thermometer, we must first determine the pressure of the gas p_{tr} at the triple point. This is a fixed value for the thermometer and is used in any measurement. To measure the temperature of a bath of extended volume, the bulb *A* is dipped in the bath. Sufficient time is allowed so that the gas in the bulb comes to thermal equilibrium with the bath. The reservoir *F* is adjusted to bring the volume of the gas to its original value and the pressure p of the gas is measured with the manometer. The temperature T on the gas scale is then obtained from equation (23.5).

One can also define a centigrade scale with gas thermometers. Suppose the pressure of the gas is p_0 when the bulb *A* is placed in melting ice (ice point) and it is p_{100} when the bulb is placed in a steam bath (steam point). We assign 0°C to the temperature of the ice point and 100°C to the steam point. The temperature t corresponding to a pressure p of the gas is defined by

$$t = \frac{p - p_0}{p_{100} - p_0} \times 100°\text{C}. \qquad \text{... (23.6)}$$

The constant volume gas thermometer allows several errors in the temperature measurement. The main sources of error are the following:

(a) The space in the capillary tube *BC* generally remains out of the heat bath in which the bulb *A* is placed. The gas in *BC* is, therefore, not at the same temperature as the gas in *A*.

(b) The volume of the glass bulb changes slightly with temperature allowing the volume of the gas to change.

Example 23.1

The pressure of air in the bulb of a constant volume gas thermometer is 73 cm *of mercury at* 0°C, 100·3 cm *of mercury at* 100°C *and* 77·8 cm *of mercury at room temperature. Find the room temperature in centigrades.*

Solution : We have $t = \dfrac{p - p_0}{p_{100} - p_0} \times 100°\text{C}$

$$= \frac{77{\cdot}8 - 73}{100{\cdot}3 - 73} \times 100°\text{C} = 17°\text{C}.$$

23.5 IDEAL GAS TEMPERATURE SCALE

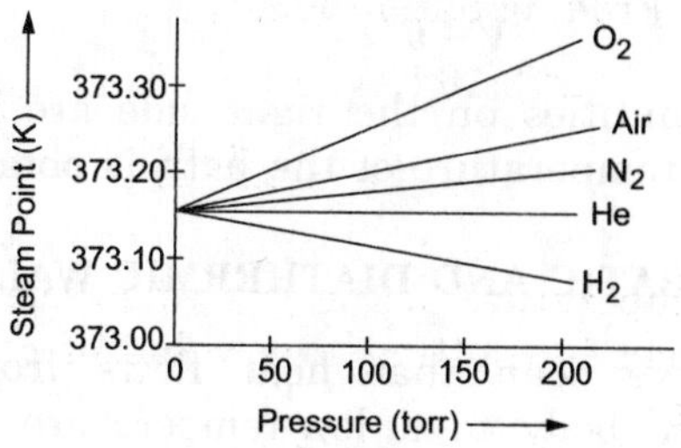

Figure 23.4

The temperature scale defined by equation (23.5) depends slightly on the gas used and its amount present in the thermometer. Figure (23.4) shows the temperature of a steam bath (steam point) as measured by placing different gases in different amounts. On the horizontal axis, we have plotted the pressure p_{tr} of the gas in the thermometer at the triple point of water. This is almost proportional to the mass of the gas present. From the figure, we see that although different gas thermometers differ in their measurement of steam point but the difference decreases as the amount of the gas and hence p_{tr} decreases. In the limit $p_{tr} \to 0$, all the different gas thermometers give the same value 373·15 K for steam point. So we define a temperature scale by the equation

$$T = \lim_{p_{tr} \to 0} \frac{p}{p_{tr}} \times 273{\cdot}16 \text{ K}. \quad \dots (23.7)$$

When we use small amount of gas in a gas thermometer, the scale (23.5) is almost identical to (23.7).

The temperature scale defined by (23.7) is called *ideal gas temperature scale* and is independent of the gas chosen. However, it may depend on the properties of gases in general. As mentioned above, it is possible to define an *absolute temperature scale* which does not depend on any property of any substance. Such a temperature scale has been defined and is in use. The unit of this temperature is called kelvin and is abbreviated as K. The ideal gas temperature scale (23.7) happens to be identical with the absolute scale and hence we have used K to denote the unit.

23.6 CELSIUS TEMPERATURE SCALE

The temperature of the ice point on the ideal gas scale is 273·15 K and of the steam point is $T = 373{\cdot}15$ K. The interval between the two is 100 K. The centigrade scale discussed earlier has 0°C for the ice point and 100°C for the steam point. However, dividing the temperature interval into 100 parts needs a thermometric substance like mercury in glass or resistance of platinum wire etc. Thus, the scales are different for different thermometers. The use of the term "centrigrade scale" is now replaced by "Celsius scale". Celsius scale is defined to have the ice point at 0°C and the steam point at 100°C. The size of a degree in Celsius scale is defined to be the same as the size of a degree in the ideal gas scale. The Celsius scale is shifted from the ideal gas scale by $-273{\cdot}15$. If θ denotes the Celsius temperature and T denotes the kelvin temperature,

$$\theta = T - 273{\cdot}15 \text{ K}. \quad \dots (23.8)$$

The mercury centigrade scale described earlier is quite close to the Celsius scale.

23.7 IDEAL GAS EQUATION

We have seen that the pressure of all gases changes with temperature in a similar fashion for low pressures. Many of the properties of gases are common at low pressures (and high temperatures, that is, far above their condensation point). The pressure, volume and the temperature in kelvin of such a gas obey the equation

$$pV = nRT, \quad \dots (23.9)$$

where n is the amount of the gas in number of moles and R is a universal constant having value $8{\cdot}314 \text{ J K}^{-1} \text{ mol}^{-1}$. The constant R is called the gas constant. Equation (23.9) is known as *ideal gas equation.* A gas obeying this equation is called an *ideal gas.*

23.8 CALLENDAR'S COMPENSATED CONSTANT PRESSURE THERMOMETER

In constant volume gas thermometer, the gas in the capillary tube connecting the bulb and the manometer remains outside the heat bath. The temperature of this part is different from the main bulk of the gas and this introduces some error. Callender's compensated constant pressure thermometer avoids this problem by a special design.

Figure (23.5) shows a schematic diagram of the Callender's thermometer. An ideal gas is filled in a bulb A connected to a manometer M and another bulb B through a capillary cd. The bulb B is filled with mercury and is graduated in volume. Mercury may be

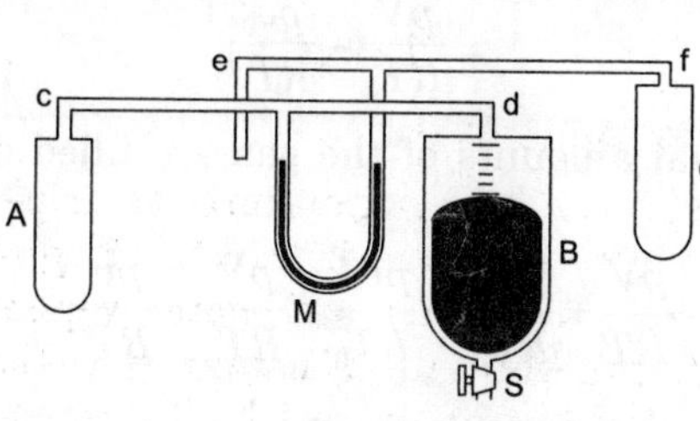

Figure 23.5

taken out from the bulb by opening a stopcock fitted in the lower part of B. The volume of the mercury taken out may be measured with the help of the graduations on B. The other arm of the manometer is connected to a capillary tube ef and a bulb C. The capillary ef and the capillary cd have equal volumes. The bulb A and the bulb C also have equal volumes.

The same ideal gas (as filled in A) is filled in the bulb C. The amount of gas in the bulb C (and the capillary ef) is kept the same as the amount in the bulb A (and the capillary cd). When all the parts of the thermometer are at the same temperature and the bulb B is completely filled with mercury, the levels of the liquid in the two arms of the manometer are equal.

To measure the temperature of a heat bath (at temperature larger than the ice point), the bulb A is placed in the heat bath and the bulbs B and C are placed in melting-ice baths. The pressure in the bulb A becomes more than the pressure in the bulb C and the levels in the manometer tubes become different. Mercury is taken out from B till the levels in the manometer tubes become equal. When mercury is taken out, the total volume of the gas in bulb A, capillary cd and bulb B increases. This decreases the pressure on this side. When sufficient amount of mercury is taken out, the pressure becomes equal to the pressure in the bulb C and hence, the levels in the manometer tubes again become equal.

Suppose,

the volume of A = volume of $C = V$,

volume of capillary cd = volume of capillary $ef = v_0$,

volume of the mercury taken out $= v'$,

temperature of the heat bath $= T$,

temperature of the ice bath $= T_0$,

and the temperature of cd and $ef = T'$.

Using $pV = nRT$, the number of moles in the bulb A, the capillary cd and the bulb B

$$= \frac{pV}{RT} + \frac{pv_0}{RT'} + \frac{pv'}{RT_0}$$

and, the number of moles in the bulb C and the capillary ef

$$= \frac{pV}{RT_0} + \frac{pv_0}{RT'}.$$

As equal amounts of the gas are filled on the two sides,

$$\frac{pV}{RT} + \frac{pv_0}{RT'} + \frac{pv'}{RT_0} = \frac{pV}{RT_0} + \frac{pv_0}{RT'}$$

or, $$\frac{V}{T} = \frac{V}{T_0} - \frac{v'}{T_0}$$

or, $$T = \frac{V}{V - v'} T_0. \qquad \dots (23.10)$$

All the quantities on the right side are known and hence, the temperature of the bath is obtained.

23.9 ADIABATIC AND DIATHERMIC WALLS

We have seen that heat flows from a high-temperature body to a low-temperature body when they are put in contact. There are certain materials which resist the flow of heat through them. When two bodies at different temperatures are separated by such a material, the heat-flow is very slow. We assume an idealised wall or separator which does not allow any heat-flow through it. The bodies on the two sides of such a wall may remain at different temperatures. Such a wall is called an *adiabatic wall*.

Opposite is the concept of a *diathermic wall* which allows heat transfer through it rapidly. If two bodies at different temperatures are separated by such a wall, their temperatures will become equal in a short time.

23.10 THERMAL EXPANSION

If the temperature of a body increases, in general, its size also increases. We used this expansion property to define a temperature scale. Now, we have an absolute scale of temperature independent of any property of any subsbstance. We can study the thermal expansion of a body as a function of temperature. Consider a rod at temperature T and suppose its length at this temperature is L. As the temperature is changed to $T + \Delta T$, the length is changed to $L + \Delta L$. We define *average coefficient of linear expansion* in the temperature range ΔT as

$$\bar{\alpha} = \frac{1}{L}\frac{\Delta L}{\Delta T}.$$

The *coefficient of linear expansion* at temperature T is limit of average coefficient as $\Delta T \to 0$, i.e.,

$$\alpha = \lim_{\Delta T \to 0} \frac{1}{L}\frac{\Delta L}{\Delta T} = \frac{1}{L}\frac{dL}{dT}.$$

Suppose the length of a rod is L_0 at 0°C and L_θ at temperature θ measured in Celsius. If α is small and constant over the given temperature interval,

$$\alpha = \frac{L_\theta - L_0}{L_0 \theta}$$

or, $$L_\theta = L_0 (1 + \alpha\theta). \qquad \dots (23.11)$$

This equation is widely used in solving problems.

The coefficient of volume expansion γ is defined in a similar way. If V is the volume of a body at temperature T, the *coefficient of volume expansion* at temperature T is

$$\gamma = \frac{1}{V}\frac{dV}{dT}.$$

It is also known as coefficient of cubical expansion.

If V_0 and V_θ denote the volumes at 0°C and θ (measured in Celsius) respectively and γ is small and constant over the given temperature range, we have

$$V_\theta = V_0(1 + \gamma\theta). \qquad \text{... (23.12)}$$

It is easy to show that $\gamma = 3\alpha$.

The change in volume of water as temperature increases is slightly complicated. Figure (23.6) shows the volume of 1 g of water as the temperature increases from 0°C to 10°C. The volume of water

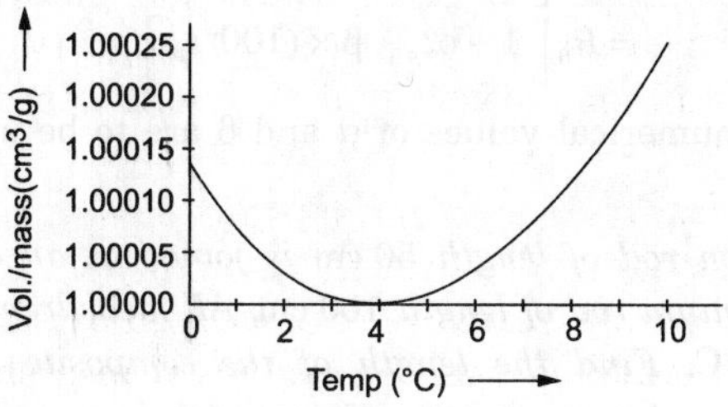

Figure 23.6

decreases from about 1·00013 cm^3 to 1·00000 cm^3 as the temperature increases from 0°C to 4°C. This means γ is negative in this temperature range. The volume again increases as the temperature is increased further from 4°C. The density (mass/volume) of water is thus maximum at 4°C.

The anomalous expansion of water has a favourable effect for animals living in water. Since the density of water is maximum at 4°C, water at the bottom of lakes remain at 4°C in winter even if that at the surface freezes. This allows marine animals to remain alive and move near the bottom.

The study of expansion of a liquid presents another difficulty due to the expansion of the container. Consider a liquid kept in a flask with a graduated stem. As the temperature is increased, the volume of the flask expands faster than the liquid in the beginning and the level of liquid in the stem goes down as if the liquid has contracted. As the temperature of the liquid increases, the volume of the liquid increases and rises in the stem. The apparent increase in the volume is equal to the real increase in the volume of the liquid minus the increase in the volume of the container.

Worked Out Examples

1. *The pressure of the gas in a constant volume gas thermometer at steam point* (373·15 K) *is* $1{\cdot}50 \times 10^4$ Pa. *What will be the pressure at the triple point of water?*

Solution : The temperature in kelvin is defined as

$$T = \frac{p}{p_{tr}} \times 273{\cdot}16 \text{ K}.$$

Thus,

$$373{\cdot}15 = \frac{1{\cdot}50 \times 10^4 \text{ Pa}}{p_{tr}} \times 273{\cdot}16$$

or,

$$p_{tr} = 1{\cdot}50 \times 10^4 \text{ Pa} \times \frac{273{\cdot}16}{373{\cdot}15}$$

$$= 1{\cdot}10 \times 10^4 \text{ Pa}.$$

2. *The pressure of air in the bulb of a constant volume gas thermometer at* 0°C *and* 100°C *are* 73·00 cm *and* 100 cm *of mercury respectively. Calculate the pressure at the room temperature* 20°C.

Solution : The room temperature on the scale measured by the thermometer is

$$t = \frac{p_t - p_0}{p_{100} - p_0} \times 100°\text{C}.$$

Thus,

$$20°\text{C} = \frac{p_t - 73{\cdot}00 \text{ cm of Hg}}{100 \text{ cm of Hg} - 73{\cdot}00 \text{ cm of Hg}} \times 100°\text{C}$$

or, $\quad p_t = 78{\cdot}4$ cm of mercury.

3. *The pressure of the gas in a constant volume gas thermometer is* 80 cm *of mercury in melting ice at* 1 atm. *When the bulb is placed in a liquid, the pressure becomes* 160 cm *of mercury. Find the temperature of the liquid.*

Solution : For an ideal gas at constant volume,

$$\frac{T_1}{T_2} = \frac{p_1}{p_2}$$

or,

$$T_2 = \frac{p_2}{p_1} T_1.$$

The temperature of melting ice at 1 atm is 273·15 K. Thus, the temperature of the liquid is

$$T_2 = \frac{160}{80} \times 273{\cdot}15 \text{ K} = 546{\cdot}30 \text{ K}.$$

4. *In a constant volume gas thermometer, the pressure of the working gas is measured by the difference in the levels of mercury in the two arms of a U-tube connected to the gas at one end. When the bulb is placed at the room temperature* 27·0°C, *the mercury column in the arm open to atmosphere stands* 5·00 cm *above the level of mercury in the other arm. When the bulb is placed in a hot liquid, the difference of mercury levels becomes* 45·0 cm. *Calculate the temperature of the liquid. (Atmospheric pressure* = 75·0 cm of mercury.)

Solution : The pressure of the gas = atmospheric pressure + the pressure due to the difference in mercury levels.

At 27°C, the pressure is 75 cm + 5 cm = 80 cm of mercury. At the liquid temperature, the pressure is 75 cm + 45 cm = 120 cm of mercury. Using $T_2 = \frac{P_2}{P_1} T_1$, the temperature of the liquid is

$$T = \frac{120}{80} \times (27{\cdot}0 + 273{\cdot}15)\ \text{K} = 450{\cdot}22\ \text{K}.$$

$$= 177{\cdot}07°\text{C} \approx 177°\text{C}.$$

5. *The resistances of a platinum resistance thermometer at the ice point, the steam point and the boiling point of sulphur are 2·50, 3·50 and 6·50 Ω respectively. Find the boiling point of sulphur on the platinum scale. The ice point and the steam point measure 0° and 100° respectively.*

Solution : The temperature on the platinum scale is defined as

$$t = \frac{R_t - R_0}{R_{100} - R_0} \times 100°.$$

The boiling point of sulphur on this scale is

$$t = \frac{6{\cdot}50 - 2{\cdot}50}{3{\cdot}50 - 2{\cdot}50} \times 100° = 400°.$$

6. *A platinum resistance thermometer reads 0° and 100° at the ice point and the boiling point of water respectively. The resistance of a platinum wire varies with Celsius temperature θ as $R_t = R_0(1 + \alpha\theta + \beta\theta^2)$, where $\alpha = 3{\cdot}8 \times 10^{-3}\ °\text{C}^{-1}$ and $\beta = -5{\cdot}6 \times 10^{-7}\ °\text{C}^{-2}$. What will be the reading of this thermometer if it is placed in a liquid bath maintained at 50°C ?*

Solution : The resistances of the wire in the thermometer at 100°C and 50°C are

$$R_{100} = R_0[1 + \alpha \times 100°\text{C} + \beta \times (100°\text{C})^2]$$

and, $$R_{50} = R_0[1 + \alpha \times 50°\text{C} + \beta \times (50°\text{C})^2].$$

The temperature t measured on the platinum thermometer is given by

$$t = \frac{R_{50} - R_0}{R_{100} - R_0} \times 100°$$

$$= \frac{\alpha \times 50°\text{C} + \beta \times (50°\text{C})^2}{\alpha \times 100°\text{C} + \beta \times (100°\text{C})^2} \times 100°$$

$$= 50{\cdot}4°.$$

7. *A platinum resistance thermometer is constructed which reads 0° at ice point and 100° at steam point. Let t_p denote the temperature on this scale and let t denote the temperature on a mercury thermometer scale. The resistance of the platinum coil varies with t as $R_t = R_0(1 + \alpha t + \beta t^2)$. Derive an expression for the resistance as a function of t_p.*

Solution : Let R_{t_p} denote the resistance of the coil at the platinum scale temperature t_p. Then

$$t_p = \frac{R_{t_p} - R_0}{R_{100} - R_0} \times 100$$

or, $$R_{t_p} = \frac{t_p}{100}\left(R_{100} - R_0\right) + R_0$$

$$= \frac{t_p}{100}\left[R_0\{1 + \alpha \times 100 + \beta \times (100)^2\} - R_0\right] + R_0$$

$$= \frac{t_p}{100}\left[\alpha \times 100 + \beta \times (100)^2\right] R_0 + R_0$$

$$= R_0\left[1 + \{\alpha \times 100 + \beta \times (100)^2\}\frac{t_p}{100}\right]$$

$$= R_0\left[1 + \alpha t_p + \beta \times (100)\, t_p\right].$$

Only numerical values of α and β are to be used.

8. *An iron rod of length 50 cm is joined at an end to an aluminium rod of length 100 cm. All measurements refer to 20°C. Find the length of the composite system at 100°C and its average coefficient of linear expansion. The coefficient of linear expansion of iron and aluminium are $12 \times 10^{-6}\ °\text{C}^{-1}$ and $24 \times 10^{-6}\ °\text{C}^{-1}$ respectively.*

Solution : The length of the iron rod at 100°C is

$$l_1 = (50\ \text{cm})\,[1 + (12 \times 10^{-6}\ °\text{C}^{-1})\,(100°\text{C} - 20°\text{C})]$$

$$= 50{\cdot}048\ \text{cm}.$$

The length of the aluminium rod at 100°C is

$$l_2 = (100\ \text{cm})\,[1 + (24 \times 10^{-6}\ °\text{C}^{-1})\,(100°\text{C} - 20°\text{C})]$$

$$= 100{\cdot}192\ \text{cm}.$$

The length of the composite system at 100°C is

$$50{\cdot}048\ \text{cm} + 100{\cdot}192\ \text{cm} = 150{\cdot}24\ \text{cm}.$$

The length of the composite system at 20°C is 150 cm. So, the average coefficient of linear expansion of the composite rod is

$$\alpha = \frac{0{\cdot}24\ \text{cm}}{150\ \text{cm} \times (100°\text{C} - 20°\text{C})}$$

$$= 20 \times 10^{-6}\ °\text{C}^{-1}.$$

9. *An iron ring measuring 15·00 cm in diameter is to be shrunk on a pulley which is 15·05 cm in diameter. All measurements refer to the room temperature 20°C. To what minimum temperature should the ring be heated to make the job possible ? Calculate the strain developed in the ring when it comes to the room temperature. Coefficient of linear expansion of iron = $12 \times 10^{-6}\ °\text{C}^{-1}$.*

Solution : The ring should be heated to increase its diameter from 15·00 cm to 15·05 cm.

Using $$l_2 = l_1(1 + \alpha\,\Delta\theta),$$

$$= \frac{0{\cdot}05 \text{ cm}}{15{\cdot}00 \text{ cm} \times 12 \times 10^{-6} \text{ °C}^{-1}}$$

$$= 278°\text{C}$$

The temperature $= 20°\text{C} + 278°\text{C} = 298°\text{C}$.

The strain developed $= \frac{l_2 - l_1}{l_1} = 3{\cdot}33 \times 10^{-3}$.

10. *A pendulum clock consists of an iron rod connected to a small, heavy bob. If it is designed to keep correct time at* 20°C, *how fast or slow will it go in* 24 hours *at* 40°C ? *Coefficient of linear expansion of iron* $= 1.2 \times 10^{-5}$ °C^{-1}.

Solution : The time period at temperature θ is

$$T = 2\pi\sqrt{l_\theta / g}$$
$$= 2\pi\sqrt{l_0(1 + \alpha\theta)/g}$$
$$= 2\pi\sqrt{l_0 / g}\,(1 + \alpha\theta)^{1/2}$$
$$\approx T_0(1 + \frac{1}{2}\alpha\theta).$$

Thus, $T_{20} = T_0[1 + \frac{1}{2}\alpha(20°\text{C})]$

and, $T_{40} = T_0[1 + \frac{1}{2}\alpha(40°\text{C})]$

or, $\frac{T_{40}}{T_{20}} = [1 + (20°\text{C})\alpha]\,[1 + (10°\text{C})\alpha]^{-1}$

$$\approx [1 + (20°\text{C})\alpha]\,[1 - (10°\text{C})\alpha]$$
$$\approx 1 + (10°\text{C})\,\alpha$$

or, $\frac{T_{40} - T_{20}}{T_{20}} = (10°\text{C})\,\alpha = 1{\cdot}2 \times 10^{-4}$. ... (i)

This is fractional loss of time. As the temperature increases, the time period also increases. Thus, the clock goes slow. The time lost in 24 hours is, by (i),

$$\Delta t = (24 \text{ hours})\,(1{\cdot}2 \times 10^{-4}) = 10{\cdot}4 \text{ s}.$$

11. *A pendulum clock having copper rod keeps correct time at* 20°C. *It gains* 15 seconds *per day if cooled to* 0°C. *Calculate the coefficient of linear expansion of copper.*

Solution : The time period at temperature θ is

$$T = 2\pi\sqrt{l_\theta / g}$$
$$\approx T_0\,(1 + \frac{1}{2}\alpha\theta)$$

Thus, $T_{20} = T_0\,[1 + \alpha\,(10°\text{C})]$

or, $\frac{(T_{20} - T_0)}{T_0} = \alpha\,(10°\text{C})$. ... (i)

T_{20} is the correct time period. The period at 0°C is smaller so that the clock runs fast. Equation (i) gives approximately the fractional gain in time. The time gained in 24 hours is

$$\Delta T = (24 \text{ hours})\,[(10°\text{C})\alpha]$$

or, $15 \text{ s} = (24 \text{ hours})\,[(10°\text{C})\alpha]$

or, $\alpha = \frac{15 \text{ s}}{(24 \text{ hours})\,(10°\text{C})}$

$$= 1{\cdot}7 \times 10^{-5} \text{ °C}^{-1}.$$

12. *A piece of metal weighs* 46 g *in air and* 30 g *in a liquid of density* $1{\cdot}24 \times 10^3$ kg m^{-3} *kept at* 27°C. *When the temperature of the liquid is raised to* 42°C, *the metal piece weighs* 30·5 g. *The density of the liquid at* 42°C *is* $1{\cdot}20 \times 10^3$ kg m^{-3}. *Calculate the coefficient of linear expansion of the metal.*

Solution : Let the volume of the metal piece be V_0 at 27°C and V_θ at 42°C. The density of the liquid at 27°C is $\rho_0 = 1{\cdot}24 \times 10^3$ kg m^{-3} and the density of the liquid at 42°C is $\rho_\theta = 1{\cdot}20 \times 10^3$ kg m^{-3}.

The weight of the liquid displaced = apparent loss in the weight of the metal piece when dipped in the liquid. Thus,

$$V_0\,\rho_0 = 46 \text{ g} - 30 \text{ g} = 16 \text{ g}$$

and, $V_\theta\,\rho_\theta = 46 \text{ g} - 30{\cdot}5 \text{ g} = 15{\cdot}5 \text{ g}$.

Thus,

$$\frac{V_\theta}{V_0} = \frac{\rho_0}{\rho_\theta} \times \frac{15{\cdot}5}{16}$$

or, $1 + 3\,\alpha\Delta\theta = \frac{1{\cdot}24 \times 10^3 \times 15{\cdot}5}{1{\cdot}20 \times 10^3 \times 16}$

or, $1 + 3\alpha(42°\text{C} - 27°\text{C}) = 1{\cdot}00104$

or, $\alpha = 2{\cdot}3 \times 10^{-5}$ °C^{-1}.

13. *A sphere of diameter* 7·0 cm *and mass* 266·5 g *floats in a bath of liquid. As the temperature is raised, the sphere begins to sink at a temperature of* 35°C. *If the density of the liquid is* 1·527 g cm^{-3} *at* 0°C, *find the coeffiecient of cubical expansion of the liquid. Neglect the expansion of the sphere.*

Solution : It is given that the expansion of the sphere is negligible as compared to the expansion of the liquid. At 0°C, the density of the liquid is $\rho_0 = 1{\cdot}527$ g cm^{-3}. At 35°C, the density of the liquid equals the density of the sphere. Thus,

$$\rho_{35} = \frac{266{\cdot}5 \text{ g}}{\frac{4}{3}\pi\,(3{\cdot}5 \text{ cm})^3}$$
$$= 1{\cdot}484 \text{ g cm}^{-3}$$

We have $\frac{\rho_\theta}{\rho_0} = \frac{V_0}{V_\theta} = \frac{1}{(1 + \gamma\theta)}$

or, $\rho_\theta = \frac{\rho_0}{1 + \gamma\theta}$.

Thus, $\gamma = \frac{\rho_0 - \rho_{35}}{\rho_{35}\,(35°\text{C})}$

$$= \frac{(1{\cdot}527 - 1{\cdot}484)\text{ g cm}^{-3}}{(1{\cdot}484\text{ g cm}^{-3})\,(35°\text{C})}$$
$$= 8{\cdot}28 \times 10^{-4}\ °\text{C}^{-1}.$$

14. *An iron rod and a copper rod lie side by side. As the temperature is changed, the difference in the lengths of the rods remains constant at a value of* 10 cm. *Find the lengths at* 0°C. *Coefficients of linear expansion of iron and copper are* $1{\cdot}1 \times 10^{-5}\ °\text{C}^{-1}$ *and* $1{\cdot}7 \times 10^{-5}\ °\text{C}^{-1}$ *respectively.*

Solution : Suppose the length of the iron rod at 0°C is l_{i0} and the length of the copper rod at 0°C is l_{c0}. The lengths at temperature θ are

$$l_{i\theta} = l_{i0}\,(1 + \alpha_i \theta) \quad \text{... (i)}$$

and $$l_{c\theta} = l_{c0}\,(1 + \alpha_c \theta). \quad \text{... (ii)}$$

Subtracting,

$$l_{i\theta} - l_{c\theta} = (l_{i0} - l_{c0}) + (l_{i0}\,\alpha_i - l_{c0}\,\alpha_c)\,\theta. \quad \text{... (iii)}$$

Now,

$$l_{i\theta} - l_{c\theta} = l_{i0} - l_{c0}\ (= 10\text{ cm}).$$

Thus, from (iii), $l_{i0}\,\alpha_i = l_{c0}\,\alpha_c$

or, $$\frac{l_{i0}}{l_{c0}} = \frac{\alpha_c}{\alpha_i}$$

or, $$\frac{l_{i0}}{l_{i0} - l_{c0}} = \frac{\alpha_c}{\alpha_c - \alpha_i}$$
$$= \frac{1{\cdot}7 \times 10^{-5}\ °\text{C}^{-1}}{0{\cdot}6 \times 10^{-5}\ °\text{C}^{-1}} = \frac{17}{6}.$$

This shows that $l_{i0} - l_{c0}$ is positive. Its value is 10 cm as given in the question.

Hence, $$l_{i0} = \frac{17}{6} \times (l_{i0} - l_{c0})$$
$$= \frac{17}{6} \times 10\text{ cm} = 28{\cdot}3\text{ cm}$$

and $$l_{c0} = l_{i0} - 10\text{ cm} = 18{\cdot}3\text{ cm}.$$

15. *A uniform steel wire of cross-sectional area* $0{\cdot}20\text{ mm}^2$ *is held fixed by clamping its two ends. Find the extra force exerted by each clamp on the wire if the wire is cooled from* 100°C *to* 0°C. *Young's modulus of steel* $= 2.0 \times 10^{11}\text{ N m}^{-2}$. *Coefficient of linear expansion of steel* $= 1{\cdot}2 \times 10^{-5}\ °\text{C}^{-1}$.

Solution : Let us assume that the tension is zero at 100°C so that l_θ is the natural length of the wire at 100°C. As the wire cools down, its natural length decreases to l_0. As the wire is fixed at the clamps, its length remains the same as the length at 100°C. Thus, the extension of the wire over its natural length at 0°C is

$$l_\theta - l_0 = l_0\,(1 + \alpha\theta) - l_0 = l_0 \alpha\theta.$$

The strain developed is $\dfrac{l_\theta - l_0}{l_\theta} \approx \dfrac{l_\theta - l_0}{l_0} = \alpha\theta.$

The stress developed = $Y \times$ strain = $Y\alpha\theta$.

The tension in the wire at 0°C is

$$T = \text{stress} \times \text{area}$$
$$= Y\alpha t \times 0{\cdot}20\text{ mm}^2$$
$$= (2{\cdot}0 \times 10^{11}\text{ N m}^{-2}) \times (1{\cdot}2 \times 10^{-5}\ °\text{C}^{-1})$$
$$\times 100°\text{C} \times (0{\cdot}20 \times 10^{-6}\text{ m}^{-2})$$
$$= 48\text{ N}.$$

This is equal to the extra force exerted by each clamp.

16. *A glass vessel of volume* 100 cm^{-3} *is filled with mercury and is heated from* 25°C *to* 75°C. *What volume of mercury will overflow ? Coefficient of linear expansion of glass* $= 1.8 \times 10^{-6}\ °\text{C}^{-1}$ *and coefficient of volume expansion of mercury is* $1.8 \times 10^{-4}\ °\text{C}^{-1}$.

Solution : The volume of mercury at 25°C is

$$V_0 = 100\text{ cm}^{-3}.$$

The coefficient of volume expansion of mercury

$$\gamma_L = 1{\cdot}8 \times 10^{-4}\ °\text{C}^{-1}.$$

The coefficient of volume expansion of glass

$$\gamma_S = 3 \times 1{\cdot}8 \times 10^{-6}\ °\text{C}^{-1}$$
$$= 5{\cdot}4 \times 10^{-6}\ °\text{C}^{-1}.$$

Thus, the volume of mercury at 75°C is

$$V_{L\theta} = V_0(1 + \gamma_L\,\Delta\theta)$$

and the volume of the vessel at 75°C is

$$V_{S\theta} = V_0\,(1 + \gamma_S\,\Delta\theta).$$

The volume of mercury overflown

$$= V_{L\theta} - V_{S\theta} = V_0\,(\gamma_L - \gamma_S)\,\Delta\theta \quad \text{... (i)}$$
$$= (100\text{ cm}^{-3})\,(1{\cdot}8 \times 10^{-4} - 5{\cdot}4 \times 10^{-6})/°\text{C} \times (50°\text{C})$$
$$= 0{\cdot}87\text{ cm}^3.$$

Note that $\gamma_a = (\gamma_L - \gamma_S)$ acts as the effective coefficient of expansion of the liquid with respect to the solid. The expansion of mercury 'as seen from the glass' can be written as

$$V_\theta - V_0 = V_0\,\gamma_a\theta$$

or, $$V_\theta = V_0(1 + \gamma_a\theta).$$

The constant γ_a is called the 'apparent coefficient of expansion' of the liquid with respect to the solid.

17. *A barometer reads* 75·0 cm *on a steel scale. The room temperature is* 30°C. *The scale is correctly graduated for* 0°C. *The coefficient of linear expansion of steel is* $\alpha = 1{\cdot}2 \times 10^{-5}\ °\text{C}^{-1}$ *and the coefficient of volume expansion of mercury is* $\gamma = 1{\cdot}8 \times 10^{-4}\ °\text{C}^{-1}$. *Find the correct atmospheric pressure.*

Solution : The 75 cm length of steel at 0°C will become l_θ at 30°C where,

$$l_\theta = (75\text{ cm})\,[1 + \alpha\,(30°\text{C})]. \quad \text{... (i)}$$

The length of mercury column at 30°C is l_θ. The atmospheric pressure is

$$P = l_\theta \rho_{30} g$$

$$= l_0 \frac{\rho_0}{1+\gamma (30°C)} g = l_1 \rho_0 g, \text{ where } l_1 = \frac{l_\theta}{1+\gamma (30°C)}$$

or, $$P = 75 \text{ cm} \frac{[1+\alpha (30°C)]}{[1+\gamma (30°C)]}$$

$$\approx 75 \text{ cm } [1+(\alpha-\gamma)(30°C)]$$

$$= 74{\cdot}62 \text{ cm}.$$

Thus, the atmospheric pressure is 74.62 cm of Hg.

□

QUESTIONS FOR SHORT ANSWER

1. If two bodies are in thermal equilibrium in one frame, will they be in thermal equilibrium in all frames?
2. Does the temperature of a body depend on the frame from which it is observed?
3. It is heard sometimes that mercury is used in defining the temperature scale because it expands uniformly with the temperature. If the temperature scale is not yet defined, is it logical to say that a substance expands uniformly with the temperature?
4. In defining the ideal gas temperature scale, it is assumed that the pressure of the gas at constant volume is proportional to the temperature T. How can we verify whether this is true or not? Are we using the kinetic theory of gases? Are we using the experimental result that the pressure is proportional to temperature?
5. Can the bulb of a thermometer be made of an adiabatic wall?
6. Why do marine animals live deep inside a lake when the surface of the lake freezes?
7. The length of a brass rod is found to be smaller on a hot summer day than on a cold winter day as measured by the same aluminium scale. Do we conclude that brass shrinks on heating?
8. If mercury and glass had equal coefficient of volume expansion, could we make a mercury thermometer in a glass tube?
9. The density of water at 4°C is supposed to be 1000 kg m^{-3}. Is it same at the sea level and at a high altitude?
10. A tightly closed metal lid of a glass bottle can be opened more easily if it is put in hot water for some time. Explain.
11. If an automobile engine is overheated, it is cooled by putting water on it. It is advised that the water should be put slowly with engine running. Explain the reason.
12. Is it possible for two bodies to be in thermal equilibrium if they are not in contact?
13. A spherical shell is heated. The volume changes according to the equation $V_\theta = V_0(1+\gamma\theta)$. Does the volume refer to the volume enclosed by the shell or the volume of the material making up the shell?

OBJECTIVE I

1. A system X is neither in thermal equilibrium with Y nor with Z. The systems Y and Z
   (a) must be in thermal equilibrium
   (b) cannot be in thermal equilibrium
   (c) may be in thermal equilibrium.
2. Which of the curves in figure (23-Q1) represents the relation between Celsius and Fahrenheit temperatures?

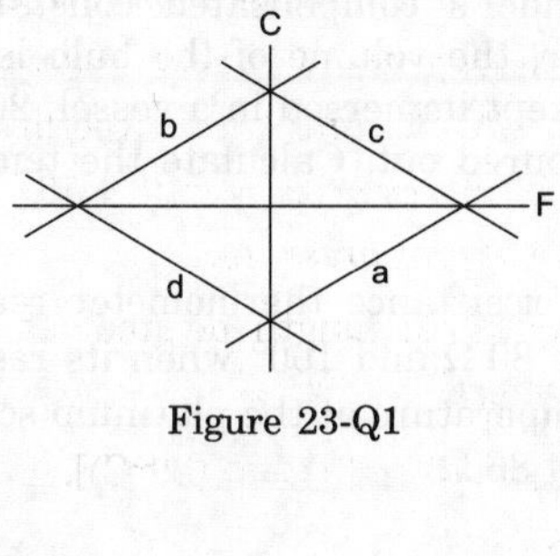

Figure 23-Q1

3. Which of the following pairs may give equal numerical values of the temperature of a body?
   (a) Fahrenheit and kelvin (b) Celsius and kelvin
   (c) Kelvin and platinum
4. For a constant volume gas thermometer, one should fill the gas at
   (a) low temperature and low pressure
   (b) low temperature and high pressure
   (c) high temperature and low pressure
   (d) high temperature and high pressure.
5. Consider the following statements.
   (A) The coefficient of linear expansion has dimension K^{-1}.
   (B) The coefficient of volume expansion has dimension K^{-1}.
   (a) A and B are both correct.
   (b) A is correct but B is wrong.

(c) B is correct but A is wrong.
(d) A and B are both wrong.

6. A metal sheet with a circular hole is heated. The hole
(a) gets larger (b) gets smaller
(c) remains of the same size (d) gets deformed.

7. Two identical rectangular strips, one of copper and the other of steel, are rivetted together to form a bimetallic strip ($\alpha_{copper} > \alpha_{steel}$). On heating, this strip will
(a) remain straight
(b) bend with copper on convex side
(c) bend with steel on convex side
(d) get twisted.

8. If the temperature of a uniform rod is slightly increased by Δt, its moment of inertia I about a perpendicular bisector increases by
(a) zero (b) $\alpha I \Delta t$ (c) $2\alpha I \Delta t$ (d) $3\alpha I \Delta t$.

9. If the temperature of a uniform rod is slightly increased by Δt, its moment of inertia I about a line parallel to itself will increase by
(a) zero (b) $\alpha I \Delta t$ (c) $2\alpha I \Delta t$ (d) $3\alpha I \Delta t$.

10. The temperature of water at the surface of a deep lake is 2°C. The temperature expected at the bottom is
(a) 0°C (b) 2°C (c) 4°C (d) 6°C.

11. An aluminium sphere is dipped into water at 10°C. If the temperature is increased, the force of buoyancy
(a) will increase (b) will decrease
(c) will remain constant
(d) may increase or decrease depending on the radius of the sphere.

OBJECTIVE II

1. A spinning wheel is brought in contact with an identical wheel spinning at identical speed. The wheels slow down under the action of friction. Which of the following energies of the first wheel decrease?
(a) Kinetic (b) Total (c) Mechanical (d) Internal

2. A spinning wheel A is brought in contact with another wheel B initially at rest. Because of the friction at contact, the second wheel also starts spinning. Which of the following energies of the wheel B increase?
(a) Kinetic (b) Total (c) Mechanical (d) Internal

3. A body A is placed on a railway platform and an identical body B in a moving train. Which of the following energies of B are greater than those of A as seen from the ground?
(a) Kinetic (b) Total (c) Mechanical (d) Internal

4. In which of the following pairs of temperature scales, the size of a degree is identical?
(a) Mercury scale and ideal gas scale
(b) Celsius scale and mercury scale
(c) Celsius scale and ideal gas scale
(d) Ideal gas scale and absolute scale

5. A solid object is placed in water contained in an adiabatic container for some time. The temperature of water falls during the period and there is no appreciable change in the shape of the object. The temperature of the solid object
(a) must have increased (b) must have decreased
(c) may have increased
(d) may have remained constant.

6. As the temperature is increased, the time period of a pendulum
(a) increases proportionately with temperature
(b) increases (c) decreases
(d) remains constant.

EXERCISES

1. The steam point and the ice point of a mercury thermometer are marked as 80° and 20°. What will be the temperature in centigrade mercury scale when this thermometer reads 32°?

2. A constant volume thermometer registers a pressure of $1{\cdot}500 \times 10^4$ Pa at the triple point of water and a pressure of $2{\cdot}050 \times 10^4$ Pa at the normal boiling point. What is the temperature at the normal boiling point?

3. A gas thermometer measures the temperature from the variation of pressure of a sample of gas. If the pressure measured at the melting point of lead is 2·20 times the pressure measured at the triple point of water, find the melting point of lead.

4. The pressure measured by a constant volume gas thermometer is 40 kPa at the triple point of water. What will be the pressure measured at the boiling point of water (100°C)?

5. The pressure of the gas in a constant volume gas thermometer is 70 kPa at the ice point. Find the pressure at the steam point.

6. The pressures of the gas in a constant volume gas thermometer are 80 cm, 90 cm and 100 cm of mercury at the ice point, the steam point and in a heated wax bath respectively. Find the temperature of the wax bath.

7. In a Callender's compensated constant pressure air thermometer, the volume of the bulb is 1800 cc. When the bulb is kept immersed in a vessel, 200 cc of mercury has to be poured out. Calculate the temperature of the vessel.

8. A platinum resistance thermometer reads 0° when its resistance is 80 Ω and 100° when its resistance is 90 Ω. Find the temperature at the platinum scale at which the resistance is 86 Ω.

9. A resistance thermometer reads $R = 20{\cdot}0\ \Omega$, $27{\cdot}5\ \Omega$, and $50{\cdot}0\ \Omega$ at the ice point (0°C), the steam point (100°C) and the zinc point (420°C) respectively. Assuming that the resistance varies with temperature as $R_\theta = R_0(1 + \alpha\theta + \beta\theta^2)$, find the values of R_0, α and β. Here θ represents the temperature on Celsius scale.

10. A concrete slab has a length of 10 m on a winter night when the temperature is 0°C. Find the length of the slab on a summer day when the temperature is 35°C. The coefficient of linear expansion of concrete is $1{\cdot}0 \times 10^{-5}\ {}^\circ\text{C}^{-1}$.

11. A metre scale made of steel is calibrated at 20°C to give correct reading. Find the distance between 50 cm mark and 51 cm mark if the scale is used at 10°C. Coefficient of linear expansion of steel is $1{\cdot}1 \times 10^{-5}\ {}^\circ\text{C}^{-1}$.

12. A railway track (made of iron) is laid in winter when the average temperature is 18°C. The track consists of sections of 12·0 m placed one after the other. How much gap should be left between two such sections so that there is no compression during summer when the maximum temperature goes to 48°C? Coefficient of linear expansion of iron $= 11 \times 10^{-6}\ {}^\circ\text{C}^{-1}$.

13. A circular hole of diameter 2·00 cm is made in an aluminium plate at 0°C. What will be the diameter at 100°C? α for aluminium $= 2{\cdot}3 \times 10^{-5}\ {}^\circ\text{C}^{-1}$.

14. Two metre scales, one of steel and the other of aluminium, agree at 20°C. Calculate the ratio aluminium-centimetre/steel-centimetre at (a) 0°C, (b) 40°C and (c) 100°C. α for steel $= 1{\cdot}1 \times 10^{-5}\ {}^\circ\text{C}^{-1}$ and for aluminium $= 2{\cdot}3 \times 10^{-5}\ {}^\circ\text{C}^{-1}$.

15. A metre scale is made up of steel and measures correct length at 16°C. What will be the percentage error if this scale is used (a) on a summer day when the temperature is 46°C and (b) on a winter day when the temperature is 6°C? Coefficient of linear expansion of steel $= 11 \times 10^{-6}\ {}^\circ\text{C}^{-1}$.

16. A metre scale made of steel reads accurately at 20°C. In a sensitive experiment, distances accurate up to 0·055 mm in 1 m are required. Find the range of temperature in which the experiment can be performed with this metre scale. Coefficient of linear expansion of steel $= 11 \times 10^{-6}\ {}^\circ\text{C}^{-1}$.

17. The density of water at 0°C is $0{\cdot}998\ \text{g cm}^{-3}$ and at 4°C is $1{\cdot}000\ \text{g cm}^{-3}$. Calculate the average coefficient of volume expansion of water in the temperature range 0 to 4°C.

18. Find the ratio of the lengths of an iron rod and an aluminium rod for which the difference in the lengths is independent of temperature. Coefficients of linear expansion of iron and aluminium are $12 \times 10^{-6}\ {}^\circ\text{C}^{-1}$ and $23 \times 10^{-6}\ {}^\circ\text{C}^{-1}$ respectively.

19. A pendulum clock gives correct time at 20°C at a place where $g = 9{\cdot}800\ \text{m s}^{-2}$. The pendulum consists of a light steel rod connected to a heavy ball. It is taken to a different place where $g = 9{\cdot}788\ \text{m s}^{-2}$. At what temperature will it give correct time? Coefficient of linear expansion of steel $= 12 \times 10^{-6}\ {}^\circ\text{C}^{-1}$.

20. An aluminium plate fixed in a horizontal position has a hole of diameter 2·000 cm. A steel sphere of diameter 2·005 cm rests on this hole. All the lengths refer to a temperature of 10°C. The temperature of the entire system is slowly increased. At what temperature will the ball fall down? Coefficient of linear expansion of aluminium is $23 \times 10^{-6}\ {}^\circ\text{C}^{-1}$ and that of steel is $11 \times 10^{-6}\ {}^\circ\text{C}^{-1}$.

21. A glass window is to be fit in an aluminium frame. The temperature on the working day is 40°C and the glass window measures exactly 20 cm × 30 cm. What should be the size of the aluminium frame so that there is no stress on the glass in winter even if the temperature drops to 0°C? Coefficients of linear expansion for glass and aluminium are $9{\cdot}0 \times 10^{-6}\ {}^\circ\text{C}^{-1}$ and $24 \times 10^{-6}\ {}^\circ\text{C}^{-1}$ respectively.

22. The volume of a glass vessel is 1000 cc at 20°C. What volume of mercury should be poured into it at this temperature so that the volume of the remaining space does not change with temperature? Coefficients of cubical expansion of mercury and glass are $1{\cdot}8 \times 10^{-4}\ {}^\circ\text{C}^{-1}$ and $9{\cdot}0 \times 10^{-6}\ {}^\circ\text{C}^{-1}$ respectively.

23. An aluminium can of cylindrical shape contains $500\ \text{cm}^3$ of water. The area of the inner cross section of the can is $125\ \text{cm}^2$. All measurements refer to 10°C. Find the rise in the water level if the temperature increases to 80°C. The coefficient of linear expansion of aluminium $= 23 \times 10^{-6}\ {}^\circ\text{C}^{-1}$ and the average coefficient of volume expansion of water $= 3.2 \times 10^{-4}\ {}^\circ\text{C}^{-1}$ respectively.

24. A glass vessel measures exactly 10 cm × 10 cm × 10 cm at 0°C. It is filled completely with mercury at this temperature. When the temperature is raised to 10°C, $1{\cdot}6\ \text{cm}^3$ of mercury overflows. Calculate the coefficient of volume expansion of mercury. Coefficient of linear expansion of glass $= 6{\cdot}5 \times 10^{-6}\ {}^\circ\text{C}^{-1}$.

25. The densities of wood and benzene at 0°C are $880\ \text{kg m}^3$ and $900\ \text{kg m}^{-3}$ respectively. The coefficients of volume expansion are $1{\cdot}2 \times 10^{-3}\ {}^\circ\text{C}^{-1}$ for wood and $1{\cdot}5 \times 10^{-3}\ {}^\circ\text{C}^{-1}$ for benzene. At what temperature will a piece of wood just sink in benzene?

26. A steel rod of length 1 m rests on a smooth horizontal base. If it is heated from 0°C to 100°C, what is the longitudinal strain developed?

27. A steel rod is clamped at its two ends and rests on a fixed horizontal base. The rod is unstrained at 20°C. Find the longitudinal strain developed in the rod if the temperature rises to 50°C. Coefficient of linear expansion of steel $= 1{\cdot}2 \times 10^{-5}\ {}^\circ\text{C}^{-1}$.

28. A steel wire of cross-sectional area $0{\cdot}5\ \text{mm}^2$ is held between two fixed supports. If the wire is just taut at 20°C, determine the tension when the temperature falls to 0°C. Coefficient of linear expansion of steel is $1{\cdot}2 \times 10^{-5}\ {}^\circ\text{C}^{-1}$ and its Young's modulus is $2{\cdot}0 \times 10^{11}\ \text{N m}^{-2}$.

29. A steel rod is rigidly clamped at its two ends. The rod is under zero tension at 20°C. If the temperature rises to 100°C, what force will the rod exert on one of the clamps? Area of cross section of the rod = 2·00 mm^2. Coefficient of linear expansion of steel = 12.0×10^{-6} °C^{-1} and Young's modulus of steel = $2·00 \times 10^{11}$ N m^{-2}.

30. Two steel rods and an aluminium rod of equal length l_o and equal cross section are joined rigidly at their ends as shown in the figure below. All the rods are in a state of zero tension at 0°C. Find the length of the system when the temperature is raised to θ. Coefficient of linear expansion of aluminium and steel are α_a and α_s respectively. Young's modulus of aluminium is Y_a and of steel is Y_s.

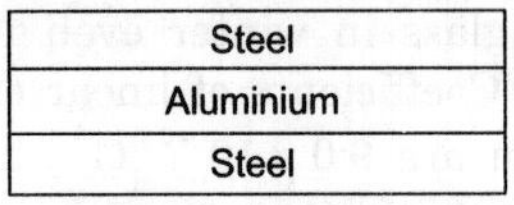

Figure 23-E1

31. A steel ball initially at a pressure of $1·0 \times 10^5$ Pa is heated from 20°C to 120°C keeping its volume constant. Find the pressure inside the ball. Coefficient of linear expansion of steel = 12×10^{-6} °C^{-1} and bulk modulus of steel = $1·6 \times 10^{11}$ N m^{-2}.

32. Show that moment of inertia of a solid body of any shape changes with temperature as $I = I_0(1 + 2\alpha\theta)$, where I_0 is the moment of inertia at 0°C and α is the coefficient of linear expansion of the solid.

33. A torsional pendulum consists of a solid disc connected to a thin wire ($\alpha = 2·4 \times 10^{-5}$ °C^{-1}) at its centre. Find the percentage change in the time period between peak winter (5°C) and peak summer (45°C).

34. A circular disc made of iron is rotated about its axis at a constant velocity ω. Calculate the percentage change in the linear speed of a particle of the rim as the disc is slowly heated from 20°C to 50°C keeping the angular velocity constant. Coefficient of linear expansion of iron = $1·2 \times 10^{-5}$ °C^{-1}.

ANSWERS

OBJECTIVE I

1. (c) 2. (a) 3. (a) 4. (c) 5. (a) 6. (a)
7. (b) 8. (c) 9. (c) 10. (c) 11. (b)

OBJECTIVE II

1. (a), (c) 2. all 3. (a), (b), (c)
4. (c), (d) 5. (a) 6. (b)

EXERCISES

1. 20°C
2. 373·3 K
3. 601 K
4. 55 kPa
5. 96 kPa
6. 200°C
7. 307 K
8. 60°
9. 20·0 Ω, $3·8 \times 10^{-3}$ °C^{-1}, $-5·6 \times 10^{-7}$ °C^{-2}
10. 10·0035 m
11. 0·99989 cm
12. 0·4 cm
13. 2·0046 cm
14. (a) 0·99977 (b) 1·00025 (c) 1·00096
15. (a) –0·033% (b) 0·011%
16. 15°C to 25°C
17. -5×10^{-4} °C^{-1}
18. 23 : 12
19. – 82°C
20. 219°C
21. 20·012 cm × 30·018 cm
22. 50 cc
23. 0·089 cm
24. $1·8 \times 10^{-4}$ °C^{-1}
25. 83°C
26. zero
27. $-3·6 \times 10^{-4}$
28. 24 N
29. 384 N
30. $l_o\left[1 + \dfrac{\alpha_a Y_a + 2\alpha_s Y_s}{Y_a + 2Y_s}\,\theta\right]$
31. $5·8 \times 10^8$ Pa
33. $9·6 \times 10^{-2}$
34. $3·6 \times 10^{-2}$

CHAPTER 24

KINETIC THEORY OF GASES

24.1 INTRODUCTION

We have seen in the previous chapter that the pressure p, the volume V and the temperature T of any gas at low densities obey the equation

$$pV = nRT,$$

where n is the number of moles in the gas and R is the gas constant having value $8{\cdot}314\ JK^{-1}mol^{-1}$. The temperature T is defined on the absolute scale. We define the term *ideal gas* to mean a gas which always obeys this equation. The real gases available to us are good approximation of an ideal gas at low density but deviate from it when the density is increased.

Any sample of a gas is made of molecules. A molecule is the smallest unit having all the chemical properties of the sample. The observed behaviour of a gas results from the detailed behaviour of its large number of molecules. The kinetic theory of gases attempts to develop a model of the molecular behaviour which should result in the observed behaviour of an ideal gas.

24.2 ASSUMPTIONS OF KINETIC THEORY OF GASES

1. All gases are made of molecules moving randomly in all directions.
2. The size of a molecule is much smaller than the average separation between the molecules.
3. The molecules exert no force on each other or on the walls of the container except during collision.
4. All collisions between two molecules or between a molecule and a wall are perfectly elastic. Also, the time spent during a collision is negligibly small.
5. The molecules obey Newton's laws of motion.
6. When a gas is left for sufficient time, it comes to a steady state. The density and the distribution of molecules with different velocities are independent of position, direction and time. This assumption may be justified if the number of molecules is very large.

The last assumption needs some explanation. Suppose there are 2×10^{19} molecules in a particular $1\ cm^3$. Our assumption means that there are 2×10^{19} molecules in any other $1\ cm^3$ in the container and this number does not change as time passes. Similarly, if there are 400 molecules having velocities nearly parallel to the x-axis in a particular $1\ cm^3$, there are 400 molecules having velocities in this direction in any other $1\ cm^3$ and this number does not change with time. Also, there are 400 molecules in $1\ cm^3$ that are going in y-direction. The fact that the distribution of molecules does not change with time has an interesting consequence. Consider a molecule in a small volume ΔV having a velocity $\vec{v}$. A collision occurs and the velocity of this molecule changes. But the number of molecules in ΔV having velocity $\vec{v}$ should not depend on time. So there must be another collision which results in a nearby molecule taking up velocity $\vec{v}$. Effectively, we may neglect both the collisions and say that the molecule continues with the same velocity $\vec{v}$. This greatly simplifies calculations.

The assumptions of kinetic theory are close to the real situation at low densities. The molecular size is roughly 100 times smaller than the average separation between the molecules at $0{\cdot}1$ atm and room temperature. The real molecules do exert electric forces on each other but these forces may be neglected as the average separation between the molecules is large as compared to their size. The collisions between real molecules are indeed elastic if no permanent deformation is caused to a molecule. This is true when the temperature is not too high. The collisions with the walls are elastic if the temperature of the walls is the same as the temperature of the gas. If the gas is left in the container for sufficient time, this assumption will be valid. The fact that the motion of molecules may be described by Newton's laws may be taken as a pure chance for the time being. The last assumption is very nearly true if the number of molecules is very large. As there are about 6×10^{23} molecules per mole, this condition is almost always true in a practical situation.

24.3 CALCULATION OF THE PRESSURE OF AN IDEAL GAS

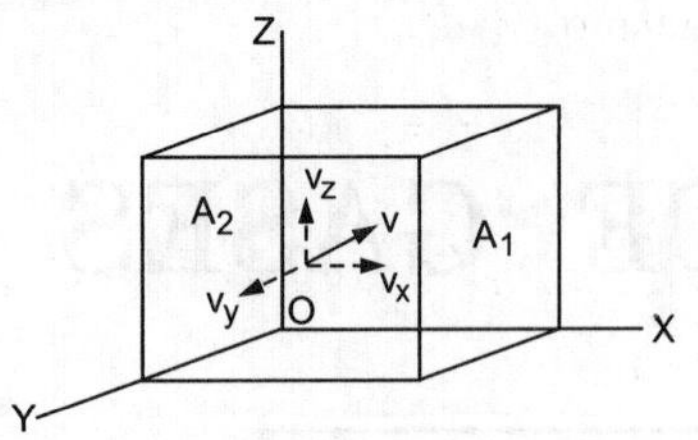

Figure 24.1

Consider an ideal gas enclosed in a cubical vessel of edge L. Take a corner of the vessel as the origin O and the x-, y-, z- axes along the edges (figure 24.1). Let A_1 and A_2 be the parallel faces perpendicular to the x-axis. Consider a molecule moving with velocity $\vec{v}$. The components of the velocity along the axes are v_x, v_y and v_z. When the molecule collides with the face A_1, the x-component of the velocity is reversed whereas the y- and the z-components remain unchanged. This follows from our assumption that the collisions of the molecules with the wall are perfectly elastic. The change in momentum of the molecule is

$$\Delta p = (-mv_x) - (mv_x) = -2mv_x.$$

As the momentum remains conserved in a collision, the change in momentum of the wall is

$$\Delta p' = 2mv_x. \qquad \text{... (i)}$$

After rebound, this molecule travels towards A_2 with the x-component of velocity equal to $-v_x$. Any collision of the molecule with any other face (except for A_2) does not change the value of v_x. So, it travels between A_1 and A_2 with a constant x-component of velocity which is equal to $-v_x$. Note that we can neglect any collision with the other molecules in view of the last assumption discussed in the previous section.

The distance travelled parallel to the x-direction between A_1 and $A_2 = L$. Thus, the time taken by the molecule to go from A_1 to $A_2 = L/v_x$. The molecule rebounds from A_2, travels towards A_1 and collides with it after another time interval L/v_x. Thus, the time between two consecutive collisions of this molecule with A_1 is $\Delta t = 2L/v_x$. The number of collisions of this molecule with A_1 in unit time is

$$n = \frac{1}{\Delta t} = \frac{v_x}{2L}. \qquad \text{... (ii)}$$

The momentum imparted per unit time to the wall by this molecule is, from (i) and (ii),

$$\Delta F = n\Delta p'$$

$$= \frac{v_x}{2L} \times 2mv_x = \frac{m}{L} v_x^2.$$

This is also the force exerted on the wall A_1 due to this molecule. The total force on the wall A_1 due to all the molecules is

$$F = \sum \frac{m}{L} v_x^2$$

$$= \frac{m}{L} \sum v_x^2. \qquad \text{... (iii)}$$

As all directions are equivalent, we have

$$\sum v_x^2 = \sum v_y^2 = \sum v_z^2$$

$$= \frac{1}{3} \sum (v_x^2 + v_y^2 + v_z^2)$$

$$= \frac{1}{3} \sum v^2.$$

Thus, from (iii), $F = \frac{1}{3} \frac{m}{L} \sum v^2$.

If N is the total number of molecules in the sample, we can write

$$F = \frac{1}{3} \frac{mN}{L} \frac{\Sigma v^2}{N}.$$

The pressure is force per unit area so that

$$p = \frac{F}{L^2}$$

$$= \frac{1}{3} \frac{mN}{L^3} \frac{\Sigma v^2}{N}$$

$$= \frac{1}{3} \frac{M}{L^3} \frac{\Sigma v^2}{N} = \frac{1}{3} \rho \frac{\Sigma v^2}{N},$$

where M is the total mass of the gas taken and ρ is its density. Also, $\Sigma v^2/N$ is the average of the speeds squared. It is written as $\overline{v^2}$ and is called *mean square speed*. Thus, the pressure is

$$p = \frac{1}{3} \rho \overline{v^2} \qquad \text{... (24.1)}$$

or, $$pV = \frac{1}{3} M\overline{v^2} \qquad \text{... (24.2)}$$

or, $$pV = \frac{1}{3} Nm\overline{v^2}. \qquad \text{... (24.3)}$$

24.4 RMS SPEED

The square root of mean square speed is called *root-mean-square speed* or rms speed. It is denoted by the symbol v_{rms}. Thus,

$$v_{rms} = \sqrt{\Sigma v^2/N}$$

or, $$\overline{v^2} = (v_{rms})^2.$$

Equation (24.1) may be written as

$$p = \frac{1}{3} \rho v_{rms}^2.$$

so that $v_{rms} = \sqrt{\frac{3p}{\rho}} = \sqrt{\frac{3pV}{M}}$.

Example 24.1

Calculate the rms speed of nitrogen at STP (pressure = 1 atm and temperature = 0°C). The density of nitrogen in these conditions is 1·25 kg m^{-3}.

Solution : At STP, the pressure is $1{\cdot}0 \times 10^5$ N m^{-2}. The rms speed is

$$v_{rms} = \sqrt{\frac{3p}{\rho}}$$

$$= \sqrt{\frac{3 \times 10^5 \text{ N m}^{-2}}{1{\cdot}25 \text{ kg m}^{-3}}}$$

$$= 490 \text{ m s}^{-1}$$

Translational Kinetic Energy of a Gas

The total translational kinetic energy of all the molecules of the gas is

$$K = \sum \frac{1}{2} mv^2 = \frac{1}{2} mN \frac{\Sigma v^2}{N} = \frac{1}{2} Mv_{rms}^2. \quad \text{... (24.4)}$$

The average kinetic energy of a molecule is

$$K/N = \frac{1}{2}\frac{M}{N} v_{rms}^2 = \frac{1}{2} mv_{rms}^2.$$

From equation (24.2),

$$pV = \frac{2}{3} \cdot \frac{1}{2} Mv_{rms}^2$$

or, $$pV = \frac{2}{3} K$$

or, $$K = \frac{3}{2} pV.$$

24.5 KINETIC INTERPRETATION OF TEMPERATURE

We know that a hotter body has larger internal energy than an otherwise similar colder body. Thus, higher temperature means higher internal energy and lower temperature means lower internal energy. According to the kinetic theory of gases, the internal energy of an ideal gas is the same as the total translational kinetic energy of its molecules which is, from equation (24.4),

$$K = \frac{1}{2} M v_{rms}^2.$$

Thus, for a given sample of a gas, higher temperature means higher value of v_{rms} and lower temperature means lower value of v_{rms}. We can write,

$$T = f(v_{rms})$$

for a given sample of a gas.

Let p and v be the pressure of the gas and the rms speed of the molecules at temperature T respectively. Let p_{tr} and v_{tr} be the values of these quantities at temperature 273·16 K, keeping the volume V the same as that at T.

From equation (24.2),

$$pV = \frac{1}{3} Mv^2$$

and $$p_{tr}V = \frac{1}{3} Mv_{tr}^2.$$

Thus, $$\frac{p}{p_{tr}} = \frac{v^2}{v_{tr}^2}. \quad \text{... (i)}$$

From the definition of absolute temperature scale,

$$\frac{p}{p_{tr}} = \frac{T}{273{\cdot}16 \text{ K}}. \quad \text{... (ii)}$$

From (i) and (ii),

$$T = \left(\frac{273{\cdot}16 \text{ K}}{v_{tr}^2}\right) v^2. \quad \text{... (24.5)}$$

Now, v_{tr} is the rms speed of the molecules at 273·16 K and hence is a constant for a given gas. Equation (24.5) shows that *the absolute temperature of a given gas is proportional to the square of the rms speed of its molecules.* As the total translational kinetic energy of the molecules is $K = \frac{1}{2} Mv_{rms}^2$, we see that $T \propto K$ for a given sample of a gas.

Thus, *the absolute temperature of a given sample of a gas is proportional to the total translational kinetic energy of its molecules.*

Now consider a mixture of two gases A and B. Let m_1 be the mass of a molecule of the first gas and m_2 be that of the second. As the molecules collide with each other, they exchange energy. On an average, the molecules with higher kinetic energy lose energy to those with lower kinetic energy. In thermal equilibrium, the average kinetic energy of all molecules are equal. If v_1 and v_2 be the rms speeds of the molecules of A and B respectively,

$$\frac{1}{2} m_1 v_1^2 = \frac{1}{2} m_2 v_2^2. \quad \text{... (24.6)}$$

We find that for different kinds of gases, it is not the rms speed but average kinetic energy of individual molecules that has a fixed value at a given temperature. The heavier molecules move with smaller rms speed and the lighter molecules move with larger rms speed.

Example 24.2

If the rms speed of nitrogen molecules is 490 m s^{-1} *at* 273 K, *find the rms speed of hydrogen molecules at the same temperature.*

Solution : The molecular weight of nitrogen is 28 g mol^{-1} and that of hydrogen is 2 g mol^{-1}. Let m_1, m_2 be the masses and v_1, v_2 be the rms speeds of a nitrogen molecule and a hydrogen molecule respectively. Then $m_1 = 14m_2$. Using equation (24.6),

$$\frac{1}{2} m_1 v_1^2 = \frac{1}{2} m_2 v_2^2$$

or, $$v_2 = v_1 \sqrt{m_1 / m_2} = 490 \text{ m s}^{-1} \times \sqrt{14} \approx 1830 \text{ m s}^{-1}.$$

24.6 DEDUCTIONS FROM KINETIC THEORY

Boyle's Law

At a given temperature, the pressure of a given mass of a gas is inversely proportional to its volume. This is known as Boyle's law.

From equation (24.3), we have

$$pV = \frac{1}{3} mN v_{rms}^2. \qquad \text{... (i)}$$

As for a given gas $v_{rms}^2 \propto T$, the value of v_{rms}^2 is constant at a given temperature. Also, for a given mass of the gas, m and N are constants. Thus, from (i),

$$pV = \text{constant}$$

or, $$p \propto \frac{1}{V}$$

which is Boyle's law.

Charles's Law

At a given pressure, the volume of a given mass of a gas is proportional to its absolute temperature. This is known as Charles's law.

From (i), if p is constant,

$$V \propto v_{rms}^2.$$

As $v_{rms}^2 \propto T$, we get $V \propto T$

which is Charles's law.

Charles's Law of Pressure

At a given volume, the pressure of a given mass of a gas is proportional to its absolute temperature. This is known as Charles's law for pressure.

In fact, this is the definition of the absolute temperature T. If one starts from the fact that $v_{rms}^2 \propto T$ and uses the fact that V is constant, one gets from (i),

$$p \propto v_{rms}^2$$

or, $$p \propto T.$$

Avogadro's Law

At the same temperature and pressure, equal volumes of all gases contain equal number of molecules. This is known as Avogadro's law.

Consider equal volumes of two gases kept at the same pressure and temperature. Let,

m_1 = mass of a molecule of the first gas
m_2 = mass of a molecule of the second gas
N_1 = number of molecules of the first gas
N_2 = number of molecules of the second gas
p = common pressure of the two gases
V = common volume of the two gases.

From equation (24.3),

$$pV = \frac{1}{3} N_1 m_1 v_1^2$$

and $$pV = \frac{1}{3} N_2 m_2 v_2^2,$$

where v_1 and v_2 are rms speeds of the molecules of the first and the second gas respectively. Thus,

$$N_1 m_1 v_1^2 = N_2 m_2 v_2^2. \qquad \text{... (i)}$$

As the temperatures of the gases are the same, the average kinetic energy of the molecules is same for the two gases (equation 24.6), i.e.,

$$\frac{1}{2} m_1 v_1^2 = \frac{1}{2} m_2 v_2^2. \qquad \text{... (ii)}$$

From (i) and (ii),

$$N_1 = N_2$$

which proves Avogadro's law.

Graham's Law of Diffusion

When two gases at the same pressure and temperature are allowed to diffuse into each other, the rate of diffusion of each gas is inversely proportional to the square root of the density of the gas. This is known as Graham's law of diffusion.

It is reasonable to assume that the rate of diffusion is proportional to the rms speed of the molecules of the gas. Then if r_1 and r_2 be the rates of diffusion of the two gases,

$$\frac{r_1}{r_2} = \frac{v_{1,rms}}{v_{2,rms}}. \qquad \text{... (i)}$$

From equation (24.1),

$$v_{rms} = \sqrt{\frac{3p}{\rho}}.$$

If the pressure of the two gases are the same,

$$\frac{v_{1,rms}}{v_{2,rms}} = \sqrt{\frac{\rho_2}{\rho_1}}$$

so that from (i)

$$\frac{r_1}{r_2} = \sqrt{\frac{\rho_2}{\rho_1}}$$

which is Graham's law.

Dalton's Law of Partial Pressure

Dalton's law of partial pressure says that *the pressure exerted by a mixture of several gases equals the sum of the pressures exerted by each gas occupying the same volume as that of the mixture.*

In kinetic theory, we assume that the pressure exerted by a gas on the walls of a container is due to the collisions of the molecules with the walls. The total force on the wall is the sum of the forces exerted by the individual molecules. Suppose there are N_1 molecules of gas 1, N_2 molecules of gas 2, etc., in the mixture.

Thus, the force on a wall of surface area A is

$$F = \text{force by } N_1 \text{ molecules of gas 1} + \text{force by } N_2 \text{ molecules of gas 2} + \dots$$

$$= F_1 + F_2 + \dots$$

Thus, the pressure is

$$p = \frac{F_1}{A} + \frac{F_2}{A} + \dots$$

If the first gas alone is kept in the container, its N_1 molecules will exert a force F_1 on the wall. If the pressure in this case is p_1,

$$p_1 = F_1 / A.$$

Similar is the case for other gases.

Thus,

$$p = p_1 + p_2 + p_3 + \dots$$

24.7 IDEAL GAS EQUATION

Consider a sample of an ideal gas at pressure P, volume V and temperature T. Let m be the mass of each molecule and v be the rms speed of the molecules. Also, let v_{tr} be the rms speed of the gas at the triple point 273·16 K. From equation (24.3),

$$pV = \frac{1}{3} N m v^2 \qquad \dots \text{(i)}$$

and from equation (24.5)

$$T = \left(\frac{273{\cdot}16\ \text{K}}{v_{tr}^2} \right) v^2$$

or,

$$v^2 = \left(\frac{v_{tr}^2}{273{\cdot}16\ \text{K}} \right) T.$$

Putting this expression for v^2 in (i),

$$pV = N \left(\frac{1}{3} \frac{m v_{tr}^2}{273{\cdot}16\ \text{K}} \right) T. \qquad \dots \text{(ii)}$$

Now $\frac{1}{2} m v_{tr}^2$ is the average kinetic energy of a molecule at the triple point 273·16 K. As the average kinetic energy of a molecule is the same for all gases at a fixed temperature (equation 24.6), $\frac{1}{2} m v_{tr}^2$ is a universal constant. Accordingly, the quantity in bracket in equation (ii) above is also a universal constant. Writing this constant as k, equation (ii) becomes,

$$pV = NkT. \qquad \dots (24.7)$$

The universal constant k is known as the *Boltzmann constant* and its value is

$$k = 1{\cdot}38 \times 10^{-23}\ \text{J K}^{-1}$$

up to three significant digits. If the gas contains n moles, the number of molecules is

$$N = n N_A$$

where $N_A = 6{\cdot}02 \times 10^{23}\ \text{mol}^{-1}$ is the Avogadro constant.

Using this, equation (24.7) becomes

$$pV = nN_A kT$$

or,

$$pV = nRT \qquad \dots (24.8)$$

where $R = N_A k$ is another universal constant known as the *universal gas constant.* Its value is

$$R = 8{\cdot}314\ \text{J K}^{-1}\ \text{mol}^{-1}.$$

Equation (24.8) is known as the *equation of state* of an ideal gas.

Example 24.3

Calculate the number of molecules in each cubic metre of a gas at 1 atm *and* 27 °C.

Solution : We have $pV = NkT$

or,

$$N = \frac{pV}{kT}$$

$$= \frac{(1{\cdot}0 \times 10^5\ \text{N m}^{-2})\,(1\ \text{m}^3)}{(1{\cdot}38 \times 10^{-23}\ \text{J K}^{-1})\,(300\ \text{K})}$$

$$\approx 2{\cdot}4 \times 10^{25}.$$

Rms Speed in Terms of Temperature

We are now in a position to write the rms speed of the molecules in terms of the absolute temperature. From equation (24.3),

$$pV = \frac{1}{3} N m v_{rms}^2$$

and from equation (24.7),

$$pV = NkT.$$

From these two,

$$\frac{1}{3} m v_{rms}^2 = kT$$

or,

$$v_{rms} = \sqrt{\frac{3kT}{m}}. \qquad \dots (24.9)$$

This may also be written as,

$$v_{rms} = \sqrt{\frac{3kN_A T}{mN_A}}$$

$$= \sqrt{\frac{3RT}{M_o}} \qquad \dots (24.10)$$

where $M_o = mN_A$ is the molecular weight.

Average Kinetic Energy of a Molecule

Average kinetic energy of a molecule is

$$\frac{1}{2} m v_{rms}^2 = \frac{1}{2} m \cdot \frac{3kT}{m}$$

$$= \frac{3}{2} kT. \qquad \dots (24.11)$$

The total kinetic energy of all the molecules is

$$U = N\left(\frac{3}{2} kT\right) = \frac{3}{2} nRT. \qquad \dots (24.12)$$

The *average speed* $\bar{v} = \Sigma v / N$ is somewhat smaller than the rms speed. It can be shown that

$$\bar{v} = \sqrt{\frac{8kT}{\pi m}} = \sqrt{\frac{8RT}{\pi M_o}}.$$

Example 24.4

Find the rms speed of oxygen molecules in a gas at 300 K.

Solution : $v_{rms} = \sqrt{\frac{3RT}{M_o}}$

$$= \sqrt{\frac{3 \times (8{\cdot}3 \text{ J K}^{-1} \text{mol}^{-1}) \times (300 \text{ K})}{32 \text{ g mol}^{-1}}}$$

$$= \sqrt{\frac{3 \times 8{\cdot}3 \times 300}{0{\cdot}032}} \text{ m s}^{-1} = 483 \text{ m s}^{-1}.$$

It should be clearly understood that the motion of molecules discussed here is truly random motion. In other words, the centre of mass of the gas is assumed to be at rest and any rotation about the centre of mass is assumed to be absent. Any systematic motion of a gas sample has no effect on temperature. For example, if we place a gas jar in a moving train, the increase in translational kinetic energy does not increase the temperature of the gas.

24.8 MAXWELL'S SPEED DISTRIBUTION LAW

The rms speed of an oxygen molecule in a sample at 300 K is about 480 m s^{-1}. This does not mean that the speed of each molecule is 480 m s^{-1}. Many of the molecules have speed less than 480 m s^{-1} and many have speed more than 480 m s^{-1}. Maxwell derived an equation giving the distribution of molecules in different speeds. If dN represents the number of molecules with speeds between v and $v + dv$ then

$$dN = 4\pi N \left(\frac{m}{2\pi kT}\right)^{3/2} v^2 e^{-mv^2/2kT} dv \qquad \dots (24.13)$$

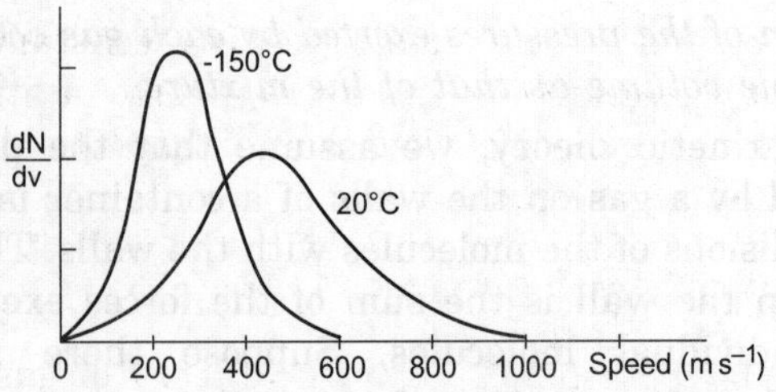

Figure 24.2

Figure (24.2) shows plots of dN/dv against v at two different temperatures. We see that there are some molecules which have speeds many times greater than the mean speed. This fact helps in making nuclear fusion reactions in a laboratory. The speed v_p at which dN/dv is maximum is called the *most probable speed*. Its value is given by

$$v_p = \sqrt{\frac{2kT}{m}}. \qquad \dots (24.14)$$

24.9 THERMODYNAMIC STATE

A given sample of a substance has a number of parameters which can be physically measured. When these parameters are uniquely specified, we say that the *thermodynamic state* of the system is specified. However, not all of these parameters are independent of each other. For example, we can measure pressure, volume, temperature, internal energy and many other parameters of an ideal gas. But if pressure and volume are specified, the rest of the parameters may be calculated. Thus, a thermodynamic state of a given sample of an ideal gas is completely described if its pressure and its volume are given. When a process is performed on a system, it passes from one thermodynamic state to another.

Equation of State

The pressure, volume and temperature of a given sample of a substance are related to each other. An equation describing this relation is called the *equation of state for that substance*. For an ideal gas it is

$$pV = nRT$$

where the symbols have their usual meanings. For a real gas the equation of state is different. The size of a molecule is not negligible in comparison to the average separation between them. Also, the molecular attraction is not negligible. Taking these two facts into account, van der Waals derived the following equation of state for a real gas:

$$\left(p + \frac{a}{V^2}\right)(V - b) = nRT \qquad \dots (24.15)$$

where a and b are small positive constants. The constant a is related to the average force of attraction between the molecules and b is related to the total volume of the molecules.

24.10 BROWNIAN MOTION

We have assumed in kinetic theory of gases that the molecules of a gas are in constant random motion, colliding with each other and with the walls of the container. This is also valid for a liquid. Robert Brown, a botanist, accidentally came across an evidence of this type of molecular motion in 1827. He was observing small pollen grains suspended in water, under a powerful microscope. He observed that although the water appeared to be at complete rest, the grains were moving randomly in the water, occasionally changing their directions of motion. A typical path of a grain looks as shown in figure (24.3). Such a phenomenon is called *Brownian motion*. The molecules strike the particles of the pollen grains and kick them to move in a direction. Another collision with some other molecules changes the direction of the grain.

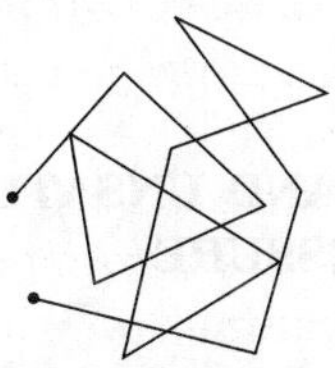

Figure 24.3

The molecules are too small to be directly seen under a normal microscope, but the grains can be seen. A piece of wood floating in water can be seen with naked eyes but its mass is so large that it does not respond quickly to the molecular collisions. Hence, to observe Brownian motion one should have light suspended particles. Brownian motion increases if we increase the temperature. Comparing between different liquids, one with smaller viscosity and smaller density will show more intense Brownian motion.

Einstein developed a theoretical model for Brownian motion in 1905 and deduced the average size of the molecules from it.

24.11 VAPOUR

The kinetic theory of gases described above is strictly valid only for ideal gases. These concepts are also useful in qualitatively understanding several behaviours of nonideal gases, liquids and even solids. We have assumed in kinetic theory that the molecules do not exert a force on each other except at the time of collision. The molecules, in fact, exert an attractive force on each other. For a gas at a low pressure and a high temperature, the average separation between the molecules is quite large. The molecular attraction is quite small and hence the associated attraction energy is small as compared to the average kinetic energy. If the pressure is increased or the temperature is decreased, the attraction energy gradually becomes more important and finally the gas liquefies. Thus, in general, a gas can be liquefied either by increasing the pressure (by compressing it) or by decreasing the temperature. However, if the temperature is sufficiently high so that the kinetic energy of the molecules is large, no amount of pressure can liquefy the gas. The temperature above which this behaviour occurs is called the *critical temperature* of the substance. A gas below its critical temperature is called *vapour*.

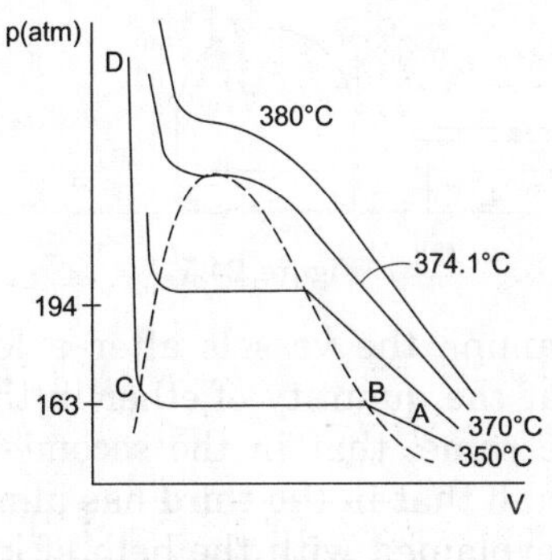

Figure 24.4

Figure (24.4) shows the gas–liquid transition of water in a p–V diagram. Each solid curve represents the variation in pressure with the volume of a sample of water while the temperature is kept fixed. It, therefore, represents an isothermal process and is called an *isotherm*. The dotted curve represents the region where the transition actually takes place. Consider the isotherm *ABCD*. Suppose the water is in its gas form at 350°C and its pressure and volume are represented by the point *A*. We say that the state of the system is represented by *A*. As the pressure is increased keeping the temperature fixed, the state changes to *B* where it enters the region bounded by the dotted curve. Liquefaction starts at 350°C at 163 atm of pressure and the volume rapidly decreases. When the entire water is converted to liquid phase, the state is represented by the point *C*. Now, a large increase in pressure is needed for even a small compression so that the part *CD* is very steep.

At 370°C, liquefaction starts at a higher pressure that is around 194 atm. If the temperature is higher than 374·1°C (say 380°C), the isotherm does not enter the region bounded by the dotted curve. This means water cannot be liquefied at a temperature greater than 374·1°C, no matter how large the pressure is. Thus, 374·1°C is the critical temperature of water. Water in its gas form at a temperature lower than 374·1°C is called *water vapour* and that above 374·1°C is *water gas*.

So, a vapour is a gas which can be liquefied by increasing the pressure without changing the temperature. Vapour obeys Dalton's law of partial pressure. Thus, the pressure exerted by the vapour present in air is the same as what it would be if the vapour were alone in the space with the same density and at the same temperature.

24.12 EVAPORATION

Let us take equal amounts of ether in three identical vessels. One is closed by a lid, one by a big jar and one is left open to air.

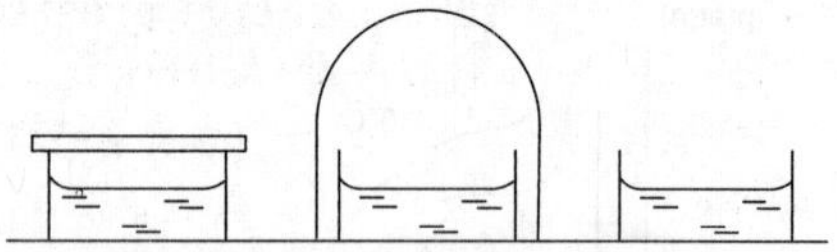

Figure 24.5

If we examine the vessels after a few hours, we shall find that the quantity of ether in the first vessel is almost the same, that in the second is reduced to some extent and that in the third has almost vanished. This can be explained with the help of kinetic theory. The molecules of ether move with random speeds and in random directions. A molecule collides frequently with other molecules and the container walls to change its direction and speed. Occasionally, a molecule starting in upward direction near the surface of the liquid may escape collisions and move out of the liquid. This process is called *evaporation*. Thus, *evaporation is a process in which molecules escape slowly from the surface of a liquid.*

We can now understand why the first vessel contains almost the same amount of ether as time passes. Surface molecules still move out of the liquid, but they cannot move very far away because of the lid. These molecules collide with the lid, with the air molecules, with the surface of the water and among themselves. Some of these molecules may be directed back into the liquid. The number going back depends on the density of the escaped molecules which keeps on increasing as more and more evaporation takes place. An equilibrium is reached when the number of molecules escaping from the liquid per second equals the number returning to the liquid. The volume of the liquid then becomes constant.

The same process takes place in the vessel covered by the jar. But now there is much more space for the escaped molecules to move around and many more molecules must escape before the equilibrium is reached.

In the vessel open to air, there is no restriction on the escaped molecules. They can go far away and never return. Occasionally, some molecules may return after colliding with an air molecule but the number escaped is always greater than the number returned. Thus, the liquid will keep on evaporating till the entire liquid is evaporated. If air blows over the liquid surface in the open vessel, the number of returning molecules is further reduced. This is because any molecule escaping from the surface is blown away from the vicinity of the liquid. This increases the rate of net evaporation. This is why clothes dry faster when a wind is blowing.

When a molecule comes out of the liquid surface, it has to oppose the attraction of the surface molecules it is leaving behind. This needs extra energy. Thus, only those molecules can escape which have kinetic energy sufficiently larger than the average. The average kinetic energy of the remaining liquid decreases and hence, its temperature goes down. This effect is used in cooling water in pitchers having porous walls.

24.13 SATURATED AND UNSATURATED VAPOUR: VAPOUR PRESSURE

Let us consider the vessel of figure (24.5) closed by the jar. After sufficient time an equilibrium is reached when the volume of the liquid becomes constant. The rate of transformation from liquid to vapour equals the rate of transformation from vapour to liquid. If we inject some vapour from outside into the space above the liquid, the rate of the returning molecules will increase while the rate of evaporation will still be the same. The net result is that the extra amount of vapour will convert into liquid. Thus, the space cannot contain more than a certain maximum amount of vapour. If the amount of vapour is less than this, the return rate is less than the rate of evaporation and the amount of vapour will increase to its maximum value.

When a space actually contains the maximum possible amount of vapour, the vapour is called *saturated*. If the amount is less than the maximum possible, the vapour is called *unsaturated*.

This maximum amount depends on the temperature. If we increase the temperature of the vessel, the liquid molecules will have higher average speed and the chances of escaping increases. Thus, the rate of evaporation increases and equilibrium is reached after more vapour has gone in the space provided.

The pressure exerted by a saturated vapour is called *saturation vapour pressure*. We shall denote it by the symbol SVP. The saturation vapour pressure of a substance is constant at a given temperature. It increases when the temperature is increased. Figure (24.6) shows the saturation vapour pressure as a function of temperature for methyl alcohol and water.

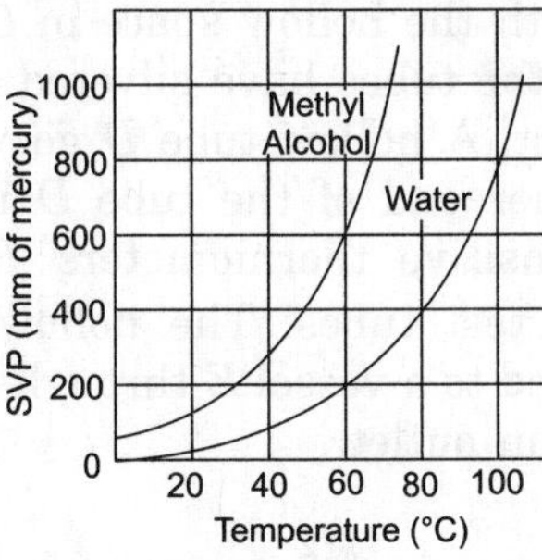

Figure 24.6

Table (24.1) gives the saturation vapour pressure of water at different temperatures.

Table 24.1 : *Saturation vapour pressure of water*

T °C	Vapour pressure torr (mmHg)	*T* °C	Vapour pressure torr (mmHg)
0	4·58	100	760
5	6·51	120	1490
10	8·94	140	2710
15	12·67	160	4630
20	17·5	180	7510
40	55·1	200	11650
60	149	220	17390
80	355		

The concept of saturated vapour is valid even if there is no liquid below. Consider a closed vessel in which we gradually inject vapour. When the amount of vapour is small, on an average, the molecules are far apart. The average attraction energy is much smaller than the average kinetic energy. As the amount is increased, the average separation decreases and the attraction energy becomes more and more important. At a certain state, the attraction becomes sufficient to draw several molecules close enough to form liquid. Thus, the vapour starts condensing. This is the case of saturation. Any vapour further injected will condense and the pressure inside the container will remain equal to the saturation vapour pressure.

In atmosphere, air and vapour are mixed with each other. If a given volume contains maximum amount of vapour possible, the air is called saturated with vapour. Otherwise, it is called unsaturated.

24.14 BOILING

The energy of a certain amount of substance is more in its vapour state than in its liquid state. This is because energy has to be supplied to separate the molecules against the attractive forces operating in the liquid phase. If we heat the liquid, the average kinetic energy of the entire liquid increases and at a certain stage the energy becomes sufficient to break the molecular attraction. The molecules anywhere in the liquid can form vapour bubbles. These bubbles float to the surface of the liquid and finally come out of the liquid. This phenomenon is called *boiling* and the temperature at which boiling occurs is called *boiling point*. Thus, in evaporation, only the molecules near the surface which have kinetic energy greater than the average escape from the liquid, whereas, in boiling, the molecules all over the liquid gain enough energy to become vapour.

The boiling point of a liquid depends on the external pressure over its surface. In fact, boiling occurs at a temperature where the SVP equals the external pressure. Thus, from figure (24.6), the boiling point of water at 1 atm (760 mm of mercury) is 100°C but at 0·5 atm it is 82°C.

Example 24.5

At what external pressure will water boil at 140°C ? *Use table (24.1) for vapour pressure data and express the answer in* atm.

Solution : The saturation vapour pressure of water at 140°C is 2710 mm of Hg. Thus, water will boil at 140°C at this pressure. Now 760 mm of Hg = 1 atm. Thus, 2710 mm of Hg $= \frac{2710}{760}$ atm = 3·56 atm.

The pressure inside a pressure cooker is of this order when it whistles. So, the temperature inside is of the order of 140°C which helps in cooking the food much faster.

24.15 DEW POINT

Table (24.1) gives the saturation vapour pressure of water as a function of temperature. Suppose air at temperature 20°C contains some vapour which exerts a pressure of 8·94 mm of mercury. The air is unsaturated because a vapour pressure of 17·5 mm of mercury is needed to saturate the air at 20°C. If we decrease the temperature from 20°C to 10°C, the air will become saturated with vapour because at 10°C the saturated vapour pressure is 8·94 mm of mercury.

The temperature at which the saturation vapour pressure is equal to the present vapour pressure is called the *dew point*.

If the temperature is decreased below the dew point, some of the vapour condenses.

24.16 HUMIDITY

The amount of water vapour present in a unit volume of air is called the *absolute humidity* of air. It is generally mentioned in terms of g m^{-3}. The ratio of the amount of water vapour present in a given volume to the amount of water vapour required to saturate the volume at the same temperature is called the *relative humidity*. Thus, relative humidity is defined as

$$RH = \frac{\text{Amount of water vapour present in a given volume of air at a given temperature}}{\text{Amount of water vapour required to saturate the same volume of air at the same temperature}} \quad \ldots (24.16)$$

Relative humidity is generally expressed as a percentage. Thus, if the above ratio is 0·6, the relative humidity is 60%. If the air is already saturated, the relative humidity is 100%.

As the pressure exerted by the vapour is directly proportional to the amount of vapour present in a given volume, the relative humidity may also be defined as

$$RH = \frac{\text{Vapour pressure of air}}{\text{SVP at the same temperature}} \cdot \quad \ldots (24.17)$$

The vapour pressure of air at the actual temperature is equal to the saturation vapour pressure at the dew point. Thus, the relative humidity may be redefined as

$$RH = \frac{\text{SVP at the dew point}}{\text{SVP at the air-temperature}} \cdot \quad \ldots (24.18)$$

Example 24.6

The vapour pressure of air at 20°C is found to be 12 mm of Hg *on a particular day. Find the relative humidity. Use the data of table (24.1).*

Solution : The saturation vapour pressure of water at 20°C is 17·5 mm of Hg. Thus, the relative humidity is

$$\frac{\text{vapour pressure of air}}{\text{SVP at the same temperature}}$$

$$= \frac{12 \text{ mm of Hg}}{17{\cdot}5 \text{ mm of Hg}} = 0{\cdot}69,$$

that is, 69%.

24.17 DETERMINATION OF RELATIVE HUMIDITY

A simple method to measure the relative humidity is to find the dew point and then use equation (24.18). We describe below the Regnault's hygrometer to find the dew point.

The apparatus consists of two test tubes *A* and *B* fitted with a hollow stand *C*. The test tube *A* can communicate with the hollow space in *C* but the tube *B* cannot. Both the tubes have silvered outer surfaces in the lower part. A hollow tube *D* goes into the test tube *A*. The other end of the tube *D* is open to the atmosphere. Sensitive thermometers T_1 and T_2 are inserted in the test tubes. The hollow space of the stand is connected to a vessel *E* through a rubber tube. The vessel has an outlet.

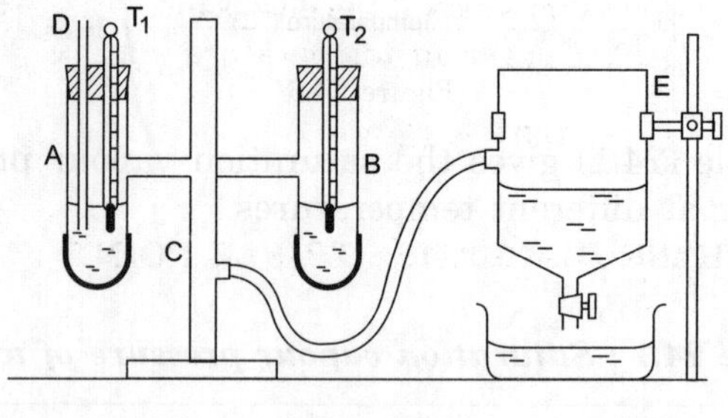

Figure 24.7

Some ether (about half the test tube) is taken in the test tube *A* and the vessel *E* is filled with water. The outlet below the vessel *E* is opened so that the water slowly comes out of the vessel. As a partial vacuum is created over the water surface, air is sucked through the tube *D*, the hollow stand and the rubber tube. Thus, air passes through the ether and evaporates it in the process. The temperature of the test tube *A* gradually decreases and becomes equal to the dew point at a certain time. The vapour in the air near the silvered surface of the test tube *A* starts condensing. Tiny water droplets in the form of *dew* appear on the silvered surface. This surface becomes hazy while the silvered surface of the test tube *B* remains shining. Both the surfaces are continuously observed from a distance (a telescope may be used for the purpose). As soon as the difference in shine is observed, the temperature of the test tube *A* is noted with the thermometer T_1. The reading of T_2 gives the air-temperature.

The outlet to the vessel *D* is closed. The evaporation stops and the temperature of *A* which had gone below the dew point, starts rising. As it just crosses the dew point, the surface again starts shining. The temperature of T_1 at which the two silvered surfaces start looking similar, is noted. The average of the two readings of T_1 is taken as the dew point.

If f and F be the saturation vapour pressures at the dew point and at the air-temperature respectively, the relative humidity is

$$\frac{f}{F} \times 100\%.$$

Example 24.7

In an experiment with Regnault's hygrometer, dew appears at 10°C *when the atmospheric temperature is* 40°C. *Using table (24.1), find the relative humidity.*

Solution : The dew point is 10°C. The saturation vapour pressure at this temperature is 8·94 mm of Hg from table (24.1). Also, the saturation vapour pressure of air at 40°C is 55·1 mm of Hg. The relative humidity expressed in percentage

$$= \frac{\text{vapour pressure at the dew point}}{\text{SVP at the air-temperature}} \times 100\%$$

$$= \frac{8{\cdot}94}{55{\cdot}1} \times 100\% = 16{\cdot}2\%.$$

24.18 PHASE DIAGRAMS : TRIPLE POINT

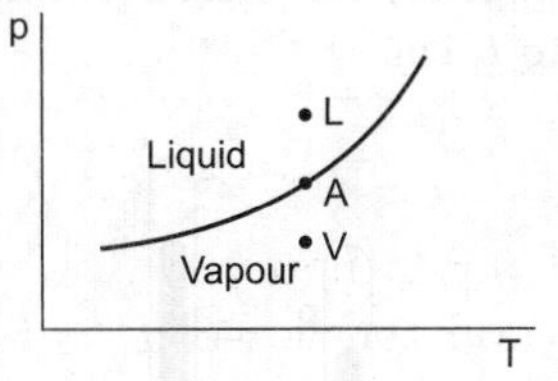

Figure 24.8

When a liquid and its vapour remain together in equilibrium, the vapour is saturated. The saturation vapour pressure depends on temperature. Figure (24.8) shows a curve representing the saturation vapour pressure as a function of temperature. If the vapour pressure and the temperature of a liquid–vapour system are represented by a point on the curve, such as A, the vapour is saturated. The liquid and the vapour can coexist in this case. Now suppose, the vapour pressure is increased by injecting more vapour into the space so that the situation is represented by the point L in figure (24.8). As the vapour is already saturated, the extra vapour will condense into liquid and the system will return to the point A. Similarly, suppose the vapour pressure is decreased by taking out some vapour from the space so that the situation is represented by the point V in figure (24.8). The vapour will become unsaturated and some liquid will evaporate to take the system back to the point A.

Thus, the liquid phase and the vapour phase can coexist only along the curve shown. At points above this curve a pure liquid can exist in equilibrium and at points below this curve a pure vapour can exist in equilibrium.

At the boiling point, the saturation vapour pressure equals the external pressure. The curve in figure (24.8), therefore, also represents the boiling point as a function of external pressure. The horizontal axis then represents the boiling point and the vertical axis represents the external pressure.

Similar curves also exist for solid–liquid transition and for solid–vapour transition. Figure (24.9) shows qualitatively these curves for water and carbon dioxide. The curve PB represents solid–liquid transition and PC represents solid–vapour transition. Solid and liquid phases may coexist along the curve PB and solid and vapour phases can coexist along PC. These curves also represent, respectively, the melting point as a function of pressure and sublimation point as a function of pressure. Thus, the p–T space is divided in three regions labelled solid, liquid and vapour.

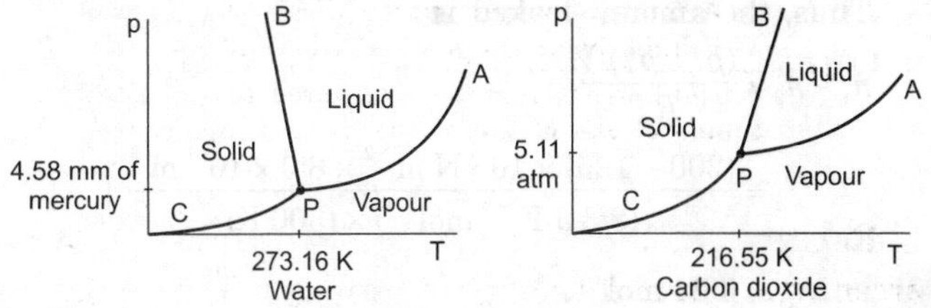

Figure 24.9

The three curves meet at one point labelled P. At the pressure and temperature corresponding to this point, all the three phases may remain together in equilibrium. This point is known as the *triple point*. For water, the triple point occurs at the pressure 4·58 mm of mercury and temperature 273·16 K.

For carbon dioxide, the temperature at the triple point is 216·55 K and the corresponding pressure is 5·11 atm. Thus, at atmospheric pressure it can remain either in solid phase or in vapour phase (figure 24.9). When solid CO_2, open to atmosphere, is heated, it becomes vapour directly without passing through the liquid phase. It is, therefore, called *dry ice*.

24.19 DEW AND FOG

In winter nights, the atmospheric temperature goes down. The surfaces of windowpanes, flowers, grass, etc., become still colder due to radiation. The air near them becomes saturated and condensation begins. The droplets condensed on such surfaces are known as *dew*.

If the temperature falls further, the whole atmosphere in that region may become saturated. Small droplets then condense on the dust particles present in the air. These droplets keep floating in the air and form a thick mist which restricts visibility. This thick mist is called *fog*.

Worked Out Examples

1. *A vessel of volume* $8{\cdot}0 \times 10^{-3}\ \mathrm{m}^3$ *contains an ideal gas at* 300 K *and* 200 kPa. *The gas is allowed to leak till the pressure falls to* 125 kPa. *Calculate the amount of the gas (in moles) leaked assuming that the temperature remains constant.*

Solution : As the gas leaks out, the volume and the temperature of the remaining gas do not change. The number of moles of the gas in the vessel is given by $n = \frac{pV}{RT}$. The number of moles in the vessel before the leakage is

$$n_1 = \frac{p_1 V}{RT}$$

and that after the leakage is

$$n_2 = \frac{p_2 V}{RT}.$$

Thus, the amount leaked is

$$n_1 - n_2 = \frac{(p_1 - p_2)\,V}{RT}$$

$$= \frac{(200 - 125) \times 10^3\ \mathrm{N\,m^{-2}} \times 8{\cdot}0 \times 10^{-3}\ \mathrm{m}^3}{(8{\cdot}3\ \mathrm{J\,K^{-1}\,mol^{-1}}) \times (300\ \mathrm{K})}$$

$$= 0{\cdot}24\ \mathrm{mol}^{-1}.$$

2. *A vessel of volume* $2000\ \mathrm{cm}^3$ *contains* 0·1 mol *of oxygen and* 0·2 mol *of carbon dioxide. If the temperature of the mixture is* 300 K, *find its pressure.*

Solution : We have $p = \frac{nRT}{V}$.

The pressure due to oxygen is

$$p_1 = \frac{(0{\cdot}1\ \mathrm{mol})\,(8{\cdot}3\ \mathrm{J\,K^{-1}\,mol^{-1}})\,(300\ \mathrm{K})}{(2000 \times 10^{-6}\ \mathrm{m^{-3}})} = 1{\cdot}25 \times 10^5\ \mathrm{Pa}.$$

Similarly, the pressure due to carbon dioxide is

$$p_2 = 2{\cdot}50 \times 10^5\ \mathrm{Pa}.$$

The total pressure in the vessel is

$$p = p_1 + p_2$$

$$= (1{\cdot}25 + 2{\cdot}50) \times 10^5\ \mathrm{Pa} = 3{\cdot}75 \times 10^5\ \mathrm{Pa}.$$

3. *A mixture of hydrogen and oxygen has volume* $2000\ \mathrm{cm}^3$, *temperature* 300 K, *pressure* 100 kPa *and mass* 0·76 g. *Calculate the masses of hydrogen and oxygen in the mixture.*

Solution : Suppose there are n_1 moles of hydrogen and n_2 moles of oxygen in the mixture. The pressure of the mixture will be

$$p = \frac{n_1 RT}{V} + \frac{n_2 RT}{V} = (n_1 + n_2)\frac{RT}{V}$$

or, $$100 \times 10^3\ \mathrm{Pa} = (n_1 + n_2)\,\frac{(8{\cdot}3\ \mathrm{J\,K^{-1}\,mol^{-1}})\,(300\ \mathrm{K})}{2000 \times 10^{-6}\ \mathrm{m^{-3}}}$$

or, $$n_1 + n_2 = 0{\cdot}08\ \mathrm{mol}. \quad \text{... (i)}$$

The mass of the mixture is

$$n_1 \times 2\ \mathrm{g\,mol^{-1}} + n_2 \times 32\ \mathrm{g\,mol^{-1}} = 0{\cdot}76\ \mathrm{g}$$

or, $$n_1 + 16 n_2 = 0{\cdot}38\ \mathrm{mol}. \quad \text{... (ii)}$$

from (i) and (ii),

$$n_1 = 0{\cdot}06\ \mathrm{mol}\ \text{and}\ n_2 = 0{\cdot}02\ \mathrm{mol}.$$

The mass of hydrogen $= 0{\cdot}06 \times 2\ \mathrm{g} = 0{\cdot}12\ \mathrm{g}$ and the mass of oxygen $= 0{\cdot}02 \times 32\ \mathrm{g} = 0{\cdot}64\ \mathrm{g}$.

4. *A mercury manometer (figure 24-W1) consists of two unequal arms of equal cross section* $1\ \mathrm{cm}^2$ *and lengths* 100 cm *and* 50 cm. *The two open ends are sealed with air in the tube at a pressure of* 80 cm of mercury. *Some amount of mercury is now introduced in the manometer through the stopcock connected to it. If mercury rises in the shorter tube to a length* 10 cm *in steady state, find the length of the mercury column risen in the longer tube.*

Solution : Let p_1 and p_2 be the pressures in centimetre of mercury in the two arms after introducing mercury in the tube. Suppose the mercury column rises in the second arm to l_0 cm.

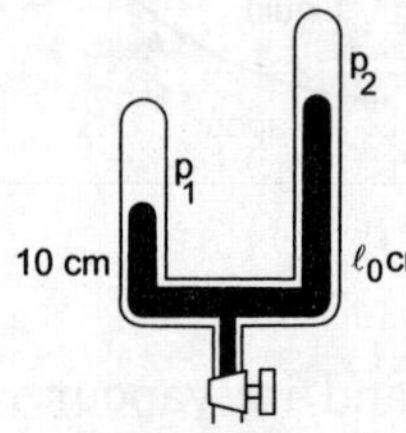

Figure 24-W1

Using pV = constant for the shorter arm,

$$(80\ \mathrm{cm})\,(50\ \mathrm{cm}) = p_1(50\ \mathrm{cm} - 10\ \mathrm{cm})$$

or, $$p_1 = 100\ \mathrm{cm}. \quad \text{... (i)}$$

Using pV = constant for the longer arm,

$$(80\ \mathrm{cm})\,(100\ \mathrm{cm}) = p_2(100 - l_0)\ \mathrm{cm}. \quad \text{... (ii)}$$

From the figure,

$$p_1 = p_2 + (l_0 - 10)\ \mathrm{cm}.$$

Thus by (i),

$$100\ \mathrm{cm} = p_2 + (\,l_0 - 10\,)\ \mathrm{cm}$$

or, $$p_2 = 110\ \mathrm{cm} - l_0\ \mathrm{cm}.$$

Putting in (ii),

$$(110 - l_0)\,(100 - l_0) = 8000$$

or, $$l_0^2 - 210 l_0 + 3000 = 0$$

or, $$l_0 = 15{\cdot}5.$$

The required length is 15·5 cm.

5. *An ideal gas has pressure* p_0, *volume* V_0 *and temperature* T_0. *It is taken through an isochoric process till its* *pressure is doubled. It is now isothermally expanded to get the original pressure. Finally, the gas is isobarically compressed to its original volume V_0. (a) Show the process on a p–V diagram. (b) What is the temperature in the isothermal part of the process ? (c) What is the volume at the end of the isothermal part of the process ?*

Solution : (a) The process is shown in a p–V diagram in figure (24-W2). The process starts from A and goes through $ABCA$.

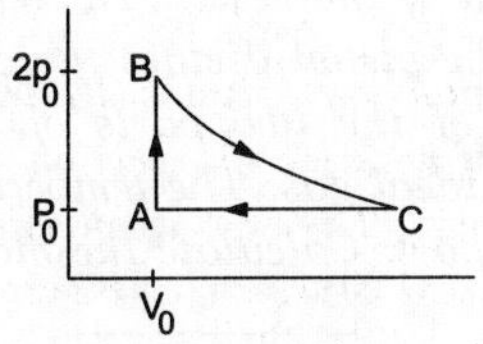

Figure 24-W2

(b) Applying $pV = nRT$ at A and B,

$$p_0V_0 = nRT_0$$

and $(2p_0)V_0 = nRT_B$.

Thus, $T_B = 2\,T_0$.

This is the temperature in the isothermal part BC.

(c) As the process BC is isothermal, $T_C = T_B = 2T_0$.

Applying $pV = nRT$ at A and C,

$$p_0V_0 = nRT_0$$

and $p_0V_C = nR(2T_0)$

or, $V_C = 2V_0$.

6. *A cyclic process ABCA shown in the V–T diagram (figure 24-W3) is performed with a constant mass of an ideal gas. Show the same process on a p–V diagram. In the figure, CA is parallel to the V-axis and BC is parallel to the T-axis.*

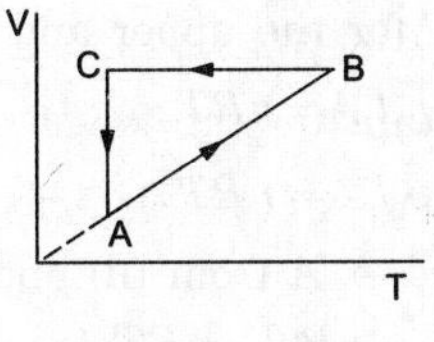

Figure 24-W3

Solution : The p–V diagram is shown in figure (24-W4). During the part AB of figure (24-W3), V is proportional to T. Thus, $\frac{V}{T}$ is constant. Using $\frac{pV}{T} = nR$, we see that the pressure p is constant in this part. This is represented by the part $A'B'$ in the p–V diagram. During the part BC, volume is constant. Thus, $\frac{p}{T}$ is constant. As the temperature decreases, pressure also decreases. This is represented by the part $B'C'$ in the p–V diagram. During the part CA, the temperature remains constant so that pV = constant. Thus, p is inversely proportional to V. This is represented by the part $C'A'$ in the p–V diagram.

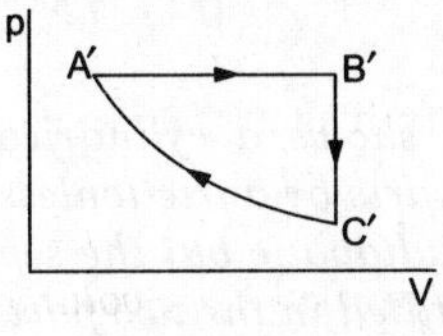

Figure 24-W4

7. *Two closed vessels of equal volume contain air at 105 kPa, 300 K and are connected through a narrow tube. If one of the vessels is now maintained at 300 K and the other at 400 K, what will be the pressure in the vessels ?*

Solution : Let the initial pressure, volume and temperature in each vessel be p_0(= 105 kPa), V_0 and T_0(= 300 K). Let the number of moles in each vessel be n. When the first vessel is maintained at temperature T_0 and the other is maintained at $T' = 400$ K, the pressures change. Let the common pressure become p' and the number of moles in the two vessels become n_1 and n_2. We have

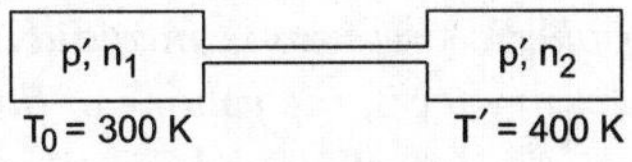

Figure 24-W5

$$p_0V_0 = nRT_0 \quad \ldots \text{(i)}$$

$$p'V_0 = n_1RT_0 \quad \ldots \text{(ii)}$$

$$p'V_0 = n_2RT' \quad \ldots \text{(iii)}$$

and $$n_1 + n_2 = 2n. \quad \ldots \text{(iv)}$$

Putting n, n_1 and n_2 from (i), (ii) and (iii) in (iv),

$$\frac{p'V_0}{RT_0} + \frac{p'V_0}{RT'} = 2\frac{p_0V_0}{RT_0}$$

or, $$p'\left(\frac{T' + T_0}{T_0T'}\right) = \frac{2p_0}{T_0}$$

or, $$p' = \frac{2p_0T'}{T' + T_0}$$

$$= \frac{2 \times 105 \text{ kPa} \times 400 \text{ K}}{400 \text{ K} + 300 \text{ K}} = 120 \text{ kPa}.$$

8. *A vessel contains 14 g of hydrogen and 96 g of oxygen at STP. (a) Find the volume of the vessel. (b) Chemical reaction is induced by passing electric spark in the vessel till one of the gases is consumed. The temperature is brought back to its starting value 273 K. Find the pressure in the vessel.*

Solution : (a) The number of moles of hydrogen = 14 g/2 g = 7 and the number of moles of oxygen = 96 g/32 g = 3. The total number of moles in the vessel = 7 + 3 = 10. The pressure is 1 atm = $1{\cdot}0 \times 10^5$ N m^{-2} and the temperature = 273 K.

Now $$pV = nRT \quad \ldots \text{(i)}$$

or, $$V = \frac{nRT}{p}$$

$$= \frac{(10\ \text{mol}) \times (8{\cdot}3\ \text{J K}^{-1}\ \text{mol}^{-1}) \times (273\ \text{K})}{1{\cdot}0 \times 10^{5}\ \text{N m}^{-2}}$$

$$= 0{\cdot}23\ \text{m}^3.$$

(b) When electric spark is passed, hydrogen reacts with oxygen to form water (H_2O). Each gram of hydrogen reacts with eight grams of oxygen. Thus, 96 g of oxygen will be totally consumed together with 12 g of hydrogen. The gas left in the vessel will be 2 g of hydrogen which is $n' = 1$ mole.

Neglecting the volume of the water formed,

$$p'V = n'RT. \quad \text{... (ii)}$$

From (i) and (ii),

$$\frac{p'}{p} = \frac{n'}{n} = \frac{1}{10}$$

or, $$p' = p \times 0{\cdot}10$$

$$= 0{\cdot}10\ \text{atm}.$$

9. *A barometer reads* 75 cm *of mercury. When* $2{\cdot}0\ \text{cm}^3$ *of air at atmospheric pressure is introduced into the space above the mercury level, the volume of this space becomes* $50\ \text{cm}^3$. *Find the length by which the mercury column descends.*

Solution : Let the pressure of the air in the barometer be p. We have,

$$p \times 50\ \text{cm}^3 = (75\ \text{cm of mercury}) \times (2{\cdot}0\ \text{cm}^3)$$

or, $$p = 3{\cdot}0\ \text{cm of mercury}.$$

The atmospheric pressure is equal to the pressure due to the mercury column plus the pressure due to the air inside. Thus, the mercury column descends by 3·0 cm.

10. *A barometer tube is* 1 m *long and* $2\ \text{cm}^2$ *in cross section. Mercury stands to a height of* 75 cm *in the tube. When a small amount of oxygen is introduced in the space above the mercury level, the level falls by* 5 cm. *Calculate the mass of the oxygen introduced. Room temperature* = 27°C, $g = 10\ \text{m s}^{-2}$ *and density of mercury* $= 13600\ \text{kg m}^{-3}$.

Solution : The pressure of oxygen in the space above the mercury level = 5 cm of mercury

$$= 0{\cdot}05\ \text{m} \times 13600\ \text{kg m}^{-3} \times 10\ \text{m s}^{-2}$$
$$= 6800\ \text{N m}^{-2}.$$

The volume of oxygen $= (2\ \text{cm}^2) \times (25\ \text{cm} + 5\ \text{cm})$

$$= 60\ \text{cm}^3 = 6 \times 10^{-5}\ \text{m}^3.$$

The temperature $= (273 + 27)\ \text{K} = 300\ \text{K}.$

The amount of oxygen is

$$n = \frac{pV}{RT}$$

$$= \frac{(6800\ \text{N m}^{-2}) \times 6 \times 10^{-5}\ \text{m}^{-3}}{(8{\cdot}3\ \text{J K}^{-1}\ \text{mol}^{-1}) \times (300\ \text{K})}$$

$$= 16{\cdot}4 \times 10^{-5}\ \text{mol}.$$

The mass of oxygen is

$$(16{\cdot}4 \times 10^{-5}\ \text{mol}) \times (32\ \text{g mol}^{-1})$$

$$= 5{\cdot}24 \times 10^{-3}\ \text{g}.$$

11. *Figure (24-W6) shows a vertical cylindrical vessel separated in two parts by a frictionless piston free to move along the length of the vessel. The length of the cylinder is* 90 cm *and the piston divides the cylinder in the ratio of* 5 : 4. *Each of the two parts of the vessel contains* 0.1 *mole of an ideal gas. The temperature of the gas is* 300 K *in each part. Calculate the mass of the piston.*

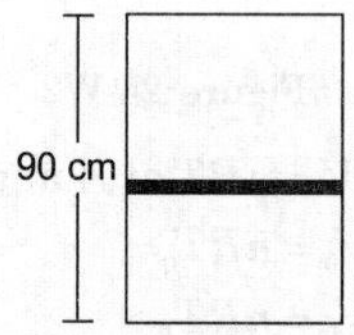

Figure 24-W6

Solution : Let l_1 and l_2 be the lengths of the upper part and the lower part of the cylinder respectively. Clearly, $l_1 = 50$ cm and $l_2 = 40$ cm. Let the pressures in the upper and lower parts be p_1 and p_2 respectively. Let the area of cross section of the cylinder be A. The temperature in both parts is $T = 300$ K.

Consider the equilibrium of the piston. The forces acting on the piston are

(a) its weight mg

(b) $p_1 A$ downward, by the upper part of the gas

and (c) $p_2 A$ upward, by the lower part of the gas.

Thus, $$p_2 A = p_1 A + mg \quad \text{... (i)}$$

Using $pV = nRT$ for the upper and the lower parts

$$p_1 l_1 A = nRT \quad \text{... (ii)}$$

and $$p_2 l_2 A = nRT. \quad \text{... (iii)}$$

Putting $p_1 A$ and $p_2 A$ from (ii) and (iii) into (i),

$$\frac{nRT}{l_2} = \frac{nRT}{l_1} + mg.$$

Thus, $$m = \frac{nRT}{g}\left[\frac{1}{l_2} - \frac{1}{l_1}\right]$$

$$= \frac{(0{\cdot}1\ \text{mol})\ (8{\cdot}3\ \text{J K}^{-1}\ \text{mol}^{-1})\ (300\ \text{K})}{9{\cdot}8\ \text{m s}^{-2}}\left[\frac{1}{0{\cdot}4\ \text{m}} - \frac{1}{0{\cdot}5\ \text{m}}\right]$$

$$= 12{\cdot}7\ \text{kg}.$$

12. *Figure (24-W7) shows a cylindrical tube of volume* V_0 *divided in two parts by a frictionless separator. The walls of the tube are adiabatic but the separator is conducting. Ideal gases are filled in the two parts. When the separator is kept in the middle, the pressures are* p_1 *and* p_2 *in the* *left part and the right part respectively. The separator is slowly slid and is released at a position where it can stay in equilibrium. Find the volumes of the two parts.*

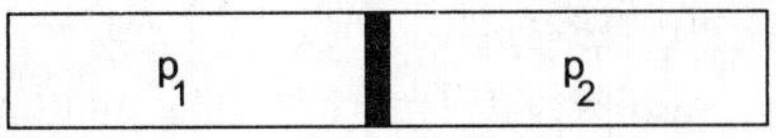

Figure 24-W7

Solution : As the separator is conducting, the temperatures in the two parts will be the same. Suppose the common temperature is T when the separator is in the middle. Let n_1 and n_2 be the number of moles of the gas in the left part and the right part respectively. Using ideal gas equation,

$$p_1\frac{V_0}{2} = n_1RT$$

and $$p_2\frac{V_0}{2} = n_2RT.$$

Thus, $$\frac{n_1}{n_2} = \frac{p_1}{p_2}. \qquad \text{... (i)}$$

The separator will stay in equilibrium at a position where the pressures on the two sides are equal. Suppose the volume of the left part is V_1 and of the right part is V_2 in this situation. Let the common pressure be p'. Also, let the common temperature in this situation be T'. Using ideal gas equation,

$$p'V_1 = n_1RT'$$

and $$p'V_2 = n_2RT'$$

or, $$\frac{V_1}{V_2} = \frac{n_1}{n_2} = \frac{p_1}{p_2}. \qquad \text{[using (i)]}$$

Also, $$V_1 + V_2 = V_0.$$

Thus, $$V_1 = \frac{p_1V_0}{p_1+p_2} \text{ and } V_2 = \frac{p_2V_0}{p_1+p_2}.$$

13. *A thin tube of uniform cross section is sealed at both ends. It lies horizontally, the middle* 5 cm *containing mercury and the parts on its two sides containing air at the same pressure p. When the tube is held at an angle of* 60° *with the vertical, the length of the air column above and below the mercury pellet are* 46 cm *and* 44·5 cm *respectively. Calculate the pressure p in* centimetres of mercury. *The temperature of the system is kept at* 30°C.

Solution : When the tube is kept inclined to the vertical, the length of the upper part is $l_1 = 46$ cm and that of the lower part is $l_2 = 44{\cdot}5$ cm. When the tube lies horizontally, the length on each side is

$$l_0 = \frac{l_1+l_2}{2} = \frac{46\text{ cm} + 44{\cdot}5\text{ cm}}{2} = 45{\cdot}25\text{ cm}.$$

Let p_1 and p_2 be the pressures in the upper and the lower parts when the tube is kept inclined. As the temperature is constant throughout, we can apply Boyle's law. For the upper part,

$$p_1l_1A = pl_0A$$

or, $$p_1 = \frac{pl_0}{l_1}. \qquad \text{... (i)}$$

Similarly, for the lower part,

$$p_2 = \frac{pl_0}{l_2}. \qquad \text{... (ii)}$$

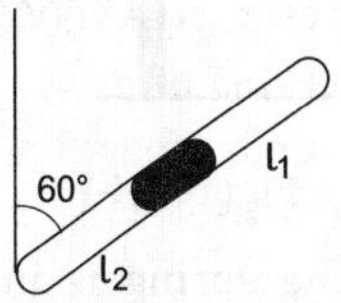

Figure 24-W8

Now consider the equilibrium of the mercury pellet when the tube is kept in inclined position. Let m be the mass of the mercury. The forces along the length of the tube are

(a) p_1A down the tube

(b) p_2A up the tube

and (c) mg cos 60° down the tube.

Thus, $$p_2 = p_1 + \frac{mg}{A}\cos 60°.$$

Putting from (i) and (ii),

$$\frac{pl_0}{l_2} = \frac{pl_0}{l_1} + \frac{mg}{2A}$$

or, $$pl_0\left(\frac{1}{l_2} - \frac{1}{l_1}\right) = \frac{mg}{2A}$$

or, $$p = \frac{mg}{2Al_0\left(\frac{1}{l_2} - \frac{1}{l_1}\right)}.$$

If the pressure p is equal to a height h of mercury,

$$p = h\rho g.$$

Also, $$m = (5\text{ cm})A\rho$$

so that $$h\rho g = \frac{(5\text{ cm})A\rho g}{2Al_0\left(\frac{1}{l_2} - \frac{1}{l_1}\right)}$$

or, $$h = \frac{(5\text{ cm})}{2(45{\cdot}25\text{ cm})\left(\frac{1}{44{\cdot}5\text{ cm}} - \frac{1}{46\text{ cm}}\right)}$$

$$= 75{\cdot}39\text{ cm}.$$

The pressure p is equal to 75·39 cm of mercury.

14. *An ideal monatomic gas is confined in a cylinder by a spring-loaded piston of cross section* $8{\cdot}0 \times 10^{-3}\text{ m}^2$. *Initially the gas is at* 300 K *and occupies a volume of* $2{\cdot}4 \times 10^{-3}\text{ m}^3$ *and the spring is in its relaxed state (figure 24-W9). The gas is heated by a small heater until the piston moves out slowly by* 0·1 m. *Calculate the final temperature of the gas. The force constant of the spring is* 8000 N m^{-1}, *and the atmospheric pressure is* $1{\cdot}0 \times 10^5\text{ N m}^{-2}$. *The cylinder and the piston are* *thermally insulated. The piston and the spring are massless and there is no friction between the piston and the cylinder. Neglect any heat-loss through the lead wires of the heater. The heat capacity of the heater coil is negligible.*

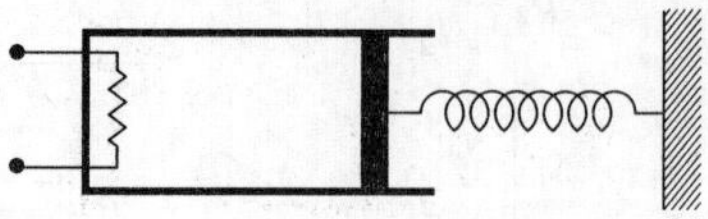

Figure 24-W9

Solution : Initially the spring is in its relaxed state. So, the pressure of the gas equals the atmospheric pressure.

Initial pressure $= p_1 = 1{\cdot}0 \times 10^5 \text{ N m}^{-2}$.

Final pressure $= p_2 = p_1 + \dfrac{kx}{A}$

$$= 1{\cdot}0 \times 10^5 \text{ N m}^{-2} + \frac{(8000 \text{ N m}^{-1})(0{\cdot}1 \text{ m})}{8{\cdot}0 \times 10^{-3} \text{ m}^2}$$

$$= 2{\cdot}0 \times 10^5 \text{ N m}^{-2}.$$

Final volume $= V_2 = V_1 + Ax$

$= 2{\cdot}4 \times 10^{-3} \text{ m}^3 + 8{\cdot}0 \times 10^{-3} \text{ m}^2 \times 0{\cdot}1 \text{ m} = 3{\cdot}2 \times 10^{-3} \text{ m}^3$.

Using $\dfrac{p_1V_1}{T_1} = \dfrac{p_2V_2}{T_2}$,

$$T_2 = \frac{p_2V_2}{p_1V_1} T_1$$

$$= \frac{(2{\cdot}0 \times 10^5 \text{ N m}^{-2})(3{\cdot}2 \times 10^{-3} \text{ m}^3)}{(1{\cdot}0 \times 10^5 \text{ N m}^{-2})(2{\cdot}4 \times 10^{-3} \text{ m}^3)} \times 300 \text{ K}$$

$$= 800 \text{ K}.$$

15. *Assume that the temperature remains essentially constant in the upper part of the atmosphere. Obtain an expression for the variation in pressure in the upper atmosphere with height. The mean molecular weight of air is M.*

Solution : Suppose the pressure at height h is p and that at $h + dh$ is $p + dp$. Then

$$dp = -\rho g\, dh. \quad \text{... (i)}$$

Now considering any small volume ΔV of air of mass Δm,

$$p\Delta V = nRT = \frac{\Delta m}{M} RT$$

or, $$p = \frac{\Delta m}{\Delta V}\frac{RT}{M} = \frac{\rho RT}{M}$$

or, $$\rho = \frac{M}{RT} p.$$

Putting in (i),

$$dp = -\frac{M}{RT} pg\, dh$$

or, $$\int_{p_0}^{p} \frac{dp}{p} = \int_0^h -\frac{M}{RT} g\, dh$$

or, $$\ln \frac{p}{p_0} = -\frac{Mgh}{RT}$$

where p_0 is the pressure at $h = 0$.

Thus, $$p = p_0 e^{-\frac{Mgh}{RT}}.$$

16. *A horizontal tube of length l closed at both ends contains an ideal gas of molecular weight M. The tube is rotated at a constant angular velocity ω about a vertical axis passing through an end. Assuming the temperature to be uniform and constant, show that*

$$p_2 = p_1 e^{\frac{M\omega^2 l^2}{2RT}},$$

where p_2 and p_1 denote the pressures at the free end and the fixed end respectively.

Solution : Consider an element of the gas between the cross sections at distances x and $x + dx$ from the fixed end (figure 24-W10). If p be the pressure at x and $p + dp$ at $x + dx$, the force acting on the element towards the centre is Adp, where A is the cross sectional area. As this element is going in a circle of radius x,

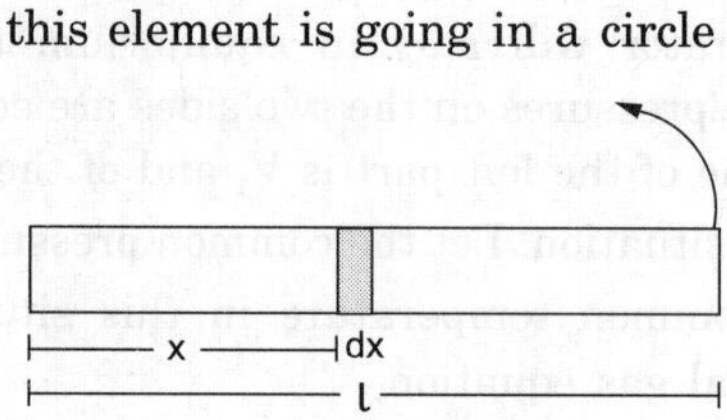

Figure 24-W10

$$Adp = (dm)\omega^2 x \quad \text{... (i)}$$

where dm = mass of the element. Using $pV = nRT$ on this element,

$$pAdx = \frac{dm}{M} RT$$

or, $$dm = \frac{MpA}{RT} dx.$$

Putting in (i),

$$Adp = \frac{MpA}{RT} \omega^2 x\, dx$$

or, $$\int_{p_1}^{p_2} \frac{dp}{p} = \int_0^l \frac{M\omega^2}{RT} x\, dx$$

or, $$\ln \frac{p_2}{p_1} = \frac{M\omega^2 l^2}{2RT}$$

or, $$p_2 = p_1 e^{\frac{M\omega^2 l^2}{2RT}}.$$

17. *A barometer tube contains a mixture of air and saturated water vapour in the space above the mercury column. It reads 70 cm when the actual atmospheric pressure is 76 cm of mercury. The saturation vapour pressure at room temperature is 1·0 cm of mercury. The tube is now lowered in the reservoir till the space above the mercury column is reduced to half its original volume. Find the* *reading of the barometer. Assume that the temperature remains constant.*

Solution : The pressure due to the air + vapour is 76 cm − 70 cm = 6 cm of mercury. The vapour is saturated and the pressure due to it is 1 cm of mercury. The pressure due to the air is, therefore, 5 cm of mercury.

As the tube is lowered and the volume above the mercury is decreased, some of the vapour will condense. The remaining vapour will again exert a pressure of 1 cm of mercury. The pressure due to air is doubled as the volume is halved. Thus, $p_{air} = 2 \times 5\text{ cm} = 10\text{ cm}$ of mercury. The pressure due to the air + vapour = 10 cm + 1 cm = 11 cm of mercury. The barometer reading is 76 cm − 11 cm = 65 cm.

18. *Find the mass of water vapour per cubic metre of air at temperature* 300 K *and relative humidity* 50%. *The saturation vapour pressure at* 300 K *is* 3·6 kPa *and the gas constant* $R = 8{\cdot}3\text{ J K}^{-1}\text{ mol}^{-1}$.

Solution : At 300 K, the saturation vapour pressure = 3·6 kPa. Considering 1 m^3 of volume,

$$pV = nRT = \frac{m}{M}RT$$

where m = mass of vapour and M = molecular weight of water.

Thus, $$m = \frac{MpV}{RT}$$

$$= \frac{(18\text{ g mol}^{-1})(3{\cdot}6 \times 10^3\text{ Pa})(1\text{ m}^3)}{(8{\cdot}3\text{ J K}^{-1}\text{ mol}^{-1})(300\text{ K})} \approx 26\text{ g}.$$

As the relative humidity is 50%, the amount of vapour present in 1 m^3 is 26 g × 0·50 = 13 g.

19. *The temperature and the relative humidity of air are* 20°C *and* 80% *on a certain day. Find the fraction of the mass of water vapour that will condense if the temperature falls to* 5°C. *Saturation vapour pressures at* 20°C *and* 5°C *are* 17·5 mm *and* 6·5 mm *of mercury respectively.*

Solution : The relative humidity is

$$\frac{\text{vapour pressure of the air}}{\text{SVP at the same temperature}}.$$

Thus, the vapour pressure at 20°C

$$= 0{\cdot}8 \times 17{\cdot}5\text{ mm of Hg}$$
$$= 14\text{ mm of Hg}.$$

Consider a volume V of air. If the vapour pressure is p and the temperature is T, the mass m of the vapour present is given by

$$pV = \frac{m}{M}RT$$

or, $$m = \frac{MV}{R}\frac{p}{T}. \quad \text{... (i)}$$

The mass present at 20°C is

$$m_1 = \frac{MV}{R}\frac{14\text{ mm of Hg}}{293\text{ K}}.$$

When the air is cooled to 5°C, some vapour condenses and the air gets saturated with the remaining vapour. The vapour pressure at 5°C is, therefore, 6·5 mm of mercury. The mass of vapour present at 5°C is, therefore,

$$m_2 = \frac{MV}{R}\frac{6{\cdot}5\text{ mm of Hg}}{278\text{ K}}.$$

The fraction condensed

$$= \frac{m_1 - m_2}{m_1} = 1 - \frac{m_2}{m_1}$$

$$= 1 - \frac{6{\cdot}5}{278} \times \frac{293}{14} = 0{\cdot}51.$$

20. *A vessel containing water is put in a dry sealed room of volume* 76 m^3 *at a temperature of* 15°C. *The saturation vapour pressure of water at* 15°C *is* 15 mm *of mercury. How much water will evaporate before the water is in equilibrium with the vapour?*

Solution : Water will be in equilibrium with its vapour when the vapour gets saturated. In this case, the pressure of vapour = saturation vapour pressure = 15 mm of mercury

$$= (15 \times 10^{-3}\text{ m})(13600\text{ kg m}^{-3})(9{\cdot}8\text{ m s}^{-2})$$
$$= 2000\text{ N m}^{-2}.$$

Using gas law, $pV = \frac{m}{M}RT$

$$m = \frac{MpV}{RT}$$

$$= \frac{(18\text{ g mol}^{-1})(2000\text{ N m}^{-2})(76\text{ m}^3)}{(8{\cdot}3\text{ J K}^{-1}\text{ mol}^{-1})(288\text{ K})}$$

$$= 1145\text{ g} = 1{\cdot}14\text{ kg}.$$

Thus, 1·14 kg of water will evaporate.

21. *A jar contains a gas and a few drops of water at absolute temperature* T_1. *The pressure in the jar is* 830 mm *of mercury. The temperature of the jar is reduced by* 1%. *The saturation vapour pressures of water at the two temperatures are* 30 mm *of mercury and* 25 mm *of mercury. Calculate the new pressure in the jar.*

Solution : At temperature T_1, the total pressure is 830 mm of mercury. Out of this, 30 mm of mercury is due to the vapour and 800 mm of mercury is due to the gas. As the temperature decreases, the pressure due to the gas decreases according to the gas law. Here the volume is constant, so,

$$\frac{p_2}{T_2} = \frac{p_1}{T_1}$$

or, $$p_2 = \frac{T_2}{T_1}p_1.$$

As T_2 is 1% less than T_1

$$T_2 = 0{\cdot}99\,T_1$$

and hence,

$$p_2 = 0{\cdot}99\,p_1$$

$= 0{\cdot}99 \times 800$ mm of mercury $= 792$ mm of mercury.

The vapour is still saturated and hence, its pressure is 25 mm of mercury. The total pressure at the reduced temperature is

$$p = (792 + 25) \text{ mm of mercury}$$
$$= 817 \text{ mm of mercury.}$$

22. *Calculate the mass of* 1 litre *of moist air at* 27°C *when the barometer reads* 753·6 mm of mercury *and the dew point is* 16·1°C. *Saturation vapour pressure of water at* 16·1°C = 13·6 mm of mercury, *density of air at STP* $= 0{\cdot}001293\ \text{g (cc)}^{-1}$, *density of saturated water vapour at STP* $= 0{\cdot}000808\ \text{g (cc)}^{-1}$.

Solution : We have $pV = \frac{m}{M}RT$

or,
$$\rho = \frac{m}{V} = \frac{Mp}{RT}. \qquad \text{... (i)}$$

The dew point is 16·1°C and the saturation vapour pressure is 13·6 mm of mercury at the dew point. This means that the present vapour pressure is 13·6 mm of mercury.

At this pressure and temperature, the density of vapour will be

$$\rho = \frac{Mp}{RT}$$
$$= \frac{(18\ \text{g mol}^{-1})\,(13{\cdot}6 \times 10^{-3}\ \text{m})\,(13600\ \text{kg m}^{-3})\,(9{\cdot}8\ \text{m s}^{-2})}{(8{\cdot}3\ \text{J K}^{-1}\ \text{mol}^{-1})\,(300\ \text{K})}$$
$$= 13{\cdot}1\ \text{g m}^{-3}.$$

Thus, 1 litre of moist air at 27°C contains 0·0131 g of vapour.

The pressure of dry air at 27°C is 753·6 mm − 13·6 mm = 740 mm of mercury. The density of air at STP is $0{\cdot}001293\ \text{g (cc)}^{-1}$. The density at 27°C is given by equation (i),

$$\frac{\rho_1}{\rho_2} = \frac{p_1/T_1}{p_2/T_2}$$

or,
$$\rho_2 = \frac{p_2 T_1}{T_2\, p_1}\,\rho_1$$
$$= \frac{740 \times 273}{300 \times 760} \times 0{\cdot}001293\ \text{g (cc)}^{-1}.$$
$$= {\cdot}001457\ \text{g (cc)}^{-1}.$$

Thus, 1 litre of moist air contains 1·145 g of dry air. The mass of 1 litre of moist air is 1·1457 g + 0·0131 g ≈ 1·159 g.

□

QUESTIONS FOR SHORT ANSWER

1. When we place a gas cylinder on a van and the van moves, does the kinetic energy of the molecules increase ? Does the temperature increase ?
2. While gas from a cooking gas cylinder is used, the pressure does not fall appreciably till the last few minutes. Why ?
3. Do you expect the gas in a cooking gas cylinder to obey the ideal gas equation ?
4. Can we define the temperature of (a) vacuum, (b) a single molecule ?
5. Comment on the following statement: the temperature of all the molecules in a sample of a gas is the same.
6. Consider a gas of neutrons. Do you expect it to behave much better as an ideal gas as compared to hydrogen gas at the same pressure and temperature ?
7. A gas is kept in a rigid cubical container. If a load of 10 kg is put on the top of the container, does the pressure increase ?
8. If it were possible for a gas in a container to reach the temperature 0 K, its pressure would be zero. Would the molecules not collide with the walls ? Would they not transfer momentum to the walls ?
9. It is said that the assumptions of kinetic theory are good for gases having low densities. Suppose a container is so evacuated that only one molecule is left in it. Which of the assumptions of kinetic theory will not be valid for such a situation ? Can we assign a temperature to this gas ?
10. A gas is kept in an enclosure. The pressure of the gas is reduced by pumping out some gas. Will the temperature of the gas decrease by Charles's law ?
11. Explain why cooking is faster in a pressure cooker.
12. If the molecules were not allowed to collide among themselves, would you expect more evaporation or less evaporation ?
13. Is it possible to boil water at room temperature, say 30°C ? If we touch a flask containing water boiling at this temperature, will it be hot ?
14. When you come out of a river after a dip, you feel cold. Explain.

OBJECTIVE I

1. Which of the following parameters is the same for molecules of all gases at a given temperature ?
(a) Mass (b) Speed
(c) Momentum (d) Kinetic energy.

2. A gas behaves more closely as an ideal gas at
(a) low pressure and low temperature
(b) low pressure and high temperature
(c) high pressure and low temperature
(d) high pressure and high temperature.

3. The pressure of an ideal gas is written as $p = \frac{2E}{3V}$. Here E refers to
(a) translational kinetic energy
(b) rotational kinetic energy
(c) vibrational kinetic energy
(d) total kinetic energy.

4. The energy of a given sample of an ideal gas depends only on its
(a) volume (b) pressure (c) density (d) temperature.

5. Which of the following gases has maximum rms speed at a given temperature ?
(a) hydrogen (b) nitrogen
(c) oxygen (d) carbon dioxide.

6. Figure 24-Q1 shows graphs of pressure vs density for an ideal gas at two temperatures T_1 and T_2.
(a) $T_1 > T_2$ (b) $T_1 = T_2$
(c) $T_1 < T_2$ (d) Any of the three is possible.

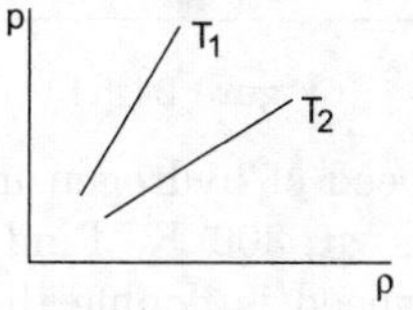

Figure 24-Q1

7. The mean square speed of the molecules of a gas at absolute temperature T is proportional to
(a) $\frac{1}{T}$ (b) $\sqrt{T}$ (c) T (d) T^2.

8. Suppose a container is evacuated to leave just one molecule of a gas in it. Let v_a and v_{rms} represent the average speed and the rms speed of the gas.
(a) $v_a > v_{rms}$ (b) $v_a < v_{rms}$
(c) $v_a = v_{rms}$ (d) v_{rms} is undefined.

9. The rms speed of oxygen at room temperature is about 500 m/s. The rms speed of hydrogen at the same temperature is about
(a) 125 m s^{-1} (b) 2000 m s^{-1} (c) 8000 m s^{-1} (d) 31 m s^{-1}.

10. The pressure of a gas kept in an isothermal container is 200 kPa. If half the gas is removed from it, the pressure will be
(a) 100 kPa (b) 200 kPa (c) 400 kPa (d) 800 kPa.

11. The rms speed of oxygen molecules in a gas is v. If the temperature is doubled and the oxygen molecules dissociate into oxygen atoms, the rms speed will become
(a) v (b) $v\sqrt{2}$ (c) $2v$ (d) $4v$.

12. The quantity $\frac{pV}{kT}$ represents
(a) mass of the gas
(b) kinetic energy of the gas
(c) number of moles of the gas
(d) number of molecules in the gas.

13. The process on an ideal gas, shown in figure (24-Q2), is
(a) isothermal (b) isobaric (c) isochoric (d) none of these.

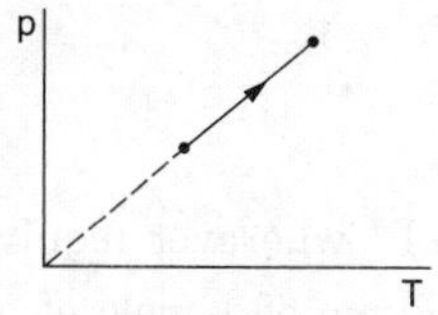

Figure 24-Q2

14. There is some liquid in a closed bottle. The amount of liquid is continuously decreasing. The vapour in the remaining part
(a) must be saturated (b) must be unsaturated
(c) may be saturated (d) there will be no vapour.

15. There is some liquid in a closed bottle. The amount of liquid remains constant as time passes. The vapour in the remaining part
(a) must be saturated (b) must be unsaturated
(c) may be unsaturated (d) there will be no vapour.

16. Vapour is injected at a uniform rate in a closed vessel which was initially evacuated. The pressure in the vessel
(a) increases continuously
(b) decreases continuously
(c) first increases and then decreases
(d) first increases and then becomes constant.

17. A vessel A has volume V and a vessel B has volume $2V$. Both contain some water which has a constant volume. The pressure in the space above water is p_a for vessel A and p_b for vessel B.
(a) $p_a = p_b$ (b) $p_a = 2p_b$
(c) $p_b = 2p_a$ (d) $p_b = 4p_a$.

OBJECTIVE II

1. Consider a collision between an oxygen molecule and a hydrogen molecule in a mixture of oxygen and hydrogen kept at room temperature. Which of the following are possible ?
(a) The kinetic energies of both the molecules increase.
(b) The kinetic energies of both the molecules decrease.

(c) kinetic energy of the oxygen molecule increases and that of the hydrogen molecule decreases.
(d) The kinetic energy of the hydrogen molecule increases and that of the oxygen molecule decreases.

2. Consider a mixture of oxygen and hydrogen kept at room temperature. As compared to a hydrogen molecule an oxygen molecule hits the wall
(a) with greater average speed
(b) with smaller average speed
(c) with greater average kinetic energy
(d) with smaller average kinetic energy.

3. Which of the following quantities is zero on an average for the molecules of an ideal gas in equilibrium ?
(a) Kinetic energy (b) Momentum
(c) Density (d) Speed.

4. Keeping the number of moles, volume and temperature the same, which of the following are the same for all ideal gases ?
(a) Rms speed of a molecule (b) Density
(c) Pressure
(d) Average magnitude of momentum.

5. The average momentum of a molecule in a sample of an ideal gas depends on
(a) temperature (b) number of moles
(c) volume (d) none of these.

6. Which of the following quantities is the same for all ideal gases at the same temperature ?
(a) The kinetic energy of 1 mole
(b) The kinetic energy of 1 g
(c) The number of molecules in 1 mole
(d) The number of molecules in 1 g

7. Consider the quantity $\frac{MkT}{pV}$ of an ideal gas where M is the mass of the gas. It depends on the
(a) temperature of the gas (b) volume of the gas
(c) pressure of the gas (d) nature of the gas.

EXERCISES

Use $R = 8·3 \text{ J K}^{-1} \text{ mol}^{-1}$ wherever required.

1. Calculate the volume of 1 mole of an ideal gas at STP.
2. Find the number of molecules of an ideal gas in a volume of $1·000 \text{ cm}^3$ at STP.
3. Find the number of molecules in 1 cm^3 of an ideal gas at 0°C and at a pressure of 10^{-5} mm of mercury.
4. Calculate the mass of 1 cm^3 of oxygen kept at STP.
5. Equal masses of air are sealed in two vessels, one of volume V_0 and the other of volume $2V_0$. If the first vessel is maintained at a temperature 300 K and the other at 600 K, find the ratio of the pressures in the two vessels.
6. An electric bulb of volume 250 cc was sealed during manufacturing at a pressure of 10^{-3} mm of mercury at 27°C. Compute the number of air molecules contained in the bulb. Avogadro constant $= 6 \times 10^{23} \text{ mol}^{-1}$, density of mercury $= 13600 \text{ kg m}^{-3}$ and $g = 10 \text{ m s}^{-2}$.
7. A gas cylinder has walls that can bear a maximum pressure of $1·0 \times 10^6$ Pa. It contains a gas at $8·0 \times 10^5$ Pa and 300 K. The cylinder is steadily heated. Neglecting any change in the volume, calculate the temperature at which the cylinder will break.
8. 2 g of hydrogen is sealed in a vessel of volume $0·02 \text{ m}^3$ and is maintained at 300 K. Calculate the pressure in the vessel.
9. The density of an ideal gas is $1·25 \times 10^{-3} \text{ g cm}^{-3}$ at STP. Calculate the molecular weight of the gas.
10. The temperature and pressure at Simla are 15·0°C and 72·0 cm of mercury and at Kalka these are 35·0°C and 76·0 cm of mercury. Find the ratio of air density at Kalka to the air density at Simla.
11. Figure (24-E1) shows a cylindrical tube with adiabatic walls and fitted with a diathermic separator. The separator can be slid in the tube by an external mechanism. An ideal gas is injected into the two sides at equal pressures and equal temperatures. The separator remains in equilibrium at the middle. It is now slid to a position where it divides the tube in the ratio of 1:3. Find the ratio of the pressures in the two parts of the vessel.

Figure 24-E1

12. Find the rms speed of hydrogen molecules in a sample of hydrogen gas at 300 K. Find the temperature at which the rms speed is double the speed calculated in the previous part.
13. A sample of 0·177 g of an ideal gas occupies 1000 cm^3 at STP. Calculate the rms speed of the gas molecules.
14. The average translational kinetic energy of air molecules is 0·040 eV ($1 \text{ eV} = 1·6 \times 10^{-19}$ J). Calculate the temperature of the air. Boltzmann constant $k = 1·38 \times 10^{-23} \text{ J K}^{-1}$.
15. Consider a sample of oxygen at 300 K. Find the average time taken by a molecule to travel a distance equal to the diameter of the earth.
16. Find the average magnitude of linear momentum of a helium molecule in a sample of helium gas at 0°C. Mass of a helium molecule $= 6·64 \times 10^{-27}$ kg and Boltzmann constant $= 1·38 \times 10^{-23} \text{ J K}^{-1}$.
17. The mean speed of the molecules of a hydrogen sample equals the mean speed of the molecules of a helium sample. Calculate the ratio of the temperature of the hydrogen sample to the temperature of the helium sample.
18. At what temperature the mean speed of the molecules of hydrogen gas equals the escape speed from the earth ?

19. Find the ratio of the mean speed of hydrogen molecules to the mean speed of nitrogen molecules in a sample containing a mixture of the two gases.

20. Figure (24-E2) shows a vessel partitioned by a fixed diathermic separator. Different ideal gases are filled in the two parts. The rms speed of the molecules in the left part equals the mean speed of the molecules in the right part. Calculate the ratio of the mass of a molecule in the left part to the mass of a molecule in the right part.

Figure 24-E2

21. Estimate the number of collisions per second suffered by a molecule in a sample of hydrogen at STP. The mean free path (average distance covered by a molecule between successive collisions) = $1{\cdot}38 \times 10^{-5}$ cm.

22. Hydrogen gas is contained in a closed vessel at 1 atm (100 kPa) and 300 K. (a) Calculate the mean speed of the molecules. (b) Suppose the molecules strike the wall with this speed making an average angle of 45° with it. How many molecules strike each square metre of the wall per second ?

23. Air is pumped into an automobile tyre's tube up to a pressure of 200 kPa in the morning when the air temperature is 20°C. During the day the temperature rises to 40°C and the tube expands by 2%. Calculate the pressure of the air in the tube at this temperature.

24. Oxygen is filled in a closed metal jar of volume $1{\cdot}0 \times 10^{-3}$ m^3 at a pressure of $1{\cdot}5 \times 10^5$ Pa and temperature 400 K. The jar has a small leak in it. The atmospheric pressure is $1{\cdot}0 \times 10^5$ Pa and the atmospheric temperature is 300 K. Find the mass of the gas that leaks out by the time the pressure and the temperature inside the jar equalise with the surrounding.

25. An air bubble of radius 2·0 mm is formed at the bottom of a 3·3 m deep river. Calculate the radius of the bubble as it comes to the surface. Atmospheric pressure $= 1{\cdot}0 \times 10^5$ Pa and density of water = 1000 kg m^{-3}.

26. Air is pumped into the tubes of a cycle rickshaw at a pressure of 2 atm. The volume of each tube at this pressure is 0·002 m^3. One of the tubes gets punctured and the volume of the tube reduces to 0·0005 m^3. How many moles of air have leaked out ? Assume that the temperature remains constant at 300 K and that the air behaves as an ideal gas.

27. 0·040 g of He is kept in a closed container initially at 100·0°C. The container is now heated. Neglecting the expansion of the container, calculate the temperature at which the internal energy is increased by 12 J.

28. During an experiment, an ideal gas is found to obey an additional law pV^2 = constant. The gas is initially at a temperature T and volume V. Find the temperature when it expands to a volume $2V$.

29. A vessel contains 1·60 g of oxygen and 2·80 g of nitrogen. The temperature is maintained at 300 K and the volume of the vessel is 0·166 m^3. Find the pressure of the mixture.

30. A vertical cylinder of height 100 cm contains air at a constant temperature. The top is closed by a frictionless light piston. The atmospheric pressure is equal to 75 cm of mercury. Mercury is slowly poured over the piston. Find the maximum height of the mercury column that can be put on the piston.

31. Figure (24-E3) shows two vessels A and B with rigid walls containing ideal gases. The pressure, temperature and the volume are p_A, T_A, V in the vessel A and p_B, T_B, V in the vessel B. The vessels are now connected through a small tube. Show that the pressure p and the temperature T satisfy

$$\frac{p}{T} = \frac{1}{2}\left(\frac{p_A}{T_A} + \frac{p_B}{T_B}\right)$$

when equilibrium is achieved.

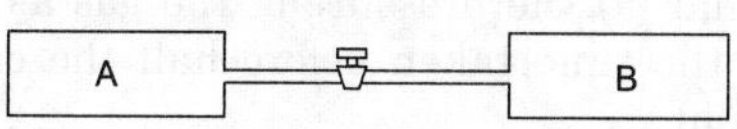

Figure 24-E3

32. A container of volume 50 cc contains air (mean molecular weight = 28·8 g) and is open to atmosphere where the pressure is 100 kPa. The container is kept in a bath containing melting ice (0°C). (a) Find the mass of the air in the container when thermal equilibrium is reached. (b) The container is now placed in another bath containing boiling water (100°C). Find the mass of air in the container. (c) The container is now closed and placed in the melting-ice bath. Find the pressure of the air when thermal equilibrium is reached.

33. A uniform tube closed at one end, contains a pellet of mercury 10 cm long. When the tube is kept vertically with the closed-end upward, the length of the air column trapped is 20 cm. Find the length of the air column trapped when the tube is inverted so that the closed-end goes down. Atmospheric pressure = 75 cm of mercury.

34. A glass tube, sealed at both ends, is 100 cm long. It lies horizontally with the middle 10 cm containing mercury. The two ends of the tube contain air at 27°C and at a pressure 76 cm of mercury. The air column on one side is maintained at 0°C and the other side is maintained at 127°C. Calculate the length of the air column on the cooler side. Neglect the changes in the volume of mercury and of the glass.

35. An ideal gas is trapped between a mercury column and the closed-end of a narrow vertical tube of uniform base containing the column. The upper end of the tube is open to the atmosphere. The atmospheric pressure equals 76 cm of mercury. The lengths of the mercury column and the trapped air column are 20 cm and 43 cm respectively. What will be the length of the air column when the tube is tilted slowly in a vertical plane through an angle of 60° ? Assume the temperature to remain constant.

36. Figure (24-E4) shows a cylindrical tube of length 30 cm which is partitioned by a tight-fitting separator. The separator is very weakly conducting and can freely slide along the tube. Ideal gases are filled in the two parts of the vessel. In the beginning, the temperatures in the parts A and B are 400 K and 100 K respectively. The separator slides to a momentary equilibrium position shown in the figure. Find the final equilibrium position of the separator, reached after a long time.

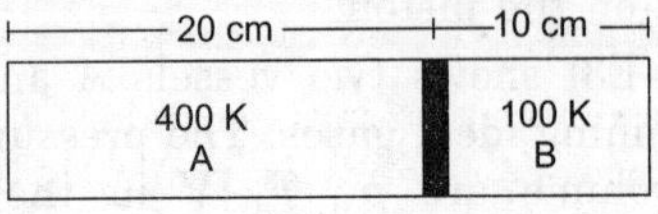

Figure 24-E4

37. A vessel of volume V_0 contains an ideal gas at pressure p_0 and temperature T. Gas is continuously pumped out of this vessel at a constant volume-rate $dV/dt = r$ keeping the temperature constant. The pressure of the gas being taken out equals the pressure inside the vessel. Find (a) the pressure of the gas as a function of time, (b) the time taken before half the original gas is pumped out.

38. One mole of an ideal gas undergoes a process

$$p = \frac{p_0}{1 + (V/V_0)^2}$$

where p_0 and V_0 are constants. Find the temperature of the gas when $V = V_0$.

39. Show that the internal energy of the air (treated as an ideal gas) contained in a room remains constant as the temperature changes between day and night. Assume that the atmospheric pressure around remains constant and the air in the room maintains this pressure by communicating with the surrounding through the windows, doors, etc.

40. Figure (24-E5) shows a cylindrical tube of radius 5 cm and length 20 cm. It is closed by a tight-fitting cork. The friction coefficient between the cork and the tube is 0·20. The tube contains an ideal gas at a pressure of 1 atm and a temperature of 300 K. The tube is slowly heated and it is found that the cork pops out when the temperature reaches 600 K. Let dN denote the magnitude of the normal contact force exerted by a small length dl of the cork along the periphery (see the figure). Assuming that the temperature of the gas is uniform at any instant, calculate $\frac{dN}{dl}$.

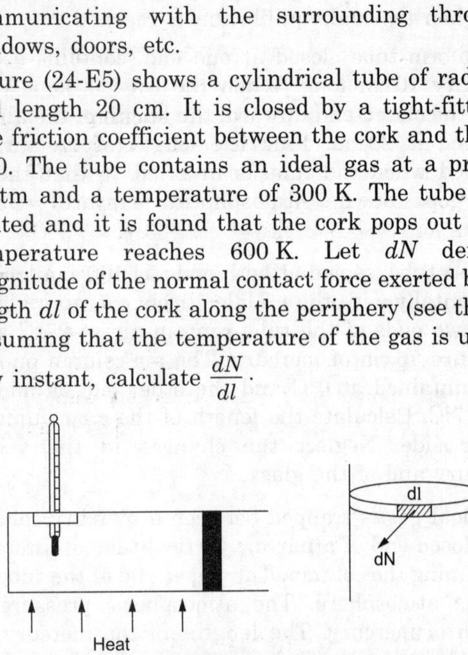

Figure 24-E5

41. Figure (24-E6) shows a cylindrical tube of cross-sectional area A fitted with two frictionless pistons. The pistons are connected to each other by a metallic wire. Initially, the temperature of the gas is T_0 and its pressure is p_0 which equals the atmospheric pressure. (a) What is the tension in the wire? (b) What will be the tension if the temperature is increased to $2T_0$?

Figure 24-E6

42. Figure (24-E7) shows a large closed cylindrical tank containing water. Initially the air trapped above the water surface has a height h_0 and pressure $2p_0$ where p_0 is the atmospheric pressure. There is a hole in the wall of the tank at a depth h_1 below the top from which water comes out. A long vertical tube is connected as shown. (a) Find the height h_2 of the water in the long tube above the top initially. (b) Find the speed with which water comes out of the hole. (c) Find the height of the water in the long tube above the top when the water stops coming out of the hole.

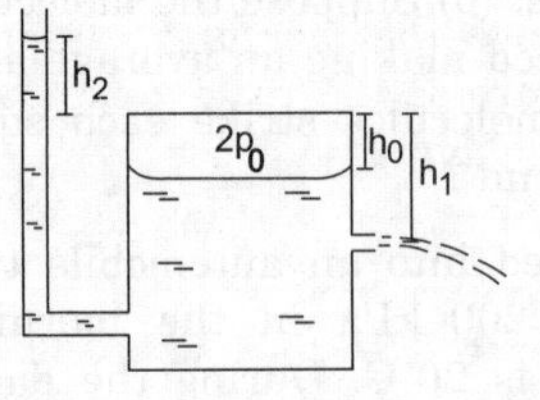

Figure 24-E7

43. An ideal gas is kept in a long cylindrical vessel fitted with a frictionless piston of cross-sectional area 10 cm^2 and weight 1 kg (figure 24-E8). The vessel itself is kept in a big chamber containing air at atmospheric pressure 100 kPa. The length of the gas column is 20 cm. If the chamber is now completely evacuated by an exhaust pump, what will be the length of the gas column? Assume the temperature to remain constant throughout the process.

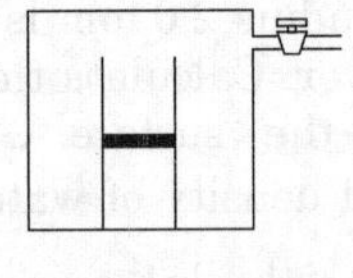

Figure 24-E8

44. An ideal gas is kept in a long cylindrical vessel fitted with a frictionless piston of cross-sectional area 10 cm^2 and weight 1 kg. The length of the gas column in the vessel is 20 cm. The atmospheric pressure is 100 kPa. The vessel is now taken into a spaceship revolving round the earth as a satellite. The air pressure in the spaceship is maintained at 100 kPa. Find the length of the gas column in the cylinder.

45. Two glass bulbs of equal volume are connected by a narrow tube and are filled with a gas at 0°C at a pressure of 76 cm of mercury. One of the bulbs is then placed in melting ice and the other is placed in a water bath maintained at 62°C. What is the new value of the pressure inside the bulbs ? The volume of the connecting tube is negligible.

46. The weather report reads, "Temperature 20°C : Relative humidity 100%". What is the dew point ?

47. The condition of air in a closed room is described as follows. Temperature = 25°C, relative humidity = 60%, pressure = 104 kPa. If all the water vapour is removed from the room without changing the temperature, what will be the new pressure? The saturation vapour pressure at 25°C = 3·2 kPa.

48. The temperature and the dew point in an open room are 20°C and 10°C. If the room temperature drops to 15°C, what will be the new dew point ?

49. Pure water vapour is trapped in a vessel of volume 10 cm^3. The relative humidity is 40%. The vapour is compressed slowly and isothermally. Find the volume of the vapour at which it will start condensing.

50. A barometer tube is 80 cm long (above the mercury reservoir). It reads 76 cm on a particular day. A small amount of water is introduced in the tube and the reading drops to 75·4 cm. Find the relative humidity in the space above the mercury column if the saturation vapour pressure at the room temperature is 1·0 cm.

51. Using figure (24.6) of the text, find the boiling point of methyl alcohol at 1 atm (760 mm of mercury) and at 0·5 atm.

52. The human body has an average temperature of 98 °F. Assume that the vapour pressure of the blood in the veins behaves like that of pure water. Find the minimum atmospheric pressure which is necessary to prevent the blood from boiling. Use figure (24.6) of the text for the vapour pressures.

53. A glass contains some water at room temperature 20°C. Refrigerated water is added to it slowly. When the temperature of the glass reaches 10°C, small droplets condense on the outer surface. Calculate the relative humidity in the room. The boiling point of water at a pressure of 17·5 mm of mercury is 20°C and at 8·9 mm of mercury it is 10°C.

54. 50 m^3 of saturated vapour is cooled down from 30°C to 20°C. Find the mass of the water condensed. The absolute humidity of saturated water vapour is 30 g m^{-3} at 30°C and 16 g m^{-3} at 20°C.

55. A barometer correctly reads the atmospheric pressure as 76 cm of mercury. Water droplets are slowly introduced into the barometer tube by a dropper. The height of the mercury column first decreases and then becomes constant. If the saturation vapour pressure at the atmospheric temperature is 0·80 cm of mercury, find the height of the mercury column when it reaches its minimum value.

56. 50 cc of oxygen is collected in an inverted gas jar over water. The atmospheric pressure is 99·4 kPa and the room temperature is 27°C. The water level in the jar is same as the level outside. The saturation vapour pressure at 27°C is 3·4 kPa. Calculate the number of moles of oxygen collected in the jar.

57. A faulty barometer contains certain amount of air and saturated water vapour. It reads 74·0 cm when the atmospheric pressure is 76·0 cm of mercury and reads 72·10 cm when the atmospheric pressure is 74·0 cm of mercury. Saturation vapour pressure at the air temperature = 1·0 cm of mercury. Find the length of the barometer tube above the mercury level in the reservoir.

58. On a winter day, the outside temperature is 0°C and relative humidity 40%. The air from outside comes into a room and is heated to 20°C. What is the relative humidity in the room ? The saturation vapour pressure at 0°C is 4·6 mm of mercury and at 20°C it is 18 mm of mercury.

59. The temperature and humidity of air are 27°C and 50% on a particular day. Calculate the amount of vapour that should be added to 1 cubic metre of air to saturate it. The saturation vapour pressure at 27°C = 3600 Pa.

60. The temperature and relative humidity in a room are 300 K and 20% respectively. The volume of the room is 50 m^3. The saturation vapour pressure at 300 K is 3·3 kPa. Calculate the mass of the water vapour present in the room.

61. The temperature and the relative humidity are 300 K and 20% in a room of volume 50 m^3. The floor is washed with water, 500 g of water sticking on the floor. Assuming no communication with the surrounding, find the relative humidity when the floor dries. The changes in temperature and pressure may be neglected. Saturation vapour pressure at 300 K = 3·3 kPa.

62. A bucket full of water is placed in a room at 15°C with initial relative humidity 40%. The volume of the room is 50 m^3. (a) How much water will evaporate ? (b) If the room temperature is increased by 5°C, how much more water will evaporate ? The saturation vapour pressure of water at 15°C and 20°C are 1·6 kPa and 2·4 kPa respectively.

□

ANSWERS

OBJECTIVE I

1. (d)	2. (b)	3. (a)	4. (d)	5. (a)	6. (a)
7. (c)	8. (c)	9. (b)	10. (a)	11. (c)	12. (d)
13. (c)	14. (b)	15. (a)	16. (d)	17. (a)	

OBJECTICE II

1. (c), (d)	2. (b)	3. (b)
4. (c)	5. (d)	6. (a), (c)
7. (d)		

EXERCISES

1. $2{\cdot}24 \times 10^{-2}\ m^3$
2. $2{\cdot}685 \times 10^{19}$
3. $3{\cdot}53 \times 10^{11}$
4. 1·43 mg
5. 1 : 1
6. $8{\cdot}0 \times 10^{15}$
7. 375 K
8. $1{\cdot}24 \times 10^{5}$ Pa
9. $28{\cdot}3\ g\ mol^{-1}$
10. 0·987
11. 3 : 1
12. $1930\ m\ s^{-1}$, 1200 K
13. $1300\ m\ s^{-1}$
14. 310 K
15. 8·0 hour
16. $8{\cdot}0 \times 10^{-24}\ kg\ m\ s^{-1}$
17. 1 : 2
18. 11800 K
19. 3·74
20. 1·18
21. $1{\cdot}23 \times 10^{10}$
22. (a) $1780\ m\ s^{-1}$ (b) $1{\cdot}2 \times 10^{28}$
23. 209 kPa
24. 0·16 g
25. 2·2 mm
26. 0·14
27. 196°C
28. *T*/2
29. $2250\ N\ m^{-2}$
30. 25 cm
32. (a) 0·058 g (b) 0·0468 g (c) 73·0 kPa
33. 15 cm
34. 36·5 cm
35. 48 cm
36. 10 cm from the left end
37. (a) $p = p_0 e^{-\gamma t/V_0}$ (b) $\dfrac{V_0 \ln 2}{\gamma}$
38. $\dfrac{p_0 V_0}{2R}\ mol^{-1}$
40. $1{\cdot}25 \times 10^{4}\ N\ m^{-1}$
41. (a) zero (b) $p_0 A$
42. (a) $\dfrac{p_0}{\rho g} - h_0$ (b) $\left[\dfrac{2}{\rho}\left(p_0 + \rho g (h_1 - h_0)\right)\right]^{1/2}$ (c) $-h_1$
43. 2·2 m
44. 22 cm
45. 84 cm of mercury
46. 20°C
47. 102 kPa
48. 10°C
49. $4{\cdot}0\ cm^3$
50. 60%
51. 65°C, 48°C
52. 50 mm of mercury
53. 51%
54. 700 g
55. 75·2 cm
56. $1{\cdot}93 \times 10^{-3}$
57. 91·1 cm
58. 9·5%
59. 13 g
60. 238 g
61. 62%
62. (a) 361 g (b) 296 g

□

CHAPTER 25

CALORIMETRY

25.1 HEAT AS A FORM OF ENERGY

When two bodies at different temperatures are placed in contact, the hotter body cools down and the colder body warms up. Energy is thus transferred from a body at higher temperature to a body at lower temperature when they are brought in contact.

The energy being transferred between two bodies or between adjacent parts of a body as a result of temperature difference is called *heat.*

Thus, heat is a form of energy. It is energy in transit whenever temperature differences exist. Once it is transferred it becomes the internal energy of the receiving body. It should be clearly understood that the word "heat" is meaningful only as long as the energy is being transferred. Thus, expressions like "heat in a body" or "heat of a body" are meaningless.

25.2 UNITS OF HEAT

As heat is just energy in transit, its unit in SI is joule. However, another unit of heat "calorie" is in wide use. This unit was formulated much before it was recognised that heat is a form of energy. The old day definition of calorie is as follows:

The amount of heat needed to increase the temperature of 1 g *of water from* 14·5°C to 15·5°C *at a pressure of* 1 atm *is called* 1 calorie.

The amount of heat needed to raise the temperature of 1 g of water by 1°C depends slightly on the actual temperature of water and the pressure. That is why, the range 14·5°C to 15·5°C and the pressure 1 atm was specified in the definition. We shall ignore this small variation and use one calorie to mean the amount of heat needed to increase the temperature of 1 g of water by 1°C at any region of temperature and pressure.

The calorie is now defined in terms of joule as 1 cal = 4·186 joule. We also use the unit kilocalorie which is equal to 1000 calorie as the name indicates.

Example 25.1

What is the kinetic energy of a 10 kg *mass moving at a speed of* 36 km h^{-1} *in calorie ?*

Solution :

The kinetic energy is

$$\frac{1}{2}mv^2 = \frac{1}{2} \times 10 \text{ kg} \times \left(\frac{36 \times 10^3 \text{ m}}{3600 \text{ s}}\right)^2$$

$$= 500 \text{ J} = \frac{500}{4 \cdot 186} \text{ cal} \approx 120 \text{ cal.}$$

25.3 PRINCIPLE OF CALORIMETRY

A simple calorimeter is a vessel generally made of copper with a stirrer of the same material. The vessel is kept in a wooden box to isolate it thermally from the surrounding. A thermometer is used to measure the temperature of the contents of the calorimeter.

Objects at different temperatures are made to come in contact with each other in the calorimeter. As a result, heat is exchanged between the objects as well as with the calorimeter. Neglecting any heat exchange with the surrounding, the principle of calorimetry states that *the total heat given by the hot objects equals the total heat received by the cold objects.*

25.4 SPECIFIC HEAT CAPACITY AND MOLAR HEAT CAPACITY

When we supply heat to a body, its temperature increases. The amount of heat absorbed depends on the mass of the body, the change in temperature, the material of the body as well as the surrounding conditions, such as pressure. We write the equation

$$Q = ms\Delta\theta \qquad \dots (25.1)$$

where $\Delta\theta$ is the change in temperature, m is the mass of the body, Q is the heat supplied, and s is a constant for the given material under the given surrounding conditions. The constant s is called *specific heat capacity* of the substance. When a solid or a liquid is kept open in the atmosphere and heated, the pressure remains constant. Table (25.1) gives the specific heat capacities of some of the solids and liquids under constant pressure condition. As can be seen from equation (25.1), the SI unit for specific heat capacity is J kg^{-1} K^{-1} which is the same as J kg^{-1} $°C^{-1}$. The specific heat capacity may also be expressed in cal g^{-1} K^{-1} (same as cal g^{-1} $°C^{-1}$). Specific heat capacity is also called *specific heat* in short.

Table 25.1 : Specific heat capacities of some materials

Material	cal g^{-1} $°C^{-1}$	J kg^{-1} K^{-1}	Material	Cal g^{-1} $°C^{-1}$	J kg^{-1} K^{-1}
Water	1·00	4186	Glass	0·1–0·2	419–837
Ethanol	0·55	2302	Iron	0·112	470
Paraffin	0·51	2135	Copper	0·093	389
Ice	0·50	2093	Mercury	0·033	138
Steam	0·46	1926	Lead	0·031	130
Aluminium	0·215	900			

The amount of substance in the given body may also be measured in terms of the number of moles. Equation (25.1) may be rewritten as

$$Q = nC\Delta\theta$$

where n is the number of moles in the sample. The constant C is called *molar heat capacity*.

Example 25.2

A copper block of mass 60 g *is heated till its temperature is increased by* 20°C. *Find the heat supplied to the block. Specific heat capacity of copper* = 0·09 cal g^{-1} $°C^{-1}$.

Solution :

The heat supplied is $Q = ms\Delta\theta$

$= (60 \text{ g}) (0·09 \text{ cal g}^{-1} °\text{C}^{-1}) (20°\text{C}) = 108 \text{ cal}.$

The quantity ms is called the *heat capacity of the body*. Its unit is J K^{-1}. The mass of water having the same heat capacity as a given body is called the *water equivalent* of the body.

25.5 DETERMINATION OF SPECIFIC HEAT CAPACITY IN LABORATORY

Figure (25.1) shows Regnault's apparatus to determine the specific heat capacity of a solid heavier than water, and insoluble in it. A wooden partition P separates a steam chamber O and a calorimeter C. The steam chamber O is a double-walled cylindrical vessel. Steam can be passed in the space between the two walls through an inlet A and it can escape through an outlet B. The upper part of the vessel is closed by a cork. The given solid may be suspended in the vessel by a thread passing through the cork. A thermometer T_1 is also inserted into the vessel to record the temperature of the solid. The steam chamber is kept on a wooden platform with a removable wooden disc D closing the bottom hole of the chamber.

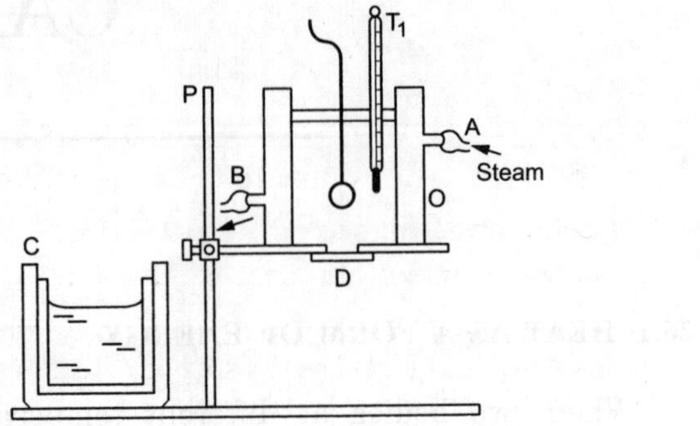

Figure 25.1

To start with, the experimental solid (in the form of a ball or a block) is weighed and then suspended in the steam chamber. Steam is prepared by boiling water in a separate boiler and is passed through the steam chamber. A calorimeter with a stirrer is weighed and sufficient amount of water is kept in it so that the solid may be completely immersed in it. The calorimeter is again weighed with water to get the mass of the water. The initial temperature of the water is noted.

When the temperature of the solid becomes constant (say for 15 minutes), the partition P is removed, the calorimeter is taken below the steam chamber, the wooden disc D is removed and the thread is cut to drop the solid in the calorimeter. The calorimeter is taken to its original place and is stirred. The maximum temperature of the mixture is noted.

Calculation:

Let the mass of the solid $= m_1$

mass of the calorimeter and the stirrer $= m_2$

mass of the water $= m_3$

specific heat capacity of the solid $= s_1$

specific heat capacity of the material of the calorimeter (and stirrer) $= s_2$

specific heat capacity of water $= s_3$

initial temperature of the solid $= \theta_1$

initial temperature of the calorimeter, stirrer and water $= \theta_2$

final temperature of the mixture $= \theta$.

We have,

heat lost by the solid $= m_1 s_1(\theta_1 - \theta)$

heat gained by the calorimeter (and the stirrer) $= m_2 s_2(\theta - \theta_2)$

and heat gained by the water $= m_3s_3(\theta - \theta_2)$.

Assuming no loss of heat to the surrounding, the heat lost by the solid goes into the calorimeter, stirrer and water. Thus,

$$m_1s_1(\theta_1 - \theta) = m_2s_2(\theta - \theta_2) + m_3s_3(\theta - \theta_2) \quad \dots \text{(i)}$$

or, $$s_1 = \frac{(m_2s_2 + m_3s_3)(\theta - \theta_2)}{m_1(\theta_1 - \theta)}.$$

Knowing the specific heat capacity of water ($s_3 = 4186 \text{ J kg}^{-1} \text{ K}^{-1}$) and that of the material of the calorimeter and the stirrer ($s_2 = 389 \text{ J kg}^{-1} \text{ K}^{-1}$ if the material be copper), one can calculate s_1.

Specific heat capacity of a liquid can also be measured with the Regnault's apparatus. Here a solid of known specific heat capacity s_1 is used and the experimental liquid is taken in the calorimeter in place of water. The solid should be denser than the liquid. Using the same procedure and with the same symbols we get an equation identical to equation (i) above, that is,

$$m_1s_1(\theta_1 - \theta) = m_2s_2(\theta - \theta_2) + m_3s_3(\theta - \theta_2)$$

in which s_3 is the specific heat capacity of the liquid. We get,

$$s_3 = \frac{m_1s_1(\theta_1 - \theta)}{m_3(\theta - \theta_2)} - \frac{m_2s_2}{m_3}.$$

25.6 SPECIFIC LATENT HEAT OF FUSION AND VAPORIZATION

Apart from raising the temperature, heat supplied to a body may cause a phase change such as solid to liquid or liquid to vapour.

During this process of melting or vaporization, the temperature remains constant. The amount of heat needed to melt a solid of mass m may be written as

$$Q = mL \quad \dots (25.2)$$

where L is a constant for the given material (and surrounding conditions). This constant L is called *specific latent heat of fusion*. The term *latent heat of fusion* is also used to mean the same thing. Equation (25.2) is also valid when a liquid changes its phase to vapour. The constant L in this case is called the *specific latent heat of vaporization* or simply *latent heat of vaporization*. When a vapour condenses or a liquid solidifies, heat is released to the surrounding.

In solids, the forces between the molecules are large and the molecules are almost fixed in their positions inside the solid. In a liquid, the forces between the molecules are weaker and the molecules may move freely inside the volume of the liquid. However, they are not able to come out of the surface. In vapours or gases, the intermolecular forces are almost negligible and the molecules may move freely anywhere in the container. When a solid melts, its molecules move apart against the strong molecular attraction. This needs energy which must be supplied from outside. Thus, the internal energy of a given body is larger in liquid phase than in solid phase. Similarly, the internal energy of a given body in vapour phase is larger than that in liquid phase.

Example 25.3

A piece of ice of mass 100 g *and at temperature* 0°C *is put in* 200 g *of water at* 25°C. *How much ice will melt as the temperature of the water reaches* 0°C ? *The specific heat capacity of water* $= 4200 \text{ J kg}^{-1} \text{ K}^{-1}$ *and the specific latent heat of fusion of ice* $= 3{\cdot}4 \times 10^5 \text{ J kg}^{-1}$.

Solution :

The heat released as the water cools down from 25°C to 0°C is

$$Q = ms\Delta\theta = (0{\cdot}2 \text{ kg})(4200 \text{ J kg}^{-1} \text{ K}^{-1})(25 \text{ K}) = 21000 \text{ J}.$$

The amount of ice melted by this much heat is given by

$$m = \frac{Q}{L} = \frac{21000 \text{ J}}{3{\cdot}4 \times 10^5 \text{ J kg}^{-1}} = 62 \text{ g}.$$

25.7 MEASUREMENT OF SPECIFIC LATENT HEAT OF FUSION OF ICE

An empty calorimeter (together with a stirrer) is weighed. About two third of the calorimeter is filled with water and is weighed again. Thus, one gets the mass of the water. The initial temperature of the water is measured with the help of a thermometer. A piece of ice is taken and as it starts melting it is dried with a blotting paper and put into the calorimeter. The water is stirred keeping the ice always fully immersed in it. The minimum temperature reached is recorded. This represents the temperature when all the ice has melted. The calorimeter with its contents is weighed again. Thus, one can get the mass of the ice that has melted in the calorimeter.

Calculation:

Let the mass of the calorimeter (with stirrer) $= m_1$

mass of water $= m_2$

mass of ice $= m_3$

initial temperature of the calorimeter and the water (in Celsius) $= \theta_1$

final temperature of the calorimeter and the water (in Celsius) $= \theta_2$

temperature of the melting ice = 0°C

specific latent heat of fusion of ice $= L$

specific heat capacity of the material of the calorimeter (and stirrer) = s_1

specific heat capacity of water = s_2.

We have,

heat lost by the calorimeter (and the stirrer)

$$= m_1 s_1(\theta_1 - \theta_2)$$

heat lost by the water kept initially in the calorimeter $= m_2 s_2(\theta_1 - \theta_2)$

heat gained by the ice during its fusion to water $= m_3 L$

heat gained by this water in coming from 0°C to θ_2

$$= m_3 s_2 \theta_2.$$

Assuming no loss of heat to the surrounding,

$$m_1 s_1(\theta_1 - \theta_2) + m_2 s_2(\theta_1 - \theta_2) = m_3 L + m_3 s_2 \theta_2$$

$$\text{or,} \quad L = \frac{(m_1 s_1 + m_2 s_2)(\theta_1 - \theta_2)}{m_3} - s_2 \theta_2.$$

Knowing the specific heat capacity of water and that of the material of the calorimeter and the stirrer, one can calculate the specific latent heat of fusion of ice L.

25.8 MEASUREMENT OF SPECIFIC LATENT HEAT OF VAPORIZATION OF WATER

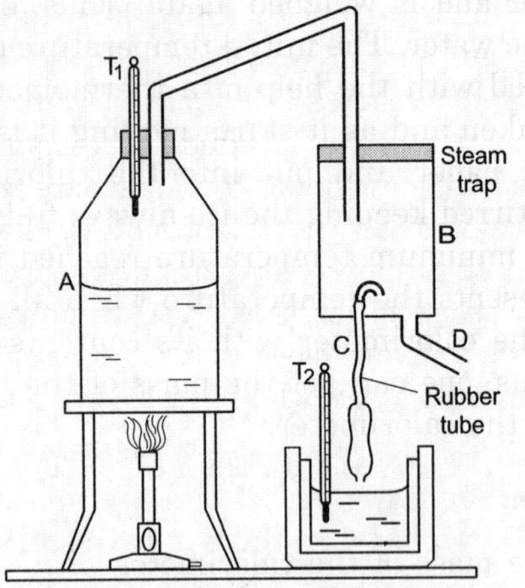

Figure 25.2

Figure (25.2) shows the arrangement used to measure the specific latent heat of vaporization of water. Steam is prepared by boiling water in a boiler A. The cork of the boiler has two holes. A thermometer T_1 is inserted into one to measure the temperature of the steam and the other contains a bent glass tube to carry the steam to a steam trap B. A tube C with one end bent and the other end terminated in a jet is fitted in the steam trap. Another tube D is fitted in the trap which is used to drain out the extra steam and water condensed at the bottom.

To start the experiment, an empty calorimeter (together with the stirrer) is weighed. About half of it is filled with water and is weighed again. Thus, one gets the mass of the water. The initial temperature of the water and the calorimeter is measured by a thermometer T_2. Water is kept in the boiler A and is heated. As it boils, the steam passes to the steam trap and then comes out through the tubes C and D. After some steam has gone out (say for 5 minutes), the temperature of the steam is noted. The calorimeter with the water is kept below the tube C so that steam goes into the calorimeter. The water in the calorimeter is continuously stirred and the calorimeter is removed after the temperature in it increases by about 5°C. The final temperature of the water in the calorimeter is noted. The calorimeter together with the water (including the water condensed) is weighed. From this, one gets the mass of the steam that condensed in the calorimeter.

Let the mass of the calorimeter (with the stirrer) $= m_1$

mass of the water $= m_2$

mass of the steam condensed $= m_3$

temperature of the steam $= \theta_1$

initial temperature of the water in the calorimeter $= \theta_2$

final temperature of the water in the calorimeter $= \theta_3$

specific latent heat of vaporization of water $= L$

specific heat capacity of the material of the calorimeter (and the stirrer) $= s_1$

specific heat capacity of water $= s_2$.

We have,

heat gained by the calorimeter (and the stirrer) $= m_1 s_1(\theta_3 - \theta_2)$

heat gained by the water kept initially in the calorimeter $= m_2 s_2(\theta_3 - \theta_2)$

heat lost by the steam in condensing $= m_3 L$

heat lost by the condensed water in cooling from temperature θ_1 to $\theta_3 = m_3 s_2(\theta_1 - \theta_3)$.

Assuming no loss of heat to the surrounding,

$$m_1 s_1(\theta_3 - \theta_2) + m_2 s_2(\theta_3 - \theta_2) = m_3 L + m_3 s_2(\theta_1 - \theta_3)$$

$$\text{or,} \quad L = \frac{(m_1 s_1 + m_2 s_2)(\theta_3 - \theta_2)}{m_3} - s_2(\theta_1 - \theta_3).$$

Knowing the specific heat capacity of water and that of the material of the calorimeter, one can calculate the specific latent heat of vaporization of water L.

Example 25.4

A calorimeter of water equivalent 15 g *contains* 165 g *of water at* 25°C. *Steam at* 100°C *is passed through the water for some time. The temperature is increased to* 30°C *and the mass of the calorimeter and its contents is increased by* 1·5 g. *Calculate the specific latent heat of vaporization of water. Specific heat capacity of water is* 1 cal g^{-1} °C^{-1}.

Solution : Let L be the specific latent heat of vaporization of water. The mass of the steam condensed is 1·5 g. Heat lost in condensation of steam is

$$Q_1 = (1{\cdot}5\ \text{g})\, L.$$

The condensed water cools from 100°C to 30°C. Heat lost in this process is

$$Q_2 = (1{\cdot}5\ \text{g})\,(1\ \text{cal g}^{-1}\,°\text{C}^{-1})\,(70°\text{C}) = 105\ \text{cal}.$$

Heat supplied to the calorimeter and to the cold water during the rise in temperature from 25°C to 30°C is

$$Q_3 = (15\ \text{g} + 165\ \text{g})\,(1\ \text{cal g}^{-1}\,°\text{C}^{-1})\,(5°\text{C}) = 900\ \text{cal}.$$

If no heat is lost to the surrounding,

$$(1{\cdot}5\ \text{g})\, L + 105\ \text{cal} = 900\ \text{cal}$$

or,
$$L = 530\ \text{cal g}^{-1}.$$

25.9 MECHANICAL EQUIVALENT OF HEAT

In early days heat was not recognised as a form of energy. Heat was supposed to be something needed to raise the temperature of a body or to change its phase. Calorie was defined as the unit of heat. A number of experiments were performed to show that the temperature may also be increased by doing mechanical work on the system. These experiments established that heat is equivalent to mechanical energy and measured how much mechanical energy is equivalent to a calorie. If mechanical work W produces the same temperature change as heat H, we write,

$$W = JH \qquad \dots (25.3)$$

where J is called *mechanical equivalent of heat*. It is clear that if W and H are both measured in the same unit then $J = 1$. If W is measured in joule (work done by a force of 1 N in displacing an object by 1 m in its direction) and H in calorie (heat required to raise the temperature of 1 g of water by 1°C) then J is expressed in joule per calorie. The value of J gives how many joules of mechanical work is needed to raise the temperature of 1 g of water by 1°C. We describe below a laboratory method to measure the mechanical equivalent of heat.

Searle's Cone Method

Figure (25.3) shows the apparatus. A conical vessel B just fits in another conical vessel A of the same material. The outer vessel A is connected to a spindle C which may be rotated at high speed by an electric motor or by hand. The number of rotations made in a given time can be recorded.

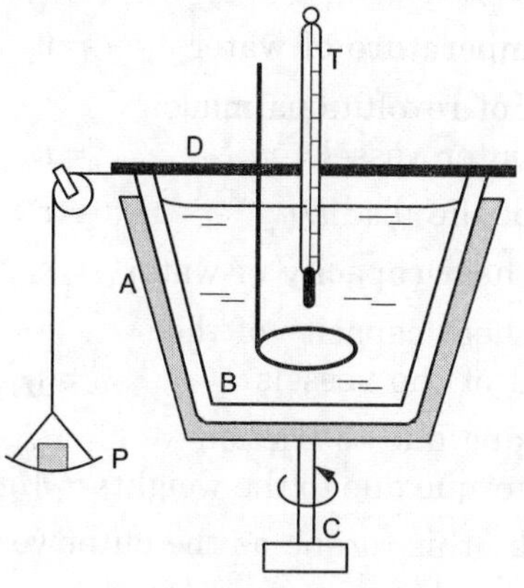

Figure 25.3

The inner vessel B is fitted with a grooved wooden disc D. A cord is wound around the groove and is connected to a hanging pan P after passing through a fixed pulley. Weights can be put on this pan.

The wooden disc D contains two holes through which a thermometer and a stirrer can pass into the inner vessel. If the outer vessel is rotated, it tries to drag the inner vessel with it due to the friction between the surfaces of the cones. The friction produces a net torque Γ about the central axis. The hanging weights also produce a torque about the central axis which is equal to Mgr where M is the total mass of the pan and the weights on it. If the direction of rotation is properly chosen, these torques may be opposite to each other. Also, the value of M may be adjusted for a given speed of the outer vessel so that $Mgr = \Gamma$. In such a case the inner vessel does not move.

To start the experiment, a measured mass of water is taken in the inner vessel and the thermometer and the stirrer are placed in their positions. The masses of the vessels A and B are also known. The outer vessel A is rotated by rotating the spindle either by a motor or by hand. The direction of rotation is chosen to make sure that the frictional torque and the torque due to the weight Mg oppose each other. The value of M is so adjusted that the inner vessel does not move. The temperature of the water is noted at an initial instant after the adjustments are made. The water is continuously stirred with the help of the stirrer and the temperature is noted at the final instant when it is increased roughly by 5°C. The number of revolutions made by the spindle during this period is noted.

Suppose,

the mass of the water taken $= m_1$

mass of the two vessels taken together $= m_2$

mass of the pan and the weights on it $= M$

initial temperature of water $= \theta_1$

final temperature of water $= \theta_2$

number of revolutions made by the outer vessel $= n$

radius of the disc D $= r$

specific heat capacity of water $= s_1$

specific heat capacity of the material of the vessels $= s_2$.

The torque due to friction

= The torque due to the weights $= Mgr$.

Work done by this torque as the outer vessel slides on the inner one $= \Gamma\theta$

$$= Mgr.2\pi n.$$

The heat needed to raise the temperature of water

$$= m_1 s_1(\theta_2 - \theta_1).$$

Heat needed to raise the temperature of the vessels

$$= m_2 s_2(\theta_2 - \theta_1).$$

The total amount of heat needed to raise the temperature is $(m_1 s_1 + m_2 s_2)(\theta_2 - \theta_1)$. Thus, the mechanical work $2\pi n\, Mgr$ produces the same effect as the heat $(m_1 s_1 + m_2 s_2)(\theta_2 - \theta_1)$.

Thus, $$2\pi n\, Mgr = J(m_1 s_1 + m_2 s_2)(\theta_2 - \theta_1)$$

or, $$J = \frac{2\pi n\, Mgr}{(m_1 s_1 + m_2 s_2)(\theta_2 - \theta_1)}.$$

Putting s_1, s_2 in cal gm^{-1} °C^{-1} (for water $s = 1$ cal g^{-1} °C^{-1}), one gets J in joule per calorie. Experiments give a value $J = 4{\cdot}186$ J cal^{-1}.

Although heat is the energy in transit due to temperature difference, the word "heat" is also used for the mechanical work that raises the temperature of a body or that which causes a phase change. Thus, if a block slides on a rough surface, its kinetic energy may be used to increase the temperature of the block and the surface. We say that "heat is developed" when the block slides on the surface. Such a use of the word "heat" is made only due to tradition, though it is not strictly correct. It is better to say that thermal energy is produced.

Worked Out Examples

1. *Calculate the amount of heat required to convert* 1·00 kg *of ice at* –10°C *into steam at* 100°C *at normal pressure. Specific heat capacity of ice* = 2100 J kg^{-1} K^{-1}, *latent heat of fusion of ice* = 3·36 × 10^{5} J kg^{-1}, *specific heat capacity of water* = 4200 J kg^{-1} K^{-1} *and latent heat of vaporization of water* = 2·25 × 10^{6} J kg^{-1}.

Solution : Heat required to take the ice from –10°C to 0°C

$$= (1\text{ kg})(2100\text{ J kg}^{-1}\text{ K}^{-1})(10\text{ K}) = 21000\text{ J}.$$

Heat required to melt the ice at 0°C to water

$$= (1\text{ kg})(3{\cdot}36 \times 10^{5}\text{ J kg}^{-1}) = 336000\text{ J}.$$

Heat required to take 1 kg of water from 0°C to 100°C

$$= (1\text{ kg})(4200\text{ J kg}^{-1}\text{ K}^{-1})(100\text{ K}) = 420000\text{ J}.$$

Heat required to convert 1 kg of water at 100°C into steam

$$= (1\text{ kg})(2{\cdot}25 \times 10^{6}\text{ J kg}^{-1}) = 2{\cdot}25 \times 10^{6}\text{ J}.$$

Total heat required = 3·03 × 10^{6} J.

2. *A* 5 g *piece of ice at* –20°C *is put into* 10 g *of water at* 30°C. *Assuming that heat is exchanged only between the ice and the water, find the final temperature of the mixture. Specific heat capacity of ice* = 2100 J kg^{-1} °C^{-1}, *specific heat capacity of water* = 4200 J kg^{-1} °C^{-1} *and latent heat of fusion of ice* = 3·36 × 10^{5} J kg^{-1}.

Solution : The heat given by the water when it cools down from 30°C to 0°C is

$$(0{\cdot}01\text{ kg})(4200\text{ J kg}^{-1}\,°\text{C}^{-1})(30°\text{C}) = 1260\text{ J}.$$

The heat required to bring the ice to 0°C is

$$(0{\cdot}005\text{ kg})(2100\text{ J kg}^{-1}\,°\text{C}^{-1})(20°\text{C}) = 210\text{ J}.$$

The heat required to melt 5 g of ice is

$$(0{\cdot}005\text{ kg})(3{\cdot}36 \times 10^{5}\text{ J kg}^{-1}) = 1680\text{ J}.$$

We see that whole of the ice cannot be melted as the required amount of heat is not provided by the water. Also, the heat is enough to bring the ice to 0°C. Thus the final temperature of the mixture is 0°C with some of the ice melted.

3. *An aluminium container of mass* 100 g *contains* 200 g *of ice at* –20°C. *Heat is added to the system at a rate of* 100 cal s^{-1}. *What is the temperature of the system after* 4 *minutes ? Draw a rough sketch showing the variation in the temperature of the system as a function of time. Specific heat capacity of ice* = 0.5 cal g^{-1} °C^{-1}, *specific heat capacity of aluminium* = 0·2 cal g^{-1} °C^{-1}, *specific heat capacity of water* = 1 cal g^{-1} °C^{-1} *and latent heat of fusion of ice* = 80 cal g^{-1}.

Solution : Total heat supplied to the system in 4 minutes is $Q = 100\ \text{cal s}^{-1} \times 240\ \text{s} = 2{\cdot}4 \times 10^{4}$ cal.

The heat required to take the system from $-20°C$ to $0°C$

$$= (100\ \text{g}) \times (0{\cdot}2\ \text{cal g}^{-1}\ °\text{C}^{-1}) \times (20°\text{C}) +$$
$$(200\ \text{g}) \times (0{\cdot}5\ \text{cal g}^{-1}\ °\text{C}^{-1}) \times (20°\text{C})$$
$$= 400\ \text{cal} + 2000\ \text{cal} = 2400\ \text{cal}.$$

The time taken in this process $= \frac{2400}{100}\ \text{s} = 24\ \text{s}.$

The heat required to melt the ice at 0°C

$$= (200\ \text{g})\ (80\ \text{cal g}^{-1}) = 16000\ \text{cal}.$$

The time taken in this process $= \frac{16000}{100}\ \text{s} = 160\ \text{s}.$

If the final temperature is θ, the heat required to take the system to the final temperature is

$$= (100\ \text{g})\ (0{\cdot}2\ \text{cal g}^{-1}\ °\text{C}^{-1})\ \theta + (200\ \text{g})\ (1\ \text{cal g}^{-1}\ °\text{C}^{-1})\ \theta.$$

Thus,

$$2{\cdot}4 \times 10^{4}\ \text{cal} = 2400\ \text{cal} + 16000\ \text{cal} + (220\ \text{cal}\ °\text{C}^{-1})\ \theta$$

or, $$\theta = \frac{5600\ \text{cal}}{220\ \text{cal}\ °\text{C}^{-1}} = 25{\cdot}5°\text{C}.$$

The variation in the temperature as a function of time is sketched in figure (25-W1).

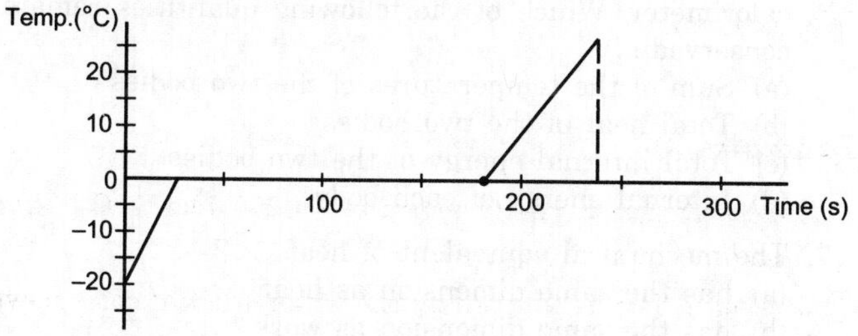

Figure 25-W1

4. *A thermally isolated vessel contains* 100 g *of water at* 0°C. *When air above the water is pumped out, some of the water freezes and some evaporates at* 0°C *itself. Calculate the mass of the ice formed if no water is left in the vessel. Latent heat of vaporization of water at* 0°C = $2{\cdot}10 \times 10^{6}\ \text{J kg}^{-1}$ *and latent heat of fusion of ice* = $3{\cdot}36 \times 10^{5}\ \text{J kg}^{-1}$.

Solution : Total mass of the water $= M = 100$ g.

Latent heat of vaporization of water at 0°C

$$= L_1 = 21{\cdot}0 \times 10^{5}\ \text{J kg}^{-1}.$$

Latent heat of fusion of ice $= L_2 = 3{\cdot}36 \times 10^{5}\ \text{J kg}^{-1}$.

Suppose, the mass of the ice formed $= m$.

Then the mass of water evaporated $= M - m$.

Heat taken by the water to evaporate $= (M - m)\ L_1$

and heat given by the water in freezing $= mL_2$.

Thus, $mL_2 = (M - m)L_1$

or, $$m = \frac{ML_1}{L_1 + L_2}$$

$$= \frac{(100\ \text{g})\ (21{\cdot}0 \times 10^{5}\ \text{J kg}^{-1})}{(21{\cdot}0 + 3{\cdot}36) \times 10^{5}\ \text{J kg}^{-1}} = 86\ \text{g}.$$

5. *A lead bullet penetrates into a solid object and melts. Assuming that 50% of its kinetic energy was used to heat it, calculate the initial speed of the bullet. The initial temperature of the bullet is 27°C and its melting point is 327°C. Latent heat of fusion of lead* = $2{\cdot}5 \times 10^{4}\ \text{J kg}^{-1}$ *and specific heat capacity of lead* = $125\ \text{J kg}^{1}\ \text{K}^{1}$.

Solution : Let the mass of the bullet = m.

Heat required to take the bullet from 27°C to 327°C

$$= m \times (125\ \text{J kg}^{-1}\ \text{K}^{-1})\ (300\ \text{K})$$
$$= m \times (3{\cdot}75 \times 10^{4}\ \text{J kg}^{-1}).$$

Heat required to melt the bullet

$$= m \times (2{\cdot}5 \times 10^{4}\ \text{J kg}^{-1}).$$

If the initial speed be v, the kinetic energy is $\frac{1}{2}mv^2$ and hence the heat developed is $\frac{1}{2}\left(\frac{1}{2}mv^2\right) = \frac{1}{4}mv^2$. Thus,

$$\frac{1}{4}mv^2 = m(3{\cdot}75 + 2{\cdot}5) \times 10^{4}\ \text{J kg}^{-1}$$

or, $$v = 500\ \text{m s}^{-1}.$$

6. *A lead ball at 30°C is dropped from a height of* 6·2 km. *The ball is heated due to the air resistance and it completely melts just before reaching the ground. The molten substance falls slowly on the ground. Calculate the latent heat of fusion of lead. Specific heat capacity of lead* = $126\ \text{J kg}^{-1}\ °\text{C}^{-1}$ *and melting point of lead* = 330°C. *Assume that any mechanical energy lost is used to heat the ball. Use* $g = 10\ \text{m s}^{-2}$.

Solution : The initial gravitational potential energy of the ball

$$= mgh$$
$$= m \times (10\ \text{m s}^{-2}) \times (6{\cdot}2 \times 10^{3}\ \text{m})$$
$$= m \times (6{\cdot}2 \times 10^{4}\ \text{m}^2\ \text{s}^{-2}) = m \times (6{\cdot}2 \times 10^{4}\ \text{J kg}^{-1}).$$

All this energy is used to heat the ball as it reaches the ground with a small velocity. Energy required to take the ball from 30°C to 330°C is

$$m \times (126\ \text{J kg}^{-1}\ °\text{C}^{-1}) \times (300°\text{C})$$
$$= m \times 37800\ \text{J kg}^{-1}$$

and energy required to melt the ball at 330°C

$$= mL$$

where L = latent heat of fusion of lead.

Thus,

$$m \times (6{\cdot}2 \times 10^{4}\ \text{J kg}^{-1}) = m \times 37800\ \text{J kg}^{-1} + mL$$

or, $$L = 2{\cdot}4 \times 10^{4}\ \text{J kg}^{-1}.$$

QUESTIONS FOR SHORT ANSWER

1. Is heat a conserved quantity ?
2. The calorie is defined as 1 cal = 4·186 joule. Why not as 1 cal = 4 J to make the conversions easy ?
3. A calorimeter is kept in a wooden box to insulate it thermally from the surroundings. Why is it necessary ?
4. In a calorimeter, the heat given by the hot object is assumed to be equal to the heat taken by the cold object. Does it mean that heat of the two objects taken together remains constant ?
5. In Regnault's apparatus for measuring specific heat capacity of a solid, there is an inlet and an outlet in the steam chamber. The inlet is near the top and the outlet is near the bottom. Why is it better than the opposite choice where the inlet is near the bottom and the outlet is near the top ?
6. When a solid melts or a liquid boils, the temperature does not increase even when heat is supplied. Where does the energy go ?
7. What is the specific heat capacity of (a) melting ice (b) boiling water ?
8. A person's skin is more severely burnt when put in contact with 1 g of steam at 100°C than when put in contact with 1 g of water at 100°C. Explain.
9. The atmospheric temperature in the cities on sea-coast change very little. Explain.
10. Should a thermometer bulb have large heat capacity or small heat capacity ?

OBJECTIVE I

1. The specific heat capacity of a body depends on
(a) the heat given (b) the temperature raised
(c) the mass of the body (d) the material of the body.
2. Water equivalent of a body is measured in
(a) kg (b) calorie (c) kelvin (d) m^3.
3. When a hot liquid is mixed with a cold liquid, the temperature of the mixture
(a) first decreases then becomes constant
(b) first increases then becomes constant
(c) continuously increases
(d) is undefined for some time and then becomes nearly constant.
4. Which of the following pairs represent units of the same physical quantity ?
(a) Kelvin and joule (b) Kelvin and calorie
(c) Newton and calorie (d) Joule and calorie
5. Which of the following pairs of physical quantities may be represented in the same unit ?
(a) Heat and temperature (b) Temperature and mole
(c) Heat and work (d) Specific heat and heat
6. Two bodies at different temperatures are mixed in a calorimeter. Which of the following quantities remains conserved ?
(a) Sum of the temperatures of the two bodies
(b) Total heat of the two bodies
(c) Total internal energy of the two bodies
(d) Internal energy of each body
7. The mechanical equivalent of heat
(a) has the same dimension as heat
(b) has the same dimension as work
(c) has the same dimension as energy
(d) is dimensionless.

OBJECTIVE II

1. The heat capacity of a body depends on
(a) the heat given (b) the temperature raised
(c) the mass of the body (d) the material of the body.
2. The ratio of specific heat capacity to molar heat capacity of a body
(a) is a universal constant
(b) depends on the mass of the body
(c) depends on the molecular weight of the body
(d) is dimensionless.
3. If heat is supplied to a solid, its temperature
(a) must increase (b) may increase
(c) may remain constant (d) may decrease.
4. The temperature of a solid object is observed to be constant during a period. In this period
(a) heat may have been supplied to the body
(b) heat may have been extracted from the body
(c) no heat is supplied to the body
(d) no heat is extracted from the body.
5. The temperature of an object is observed to rise in a period. In this period
(a) heat is certainly supplied to it
(b) heat is certainly not supplied to it
(c) heat may have been supplied to it
(d) work may have been done on it.
6. Heat and work are equivalent. This means,
(a) when we supply heat to a body we do work on it
(b) when we do work on a body we supply heat to it
(c) the temperature of a body can be increased by doing work on it
(d) a body kept at rest may be set into motion along a line by supplying heat to it.

EXERCISES

1. An aluminium vessel of mass 0·5 kg contains 0·2 kg of water at 20°C. A block of iron of mass 0·2 kg at 100°C is gently put into the water. Find the equilibrium temperature of the mixture. Specific heat capacities of aluminium, iron and water are $910\ \mathrm{J\ kg^{-1}\ K^{-1}}$, $470\ \mathrm{J\ kg^{-1}\ K^{-1}}$ and $4200\ \mathrm{J\ kg^{-1}\ K^{-1}}$ respectively.
2. A piece of iron of mass 100 g is kept inside a furnace for a long time and then put in a calorimeter of water equivalent 10 g containing 240 g of water at 20°C. The mixture attains an equilibrium temperature of 60°C. Find the temperature of the furnace. Specific heat capacity of iron $= 470\ \mathrm{J\ kg^{-1}\ {}^\circ C^{-1}}$.
3. The temperatures of equal masses of three different liquids *A*, *B* and *C* are 12°C, 19°C and 28°C respectively. The temperature when *A* and *B* are mixed is 16°C, and when *B* and *C* are mixed, it is 23°C. What will be the temperature when *A* and *C* are mixed?
4. Four 2 cm × 2 cm × 2 cm cubes of ice are taken out from a refrigerator and are put in 200 ml of a drink at 10°C. (a) Find the temperature of the drink when thermal equilibrium is attained in it. (b) If the ice cubes do not melt completely, find the amount melted. Assume that no heat is lost to the outside of the drink and that the container has negligible heat capacity. Density of ice $= 900\ \mathrm{kg\ m^{-3}}$, density of the drink $= 1000\ \mathrm{kg\ m^{-3}}$, specific heat capacity of the drink $= 4200\ \mathrm{J\ kg^{-1}\ K^{-1}}$, latent heat of fusion of ice $= 3{\cdot}4 \times 10^{5}\ \mathrm{J\ kg^{-1}}$.
5. Indian style of cooling drinking water is to keep it in a pitcher having porous walls. Water comes to the outer surface very slowly and evaporates. Most of the energy needed for evaporation is taken from the water itself and the water is cooled down. Assume that a pitcher contains 10 kg of water and 0·2 g of water comes out per second. Assuming no backward heat transfer from the atmosphere to the water, calculate the time in which the temperature decreases by 5°C. Specific heat capacity of water $= 4200\ \mathrm{J\ kg^{-1}\ {}^\circ C^{-1}}$ and latent heat of vaporization of water $= 2{\cdot}27 \times 10^{6}\ \mathrm{J\ kg^{-1}}$.
6. A cube of iron (density $= 8000\ \mathrm{kg\ m^{-3}}$, specific heat capacity $= 470\ \mathrm{J\ kg^{-1}\ K^{-1}}$) is heated to a high temperature and is placed on a large block of ice at 0°C. The cube melts the ice below it, displaces the water and sinks. In the final equilibrium position, its upper surface just goes inside the ice. Calculate the initial temperature of the cube. Neglect any loss of heat outside the ice and the cube. The density of ice $= 900\ \mathrm{kg\ m^{-3}}$ and the latent heat of fusion of ice $= 3{\cdot}36 \times 10^{5}\ \mathrm{J\ kg^{-1}}$.
7. 1 kg of ice at 0°C is mixed with 1 kg of steam at 100°C. What will be the composition of the system when thermal equilibrium is reached? Latent heat of fusion of ice $= 3{\cdot}36 \times 10^{5}\ \mathrm{J\ kg^{-1}}$ and latent heat of vaporization of water $= 2{\cdot}26 \times 10^{6}\ \mathrm{J\ kg^{-1}}$.
8. Calculate the time required to heat 20 kg of water from 10°C to 35°C using an immersion heater rated 1000 W. Assume that 80% of the power input is used to heat the water. Specific heat capacity of water $= 4200\ \mathrm{J\ kg^{-1}\ K^{-1}}$.
9. On a winter day the temperature of the tap water is 20°C whereas the room temperature is 5°C. Water is stored in a tank of capacity $0{\cdot}5\ \mathrm{m^{3}}$ for household use. If it were possible to use the heat liberated by the water to lift a 10 kg mass vertically, how high can it be lifted as the water comes to the room temperature? Take $g = 10\ \mathrm{m\ s^{-2}}$.
10. A bullet of mass 20 g enters into a fixed wooden block with a speed of $40\ \mathrm{m\ s^{-1}}$ and stops in it. Find the change in internal energy during the process.
11. A 50 kg man is running at a speed of $18\ \mathrm{km\ h^{-1}}$. If all the kinetic energy of the man can be used to increase the temperature of water from 20°C to 30°C, how much water can be heated with this energy?
12. A brick weighing 4·0 kg is dropped into a 1·0 m deep river from a height of 2·0 m. Assuming that 80% of the gravitational potential energy is finally converted into thermal energy, find this thermal energy in calorie.
13. A van of mass 1500 kg travelling at a speed of $54\ \mathrm{km\ h^{-1}}$ is stopped in 10 s. Assuming that all the mechanical energy lost appears as thermal energy in the brake mechanism, find the average rate of production of thermal energy in $\mathrm{cal\ s^{-1}}$.
14. A block of mass 100 g slides on a rough horizontal surface. If the speed of the block decreases from $10\ \mathrm{m\ s^{-1}}$ to $5\ \mathrm{m\ s^{-1}}$, find the thermal energy developed in the process.
15. Two blocks of masses 10 kg and 20 kg moving at speeds of $10\ \mathrm{m\ s^{-1}}$ and $20\ \mathrm{m\ s^{-1}}$ respectively in opposite directions, approach each other and collide. If the collision is completely inelastic, find the thermal energy developed in the process.
16. A ball is dropped on a floor from a height of 2·0 m. After the collision it rises up to a height of 1·5 m. Assume that 40% of the mechanical energy lost goes as thermal energy into the ball. Calculate the rise in the temperature of the ball in the collision. Heat capacity of the ball is $800\ \mathrm{J\ K^{-1}}$.
17. A copper cube of mass 200 g slides down on a rough inclined plane of inclination 37° at a constant speed. Assume that any loss in mechanical energy goes into the copper block as thermal energy. Find the increase in the temperature of the block as it slides down through 60 cm. Specific heat capacity of copper $= 420\ \mathrm{J\ kg^{-1}\ K^{-1}}$.
18. A metal block of density $6000\ \mathrm{kg\ m^{-3}}$ and mass 1·2 kg is suspended through a spring of spring constant $200\ \mathrm{N\ m^{-1}}$. The spring–block system is dipped in water kept in a vessel. The water has a mass of 260 g and the block is at a height 40 cm above the bottom of the vessel. If the support to the spring is broken, what will be the rise in the temperature of the water. Specific heat capacity of the block is $250\ \mathrm{J\ kg^{-1}\ K^{-1}}$ and that of water is $4200\ \mathrm{J\ kg^{-1}\ K^{-1}}$. Heat capacities of the vessel and the spring are negligible.

ANSWERS

OBJECTIVE I

1. (d) 2. (a) 3. (d) 4. (d) 5. (c) 6. (c)
7. (d)

OBJECTIVE II

1. (c), (d) 2. (c) 3. (b), (c)
4. (a), (b) 5. (c), (d) 6. (c)

EXERCISES

1. 25°C
2. 950°C
3. 20·3°C
4. (a) 0°C (b) 25 g
5. 7·7 min
6. 80°C
7. 665 g steam and 1·335 kg water
8. 44 min
9. 315 km
10. 16 J
11. 15 g
12. 23 cal
13. 4000 cal s^{-1}
14. 3·75 J
15. 3000 J
16. $2·5 \times 10^{-3}$°C
17. $8·6 \times 10^{-3}$°C
18. 0·003°C

□

CHAPTER 26

LAWS OF THERMODYNAMICS

26.1 THE FIRST LAW OF THERMODYNAMICS

We have seen that heat is just a form of energy. A system can be given energy either by supplying heat to it (by placing it in contact with a hotter object) or by doing mechanical work on it. Consider an ideal gas in a cylindrical container fitted with a piston (figure 26.1). Suppose the piston is fixed in its position and the walls of the cylinder are kept at a temperature higher than that of the gas. The gas molecules strike the wall and rebound. The average kinetic energy of a wall molecule is larger than the average kinetic energy of a gas molecule. Thus, on collision, the gas molecules receive energy from the wall molecules. This increased kinetic energy is shared by other molecules of the gas and in this way the total internal energy of the gas increases.

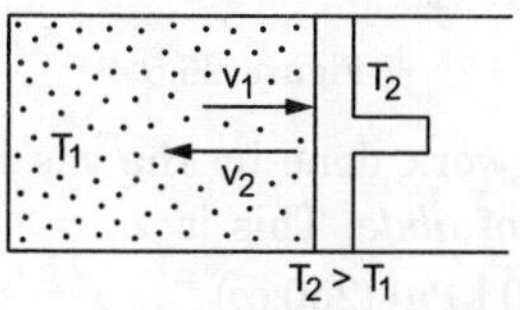

Figure 26.1

Next, consider the same initial situation but now the walls are at the same temperature as the gas. Suppose the piston is pushed slowly to compress the gas. As a gas molecule collides with the piston coming towards it, the speed of the molecule increases on collision (assuming elastic collision, $v_2 = v_1 + 2u$ in figure 26.2). This way the internal energy of the molecules increases as the piston is pushed in.

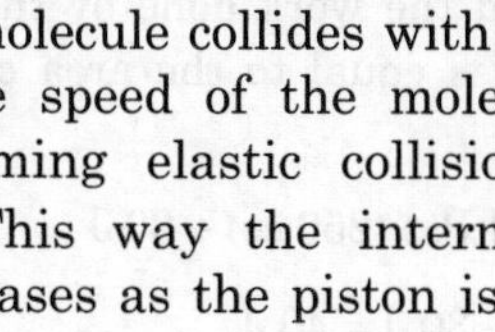

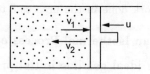

Figure 26.2

We see that the total internal energy of the gas may be increased because of the temperature difference between the walls and the gas (heat transfer) or because of the motion of the piston (work done on the gas).

In a general situation both modes of energy transfer may go together. As an example, consider a gas kept in a cylindrical can fitted with a movable piston. If the can is put on a hot stove, heat is supplied by the hot bottom to the gas and the piston is pushed out to some distance. As the piston moves out, work is done by the gas on it and the gas loses this much amount of energy. Thus, the gas gains energy as heat is supplied to it and it loses energy as work is done by it.

Suppose, in a process, an amount ΔQ of heat is given to the gas and an amount ΔW of work is done by it. The total energy of the gas must increase by $\Delta Q - \Delta W$. As a result, the entire gas together with its container may start moving (systematic motion) or the internal energy (random motion of the molecules) of the gas may increase. If the energy does not appear as a systematic motion of the gas then this net energy $\Delta Q - \Delta W$ must go in the form of its internal energy. If we denote the change in internal energy by ΔU, we get

$$\Delta U = \Delta Q - \Delta W$$

or, $$\Delta Q = \Delta U + \Delta W. \qquad \dots (26.1)$$

Equation (26.1) is the statement of the *first law of thermodynamics.* In an ideal monatomic gas, the internal energy of the gas is simply translational kinetic energy of all its molecules. In general, the internal energy may get contributions from the vibrational kinetic energy of molecules, rotational kinetic energy of molecules as well as from the potential energy corresponding to the molecular forces. Equation (26.1) represents a statement of conservation of energy and is applicable to any system, however complicated.

Example 26.1

A gas is contained in a vessel fitted with a movable piston. The container is placed on a hot stove. A total of

100 cal of heat is given to the gas and the gas does 40 J of work in the expansion resulting from heating. Calculate the increase in internal energy in the process.

Solution : Heat given to the gas is $\Delta Q = 100 \text{ cal} = 418 \text{ J}$.

Work done by the gas is $\Delta W = 40 \text{ J}$.

The increase in internal energy is

$$\Delta U = \Delta Q - \Delta W$$
$$= 418 \text{ J} - 40 \text{ J} = 378 \text{ J}.$$

First law of thermodynamics may be viewed from different angles. Equation (26.1) tells us that if we take a system from an initial state i to a final state f by several different processes, $\Delta Q - \Delta W$ should be identical in all the processes. This is because $\Delta Q - \Delta W = \Delta U = U_f - U_i$ depends only on the end states i and f. Both ΔQ and ΔW may be different in different processes, but $\Delta Q - \Delta W$ is the same for all the processes taking the system from i to f. Thus, we do not write $\Delta Q = Q_f - Q_i$ or we do not write $\Delta W = W_f - W_i$, but we do write $\Delta U = U_f - U_i$. The first law may be taken as a statement that there exists an internal energy function U that has a fixed value in a given state.

It should be remembered that when work is done *by* the system, ΔW is positive. If work is done *on* the system, ΔW is negative. When heat is given *to* the system, ΔQ is positive. If heat is given *by* the system, ΔQ is negative. A positive ΔW decreases the internal energy and a positive ΔQ increases it.

26.2 WORK DONE BY A GAS

Consider a gas contained in a cylinder of cross-sectional area A fitted with a movable piston. Let the pressure of the gas be p. The force exerted by the gas on the piston is pA in outward direction. Suppose the gas expands a little and the piston is pushed out by a small distance Δx. The work done by the gas on the piston is

$$\Delta W = (pA)(\Delta x) = p\,\Delta V,$$

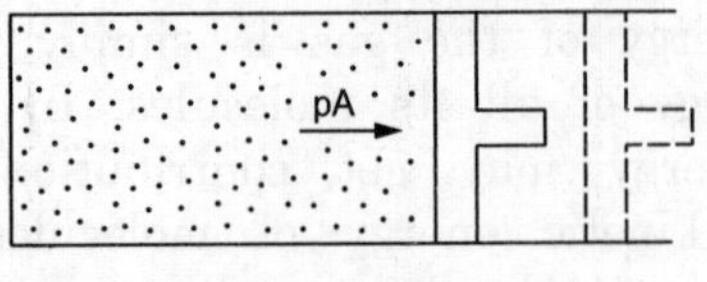

Figure 26.3

where $\Delta V = A\,\Delta x$ is the change in the volume of the gas. For a finite change of volume from V_1 to V_2, the pressure may not be constant. We can divide the whole process of expansion in small steps and add the work done in each step. Thus, the total work done by the gas in the process is

$$W = \int_{V_1}^{V_2} p\,dV. \qquad \ldots (26.2)$$

If we show the process in a p–V diagram, the work done is equal to the area bounded by the p–V curve, the V-axis and the ordinates $V = V_1$ and $V = V_2$.

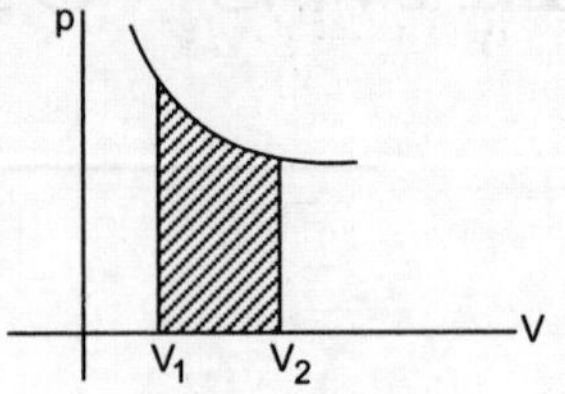

Figure 26.4

Equation (26.2) is derived for a cylindrical vessel only for mathematical simplicity. It is equally true for any shape of the vessel. It is also true for the expansion of solids and liquids or even in phase-changes.

Example 26.2

Calculate the work done by a gas as it is taken from the state a to b, b to c and c to a as shown in figure (26.5).

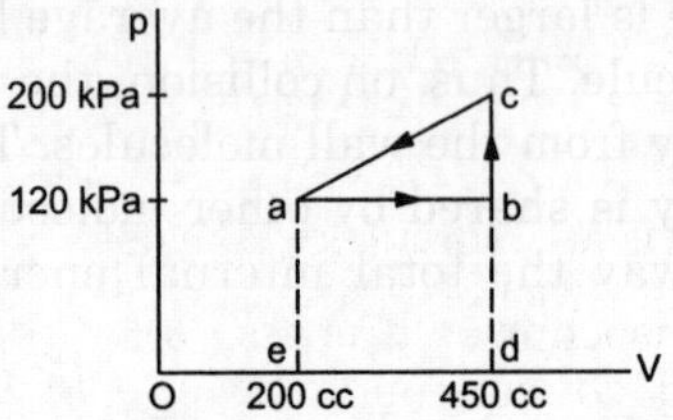

Figure 26.5

Solution : The work done by the gas in the process a to b is the area of *abde*. This is

$$W_{ab} = (120 \text{ kPa})(250 \text{ cc})$$
$$= 120 \times 10^3 \times 250 \times 10^{-6} \text{ J} = 30 \text{ J}.$$

In the process b to c the volume remains constant and the work done is zero.

In the process c to a the gas is compressed. The volume is decreased and the work done by the gas is negative. The magnitude is equal to the area of *caed*. This area is *cab* + *baed*

$$= \frac{1}{2}(80 \text{ kPa})(250 \text{ cc}) + 30 \text{ J}$$
$$= 10 \text{ J} + 30 \text{ J} = 40 \text{ J}.$$

Thus, the work done in the process c to a is -40 J.

Work Done in an Isothermal Process on an Ideal Gas

Suppose an ideal gas has initial pressure, volume and temperature as p_1, V_1 and T respectively. In a process, the temperature is kept constant and its pressure and volume are changed from p_1, V_1 to p_2, V_2. The work done by the gas is

$$W = \int_{V_1}^{V_2} p\, dV.$$

As $pV = nRT$, we have $p = \frac{nRT}{V}$.

$$\text{Thus,} \quad W = \int_{V_1}^{V_2} \frac{nRT}{V}\, dV$$

$$= nRT \int_{V_1}^{V_2} \frac{dV}{V}$$

$$= nRT \ln\left(\frac{V_2}{V_1}\right). \quad \text{... (26.3)}$$

Work Done in an Isobaric Process

Suppose the pressure of a system remains constant at a value p and the volume changes from V_1 to V_2. The work done by the system is

$$W = \int_{V_1}^{V_2} p\, dV$$

$$= p \int_{V_1}^{V_2} dV = p\,(V_2 - V_1).$$

Work Done in an Isochoric Process

In an isochoric process the volume remains constant and no work is done by the system.

26.3 HEAT ENGINES

We have seen that when mechanical work is done on a system, its internal energy increases (remember, we assume that the system does not have any systematic motion). The reverse process in which mechanical work is obtained at the expense of internal energy is also possible. Heat engines are devices to perform this task. The basic activity of a heat engine is shown in figure (26.6). It takes some heat from bodies at higher temperature, converts a part of it into the mechanical work and delivers the rest to bodies at lower temperature.

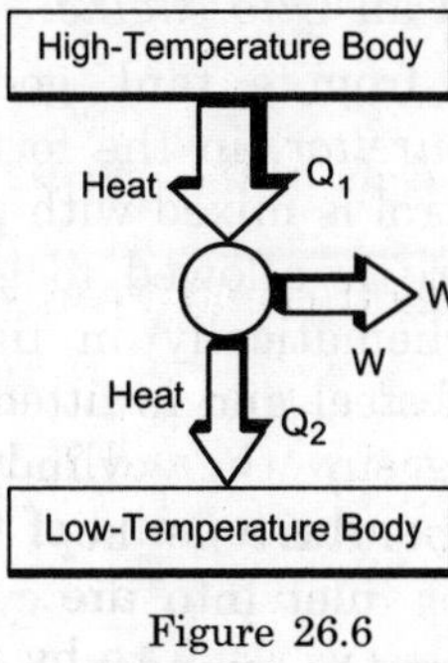

Figure 26.6

The substance inside the engine comes back to the original state. A process in which the final state of a system is the same as its initial state, is called a *cyclic process*. An engine works in cyclic process.

Efficiency

Suppose an engine takes an amount Q_1 of heat from high-temperature bodies, converts a part W of it into work and rejects an amount Q_2 of heat to low-temperature bodies. If the final state of the substance inside the engine is the same as the initial state, there is no change in its internal energy. By first law of thermodynamics, $W = Q_1 - Q_2$.

The efficiency of the engine is defined as

$$\eta = \frac{\text{work done by the engine}}{\text{heat supplied to it}}$$

$$= \frac{W}{Q_1} = \frac{Q_1 - Q_2}{Q_1} = 1 - \frac{Q_2}{Q_1}. \quad \text{... (26.4)}$$

We now describe some of the heat engines in use.

Steam Engine

A steam engine takes heat from steam and converts a part of it into mechanical motion of a piston which is then used to move heavy objects, such as trains. It is said that James Watt got the idea of steam engine while watching the lid of a kettle being pushed by the steam produced in the kettle in his kitchen. There have been a number of important changes in the design of steam engines, but the essential features remain the same. The main parts of a steam engine are shown in figure (26.7a).

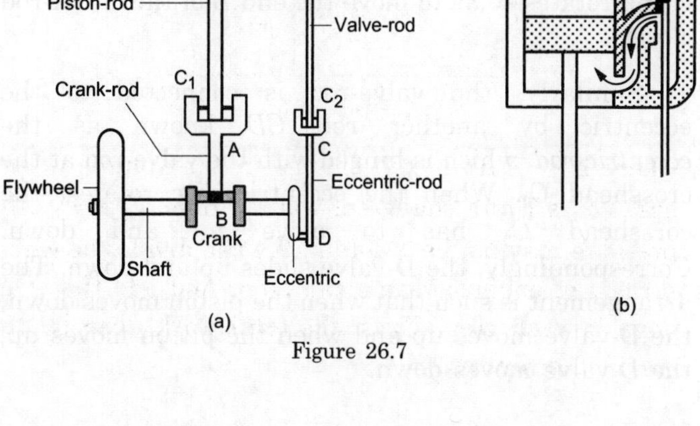

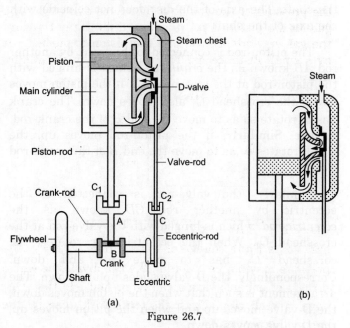

Figure 26.7

Description

It consists of a stout cylindrical vessel known as the *main cylinder*. A tight-fitting, movable piston separates the cylinder into two parts: upper part and lower part. The piston is connected to a rod, known as the *piston-rod* which comes out of the main cylinder.

Adjacent to the main cylinder, there is another stout chamber known as the *steam chest*. The steam chest and the cylinder have a common wall in which there are three holes. The upper and the lower holes open in the upper and the lower parts of the cylinder. The middle hole is connected to a *condenser* (not shown in the figure) through a pipe. Condenser is just a vessel in which the steam cools down and condenses.

The steam chest contains a valve of the shape of an open box. It slides on the surface of the common wall between the steam chest and the main cylinder. Together with the wall, the valve forms the shape of "D" and hence it is called a *D-Valve*. Its size is such that at any time it covers either the upper or the lower hole and leaves the other open. The middle hole is always covered. In the situation shown in the figure, the upper hole is open and the middle and the lower holes are covered. The valve is connected to a *valve-rod* which comes out of the steam chest.

A *flywheel* is connected to a *crankshaft*. A *crank* is fixed to this shaft. If a force is applied to the crank in such a way that the force does not intersect the axis of the shaft, a torque acts on the shaft and it rotates. The flywheel and the crank also rotate with it.

A circular disc called *eccentric* is also connected to the shaft. The axis of the disc does not coincide with the axis of the shaft.

The piston-rod is connected to the crank by another rod *AB* known as the *crank-rod*, which is hinged with the piston-rod at the crosshead C_1. If the piston moves down, the crosshead C_1 also moves down. The crank has to rotate so as to move the end *B* of the crank-rod, farther. Similarly, if the piston-rod moves up, the crank rotates so as to move the end *B* of the crank-rod closer.

Similarly, the valve-rod is connected to the eccentric by another rod *CD* known as the *eccentric-rod*, which is hinged with the valve-rod at the crosshead C_2. When the eccentric disc rotates, the corsshead C_2 has to move up and down. Correspondingly, the D-valve slides up and down. The arrangement is such that when the piston moves down, the D-valve moves up and when the piston moves up, the D-valve moves down.

Working

Water is boiled in a big boiler and the steam so prepared is allowed to go into the steam chest. The flow of steam into the steam chest is controlled by a valve.

In the position shown in figure (26.7a), the piston is near the top end of the cylinder and the D-valve is near its lowest position. Steam is forced into the upper part of the cylinder through the upper hole. The piston is pushed down and the steam in the lower part passes through the lower hole and then through the middle hole to the condenser. As the piston comes down, the crank rotates the shaft and the D-valve slides up. When the piston reaches near the bottom end, the D-valve closes the upper hole and opens the lower hole (figure 26.7b). Thus, steam is forced into the lower part of the cylinder which pushes the piston up. The steam in the upper part passes through the upper hole and then through the middle hole to the condenser. The D-valve slides down. This process is repeated continuously. The piston thus keeps on moving up and down rotating the shaft and the flywheel. The kinetic energy of the piston, flywheel and any part connected to the engine comes from the internal energy of the steam. Thus, a part of the internal energy is converted into mechanical energy.

The efficiency of a steam engine is often measured as the ratio of the mechanical work obtained to the heat that could be produced in burning the fuel (to produce steam in this case). The efficiency of a steam engine is typically of the order of 3 to 10%.

Internal Combustion Engine

In a steam engine, there is a separate furnace to boil water. There are engines in which there is no separate furnace and heat is produced in the main cylinder itself. Such engines are called *internal combustion engines*. We will describe two types of internal combustion engines: *petrol engine* and *diesel engine*.

Petrol Engine

This engine was designed by Otto in 1876 and hence is also called an *Otto engine*.

In this, petrol from a tank goes to a chamber known as the *carburettor*, in the form of jets. In the carburettor, the petrol is mixed with proper amount of air and the mixture is allowed to go into the main cylinder shown schematically in figure (26.8). The cylinder is made of steel and is fitted with a movable piston just fitting in the cylinder. Two valves V_1 and V_2 are fixed at the top end of the cylinder. The valve V_1 is used for inlet into the cylinder and V_2 is used for outlet from the cylinder. Valves are opened and closed at proper times. The piston is rigidly connected to a piston-rod which is connected to a crankshaft much like that in a steam engine.

A spark plug is placed in the main cylinder and is used to produce electric sparks. These sparks burn the petrol–air mixture.

The working of the engine may be described in four steps known as four strokes. Figure (26.8) is used to explain these strokes.

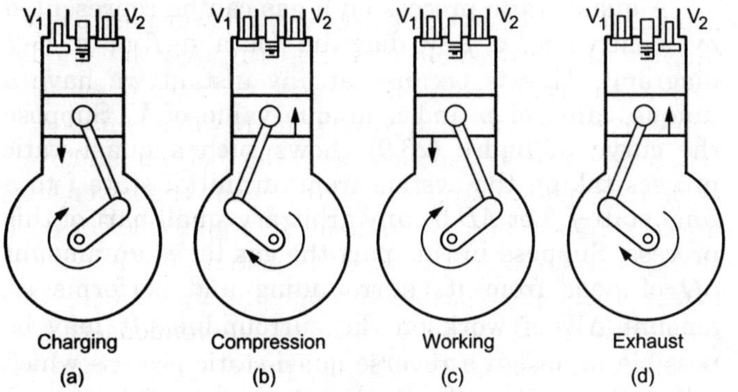

Figure 26.8

(a) Charging Stroke

The valve V_1 is opened and the mixture of petrol vapour and air enters into the cylinder. The piston goes down.

(b) Compression Stroke

Both the inlet and the outlet valves are closed and the piston moves up in the cylinder. This compresses the mixture to a high pressure and the temperature increases to about 500°C.

(c) Working Stroke

The spark plug produces a spark at the end of the compression stroke. Both the valves are closed. The fuel mixture ignites. The temperature increases to about 2000°C and the pressure to about 15 atm. The piston is pushed down and this rotates the crankshaft and the flywheel connected to it. This stroke provides a large amount of mechanical energy and, therefore, is called the working stroke.

(d) Exhaust Stroke

In this stroke, the valve V_2 is opened and the burnt gases are flushed out. The piston moves in and the cycle is completed.

Diesel Engine

In a diesel engine, diesel is used as a fuel. Its construction and working is similar to that of a petrol engine.

The main action takes place in a cylinder fitted with an inlet valve, an outlet valve and a valve that allows the fuel to come into the cylinder. No spark plug is used in it. The inlet valve is opened and air is sucked in due to the forward motion of the piston. When the piston moves backward, the inlet valve is closed and the air gets compressed. Due to the compression, the temperature rises to about 1000°C and the pressure to about 36 atm. The fuel valve is opened at this moment and fuel is injected into the cylinder. The fuel ignites readily due to the high temperature. The piston is pushed forward with a great force. This is the working stroke of the engine in which large amount of mechanical energy is obtained. At the end of this stroke the outlet valve opens and the burnt gases are expelled by the backward motion of the piston.

Internal combustion engines have better efficiency than steam engines. They occupy small space and are used with scooters, motorcycles, etc.

26.4 THE SECOND LAW OF THERMODYNAMICS

When a body at 100°C is kept in contact with a similar body at 0°C, heat flows from the hotter body to the colder body and both come to 50°C. Is the reverse process possible ? That is, if we put two similar bodies both at 50°C in contact, can heat flow from one body to the other so that one body reaches 0°C and the other 100°C ? A block moving at a speed v_0 on a rough table eventually stops and the table and the block warm up. The kinetic energy of the block appears as the internal energy of the table and the block. Can the reverse process be possible ? That is, we heat the block and the table and put the block on the table. Can the bodies cool down and the block start sliding with speed v_0 on the table converting the internal energy into kinetic energy ? Consider a container with rigid walls divided in two parts by a partition having a valve. A gas is put in one part and vacuum is created in the other part. The valve is now opened. The gas eventually occupies both the parts of the container. Is the reverse process possible ? We put the gas distributed in both the parts with the valve open. Can the gas go into one part evacuating the other part all by itself ?

The answer to all these questions is NO. Of course, the first law of thermodynamics is not violated in any of these proposed reverse processes. The energy is conserved in the direct process as well as in the reverse process. Still the reverse process is not possible. There must be a law of nature other than the first law which decides, whether a given process, allowed by the first law, will actually take place or not. This law is the second law of thermodynamics. This law may be stated in various ways. We give here one statement in terms of working of heat engines. We know that a heat engine takes Q_1 amount of heat energy from a hot body, converts a part of it into mechanical work and rejects the rest amount Q_2 to a cold body. The efficiency of the engine is $1 - Q_2/Q_1$. The efficiency would be 1, that is, 100% if $Q_2 = 0$. Such an engine would not need any "low-temperature body" to which it needs to reject heat. Hence, it needs only one body at a single temperature, from which it will take heat and convert it completely into mechanical work. This temperature can even be the temperature of the surrounding and hence we will not have to burn any fuel to prepare steam or gases at high temperature to run the engine. A scooter could be run by an engine taking heat from the body of the scooter without needing any petrol. A ship could be run by an engine taking heat from the ocean. However, all attempts to construct such a 100% efficient engine failed. In fact, it is not possible to have such an engine and this is one form of the second law of thermodynamics stated more precisely as follows:

It is not possible to design a heat engine which works in cyclic process and whose only result is to take heat from a body at a single temperature and convert it completely into mechanical work.

This statement of the second law is called the *Kelvin–Planck statement.*

One can convert mechanical work completely into heat but one cannot convert heat completely into mechanical work. In this respect, heat and work are not equivalent. We shall now study some other aspects of the second law of thermodynamics.

26.5 REVERSIBLE AND IRREVERSIBLE PROCESSES

Consider a sample of an ideal gas kept in an enclosure. The state of the gas is described by specifying its pressure p, volume V and temperature T. If these parameters can be uniquely specified at a time, we say that the gas is in *thermodynamic equilibrium*. If we put the enclosure on a hot stove, the temperature of various parts of the gas will be different and we will not be able to specify a unique temperature of the gas. The gas is not in thermodynamic equilibrium in such a case.

When we perform a process on a given system, its state is, in general, changed. Suppose the initial state of the system is described by the values p_1, V_1, T_1 and the final state by p_2, V_2, T_2. If the process is performed in such a way that at any instant during the process, the system is very nearly in thermodynamic equilibrium, the process is called *quasi-static*. This means, we can specify the parameters p, V, T uniquely at any instant during such a process.

Actual processes are not quasi-static. To change the pressure of a gas, we can move a piston inside the enclosure. The gas near the piston is acted upon by greater force as compared to the gas away from the piston. The pressure of the gas may not be uniform everywhere while the piston is moving. However, we can move the piston very slowly to make the process as close to quasi-static as we wish. Thus, a *quasi-static process is an idealised process in which all changes take place infinitely slowly.*

A quasi-static process on a gas can be represented by a curve on a p–V diagram (or a p–T or a V–T diagram). This is because at any instant we have a unique value of p and a unique value of V. Suppose the curve in figure (26.9) shows such a quasi-static process taking the system from an initial state i to a final state f. Let AB be any arbitrary small part of this process. Suppose in this part the gas takes an amount ΔQ of heat from its surrounding and performs an amount ΔW of work on the surrounding. It may be possible to design a reverse quasi-static process which takes the system from the state f to the state i satisfying the following conditions:

(a) the reverse process is represented by the same curve as the direct process, with the arrow inverted,

(b) in the part BA, the system gives an amount ΔQ of heat to the surrounding and an amount ΔW of work is performed on the system.

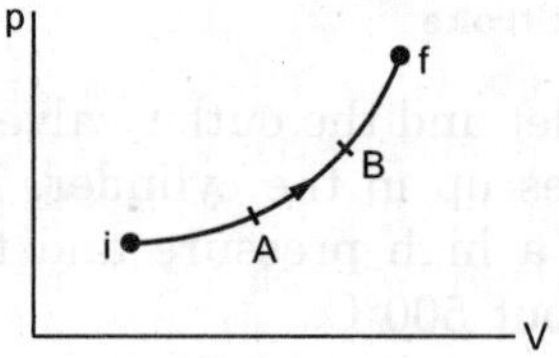

Figure 26.9

If such a reverse process is possible, the original process is called *reversible process*. In the direct process the system has passed through certain equilibrium states in a sequence. When the process is reversed, the system passes through the same states in the reverse sequence. Also, in any small part of the reverse process, it returns the same amount of heat to the surrounding as was taken during the corresponding part in the direct process. Similarly, any work done by the system in the direct process is compensated by the equal work done on the system in the corresponding reverse process.

A process can be reversible if it satisfies two conditions. The process must be quasi-static and it should be nondissipative. This means, friction, viscosity, etc., should be completely absent.

All processes described in this and the following chapters will be assumed to be reversible unless stated otherwise.

Reversible Cycle

We know that if the state of a system at the end of a process is the same as the state of the system at the beginning, the process is called a cyclic process. If all parts of a cyclic process are reversible, it is called a *reversible cycle.*

26.6 ENTROPY

Like pressure, volume, temperature, internal energy, etc., we have another thermodynamic variable of a system, named *entropy*. In a given equilibrium state, the system has a definite value of entropy. If the system has a temperature T (in absolute scale) and a small amount of heat ΔQ is given to it, we define the change in the entropy of the system as

$$\Delta S = \frac{\Delta Q}{T} \cdot \qquad \dots (26.5)$$

In general, the temperature of the system may change during a process. If the process is reversible, the change in entropy is defined as

$$S_f - S_i = \int_i^f \frac{\Delta Q}{T} \cdot \qquad \dots (26.6)$$

In an adiabatic reversible process, no heat is given to the system. The entropy of the system remains constant in such a process.

Entropy is related to the *disorder* in the system. Thus, if all the molecules in a given sample of a gas are made to move in the same direction with the same velocity, the entropy will be smaller than that in the actual situation in which the molecules move randomly in all directions.

An interesting fact about entropy is that it is not a conserved quantity. More interesting is the fact that entropy can be created but cannot be destroyed. Once some entropy is created in a process, the universe has to carry the burden of that entropy for ever. The second law of thermodynamics may be stated in terms of entropy as follows:

It is not possible to have a process in which the entropy of an isolated system is decreased.

26.7 CARNOT ENGINE

The French scientist N L Sadi Carnot, in 1824, suggested an idealised engine which we call *Carnot engine* and which has an intimate relation with the second law of thermodynamics. To understand the principle, let us consider an ideal gas taken in a cylinder. The bottom of the cylinder is diathermic whereas rest of it is adiabatic. An adiabatic piston is fitted into the cylinder. Also, suppose we have two large bodies, one at a constant high temperature T_1 and the other at a lower temperature T_2.

Figure (26.10a) shows the basic process of a Carnot engine on a p–V diagram. The other parts of the figure represent the process schematically. Suppose, the cylinder is kept in contact with the high-temperature body at temperature T_1 in a compressed state. This state is represented by the point a in the p–V diagram. The gas is isothermally expanded to a state b (figure 26.10b). Work is done by the gas and Q_1 amount of heat is supplied to it by the body at temperature T_1. The cylinder is now kept on an adiabatic platform and the gas is allowed to expand further to the state c (figure 26.10c). This is an adiabatic expansion and the temperature falls from T_1 to T_2. Work is done by the gas. At this stage, the cylinder is put in contact with the lower temperature body at temperature T_2. It is isothermally compressed to a state d (figure 26.10d). Work is done on the gas and the gas rejects an amount Q_2 of heat to the body at the lower temperature T_2. Finally, it is kept on the adiabatic platform and is further compressed to reach the state a where the temperature is T_1 (figure 26.10e).

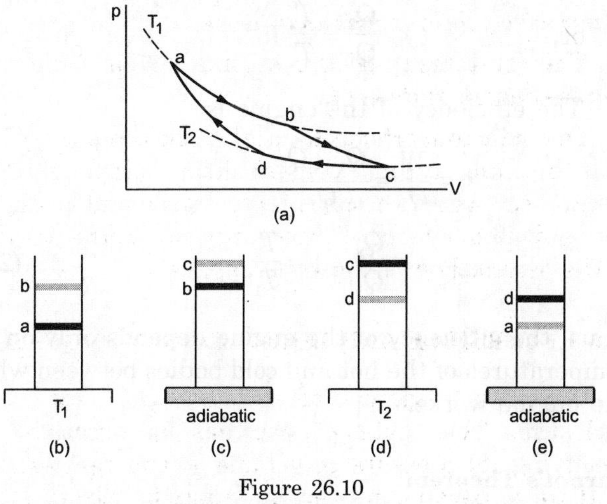

Figure 26.10

The process represented by *abcda* in figure (26.10a) is a cyclic process. If the piston is frictionless and is always moved very slowly, the process is a reversible cyclic process.

Efficiency of a Carnot Engine

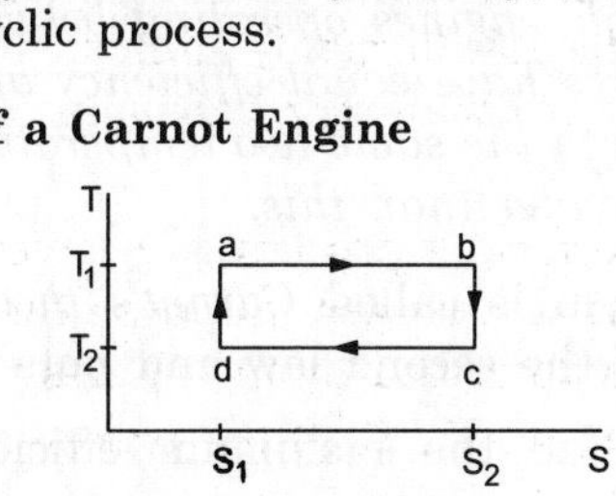

Figure 26.11

The basic process of a Carnot engine, described above, is again shown in figure (26.11) in a T–S (temperature–entropy) diagram. The points a, b, c and

d represent the same states as in figure (26.10a). Let the entropy in state a be S_1. An amount Q_1 of heat is supplied to the system in the isothermal process ab at the temperature T_1. The entropy increases in this part as heat is supplied to the system. Also, by definition,

$$S_2 - S_1 = \frac{Q_1}{T_1} \quad \dots \text{(i)}$$

The entropy remains constant in the part bc as it describes an adiabatic process. So the entropy in state c is S_2. In the part cd, the system gives a heat Q_2 at the lower temperature T_2 and its entropy is decreased. The part da represents an adiabatic process and the entropy remains constant. As the entropy in state a is S_1, the entropy in state d is also S_1. Using the definition of change in entropy for the process cd,

$$S_1 - S_2 = \frac{-Q_2}{T_2} \quad \dots \text{(ii)}$$

From (i) and (ii),

$$\frac{Q_1}{T_1} = \frac{Q_2}{T_2}$$

or,

$$\frac{Q_2}{Q_1} = \frac{T_2}{T_1}.$$

The efficiency of the engine is

$$\eta = \frac{W}{Q_1} = \frac{Q_1 - Q_2}{Q_1}$$

$$= 1 - \frac{Q_2}{Q_1} = 1 - \frac{T_2}{T_1}. \quad \dots (26.7)$$

Thus, the efficiency of the engine depends only on the temperatures of the hot and cold bodies between which the engine works.

Carnot's Theorem

Carnot engine is a reversible engine. It can be proved from the second law of thermodynamics that:

All reversible engines operating between the same two temperatures have equal efficiency and no engine operating between the same two temperatures can have an efficiency greater than this.

This theorem is called *Carnot's theorem*. It is a consequence of the second law and puts a theoretical limit $\eta = 1 - \frac{T_2}{T_1}$ to the maximum efficiency of heat engines.

Refrigerator or Heat Pump

A heat engine takes heat from a hot body, converts part of it into work and rejects the rest to a cold body. The reverse operation is done by a *refrigerator* also known as a *heat pump*. It takes an amount Q_2 of heat from a cold body, an amount W of work is done on it by the surrounding and the total energy $Q_1 = Q_2 + W$ is supplied to a hot body in the form of heat. Thus, heat is passed from the cold body to the hot body. Figure (26.12) shows the process schematically. If the heat is taken at a single low temperature T_2, it is rejected at a single high temperature T_1 and all the parts of the process are carried out reversibly, we get a *Carnot refrigerator*. If the operating temperatures are fixed, a Carnot refrigerator needs minimum amount of work done to extract a given amount Q_2 of heat from the colder body.

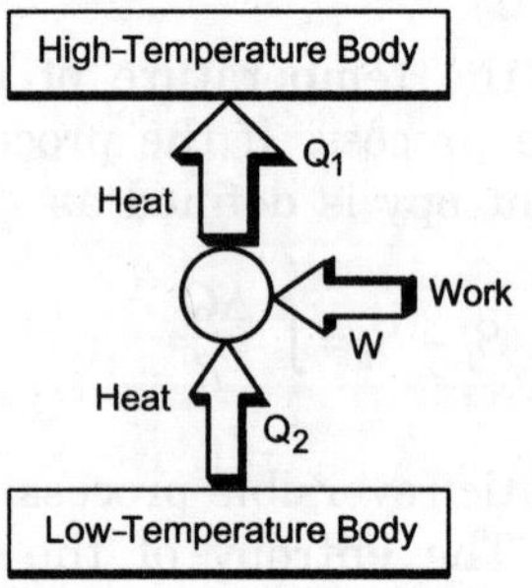

Figure 26.12

In this case,

$$\frac{Q_1}{Q_2} = \frac{T_1}{T_2}$$

or,

$$\frac{Q_2 + W}{Q_2} = \frac{T_1}{T_2}$$

or,

$$W = Q_2\left(\frac{T_1}{T_2} - 1\right).$$

A minimum of this much work has to be done by the surrounding, if we wish to transfer heat Q_2 from the low-temperature body to the high-temperature body. This leads to another statement of second law of thermodynamics as follows:

It is not possible to design a refrigerator which works in cyclic process and whose only result is to transfer heat from a body to a hotter body.

This is known as the *Claussius statement* of the second law.

Worked Out Examples

1. *A sample of an ideal gas is taken through the cyclic process abca (figure 26-W1). It absorbs* 50 J *of heat during the part ab, no heat during bc and rejects* 70 J *of heat during ca.* 40 J *of work is done on the gas during the part bc. (a) Find the internal energy of the gas at b and c if it is* 1500 J *at a. (b) Calculate the work done by the gas during the part ca.*

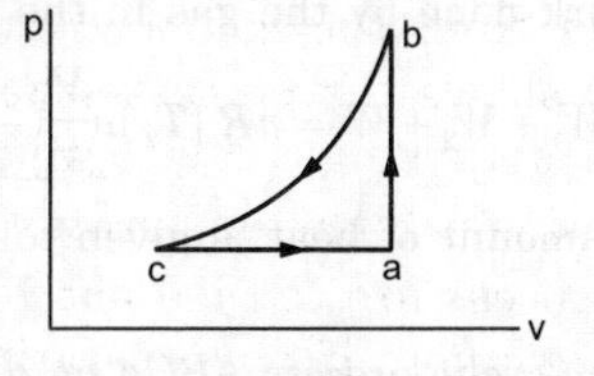

Figure 26-W1

Solution : (a) In the part *ab* the volume remains constant. Thus, the work done by the gas is zero. The heat absorbed by the gas is 50 J. The increase in internal energy from *a* to *b* is

$$\Delta U = \Delta Q = 50 \text{ J}.$$

As the internal energy is 1500 J at *a*, it will be 1550 J at *b*. In the part *bc*, the work done by the gas is $\Delta W = -40$ J and no heat is given to the system. The increase in internal energy from *b* to *c* is

$$\Delta U = -\Delta W = 40 \text{ J}.$$

As the internal energy is 1550 J at *b*, it will be 1590 J at *c*.

(b) The change in internal energy from *c* to *a* is

$$\Delta U = 1500 \text{ J} - 1590 \text{ J} = -90 \text{ J}.$$

The heat given to the system is $\Delta Q = -70$ J.

Using $\Delta Q = \Delta U + \Delta W$,

$$\Delta W = \Delta Q - \Delta U$$

$$= -70 \text{ J} + 90 \text{ J} = 20 \text{ J}.$$

2. *A thermodynamic system is taken through the cycle abcda (figure 26-W2). (a) Calculate the work done by the gas during the parts ab, bc, cd and da. (b) Find the total heat rejected by the gas during the process.*

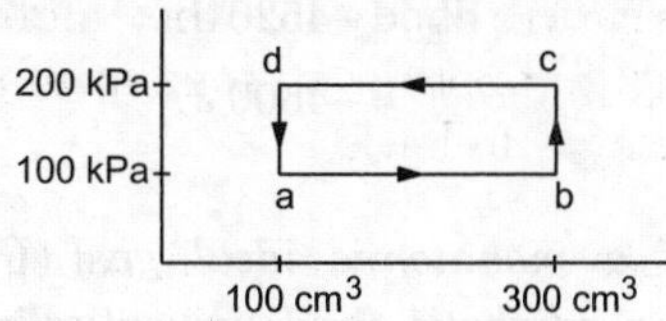

Figure 26-W2

Solution : (a) The work done during the part *ab*,

$$= \int_a^b p\, dV = (100 \text{ kPa}) \int_a^b dV$$

$$= (100 \text{ kPa})\,(300 \text{ cm}^3 - 100 \text{ cm}^3)$$

$$= 20 \text{ J}.$$

The work done during *bc* is zero as the volume does not change. The work done during *cd*

$$= \int_c^d p\, dV = (200 \text{ kPa})\,(100 \text{ cm}^3 - 300 \text{ cm}^3)$$

$$= -40 \text{ J}.$$

The work done during *da* is zero as the volume does not change.

(b) The total work done by the system during the cycle *abcda*

$$\Delta W = 20 \text{ J} - 40 \text{ J} = -20 \text{ J}.$$

The change in internal energy $\Delta U = 0$ as the initial state is the same as the final state. Thus $\Delta Q = \Delta U + \Delta W = -20$ J. So the system rejects 20 J of heat during the cycle.

3. *Calculate the increase in internal energy of* 1 kg *of water at* 100°C *when it is converted into steam at the same temperature and at* 1 atm (100 kPa). *The density of water and steam are* 1000 kg m^{-3} *and* 0·6 kg m^{-3} *respectively. The latent heat of vaporization of water* $= 2{\cdot}25 \times 10^6$ J kg^{-1}.

Solution : The volume of 1 kg of water

$$= \frac{1}{1000} \text{ m}^3 \text{ and of 1 kg of steam} = \frac{1}{0{\cdot}6} \text{ m}^3.$$

The increase in volume

$$= \frac{1}{0{\cdot}6} \text{ m}^3 - \frac{1}{1000} \text{ m}^3$$

$$= (1{\cdot}7 - 0{\cdot}001) \text{ m}^3 \approx 1{\cdot}7 \text{ m}^3.$$

The work done by the system is $p\Delta V$

$$= (100 \text{ kPa})\,(1{\cdot}7 \text{ m}^3)$$

$$= 1{\cdot}7 \times 10^5 \text{ J}.$$

The heat given to convert 1 kg of water into steam

$$= 2{\cdot}25 \times 10^6 \text{ J}.$$

The change in internal energy is

$$\Delta U = \Delta Q - \Delta W$$

$$= 2{\cdot}25 \times 10^6 \text{ J} - 1{\cdot}7 \times 10^5 \text{ J}$$

$$= 2{\cdot}08 \times 10^6 \text{ J}.$$

4. *The internal energy of a monatomic ideal gas is* 1·5 *nRT. One mole of helium is kept in a cylinder of cross section* 8·5 cm^2. *The cylinder is closed by a light frictionless piston. The gas is heated slowly in a process during which a total of* 42 J *heat is given to the gas. If the temperature rises through* 2°C, *find the distance moved by the piston. Atmospheric pressure* = 100 kPa.

Solution : The change in internal energy of the gas is

$$\Delta U = 1{\cdot}5\ nR\,(\Delta T)$$
$$= 1{\cdot}5\ (1\ \text{mol})\ (8{\cdot}3\ \text{J K}^{-1}\ \text{mol}^{-1})\ (2\ \text{K})$$
$$= 24{\cdot}9\ \text{J}.$$

The heat given to the gas = 42 J.

The work done by the gas is

$$\Delta W = \Delta Q - \Delta U$$
$$= 42\ \text{J} - 24{\cdot}9\ \text{J} = 17{\cdot}1\ \text{J}.$$

If the distance moved by the piston is x, the work done is

$$\Delta W = (100\ \text{kPa})\ (8{\cdot}5\ \text{cm}^2)\ x.$$

Thus,

$$(10^5\ \text{N m}^{-2})\ (8{\cdot}5 \times 10^{-4}\ \text{m}^{-2})\ x = 17{\cdot}1\ \text{J}$$

or, $x = 0{\cdot}2\ \text{m} = 20\ \text{cm}.$

5. *A steam engine intakes* 100 g *of steam at* 100°C *per minute and cools it down to* 20°C. *Calculate the heat rejected by the steam engine per minute. Latent heat of vaporization of steam* = 540 cal g^{-1}.

Solution : Heat rejected during the condensation of steam in one minute

$$= (100\ \text{g}) \times (540\ \text{cal g}^{-1}) = 5{\cdot}4 \times 10^4\ \text{cal}.$$

Heat rejected during the cooling of water

$$= (100\ \text{g}) \times (1\ \text{cal g}^{-1}\ {}^\circ\text{C}^{-1})\ (100^\circ\text{C} - 20^\circ\text{C})$$
$$= 8000\ \text{cal}.$$

Thus, heat rejected by the engine per minute

$$= 5{\cdot}4 \times 10^4\ \text{cal} + 0{\cdot}8 \times 10^4\ \text{cal}$$
$$= 6{\cdot}2 \times 10^4\ \text{cal}.$$

6. *Figure (26-W3) shows a process ABCA performed on an ideal gas. Find the net heat given to the system during the process.*

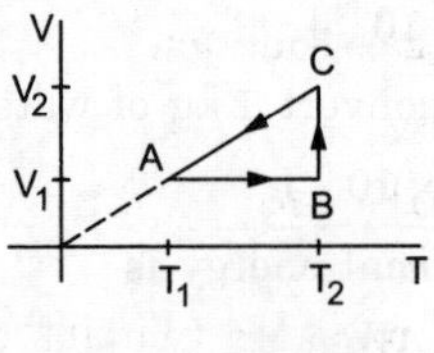

Figure 26-W3

Solution : As the process is cyclic, the change in internal energy is zero. The heat given to the system is then equal to the work done by it.

The work done in part AB is $W_1 = 0$ as the volume remains constant. The part BC represents an isothermal process so that the work done by the gas during this part is

$$W_2 = nR\,T_2 \ln(V_2/V_1).$$

During the part CA,

$$V \propto T.$$

So, V/T is constant and hence,

$$p = \frac{nRT}{V} \text{ is constant.}$$

The work done by the gas during the part CA is

$$W_3 = p\,(V_1 - V_2)$$
$$= nRT_1 - nRT_2$$
$$= -nR\,(T_2 - T_1).$$

The net work done by the gas in the process $ABCA$ is

$$W = W_1 + W_2 + W_3 = nR\,[T_2 \ln\frac{V_2}{V_1} - (T_2 - T_1)].$$

The same amount of heat is given to the gas.

7. *Consider the cyclic process ABCA on a sample of* 2·0 mol *of an ideal gas as shown in figure (26-W4). The temperatures of the gas at A and B are* 300 K *and* 500 K *respectively. A total of* 1200 J *heat is withdrawn from the sample in the process. Find the work done by the gas in part BC. Take* $R = 8{\cdot}3\ \text{J K}^{-1}\ \text{mol}^{-1}$.

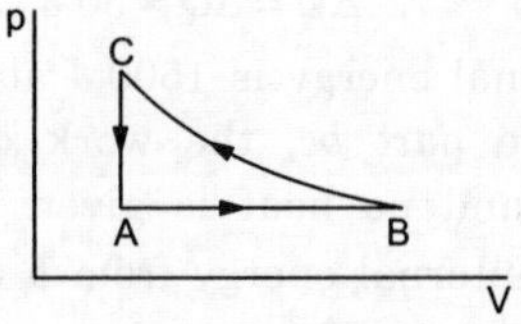

Figure 26-W4

Solution : The change in internal energy during the cyclic process is zero. Hence, the heat supplied to the gas is equal to the work done by it. Hence,

$$W_{AB} + W_{BC} + W_{CA} = -1200\ \text{J}. \quad \text{... (i)}$$

The work done during the process AB is

$$W_{AB} = p_A(V_B - V_A)$$
$$= nR(T_B - T_A)$$
$$= (2{\cdot}0\ \text{mol})\ (8{\cdot}3\ \text{J K}^{-1}\ \text{mol}^{-1})\ (200\ \text{K})$$
$$= 3320\ \text{J}.$$

The work done by the gas during the process CA is zero as the volume remains constant. From (i),

$$3320\ \text{J} + W_{BC} = -1200\ \text{J}$$

or, $W_{BC} = -4520\ \text{J}.$

$$\approx -4500\ \text{J}.$$

8. 2·00 mol *of a monatomic ideal gas* ($U = 1{\cdot}5\ nRT$) *is enclosed in an adiabatic, fixed, vertical cylinder fitted with a smooth, light adiabatic piston. The piston is connected to a vertical spring of spring constant* 200 N m^{-1} *as shown in figure (26-W5). The area of cross section of the cylinder is* 20.0 cm^2. *Initially, the spring is at its natural length and the temperature of the gas is* 300 K. *The atmospheric pressure is* 100 kPa. *The gas is heated slowly for some time by means of an electric heater so as to move the* *piston up through* 10 cm. *Find (a) the work done by the gas (b) the final temperature of the gas and (c) the heat supplied by the heater.*

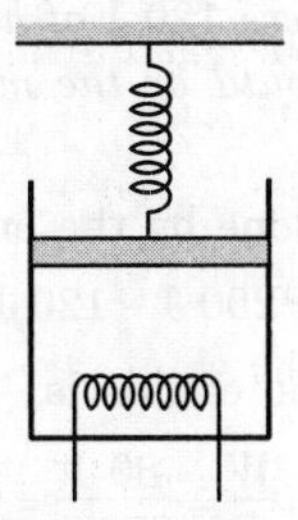

Figure 26-W5

Solution : (a) The force by the gas on the piston is

$$F = p_0 A + kx$$

where $p_0 = 100$ kPa is the atmospheric pressure, $A = 20\ \text{cm}^2$ is the area of cross section, $k = 200\ \text{N m}^{-1}$ is the spring constant and x is the compression of the spring. The work done by the gas as the piston moves through $l = 10$ cm is

$$W = \int_0^l F\,dx$$

$$= p_0 A l + \frac{1}{2} k l^2$$

$$= (100 \times 10^3\ \text{Pa}) \times (20 \times 10^{-4}\ \text{m}^2) \times (10 \times 10^{-2}\ \text{m})$$

$$+ \frac{1}{2} (200\ \text{N m}^{-1}) \times (100 \times 10^{-4}\ \text{m}^2)$$

$$= 20\ \text{J} + 1\ \text{J} = 21\ \text{J}.$$

(b) The initial temperature is $T_1 = 300$ K. Let the final temperature be T_2. We have

$$nRT_1 = p_0 V_0$$

and $$nRT_2 = pV_2 = \left(p_0 + \frac{kl}{A}\right)(V_0 + Al)$$

$$= nRT_1 + p_0 Al + kl^2 + \frac{kl\,nRT_1}{A\,p_0}$$

or, $$T_2 = T_1 + \frac{p_0 Al + kl^2}{nR} + \frac{klT_1}{Ap_0}$$

$$= (300\ \text{K}) + \frac{20\ \text{J} + 2\ \text{J}}{(2{\cdot}0\ \text{mol})\,(8{\cdot}3\ \text{J K}^{-1}\ \text{mol}^{-1})}$$

$$+ \frac{(200\ \text{N m}^{-1}) \times (10 \times 10^{-2}\ \text{m}) \times (300\ \text{K})}{(20 \times 10^{-4}\ \text{m}^2) \times (100 \times 10^3\ \text{Pa})}$$

$$= 300\ \text{K} + 1{\cdot}325\ \text{K} + 30\ \text{K}$$

$$\approx 331\ \text{K}.$$

(c) The internal energy is $U = 1{\cdot}5\, nRT$.

The change in internal energy is

$$\Delta U = 1{\cdot}5\, nR\, \Delta T$$

$$= 1{\cdot}5 \times (2{\cdot}00\ \text{mol}) \times (8{\cdot}3\ \text{J K}^{-1}\ \text{mol}^{-1}) \times (31\ \text{K})$$

$$= 772\ \text{J}.$$

From the first law,

$$\Delta Q = \Delta U + \Delta W$$

$$= 772\ \text{J} + 21\ \text{J} = 793\ \text{J}.$$

9. *A sample of an ideal gas has pressure* p_0, *volume* V_0 *and temperature* T_0. *It is isothermally expanded to twice its original volume. It is then compressed at constant pressure to have the original volume* V_0. *Finally, the gas is heated at constant volume to get the original temperature. (a) Show the process in a V–T diagram (b) Calculate the heat absorbed in the process.*

Solution :

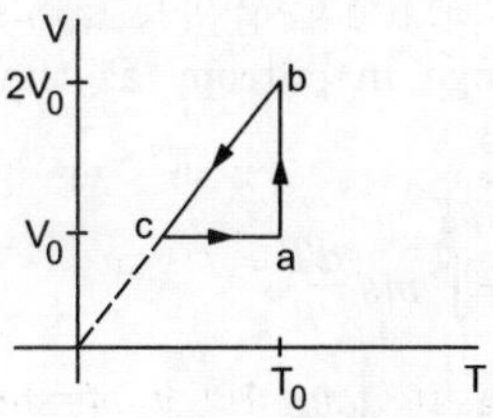

Figure 26-W6

(a) The V–T diagram for the process is shown in figure (26-W6). The initial state is represented by the point *a*. In the first step, it is isothermally expanded to a volume $2V_0$. This is shown by *ab*. Then the pressure is kept constant and the gas is compressed to the volume V_0. From the ideal gas equation, V/T is constant at constant pressure. Hence, the process is shown by a line *bc* which passes through the origin. At point *c*, the volume is V_0. In the final step, the gas is heated at constant volume to a temperature T_0. This is shown by *ca*. The final state is the same as the inital state.

(b) The process is cyclic so that the change in internal energy is zero. The heat supplied is, therefore, equal to the work done by the gas. The work done during *ab* is

$$W_1 = nRT_0 \ln \frac{2V_0}{V_0} = nRT_0 \ln 2 = p_0 V_0 \ln 2.$$

Also from the ideal gas equation,

$$p_a V_a = p_b V_b$$

or, $$p_b = \frac{p_a V_a}{V_b} = \frac{p_0 V_0}{2V_0} = \frac{p_0}{2}.$$

In the step *bc*, the pressure remains constant. Hence, the work done is,

$$W_2 = \frac{p_0}{2}(V_0 - 2V_0) = -\frac{p_0 V_0}{2}.$$

In the step *ca*, the volume remains constant and so the work done is zero. The net work done by the gas in the cyclic process is

$$W = W_1 + W_2$$

$$= p_0 V_0\, [\ln 2 - 0{\cdot}5]$$

$$= 0{\cdot}193\, p_0 V_0.$$

Hence, the heat supplied to the gas is $0{\cdot}193\, p_0 V_0$.

10. *A sample of 100 g water is slowly heated from 27°C to 87°C. Calculate the change in the entropy of the water. Specific heat capacity of water* = $4200 \text{ J kg}^{-1} \text{ K}^{-1}$.

Solution : The heat supplied to increase the temperature of the sample from T to $T + \Delta T$ is

$$\Delta Q = ms\,\Delta T,$$

where $m = 100 \text{ g} = 0{\cdot}1 \text{ kg}$ and $C = 4200 \text{ J kg}^{-1} \text{ K}^{-1}$.

The change in entropy during this process is

$$\Delta S = \frac{\Delta Q}{T} = ms\,\frac{\Delta T}{T}.$$

The total change in entropy as the temperature rises from T_1 to T_2 is,

$$S_2 - S_1 = \int_{T_1}^{T_2} ms\,\frac{dT}{T}$$

$$= ms \ln \frac{T_2}{T_1}.$$

Putting $T_1 = 27°\text{C} = 300 \text{ K}$ and $T_2 = 87°\text{C} = 360 \text{ K}$,

$$S_2 - S_1 = (0{\cdot}1 \text{ kg})\,(4200 \text{ J kg}^{-1} \text{ K}^{-1}) \ln \frac{360}{300}$$

$$= 76{\cdot}6 \text{ J K}^{-1}.$$

11. *A heat engine operates between a cold reservoir at temperature* $T_2 = 300 \text{ K}$ *and a hot reservoir at temperature* T_1. *It takes* 200 J *of heat from the hot reservoir and delivers* 120 J *of heat to the cold reservoir in a cycle. What could be the minimum temperature of the hot reservoir ?*

Solution : The work done by the engine in a cycle is

$$W = 200 \text{ J} - 120 \text{ J} = 80 \text{ J}.$$

The efficiency of the engine is

$$\eta = \frac{W}{Q} = \frac{80 \text{ J}}{200 \text{ J}} = 0{\cdot}40.$$

From Carnot's theorem, no engine can have an efficiency greater than that of a Carnot engine.

Thus, $$0{\cdot}40 \le 1 - \frac{T_2}{T_1} = 1 - \frac{300 \text{ K}}{T_1}$$

or, $$\frac{300 \text{ K}}{T_1} \le 1 - 0{\cdot}40 = 0{\cdot}60$$

or, $$T_1 \ge \frac{300 \text{ K}}{0{\cdot}60}$$

or, $$T_1 \ge 500 \text{ K}.$$

The minimum temperature of the hot reservoir has to be 500 K.

□

QUESTIONS FOR SHORT ANSWER

1. Should the internal energy of a system necessarily increase if heat is added to it ?
2. Should the internal energy of a system necessarily increase if its temperature is increased ?
3. A cylinder containing a gas is lifted from the first floor to the second floor. What is the amount of work done on the gas ? What is the amount of work done by the gas ? Is the internal energy of the gas increased ? Is the temperature of the gas increased ?
4. A force F is applied on a block of mass M. The block is displaced through a distance d in the direction of the force. What is the work done by the force on the block ? Does the internal energy change because of this work ?
5. The outer surface of a cylinder containing a gas is rubbed vigorously by a polishing machine. The cylinder and its gas become warm. Is the energy transferred to the gas heat or work ?
6. When we rub our hands they become warm. Have we supplied heat to the hands ?
7. A closed bottle contains some liquid. The bottle is shaken vigorously for 5 minutes. It is found that the temperature of the liquid is increased. Is heat transferred to the liquid ? Is work done on the liquid ? Neglect expansion on heating.
8. The final volume of a system is equal to the initial volume in a certain process. Is the work done by the system necessarily zero ? Is it necessarily nonzero ?
9. Can work be done by a system without changing its volume ?
10. An ideal gas is pumped into a rigid container having diathermic walls so that the temperature remains constant. In a certain time interval, the pressure in the container is doubled. Is the internal energy of the contents of the container also doubled in the interval ?
11. When a tyre bursts, the air coming out is cooler than the surrounding air. Explain.
12. When we heat an object, it expands. Is work done by the object in this process ? Is heat given to the object equal to the increase in its internal energy ?
13. When we stir a liquid vigorously, it becomes warm. Is it a reversible process ?
14. What should be the condition for the efficiency of a Carnot engine to be equal to 1 ?
15. When an object cools down, heat is withdrawn from it. Does the entropy of the object decrease in this process ? If yes, is it a violation of the second law of thermodynamics stated in terms of increase in entropy ?

OBJECTIVE I

1. The first law of thermodynamics is a statement of
(a) conservation of heat
(b) conservation of work
(c) conservation of momentum
(d) conservation of energy.

2. If heat is supplied to an ideal gas in an isothermal process,
(a) the internal energy of the gas will increase
(b) the gas will do positive work
(c) the gas will do negative work
(d) the said process is not possible.

3. Figure (26-Q1) shows two processes A and B on a system. Let ΔQ_1 and ΔQ_2 be the heat given to the system in processes A and B respectively. Then
(a) $\Delta Q_1 > \Delta Q_2$ (b) $\Delta Q_1 = \Delta Q_2$ (c) $\Delta Q_1 < \Delta Q_2$ (d) $\Delta Q_1 \leq \Delta Q_2$.

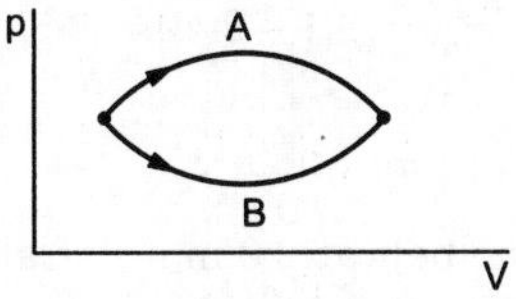

Figure 26-Q1

4. Refer to figure (26-Q1). Let ΔU_1 and ΔU_2 be the changes in internal energy of the system in the processes A and B. Then
(a) $\Delta U_1 > \Delta U_2$ (b) $\Delta U_1 = \Delta U_2$
(c) $\Delta U_1 < \Delta U_2$ (d) $\Delta U_1 \neq \Delta U_2$.

5. Consider the process on a system shown in figure (26-Q2). During the process, the work done by the system
(a) continuously increases
(b) continuously decreases
(c) first increases then decreases
(d) first decreases then increases.

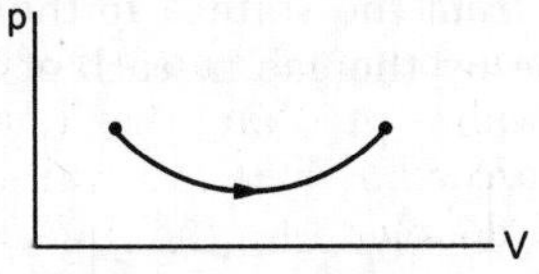

Figure 26-Q2

6. Consider the following two statements.
(A) If heat is added to a system, its temperature must increase.
(B) If positive work is done by a system in a thermodynamic process, its volume must increase.
(a) Both A and B are correct.
(b) A is correct but B is wrong.
(c) B is correct but A is wrong.
(d) Both A and B are wrong.

7. An ideal gas goes from the state i to the state f as shown in figure (26-Q3). The work done by the gas during the process
(a) is positive (b) is negative (c) is zero
(d) cannot be obtained from this information.

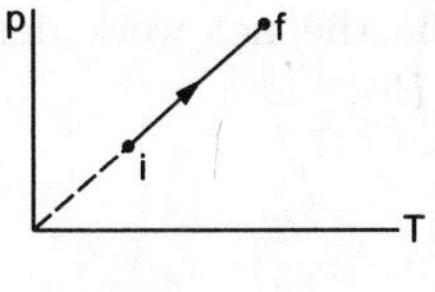

Figure 26-Q3

8. Consider two processes on a system as shown in figure (26-Q4).

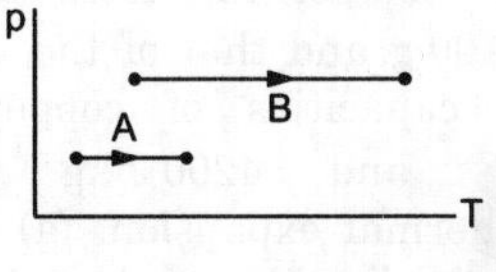

Figure 26-Q4

The volumes in the initial states are the same in the two processes and the volumes in the final states are also the same. Let ΔW_1 and ΔW_2 be the work done by the system in the processes A and B respectively.
(a) $\Delta W_1 > \Delta W_2$. (b) $\Delta W_1 = \Delta W_2$. (c) $\Delta W_1 < \Delta W_2$.
(d) Nothing can be said about the relation between ΔW_1 and ΔW_2.

9. A gas is contained in a metallic cylinder fitted with a piston. The piston is suddenly moved in to compress the gas and is maintained at this position. As time passes the pressure of the gas in the cylinder
(a) increases (b) decreases
(c) remains constant
(d) increases or decreases depending on the nature of the gas.

OBJECTIVE II

1. The pressure p and volume V of an ideal gas both increase in a process.

(a) Such a process is not possible.

(b) The work done by the system is positive.

(c) The temperature of the system must increase.

(d) Heat supplied to the gas is equal to the change in internal energy.

2. In a process on a system, the initial pressure and volume are equal to the final pressure and volume.

(a) The initial temperature must be equal to the final temperature.

(b) The initial internal energy must be equal to the final internal energy.
(c) The net heat given to the system in the process must be zero.
(d) The net work done by the system in the process must be zero.

3. A system can be taken from the initial state p_1, V_1 to the final state p_2, V_2 by two different methods. Let ΔQ and ΔW represent the heat given to the system and the work done by the system. Which of the following must be the same in both the methods ?
(a) ΔQ (b) ΔW (c) $\Delta Q + \Delta W$ (d) $\Delta Q - \Delta W$.

4. Refer to figure (26-Q5). Let ΔU_1 and ΔU_2 be the change in internal energy in processes A and B respectively, ΔQ be the net heat given to the system in process $A+B$ and ΔW be the net work done by the system in the process $A+B$.

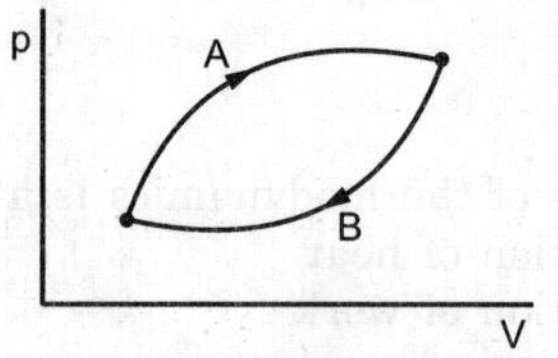

Figure 26-Q5

(a) $\Delta U_1 + \Delta U_2 = 0$. (b) $\Delta U_1 - \Delta U_2 = 0$.
(c) $\Delta Q - \Delta W = 0$. (d) $\Delta Q + \Delta W = 0$.

5. The internal energy of an ideal gas decreases by the same amount as the work done by the system.
(a) The process must be adiabatic.
(b) The process must be isothermal.
(c) The process must be isobaric.
(d) The temperature must decrease.

EXERCISES

1. A thermally insulated, closed copper vessel contains water at 15°C. When the vessel is shaken vigorously for 15 minutes, the temperature rises to 17°C. The mass of the vessel is 100 g and that of the water is 200 g. The specific heat capacities of copper and water are 420 J kg^{-1} K^{-1} and 4200 J kg^{-1} K^{-1} respectively. Neglect any thermal expansion. (a) How much heat is transferred to the liquid–vessel system ? (b) How much work has been done on this system ? (c) How much is the increase in internal energy of the system ?

2. Figure (26-E1) shows a paddle wheel coupled to a mass of 12 kg through fixed frictionless pulleys. The paddle is immersed in a liquid of heat capacity 4200 J K^{-1} kept in an adiabatic container. Consider a time interval in which the 12 kg block falls slowly through 70 cm. (a) How much heat is given to the liquid ? (b) How much work is done on the liquid ? (c) Calculate the rise in the temperature of the liquid neglecting the heat capacity of the container and the paddle.

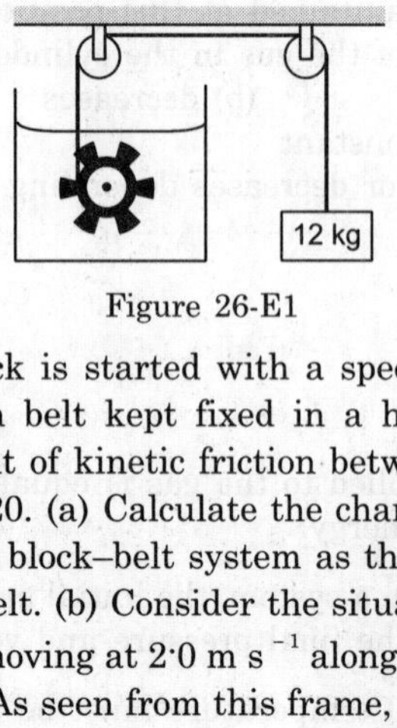

Figure 26-E1

3. A 100 kg block is started with a speed of 2·0 m s^{-1} on a long, rough belt kept fixed in a horizontal position. The coefficient of kinetic friction between the block and the belt is 0·20. (a) Calculate the change in the internal energy of the block–belt system as the block comes to a stop on the belt. (b) Consider the situation from a frame of reference moving at 2·0 m s^{-1} along the initial velocity of the block. As seen from this frame, the block is gently put on a moving belt and in due time the block starts moving with the belt at 2·0 m s^{-1}. Calculate the increase in the kinetic energy of the block as it stops slipping past the belt. (c) Find the work done in this frame by the external force holding the belt.

4. Calculate the change in internal energy of a gas kept in a rigid container when 100 J of heat is supplied to it.

5. The pressure of a gas changes linearly with volume from 10 kPa, 200 cc to 50 kPa, 50 cc. (a) Calculate the work done by the gas. (b) If no heat is supplied or extracted from the gas, what is the change in the internal energy of the gas ?

6. An ideal gas is taken from an initial state i to a final state f in such a way that the ratio of the pressure to the absolute temperature remains constant. What will be the work done by the gas ?

7. Figure (26-E2) shows three paths through which a gas can be taken from the state A to the state B. Calculate the work done by the gas in each of the three paths.

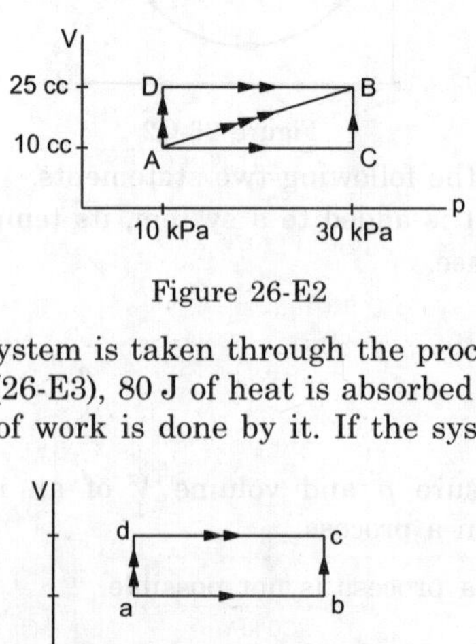

Figure 26-E2

8. When a system is taken through the process abc shown in figure (26-E3), 80 J of heat is absorbed by the system and 30 J of work is done by it. If the system does 10 J

Figure 26-E3

of work during the process *adc*, how much heat flows into it during the process ?

9. 50 cal of heat should be supplied to take a system from the state *A* to the state *B* through the path *ACB* as shown in figure (26-E4). Find the quantity of heat to be supplied to take it from *A* to *B* via *ADB*.

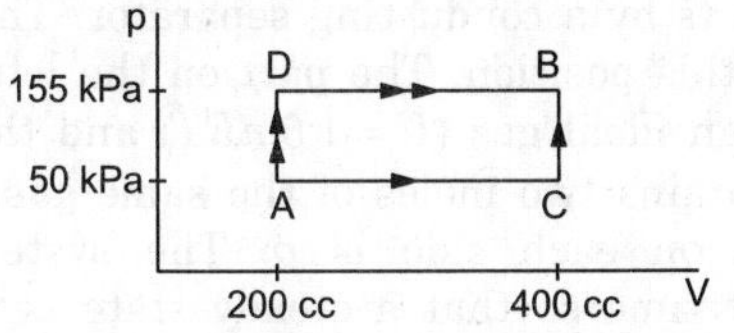

Figure 26-E4

10. Calculate the heat absorbed by a system in going through the cyclic process shown in figure (26-E5).

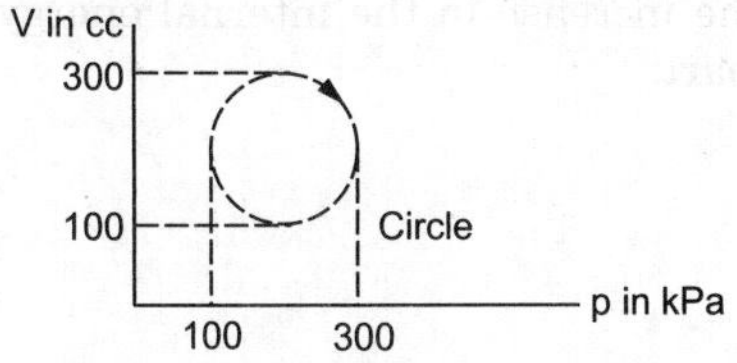

Figure 26-E5

11. A gas is taken through a cyclic process *ABCA* as shown in figure (26-E6). If 2·4 cal of heat is given in the process, what is the value of *J* ?

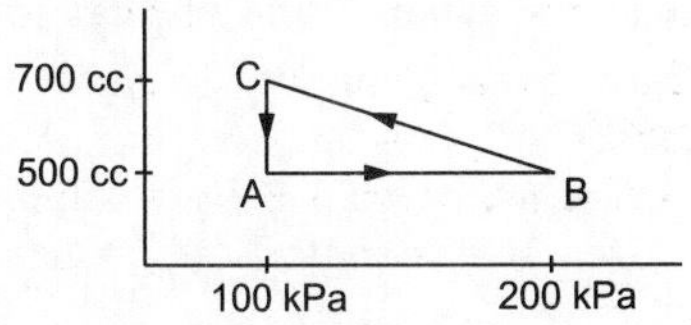

Figure 26-E6

12. A substance is taken through the process *abc* as shown in figure (26-E7). If the internal energy of the substance increases by 5000 J and a heat of 2625 cal is given to the system, calculate the value of *J*.

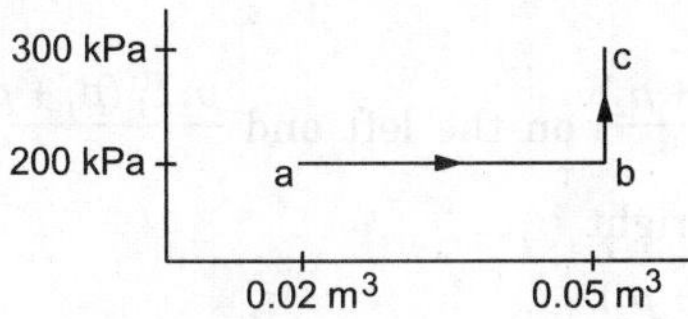

Figure 26-E7

13. A gas is taken along the path *AB* as shown in figure (26-E8). If 70 cal of heat is extracted from the gas in the process, calculate the change in the internal energy of the system.

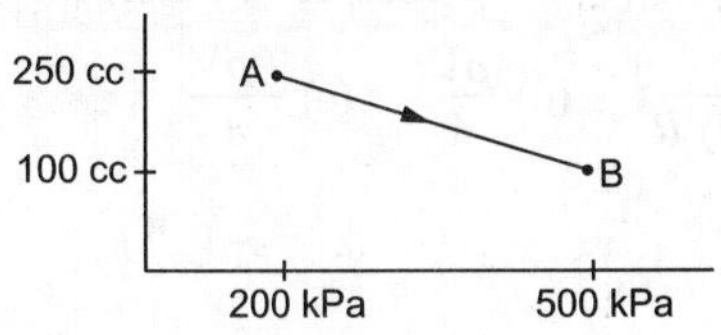

Figure 26-E8

14. The internal energy of a gas is given by $U = 1{\cdot}5\,pV$. It expands from 100 cm^3 to 200 cm^3 against a constant pressure of $1{\cdot}0 \times 10^5$ Pa. Calculate the heat absorbed by the gas in the process.

15. A gas is enclosed in a cylindrical vessel fitted with a frictionless piston. The gas is slowly heated for some time. During the process, 10 J of heat is supplied and the piston is found to move out 10 cm. Find the increase in the internal energy of the gas. The area of cross section of the cylinder = 4 cm^2 and the atmospheric pressure = 100 kPa.

16. A gas is initially at a pressure of 100 kPa and its volume is 2·0 m^3. Its pressure is kept constant and the volume is changed from 2·0 m^3 to 2·5 m^3. Its volume is now kept constant and the pressure is increased from 100 kPa to 200 kPa. The gas is brought back to its initial state, the pressure varying linearly with its volume. (a) Whether the heat is supplied to or extracted from the gas in the complete cycle ? (b) How much heat was supplied or extracted ?

17. Consider the cyclic process *ABCA*, shown in figure (26-E9), performed on a sample of 2·0 mol of an ideal gas. A total of 1200 J of heat is withdrawn from the sample in the process. Find the work done by the gas during the part *BC*.

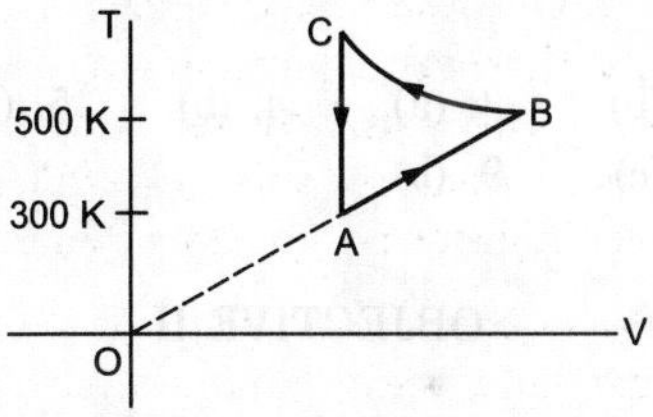

Figure 26-E9

18. Figure (26-E10) shows the variation in the internal energy *U* with the volume *V* of 2·0 mol of an ideal gas in a cyclic process *abcda*. The temperatures of the gas at *b* and *c* are 500 K and 300 K respectively. Calculate the heat absorbed by the gas during the process.

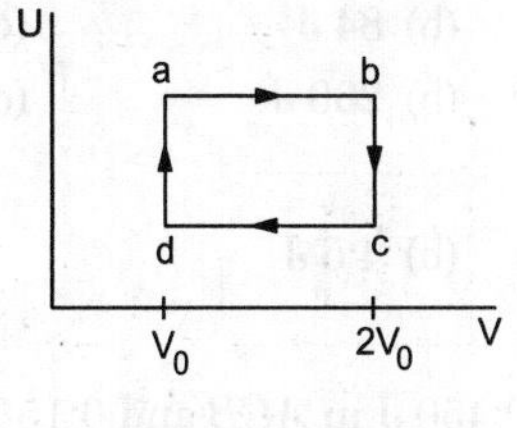

Figure 26-E10

19. Find the change in the internal energy of 2 kg of water as it is heated from 0°C to 4°C. The specific heat capacity of water is 4200 J kg^{-1} K^{-1} and its densities at 0°C and 4°C are 999·9 kg m^{-3} and 1000 kg m^{-3} respectively. Atmospheric pressure = 10^5 Pa.

20. Calculate the increase in the internal energy of 10 g of water when it is heated from 0°C to 100°C and converted into steam at 100 kPa. The density of steam = 0·6 kg m^{-3}. Specific heat capacity of water = 4200 J kg^{-1} °C^{-1} and the latent heat of vaporization of water = 2.25 × 10 6 J kg^{-1}.

21. Figure (26-E11) shows a cylindrical tube of volume V with adiabatic walls containing an ideal gas. The internal energy of this ideal gas is given by 1·5 nRT. The tube is divided into two equal parts by a fixed diathermic wall. Initially, the pressure and the temperature are p_1, T_1 on the left and p_2, T_2 on the right. The system is left for sufficient time so that the temperature becomes equal on the two sides. (a) How much work has been done by the gas on the left part? (b) Find the final pressures on the two sides. (c) Find the final equilibrium temperature. (d) How much heat has flown from the gas on the right to the gas on the left?

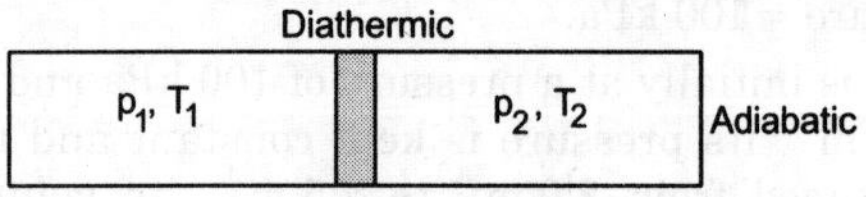

Figure 26-E11

22. An adiabatic vessel of total volume V is divided into two equal parts by a conducting separator. The separator is fixed in this position. The part on the left contains one mole of an ideal gas (U = 1·5 nRT) and the part on the right contains two moles of the same gas. Initially, the pressure on each side is p. The system is left for sufficient time so that a steady state is reached. Find (a) the work done by the gas in the left part during the process, (b) the temperature on the two sides in the beginning, (c) the final common temperature reached by the gases, (d) the heat given to the gas in the right part and (e) the increase in the internal energy of the gas in the left part.

□

ANSWERS

OBJECTIVE I

1. (d) 2. (b) 3. (a) 4. (b) 5. (a) 6. (c)
7. (c) 8. (c) 9. (b)

OBJECTIVE II

1. (b), (c) 2. (a), (b) 3. (d) 4. (a), (c)
5. (a), (d)

EXERCISES

1. (a) zero (b) 1764 J (c) 1764 J
2. (a) zero (b) 84 J (c) 0·02°C
3. (a) 200 J (b) 200 J (c) 400 J
4. 100 J
5. (a) −4·5 J (b) 4·5 J
6. zero
7. 0·30 J in AB, 0·450 J in ACB and 0·150 J in ADB
8. 60 J
9. 55 cal
10. 31·4 J
11. 4·17 J cal^{-1}
12. 4·19 J cal^{-1}
13. −241 J
14. 25 J
15. 6 J
16. (a) extracted (b) 25000 J
17. −4520 J
18. 2300 J
19. (33600 − 0·02) J
20. 2·5 × 10^4 J
21. (a) zero
(b) $\frac{p_1 T_2 (p_1 + p_2)}{\lambda}$ on the left and $\frac{p_2 T_1 (p_1 + p_2)}{\lambda}$ on the right
(c) $\frac{T_1 T_2 (p_1 + p_2)}{\lambda}$
(d) $\frac{3 p_1 p_2 (T_2 - T_1) V}{4\lambda}$ where $\lambda = p_1 T_2 + p_2 T_1$
22. (a) zero (b) $\frac{pV}{(2 \text{ mol}) R}$, $\frac{pV}{(4 \text{ mol}) R}$
(c) $\frac{pV}{(3 \text{ mol}) R}$ (d) $\frac{pV}{4}$ (e) $\frac{-pV}{4}$

□

CHAPTER 27

SPECIFIC HEAT CAPACITIES OF GASES

27.1 TWO KINDS OF SPECIFIC HEAT CAPACITIES OF GASES

The specific heat capacity of a substance is defined as the heat supplied per unit mass of the substance per unit rise in the temperature. If an amount ΔQ of heat is given to a mass m of the substance and its temperature rises by ΔT, the specific heat capacity s is given by the equation

$$s = \frac{\Delta Q}{m\,\Delta T} \cdot \qquad \text{... (27.1)}$$

This definition applies to any mode of the substance, solid, liquid or gas.

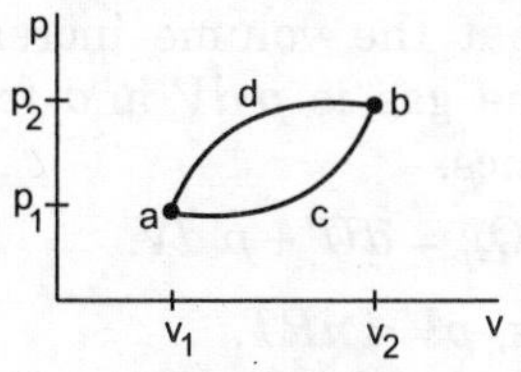

Figure 27.1

Consider a mass m of a gas at pressure p_1, volume V_1 and temperature T_1. We show this state by the point a in the p–V diagram of figure (27.1). The point b represents another state in which the pressure is p_2, the volume is V_2 and the temperature is T_2. The change in temperature as the system is taken from a to b is $\Delta T = T_2 - T_1$. The internal energy of the gas at a is U_1 and at b it is U_2. The change in internal energy as the system is taken from a to b is $\Delta U = U_2 - U_1$. If the work done by the gas in taking it from a to b is ΔW and the heat supplied is ΔQ, from the first law of thermodynamics,

$$\Delta Q = \Delta U + \Delta W.$$

Now, the work done ΔW depends on the process by which the gas is taken from a to b. For example, the work done is smaller if the gas is taken through the process acb and is larger if the process is adb. Accordingly, ΔQ is smaller in the process acb and is larger in the process adb. In both these processes, the change in temperature ΔT is the same. So the heat ΔQ given to raise the temperature of a gas by ΔT, depends on the process involved. From equation (27.1), the specific heat capacity s also depends on the process. Thus, to define the specific heat capacity of a gas the process should also be specified.

Suppose, the volume of a gas of mass m is kept constant and heat ΔQ is given to it. If its temperature rises by ΔT, the specific heat capacity given by equation (27.1) is called the *specific heat capacity at constant volume* and is denoted by the symbol s_V. Thus,

$$s_V = \left(\frac{\Delta Q}{m\,\Delta T}\right)_{\text{constant volume}} \cdot \qquad \text{... (27.2)}$$

Next suppose, the pressure of a gas of mass m is kept constant and heat ΔQ is given to it. If the temperature rises by ΔT, the specific heat capacity given by equation (27.1) is called the *specific heat capacity at constant pressure* and is denoted by the symbol s_p. Thus,

$$s_p = \left(\frac{\Delta Q}{m\,\Delta T}\right)_{\text{constant pressure}} \cdot \qquad \text{... (27.3)}$$

There can be many more processes, but these two are more important and correspondingly two specific heat capacities are defined for gases.

The above discussion is also valid for solids and liquids. However, in these systems the expansion is quite small and hence the work done in a process is small. Thus, the specific heat capacity depends only slightly on the process and the process is generally not mentioned.

The molar heat capacities of a gas are defined as the heat given per mole of the gas per unit rise in the temperature. The *molar heat capacity at constant volume*, denoted by C_V, is

$$C_V = \left(\frac{\Delta Q}{n\,\Delta T}\right)_{\text{constant volume}} \qquad \text{... (27.4)}$$

and the *molar heat capacity at constant pressure*, denoted by C_p, is

$$C_p = \left(\frac{\Delta Q}{n\,\Delta T}\right)_{\text{constant pressure}} \quad \dots \quad (27.5)$$

where n is the amount of the gas in number of moles. Quite often, the term *specific heat capacity* or *specific heat* is used for molar heat capacity. It is advised that the unit be carefully noted to determine the actual meaning. The unit of specific heat capacity is J kg^{-1} K^{-1} whereas that of molar heat capacity is J K^{-1} mol^{-1}.

Example 27.1

0·32 g of oxygen is kept in a rigid container and is heated. Find the amount of heat needed to raise the temperature from 25°C to 35°C. The molar heat capacity of oxygen at constant volume is 20 J K^{-1} mol^{-1}.

Solution : The molecular weight of oxygen = 32 g mol^{-1}.

The amount of the gas in moles is

$$n = \frac{0{\cdot}32 \text{ g}}{32 \text{ g mol}^{-1}} = 0{\cdot}01 \text{ mol.}$$

The amount of heat needed is $Q = nC_V\,\Delta T$

$$= (0{\cdot}01 \text{ mol})\,(20 \text{ J K}^{-1} \text{ mol}^{-1})\,(10 \text{ K}) = 2{\cdot}0 \text{ J.}$$

Example 27.2

A tank of volume 0·2 m^3 contains helium gas at a temperature of 300 K and pressure 1·0 × 10^5 N m^{-2}. Find the amount of heat required to raise the temperature to 400 K. The molar heat capacity of helium at constant volume is 3·0 cal K^{-1} mol^{-1}. Neglect any expansion in the volume of the tank.

Solution : The amount of the gas in moles is

$$n = \frac{pV}{RT}$$

$$= \frac{(1{\cdot}0 \times 10^5 \text{ N m}^{-2})\,(0{\cdot}2 \text{ m}^3)}{(8{\cdot}31 \text{ J K}^{-1} \text{ mol}^{-1})\,(300 \text{ K})} = 8{\cdot}0 \text{ mol.}$$

The amount of heat required is

$$\Delta Q = nC_V\,\Delta T$$

$$= (8{\cdot}0 \text{ mol})\,(3{\cdot}0 \text{ cal mol}^{-1} \text{ K}^{-1})\,(100 \text{ K}) = 2400 \text{ cal.}$$

27.2 RELATION BETWEEN C_P AND C_V FOR AN IDEAL GAS

Suppose, the volume of a gas is kept constant and heat is supplied to it. The work done by the gas is zero. The entire heat supplied goes as internal energy of the gas and is used to increase the temperature. Now consider a process in which the pressure is kept constant. If heat is supplied to the gas, its volume increases. A part of the heat supplied is used by the gas to do work in the expansion. Only the remaining part goes as increase in the internal energy which increases the temperature. Thus, for a given amount ΔQ of heat, the rise in temperature of a gas at constant pressure is smaller than the rise in temperature at constant volume. Thus, $C_p > C_V$.

Consider an amount n (in moles) of an ideal gas kept in a rigid container at an initial pressure p, volume V and temperature T. An amount $(dQ)_V$ of heat is supplied to the gas. Its temperature rises from T to $T + dT$ whereas the volume remains constant. The work done by the gas is $dW = 0$. From the first law of thermodynamics, the internal energy changes by dU such that

$$(dQ)_V = dU. \quad \dots \quad \text{(i)}$$

Now suppose, the same sample of the gas is taken in a vessel with a movable light piston of cross-sectional area A (figure 27.2). The initial pressure, volume and temperature are p, V and T. The piston is pushed by a constant external force $F = pA$. The pressure inside the gas thus remains constant at the value p.

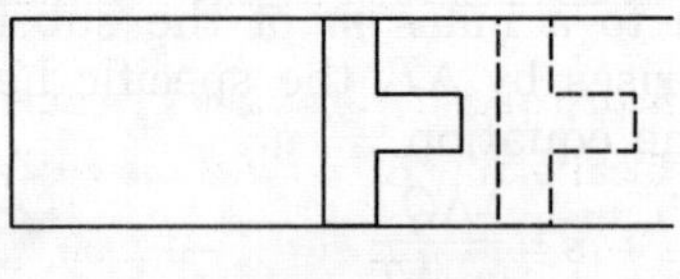

Figure 27.2

The gas is given heat $(dQ)_p$ which raises the temperature by the same amount dT. The piston moves out so that the volume increases by dV. The work done by the gas is $p\,dV$ and from the first law of thermodynamics,

$$(dQ)_p = dU' + p\,dV. \quad \dots \quad \text{(ii)}$$

For an ideal gas, $pV = nRT$.

As the pressure remains constant,

$$p(V + dV) = nR(T + dT)$$

and hence,

$$p\,dV = nR dT.$$

From (ii),

$$(dQ)_p = dU' + nR\,dT. \quad \dots \quad \text{(iii)}$$

As the temperature rises by the same amount in the two cases and the internal energy of an ideal gas depends only on its temperature,

$$dU = dU'.$$

Thus, from (i) and (iii),

$$(dQ)_p = (dQ)_V + nR\,dT$$

or,

$$\frac{1}{n}\frac{(dQ)_p}{dT} = \frac{1}{n}\frac{(dQ)_V}{dT} + R. \quad \dots \quad \text{(iv)}$$

But $(dQ)_p$ is the heat given to increase the temperature of the gas by dT at constant pressure. Thus, by definition,

$$C_p = \frac{1}{n}\frac{(dQ)_p}{dT}.$$

Similarly, $C_V = \dfrac{1}{n}\dfrac{(dQ)_V}{dT}$

and (iv) becomes

$$C_p = C_V + R$$

or, $$C_p - C_V = R. \quad \text{... (27.6)}$$

Relations of C_V with energy

From (i), $(dQ)_V = dU$

or, $$\frac{1}{n}\frac{(dQ)_V}{dT} = \frac{1}{n}\frac{dU}{dT}$$

or, $$C_V = \frac{1}{n}\frac{dU}{dT} \quad \text{... (27.7)}$$

or, $$dU = nC_V\, dT.$$

Taking the energy to be zero at $T = 0$,

$$U = nC_V T. \quad \text{... (27.8)}$$

Example 27.3

The molar heat capacity of a gas at constant volume is found to be 5 cal mol^{-1} K^{-1}. *Find the ratio* $\gamma = C_p/C_V$ *for the gas. The gas constant* $R = 2$ cal mol^{-1} K^{-1}.

Solution : We have $C_V = 5$ cal mol^{-1} K^{-1}.

Thus, $C_p = C_V + R = 5$ cal mol^{-1} K^{-1} + 2 cal mol^{-1} K^{-1}

= 7 cal mol^{-1} K^{-1}

or, $$\frac{C_p}{C_V} = \frac{7}{5} = 1{\cdot}4.$$

27.3 DETERMINATION OF C_p OF A GAS

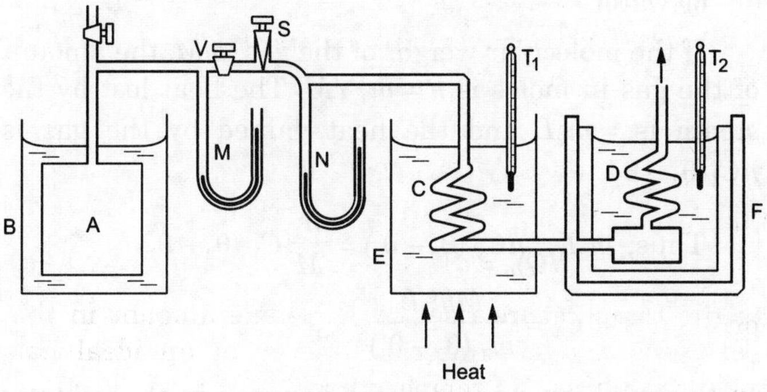

Figure 27.3

Figure (27.3) shows a schematic diagram of the Regnault's apparatus to measure C_p of a gas. The experimental gas is taken at a high pressure in a large tank A immersed in water at a constant temperature. The tank is connected through a tube to two copper coils C and D. A valve V in the tube opens or closes the path for the gas to flow. The rate of flow can be increased or decreased by adjusting a screw valve S. The first copper coil C is immersed in a hot oil bath E and the second copper coil D is immersed in a calorimeter F containing water. Thermometers T_1 and T_2 are provided in the bath E and the calorimeter F. A manometer M connected close to the tank measures the pressure of the gas in the tank. Another manometer N connected after the screw valve S measures the pressure of the gas flowing in the calorimeter.

To do the experiment, the oil bath is heated with a burner to keep it at a high temperature which is measured by the thermometer T_1. A measured mass m of water is taken in the calorimeter. The calorimeter should be almost full with water so that the gas flowing through the coil D gets maximum time to exchange heat with the water. The initial temperature of the water is measured by T_2. The difference in the heights of mercury in the two arms of the manometer M is noted. The valve V is opened to allow the gas to flow through the system. As the amount of the gas in the tank reduces, the pressure in it decreases and the rate of flow tends to decrease. The screw valve S is continuously adjusted to keep the rate of flow constant. This is decided by keeping the difference in the levels of mercury in manometer N constant. The pressure of the gas going in the coil then remains constant. The gas is allowed to flow for some time and the final temperature of water and the final difference in the mercury levels in the manometer M are noted.

Let the water equivalent of the calorimeter together with the coil D $= W$

mass of the water $= m$

temperature of the oil bath $= \theta_1$

initial temperature of water $= \theta_2$

final temperature of water $= \theta_3$

and the amount of the gas (in moles) passed through the water $= n$.

The gas at temperature θ_1 enters the coil D. In the beginning of the experiment, the gas leaves the coil D at temperature θ_2. This temperature gradually increases and at the end of the experiment it becomes θ_3. The average temperature of the gas leaving the coil D is, therefore, $\frac{\theta_2 + \theta_3}{2}$. The heat lost by the gas is

$$\Delta Q = n\, C_p\left[\theta_1 - \frac{\theta_2 + \theta_3}{2}\right]. \quad \text{... (i)}$$

This heat is used to increase the temperature of the calorimeter, the water and the coil D from θ_2 to θ_3. The heat received by them is

$$\Delta Q = (W + m)s\,(\theta_3 - \theta_2) \quad \text{... (ii)}$$

where s is the specific heat capacity of water. From (i) and (ii),

$$nC_p\left[\theta_1 - \frac{\theta_2 + \theta_3}{2}\right] = (W + m)s\,(\theta_3 - \theta_2)$$

$$\text{or,}\quad C_p = \frac{(W+m)s\,(\theta_3 - \theta_2)}{n\left[\theta_1 - \dfrac{\theta_2 + \theta_3}{2}\right]} \cdot \quad \dots \text{(iii)}$$

Determination of *n*

Suppose the difference in the mercury levels in the manometer M is h and the atmospheric pressure is equal to a height H of mercury. The pressure in the tank is p, equal to a height $H+h$ of mercury. By noting the difference h at the beginning and at the end of the experiment, the initial pressure p_1 and the final pressure p_2 are determined. Assuming the gas to be ideal,

$$p_1 V = n_1 RT$$

$$\text{and}\quad p_2 V = n_2 RT.$$

Here n_1, n_2 are the amounts of the gas (in moles) in the tank at the beginning and at the end respectively, V is the volume of the tank and T is the absolute temperature of the tank. Thus,

$$(p_1 - p_2)V = (n_1 - n_2)RT$$

$$\text{or,}\quad n = n_1 - n_2 = \frac{(p_1 - p_2)V}{RT} \cdot$$

Putting in (iii), one can find the value of C_p.

27.4 DETERMINATION OF C_V OF A GAS

Figure (27.4) shows a schematic diagram of Joly's differential steam calorimeter used to measure C_v of a gas. Two hollow copper spheres A and B are suspended from the pans of a sensitive balance. The spheres are enclosed in a steam chamber. The balance is placed over the steam chamber. Two pans C and D are fitted below the spheres.

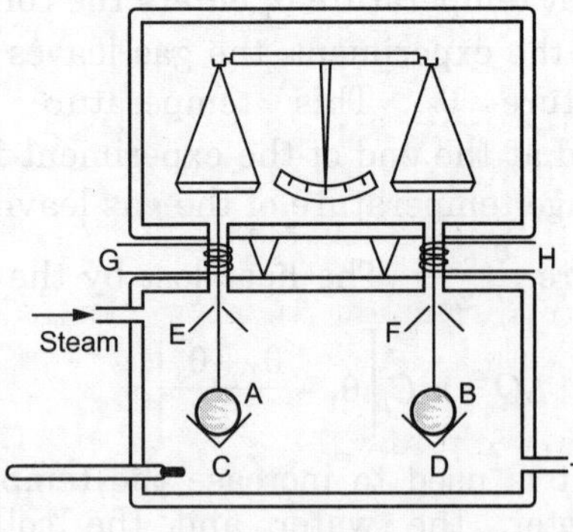

Figure 27.4

Umbrella-like shields E, F are provided over the spheres. Plaster of paris tubes are provided at the holes in the steam chamber through which the suspension wires pass. These are heated electrically by the coils G, H. This ensures that when steam is sent into the steam chamber, no drops are formed on the wires and they move freely as the balance pans oscillate. The shields E, F do not allow the drops to fall on the spheres or on the pans. A thermometer is fitted in the steam chamber.

To do the experiment, air is pumped out of the spheres and the spheres are balanced. The experimental gas is filled in one of the spheres, say B, and additional weights are put on the balance pan so that the spheres are again balanced. This gives the mass of the gas. The temperature of the steam chamber is noted. This gives the initial temperature of the gas.

Steam is now passed through the steam chamber. The steam condenses on the spheres and the water formed is collected in the pans C and D. The temperatures of the spheres rise. More steam condenses on the pan which is below the sphere containing the gas. This is because the steam has to raise the temperature of the sphere as well as of the gas. When the temperature becomes steady, the spheres are again balanced by putting extra weights. This extra weight gives the amount of steam needed to raise the temperature of the gas only. The final temperature in steady state is noted.

Suppose,

the mass of the gas taken $= m_1$
the mass of the extra steam condensed $= m_2$
initial temperature of the gas $= \theta_1$
final temperature of the gas $= \theta_2$
specific latent heat of vaporization of water $= L$.

If the molecular weight of the gas is M, the amount of the gas in moles is $n = m_1 / M$. The heat lost by the steam is $= m_2 L$ and the heat gained by the gas is $nC_V(\theta_2 - \theta_1)$.

$$\text{Thus,}\quad m_2 L = nC_V(\theta_2 - \theta_1) = \frac{m_1}{M} C_V(\theta_2 - \theta_1)$$

$$\text{or,}\quad C_V = \frac{Mm_2 L}{m_1(\theta_2 - \theta_1)} \cdot$$

In this we have neglected the increase in the volumes of the spheres as the temperature rises.

27.5 ISOTHERMAL AND ADIABATIC PROCESSES

Isothermal Process

A process on a system is called isothermal if the temperature of the system remains constant. In case of an ideal gas the internal energy remains constant in such a process. The amount of heat supplied is equal to the work done by the gas. The gas obeys Boyle's law and the work done by the gas is

$$W = \int_{V_i}^{V_f} p\,dV = \int_{V_i}^{V_f} n\frac{RT}{V}\,dV = nRT\ln(V_f / V_i).$$

This is also the amount of heat given as the volume of the gas is changed from V_i to V_f. As the change in temperature is zero, the molar heat capacity in such a process is

$$C_{isothermal} = \frac{\Delta Q}{n\,\Delta T} = \text{infinity}.$$

An isothermal process may be achieved by immersing the system in a large reservoir and performing the process very slowly. The temperature of the system then remains equal to the temperature of the reservoir. Heat may be exchanged between the reservoir and the system if necessary.

As an example, if a gas is taken in a metal cylinder (good conductor of heat) fitted with a piston and the piston is moved slowly, the temperature of the gas does not change. It remains equal to the temperature of the surrounding air. If the temperature tends to increase, heat is conducted from the gas to the air through the metallic walls. Similarly, if the temperature tends to decrease, heat is conducted from the surrounding air to the gas through the metallic walls. Here the surrounding air acts as a large reservoir.

Adiabatic Process

A process on a system is called adiabatic if no heat is supplied to it or extracted from it. In such a case, the temperature changes without adding any heat. The molar heat capacity in such a process is

$$C_{adiabatic} = \frac{\Delta Q}{n\,\Delta T} = \text{zero}.$$

The work done by the gas in an adiabatic process equals the decrease in its internal energy. Thus, if a gas enclosed in a container with adiabatic walls expands, the internal energy decreases and hence the temperature falls. If the gas is compressed adiabatically, the temperature rises.

27.6 RELATIONS BETWEEN p, V, T IN A REVERSIBLE ADIABATIC PROCESS

Relation between p and V

Consider an adiabatic process on an ideal gas. During a short part of the process, the pressure, the volume and the temperature change from p, V, T to $p + dp$, $V + dV$ and $T + dT$ respectively. The internal energy changes from U to $U + dU$. As the amount of heat supplied is zero, the first law of thermodynamics gives

$$0 = dU + p\,dV. \quad \text{... (i)}$$

We have, $C_V = \dfrac{1}{n}\dfrac{dU}{dT}$

or, $dU = nC_V dT$.

Thus, from (i),

$$nC_V dT + p\,dV = 0. \quad \text{... (ii)}$$

As the gas is ideal,

$$pV = nRT$$

or, $p\,dV + V\,dp = nR\,dT$

or, $dT = \dfrac{p\,dV + V\,dp}{nR}$.

Substituting this expression for dT in (ii),

$$C_V\left(\frac{p\,dV + V\,dp}{R}\right) + p\,dV = 0$$

or, $(C_V + R)\,p\,dV + C_V\,V\,dp = 0$

or, $C_p\,p\,dV + C_V\,V\,dp = 0$

or, $\dfrac{C_p}{C_V}\dfrac{dV}{V} + \dfrac{dp}{p} = 0$

or, $\gamma\dfrac{dV}{V} = -\dfrac{dp}{p}$

where $\gamma = C_p / C_V$.

Let the initial pressure and volume be p_i and V_i respectively and the final pressure and volume be p_f and V_f respectively. Then

$$\int_{V_i}^{V_f} \gamma\frac{dV}{V} = -\int_{p_i}^{p_f} \frac{dp}{p}.$$

or, $\gamma \ln\dfrac{V_f}{V_i} = -\ln\dfrac{p_f}{p_i}$

or, $\ln\left(\dfrac{V_f}{V_i}\right)^{\gamma} = \ln\left(\dfrac{p_i}{p_f}\right)$

or, $\dfrac{V_f^{\gamma}}{V_i^{\gamma}} = \dfrac{p_i}{p_f}$

or, $p_i V_i^{\gamma} = p_f V_f^{\gamma}$

or, $pV^{\gamma} = \text{constant}. \quad \text{... (27.9)}$

Thus, pV^{γ} remains constant in a reversible adiabatic process.

Relation between p and T

We have $pV = nRT$

or, $V = \dfrac{nRT}{p}$.

Putting in (27.9),

$$p\left(\frac{nRT}{p}\right)^{\gamma} = \text{constant}$$

or, $p^{1-\gamma}\,T^{\gamma} = \text{constant}$

or, $$\frac{T^{\gamma}}{p^{\gamma-1}} = \text{constant.} \quad \ldots (27.10)$$

Relation between *V* and *T*

We have $$pV = nRT$$

or, $$p = \frac{nRT}{V}.$$

Putting in (27.9),

$$\left(\frac{nRT}{V}\right)V^{\gamma} = \text{constant}$$

or, $$TV^{\gamma-1} = \text{constant.} \quad \ldots (27.11)$$

Example 27.4

Dry air at 15°C *and* 10 atm *is suddenly released at atmospheric pressure. Find the final temperature of the air* $[C_p/C_V = 1{\cdot}41]$.

Solution : As the air is suddenly released, it does not get time to exchange heat with the surrounding. Thus the process is adiabatic. Assuming the process to be reversible,

$$\frac{T^{\gamma}}{p^{\gamma-1}} = \text{constant}$$

or, $$\frac{T_1^{\gamma}}{p_1^{\gamma-1}} = \frac{T_2^{\gamma}}{p_2^{\gamma-1}}$$

or, $$\left(\frac{T_2}{T_1}\right)^{\gamma} = \left(\frac{p_2}{p_1}\right)^{\gamma-1}$$

or, $$T_2 = T_1\left(\frac{p_2}{p_1}\right)^{\frac{\gamma-1}{\gamma}}.$$

Taking $p_1 = 10$ atm, $p_2 = 1$ atm, $\gamma = 1{\cdot}41$ and $T_1 = (273 + 15)$ K $= 288$ K, the final temperature is $T_2 = 148$ K.

27.7 WORK DONE IN AN ADIABATIC PROCESS

Suppose a sample of gas has initial pressure p_1 and initial volume V_1. In an adiabatic process, the pressure and volume change to p_2 and V_2. We have

$$pV^{\gamma} = p_1V_1^{\gamma} = p_2V_2^{\gamma} = K. \quad \ldots (i)$$

Thus, $$p = \frac{K}{V^{\gamma}}.$$

The work done by the gas in the process is

$$W = \int_{V_1}^{V_2} p\,dV = \int_{V_1}^{V_2} \frac{K}{V^{\gamma}}\,dV$$

$$= \frac{1}{1-\gamma}\left[\frac{K}{V_2^{\gamma-1}} - \frac{K}{V_1^{\gamma-1}}\right].$$

From (i), $\frac{K}{V_2^{\gamma}} = p_2$ and $\frac{K}{V_1^{\gamma}} = p_1$.

Thus, $$W = -\frac{1}{\gamma-1}(p_2V_2 - p_1V_1)$$

$$= \frac{p_1V_1 - p_2V_2}{\gamma - 1}. \quad \ldots (27.12)$$

27.8 EQUIPARTITION OF ENERGY

When we assume the molecules of a gas to be like hard spheres of negligible size, the energy of each molecule may be written as

$$E = \frac{1}{2}mv_x^2 + \frac{1}{2}mv_y^2 + \frac{1}{2}mv_z^2.$$

There are three terms in this expression and each may be treated independently. The above picture is suitable for monatomic gases. In diatomic gases the molecules are assumed to be in the shape of dumbbells, two hard spheres of negligible size at a separation. Apart from translational motion, the molecule can rotate about its centre. The energy is the sum of translational kinetic energy and rotational kinetic energy. If the line joining the two particles is taken as the *z*-axis, the rotational kinetic energy may be written as

$$\frac{1}{2}I_x\omega_x^2 + \frac{1}{2}I_y\omega_y^2,$$

the first term describing the energy of rotation about the *x*-axis and the second term describing the energy of rotation about the *y*-axis. As the size of each atom is assumed negligible, the moment of inertia I_z is negligible and no term like $\frac{1}{2}I_z\omega_z^2$ is added. The total energy is then

$$E = \frac{1}{2}mv_x^2 + \frac{1}{2}mv_y^2 + \frac{1}{2}mv_z^2 + \frac{1}{2}I_x\omega_x^2 + \frac{1}{2}I_y\omega_y^2.$$

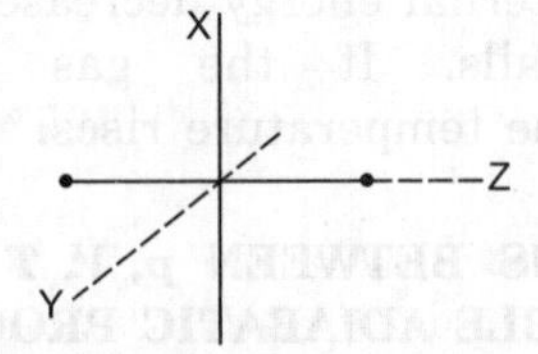

Figure 27.5

The number of independent terms in this expression is 5. If the two atoms of a diatomic molecule vibrate along its length, additional energy results. Such a vibration involves kinetic energy of vibration as well as the potential energy of the pair of atoms. The energy of vibration will be of the form

$$\frac{1}{2}\mu u^2 + \frac{1}{2}kr^2$$

where r is the separation between the atoms and $v = (dr/dt)$. The constant μ is related to the mass of the molecule and k is related to the force constant of the system. The total energy of a molecule is

$$E = \frac{1}{2}mv_x^2 + \frac{1}{2}mv_y^2 + \frac{1}{2}mv_z^2 + \frac{1}{2}I_x\omega_x^2 + \frac{1}{2}I_y\omega_y^2 + \frac{1}{2}\mu v^2 + \frac{1}{2}kr^2.$$

There are 7 independent terms.

For a polyatomic molecule, the number of terms in the rotational and vibrational energy depends on the actual arrangement of atoms in the molecule.

The number of independent terms in the expression of energy of a molecule is called its *degree of freedom*. Thus, the degree of freedom is 3 for a monatomic gas molecule, it is 5 for a diatomic molecule if the molecule does not vibrate and is 7 if it vibrates.

Equipartition of energy states that *the average energy of a molecule in a gas associated with each degree of freedom is* $\frac{1}{2}kT$ *where k is the Boltzmann constant and T is its absolute temperature.*

The theorem may be proved using more advanced techniques of statistical mechanics.

According to the equipartition theorem, the average energy of a molecule in a monatomic gas is $\frac{3}{2}kT$ as the degree of freedom is 3. This is also the result of the kinetic theory of gases.

For diatomic gases, the average energy per molecule is $\frac{5}{2}kT$ if the molecules translate and rotate but do not vibrate, and is $\frac{7}{2}kT$ if they vibrate also.

Now, consider a sample of amount n (in moles) of an ideal gas. The total number of molecules is nN_A where N_A is the Avogadro number. If the gas is monatomic, the internal energy of the gas is

$$U = nN_A\left(\frac{3}{2}kT\right) = n\frac{3}{2}RT.$$

The molar heat capacity at constant volume is

$$C_V = \frac{1}{n}\frac{dU}{dT} = \frac{3}{2}R.$$

The molar heat capacity at constant pressure is

$$C_p = C_V + R = \frac{3}{2}R + R = \frac{5}{2}R.$$

Thus, $$\gamma = \frac{C_p}{C_V} = \frac{5}{3} = 1{\cdot}67.$$

For a sample of a diatomic gas,

$$U = nN_A\left(\frac{5}{2}kT\right) = n\frac{5}{2}RT$$

if the molecules do not vibrate. In this case,

$$C_V = \frac{1}{n}\frac{dU}{dT} = \frac{5}{2}R \text{ and } C_p = C_V + R = \frac{5}{2}R + R = \frac{7}{2}R.$$

Thus, $\gamma = \frac{C_p}{C_V} = \frac{7}{5} = 1{\cdot}40.$

If the molecules do vibrate, $U = n\frac{7}{2}RT$

so that, $C_V = \frac{7}{2}R$, $C_p = \frac{9}{2}R$ and $\gamma = \frac{C_p}{C_V} = \frac{9}{7} = 1{\cdot}29.$

Our expectations about C_V, C_p and γ are summarized in table (27.1a) and the experimental values for a number of gases are given in table (27.1b).

Table 27.1a: *Expected values of C_V, C_p and γ*

Nature of the gas	C_V (J K^{-1} mol^{-1})	C_p (J K^{-1} mol^{-1})	$C_p - C_V$ (J K^{-1} mol^{-1})	γ
Monatomic	12·5	20·8	8·31	1·67
Diatomic, assuming no vibrations	20·8	29·1	8·31	1·40
Diatomic, assuming vibrations	29·1	37·4	8·31	1·29

Table 27.1b: *Experimental values of C_V, C_p and γ*

Gas (15°C)	C_V (J K^{-1} mol^{-1})	C_p (J K^{-1} mol^{-1})	$C_p - C_V$ (J K^{-1} mol^{-1})	γ
He	12·5	20·8	8·30	1·66
Ne	12·7	20·8	8·12	1·64
Ar	12·5	20·8	8·30	1·67
Kr	12·3	20·8	8·49	1·69
Xe	12·6	21·0	8·36	1·67
H_2	20·4	28·8	8·45	1·41
O_2	21·0	29·3	8·32	1·40
N_2	20·8	29·1	8·32	1·40
CO	20·6	29·0	8·45	1·41
HCl	21·0	29·6	8·61	1·41
CO_2	28·2	36·5	8·32	1·30
H_2O (200°C)	27·0	35·4	8·35	1·31
CH_4	27·1	35·4	8·36	1·31

We find excellent agreement between the prediction of the equipartition theorem and the experimental values. The results also suggest that diatomic molecules do not vibrate at ordinary temperatures. The table suggests that the degree of freedom of polyatomic molecules CO_2, H_2O and CH_4 is 6.

According to the equipartition theorem, the molar heat capacities should be independent of temperature. However, variations in C_V and C_p are observed as the temperature changes. At very high temperatures, vibrations are also important and that affects the values of C_V and C_p for diatomic and polyatomic gases.

While H_2O and CH_4 are nonlinear molecules, CO_2 is linear. Because of this the degree of freedom of CO_2 corresponding to rotation should be 2 just like H_2O and CH_4. Then how can the specific heat capacities of CO_2 be similar to CH_4 and H_2O? For CO_2, some fraction of molecules get into vibrations even at room temperature or so. This extra contribution from vibrations increases the specific heats and it looks like having degree of freedom 6.

Example 27.5

Calculate the internal energy of 1 g of oxygen at STP.

Solution : Oxygen is a diatomic gas. The average energy per molecule is, therefore, $\frac{5}{2}kT$ and the average energy per mole is $\frac{5}{2}RT$. As the molecular weight of oxygen is $32\ \mathrm{g\ mol^{-1}}$, 1 g of oxygen has

$$n = \frac{1\ \mathrm{g}}{32\ \mathrm{g\ mol^{-1}}} = \frac{1}{32}\ \mathrm{mol}.$$

The temperature of oxygen is 273 K. Thus, the internal energy is

$$U = n\left(\frac{5}{2}RT\right)$$

$$= \left(\frac{1}{32}\ \mathrm{mol}\right)\left(\frac{5}{2}\right)(8.31\ \mathrm{J\ K^{-1}\ mol^{-1}})\ (273\ \mathrm{K})$$

$$= 177\ \mathrm{J}.$$

Worked Out Examples

1. *Calculate the value of mechanical equivalent of heat from the following data. Specific heat capacity of air at constant volume* $= 170\ \mathrm{cal\ kg^{-1}\ K^{-1}}$, $\gamma = C_p/C_V = 1.4$ *and the density of air at STP is* $1.29\ \mathrm{kg\ m^{-3}}$. *Gas constant* $R = 8.3\ \mathrm{J\ K^{-1}\ mol^{-1}}$.

Solution : Using $pV = nRT$, the volume of 1 mole of air at STP is

$$V = \frac{nRT}{p} = \frac{(1\ \mathrm{mol}) \times (8.3\ \mathrm{J\ K^{-1}\ mol^{-1}}) \times (273\ \mathrm{K})}{1.0 \times 10^5\ \mathrm{N\ m^{-2}}}$$

$$= 0.0224\ \mathrm{m^3}.$$

The mass of 1 mole is, therefore,

$$(1.29\ \mathrm{kg\ m^{-3}}) \times (0.0224\ \mathrm{m^3}) = 0.029\ \mathrm{kg}.$$

The number of moles in 1 kg is $\frac{1}{0.029}$. The molar heat capacity at constant volume is

$$C_V = \frac{170\ \mathrm{cal}}{(1/0.029)\ \mathrm{mol\ K^{-1}}}$$

$$= 4.93\ \mathrm{cal\ K^{-1}\ mol^{-1}}.$$

Hence, $C_p = \gamma C_V = 1.4 \times 4.93\ \mathrm{cal\ K^{-1}\ mol^{-1}}$

or, $C_p - C_V = 0.4 \times 4.93\ \mathrm{cal\ K^{-1}\ mol^{-1}}$

$$= 1.97\ \mathrm{cal\ K^{-1}\ mol^{-1}}$$

Also, $C_p - C_V = R = 8.3\ \mathrm{J\ K^{-1}\ mol^{-1}}$.

Thus, $8.3\ \mathrm{J} = 1.97\ \mathrm{cal}$.

The mechanical equivalent of heat is

$$\frac{8.3\ \mathrm{J}}{1.97\ \mathrm{cal}} = 4.2\ \mathrm{J\ cal^{-1}}.$$

2. *An ideal gas has a molar heat capacity at constant pressure* $C_p = 2.5\,R$. *The gas is kept in a closed vessel of volume* $0.0083\ \mathrm{m^3}$, *at a temperature of* 300 K *and a pressure of* $1.6 \times 10^6\ \mathrm{N\ m^{-2}}$. *An amount* 2.49×10^4 J *of heat energy is supplied to the gas. Calculate the final temperature and pressure of the gas.*

Solution : We have

$$C_V = C_p - R = 2.5\,R - R = 1.5\,R.$$

The amount of the gas (in moles) is $n = \frac{pV}{RT}$

$$= \frac{(1.6 \times 10^6\ \mathrm{N\ m^{-2}}) \times (0.0083\ \mathrm{m^3})}{(8.3\ \mathrm{J\ K^{-1}\ mol^{-1}})\ (300\ \mathrm{K})} = 5.3\ \mathrm{mol}.$$

As the gas is kept in a closed vessel, its volume is constant. Thus, we have

$$\Delta Q = n\,C_V\,\Delta T$$

or, $\Delta T = \frac{\Delta Q}{nC_V}$

$$= \frac{2.49 \times 10^4\ \mathrm{J}}{(5.3\ \mathrm{mol})\ (1.5 \times 8.3\ \mathrm{J\ K^{-1}\ mol^{-1}})} = 377\ \mathrm{K}.$$

The final temperature is 300 K + 377 K = 677 K.

We have,

$$\frac{p_1V_1}{T_1} = \frac{p_2V_2}{T_2}.$$

Here $V_1 = V_2$. Thus,

$$p_2 = \frac{T_2}{T_1}p_1 = \frac{677}{300} \times 1.6 \times 10^6\ \mathrm{N\ m^{-2}}$$

$$= 3.6 \times 10^6\ \mathrm{N\ m^{-2}}.$$

3. *A sample of ideal gas* ($\gamma = 1.4$) *is heated at constant pressure. If an amount* 140 J *of heat is supplied to the gas, find (a) the change in internal energy of the gas, (b) the work done by the gas.*

Solution : Suppose the sample contains n moles. Also, suppose the volume changes from V_1 to V_2 and the temperature changes from T_1 to T_2.

The heat supplied is

$$\Delta Q = nC_p(T_2 - T_1).$$

(a) The change in internal energy is

$$\Delta U = nC_V(T_2 - T_1) = \frac{C_V}{C_p} nC_p(T_2 - T_1)$$

$$= \frac{C_V}{C_p}\Delta Q = \frac{140 \text{ J}}{1{\cdot}4} = 100 \text{ J}.$$

(b) The work done by the gas is

$$\Delta W = \Delta Q - \Delta U$$

$$= 140 \text{ J} - 100 \text{ J} = 40 \text{ J}.$$

4. *An experiment is performed to measure the molar heat capacity of a gas at constant pressure using Regnault's method. The gas is initially contained in a cubical reservoir of size* 40 cm × 40 cm × 40 cm *at* 600 kPa *at* 27°C. *A part of the gas is brought out, heated to* 100°C *and is passed through a calorimeter at constant pressure. The water equivalent of the calorimeter and its contents is* 100 g. *The temperature of the calorimeter and its contents increases from* 20°C *to* 30°C *during the experiment and the pressure in the reservoir decreases to* 525 kPa. *Specific heat capacity of water* = 4200 J kg^{-1} K^{-1}. *Calculate the molar heat capacity* C_p *from these data.*

Solution : We have $pV = nRT$ or, $n = \frac{pV}{RT}$. The amount of the gas in the reservoir is $n_1 = \frac{p_1V}{RT}$ before the gas is taken out and $n_2 = \frac{p_2V}{RT}$ after the gas is taken out. The amount taken out is

$$\Delta n = n_1 - n_2 = (p_1 - p_2)\frac{V}{RT}$$

$$= \frac{(600 - 525) \times 10^3 \text{ N m}^{-2} \times (40 \times 10^{-2} \text{ m})^3}{(8{\cdot}3 \text{ J K}^{-1} \text{ mol}^{-1}) \times (300 \text{ K})}$$

$$= 1{\cdot}925 \text{ mol}.$$

The gas is heated to 100°C and cools down as it passes through the calorimeter. The average final temperature of the gas is $\frac{20°\text{C} + 30°\text{C}}{2} = 25°\text{C}$. Thus, the average decrease in temperature of the gas is

$$\Delta T = (100°\text{C} - 25°\text{C}) = 75°\text{C}$$

or, $\Delta T = 75$ K.

The heat lost by the gas is

$$\Delta Q = \Delta n\, C_p\, \Delta T.$$

The heat gained by the calorimeter and its contents is

(100 g) (4200 J kg^{-1} K^{-1}) (30 − 20)°C = 4200 J.

Thus, $\Delta n\, C_p\, \Delta T = 4200$ J

or, $$C_p = \frac{4200 \text{ J}}{(1{\cdot}925 \text{ mol})(75 \text{ K})} = 29 \text{ J K}^{-1} \text{ mol}^{-1}.$$

5. *A quantity of air is kept in a container having walls which are slightly conducting. The initial temperature and volume are* 27°C *(equal to the temperature of the surrounding) and* 800 cm^3 *respectively. Find the rise in the temperature if the gas is compressed to* 200 cm^3 *(a) in a short time (b) in a long time. Take* $\gamma = 1{\cdot}4$.

Solution : (a) When the gas is compressed in a short time, the process is adiabatic. Thus,

$$T_2V_2^{\gamma - 1} = T_1V_1^{\gamma - 1}$$

or, $$T_2 = T_1\left(\frac{V_1}{V_2}\right)^{\gamma - 1}$$

$$= (300 \text{ K}) \times \left[\frac{800}{200}\right]^{0{\cdot}4} = 522 \text{ K}.$$

Rise in temperature $= T_2 - T_1 = 222$ K.

(b) When the gas is compressed in a long time, the process is isothermal. Thus, the temperature remains equal to the temperature of the surrounding that is 27°C. The rise in temperature = 0.

6. *A sample of gas* ($\gamma = 1{\cdot}5$) *is taken through an adiabatic process in which the volume is compressed from* 1600 cm^3 *to* 400 cm^3. *If the initial pressure is* 150 kPa, *(a) what is the final pressure and (b) how much work is done by the gas in the process ?*

Solution : (a) For an adiabatic process,

$$p_1V_1^\gamma = p_2V_2^\gamma.$$

Thus,

$$p_2 = p_1\left(\frac{V_1}{V_2}\right)^\gamma$$

$$= (150 \text{ kPa})\left(\frac{1600 \text{ cm}^3}{400 \text{ cm}^3}\right)^{3/2} = 1200 \text{ kPa}.$$

(b) Work done by the gas in an adiabatic process is

$$W = \frac{p_1V_1 - p_2V_2}{\gamma - 1}$$

$$= \frac{(150 \text{ kPa})(1600 \text{ cm}^3) - (1200 \text{ kPa})(400 \text{ cm}^3)}{1{\cdot}5 - 1}$$

$$= \frac{240 \text{ J} - 480 \text{ J}}{0{\cdot}5} = -480 \text{ J}.$$

7. *Two moles of helium gas* ($\gamma = 5/3$) *are initially at* 27°C *and occupy a volume of* 20 *litres. The gas is first expanded at constant pressure until the volume is doubled. Then it undergoes an adiabatic change until the temperature returns to its initial value. (a) Sketch the process in a p–V diagram. (b) What is the final volume and pressure of the gas ? (c) What is the work done by the gas ?*

Solution : (a) The process is shown in figure (27-W1). During the part *ab*, the pressure is constant. We have,

$$\frac{p_aV_a}{T_a} = \frac{p_bV_b}{T_b}$$

or, $$T_b = \frac{V_b}{V_a} T_a = 2T_a = 600 \text{ K}.$$

During the part bc, the gas is adiabatically returned to the temperature T_a. The point a and the point c are on the same isotherm. Thus, we draw an adiabatic curve from b and an isotherm from a and look for the point of intersection c. That is the final state.

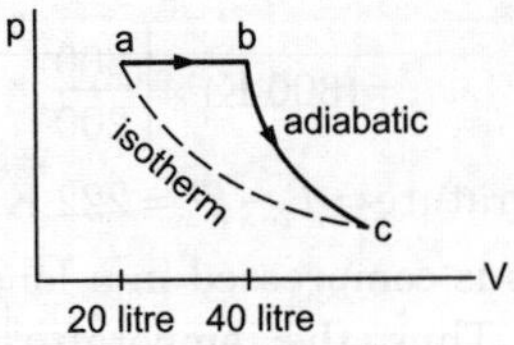

Figure 27-W1

(b) From the isotherm ac,

$$p_a V_a = p_c V_c \quad \text{... (i)}$$

and from the adiabatic curve bc,

$$p_b V_b^{\gamma} = p_c V_c^{\gamma}$$

or, $$p_a (2V_a)^{\gamma} = p_c V_c^{\gamma}. \quad \text{... (ii)}$$

Dividing (ii) by (i),

$$2^{\gamma} (V_a)^{\gamma - 1} = (V_c)^{\gamma - 1}$$

or, $$V_c = 2^{\gamma/(\gamma - 1)} V_a = 4\sqrt{2} V_a = 113 \text{ litres}.$$

From (i), $$p_c = \frac{p_a V_a}{V_c} = \frac{nRT_a}{V_c}$$

$$= \frac{2 \text{ mol} \times (8{\cdot}3 \text{ J K}^{-1} \text{ mol}^{-1}) \times (300 \text{ K})}{113 \times 10^{-3} \text{ m}^3}$$

$$= 4{\cdot}4 \times 10^4 \text{ Pa}.$$

(c) Work done by the gas in the part ab

$$= p_a (V_b - V_a)$$

$$= p_b V_b - p_a V_a$$

$$= nRT_2 - nRT_1$$

$$= 2 \text{ mol} \times (8{\cdot}3 \text{ J K}^{-1} \text{ mol}^{-1}) \times (600 \text{ K} - 300 \text{ K})$$

$$= 4980 \text{ J}.$$

The work done in the adiabatic part bc

$$= \frac{p_b V_b - p_c V_c}{\gamma - 1}$$

$$= \frac{nR(T_2 - T_1)}{\gamma - 1}$$

$$= \frac{4980 \text{ J}}{5/3 - 1} = 7470 \text{ J}.$$

The net work done by the gas

$$= 4980 \text{ J} + 7470 \text{ J} = 12450 \text{ J}.$$

8. *An ideal gas enclosed in a vertical cylindrical container supports a freely moving piston of mass M. The piston and the cylinder have equal cross-sectional area A. When the piston is in equilibrium, the volume of the gas is V_0 and its pressure is p_0. The piston is slightly displaced from the equilibrium position and released. Assuming that the system is completely isolated from its surrounding, show that the piston executes simple harmonic motion and find the frequency of oscillations.*

Solution : Suppose the piston is displaced through a distance x above the equilibrium position. The volume of the gas increases by $\Delta V = Ax$. As the system is completely isolated from its surrounding, the process is adiabatic. Thus,

$$pV^{\gamma} = \text{constant}$$

or, $$\ln p + \gamma \ln V = \text{constant}$$

or, $$\frac{\Delta p}{p} + \gamma \frac{\Delta V}{V} = 0$$

or, $$\Delta p = -\frac{\gamma p}{V} \Delta V.$$

As the piston is only slightly pushed, we can write

$$\Delta p = -\frac{\gamma p_0}{V_0} \Delta V.$$

The resultant force acting on the piston in this position is

$$F = A \Delta p = -A \frac{\gamma p_0}{V_0} \Delta V$$

$$= -\frac{A^2 \gamma p_0}{V_0} x = -kx$$

where $k = \dfrac{A^2 \gamma p_0}{V_0}$.

Thus, the motion of the piston is simple harmonic. The angular frequency ω is given by

$$\omega = \sqrt{\frac{k}{M}} = \sqrt{\frac{A^2 \gamma p_0}{MV_0}}$$

and the frequency is $$\nu = \frac{\omega}{2\pi} = \frac{1}{2\pi} \sqrt{\frac{A^2 \gamma p_0}{MV_0}}.$$

9. *Two vessels of volumes V_1 and V_2 contain the same ideal gas. The pressures in the vessels are p_1 and p_2 and the temperatures are T_1 and T_2 respectively. The two vessels are now connected to each other through a narrow tube. Assuming that no heat is exchanged between the surrounding and the vessels, find the common pressure and temperature attained after the connection.*

Solution :

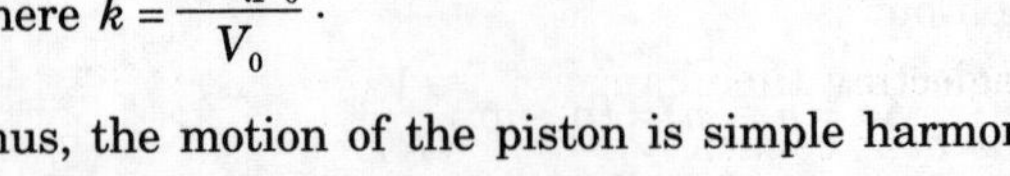

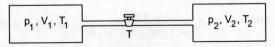

Figure 27-W2

The amount of the gas in vessel 1 is $n_1 = \dfrac{p_1 V_1}{RT_1}$

and that in vessel 2 is $n_2 = \dfrac{p_2 V_2}{R T_2}$.

If p' and T' be the common pressure and temperature after the connection is made, the amounts are

$$n_1' = \frac{p' V_1}{R T'} \text{ and } n_2' = \frac{p' V_2}{R T'}$$

We have $n_1 + n_2 = n_1' + n_2'$

$$\text{or,} \quad \frac{p_1 V_1}{R T_1} + \frac{p_2 V_2}{R T_2} = \frac{p' V_1}{R T'} + \frac{p' V_2}{R T'}$$

$$\text{or,} \quad \frac{p'}{T'} = \frac{1}{V_1 + V_2}\left(\frac{p_1 V_1}{T_1} + \frac{p_2 V_2}{T_2}\right)$$

$$\text{or,} \quad \frac{T'}{p'} = \frac{T_1 T_2 (V_1 + V_2)}{p_1 V_1 T_2 + p_2 V_2 T_1}. \quad \text{... (i)}$$

As the vessels have fixed volume, no work is done by the gas plus the vessels system. Also, no heat is exchanged with the surrounding. Thus, the internal energy of the total system remains constant.

The internal energy of an ideal gas is

$$U = n C_V T$$

$$= C_V \frac{pV}{R}$$

The internal energy of the gases before the connection

$$= \frac{C_V p_1 V_1}{R} + \frac{C_V p_2 V_2}{R}$$

and after the connection

$$= \frac{C_V p' (V_1 + V_2)}{R}.$$

Neglecting the change in internal energy of the vessels (the heat capacity of the vessels is assumed negligible),

$$\frac{C_V p_1 V_1}{R} + \frac{C_V p_2 V_2}{R} = \frac{C_V p' (V_1 + V_2)}{R}$$

$$\text{or,} \quad p' = \frac{p_1 V_1 + p_2 V_2}{V_1 + V_2}.$$

$$\text{From (i),} \quad T' = \frac{T_1 T_2 (p_1 V_1 + p_2 V_2)}{p_1 V_1 T_2 + p_2 V_2 T_1}.$$

10. 4 mol *of an ideal gas having* $\gamma = 1{\cdot}67$ *are mixed with* 2 mol *of another ideal gas having* $\gamma = 1{\cdot}4$. *Find the equivalent value of* γ *for the mixture.*

Solution : Let,

C'_V = molar heat capacity of the first gas,

C''_V = molar heat capacity of the second gas,

C_V = molar heat capacity of the mixture

and similar symbols for other quantities. Then,

$$\gamma = \frac{C'_p}{C'_V} = 1{\cdot}67$$

$$\text{and} \quad C'_p = C'_V + R.$$

This gives $C'_V = \dfrac{3}{2} R$ and $C'_p = \dfrac{5}{2} R$.

Similarly, $\gamma = 1{\cdot}4$ gives $C''_V = \dfrac{5}{2} R$ and $C''_p = \dfrac{7}{2} R$.

Suppose the temperature of the mixture is increased by dT. The increase in the internal energy of the first gas $= n_1 C'_V dT$. The increase in internal energy of the second gas $= n_2 C''_V dT$ and the increase in internal energy of the mixture $= (n_1 + n_2) C_V dT$. Thus,

$$(n_1 + n_2) C_V dT = n_1 C'_V dT + n_2 C''_V dT$$

$$\text{or,} \quad C_V = \frac{n_1 C'_V + n_2 C''_V}{n_1 + n_2}. \quad \text{... (i)}$$

$$C_p = C_V + R = \frac{n_1 C'_V + n_2 C''_V}{n_1 + n_2} + R$$

$$= \frac{n_1 (C'_V + R) + n_2 (C''_V + R)}{n_1 + n_2}$$

$$= \frac{n_1 C'_p + n_2 C''_p}{n_1 + n_2}. \quad \text{... (ii)}$$

$$\text{From (i) and (ii),} \quad \gamma = \frac{C_p}{C_V} = \frac{n_1 C'_p + n_2 C''_p}{n_1 C'_V + n_2 C''_V}$$

$$= \frac{4 \times \frac{5}{2} R + 2 \times \frac{7}{2} R}{4 \times \frac{3}{2} R + 2 \times \frac{5}{2} R} = 1{\cdot}54.$$

11. *A diatomic gas* ($\gamma = 1{\cdot}4$) *does* 200 J *of work when it is expanded isobarically. Find the heat given to the gas in the process.*

Solution : For a diatomic gas, $C_V = \frac{5}{2} R$ and $C_p = \frac{7}{2} R$. The work done in an isobaric process is

$$W = p(V_2 - V_1)$$

$$= nRT_2 - nRT_1$$

$$\text{or,} \quad T_2 - T_1 = \frac{W}{nR}.$$

The heat given in an isobaric process is

$$Q = n C_p (T_2 - T_1)$$

$$= n C_p \frac{W}{nR} = \frac{7}{2} W$$

$$= \frac{7}{2} \times 200 \text{ J} = 700 \text{ J}.$$

12. *Calculate the ratio* C_p / C_V *of oxygen from the following data. Speed of sound in oxygen at* $0°\text{C} = 315 \text{ m s}^{-1}$, *molecular weight of oxygen* $= 32 \text{ g mol}^{-1}$ *and the gas constant* $R = 8{\cdot}3 \text{ J K}^{-1} \text{ mol}^{-1}$.

Solution : The speed of sound in a gas is given by

$$v = \sqrt{\frac{\gamma P}{\rho}} = \sqrt{\frac{\gamma R T}{M}}$$

$$\text{or,} \quad \gamma = \frac{M v^2}{RT}$$

$$= \frac{(32 \times 10^{-3} \text{ kg mol}^{-1})(315 \text{ m s}^{-1})^2}{(8{\cdot}3 \text{ J K}^{-1} \text{ mol}^{-1})(273 \text{ K})} = 1{\cdot}4.$$

□

QUESTIONS FOR SHORT ANSWER

1. Does a gas have just two specific heat capacities or more than two ? Is the number of specific heat capacities of a gas countable ?
2. Can we define specific heat capacity at constant temperature ?
3. Can we define specific heat capacity for an adiabatic process ?
4. Does a solid also have two kinds of molar heat capacities C_p and C_V ? If yes, do we have $C_p > C_V$? Is $C_p - C_V = R$?
5. In a real gas the internal energy depends on temperature and also on volume. The energy increases when the gas expands isothermally. Looking into the derivation of $C_p - C_V = R$, find whether $C_p - C_V$ will be more than R, less than R or equal to R for a real gas.
6. Can a process on an ideal gas be both adiabatic and isothermal ?
7. Show that the slope of p–V diagram is greater for an adiabatic process as compared to an isothermal process.
8. Is a slow process always isothermal ? Is a quick process always adiabatic ?
9. Can two states of an ideal gas be connected by an isothermal process as well as an adiabatic process ?
10. The ratio C_p/C_V for a gas is 1·29. What is the degree of freedom of the molecules of this gas ?

OBJECTIVE I

1. Work done by a sample of an ideal gas in a process A is double the work done in another process B. The temperature rises through the same amount in the two processes. If C_A and C_B be the molar heat capacities for the two processes,
(a) $C_A = C_B$ (b) $C_A < C_B$
(c) $C_A > C_B$ (d) C_A and C_B cannot be defined.
2. For a solid with a small expansion coefficient,
(a) $C_p - C_V = R$ (b) $C_p = C_V$
(c) C_p is slightly greater than C_V
(d) C_p is slightly less than C_V.
3. The value of $C_p - C_V$ is 1·00 R for a gas sample in state A and is 1·08 R in state B. Let p_A, p_B denote the pressures and T_A and T_B denote the temperatures of the states A and B respectively. Most likely
(a) $p_A < p_B$ and $T_A > T_B$ (b) $p_A > p_B$ and $T_A < T_B$
(c) $p_A = p_B$ and $T_A < T_B$ (d) $p_A > p_B$ and $T_A = T_B$
4. Let C_V and C_p denote the molar heat capacities of an ideal gas at constant volume and constant pressure respectively. Which of the following is a universal constant ?
(a) $\frac{C_p}{C_V}$ (b) C_pC_V (c) $C_p - C_V$ (d) $C_p + C_V$
5. 70 calories of heat is required to raise the temperature of 2 mole of an ideal gas at constant pressure from 30°C to 35°C. The amount of heat required to raise the temperature of the same gas through the same range at constant volume is
(a) 30 calories (b) 50 calories
(c) 70 calories (d) 90 calories.

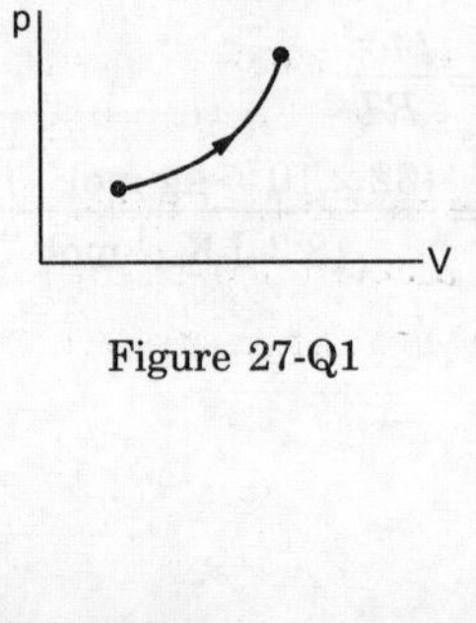

Figure 27-Q1

6. Figure (27-Q1) shows a process on a gas in which pressure and volume both change. The molar heat capacity for this process is C.
(a) $C = 0$ (b) $C = C_V$ (c) $C > C_V$ (d) $C < C_V$
7. The molar heat capacity for the process shown in figure (27-Q2) is
(a) $C = C_p$ (b) $C = C_V$ (c) $C > C_V$ (d) $C = 0$.

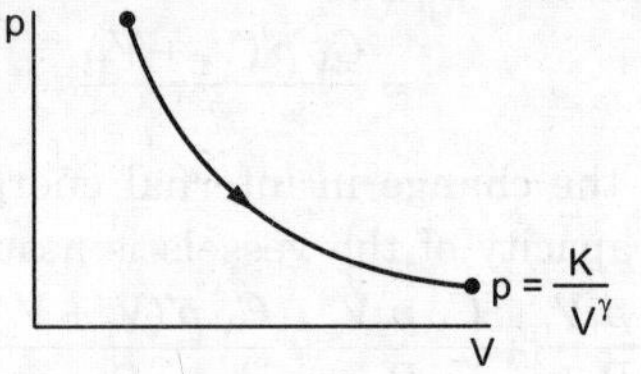

Figure 27-Q2

8. In an isothermal process on an ideal gas, the pressure increases by 0·5%. The volume decreases by about
(a) 0·25% (b) 0·5% (c) 0·7% (d) 1%.
9. In an adiabatic process on a gas with $\gamma = 1{\cdot}4$, the pressure is increased by 0·5%. The volume decreases by about
(a) 0·36% (b) 0·5% (c) 0·7% (d) 1%.
10. Two samples A and B are initially kept in the same state. The sample A is expanded through an adiabatic process and the sample B through an isothermal process. The final volumes of the samples are the same. The final pressures in A and B are p_A and p_B respectively.
(a) $p_A > p_B$ (b) $p_A = p_B$ (c) $p_A < p_B$
(d) The relation between p_A and p_B cannot be deduced.
11. Let T_a and T_b be the final temperatures of the samples A and B respectively in the previous question.
(a) $T_a < T_b$ (b) $T_a = T_b$ (c) $T_a > T_b$
(d) The relation between T_a and T_b cannot be deduced.
12. Let ΔW_a and ΔW_b be the work done by the systems A and B respectively in the previous question.
(a) $\Delta W_a > \Delta W_b$ (b) $\Delta W_a = \Delta W_b$ (c) $\Delta W_a < \Delta W_b$

(d) The relation between ΔW_a and ΔW_b cannot be deduced.

13. The molar heat capacity of oxygen gas at STP is nearly $2{\cdot}5\,R$. As the temperature is increased, it gradually increases and approaches $3{\cdot}5\,R$. The most appropriate reason for this behaviour is that at high temperatures

(a) oxygen does not behave as an ideal gas
(b) oxygen molecules dissociate in atoms
(c) the molecules collide more frequently
(d) molecular vibrations gradually become effective.

OBJECTIVE II

1. A gas kept in a container of finite conductivity is suddenly compressed. The process
(a) must be very nearly adiabatic
(b) must be very nearly isothermal
(c) may be very nearly adiabatic
(d) may be very nearly isothermal.

2. Let Q and W denote the amount of heat given to an ideal gas and the work done by it in an isothermal process.
(a) $Q = 0$ (b) $W = 0$ (c) $Q \neq W$ (d) $Q = W$

3. Let Q and W denote the amount of heat given to an ideal gas and the work done by it in an adiabatic process.
(a) $Q = 0$ (b) $W = 0$ (c) $Q = W$ (d) $Q \neq W$

4. Consider the processes A and B shown in figure (27-Q3). It is possible that

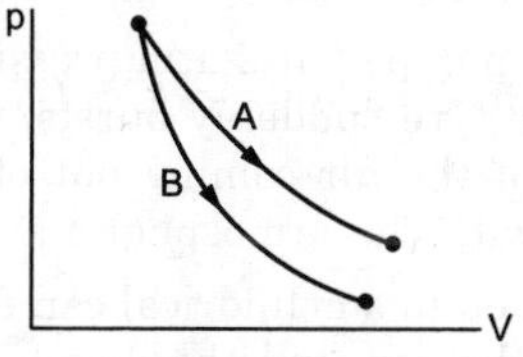

Figure 27-Q3

(a) both the processes are isothermal
(b) both the processes are adiabatic
(c) A is isothermal and B is adiabatic
(d) A is adiabatic and B is isothermal.

5. Three identical adiabatic containers A, B and C contain helium, neon and oxygen respectively at equal pressure. The gases are pushed to half their original volumes.
(a) The final temperatures in the three containers will be the same.
(b) The final pressures in the three containers will be the same.
(c) The pressures of helium and neon will be the same but that of oxygen will be different.
(d) The temperatures of helium and neon will be the same but that of oxygen will be different.

6. A rigid container of negligible heat capacity contains one mole of an ideal gas. The temperature of the gas increases by 1°C if 3·0 cal of heat is added to it. The gas may be
(a) helium (b) argon (c) oxygen (d) carbon dioxide.

7. Four cylinders contain equal number of moles of argon, hydrogen, nitrogen and carbon dioxide at the same temperature. The energy is minimum in
(a) argon (b) hydrogen (c) nitrogen (d) carbon dioxide.

EXERCISES

1. A vessel containing one mole of a monatomic ideal gas (molecular weight = 20 g mol^{-1}) is moving on a floor at a speed of 50 m s^{-1}. The vessel is stopped suddenly. Assuming that the mechanical energy lost has gone into the internal energy of the gas, find the rise in its temperature.

2. 5 g of a gas is contained in a rigid container and is heated from 15°C to 25°C. Specific heat capacity of the gas at constant volume is 0·172 cal g^{-1} °C^{-1} and the mechanical equivalent of heat is 4·2 J cal^{-1}. Calculate the change in the internal energy of the gas.

3. Figure (27-E1) shows a cylindrical container containing oxygen ($\gamma = 1{\cdot}4$) and closed by a 50 kg frictionless piston. The area of cross section is 100 cm^2, atmospheric pressure is 100 kPa and g is 10 m s^{-2}. The cylinder is slowly heated for some time. Find the amount of heat supplied to the gas if the piston moves out through a distance of 20 cm.

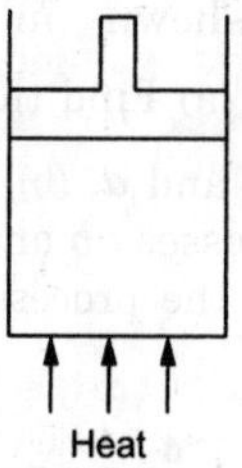

Figure 27-E1

4. The specific heat capacities of hydrogen at constant volume and at constant pressure are 2·4 cal g^{-1} °C^{-1} and 3·4 cal g^{-1} °C^{-1} respectively. The molecular weight of hydrogen is 2 g mol^{-1} and the gas constant $R = 8{\cdot}3 \times 10^7$ erg °C^{-1} mol^{-1}. Calculate the value of J.

5. The ratio of the molar heat capacities of an ideal gas is $C_p/C_V = 7/6$. Calculate the change in internal energy of 1·0 mole of the gas when its temperature is raised by

50 K (a) keeping the pressure constant, (b) keeping the volume constant and (c) adiabatically.

6. A sample of air weighing 1·18 g occupies $1 \cdot 0 \times 10^3$ cm^3 when kept at 300 K and $1 \cdot 0 \times 10^5$ Pa. When 2·0 cal of heat is added to it at constant volume, its temperature increases by 1°C. Calculate the amount of heat needed to increase the temperature of air by 1°C at constant pressure if the mechanical equivalent of heat is 4.2×10^{-7} erg cal^{-1}. Assume that air behaves as an ideal gas.

7. An ideal gas expands from 100 cm^3 to 200 cm^3 at a constant pressure of $2 \cdot 0 \times 10^5$ Pa when 50 J of heat is supplied to it. Calculate (a) the change in internal energy of the gas, (b) the number of moles in the gas if the initial temperature is 300 K, (c) the molar heat capacity C_p at constant pressure and (d) the molar heat capacity C_V at constant volume.

8. An amount Q of heat is added to a monatomic ideal gas in a process in which the gas performs a work $Q/2$ on its surrounding. Find the molar heat capacity for the process.

9. An ideal gas is taken through a process in which the pressure and the volume are changed according to the equation $p = kV$. Show that the molar heat capacity of the gas for the process is given by $C = C_V + \frac{R}{2} \cdot$

10. An ideal gas ($C_p / C_V = \gamma$) is taken through a process in which the pressure and the volume vary as $p = aV^b$. Find the value of b for which the specific heat capacity in the process is zero.

11. Two ideal gases have the same value of $C_p / C_V = \gamma$. What will be the value of this ratio for a mixture of the two gases in the ratio 1 : 2 ?

12. A mixture contains 1 mole of helium ($C_p = 2 \cdot 5\, R$, $C_V = 1 \cdot 5\, R$) and 1 mole of hydrogen ($C_p = 3 \cdot 5\, R$, $C_V = 2 \cdot 5\, R$). Calculate the values of C_p, C_V and γ for the mixture.

13. Half mole of an ideal gas ($\gamma = 5/3$) is taken through the cycle $abcda$ as shown in figure (27-E2). Take $R = \frac{25}{3}$ J K^{-1} mol^{-1}. (a) Find the temperature of the gas in the states a, b, c and d. (b) Find the amount of heat supplied in the processes ab and bc. (c) Find the amount of heat liberated in the processes cd and da.

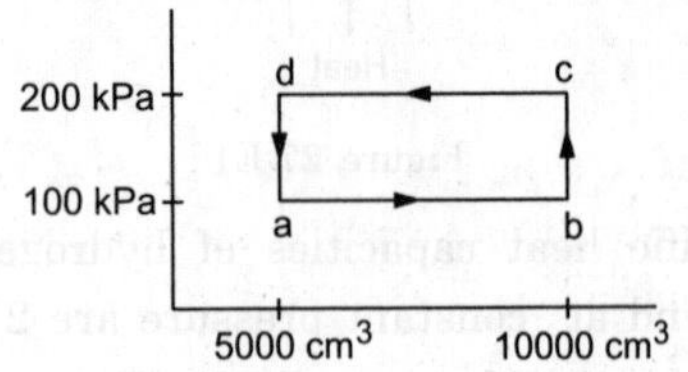

Figure 27-E2

14. An ideal gas ($\gamma = 1 \cdot 67$) is taken through the process abc shown in figure (27-E3). The temperature at the point a is 300 K. Calculate (a) the temperatures at b and c, (b) the work done in the process, (c) the amount of heat supplied in the path ab and in the path bc and (d) the change in the internal energy of the gas in the process.

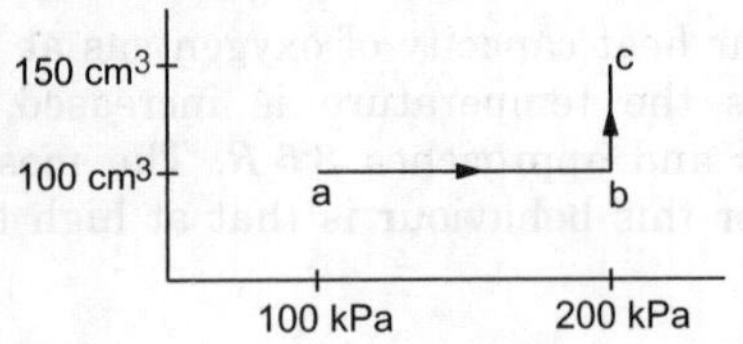

Figure 27-E3

15. In Joly's differential steam calorimeter, 3 g of an ideal gas is contained in a rigid closed sphere at 20°C. The sphere is heated by steam at 100°C and it is found that an extra 0·095 g of steam has condensed into water as the temperature of the gas becomes constant. Calculate the specific heat capacity of the gas in J g^{-1} K^{-1}. The latent heat of vaporization of water = 540 cal g^{-1}.

16. The volume of an ideal gas ($\gamma = 1 \cdot 5$) is changed adiabatically from 4·00 litres to 3·00 litres. Find the ratio of (a) the final pressure to the initial pressure and (b) the final temperature to the initial temperature.

17. An ideal gas at pressure $2 \cdot 5 \times 10^5$ Pa and temperature 300 K occupies 100 cc. It is adiabatically compressed to half its original volume. Calculate (a) the final pressure, (b) the final temperature and (c) the work done by the gas in the process. Take $\gamma = 1 \cdot 5$.

18. Air ($\gamma = 1 \cdot 4$) is pumped at 2 atm pressure in a motor tyre at 20°C. If the tyre suddenly bursts, what would be the temperature of the air coming out of the tyre. Neglect any mixing with the atmospheric air.

19. A gas is enclosed in a cylindrical can fitted with a piston. The walls of the can and the piston are adiabatic. The initial pressure, volume and temperature of the gas are 100 kPa, 400 cm^3 and 300 K respectively. The ratio of the specific heat capacities of the gas is $C_p / C_V = 1 \cdot 5$. Find the pressure and the temperature of the gas if it is (a) suddenly compressed (b) slowly compressed to 100 cm^3.

20. The initial pressure and volume of a given mass of a gas ($C_p / C_V = \gamma$) are p_0 and V_0. The gas can exchange heat with the surrounding. (a) It is slowly compressed to a volume $V_0/2$ and then suddenly compressed to $V_0/4$. Find the final pressure. (b) If the gas is suddenly compressed from the volume V_0 to $V_0/2$ and then slowly compressed to $V_0/4$, what will be the final pressure ?

21. Consider a given sample of an ideal gas ($C_p / C_V = \gamma$) having initial pressure p_0 and volume V_0. (a) The gas is isothermally taken to a pressure $p_0/2$ and from there adiabatically to a pressure $p_0/4$. Find the final volume. (b) The gas is brought back to its initial state. It is adiabatically taken to a pressure $p_0/2$ and from there isothermally to a pressure $p_0/4$. Find the final volume.

22. A sample of an ideal gas ($\gamma = 1 \cdot 5$) is compressed adiabatically from a volume of 150 cm^3 to 50 cm^3. The initial pressure and the initial temperature are 150 kPa and 300 K. Find (a) the number of moles of the gas in the sample, (b) the molar heat capacity at constant volume, (c) the final pressure and temperature, (d) the

work done by the gas in the process and (e) the change in internal energy of the gas.

23. Three samples A, B and C of the same gas ($\gamma = 1{\cdot}5$) have equal volumes and temperatures. The volume of each sample is doubled, the process being isothermal for A, adiabatic for B and isobaric for C. If the final pressures are equal for the three samples, find the ratio of the initial pressures.

24. Two samples A and B of the same gas have equal volumes and pressures. The gas in sample A is expanded isothermally to double its volume and the gas in B is expanded adiabatically to double its volume. If the work done by the gas is the same for the two cases, show that γ satisfies the equation $1 - 2^{1-\gamma} = (\gamma - 1)\ln 2$.

25. 1 litre of an ideal gas ($\gamma = 1{\cdot}5$) at 300 K is suddenly compressed to half its original volume. (a) Find the ratio of the final pressure to the initial pressure. (b) If the original pressure is 100 kPa, find the work done by the gas in the process. (c) What is the change in internal energy ? (d) What is the final temperature ? (e) The gas is now cooled to 300 K keeping its pressure constant. Calculate the work done during the process. (f) The gas is now expanded isothermally to achieve its original volume of 1 litre. Calculate the work done by the gas. (g) Calculate the total work done in the cycle.

26. Figure (27-E4) shows a cylindrical tube with adiabatic walls and fitted with an adiabatic separator. The separator can be slid into the tube by an external mechanism. An ideal gas ($\gamma = 1{\cdot}5$) is injected in the two sides at equal pressures and temperatures. The separator remains in equilibrium at the middle. It is now slid to a position where it divides the tube in the ratio 1 : 3. Find the ratio of the temperatures in the two parts of the vessel.

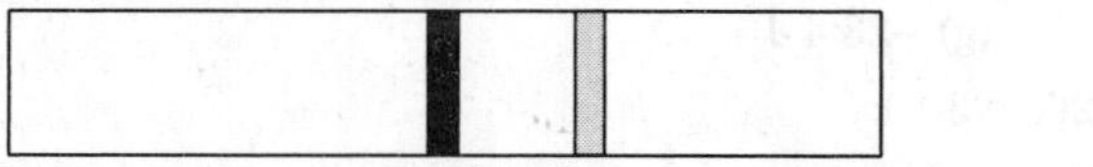

Figure 27-E4

27. Figure (27-E5) shows two rigid vessels A and B, each of volume 200 cm^3 containing an ideal gas ($C_V = 12{\cdot}5$ J K^{-1} mol^{-1}). The vessels are connected to a manometer tube containing mercury. The pressure in both the vessels is 75 cm of mercury and the temperature is 300 K. (a) Find the number of moles of the gas in each vessel. (b) 5·0 J of heat is supplied to the gas in the vessel A and 10 J to the gas in the vessel B. Assuming no appreciable transfer of heat from A to B calculate the difference in the heights of mercury in the two sides of the manometer. Gas constant $R = 8{\cdot}3$ J K^{-1} mol^{-1}.

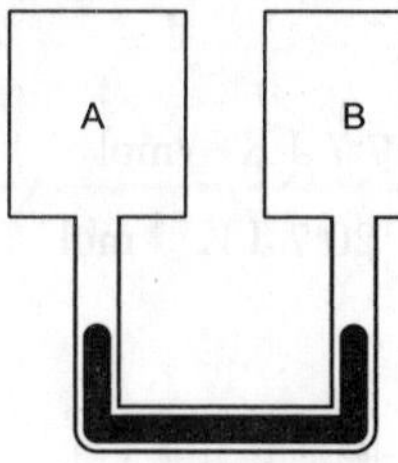

Figure 27-E5

28. Figure (27-E6) shows two vessels with adiabatic walls, one containing 0·1 g of helium ($\gamma = 1{\cdot}67$, $M = 4$ g mol^{-1}) and the other containing some amount of hydrogen ($\gamma = 1{\cdot}4$, $M = 2$ g mol^{-1}). Initially, the temperatures of the two gases are equal. The gases are electrically heated for some time during which equal amounts of heat are given to the two gases. It is found that the temperatures rise through the same amount in the two vessels. Calculate the mass of hydrogen.

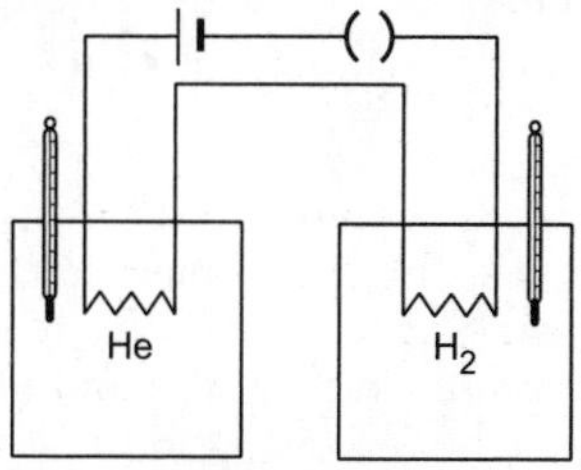

Figure 27-E6

29. Two vessels A and B of equal volume V_0 are connected by a narrow tube which can be closed by a valve. The vessels are fitted with pistons which can be moved to change the volumes. Initially, the valve is open and the vessels contain an ideal gas ($C_p / C_V = \gamma$) at atmospheric pressure p_0 and atmospheric temperature T_0. The walls of the vessel A are diathermic and those of B are adiabatic. The valve is now closed and the pistons are slowly pulled out to increase the volumes of the vessels to double the original value. (a) Find the temperatures and pressures in the two vessels. (b) The valve is now opened for sufficient time so that the gases acquire a common temperature and pressure. Find the new values of the temperature and the pressure.

30. Figure (27-E7) shows an adiabatic cylindrical tube of volume V_0 divided in two parts by a frictionless adiabatic separator. Initially, the separator is kept in the middle, an ideal gas at pressure p_1 and temperature T_1 is injected into the left part and another ideal gas at pressure p_2 and temperature T_2 is injected into the right part. $C_p / C_V = \gamma$ is the same for both the gases. The separator is slid slowly and is released at a position where it can stay in equilibrium. Find (a) the volumes of the two parts, (b) the heat given to the gas in the left part and (c) the final common pressure of the gases.

Figure 27-E7

31. An adiabatic cylindrical tube of cross-sectional area 1 cm^2 is closed at one end and fitted with a piston at the other end. The tube contains 0·03 g of an ideal gas. At 1 atm pressure and at the temperature of the surrounding, the length of the gas column is 40 cm. The piston is suddenly pulled out to double the length of the column. The pressure of the gas falls to 0·355 atm. Find the speed of sound in the gas at atmospheric temperature.

32. The speed of sound in hydrogen at 0°C is $1280\ m\ s^{-1}$. The density of hydrogen at STP is $0·089\ kg\ m^{-3}$. Calculate the molar heat capacities C_p and C_V of hydrogen.

33. 4·0 g of helium occupies $22400\ cm^3$ at STP. The specific heat capacity of helium at constant pressure is $5·0\ cal\ K^{-1}\ mol^{-1}$. Calculate the speed of sound in helium at STP.

34. An ideal gas having density $1·7 \times 10^{-3}\ g\ cm^{-3}$ at a pressure $1·5 \times 10^5$ Pa is filled in a Kundt tube. When the gas is resonated at a frequency of 3·0 kHz, nodes are formed at a separation of 6·0 cm. Calculate the molar heat capacities C_p and C_V of the gas.

35. Standing waves of frequency 5·0 kHz are produced in a tube filled with oxygen at 300 K. The separation between the consecutive nodes is 3·3 cm. Calculate the specific heat capacities C_p and C_V of the gas.

□

ANSWERS

OBJECTIVE I

1. (c)	2. (c)	3. (a)	4. (c)	5. (b)	6. (c)
7. (d)	8. (b)	9. (a)	10. (c)	11. (a)	12. (c)
13. (d)					

OBJECTIVE II

1. (c), (d)	2. (d)	3. (a, (d)
4. (c)	5. (c), (d)	6. (a), (b)
7. (a)		

EXERCISES

1. 2·0 K
2. 36 J
3. 1050 J
4. $4·15 \times 10^7\ erg\ cal^{-1}$
5. 2490 J in all cases
6. 2·08 cal
7. (a) 30 J (b) 0·008
   (c) $20·8\ J\ K^{-1}\ mol^{-1}$ (d) $12·5\ J\ K^{-1}\ mol^{-1}$
8. $3R$
10. $-\gamma$
11. γ
12. $3R$, $2R$, 1·5
13. (a) 120 K, 240 K, 480 K, 240 K
    (b) 1250 J, 1500 J (c) 2500 J, 750 J
14. (a) 600 K, 900 K (b) 10 J
    (c) 14·9 J, 24·9 J (d) 29·8 J
15. $0·90\ J\ g^{-1}\ K^{-1}$
16. (a) 1·54 (b) 1·15
17. (a) $7·1 \times 10^5$ Pa (b) 424 K (c) − 21 J
18. 240 K
19. 800 kPa, 600 K in both cases
20. $2^{\gamma+1}\ p_0$ in both cases
21. $2^{(\gamma+1)/\gamma}\ V_0$ in each case
22. (a) 0·009 (b) $2R = 16·6\ J\ K^{-1}\ mol^{-1}$
    (c) 780 kPa, 520 K (d) −33 J (e) 33 J
23. $2 : 2\sqrt{2} : 1$
25. (a) $2\sqrt{2}$ (b) −82 J
    (c) 82 J (d) 424 K
    (e) −41·4 J (f) 103 J
    (g) −23·4 J
26. $\sqrt{3} : 1$
27. (a) 0·008 (b) 12·5 cm
28. 0·03 g
29. (a) T_0, $\frac{p_0}{2}$ in vessel A and $T_0/2^{\gamma-1}$, $p_0/2^{\gamma}$ in vessel B
    (b) T_0, $p_0/2$
30. (a) $\frac{p_1^{1/\gamma}V_0}{A}$, $\frac{p_2^{1/\gamma}V_0}{A}$ (b) zero
    (c) $(A/2)^{\gamma}$ where $A = p_1^{1/\gamma} + p_2^{1/\gamma}$
31. $447\ m\ s^{-1}$
32. $18·0\ J\ K^{-1}\ mol^{-1}$, $26·3\ J\ K^{-1}\ mol^{-1}$
33. $960\ m\ s^{-1}$
34. $26\ J\ K^{-1}\ mol^{-1}$, $17·7\ J\ K^{-1}\ mol^{-1}$
35. $29·0\ J\ K^{-1}\ mol^{-1}$, $20·7\ J\ K^{-1}\ mol^{-1}$

□

CHAPTER 28

HEAT TRANSFER

Heat can be transferred from one place to another by three different methods, namely, conduction, convection and radiation. Conduction usually takes place in solids, convection in liquids and gases, and no medium is required for radiation.

28.1 THERMAL CONDUCTION

If one end of a metal rod is placed in a stove, the temperature of the other end gradually increases. Heat is transferred from one end of the rod to the other end. This transfer takes place due to molecular collisions and the process is called *heat conduction.* The molecules at one end of the rod gain heat from the stove and their average kinetic energy increases. As these molecules collide with the neighbouring molecules having less kinetic energy, the energy is shared between these two groups. The kinetic energy of these neighbouring molecules increases. As they collide with their neighbours on the colder side, they transfer energy to them. This way, heat is passed along the rod from molecule to molecule. The average position of a molecule does not change and hence, there is no mass movement of matter.

Thermal Conductivity

The ability of a material to conduct heat is measured by *thermal conductivity* (defined below) of the material.

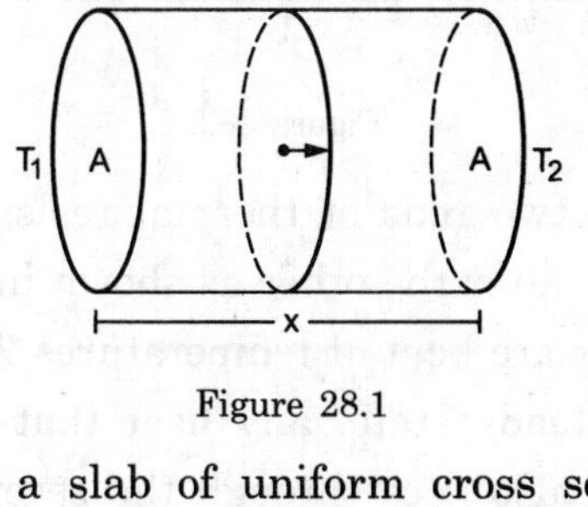

Figure 28.1

Consider a slab of uniform cross section A and length x. Let one face of the slab be maintained at temperature T_1 and the other at T_2. Also, suppose the remaining surface is covered with a nonconducting material so that no heat is transferred through the sides. After sufficient time, steady state is reached and the temperature at any point remains unchanged as time passes. In such a case, the amount of heat crossing per unit time through any cross section of the slab is equal. If ΔQ amount of heat crosses through any cross section in time Δt, $\Delta Q/\Delta t$ is called the *heat current.* It is found that in steady state the heat current is proportional to the area of cross section A, proportional to the temperature difference $(T_1 - T_2)$ between the ends and inversely proportional to the length x. Thus,

$$\frac{\Delta Q}{\Delta t} = K\frac{A(T_1 - T_2)}{x} \qquad \dots (28.1)$$

where K is a constant for the material of the slab and is called the *thermal conductivity* of the material.

If the area of cross section is not uniform or if the steady-state conditions are not reached, the equation can only be applied to a thin layer of material perpendicular to the heat flow. If A be the area of cross section at a place, dx be a small thickness along the direction of heat flow, and dT be the temperature difference across the layer of thickness dx, the heat current through this cross section is

$$\frac{\Delta Q}{\Delta t} = -KA\frac{dT}{dx} \cdot \qquad \dots (28.2)$$

The quantity dT/dx is called the *temperature gradient.* The minus sign indicates that dT/dx is negative along the direction of the heat flow.

The unit of thermal conductivity can be easily worked out using equation (28.1) or (28.2). The SI unit is $Js^{-1}m^{-1}K^{-1}$ or $Wm^{-1}K^{-1}$. As a change of 1 K and a change of 1°C are the same, the unit may also be written as $Wm^{-1}°C^{-1}$.

Example 28.1

One face of a copper cube of edge 10 cm *is maintained at* 100°C *and the opposite face is maintained at* 0°C. *All other surfaces are covered with an insulating material.*

Find the amount of heat flowing per second through the cube. Thermal conductivity of copper is 385 Wm^{-1}°C^{-1}.

Solution : The heat flows from the hotter face towards the colder face. The area of cross section perpendicular to the heat flow is

$$A = (10 \text{ cm})^2.$$

The amount of heat flowing per second is

$$\frac{\Delta Q}{\Delta t} = KA\frac{T_1 - T_2}{x}$$

$$= (385 \text{ Wm}^{-1}\text{°C}^{-1}) \times (0{\cdot}1 \text{ m})^2 \times \frac{(100\text{°C} - 0\text{°C})}{0{\cdot}1 \text{ m}}$$

$$= 3850 \text{ W}.$$

In general, solids are better conductors than liquids and liquids are better conductors than gases. Metals are much better conductors than nonmetals. This is because, in metals we have a large number of "free electrons" which can move freely anywhere in the body of the metal. These free electrons help in carrying the thermal energy from one place to another in a metal.

Table (28.1) gives thermal conductivities of some materials.

Table 28.1 : ***Thermal conductivities***

Material	K(Wm^{-1}K^{-1})
Aluminium	209
Brass	109
Copper	385
Silver	414
Steel	46·0
Water	0·585
Transformer oil	0·176
Air	0·0238
Hydrogen	0·167
Oxygen	0·0242
Brick	0·711
Celotex (Sugarcane fibre)	0·50
Concrete	1·30
Glass	0·669
Masonite	0·046
Rock & Galls wool	0·042
Wood (oak)	0·146
Wood (pine)	0·117

We can now understand why cooking utensils are made of metals whereas their handles are made of plastic or wood. When a rug is placed in bright sun on a tiled floor, both the rug and the floor acquire the same temperature. But it is much more difficult to stay bare foot on the tiles than to stay on the rug. This is because the conductivity of the rug is lesser than the tiles, and hence, the heat current going into the foot is smaller.

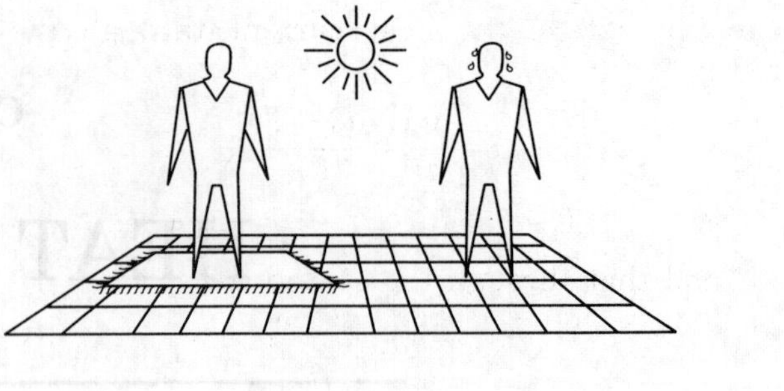

Figure 28.2

Thermal Resistance

The quantity $\frac{x}{KA}$ in equation (28.1) is called the *thermal resistance* R. Writing the heat current $\Delta Q/\Delta t$ as i, we have

$$i = \frac{T_1 - T_2}{R}. \quad \ldots \ (28.3)$$

This is mathematically equivalent to Ohm's law to be introduced in a later chapter. Many results derived from Ohm's law are also valid for thermal conduction.

Example 28.2

Find the thermal resistance of an aluminium rod of length 20 cm *and area of cross section* 1 cm^2. *The heat current is along the length of the rod. Thermal conductivity of aluminium* = 200 Wm^{-1}K^{-1}.

Solution : The thermal resistance is

$$R = \frac{x}{KA} = \frac{20 \times 10^{-2} \text{ m}}{(200 \text{ Wm}^{-1}\text{K}^{-1})(1 \times 10^{-4} \text{ m}^2)} = 10 \text{ KW}^{-1}.$$

28.2 SERIES AND PARALLEL CONNECTION OF RODS

(a) Series Connection

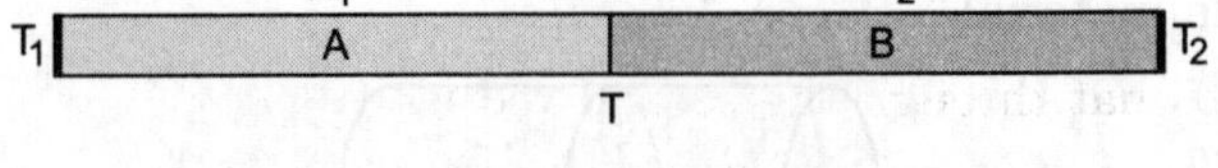

Figure 28.3

Consider two rods of thermal resistances R_1 and R_2 joined one after the other as shown in figure (28.3). The free ends are kept at temperatures T_1 and T_2 with $T_1 > T_2$. In steady state, any heat that goes through the first rod also goes through the second rod. Thus, the same heat current passes through the two rods. Such a connection of rods is called a *series connection*. Suppose, the temperature of the junction is T. From equation (28.3), the heat current through the first rod is

$$i = \frac{\Delta Q}{\Delta t} = \frac{T_1 - T}{R_1}$$

or, $$T_1 - T = R_1 i \qquad \ldots \text{(i)}$$

and that through the second rod is

$$i = \frac{\Delta Q}{\Delta t} = \frac{T - T_2}{R_2}$$

or, $$T - T_2 = R_2 i. \qquad \ldots \text{(ii)}$$

Adding (i) and (ii),

$$T_1 - T_2 = (R_1 + R_2)\, i$$

or, $$i = \frac{T_1 - T_2}{R_1 + R_2}.$$

Thus, the two rods together is equivalent to a single rod of thermal resistance $R_1 + R_2$.

If more than two rods are joined in series, the equivalent thermal resistance is given by

$$R = R_1 + R_2 + R_3 + \ldots$$

(b) Parallel Connection

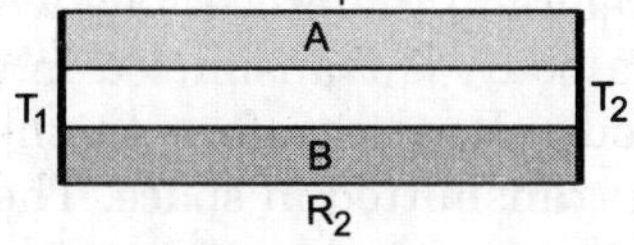

Figure 28.4

Now, suppose the two rods are joined at their ends as shown in figure (28.4). The left ends of both the rods are kept at temperature T_1 and the right ends are kept at temperature T_2. So the same temperature difference is maintained between the ends of each rod. Such a connection of rods is called a *parallel connection*. The heat current going through the first rod is

$$i_1 = \frac{\Delta Q_1}{\Delta t} = \frac{T_1 - T_2}{R_1}$$

and that through the second rod is

$$i_2 = \frac{\Delta Q_2}{\Delta t} = \frac{T_1 - T_2}{R_2}.$$

The total heat current going through the left end is

$$i = i_1 + i_2$$

$$= (T_1 - T_2)\left(\frac{1}{R_1} + \frac{1}{R_2}\right)$$

or, $$i = \frac{T_1 - T_2}{R}$$

where $$\frac{1}{R} = \frac{1}{R_1} + \frac{1}{R_2}. \qquad \ldots \text{(i)}$$

Thus, the system of the two rods is equivalent to a single rod of thermal resistance R given by (i).

If more than two rods are joined in parallel, the equivalent thermal resistance R is given by

$$\frac{1}{R} = \frac{1}{R_1} + \frac{1}{R_2} + \frac{1}{R_3} + \ldots$$

28.3 MEASUREMENT OF THERMAL CONDUCTIVITY OF A SOLID

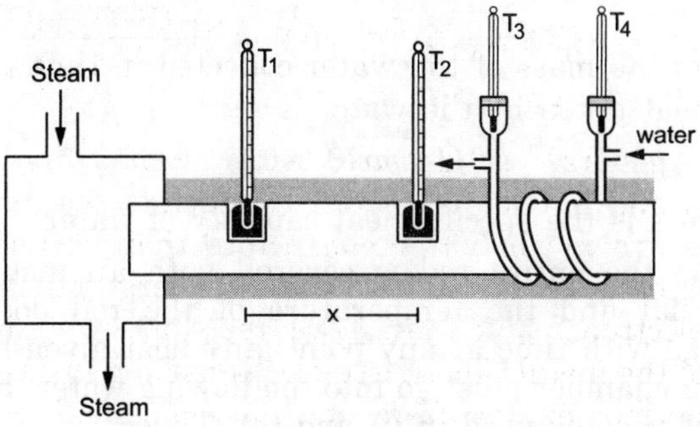

Figure 28.5

Figure (28.5) shows Searle's apparatus to measure the thermal conductivity of a solid. The solid is taken in the form of a cylindrical rod. One end of the rod goes into a steam chamber. A copper tube is coiled around the rod near the other end of the rod. A steady flow of water is maintained in the copper tube. Water enters the tube at the end away from the steam chamber and it leaves at the end nearer to it. Thermometers T_3 and T_4 are provided to measure the temperatures of the outgoing and incoming water. Two holes are drilled in the rod and mercury is filled in these holes to measure the temperature of the rod at these places with the help of thermometers T_1 and T_2. The whole apparatus is covered properly with layers of an insulating material like wool or felt so as to prevent any loss of heat from the sides.

Steam is passed in the steam chamber and a steady flow of water is maintained. The temperatures of all the four thermometers rise initially and ultimately become constant in time as the steady state is reached. The readings θ_1, θ_2, θ_3 and θ_4 are noted in steady state.

A beaker is weighed and the water coming out of the copper tube is collected in it for a fixed time t measured by a stop clock. The beaker together with the water is weighed. The mass m of the water collected is then calculated. The area of cross section of the rod is calculated by measuring its radius with a slide calipers. The distance between the holes in the rod is measured with the help of a divider and a metre scale.

Let the length of the rod between the holes be x and the area of cross section of the rod be A. If the thermal conductivity of the material of the rod is K, the rate of heat flow (heat current) from the steam chamber to the rod is

$$\frac{\Delta Q}{\Delta t} = K\frac{A(\theta_1 - \theta_2)}{x}.$$

In a time t, the chamber supplies a heat

$$Q = K\frac{A(\theta_1 - \theta_2)}{x}t. \quad \dots \text{(i)}$$

As the mass of the water collected in time t is m, the heat taken by the water is

$$Q = ms(\theta_3 - \theta_4) \quad \dots \text{(ii)}$$

where s is the specific heat capacity of water.

As the entire rod is covered with an insulating material and the temperature of the rod does not change with time at any point, any heat given by the steam chamber must go into the flowing water. Hence, the same Q is used in (i) and (ii). Thus,

$$K\frac{A(\theta_1 - \theta_2)}{x}t = ms(\theta_3 - \theta_4)$$

or,
$$K = \frac{x\, ms(\theta_3 - \theta_4)}{A(\theta_1 - \theta_2)t}. \quad \dots \text{(28.4)}$$

28.4 CONVECTION

In convection, heat is transferred from one place to the other by the actual motion of heated material. For example, in a hot air blower, air is heated by a heating element and is blown by a fan. The air carries the heat wherever it goes. When water is kept in a vessel and heated on a stove, the water at the bottom gets heat due to conduction through the vessel's bottom. Its density decreases and consequently it rises. Thus, the heat is carried from the bottom to the top by the actual movement of the parts of the water. If the heated material is forced to move, say by a blower or a pump, the process of heat transfer is called *forced convection*. If the material moves due to difference in density, it is called *natural* or *free convection*.

Natural convection and the anomalous expansion of water play important roles in saving the lives of aquatic animals like fishes when the atmospheric temperature goes below 0°C. As the water at the surface is cooled, it becomes denser and goes down. The less cold water from the bottom rises up to the surface and gets cooled. This way the entire water is cooled to 4°C. As the water at the surface is further cooled, it expands and the density decreases. Thus, it remains at the surface and gets further cooled. Finally, it starts freezing. Heat is now lost to the atmosphere by the water only due to conduction through the ice. As ice is a poor conductor of heat, the further freezing is very slow. The temperature of the water at the bottom remains constant at 4°C for a large period of time. The atmospheric temperature ultimately improves and the animals are saved.

The main mechanism for heat transfer inside a human body is forced convection. Heart serves as the pump and blood as the circulating fluid. Heat is lost to the atmosphere through all the three processes conduction, convection and radiation. The rate of loss depends on the clothing, the tiredness and perspiration, atmospheric temperature, air current, humidity and several other factors. The system, however, transports the just required amount of heat and hence maintains a remarkably constant body temperature.

28.5 RADIATION

The process of radiation does not need any material medium for heat transfer. Energy is emitted by a body and this energy travels in the space just like light. When it falls on a material body, a part is absorbed and the thermal energy of the receiving body is increased. The energy emitted by a body in this way is called *radiant energy, thermal radiation* or simply *radiation*. Thus, the word "radiation" is used in two meanings. It refers to the process by which the energy is emitted by a body, is transmitted in space and falls on another body. It also refers to the energy itself which is being transmitted in space. The heat from the sun reaches the earth by this process, travelling millions of kilometres of empty space.

28.6 PRÉVOST THEORY OF EXCHANGE

Way back in 1792, Pierre Prévost put forward the theory of radiation in a systematic way now known as the *theory of exchange*. According to this theory, all bodies radiate thermal radiation at all temperatures. The amount of thermal radiation radiated per unit time depends on the nature of the emitting surface, its area and its temperature. The rate is faster at higher temperatures. Besides, a body also absorbs part of the thermal radiation emitted by the surrounding bodies when this radiation falls on it. If a body radiates more than what it absorbs, its temperature falls. If a body radiates less than what it absorbs, its temperature rises.

Now, consider a body kept in a room for a long time. One finds that the temperature of the body remains constant and is equal to the room temperature. The body is still radiating thermal radiation. But it is also absorbing part of the radiation emitted by the surrounding objects, walls, etc. We thus conclude that when the temperature of a body is equal to the temperature of its surroundings, it radiates at the same rate as it absorbs. If we place a hotter body in the room, it radiates at a faster rate than the rate at which it absorbs. Thus, the body suffers a net loss of thermal energy in any given time and its temperature decreases. Similarly, if a colder body is kept in a warm surrounding, it radiates less to the surrounding than what it absorbs from the surrounding. Consequently, there is a net increase in the thermal energy of the body and the temperature rises.

28.7 BLACKBODY RADIATION

Consider two bodies of equal surface areas suspended in a room. One of the bodies has polished surface and the other is painted black. After sufficient time, the temperature of both the bodies will be equal to the room temperature. As the surface areas of the bodies are the same, equal amount of radiation falls on the two surfaces. The polished surface reflects a large part of it and absorbs a little, while the black-painted surface reflects a little and absorbs a large part of it. As the temperature of each body remains constant, we conclude that the polished surface radiates at a slower rate and the black-painted surface radiates at a faster rate. So, good absorbers of radiation are also good emitters.

A body that absorbs all the radiation falling on it is called a *blackbody*. Such a body will emit radiation at the fastest rate. The radiation emitted by a blackbody is called *blackbody radiation*. The radiation inside an enclosure with its inner walls maintained at a constant temperature has the same properties as the blackbody radiation and is also called blackbody radiation. A blackbody is also called an *ideal radiator*. A perfect blackbody, absorbing 100% of the radiation falling on it, is only an ideal concept. Among the materials, lampblack is close to a blackbody. It reflects only about 1% of the radiation falling on it. If an enclosure is painted black from inside and a small hole is made in the wall (figure 28.6) the hole acts as a very good blackbody.

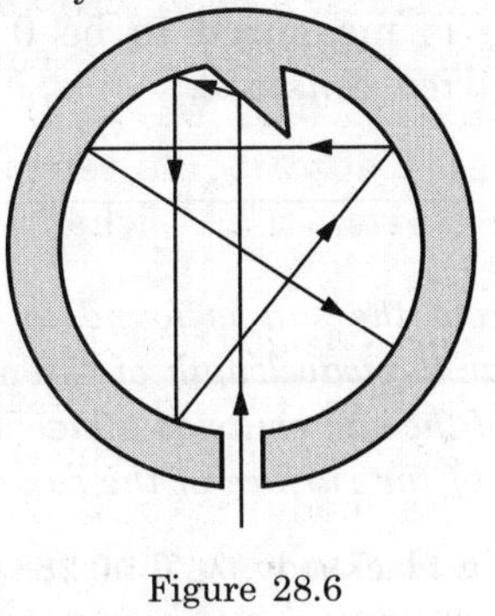

Figure 28.6

Any radiation that falls on the hole goes inside. This radiation has little chance to come out of the hole again and it gets absorbed after multiple reflections. The cone directly opposite to the hole (figure 28.6) ensures that the incoming radiation is not directly reflected back to the hole.

28.8 KIRCHHOFF'S LAW

We have learnt that good absorbers of radiation are also good radiators. This aspect is described quantitatively by Kirchhoff's law of radiation. Before stating the law let us define certain terms.

Emissive Power

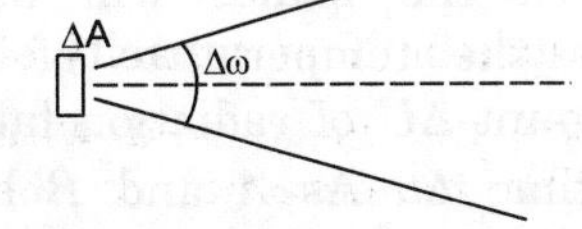

Figure 28.7

Consider a small area ΔA of a body emitting thermal radiation. Consider a small solid angle $\Delta\omega$ (see the chapter "Gauss's Law") about the normal to the radiating surface. Let the energy radiated by the area ΔA of the surface in the solid angle $\Delta\omega$ in time Δt be ΔU. We define *emissive power* of the body as

$$E = \frac{\Delta U}{(\Delta A)\,(\Delta\omega)\,(\Delta t)}\,.$$

Thus, emissive power denotes the energy radiated per unit area per unit time per unit solid angle along the normal to the area.

Absorptive Power

Absorptive power of a body is defined as the fraction of the incident radiation that is absorbed by the body. If we denote the absorptive power by a,

$$a = \frac{\text{energy absorbed}}{\text{energy incident}}\,.$$

As all the radiation incident on a blackbody is absorbed, the absorptive power of a blackbody is unity.

Note that the absorptive power is a dimensionless quantity but the emissive power is not.

Kirchhoff's Law

The ratio of emissive power to absorptive power is the same for all bodies at a given temperature and is equal to the emissive power of a blackbody at that temperature. Thus,

$$\frac{E(\text{body})}{a(\text{body})} = E(\text{blackbody})\,.$$

Kirchhoff's law tells that if a body has high emissive power, it should also have high absorptive power to have the ratio E/a same. Similarly, a body having low emissive power should have low absorptive power. Kirchhoff's law may be easily proved by a simple argument as described below.

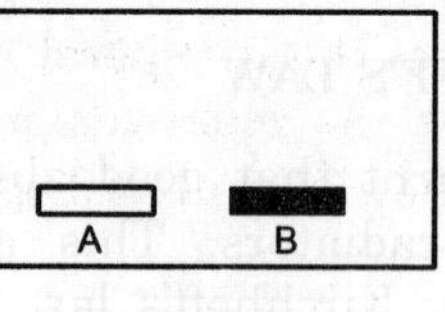

Figure 28.8

Consider two bodies A and B of identical geometrical shapes placed in an enclosure. Suppose A is an arbitrary body and B is a blackbody. In thermal equilibrium, both the bodies will have the same temperature as the temperature of the enclosure. Suppose an amount ΔU of radiation falls on the body A in a given time Δt. As A and B have the same geometrical shapes, the radiation falling on the blackbody B is also ΔU. The blackbody absorbs all of this ΔU. As the temperature of the blackbody remains constant, it also emits an amount ΔU of radiation in that time. If the emissive power of the blackbody is E_0, we have

$$\Delta U \propto E_0 \text{ or } \Delta U = kE_0 \quad \dots \text{(i)}$$

where k is a constant.

Let the absorptive power of A be a. Thus, it absorbs an amount $a\Delta U$ of the radiation falling on it in time Δt. As its temperature remains constant, it must also emit the same amount $a\Delta U$ in that time. If the emissive power of the body A is E, we have

$$a\Delta U = kE. \quad \dots \text{(ii)}$$

The same proportionality constant k is used in (i) and (ii) because the two bodies have identical geometrical shapes and radiation emitted in the same time Δt is considered.

From (i) and (ii),

$$a = \frac{E}{E_0}$$

or, $$\frac{E}{a} = E_0$$

or, $$\frac{E(\text{body})}{a(\text{body})} = E(\text{blackbody}).$$

This proves Kirchhoff's law.

28.9 NATURE OF THERMAL RADIATION

Thermal radiation, once emitted, is an electromagnetic wave like light. It, therefore, obeys all the laws of wave theory. The wavelengths are still small compared to the dimensions of usual obstacles encountered, so the rules of geometrical optics are valid, i.e., it travels in a straight line, casts shadow, is reflected and refracted at the change of medium, etc. The radiation emitted by a body is a mixture of waves of different wavelengths. However, only a small range of wavelength has significant contribution in the total radiation. The radiation emitted by a body at a temperature of 300 K (room temperature) has significant contribution from wavelengths around 9550 nm which is in long infrared region (visible light has a range of about 380–780 nm). As the temperature of the emitter increases, this dominant wavelength decreases. At around 1100 K, the radiation has a good contribution from red region of wavelengths and the object appears red. At temperatures around 3000 K, the radiation contains enough shorter wavelengths and the object appears white. Even at such a high temperature most significant contributions come from wavelengths around 950 nm.

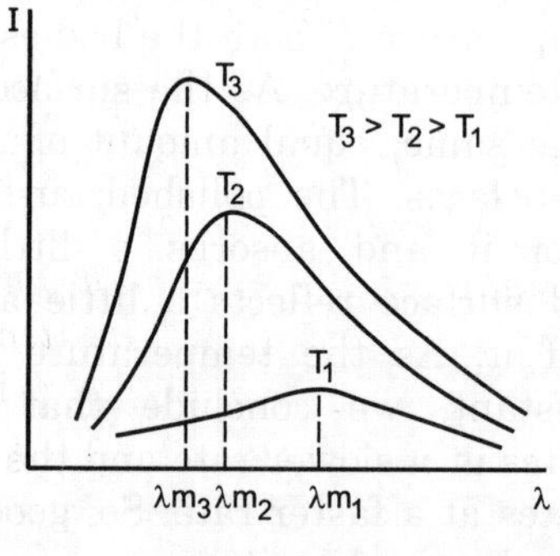

Figure 28.9

The relative importance of different wavelengths in a thermal radiation can be studied qualitatively from figure (28.9). Here the intensity of radiation near a given wavelength is plotted against the wavelength for different temperatures. We see that as the temperature is increased, the wavelength corresponding to the highest intensity decreases. In fact, this wavelength λ_m is inversely proportional to the absolute temperature of the emitter. So,

$$\lambda_m T = b \quad \dots (28.5)$$

where b is a constant.

This equation is known as the *Wien's displacement law.* For a blackbody, the constant b appearing in equation (28.5) is measured to be 0·288 cmK and is known as the *Wien constant.*

Example 28.3

The light from the sun is found to have a maximum intensity near the wavelength of 470 nm. *Assuming that the surface of the sun emits as a blackbody, calculate the temperature of the surface of the sun.*

Solution : For a blackbody, $\lambda_m T = 0{\cdot}288$ cmK.

Thus, $T = \dfrac{0{\cdot}288 \text{ cmK}}{470 \text{ nm}} = 6130$ K.

Distribution of radiant energy among different wavelengths has played a very significant role in the development of quantum mechanics and in our understanding of nature in a new way. Classical physics had predicted a very different and unrealistic wavelength distribution. Planck put forward a bold hypothesis that radiation can be emitted or absorbed only in discrete steps, each step involving an amount of energy given by $E = nh\nu$ where ν is the frequency of the radiation and n is an integer. A new fundamental constant h named as *Planck constant* was introduced in physics. This opened the gateway of modern physics through which we look into the atomic and subatomic world.

28.10 STEFAN–BOLTZMANN LAW

The energy of thermal radiation emitted per unit time by a blackbody of surface area A is given by

$$u = \sigma A T^4 \qquad \dots (28.6)$$

where σ is a universal constant known as Stefan–Boltzmann constant and T is its temperature on absolute scale. The measured value of σ is $5{\cdot}67 \times 10^{-8}$ $\mathrm{W m^{-2} K^{-4}}$. Equation (28.6) itself is called the *Stefan–Boltzmann law.* Stefan had suggested this law from experimental data available on radiation and Boltzmann derived it from thermodynamical considerations. The law is also quoted as *Stefan's law* and the constant σ as *Stefan constant.*

A body which is not a blackbody, emits less radiation than given by equation (28.6). It is, however, proportional to T^4. The energy emitted by such a body per unit time is written as

$$u = e\sigma A T^4 \qquad \dots (28.7)$$

where e is a constant for the given surface having a value between 0 and 1. This constant is called the *emissivity* of the surface. It is zero for completely reflecting surface and is unity for a blackbody.

Using Kirchhoff's law,

$$\frac{E(\text{body})}{E(\text{blackbody})} = a \qquad \dots (\text{i})$$

where a is the absorptive power of the body. The emissive power E is proportional to the energy radiated per unit time, that is, proportional to u. Using equations (28.6) and (28.7) in (i),

$$\frac{e\sigma A T^4}{\sigma A T^4} = a \quad \text{or} \quad e = a.$$

Thus, emissivity and absorptive power have the same value.

Consider a body of emissivity e kept in thermal equilibrium in a room at temperature T_0. The energy of radiation absorbed by it per unit time should be equal to the energy emitted by it per unit time. This is because the temperature remains constant. Thus, the energy of the radiation absorbed per unit time is

$$u = e\sigma A T_0^4.$$

Now, suppose the temperature of the body is changed to T but the room temperature remains T_0. The energy of the thermal radiation emitted by the body per unit time is

$$u = e\sigma A T^4.$$

The energy absorbed per unit time by the body is

$$u_0 = e\sigma A T_0^4.$$

Thus, the net loss of thermal energy per unit time is

$$\Delta u = u - u_0$$

$$= e\sigma A(T^4 - T_0^4). \qquad \dots (28.8)$$

Example 28.4

A blackbody of surface area $10\ \mathrm{cm}^2$ *is heated to* 127°C *and is suspended in a room at temperature* 27°C. *Calculate the initial rate of loss of heat from the body to the room.*

Solution : For a blackbody at temperature T, the rate of emission is $u = \sigma A T^4$. When it is kept in a room at temperature T_0, the rate of absorption is $u_0 = \sigma A T_0^4$. The net rate of loss of heat is $u - u_0 = \sigma A(T^4 - T_0^4)$. Here $A = 10 \times 10^{-4}\ \mathrm{m}^2$, $T = 400$ K and $T_0 = 300$ K . Thus,

$u - u_0$

$= (5{\cdot}67 \times 10^{-8}\ \mathrm{W m^{-2} K^{-4}})\ (10 \times 10^{-4}\ \mathrm{m}^2)\ (400^4 - 300^4)\ \mathrm{K}^4$

$= 0{\cdot}99$ W.

28.11 NEWTON'S LAW OF COOLING

Suppose, a body of surface area A at an absolute temperature T is kept in a surrounding having a lower temperature T_0. The net rate of loss of thermal energy from the body due to radiation is

$$\Delta u_1 = e\sigma A(T^4 - T_0^4).$$

If the temperature difference is small, we can write

$$T = T_0 + \Delta T$$

or,

$$T^4 - T_0^4 = (T_0 + \Delta T)^4 - T_0^4$$

$$= T_0^4\left(1 + \frac{\Delta T}{T_0}\right)^4 - T_0^4$$

$$= T_0^4\left[1 + 4\frac{\Delta T}{T_0} + \text{higher powers of } \frac{\Delta T}{T_0}\right] - T_0^4$$

$$\approx 4\,T_0^3 \Delta T = 4\,T_0^3(T - T_0).$$

Thus,

$$\Delta u_1 = 4\,e\sigma A T_0^3(T - T_0)$$

$$= b_1 A(T - T_0).$$

The body may also lose thermal energy due to convection in the surrounding air. For small temperature difference, the rate of loss of heat due to convection is also proportional to the temperature difference and the area of the surface. This rate may, therefore, be written as

$$\Delta u_2 = b_2 A(T - T_0).$$

The net rate of loss of thermal energy due to convection and radiation is

$$\Delta u = \Delta u_1 + \Delta u_2 = (b_1 + b_2)A(T - T_0).$$

If s be the specific heat capacity of the body and m its mass, the rate of fall of temperature is

$$\frac{-dT}{dt} = \frac{\Delta u}{ms} = \frac{b_1 + b_2}{ms} A(T - T_0)$$

$$= bA(T - T_0).$$

Thus, for small temperature difference between a body and its surrounding, the rate of cooling of the body is directly proportional to the temperature difference and the surface area exposed. We can write

$$\frac{dT}{dt} = - bA(T - T_0). \quad \dots (28.9)$$

This is known as *Newton's law of cooling*. The constant b depends on the nature of the surface involved and the surrounding conditions. The minus sign indicates that if $T > T_0$, dT/dt is negative, that is, the temperature decreases with time. As the difference in temperature is the same for absolute and Celsius scale, equation (28.9) may also be written as

$$\frac{d\theta}{dt} = - bA(\theta - \theta_0) = -k(\theta - \theta_0)$$

where θ refers to temperature in Celsius scale.

Example 28.5

A liquid cools from 70°C *to* 60°C *in* 5 minutes . *Calculate the time taken by the liquid to cool from* 60°C *to* 50°C, *if the temperature of the surrounding is constant at* 30°C.

Solution : The average temperature of the liquid in the first case is

$$\theta_1 = \frac{70°C + 60°C}{2} = 65°C.$$

The average temperature difference from the surrounding is

$$\theta_1 - \theta_0 = 65°C - 30°C = 35°C.$$

The rate of fall of temperature is

$$-\frac{d\theta_1}{dt} = \frac{70°C - 60°C}{5 \text{ min}} = 2°C \text{ min}^{-1}.$$

From Newton's law of cooling,

$$2°C \text{ min}^{-1} = bA(35°C)$$

or, $$bA = \frac{2}{35 \text{ min}}. \quad \dots \text{(i)}$$

In the second case, the average temperature of the liquid is

$$\theta_2 = \frac{60°C + 50°C}{2} = 55°C$$

so that, $\theta_2 - \theta_0 = 55°C - 30°C = 25°C.$

If it takes a time t to cool down from 60°C to 50°C, the rate of fall of temperature is

$$-\frac{d\theta_2}{dt} = \frac{60°C - 50°C}{t} = \frac{10°C}{t}.$$

From Newton's law of cooling and (i),

$$\frac{10°C}{t} = \frac{2}{35 \text{ min}} \times 25°C$$

or, $t = 7$ min.

28.12 DETECTION AND MEASUREMENT OF RADIATION

Several instruments are used to detect and measure the amount of thermal radiation. We describe two of them here, a bolometer and a thermopile.

Bolometer

The bolometer is based on the theory of Wheatstone bridge which was introduced while discussing resistance thermometer. A thin (a small fraction of a millimetre) foil of platinum is taken and strips are cut from it to leave a grid-type structure as shown in figure (28.10a). Four such grids, identical in all respect, are prepared and joined with a battery and a galvanometer to form a Wheatstone bridge (figure 28.10b). Grid 1 faces the radiation to be detected or measured. The particular arrangement of the four grids ensures that the radiation passing through the empty spaces in grid 1 falls on the strips of grid 4. Grids 2 and 3 are protected from the radiation.

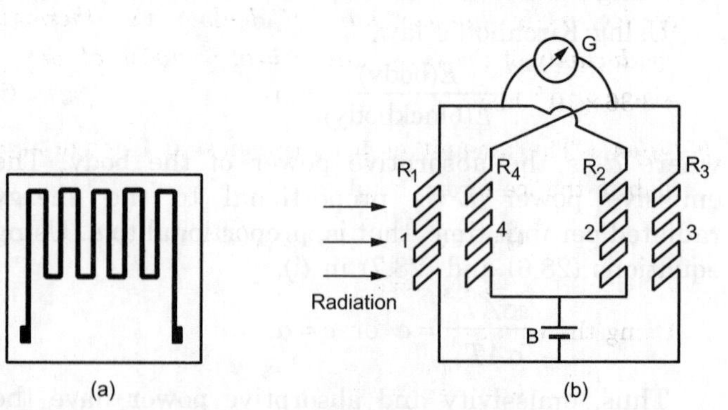

Figure 28.10

When no radiation falls on the bolometer, all the grids have the same resistance so that

$R_1 = R_2 = R_3 = R_4$. Thus, $\frac{R_1}{R_2} = \frac{R_3}{R_4}$ and the bridge is balanced. There is no deflection in the galvanometer. When radiation falls on the bolometer, grids 1 and 4 get heated. As the temperature increases, the resistances R_1 and R_4 increase and hence the product $R_1 R_4$ increases. On the other hand, $R_2 R_3$ remains unchanged. Thus,

$$R_1 R_4 > R_2 R_3$$

or, $$\frac{R_1}{R_2} > \frac{R_3}{R_4}.$$

The bridge becomes unbalanced and there is a deflection in the galvanometer which indicates the presence of radiation. The magnitude of deflection is related to the amount of radiation falling on the bolometer.

The bolometer is usually enclosed in a glass bulb evacuated to low pressures. This increases the sensitivity.

Thermopile

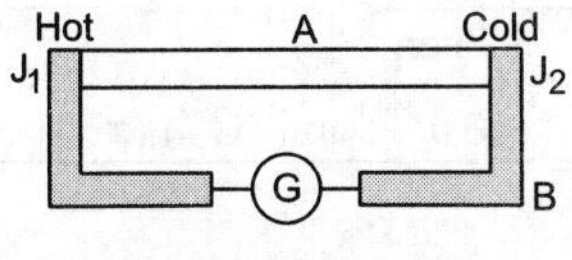

Figure 28.11

A thermopile is based on the principle of *Seebeck effect.* Figure (28.11) illustrates the principle. Two dissimilar metals A and B are joined to form two junctions J_1 and J_2. A galvanometer is connected between the junctions through the metal B. If the junctions are at the same temperature, there is no deflection in the galvanometer. But if the temperatures of the junctions are different, the galvanometer deflects. Such an instrument is called a *thermocouple.*

In a thermopile, a number of thermocouples are joined in series. The thermocouples are made from antimony and bismuth metals. The free ends are joined to a galvanometer (figure 28.12). The series connection of thermocouples increases the sensitivity of the system.

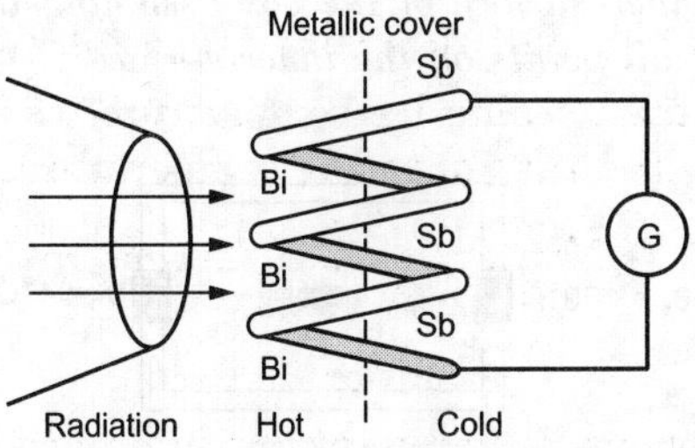

Figure 28.12

The junctions are arranged in such a way that all the hot junctions lie on a plane face and all the cold junctions lie on the opposite plane face. The face of the hot junctions is blackened so that it may absorb large fraction of radiation falling on it. This face is exposed to the radiation and the other face is protected from it by a metallic cover. A metallic cone generally concentrates the radiation on the hot face.

The radiation is detected and measured by observing the deflection in the galvanometer.

Worked Out Examples

1. *The lower surface of a slab of stone of face-area* 3600 cm^2 *and thickness* 10 cm *is exposed to steam at* 100°C. *A block of ice at* 0°C *rests on the upper surface of the slab.* 4·8 g *of ice melts in one hour. Calculate the thermal conductivity of the stone. Latent heat of fusion of ice* = 3·36 × 10^5 J kg^{-1}.

Solution : The amount of heat transferred through the slab to the ice in one hour is

$$Q = (4{\cdot}8 \times 10^{-3}\ \text{kg}) \times (3{\cdot}36 \times 10^5\ \text{J kg}^{-1})$$

$$= 4{\cdot}8 \times 336\ \text{J}.$$

Using the equation

$$Q = \frac{KA(\theta_1 - \theta_2)t}{x},$$

$$4{\cdot}8 \times 336\ \text{J} = \frac{K(3600\ \text{cm}^2)(100°\text{C}) \times (3600\ \text{s})}{10\ \text{cm}}$$

or, $$K = 1{\cdot}24 \times 10^{-3}\ \text{W m}^{-1}\,°\text{C}^{-1}.$$

2. *An icebox made of* 1·5 cm *thick styrofoam has dimensions* 60 cm × 60 cm × 30 cm. *It contains ice at* 0°C *and is kept in a room at* 40°C. *Find the rate at which the ice is melting. Latent heat of fusion of ice* = 3·36 × 10^5 J kg^{-1}. *and thermal conductivity of styrofoam* = 0·04 W m^{-1}°C^{-1}.

Solution : The total surface area of the walls

$$= 2(60\ \text{cm} \times 60\ \text{cm} + 60\ \text{cm} \times 30\ \text{cm} + 60\ \text{cm} \times 30\ \text{cm})$$
$$= 1{\cdot}44\ \text{m}^2.$$

The thickness of the walls = 1·5 cm = 0·015 m.

The rate of heat flow into the box is

$$\frac{\Delta Q}{\Delta t} = \frac{KA(\theta_1 - \theta_2)}{x}$$

$$= \frac{(0{\cdot}04\ \text{W m}^{-1}°\text{C}^{-1})(1{\cdot}44\ \text{m}^2)(40°\text{C})}{0{\cdot}015\ \text{m}} = 154\ \text{W}.$$

The rate at which the ice melts is

$$= \frac{154\ \text{W}}{3{\cdot}36 \times 10^5\ \text{J kg}^{-1}} = 0{\cdot}46\ \text{g s}^{-1}.$$

3. *A closed cubical box is made of perfectly insulating material and the only way for heat to enter or leave the box is through two solid cylindrical metal plugs, each of cross sectional area* 12 cm^2 *and length* 8 cm *fixed in the opposite walls of the box. The outer surface of one plug is kept at a temperature of* 100°C *while the outer surface of the other plug is maintained at a temperature of* 4°C. *The thermal conductivity of the material of the plug is* 2·0 Wm^{-1}°C^{-1}. *A source of energy generating* 13 W *is enclosed inside the box. Find the equilibrium temperature of the inner surface of the box assuming that it is the same at all points on the inner surface.*

Solution :

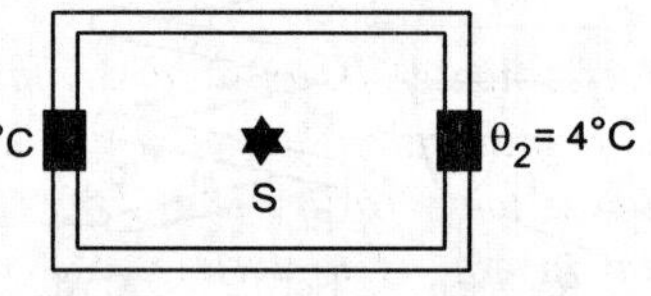

Figure 28-W1

The situation is shown in figure (28-W1). Let the temperature inside the box be θ. The rate at which heat enters the box through the left plug is

$$\frac{\Delta Q_1}{\Delta t} = \frac{KA(\theta_1 - \theta)}{x}$$

The rate of heat generation in the box = 13 W. The rate at which heat flows out of the box through the right plug is

$$\frac{\Delta Q_2}{\Delta t} = \frac{KA(\theta - \theta_2)}{x}.$$

In the steady state

$$\frac{\Delta Q_1}{\Delta t} + 13\text{ W} = \frac{\Delta Q_2}{\Delta t}$$

or, $$\frac{KA}{x}(\theta_1 - \theta) + 13\text{ W} = \frac{KA}{x}(\theta - \theta_2)$$

or, $$2\frac{KA}{x}\theta = \frac{KA}{x}(\theta_1 + \theta_2) + 13\text{ W}$$

or, $$\theta = \frac{\theta_1 + \theta_2}{2} + \frac{(13\text{ W})\,x}{2KA}$$

$$= \frac{100°\text{C} + 4°\text{C}}{2} + \frac{(13\text{ W}) \times 0{\cdot}08\text{ m}}{2 \times (2{\cdot}0\text{ W m}^{-1}°\text{C}^{-1})(12 \times 10^{-4}\text{ m}^2)}$$

$$= 52°\text{C} + 216{\cdot}67°\text{C} \approx 269°\text{C}.$$

4. *A bar of copper of length* 75 cm *and a bar of steel of length* 125 cm *are joined together end to end. Both are of circular cross section with diameter* 2 cm. *The free ends of the copper and the steel bars are maintained at* 100°C *and* 0°C *respectively. The curved surfaces of the bars are thermally insulated. What is the temperature of the copper–steel junction? What is the amount of heat transmitted per unit time across the junction? Thermal conductivity of copper is* 386 J s^{-1} m^{-1}°C^{-1} *and that of steel is* 46 J s^{-1} m^{-1}°C^{-1}.

Solution :

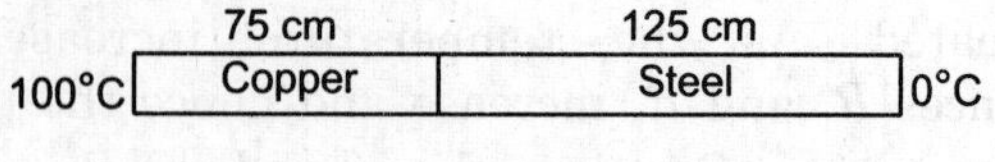

Figure 28-W2

The situation is shown in figure (28-W2). Let the temperature at the junction be θ (on Celsius scale). The same heat current passes through the copper and the steel rods. Thus,

$$\frac{\Delta Q}{\Delta t} = \frac{K_{cu}\,A(100°\text{C} - \theta)}{75\text{ cm}} = \frac{K_{steel}\,A\theta}{125\text{ cm}}$$

or, $$\frac{K_{cu}\,(100°\text{C} - \theta)}{75} = \frac{K_{steel}\,\theta}{125}$$

or, $$\frac{100°\text{C} - \theta}{\theta} = \frac{75\,K_{steel}}{125\,K_{cu}} = \frac{3}{5} \times \frac{46}{386}$$

or, $$\theta = 93°\text{C}.$$

The rate of heat flow is

$$\frac{\Delta Q}{\Delta t} = \frac{K_{steel}A\theta}{125\text{ cm}}$$

$$= \frac{(46\text{ J s}^{-1}\text{ m}^{-1}°\text{C}^{-1})\,(\pi \times 1\text{ cm}^2) \times 93°\text{C}}{125\text{ cm}}$$

$$= 1{\cdot}07\text{ J s}^{-1}.$$

5. *Two parallel plates A and B are joined together to form a compound plate (figure 28-W3). The thicknesses of the plates are* 4·0 cm *and* 2·5 cm *respectively and the area of cross section is* 100 cm^2 *for each plate. The thermal conductivities are* K_A = 200 W m^{-1}°C^{-1} *for the plate A and* K_B = 400 W m^{-1}°C^{-1} *for the plate B. The outer surface of the plate A is maintained at* 100°C *and the outer surface of the plate B is maintained at* 0°C. *Find (a) the rate of heat flow through any cross section, (b) the temperature at the interface and (c) the equivalent thermal conductivity of the compound plate.*

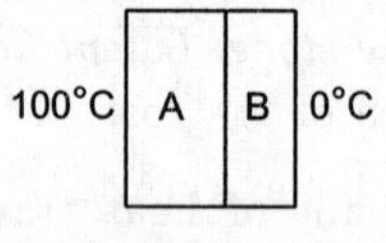

Figure 28-W3

Solution : (a) Let the temperature of the interface be θ. The area of cross section of each plate is A = 100 cm^2 = 0·01 m^2. The thicknesses are x_A = 0·04 m and x_B = 0·025 m.

The thermal resistance of the plate A is

$$R_1 = \frac{1}{K_A}\frac{x_A}{A}$$

and that of the plate B is

$$R_2 = \frac{1}{K_B}\frac{x_B}{A}.$$

The equivalent thermal resistance is

$$R = R_1 + R_2 = \frac{1}{A}\left(\frac{x_A}{K_A} + \frac{x_B}{K_B}\right). \quad \ldots \text{(i)}$$

Thus, $\frac{\Delta Q}{\Delta t} = \frac{\theta_1 - \theta_2}{R}$

$$= \frac{A(\theta_1 - \theta_2)}{x_A/K_A + x_B/K_B}$$

$$= \frac{(0{\cdot}01 \text{ m}^2)(100°\text{C})}{(0{\cdot}04 \text{ m})/(200 \text{ W m}^{-1}°\text{C}^{-1}) + (0{\cdot}025 \text{ m})/(400 \text{ W m}^{-1}°\text{C}^{-1})}$$

$= 3810$ W.

(b) We have $\frac{\Delta Q}{\Delta t} = \frac{A(\theta - \theta_2)}{x_B/K_B}$

or, $3810 \text{ W} = \frac{(0{\cdot}01 \text{ m}^2)(\theta - 0°\text{C})}{(0{\cdot}025 \text{ m})/(400 \text{ W m}^{-1}°\text{C}^{-1})}$

or, $\theta = 24°$C.

(c) If K is the equivalent thermal conductivity of the compound plate, its thermal resistance is

$$R = \frac{1}{A}\frac{x_A + x_B}{K}.$$

Comparing with (i),

$$\frac{x_A + x_B}{K} = \frac{x_A}{K_A} + \frac{x_B}{K_B}$$

or, $K = \frac{x_A + x_B}{x_A/K_A + x_B/K_B}$

$= 248 \text{ W m}^{-1}°\text{C}^{-1}$.

6. *A room has a 4 m × 4 m × 10 cm concrete roof ($K = 1{\cdot}26$ $\text{Wm}^{-1}°\text{C}^{-1}$). At some instant, the temperature outside is 46°C and that inside is 32°C. (a) Neglecting convection, calculate the amount of heat flowing per second into the room through the roof. (b) Bricks ($K = 0{\cdot}65 \text{ Wm}^{-1}°\text{C}^{-1}$) of thickness 7·5 cm are laid down on the roof. Calculate the new rate of heat flow under the same temperature conditions.*

Solution : The area of the roof

$= 4 \text{ m} \times 4 \text{ m} = 16 \text{ m}^2$.

The thickness $x = 10 \text{ cm} = 0{\cdot}10$ m.

(a) The thermal resistance of the roof is

$$R_1 = \frac{1}{K}\frac{x}{A} = \frac{1}{1{\cdot}26 \text{ W m}^{-1}°\text{C}^{-1}}\frac{0{\cdot}10 \text{ m}}{16 \text{ m}^2}$$

$$= 4{\cdot}96 \times 10^{-3} \text{ °C W}^{-1}.$$

The heat current is

$$\frac{\Delta Q}{\Delta t} = \frac{\theta_1 - \theta_2}{R_1} = \frac{46°\text{C} - 32°\text{C}}{4{\cdot}96 \times 10^{-3} \text{ °C W}^{-1}}$$

$= 2822$ W.

(b) The thermal resistance of the brick layer is

$$R_2 = \frac{1}{K}\frac{x}{A} = \frac{1}{0{\cdot}65 \text{ W m}^{-1}°\text{C}^{-1}}\frac{7{\cdot}5 \times 10^{-2} \text{ m}}{16 \text{ m}^2}$$

$$= 7{\cdot}2 \times 10^{-3} \text{ °C W}^{-1}.$$

The equivalent thermal resistance is

$$R = R_1 + R_2 = (4{\cdot}96 + 7{\cdot}2) \times 10^{-3} \text{ °C W}^{-1}$$

$$= 1{\cdot}216 \times 10^{-2} \text{ °C W}^{-1}.$$

The heat current is

$$\frac{\Delta Q}{\Delta t} = \frac{\theta_1 - \theta_2}{R} = \frac{46°\text{C} - 32°\text{C}}{1{\cdot}216 \times 10^{-2} \text{ °C W}^{-1}}.$$

$= 1152$ W.

7. *An electric heater is used in a room of total wall area 137 m² to maintain a temperature of 20°C inside it, when the outside temperature is – 10°C. The walls have three different layers of materials. The innermost layer is of wood of thickness 2·5 cm, the middle layer is of cement of thickness 1·0 cm and the outermost layer is of brick of thickness 25·0 cm. Find the power of the electric heater. Assume that there is no heat loss through the floor and the ceiling. The thermal conductivities of wood, cement and brick are $0{\cdot}125 \text{ Wm}^{-1}°\text{C}^{-1}$, $1{\cdot}5 \text{ Wm}^{-1}°\text{C}^{-1}$ and $1{\cdot}0 \text{ Wm}^{-1}°\text{C}^{-1}$ respectively.*

Solution :

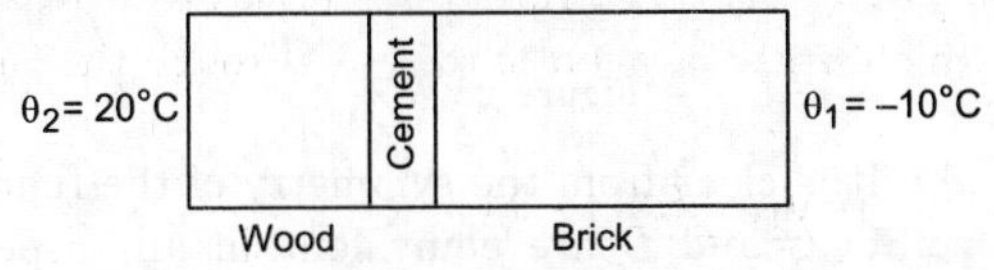

Figure 28-W4

The situation is shown in figure (28-W4).

The thermal resistances of the wood, the cement and the brick layers are

$$R_W = \frac{1}{K}\frac{x}{A}$$

$$= \frac{1}{0{\cdot}125 \text{ W m}^{-1}°\text{C}^{-1}}\frac{2{\cdot}5 \times 10^{-2} \text{ m}}{137 \text{ m}^2}$$

$$= \frac{0{\cdot}20}{137} \text{ °C W}^{-1},$$

$$R_C = \frac{1}{1{\cdot}5 \text{ W m}^{-1}°\text{C}^{-1}}\frac{1{\cdot}0 \times 10^{-2} \text{ m}}{137 \text{ m}^2}$$

$$= \frac{0{\cdot}0067}{137} \text{ °C W}^{-1}$$

and $R_B = \frac{1}{1{\cdot}0 \text{ W m}^{-1}°\text{C}^{-1}}\frac{25{\cdot}0 \times 10^{-2} \text{ m}}{137 \text{ m}^2}$

$$= \frac{0{\cdot}25}{137} \text{ °C W}^{-1}.$$

As the layers are connected in series, the equivalent thermal resistance is

$$R = R_W + R_C + R_B$$

$$= \frac{0{\cdot}20 + 0{\cdot}0067 + 0{\cdot}25}{137}\ °\text{C W}^{-1}$$

$$= 3{\cdot}33 \times 10^{-3}\ °\text{C W}^{-1}.$$

The heat current is

$$i = \frac{\theta_1 - \theta_2}{R}$$

$$= \frac{20°\text{C} - (-10°\text{C})}{3{\cdot}33 \times 10^{-3}\ °\text{C W}^{-1}} \approx 9000\ \text{W}.$$

The heater must supply 9000 W to compensate the outflow of heat.

8. *Three rods of material x and three of material y are connected as shown in figure (28-W5). All the rods are identical in length and cross sectional area. If the end A is maintained at 60°C and the junction E at 10°C, calculate the temperature of the junction B. The thermal conductivity of x is 800 W m^{-1}°C^{-1} and that of y is 400 W m^{-1}°C^{-1}.*

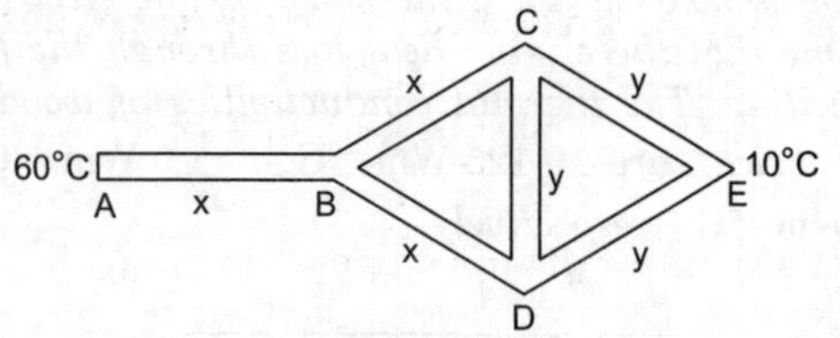

Figure 28-W5

Solution : It is clear from the symmetry of the figure that the points C and D are equivalent in all respect and hence, they are at the same temperature, say θ. No heat will flow through the rod CD. We can, therefore, neglect this rod in further analysis.

Let l and A be the length and the area of cross section of each rod. The thermal resistances of AB, BC and BD are equal. Each has a value

$$R_1 = \frac{1}{K_x}\frac{l}{A}. \qquad \text{... (i)}$$

Similarly, thermal resistances of CE and DE are equal, each having a value

$$R_2 = \frac{1}{K_y}\frac{l}{A}. \qquad \text{... (ii)}$$

As the rod CD has no effect, we can say that the rods BC and CE are joined in series. Their equivalent thermal resistance is

$$R_3 = R_{BC} + R_{CE} = R_1 + R_2.$$

Also, the rods BD and DE together have an equivalent thermal resistance $R_4 = R_{BD} + R_{DE} = R_1 + R_2$.

The resistances R_3 and R_4 are joined in parallel and hence their equivalent thermal resistance is given by

$$\frac{1}{R_5} = \frac{1}{R_3} + \frac{1}{R_4} = \frac{2}{R_3}$$

or, $$R_5 = \frac{R_3}{2} = \frac{R_1 + R_2}{2}.$$

This resistance R_5 is connected in series with AB. Thus, the total arrangement is equivalent to a thermal resistance

$$R = R_{AB} + R_5 = R_1 + \frac{R_1 + R_2}{2} = \frac{3R_1 + R_2}{2}.$$

Figure (28-W6) shows the successive steps in this reduction.

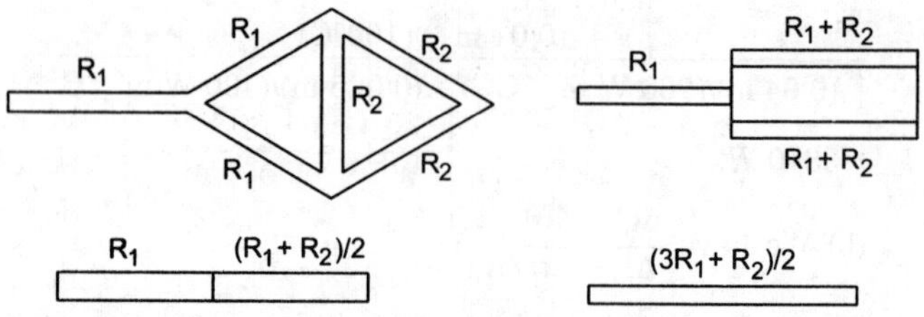

Figure 28-W6

The heat current through A is

$$i = \frac{\theta_A - \theta_E}{R} = \frac{2(\theta_A - \theta_E)}{3R_1 + R_2}.$$

This current passes through the rod AB. We have

$$i = \frac{\theta_A - \theta_B}{R_{AB}}$$

or, $$\theta_A - \theta_B = (R_{AB})i$$

$$= R_1 \frac{2(\theta_A - \theta_E)}{3R_1 + R_2}.$$

Putting from (i) and (ii),

$$\theta_A - \theta_B = \frac{2K_y(\theta_A - \theta_E)}{K_x + 3K_y}$$

$$= \frac{2 \times 400}{800 + 3 \times 400} \times 50°\text{C} = 20°\text{C}$$

or, $$\theta_B = \theta_A - 20°\text{C} = 40°\text{C}.$$

9. *A rod CD of thermal resistance 5·0 K W^{-1} is joined at the middle of an identical rod AB as shown in figure (28-W7). The ends A, B and D are maintained at 100°C, 0°C and 25°C respectively. Find the heat current in CD.*

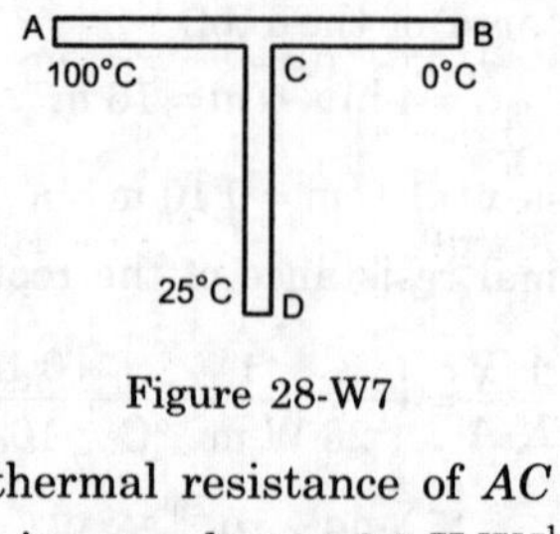

Figure 28-W7

Solution : The thermal resistance of AC is equal to that of CB and is equal to 2·5 K W^{-1}. Suppose, the temperature at C is θ. The heat currents through AC, CB and CD are

$$\frac{\Delta Q_1}{\Delta t} = \frac{100°\text{C} - \theta}{2{\cdot}5\ \text{K W}^{-1}},$$

$$\frac{\Delta Q_2}{\Delta t} = \frac{\theta - 0°C}{2{\cdot}5\ K\ W^{-1}}$$

and $$\frac{\Delta Q_3}{\Delta t} = \frac{\theta - 25°C}{5{\cdot}0\ K\ W^{-1}}.$$

We also have

$$\frac{\Delta Q_1}{\Delta t} = \frac{\Delta Q_2}{\Delta t} + \frac{\Delta Q_3}{\Delta t}$$

or, $$\frac{100°C - \theta}{2{\cdot}5} = \frac{\theta - 0°C}{2{\cdot}5} + \frac{\theta - 25°C}{5}$$

or, $$225°C = 5\theta$$

or, $$\theta = 45°C.$$

Thus, $$\frac{\Delta Q_3}{\Delta t} = \frac{45°C - 25°C}{5{\cdot}0\ K\ W^{-1}} = \frac{20\ K}{5{\cdot}0\ K\ W^{-1}}$$

$$= 4{\cdot}0\ W.$$

10. *Two thin metallic spherical shells of radii r_1 and r_2 ($r_1 < r_2$) are placed with their centres coinciding. A material of thermal conductivity K is filled in the space between the shells. The inner shell is maintained at temperature θ_1 and the outer shell at temperature θ_2 ($\theta_1 < \theta_2$). Calculate the rate at which heat flows radially through the material.*

Solution :

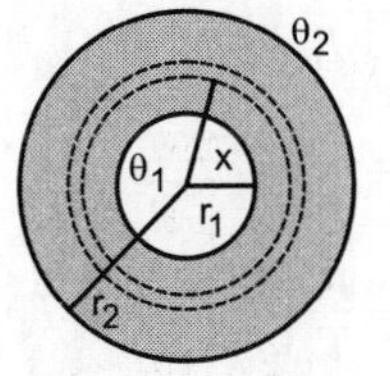

Figure 28-W8

Let us draw two spherical shells of radii x and $x + dx$ concentric with the given system. Let the temperatures at these shells be θ and $\theta + d\theta$ respectively. The amount of heat flowing radially inward through the material between x and $x + dx$ is

$$\frac{\Delta Q}{\Delta t} = \frac{K\, 4\pi x^2\, d\theta}{dx}.$$

Thus,

$$K\, 4\pi \int_{\theta_1}^{\theta_2} d\theta = \frac{\Delta Q}{\Delta t} \int_{r_1}^{r_2} \frac{dx}{x^2}$$

or, $$K\, 4\pi(\theta_2 - \theta_1) = \frac{\Delta Q}{\Delta t}\left(\frac{1}{r_1} - \frac{1}{r_2}\right)$$

or, $$\frac{\Delta Q}{\Delta t} = \frac{4\pi K r_1 r_2 (\theta_2 - \theta_1)}{r_2 - r_1}.$$

11. *On a cold winter day, the atmospheric temperature is $-\theta$ (on Celsius scale) which is below 0°C. A cylindrical drum of height h made of a bad conductor is completely filled with water at 0°C and is kept outside without any lid. Calculate the time taken for the whole mass of water to freeze. Thermal conductivity of ice is K and its latent heat of fusion is L. Neglect expansion of water on freezing.*

Solution :

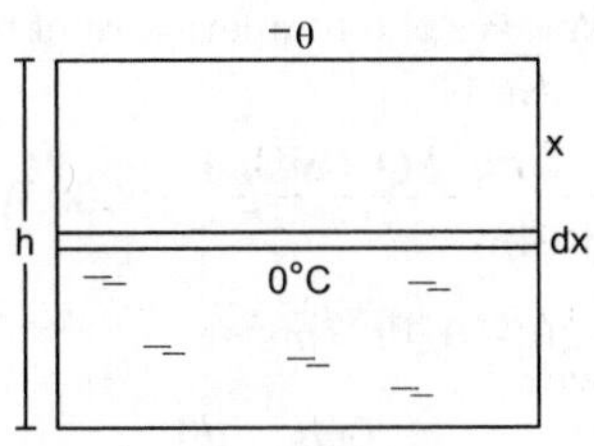

Figure 28-W9

Suppose, the ice starts forming at time $t = 0$ and a thickness x is formed at time t. The amount of heat flown from the water to the surrounding in the time interval t to $t + dt$ is

$$\Delta Q = \frac{KA\theta}{x}\, dt.$$

The mass of the ice formed due to the loss of this amount of heat is

$$dm = \frac{\Delta Q}{L} = \frac{KA\theta}{xL}\, dt.$$

The thickness dx of ice formed in time dt is

$$dx = \frac{dm}{A\rho} = \frac{K\theta}{\rho x L}\, dt$$

or, $$dt = \frac{\rho L}{K\theta}\, x\, dx.$$

Thus, the time T taken for the whole mass of water to freeze is given by

$$\int_0^T dt = \frac{\rho L}{K\theta} \int_0^h x\, dx$$

or, $$T = \frac{\rho L h^2}{2K\theta}.$$

12. *Figure (28-W10) shows a large tank of water at a constant temperature θ_0 and a small vessel containing a mass m of water at an initial temperature $\theta_1 (< \theta_0)$. A metal rod of length L, area of cross section A and thermal conductivity K connects the two vessels. Find the time taken for the temperature of the water in the smaller vessel to become $\theta_2 (\theta_1 < \theta_2 < \theta_0)$. Specific heat capacity of water is s and all other heat capacities are negligible.*

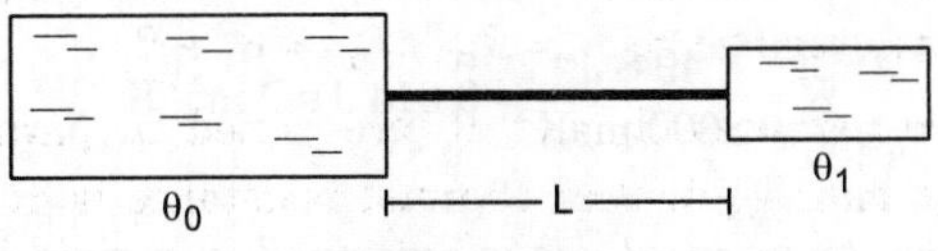

Figure 28-W10

Solution : Suppose, the temperature of the water in the smaller vessel is θ at time t. In the next time interval dt, a heat ΔQ is transferred to it where

$$\Delta Q = \frac{KA}{L}(\theta_0 - \theta)\, dt. \qquad \text{... (i)}$$

This heat increases the temperature of the water of mass m to $\theta + d\theta$ where

$$\Delta Q = ms\, d\theta. \qquad \text{... (ii)}$$

From (i) and (ii),

$$\frac{KA}{L}(\theta_0 - \theta)\, dt = ms\, d\theta$$

or,
$$dt = \frac{Lms}{KA}\frac{d\theta}{\theta_0 - \theta}$$

or,
$$\int_0^T dt = \frac{Lms}{KA}\int_{\theta_1}^{\theta_2}\frac{d\theta}{\theta_0 - \theta}$$

where T is the time required for the temperature of the water to become θ_2.

Thus,
$$T = \frac{Lms}{KA}\ln\frac{\theta_0 - \theta_1}{\theta_0 - \theta_2}.$$

13. *One mole of an ideal monatomic gas is kept in a rigid vessel. The vessel is kept inside a steam chamber whose tempreature is 97°C. Initially, the temperature of the gas is 5·0°C. The walls of the vessel have an inner surface of area 800 cm^2 and thickness 1·0 cm. If the temperature of the gas increases to 9·0°C in 5·0 seconds, find the thermal conductivity of the material of the walls.*

Solution : The initial temperature difference is 97°C − 5°C = 92°C and at 5·0 s the temperature difference becomes 97°C − 9°C = 88°C. As the change in the temperature difference is small, we work with the average temperature difference

$$\frac{92°C + 88°C}{2} = 90°C = 90 \text{ K}.$$

The rise in the temperature of the gas is

$$9·0°C - 5·0°C = 4°C = 4 \text{ K}.$$

The heat supplied to the gas in 5·0 s is

$$\Delta Q = nC_v\,\Delta T$$

$$= (1 \text{ mol}) \times \left(\frac{3}{2} \times 8·3 \text{ JK}^{-1}\text{ mol}^{-1}\right) \times (4 \text{ K})$$

$$= 49·8 \text{ J}.$$

If the thermal conductivity is K,

$$49·8 \text{ J} = \frac{K(800 \times 10^{-4}\text{ m}^2) \times (90 \text{ K})}{1·0 \times 10^{-2}\text{ m}} \times 5·0 \text{ s}$$

or,
$$K = \frac{49·8 \text{ J}}{3600 \text{ msK}} = 0·014 \text{ J s}^{-1}\text{ m}^{-1}\text{ K}^{-1}.$$

14. *A monatomic ideal gas is contained in a rigid container of volume V with walls of total inner surface area A, thickness x and thermal conductivity K. The gas is at an initial temperature T_0 and pressure p_0. Find the pressure of the gas as a function of time if the temperature of the surrounding air is T_s. All temperatures are in absolute scale.*

Solution : As the volume of the gas is constant, a heat ΔQ given to the gas increases its temperature by $\Delta T = \Delta Q / C_v$. Also, for a monatomic gas, $C_v = \frac{3}{2}R$. If the temperature of the gas at time t is T, the heat current into the gas is

$$\frac{\Delta Q}{\Delta t} = \frac{KA(T_s - T)}{x}$$

or,
$$\frac{\Delta T}{\Delta t} = \frac{2\,KA}{3\,xR}(T_s - T)$$

or,
$$\int_{T_0}^{T}\frac{dT}{T_s - T} = \int_0^t \frac{2\,KA}{3\,xR}\,dt$$

or,
$$\ln\frac{T_s - T_0}{T_s - T} = \frac{2\,KA}{3\,xR}t$$

or,
$$T_s - T = (T_s - T_0)\, e^{-\frac{2\,KA}{3xR}t}$$

or,
$$T = T_s - (T_s - T_0)\, e^{-\frac{2\,KA}{3xR}t}.$$

As the volume remains constant,

$$\frac{p}{T} = \frac{p_0}{T_0}$$

or,
$$p = \frac{p_0}{T_0}T$$

$$= \frac{p_0}{T_0}\left[T_s - (T_s - T_0)\, e^{-\frac{2\,KA}{3\,xR}t}\right].$$

15. *Consider a cubical vessel of edge a having a small hole in one of its walls. The total thermal resistance of the walls is r. At time t = 0, it contains air at atmospheric pressure p_a and temperature T_0. The temperature of the surrounding air is $T_a (> T_0)$. Find the amount of the gas (in moles) in the vessel at time t. Take C_v of air to be 5 R/2.*

Solution : As the gas can leak out of the hole, the pressure inside the vessel will be equal to the atmospheric pressure p_a. Let n be the amount of the gas (moles) in the vessel at time t. Suppose an amount ΔQ of heat is given to the gas in time dt. Its temperature increases by dT where

$$\Delta Q = nC_p dT.$$

If the temperature of the gas is T at time t, we have

$$\frac{\Delta Q}{dt} = \frac{T_a - T}{r}$$

or,
$$(C_p r)n\, dT = (T_a - T)dt. \qquad \text{... (i)}$$

We have,
$$p_a\, a^3 = nRT$$

or,
$$n\, dT + T\, dn = 0$$

or,
$$n\, dT = -T\, dn. \qquad \text{... (ii)}$$

Also, $$T = \frac{p_a a^3}{nR}. \qquad \ldots \text{(iii)}$$

Using (ii) and (iii) in (i),

$$\frac{-C_p r p_a a^3}{nR} dn = \left(T_a - \frac{p_a a^3}{nR} \right) dt$$

or, $$\frac{dn}{nR\left(T_a - \frac{p_a a^3}{nR} \right)} = -\frac{dt}{C_p r p_a a^3}$$

or, $$\int_{n_0}^{n} \frac{dn}{nRT_a - p_a a^3} = -\int_0^t \frac{dt}{C_p r p_a a^3}$$

where $n_0 = \frac{p_a a^3}{RT_0}$ is the initial amount of the gas in the vessel. Thus,

$$\frac{1}{RT_a} \ln \frac{nRT_a - p_a a^3}{n_0 RT_a - p_a a^3} = -\frac{t}{C_p r p_a a^3}$$

or, $$nRT_a - p_a a^3 = (n_0 RT_a - p_a a^3)\, e^{-\frac{RT_a}{C_p r p_a a^3} t}.$$

Writing $$n_0 = \frac{p_a a^3}{RT_0} \text{ and } C_p = C_v + R = \frac{7R}{2},$$

$$n = \frac{p_a a^3}{RT_a}\left[1 + \left(\frac{T_a}{T_0} - 1 \right) e^{-\frac{2T_a}{7 r p_a a^3} t} \right].$$

16 *A blackbody of surface area* 1 cm^2 *is placed inside an enclosure. The enclosure has a constant temperature* 27°C *and the blackbody is maintained at* 327°C *by heating it electrically. What electric power is needed to maintain the temperature?* $\sigma = 6{\cdot}0 \times 10^{-8}$ W m^{-2} K^{-4}.

Solution : The area of the blackbody is $A = 10^{-4}$ m^2, its temperature is $T_1 = 327°\text{C} = 600$ K and the temperature of the enclosure is $T_2 = 27°\text{C} = 300$ K. The blackbody emits radiation at the rate of $A\sigma T_1^4$. The radiation falls on it (and gets absorbed) at the rate of $A\sigma T_2^4$. The net rate of loss of energy is $A\sigma(T_1^4 - T_2^4)$. The heater must supply this much of power. Thus, the power needed is

$$A\sigma(T_1^4 - T_2^4)$$
$$= (10^{-4} \text{ m}^2)(6{\cdot}0 \times 10^{-8} \text{ W m}^{-2} \text{ K}^{-4})\,[(600 \text{ K})^4 - (300 \text{ K})^4]$$
$$= 0{\cdot}73 \text{ W}.$$

17. *An electric heater emits* 1000 W *of thermal radiation. The coil has a surface area of* 0·020 m^2. *Assuming that the coil radiates like a blackbody, find its temperature.* $\sigma = 6{\cdot}00 \times 10^{-8}$ W m^{-2} K^{-4}.

Solution : Let the temperature of the coil be T. The coil will emit radiation at a rate $A\sigma T^4$. Thus,

$$1000 \text{ W} = (0{\cdot}020 \text{ m}^2) \times (6{\cdot}0 \times 10^{-8} \text{ W m}^{-2} \text{ K}^{-4}) \times T^4$$

or, $$T^4 = \frac{1000}{0{\cdot}020 \times 6{\cdot}00 \times 10^{-8}} \text{ K}^4$$
$$= 8{\cdot}33 \times 10^{11} \text{ K}^4$$

or, $$T = 955 \text{ K}.$$

18. *The earth receives solar radiation at a rate of* 8·2 J cm^{-2} min^{-1}. *Assuming that the sun radiates like a blackbody, calculate the surface temperature of the sun. The angle subtended by the sun on the earth is* 0·53° *and the Stefan constant* $\sigma = 5{\cdot}67 \times 10^{-8}$ W m^{-2} K^{-4}.

Solution :

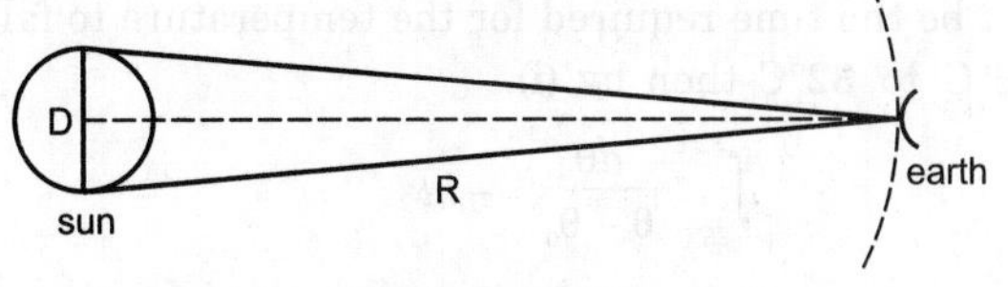

Figure 28-W11

Let the diameter of the sun be D and its distance from the earth be R. From the question,

$$\frac{D}{R} \approx 0{\cdot}53 \times \frac{\pi}{180}$$
$$= 9{\cdot}25 \times 10^{-3}. \qquad \ldots \text{(i)}$$

The radiation emitted by the surface of the sun per unit time is

$$4\pi\left(\frac{D}{2}\right)^2 \sigma T^4 = \pi D^2 \sigma T^4.$$

At distance R, this radiation falls on an area $4\pi R^2$ in unit time. The radiation received at the earth's surface per unit time per unit area is, therefore,

$$\frac{\pi D^2 \sigma T^4}{4\pi R^2} = \frac{\sigma T^4}{4}\left(\frac{D}{R}\right)^2.$$

Thus, $$\frac{\sigma T^4}{4}\left(\frac{D}{R}\right)^2 = 8{\cdot}2 \text{ J cm}^{-2} \text{ min}^{-1}$$

or, $$\frac{1}{4} \times (5{\cdot}67 \times 10^{-8} \text{ W m}^{-2} \text{ K}^{-4})\, T^4 \times (9{\cdot}25 \times 10^{-3})^2$$
$$= \frac{8{\cdot}2}{10^{-4} \times 60} \text{ W m}^{-2}$$

or, $$T = 5794 \text{ K} \approx 5800 \text{ K}.$$

19. *The temperature of a body falls from* 40°C *to* 36°C *in* 5 *minutes when placed in a surrounding of constant temperature* 16°C. *Find the time taken for the temperature of the body to become* 32°C.

Solution : As the temperature differences are small, we can use Newton's law of cooling.

$$\frac{d\theta}{dt} = -k(\theta - \theta_0)$$

or, $$\frac{d\theta}{\theta - \theta_0} = -k\,dt \qquad \ldots \text{(i)}$$

where k is a constant, θ is the temperature of the body at time t and $\theta_0 = 16°\text{C}$ is the temperature of the surrounding. We have,

$$\int_{40^\circ C}^{36^\circ C} \frac{d\theta}{\theta - \theta_0} = -k(5\text{ min})$$

or, $$\ln \frac{36^\circ C - 16^\circ C}{40^\circ C - 16^\circ C} = -k(5\text{ min})$$

or, $$k = -\frac{\ln(5/6)}{5\text{ min}}.$$

If t be the time required for the temperature to fall from 36°C to 32°C then by (i),

$$\int_{36^\circ C}^{32^\circ C} \frac{d\theta}{\theta - \theta_0} = -kt$$

or, $$\ln \frac{32^\circ C - 16^\circ C}{36^\circ C - 16^\circ C} = \frac{\ln(5/6)t}{5\text{ min}}$$

or, $$t = \frac{\ln(4/5)}{\ln(5/6)} \times 5\text{ min}$$

$$= 6{\cdot}1\text{ min}.$$

Alternative method

The mean temperature of the body as it cools from 40°C to 36°C is $\frac{40^\circ C + 36^\circ C}{2} = 38^\circ C$. The rate of decrease of temperature is $\frac{40^\circ C - 36^\circ C}{5\text{ min}} = 0{\cdot}80^\circ C\text{ min}^{-1}$.

Newton's law of cooling is

$$\frac{d\theta}{dt} = -k(\theta - \theta_0)$$

or, $$-0{\cdot}8^\circ C\text{ min}^{-1} = -k(38^\circ C - 16^\circ C) = -k(22^\circ C)$$

or, $$k = \frac{0{\cdot}8}{22}\text{ min}^{-1}.$$

Let the time taken for the temperature to become 32°C be t.

During this period,

$$\frac{d\theta}{dt} = -\frac{36^\circ C - 32^\circ C}{t} = -\frac{4^\circ C}{t}.$$

The mean temperature is $\frac{36^\circ C + 32^\circ C}{2} = 34^\circ C$.

Now,

$$\frac{d\theta}{dt} = -k(\theta - \theta_0)$$

or, $$\frac{-4^\circ C}{t} = -\frac{0{\cdot}8}{22} \times (34^\circ C - 16^\circ C)\text{ min}^{-1}$$

or, $$t = \frac{22 \times 4}{0{\cdot}8 \times 18}\text{ min} = 6{\cdot}1\text{ min}.$$

20. *A hot body placed in air is cooled down according to Newton's law of cooling, the rate of decrease of temperature being k times the temperature difference from the surrounding. Starting from t = 0, find the time in which the body will lose half the maximum heat it can lose.*

Solution : We have,

$$\frac{d\theta}{dt} = -k(\theta - \theta_0)$$

where θ_0 is the temperature of the surrounding and θ is the temperature of the body at time t. Suppose $\theta = \theta_1$ at $t = 0$.

Then,

$$\int_{\theta_1}^{\theta} \frac{d\theta}{\theta - \theta_0} = -k\int_0^t dt$$

or, $$\ln \frac{\theta - \theta_0}{\theta_1 - \theta_0} = -kt$$

or, $$\theta - \theta_0 = (\theta_1 - \theta_0)\,e^{-kt}. \quad \text{... (i)}$$

The body continues to lose heat till its temperature becomes equal to that of the surrounding. The loss of heat in this entire period is

$$\Delta Q_m = ms(\theta_1 - \theta_0).$$

This is the maximum heat the body can lose. If the body loses half this heat, the decrease in its temperature will be,

$$\frac{\Delta Q_m}{2\,ms} = \frac{\theta_1 - \theta_0}{2}.$$

If the body loses this heat in time t_1, the temperature at t_1 will be

$$\theta_1 - \frac{\theta_1 - \theta_0}{2} = \frac{\theta_1 + \theta_0}{2}.$$

Putting these values of time and temperature in (i),

$$\frac{\theta_1 + \theta_0}{2} - \theta_0 = (\theta_1 - \theta_0)\,e^{-kt_1}$$

or, $$e^{-kt_1} = \frac{1}{2}$$

or, $$t_1 = \frac{\ln 2}{k}.$$

□

QUESTIONS FOR SHORT ANSWER

1. The heat current is written as $\frac{\Delta Q}{\Delta t}$. Why don't we write $\frac{dQ}{dt}$?

2. Does a body at 20°C radiate in a room, where the room temperature is 30°C ? If yes, why does its temperature not fall further ?

3. Why does blowing over a spoonful of hot tea cools it ? Does evaporation play a role ? Does radiation play a role ?
4. On a hot summer day we want to cool our room by opening the refrigerator door and closing all the windows and doors. Will the process work ?
5. On a cold winter night you are asked to sit on a chair. Would you like to choose a metal chair or a wooden chair ? Both are kept in the same lawn and are at the same temperature.
6. Two identical metal balls one at $T_1 = 300$ K and the other at $T_2 = 600$ K are kept at a distance of 1 m in vacuum. Will the temperatures equalise by radiation ? Will the rate of heat gained by the colder sphere be proportional to $T_2^4 - T_1^4$ as may be expected from the Stefan's law ?
7. An ordinary electric fan does not cool the air, still it gives comfort in summer. Explain.
8. The temperature of the atmosphere at a high altitude is around 500°C. Yet an animal there would freeze to death and not boil. Explain.
9. Standing in the sun is more pleasant on a cold winter day than standing in shade. Is the temperature of air in the sun considerably higher than that of the air in shade ?
10. Cloudy nights are warmer than the nights with clean sky. Explain.
11. Why is a white dress more comfortable than a dark dress in summer ?

OBJECTIVE I

1. The thermal conductivity of a rod depends on
(a) length (b) mass
(c) area of cross section (d) material of the rod.
2. In a room containing air, heat can go from one place to another
(a) by conduction only (b) by convection only
(c) by radiation only (d) by all the three modes.
3. A solid at temperature T_1 is kept in an evacuated chamber at temperature $T_2 > T_1$. The rate of increase of temperature of the body is proportional to
(a) $T_2 - T_1$ (b) $T_2^2 - T_1^2$
(c) $T_2^3 - T_1^3$ (d) $T_2^4 - T_1^4$.
4. The thermal radiation emitted by a body is proportional to T^n where T is its absolute temperature. The value of n is exactly 4 for
(a) a blackbody (b) all bodies
(c) bodies painted black only (d) polished bodies only.
5. Two bodies A and B having equal surface areas are maintained at temperatures 10°C and 20°C. The thermal radiation emitted in a given time by A and B are in the ratio
(a) 1 : 1·15 (b) 1 : 2
(c) 1 : 4 (d) 1 : 16.
6. One end of a metal rod is kept in a furnace. In steady state, the temperature of the rod
(a) increases (b) decreases
(c) remains constant (d) is nonuniform.
7. Newton's law of cooling is a special case of
(a) Wien's displacement law (b) Kirchhoff's law
(c) Stefan's law (d) Planck's law.
8. A hot liquid is kept in a big room. Its temperature is plotted as a function of time. Which of the following curves may represent the plot ?

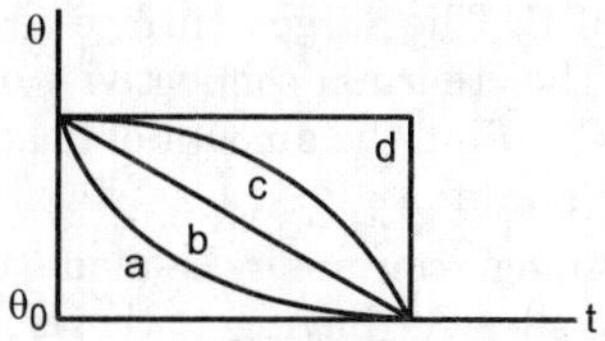

Figure 28-Q1

9. A hot liquid is kept in a big room. The logarithm of the numerical value of the temperature difference between the liquid and the room is plotted against time. The plot will be very nearly
(a) a straight line (b) a circular arc
(c) a parabola (d) an ellipse.
10. A body cools down from 65°C to 60°C in 5 minutes. It will cool down from 60°C to 55°C in
(a) 5 minutes (b) less than 5 minutes
(c) more than 5 minutes
(d) less than or more than 5 minutes depending on whether its mass is more than or less than 1 kg.

OBJECTIVE II

1. One end of a metal rod is dipped in boiling water and the other is dipped in melting ice.
(a) All parts of the rod are in thermal equilibrium with each other.
(b) We can assign a temperature to the rod.
(c) We can assign a temperature to the rod after steady state is reached.
(d) The state of the rod does not change after steady state is reached.
2. A blackbody does not
(a) emit radiation (b) absorb radiation
(c) reflect radiation (d) refract radiation.

3. In summer, a mild wind is often found on the shore of a calm river. This is caused due to
(a) difference in thermal conductivity of water and soil
(b) convection currents
(c) conduction between air and the soil
(d) radiation from the soil.

4. A piece of charcoal and a piece of shining steel of the same surface area are kept for a long time in an open lawn in bright sun.
(a) The steel will absorb more heat than the charcoal.
(b) The temperature of the steel will be higher than that of the charcoal.
(c) If both are picked up by bare hands, the steel will be felt hotter than the charcoal.
(d) If the two are picked up from the lawn and kept in a cold chamber, the charcoal will lose heat at a faster rate than the steel.

5. A heated body emits radiation which has maximum intensity near the frequency ν_0. The emissivity of the material is 0·5. If the absolute temperature of the body is doubled,
(a) the maximum intensity of radiation will be near the frequency $2\nu_0$
(b) the maximum intensity of radiation will be near the frequency $\nu_0/2$
(c) the total energy emitted will increase by a factor of 16
(d) the total energy emitted will increase by a factor of 8.

6. A solid sphere and a hollow sphere of the same material and of equal radii are heated to the same temperature.
(a) Both will emit equal amount of radiation per unit time in the biginning.
(b) Both will absorb equal amount of radiation from the surrounding in the biginning.
(c) The initial rate of cooling (dT/dt) will be the same for the two spheres.
(d) The two spheres will have equal temperatures at any instant.

EXERCISES

1. A uniform slab of dimension 10 cm × 10 cm × 1 cm is kept between two heat reservoirs at temperatures 10°C and 90°C. The larger surface areas touch the reservoirs. The thermal conductivity of the material is 0·80 W m^{-1}°C^{-1}. Find the amount of heat flowing through the slab per minute.

2. A liquid-nitrogen container is made of a 1-cm thick styrofoam sheet having thermal conductivity 0·025 J s^{-1} m^{-1}°C^{-1}. Liquid nitrogen at 80 K is kept in it. A total area of 0·80 m^2 is in contact with the liquid nitrogen. The atmospheric temperature is 300 K. Calculate the rate of heat flow from the atmosphere to the liquid nitrogen.

3. The normal body-temperature of a person is 97°F. Calculate the rate at which heat is flowing out of his body through the clothes assuming the following values. Room temperature = 47°F, surface of the body under clothes = 1·6 m^2, conductivity of the cloth = 0·04 J s^{-1} m^{-1}°C^{-1}, thickness of the cloth = 0·5 cm.

4. Water is boiled in a container having a bottom of surface area 25 cm^2, thickness 1·0 mm and thermal conductivity 50 W m^{-1}°C^{-1}. 100 g of water is converted into steam per minute in the steady state after the boiling starts. Assuming that no heat is lost to the atmosphere, calculate the temperature of the lower surface of the bottom. Latent heat of vaporization of water = 2·26 × 10^6 J kg^{-1}.

5. One end of a steel rod (K = 46 J s^{-1} m^{-1}°C^{-1}) of length 1·0 m is kept in ice at 0°C and the other end is kept in boiling water at 100°C. The area of cross section of the rod is 0·04 cm^2. Assuming no heat loss to the atmosphere, find the mass of the ice melting per second. Latent heat of fusion of ice = 3·36 × 10^5 J kg^{-1}.

6. An icebox almost completely filled with ice at 0°C is dipped into a large volume of water at 20°C. The box has walls of surface area 2400 cm^2, thickness 2·0 mm and thermal conductivity 0·06 W m^{-1}°C^{-1}. Calculate the rate at which the ice melts in the box. Latent heat of fusion of ice = 3·4 × 10^5 J kg^{-1}.

7. A pitcher with 1-mm thick porous walls contains 10 kg of water. Water comes to its outer surface and evaporates at the rate of 0·1 g s^{-1}. The surface area of the pitcher (one side) = 200 cm^2. The room temperature = 42°C, latent heat of vaporization = 2·27 × 10^6 J kg^{-1}, and the thermal conductivity of the porous walls = 0·80 J s^{-1} m^{-1}°C^{-1}. Calculate the temperature of water in the pitcher when it attains a constant value.

8. A steel frame (K = 45 W m^{-1}°C^{-1}) of total length 60 cm and cross sectional area 0·20 cm^2, forms three sides of a square. The free ends are maintained at 20°C and 40°C. Find the rate of heat flow through a cross section of the frame.

9. Water at 50°C is filled in a closed cylindrical vessel of height 10 cm and cross sectional area 10 cm^2. The walls of the vessel are adiabatic but the flat parts are made of 1-mm thick aluminium (K = 200 J s^{-1} m^{-1}°C^{-1}). Assume that the outside temperature is 20°C. The density of water is 1000 kg m^{-3}, and the specific heat capacity of water = 4200 J kg^{-1}°C^{-1}. Estimate the time taken for the temperature to fall by 1·0°C. Make any simplifying assumptions you need but specify them.

10. The left end of a copper rod (length = 20 cm, area of cross section = 0·20 cm^2) is maintained at 20°C and the right end is maintained at 80°C. Neglecting any loss of heat through radiation, find (a) the temperature at a point 11 cm from the left end and (b) the heat current through the rod. Thermal conductivity of copper = 385 W m^{-1}°C^{-1}.

11. The ends of a metre stick are maintained at 100°C and 0°C. One end of a rod is maintained at 25°C. Where should its other end be touched on the metre stick so that there is no heat current in the rod in steady state ?

12. A cubical box of volume $216\ \mathrm{cm}^3$ is made up of 0·1 cm thick wood. The inside is heated electrically by a 100 W heater. It is found that the temperature difference between the inside and the outside surface is 5°C in steady state. Assuming that the entire electrical energy spent appears as heat, find the thermal conductivity of the material of the box.

13. Figure (28-E1) shows water in a container having 2·0-mm thick walls made of a material of thermal conductivity $0{\cdot}50\ \mathrm{W\ m^{-1}{}^\circ C^{-1}}$. The container is kept in a melting-ice bath at 0°C. The total surface area in contact with water is $0{\cdot}05\ \mathrm{m}^2$. A wheel is clamped inside the water and is coupled to a block of mass M as shown in the figure. As the block goes down, the wheel rotates. It is found that after some time a steady state is reached in which the block goes down with a constant speed of $10\ \mathrm{cm\ s^{-1}}$ and the temperature of the water remains constant at 1·0°C. Find the mass M of the block. Assume that the heat flows out of the water only through the walls in contact. Take $g = 10\ \mathrm{m\ s^{-2}}$.

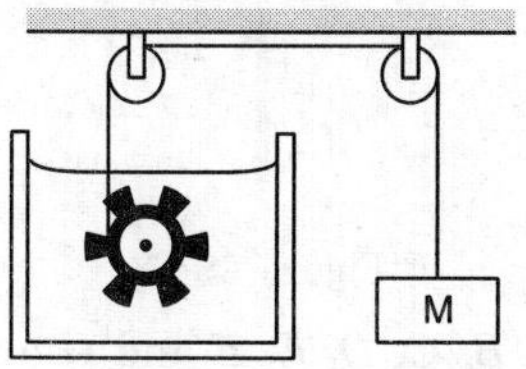

Figure 28-E1

14. On a winter day when the atmospheric temperature drops to −10°C, ice forms on the surface of a lake. (a) Calculate the rate of increase of thickness of the ice when 10 cm of ice is already formed. (b) Calculate the total time taken in forming 10 cm of ice. Assume that the temperature of the entire water reaches 0°C before the ice starts forming. Density of water = $1000\ \mathrm{kg\ m^{-3}}$, latent heat of fusion of ice = $3{\cdot}36\times10^5\ \mathrm{J\ kg^{-1}}$ and thermal conductivity of ice = $1{\cdot}7\ \mathrm{W\ m^{-1}{}^\circ C^{-1}}$. Neglect the expansion of water on freezing.

15. Consider the situation of the previous problem. Assume that the temperature of the water at the bottom of the lake remains constant at 4°C as the ice forms on the surface (the heat required to maintain the temperature of the bottom layer may come from the bed of the lake). The depth of the lake is 1·0 m. Show that the thickness of the ice formed attains a steady state maximum value. Find this value. The thermal conductivity of water = $0{\cdot}50\ \mathrm{W\ m^{-1}{}^\circ C^{-1}}$. Take other relevant data from the previous problem.

16. Three rods of lengths 20 cm each and area of cross section $1\ \mathrm{cm}^2$ are joined to form a triangle ABC. The conductivities of the rods are $K_{AB} = 50\ \mathrm{J\ s^{-1}\ m^{-1}{}^\circ C^{-1}}$, $K_{BC} = 200\ \mathrm{J\ s^{-1}\ m^{-1}{}^\circ C^{-1}}$ and $K_{AC} = 400\ \mathrm{J\ s^{-1}\ m^{-1}{}^\circ C^{-1}}$. The junctions A, B and C are maintained at 40°C, 80°C and 80°C respectively. Find the rate of heat flowing through the rods AB, AC and BC.

17. A semicircular rod is joined at its end to a straight rod of the same material and the same cross-sectional area. The straight rod forms a diameter of the other rod. The junctions are maintained at different temperatures. Find the ratio of the heat transferred through a cross section of the semicircular rod to the heat transferred through a cross section of the straight rod in a given time.

18. A metal rod of cross sectional area $1{\cdot}0\ \mathrm{cm}^2$ is being heated at one end. At one time, the temperature gradient is $5{\cdot}0\ \mathrm{{}^\circ C\ cm^{-1}}$ at cross section A and is $2{\cdot}5\ \mathrm{{}^\circ C cm^{-1}}$ at cross section B. Calculate the rate at which the temperature is increasing in the part AB of the rod. The heat capacity of the part $AB = 0{\cdot}40\ \mathrm{J{}^\circ C^{-1}}$, thermal conductivity of the material of the rod = $200\ \mathrm{W\ m^{-1}{}^\circ C^{-1}}$. Neglect any loss of heat to the atmosphere.

19. Steam at 120°C is continuously passed through a 50-cm long rubber tube of inner and outer radii 1·0 cm and 1·2 cm. The room temperature is 30°C. Calculate the rate of heat flow through the walls of the tube. Thermal conductivity of rubber = $0{\cdot}15\ \mathrm{J\ s^{-1}\ m^{-1}{}^\circ C^{-1}}$.

20. A hole of radius r_1 is made centrally in a uniform circular disc of thickness d and radius r_2. The inner surface (a cylinder of length d and radius r_1) is maintained at a temperature θ_1 and the outer surface (a cylinder of length d and radius r_2) is maintained at a temperature $\theta_2(\theta_1 > \theta_2)$. The thermal conductivity of the material of the disc is K. Calculate the heat flowing per unit time through the disc.

21. A hollow tube has a length l, inner radius R_1 and outer radius R_2. The material has a thermal conductivity K. Find the heat flowing through the walls of the tube if (a) the flat ends are maintained at temperatures T_1 and $T_2 (T_2 > T_1)$ (b) the inside of the tube is maintained at temperature T_1 and the outside is maintained at T_2.

22. A composite slab is prepared by pasting two plates of thicknesses L_1 and L_2 and thermal conductivities K_1 and K_2. The slabs have equal cross-sectional area. Find the equivalent conductivity of the composite slab.

23. Figure (28-E2) shows a copper rod joined to a steel rod. The rods have equal length and equal cross sectional area. The free end of the copper rod is kept at 0°C and that of the steel rod is kept at 100°C. Find the temperature at the junction of the rods. Conductivity of copper = $390\ \mathrm{W\ m^{-1}{}^\circ C^{-1}}$ and that of steel = $46\ \mathrm{W\ m^{-1}{}^\circ C^{-1}}$.

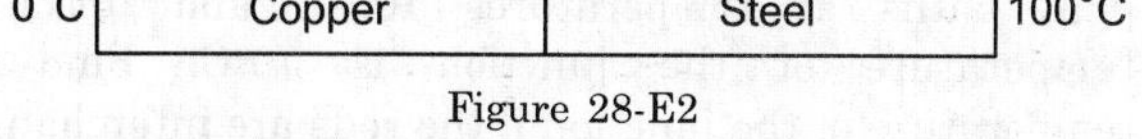

Figure 28-E2

24. An aluminium rod and a copper rod of equal length 1·0 m and cross-sectional area $1\ \mathrm{cm}^2$ are welded together as shown in figure (28-E3). One end is kept at a temperature of 20°C and the other at 60°C. Calculate the amount of heat taken out per second from the hot end. Thermal conductivity of aluminium = $200\ \mathrm{W m^{-1}{}^\circ C^{-1}}$ and of copper = $390\ \mathrm{W\ m^{-1}{}^\circ C^{-1}}$.

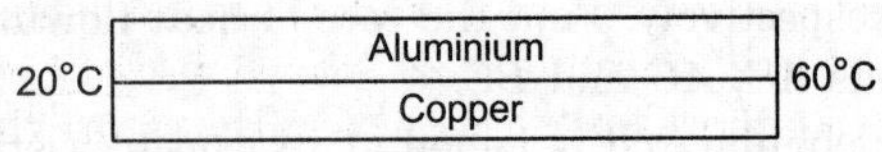

Figure 28-E3

25. Figure (28-E4) shows an aluminium rod joined to a copper rod. Each of the rods has a length of 20 cm and area of cross section $0{\cdot}20\ \text{cm}^2$. The junction is maintained at a constant temperature 40°C and the two ends are maintained at 80°C. Calculate the amount of heat taken out from the cold junction in one minute after the steady state is reached. The conductivities are $K_{Al} = 200\ \text{W m}^{-1}{}^\circ\text{C}^{-1}$ and $K_{Cu} = 400\ \text{W m}^{-1}{}^\circ\text{C}^{-1}$.

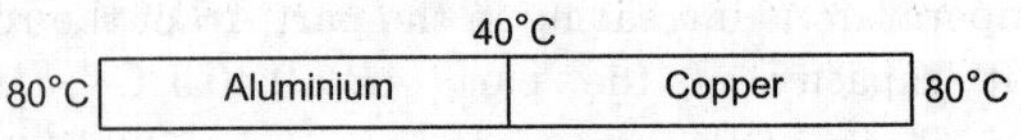

Figure 28-E4

26. Consider the situation shown in figure (28-E5). The frame is made of the same material and has a uniform cross-sectional area everywhere. Calculate the amount of heat flowing per second through a cross section of the bent part if the total heat taken out per second from the end at 100°C is 130 J.

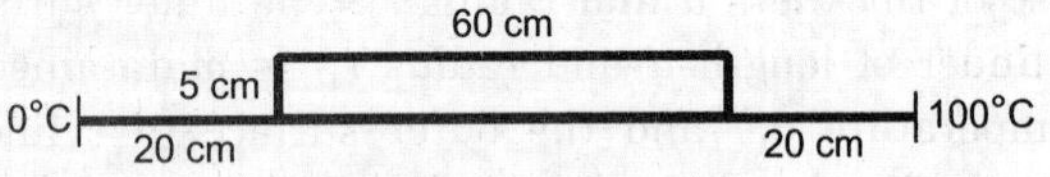

Figure 28-E5

27. Suppose the bent part of the frame of the previous problem has a thermal conductivity of $780\ \text{J s}^{-1}\ \text{m}^{-1}{}^\circ\text{C}^{-1}$ whereas it is $390\ \text{J s}^{-1}\ \text{m}^{-1}{}^\circ\text{C}^{-1}$ for the straight part. Calculate the ratio of the rate of heat flow through the bent part to the rate of heat flow through the straight part.

28. A room has a window fitted with a single $1{\cdot}0\ \text{m} \times 2{\cdot}0\ \text{m}$ glass of thickness 2 mm. (a) Calculate the rate of heat flow through the closed window when the temperature inside the room is 32°C and that outside is 40°C. (b) The glass is now replaced by two glasspanes, each having a thickness of 1 mm and separated by a distance of 1 mm. Calculate the rate of heat flow under the same conditions of temperature. Thermal conductivity of window glass $= 1{\cdot}0\ \text{J s}^{-1}\ \text{m}^{-1}{}^\circ\text{C}^{-1}$ and that of air $= 0{\cdot}025\ \text{J s}^{-1}\ \text{m}^{-1}{}^\circ\text{C}^{-1}$.

29. The two rods shown in figure (28-E6) have identical geometrical dimensions. They are in contact with two heat baths at temperatures 100°C and 0°C. The temperature of the junction is 70°C. Find the temperature of the junction if the rods are interchanged.

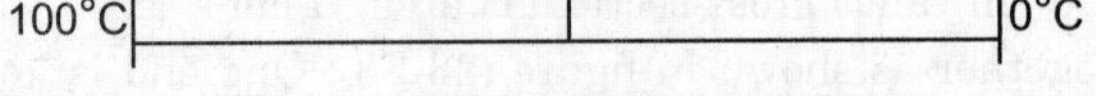

Figure 28-E6

30. The three rods shown in figure (28-E7) have identical geometrical dimensions. Heat flows from the hot end at a rate of 40 W in the arrangement (a). Find the rates of heat flow when the rods are joined as in arrangement (b) and in (c). Thermal conductivities of aluminium and copper are $200\ \text{W m}^{-1}{}^\circ\text{C}^{-1}$ and $400\ \text{W m}^{-1}{}^\circ\text{C}^{-1}$ respectively.

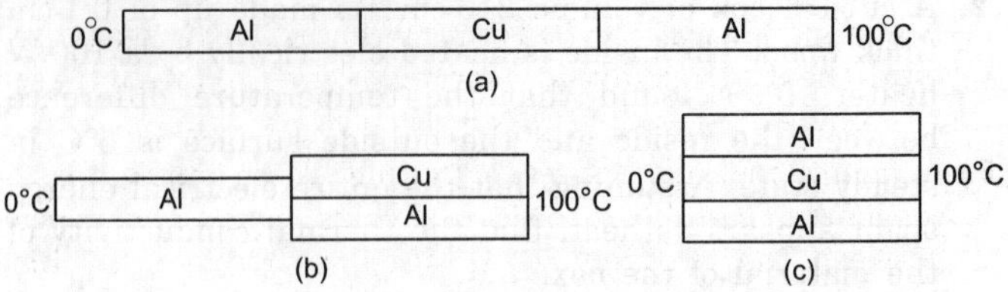

Figure 28-E7

31. Four identical rods *AB*, *CD*, *CF* and *DE* are joined as shown in figure (28-E8). The length, cross-sectional area and thermal conductivity of each rod are *l*, *A* and *K* respectively. The ends *A*, *E* and *F* are maintained at temperatures T_1, T_2 and T_3 respectively. Assuming no loss of heat to the atmosphere, find the temperature at *B*.

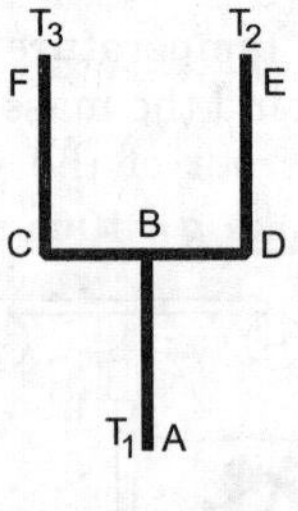

Figure 28-E8

32. Seven rods *A*, *B*, *C*, *D*, *E*, *F* and *G* are joined as shown in figure (28-E9). All the rods have equal cross-sectional area *A* and length *l*. The thermal conductivities of the rods are $K_A = K_C = K_0$, $K_B = K_D = 2K_0$, $K_E = 3K_0$, $K_F = 4K_0$ and $K_G = 5K_0$. The rod *E* is kept at a constant temperature T_1 and the rod *G* is kept at a constant temperature $T_2 (T_2 > T_1)$. (a) Show that the rod *F* has a uniform temperature $T = (T_1 + 2T_2)/3$. (b) Find the rate of heat flowing from the source which maintains the temperature T_2.

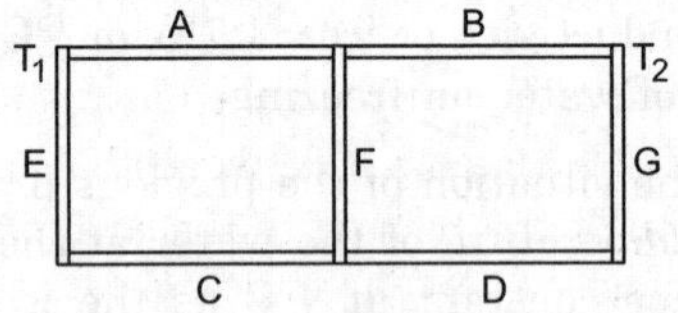

Figure 28-E9

33. Find the rate of heat flow through a cross section of the rod shown in figure (28-E10) $(\theta_2 > \theta_1)$. Thermal conductivity of the material of the rod is *K*.

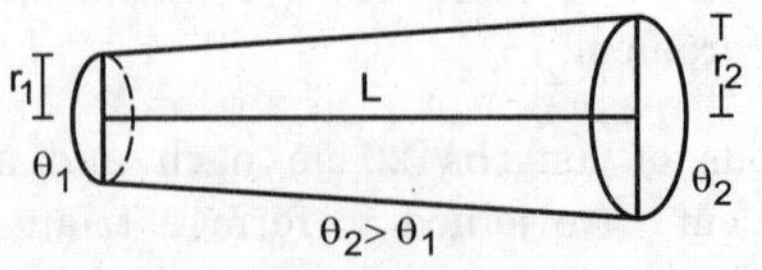

Figure 28-E10

34. A rod of negligible heat capacity has length 20 cm, area of cross section 1·0 cm^2 and thermal conductivity 200 W m^{-1}°C^{-1}. The temperature of one end is maintained at 0°C and that of the other end is slowly and linearly varied from 0°C to 60°C in 10 minutes. Assuming no loss of heat through the sides, find the total heat transmitted through the rod in these 10 minutes.

35. A hollow metallic sphere of radius 20 cm surrounds a concentric metallic sphere of radius 5 cm. The space between the two spheres is filled with a nonmetallic material. The inner and outer spheres are maintained at 50°C and 10°C respectively and it is found that 100 J of heat passes from the inner sphere to the outer sphere per second. Find the thermal conductivity of the material between the spheres.

36. Figure (28-E11) shows two adiabatic vessels, each containing a mass m of water at different temperatures. The ends of a metal rod of length L, area of cross section A and thermal conductivity K, are inserted in the water as shown in the figure. Find the time taken for the difference between the temperatures in the vessels to become half of the original value. The specific heat capacity of water is s. Neglect the heat capacity of the rod and the container and any loss of heat to the atmosphere.

Figure 28-E11

37. Two bodies of masses m_1 and m_2 and specific heat capacities s_1 and s_2 are connected by a rod of length l, cross-sectional area A, thermal conductivity K and negligible heat capacity. The whole system is thermally insulated. At time $t = 0$, the temperature of the first body is T_1 and the temperature of the second body is T_2 ($T_2 > T_1$). Find the temperature difference between the two bodies at time t.

38. An amount n (in moles) of a monatomic gas at an initial temperature T_0 is enclosed in a cylindrical vessel fitted with a light piston. The surrounding air has a temperature $T_s (> T_0)$ and the atmospheric pressure is p_a. Heat may be conducted between the surrounding and the gas through the bottom of the cylinder. The bottom has a surface area A, thickness x and thermal conductivity K. Assuming all changes to be slow, find the distance moved by the piston in time t.

39. Assume that the total surface area of a human body is 1·6 m^2 and that it radiates like an ideal radiator. Calculate the amount of energy radiated per second by the body if the body temperature is 37°C. Stefan constant σ is 6·0 × 10^{-8} W m^{-2} K^{-4}.

40. Calculate the amount of heat radiated per second by a body of surface area 12 cm^2 kept in thermal equilibrium in a room at temperature 20°C. The emissivity of the surface = 0·80 and σ = 6·0 × 10^{-8} W m^{-2} K^{-4}.

41. A solid aluminium sphere and a solid copper sphere of twice the radius are heated to the same temperature and are allowed to cool under identical surrounding temperatures. Assume that the emissivity of both the spheres is the same. Find the ratio of (a) the rate of heat loss from the aluminium sphere to the rate of heat loss from the copper sphere and (b) the rate of fall of temperature of the aluminium sphere to the rate of fall of temperature of the copper sphere. The specific heat capacity of aluminium = 900 J kg^{-1}°C^{-1} and that of copper = 390 J kg^{-1}°C^{-1}. The density of copper = 3·4 times the density of aluminium.

42. A 100 W bulb has tungsten filament of total length 1·0 m and radius 4 × 10^{-5} m. The emissivity of the filament is 0·8 and σ = 6·0 × 10^{-8} W m^{-2} K^4. Calculate the temperature of the filament when the bulb is operating at correct wattage.

43. A spherical ball of surface area 20 cm^2 absorbs any radiation that falls on it. It is suspended in a closed box maintained at 57°C. (a) Find the amount of radiation falling on the ball per second. (b) Find the net rate of heat flow to or from the ball at an instant when its temperature is 200°C. Stefan constant = 6·0 × 10^{-8} W m^{-2} K^{-4}.

44. A spherical tungsten piece of radius 1·0 cm is suspended in an evacuated chamber maintained at 300 K. The piece is maintained at 1000 K by heating it electrically. Find the rate at which the electrical energy must be supplied. The emissivity of tungsten is 0·30 and the Stefan constant σ is 6·0 × 10^{-8} W m^{-2} K^{-4}.

45. A cubical block of mass 1·0 kg and edge 5·0 cm is heated to 227°C. It is kept in an evacuated chamber maintained at 27°C. Assuming that the block emits radiation like a blackbody, find the rate at which the temperature of the block will decrease. Specific heat capacity of the material of the block is 400 J kg^{-1} K^{-1}.

46. A copper sphere is suspended in an evacuated chamber maintained at 300 K. The sphere is maintained at a constant temperature of 500 K by heating it electrically. A total of 210 W of electric power is needed to do it. When the surface of the copper sphere is completely blackened, 700 W is needed to maintain the same temperature of the sphere. Calculate the emissivity of copper.

47. A spherical ball A of surface area 20 cm^2 is kept at the centre of a hollow spherical shell B of area 80 cm^2. The surface of A and the inner surface of B emit as blackbodies. Both A and B are at 300 K. (a) How much is the radiation energy emitted per second by the ball A? (b) How much is the radiation energy emitted per second by the inner surface of B? (c) How much of the energy emitted by the inner surface of B falls back on this surface itself ?

48. A cylindrical rod of length 50 cm and cross sectional area 1 cm^2 is fitted between a large ice chamber at 0°C and an evacuated chamber maintained at 27°C as shown in figure (28-E12). Only small portions of the rod are inside the chambers and the rest is thermally insulated from the surrounding. The cross section going into the evacuated chamber is blackened so that it completely absorbs any radiation falling on it. The temperature of the blackened end is 17°C when steady state is reached. Stefan constant $\sigma = 6 \times 10^{-8}\ \mathrm{W\ m^{-2}\ K^{-4}}$. Find the thermal conductivity of the material of the rod.

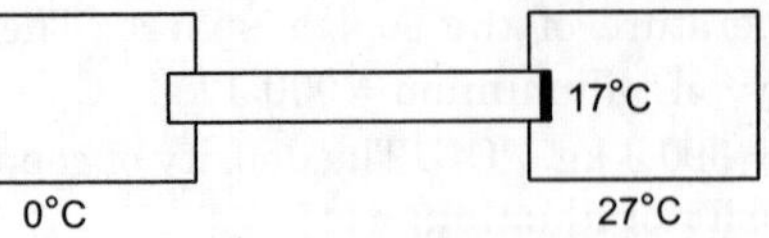

Figure 28-E12

49. One end of a rod of length 20 cm is inserted in a furnace at 800 K. The sides of the rod are covered with an insulating material and the other end emits radiation like a blackbody. The temperature of this end is 750 K in the steady state. The temperature of the surrounding air is 300 K. Assuming radiation to be the only important mode of energy transfer between the surrounding and the open end of the rod, find the thermal conductivity of the rod. Stefan constant $\sigma = 6{\cdot}0 \times 10^{-8}\ \mathrm{W\ m^{-2}\ K^{-4}}$.

50. A calorimeter of negligible heat capacity contains 100 cc of water at 40°C. The water cools to 35°C in 5 minutes. The water is now replaced by K-oil of equal volume at 40°C. Find the time taken for the temperature to become 35°C under similar conditions. Specific heat capacities of water and K-oil are $4200\ \mathrm{J\ kg^{-1}\ K^{-1}}$ and $2100\ \mathrm{J\ kg^{-1}\ K^{-1}}$ respectively. Density of K-oil $= 800\ \mathrm{kg\ m^{-3}}$.

51. A body cools down from 50°C to 45°C in 5 minutes and to 40°C in another 8 minutes. Find the temperature of the surrounding.

52. A calorimeter contains 50 g of water at 50°C. The temperature falls to 45°C in 10 minutes. When the calorimeter contains 100 g of water at 50°C, it takes 18 minutes for the temperature to become 45°C. Find the water equivalent of the calorimeter.

53. A metal ball of mass 1 kg is heated by means of a 20 W heater in a room at 20°C. The temperature of the ball becomes steady at 50°C. (a) Find the rate of loss of heat to the surrounding when the ball is at 50°C. (b) Assuming Newton's law of cooling, calculate the rate of loss of heat to the surrounding when the ball is at 30°C. (c) Assume that the temperature of the ball rises uniformly from 20°C to 30°C in 5 minutes. Find the total loss of heat to the surrounding during this period. (d) Calculate the specific heat capacity of the metal.

54. A metal block of heat capacity $80\ \mathrm{J°C^{-1}}$ placed in a room at 20°C is heated electrically. The heater is switched off when the temperature reaches 30°C. The temperature of the block rises at the rate of $2\ \mathrm{°C\ s^{-1}}$ just after the heater is switched on and falls at the rate of $0{\cdot}2\ \mathrm{°C\ s^{-1}}$ just after the heater is switched off. Assume Newton's law of cooling to hold. (a) Find the power of the heater. (b) Find the power radiated by the block just after the heater is switched off. (c) Find the power radiated by the block when the temperature of the block is 25°C. (d) Assuming that the power radiated at 25°C represents the average value in the heating process, find the time for which the heater was kept on.

55. A hot body placed in a surrounding of temperature θ_0 obeys Newton's law of cooling $\frac{d\theta}{dt} = -k(\theta - \theta_0)$. Its temperature at $t = 0$ is θ_1. The specific heat capacity of the body is s and its mass is m. Find (a) the maximum heat that the body can lose and (b) the time starting from $t = 0$ in which it will lose 90% of this maximum heat.

□

ANSWERS

OBJECTIVE I

1. (d) 2. (d) 3. (d) 4. (b) 5. (a) 6. (d)
7. (c) 8. (a) 9. (a) 10. (c)

OBJECTIVE II

1. (d) 2. (c), (d) 3. (b)
4. (c), (d) 5. (a), (c) 6. (a), (b)

EXERCISES

1. 3840 J
2. 440 W
3. $356\ \mathrm{J\ s^{-1}}$
4. 130°C
5. $5{\cdot}5 \times 10^{-5}$ g
6. $1{\cdot}5\ \mathrm{kg\ h^{-1}}$
7. 28°C
8. 0·03 W
9. 0·035 s
10. (a) 53°C (b) $2{\cdot}31\ \mathrm{J\ s^{-1}}$
11. 25 cm from the cold end
12. $0{\cdot}92\ \mathrm{W\ m^{-1}°C^{-1}}$
13. 12·5 kg

14. (a) $5{\cdot}0 \times 10^{-7}$ m s^{-1} (b) 27·5 hours
15. 89 cm
16. 1 W, 8 W, zero
17. $2 : \pi$
18. 12·5°C s^{-1}
19. 233 J s^{-1}
20. $\dfrac{2\pi Kd(\theta_1 - \theta_2)}{\ln(r_2/r_1)}$
21. (a) $\dfrac{K\pi(R_2^2 - R_1^2)(T_2 - T_1)}{l}$ (b) $\dfrac{2\pi Kl(T_2 - T_1)}{\ln(R_2/R_1)}$
22. $\dfrac{K_1K_2(L_1 + L_2)}{L_1K_2 + L_2K_1}$
23. 10·6°C
24. 2·36 J
25. 144 J
26. 60 J
27. 12 : 7
28. (a) 8000 J s^{-1} (b) 381 J s^{-1}
29. 30°C
30. 75 W, 400 W
31. $\dfrac{3\,T_1 + 2(T_2 + T_3)}{7}$
32. (b) $\dfrac{4\,K_0\,A(T_2 - T_1)}{3l}$
33. $\dfrac{K\pi r_1 r_2(\theta_2 - \theta_1)}{L}$
34. 1800 J
35. 3·0 W m^{-1}°C^{-1}
36. $\dfrac{Lms}{2KA}\ln 2$
37. $(T_2 - T_1)\,e^{-\lambda t}$ where $\lambda = \dfrac{KA(m_1s_1 + m_2s_2)}{lm_1m_2s_1s_2}$
38. $\dfrac{nR}{P_aA}(T_s - T_0)(1 - e^{-2KAt/5Rnx})$
39. 887 J
40. 0·42 J
41. (a) 1 : 4 (b) 2·9 : 1
42. 1700 K
43. (a) 1·4 J (b) 4·58 W from the ball
44. 22 W
45. 0·12°C s^{-1}
46. 0·3
47. (a) 0.94 J (b) 3.8 J (c) 2.8 J
48. 1·8 W m^{-1}°C^{-1}
49. 74 W m^{-1} K^{-1}
50. 2 min
51. 34°C
52. 12·5 g
53. (a) 20 W (b) $\dfrac{20}{3}$ W (c) 1000 J (d) 500 J kg^{-1} K^{-1}
54. (a) 160 W (b) 16 W (c) 8 W (d) 5·2 s
55. (a) $ms(\theta_1 - \theta_0)$ (b) $\dfrac{\ln 10}{k}$

□

CHAPTER 29

ELECTRIC FIELD AND POTENTIAL

29.1 WHAT IS ELECTRIC CHARGE ?

Matter is made of certain elementary particles. With the advancement in technology, we have discovered hundreds of elementary particles. Many of them are rare and of no concern to us in the present course. The three most common elementary particles are electrons, protons and neutrons having masses $m_e = 9{\cdot}10940 \times 10^{-31}$ kg, $m_p = 1{\cdot}67262 \times 10^{-27}$ kg and $m_n = 1{\cdot}67493 \times 10^{-27}$ kg. Because of their mass these particles attract each other by gravitational forces. Thus, an electron attracts another electron, placed 1 cm away, with a gravitational force

$$F = \frac{Gm_1m_2}{r^2}$$

$$= \frac{(6{\cdot}67 \times 10^{-11}\ \text{N m}^2\ \text{kg}^{-2}) \times (9{\cdot}1 \times 10^{-31}\ \text{kg})^2}{(10^{-2}\ \text{m})^2}$$

$$= 5{\cdot}5 \times 10^{-67}\ \text{N}.$$

However, an electron is found to repel another electron at 1 cm with a force of $2{\cdot}3 \times 10^{-24}$ N. This extra force is called the *electric force*. The electric force is very large as compared to the gravitational force. The electrons must have some additional property, apart from their mass, which is responsible for the electric force. We call this property *charge*. Just as masses are responsible for the gravitational force, charges are responsible for the electric force. Two protons placed at a distance of 1 cm also repel each other with a force of $2{\cdot}3 \times 10^{-24}$ N. Thus, protons also have charge. Two neutrons placed at a distance of 1 cm attract each other with a force of $1{\cdot}9 \times 10^{-60}$ N which is equal to $\frac{Gm_1m_2}{r^2}\cdot$ Thus, neutrons exert only gravitational force on each other and experience no electric force. The neutrons have mass but no charge.

Two Kinds of Charges

As mentioned above, the electric force between two electrons is the same as the electric force between two protons placed at the same separation. We may guess that the amount of charge on an electron is the same as that on a proton. However, if a proton and an electron are placed 1 cm apart, they attract each other with a force of $2{\cdot}3 \times 10^{-24}$ N. Certainly this force is electric, but it is attractive and not repulsive. The charge on an electron repels the charge on another electron but attracts the charge on a proton. Thus, although the charge on an electron and that on a proton have the same strength, they are of two different nature. Also, if we pack a proton and an electron together in a small volume, the combination does not attract or repel another electron or proton placed at a distance. The net charge on the proton–electron system seems to be zero. It is, therefore, convenient to define one charge as positive and the other as negative. We arbitrarily call the charge on a proton as positive and that on an electron as negative. This assignment of positive and negative signs to the proton charge and the electron charge is purely a convention. It does not mean that the charge on an electron is "less" than the charge on a proton.

Unit of Charge

The above discussion suggests that charge is a basic property associated with the elementary particles and its definition is as difficult as the definition of mass or time or length. We can measure the charge on a system by comparing it with the charge on a standard body but we do not know what exactly it is that we intend to measure. The SI unit of charge is coulomb abbreviated as C. 1 coulomb is the charge flowing through a wire in 1 *s* if the electric current in it is 1 A. The charge on a proton is

$$e = 1{\cdot}60218 \times 10^{-19}\ \text{C}.$$

The charge on an electron is the negative of this value.

Charge is Quantized

If protons and electrons are the only charge carriers in the universe, all observable charges must be integral multiples of e. If an object contains n_1 protons and n_2 electrons, the net charge on the object is

$$n_1(e) + n_2(-e) = (n_1 - n_2)e.$$

Indeed, there are elementary particles other than protons and electrons, which carry charge. However, they all carry charges which are integral multiples of e. Thus, the charge on any object is always an integral multiple of e and can be changed only in steps of e, i.e., charge is quantized.

The step size e is usually so small that we can easily neglect the quantization. If we rub a glass rod with a silk cloth, typically charges of the order of a microcoulomb appear on the rubbed objects. Now, 1 μC contains n units of basic charge e where

$$n = \frac{1\ \mu\text{C}}{1{\cdot}6 \times 10^{-19}\ \text{C}} \approx 6 \times 10^{12}.$$

The step size is thus very small as compared to the charges usually found and in many cases we can assume a continuous charge variation.

Charge is Conserved

The charge of an isolated system is conserved. It is possible to create or destroy charged particles but it is not possible to create or destroy *net charge*. In a beta decay process, a neutron converts itself into a proton and a fresh electron is created. The charge however, remains zero before and after the event.

Frictional Electricity : Induction

The simplest way to experience electric charges is to rub certain solid bodies against each other. Long ago, around 600 BC, the Greeks knew that when amber is rubbed with wool, it acquires the property of attracting light objects such as small pieces of paper. This is because amber becomes electrically charged. If we pass a comb through dry hair, the comb becomes electrically charged and can attract small pieces of paper. An automobile becomes charged when it travels through the air. A paper sheet becomes charged when it passes through a printing machine. A gramophone record becomes charged when cleaned with a dry cloth.

The explanation of appearance of electric charge on rubbing is simple. All material bodies contain large number of electrons and equal number of protons in their normal state. When rubbed against each other, some electrons from one body may pass on to the other body. The body that receives the extra electrons, becomes negatively charged. The body that donates the electrons, becomes positively charged because it has more protons than electrons. Thus, when a glass rod is rubbed with a silk cloth, electrons are transferred from the glass rod to the silk cloth. The glass rod becomes positively charged and the silk cloth becomes negatively charged.

If we take a positively charged glass rod near small pieces of paper, the rod attracts the pieces. Why does the rod attract paper pieces which are uncharged ? This is because the positively charged rod attracts the electrons of a paper piece towards itself. Some of the electrons accumulate at that edge of the paper piece which is closer to the rod. At the farther end of the piece there is a deficiency of electrons and hence positive charge appears there. Such a redistribution of charge in a material, due to the presence of a nearby charged body, is called *induction*. The rod exerts larger attraction on the negative charges of the paper piece as compared to the repulsion on the positive charges. This is because the negative charges are closer to the rod. Hence, there is a net attraction between the rod and the paper piece.

29.2 COULOMB'S LAW

The experiments of Coulomb and others established that the force exerted by a charged particle on the other is given by

$$F = \frac{kq_1q_2}{r^2}, \qquad \dots (29.1)$$

where q_1 and q_2 are the charges on the particles, r is the separation between them and k is a constant. The force is attractive if the charges are of opposite signs and is repulsive if they are of the same sign. We can write Coulomb's law as

$$\vec{F} = \frac{kq_1q_2\,\vec{r}}{r^3},$$

where $\vec{r}$ is the position vector of the force-experiencing particle with respect to the force-exerting particle. In this form, the equation includes the direction of the force.

Figure 29.1

As F, q_1, q_2 and r are all independently defined quantities, the constant k can be measured experimentally. In SI units, the constant k is measured to be $8{\cdot}98755 \times 10^{9}\ \text{N m}^2\ \text{C}^{-2}$.

The constant k is often written as $\frac{1}{4\pi\varepsilon_0}$ so that equation (29.1) becomes

$$F = \frac{1}{4\pi\varepsilon_0}\frac{q_1q_2}{r^2}. \qquad \dots (29.2)$$

The constant ε_0 is called the *permittivity of free space* and its value is

$$\varepsilon_0 = \frac{1}{4\pi k} = 8{\cdot}85419 \times 10^{-12}\ \text{C}^2\ \text{N}^{-1}\ \text{m}^{-2}.$$

29.3 ELECTRIC FIELD

We have already discussed in the chapter on gravitation that a particle cannot directly interact with another particle kept at a distance. A particle creates a gravitational field around it and this field exerts force on another particle placed in it. The electric force between two charged particles is also seen as a two-step process. A charge produces something called an *electric field* in the space around it and this electric field exerts a force on any charge (except the source charge itself) placed in it. The electric field has its own existence and is present even if there is no additional charge to experience the force. The field takes finite time to propagate. Thus, if a charge is displaced from its position, the field at a distance r will change after a time $t = r/c$, where c is the speed of light. We define the *intensity of electric field* at a point as follows:

Bring a charge q at the given point without disturbing any other charge that has produced the field. If the charge q experiences an electric force $\vec{F}$, we define the intensity of electric field at the given point as

$$\vec{E} = \frac{\vec{F}}{q} \cdot \qquad \text{... (29.3)}$$

The charge q used to define $\vec{E}$ is called a *test charge.*

One way to ensure that the test charge q does not disturb other charges is to keep its magnitude very small. If this magnitude is not small, the positions of the other charges may change. Equation (29.3) then gives the electric field due to the charges in the changed positions. The intensity of electric field is often abbreviated as *electric field.*

The electric field at a point is a vector quantity. Suppose, $\vec{E}_1$ is the field at a point due to a charge Q_1 and $\vec{E}_2$ is the field at the same point due to a charge Q_2. The resultant field when both the charges are present, is $\vec{E} = \vec{E}_1 + \vec{E}_2$.

Electric Field due to a Point Charge

Consider a point charge Q placed at a point A (figure 29.2). We are interested in the electric field $\vec{E}$ at a point P at a distance r from Q. Let us imagine a test charge q placed at P. The charge Q creates a field $\vec{E}$ at P and this field exerts a force $\vec{F} = q\vec{E}$ on the charge q. But, from Coulomb's law the force on the charge q in the given situation is

$$F = \frac{Qq}{4\pi\varepsilon_0 r^2}$$

along AP. The electric field at P is, therefore,

$$E = \frac{F}{q} = \frac{Q}{4\pi\varepsilon_0 r^2} \qquad \text{... (29.4)}$$

along AP.

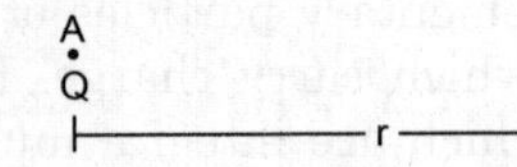

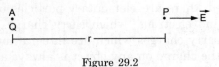

Figure 29.2

The electric field due to a set of charges may be obtained by finding the fields due to each individual charge and then adding these fields according to the rules of vector addition.

Example 29.1

Two charges 10 μC *and* −10 μC *are placed at points A and B separated by a distance of* 10 cm. *Find the electric field at a point P on the perpendicular bisector of AB at a distance of* 12 cm *from its middle point.*

Solution :

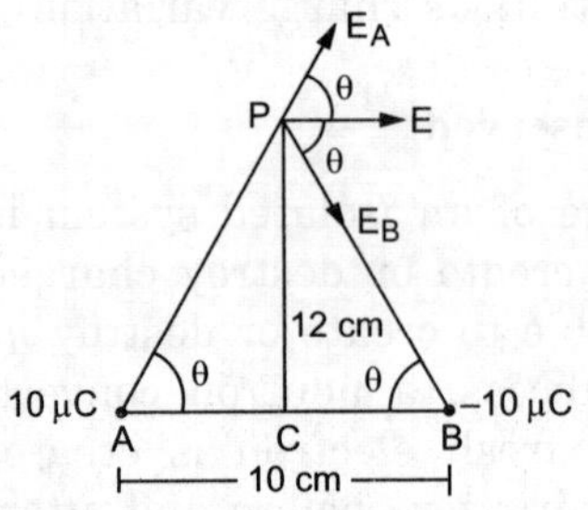

Figure 29.3

The situation is shown in figure (29.3). The distance

$AP = BP = \sqrt{(5\text{ cm})^2 + (12\text{ cm})^2} = 13\text{ cm}.$

The field at the point P due to the charge 10 μC is

$$E_A = \frac{10\ \mu\text{C}}{4\pi\varepsilon_0 (13\text{ cm})^2} = \frac{(10\times 10^{-6}\text{ C})\times(9\times 10^9\text{ N m}^2\text{ C}^{-2})}{169\times 10^{-4}\text{ m}^2}$$

$$= 5{\cdot}3\times 10^6\text{ N C}^{-1}.$$

This field is along AP. The field due to −10 μC at P is $E_B = 5{\cdot}3\times 10^6\text{ N C}^{-1}$ along PB. As E_A and E_B are equal in magnitude, the resultant will bisect the angle between the two. The geometry of the figure shows that this resultant is parallel to the base AB. The magnitude of the resultant field is

$$E = E_A\cos\theta + E_B\cos\theta$$

$$= 2\times(5{\cdot}3\times 10^6\text{ N C}^{-1})\times\frac{5}{13}$$

$$= 4{\cdot}1\times 10^6\text{ N C}^{-1}.$$

If a given charge distribution is continuous, we can use the technique of integration to find the resultant electric field at a point. A small element dQ is chosen in the distribution and the field $d\vec{E}$ due to dQ is calculated. The resultant field is then calculated by integrating the components of $d\vec{E}$ under proper limits.

Example 29.2

A ring of radius a contains a charge q distributed uniformly over its length. Find the electric field at a point on the axis of the ring at a distance x from the centre.

Solution :

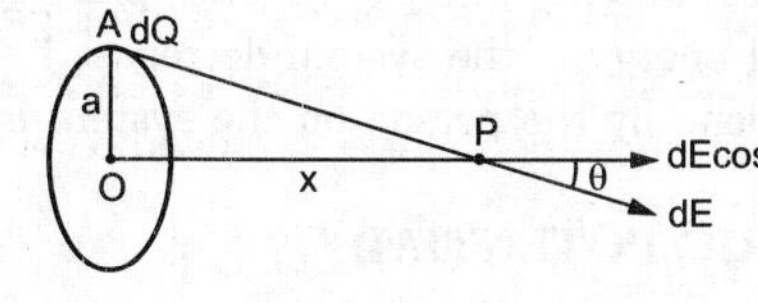

Figure 29.4

Figure (29.4) shows the situation. Let us consider a small element of the ring at the point A having a charge dQ. The field at P due to this element is

$$dE = \frac{dQ}{4\pi\varepsilon_0 (AP)^2}.$$

By symmetry, the field at P will be along the axis OP. The component of dE along this direction is

$$dE\cos\theta = \frac{dQ}{4\pi\varepsilon_0 (AP)^2}\left(\frac{OP}{AP}\right)$$

$$= \frac{x\,dQ}{4\pi\varepsilon_0 (a^2 + x^2)^{3/2}}.$$

The net field at P is

$$E = \int dE\cos\theta = \int \frac{x\,dQ}{4\pi\varepsilon_0 (a^2 + x^2)^{3/2}}$$

$$= \frac{x}{4\pi\varepsilon_0 (a^2 + x^2)^{3/2}} \int dQ = \frac{xQ}{4\pi\varepsilon_0 (a^2 + x^2)^{3/2}}.$$

29.4 LINES OF ELECTRIC FORCE

The electric field in a region can be graphically represented by drawing certain curves known as *lines of electric force* or *electric field lines*. Lines of force are drawn in such a way that the tangent to a line of force gives the direction of the resultant electric field there. Thus, the electric field due to a positive point charge is represented by straight lines originating from the charge (figure 29.5a). The electric field due to a negative point charge is represented by straight lines terminating at the charge (figure 29.5b). If we draw the lines isotropically (the lines are drawn uniformly in all directions, originating from the point charge), we can compare the intensities of the field at two points by just looking at the distribution of the lines of force.

Consider two points P_1 and P_2 in figure (29.5). Draw equal small areas through P_1 and P_2 perpendicular to the lines. More number of lines pass through the area at P_1 and less number of lines pass through the area at P_2. Also, the intensity of electric field is more at P_1 than at P_2. In fact, the electric field is proportional to the lines per unit area if the lines originate isotropically from the charge.

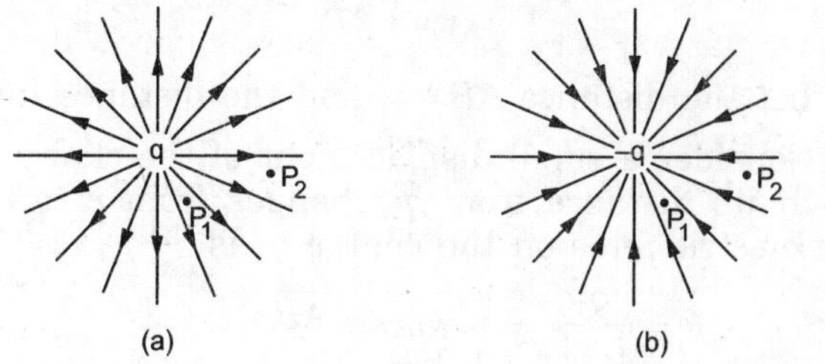

Figure 29.5

We can draw the lines of force for a charge distribution containing more than one charge. From each charge we can draw the lines isotropically. The lines may not be straight as one moves away from a charge. Figure (29.6) shows the shapes of these lines for some charge distributions.

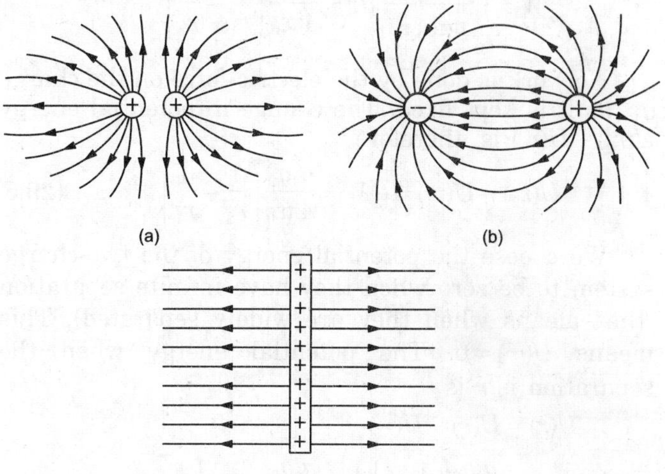

Figure 29.6

The lines of force are purely a geometrical construction which help us to visualise the nature of electric field in a region. They have no physical existence.

29.5 ELECTRIC POTENTIAL ENERGY

Consider a system of charges. The charges of the system exert electric forces on each other. If the position of one or more charges is changed, work may be done by these electric forces. We define *change in electric potential energy* of the system as negative of the work done by the electric forces as the configuration of the system changes.

Consider a system of two charges q_1 and q_2. Suppose, the charge q_1 is fixed at a point A and the charge q_2 is taken from a point B to a point C along the line ABC (figure 29.7).

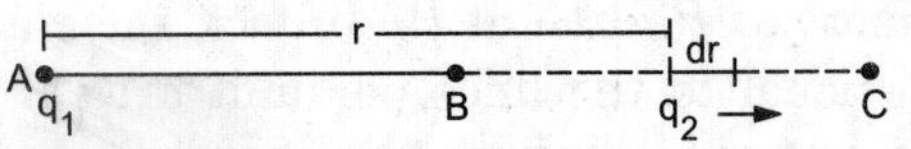

Figure 29.7

Let the distance $AB = r_1$ and the distance $AC = r_2$.

Consider a small displacement of the charge q_2 in which its distance from q_1 changes from r to $r + dr$. The electric force on the charge q_2 is

$$F = \frac{q_1 q_2}{4\pi\varepsilon_0 r^2} \text{ towards } \overrightarrow{AB}.$$

The work done by this force in the small displacement dr is

$$dW = \frac{q_1 q_2}{4\pi\varepsilon_0 r^2} dr.$$

The total work done as the charge q_2 moves from B to C is

$$W = \int_{r_1}^{r_2} \frac{q_1 q_2}{4\pi\varepsilon_0 r^2} dr = \frac{q_1 q_2}{4\pi\varepsilon_0}\left(\frac{1}{r_1} - \frac{1}{r_2}\right).$$

No work is done by the electric force on the charge q_1 as it is kept fixed. The change in potential energy $U(r_2) - U(r_1)$ is, therefore,

$$U(r_2) - U(r_1) = -W = \frac{q_1 q_2}{4\pi\varepsilon_0}\left(\frac{1}{r_2} - \frac{1}{r_1}\right). \quad \ldots (29.5)$$

We choose the potential energy of the two-charge system to be zero when they have infinite separation (that means when they are widely separated). This means $U(\infty) = 0$. The potential energy when the separation is r is

$$U(r) = U(r) - U(\infty)$$

$$= \frac{q_1 q_2}{4\pi\varepsilon_0}\left(\frac{1}{r} - \frac{1}{\infty}\right) = \frac{q_1 q_2}{4\pi\varepsilon_0 r}. \quad \ldots (29.6)$$

The above equation is derived by assuming that one of the charges is fixed and the other is displaced. However, the potential energy depends essentially on the separation between the charges and is independent of the spatial location of the charged particles. Equations (29.5) and (29.6) are, therefore, general.

Equation (29.6) gives the electric potential energy of a pair of charges. If there are three charges q_1, q_2 and q_3, there are three pairs. Similarly for an N-particle system, the potential energy of the system is equal to the sum of the potential energies of all the pairs of the charged particles.

Example 29.3

Three particles, each having a charge of 10 μC, *are placed at the vertices of an equilateral triangle of side* 10 cm. *Find the work done by a person in pulling them apart to infinite separations.*

Solution : The potential energy of the system in the initial condition is

$$U = \frac{3 \times (10\ \mu\text{C}) \times (10\ \mu\text{C})}{4\pi\varepsilon_0\ (10\ \text{cm})}$$

$$= \frac{(3 \times 10^{-10}\ \text{C}^2) \times (9 \times 10^9\ \text{N m}^2\ \text{C}^{-2})}{0{\cdot}1\ \text{m}} = 27\ \text{J}.$$

When the charges are infinitely separated, the potential energy is reduced to zero. If we assume that the charges do not get kinetic energy in the process, the total mechanical energy of the system decreases by 27 J. Thus, the work done by the person on the system is –27 J.

29.6 ELECTRIC POTENTIAL

The electric field in a region of space is described by assigning a vector quantity $\vec{E}$ at each point. The same field can also be described by assigning a scalar quantity V at each point. We now define this scalar quantity known as *electric potential*.

Suppose, a test charge q is moved in an electric field from a point A to a point B while all the other charges in question remain fixed. If the electric potential energy changes by $U_B - U_A$ due to this displacement, we define the *potential difference* between the point A and the point B as

$$V_B - V_A = \frac{U_B - U_A}{q}. \quad \ldots (29.7)$$

Conversely, if a charge q is taken through a potential difference $V_B - V_A$, the electric potential energy changes by $U_B - U_A = q(V_B - V_A)$. This equation defines potential difference between any two points in an electric field. We can define absolute electric potential at any point by choosing a reference point P and saying that the potential at this point is zero. The electric potential at a point A is then given by (equation 29.7)

$$V_A = V_A - V_P = \frac{U_A - U_P}{q}. \quad \ldots (29.8)$$

So, *the potential at a point A is equal to the change in electric potential energy per unit test charge when it is moved from the reference point to the point A.*

Suppose, the test charge is moved in an electric field without changing its kinetic energy. The total work done on the charge should be zero from the work–energy theorem. If W_{ext} and W_{el} be the work done by the external agent and by the electric field as the charge moves, we have,

$$W_{ext} + W_{el} = 0$$

or, $$W_{ext} = -W_{el} = \Delta U,$$

where ΔU is the change in electric potential energy. Using this equation and equation (29.8), the potential at a point A may also be defined as follows:

The potential at a point A is equal to the work done per unit test charge by an external agent in moving the test charge from the reference point to the point A (without changing its kinetic energy).

The choice of reference point is purely ours. Generally, a point widely separated from all charges in question is taken as the reference point. Such a point is assumed to be at infinity.

As potential energy is a scalar quantity, potential is also a scalar quantity. Thus, if V_1 is the potential at a given point due to a charge q_1 and V_2 is the potential at the same point due to a charge q_2, the potential due to both the charges is $V_1 + V_2$.

29.7 ELECTRIC POTENTIAL DUE TO A POINT CHARGE

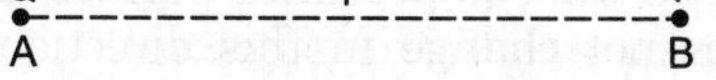

Figure 29.8

Consider a point charge Q placed at a point A (figure 29.8). We have to find the electric potential at a point P where $AP = r$. Let us take the reference point at $r = \infty$. Suppose, a test charge q is moved from $r = \infty$ to the point P. The change in electric potential energy of the system is, from equation (29.6),

$$U_P - U_\infty = \frac{Qq}{4\pi\varepsilon_0 r}.$$

The potential at P is, from equation (29.8),

$$V_P = \frac{U_P - U_\infty}{q} = \frac{Q}{4\pi\varepsilon_0 r}. \quad \ldots (29.9)$$

The electric potential due to a system of charges may be obtained by finding potentials due to the individual charges using equation (29.9) and then adding them. Thus,

$$V = \frac{1}{4\pi\varepsilon_0}\sum_i \frac{Q_i}{r_i}.$$

Example 29.4

Two charges $+10\,\mu C$ *and* $+20\,\mu C$ *are placed at a separation of* 2 cm. *Find the electric potential due to the pair at the middle point of the line joining the two charges.*

Solution : Using the equation $V = \frac{Q}{4\pi\varepsilon_0 r}$, the potential due to $+10\,\mu C$ is

$$V_1 = \frac{(10\times 10^{-6}\,\mathrm{C})\times(9\times 10^{9}\,\mathrm{N\,m^2C^{-2}})}{1\times 10^{-2}\,\mathrm{m}} = 9\,\mathrm{MV}.$$

The potential due to $+20\,\mu C$ is

$$V_2 = \frac{(20\times 10^{-6}\,\mathrm{C})\times(9\times 10^{9}\,\mathrm{N\,m^2C^{-2}})}{1\times 10^{-2}\,\mathrm{m}} = 18\,\mathrm{MV}.$$

The net potential at the given point is

$$9\,\mathrm{MV} + 18\,\mathrm{MV} = 27\,\mathrm{MV}.$$

If the charge distribution is continuous, we may use the technique of integration to find the electric potential.

29.8 RELATION BETWEEN ELECTRIC FIELD AND POTENTIAL

Suppose, the electric field at a point $\vec{r}$ due to a charge distribution is $\vec{E}$ and the electric potential at the same point is V. Suppose, a point charge q is displaced slightly from the point $\vec{r}$ to $\vec{r} + \vec{dr}$. The force on the charge is

$$\vec{F} = q\vec{E}$$

and the work done by the electric field during the displacement is

$$dW = \vec{F}\cdot\vec{dr} = q\vec{E}\cdot\vec{dr}.$$

The change in potential energy is

$$dU = -\,dW = -\,q\vec{E}\cdot\vec{dr}.$$

The change in potential is

$$dV = \frac{dU}{q}$$

or, $$dV = -\,\vec{E}\cdot\vec{dr}. \quad \ldots (29.10)$$

Integrating between the points $\vec{r}_1$ and $\vec{r}_2$, we get

$$V_2 - V_1 = -\int_{\vec{r}_1}^{\vec{r}_2} \vec{E}\cdot\vec{dr} \quad \ldots (29.11)$$

where V_1 and V_2 are the potentials at $\vec{r}_1$ and $\vec{r}_2$ respectively. If we choose $\vec{r}_1$, at the reference point (say at infinity) and $\vec{r}_2$ at $\vec{r}$, equation (29.11) becomes

$$V(\vec{r}) = -\int_{\infty}^{\vec{r}} \vec{E}\cdot\vec{dr}. \quad \ldots (29.12)$$

Example 29.5

Figure (29.9) shows two metallic plates A and B placed parallel to each other at a separation d. A uniform electric field E exists between the plates in the direction from plate B to plate A. Find the potential difference between the plates.

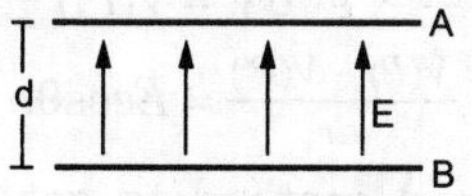

Figure 29.9

Solution : Let us take the origin at plate A and x-axis along the direction from plate A to plate B. We have

$$V_B - V_A = -\int_{\vec{r}_A}^{\vec{r}_B} \vec{E}\cdot d\vec{r} = -\int_0^d - E\,dx = Ed.$$

If we work in Cartesian coordinate system

$$\vec{E} = E_x \vec{i} + E_y \vec{j} + E_z \vec{k}$$

and $$d\vec{r} = dx\,\vec{i} + dy\,\vec{j} + dz\,\vec{k}.$$

Thus, from (29.10)

$$dV = -E_x\,dx - E_y\,dy - E_z\,dz. \quad \ldots \text{(i)}$$

If we change x to $x + dx$ keeping y and z constant, $dy = dz = 0$ and from (i),

$$E_x = -\frac{\partial V}{\partial x}.$$

Similarly, $$E_y = -\frac{\partial V}{\partial y} \quad \ldots \text{(29.13)}$$

and $$E_z = -\frac{\partial V}{\partial z}$$

The symbols $\frac{\partial}{\partial x}, \frac{\partial}{\partial y}$, etc., are used to indicate that while differentiating with respect to one coordinate, the others are kept constant.

If we know the electric field in a region, we can find the electric potential using equation (29.12) and if we know the electric potential in a region, we can find the electric field using (29.13).

Equation (29.10) may also be written as

$$dV = E\,dr\cos\theta$$

where θ is the angle between the field $\vec{E}$ and the small displacement $d\vec{r}$. Thus,

$$-\frac{dV}{dr} = E\cos\theta. \quad \ldots \text{(29.14)}$$

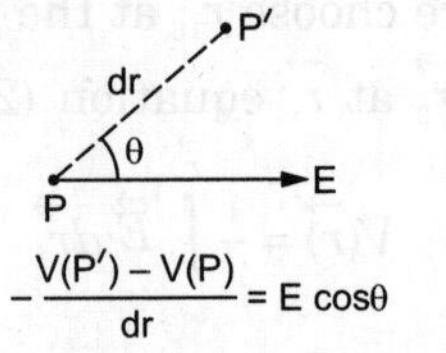

Figure 29.10

We see that, $-\frac{dV}{dr}$ gives the component of the electric field in the direction of displacement $d\vec{r}$. In figure (29.10), we show a small displacement $PP' = dr$. The electric field is E making an angle θ with PP'. We have

$$dV = V(P') - V(P)$$

so that $$\frac{V(P) - V(P')}{dr} = E\cos\theta.$$

This gives us a method to get the component of the electric field in any given direction if we know the potential. Move a small distance dr in the given direction and see the change dV in the potential. The component of electric field along that direction is $-\frac{dV}{dr}$.

If we move a distance dr in the direction of the field, θ is zero and $-\frac{dV}{dr} = E$ is maximum. Thus, *the electric field is along the direction in which the potential decreases at the maximum rate.*

If a small displacement $d\vec{r}$ perpendicular to the electric field is considered, $\theta = 90°$ and $dV = -\vec{E}\cdot d\vec{r} = 0$. The potential does not vary in a direction perpendicular to the electric field.

Equipotential Surfaces

If we draw a surface in such a way that the electric potential is the same at all the points of the surface, it is called an *equipotential surface*. The component of electric field parallel to an equipotential surface is zero, as the potential does not change in this direction. Thus, the electric field is perpendicular to the equipotential surface at each point of the surface. For a point charge, the electric field is radial and the equipotential surfaces are concentric spheres with centres at the charge (figure 29.11).

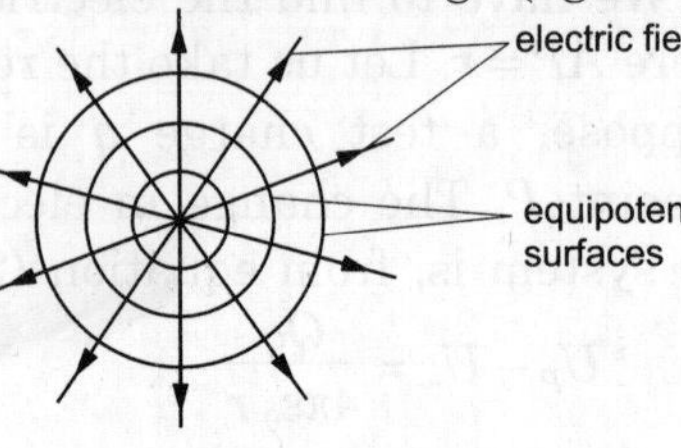

Figure 29.11

29.9 ELECTRIC DIPOLE

A combination of two charges $+q$ and $-q$ separated by a small distance d constitutes an *electric dipole*. The *electric dipole moment* of this combination is defined as a vector

$$\vec{p} = q\vec{d}, \quad \ldots \text{(29.15)}$$

where $\vec{d}$ is the vector joining the negative charge to the positive charge. The line along the direction of the dipole moment is called the *axis of the dipole.*

Electric Potential due to a Dipole

Suppose, the negative charge $-q$ is placed at a point A and the positive charge q is placed at a point

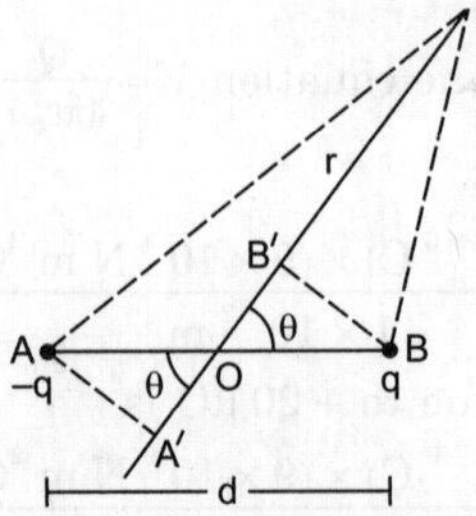

Figure 29.12

B (figure 29.12), the separation $AB = d$. The middle point of AB is O. The potential is to be evaluated at a point P where $OP = r$ and $\angle POB = \theta$. Also, let $r \gg d$.

Let AA' be the perpendicular from A to PO and BB' be the perpendicular from B to PO. As d is very small compared to r,

$$AP \approx A'P = OP + OA'$$

$$= OP + AO\cos\theta = r + \frac{d}{2}\cos\theta.$$

Similarly, $BP \approx B'P = OP - OB'$

$$= r - \frac{d}{2}\cos\theta.$$

The potential at P due to the charge $-q$ is

$$V_1 = -\frac{1}{4\pi\varepsilon_0}\frac{q}{AP} \approx -\frac{1}{4\pi\varepsilon_0}\frac{q}{r + \frac{d}{2}\cos\theta}$$

and that due to the charge $+q$ is

$$V_2 = \frac{1}{4\pi\varepsilon_0}\frac{q}{BP} \approx \frac{1}{4\pi\varepsilon_0}\frac{q}{r - \frac{d}{2}\cos\theta}.$$

The net potential at P due to the dipole is

$$V = V_1 + V_2$$

$$= \frac{1}{4\pi\varepsilon_0}\left[\frac{q}{r - \frac{d}{2}\cos\theta} - \frac{q}{r + \frac{d}{2}\cos\theta}\right]$$

$$= \frac{1}{4\pi\varepsilon_0}\frac{q\,d\cos\theta}{r^2 - \frac{d^2}{4}\cos^2\theta}$$

$$\approx \frac{1}{4\pi\varepsilon_0}\frac{q\,d\cos\theta}{r^2}$$

or, $$V = \frac{1}{4\pi\varepsilon_0}\frac{p\cos\theta}{r^2}. \qquad \ldots (29.16)$$

Generalised Definition of Electric Dipole

The potential at a distance r from a point charge q is given by

$$V = \frac{1}{4\pi\varepsilon_0}\frac{q}{r}.$$

It is inversely proportional to r and is independent of direction. The potential due to a dipole is inversely proportional to r^2 and depends on direction as shown by the term $\cos\theta$ in equation (29.16). In general, any charge distribution that produces electric potential given by

$$V = \frac{1}{4\pi\varepsilon_0}\frac{p\cos\theta}{r^2}$$

is called an electric dipole. The constant p is called its dipole moment and the direction from which the angle θ is measured to get the above equation is called the direction of the dipole moment.

Electric Field due to a Dipole

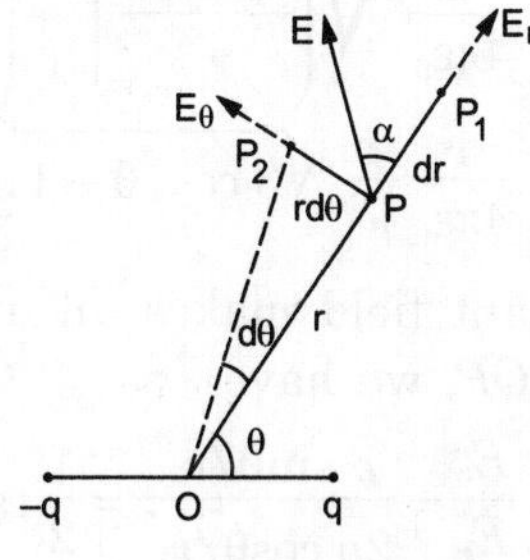

Figure 29.13

We can find the electric field due to an electric dipole using the expression (29.16) for the electric potential. In figure (29.13), PP_1 is a small displacement in the direction of OP and PP_2 is a small displacement perpendicular to OP. Thus, PP_1 is in radial direction and PP_2 is in transverse direction. In going from P to P_1, the angle θ does not change and the distance OP changes from r to $r + dr$. Thus, $PP_1 = dr$. In going from P to P_2, the angle θ changes from θ to $\theta + d\theta$ while the distance r remains almost constant. Thus, $PP_2 = r\,d\theta$. From equation (29.14), the component of the electric field at P in the radial direction PP_1 is

$$E_r = -\frac{dV}{PP_1} = -\frac{dV}{dr} = -\frac{\partial V}{\partial r}. \qquad \ldots (i)$$

The symbol ∂ specifies that θ should be treated as constant while differentiating with respect to r.

Similarly, the component of the electric field at P in the transverse direction PP_2 is

$$E_\theta = -\frac{dV}{PP_2} = -\frac{dV}{r d\theta} = -\frac{1}{r}\frac{\partial V}{\partial \theta}. \qquad \ldots (ii)$$

As $$V = \frac{1}{4\pi\varepsilon_0}\frac{p\cos\theta}{r^2},$$

$$E_r = -\frac{\partial V}{\partial r} = -\frac{1}{4\pi\varepsilon_0}\frac{\partial}{\partial r}\left(\frac{p\cos\theta}{r^2}\right)$$

$$= -\frac{1}{4\pi\varepsilon_0}(p\cos\theta)\frac{d}{dr}\left(\frac{1}{r^2}\right)$$

$$= \frac{1}{4\pi\varepsilon_0}\frac{2p\cos\theta}{r^3} \qquad \ldots (iii)$$

and $$E_\theta = -\frac{1}{r}\frac{\partial V}{\partial \theta} = -\frac{1}{r}\frac{1}{4\pi\varepsilon_0}\frac{\partial}{\partial \theta}\left(\frac{p\cos\theta}{r^2}\right)$$

$$= -\frac{1}{4\pi\varepsilon_0}\frac{p}{r^3}\frac{d}{d\theta}(\cos\theta)$$

$$= \frac{1}{4\pi\varepsilon_0}\frac{p\sin\theta}{r^3}. \qquad \ldots (iv)$$

The resultant electric field at P (figure 29.13) is

$$E=\sqrt{E_r^2+E_\theta^2}$$

$$=\frac{1}{4\pi\varepsilon_0}\sqrt{\left(\frac{2p\cos\theta}{r^3}\right)^2+\left(\frac{p\sin\theta}{r^3}\right)^2}$$

$$=\frac{1}{4\pi\varepsilon_0}\frac{p}{r^3}\sqrt{3\cos^2\theta+1}. \quad \ldots (29.17)$$

If the resultant field makes an angle α with the radial direction OP, we have

$$\tan\alpha=\frac{E_\theta}{E_r}=\frac{p\sin\theta/r^3}{2p\cos\theta/r^3}=\frac{1}{2}\tan\theta$$

or, $$\alpha=\tan^{-1}\left(\frac{1}{2}\tan\theta\right). \quad \ldots (29.18)$$

Special Cases

(a) $\theta=0$

In this case, the point P is on the axis of the dipole. From equation (29.16), the electric potential is $V=\frac{1}{4\pi\varepsilon_0}\frac{p}{r^2}$.

The field at such a point is, from equation (29.17), $E=\frac{1}{4\pi\varepsilon_0}\frac{2p}{r^3}$ along the axis. Such a position of the point P is called an *end-on position.*

(b) $\theta=90°$

In this case the point P is on the perpendicular bisector of the dipole. The potential here is zero while the field is, from equation (29.17), $E=\frac{1}{4\pi\varepsilon_0}\frac{p}{r^3}$.

The angle α is given by

$$\tan\alpha=\frac{\tan\theta}{2}=\infty$$

or, $$\alpha=90°.$$

The field is antiparallel to the dipole axis. Such a position of the point P is called a *broadside-on position.*

29.10 TORQUE ON AN ELECTRIC DIPOLE PLACED IN AN ELECTRIC FIELD

Consider an electric dipole placed in a uniform electric field $\vec{E}$. The dipole consists of charges $-q$ placed at A and $+q$ placed at B (figure 29.14). The mid-point of AB is O and the length $AB=d$. Suppose the axis of the dipole AB makes an angle θ with the electric field at a certain instant.

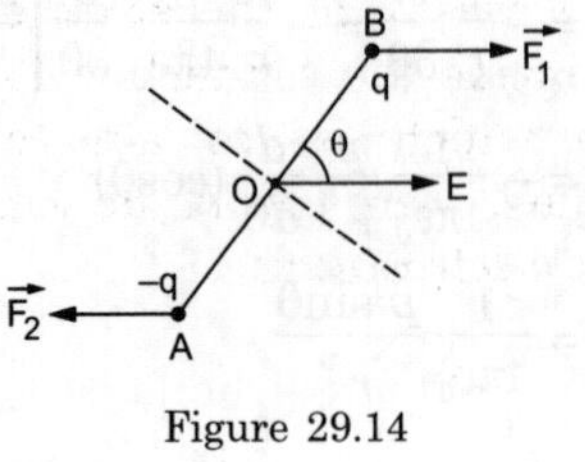

Figure 29.14

The force on the charge $+q$ is $\vec{F_1}=q\vec{E}$ and the force on the charge $-q$ is $\vec{F_2}=-q\vec{E}$. Let us calculate the torques $(\vec{r}\times\vec{F})$ of these forces about O.

The torque of $\vec{F_1}$ about O is

$$\vec{\Gamma}_1=\vec{OB}\times\vec{F_1}=q(\vec{OB}\times\vec{E})$$

and the torque of $\vec{F_2}$ about O is

$$\vec{\Gamma}_2=\vec{OA}\times\vec{F_2}=-q(\vec{OA}\times\vec{E})=q(\vec{AO}\times\vec{E}).$$

The net torque acting on the dipole is

$$\vec{\Gamma}=\vec{\Gamma}_1+\vec{\Gamma}_2$$

$$=q(\vec{OB}\times\vec{E})+q(\vec{AO}\times\vec{E})$$

$$=q(\vec{OB}+\vec{AO})\times\vec{E}$$

$$=q\,\vec{AB}\times\vec{E}=\vec{p}\times\vec{E}. \quad \ldots (29.19)$$

The direction of the torque is perpendicular to the plane containing the dipole axis and the electric field. In figure (29.14), this is perpendicular to the plane of paper and is going into the page. The magnitude is $\Gamma=|\vec{\Gamma}|=pE\sin\theta$.

29.11 POTENTIAL ENERGY OF A DIPOLE PLACED IN A UNIFORM ELECTRIC FIELD

When an electric dipole is placed in an electric field $\vec{E}$, a torque $\vec{\Gamma}=\vec{p}\times\vec{E}$ acts on it (figure 29.14). If we rotate the dipole through a small angle $d\theta$, the work done by the torque is

$$dW=\Gamma d\theta$$

$$=-pE\sin\theta\, d\theta.$$

The work is negative as the rotation $d\theta$ is opposite to the torque.

The change in electric potential energy of the dipole is, therefore,

$$dU=-dW=pE\sin\theta\, d\theta.$$

If the angle θ is changed from 90° to θ, the change in potential energy is

$$U(\theta)-U(90°)=\int_{90°}^{\theta}pE\sin\theta\, d\theta$$

$$=pE\left[-\cos\theta\right]_{90°}^{\theta}$$

$$=-pE\cos\theta=-\vec{p}\cdot\vec{E}.$$

If we choose the potential energy of the dipole to be zero when $\theta=90°$ (dipole axis is perpendicular to the field), $U(90°)=0$ and the above equation becomes

$$U(\theta)=-\vec{p}\cdot\vec{E}. \quad \ldots (29.20)$$

29.12 CONDUCTORS, INSULATORS AND SEMICONDUCTORS

Any piece of matter of moderate size contains millions and millions of atoms or molecules. Each atom contains a positively charged nucleus and several electrons going round it.

In gases, the atoms or molecules almost do not interact with each other. In solids and liquids, the interaction is comparatively stronger. It turns out that the materials may be broadly divided into three categories according to their behaviour when they are placed in an electric field.

In some materials, the outer electrons of each atom or molecule are only weakly bound to it. These electrons are almost free to move throughout the body of the material and are called *free electrons*. They are also known as *conduction electrons*. When such a material is placed in an electric field, the free electrons move in a direction opposite to the field. Such materials are called *conductors*.

Another class of materials is called *insulators* in which all the electrons are tightly bound to their respective atoms or molecules. Effectively, there are no *free electrons*. When such a material is placed in an electric field, the electrons may slightly shift opposite to the field but they can't leave their parent atoms or molecules and hence can't move through long distances. Such materials are also called *dielectrics*.

In *semiconductors*, the behaviour is like an insulator at the temperature 0 K. But at higher temperatures, a small number of electrons are able to free themselves and they respond to the applied electric field. As the number of free electrons in a semiconductor is much smaller than that in a conductor, its behaviour is in between a conductor and an insulator and hence, the name semiconductor. A freed electron in a semiconductor leaves a vacancy in its normal bound position. These vacancies also help in conduction.

We shall learn more about conductivity in later chapters. At the moment we accept the simple approximate model described above. The conductors have large number of free electrons everywhere in the material whereas the insulators have none. The discussion of semiconductors is deferred to a separate chapter.

Roughly speaking, the metals are conductors and the nonmetals are insulators. The above discussion may be extended to liquids and gases. Some of the liquids, such as mercury, and ionized gases are conductors.

29.13 THE ELECTRIC FIELD INSIDE A CONDUCTOR

Consider a conducting plate placed in a region. Initially, there is no electric field and the conduction electrons are almost uniformly distributed within the plate (shown by dots in figure 29.15a). In any small volume (which contains several thousand molecules) the number of electrons is equal to the number of protons in the nuclei. The net charge in the volume is zero.

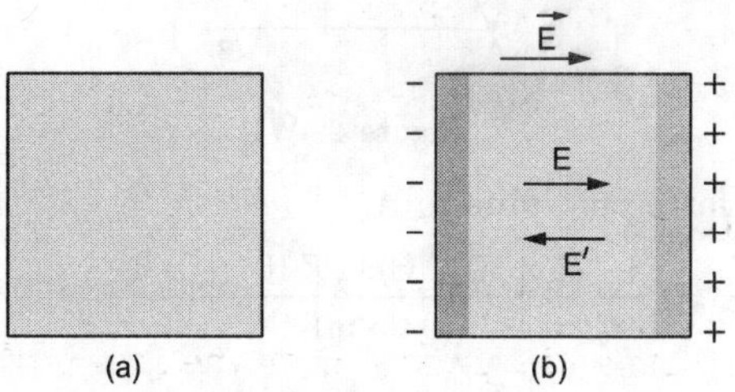

Figure 29.15

Now, suppose an electric field $\vec{E}$ is created in the direction left to right (figure 29.15b). This field exerts force on the free electrons from right to left. The electrons move towards left, the number of electrons on the left face increases and the number on the right face decreases. The left face becomes negatively charged and the right face becomes positively charged. These extra charges produce an extra electric field E' inside the plate from right to left. The electrons continue to drift and the internal field $\vec{E'}$ becomes stronger and stronger. A situation comes when the field $\vec{E'}$ due to the redistribution of free electrons becomes equal in magnitude to $\vec{E}$. The net electric field inside the plate is then zero. The free electrons there do not experience any net force and the process of further drifting stops. Thus, a steady state is reached in which some positive and negative charges appear at the surface of the plate and there is no electric field inside the plate.

Whenever a conductor is placed in an electric field some of the free electrons redistribute themselves on the surface of the conductor. The redistribution takes place in such a way that the electric field is zero at all the points inside the conductor. The redistribution takes a time which is, in general, less than a millisecond. Thus, *there can be no electric field inside a conductor in electrostatics.*

Worked Out Examples

1. *Charges* $5{\cdot}0\times10^{-7}$ C, $-2{\cdot}5\times10^{-7}$ C *and* $1{\cdot}0\times10^{-7}$ C *are held fixed at the three corners A, B, C of an equilateral triangle of side* 5·0 cm. *Find the electric force on the charge at C due to the rest two.*

Solution :

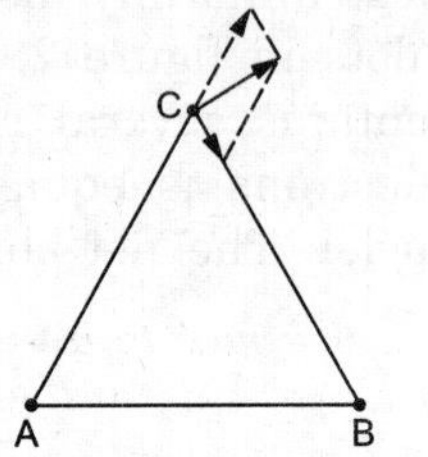

Figure 29-W1

The force on C due to A

$$=\frac{1}{4\pi\varepsilon_0}\frac{(5\times10^{-7}\text{ C})(1\times10^{-7}\text{ C})}{(0{\cdot}05\text{ m})^2}$$

$$=9\times10^9\text{ Nm}^2\text{C}^{-2}\times\frac{5\times10^{-14}\text{ C}^2}{25\times10^{-4}\text{ m}^2}=0{\cdot}18\text{ N}.$$

This force acts along AC. The force on C due to B

$$=\frac{1}{4\pi\varepsilon_0}\frac{(2{\cdot}5\times10^{-7}\text{ C})(1\times10^{-7}\text{ C})}{(0{\cdot}05\text{ m})^2}=0{\cdot}09\text{ N}.$$

This attractive force acts along CB. As the triangle is equilateral, the angle between these two forces is 120°. The resultant electric force on C is

$$[(0{\cdot}18\text{ N})^2+(0{\cdot}09\text{ N})^2+2(0{\cdot}18\text{ N})(0{\cdot}09\text{ N})(\cos120°)]^{1/2}$$

$$=0{\cdot}16\text{ N}.$$

The angle made by this resultant with CB is

$$\tan^{-1}\frac{0{\cdot}18\sin120°}{0{\cdot}09+0{\cdot}18\cos120°}=90°.$$

2. *Two particles A and B having charges* $8{\cdot}0\times10^{-6}$ C *and* $-2{\cdot}0\times10^{-6}$ C *respectively are held fixed with a separation of* 20 cm. *Where should a third charged particle be placed so that it does not experience a net electric force?*

Solution : As the net electric force on C should be equal to zero, the force due to A and B must be opposite in direction. Hence, the particle should be placed on the line AB. As A and B have charges of opposite signs, C cannot be between A and B. Also, A has larger magnitude of charge than B. Hence, C should be placed closer to B than A. The situation is shown in figure (29-W2).

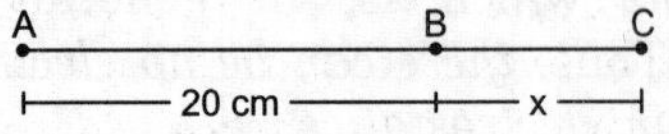

Figure 29-W2

Suppose $BC=x$ and the charge on C is Q.

The force due to $A=\dfrac{(8{\cdot}0\times10^{-6}\text{ C})Q}{4\pi\varepsilon_0(20\text{ cm}+x)^2}$.

The force due to $B=\dfrac{(2{\cdot}0\times10^{-6}\text{ C})Q}{4\pi\varepsilon_0x^2}$.

They are oppositely directed and to have a zero resultant, they should be equal in magnitude. Thus,

$$\frac{8}{(20\text{ cm}+x)^2}=\frac{2}{x^2}$$

or, $$\frac{20\text{ cm}+x}{x}=2,\text{ giving }x=20\text{ cm}.$$

3. *Three equal charges, each having a magnitude of* $2{\cdot}0\times10^{-6}$ C, *are placed at the three corners of a right-angled triangle of sides* 3 cm, 4 cm *and* 5 cm. *Find the force on the charge at the right-angle corner.*

Solution :

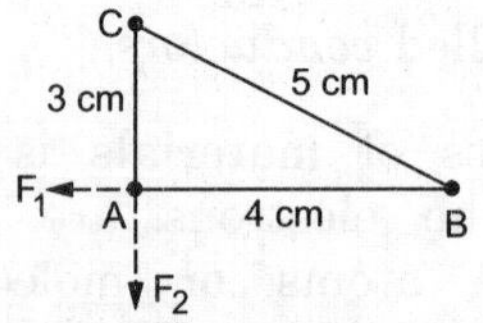

Figure 29-W3

The situation is shown in figure (29-W3). The force on A due to B is

$$F_1=\frac{(2{\cdot}0\times10^{-6}\text{ C})(2{\cdot}0\times10^{-6}\text{ C})}{4\pi\varepsilon_0(4\text{ cm})^2}$$

$$=9\times10^9\text{ N m}^2\text{C}^{-2}\times4\times10^{-12}\text{ C}^2\times\frac{1}{16\times10^{-4}\text{ m}^2}$$

$$=22{\cdot}5\text{ N}.$$

This force acts along BA. Similarly, the force on A due to C is $F_2=40$ N in the direction of CA. Thus, the net electric force on A is

$$F=\sqrt{F_1^2+F_2^2}$$

$$=\sqrt{(22{\cdot}5\text{ N})^2+(40\text{ N})^2}=45{\cdot}9\text{ N}.$$

This resultant makes an angle θ with BA where

$$\tan\theta=\frac{40}{22{\cdot}5}=\frac{16}{9}.$$

4. *Two small iron particles, each of mass* 280 mg, *are placed at a distance* 10 cm *apart. If* 0·01% *of the electrons of one particle are transferred to the other, find the electric force between them. Atomic weight of iron is* 56 g mol^{-1} *and there are 26 electrons in each atom of iron.*

Solution : The atomic weight of iron is 56 g mol^{-1}. Thus, 56 g of iron contains 6×10^{23} atoms and each atom contains 26 electrons. Hence, 280 mg of iron contains

$$\frac{280\text{ mg}\times 6\times 10^{23}\times 26}{56\text{ g}}=7\cdot 8\times 10^{22}\text{ electrons.}$$

The number of electrons transferred from one particle to another

$$=\frac{0\cdot 01}{100}\times 7\cdot 8\times 10^{22}=7\cdot 8\times 10^{18}.$$

The charge transferred is, therefore,

$$1\cdot 6\times 10^{-19}\text{ C}\times 7\cdot 8\times 10^{18}=1\cdot 2\text{ C}.$$

The electric force between the particles is

$$(9\times 10^{9}\text{ N m}^2\text{ C}^{-2})\frac{(1\cdot 2\text{ C})^2}{(10\times 10^{-2}\text{ m})^2}$$

$$=1\cdot 3\times 10^{12}\text{ N}.$$

This equals the load of approximately 2000 million grown-up persons !

5. *A charge Q is to be divided on two objects. What should be the values of the charges on the objects so that the force between the objects can be maximum ?*

Solution : Suppose one object receives a charge q and the other $Q-q$. The force between the objects is

$$F=\frac{q(Q-q)}{4\pi\varepsilon_0 d^2},$$

where d is the separation between them. For F to be maximum, the quantity

$$y=q(Q-q)=Qq-q^2$$

should be maximum. This is the case when,

$$\frac{dy}{dq}=0\ \text{ or, }\ Q-2q=0\ \text{ or, }\ q=Q/2.$$

Thus, the charge should be divided equally on the two objects.

6. *Two particles, each having a mass of* 5 g *and charge* $1\cdot 0\times 10^{-7}$ C, *stay in limiting equilibrium on a horizontal table with a separation of* 10 cm *between them. The coefficient of friction between each particle and the table is the same. Find the value of this coefficient.*

Solution : The electric force on one of the particles due to the other is

$$F=(9\times 10^9\text{ N m}^2\text{ C}^{-2})\times(1\cdot 0\times 10^{-7}\text{C})^2\times\frac{1}{(0\cdot 10\text{ m})^2}$$

$$=0\cdot 009\text{ N}.$$

The frictional force in limiting equilibrium

$$f=\mu\times(5\times 10^{-3}\text{ kg})\times 9\cdot 8\text{ m s}^{-2}$$

$$=(0\cdot 049\ \mu)\text{ N}.$$

As these two forces balance each other,

$$0\cdot 049\ \mu=0\cdot 009$$

or, $\mu=0\cdot 18.$

7. *A vertical electric field of magnitude* $4\cdot 00\times 10^5\text{ N C}^{-1}$ *just prevents a water droplet of mass* $1\cdot 00\times 10^{-4}$ kg *from falling. Find the charge on the droplet.*

Solution : The forces acting on the droplet are

(i) the electric force $q\vec{E}$ and

(ii) the force of gravity $m\vec{g}$.

To just prevent from falling, these two forces should be equal and opposite. Thus,

$$q(4\cdot 00\times 10^5\text{ N C}^{-1})=(1\cdot 00\times 10^{-4}\text{ kg})\times(9\cdot 8\text{ m s}^{-2})$$

or, $q=2\cdot 45\times 10^{-9}$ C.

8. *Three charges, each equal to q, are placed at the three corners of a square of side a. Find the electric field at the fourth corner.*

Solution :

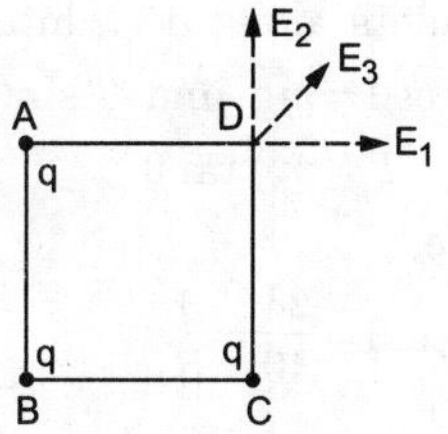

Figure 29-W4

Let the charges be placed at the corners A, B and C (figure 29-W4). We shall calculate the electric field at the fourth corner D. The field E_1 due to the charge at A will have the magnitude $\frac{q}{4\pi\varepsilon_0 a^2}$ and will be along AD. The field E_2 due to the charge at C will have the same magnitude and will be along CD.

The field E_3 due to the charge at B will have the magnitude $\frac{q}{4\pi\varepsilon_0(\sqrt{2}a)^2}$ and will be along BD. As E_1 and E_2 are equal in magnitude, their resultant will be along the bisector of the angle between E_1, E_2 and hence along E_3. The magnitude of this resultant is $\sqrt{E_1^2+E_2^2}$ as the angle between E_1 and E_2 is $\pi/2$. The resultant electric field at D is, therefore, along E_3 and has magnitude

$$\sqrt{E_1^2+E_2^2}+E_3$$

$$=\sqrt{\left(\frac{q}{4\pi\varepsilon_0 a^2}\right)^2+\left(\frac{q}{4\pi\varepsilon_0 a^2}\right)^2}+\frac{q}{4\pi\varepsilon_0(\sqrt{2}a)^2}$$

$$=\frac{q}{4\pi\varepsilon_0}\left[\frac{\sqrt{2}}{a^2}+\frac{1}{2a^2}\right]=(2\sqrt{2}+1)\frac{q}{8\pi\varepsilon_0 a^2}.$$

9. *A charged particle of mass* $1\cdot 0$ g *is suspended through a silk thread of length* 40 cm *in a horizontal electric field of* $4\cdot 0\times 10^4\text{ N C}^{-1}$. *If the particle stays at a distance of* 24 cm *from the wall in equilibrium, find the charge on the particle.*

Solution :

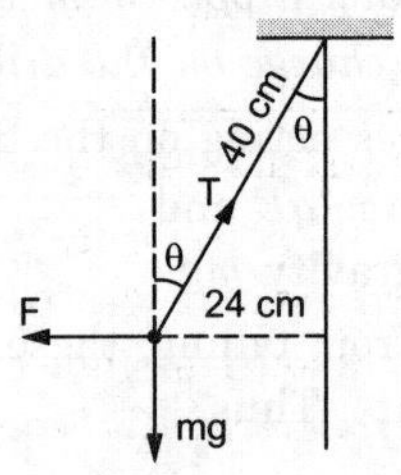

Figure 29-W5

The situation is shown in figure (29-W5).

The forces acting on the particle are
(i) the electric force $F = qE$ horizontally,
(ii) the force of gravity mg downward and
(iii) the tension T along the thread.

As the particle is at rest, these forces should add to zero. Taking components along horizontal and vertical,

$$T\cos\theta = mg \text{ and } T\sin\theta = F$$

or, $$F = mg\tan\theta \quad \text{... (i)}$$

From the figure,

$$\sin\theta = \frac{24}{40} = \frac{3}{5}.$$

Thus, $\tan\theta = \frac{3}{4}$. From (i),

$$q(4{\cdot}0 \times 10^{4}\ \text{N C}^{-1}) = (1{\cdot}0 \times 10^{-3}\ \text{kg})\ (9{\cdot}8\ \text{m s}^{-2})\ \frac{3}{4},$$

giving $q = 1{\cdot}8 \times 10^{-7}\ \text{C}$.

10. *A particle A having a charge of* $5{\cdot}0 \times 10^{-7}$ C *is fixed in a vertical wall. A second particle B of mass* 100 g *and having equal charge is suspended by a silk thread of length* 30 cm *from the wall. The point of suspension is* 30 cm *above the particle A. Find the angle of the thread with the vertical when it stays in equilibrium.*

Solution :

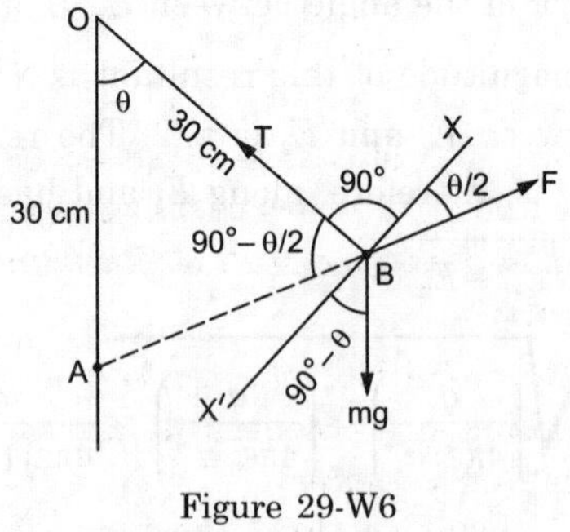

Figure 29-W6

The situation is shown in figure (29-W6). Suppose the point of suspension is O and let θ be the angle between the thread and the vertical. Forces on the particle B are
(i) weight mg downward
(ii) tension T along the thread and
(iii) electric force of repulsion F along AB.

For equilibrium, these forces should add to zero. Let $X'BX$ be the line perpendicular to OB. We shall take the components of the forces along BX. This will give a relation between F, mg and θ.

The various angles are shown in the figure. As

$$OA = OB,\ \angle OBA = \angle OAB = 90° - \frac{\theta}{2}.$$

The other angles can be written down directly.
Taking components along BX, we get

$$F\cos\frac{\theta}{2} = mg\cos(90° - \theta)$$

$$= 2\,mg\sin\frac{\theta}{2}\cos\frac{\theta}{2}$$

or, $$\sin\frac{\theta}{2} = \frac{F}{2\,mg}. \quad \text{... (i)}$$

Now, $$F = (9 \times 10^{9}\ \text{N m}^2\ \text{C}^{-2}) \times (5{\cdot}0 \times 10^{-7}\ \text{C})^2 \times \frac{1}{AB^2}$$

and $$AB = 2(OA)\sin\frac{\theta}{2}.$$

Thus, $$F = \frac{9 \times 10^{9} \times 25 \times 10^{-14}}{4 \times (30 \times 10^{-2})^2 \times \sin^2\frac{\theta}{2}}\ \text{N}. \quad \text{... (ii)}$$

From (i) and (ii),

$$\sin\frac{\theta}{2} = \frac{F}{2\,mg} = \frac{9 \times 10^{9} \times 25 \times 10^{-14}\ \text{N}}{4 \times (30 \times 10^{-2})^2 \times \sin^2\frac{\theta}{2}} \cdot \frac{1}{2\,mg}$$

or,

$$\sin^3\frac{\theta}{2} = \frac{9 \times 10^{9} \times 25 \times 10^{-14}\ \text{N}}{4 \times 9 \times 10^{-2} \times 2 \times (100 \times 10^{-3}\ \text{kg}) \times 9{\cdot}8\ \text{m s}^{-2}}$$

$$= 0{\cdot}0032$$

or, $\sin\frac{\theta}{2} = 0{\cdot}15$, giving $\theta = 17°$.

11. *Four particles, each having a charge q, are placed on the four vertices of a regular pentagon. The distance of each corner from the centre is a. Find the electric field at the centre of the pentagon.*

Solution :

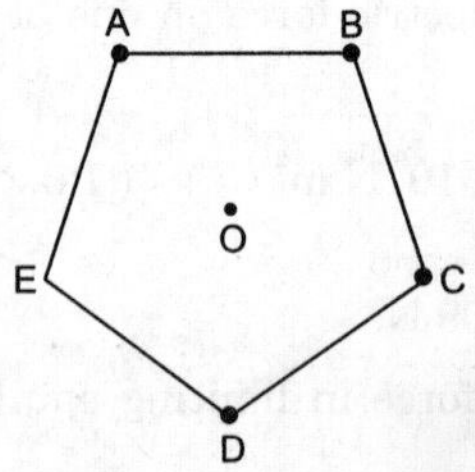

Figure 29-W7

Let the charges be placed at the vertices A, B, C and D of the pentagon $ABCDE$. If we put a charge q at the corner E also, the field at O will be zero by symmetry. Thus, the field at the centre due to the charges at A, B,

C and D is equal and opposite to the field due to the charge q at E alone.

The field at O due to the charge q at E is

$$\frac{q}{4\pi\varepsilon_0 a^2} \text{ along } EO.$$

Thus, the field at O due to the given system of charges is $\frac{q}{4\pi\varepsilon_0 a^2}$ along OE.

12. *Find the electric field at a point P on the perpendicular bisector of a uniformly charged rod. The length of the rod is L, the charge on it is Q and the distance of P from the centre of the rod is a.*

Solution **:**

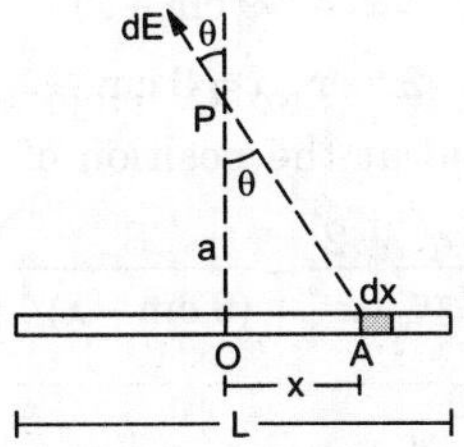

Figure 29-W8

Let us take an element of length dx at a distance x from the centre of the rod (figure 29-W8). The charge on this element is

$$dQ = \frac{Q}{L}dx.$$

The electric field at P due to this element is

$$dE = \frac{dQ}{4\pi\varepsilon_0 (AP)^2}.$$

By symmetry, the resultant field at P will be along OP (if the charge is positive). The component of dE along OP is

$$dE\cos\theta = \frac{dQ}{4\pi\varepsilon_0 (AP)^2} \cdot \frac{OP}{AP} = \frac{a\,Q\,dx}{4\pi\varepsilon_0 L(a^2 + x^2)^{3/2}}$$

Thus, the resultant field at P is

$$E = \int dE\cos\theta$$

$$= \frac{aQ}{4\pi\varepsilon_0 L}\int_{-L/2}^{L/2} \frac{dx}{(a^2 + x^2)^{3/2}}. \qquad \text{... (i)}$$

We have $x = a\tan\theta$ or $dx = a\sec^2\theta\, d\theta$.

$$\text{Thus, } \int \frac{dx}{(a^2 + x^2)^{3/2}} = \int \frac{a\sec^2\theta\, d\theta}{a^3\sec^3\theta}$$

$$= \frac{1}{a^2}\int \cos\theta\, d\theta = \frac{1}{a^2}\sin\theta = \frac{1}{a^2}\frac{x}{(x^2 + a^2)^{1/2}}.$$

From (i),

$$E = \frac{aQ}{4\pi\varepsilon_0 La^2}\left[\frac{x}{(x^2 + a^2)^{1/2}}\right]_{-L/2}^{L/2}$$

$$= \frac{aQ}{4\pi\varepsilon_0 La^2}\left[\frac{2L}{(L^2 + 4a^2)^{1/2}}\right]$$

$$= \frac{Q}{2\pi\varepsilon_0 a\sqrt{L^2 + 4a^2}}.$$

13. *A uniform electric field E is created between two parallel, charged plates as shown in figure (29-W9). An electron enters the field symmetrically between the plates with a speed v_0. The length of each plate is l. Find the angle of deviation of the path of the electron as it comes out of the field.*

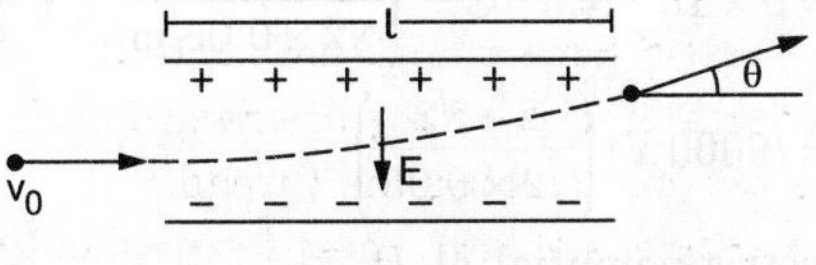

Figure 29-W9

Solution **:** The acceleration of the electron is $a = \frac{eE}{m}$ in the upward direction. The horizontal velocity remains v_0 as there is no acceleration in this direction. Thus, the time taken in crossing the field is

$$t = \frac{l}{v_0}. \qquad \text{... (i)}$$

The upward component of the velocity of the electron as it emerges from the field region is

$$v_y = at = \frac{eEl}{mv_0}.$$

The horizontal component of the velocity remains

$$v_x = v_0.$$

The angle θ made by the resultant velocity with the original direction is given by

$$\tan\theta = \frac{v_y}{v_x} = \frac{eEl}{mv_0^2}.$$

Thus, the electron deviates by an angle

$$\theta = \tan^{-1}\frac{eEl}{mv_0^2}.$$

14. *In a circuit,* 10 C *of charge is passed through a battery in a given time. The plates of the battery are maintained at a potential difference of* 12 V. *How much work is done by the battery ?*

Solution **:** By definition, the work done to transport a charge q through a potential difference V is qV. Thus, work done by the battery

$$= 10\text{ C} \times 12\text{ V} = 120\text{ J}.$$

15. *Charges* $2{\cdot}0 \times 10^{-6}$ C *and* $1{\cdot}0 \times 10^{-6}$ C *are placed at corners A and B of a square of side* 5·0 cm *as shown in figure (29-W10). How much work will be done against the electric field in moving a charge of* $1{\cdot}0 \times 10^{-6}$ C *from C to D ?*

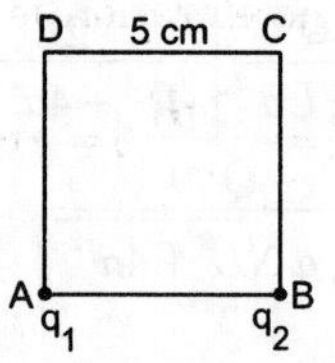

Figure 29-W10

Solution : The electric potential at C

$$= \frac{1}{4\pi\varepsilon_0}\left(\frac{q_1}{AC} + \frac{q_2}{BC}\right)$$

$$= 9\times 10^9 \text{ Nm}^{-2}\text{C}^{-2}\left(\frac{2{\cdot}0\times 10^{-6}\text{ C}}{\sqrt{2}\times 0{\cdot}05\text{ m}} + \frac{1{\cdot}0\times 10^{-6}\text{ C}}{0{\cdot}05\text{ m}}\right)$$

$$= (9000\text{ V})\left(\frac{2+\sqrt{2}}{\sqrt{2}\times 0{\cdot}05}\right).$$

The electric potential at D

$$= \frac{1}{4\pi\varepsilon_0}\left(\frac{q_1}{AD} + \frac{q_2}{BD}\right)$$

$$= 9\times 10^9 \text{ Nm}^{-2}\text{C}^{-2}\left(\frac{2{\cdot}0\times 10^{-6}\text{ C}}{0{\cdot}05\text{ m}} + \frac{1{\cdot}0\times 10^{-6}\text{ C}}{\sqrt{2}\times 0{\cdot}05\text{ m}}\right)$$

$$= (9000\text{ V})\left(\frac{2\sqrt{2}+1}{\sqrt{2}\times 0{\cdot}05}\right).$$

The work done against the electric field in moving the charge $1{\cdot}0\times 10^{-6}$ C from C to D is $q(V_D - V_C)$

$$= (1{\cdot}0\times 10^{-6}\text{ C})\,(9000\text{ V})\left(\frac{2\sqrt{2}+1-2-\sqrt{2}}{\sqrt{2}\times 0{\cdot}05}\right)$$

$$= 0{\cdot}053\text{ J}.$$

16. *The electric field in a region is given by $\vec{E} = (A/x^3)\,\vec{i}$. Write a suitable SI unit for A. Write an expression for the potential in the region assuming the potential at infinity to be zero.*

Solution : The SI unit of electric field is N C^{-1} or V m^{-1}. Thus, the unit of A is N m^3 C^{-1} or V m^{-2}.

$$V(x, y, z) = -\int_{\infty}^{(x, y, z)} \vec{E}\cdot d\vec{r}$$

$$= -\int_{\infty}^{(x, y, z)} \frac{A\,dx}{x^3} = \frac{A}{2x^2}.$$

17. *Three point charges q, 2q and 8q are to be placed on a 9 cm long straight line. Find the positions where the charges should be placed such that the potential energy of this system is minimum. In this situation, what is the electric field at the charge q due to the other two charges?*

Solution : The maximum contribution may come from the charge $8q$ forming pairs with others. To reduce its effect, it should be placed at a corner and the smallest charge q in the middle. This arrangement shown in figure (29-W11) ensures that the charges in the strongest pair $2q$, $8q$ are at the largest separation.

Figure 29-W11

The potential energy is

$$U = \frac{q^2}{4\pi\varepsilon_0}\left[\frac{2}{x} + \frac{16}{9\text{ cm}} + \frac{8}{9\text{ cm} - x}\right].$$

This will be minimum if

$$A = \frac{2}{x} + \frac{8}{9\text{ cm} - x} \text{ is minimum.}$$

For this, $$\frac{dA}{dx} = -\frac{2}{x^2} + \frac{8}{(9\text{ cm} - x)^2} = 0 \qquad \text{... (i)}$$

or, $9\text{ cm} - x = 2x$ or, $x = 3$ cm.

The electric field at the position of charge q is

$$\frac{q}{4\pi\varepsilon_0}\left(\frac{2}{x^2} - \frac{8}{(9\text{ cm} - x)^2}\right)$$

$$= 0 \qquad \text{from (i).}$$

18. *An* HCl *molecule has a dipole moment of* $3{\cdot}4\times 10^{-30}$ Cm. *Assuming that equal and opposite charges lie on the two atoms to form a dipole, what is the magnitude of this charge? The separation between the two atoms of* HCl *is* $1{\cdot}0\times 10^{-10}$ m.

Solution : If the charges on the two atoms are q, $-q$,

$$q(1{\cdot}0\times 10^{-10}\text{ m}) = 3{\cdot}4\times 10^{-30}\text{ Cm}$$

or, $$q = 3{\cdot}4\times 10^{-20}\text{ C}.$$

Note that this is less than the charge of a proton. Can you explain, how such a charge can appear on an atom?

19. *Figure (29-W12) shows an electric dipole formed by two particles fixed at the ends of a light rod of length l. The mass of each particle is m and the charges are $-q$ and $+q$. The system is placed in such a way that the dipole axis is parallel to a uniform electric field E that exists in the region. The dipole is slightly rotated about its centre and released. Show that for small angular displacement, the motion is angular simple harmonic and find its time period.*

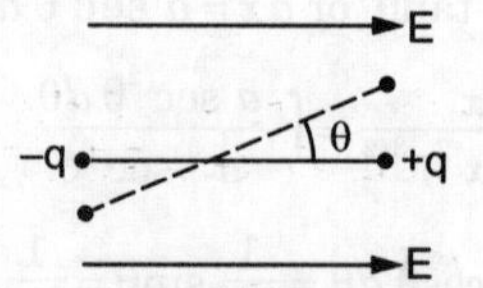

Figure 29-W12

Solution : Suppose, the dipole axis makes an angle θ with the electric field at an instant. The magnitude of the torque on it is

$$|\tau| = |\vec{p} \times \vec{E}|$$
$$= qlE \sin\theta.$$

This torque will tend to rotate the dipole back towards the electric field. Also, for small angular displacement $\sin\theta \approx \theta$ so that

$$\tau = -qlE\theta.$$

The moment of inertia of the system about the axis of rotation is

$$I = 2 \times m\left(\frac{l}{2}\right)^2 = \frac{ml^2}{2}.$$

Thus, the angular acceleration is

$$\alpha = \frac{\tau}{I} = -\frac{2qE}{ml}\theta = -\omega^2\theta$$

where $\omega^2 = \frac{2qE}{ml}$.

Thus, the motion is angular simple harmonic and the time period is $T = 2\pi\sqrt{\frac{ml}{2qE}}$. □

QUESTIONS FOR SHORT ANSWER

1. The charge on a proton is $+1{\cdot}6 \times 10^{-19}$ C and that on an electron is $-1{\cdot}6 \times 10^{-19}$ C. Does it mean that the electron has a charge $3{\cdot}2 \times 10^{-19}$ C less than the charge of a proton ?
2. Is there any lower limit to the electric force between two particles placed at a separation of 1 cm ?
3. Consider two particles A and B having equal charges and placed at some distance. The particle A is slightly displaced towards B. Does the force on B increase as soon as the particle A is displaced ? Does the force on the particle A increase as soon as it is displaced ?
4. Can a gravitational field be added vectorially to an electric field to get a total field ?
5. Why does a phonograph-record attract dust particles just after it is cleaned ?
6. Does the force on a charge due to another charge depend on the charges present nearby ?
7. In some old texts it is mentioned that 4π lines of force originate from each unit positive charge. Comment on the statement in view of the fact that 4π is not an integer.
8. Can two equipotential surfaces cut each other ?
9. If a charge is placed at rest in an electric field, will its path be along a line of force ? Discuss the situation when the lines of force are straight and when they are curved.
10. Consider the situation shown in figure (29-Q1). What are the signs of q_1 and q_2 ? If the lines are drawn in proportion to the charge, what is the ratio q_1/q_2 ?

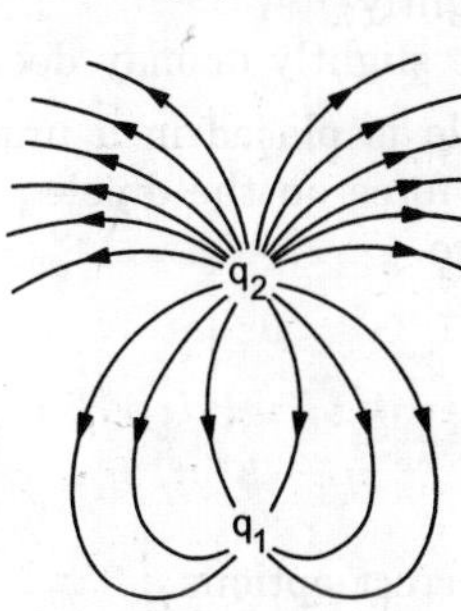

Figure 29-Q1

11. A point charge is taken from a point A to a point B in an electric field. Does the work done by the electric field depend on the path of the charge ?
12. It is said that the separation between the two charges forming an electric dipole should be small. Small compared to what ?
13. The number of electrons in an insulator is of the same order as the number of electrons in a conductor. What is then the basic difference between a conductor and an insulator ?
14. When a charged comb is brought near a small piece of paper, it attracts the piece. Does the paper become charged when the comb is brought near it ?

OBJECTIVE I

1. Figure (29-Q2) shows some of the electric field lines corresponding to an electric field. The figure suggests that

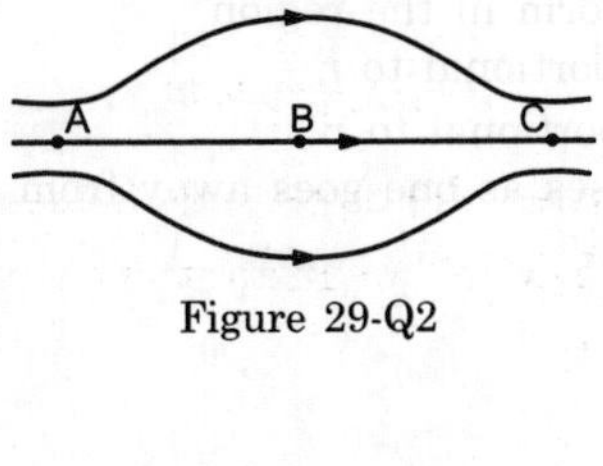

Figure 29-Q2

(a) $E_A > E_B > E_C$ (b) $E_A = E_B = E_C$
(c) $E_A = E_C > E_B$ (d) $E_A = E_C < E_B$.

2. When the separation between two charges is increased, the electric potential energy of the charges
(a) increases (b) decreases
(c) remains the same (d) may increase or decrease.
3. If a positive charge is shifted from a low-potential region to a high-potential region, the electric potential energy

(a) increases (b) decreases
(c) remains the same (d) may increase or decrease.

4. Two equal positive charges are kept at points A and B. The electric potential at the points between A and B (excluding these points) is studied while moving from A to B. The potential
(a) continuously increases
(b) continuously decreases
(c) increases then decreases
(d) decreases then increases.

5. The electric field at the origin is along the positive x-axis. A small circle is drawn with the centre at the origin cutting the axes at points A, B, C and D having coordinates $(a, 0)$, $(0, a)$, $(-a, 0)$, $(0, -a)$ respectively. Out of the points on the periphery of the circle, the potential is minimum at
(a) A (b) B (c) C (d) D.

6. If a body is charged by rubbing it, its weight
(a) remains precisely constant
(b) increases slightly
(c) decreases slightly
(d) may increase slightly or may decrease slightly.

7. An electric dipole is placed in a uniform electric field. The net electric force on the dipole
(a) is always zero
(b) depends on the orientation of the dipole
(c) can never be zero
(d) depends on the strength of the dipole.

8. Consider the situation of figure (29-Q3). The work done in taking a point charge from P to A is W_A, from P to B is W_B and from P to C is W_C.
(a) $W_A < W_B < W_C$ (b) $W_A > W_B > W_C$
(c) $W_A = W_B = W_C$ (d) None of these

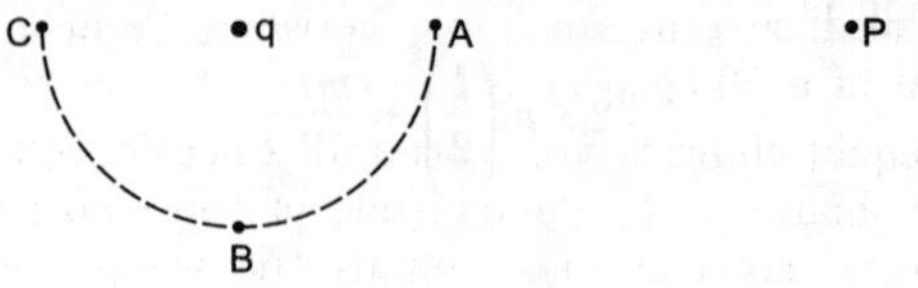

Figure 29-Q3

9. A point charge q is rotated along a circle in the electric field generated by another point charge Q. The work done by the electric field on the rotating charge in one complete revolution is
(a) zero (b) positive (c) negative
(d) zero if the charge Q is at the centre and nonzero otherwise.

OBJECTIVE II

1. Mark out the correct options.
(a) The total charge of the universe is constant.
(b) The total positive charge of the universe is constant.
(c) The total negative charge of the universe is constant.
(d) The total number of charged particles in the universe is constant.

2. A point charge is brought in an electric field. The electric field at a nearby point
(a) will increase if the charge is positive
(b) will decrease if the charge is negative
(c) may increase if the charge is positive
(d) may decrease if the charge is negative.

3. The electric field and the electric potential at a point are E and V respectively.
(a) If $E = 0$, V must be zero.
(b) If $V = 0$, E must be zero.
(c) If $E \neq 0$, V cannot be zero.
(d) If $V \neq 0$, E cannot be zero.

4. The electric potential decreases uniformly from 120 V to 80 V as one moves on the x-axis from $x = -1$ cm to $x = +1$ cm. The electric field at the origin
(a) must be equal to 20 Vcm^{-1}
(b) may be equal to 20 Vcm^{-1}
(c) may be greater than 20 Vcm^{-1}
(d) may be less than 20 Vcm^{-1}.

5. Which of the following quantities do not depend on the choice of zero potential or zero potential energy?
(a) Potential at a point
(b) Potential difference between two points
(c) Potential energy of a two-charge system
(d) Change in potential energy of a two-charge system.

6. An electric dipole is placed in an electric field generated by a point charge.
(a) The net electric force on the dipole must be zero.
(b) The net electric force on the dipole may be zero.
(c) The torque on the dipole due to the field must be zero.
(d) The torque on the dipole due to the field may be zero.

7. A proton and an electron are placed in a uniform electric field.
(a) The electric forces acting on them will be equal.
(b) The magnitudes of the forces will be equal.
(c) Their accelerations will be equal.
(d) The magnitudes of their accelerations will be equal.

8. The electric field in a region is directed outward and is proportional to the distance r from the origin. Taking the electric potential at the origin to be zero,
(a) it is uniform in the region
(b) it is proportional to r
(c) it is proportional to r^2
(d) it increases as one goes away from the origin.

EXERCISES

1. Find the dimensional formula of ε_0.

2. A charge of 1·0 C is placed at the top of your college building and another equal charge at the top of your house. Take the separation between the two charges to be 2·0 km. Find the force exerted by the charges on each other. How many times of your weight is this force ?

3. At what separation should two equal charges, 1·0 C each, be placed so that the force between them equals the weight of a 50 kg person ?

4. Two equal charges are placed at a separation of 1·0 m. What should be the magnitude of the charges so that the force between them equals the weight of a 50 kg person ?

5. Find the electric force between two protons separated by a distance of 1 fermi (1 fermi = 10^{-15} m). The protons in a nucleus remain at a separation of this order.

6. Two charges $2{\cdot}0 \times 10^{-6}$ C and $1{\cdot}0 \times 10^{-6}$ C are placed at a separation of 10 cm. Where should a third charge be placed such that it experiences no net force due to these charges ?

7. Suppose the second charge in the previous problem is $-1{\cdot}0 \times 10^{-6}$ C. Locate the position where a third charge will not experience a net force.

8. Two charged particles are placed at a distance 1·0 cm apart. What is the minimum possible magnitude of the electric force acting on each charge ?

9. Estimate the number of electrons in 100 g of water. How much is the total negative charge on these electrons ?

10. Suppose all the electrons of 100 g water are lumped together to form a negatively charged particle and all the nuclei are lumped together to form a positively charged particle. If these two particles are placed 10·0 cm away from each other, find the force of attraction between them. Compare it with your weight.

11. Consider a gold nucleus to be a sphere of radius 6·9 fermi in which protons and neutrons are distributed. Find the force of repulsion between two protons situated at largest separation. Why do these protons not fly apart under this repulsion ?

12. Two insulating small spheres are rubbed against each other and placed 1 cm apart. If they attract each other with a force of 0·1 N, how many electrons were transferred from one sphere to the other during rubbing ?

13. NaCl molecule is bound due to the electric force between the sodium and the chlorine ions when one electron of sodium is transferred to chlorine. Taking the separation between the ions to be $2{\cdot}75 \times 10^{-8}$ cm, find the force of attraction between them. State the assumptions (if any) that you have made.

14. Find the ratio of the electric and gravitational forces between two protons.

15. Suppose an attractive nuclear force acts between two protons which may be written as $F = Ce^{-kr}/r^2$. (a) Write down the dimensional formulae and appropriate SI units of C and k. (b) Suppose that $k = 1$ fermi^{-1} and that the repulsive electric force between the protons is just balanced by the attractive nuclear force when the separation is 5 fermi. Find the value of C.

16. Three equal charges, $2{\cdot}0 \times 10^{-6}$ C each, are held fixed at the three corners of an equilateral triangle of side 5 cm. Find the Coulomb force experienced by one of the charges due to the rest two.

17. Four equal charges $2{\cdot}0 \times 10^{-6}$ C each are fixed at the four corners of a square of side 5 cm. Find the Coulomb force experienced by one of the charges due to the rest three.

18. A hydrogen atom contains one proton and one electron. It may be assumed that the electron revolves in a circle of radius 0·53 angstrom (1 angstrom = 10^{-10} m and is abbreviated as Å) with the proton at the centre. The hydrogen atom is said to be in the ground state in this case. Find the magnitude of the electric force between the proton and the electron of a hydrogen atom in its ground state.

19. Find the speed of the electron in the ground state of a hydrogen atom. The description of ground state is given in the previous problem.

20. Ten positively charged particles are kept fixed on the x-axis at points $x = 10$ cm, 20 cm, 30 cm, ..., 100 cm. The first particle has a charge $1{\cdot}0 \times 10^{-8}$ C, the second 8×10^{-8} C, the third 27×10^{-8} C and so on. The tenth particle has a charge 1000×10^{-8} C. Find the magnitude of the electric force acting on a 1 C charge placed at the origin.

21. Two charged particles having charge $2{\cdot}0 \times 10^{-8}$ C each are joined by an insulating string of length 1 m and the system is kept on a smooth horizontal table. Find the tension in the string.

22. Two identical balls, each having a charge of $2{\cdot}00 \times 10^{-7}$ C and a mass of 100 g, are suspended from a common point by two insulating strings each 50 cm long. The balls are held at a separation 5·0 cm apart and then released. Find (a) the electric force on one of the charged balls (b) the components of the resultant force on it along and perpendicular to the string (c) the tension in the string (d) the acceleration of one of the balls. Answers are to be obtained only for the instant just after the release.

23. Two identical pith balls are charged by rubbing against each other. They are suspended from a horizontal rod through two strings of length 20 cm each, the separation between the suspension points being 5 cm. In equilibrium, the separation between the balls is 3 cm. Find the mass of each ball and the tension in the strings. The charge on each ball has a magnitude $2{\cdot}0 \times 10^{-8}$ C.

24. Two small spheres, each having a mass of 20 g, are suspended from a common point by two insulating strings of length 40 cm each. The spheres are identically charged and the separation between the balls at equilibrium is found to be 4 cm. Find the charge on each sphere.

25. Two identical pith balls, each carrying a charge q, are suspended from a common point by two strings of equal length l. Find the mass of each ball if the angle between the strings is 2θ in equilibrium.

26. A particle having a charge of $2{\cdot}0 \times 10^{-4}$ C is placed directly below and at a separation of 10 cm from the bob of a simple pendulum at rest. The mass of the bob is 100 g. What charge should the bob be given so that the string becomes loose?

27. Two particles A and B having charges q and $2q$ respectively are placed on a smooth table with a separation d. A third particle C is to be clamped on the table in such a way that the particles A and B remain at rest on the table under electrical forces. What should be the charge on C and where should it be clamped?

28. Two identically charged particles are fastened to the two ends of a spring of spring constant 100 N m^{-1} and natural length 10 cm. The system rests on a smooth horizontal table. If the charge on each particle is $2{\cdot}0 \times 10^{-8}$ C, find the extension in the length of the spring. Assume that the extension is small as compared to the natural length. Justify this assumption after you solve the problem.

29. A particle A having a charge of $2{\cdot}0 \times 10^{-6}$ C is held fixed on a horizontal table. A second charged particle of mass 80 g stays in equilibrium on the table at a distance of 10 cm from the first charge. The coefficient of friction between the table and this second particle is $\mu = 0{\cdot}2$. Find the range within which the charge of this second particle may lie.

30. A particle A having a charge of $2{\cdot}0 \times 10^{-6}$ C and a mass of 100 g is placed at the bottom of a smooth inclined plane of inclination 30°. Where should another particle B, having same charge and mass, be placed on the incline so that it may remain in equilibrium?

31. Two particles A and B, each having a charge Q, are placed a distance d apart. Where should a particle of charge q be placed on the perpendicular bisector of AB so that it experiences maximum force? What is the magnitude of this maximum force?

32. Two particles A and B, each carrying a charge Q, are held fixed with a separation d between them. A particle C having mass m and charge q is kept at the middle point of the line AB. (a) If it is displaced through a distance x perpendicular to AB, what would be the electric force experienced by it. (b) Assuming $x << d$, show that this force is proportional to x. (c) Under what conditions will the particle C execute simple harmonic motion if it is released after such a small displacement? Find the time period of the oscillations if these conditions are satisfied.

33. Repeat the previous problem if the particle C is displaced through a distance x along the line AB.

34. The electric force experienced by a charge of $1{\cdot}0 \times 10^{-6}$ C is $1{\cdot}5 \times 10^{-3}$ N. Find the magnitude of the electric field at the position of the charge.

35. Two particles A and B having charges of $+2{\cdot}00 \times 10^{-6}$ C and of $-4{\cdot}00 \times 10^{-6}$ C respectively are held fixed at a separation of 20·0 cm. Locate the point(s) on the line AB where (a) the electric field is zero (b) the electric potential is zero.

36. A point charge produces an electric field of magnitude 5·0 N C^{-1} at a distance of 40 cm from it. What is the magnitude of the charge?

37. A water particle of mass 10·0 mg and having a charge of $1{\cdot}50 \times 10^{-6}$ C stays suspended in a room. What is the magnitude of electric field in the room? What is its direction?

38. Three identical charges, each having a value $1{\cdot}0 \times 10^{-8}$ C, are placed at the corners of an equilateral triangle of side 20 cm. Find the electric field and potential at the centre of the triangle.

39. Positive charge Q is distributed uniformly over a circular ring of radius R. A particle having a mass m and a negative charge q, is placed on its axis at a distance x from the centre. Find the force on the particle. Assuming $x << R$, find the time period of oscillation of the particle if it is released from there.

40. A rod of length L has a total charge Q distributed uniformly along its length. It is bent in the shape of a semicircle. Find the magnitude of the electric field at the centre of curvature of the semicircle.

41. A 10-cm long rod carries a charge of +50 μC distributed uniformly along its length. Find the magnitude of the electric field at a point 10 cm from both the ends of the rod.

42. Consider a uniformly charged ring of radius R. Find the point on the axis where the electric field is maximum.

43. A wire is bent in the form of a regular hexagon and a total charge q is distributed uniformly on it. What is the electric field at the centre? You may answer this part without making any numerical calculations.

44. A circular wire-loop of radius a carries a total charge Q distributed uniformly over its length. A small length dL of the wire is cut off. Find the electric field at the centre due to the remaining wire.

45. A positive charge q is placed in front of a conducting solid cube at a distance d from its centre. Find the electric field at the centre of the cube due to the charges appearing on its surface.

46. A pendulum bob of mass 80 mg and carrying a charge of 2×10^{-8} C is at rest in a uniform, horizontal electric field of 20 kVm^{-1}. Find the tension in the thread.

47. A particle of mass m and charge q is thrown at a speed u against a uniform electric field E. How much distance will it travel before coming to momentary rest?

48. A particle of mass 1 g and charge $2{\cdot}5 \times 10^{-4}$ C is released from rest in an electric field of $1{\cdot}2 \times 10^{4}$ N C^{-1}. (a) Find the electric force and the force of gravity acting on this particle. Can one of these forces be neglected in comparison with the other for approximate analysis? (b) How long will it take for the particle to travel a distance of 40 cm? (c) What will be the speed of the particle after travelling this distance? (d) How much is the work done by the electric force on the particle during this period?

49. A ball of mass 100 g and having a charge of $4{\cdot}9 \times 10^{-5}$ C is released from rest in a region where a horizontal electric field of $2{\cdot}0 \times 10^{4}$ N C^{-1} exists. (a) Find the resultant force acting on the ball. (b) What will be the path of the ball ? (c) Where will the ball be at the end of 2 s ?

50. The bob of a simple pendulum has a mass of 40 g and a positive charge of $4{\cdot}0 \times 10^{-6}$ C. It makes 20 oscillations in 45 s. A vertical electric field pointing upward and of magnitude $2{\cdot}5 \times 10^{4}$ N C^{-1} is switched on. How much time will it now take to complete 20 oscillations ?

51. A block of mass m having a charge q is placed on a smooth horizontal table and is connected to a wall through an unstressed spring of spring constant k as shown in figure (29-E1). A horizontal electric field E parallel to the spring is switched on. Find the amplitude of the resulting SHM of the block.

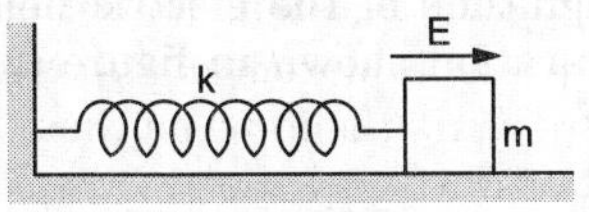

Figure 29-E1

52. A block of mass m containing a net positive charge q is placed on a smooth horizontal table which terminates in a vertical wall as shown in figure (29-E2). The distance of the block from the wall is d. A horizontal electric field E towards right is switched on. Assuming elastic collisions (if any) find the time period of the resulting oscillatory motion. Is it a simple harmonic motion ?

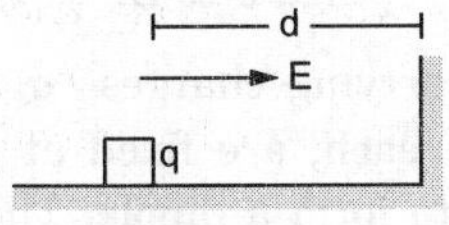

Figure 29-E2

53. A uniform electric field of 10 N C^{-1} exists in the vertically downward direction. Find the increase in the electric potential as one goes up through a height of 50 cm.

54. 12 J of work has to be done against an existing electric field to take a charge of 0·01 C from A to B. How much is the potential difference $V_B - V_A$?

55. Two equal charges, $2{\cdot}0 \times 10^{-7}$ C each, are held fixed at a separation of 20 cm. A third charge of equal magnitude is placed midway between the two charges. It is now moved to a point 20 cm from both the charges. How much work is done by the electric field during the process ?

56. An electric field of 20 N C^{-1} exists along the x-axis in space. Calculate the potential difference $V_B - V_A$ where the points A and B are given by,
(a) $A = (0, 0)$; $B = (4\text{ m}, 2\text{ m})$
(b) $A = (4\text{ m}, 2\text{ m})$; $B = (6\text{ m}, 5\text{ m})$
(c) $A = (0, 0)$; $B = (6\text{ m}, 5\text{ m})$.
Do you find any relation between the answers of parts (a), (b) and (c) ?

57. Consider the situation of the previous problem. A charge of $-2{\cdot}0 \times 10^{-4}$ C is moved from the point A to the point B. Find the change in electrical potential energy $U_B - U_A$ for the cases (a), (b) and (c).

58. An electric field $\vec{E} = (\vec{i}\,20 + \vec{j}\,30)$ N C^{-1} exists in the space. If the potential at the origin is taken to be zero, find the potential at (2 m, 2 m).

59. An electric field $\vec{E} = \vec{i}Ax$ exists in the space, where $A = 10$ V m^{-2}. Take the potential at (10 m, 20 m) to be zero. Find the potential at the origin.

60. The electric potential existing in space is $V(x, y, z) = A(xy + yz + zx)$. (a) Write the dimensional formula of A. (b) Find the expression for the electric field. (c) If A is 10 SI units, find the magnitude of the electric field at (1 m, 1 m, 1 m).

61. Two charged particles, having equal charges of $2{\cdot}0 \times 10^{-5}$ C each, are brought from infinity to within a separation of 10 cm. Find the increase in the electric potential energy during the process.

62. Some equipotential surfaces are shown in figure (29-E3). What can you say about the magnitude and the direction of the electric field ?

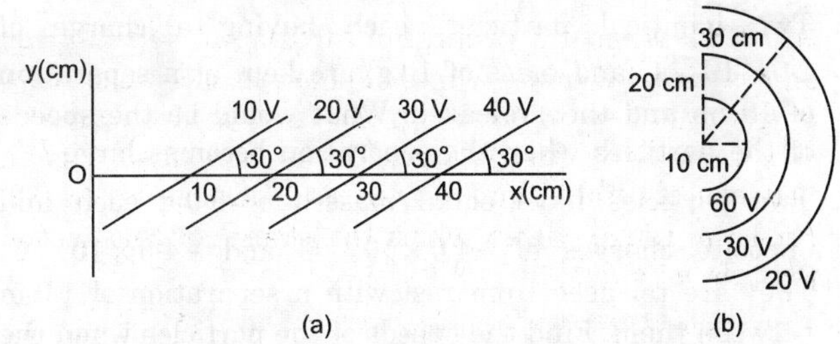

Figure 29-E3

63. Consider a circular ring of radius r, uniformly charged with linear charge density λ. Find the electric potential at a point on the axis at a distance x from the centre of the ring. Using this expression for the potential, find the electric field at this point.

64. An electric field of magnitude 1000 N C^{-1} is produced between two parallel plates having a separation of 2·0 cm as shown in figure (29-E4). (a) What is the potential difference between the plates ? (b) With what minimum speed should an electron be projected from the lower plate in the direction of the field so that it may reach the upper plate ? (c) Suppose the electron is projected from the lower plate with the speed calculated in part (b). The direction of projection makes an angle of 60° with the field. Find the maximum height reached by the electron.

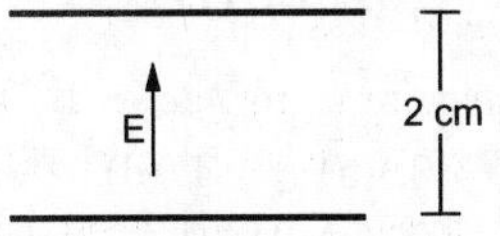

Figure 29-E4

65. A uniform field of 2·0 N C^{-1} exists in space in x-direction. (a) Taking the potential at the origin to be zero, write an expression for the potential at a general point (x, y, z). (b) At which points, the potential is 25 V ? (c) If the potential at the origin is taken to be 100 V, what will be the expression for the potential at a general point ? (d) What will be the potential at the origin if the potential at infinity is taken to be zero ? Is it practical to choose the potential at infinity to be zero ?

66. How much work has to be done in assembling three charged particles at the vertices of an equilateral triangle as shown in figure (29-E5) ?

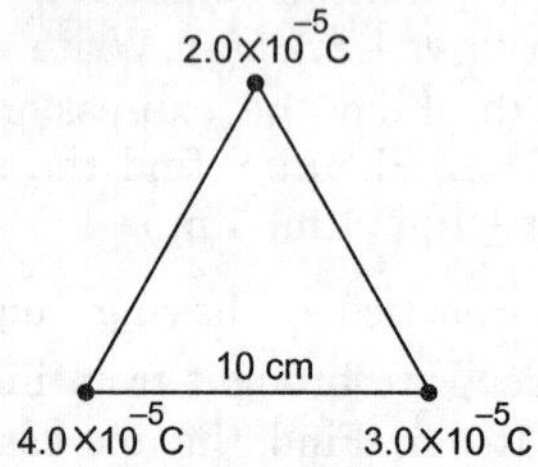

Figure 29-E5

67. The kinetic energy of a charged particle decreases by 10 J as it moves from a point at potential 100 V to a point at potential 200 V. Find the charge on the particle.

68. Two identical particles, each having a charge of $2{\cdot}0 \times 10^{-4}$ C and mass of 10 g, are kept at a separation of 10 cm and then released. What would be the speeds of the particles when the separation becomes large ?

69. Two particles have equal masses of 5·0 g each and opposite charges of $+4{\cdot}0 \times 10^{-5}$ C and $-4{\cdot}0 \times 10^{-5}$ C. They are released from rest with a separation of 1·0 m between them. Find the speeds of the particles when the separation is reduced to 50 cm.

70. A sample of HCl gas is placed in an electric field of $2{\cdot}5 \times 10^{4}$ N C^{-1}. The dipole moment of each HCl molecule is $3{\cdot}4 \times 10^{-30}$ Cm. Find the maximum torque that can act on a molecule.

71. Two particles A and B, having opposite charges $2{\cdot}0 \times 10^{-6}$ C and $-2{\cdot}0 \times 10^{-6}$ C, are placed at a separation of 1·0 cm. (a) Write down the electric dipole moment of this pair. (b) Calculate the electric field at a point on the axis of the dipole 1·0 m away from the centre. (c) Calculate the electric field at a point on the perpendicular bisector of the dipole and 1·0 m away from the centre.

72. Three charges are arranged on the vertices of an equilateral triangle as shown in figure (29-E6). Find the dipole moment of the combination.

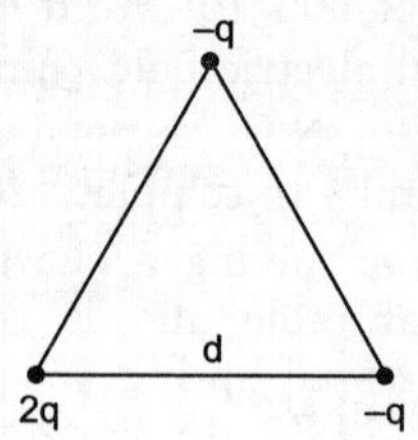

Figure 29-E6

73. Find the magnitude of the electric field at the point P in the configuration shown in figure (29-E7) for $d >> a$. Take $2qa = p$.

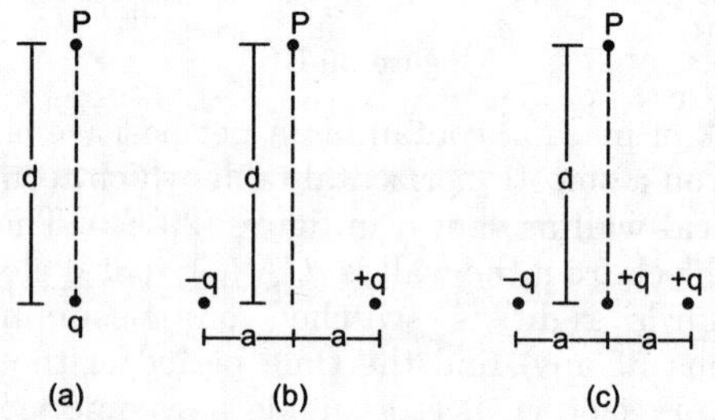

Figure 29-E7

74. Two particles, carrying charges $-q$ and $+q$ and having equal masses m each, are fixed at the ends of a light rod of length a to form a dipole. The rod is clamped at an end and is placed in a uniform electric field E with the axis of the dipole along the electric field. The rod is slightly tilted and then released. Neglecting gravity find the time period of small oscillations.

75. Assume that each atom in a copper wire contributes one free electron. Estimate the number of free electrons in a copper wire having a mass of 6·4 g (take the atomic weight of copper to be 64 g mol^{-1}).

□

ANSWERS

OBJECTIVE I

1. (c)	2. (d)	3. (a)	4. (d)	5. (a)	6. (d)
7. (a)	8. (c)	9. (a)			

OBJECTIVE II

1. (a)	2. (c), (d)	3. none
4. (b), (c)	5. (b), (d)	6. (d)
7. (b)	8. (c)	

EXERCISES

1. $I^2M^{-1}L^{-3}T^4$
2. $2·25 \times 10^3$ N
3. $4·3 \times 10^3$ m
4. $2·3 \times 10^{-4}$ C
5. 230 N
6. 5·9 cm from the larger charge in between the two charges
7. 34·1 cm from the larger charge on the line joining the charge in the side of the smaller charge
8. $2·3 \times 10^{-24}$ N
9. $3·35 \times 10^{25}$, $5·35 \times 10^6$ C
10. $2·56 \times 10^{25}$ N
11. 1·2 N
12. 2×10^{11}
13. $3·05 \times 10^{-9}$ N
14. $1·23 \times 10^{36}$
15. (a) ML^3T^{-2}, L^{-1}, N m^2, m^{-1} (b) $3·4 \times 10^{-26}$ N m^2
16. 24·9 N at 30° with the extended sides from the charge under consideration
17. 27·5 N at 45° with the extended sides of the square from the charge under consideration
18. $8·2 \times 10^{-8}$ N
19. $2·18 \times 10^6$ m s^{-1}
20. $4·95 \times 10^5$ N
21. $3·6 \times 10^{-6}$ N
22. (a) 0·144 N
    (b) zero, 0·095 N away from the other charge
    (c) 0·986 N and (d) 0·95 m s^{-2} perpendicular to the string and going away from the other charge
23. 8·2 g, $8·2 \times 10^{-2}$ N
24. $4·17 \times 10^{-8}$ C
25. $\dfrac{q^2 \cot\theta}{16\pi\varepsilon_0 gl^2 \sin^2\theta}$
26. $5·4 \times 10^{-9}$ C
27. $-(6 - 4\sqrt{2})\, q$, between q and $2q$ at a distance of $(\sqrt{2} - 1)\, d$ from q
28. $3·6 \times 10^{-6}$ m
29. between $\pm\, 8·71 \times 10^{-8}$ C
30. 27 cm from the bottom
31. $d/2\sqrt{2}$, $3·08 \dfrac{Qq}{4\pi\varepsilon_0 d^2}$
32. (a) $\dfrac{Qqx}{2\pi\varepsilon_0 \left(x^2 + \dfrac{d^2}{4}\right)^{3/2}}$ (c) $\left[\dfrac{m\pi^3\varepsilon_0 d^3}{Qq}\right]^{\frac{1}{2}}$
33. time period $= \left[\dfrac{\pi^3\varepsilon_0 md^3}{2Qq}\right]^{\frac{1}{2}}$
34. $1·5 \times 10^3$ N C^{-1}
35. (a) 48·3 cm from A along BA
    (b) 20 cm from A along BA and $\dfrac{20}{3}$ cm from A along AB
36. $8·9 \times 10^{-11}$ C
37. 65·3 N C^{-1}, upward
38. zero, $2·3 \times 10^3$ V
39. $\left[\dfrac{16\pi^3\varepsilon_0 mR^3}{Qq}\right]^{1/2}$
40. $\dfrac{Q}{2\varepsilon_0 L^2}$
41. $5·2 \times 10^7$ N C^{-1}
42. $R/\sqrt{2}$
43. zero
44. $\dfrac{QdL}{8\pi^2\varepsilon_0 a^3}$
45. $\dfrac{q}{4\pi\varepsilon_0 d^2}$ towards the charge q
46. $8·8 \times 10^{-4}$ N
47. $\dfrac{mu^2}{2qE}$
48. (a) 3·0 N, $9·8 \times 10^{-3}$ N (b) $1·63 \times 10^{-2}$ s
    (c) 49·0 m s^{-1} (d) 1·20 J
49. (a) 1·4 N making an angle of 45° with $\vec{g}$ and $\vec{E}$
    (b) straight line along the resultant force
    (c) 28 m from the starting point on the line of motion
50. 52 s
51. qE/k
52. $\sqrt{\dfrac{8\,md}{qE}}$
53. 5 V
54. 1200 volts
55. $3·6 \times 10^{-3}$ J
56. (a) −80 V (b) −40 V (c) −120 V
57. 0·016 J, 0·008 J, 0·024 J
58. −100 V
59. 500 V
60. (a) $MT^{-3}I^{-1}$ (b) $-A\,\{\vec{i}\,(y+z) + \vec{j}\,(z+x) + \vec{k}\,(x+y)\}$
    (c) 35 N C^{-1}
61. 36 J
62. (a) 200 V m^{-1} making an angle 120° with the x-axis
    (b) radially outward, decreasing with distance as $E = \dfrac{6\ \text{Vm}}{r^2}$.
63. $\dfrac{r\lambda}{2\varepsilon_0 (r^2 + x^2)^{1/2}}$, $\dfrac{r\lambda x}{2\varepsilon_0 (r^2 + x^2)^{3/2}}$

64. (a) 20 V (b) $2{\cdot}65 \times 10^{6}$ m s^{-1} (c) 0·50 cm

65. (a) $-(2{\cdot}0 \text{ V m}^{-1})\, x$
 (b) points on the plane $x = -12{\cdot}5$ m
 (c) $100 \text{ V} - (2{\cdot}0 \text{ V m}^{-1})\, x$
 (d) infinity

66. 234 J

67. 0·1 C

68. 600 m s^{-1}

69. 54 m s^{-1} for each particle

70. $8{\cdot}5 \times 10^{-26}$ Nm

71. (a) $2{\cdot}0 \times 10^{-8}$ Cm (b) 360 N C^{-1} (c) 180 N C^{-1}

72. $qd\sqrt{3}$, along the bisector of the angle at $2q$, away from the triangle

73. (a) $\dfrac{q}{4\pi\varepsilon_0 d^2}$ (b) $\dfrac{p}{4\pi\varepsilon_0 d^3}$ (c) $\dfrac{1}{4\pi\varepsilon_0 d^3}\sqrt{q^2 d^2 + p^2}$

74. $2\pi\sqrt{\dfrac{ma}{qE}}$

75. 6×10^{22}

□

CHAPTER 30

GAUSS'S LAW

Gauss's law is one of the fundamental laws of physics. It relates the electric field to the charge distribution which has produced this field. In section (30.1) we define the flux of an electric field and in the next section we discuss the concept of a solid angle. These will be needed to state and understand Gauss's law.

30.1 FLUX OF AN ELECTRIC FIELD THROUGH A SURFACE

Consider a hypothetical plane surface of area ΔS and suppose a uniform electric field $\vec{E}$ exists in the space (figure 30.1). Draw a line perpendicular to the surface and call one side of it, the positive normal to the surface. Suppose, the electric field $\vec{E}$ makes an angle θ with the positive normal.

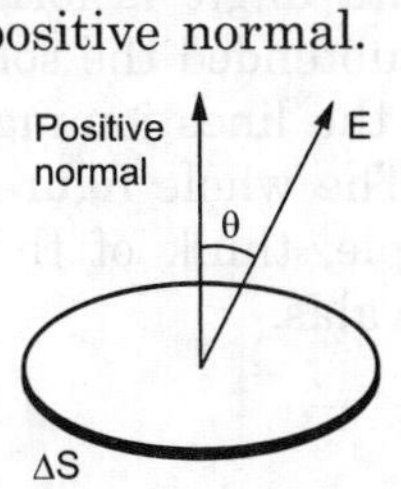

Figure 30.1

The quantity

$$\Delta\Phi = E\,\Delta S\cos\theta$$

is called *the flux of the electric field through the chosen surface.* If we draw a vector of magnitude ΔS along the positive normal, it is called the *area-vector* $\Delta\vec{S}$ corresponding to the area ΔS. One can then write

$$\Delta\Phi = \vec{E}\cdot\Delta\vec{S}.$$

Remember, the direction of the area-vector is always along the normal to the corresponding surface. If the field $\vec{E}$ is perpendicular to the surface, it is parallel to the area-vector. If $\vec{E}$ is along the positive normal, $\theta = 0$, and $\Delta\Phi = E\,\Delta S$. If it is opposite to the positive normal, $\theta = \pi$, and $\Delta\Phi = -E\,\Delta S$. If the electric field is parallel to the surface, $\theta = \pi/2$, and $\Delta\Phi = 0$.

Flux is a scalar quantity and may be added using the rules of scalar addition. Thus, if the surface ΔS has two parts ΔS_1 and ΔS_2, the flux through ΔS equals the flux through ΔS_1 plus the flux through ΔS_2. This gives us a clue to define the flux through surfaces which are not plane, as well as the flux when the field is not uniform. We divide the given surface into smaller parts so that each part is approximately plane and the variation of electric field over each part can be neglected. We calculate the flux through each part separately, using the relation $\Delta\Phi = \vec{E}\cdot\Delta\vec{S}$ and then add the flux through all the parts. Using the techniques of integration, the flux is

$$\Phi = \int \vec{E}\cdot d\vec{S}$$

where integration has to be performed over the entire surface through which the flux is required.

The surface under consideration may be a closed one, enclosing a volume, such as a spherical surface. A hemispherical surface is an open surface. A cylindrical surface is also open. A cylindrical surface plus two plane surfaces perpendicular to the axis enclose a volume and these three taken together form a closed surface. When flux through a closed surface is required, we use a small circular sign on the integration symbol;

$$\Phi = \oint \vec{E}\cdot d\vec{S}.$$

It is customary to take the outward normal as positive in this case.

Example 30.1

A square frame of edge 10 cm *is placed with its positive normal making an angle of* 60° *with a uniform electric field of* $20\ \mathrm{V\,m^{-1}}$. *Find the flux of the electric field through the surface bounded by the frame.*

Solution : The surface considered is plane and the electric field is uniform (figure 30.2). Hence, the flux is

$$\Delta\Phi = \vec{E}\cdot\Delta\vec{S}$$
$$= E\,\Delta S\cos 60°$$

$$= (20\ \text{V m}^{-1})\ (0{\cdot}01\ \text{m}^2)\left(\frac{1}{2}\right) = 0{\cdot}1\ \text{Vm}.$$

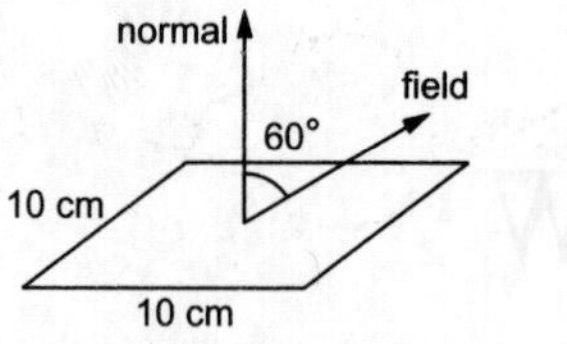

Figure 30.2

Example 30.2

A charge q is placed at the centre of a sphere. Taking outward normal as positive, find the flux of the electric field through the surface of the sphere due to the enclosed charge.

Solution :

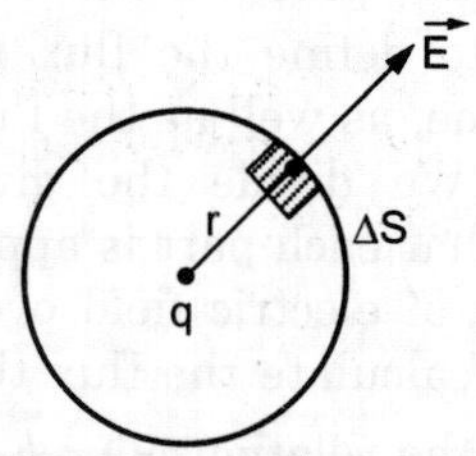

Figure 30.3

Let us take a small element ΔS on the surface of the sphere (Figure 30.3). The electric field here is radially outward and has the magnitude

$$\frac{q}{4\pi\varepsilon_0 r^2},$$

where r is the radius of the sphere. As the positive normal is also outward, $\theta = 0$ and the flux through this part is

$$\Delta\Phi = \vec{E}{\cdot}\Delta\vec{S} = \frac{q}{4\pi\varepsilon_0 r^2}\,\Delta S.$$

Summing over all the parts of the spherical surface,

$$\Phi = \sum \Delta\Phi = \frac{q}{4\pi\varepsilon_0 r^2}\sum \Delta S = \frac{q}{4\pi\varepsilon_0 r^2}\,4\pi r^2 = \frac{q}{\varepsilon_0}.$$

Example 30.3

A uniform electric field exists in space. Find the flux of this field through a cylindrical surface with the axis parallel to the field.

Solution :

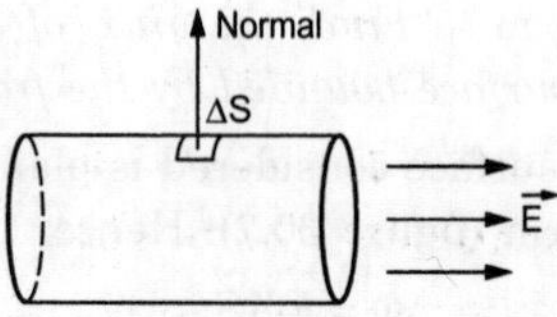

Figure 30.4

Consider figure (30.4) and take a small area ΔS on the cylindrical surface. The normal to this area will be perpendicular to the axis of the cylinder. But the electric field is parallel to the axis and hence

$$\Delta\Phi = \vec{E}{\cdot}\Delta\vec{S} = E\,\Delta S\cos(\pi/2) = 0.$$

This is true for each small part of the cylindrical surface. Summing over the entire surface, the total flux is zero.

30.2 SOLID ANGLE

Solid angle is a generalisation of the plane angle. In figure (30.5a) we show a plane curve AB. The end points A and B are joined to the point O. We say that the curve AB subtends an *angle* or a *plane angle* at O. An angle is formed at O by the two lines OA and OB passing through O.

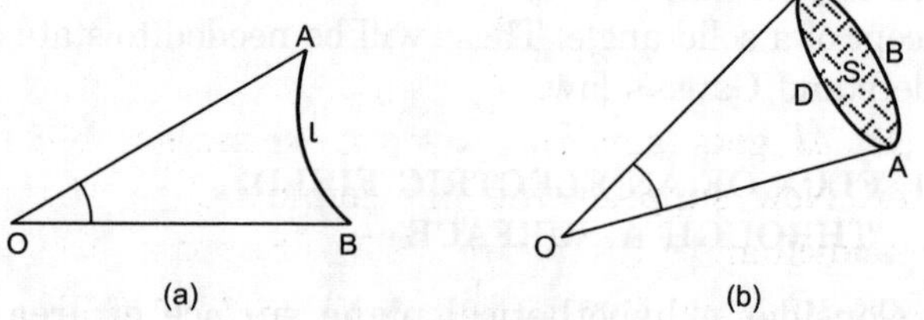

Figure 30.5

To construct a solid angle, we start with a surface S (figure 30.5b) and join all the points on the periphery such as A, B, C, D, etc., with the given point O. We then say that a *solid angle* is formed at O and that the surface S has subtended the solid angle. The solid angle is formed by the lines joining the points on the periphery with O. The whole figure looks like a cone. As a typical example, think of the paper containers used by Moongfaliwalas.

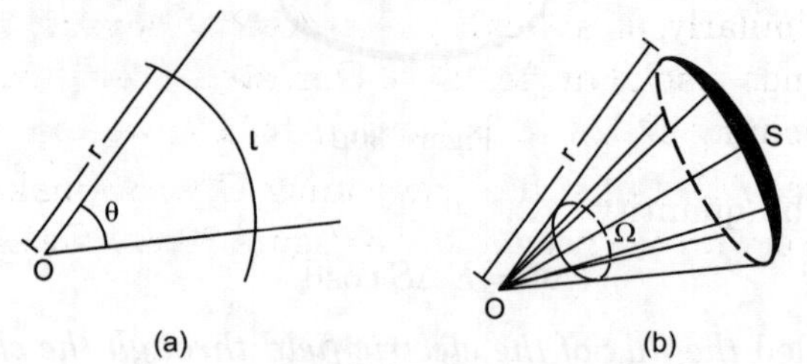

Figure 30.6

How do we measure a solid angle ? Let us consider how do we measure a plane angle. See figure (30.6a). We draw a circle of any radius r with the centre at O and measure the length l of the arc intercepted by the angle. The angle θ is then defined as $\theta = l/r$. In order to measure a solid angle at the point O (figure 30.6b), we draw a sphere of any radius r with O as the centre and measure the area S of the part of the sphere intercepted by the cone. The solid angle Ω is then defined as

$$\Omega = S/r^2.$$

Note that this definition makes the solid angle a dimensionless quantity. It is independent of the radius of the sphere drawn.

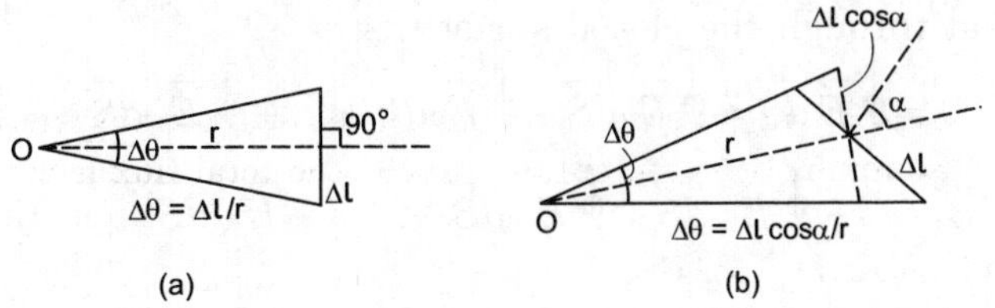

Figure 30.7

Next, consider a plane angle subtended at a point O by a small line segment Δl (figure 30.7a). Suppose, the line joining O to the middle point of Δl is perpendicular to Δl. As the segment is small, we can approximately write

$$\Delta\theta = \frac{\Delta l}{r}.$$

As Δl gets smaller, the approximation becomes better. Now suppose, the line joining O to Δl is not perpendicluar to Δl (figure 30.7b). Suppose, this line makes an angle α with the perpendicular to Δl. The angle subtended by Δl at O is

$$\Delta\theta = \frac{\Delta l \cos\alpha}{r}.$$

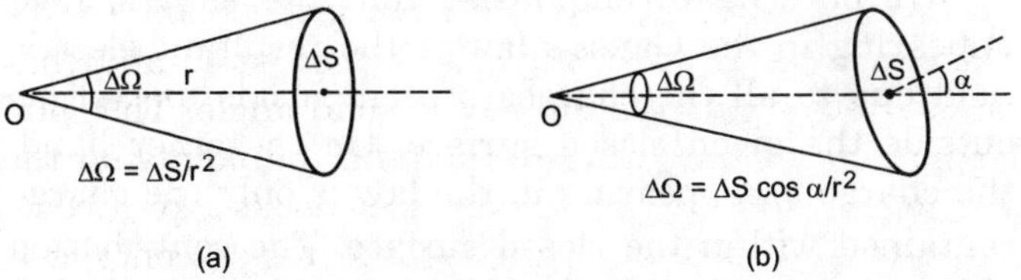

Figure 30.8

Similarly, if a small plane area ΔS (figure 30.8a) subtends a solid angle $\Delta\Omega$ at O in such a way that the line joining O to ΔS is normal to ΔS, we can write $\Delta\Omega = \Delta S/r^2$. But if the line joining O to ΔS makes an angle α with the normal to ΔS (figure 30.8b), we should write

$$\Delta\Omega = \frac{\Delta S \cos\alpha}{r^2}.$$

A complete circle subtends an angle

$$\theta = \frac{l}{r} = \frac{2\pi r}{r} = 2\pi$$

at the centre. In fact, any closed curve subtends an angle 2π at any of the internal points. Similarly, a complete sphere subtends a solid angle

$$\Omega = \frac{S}{r^2} = \frac{4\pi r^2}{r^2} = 4\pi$$

at the centre. Also, any closed surface subtends a solid angle 4π at any internal point.

How much is the angle subtended by a closed plane curve at an external point ?

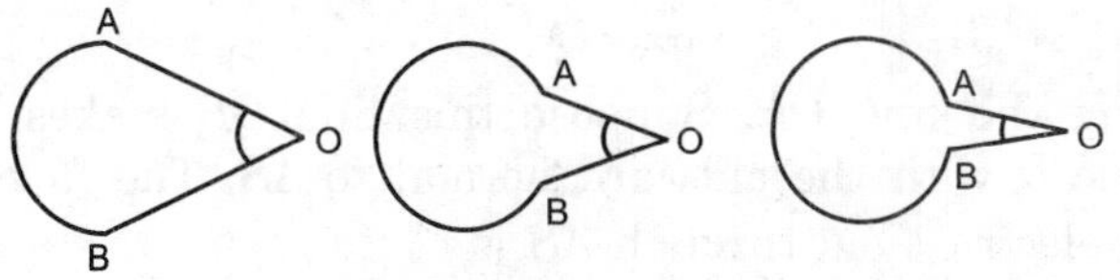

Figure 30.9

See figure (30.9). As we gradually close the curve, the angle finally diminishes to zero. A closed curve subtends zero angle at an external point. Similarly, a closed surface subtends zero solid angle at an external point.

30.3 GAUSS'S LAW AND ITS DERIVATION FROM COULOMB'S LAW

The statement of the Gauss's law may be written as follows:

The flux of the net electric field through a closed surface equals the net charge enclosed by the surface divided by ε_0. In symbols,

$$\oint \vec{E}\cdot d\vec{S} = \frac{q_{in}}{\varepsilon_0} \qquad \ldots (30.1)$$

where q_{in} is the net charge enclosed by the surface through which the flux is calculated.

It should be carefully noted that the electric field on the left-hand side of equation (30.1) is the resultant electric field due to all the charges existing in the space, whereas, the charge appearing on the right-hand side includes only those which are inside the closed surface.

Gauss's law is taken as a fundamental law of nature, a law whose validity is shown by experiments. However, historically Coulomb's law was discovered before Gauss's law and it is possible to derive Gauss's law from Coulomb's law.

Proof of Gauss's Law (Assuming Coulomb's Law)

Flux due to an internal charge

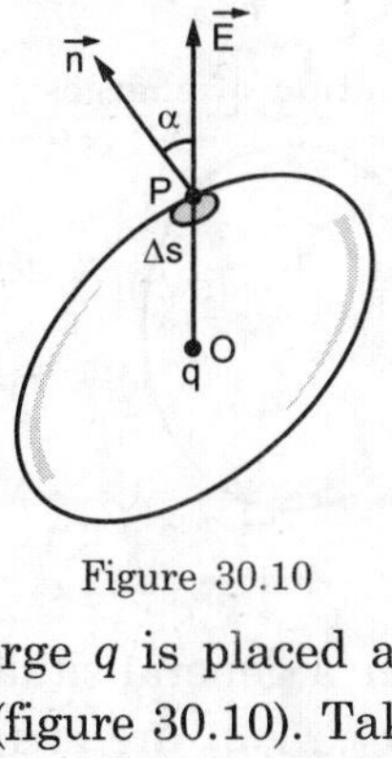

Figure 30.10

Suppose a charge q is placed at a point O inside a "closed" surface (figure 30.10). Take a point P on the surface and consider a small area ΔS on the surface around P. Let $OP = r$. The electric field at P due to the charge q is

$$E = \frac{q}{4\pi\varepsilon_0 r^2}$$

along the line OP. Suppose this line OP makes an angle α with the outward normal to ΔS. The flux of the electric field through ΔS is

$$\Delta\Phi = \vec{E}\cdot\Delta\vec{S} = E\,\Delta S\cos\alpha$$

$$= \frac{q}{4\pi\varepsilon_0 r^2}\Delta S\cos\alpha$$

$$= \frac{q}{4\pi\varepsilon_0}\Delta\Omega$$

where $\Delta\Omega = \frac{\Delta S\cos\alpha}{r^2}$ is the solid angle subtended by ΔS at O. The flux through the entire surface is

$$\Phi = \Sigma\frac{q}{4\pi\varepsilon_0}\Delta\Omega = \frac{q}{4\pi\varepsilon_0}\Sigma\,\Delta\Omega.$$

The sum over $\Delta\Omega$ is the total solid angle subtended by the closed surface at the internal point O and hence is equal to 4π.

The total flux of the electric field due to the internal charge q through the closed surface is, therefore,

$$\Phi = \frac{q}{4\pi\varepsilon_0}4\pi = \frac{q}{\varepsilon_0}. \quad \ldots \text{(i)}$$

Flux due to an external charge

Now, suppose a charge q is placed at a point O outside the closed surface. The flux of the electric field due to q through the small area ΔS is again

$$\Delta\Phi = \frac{q}{4\pi\varepsilon_0}\frac{\Delta S\cos\alpha}{r^2} = \frac{q}{4\pi\varepsilon_0}\Delta\Omega.$$

When we sum over all the small area elements of the closed surface we get $\Sigma\Delta\Omega = 0$ as this is the total solid angle subtended by the closed surface at an external point. Hence,

$$\Phi = 0. \quad \ldots \text{(ii)}$$

Flux due to a combination of charges

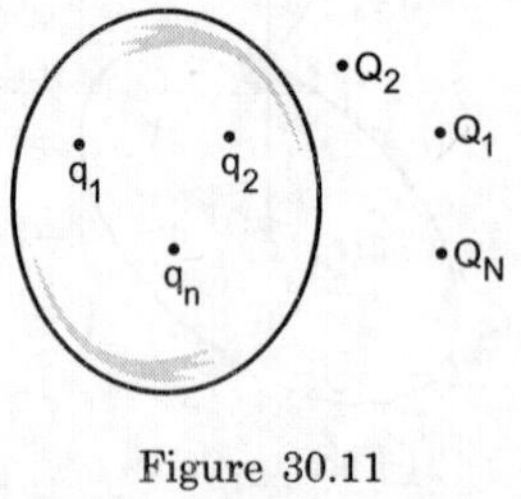

Figure 30.11

Finally, consider a general situation (figure 30.11) where charges q_1, q_2, …, q_n are inside a closed surface and charges Q_1, Q_2, …, Q_N are outside it. The resultant electric field at any point is

$$\vec{E} = \vec{E}_1 + \vec{E}_2 + \ldots + \vec{E}_n + \vec{E'}_1 + \vec{E'}_2 + \ldots + \vec{E'}_N$$

where E_i and E'_i are the fields due to q_i and Q_i respectively. Thus, the flux of the resultant electric field through the closed surface is

$$\Phi = \oint \vec{E}\cdot d\vec{S} = \oint \vec{E}_1\cdot d\vec{S} + \oint \vec{E}_2\cdot d\vec{S} + \ldots + \oint \vec{E}_n\cdot d\vec{S}$$

$$+ \oint \vec{E'}_1\cdot d\vec{S} + \oint \vec{E'}_2\cdot d\vec{S} + \ldots + \oint \vec{E'}_N\cdot d\vec{S}. \quad \ldots \text{(iii)}$$

Now, $\oint \vec{E}_i\cdot d\vec{S}$ is the flux of the electric field due to the charge q_i only. As this charge is inside the closed surface, from (i), it is equal to q_i/ε_0. Also, $\oint \vec{E'}_i\cdot d\vec{S}$ is the flux of the electric field due to the charge Q_i which is outside the closed surface. This flux is, therefore, zero from (ii). Using these results in (iii),

$$\Phi = \frac{q_1}{\varepsilon_0} + \frac{q_2}{\varepsilon_0} + \ldots + \frac{q_n}{\varepsilon_0} + 0 + \ldots + 0$$

or, $$\Phi = \frac{1}{\varepsilon_0}\Sigma\, q_i$$

or, $$\oint \vec{E}\cdot d\vec{S} = \frac{q_{in}}{\varepsilon_0}.$$

This completes the derivation of Gauss's law (equation 30.1).

We once again emphasise that the electric field appearing in the Gauss's law is the resultant electric field due to all the charges present inside as well as outside the given closed surface. On the other hand, the charge q_{in} appearing in the law is only the charge contained within the closed surface. The contribution of the charges outside the closed surface in producing the flux is zero. A surface on which Gauss's law is applied, is sometimes called the *Gaussian surface.*

Example 30.4

A charge Q is distributed uniformly on a ring of radius r. A sphere of equal radius r is constructed with its centre at the periphery of the ring (figure 30.12). Find the flux of the electric field through the surface of the sphere.

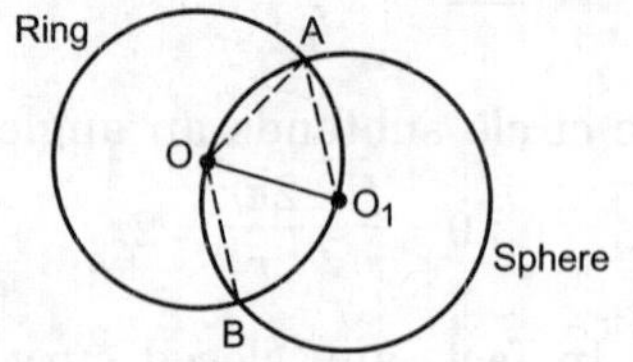

Figure 30.12

Solution : From the geometry of the figure, $OA = OO_1$ and $O_1A = O_1O$. Thus, OAO_1 is an equilateral triangle. Hence $\angle AOO_1 = 60°$ or $\angle AOB = 120°$.

The arc AO_1B of the ring subtends an angle 120° at the centre O. Thus, one third of the ring is inside the sphere.

The charge enclosed by the sphere $= \frac{Q}{3}$. From Gauss's law, the flux of the electric field through the surface of the sphere is $\frac{Q}{3\,\varepsilon_0}$.

30.4 APPLICATIONS OF GAUSS'S LAW

(A) Charged Conductor

As discussed earlier, an electric conductor has a large number of free electrons and when placed in an electric field, these electrons redistribute themselves to make the field zero at all the points inside the conductor.

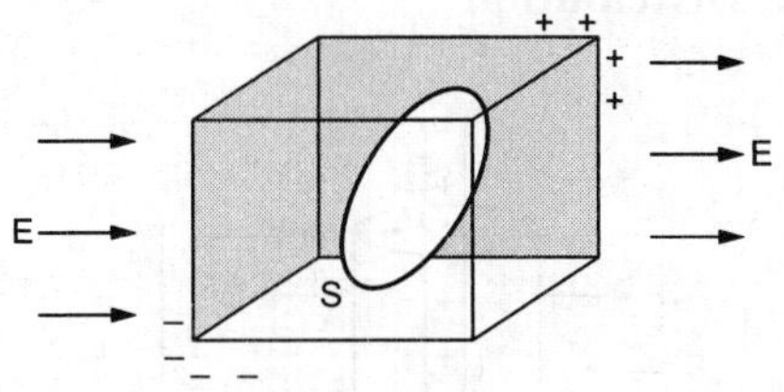

Figure 30.13

Consider a charged conductor placed in an electric field (figure 30.13). We assume that the redistribution of free electrons (if any) is complete. Draw a closed surface S going through the interior points only. As the electric field at all the points of this surface is zero (they are interior points), the flux $\oint \vec{E} \cdot d\vec{S}$ is also zero. But from Gauss's law, this equals the charge contained inside the surface divided by ε_0. Hence, the charge enclosed by the surface is zero. This shows that any volume completely inside a conductor is electrically neutral. If a charge is injected anywhere in the conductor, it must come over to the surface of the conductor so that the interior is always charge free. Also, if the conductor has a cavity, the charge must come over to the outer surface.

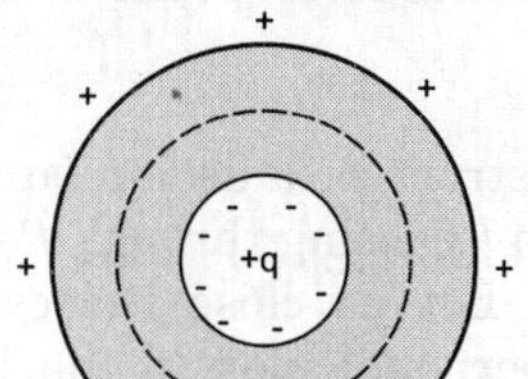

Figure 30.14

However, if a charge is placed within the cavity as in figure (30.14), the inner surface cannot be charge free. Taking the Gaussian surface S as shown, $\vec{E} = 0$ at all the points of this surface and hence $\oint \vec{E} \cdot d\vec{S} = 0$. This ensures that the charge contained in S is zero and if a charge $+q$ is placed in the cavity, there must be a charge $-q$ on the inner surface of the conductor. If the conductor is neutral, i.e., no charge is placed on it, a charge $+q$ will appear on the outer surface.

If there is a cavity in the conductor and no charge is placed in the cavity, the electric field at all the points in the cavity is zero. This can be proved using a little more advanced mathematics.

(B) Electric Field due to a Uniformly Charged Sphere

Suppose a total charge Q is uniformly distributed in a spherical volume of radius R and we are required to find the electric field at a point P which is at a distance r from the centre of the charge distribution.

Field at an outside point

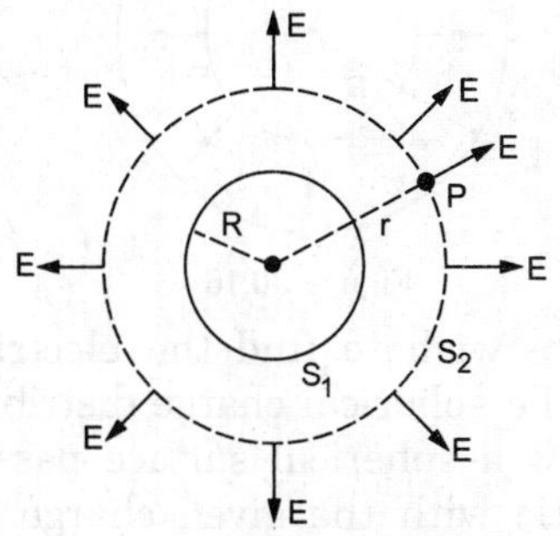

Figure 30.15

For a point P outside the charge distribution (figure 30.15), we have $r > R$. Draw a spherical surface passing through the point P and concentric with the charge distribution. Take this to be the Gaussian surface. The electric field is radial by symmetry and if Q is positive the field is outward. Also, its magnitude at all the points of the Gaussian surface must be equal. Let this magnitude be E. This is also the magnitude of the field at P. As the field $\vec{E}$ is normal to the surface element everywhere, $\vec{E} \cdot d\vec{S} = E\,dS$ for each element. The flux of the electric field through this closed surface is

$$\Phi = \oint \vec{E} \cdot d\vec{S}$$

$$= \oint E\,dS = E \oint dS = E\,4\pi r^2.$$

This should be equal to the charge contained inside the Gaussian surface divided by ε_0. As the entire charge Q is contained inside the Gaussian surface, we get

$$E\,4\pi r^2 = Q/\varepsilon_0$$

or, $$E = \frac{Q}{4\pi\varepsilon_0 r^2}. \qquad \ldots (30.2)$$

The electric field due to a uniformly charged sphere at a point outside it, is identical with the field due to an equal point charge placed at the centre.

Notice the use of the argument of symmetry. All the points of the sphere through P are equivalent. No point on this surface has any special property which a different point does not have. That is why we could say that the field has the same magnitude E at all these points. Also, the field is radial at all the points. We have wisely chosen the Gaussian surface which has these properties. We could then easily evaluate the flux $\oint \vec{E} \cdot d\vec{S} = E\, 4\pi r^2$.

Field at an internal point

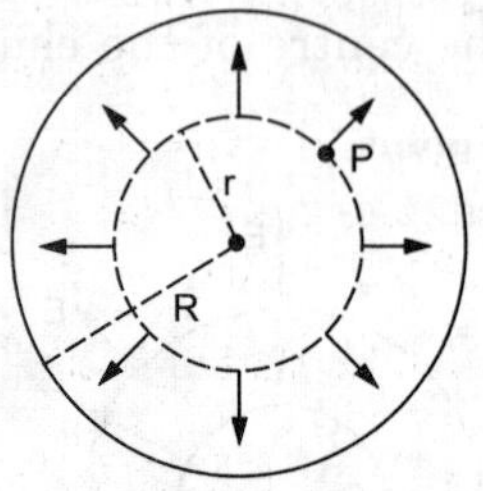

Figure 30.16

Suppose, we wish to find the electric field at a point P inside the spherical charge distribution (figure 30.16). We draw a spherical surface passing through P and concentric with the given charge distribution. The radius of this sphere will be r. All the points of this sphere are equivalent. By symmetry, the field is radial at all the points of this surface and has a constant magnitude E. The flux through this spherical surface is

$$\Phi = \oint \vec{E} \cdot d\vec{S}$$

$$= \oint E\, dS = E \oint dS = E\, 4\pi r^2. \quad \ldots \text{(i)}$$

Let us now calculate the total charge contained inside this spherical surface. As the charge is uniformly distributed within the given spherical volume, the charge per unit volume is $\frac{Q}{\frac{4}{3}\pi R^3}$. The volume enclosed by the Gaussian surface, through which the flux is calculated, is $\frac{4}{3}\pi r^3$. Hence, the charge enclosed is

$$\frac{Q}{\frac{4}{3}\pi R^3} \cdot \frac{4}{3}\pi r^3 = \frac{Q r^3}{R^3}.$$

Using Gauss's law and (i),

$$E\, 4\pi r^2 = \frac{Qr^3}{\varepsilon_0 R^3}$$

or, $$E = \frac{Qr}{4\pi\varepsilon_0 R^3}. \quad \ldots (30.3)$$

The electric field due to a uniformly charged sphere at an internal point is $\frac{Qr}{4\pi\varepsilon_0 R^3}$ *in radial direction.*

At the centre, $r = 0$ and hence $E = 0$. This is clear from the symmetry arguments as well. At the centre, all directions are equivalent. If the electric field is not zero, what can be its direction ? You cannot choose a unique direction. The field has to be zero. It is proportional to the distance r from the centre for the internal points. Equations (30.2) and (30.3) give the same value of the field at the surface, where $r = R$.

(C) Electric Field due to a Linear Charge Distribution

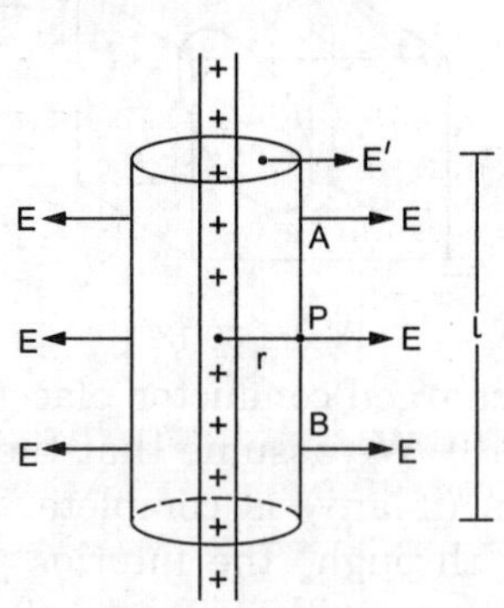

Figure 30.17

Consider a long line charge with a linear charge density (that is, charge per unit length) λ. We have to calculate the electric field at a point P which is at a distance r from the line charge (figure 30.17). What can be the direction of the electric field at P ? Can it be along PA ? If yes, then why not along PB ? PA and PB are equivalent to each other. In fact, the only unique direction through P is along the perpendicular to the line charge. The electric field must be along this direction. If the charge is positive, the field will be outward.

Now, we construct a Gaussian surface. We draw a cylinder of length l passing through P and coaxial with the line charge. Let us close the cylinder with two plane surfaces perpendicular to the line charge. The curved surface of the cylinder together with the two plane parallel surfaces constitutes a closed surface as shown in figure (30.17). We use this surface as the Gaussian surface.

All the points on the curved part of this Gaussian surface are at the same perpendicular distance from the line charge. All these points are equivalent. The electric field at all these points will have the same magnitude E as that at P. Also, the direction of the field at any point on the curved surface is normal to the line and hence normal to the cylindrical surface element there. The flux through the curved part is, therefore,

$$\int \vec{E}\cdot d\vec{S} = \int E\,dS = E\int dS = E\,2\pi rl.$$

Now, consider the flat parts of the Gaussian surface, that is, the lids of the cylinder. The electric field at any point is perpendicular to the line charge. The normal to any element on these plane surfaces is parallel to the line charge. Hence, the field and the area-vector make an angle of 90° with each other so that $\int \vec{E}\cdot d\vec{S} = 0$ on these parts. The total flux through the closed Gaussian surface is, therefore,

$$\oint \vec{E}\cdot d\vec{S} = E\,2\pi rl. \qquad \text{... (i)}$$

The charge enclosed in the Gaussian surface is λl as a length l of the line charge is inside the closed surface. Using Gauss's law and (i),

$$E\,2\pi rl = (\lambda l)/\varepsilon_0$$

or, $$E = \frac{\lambda}{2\pi\varepsilon_0\, r}\cdot \qquad \text{... (30.4)}$$

This is the field at a distance r from the line. It is directed away from the line if the charge is positive and towards the line if the charge is negative.

(D) Electric Field due to a Plane Sheet of Charge

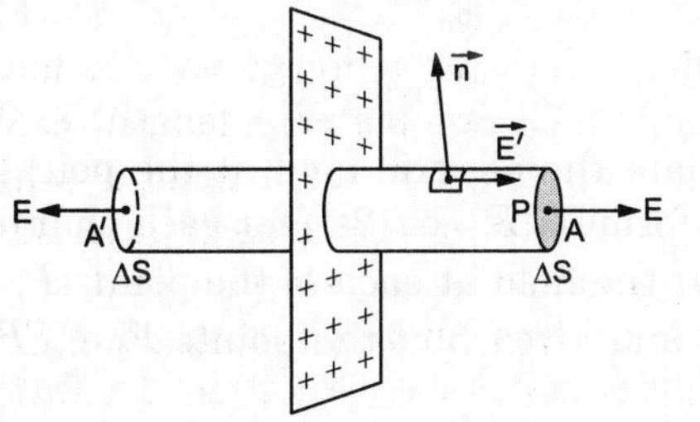

Figure 30.18

Consider a large plane sheet of charge with surface charge density (charge per unit area) σ. We have to find the electric field E at a point P in front of the sheet (Figure 30.18). What can be the direction of the electric field at P? The only unique direction we can identify is along the perpendicular to the plane. The field must be along this line. If the charge is positive, the field is away from the plane. Same is true for all points near the plane provided the sheet is large and the charge density is uniform. If these conditions are not fulfilled, the argument of symmetry may fail.

To calculate the field E at P, we choose a Gaussian surface as follows. Draw a plane surface A passing through P and parallel to the charge sheet. Draw a cylinder with this surface as a cross section and extend it to the other side of the plane charge sheet. Close the cylinder on the other side by a cross section A' such that A and A' are equidistant from the sheet. Also, A and A' have equal area ΔS. The cylinder together with its cross sectional areas forms a closed surface and we apply Gauss's law to this surface.

The electric field at all the points of A has the same magnitude E. The direction is along the positive normal to A. Thus, the flux of the electric field through A is

$$\Phi = \vec{E}\cdot\Delta\vec{S} = E\,\Delta S.$$

Note that the two sides of the charge sheet are equivalent in all respect. As A and A' are equidistant from the sheet, the electric field at any point of A' is also equal to E and is along the positive normal (that is, the outward normal) to A'. Hence, the flux of the electric field through A' is also $E\,\Delta S$. At the points on the curved surface, the field and the outward normal make an angle of 90° with each other and hence $\vec{E}\cdot\Delta\vec{S} = 0$. The total flux through the closed surface is

$$\Phi = \oint \vec{E}\cdot d\vec{S} = E\,\Delta S + E\,\Delta S + 0 = 2\,E\,\Delta S.$$

The area of the sheet enclosed in the cylinder is ΔS. The charge contained in the cylinder is, therefore, $\sigma\,\Delta S$. Hence from Gauss's law,

$$2\,E\Delta S = \frac{\sigma\,\Delta S}{\varepsilon_0}$$

or, $$E = \frac{\sigma}{2\varepsilon_0}\cdot \qquad \text{... (30.5)}$$

We see that the field is uniform and does not depend on the distance from the charge sheet. This is true as long as the sheet is large as compared to its distance from P.

(E) Electric Field near a Charged Conducting Surface

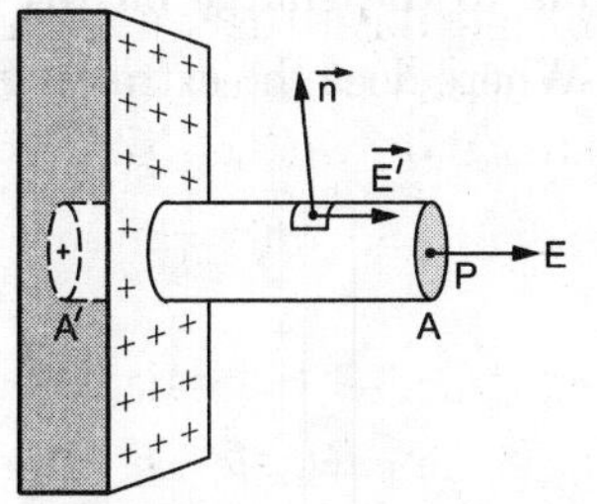

Figure 30.19

In figure (30.19), we show a large, plane conducting sheet. The surface on right has a uniform surface charge density σ. We have to find the electric field at a point P near this surface and outside the conductor. As we know, the conducting surface is an equipotential surface and the electric field near the surface is perpendicular to the surface. For positive charge on the surface, the field is away from the surface. To find the electric field, we construct a Gaussian surface as follows. Take a small plane surface A passing through the point P and parallel to the given conducting surface. Draw a cylinder with A as a cross section and terminate it with another plane surface A' parallel to A and lying in the interior of the conducting sheet.

If the electric field at P is E, the flux through the plane surface A is

$$\Phi = E\,\Delta S,$$

where ΔS is the area of A. At the curved parts of the cylinder, the electric field is either zero (inside the conductor) or is parallel to the curved surface (outside the conductor). The field $\vec{E}$ and the area-vector $\Delta\vec{S}$ are perpendicular to each other making $\vec{E}\cdot\Delta\vec{S} = 0$ at these outside points. The flux on the curved part is, therefore, zero. Also, the flux on A' is zero as the field inside the conductor is zero.

The total flux through the Gaussian surface constructed is, therefore, $E\,\Delta S$. The charge enclosed inside the closed surface is $\sigma\,\Delta S$ and hence from Gauss's law,

$$E\,\Delta S = \frac{\sigma\,\Delta S}{\varepsilon_0}$$

or, $$E = \frac{\sigma}{\varepsilon_0}\cdot \qquad \ldots (30.6)$$

The electric field near a charged conducting surface is σ/ε_0 *and it is normal to the surface.*

Compare this result with the field due to a plane sheet of charge of surface density σ (equation 30.5). The field E had a magnitude $\sigma/(2\varepsilon_0)$ in that case. Apparently, for a conductor also we have a plane sheet of charge of the same density but the field derived is σ/ε_0 and not $\sigma/(2\varepsilon_0)$. Consider the conducting sheet shown in figure (30.20). In fact, the field due to the charge on the right surface is indeed $\frac{\sigma}{2\varepsilon_0}$ at P. Where does the extra $\frac{\sigma}{2\varepsilon_0}$ field come from ?

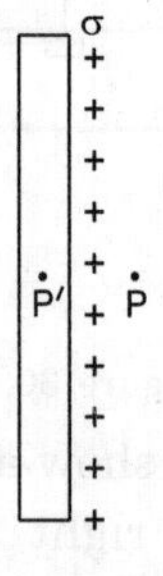

Figure 30.20

Consider a point P' inside the sheet as shown in figure (30.20). The electric field at this point due to the charge sheet on the right surface of the conductor is $\sigma/(2\varepsilon_0)$ towards left. But P' is a point inside the conductor and hence the field here must be zero. This means that the charge distribution shown in figure (30.20) is not complete as it does not ensure zero field inside the conductor. Apart from the surface charge of density σ shown in the figure, there must be other charges nearby. These other nearby charges must create a field at P' towards right so that the resultant field at P' becomes zero. These other charges also create a field $\sigma/(2\varepsilon_0)$ towards right at P which adds to the field due to the surface charge shown in figure (30.20). Thus, the field at P becomes

$$\frac{\sigma}{2\varepsilon_0} + \frac{\sigma}{2\varepsilon_0} = \frac{\sigma}{\varepsilon_0}$$

towards right. As Gauss's law gives the net field, equation (30.6) gives $E = \sigma/\varepsilon_0$ which is the actual field due to all the charges and not the field due to the surface charge only. As examples, we give in figure (30.21) some of the possible complete charge distributions which ensure zero field inside the conductor.

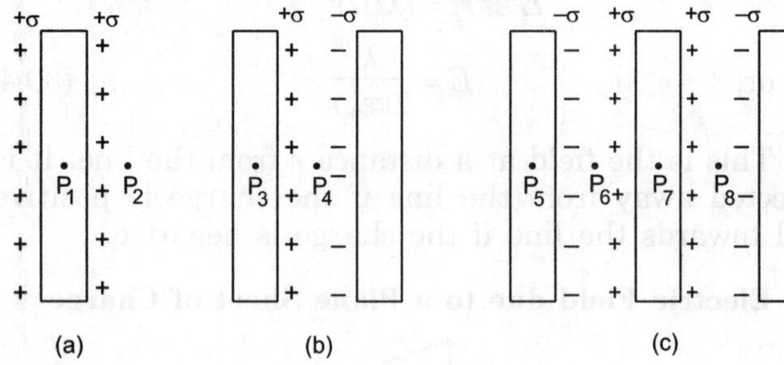

Figure 30.21

Calculate the electric field at the points indicated using the formula $E = \sigma/(2\varepsilon_0)$ for each charged surface. Verify that the field at each of the points P_1, P_3, P_5 and P_7 is zero and at each of the points P_2, P_4, P_6 and P_8 is σ/ε_0.

Note that electric field changes discontinuously at the surface of a conductor. Just outside the conductor it is σ/ε_0 and inside the conductor it is zero. In fact, the field gradually decreases from σ/ε_0 to zero in a small thickness of about 4–5 atomic layers at the surface. When we say 'the surface of a conductor' we actually mean this small thickness.

30.5 SPHERICAL CHARGE DISTRIBUTIONS

We have seen that the electric field due to a uniformly charged sphere at an external point is the same as that due to an equal point charge placed at the centre. Similar result was obtained for the gravitational field due to a uniform sphere. This similarity is expected because the Coulomb force

$$F = \frac{q_1 q_2}{4\pi\varepsilon_0\, r^2}$$

and the gravitational force

$$F = \frac{Gm_1m_2}{r^2}$$

have similar mathematical structure.

Many of the results derived for gravitational field, potential and potential energy may, therefore, be used for the corresponding electrical quantities. We state some of the useful results for a spherical charge distribution of radius R.

(a) The electric field due to a uniformly charged, thin spherical shell at an external point is the same as that due to an equal point charge placed at the centre of the shell, $E = Q/(4\pi\varepsilon_0 r^2)$.

(b) The electric field due to a uniformly charged thin spherical shell at an internal point is zero.

(c) The electric field due to a uniformly charged sphere at an external point is the same as that due to an equal point charge placed at the centre of the sphere.

(d) The electric field due to a uniformly charged sphere at an internal point is proportional to the distance of the point from the centre of the sphere. Thus, it is zero at the centre and increases linearly as one moves out towards the surface.

(e) The electric potential due to a uniformly charged, thin spherical shell at an external point is the same as that due to an equal point charge placed at the centre, $V = Q/(4\pi\varepsilon_0 r)$.

(f) The electric potential due to a uniformly charged, thin spherical shell at an internal point is the same everywhere and is equal to that at the surface, $V = Q/(4\pi\varepsilon_0 R)$.

(g) The electric potential due to a uniformly charged sphere at an external point is the same as that due to an equal point charge placed at the centre, $V = Q/(4\pi\varepsilon_0 r)$.

Electric Potential Energy of a Uniformly Charged Sphere

Consider a uniformly charged sphere of radius R having a total charge Q. The electric potential energy of this sphere is equal to the work done in bringing the charges from infinity to assemble the sphere. Let us assume that at some instant, charge is assembled up to a radius x. In the next step, we bring some charge from infinity and put it on this sphere to increase the radius from x to $x + dx$. The entire sphere is assembled as x varies from 0 to R.

The charge density is

$$\rho = \frac{3Q}{4\pi R^3}.$$

When the radius of the sphere is x, the charge contained in it is,

$$q = \frac{4}{3}\pi x^3 \rho = \frac{Q}{R^3} x^3.$$

The potential at the surface is

$$V = \frac{q}{4\pi\varepsilon_0 x} = \frac{Q}{4\pi\varepsilon_0 R^3} x^2.$$

The charge needed to increase the radius from x to $x + dx$ is

$$dq = (4\pi x^2 dx)\rho = \frac{3Q}{R^3} x^2 dx.$$

The work done in bringing the charge dq from infinity to the surface of the sphere of radius x is

$$dW = V(dq) = \frac{3Q^2}{4\pi\varepsilon_0 R^6} x^4 dx.$$

The total work done in assembling the charged sphere of radius R is

$$W = \frac{3Q^2}{4\pi\varepsilon_0 R^6}\int_0^R x^4 dx = \frac{3Q^2}{20\pi\varepsilon_0 R}.$$

This is the electric potential energy of the charged sphere.

Electric Potential Energy of a Uniformly Charged, Thin Spherical Shell

Consider a uniformly charged, thin spherical shell of radius R having a total charge Q. The electric potential energy is equal to the work done in bringing charges from infinity and put them on the shell. Suppose at some instant, a charge q is placed on the shell. The potential at the surface is

$$V = \frac{q}{4\pi\varepsilon_0 R}.$$

The work done in bringing a charge dq from infinity to this shell is

$$dW = V(dq) = \frac{q\,dq}{4\pi\varepsilon_0 R}.$$

The total work done in assembling the charge on the shell is

$$W = \int_0^Q \frac{qdq}{4\pi\varepsilon_0 R} = \frac{Q^2}{8\pi\varepsilon_0 R}.$$

This is the electric potential energy of the charged spherical shell.

30.6 EARTHING A CONDUCTOR

The earth is a good conductor of electricity. If we assume that the earth is uncharged, its potential will be zero. In fact, the earth's surface has a negative charge of about 1 nC m^{-2} and hence is at a constant potential V. All conductors which are not given any external charge, are also very nearly at the same potential. In turns out that for many practical calculations, we can ignore the charge on the earth. The potential of the earth can then be taken as the same as that of a point far away from all charges, i.e., at infinity. So, the potential of the earth is often taken to be zero. Also, if a small quantity of charge is given to the earth or is taken away from it, the potential does not change by any appreciable extent. This is because of the large size of the earth.

If a conductor is connected to the earth, the potential of the conductor becomes equal to that of the earth, i.e., zero. If the conductor was at some other potential, charges will flow from it to the earth or from the earth to it to bring its potential to zero.

When a conductor is connected to the earth, the conductor is said to be *earthed* or *grounded*. Figure (30.22a) shows the symbol for earthing.

Suppose a spherical conductor of radius R is given a charge Q. The charge will be distributed uniformly on the surface. So it is equivalent to a uniformly charged, thin spherical shell. Its potential will, therefore, become $Q/(4\pi\varepsilon_0 R)$. If this conductor is connected to the earth, the charge Q will be transferred to the earth so that the potential will become zero.

Next suppose, a charge $+Q$ is placed at the centre of a spherical conducting shell. A charge $-Q$ will appear on its inner surface and $+Q$ on its outer surface (figure 30.22b). The potential of the sphere due to the charge at the centre and that due to the charge at the inner surface are $\frac{Q}{4\pi\varepsilon_0 R}$ and $\frac{-Q}{4\pi\varepsilon_0 R}$ respectively. The potential due to the charge on the outer surface is $\frac{Q}{4\pi\varepsilon_0 R}$. The net potential of the sphere is, therefore, $\frac{Q}{4\pi\varepsilon_0 R}$. If this sphere is now connected to the earth (figure 30.22c), the charge Q on the outer surface flows to the earth and the potential of the sphere becomes zero.

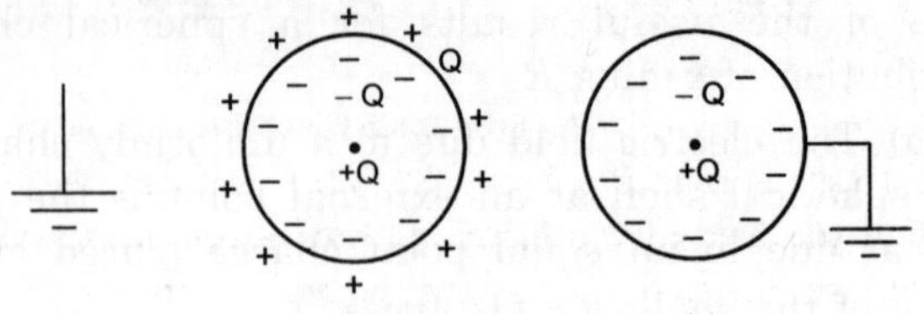

Figure 30.22

Earthing a conductor is a technical job. A thick metal plate is buried deep into the earth and wires are drawn from this plate. The electric wiring in our houses has three wires: live, neutral and earth. The live and neutral wires carry electric currents which come from the power station. The earth wire is connected to the metal plate buried in the earth. The metallic bodies of electric appliances such as electric iron, refrigerator, etc. are connected to the earth wire. This ensures that the metallic body remains at zero potential while an appliance is being used. If by any fault, the live wire touches the metallic body, charge flows to the earth and the potential of the metallic body remains zero. If it is not connected to the earth, the user may get an electric shock.

Worked Out Examples

1. *A uniform electric field of magnitude* $E = 100\ \mathrm{N\,C^{-1}}$ *exists in the space in x-direction. Calculate the flux of this field through a plane square area of edge* 10 cm *placed in the y–z plane. Take the normal along the positive x-axis to be positive.*

Solution : The flux $\Phi = \int E\cos\theta\, dS$. As the normal to the area points along the electric field, $\theta = 0$. Also, E is uniform, so

$$\Phi = E\,\Delta S$$

$$= (100\ \mathrm{N\,C^{-1}})\,(0{\cdot}10\ \mathrm{m})^2 = 1{\cdot}0\ \mathrm{N\,m^2C^{-1}}.$$

2. *A large plane charge sheet having surface charge density* $\sigma = 2{\cdot}0 \times 10^{-6}\ \mathrm{C\,m^{-2}}$ *lies in the x–y plane. Find the flux of the electric field through a circular area of radius* 1 cm *lying completely in the region where x, y, z are all positive and with its normal making an angle of* 60° *with the z-axis.*

Solution : The electric field near the plane charge sheet is $E = \sigma/2\varepsilon_0$ in the direction away from the sheet. At the given area, the field is along the z-axis.

The area $= \pi r^2 = 3{\cdot}14 \times 1\ \mathrm{cm}^2 = 3{\cdot}14 \times 10^{-4}\ \mathrm{m}^2$.

The angle between the normal to the area and the field is 60°.

Hence, the flux $= \vec{E}\cdot\Delta\vec{S} = E\,\Delta S\cos\theta = \frac{\sigma}{2\varepsilon_0}\pi r^2\cos 60°$

$$= \frac{2{\cdot}0 \times 10^{-6}\ \mathrm{C\,m^{-2}}}{2 \times 8{\cdot}85 \times 10^{-12}\ \mathrm{C^2\,N\,m^{-2}}} \times (3{\cdot}14 \times 10^{-4}\ \mathrm{m^2})\,\frac{1}{2}$$

$$= 17{\cdot}5\ \mathrm{N\,m^2\,C^{-1}}.$$

3. *A charge of* $4 \times 10^{-8}\ \mathrm{C}$ *is distributed uniformly on the surface of a sphere of radius* 1 cm. *It is covered by a concentric, hollow conducting sphere of radius* 5 cm. *(a) Find the electric field at a point* 2 cm *away from the centre. (b) A charge of* $6 \times 10^{-8}\ \mathrm{C}$ *is placed on the hollow sphere. Find the surface charge density on the outer surface of the hollow sphere.*

Solution :

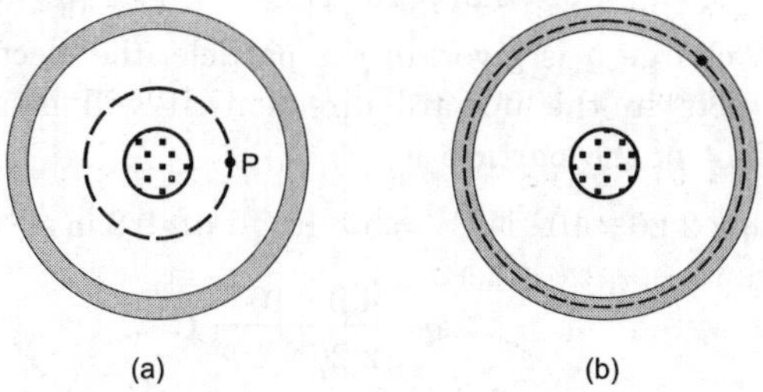

Figure 30-W1

(a) Let us consider figure (30-W1a). Suppose, we have to find the field at the point P. Draw a concentric spherical surface through P. All the points on this surface are equivalent and by symmetry, the field at all these points will be equal in magnitude and radial in direction.

The flux through this surface $= \oint \vec{E} \cdot d\vec{S}$

$$= \oint E\, dS = E \oint dS$$

$$= 4\pi x^2 E,$$

where $\quad x = 2 \text{ cm} = 2 \times 10^{-2} \text{ m}.$

From Gauss's law, this flux is equal to the charge q contained inside the surface divided by ε_0. Thus,

$$4\pi x^2 E = q/\varepsilon_0$$

or, $$E = \frac{q}{4\pi\varepsilon_0 x^2}$$

$$= (9 \times 10^9 \text{ N m}^2 \text{ C}^{-2}) \times \frac{4 \times 10^{-8} \text{ C}}{4 \times 10^{-4} \text{ m}^2}$$

$$= 9 \times 10^5 \text{ N C}^{-1}.$$

(b) See figure (30-W1b). Take a Gaussian surface through the material of the hollow sphere. As the electric field in a conducting material is zero, the flux $\oint \vec{E} \cdot d\vec{S}$ through this Gaussian surface is zero. Using Gauss's law, the total charge enclosed must be zero. Hence, the charge on the inner surface of the hollow sphere is -4×10^{-8} C. But the total charge given to this hollow sphere is 6×10^{-8} C. Hence, the charge on the outer surface will be 10×10^{-8} C.

4. *Figure (30-W2a) shows three concentric thin spherical shells A, B and C of radii a, b and c respectively. The shells A and C are given charges q and –q respectively and the shell B is earthed. Find the charges appearing on the surfaces of B and C.*

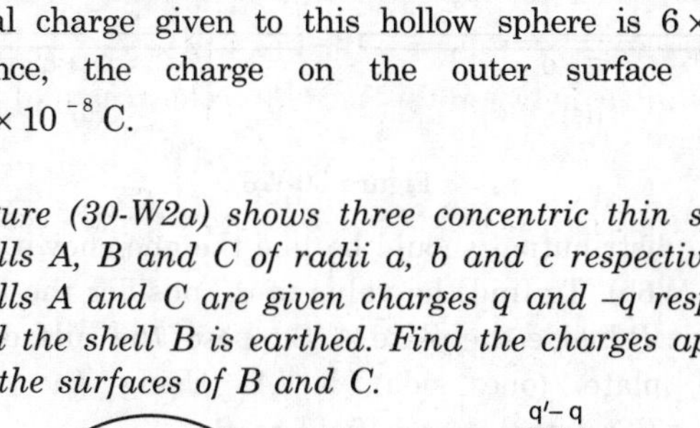

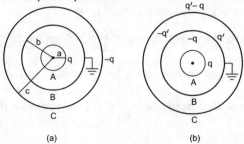

Figure 30-W2

Solution :

As shown in the previous worked out example, the inner surface of B must have a charge $-q$ from the Gauss's law. Suppose, the outer surface of B has a charge q'. The inner surface of C must have a charge $-q'$ from the Gauss's law. As the net charge on C must be $-q$, its outer surface should have a charge $q' - q$. The charge distribution is shown in figure (30-W2b).

The potential at B due to the charge q on A

$$= \frac{q}{4\pi\varepsilon_0 b},$$

due to the charge $-q$ on the inner surface of B

$$= \frac{-q}{4\pi\varepsilon_0 b},$$

due to the charge q' on the outer surface of B

$$= \frac{q'}{4\pi\varepsilon_0 b},$$

due to the charge $-q'$, on the inner surface of C

$$= \frac{-q'}{4\pi\varepsilon_0 c}$$

and due to the charge $q' - q$ on the outer surface of C

$$= \frac{q' - q}{4\pi\varepsilon_0 c}.$$

The net potential is

$$V_B = \frac{q'}{4\pi\varepsilon_0 b} - \frac{q}{4\pi\varepsilon_0 c}.$$

This should be zero as the shell B is earthed. Thus,

$$q' = \frac{b}{c} q.$$

The charges on various surfaces are as shown in figure (30-W3).

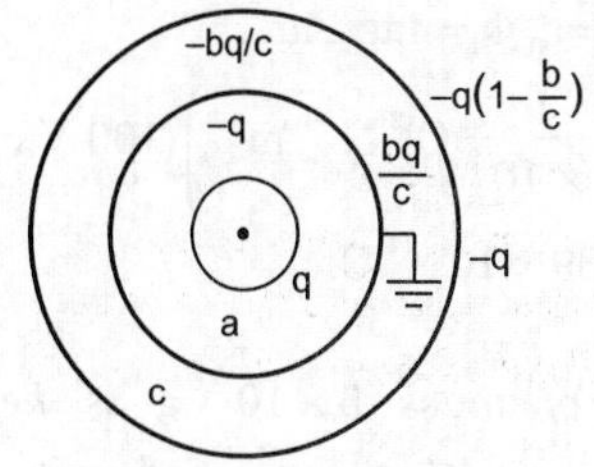

Figure 30-W3

5. *An electric dipole consists of charges* $\pm 2{\cdot}0 \times 10^{-8}$ C *separated by a distance of* $2{\cdot}0 \times 10^{-3}$ m. *It is placed near a long line charge of linear charge density* $4{\cdot}0 \times 10^{-4} \text{ C m}^{-1}$ *as shown in figure (30-W4), such that the negative charge is at a distance of* $2{\cdot}0$ cm *from the line charge. Find the force acting on the dipole.*

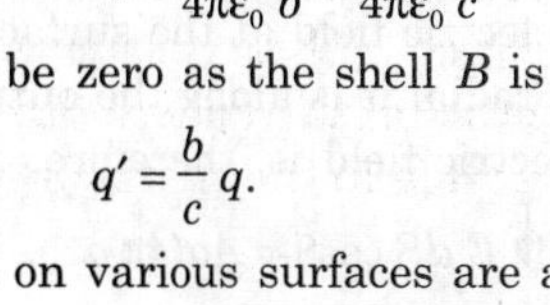

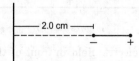

Figure 30-W4

Solution : The electric field at a distance r from the line charge of linear density λ is given by

$$E = \frac{\lambda}{2\pi\varepsilon_0 r} .$$

Hence, the field at the negative charge is

$$E_1 = \frac{(4{\cdot}0 \times 10^{-4}\ \mathrm{C\ m^{-1}})\ (2 \times 9 \times 10^{9}\ \mathrm{N\ m^2\ C^{-2}})}{0{\cdot}02\ \mathrm{m}}$$

$$= 3{\cdot}6 \times 10^{8}\ \mathrm{N\ C^{-1}}.$$

The force on the negative charge is

$$F_1 = (3{\cdot}6 \times 10^{8}\ \mathrm{N\ C^{-1}})\ (2{\cdot}0 \times 10^{-8}\ \mathrm{C}) = 7{\cdot}2\ \mathrm{N}$$

towards the line charge.

Similarly, the field at the positive charge, i.e., at $r = 0{\cdot}022$ m is

$$E_2 = 3{\cdot}3 \times 10^{8}\ \mathrm{N\ C^{-1}}.$$

The force on the positive charge is

$$F_2 = (3{\cdot}3 \times 10^{8}\ \mathrm{N\ C^{-1}}) \times (2{\cdot}0 \times 10^{-8}\ \mathrm{C})$$

$$= 6{\cdot}6\ \mathrm{N}\ \text{ away from the line charge}.$$

Hence, the net force on the dipole = (7·2 − 6·6) N

= 0·6 N towards the line charge.

6. *The electric field in a region is radially outward with magnitude $E = Ar$. Find the charge contained in a sphere of radius a centred at the origin. Take $A = 100\ \mathrm{V\ m^{-2}}$ and $a = 20{\cdot}0$ cm.*

Solution : The electric field at the surface of the sphere is Aa and being radial it is along the outward normal. The flux of the electric field is, therefore,

$$\Phi = \oint E\, dS \cos\theta = Aa(4\pi\, a^2).$$

The charge contained in the sphere is, from Gauss's law,

$$Q_{inside} = \varepsilon_0\, \Phi = 4\pi\varepsilon_0\, Aa^3$$

$$= \left(\frac{1}{9 \times 10^{9}}\ \mathrm{C^2\ N^{-1}\ m^{-2}}\right)(100\ \mathrm{V\ m^{-2}})\ (0{\cdot}20\ \mathrm{m})^3$$

$$= 8{\cdot}89 \times 10^{-11}\ \mathrm{C}.$$

7. *A particle of mass 5×10^{-6} g is kept over a large horizontal sheet of charge of density $4{\cdot}0 \times 10^{-6}\ \mathrm{C\ m^{-2}}$ (figure 30-W5). What charge should be given to this particle so that if released, it does not fall down ? How many electrons are to be removed to give this charge ? How much mass is decreased due to the removal of these electrons ?*

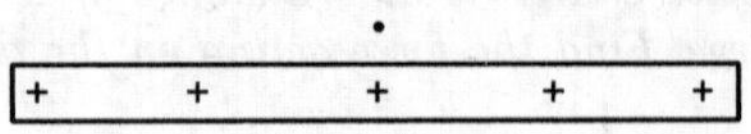

Figure 30-W5

Solution : The electric field in front of the sheet is

$$E = \frac{\sigma}{2\varepsilon_0} = \frac{4{\cdot}0 \times 10^{-6}\ \mathrm{C\ m^{-2}}}{2 \times 8{\cdot}85 \times 10^{-12}\ \mathrm{C^2\ N^{-1}\ m^{-2}}}$$

$$= 2{\cdot}26 \times 10^{5}\ \mathrm{N\ C^{-1}}.$$

If a charge q is given to the particle, the electric force qE acts in the upward direction. It will balance the weight of the particle if

$$q \times 2{\cdot}26 \times 10^{5}\ \mathrm{N\ C^{-1}} = 5 \times 10^{-9}\ \mathrm{kg} \times 9{\cdot}8\ \mathrm{m\ s^{-2}}$$

or,
$$q = \frac{4{\cdot}9 \times 10^{-8}}{2{\cdot}26 \times 10^{5}}\ \mathrm{C}$$

$$= 2{\cdot}21 \times 10^{-13}\ \mathrm{C}.$$

The charge on one electron is $1{\cdot}6 \times 10^{-19}$ C. The number of electrons to be removed

$$= \frac{2{\cdot}21 \times 10^{-13}\ \mathrm{C}}{1{\cdot}6 \times 10^{-19}\ \mathrm{C}} = 1{\cdot}4 \times 10^{6}.$$

Mass decreased due to the removal of these electrons

$$= 1{\cdot}4 \times 10^{6} \times 9{\cdot}1 \times 10^{-31}\ \mathrm{kg}$$

$$= 1{\cdot}3 \times 10^{-24}\ \mathrm{kg}.$$

8. *Two conducting plates A and B are placed parallel to each other. A is given a charge Q_1 and B a charge Q_2. Find the distribution of charges on the four surfaces.*

Solution : Consider a Gaussian surface as shown in figure (30-W6a). Two faces of this closed surface lie completely inside the conductor where the electric field is zero. The flux through these faces is, therefore, zero. The other parts of the closed surface which are outside the conductor are parallel to the electric field and hence the flux on these parts is also zero. The total flux of the electric field through the closed surface is, therefore, zero. From Gauss's law, the total charge inside this closed surface should be zero. The charge on the inner surface of A should be equal and opposite to that on the inner surface of B.

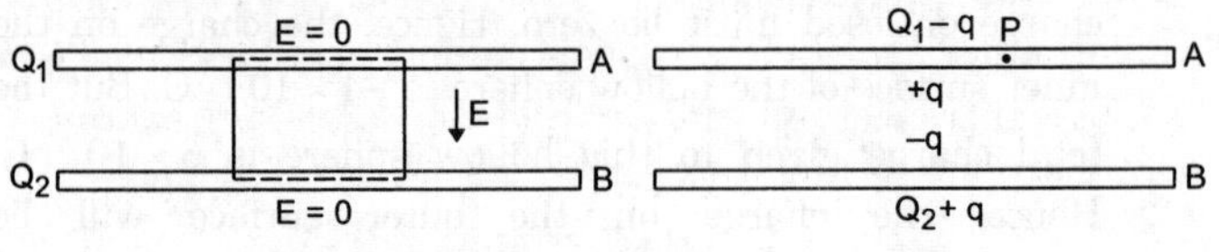

Figure 30-W6

The distribution should be like the one shown in figure (30-W6b). To find the value of q, consider the field at a point P inside the plate A. Suppose, the surface area of the plate (one side) is A. Using the equation $E = \sigma/(2\varepsilon_0)$, the electric field at P

due to the charge $Q_1 - q = \dfrac{Q_1 - q}{2A\varepsilon_0}$ (downward),

due to the charge $+q = \dfrac{q}{2A\varepsilon_0}$ (upward),

due to the charge $-q = \dfrac{q}{2A\varepsilon_0}$ (downward), and due to the charge $Q_2 + q = \dfrac{Q_2 + q}{2A\varepsilon_0}$ (upward).

The net electric field at P due to all the four charged surfaces is (in the downward direction)

$$\frac{Q_1 - q}{2A\varepsilon_0} - \frac{q}{2A\varepsilon_0} + \frac{q}{2A\varepsilon_0} - \frac{Q_2 + q}{2A\varepsilon_0}.$$

As the point P is inside the conductor, this field should be zero. Hence,

$$Q_1 - q - Q_2 - q = 0$$

or, $$q = \frac{Q_1 - Q_2}{2}. \quad \text{... (i)}$$

Thus, $$Q_1 - q = \frac{Q_1 + Q_2}{2} \quad \text{... (ii)}$$

and $$Q_2 + q = \frac{Q_1 + Q_2}{2}.$$

Using these equations, the distribution shown in the figure (30-W6) can be redrawn as in figure (30-W7).

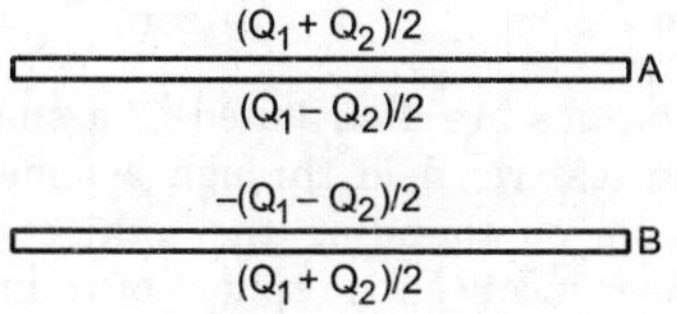

Figure 30-W7

This result is a special case of the following result. When charged conducting plates are placed parallel to each other, the two outermost surfaces get equal charges and the facing surfaces get equal and opposite charges.

□

QUESTIONS FOR SHORT ANSWER

1. A small plane area is rotated in an electric field. In which orientation of the area is the flux of electric field through the area maximum ? In which orientation is it zero ?
2. A circular ring of radius r made of a nonconducting material is placed with its axis parallel to a uniform electric field. The ring is rotated about a diameter through 180°. Does the flux of electric field change ? If yes, does it decrease or increase ?
3. A charge Q is uniformly distributed on a thin spherical shell. What is the field at the centre of the shell ? If a point charge is brought close to the shell, will the field at the centre change ? Does your answer depend on whether the shell is conducting or nonconducting ?
4. A spherical shell made of plastic, contains a charge Q distributed uniformly over its surface. What is the electric field inside the shell ? If the shell is hammered to deshape it without altering the charge, will the field inside be changed ? What happens if the shell is made of a metal ?
5. A point charge q is placed in a cavity in a metal block. If a charge Q is brought outside the metal, will the charge q feel an electric force ?
6. A rubber balloon is given a charge Q distributed uniformly over its surface. Is the field inside the balloon zero everywhere if the balloon does not have a spherical surface ?
7. It is said that any charge given to a conductor comes to its surface. Should all the protons come to the surface ? Should all the electrons come to the surface ? Should all the free electrons come to the surface ?

OBJECTIVE I

1. A charge Q is uniformly distributed over a large plastic plate. The electric field at a point P close to the centre of the plate is 10 V m^{-1}. If the plastic plate is replaced by a copper plate of the same geometrical dimensions and carrying the same charge Q, the electric field at the point P will become
(a) zero (b) 5 V m^{-1} (c) 10 V m^{-1} (d) 20 V m^{-1}.
2. A metallic particle having no net charge is placed near a finite metal plate carrying a positive charge. The electric force on the particle will be
(a) towards the plate (b) away from the plate
(c) parallel to the plate (d) zero.
3. A thin, metallic spherical shell contains a charge Q on it. A point charge q is placed at the centre of the shell and another charge q_1 is placed outside it as shown in figure (30-Q1). All the three charges are positive. The force on the charge at the centre is

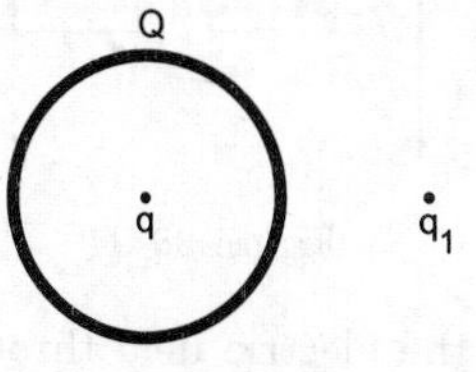

Figure 30-Q1

(a) towards left (b) towards right
(c) upward (d) zero.

4. Consider the situation of the previous problem. The force on the central charge due to the shell is
(a) towards left (b) towards right
(c) upward (d) zero.

5. Electric charges are distributed in a small volume. The flux of the electric field through a spherical surface of radius 10 cm surrounding the total charge is 25 V m. The flux over a concentric sphere of radius 20 cm will be
(a) 25 V m (b) 50 V m (c) 100 V m (d) 200 V m.

6. Figure (30-Q2a) shows an imaginary cube of edge $L/2$. A uniformly charged rod of length L moves towards left at a small but constant speed v. At $t = 0$, the left end just touches the centre of the face of the cube opposite it. Which of the graphs shown in figure (30-Q2b) represents the flux of the electric field through the cube as the rod goes through it ?

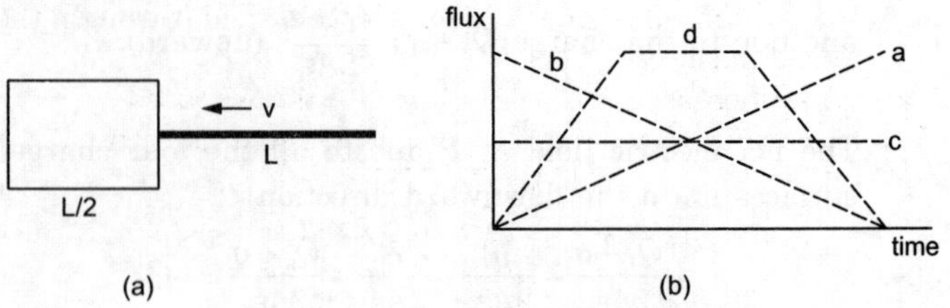

Figure 30-Q2

7. A charge q is placed at the centre of the open end of a cylindrical vessel (figure 30-Q3). The flux of the electric field through the surface of the vessel is
(a) zero (b) q/ε_0 (c) $q/2\varepsilon_0$ (d) $2q/\varepsilon_0$.

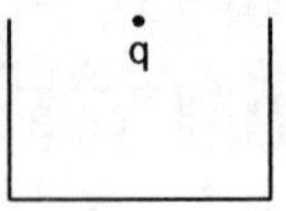

Figure 30-Q3

OBJECTIVE II

1. Mark the correct options:
(a) Gauss's law is valid only for symmetrical charge distributions.
(b) Gauss's law is valid only for charges placed in vacuum.
(c) The electric field calculated by Gauss's law is the field due to the charges inside the Gaussian surface.
(d) The flux of the electric field through a closed surface due to all the charges is equal to the flux due to the charges enclosed by the surface.

2. A positive point charge Q is brought near an isolated metal cube.
(a) The cube becomes negatively charged.
(b) The cube becomes positively charged.
(c) The interior becomes positively charged and the surface becomes negatively charged.
(d) The interior remains charge free and the surface gets nonuniform charge distribution.

3. A large nonconducting sheet M is given a uniform charge density. Two uncharged small metal rods A and B are placed near the sheet as shown in figure (30-Q4).
(a) M attracts A. (b) M attracts B.
(c) A attracts B. (d) B attracts A.

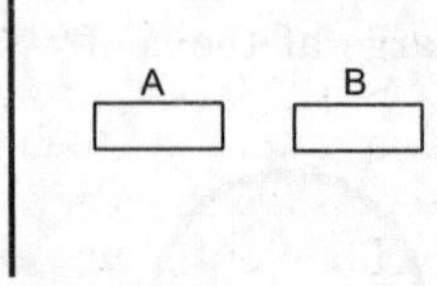

Figure 30-Q4

4. If the flux of the electric field through a closed surface is zero,
(a) the electric field must be zero everywhere on the surface
(b) the electric field may be zero everywhere on the surface
(c) the charge inside the surface must be zero
(d) the charge in the vicinity of the surface must be zero.

5. An electric dipole is placed at the centre of a sphere. Mark the correct options:
(a) The flux of the electric field through the sphere is zero.
(b) The electric field is zero at every point of the sphere.
(c) The electric field is not zero anywhere on the sphere.
(d) The electric field is zero on a circle on the sphere.

6. Figure (30-Q5) shows a charge q placed at the centre of a hemisphere. A second charge Q is placed at one of the positions A, B, C and D. In which position(s) of this second charge, the flux of the electric field through the hemisphere remains unchanged ?
(a) A (b) B (c) C (d) D.

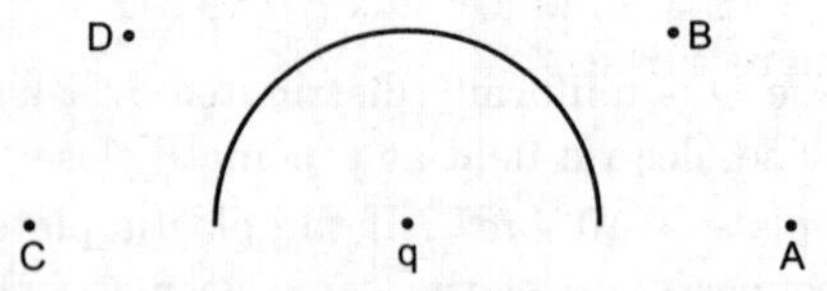

Figure 30-Q5

7. A closed surface S is constructed around a conducting wire connected to a battery and a switch (figure 30-Q6). As the switch is closed, the free electrons in the wire start moving along the wire. In any time interval, the number of electrons entering the closed surface S is equal to the number of electrons leaving it. On closing

the switch, the flux of the electric field through the closed surface
(a) is increased (b) is decreased
(c) remains unchanged (d) remains zero.

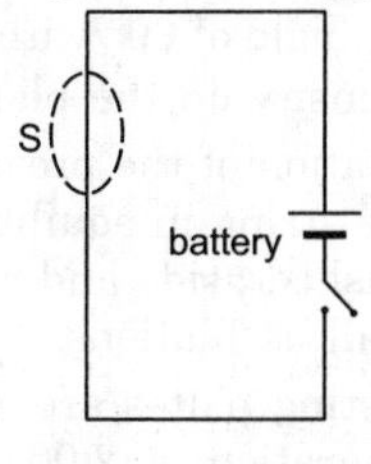

Figure 30-Q6

8. Figure (30-Q7) shows a closed surface which intersects a conducting sphere. If a positive charge is placed at the point P, the flux of the electric field through the closed surface
(a) will remain zero (b) will become positive
(c) will become negative (d) will become undefined.

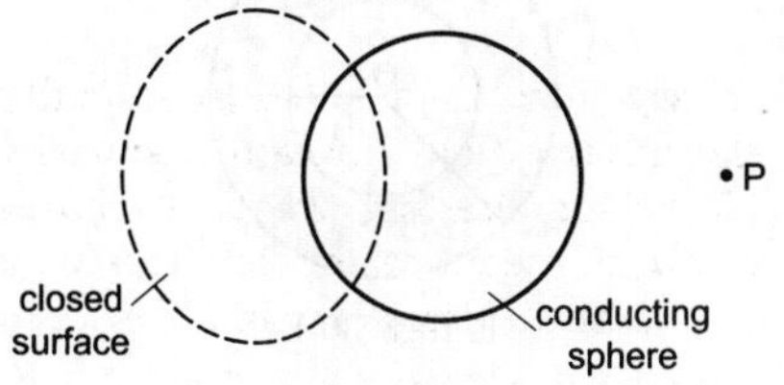

Figure 30-Q7

EXERCISES

1. The electric field in a region is given by $\vec{E} = \frac{3}{5} E_0 \vec{i} + \frac{4}{5} E_0 \vec{j}$ with $E_0 = 2{\cdot}0 \times 10^{3}\ \mathrm{N\,C^{-1}}$. Find the flux of this field through a rectangular surface of area $0{\cdot}2\ \mathrm{m}^2$ parallel to the y–z plane.

2. A charge Q is uniformly distributed over a rod of length l. Consider a hypothetical cube of edge l with the centre of the cube at one end of the rod. Find the minimum possible flux of the electric field through the entire surface of the cube.

3. Show that there can be no net charge in a region in which the electric field is uniform at all points.

4. The electric field in a region is given by $\vec{E} = \frac{E_0 x}{l} \vec{i}$. Find the charge contained inside a cubical volume bounded by the surfaces $x = 0$, $x = a$, $y = 0$, $y = a$, $z = 0$ and $z = a$. Take $E_0 = 5 \times 10^{3}\ \mathrm{N\,C^{-1}}$, $l = 2$ cm and $a = 1$ cm.

5. A charge Q is placed at the centre of a cube. Find the flux of the electric field through the six surfaces of the cube.

6. A charge Q is placed at a distance $a/2$ above the centre of a horizontal, square surface of edge a as shown in figure (30-E1). Find the flux of the electric field through the square surface.

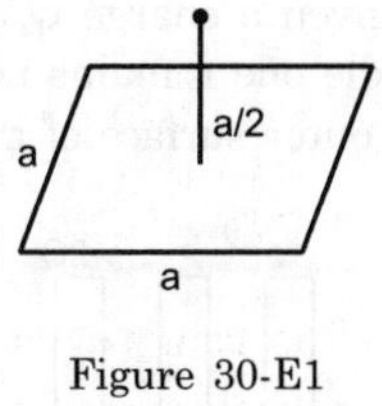

Figure 30-E1

7. Find the flux of the electric field through a spherical surface of radius R due to a charge of 10^{-7} C at the centre and another equal charge at a point $2R$ away from the centre (figure 30-E2).

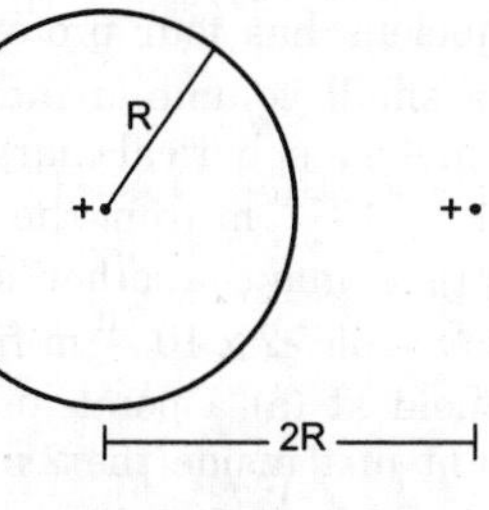

Figure 30-E2

8. A charge Q is placed at the centre of an imaginary hemispherical surface. Using symmetry arguments and the Gauss's law, find the flux of the electric field due to this charge through the surface of the hemisphere (figure 30-E3).

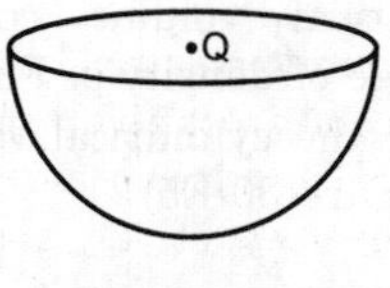

Figure 30-E3

9. A spherical volume contains a uniformly distributed charge of density $2{\cdot}0 \times 10^{-4}\ \mathrm{C\,m^{-3}}$. Find the electric field at a point inside the volume at a distance 4·0 cm from the centre.

10. The radius of a gold nucleus ($Z = 79$) is about $7{\cdot}0 \times 10^{-15}$ m. Assume that the positive charge is distributed uniformly throughout the nuclear volume. Find the strength of the electric field at (a) the surface of the nucleus and (b) at the middle point of a radius. Remembering that gold is a conductor, is it justified to assume that the positive charge is uniformly distributed over the entire volume of the nucleus and does not come to the outer surface ?

11. A charge Q is distributed uniformly within the material of a hollow sphere of inner and outer radii r_1 and r_2 (figure 30-E4). Find the electric field at a point P a

distance x away from the centre for $r_1 < x < r_2$. Draw a rough graph showing the electric field as a function of x for $0 < x < 2r_2$ (figure 30-E4).

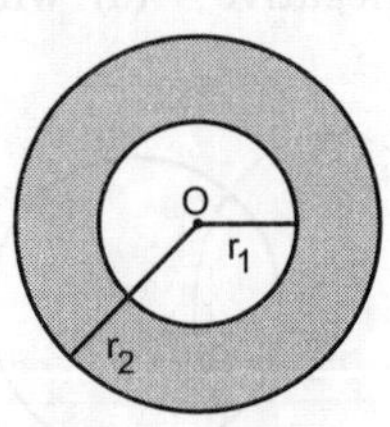

Figure 30-E4

12. A charge Q is placed at the centre of an uncharged, hollow metallic sphere of radius a. (a) Find the surface charge density on the inner surface and on the outer surface. (b) If a charge q is put on the sphere, what would be the surface charge densities on the inner and the outer surfaces? (c) Find the electric field inside the sphere at a distance x from the centre in the situations (a) and (b).

13. Consider the following very rough model of a beryllium atom. The nucleus has four protons and four neutrons confined to a small volume of radius 10^{-15} m. The two $1s$ electrons make a spherical charge cloud at an average distance of $1{\cdot}3 \times 10^{-11}$ m from the nucleus, whereas the two $2s$ electrons make another spherical cloud at an average distance of $5{\cdot}2 \times 10^{-11}$ m from the nucleus. Find the electric field at (a) a point just inside the $1s$ cloud and (b) a point just inside the $2s$ cloud.

14. Find the magnitude of the electric field at a point 4 cm away from a line charge of density 2×10^{-6} C m^{-1}.

15. A long cylindrical wire carries a positive charge of linear density $2{\cdot}0 \times 10^{-8}$ C m^{-1}. An electron revolves around it in a circular path under the influence of the attractive electrostatic force. Find the kinetic energy of the electron. Note that it is independent of the radius.

16. A long cylindrical volume contains a uniformly distributed charge of density ρ. Find the electric field at a point P inside the cylindrical volume at a distance x from its axis (figure 30-E5)

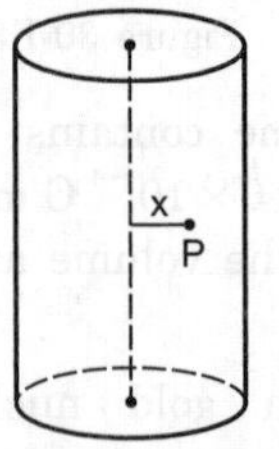

Figure 30-E5

17. A nonconducting sheet of large surface area and thickness d contains uniform charge distribution of density ρ. Find the electric field at a point P inside the plate, at a distance x from the central plane. Draw a qualitative graph of E against x for $0 < x < d$.

18. A charged particle having a charge of $-2{\cdot}0 \times 10^{-6}$ C is placed close to a nonconducting plate having a surface charge density $4{\cdot}0 \times 10^{-6}$ C m^{-2}. Find the force of attraction between the particle and the plate.

19. One end of a 10 cm long silk thread is fixed to a large vertical surface of a charged nonconducting plate and the other end is fastened to a small ball having a mass of 10 g and a charge of $4{\cdot}0 \times 10^{-6}$ C. In equilibrium, the thread makes an angle of 60° with the vertical. Find the surface charge density on the plate.

20. Consider the situation of the previous problem. (a) Find the tension in the string in equilibrium. (b) Suppose the ball is slightly pushed aside and released. Find the time period of the small oscillations.

21. Two large conducting plates are placed parallel to each other with a separation of 2·00 cm between them. An electron starting from rest near one of the plates reaches the other plate in 2·00 microseconds. Find the surface charge density on the inner surfaces.

22. Two large conducting plates are placed parallel to each other and they carry equal and opposite charges with surface density σ as shown in figure (30-E6). Find the electric field (a) at the left of the plates, (b) in between the plates and (c) at the right of the plates.

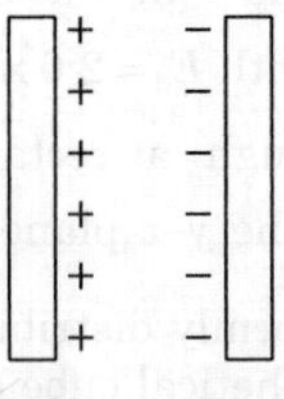

Figure 30-E6

23. Two conducting plates X and Y, each having large surface area A (on one side), are placed parallel to each other as shown in figure (30-E7). The plate X is given a charge Q whereas the other is neutral. Find (a) the surface charge density at the inner surface of the plate X, (b) the electric field at a point to the left of the plates, (c) the electric field at a point in between the plates and (d) the electric field at a point to the right of the plates.

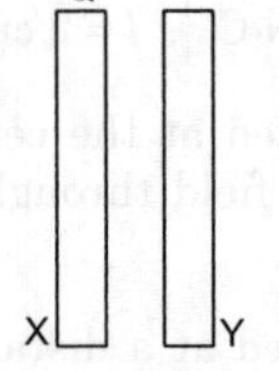

Figure 30-E7

24. Three identical metal plates with large surface areas are kept parallel to each other as shown in figure (30-E8). The leftmost plate is given a charge Q, the rightmost a charge $-2Q$ and the middle one remains neutral. Find the charge appearing on the outer surface of the rightmost plate.

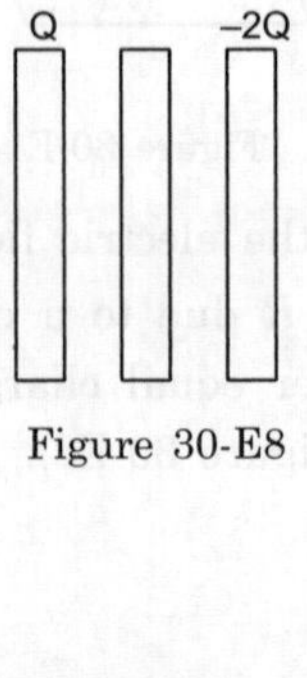

Figure 30-E8

ANSWERS

OBJECTIVE I

1. (c) 2. (a) 3. (d) 4. (b) 5. (a) 6. (d)
7. (c)

OBJECTIVE II

1. (d) 2. (d) 3. (c), (d)
4. (b), (c) 5. (a), (c) 6. (a), (c)
7. (c), (d) 8. (b)

EXERCISES

1. $240\ \text{N m}^2\ \text{C}^{-1}$
2. $Q/(2\varepsilon_0)$
4. $2{\cdot}2 \times 10^{-12}$ C
5. Q/ε_0
6. $Q/(6\varepsilon_0)$
7. $1{\cdot}1 \times 10^4\ \text{N m}^{-2}\ \text{C}^{-1}$
8. $Q/(2\varepsilon_0)$
9. $3{\cdot}0 \times 10^5\ \text{N C}^{-1}$
10. (a) $2{\cdot}32 \times 10^{21}\ \text{N C}^{-1}$ (b) $1{\cdot}16 \times 10^{21}\ \text{N C}^{-1}$
11. $\dfrac{Q(x^3 - r_1^3)}{4\pi\varepsilon_0 x^2 (r_2^3 - r_1^3)}$
12. (a) $\dfrac{Q}{4\pi a^2}, \dfrac{Q}{4\pi a^2}$ (b) $-\dfrac{Q}{4\pi a^2}, \dfrac{Q+q}{4\pi a^2}$
(c) $\dfrac{Q}{4\pi\varepsilon_0 x^2}$ in both situations
13. (a) $3{\cdot}4 \times 10^{13}\ \text{N C}^{-1}$ (b) $1{\cdot}1 \times 10^{12}\ \text{N C}^{-1}$
14. $9 \times 10^5\ \text{N C}^{-1}$
15. $2{\cdot}88 \times 10^{-17}$ J
16. $\rho x/(2\varepsilon_0)$
17. $\rho x/\varepsilon_0$
18. 0·45 N
19. $7{\cdot}5 \times 10^{-7}\ \text{C m}^{-2}$
20. (a) 0·20 N (b) 0·45 s
21. $0{\cdot}505 \times 10^{-12}\ \text{C m}^{-2}$
22. (a) zero (b) σ/ε_0 (c) zero
23. (a) $\dfrac{Q}{2A}$ (b) $\dfrac{Q}{2A\varepsilon_0}$ towards left (c) $\dfrac{Q}{2A\varepsilon_0}$ towards right
(d) $\dfrac{Q}{2A\varepsilon_0}$ towards right
24. $-Q/2$

□

CHAPTER 31

CAPACITORS

31.1 CAPACITOR AND CAPACITANCE

A combination of two conductors placed close to each other is called a *capacitor*. One of the conductors is given a positive charge and the other is given an equal negative charge. The conductor with the positive charge is called the *positive plate* and the other is called the *negative plate*. The charge on the positive plate is called *the charge on the capacitor* and the potential difference between the plates is called the *potential of the capacitor*. Figure (31.1a) shows two conductors. One of the conductors has a positive charge $+Q$ and the other has an equal, negative charge $-Q$. The first one is at a potential V_+ and the other is at a potential V_-. The charge on the capacitor is Q and the potential of the capacitor is $V = V_+ - V_-$. Note that the term *charge on a capacitor* does not mean the total charge given to the capacitor. This total charge is $+Q - Q = 0$. Figure (31.1b) shows the symbol used to represent a capacitor.

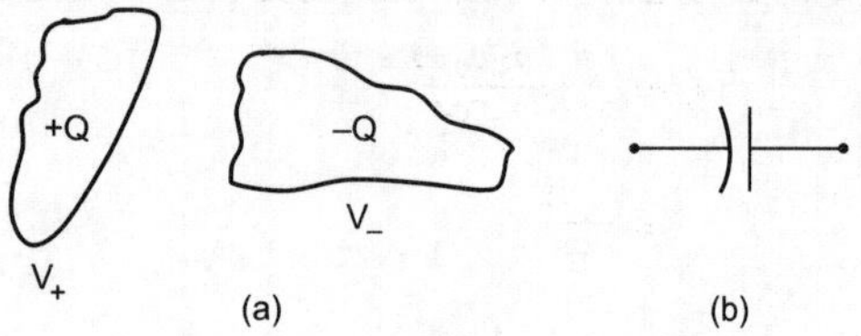

Figure 31.1

For a given capacitor, the charge Q on the capacitor is proportional to the potential difference V between the plates

Thus, $$Q \propto V$$

or, $$Q = CV. \quad \ldots (31.1)$$

The proportionality constant C is called the *capacitance* of the capacitor. It depends on the shape, size and geometrical placing of the conductors and the medium between them.

The SI unit of capacitance is coulomb per volt which is written as farad. The symbol F is used for it. This is a large unit on normal scales and microfarad (μF) is used more frequently.

To put equal and opposite charges on the two conductors, they may be connected to the terminals of a *battery*. We shall discuss in somewhat greater detail about the battery in the next chapter. Here we state the following properties of an ideal battery.

(a) A battery has two terminals.

(b) The potential difference V between the terminals is constant for a given battery. The terminal with higher potential is called the *positive terminal* and that with lower potential is called the *negative terminal*.

(c) The value of this fixed potential difference is equal to the *electromotive force* or *emf* of the battery. If a conductor is connected to a terminal of a battery, the potential of the conductor becomes equal to the potential of the terminal. When the two plates of a capacitor are connected to the terminals of a battery, the potential difference between the plates of the capacitor becomes equal to the emf of the battery.

(d) The total charge in a battery always remains zero. If its positive terminal supplies a charge Q, its negative terminal supplies an equal, negative charge $-Q$.

(e) When a charge Q passes through a battery of emf $\mathcal{E}$ from the negative terminal to the positive terminal, an amount $Q\mathcal{E}$ of work is done by the battery.

An ideal battery is represented by the symbol shown in figure (31.2). The potential difference between the facing parallel lines is equal to the emf $\mathcal{E}$ of the battery. The longer line is at the higher potential.

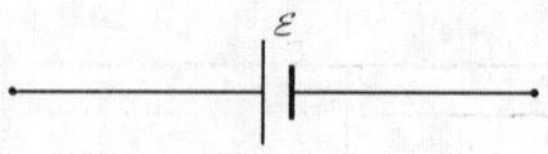

Figure 31.2

Example 31.1

A capacitor gets a charge of 60 μC *when it is connected to a battery of emf* 12 V. *Calculate the capacitance of the capacitor.*

Solution : The potential difference between the plates is the same as the emf of the battery which is 12 V. Thus, the capacitance is

$$C = \frac{Q}{V} = \frac{60\ \mu C}{12\ V} = 5\ \mu F.$$

31.2 CALCULATION OF CAPACITANCE

The procedure to calculate the capacitance of a given capacitor is simple. We assume that a charge $+Q$ is placed on the positive plate and a charge $-Q$ is placed on the negative plate of the capacitor. We calculate the electric field between the plates and from this the potential difference between the plates. The capacitance is then obtained using equation (31.1).

Parallel-plate Capacitor

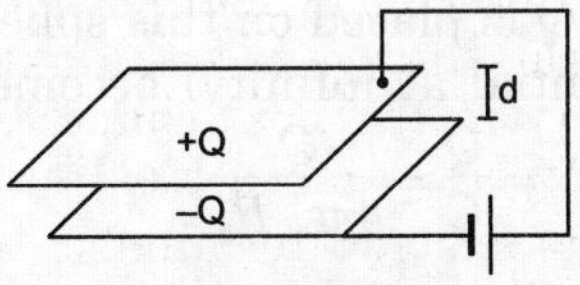

Figure 31.3

A parallel-plate capacitor consists of two large plane plates placed parallel to each other with a small separation between them (figure 31.3). Suppose, the area of each of the facing surfaces is A and the separation between the two plates is d. Also, assume that the space between the plates contains vacuum.

Let us put a charge Q on one plate and a charge $-Q$ on the other. The charges will appear on the facing surfaces. The charge density on each of these surfaces has a magnitude

$$\sigma = \frac{Q}{A}.$$

Suppose that the plates are large as compared to the separation between them. This means that any linear dimension of the plates is much larger than the separation d. For example, if the plates are square in shape, the length of a side should be much larger than d. If we use circular plates, the diameter should be much larger than d. The electric field between the plates is then uniform and perpendicular to the plates except for a small region near the edge. The magnitude of this uniform field E may be calculated using Gauss's law.

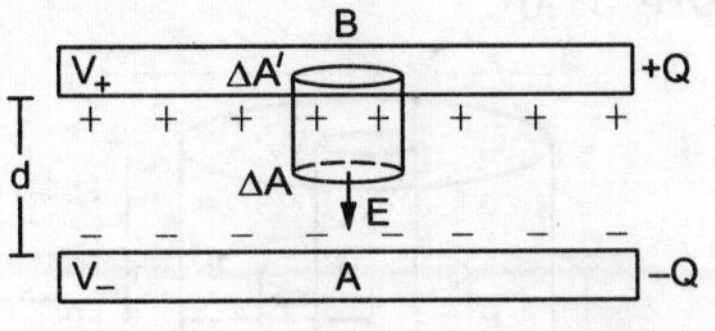

Figure 31.4

Let us draw a small area ΔA parallel to the plates and in between them (figure 31.4). Draw a cylinder with ΔA as a cross-section and terminate it by another symmetrically situated area $\Delta A'$ inside the positive plate. The cylinder and the two cross-sections ΔA and $\Delta A'$ form a Gaussian surface. The flux through $\Delta A'$ and through the curved part inside the plate is zero as the electric field is zero inside a conductor. The flux through the curved part outside the plates is also zero as the direction of the field E is parallel to this surface. The flux through ΔA is

$$\Phi = \vec{E} \cdot \Delta \vec{A} = E\,\Delta A.$$

The only charge inside the Gaussian surface is

$$\Delta Q = \sigma\,\Delta A = \frac{Q}{A}\,\Delta A.$$

From Gauss's law,

$$\oint \vec{E} \cdot d\vec{S} = Q_{in}/\varepsilon_0$$

or, $$E\,\Delta A = \frac{Q}{\varepsilon_0 A}\,\Delta A$$

or, $$E = \frac{Q}{\varepsilon_0 A}.$$

The potential difference between the plates is

$$V = V_+ - V_- = -\int_A^B \vec{E} \cdot d\vec{r}.$$

As one goes from A to B, the field $\vec{E}$ and the displacement $d\vec{r}$ are opposite in direction. Thus, $\vec{E} \cdot d\vec{r} = -E\,dr$ and

$$V = \int_A^B E\,dr$$

$$= Ed = \frac{Qd}{\varepsilon_0 A}.$$

The capacitance of the parallel-plate capacitor is

$$C = \frac{Q}{V} = \frac{Q\varepsilon_0 A}{Qd}$$

$$= \frac{\varepsilon_0 A}{d}. \quad \text{... (31.2)}$$

Example 31.2

Show that the SI unit of ε_0 may be written as farad metre^{-1}.

Solution :

We have $C = \dfrac{\varepsilon_0 A}{d}$

or, $$\varepsilon_0 = \frac{Cd}{A}.$$

As the SI units of C, d and A are farad, metre and metre^2 respectively, the SI unit of ε_0 is farad metre^{-1}.

Example 31.3

Calculate the capacitance of a parallel-plate capacitor having 20 cm × 20 cm *square plates separated by a distance of* 1·0 mm.

Solution : The capacitance is

$$C=\frac{\varepsilon_0 A}{d}$$

$$=\frac{8{\cdot}85\times10^{-12}\ \mathrm{F\ m^{-1}}\times400\times10^{-4}\ \mathrm{m}^2}{1\times10^{-3}\ \mathrm{m}}$$

$$=3{\cdot}54\times10^{-10}\ \mathrm{F}\approx350\ \mathrm{pF}.$$

Spherical Capacitor

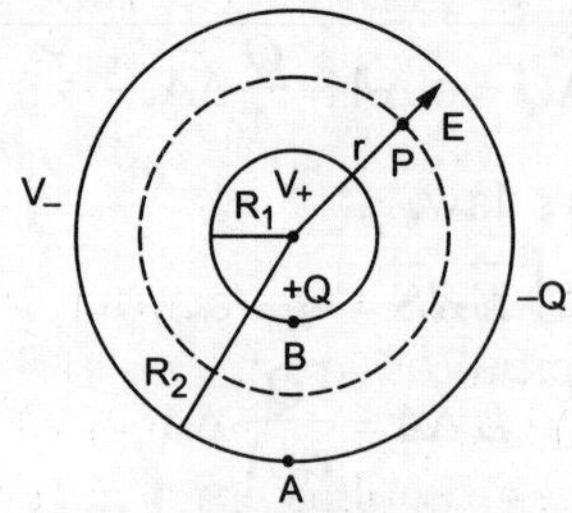

Figure 31.5

A spherical capacitor consists of a solid or a hollow spherical conductor surrounded by another concentric hollow spherical conductor. Suppose, the inner sphere has a radius R_1 and the outer sphere has a radius R_2. Suppose, the inner sphere is given a positive charge Q and the outer is given a negative charge $-Q$.

The field at any point P between the spheres is radially outward and its magnitude depends only on its distance r from the centre. Let us draw a sphere through P concentric with the given system. The flux of the electric field through this sphere is

$$\Phi=\oint\vec{E}\cdot d\vec{S}=\oint E\,dS$$

$$=E\oint dS=E\,4\pi r^2.$$

The charge enclosed in this sphere is Q. Thus, from Gauss's law,

$$E\,4\pi r^2=\frac{Q}{\varepsilon_0}$$

or, $$E=\frac{Q}{4\pi\varepsilon_0 r^2}.$$

The potential difference between the two conductors is

$$V=V_+-V_-=-\int_A^B\vec{E}\cdot d\vec{r}$$

$$=-\int_{R_2}^{R_1}\frac{Q}{4\pi\varepsilon_0 r^2}\,dr$$

$$=\frac{Q}{4\pi\varepsilon_0}\left(\frac{1}{R_1}-\frac{1}{R_2}\right)=\frac{Q(R_2-R_1)}{4\pi\varepsilon_0 R_1R_2}.$$

The capacitance of the spherical capacitor is

$$C=\frac{Q}{V}$$

$$=\frac{4\pi\varepsilon_0 R_1R_2}{R_2-R_1}. \quad \ldots (31.3)$$

Isolated sphere

If we assume that the outer sphere is at infinity, we get an isolated single sphere of radius R_1. The capacitance of such a single sphere can be obtained from equation (31.3) by taking the limit as $R_2\to\infty$. Then

$$C=\frac{4\pi\varepsilon_0 R_1R_2}{R_2-R_1}$$

$$\approx\frac{4\pi\varepsilon_0 R_1R_2}{R_2}=4\pi\varepsilon_0 R_1.$$

If a charge Q is placed on this sphere, its potential (with zero potential at infinity) becomes

$$V=\frac{Q}{C}=\frac{Q}{4\pi\varepsilon_0 R_1}.$$

Parallel limit

If both R_1 and R_2 are made large but $R_2-R_1=d$ is kept fixed, we can write

$$4\pi R_1R_2\approx4\pi R^2=A$$

where R is approximately the radius of each sphere and A is the area. Equation (31.3) then becomes

$$C=\frac{\varepsilon_0 A}{d}$$

which is the same as the equation for the capacitance of a parallel-plate capacitor.

Cylindrical Capacitor

A cylindrical capacitor consists of a solid or a hollow cylindrical conductor surrounded by another coaxial hollow cylindrical conductor. Let the length of the cylinders be l and the radii of the inner and outer cylinders be R_1 and R_2 respectively. Suppose, a positive charge Q is placed on the inner cylinder and a negative charge $-Q$ is placed on the outer cylinder. If the cylinders are long as compared to the separation between them, the electric field at a point between the cylinders will be radial and its magnitude will depend only on the distance of the point from the axis. Let P be a point between the cylinders at a distance r from the axis (figure 31.6).

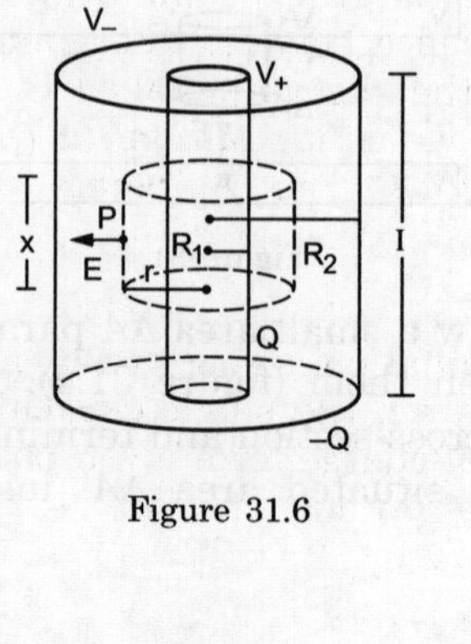

Figure 31.6

To calculate the electric field at the point P, let us draw a coaxial cylinder of length x through the point P. This cylinder together with its two cross sections forms a Gaussian surface. The flux through the cross sections is zero because the electric field is radial wherever it exists and hence is parallel to the cross sections. The flux through the curved part is

$$\Phi = \oint \vec{E} \cdot d\vec{S}$$

$$= \int E\, dS$$

$$= E \int dS = E\, 2\pi rx.$$

The charge enclosed by the Gaussian surface is

$$Q_{in} = \frac{Q}{l} x.$$

Thus, from Gauss's law,

$$E\, 2\pi rx = \left(\frac{Q}{l} x\right) / \varepsilon_0$$

or,
$$E = \frac{Q}{2\pi\varepsilon_0 rl}.$$

The potential difference between the cylinders is

$$V = V_+ - V_-$$

$$= -\int_A^B \vec{E} \cdot d\vec{r} = -\int_{R_2}^{R_1} E\, dr$$

$$= -\int_{R_2}^{R_1} \frac{Q}{2\pi\varepsilon_0 rl} dr$$

$$= \frac{Q}{2\pi\varepsilon_0 l} \ln \frac{R_2}{R_1}.$$

The capacitance is

$$C = \frac{Q}{V} = \frac{2\pi\varepsilon_0 l}{\ln(R_2/R_1)}. \quad \dots (31.4)$$

31.3 COMBINATION OF CAPACITORS

Two or more capacitors may be connected in a number of ways. The combination should have two points which may be connected to a battery to apply a potential difference. The battery supplies positive and negative charges to the system. If V be the potential difference between the points and Q be the magnitude of the charge supplied by either terminal of the battery, we define *equivalent capacitance* of the combination *between the two points* to be

$$C = \frac{Q}{V}.$$

If the combination is replaced by a single capacitor of this capacitance, the single capacitor will store the same amount of charge for a given potential difference as the combination does.

Two special methods of combination are frequently used, one known as *series* combination and the other as *parallel* combination.

Series Combination

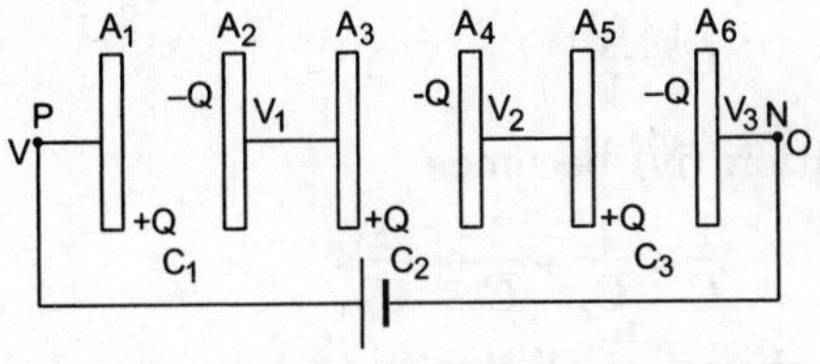

Figure 31.7

Figure (31.7) shows three capacitors connected in series. The capacitances are C_1, C_2 and C_3. The points P and N serve as the points through which a potential difference may be applied and a charge may be supplied to the combination. Let us connect the point P to the positive terminal and the point N to the negative terminal of a battery. The battery supplies a charge $+Q$ to the plate A_1 and a charge $-Q$ to the plate A_6. The charge $+Q$ given by the battery appears on the right surface of the plate A_1. The facing surface of A_2 must have a charge $-Q$ on it.

The plates A_2 and A_3 are connected and they together are isolated from everything else. The charge $-Q$ appearing on A_2 comes from the electrons drifted from the plate A_3 to A_2. This leaves a positive charge $+Q$ on the plate A_3. The facing surface of A_4 gets a charge $-Q$ from A_5 and a charge $+Q$ appears on the right surface of A_5. The facing surface of A_6 gets a charge $-Q$ from the battery. This completes the charge distribution. *In series combination, each capacitor has equal charge for any value of capacitances.*

Let us take the potential of the point N to be zero. The potential of the plate A_6 is also zero as it is connected to N by a conducting wire. The potential of the point P as well as that of the plate A_1 is V. The plates A_2 and A_3 are at the same potential, say, V_1. Similarly, A_4 and A_5 are at the same potential, say, V_2.

The charge on the first capacitor is Q and the potential difference is $V - V_1$. As the capacitance of this capacitor is C_1, we have

$$Q = C_1(V - V_1)$$

or,
$$V - V_1 = \frac{Q}{C_1}. \quad \dots \text{(i)}$$

Similarly, considering the other capacitors,

$$V_1 - V_2 = \frac{Q}{C_2} \quad \dots \text{(ii)}$$

and
$$V_2 - 0 = \frac{Q}{C_3}. \quad \dots \text{(iii)}$$

Adding (i), (ii) and (iii);

$$V = Q\left(\frac{1}{C_1} + \frac{1}{C_2} + \frac{1}{C_3}\right). \quad \dots \text{(iv)}$$

If the equivalent capacitance of the combination between the points P and N is C, we have

$$C = \frac{Q}{V}$$

and equation (iv) becomes

$$\frac{1}{C} = \frac{1}{C_1} + \frac{1}{C_2} + \frac{1}{C_3}.$$

The above analysis may be extended to any number of capacitors, the equivalent capacitance C is given by

$$\frac{1}{C} = \frac{1}{C_1} + \frac{1}{C_2} + \frac{1}{C_3} + \dots \quad \dots \text{(31.5)}$$

Example 31.4

Calculate the charge on each capacitor shown in figure (31.8).

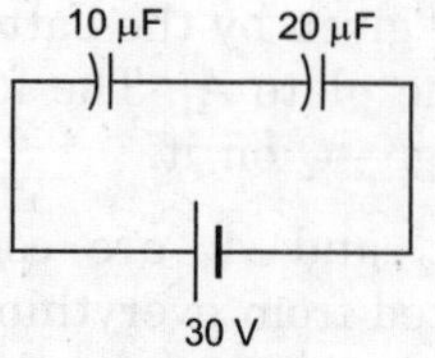

Figure 31.8

Solution : The two capacitors are joined in series. Their equivalent capacitance is given by $\frac{1}{C} = \frac{1}{C_1} + \frac{1}{C_2}$

or, $$C = \frac{C_1 C_2}{C_1 + C_2} = \frac{(10\ \mu\text{F})\ (20\ \mu\text{F})}{30\ \mu\text{F}} = \frac{20}{3}\ \mu\text{F}.$$

The charge supplied by the battery is

$$Q = CV$$
$$= \left(\frac{20}{3}\ \mu\text{F}\right)(30\ \text{V}) = 200\ \mu\text{C}.$$

In series combination, each capacitor has equal charge and this charge equals the charge supplied by the battery. Thus, each capacitor has a charge of 200 μC.

Parallel Combination

Figure (31.9) shows three capacitors connected in parallel. The capacitances are C_1, C_2 and C_3. The points

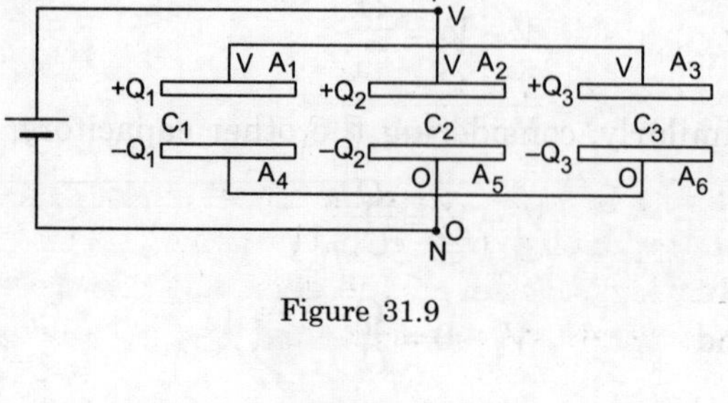

Figure 31.9

P and N are the two points through which a potential difference can be applied and charge can be supplied. Let us connect the point P to the positive terminal of a battery and the point N to its negative terminal. The battery supplies a charge $+Q$ which is distributed on the three positive plates A_1, A_2 and A_3 of the capacitors. Let the charges on the three plates A_1, A_2 and A_3 be Q_1, Q_2 and Q_3 respectively. The battery also supplies a charge $-Q$ which is distributed on the three plates A_4, A_5 and A_6. These plates must receive charges $-Q_1$, $-Q_2$ and $-Q_3$ respectively because the facing surfaces must have equal and opposite charges. We have

$$Q = Q_1 + Q_2 + Q_3. \quad \dots \text{(i)}$$

Let us take the potential of the point N to be zero. The potentials of the plates A_4, A_5 and A_6 are also zero as they are all connected to N by conducting wires. Let the potential of the point P be V. This will also be the potential of the plates A_1, A_2 and A_3. Thus, *the potential differences of the capacitors connected in parallel are equal for any value of capacitances.* Using the equation $Q = CV$ for the three capacitors,

$$Q_1 = C_1 V \quad \dots \text{(ii)}$$
$$Q_2 = C_2 V \quad \dots \text{(iii)}$$
and $$Q_3 = C_3 V. \quad \dots \text{(iv)}$$

Adding (ii), (iii) and (iv) and using (i),

$$Q = (C_1 + C_2 + C_3)V$$

or, $$\frac{Q}{V} = C_1 + C_2 + C_3.$$

But Q/V is the equivalent capacitance of the given combination. Thus,

$$C = C_1 + C_2 + C_3. \quad \dots \text{(31.6)}$$

In parallel combination, all the positive plates are at the same potential and all the negative plates are at the same potential. The potential difference on each capacitor is the same in parallel combination but the charges on the capacitors may be different. In series combination, the charges on the capacitors are equal, the potential differences may be different.

Example 31.5

Find the equivalent capacitance of the combination shown in figure (31.10) between the points P and N.

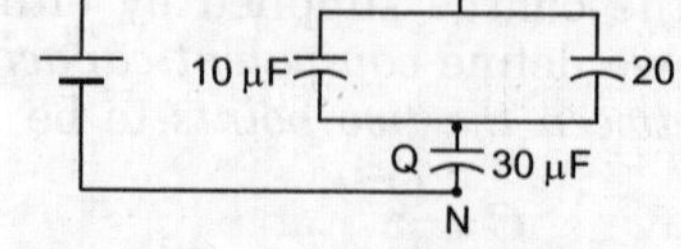

Figure 31.10

Solution : The 10 μF and 20 μF capacitors are connected in parallel. Their equivalent capacitance is

$10 \mu F + 20 \mu F = 30 \mu F$. We can replace the 10 μF and the 20 μF capacitors by a single capacitor of capacitance 30 μF between P and Q. This is connected in series with the given 30 μF capacitor. The equivalent capacitance C of this combination is given by

$$\frac{1}{C} = \frac{1}{30\ \mu F} + \frac{1}{30\ \mu F} \quad \text{or,} \quad C = 15\ \mu F.$$

We have used series–parallel combination to solve the above example. Sometimes it may not be easy to find the equivalent capacitance of a combination using the equations for series–parallel combinations. We may then use the general method which was applied to derive the equivalent capacitance in series and parallel combinations. For any given combination, one may proceed as follows:

Step 1

Identify the two points between which the equivalent capacitance is to be calculated. Call any one of them as P and the other as N.

Step 2

Connect (mentally) a battery between P and N with the positive terminal connected to P and the negative terminal to N. Send a charge $+Q$ from the positive terminal of the battery and $-Q$ from the negative terminal of the battery.

Step 3

Write the charges appearing on each of the plates of the capacitors. The charge conservation principle may be used. The facing surfaces of a capacitor will always have equal and opposite charges. Assume variables Q_1, Q_2 ..., etc., for charges wherever needed.

Step 4

Take the potential of the negative terminal N to be zero and that of the positive terminal P to be V. Write the potential of each of the plates. If necessary, assume variables V_1, V_2 ... .

Step 5

Write the capacitor equation $Q = CV$ for each capacitor. Eliminate Q_1, Q_2, ... and V_1, V_2, ..., etc., to obtain the equivalent capacitance $C = Q/V$.

Example 31.6

Find the equivalent capacitance of the combination shown in figure (31.11a) between the points P and N.

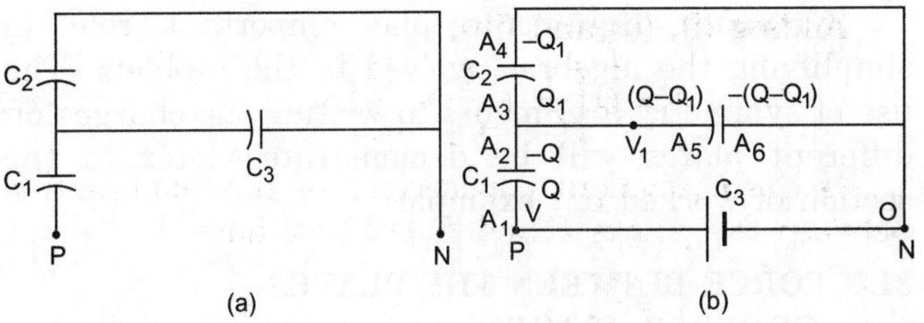

Figure 31.11

Solution : Let us connect a battery between the points P and N. The charges and the potentials are shown in figure (31.11b). The positive terminal of the battery supplies a charge $+Q$ which appears on the plate A_1. The facing plate A_2 gets a charge $-Q$. The plates A_2, A_3 and A_5 taken together form an isolated system. The total charge on these three plates should be zero. Let a charge Q_1 appear on A_3, then a charge $Q - Q_1$ will appear on A_5 to make the total charge zero on the three plates. The plate A_4 will get a charge $-Q_1$ (facing plate of A_3) and A_6 will get a charge $-(Q - Q_1)$ (facing plate of A_5). The total charge $-Q$ on A_4 and A_6 is supplied by the negative terminal of the battery. This completes the charge distribution.

Next, suppose the potential at the point N is zero and at P it is V. The potential of the plates A_4 and A_6 is also zero. The potential of the plate A_1 is V. The plates A_2, A_3 and A_5 are at the same potential. Let this common potential be V_1. This completes the potential distribution.

Applying the capacitor equation $Q = CV$ to the three capacitors,

$$Q = C_1(V - V_1) \quad \text{... (i)}$$

$$Q_1 = C_2 V_1 \quad \text{... (ii)}$$

and $$Q - Q_1 = C_3 V_1. \quad \text{... (iii)}$$

Adding (ii) and (iii),

$$Q = (C_2 + C_3)V_1$$

or, $$\frac{Q}{C_2 + C_3} = V_1. \quad \text{... (iv)}$$

From (i), $$\frac{Q}{C_1} = V - V_1. \quad \text{... (v)}$$

Adding (iv) and (v),

$$\frac{Q}{C_2 + C_3} + \frac{Q}{C_1} = V$$

or, $$\frac{(C_1 + C_2 + C_3)Q}{C_1(C_2 + C_3)} = V$$

or, $$C = \frac{Q}{V} = \frac{C_1(C_2 + C_3)}{C_1 + C_2 + C_3}.$$

It may be noted that the above example could be solved by using the equations for series–parallel combinations. However, the general method was used to demonstrate its application.

Symmetry arguments play important role in simplifying the algebra involved in the problem. The use of symmetry arguments in writing the charges on different plates will be demonstrated later in the section of worked out examples.

31.4 FORCE BETWEEN THE PLATES OF A CAPACITOR

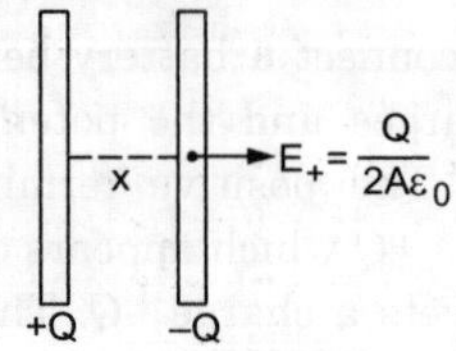

Figure 31.12

Consider a parallel-plate capacitor with plate area A. Suppose a positive charge $+Q$ is given to one plate and a negative charge $-Q$ to the other plate. The electric field due to only the positive plate is

$$E_+ = \frac{\sigma}{2\varepsilon_0} = \frac{Q}{2A\varepsilon_0}$$

at all points if the plate is large. The negative charge $-Q$ finds itself in the field of this positive charge. The force on $-Q$ is, therefore,

$$F = -QE_+$$

$$= (-Q)\frac{Q}{2A\varepsilon_0} = -\frac{Q^2}{2A\varepsilon_0}.$$

The magnitude of the force is

$$F = \frac{Q^2}{2A\varepsilon_0}.$$

This is the force with which the positive plate attracts the negative plate. This is also the force of attraction on the positive plate by the negative plate. Thus, the plates of a parallel-plate capacitor attract each other with a force

$$F = \frac{Q^2}{2A\varepsilon_0}. \qquad \text{... (31.7)}$$

31.5 ENERGY STORED IN A CAPACITOR AND ENERGY DENSITY IN ELECTRIC FIELD

Let us consider a parallel-plate capacitor of plate area A (figure 31.13). Suppose the plates of the capacitor are almost touching each other and a charge Q is given to the capacitor. One of the plates, say a, is kept fixed and the other, say b, is slowly pulled away from a to increase the separation from zero to d. The attractive force on the plate b at any instant due to the first plate is, from equation (31.7),

$$F = \frac{Q^2}{2A\varepsilon_0}.$$

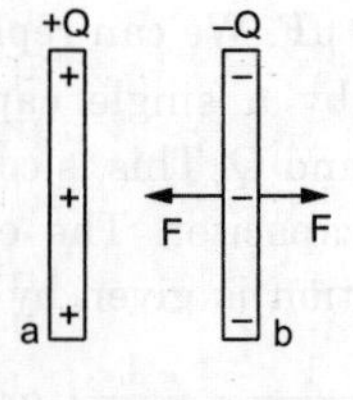

Figure 31.13

The person pulling the plate b must apply an equal force F in the opposite direction if the plate is only slowly moved.

The work done by the person during the displacement of the second plate is

$$W = Fd$$

$$= \frac{Q^2 d}{2A\varepsilon_0} = \frac{Q^2}{2\,C}$$

where C is the capacitance of the capacitor in the final position. The work done by the person must be equal to the increase in the energy of the system. Thus, a capacitor of capacitance C has a stored energy

$$U = \frac{Q^2}{2\,C} \qquad \text{... (31.8)}$$

where Q is the charge given to it. Using $Q = CV$, the above equation may also be written as

$$U = \frac{1}{2}CV^2 \qquad \text{... (31.9)}$$

or, $$U = \frac{1}{2}QV. \qquad \text{... (31.10)}$$

Example 31.7

Find the energy stored in a capacitor of capacitance 100 μF *when it is charged to a potential difference of* 20 V.

Solution : The energy stored in the capacitor is

$$U = \frac{1}{2}CV^2 = \frac{1}{2}(100\ \mu\text{F})\ (20\ \text{V})^2 = 0{\cdot}02\ \text{J}.$$

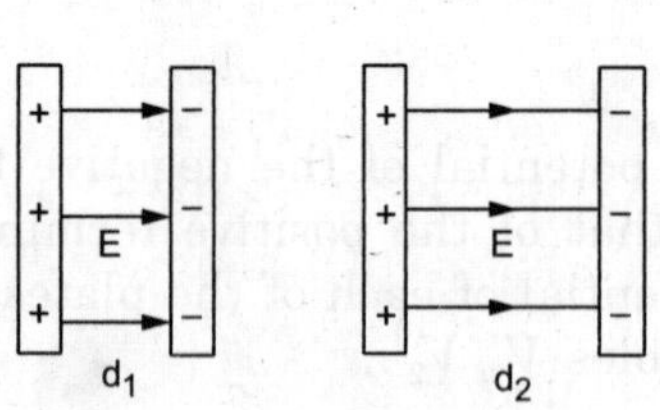

Figure 31.14

The energy stored in a capacitor is electrostatic potential energy. When we pull the plates of a capacitor apart, we have to do work against the electrostatic attraction between the plates. In which region of space is the energy stored ? When we increase the separation between the plates from d_1 to d_2, an amount $\frac{Q^2}{2A\varepsilon_0}(d_2 - d_1)$ of work is performed by us and this much energy goes into the capacitor. On the other hand, new electric field is created in a volume $A(d_2 - d_1)$ (figure 31.14). We conclude that the energy $\frac{Q^2}{2A\varepsilon_0}(d_2 - d_1)$ is stored in the volume $A(d_2 - d_1)$ which is now filled with the electric field. Thus, an electric field has energy associated with it. The energy stored per unit volume in the electric field is

$$u = \frac{\frac{Q^2(d_2 - d_1)}{2A\varepsilon_0}}{A(d_2 - d_1)} = \frac{Q^2}{2A^2\varepsilon_0}$$

$$= \frac{1}{2}\varepsilon_0\left(\frac{Q}{A\varepsilon_0}\right)^2 = \frac{1}{2}\varepsilon_0 E^2$$

where E is the intensity of the electric field.

Once it is established that a region containing electric field E has energy $\frac{1}{2}\varepsilon_0 E^2$ per unit volume, the result can be used for any electric field whether it is due to a capacitor or otherwise.

31.6 DIELECTRICS

In dielectric materials, effectively there are no free electrons. The monatomic materials are made of atoms. Each atom consists of a positively charged nucleus surrounded by electrons. In general, the centre of the negative charge coincides with the centre of the positive charge. Polyatomic materials, on the other hand, are made of molecules. The centre of the negative charge distribution in a molecule may or may not coincide with the centre of the positive charge distribution. If it does not coincide, each molecule has a permanent dipole moment $\vec{p}$. Such materials are known as *polar materials.* However, different molecules have different directions of the dipole moment because of the random thermal agitation in the material. In any volume containing a large number of molecules (say more than a thousand), the net dipole moment is zero. If such a material is placed in an electric field, the individual dipoles experience torque due to the field and they try to align along the field. On the other hand, thermal agitation tries to randomise the orientation and hence, there is a partial alignment. As a result, we get a net dipole moment in any volume of the material.

In nonpolar materials, the centre of the positive charge distribution in an atom or a molecule coincides with the centre of the negative charge distribution. The atoms or the molecules do not have any permanent dipole moment. If such a material is placed in an electric field, the electron charge distribution is slightly shifted opposite to the electric field. This induces dipole moment in each atom or molecule and thus, we get a dipole moment in any volume of the material.

Thus, when a dielectric material is placed in an electric field, dipole moment appears in any volume in it. This fact is known as *polarization* of the material. The *polarization vector* $\vec{P}$ is defined as the dipole moment per unit volume. Its magnitude P is often referred to as the polarization.

Consider a rectangular slab of a dielectric. The individual dipole moments are randomly oriented (figure 31.15a). In any volume containing a large number of molecules, the net charge is zero. When an electric field is applied, the dipoles get aligned along the field. Figure (31.15b) and (31.15c) show the effect of dipole alignment when a field is applied from left to right. We see that the interior is still charge free but the left surface of the slab gets negative charge and the right surface gets positive charge. The situation may be represented as in figure (31.15d). The charge appearing on the surface of a dielectric when placed in an electric field is called *induced charge.* As the induced charge appears due to a shift in the electrons bound to the nuclei, this charge is also called *bound charge.*

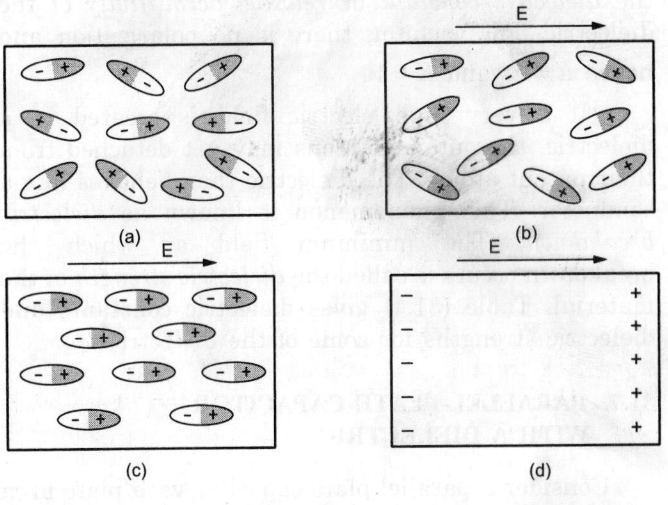

Figure 31.15

The surface charge density of the induced charge has a simple relationship with the polarization P. Suppose, the rectangular slab of figure (31.15) has a length l and area of cross-section A. Let σ_p be the magnitude of the induced charge per unit area on the faces. The dipole moment of the slab is then $(\sigma_p A)l = \sigma_p(Al)$. The polarization is dipole moment induced per unit volume. Thus,

$$P = \frac{\sigma_p(Al)}{Al} = \sigma_p. \qquad \text{... (31.11)}$$

Although this result is deduced for a rectangular slab, it is true in general. The induced surface charge density is equal in magnitude to the polarization P.

Dielectric Constant

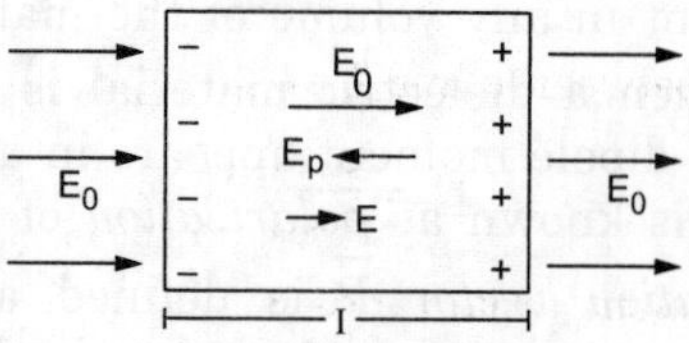

Figure 31.16

Because of the induced charges, an extra electric field is produced inside the material. Let $\vec{E}_0$ be the applied field due to external sources and $\vec{E}_p$ be the field due to polarization (figure 31.16). The resultant field is $\vec{E} = \vec{E}_0 + \vec{E}_p$. For homogeneous and isotropic dielectrics, the direction of $\vec{E}_p$ is opposite to the direction of $\vec{E}_0$. The resultant field $\vec{E}$ is in the same direction as the applied field $\vec{E}_0$ but its magnitude is reduced. We can write

$$\vec{E} = \frac{\vec{E}_0}{K}$$

where K is a constant for the given dielectric which has a value greater than one. This constant K is called the *dielectric constant* or *relative permittivity* of the dielectric. For vacuum, there is no polarization and hence $\vec{E} = \vec{E}_0$ and $K = 1$.

If a very high electric field is created in a dielectric, the outer electrons may get detached from their parent atoms. The dielectric then behaves like a conductor. This phenomenon is known as *dielectric breakdown*. The minimum field at which the breakdown occurs is called the *dielectric strength* of the material. Table (31.1) gives dielectric constants and dielectric strengths for some of the dielectrics.

31.7. PARALLEL-PLATE CAPACITOR WITH A DIELECTRIC

Consider a parallel-plate capacitor with plate area A and separation d between the plates (figure 31.17). A dielectric slab of dielectric constant K is inserted in the space between the plates. Suppose, the slab almost completely fills the space between the plates. A charge Q is given to the positive plate and $-Q$ to the negative plate of the capacitor. The electric field polarizes the dielectric so that induced charges $+Q_p$ and $-Q_p$ appear on the two faces of the slab.

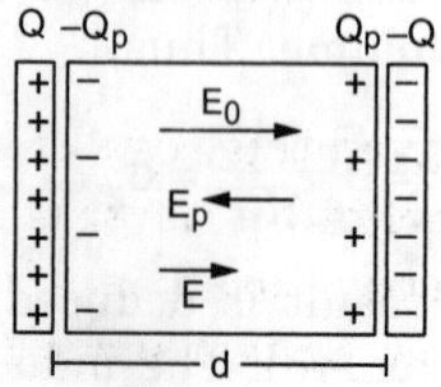

Figure 31.17

Table 31.1 : *Dielectric constants and dielectric strengths*

Material	Dielectric constant	Dielectric strength (kVmm^{-1})
Vacuum	1	∞
Pyrex Glass	5·6	≈ 14
Mica	3–6	12
Neoprene rubber	6·9	12
Bakelite	4·9	24
Plexiglas	3·40	40
Fused quartz	3·8	8
Paper	3·5	14
Polystyrene	2·6	25
Teflon	2·1	60
Strontium titanate	310	8
Titanium dioxide	100	6
Water	80	–
Glycerin	42·5	–
Benzene	2·3	–
Air (1 atm)	1·00059	3
Air (100 atm)	1·0548	–

The electric field at a point between the plates due to the charges $+Q$, $-Q$ on the capacitor plates is

$$E_0 = \frac{\sigma}{\varepsilon_0} = \frac{Q}{A\varepsilon_0} \quad \text{... (i)}$$

in a direction left to right in the figure (31.17).

From the definition of dielectric constant, the resultant field is

$$E = \frac{E_0}{K} = \frac{Q}{\varepsilon_0 AK} \cdot \quad \text{... (ii)}$$

The potential difference between the plates is

$$V = Ed$$

$$= \frac{Qd}{\varepsilon_0 AK} \cdot$$

The capacitance is

$$C = \frac{Q}{V} = \frac{K\varepsilon_0 A}{d} = KC_0 \quad \text{... (31.12)}$$

where $C_0 = \frac{\varepsilon_0 A}{d}$ is the capacitance without the dielectric. Thus,

The capacitance of a capacitor is increased by a factor of K when the space between the plates is filled with a dielectric of dielectric constant K.

This result is often taken as the definition of the dielectric constant.

Magnitude of the Induced Charge

From (i), the electric field at a point between the plates due to the charges $+Q$, $-Q$ is

$$E_0 = \frac{Q}{A\varepsilon_0} \cdot$$

The field due to the charges Q_p, $-Q_p$ is directed oppositely and has magnitude

$$E_p = \frac{\sigma_p}{\varepsilon_0} = \frac{Q_p}{A\varepsilon_0} .$$

The resultant field is

$$E = E_0 - E_p$$

$$= \frac{Q - Q_p}{A\varepsilon_0} . \quad \text{... (iii)}$$

From equations (ii) and (iii),

$$\frac{Q - Q_p}{\varepsilon_0 A} = \frac{Q}{\varepsilon_0 AK}$$

or, $$Q - Q_p = \frac{Q}{K}$$

or, $$Q_p = Q\left(1 - \frac{1}{K}\right) . \quad \text{... (31.13)}$$

Example 31.8

Two parallel-plate capacitors, each of capacitance 40 μF, are connected in series. The space between the plates of one capacitor is filled with a dielectric material of dielectric constant $K = 4$. Find the equivalent capacitance of the system.

Solution : The capacitance of the capacitor with the dielectric is

$$C_1 = KC_0 = 4 \times 40\ \mu\text{F} = 160\ \mu\text{F}.$$

The other capacitor has capacitance $C_2 = 40\ \mu\text{F}$. As they are connected in series, the equivalent capacitance is

$$C = \frac{C_1 C_2}{C_1 + C_2} = \frac{(160\ \mu\text{F})\ (40\ \mu\text{F})}{200\ \mu\text{F}} = 32\ \mu\text{F}.$$

Example 31.9

A parallel-plate capacitor has plate area A and plate separation d. The space between the plates is filled up to a thickness x (< d) with a dielectric of dielectric constant K. Calculate the capacitance of the system.

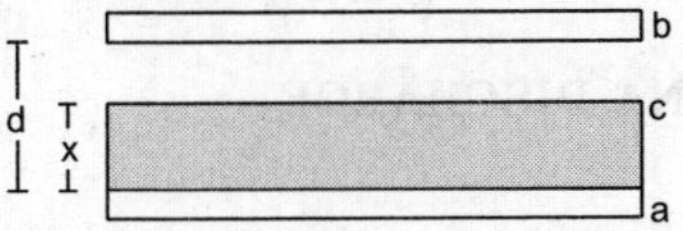

Figure 31.18

Solution :

The situation is shown in figure (31.18). The given system is equivalent to the series combination of two capacitors, one between a and c and the other between c and b. Here c represents the upper surface of the dielectric. This is because the potential at the upper surface of the dielectric is constant and we can imagine a thin metal plate being placed there.

The capacitance of the capacitor between a and c is

$$C_1 = \frac{K\varepsilon_0 A}{x}$$

and that between c and b is

$$C_2 = \frac{\varepsilon_0 A}{d - x} .$$

The equivalent capacitance is

$$C = \frac{C_1 C_2}{C_1 + C_2} = \frac{K\varepsilon_0 A}{Kd - x(K - 1)} .$$

31.8 AN ALTERNATIVE FORM OF GAUSS'S LAW

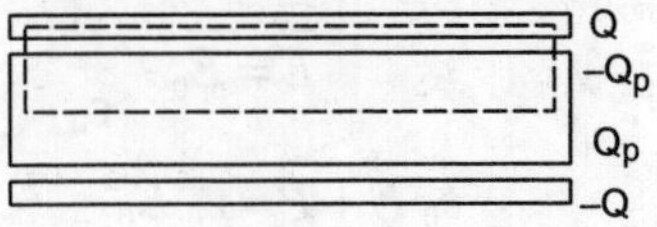

Figure 31.19

Let us again consider a parallel-plate capacitor with a charge Q. The space between the plates is filled with a dielectric slab of dielectric constant K. Let us consider a Gaussian surface as shown in figure (31.19). The charge enclosed by the surface is $Q - Q_p$. From Gauss's law,

$$\oint \vec{E} \cdot d\vec{S} = \frac{Q - Q_p}{\varepsilon_0} \quad \text{... (i)}$$

$$= \frac{1}{\varepsilon_0}\left[Q - Q\left(1 - \frac{1}{K}\right)\right] = \frac{Q}{\varepsilon_0 K}$$

or, $$\oint K\vec{E} \cdot d\vec{S} = \frac{Q_{free}}{\varepsilon_0} . \quad \text{... (31.14)}$$

Q_{free} is used in place of Q to emphasise that it is the free charge given to the plates and does not include the bound charge appearing due to polarization.

Equation (31.14) is taken as another form of Gauss's law. This form differs from the usual form of Gauss's law in two respects. Firstly, the charge Q_{free} appearing on the right-hand side is not the total charge inside the Gaussian surface. It is the free charge or external charge inside the Gaussian surface. The bound charge Q_p appearing due to polarization of the dielectric is left out. Secondly, an extra factor K appears on the left-hand side. The two differences compensate the effects of each other and the two forms of Gauss's law are identical. Either of the two may be used in any case.

Though we derived this result for a special case of parallel-plate capacitor, it is true in any situation where the dielectric used is homogeneous and isotropic. Let us now write Gauss's law in yet another form valid for any case.

Displacement Vector

The field due to the polarization is

$$E_p = \frac{\sigma_p}{\varepsilon_0} = \frac{P}{\varepsilon_0}$$

where P is the polarization (the dipole moment per unit volume). As the direction of E_p is opposite to the polarization vector $\vec{P}$, we write

$$\vec{E}_p = -\frac{\vec{P}}{\varepsilon_0}.$$

Now, $\vec{E} = \vec{E}_0 + \vec{E}_p$

or, $\vec{E} = \vec{E}_0 - \frac{\vec{P}}{\varepsilon_0}$

or, $\varepsilon_0 \vec{E} + \vec{P} = \varepsilon_0 \vec{E}_0$ ... (i)

or, $\oint (\varepsilon_0 \vec{E} + \vec{P}) \cdot d\vec{S} = \oint \varepsilon_0 \vec{E}_0 \cdot d\vec{S}$

over any closed surface. As $\vec{E}_0$ is the field produced by the free charge Q_{free}, $\oint \varepsilon_0 \vec{E}_0 \cdot d\vec{S} = Q_{free}$ from Gauss's law. Thus,

$$\oint (\varepsilon_0 \vec{E} + \vec{P}) \cdot d\vec{S} = Q_{free}. \quad \text{... (ii)}$$

The quantity $\varepsilon_0 \vec{E} + \vec{P}$ is known as the *electric displacement vector* $\vec{D}$. Equation (ii) above may be written in terms of $\vec{D}$ as

$$\oint \vec{D} \cdot d\vec{S} = Q_{free} \quad \text{... (31.15)}$$

which is another form of Gauss's law.

If there is no polarization, $\vec{D} = \varepsilon_0 \vec{E}$ and Q_{free} is equal to the total charge inside the Gaussian surface. Equation (31.15) then reduces to the usual form of Gauss's law.

In case of homogeneous and isotropic dielectrics, $\vec{E}_0 = K\vec{E}$ so that equation (i) above gives $\vec{D} = \varepsilon_0 K\vec{E}$ and equation (31.15) reduces to (31.14).

31.9 ELECTRIC FIELD DUE TO A POINT CHARGE q PLACED IN AN INFINITE DIELECTRIC

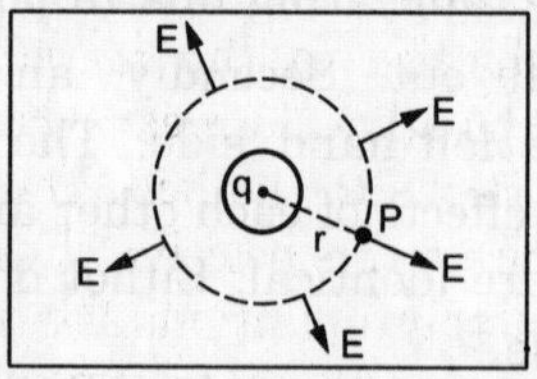

Figure 31.20

Suppose, a point charge q is placed inside an infinite dielectric and we wish to calculate the electric field at a point P at a distance r from the charge q (figure 31.20). We draw a spherical surface through P with the centre at q. From Gauss's law,

$$\oint K\,\vec{E} \cdot d\vec{S} = \frac{q}{\varepsilon_0}$$

or, $$KE\,4\pi r^2 = \frac{q}{\varepsilon_0}$$

or, $$E = \frac{q}{4\pi\varepsilon_0 K r^2}. \quad \text{... (31.16)}$$

The field is radially away from the charge. Note that q is the total *free charge* inside the Gaussian surface.

It should be clear that the field $\frac{q}{4\pi\varepsilon_0 K r^2}$ is due to the free charge q and the polarization charges induced in the dielectric medium. Because of the radially outward field (assuming q to be positive), negative charges shift inward. This produces an induced charge $-q\left(1 - \frac{1}{K}\right)$ on the surface of the cavity in the dielectric in which the charge q is residing. The effective charge is, therefore, $q - q\left(1 - \frac{1}{K}\right) = q/K$ and hence the field is $\frac{q}{4\pi\varepsilon_0 K r^2}$.

31.10 ENERGY IN THE ELECTRIC FIELD IN A DIELECTRIC

Consider a parallel-plate capacitor filled with a dielectric of dielectric constant K. The energy stored in the capacitor is $U = \frac{1}{2} CV^2$. The energy density in the volume between the plates is

$$u = \frac{U}{Ad} = \frac{\frac{1}{2}\left(\frac{K\varepsilon_0 A}{d}\right)V^2}{Ad} = \frac{1}{2} K\varepsilon_0 \left(\frac{V}{d}\right)^2 = \frac{1}{2} K\varepsilon_0 E^2$$

where $E = V/d$ is the electric field between the plates.

We see that the energy density in dielectrics is greater than that in vacuum for the same electric field. The dipole moments interact with each other so as to give this additional energy.

31.11 CORONA DISCHARGE

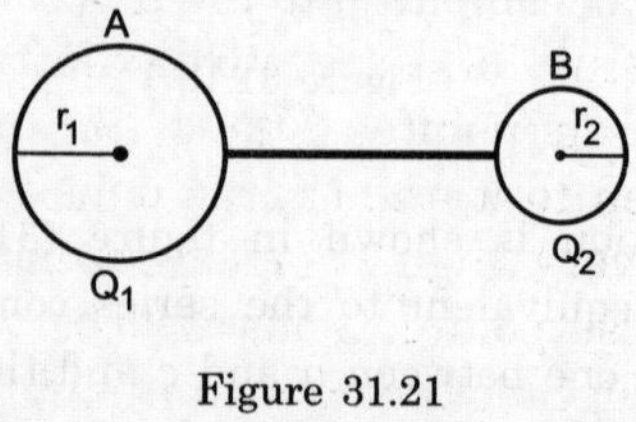

Figure 31.21

Let us consider two conducting spheres A and B connected to each other by a conducting wire. The radius of A is r_1 which is larger than the radius r_2 of B. A charge Q is given to this system. Suppose a part

Q_1 resides on the surface of A and the rest Q_2 on the surface of B. The potential of the sphere A is

$$V_1 = \frac{Q_1}{4\pi\varepsilon_0 r_1}$$

and that of the sphere B is

$$V_2 = \frac{Q_2}{4\pi\varepsilon_0 r_2}.$$

As the two spheres are connected by a conducting wire, their potentials must be the same. Thus,

$$\frac{Q_1}{4\pi\varepsilon_0 r_1} = \frac{Q_2}{4\pi\varepsilon_0 r_2}$$

or, $$\sigma_1 r_1 = \sigma_2 r_2$$

or, $$\frac{\sigma_1}{\sigma_2} = \frac{r_2}{r_1} \qquad \dots (31.17)$$

where σ_1 and σ_2 are charge densities on the two spheres. We see that the sphere with smaller radius has larger charge density to maintain the same potential.

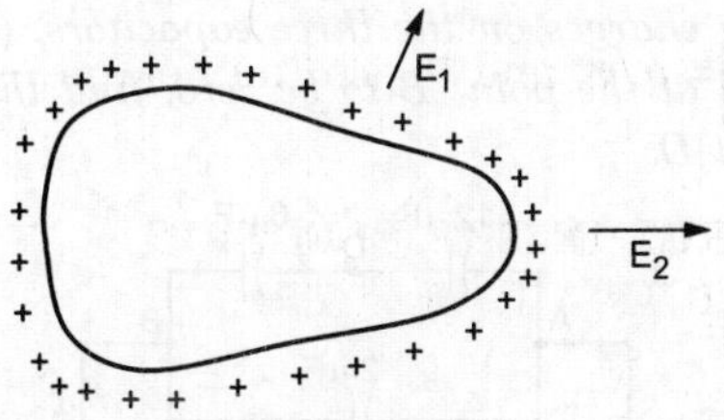

Figure 31.22

Now consider a single conductor with a nonspherical shape. If a charge is given to this conductor (figure 31.22), the charge density will not be uniform on the entire surface. A portion where the surface is more "flat" may be considered as part of a sphere of larger radius. The charge density at such a portion will be smaller from equation (31.17). At portions where the surface is more curved, the charge density will be larger. More precisely, the charge density will be larger where the radius of curvature is small.

The electric field just outside the surface of a conductor is σ/ε_0. Thus, the electric field near the portions of small radius of curvature (more curved part) is large as compared to the field near the portions of large radius of curvature (flatter part). If a conductor has a pointed shape like a needle and a charge is given to it, the charge density at the pointed end will be very high. Correspondingly, the electric field near these pointed ends will be very high which may cause dielectric breakdown in air. The charge may jump from the conductor to the air because of increased conductivity of the air. Often this discharge of air is accompanied by a visible glow surrounding the pointed end. This phenomenon is called *corona discharge.*

31.12 HIGH-VOLTAGE GENERATOR

In 1929, Robert J van de Graaff designed a machine which could produce large electrostatic potential difference, of the order of 10^7 volts. This machine, known as *van de Graaff generator,* is now described.

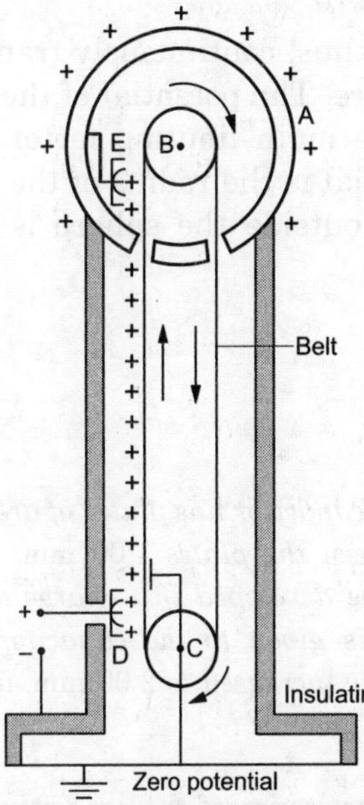

Figure 31.23

A hollow, metallic sphere A is mounted on an insulating stand. A pulley B is mounted at the centre of the sphere and another pulley C is mounted near the bottom. A belt of insulating material (such as silk) goes over the pulleys. The pulley C is continuously driven by an electric motor, or by hand for a smaller machine used for demonstration. The belt, therefore, continuously moves. Two comb-shaped conductors D and E, having a number of metallic needles, are mounted near the pulleys. The needles point towards the belt. The lower comb D is maintained at a positive potential of the order of 10^4 volts by a power supply system. The upper comb E is connected to the metallic sphere A.

Because of the high electric field near the needles of D, the air becomes conducting (corona discharge). The negative charges in the air move towards the needles and the positive charges towards the belt. This positive charge sticks to the belt. The negative charge neutralises some of the positive charge on the comb D. The power supply maintains the positive potential of the needles by supplying more positive charge to it. Effectively, positive charge is transferred from the power supply to the belt. As the belt moves, this positive charge is physically carried upwards. When it reaches near the upper comb E, corona discharge takes place and the air becomes conducting. The negative charges of the air move towards the belt and the positive charges towards the needles of the comb. The negative charges neutralise the positive charge on the belt. The positive charges of the air which have moved to the comb are transferred to the sphere. Effectively, the positive charge on the belt is transferred to the sphere. This positive charge quickly goes to the outer surface of the sphere.

The machine, thus, continuously transfers positive charge to the sphere. The potential of the sphere keeps on increasing. The main limiting factor on the value of this high potential is the radius of the sphere. If the electric field just outside the sphere is sufficient for dielectric breakdown of air, no more charge can be transferred to it. The dielectric strength of air is $3\times10^{6}\ \mathrm{V\,m^{-1}}$. For a conducting sphere, the electric field just outside the sphere is $E=\frac{Q}{4\pi\varepsilon_0 R^2}$ and the potential of the sphere is $V=\frac{Q}{4\pi\varepsilon_0 R}$. Thus, $V=ER$. To have a field of $3\times10^{6}\ \mathrm{V\,m^{-1}}$ with a sphere of radius 1 m, its potential should be 3×10^{6} V. Thus, the potential of a sphere of radius 1 m can be raised to 3×10^{6} V by this method. The potential can be increased by enclosing the sphere in a highly evacuated chamber.

Worked Out Examples

1. *A parallel-plate capacitor has plates of area 200 cm² and separation between the plates 1·00 mm. What potential difference will be developed if a charge of 1·00 nC (i.e., $1{\cdot}00\times10^{-9}$ C) is given to the capacitor? If the plate separation is now increased to 2·00 mm, what will be the new potential difference?*

Solution : The capacitance of the capacitor is $C=\frac{\varepsilon_0 A}{d}$

$$=8{\cdot}85\times10^{-12}\ \mathrm{Fm^{-1}}\times\frac{200\times10^{-4}\ \mathrm{m^2}}{1\times10^{-3}\ \mathrm{m}}$$

$$=0{\cdot}177\times10^{-9}\ \mathrm{F}=0{\cdot}177\ \mathrm{nF}.$$

The potential difference between the plates is

$$V=\frac{Q}{C}=\frac{1\ \mathrm{nC}}{0{\cdot}177\ \mathrm{nF}}=5{\cdot}65\ \text{volts}.$$

If the separation is increased from 1·00 mm to 2·00 mm, the capacitance is decreased by a factor of 2. If the charge remains the same, the potential difference will increase by a factor of 2. Thus, the new potential difference will be

$$5{\cdot}65\ \text{volts}\times2=11{\cdot}3\ \text{volts}.$$

2. *An isolated sphere has a capacitance of 50 pF. (a) Calculate its radius. (b) How much charge should be placed on it to raise its potential to 10^4 V?*

Solution : (a) The capacitance of an isolated sphere is $C=4\pi\varepsilon_0 R$. Thus,

$$50\times10^{-12}\ \mathrm{F}=\frac{R}{9\times10^{9}\ \mathrm{mF^{-1}}}$$

or, $$R=50\times10^{-12}\times9\times10^{9}\ \mathrm{m}=45\ \mathrm{cm}.$$

(b) $$Q=CV$$

$$=50\times10^{-12}\ \mathrm{F}\times10^{4}\ \mathrm{V}=0{\cdot}5\ \mu\mathrm{C}.$$

3. *Consider the connections shown in figure (31-W1). (a) Find the capacitance between the points A and B. (b) Find the charges on the three capacitors. (c) Taking the potential at the point B to be zero, find the potential at the point D.*

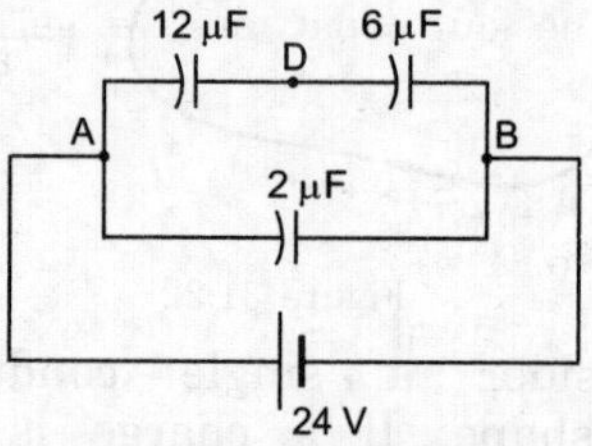

Figure 31-W1

Solution : (a) The 12 μF and 6 μF capacitors are joined in series. The equivalent of these two will have a capacitance given by

$$\frac{1}{C}=\frac{1}{12\ \mu\mathrm{F}}+\frac{1}{6\ \mu\mathrm{F}},$$

or, $$C=4\ \mu\mathrm{F}.$$

The combination of these two capacitors is joined in parallel with the 2 μF capacitor. Thus, the equivalent capacitance between A and B is

$$4\ \mu\mathrm{F}+2\ \mu\mathrm{F}=6\ \mu\mathrm{F}.$$

(b) The charge supplied by the battery is

$$Q=CV=6\ \mu\mathrm{F}\times24\ \mathrm{V}=144\ \mu\mathrm{C}.$$

The potential difference across the 2 μF capacitor is 24 V. The charge on this capacitor is, therefore,

$$2\ \mu\mathrm{F}\times24\ \mathrm{V}=48\ \mu\mathrm{C}.$$

The charge on the 12 μF and 6 μF capacitor is, therefore,

$$144\ \mu\mathrm{C}-48\ \mu\mathrm{C}=96\ \mu\mathrm{C}.$$

(c) The potential difference across the 6 μF capacitor is

$$\frac{96\ \mu\mathrm{C}}{6\ \mu\mathrm{F}}=16\ \mathrm{V}.$$

As the potential at the point B is taken to be zero, the potential at the point D is 16 V.

4. *If 100 volts of potential difference is applied between a and b in the circuit of figure (31-W2a), find the potential difference between c and d.*

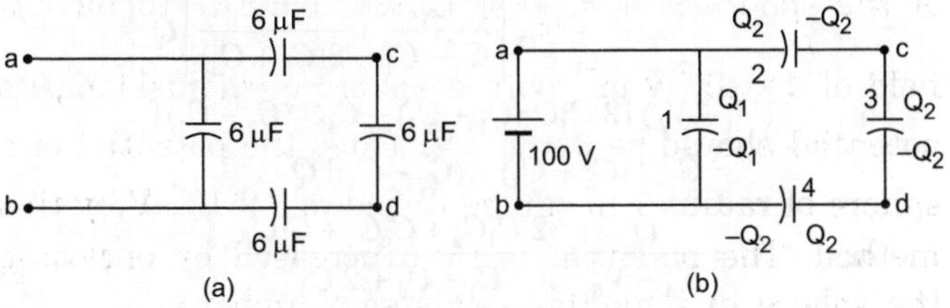

Figure 31-W2

Solution : The charge distribution on different plates is shown in figure (31-W2b). Suppose charge $Q_1 + Q_2$ is given by the positive terminal of the battery, out of which Q_1 resides on the positive plate of capacitor (1) and Q_2 on that of (2). The remaining plates will have charges as shown in the figure.

Take the potential at the point b to be zero. The potential at a will be 100 V. Let the potentials at points c and d be V_c and V_d respectively. Writing the equation $Q = CV$ for the four capacitors, we get,

$$Q_1 = 6\ \mu F \times 100\ V = 600\ \mu C \qquad \text{... (i)}$$

$$Q_2 = 6\ \mu F \times (100\ V - V_c) \qquad \text{... (ii)}$$

$$Q_2 = 6\ \mu F \times (V_c - V_d) \qquad \text{... (iii)}$$

$$Q_2 = 6\ \mu F \times V_d. \qquad \text{... (iv)}$$

From (ii) and (iii),

$$100\ V - V_c = V_c - V_d$$

or, $$2\ V_c - V_d = 100\ V \qquad \text{... (v)}$$

and from (iii) and (iv),

$$V_c - V_d = V_d$$

or, $$V_c = 2\ V_d. \qquad \text{... (vi)}$$

From (v) and (vi),

$$V_d = \frac{100}{3}\ V \text{ and } V_c = \frac{200}{3}\ V$$

so that $V_c - V_d = \dfrac{100}{3}$ V.

5. *Find the charges on the three capacitors shown in figure (31-W3a).*

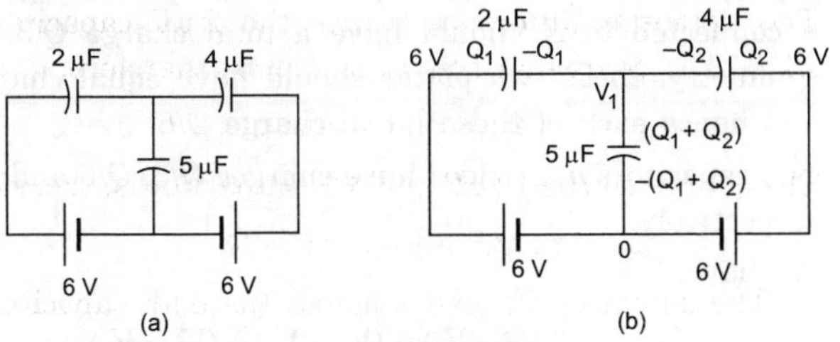

Figure 31-W3

Solution : Take the potential at the junction of the batteries to be zero. Let the left battery supply a charge Q_1 and the right battery a charge Q_2. The charge on the 5 μF capacitor will be $Q_1 + Q_2$. Let the potential at the junction of the capacitors be V_1. The charges at different plates and potentials at different points are shown in figure (31-W3b).

Note that the charges on the three plates which are in contact add to zero. It should be so, because, these plates taken together form an isolated system which cannot receive charges from the batteries. Applying the equation $Q = CV$ to the three capacitors, we get,

$$Q_1 = 2\ \mu F(6\ V - V_1) \qquad \text{... (i)}$$

$$Q_2 = 4\ \mu F(6\ V - V_1) \qquad \text{... (ii)}$$

and $$Q_1 + Q_2 = 5\ \mu F(V_1 - 0). \qquad \text{... (iii)}$$

From (i) and (ii),

$$2\ Q_1 - Q_2 = 0 \text{ or, } Q_2 = 2\ Q_1.$$

From (ii) and (iii),

$$5\ Q_2 + 4(Q_1 + Q_2) = 20\ \mu F \times 6\ V$$

or, $$4\ Q_1 + 9\ Q_2 = 120\ \mu C$$

or, $$4\ Q_1 + 18\ Q_1 = 120\ \mu C$$

or, $$Q_1 = 5{\cdot}45\ \mu C \text{ and } Q_2 = 10{\cdot}9\ \mu C.$$

Thus, the charges on the 2 μF, 4 μF and 5 μF capacitors are 5·45 μC, 10·9 μC and 16·35 μC respectively.

6. *Find the equivalent capacitance of the system shown in figure (31-W4a) between the points a and b.*

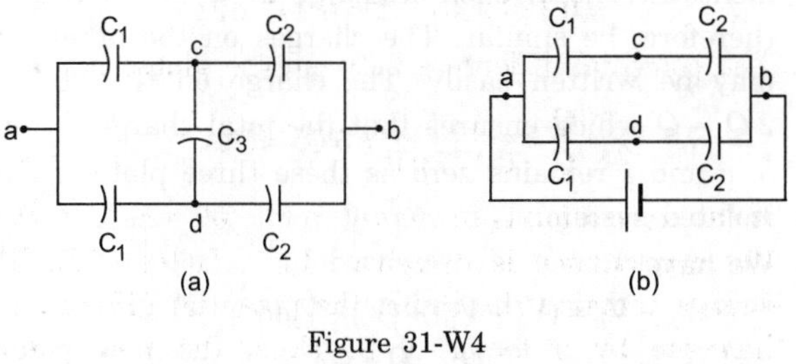

Figure 31-W4

Solution : Suppose, the capacitor C_3 is removed from the given system and a battery is connected between a and b. The remaining system is shown in figure (31-W4b). From the symmetry of the figure, the potential at c will be the same as the potential at d. Thus, if the capacitor C_3 is connected between c and d, it will have no charge. The charges of all the remaining four capacitors will remain unchanged. Thus, the system of capacitors in figure (31-W4a) is equivalent to that in the figure (31-W4b). The equivalent capacitance of the system in figure (31-W4b) can be calculated by applying the formulae for series and parallel combinations. C_1 and C_2 are connected in series. Their equivalent capacitance is

$$C = \frac{C_1 C_2}{C_1 + C_2} \cdot$$

Two such capacitors are joined in parallel. So the equivalent capacitance of the given system is

$$2C = \frac{2\,C_1C_2}{C_1 + C_2}.$$

7. *Find the equivalent capacitance between the point A and B in figure (31-W5a).*

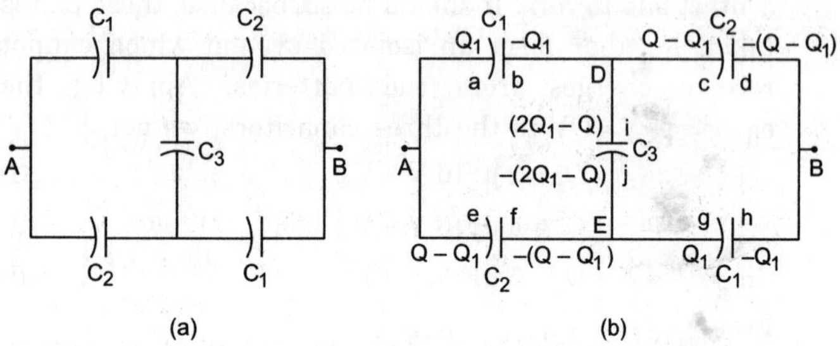

Figure 31-W5

Solution : Let us connect a battery between the points *A* and *B*. The charge distribution is shown in figure (31-W5b). Suppose the positive terminal of the battery supplies a charge $+Q$ and the negative terminal a charge $-Q$. The charge Q is divided between plates *a* and *e*. A charge Q_1 goes to the plate *a* and the rest $Q - Q_1$ goes to the plate *e*. The charge $-Q$ supplied by the negative terminal is divided between plates *d* and *h*. Using the symmetry of the figure, charge $-Q_1$ goes to the plate *h* and $-(Q - Q_1)$ to the plate *d*. This is because if you look into the circuit from *A* or from *B*, the circuit looks identical. The division of charge at *A* and at *B* should, therefore, be similar. The charges on the other plates may be written easily. The charge on the plate *i* is $2\,Q_1 - Q$ which ensures that the total charge on plates *b, c* and *i* remains zero as these three plates form an isolated system.

We have,

$$V_A - V_B = (V_A - V_D) + (V_D - V_B)$$

$$= \frac{Q_1}{C_1} + \frac{Q - Q_1}{C_2} \qquad \text{... (i)}$$

Also, $$V_A - V_B = (V_A - V_D) + (V_D - V_E) + (V_E - V_B)$$

$$= \frac{Q_1}{C_1} + \frac{2\,Q_1 - Q}{C_3} + \frac{Q_1}{C_1}. \qquad \text{... (ii)}$$

We have to eliminate Q_1 from these equations to get the equivalent capacitance $Q/(V_A - V_B)$.

The first equation may be written as

$$V_A - V_B = Q_1\left(\frac{1}{C_1} - \frac{1}{C_2}\right) + \frac{Q}{C_2}$$

or, $$\frac{C_1C_2}{C_2 - C_1}(V_A - V_B) = Q_1 + \frac{C_1}{C_2 - C_1}Q. \qquad \text{... (iii)}$$

The second equation may be written as

$$V_A - V_B = 2\,Q_1\left(\frac{1}{C_1} + \frac{1}{C_3}\right) - \frac{Q}{C_3}$$

or, $$\frac{C_1C_3}{2(C_1 + C_3)}(V_A - V_B) = Q_1 - \frac{C_1}{2(C_1 + C_3)}Q. \qquad \text{... (iv)}$$

Subtracting (iv) from (iii),

$$(V_A - V_B)\left[\frac{C_1C_2}{C_2 - C_1} - \frac{C_1C_3}{2(C_1 + C_3)}\right]$$

$$= \left[\frac{C_1}{C_2 - C_1} + \frac{C_1}{2(C_1 + C_3)}\right]Q$$

or, $$(V_A - V_B)\,[2\,C_1C_2(C_1 + C_3) - C_1C_3(C_2 - C_1)]$$

$$= C_1[2\,(C_1 + C_3) + (C_2 - C_1)]\,Q$$

or, $$C = \frac{Q}{V_A - V_B} = \frac{2\,C_1C_2 + C_2C_3 + C_3C_1}{C_1 + C_2 + 2\,C_3}.$$

8. *Twelve capacitors, each having a capacitance C, are connected to form a cube (figure 31-W6a). Find the equivalent capacitance between the diagonally opposite corners such as A and B.*

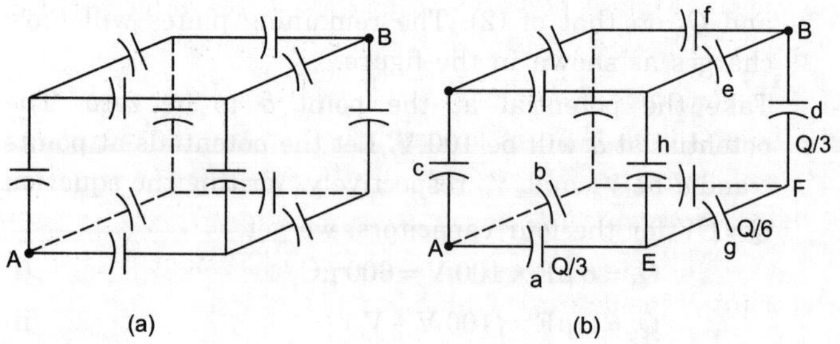

Figure 31-W6

Solution : Suppose the points *A* and *B* are connected to a battery. The charges appearing on some of the capacitors are shown in figure (31-W6b). Suppose the positive terminal of the battery supplies a charge $+Q$ through the point *A*. This charge is divided on the three plates connected to *A*. Looking from *A*, the three sides of the cube have identical properties and hence, the charge will be equally distributed on the three plates. Each of the capacitors *a*, *b* and *c* will receive a charge $Q/3$.

The negative terminal of the battery supplies a charge $-Q$ through the point *B*. This is again divided equally on the three plates connected to *B*. Each of the capacitors *d, e* and *f* gets equal charge $Q/3$.

Now consider the capacitors *g* and *h*. As the three plates connected to the point *E* form an isolated system, their total charge must be zero. The negative plate of the capacitor *a* has a charge $-Q/3$. The two plates of *g* and *h* connected to *E* should have a total charge $Q/3$. By symmetry, these two plates should have equal charges and hence each of these has a charge $Q/6$.

The capacitors *a*, *g* and *d* have charges $Q/3$, $Q/6$ and $Q/3$ respectively.

We have,

$$V_A - V_B = (V_A - V_E) + (V_E - V_F) + (V_F - V_B)$$

$$= \frac{Q/3}{C} + \frac{Q/6}{C} + \frac{Q/3}{C} = \frac{5Q}{6C}$$

or, $$C_{eq} = \frac{Q}{V_A - V_B} = \frac{6}{5} C.$$

9. *The negative plate of a parallel plate capacitor is given a charge of* -20×10^{-8} C. *Find the charges appearing on the four surfaces of the capacitor plates.*

Solution :

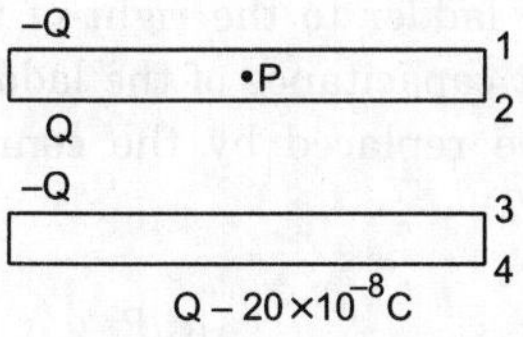

Figure 31-W7

Let the charge appearing on the inner surface of the negative plate be $-Q$. The charge on its outer surface will be $Q - 20 \times 10^{-8}$ C.

The charge on the inner surface of the positive plate will be $+Q$ from Gauss's law and that on the outer surface will be $-Q$ as the positive plate is electrically neutral. The distribution is shown in figure (31-W7).

To obtain the value of Q, consider the electric field at a point P inside the upper plate.

Field due to surface (1) $= \frac{Q}{2\varepsilon_0 A}$ upward,

due to surface (2) $= \frac{Q}{2\varepsilon_0 A}$ upward,

due to surface (3) $= \frac{Q}{2\varepsilon_0 A}$ downward

and due to surface (4) $= \frac{Q - 20 \times 10^{-8}\text{ C}}{2\varepsilon_0 A}$ upward.

As P is a point inside the conductor, the field here must be zero. Thus,

$$Q = -Q + 20 \times 10^{-8}\text{ C}$$

or, $$Q = 10 \times 10^{-8}\text{ C}.$$

The charges on the four surfaces may be written immediately from figure (31-W7).

10. *Three capacitors of capacitances* 2 μF, 3 μF *and* 6 μF *are connected in series with a* 12 V *battery. All the connecting wires are disconnected, the three positive plates are connected together and the three negative plates are connected together. Find the charges on the three capacitors after the reconnection.*

Solution : The equivalent capacitance of the three capacitors joined in series is given by

$$\frac{1}{C} = \frac{1}{2\ \mu\text{F}} + \frac{1}{3\ \mu\text{F}} + \frac{1}{6\ \mu\text{F}}$$

or, $$C = 1\ \mu\text{F}.$$

The charge supplied by the battery = 1 μF × 12 V = 12 μC.

As the capacitors are connected in series, 12 μC charge appears on each of the positive plates and −12 μC on each of the negative plates. The charged capacitors are now connected as shown in figure (31-W8).

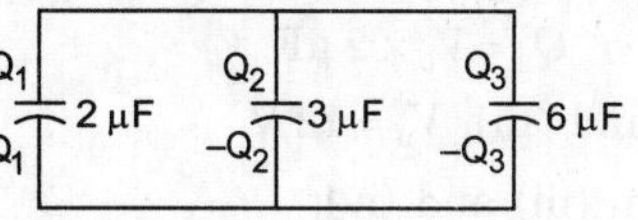

Figure 31-W8

The 36 μC charge on the three positive plates now redistribute as Q_1, Q_2 and Q_3 on the three connected positive plates. Similarly, −36 μC redistributes as $-Q_1$, $-Q_2$ and $-Q_3$. The three positive plates are now at a common potential and the three negative plates are also at a common potential. Let the potential difference across each capacitor be V. Then

$$Q_1 = (2\ \mu\text{F})\,V,$$

$$Q_2 = (3\ \mu\text{F})\,V,$$

and $$Q_3 = (6\ \mu\text{F})\,V.$$

Also, $$Q_1 + Q_2 + Q_3 = 36\ \mu\text{C}.$$

Solving these equations,

$$Q_1 = \frac{72}{11}\ \mu\text{C},\ Q_2 = \frac{108}{11}\ \mu\text{C} \text{ and } Q_3 = \frac{216}{11}\ \mu\text{C}.$$

11. *The connections shown in figure (31-W9a) are established with the switch S open. How much charge will flow through the switch if it is closed?*

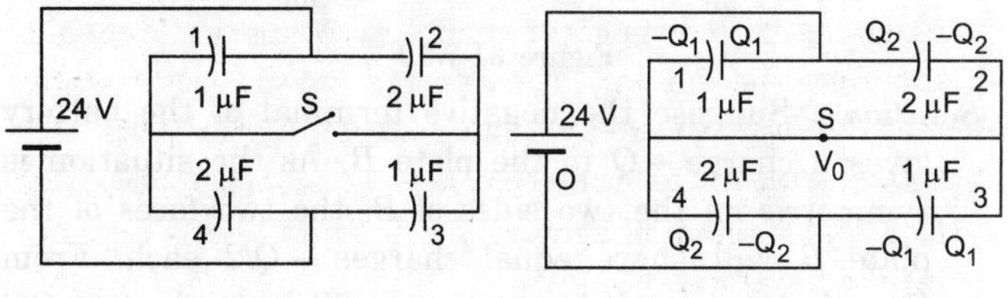

Figure 31-W9

Solution : When the switch is open, capacitors (2) and (3) are in series. Their equivalent capacitance is $\frac{2}{3}$ μF. The charge appearing on each of these capacitors is, therefore, $24\text{ V} \times \frac{2}{3}\ \mu\text{F} = 16\ \mu\text{C}$.

The equivalent capacitance of (1) and (4), which are also connected in series, is also $\frac{2}{3}$ μF and the charge on each of these capacitors is also 16 μC. The total charge on the two plates of (1) and (4) connected to the switch is, therefore, zero.

The situation when the switch S is closed is shown in figure (31-W9b). Let the charges be distributed as shown in the figure. Q_1 and Q_2 are arbitrarily chosen for the positive plates of (1) and (2). The same magnitude of charges will appear at the negative plates of (3) and (4).

Take the potential at the negative terminal to be zero and at the switch to be V_0.

Writing equations for the capacitors (1), (2), (3) and (4),

$$Q_1 = (24\ \text{V} - V_0) \times 1\ \mu\text{F} \quad \ldots \text{(i)}$$

$$Q_2 = (24\ \text{V} - V_0) \times 2\ \mu\text{F} \quad \ldots \text{(ii)}$$

$$Q_1 = V_0 \times 1\ \mu\text{F} \quad \ldots \text{(iii)}$$

$$Q_2 = V_0 \times 2\ \mu\text{F}. \quad \ldots \text{(iv)}$$

From (i) and (iii), $V_0 = 12$ V.

Thus, from (iii) and (iv),

$$Q_1 = 12\ \mu\text{C} \text{ and } Q_2 = 24\ \mu\text{C}.$$

The charge on the two plates of (1) and (4) which are connected to the switch is, therefore, $Q_2 - Q_1 = 12\ \mu$C. When the switch was open, this charge was zero. Thus, 12 μC of charge has passed through the switch after it was closed.

12. *Each of the three plates shown in figure (31-W10a) has an area of 200 cm² on one side and the gap between the adjacent plates is 0·2 mm. The emf of the battery is 20 V. Find the distribution of charge on various surfaces of the plates. What is the equivalent capacitance of the system between the terminal points?*

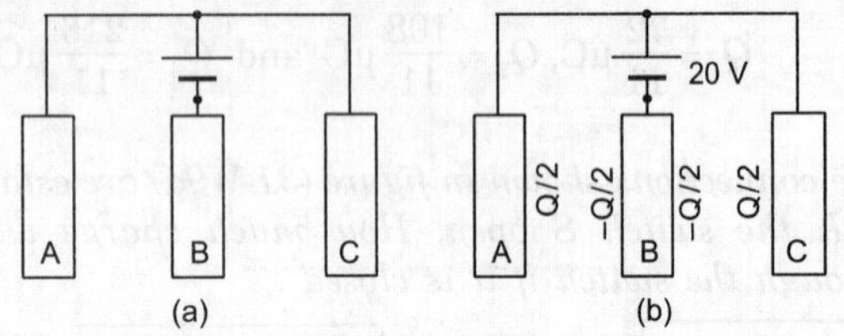

Figure 31-W10

Solution : Suppose the negative terminal of the battery gives a charge $-Q$ to the plate B. As the situation is symmetric on the two sides of B, the two faces of the plate B will share equal charges $-Q/2$ each. From Gauss's law, the facing surfaces will have charges $Q/2$ each. As the positive terminal of the battery has supplied just this much charge ($+Q$) to A and C, the outer surfaces of A and C will have no charge. The distribution will be as shown in figure (31-W10b).

The capacitance between the plates A and B is

$$8{\cdot}85 \times 10^{-12}\ \text{F m}^{-1} \times \frac{200 \times 10^{-4}\ \text{m}^2}{2 \times 10^{-4}\ \text{m}}$$

$$= 8{\cdot}85 \times 10^{-10}\ \text{F} = 0{\cdot}885\ \text{nF}.$$

Thus, $\quad \dfrac{Q}{2} = 0{\cdot}885\ \text{nF} \times 20\ \text{V} = 17{\cdot}7\ \text{nC}.$

The distribution of charge on various surfaces may be written from figure (31-W10b).

The equivalent capacitance is

$$\frac{Q}{20\ \text{V}} = 1{\cdot}77\ \text{nF}.$$

13. *Find the capacitance of the infinite ladder shown in figure (31-W11).*

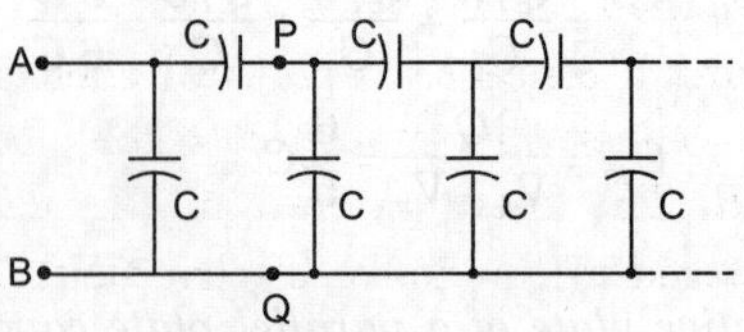

Figure 31-W11

Solution : As the ladder is infinitely long, the capacitance of the ladder to the right of the points P, Q is the same as that of the ladder to the right of the points A, B. If the equivalent capacitance of the ladder is C_1, the given ladder may be replaced by the connections shown in figure (31-W12).

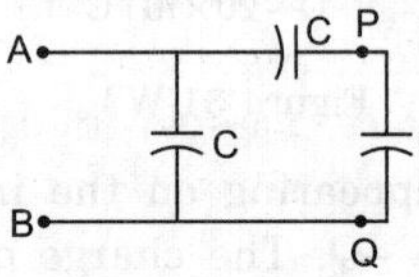

Figure 31-W12

The equivalent capacitance between A and B is easily found to be $C + \dfrac{CC_1}{C + C_1}$. But being equivalent to the original ladder, the equivalent capacitance is also C_1.

Thus, $$C_1 = C + \frac{CC_1}{C + C_1}$$

or, $$C_1 C + C_1^2 = C^2 + 2\, CC_1$$

or, $$C_1^2 - CC_1 - C^2 = 0$$

giving $$C_1 = \frac{C + \sqrt{C^2 + 4\, C^2}}{2} = \frac{1 + \sqrt{5}}{2}\, C.$$

Negative value of C_1 is rejected.

14. *Find the energy stored in the electric field produced by a metal sphere of radius R containing a charge Q.*

Solution : Consider a thin spherical shell of radius x ($> R$) and thickness dx concentric with the given metal sphere. The energy density in the shell is

$$u = \frac{1}{2}\, \varepsilon_0 E^2 = \frac{1}{2}\, \varepsilon_0 \left(\frac{Q}{4\pi\varepsilon_0 x^2} \right)^2.$$

The volume of the shell is $4\pi x^2 dx$. The energy contained in the shell is, therefore,

$$dU = \frac{1}{2}\, \varepsilon_0 \left(\frac{Q}{4\pi\varepsilon_0 x^2} \right)^2 \times 4\pi x^2 dx = \frac{Q^2 dx}{8\pi\varepsilon_0 x^2}.$$

The energy contained in the whole space outside the sphere is

$$U = \int_R^{\infty} \frac{Q^2 dx}{8\pi\varepsilon_0 x^2} = \frac{Q^2}{8\pi\varepsilon_0 R}.$$

As the field inside the sphere is zero, this is also the total energy stored in the field.

Alternative Method

Considering a concentric spherical shell at infinity, we have a spherical capacitor. The capacitance is $C = 4\pi\varepsilon_0 R$. The energy stored in this capacitor is the energy stored in the entire electric field. This energy is

$$U = \frac{Q^2}{2C} = \frac{Q^2}{8\pi\varepsilon_0 R}.$$

15. *A capacitor of capacitance C is charged by connecting it to a battery of emf $\mathcal{E}$. The capacitor is now disconnected and reconnected to the battery with the polarity reversed. Calculate the heat developed in the connecting wires.*

Solution : When the capacitor is connected to the battery, a charge $Q = C\mathcal{E}$ appears on one plate and $-Q$ on the other. When the polarity is reversed, a charge $-Q$ appears on the first plate and $+Q$ on the second. A charge $2Q$, therefore, passes through the battery from the negative to the positive terminal. The battery does a work

$$W = (2Q)\mathcal{E} = 2C\mathcal{E}^2$$

in the process. The energy stored in the capacitor is the same in the two cases. Thus, the work done by the battery appears as heat in the connecting wires. The heat produced is, therefore, $2C\mathcal{E}^2$.

16. *An uncharged capacitor is connected to a battery. Show that half the energy supplied by the battery is lost as heat while charging the capacitor.*

Solution : Suppose the capacitance of the capacitor is C and the emf of the battery is V. The charge given to the capacitor is $Q = CV$. The work done by the battery is

$$W = QV.$$

The battery supplies this energy. The energy stored in the capacitor is

$$U = \frac{1}{2}CV^2 = \frac{1}{2}QV.$$

The remaining energy $QV - \frac{1}{2}QV = \frac{1}{2}QV$ is lost as heat. Thus, half the energy supplied by the battery is lost as heat.

17. *A parallel-plate capacitor having plate area 100 cm^2 and separation 1·0 mm holds a charge of 0·12 μC when connected to a 120 V battery. Find the dielectric constant of the material filling the gap.*

Solution :

The capacitance of the capacitor is

$$\frac{0{\cdot}12\ \mu\text{C}}{120\ \text{V}} = 1{\cdot}0 \times 10^{-9}\ \text{F}.$$

If K be the dielectric constant, the capacitance is also given by $\frac{K\varepsilon_0 A}{d}$. Thus,

$$\frac{K \times 8{\cdot}85 \times 10^{-12}\ \text{F m}^{-1} \times 100 \times 10^{-4}\ \text{m}^2}{1{\cdot}0 \times 10^{-3}\ \text{m}} = 1{\cdot}0 \times 10^{-9}\ \text{F}$$

or, $$K = 11{\cdot}3.$$

18. *A parallel-plate capacitor is formed by two plates, each of area 100 cm^2, separated by a distance of 1 mm. A dielectric of dielectric constant 5·0 and dielectric strength $1{\cdot}9 \times 10^7$ V m^{-1} is filled between the plates. Find the maximum charge that can be stored on the capacitor without causing any dielectric breakdown.*

Solution : If Q be the charge on the capacitor, the surface charge density is $\sigma = Q/A$ and the electric field is $\frac{Q}{KA\varepsilon_0}$. This should not exceed the dielectric strength $1{\cdot}9 \times 10^7$ V m^{-1}. Thus, the maximum charge is given by

$$\frac{Q}{KA\varepsilon_0} = 1{\cdot}9 \times 10^7\ \text{V m}^{-1}$$

or, $$Q = KA\varepsilon_0 \times 1{\cdot}9 \times 10^7\ \text{V m}^{-1}$$

$$= (5{\cdot}0)\,(10^{-2}\ \text{m}^2)\,(8{\cdot}85 \times 10^{-12}\ \text{F m}^{-1}) \times (1{\cdot}9 \times 10^7\ \text{V m}^{-1})$$
$$= 8{\cdot}4 \times 10^{-6}\ \text{C}.$$

19. *The space between the plates of a parallel-plate capacitor of capacitance C is filled with three dielectric slabs of identical size as shown in figure (31-W13). If the dielectric constants of the three slabs are K_1, K_2 and K_3, find the new capacitance.*

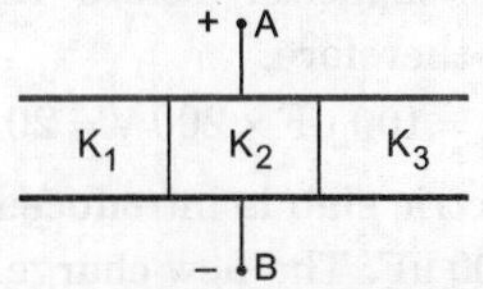

Figure 31-W13

Solution : Consider each one third of the assembly as a separate capacitor. The three positive plates are connected together at point A and the three negative plates are connected together at point B. Thus, the three capacitors are joined in parallel. As the plate area is one third of the original for each part, the capacitances of these parts will be $K_1C/3$, $K_2C/3$ and $K_3C/3$. The equivalent capacitance is, therefore,

$$C_{eq} = (K_1 + K_2 + K_3)\frac{C}{3}.$$

20. *Figure (31-W14a) shows a parallel-plate capacitor having square plates of edge a and plate-separation d. The gap between the plates is filled with a dielectric of dielectric constant K which varies parallel to an edge as*

$$K = K_0 + \alpha x$$

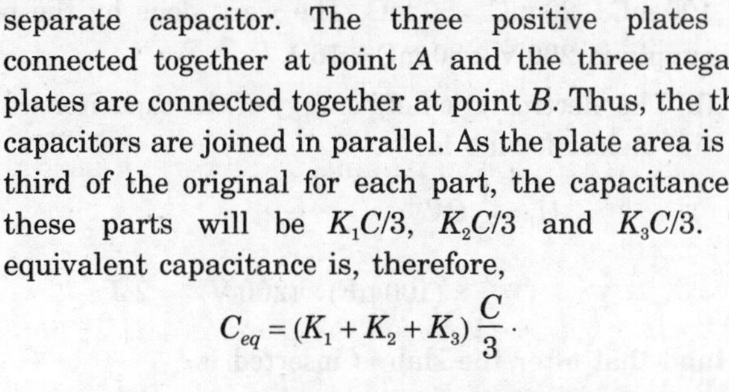

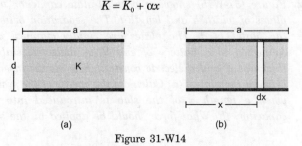

Figure 31-W14

where K and α are constants and x is the distance from the left end. Calculate the capacitance.

Solution :

Consider a small strip of width dx at a separation x from the left end (figure 31-W14b). This strip forms a small capacitor of plate area adx. Its capacitance is

$$dC = \frac{(K_0 + \alpha x)\varepsilon_0\, a\, dx}{d}.$$

The given capacitor may be divided into such strips with x varying from 0 to a. All these strips are connected in parallel. The capacitance of the given capacitor is,

$$C = \int_0^a \frac{(K_0 + \alpha x)\varepsilon_0\, a dx}{d}$$

$$= \frac{\varepsilon_0\, a^2}{d}\left(K_0 + \frac{a\alpha}{2}\right).$$

21. *A parallel-plate capacitor of capacitance 100 μF is connected to a power supply of 200 V. A dielectric slab of dielectric constant 5 is now inserted into the gap between the plates. (a) Find the extra charge flown through the power supply and the work done by the supply. (b) Find the change in the electrostatic energy of the electric field in the capacitor.*

Solution : (a) The original capacitance was 100 μF. The charge on the capacitor before the insertion of the dielectric was, therefore,

$$Q_1 = 100\ \mu\text{F} \times 200\ \text{V} = 20\ \text{mC}.$$

After the dielectric slab is introduced, the capacitance is increased to 500 μF. The new charge on the capacitor is, therefore, 500 μF × 200 V = 100 mC. The charge flown through the power supply is, therefore, 100 mC − 20 mC = 80 mC. The work done by the power supply is 200 V × 80 mC = 16 J.

(b) The electrostatic field energy of the capacitor without the dielectric slab is

$$U_1 = \frac{1}{2}CV^2$$

$$= \frac{1}{2} \times (100\ \mu\text{F}) \times (200\ \text{V})^2 = 2\ \text{J}$$

and that after the slab is inserted is

$$U_2 = \frac{1}{2} \times (500\ \mu\text{F}) \times (200\ \text{V})^2 = 10\ \text{J}.$$

Thus, the energy is increased by 8 J.

22. *Figure (31-W15) shows a parallel-plate capacitor with plates of width b and length l. The separation between the plates is d. The plates are rigidly clamped and connected to a battery of emf V. A dielectric slab of thickness d and dielectric constant K is slowly inserted between the plates. (a) Calculate the energy of the system when a length x of the slab is introduced into the capacitor. (b) What force should be applied on the slab*

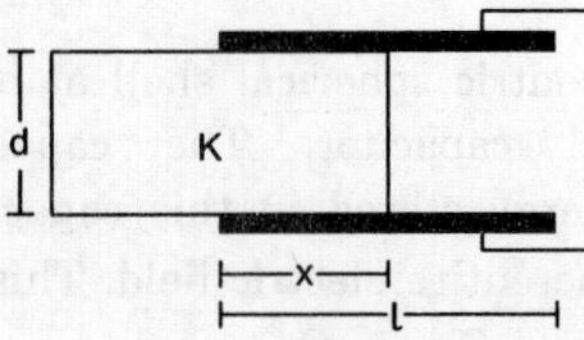

Figure 31-W15

to ensure that it goes slowly into the capacitor? Neglect any effect of friction or gravity.

Solution : (a) The plate area of the part with the dielectric is bx. Its capacitance is

$$C_1 = \frac{K\varepsilon_0\, bx}{d}.$$

Similarly, the capacitance of the part without the dielectric is

$$C_2 = \frac{\varepsilon_0\, b(l - x)}{d}.$$

These two parts are connected in parallel. The capacitance of the system is, therefore,

$$C = C_1 + C_2$$

$$= \frac{\varepsilon_0\, b}{d}[l + x\,(K - 1)]. \quad \text{... (i)}$$

The energy of the capacitor is

$$U = \frac{1}{2}CV^2 = \frac{\varepsilon_0\, bV^2}{2\,d}[l + x\,(K - 1)].$$

(b) Suppose, the electric field attracts the dielectric slab with a force F. An external force of equal magnitude F should be applied in opposite direction so that the plate moves slowly (no acceleration).

Consider the part of motion in which the dielectric moves a distance dx further inside the capacitor. The capacitance increases to $C + dC$. As the potential difference remains constant at V, the battery has to supply a further charge

$$dQ = (dC)V$$

to the capacitor. The work done by the battery is, therefore,

$$dW_b = V\,dQ = (dC)V^2.$$

The external force F does a work

$$dW_e = (-F\,dx)$$

during the displacement. The total work done on the capacitor is

$$dW_b + dW_e = (dC)V^2 - Fdx.$$

This should be equal to the increase dU in the stored energy. Thus,

$$\frac{1}{2}(dC)V^2 = (dC)V^2 - Fdx$$

or,
$$F = \frac{1}{2}V^2\frac{dC}{dx}.$$

Using equation (i),

$$F = \frac{\varepsilon_0 bV^2(K-1)}{2d}.$$

Thus, the electric field attracts the dielectric into the capacitor with a force $\frac{\varepsilon_0 bV^2(K-1)}{2d}$ and this much force should be applied in the opposite direction.

23. *A parallel-plate capacitor is placed in such a way that its plates are horizontal and the lower plate is dipped into a liquid of dielectric constant K and density ρ. Each plate has an area A. The plates are now connected to a battery which supplies a positive charge of magnitude Q to the upper plate. Find the rise in the level of the liquid in the space between the plates.*

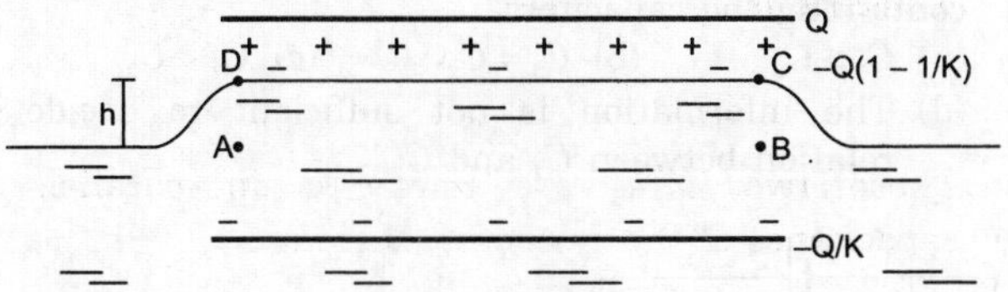

Figure 31-W16

Solution :

The situation is shown in figure (31-W16). A charge $-Q\left(1-\frac{1}{K}\right)$ is induced on the upper surface of the liquid and $Q\left(1-\frac{1}{K}\right)$ at the surface in contact with the lower plate. The net charge on the lower plate is $-Q+Q\left(1-\frac{1}{K}\right)=-\frac{Q}{K}$. Consider the equilibrium of the liquid in the volume $ABCD$. The forces on this liquid are

(a) the force due to the electric field at CD,
(b) the weight of the liquid,
(c) the force due to atmospheric pressure and
(d) the force due to the pressure of the liquid below AB.

As AB is in the same horizontal level as the outside surface, the pressure here is the same as the atmospheric pressure. The forces in (c) and (d), therefore, balance each other. Hence, for equilibrium, the forces in (a) and (b) should balance each other.

The electric field at CD due to the charge Q is

$$E_1 = \frac{Q}{2A\varepsilon_0}$$

in the downward direction. The field at CD due to the charge $-Q/K$ is

$$E_2 = \frac{Q}{2A\varepsilon_0 K}$$

also in the downward direction. The net field at CD is

$$E_1 + E_2 = \frac{(K+1)Q}{2A\varepsilon_0 K}.$$

The force on the charge $-Q\left(1-\frac{1}{K}\right)$ at CD is

$$F = Q\left(1-\frac{1}{K}\right)\frac{(K+1)Q}{2A\varepsilon_0 K}$$

$$= \frac{(K^2-1)Q^2}{2A\varepsilon_0 K^2}$$

in the upward direction. The weight of the liquid considered is $hA\rho g$. Thus,

$$hA\rho g = \frac{(K^2-1)Q^2}{2A\varepsilon_0 K^2}$$

or,
$$h = \frac{(K^2-1)Q^2}{2A^2K^2\varepsilon_0 \rho g}.$$

□

QUESTIONS FOR SHORT ANSWER

1. Suppose a charge $+Q_1$ is given to the positive plate and a charge $-Q_2$ to the negative plate of a capacitor. What is the "charge on the capacitor" ?
2. As $C = \left(\frac{1}{V}\right)Q$, can you say that the capacitance C is proportional to the charge Q ?
3. A hollow metal sphere and a solid metal sphere of equal radii are given equal charges. Which of the two will have higher potential ?
4. The plates of a parallel-plate capacitor are given equal positive charges. What will be the potential difference between the plates ? What will be the charges on the facing surfaces and on the outer surfaces ?
5. A capacitor has capacitance C. Is this information sufficient to know what maximum charge the capacitor can contain ? If yes, what is this charge ? If no, what other information is needed ?
6. The dielectric constant decreases if the temperature is increased. Explain this in terms of polarization of the material.
7. When a dielectric slab is gradually inserted between the plates of an isolated parallel-plate capacitor, the energy of the system decreases. What can you conclude about the force on the slab exerted by the electric field ?

OBJECTIVE I

1. A capacitor of capacitance C is charged to a potential V. The flux of the electric field through a closed surface enclosing the capacitor is
(a) $\frac{CV}{\varepsilon_0}$ (b) $\frac{2CV}{\varepsilon_0}$ (c) $\frac{CV}{2\varepsilon_0}$ (d) zero.

2. Two capacitors each having capacitance C and breakdown voltage V are joined in series. The capacitance and the breakdown voltage of the combination will be
(a) $2C$ and $2V$ (b) $C/2$ and $V/2$
(c) $2C$ and $V/2$ (d) $C/2$ and $2V$.

3. If the capacitors in the previous question are joined in parallel, the capacitance and the breakdown voltage of the combination will be
(a) $2C$ and $2V$ (b) C and $2V$
(c) $2C$ and V (d) C and V.

4. The equivalent capacitance of the combination shown in figure (31-Q1) is
(a) C (b) $2C$ (c) $C/2$ (d) none of these.

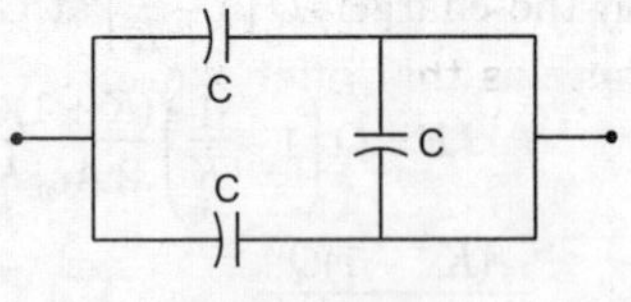

Figure 31-Q1

5. A dielectric slab is inserted between the plates of an isolated capacitor. The force between the plates will
(a) increase (b) decrease
(c) remain unchanged (d) become zero.

6. The energy density in the electric field created by a point charge falls off with the distance from the point charge as
(a) $\frac{1}{r}$ (b) $\frac{1}{r^2}$ (c) $\frac{1}{r^3}$ (d) $\frac{1}{r^4}$.

7. A parallel-plate capacitor has plates of unequal area. The larger plate is connected to the positive terminal of the battery and the smaller plate to its negative terminal. Let Q_+ and Q_- be the charges appearing on the positive and negative plates respectively.
(a) $Q_+ > Q_-$ (b) $Q_+ = Q_-$ (c) $Q_+ < Q_-$
(d) The information is not sufficient to decide the relation between Q_+ and Q_-.

8. A thin metal plate P is inserted between the plates of a parallel-plate capacitor of capacitance C in such a way that its edges touch the two plates (figure 31-Q2). The capacitance now becomes
(a) $C/2$ (b) $2C$ (c) 0 (d) indeterminate.

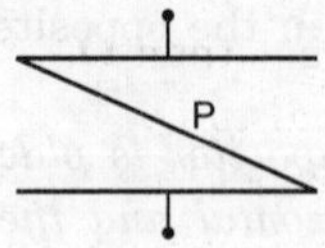

Figure 31-Q2

9. Figure (31-Q3) shows two capacitors connected in series and joined to a battery. The graph shows the variation in potential as one moves from left to right on the branch containing the capacitors.
(a) $C_1 > C_2$ (b) $C_1 = C_2$ (c) $C_1 < C_2$
(d) The information is not sufficient to decide the relation between C_1 and C_2.

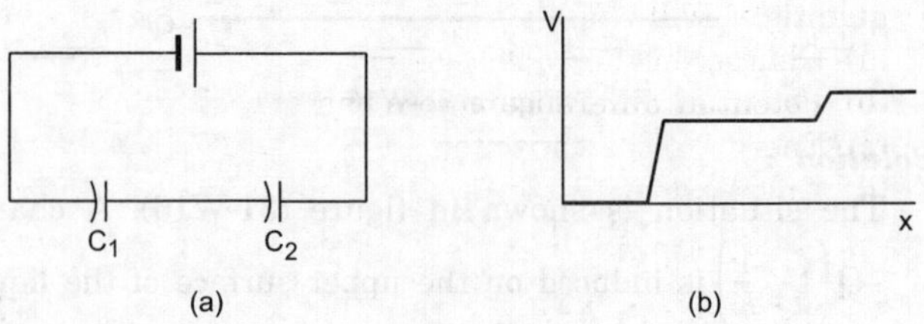

Figure 31-Q3

10. Two metal plates having charges Q, $-Q$ face each other at some separation and are dipped into an oil tank. If the oil is pumped out, the electric field between the plates will
(a) increase (b) decrease
(c) remain the same (d) become zero.

11. Two metal spheres of capacitances C_1 and C_2 carry some charges. They are put in contact and then separated. The final charges Q_1 and Q_2 on them will satisfy
(a) $\frac{Q_1}{Q_2} < \frac{C_1}{C_2}$ (b) $\frac{Q_1}{Q_2} = \frac{C_1}{C_2}$ (c) $\frac{Q_1}{Q_2} > \frac{C_1}{C_2}$ (d) $\frac{Q_1}{Q_2} = \frac{C_2}{C_1}$.

12. Three capacitors of capacitances 6 μF each are available. The minimum and maximum capacitances, which may be obtained are
(a) 6 μF, 18 μF (b) 3 μF, 12 μF
(c) 2 μF, 12 μF (d) 2 μF, 18 μF.

OBJECTIVE II

1. The capacitance of a capacitor does not depend on
(a) the shape of the plates
(b) the size of the plates
(c) the charges on the plates
(d) the separation between the plates.

2. A dielectric slab is inserted between the plates of an isolated charged capacitor. Which of the following quantities will remain the same?
(a) The electric field in the capacitor
(b) The charge on the capacitor

(c) The potential difference between the plates
(d) The stored energy in the capacitor

3. A dielectric slab is inserted between the plates of a capacitor. The charge on the capacitor is Q and the magnitude of the induced charge on each surface of the dielectric is Q'.
(a) Q' may be larger than Q.
(b) Q' must be larger than Q.
(c) Q' must be equal to Q.
(d) Q' must be smaller than Q.

4. Each plate of a parallel plate capacitor has a charge q on it. The capacitor is now connected to a battery. Now,
(a) the facing surfaces of the capacitor have equal and opposite charges
(b) the two plates of the capacitor have equal and opposite charges
(c) the battery supplies equal and opposite charges to the two plates
(d) the outer surfaces of the plates have equal charges

5. The separation between the plates of a charged parallel-plate capacitor is increased. Which of the following quantities will change ?
(a) Charge on the capacitor
(b) Potential difference across the capacitor
(c) Energy of the capacitor
(d) Energy density between the plates

6. A parallel-plate capacitor is connected to a battery. A metal sheet of negligible thickness is placed between the plates. The sheet remains parallel to the plates of the capacitor.
(a) The battery will supply more charge.
(b) The capacitance will increase.
(c) The potential difference between the plates will increase.
(d) Equal and opposite charges will appear on the two faces of the metal plate.

7. Following operations can be performed on a capacitor:
X – connect the capacitor to a battery of emf $\mathcal{E}$.
Y – disconnect the battery.
Z – reconnect the battery with polarity reversed.
W – insert a dielectric slab in the capacitor.
(a) In XYZ (perform X, then Y, then Z) the stored electric energy remains unchanged and no thermal energy is developed.
(b) The charge appearing on the capacitor is greater after the action XWY than after the action XYW.
(c) The electric energy stored in the capacitor is greater after the action WXY than after the action XYW.
(d) The electric field in the capacitor after the action XW is the same as that after WX.

EXERCISES

1. When $1{\cdot}0 \times 10^{12}$ electrons are transferred from one conductor to another, a potential difference of 10 V appears between the conductors. Calculate the capacitance of the two-conductor system.

2. The plates of a parallel-plate capacitor are made of circular discs of radii 5·0 cm each. If the separation between the plates is 1·0 mm, what is the capacitance ?

3. Suppose, one wishes to construct a 1·0 farad capacitor using circular discs. If the separation between the discs be kept at 1·0 mm, what would be the radius of the discs ?

4. A parallel-plate capacitor having plate area 25 cm^2 and separation 1·00 mm is connected to a battery of 6·0 V. Calculate the charge flown through the battery. How much work has been done by the battery during the process ?

5. A parallel-plate capacitor has plate area 25·0 cm^2 and a separation of 2·00 mm between the plates. The capacitor is connected to a battery of 12·0 V. (a) Find the charge on the capacitor. (b) The plate separation is decreased to 1·00 mm. Find the extra charge given by the battery to the positive plate.

6. Find the charges on the three capacitors connected to a battery as shown in figure (31-E1). Take $C_1 = 2{\cdot}0\ \mu F$, $C_2 = 4{\cdot}0\ \mu F$, $C_3 = 6{\cdot}0\ \mu F$ and $V = 12$ volts.

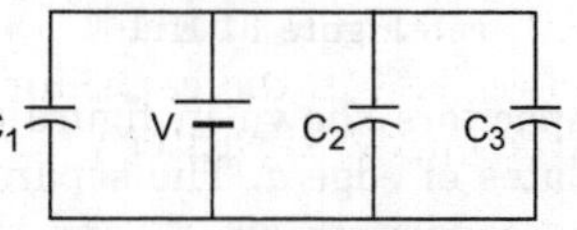

Figure 31-E1

7. Three capacitors having capacitances 20 μF, 30 μF and 40 μF are connected in series with a 12 V battery. Find the charge on each of the capacitors. How much work has been done by the battery in charging the capacitors ?

8. Find the charge appearing on each of the three capacitors shown in figure (31-E2).

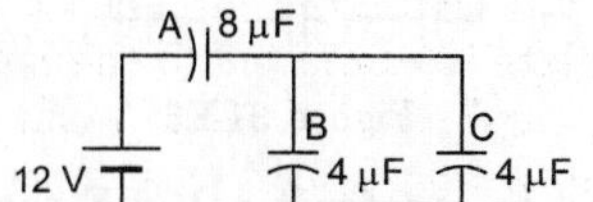

Figure 31-E2

9. Take $C_1 = 4{\cdot}0\ \mu F$ and $C_2 = 6{\cdot}0\ \mu F$ in figure (31-E3). Calculate the equivalent capacitance of the combination between the points indicated.

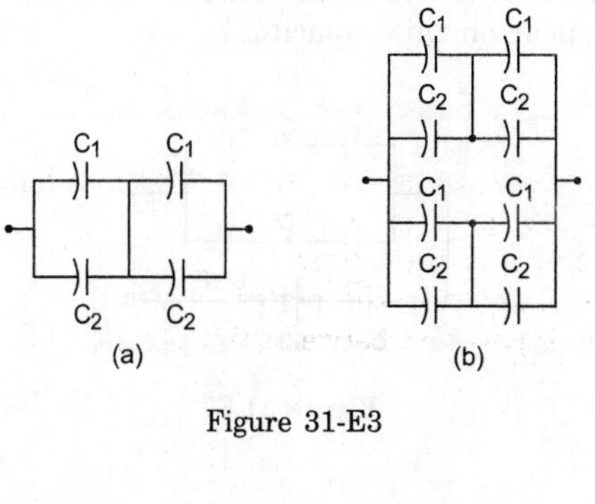

Figure 31-E3

10. Find the charge supplied by the battery in the arrangement shown in figure (31-E4).

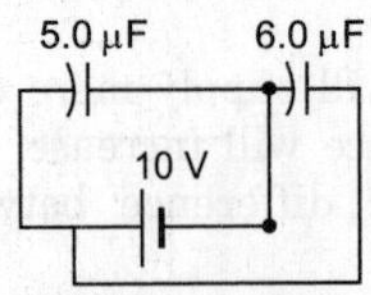

Figure 31-E4

11. The outer cylinders of two cylindrical capacitors of capacitance 2·2 μF each, are kept in contact and the inner cylinders are connected through a wire. A battery of emf 10 V is connected as shown in figure (31-E5). Find the total charge supplied by the battery to the inner cylinders.

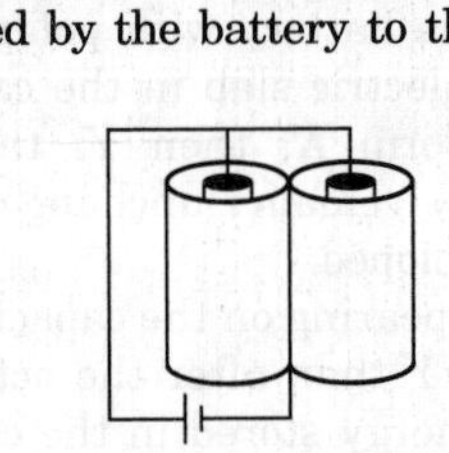

Figure 31-E5

12. Two conducting spheres of radii R_1 and R_2 are kept widely separated from each other. What are their individual capacitances ? If the spheres are connected by a metal wire, what will be the capacitance of the combination ? Think in terms of series–parallel connections.

13. Each of the capacitors shown in figure (31-E6) has a capacitance of 2 μF. Find the equivalent capacitance of the assembly between the points *A* and *B*. Suppose, a battery of emf 60 volts is connected between *A* and *B*. Find the potential difference appearing on the individual capacitors.

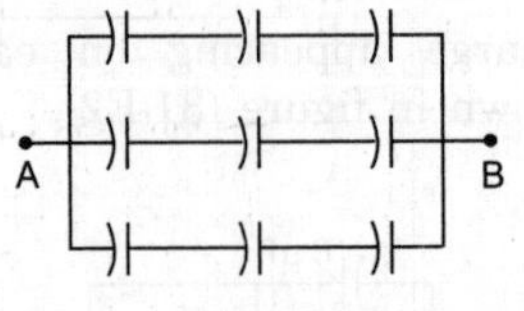

Figure 31-E6

14. It is required to construct a 10 μF capacitor which can be connected across a 200 V battery. Capacitors of capacitance 10 μF are available but they can withstand only 50 V. Design a combination which can yield the desired result.

15. Take the potential of the point *B* in figure (31-E7) to be zero. (a) Find the potentials at the points *C* and *D*. (b) If a capacitor is connected between *C* and *D*, what charge will appear on this capacitor ?

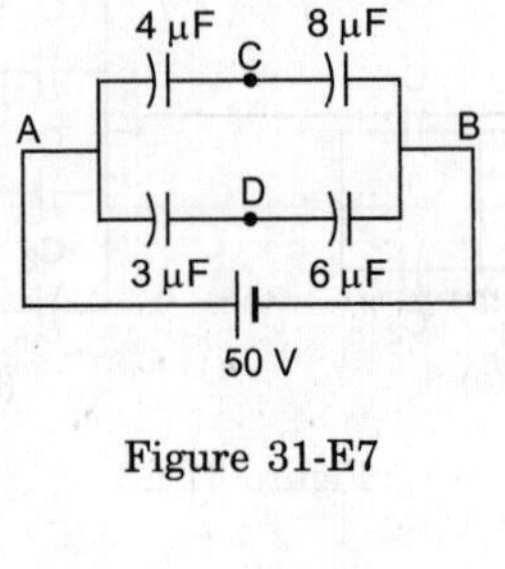

Figure 31-E7

16. Find the equivalent capacitance of the system shown in figure (31-E8) between the points *a* and *b*.

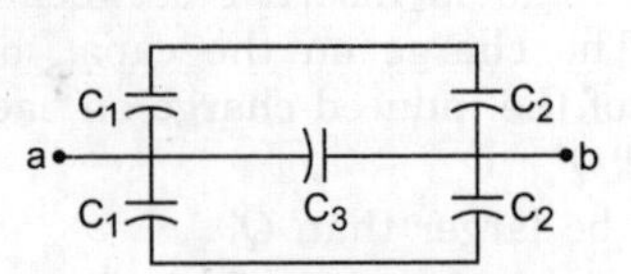

Figure 31-E8

17. A capacitor is made of a flat plate of area *A* and a second plate having a stair-like structure as shown in figure (31-E9). The width of each stair is *a* and the height is *b*. Find the capacitance of the assembly.

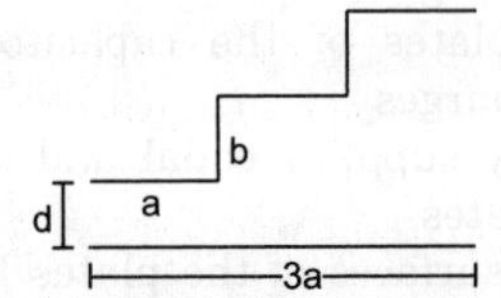

Figure 31-E9

18. A cylindrical capacitor is constructed using two coaxial cylinders of the same length 10 cm and of radii 2 mm and 4 mm. (a) Calculate the capacitance. (b) Another capacitor of the same length is constructed with cylinders of radii 4 mm and 8 mm. Calculate the capacitance.

19. A 100 pF capacitor is charged to a potential difference of 24 V. It is connected to an uncharged capacitor of capacitance 20 pF. What will be the new potential difference across the 100 pF capacitor ?

20. Each capacitor shown in figure (31-E10) has a capacitance of 5·0 μF. The emf of the battery is 50 V. How much charge will flow through *AB* if the switch *S* is closed ?

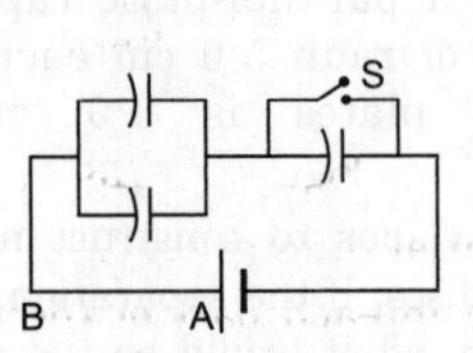

Figure 31-E10

21. The particle *P* shown in figure (31-E11) has a mass of 10 mg and a charge of – 0·01 μC. Each plate has a surface area 100 cm ^{2} on one side. What potential difference *V* should be applied to the combination to hold the particle *P* in equilibrium ?

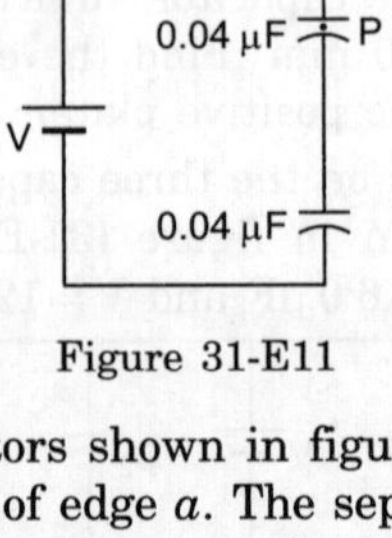

Figure 31-E11

22. Both the capacitors shown in figure (31-E12) are made of square plates of edge *a*. The separations between the plates of the capacitors are d_1 and d_2 as shown in the

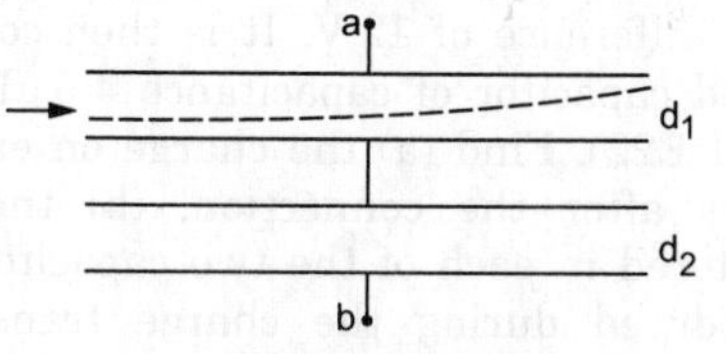

Figure 31-E12

figure. A potential difference V is applied between the points a and b. An electron is projected between the plates of the upper capacitor along the central line. With what minimum speed should the electron be projected so that it does not collide with any plate ? Consider only the electric forces.

23. The plates of a capacitor are 2·00 cm apart. An electron–proton pair is released somewhere in the gap between the plates and it is found that the proton reaches the negative plate at the same time as the electron reaches the positive plate. At what distance from the negative plate was the pair released ?

24. Convince yourself that parts (a), (b) and (c) of figure (31-E13) are identical. Find the capacitance between the points A and B of the assembly.

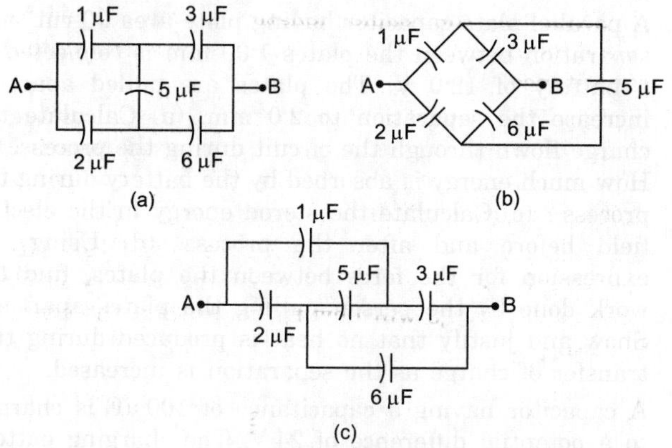

Figure 31-E13

25. Find the potential difference $V_a - V_b$ between the points a and b shown in each part of the figure (31-E14).

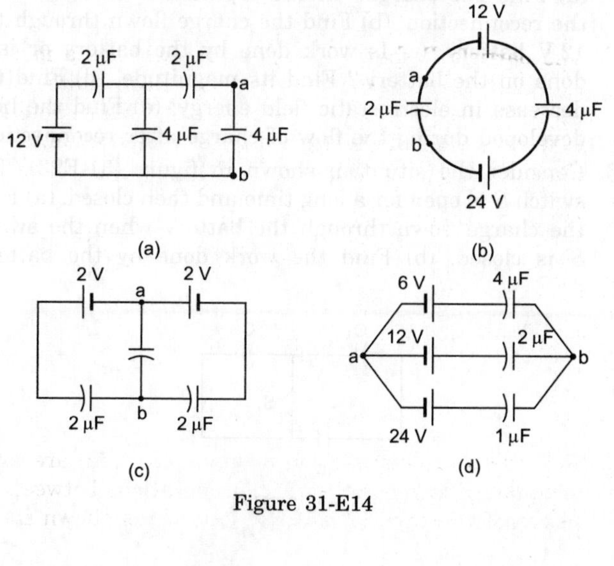

Figure 31-E14

26. Find the equivalent capacitances of the combinations shown in figure (31-E15) between the indicated points.

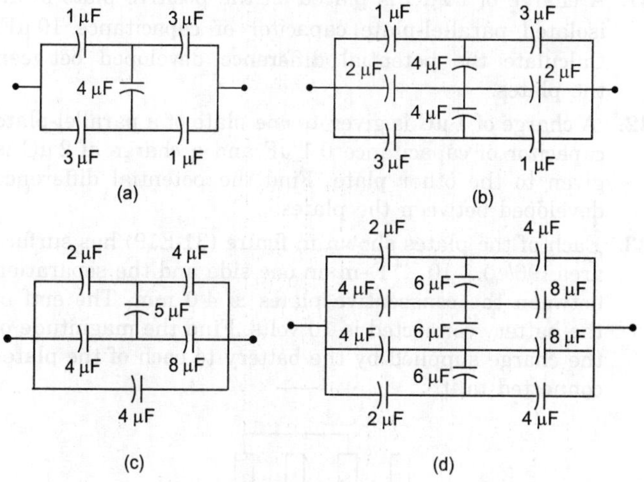

Figure 31-E15

27. Find the capacitance of the combination shown in figure (31-E16) between A and B.

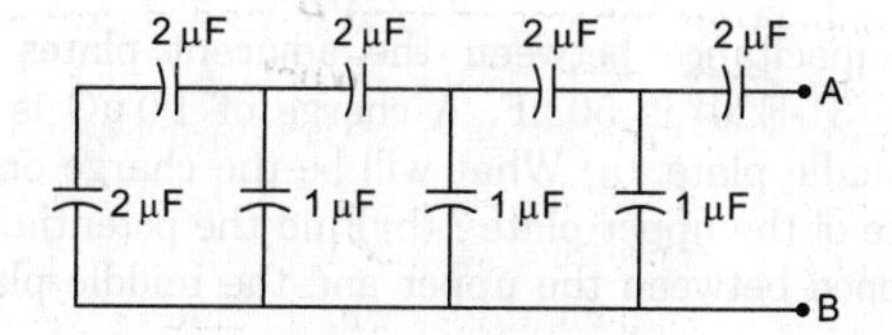

Figure 31-E16

28. Find the equivalent capacitance of the infinite ladder shown in figure (31-E17) between the points A and B.

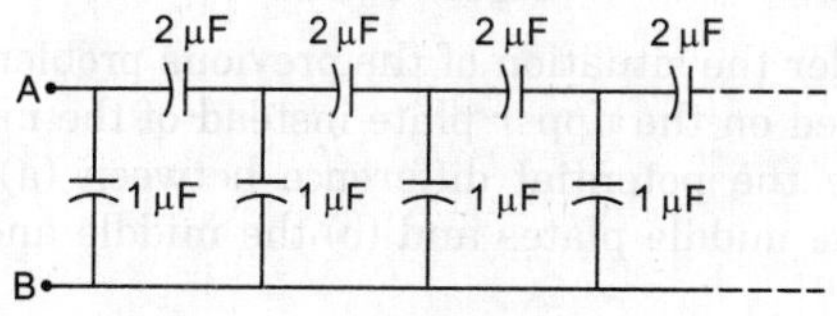

Figure 31-E17

29. A finite ladder is constructed by connecting several sections of 2 μF, 4 μF capacitor combinations as shown in figure (31-E18). It is terminated by a capacitor of capacitance C. What value should be chosen for C, such that the equivalent capacitance of the ladder between the points A and B becomes independent of the number of sections in between ?

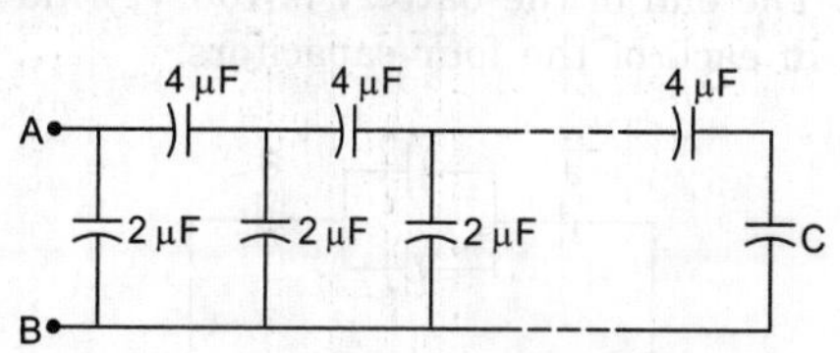

Figure 31-E18

30. A charge of $+ 2{\cdot}0 \times 10^{-8}$ C is placed on the positive plate and a charge of $- 1{\cdot}0 \times 10^{-8}$ C on the negative plate of a parallel-plate capacitor of capacitance $1{\cdot}2 \times 10^{-3}$ μF.

Calculate the potential difference developed between the plates.

31. A charge of 20 μC is placed on the positive plate of an isolated parallel-plate capacitor of capacitance 10 μF. Calculate the potential difference developed between the plates.

32. A charge of 1 μC is given to one plate of a parallel-plate capacitor of capacitance 0·1 μF and a charge of 2 μC is given to the other plate. Find the potential difference developed between the plates.

33. Each of the plates shown in figure (31-E19) has surface area $(96/\varepsilon_0) \times 10^{-12}$ F–m on one side and the separation between the consecutive plates is 4·0 mm. The emf of the battery connected is 10 volts. Find the magnitude of the charge supplied by the battery to each of the plates connected to it.

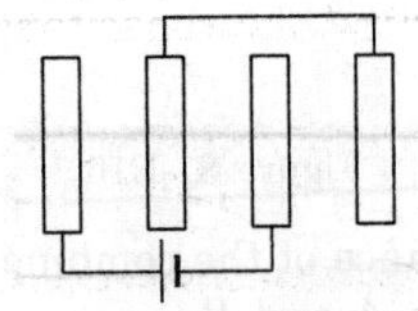

Figure 31-E19

34. The capacitance between the adjacent plates shown in figure (31-E20) is 50 nF. A charge of 1·0 μC is placed on the middle plate. (a) What will be the charge on the outer surface of the upper plate ? (b) Find the potential difference developed between the upper and the middle plates.

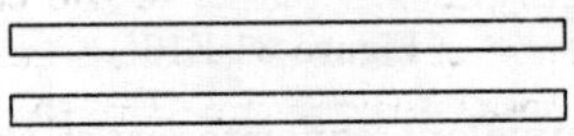

Figure 31-E20

35. Consider the situation of the previous problem. If 1·0 μC is placed on the upper plate instead of the middle, what will be the potential difference between (a) the upper and the middle plates and (b) the middle and the lower plates ?

36. Two capacitors of capacitances 20·0 pF and 50·0 pF are connected in series with a 6·00 V battery. Find (a) the potential difference across each capacitor and (b) the energy stored in each capacitor.

37. Two capacitors of capacitances 4·0 μF and 6·0 μF are connected in series with a battery of 20 V. Find the energy supplied by the battery.

38. Each capacitor in figure (31-E21) has a capacitance of 10 μF. The emf of the battery is 100 V. Find the energy stored in each of the four capacitors.

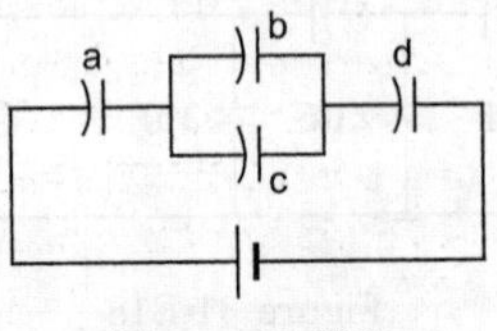

Figure 31-E21

39. A capacitor with stored energy 4·0 J is connected with an identical capacitor with no electric field in between. Find the total energy stored in the two capacitors.

40. A capacitor of capacitance 2·0 μF is charged to a potential difference of 12 V. It is then connected to an uncharged capacitor of capacitance 4·0 μF as shown in figure (31-E22). Find (a) the charge on each of the two capacitors after the connection, (b) the electrostatic energy stored in each of the two capacitors and (c) the heat produced during the charge transfer from one capacitor to the other.

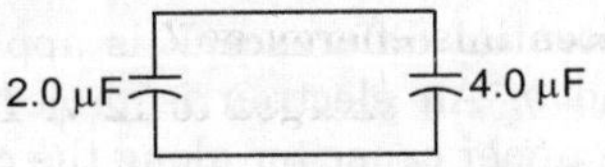

Figure 31-E22

41. A point charge Q is placed at the origin. Find the electrostatic energy stored outside the sphere of radius R centred at the origin.

42. A metal sphere of radius R is charged to a potential V. (a) Find the electrostatic energy stored in the electric field within a concentric sphere of radius $2R$. (b) Show that the electrostatic field energy stored outside the sphere of radius $2R$ equals that stored within it.

43. A large conducting plane has a surface charge density $1{\cdot}0 \times 10^{-4}$ C m^{-2}. Find the electrostatic energy stored in a cubical volume of edge 1·0 cm in front of the plane.

44. A parallel-plate capacitor having plate area 20 cm^2 and separation between the plates 1·00 mm is connected to a battery of 12·0 V. The plates are pulled apart to increase the separation to 2·0 mm. (a) Calculate the charge flown through the circuit during the process. (b) How much energy is absorbed by the battery during the process ? (c) Calculate the stored energy in the electric field before and after the process. (d) Using the expression for the force between the plates, find the work done by the person pulling the plates apart. (e) Show and justify that no heat is produced during this transfer of charge as the separation is increased.

45. A capacitor having a capacitance of 100 μF is charged to a potential difference of 24 V. The charging battery is disconnected and the capacitor is connected to another battery of emf 12 V with the positive plate of the capacitor joined with the positive terminal of the battery. (a) Find the charges on the capacitor before and after the reconnection. (b) Find the charge flown through the 12 V battery. (c) Is work done by the battery or is it done on the battery ? Find its magnitude. (d) Find the decrease in electrostatic field energy. (e) Find the heat developed during the flow of charge after reconnection.

46. Consider the situation shown in figure (31-E23). The switch S is open for a long time and then closed. (a) Find the charge flown through the battery when the switch S is closed. (b) Find the work done by the battery.

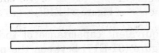

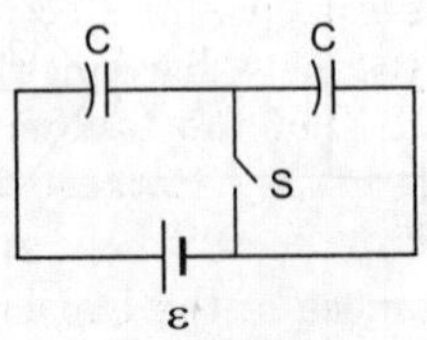

Figure 31-E23

(c) Find the change in energy stored in the capacitors. (d) Find the heat developed in the system.

47. A capacitor of capacitance 5·00 μF is charged to 24·0 V and another capacitor of capacitance 6·0 μF is charged to 12·0 V. (a) Find the energy stored in each capacitor. (b) The positive plate of the first capacitor is now connected to the negative plate of the second and vice versa. Find the new charges on the capacitors. (c) Find the loss of electrostatic energy during the process. (d) Where does this energy go ?

48. A 5·0 μF capacitor is charged to 12 V. The positive plate of this capacitor is now connected to the negative terminal of a 12 V battery and vice versa. Calculate the heat developed in the connecting wires.

49. The two square faces of a rectangular dielectric slab (dielectric constant 4·0) of dimensions 20 cm × 20 cm × 1·0 mm are metal-coated. Find the capacitance between the coated surfaces.

50. If the above capacitor is connected across a 6·0 V battery, find (a) the charge supplied by the battery, (b) the induced charge on the dielectric and (c) the net charge appearing on one of the coated surfaces.

51. The separation between the plates of a parallel-plate capacitor is 0·500 cm and its plate area is 100 cm^2. A 0·400 cm thick metal plate is inserted into the gap with its faces parallel to the plates. Show that the capacitance of the assembly is independent of the position of the metal plate within the gap and find its value.

52. A capacitor stores 50 μC charge when connected across a battery. When the gap between the plates is filled with a dielectric, a charge of 100 μC flows through the battery. Find the dielectric constant of the material inserted.

53. A parallel-plate capacitor of capacitance 5 μF is connected to a battery of emf 6 V. The separation between the plates is 2 mm. (a) Find the charge on the positive plate. (b) Find the electric field between the plates. (c) A dielectric slab of thickness 1 mm and dielectric constant 5 is inserted into the gap to occupy the lower half of it. Find the capacitance of the new combination. (d) How much charge has flown through the battery after the slab is inserted ?

54. A parallel-plate capacitor has plate area 100 cm^2 and plate separation 1·0 cm. A glass plate (dielectric constant 6·0) of thickness 6·0 mm and an ebonite plate (dielectric constant 4·0) are inserted one over the other to fill the space between the plates of the capacitor. Find the new capacitance.

55. A parallel-plate capacitor having plate area 400 cm^2 and separation between the plates 1·0 mm is connected to a power supply of 100 V. A dielectric slab of thickness 1·0 mm and dielectric constant 5·0 is inserted into the gap. (a) Find the increase in electrostatic energy. (b) If the power supply is now disconnected and the dielectric slab is taken out, find the further increase in energy. (c) Why does the energy increase in inserting the slab as well as in taking it out ?

56. Find the capacitances of the capacitors shown in figure (31-E24). The plate area is A and the separation between the plates is d. Different dielectric slabs in a particular part of the figure are of the same thickness and the entire gap between the plates is filled with the dielectric slabs.

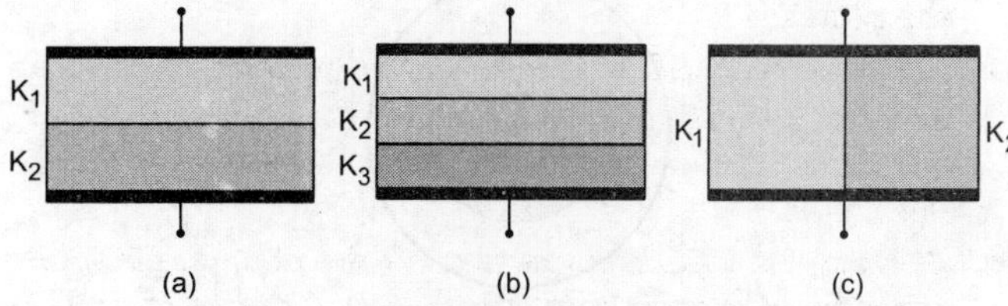

Figure 31-E24

57. A capacitor is formed by two square metal-plates of edge a, separated by a distance d. Dielectrics of dielectric constants K_1 and K_2 are filled in the gap as shown in figure (31-E25). Find the capacitance.

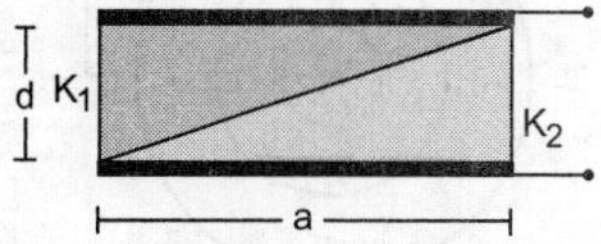

Figure 31-E25

58. Figure (31-E26) shows two identical parallel plate capacitors connected to a battery through a switch S. Initially, the switch is closed so that the capacitors are completely charged. The switch is now opened and the free space between the plates of the capacitors is filled with a dielectric of dielectric constant 3. Find the ratio of the initial total energy stored in the capacitors to the final total energy stored.

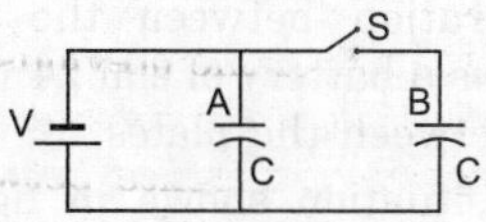

Figure 31-E26

59. A parallel-plate capacitor of plate area A and plate separation d is charged to a potential difference V and then the battery is disconnected. A slab of dielectric constant K is then inserted between the plates of the capacitor so as to fill the space between the plates. Find the work done on the system in the process of inserting the slab.

60. A capacitor having a capacitance of 100 μF is charged to a potential difference of 50 V. (a) What is the magnitude of the charge on each plate ? (b) The charging battery is disconnected and a dielectric of dielectric constant 2·5 is inserted. Calculate the new potential difference between the plates. (c) What charge would have produced this potential difference in absence of the dielectric slab. (d) Find the charge induced at a surface of the dielectric slab.

61. A sphercial capacitor is made of two conducting spherical shells of radii a and b. The space between the shells is filled with a dielectric of dielectric constant K

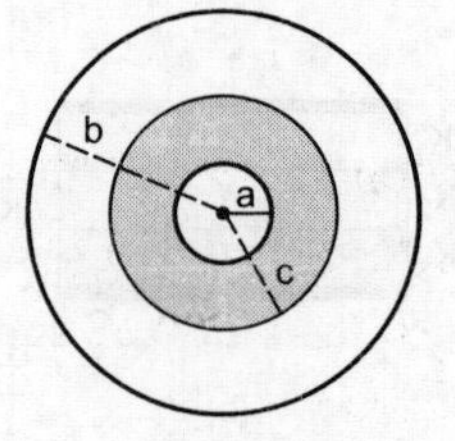

Figure 31-E27

up to a radius c as shown in figure (31-E27). Calculate the capacitance.

62. Consider an assembly of three conducting concentric spherical shells of radii *a*, *b* and *c* as shown in figure (31-E28). Find the capacitance of the assembly between the points *A* and *B*.

63. Suppose the space between the two inner shells of the

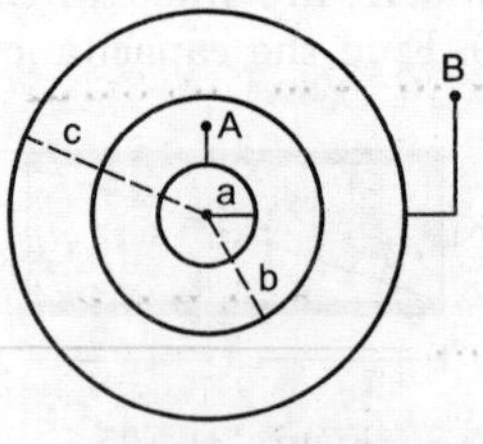

Figure 31-E28

previous problem is filled with a dielectric of dielectric constant *K*. Find the capacitance of the system between *A* and *B*.

64. An air-filled parallel-plate capacitor is to be constructed which can store 12 μC of charge when operated at 1200 V. What can be the minimum plate area of the capacitor? The dielectric strength of air is 3×10^6 V m^{-1}.

65. A parallel-plate capacitor with the plate area 100 cm^2 and the separation between the plates 1·0 cm is connected across a battery of emf 24 volts. Find the force of attraction between the plates.

66. Consider the situation shown in figure (31-E29). The width of each plate is b. The capacitor plates are rigidly clamped in the laboratory and connected to a battery of emf $\mathcal{E}$. All surfaces are frictionless. Calculate the value of *M* for which the dielectric slab will stay in equilibrium.

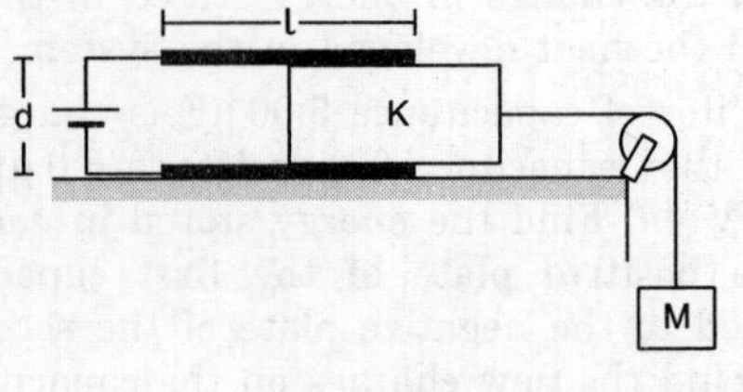

Figure 31-E29

67. Figure (31-E30) shows two parallel plate capacitors with fixed plates and connected to two batteries. The separation between the plates is the same for the two capacitors. The plates are rectangular in shape with width *b* and lengths l_1 and l_2. The left half of the dielectric slab has a dielectric constant K_1 and the right half K_2. Neglecting any friction, find the ratio of the emf of the left battery to that of the right battery for which the dielectric slab may remain in equilibrium.

68. Consider the situation shown in figure (31-E31). The

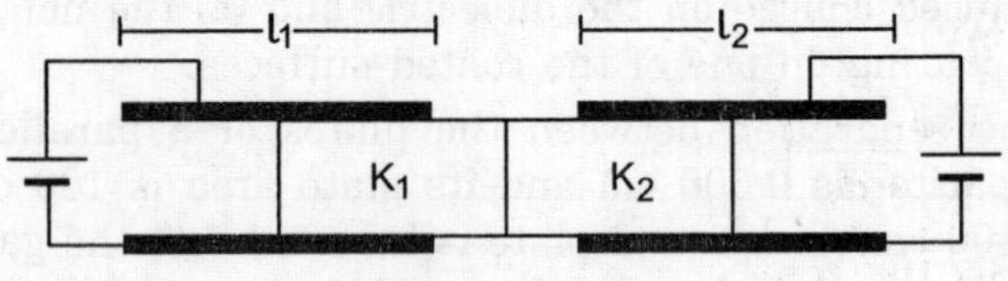

Figure 31-E30

plates of the capacitor have plate area *A* and are clamped in the laboratory. The dielectric slab is released from rest with a length *a* inside the capacitor. Neglecting any effect of friction or gravity, show that the slab will execute periodic motion and find its time period.

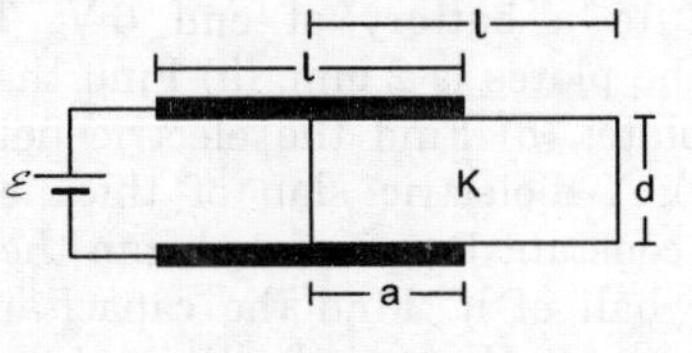

Figure 31-E31

□

ANSWERS

OBJECTIVE I

1. (d)	2. (d)	3. (c)	4. (b)	5. (c)	6. (d)
7. (b)	8. (d)	9. (c)	10. (a)	11. (b)	12. (d)

OBJECTIVE II

1. (c)	2. (b)	3. (d)	4. (a), (c), (d)	5. (b), (c)
6. (d)	7. (b), (c), (d)			

EXERCISES

1. $1·6 \times 10^{-8}$ F
2. $6·95 \times 10^{-5}$ μF
3. 6 km
4. $1·33 \times 10^{-10}$ C, $8·0 \times 10^{-10}$ J
5. (a) $1·33 \times 10^{-10}$ C (b) $1·33 \times 10^{-10}$ C

6. 24 μC, 48 μC, 72 μC
7. 110 μC on each, $1{\cdot}33 \times 10^{-3}$ J
8. 48 μC on the 8 μF capacitor and 24 μC on each of the 4 μF capacitors
9. (a) 5 μF (b) 10 μF
10. 110 μC
11. 44 μC
12. $4\pi\varepsilon_0 R_1$, $4\pi\varepsilon_0 R_2$; $4\pi\varepsilon_0 (R_1 + R_2)$
13. 2 μF, 20 V
15. (a) 50/3 μV at each point (b) zero
16. $C_3 + \dfrac{2\,C_1C_2}{C_1 + C_2}$
17. $\dfrac{\varepsilon_0 A(3\,d^2 + 6\,bd + 2\,b^2)}{3\,d(d+b)\,(d+2\,b)}$
18. (a) 8 pF (b) same as in (a)
19. 20 V
20. $3{\cdot}3 \times 10^{-4}$ C
21. 43 mV
22. $\left(\dfrac{Vea^2}{md_1(d_1+d_2)}\right)^{1/2}$
23. $1{\cdot}08 \times 10^{-3}$ cm
24. 2·25 μF
25. (a) $\dfrac{12}{11}$ V (b) − 8 V (c) zero (d) − 10·3 V
26. (a) $\dfrac{11}{6}$ μF (b) $\dfrac{11}{4}$ μF (c) 8 μF (d) 8 μF
27. 1 μF
28. 2 μF
29. 4 μF
30. 12·5 V
31. 1 V
32. 5 V
33. 0·16 μC
34. (a) 0·50 μC (b) 10 V
35. (a) 10 V (b) 10 V
36. (a) 1·71 V, 4·29 V (b) 184 pJ, 73·5 pJ
37. 960 μJ
38. 8 mJ in (a) and (d), 2 mJ in (b) and (c)
39. 2·0 J
40. (a) 8 μC, 16 μC (b) 16 μJ, 32 μJ, (c) 96 μJ
41. $\dfrac{Q^2}{8\pi\varepsilon_0 R}$
42. (a) $\pi\varepsilon_0 RV^2$
43. $5{\cdot}6 \times 10^{-4}$ J
44. (a) $1{\cdot}06 \times 10^{-10}$ C (b) $12{\cdot}7 \times 10^{-10}$ J (c) $12{\cdot}7 \times 10^{-10}$ J, $6{\cdot}35 \times 10^{-10}$ J (d) $6{\cdot}35 \times 10^{-10}$ J
45. (a) 2400 μC, 1200 μC (b) 1200 μC (c) 14·4 mJ (d) 21·6 mJ (e) 7·2 mJ
46. (a) $C\mathcal{E}/2$, (b) $C\mathcal{E}^2/2$ (c) $C\mathcal{E}^2/4$ (d) $C\mathcal{E}^2/4$
47. (a) 1·44 mJ, 0·432 mJ (b) 21·8 μC, 26·2 μC, (c) 1·77 mJ
48. 1·44 mJ
49. 1·42 nF
50. (a) 8·5 nC (b) 6·4 nC (c) 2·1 nC
51. 88 pF
52. 3
53. (a) 30 μC (b) 3×10^3 V m^{-1} (c) 8·3 μF (d) 20 μC
54. 44 pF
55. (a) 1·18 μJ (b) 1·97 μJ
56. (a) $\dfrac{2\,K_1K_2\varepsilon_0 A}{d(K_1+K_2)}$ (b) $\dfrac{3\varepsilon_0 A\,K_1K_2K_3}{d(K_1K_2 + K_2K_3 + K_3K_1)}$ (c) $\dfrac{\varepsilon_0 A}{2\,d}(K_1 + K_2)$
57. $\dfrac{\varepsilon_0 K_1K_2a^2 \ln \dfrac{K_1}{K_2}}{(K_1 - K_2)d}$
58. 3 : 5
59. $\dfrac{\varepsilon_0 AV^2}{2\,d}\left(\dfrac{1}{K} - 1\right)$
60. (a) 5 mC (b) 20 V (c) 2 mC (d) 3 mC
61. $\dfrac{4\pi\varepsilon_0 Kabc}{Ka(b-c) + b(c-a)}$
62. $\dfrac{4\pi\varepsilon_0 ac}{c-a}$
63. $\dfrac{4\pi\varepsilon_0 Kabc}{Ka(c-b) + c(b-a)}$
64. 0·45 m^2
65. $2{\cdot}5 \times 10^{-7}$ N
66. $\dfrac{\varepsilon_0 b\,\mathcal{E}^2(K-1)}{2\,dg}$
67. $\sqrt{\dfrac{K_2 - 1}{K_1 - 1}}$
68. $8\sqrt{\dfrac{(l-a)\,lmd}{\varepsilon_0 A\mathcal{E}^2(K-1)}}$

□

CHAPTER 32

ELECTRIC CURRENT IN CONDUCTORS

32.1 ELECTRIC CURRENT AND CURRENT DENSITY

When there is a transfer of charge from one side of an area to the other, we say that there is an *electric current* through the area. If the moving charges are positive, the current is in the direction of motion. If they are negative, the current is opposite to the direction of motion. If a charge ΔQ crosses an area in time Δt, we define the average electric current through the area during this time as

$$\bar{i} = \frac{\Delta Q}{\Delta t}.$$

The current at time t is

$$i = \lim_{\Delta t \to 0} \frac{\Delta Q}{\Delta t} = \frac{dQ}{dt}. \quad \ldots (32.1)$$

Thus, electric current through an area is the rate of transfer of charge from one side of the area to the other. The SI unit of current is ampere. If one coulomb of charge crosses an area in one second, the current is one ampere. It is one of the seven base units accepted in SI.

We shall now define a vector quantity known as *electric current density* at a point. To define the current density at a point P, we draw a small area ΔS through P perpendicular to the flow of charges (figure 32.1a). If Δi be the current through the area ΔS, the average current density is

$$\bar{j} = \frac{\Delta i}{\Delta S}.$$

The current density at the point P is

$$j = \lim_{\Delta S \to 0} \frac{\Delta i}{\Delta S} = \frac{di}{dS}.$$

The direction of the current density is the same as the direction of the current. Thus, it is along the motion of the moving charges if the charges are positive and opposite to the motion of the charges if the charges are negative. If a current i is uniformly distributed over an area S and is perpendicular to it,

$$j = \frac{i}{S}. \quad \ldots (32.2)$$

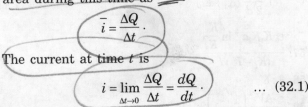

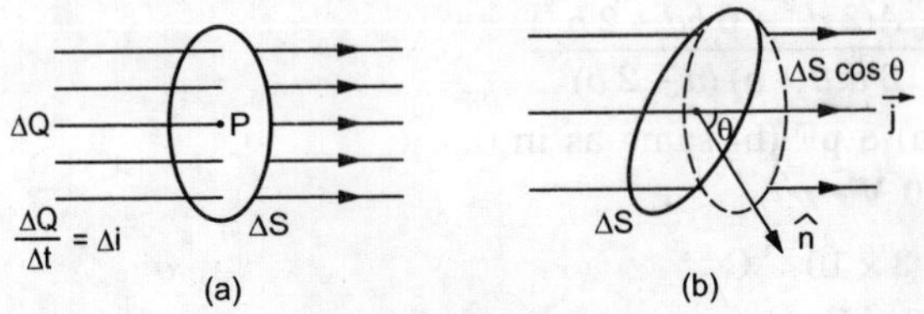

Figure 32.1

Now let us consider an area ΔS which is not necessarily perpendicular to the current (figure 32-1b). If the normal to the area makes an angle θ with the direction of the current, the current density is,

$$j = \frac{\Delta i}{\Delta S \cos\theta}$$

or,

$$\Delta i = j\, \Delta S \cos\theta$$

where Δi is the current through ΔS. If $\vec{\Delta S}$ be the *area-vector* corresponding to the area ΔS, we have

$$\Delta i = \vec{j} \cdot \vec{\Delta S}.$$

For a finite area,

$$i = \int \vec{j} \cdot d\vec{S}. \quad \ldots (32.3)$$

Note carefully that an electric current has direction as well as magnitude but it is not a vector quantity. It does not add like vectors. The current density is a vector quantity.

Example 32.1

An electron beam has an aperture $1 \cdot 0$ mm^2. A total of $6 \cdot 0 \times 10^{16}$ electrons go through any perpendicular cross section per second. Find (a) the current and (b) the current density in the beam.

Solution :

(a) The total charge crossing a perpendicular cross section in one second is

$$q = ne$$
$$= 6 \cdot 0 \times 10^{16} \times 1 \cdot 6 \times 10^{-19}\ \text{C}$$
$$= 9 \cdot 6 \times 10^{-3}\ \text{C}.$$

The current is

$$i = \frac{q}{t}$$

$$= \frac{9{\cdot}6 \times 10^{-3}\ \mathrm{C}}{1\ \mathrm{s}} = 9{\cdot}6 \times 10^{-3}\ \mathrm{A}.$$

As the charge is negative, the current is opposite to the direction of motion of the beam.

(b) The current density is

$$j = \frac{i}{S} = \frac{9{\cdot}6 \times 10^{-3}\ \mathrm{A}}{1{\cdot}0\ \mathrm{mm}^2} = 9{\cdot}6 \times 10^{3}\ \mathrm{A\ m^{-2}}.$$

Electric current can be obtained in a variety of ways. When a metal is heated to high temperatures, it emits electrons. These electrons travel in space. Considering any area perpendicular to their velocity, there is a current through it.

In many solutions, positive and negative ions wander. If the solution is placed in an electric field, the positive ions move (inside the solution) along the field and the negative ions move opposite to the field. Both movements contribute to a current in the direction of the field.

When a battery is connected across a capacitor, charges flow from the battery to the capacitor through the connecting wires. There is a current through any cross section of the wires as long as the charges keep going to the plates.

In this chapter, we shall study the electric current in a conductor when an electric field is established inside it.

32.2 DRIFT SPEED

A conductor contains a large number of loosely bound electrons which we call *free electrons* or *conduction electrons*. The remaining material is a collection of relatively heavy positive ions which we call *lattice*. These ions keep on vibrating about their mean positions. The average amplitude depends on the temperature. Occasionally, a free electron collides or interacts in some other fashion with the lattice. The speed and direction of the electron changes randomly at each such event. As a result, the electron moves in a zig-zag path. As there is a large number of free electrons moving in random directions, the number of electrons crossing an area ΔS from one side very nearly equals the number crossing from the other side in any given time interval. The electric current through the area is, therefore, zero.

When there is an electric field inside the conductor, a force acts on each electron in the direction opposite to the field. The electrons get biased in their random motion in favour of the force. As a result, the electrons drift slowly in this direction. At each collision, the electron starts afresh in a random direction with a random speed but gains an additional velocity v' due to the electric field. This velocity v' increases with time and suddenly becomes zero as the electron makes a collision with the lattice and starts afresh with a random velocity. As the time t between successive collisions is small, the electron slowly and steadily drifts opposite to the applied field (figure 32.2). If the electron drifts a distance l in a long time t, we define drift speed as

$$v_d = \frac{l}{t}.$$

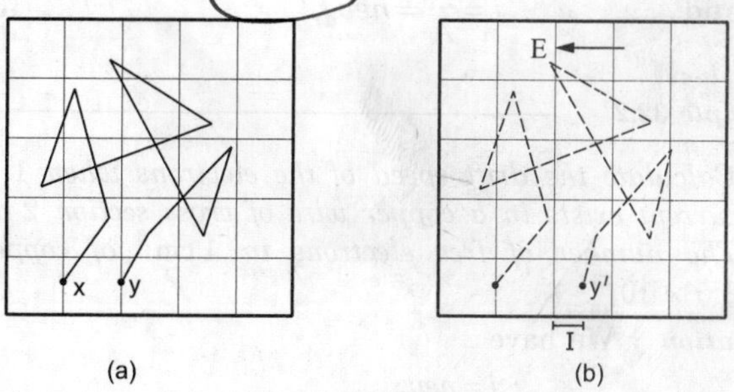

Figure 32.2

If τ be the average time between successive collisions, the distance drifted during this period is

$$l = \frac{1}{2}a(\tau)^2 = \frac{1}{2}\left(\frac{eE}{m}\right)(\tau)^2.$$

The drift speed is

$$v_d = \frac{l}{\tau} = \frac{1}{2}\left(\frac{eE}{m}\right)\tau.$$

It is proportional to the electric field E and to the average collision-time τ.

The random motion of free electrons does not contribute to the drift of these electrons. Also, the average collision-time is constant for a given material at a given temperature. We, therefore, make the following assumption for our present purpose of discussing electric current.

When no electric field exists in a conductor, the free electrons stay at rest ($v_d = 0$) and when a field E exists, they move with a constant velocity

$$v_d = \frac{e\tau}{2\,m}E = kE \qquad \ldots (32.4)$$

opposite to the field. The constant k depends on the material of the conductor and its temperature.

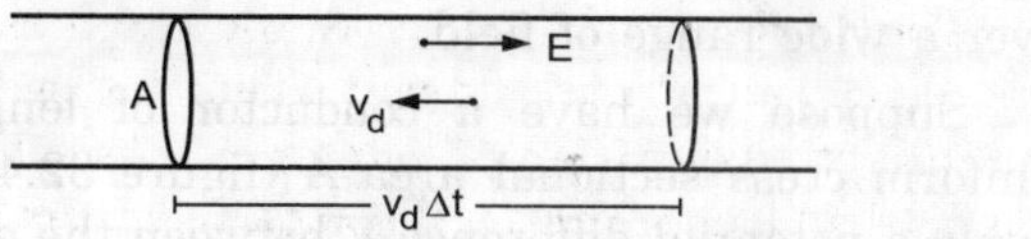

Figure 32.3

Let us now find the relation between the current density and the drift speed. Consider a cylindrical conductor of cross-sectional area A in which an electric field E exists. Consider a length $v_d \, \Delta t$ of the conductor (figure 32.3). The volume of this portion is $A v_d \Delta t$. If there are n free electrons per unit volume of the wire, the number of free electrons in this portion is $n A v_d \, \Delta t$. All these electrons cross the area A in time Δt. Thus, the charge crossing this area in time Δt is

$$\Delta Q = n A v_d \, \Delta t \, e$$

or, $$i = \frac{\Delta Q}{\Delta t} = n A v_d \, e$$

and $$j = \frac{i}{A} = n e v_d. \qquad \text{... (32.5)}$$

Example 32.2

Calculate the drift speed of the electrons when 1 A of current exists in a copper wire of cross section 2 mm^2. The number of free electrons in 1 cm^3 of copper is $8{\cdot}5 \times 10^{22}$.

Solution : We have

$$j = n e v_d$$

or, $$v_d = \frac{j}{n\,e} = \frac{i}{A\,ne}$$

$$= \frac{1 \text{ A}}{(2 \times 10^{-6} \text{ m}^2)\,(8{\cdot}5 \times 10^{22} \times 10^6 \text{ m}^{-3})\,(1{\cdot}6 \times 10^{-19} \text{ C})}$$

$$= 0{\cdot}036 \text{ mm s}^{-1}.$$

We see that the drift speed is indeed small.

32.3 OHM'S LAW

Using equations (32.4) and (32.5),

$$j = n e v_d = \frac{n e^2 \tau}{2\,m} E$$

or, $$j = \sigma E \qquad \text{... (32.6)}$$

where σ depends only on the material of the conductor and its temperature. This constant is called the *electrical conductivity* of the material. Equation (32.6) is known as *Ohm's law*.

The *resistivity* of a material is defined as

$$\rho = \frac{1}{\sigma}. \qquad \text{... (32.7)}$$

Ohm's law tells us that the conductivity (or resistivity) of a material is independent of the electric field existing in the material. This is valid for conductors over a wide range of field.

Suppose we have a conductor of length l and uniform cross sectional area A (figure 32.4a). Let us apply a potential difference V between the ends of the conductor. The electric field inside the conductor is $E = V/l$. If the current in the conductor is i, the current density is $j = \frac{i}{A}$. Ohm's law $j = \sigma E$ then becomes

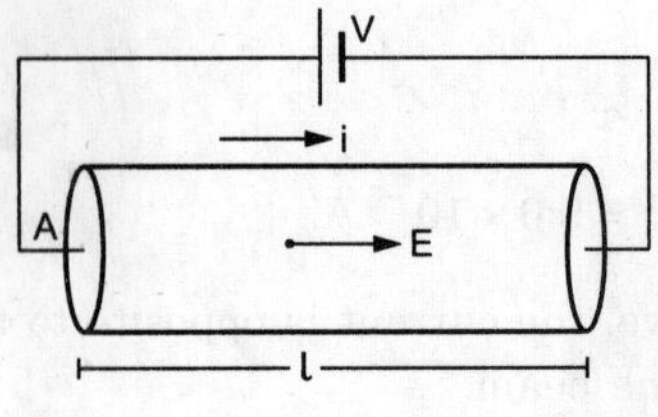

(a)

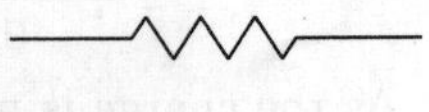
(b)

Figure 32.4

$$\frac{i}{A} = \sigma \frac{V}{l}$$

or, $$V = \frac{1}{\sigma}\frac{l}{A} i = \rho \frac{l}{A} i$$

or, $$V = R\,i \qquad \text{... (32.8)}$$

where $$R = \rho \frac{l}{A} \qquad \text{... (32.9)}$$

is called the *resistance* of the given conductor. The quantity $1/R$ is called *conductance*.

Equation (32.8) is another form of Ohm's law which is widely used in circuit analysis. The unit of resistance is called ohm and is denoted by the symbol Ω. An object of conducting material, having a resistance of desired value, is called a *resistor*. A resistor is represented by the symbol shown in figure (32.4b).

From equation (32.9), the unit of resistivity ρ is ohm metre, also written as Ωm. The unit of conductivity (σ) is (ohm m)$^{-1}$ written as mho m^{-1}.

Example 32.3

Calculate the resistance of an aluminium wire of length 50 cm and cross sectional area 2·0 mm^2. The resistivity of aluminium is $\rho = 2{\cdot}6 \times 10^{-8}$ Ωm.

Solution :

The resistance is $R = \rho \frac{l}{A}$

$$= \frac{(2{\cdot}6 \times 10^{-8} \ \Omega\text{m}) \times (0{\cdot}50 \text{ m})}{2 \times 10^{-6} \text{ m}^2} = 0{\cdot}0065 \ \Omega.$$

We arrived at Ohm's law (equation 32.6 or 32.8) by making several assumptions about the existence and behaviour of the free electrons. These assumptions are not valid for semiconductors, insulators, solutions, etc. Ohm's law cannot be applied in such cases.

Colour Code for Resistors

Resistors of different values are commercially available. To make a resistor, carbon with a suitable binding agent is molded into a cylinder. Wire leads are

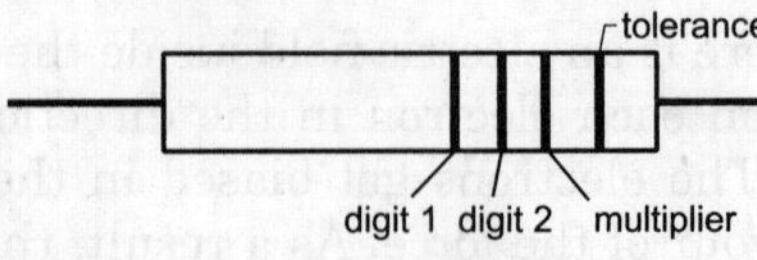

Figure 32.5

attached to this cylinder and the entire resistor is encased in a ceramic or plastic jacket. The two leads connect the resistor to a circuit. These resistors are widely used in electronic circuits such as those for radios, amplifiers, etc. The value of the resistance is indicated by four coloured-bands, marked on the surface of the cylinder (figure 32.5). The meanings of the four positions of the bands are shown in figure (32.5) and the meanings of different colours are given in table (32.1).

Table 32.1 : *Resistance codes (resistance given in ohm)*

Colour	Digit	Multiplier	Tolerance
Black	0	1	
Brown	1	10	
Red	2	10^2	
Orange	3	10^3	
Yellow	4	10^4	
Green	5	10^5	
Blue	6	10^6	
Violet	7	10^7	
Gray	8	10^8	
White	9	10^9	
Gold		0·1	5%
Silver		0·01	10%

For example, suppose the colours on the resistor shown in figure (32.5) are brown, yellow, green and gold as read from left to right. Using table (32.1), the resistance is

$$(14 \times 10^5 \pm 5\%)\Omega = (1{\cdot}4 \pm 0{\cdot}07)\ \text{M}\Omega.$$

Sometimes, the tolerance band is missing from the code so that there are only three bands. This means the tolerance is 20%.

32.4 TEMPERATURE DEPENDENCE OF RESISTIVITY

As the temperature of a conductor is increased, the thermal agitation increases and the collisions become more frequent. The average time τ between the successive collisions decreases and hence the drift speed decreases. Thus, the conductivity decreases and the resistivity increases as the temperature increases. For small temperature variations, we can write for most of the materials,

$$\rho(T) = \rho(T_0)\,[1 + \alpha(T - T_0)]$$

where $\rho(T)$ and $\rho(T_0)$ are resistivities at temperatures T and T_0 respectively and α is a constant for the given material. In fact, α depends to a small extent on the temperature. The constant α is called the *temperature coefficient of resistivity*. Table (32.2) lists the resistivity at room temperature and the average value of α for some materials.

Table 32.2 : *Resistivities of different materials*

Material	$\rho(\Omega\text{m})$	$\alpha(\text{K}^{-1})$
Silver	$1{\cdot}47 \times 10^{-8}$	0·0038
Copper	$1{\cdot}72 \times 10^{-8}$	0·0039
Gold	$2{\cdot}35 \times 10^{-8}$	0·0034
Aluminium	$2{\cdot}63 \times 10^{-8}$	0·0039
Tungsten	$5{\cdot}51 \times 10^{-8}$	0·0045
Nickel	$86{\cdot}84 \times 10^{-8}$	0·0060
Iron	$9{\cdot}71 \times 10^{-8}$	0·0050
Magnesium	44×10^{-8}	0·0000
Mercury	96×10^{-8}	0·0009
Nichrome	100×10^{-8}	0·0004
Silicon	640	− 0·075
Germanium	0·46	− 0·048
Fused quartz	$7{\cdot}5 \times 10^{17}$	

The resistance of a given conductor depends on its length and area of cross section besides the resistivity (equation 32.9). As temperature changes, the length and the area also change. But these changes are quite small and the factor l/A may be treated as constant. Then $R \propto \rho$ and hence

$$R(T) = R(T_0)\,[1 + \alpha(T - T_0)].$$

From table (32.2), we see that resistivity varies over a wide range. We have metals with resistivity of the order of 10^{-8} Ωm. They are good conductors of electricity. Fused quartz has resistivity as high as $7{\cdot}5 \times 10^{17}$ Ωm. This is an *insulator*. Then we have materials like silicon and germanium which have resistivity much smaller than that of insulators but much larger than that of the metals. They are called *semiconductors*.

Thermistor

The temperature coefficient of resistivity is negative for semiconductors. This means that the resistivity decreases as we raise the temperature of such a material. The picture of a large number of free electrons colliding with each other and with the lattice is not adequate for semiconductors. The magnitude of the temperature coefficient of resistivity is often quite large for a semiconducting material. This fact is used to construct thermometers to detect small changes in temperatures. Such a device is called a *thermistor*. Thermistors are usually prepared from oxides of various metals such as nickel, iron, cobalt, copper, etc. These compounds are also semiconductors. A thermistor is usually enclosed in a capsule with epoxy surface. The thermistor is dipped in the bath whose temperature is to be measured. The circuit is completed by connecting a battery. The current through the thermistor is measured. If the temperature increases, the current also increases because of the decrease in resistivity. Thus, by noting the change in the current, one can find the change in temperature. A typical thermistor can easily measure a change in temperature of the order of 10^{-3} °C.

Superconductors

There are certain materials for which the resistivity suddenly becomes zero below a certain temperature. This temperature is called the *critical temperature* for this transition. The material in this state is called a *superconductor*. Above the critical temperature, the resistivity follows the trend of a normal metal (figure 32.6). This phenomenon was observed for mercury in 1911 by H Kamerlingh Onnes. The critical temperature for mercury is 4·2 K.

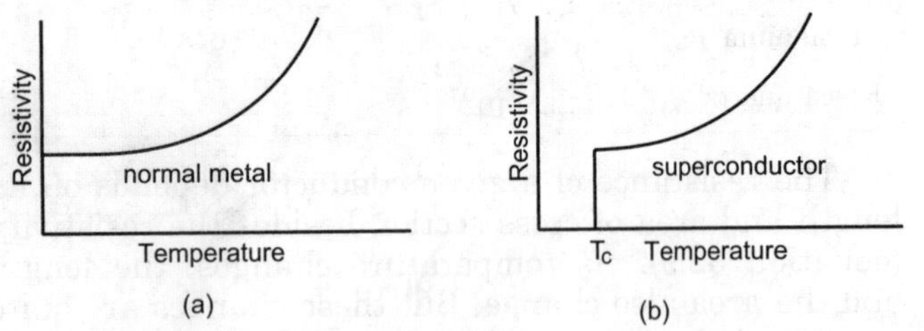

Figure 32.6

If an electric current is set up in a superconducting material, it can persist for long time without any applied emf. Steady currents have been observed for several years in superconducting loops without any observable decrease. Superconductors are used to construct very strong magnets. This has useful applications in material science research and high-energy particle physics. Possible applications of superconductors are ultrafast computer switches and transmission of electric power through superconducting power lines. However, the requirement of low temperature is posing difficulty. Scientists are putting great effort to construct compounds and alloys which would be superconducting at room temperature (300 K). Superconductivity at around 125 K has already been achieved and efforts are on to improve upon this.

32.5 BATTERY AND EMF

A battery is a device which maintains a potential difference between its two terminals A and B. Figure (32.7) shows a schematic diagram of a battery. Some internal mechanism exerts forces on the charges of the battery material. This force drives the positive charges of the battery material towards A and the negative charges of the battery material towards B. We show the force on a positive charge q as $\vec{F_b}$. As positive charge accumulates on A and negative charge on B, a potential difference develops and grows between A and B. An electric field $\vec{E}$ is developed in the battery material from A to B and exerts a force $\vec{F_e} = q\vec{E}$ on a charge q. The direction of this force is opposite to that of $\vec{F_b}$. In steady state, the charge accumulation on A and B is such that $F_b = F_e$. No further accumulation takes place.

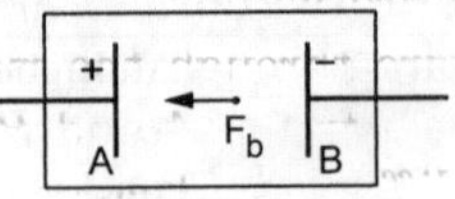

Figure 32.7

If a charge q is taken from the terminal B to the terminal A, the work done by the battery force F_b is $W = F_b\, d$ where d is the distance between A and B. The work done by the battery force per unit charge is

$$\mathcal{E} = \frac{W}{q} = \frac{F_b d}{q} . \qquad \text{... (32.10)}$$

This quantity is called the *emf* of the battery. The full form of emf is *electromotive force*. The name is misleading in the sense that emf is not a force, it is work done/charge. We shall continue to denote this quantity by the short name emf. If nothing is connected externally between A and B,

$$F_b = F_e = qE$$

or, $$F_b d = qEd = qV,$$

where $V = Ed$ is the potential difference between the terminals. Thus,

$$\mathcal{E} = \frac{F_b d}{q} = V.$$

Thus, *the emf of a battery equals the potential difference between its terminals when the terminals are not connected externally.*

Potential difference and emf are two different quantities whose magnitudes may be equal in certain conditions. The emf is the work done per unit charge by the battery force F_b which is nonelectrostatic in nature. The potential difference originates from the electrostatic field created by the charges accumulated on the terminals of the battery.

A battery is often prepared by putting two rods or plates of different metals in a chemical solution. Such a battery, using chemical reactions to generate emf, is often called a *cell*.

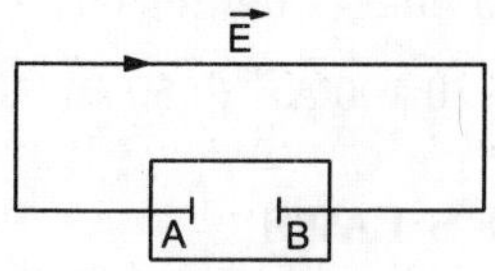

Figure 32.8

Now suppose the terminals of a battery are connected by a conducting wire as shown in figure (32.8). As the terminal A is at a higher potential than B, there is an electric field in the wire in the direction shown in the figure. The free electrons in the wire move in the opposite direction and enter the battery at the terminal A. Some electrons are withdrawn from the terminal B which enter the wire through the right end. Thus, the potential difference between A and B tends to decrease. If this potential difference decreases, the electrostatic force F_e inside the battery also decreases. The force F_b due to the battery mechanism remains the same. Thus, there is a net force on the positive charges of the battery material from B to A. The positive charges rush towards A and neutralise the effect of the electrons coming at A from the wire. Similarly, the negative charges rush towards B. Thus, the potential difference between A and B is maintained.

For calculation of current, motion of a positive charge in one direction is equivalent to the motion of a negative charge in opposite direction. Using this fact, we can describe the above situation by a simpler model. The positive terminal of the battery supplies positive charges to the wire. These charges are pushed through the wire by the electric field and they reach the negative terminal of the battery. The battery mechanism drives these charges back to the positive terminal against the electric field existing in the battery and the process continues. This maintains a steady current in the circuit.

Current can also be driven into a battery in the reverse direction. In such a case, positive charge enters the battery at the positive terminal, moves inside the battery to the negative terminal and leaves the battery from the negative terminal. Such a process is called *charging* of the battery. The more common process in which the positive charge comes out of the battery from the positive terminal is called *discharging* of the battery.

32.6 ENERGY TRANSFER IN AN ELECTRIC CIRCUIT

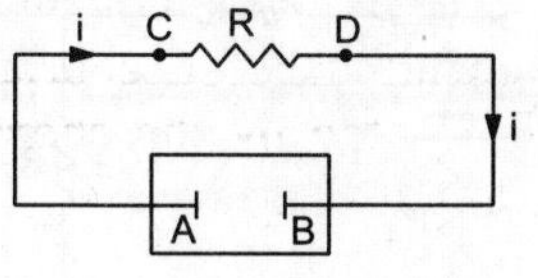

Figure 32.9

Figure (32.9) shows a simple circuit in which a resistor CD having a resistance R is connected to a battery of emf $\mathcal{E}$ through two connecting wires CA and DB. The connecting wires are assumed to have negligible resistance. This ensures that potential differences across AC and across BD are zero even when there is a current through them. The potential difference across the resistor is the same as that across the battery. If the current in the circuit is i, this potential difference is

$$V = V_A - V_B = V_C - V_D = iR.$$

Thermal Energy Produced in the Resistor

In time t, a charge $q = it$ goes through the circuit. As this charge moves from C to D, the electric potential energy decreases by

$$U = qV = (it)\,(iR) = i^2Rt. \quad \ldots \text{(32.11)}$$

This loss in electric potential energy appears as increased thermal energy of the resistor. Thus, a current i for a time t through a resistance R increases the thermal energy by i^2Rt. The power developed is

$$P = \frac{U}{t} = i^2R. \quad \ldots \text{(32.12)}$$

Using Ohm's law, this can also be written as

$$P = \frac{V^2}{R} = Vi.$$

Example 32.4

A resistor develops 400 J *of thermal energy in* 10 s *when a current of* 2 A *is passed through it. (a) Find its resistance. (b) If the current is increased to* 4 A, *what will be the energy developed in* 10 s.

Solution :

(a) Using $\quad U = i^2Rt,$

$$400 \text{ J} = (2 \text{ A})^2 R(10 \text{ s})$$

or, $\quad R = 10\ \Omega.$

(b) The thermal energy developed, when the current is 4 A, is

$$U = i^2Rt$$
$$= (4 \text{ A})^2 \times (10\ \Omega) \times (10 \text{ s}) = 1600 \text{ J}.$$

Internal Resistance of a Battery

As the charge $q = it$ goes through the battery from the negative terminal B to the positive terminal A, work is done by the nonelectrostatic battery force F_b. This work is $U_1 = q\mathcal{E} = \mathcal{E}it$. As the potential of A is higher than the potential of B by an amount V, the electric potential energy increases by an amount

$$U_2 = V(it).$$

The remaining energy $U_1 - U_2$ appears as thermal energy of the battery material. The fraction appearing as thermal energy depends on the battery material and the battery mechanism. If no thermal energy is developed as the charge goes through the battery,

$$\mathcal{E} it = Vit$$

or, $$\mathcal{E} = V.$$

Such a battery is called an *ideal battery*. The potential difference between the terminals of an ideal battery remains equal to its emf even if there is a current through it. As discussed earlier, an ideal battery is denoted by the symbol shown in figure (32.10a). The potential difference between the facing parallel lines is $V = \mathcal{E}$, the longer line being at the higher potential.

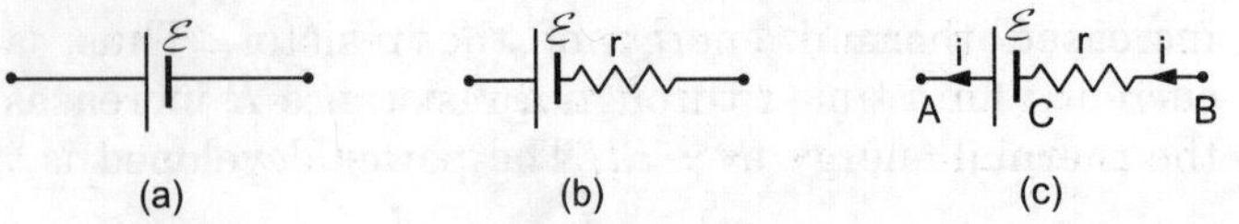

Figure 32.10

A nonideal battery develops thermal energy as a current passes through it and the potential difference between the terminals is smaller than the emf. Such a battery may be represented by the symbol shown in figure (32.10b). This is a combination of an ideal battery of emf $\mathcal{E}$ and a resistance r. If there is a current i through the battery in the direction indicated in figure (32.10c), the potential difference between the terminals is

$$V_A - V_B = (V_A - V_C) - (V_B - V_C)$$
$$= \mathcal{E} - ir.$$

The thermal energy developed in time t is i^2rt. The addition of a resistance r accounts for the difference between $\mathcal{E}$ and V as well as for the thermal energy developed in the battery. This resistance is called the *internal resistance* of the battery.

Example 32.5

A battery of emf 2·0 V *and internal resistance* 0·50 Ω *supplies a current of* 100 mA. *Find (a) the potential difference across the terminals of the battery and (b) the thermal energy developed in the battery in* 10 s.

Solution : The situation is the same as that shown in figure (32.10c).

(a) The potential difference across the terminals is

$$V_A - V_B = (V_A - V_C) - (V_B - V_C)$$
$$= \mathcal{E} - ir$$
$$= 2{\cdot}0\ \text{V} - (0{\cdot}100\ \text{A})\,(0{\cdot}50\ \Omega) = 1{\cdot}95\ \text{V}.$$

(b) The thermal energy developed in the battery is

$$U = i^2rt = (0{\cdot}100\ \text{A})^2\,(0{\cdot}50\ \Omega)\,(10\ \text{s}) = 0{\cdot}05\ \text{J}.$$

32.7 KIRCHHOFF'S LAWS

The Junction Law

The sum of all the currents directed towards a point in a circuit is equal to the sum of all the currents directed away from the point.

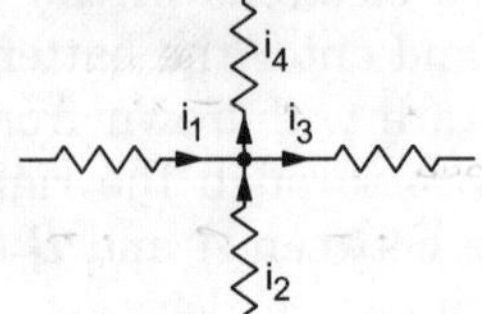

Figure 32.11

Thus, in figure (32.11),

$$i_1 + i_2 = i_3 + i_4. \quad \text{... (i)}$$

If we take the current directed towards a point as positive and that directed away from the point as negative, we can restate the junction law as, *the algebraic sum of all the currents directed towards a point is zero.*

In figure (32.11), the currents directed towards the junction point are i_1, i_2, $-i_3$ and $-i_4$.

Thus,

$$i_1 + i_2 + (-i_3) + (-i_4) = 0$$

which is the same as (i).

The junction law follows from the fact that no point in a circuit keeps on accumulating charge or keeps on supplying charge. Charges pass through the point. So, the net charge coming towards the point should be equal to that going away from it in the same time.

The Loop Law

The algebraic sum of all the potential differences along a closed loop in a circuit is zero.

While using this rule, one starts from a point on the loop and goes along the loop, either clockwise or anticlockwise, to reach the same point again. Any potential *drop* encountered is taken to be positive and any potential *rise* is taken to be negative. The net

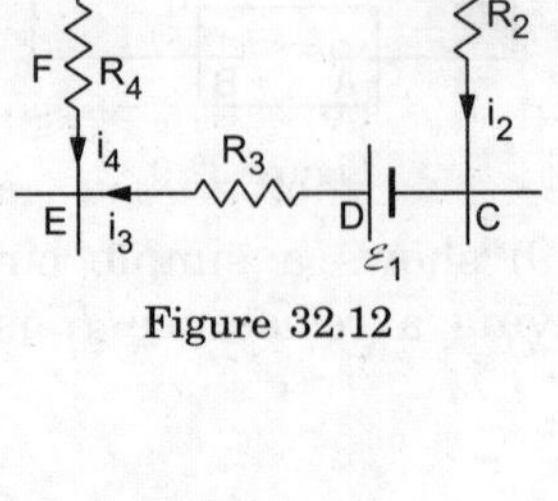

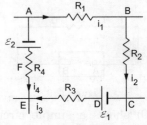

Figure 32.12

sum of all these potential differences should be zero. In figure (32.12), we show a loop *ABCDEFA* of a circuit. As we start from *A* and go along the loop clockwise to reach the same point *A*, we get the following potential differences:

$$V_A - V_B = i_1R_1$$
$$V_B - V_C = i_2R_2$$
$$V_C - V_D = -\mathcal{E}_1$$
$$V_D - V_E = i_3R_3$$
$$V_E - V_F = -i_4R_4$$
$$V_F - V_A = \mathcal{E}_2.$$

Adding all these,

$$0 = i_1R_1 + i_2R_2 - \mathcal{E}_1 + i_3R_3 - i_4R_4 + \mathcal{E}_2.$$

The loop law follows directly from the fact that electrostatic force is a conservative force and the work done by it in any closed path is zero.

32.8 COMBINATION OF RESISTORS IN SERIES AND PARALLEL

Several resistors may be combined to form a network. The combination should have two end points to connect it with a battery or other circuit elements. If a potential difference V is applied to the combination, it draws some current i. We define *equivalent resistance* of the combination as

$$R_{eq} = V/i.$$

This single resistance draws the same current as the given combination when the same potential difference is applied across the end points.

Series Combination

Two or more resistors are said to be connected in series if the same current passes through all the resistors.

Figure (32.13) shows three resistors having resistances R_1, R_2 and R_3 connected in series. The combination has two points *P* and *N* through which it can be connected to a battery or other circuit elements. Any current going through R_1 also goes through R_2 and R_3.

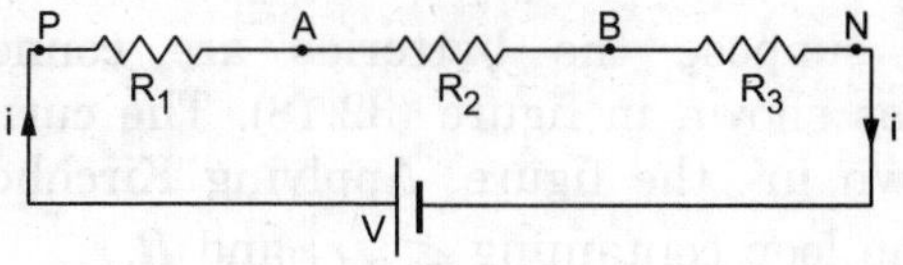

Figure 32.13

Suppose we apply a potential difference V between the points *P* and *N*. A current i passes through all the resistors. Using Kirchhoff's loop law for the loop *PABNP*,

$$iR_1 + iR_2 + iR_3 - V = 0$$

or, $$i = \frac{V}{R_1 + R_2 + R_3}$$

or, $$\frac{V}{i} = R_1 + R_2 + R_3.$$

Thus, the equivalent resistance is

$$R_{eq} = R_1 + R_2 + R_3.$$

This argument may be extended for any number of resistors connected in series.

$$R_{eq} = R_1 + R_2 + R_3 + \dots \qquad \dots (32.13)$$

Parallel Combination

Two or more resistors are said to be connected in parallel if the same potential difference exists across all the resistors.

Figure (32.14) shows three resistors having resistances R_1, R_2 and R_3 connected in parallel. The combination has two end points *P* and *N*. One end of each resistor is joined to *P* and other end to *N*. Thus, the potential difference across any resistor is the same.

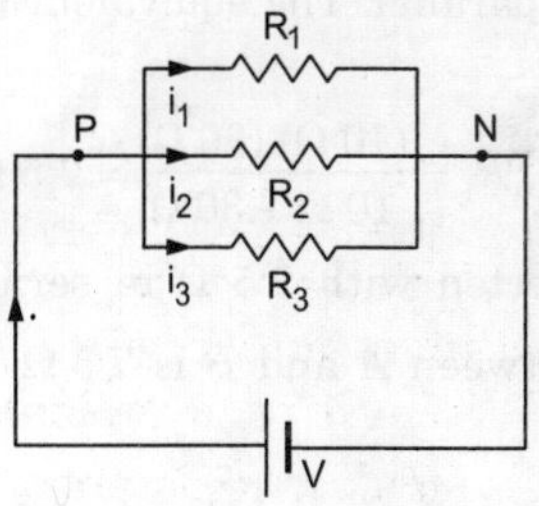

Figure 32.14

To find the equivalent resistance of the combination, let us apply a potential difference V between the points *P* and *N*. If the current through *P* is i, the equivalent resistance is

$$R_{eq} = V/i. \qquad \dots \text{(i)}$$

The current i is divided at the junction *P*. Suppose a current i_1 goes through R_1, i_2 through R_2 and i_3 through R_3. These combine at *N* to give a total current i. Using Kirchhoff's junction law at *P*,

$$i = i_1 + i_2 + i_3. \qquad \dots \text{(ii)}$$

The potential difference across each resistor is $V_P - V_N = V$. Using Ohm's law for the resistances R_1, R_2 and R_3 separately;

$$i_1 = \frac{V}{R_1}, \; i_2 = \frac{V}{R_2} \text{ and } i_3 = \frac{V}{R_3}.$$

Adding the above three equations and using (ii),

$$i = V\left(\frac{1}{R_1} + \frac{1}{R_2} + \frac{1}{R_3}\right).$$

Using (i),

$$\frac{1}{R_{eq}} = \frac{1}{R_1} + \frac{1}{R_2} + \frac{1}{R_3}.$$

The process may be generalised for any number of resistors connected in parallel, so that

$$\frac{1}{R_{eq}} = \frac{1}{R_1} + \frac{1}{R_2} + \frac{1}{R_3} + \cdots \qquad \ldots (32.14)$$

For two resistors in parallel,

$$\frac{1}{R_{eq}} = \frac{1}{R_1} + \frac{1}{R_2} \text{ or, } R_{eq} = \frac{R_1 R_2}{R_1 + R_2}.$$

Note that the equivalent resistance is smaller than the smallest individual resistance.

Example 32.6

Find the equivalent resistance of the network shown in figure (32.15) between the points A and B.

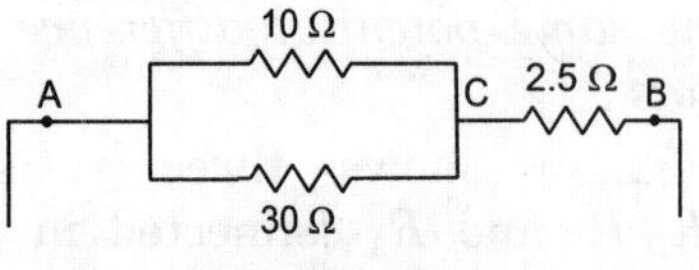

Figure 32.15

Solution : The 10 Ω resistor and the 30 Ω resistor are connected in parallel. The equivalent resistance between A and C is

$$R_1 = \frac{(10\ \Omega)\ (30\ \Omega)}{10\ \Omega + 30\ \Omega} = 7{\cdot}5\ \Omega.$$

This is connected with 2·5 Ω in series. The equivalent resistance between A and B is $7{\cdot}5\ \Omega + 2{\cdot}5\ \Omega = 10\ \Omega$.

Division of Current in Resistors Joined in Parallel

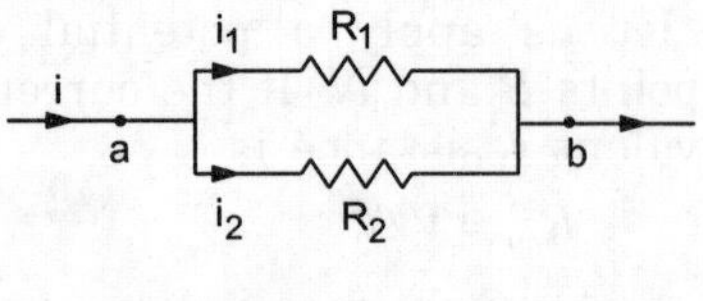

Figure 32.16

Consider the situation shown in figure (32.16). Using Ohm's law on resistors R_1 and R_2,

$$V_a - V_b = i_1 R_1 \text{ and } V_a - V_b = i_2 R_2.$$

Thus, $\quad i_1 R_1 = i_2 R_2$

or, $$\frac{i_1}{i_2} = \frac{R_2}{R_1}. \qquad \ldots \text{(i)}$$

We see that the current is divided in resistors, connected in parallel, in inverse ratio of the resistances.

From (i), $$\frac{i_1}{i_1 + i_2} = \frac{R_2}{R_1 + R_2}$$

or, $$\frac{i_1}{i} = \frac{R_2}{R_1 + R_2}$$

or, $$i_1 = \frac{R_2}{R_1 + R_2}\, i.$$

Similarly, $$i_2 = \frac{R_1}{R_1 + R_2}\, i.$$

32.9 GROUPING OF BATTERIES

Series Connection

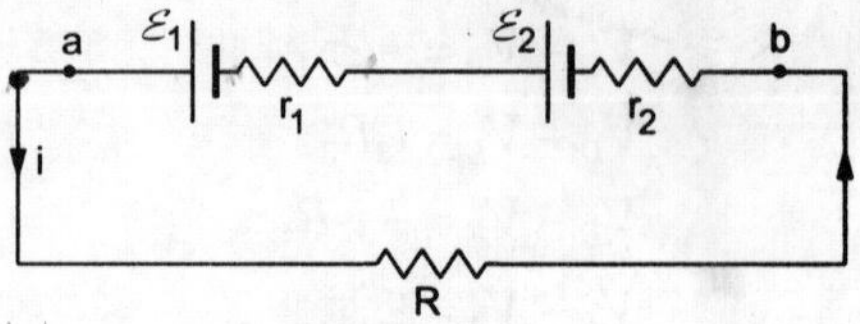

Figure 32.17

Suppose two batteries having emfs $\mathcal{E}_1$ and $\mathcal{E}_2$ and internal resistances r_1 and r_2 are connected in series as shown in figure (32.17). The points a and b act as the terminals of the combination. Suppose an external resistance R is connected across the combination. From Kirchhoff's loop law,

$$Ri + r_2 i - \mathcal{E}_2 + r_1 i - \mathcal{E}_1 = 0$$

or, $$i = \frac{\mathcal{E}_1 + \mathcal{E}_2}{R + (r_1 + r_2)} = \frac{\mathcal{E}_0}{R + r_0}.$$

where i is the current through the resistance R.

We see that the combination acts as a battery of emf $\mathcal{E}_0 = \mathcal{E}_1 + \mathcal{E}_2$ having an internal resistance $r_0 = r_1 + r_2$.

If the polarity of one of the batteries is reversed, the equivalent emf will be $|\mathcal{E}_1 - \mathcal{E}_2|$.

Parallel Connection

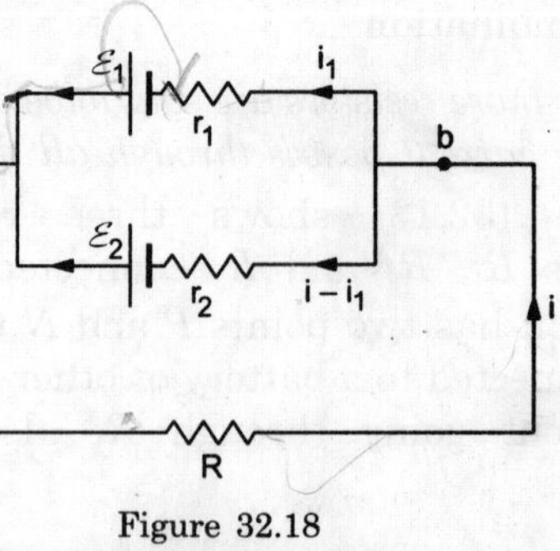

Figure 32.18

Now suppose the batteries are connected in parallel as shown in figure (32.18). The currents are also shown in the figure. Applying Kirchhoff's loop law in the loop containing $\mathcal{E}_1$, r_1 and R,

$$Ri + r_1 i_1 - \mathcal{E}_1 = 0. \qquad \ldots \text{(i)}$$

Similarly, applying Kirchhoff's law in the loop containing $\mathcal{E}_2$, r_2 and R,

$$Ri + r_2(i - i_1) - \mathcal{E}_2 = 0 \qquad \ldots \text{(ii)}$$

Multiply (i) by r_2, (ii) by r_1 and add. This gives,

$$iR(r_1+r_2)+r_1r_2i-\mathcal{E}_1r_2-\mathcal{E}_2r_1=0$$

$$\text{or,}\quad i=\frac{\mathcal{E}_1r_2+\mathcal{E}_2r_1}{R(r_1+r_2)+r_1r_2}=\frac{\dfrac{\mathcal{E}_1r_2+\mathcal{E}_2r_1}{r_1+r_2}}{R+\dfrac{r_1r_2}{r_1+r_2}}=\frac{\mathcal{E}_0}{R+r_0}.$$

We see that the combination acts as a battery of emf

$$\mathcal{E}_0=\frac{\mathcal{E}_1r_2+\mathcal{E}_2r_1}{r_1+r_2}$$

and internal resistance

$$r_0=\frac{r_1r_2}{r_1+r_2}.$$

If $\mathcal{E}_1=\mathcal{E}_2=\mathcal{E}$ and $r_1=r_2=r$, $\mathcal{E}_0=\mathcal{E}$ and $r_0=r/2$.

32.10 WHEATSTONE BRIDGE

Wheatstone bridge is an arrangement of four resistances which can be used to measure one of them in terms of the rest.

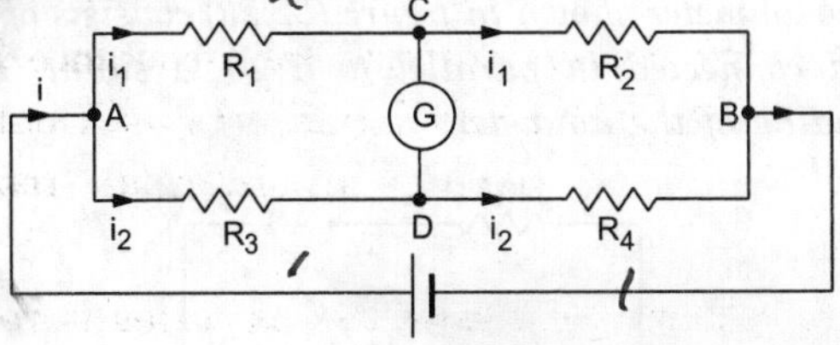

Figure 32.19

The arrangement is shown in figure (32.19). Four resistors with resistances R_1, R_2, R_3 and R_4 are connected to form a loop. There are four joints *A*, *B*, *C* and *D*. A battery is connected between two opposite joints *A* and *B* and a galvanometer is connected between the other two opposite joints *C* and *D*.

We shall discuss the construction and working of a galvanometer later. Here, we only state that a galvanometer has a needle which deflects when an electric current passes through the galvanometer. The needle deflects towards left if the current passes in one direction and towards right if the current is reversed.

The current i from the battery is divided at A in two parts. A part i_1 goes through R_1 and the rest i_2 goes through R_3. For a particular relation between the resistances, there is no current through the galvanometer. The Wheatstone bridge is then said to be *balanced*. In this case, the current in R_2 is the same as the current in R_1 and the current in R_4 is the same as that in R_3. As there is no current through the galvanometer, the potential difference across its terminals is zero. Thus,

$$V_C=V_D.$$

Applying Ohm's law to R_1 and R_2,

$$V_A-V_C=i_1R_1$$

and $$V_C-V_B=i_1R_2.$$

Thus, $$\frac{V_A-V_C}{V_C-V_B}=\frac{R_1}{R_2}. \quad \text{... (ii)}$$

Applying Ohm's law to R_3 and R_4,

$$V_A-V_D=i_2R_3$$

and $$V_D-V_B=i_2R_4.$$

Thus, $$\frac{V_A-V_D}{V_D-V_B}=\frac{R_3}{R_4}. \quad \text{... (iii)}$$

As $V_C=V_D$, left sides of (ii) and (iii) are equal. Thus,

$$\frac{R_1}{R_2}=\frac{R_3}{R_4}. \quad \text{... (32.15)}$$

This is the condition for which a Wheatstone bridge is balanced.

To measure the resistance of a resistor, it is connected as one of the four resistors in the bridge. One of the other three should be a variable resistor. Let us suppose R_4 is the resistance to be measured and R_3 is the variable resistance. When the Wheatstone bridge is connected, in general, there will be a deflection in the galvanometer. The value of the variable resistance R_3 is adjusted so that the deflection in the galvanometer becomes zero. In this case, the bridge is balanced and from equation (32.15),

$$R_4=\frac{R_2}{R_1}R_3.$$

Knowing R_1, R_2 and R_3, the value of R_4 is calculated.

Example 32.7

Find the value of R in figure (32.20) so that there is no current in the 50 Ω resistor.

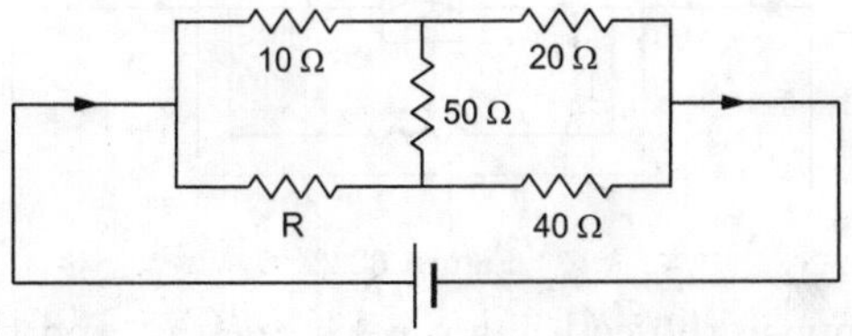

Figure 32.20

Solution :

This is a Wheatstone bridge with the galvanometer replaced by the 50 Ω resistor. There will be no current in the 50 Ω resistor if the bridge is balanced.

In this case,

$$\frac{10\ \Omega}{20\ \Omega} = \frac{R}{40\ \Omega}$$

or, $R = 20\ \Omega$.

32.11 AMMETER AND VOLTMETER

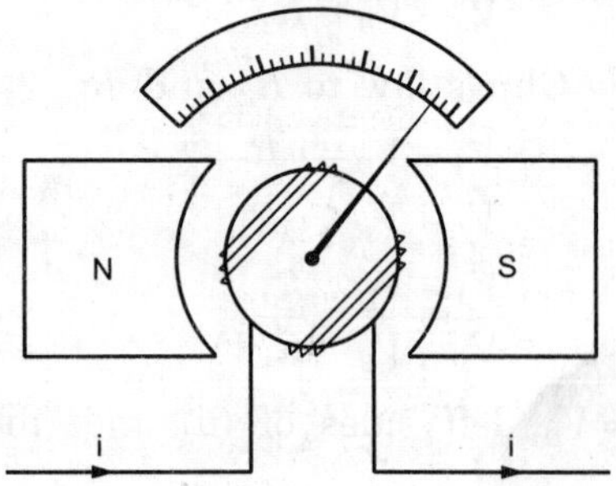

Figure 32.21

Ammeter is a device to measure an electric current and *voltmeter* is a device to measure a potential difference. In both the instruments there is a coil, suspended between the poles of a magnet. When a current is passed through the coil, it deflects. The angle of deflection is proportional to the current going through the coil. A needle is fixed to the coil. When the coil deflects, the needle moves on a graduated scale.

Ammeter

In an ammeter, a resistor having a small resistance is connected in parallel with the coil. This resistor is called the *shunt*. The current to be measured is passed through the ammeter by connecting it in series with the segment which carries the current. Plus and minus signs are marked near the terminals of the ammeter. The current should enter the ammeter through the terminal marked "plus". When no current passes through the ammeter, the needle stays at zero which is marked at the left extreme of the scale.

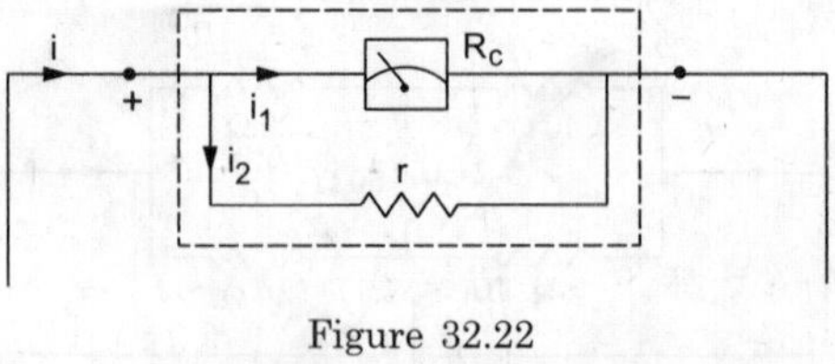

Figure 32.22

Suppose the coil has a resistance R_c and the small resistance connected in parallel (shunt) has a value r. When a current i is sent through the ammeter, the current gets divided in two parts. A part i_1 goes through the coil and the rest, $i - i_1$, through the shunt. As the potential difference across R_c is the same as that across r,

$$i_1 R_c = (i - i_1) r$$

or, $$i_1 = \frac{r}{R_c + r}\, i. \quad \dots \text{(i)}$$

The deflection is proportional to i_1 and hence to i. The scale is graduated to read the value of i directly.

The equivalent resistance of an ammeter is given by

$$R_{eq} = \frac{R_c r}{R_c + r}.$$

When the ammeter is connected in a segment of a circuit, the resistance of the segment increases by this amount R_{eq}. This reduces the main current which we wish to measure. To minimise this error, the equivalent resistant R_{eq} should be small. This is one reason why the shunt having a small resistance r is connected in parallel to the coil. This makes R_{eq} small.

Galvanometer is very similar to an ammeter in construction. When no current passes through it, the needle stays in the middle of the graduated scale. This point is marked zero. Current can be passed through the galvanometer in either direction. The needle deflects accordingly towards left or towards right.

Example 32.8

The ammeter shown in figure (32.23) consists of a 480 Ω *coil connected in parallel to a* 20 Ω *shunt. Find the reading of the ammeter.*

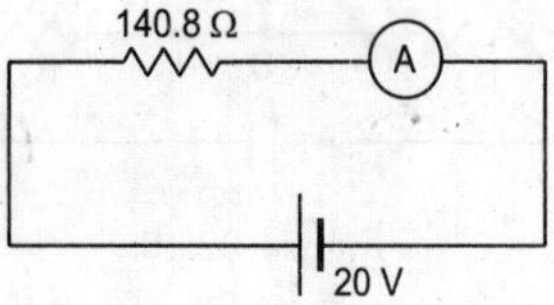

Figure 32.23

Solution : The equivalent resistance of the ammeter is

$$\frac{(480\ \Omega)(20\ \Omega)}{480\ \Omega + 20\ \Omega} = 19{\cdot}2\ \Omega.$$

The equivalent resistance of the circuit is

$$140{\cdot}8\ \Omega + 19{\cdot}2\ \Omega = 160\ \Omega.$$

The current is $i = \dfrac{20\ \text{V}}{160\ \Omega} = 0{\cdot}125\ \text{A}$.

This current goes through the ammeter and hence the reading of the ammeter is 0·125 A.

Voltmeter

In a voltmeter, a resistor having a high resistance R is connected in series with the coil. The end points (terminals) are connected to the points A and B between which the potential difference is to be measured. Plus and minus signs are marked on the terminals. The terminal marked "plus" should be connected to the point at higher potential. When no potential difference is applied between the terminals, the needle stays at zero which is marked at the left extreme of the scale. When the potential difference is applied, a current passes through the coil and the high resistance. If R_c be the resistance of the coil and V be the potential difference applied to the voltmeter, the current in the coil is

$$i = \frac{V}{R_c + R}.$$

The deflection is proportional to the current i and hence to V. The scale is graduated to read the potential difference directly.

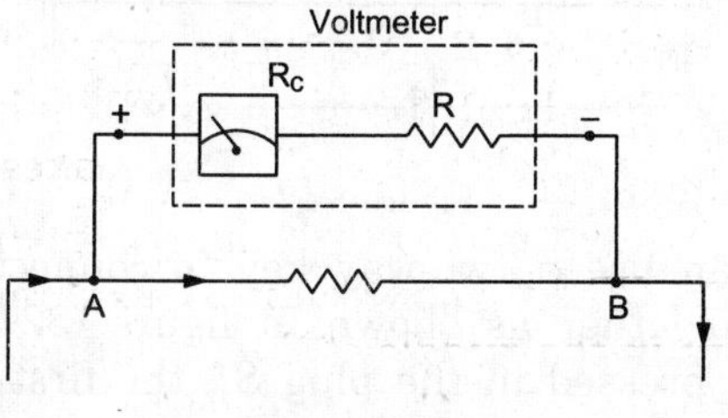

Figure 32.24

When the voltmeter is used in a circuit, its resistance $R_{eq} = R_c + R$ is connected in parallel to some element of the circuit. This changes the overall current in the circuit and hence, the potential difference to be measured is also changed. To minimise the error due to this, the equivalent resistance R_{eq} of the voltmeter should be large. (When a large resistance is connected in parallel to a small resistance, the equivalent resistance is only slightly less than the smaller one.) That is why, a large resistance R is added in series with the coil of a voltmeter.

32.12 STRETCHED-WIRE POTENTIOMETER

An ideal voltmeter which does not change the original potential difference, should have infinite resistance. But in the design described above, the resistance cannot be made infinite. *Potentiometer* is a device which does not draw any current from the given circuit and still measures the potential difference. Thus, it is equivalent to an ideal voltmeter.

The stretched-wire potentiometer consists of a long wire AB, usually 5 to 10 metres long, fixed on a wooden platform (figure 32.25). The wire has a uniform cross section. Usually, separate pieces of wire, each 1 m long, are fixed parallel to each other on the platform. The wires are joined to each other by thick copper strips so that the combination acts as a single wire of desired length (5 to 10 metres). The ends A and B are connected to a driving circuit consisting of a strong battery, a plug key and a rheostat. The driving circuit sends a constant current i through the wire AB. Thus, the potential gradually decreases from A to B. One end of a galvanometer is connected to a metal rod fixed on

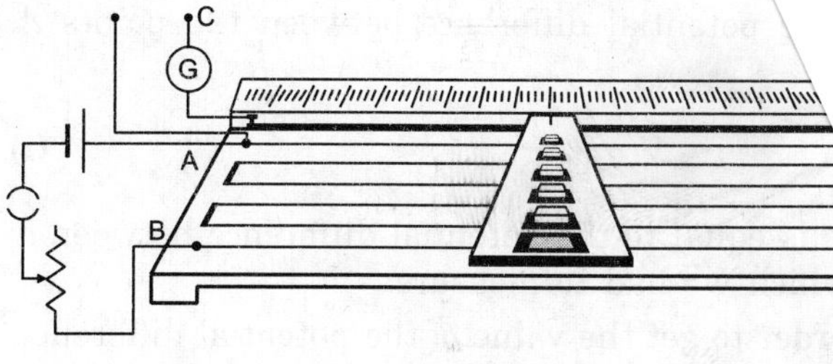

Figure 32.25

the wooden platform. A "jockey" may be slid on this metal rod and may touch the wire AB at any desired point. In this way the galvanometer gets connected to the point of AB which is touched by the jockey. The length of the wire between the end A and this point can be measured with the help of a metre scale fixed on the platform. The other end C of the galvanometer and the high-potential end A of the wire, form the two end points (terminals) of the potentiometer. These points are connected to the points between which the potential difference is to be measured.

Suppose, we have to measure the potential difference between the points a and b. Also let a be at a higher potential and b at a lower potential. The end A of the wire AB is connected to the point a and the end C of the galvanometer is connected to the point b. The circuit is represented schematically in figure (35.26).

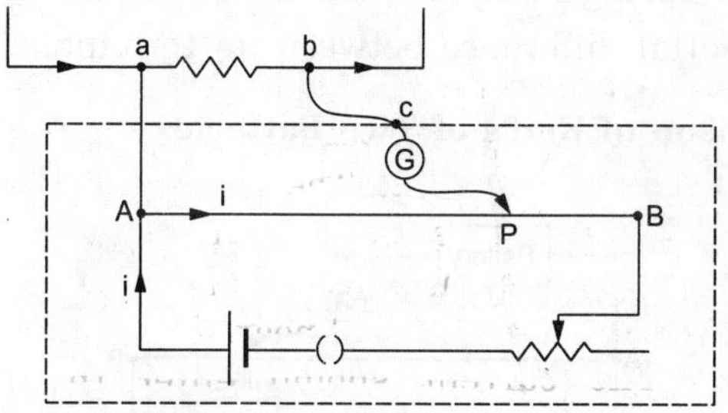

Figure 32.26

The connecting wire Aa has a negligible resistance and hence potentials of A and a are equal. Suppose, the potential drop across ab is smaller than the potential drop across AB. Then there will be a point P on AB which will have the same potential as b. If the jockey is slid to touch the wire at this point P, the potential difference across the galvanometer is zero and there will be no current through it. The process of measurement is to search for a point P so that there is no deflection in the galvanometer.

Suppose, the driving circuit sets up a potential difference V_0 between the ends A and B of the potentiometer wire. As the wire is uniform, the resistance of a piece of the wire is proportional to its length. Hence, the potential difference across a piece of wire is also proportional to its length. If $AB = L$ and

$AP = l$, the potential difference between the points A and P is

$$V = V_0 \frac{l}{L} . \quad \text{... (i)}$$

This is equal to the potential difference between a and b which we had to measure.

In order to get the value of the potential difference V, the total potential drop V_0 on AB must be known. One way to do this is to use a standard cell having known and constant emf in place of ab. If the emf of the standard cell is $\mathcal{E}$ and the potentiometer is balanced (no deflection in the galvanometer) when $AP = l_0$, we have, from (i),

$$\mathcal{E} = V_0 \frac{l_0}{L}$$

or, $$V_0 = \frac{L}{l_0} \mathcal{E} .$$

The potential difference V between a and b is, from (i)

$$V = \frac{l}{l_0} \mathcal{E} .$$

This process of finding V_0 is called *calibration of the potentiometer*. Note that there is no current through the standard cell when the potentiometer is balanced during its calibration. Thus, the emf $\mathcal{E}$ equals the potential difference between its terminals.

Comparison of Emf's of Two Batteries

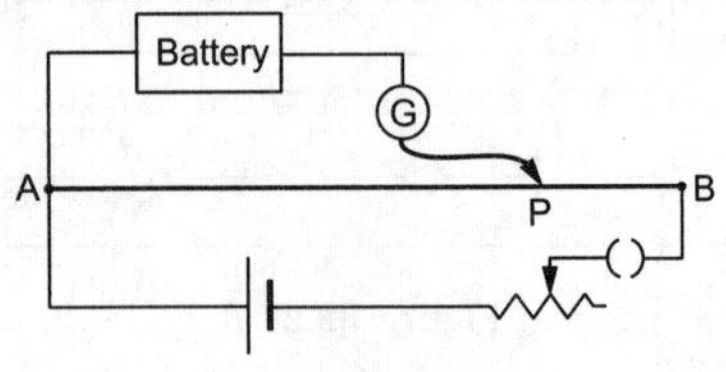

Figure 32.27

The driving circuit of the potentiometer is set up with a strong battery so that the potential difference V_0 across AB is larger than the emf of either battery. One of the batteries is connected between the positive end A and the galvanometer. The jockey is adjusted to touch the wire at a point P_1 so that there is no deflection in the galvanometer. The length $AP_1 = l_1$ is noted. Now, the first battery is replaced by the second and the length $AP_2 = l_2$ for the balance is noted. If the length $AB = L$, the emf of the first battery is, from (i) above,

$$\mathcal{E}_1 = \frac{l_1}{L} V_0$$

and that of the second battery is

$$\mathcal{E}_2 = \frac{l_2}{L} V_0 .$$

Thus, $$\frac{\mathcal{E}_1}{\mathcal{E}_2} = \frac{l_1}{l_2} .$$

Note that no calibration is needed in this case.

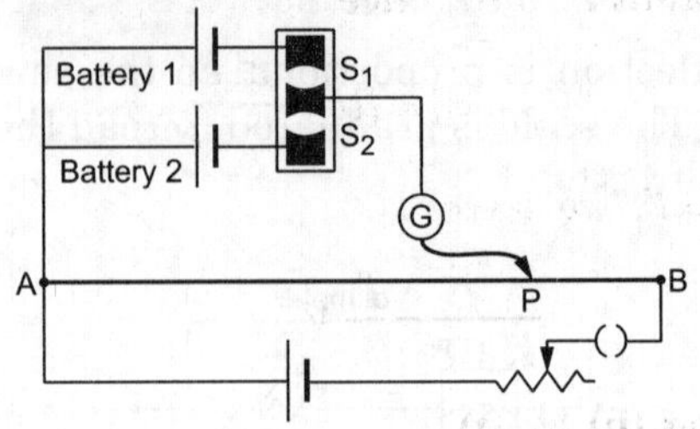

Figure 32.28

One can use a two-way key to connect both the batteries together as shown in figure (32.28). When the key is pressed in the plug S_1, the first battery is brought into the circuit. When the key is taken out from S_1 and pressed in the plug S_2, the second battery is brought into the circuit.

The value of emf of a battery can also be obtained by this same method by taking the other battery to be a standard cell. The emf of the standard cell is known and hence the emf of the given battery can be obtained.

Measurement of Internal Resistance of a Battery

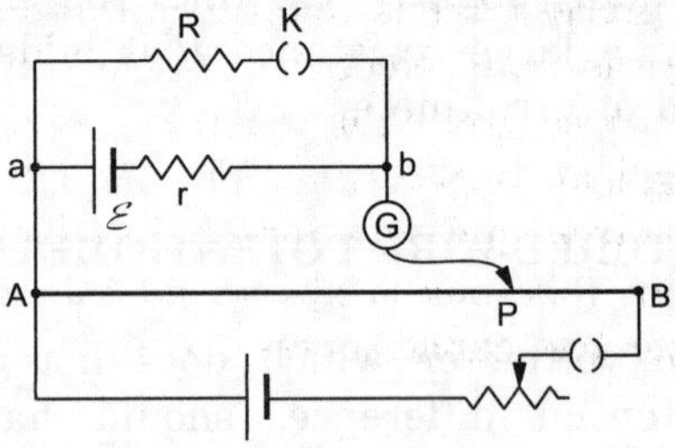

Figure 32.29

Figure (32.29) shows the arrangement for measuring the internal resistance of a battery. The emf of the battery is $\mathcal{E}$ and its internal resistance is r. A known resistance R is connected across the battery together with a plug key K. The potentiometer circuit is set up as usual. The plug key K is opened and the balance point P is searched on the wire AB so that there is no deflection in the galvanometer. As the key is open, there is no current through the resistance R. Hence, there is no current through the battery and the potential difference across the terminals a, b is the same as the emf $\mathcal{E}$ of the battery. If $AP = l$, we have

$$\mathcal{E} = \frac{l}{L} V_0 \quad \text{... (i)}$$

with the symbols having their usual meanings.

Now the key K is closed and the new balance point P' is searched. There is a current

$$i = \frac{\mathcal{E}}{R+r} \text{ through the battery.}$$

The potential difference between a and b is

$$V_a - V_b = Ri = \frac{\mathcal{E}R}{R+r}.$$

If $AP' = l'$, we have

$$\frac{\mathcal{E}R}{R+r} = \frac{l'}{L} V_0. \qquad \dots \text{ (ii)}$$

Dividing (ii) by (i),

$$\frac{R}{R+r} = \frac{l'}{l}$$

or,
$$r = \frac{R(l-l')}{l'}.$$

32.13 CHARGING AND DISCHARGING OF CAPACITORS

Charging

When a capacitor is connected to a battery, positive charge appears on one plate and negative charge on the other. The potential difference between the plates ultimately becomes equal to the emf of the battery. The whole process takes some time and during this time there is an electric current through the connecting wires and the battery. Figure (32.30a) shows a typical connection. The resistance of the connecting wires and the internal resistance of the battery taken together is shown as the resistance R. The capacitor has capacitance C.

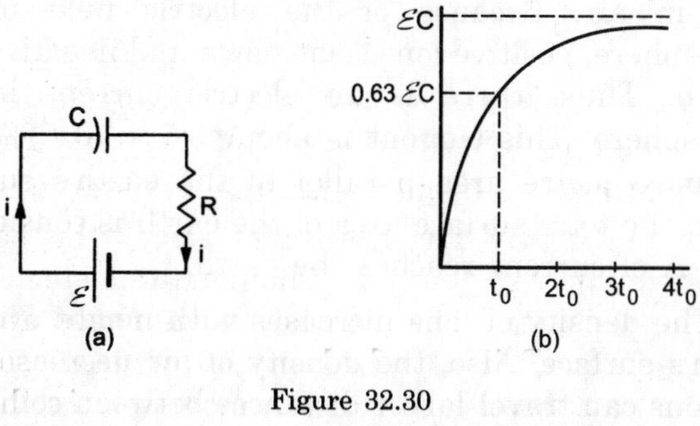

Figure 32.30

Suppose, the battery is connected at $t = 0$. Suppose the charge on the capacitor and the current in the circuit are q and i respectively at time t. The potential drop on the capacitor is q/C and on the resistor it is Ri. Also, the charge deposited on the positive plate in time dt is $dq = i\,dt$

so that
$$i = \frac{dq}{dt}.$$

Using Kirchhoff's loop law,

$$\frac{q}{C} + Ri - \mathcal{E} = 0$$

or,
$$Ri = \mathcal{E} - \frac{q}{C}$$

or,
$$R\frac{dq}{dt} = \frac{\mathcal{E}C - q}{C}$$

or,
$$\int_0^q \frac{dq}{\mathcal{E}C - q} = \int_0^t \frac{1}{CR}\,dt$$

or,
$$-\ln \frac{\mathcal{E}C - q}{\mathcal{E}C} = \frac{t}{CR}$$

or,
$$1 - \frac{q}{\mathcal{E}C} = e^{-t/CR}$$

or,
$$q = \mathcal{E}C(1 - e^{-t/CR}). \qquad \dots \text{ (32.16)}$$

This gives the charge on the capacitor at time t. As t increases, q also increases. The maximum charge is obtained, in principle, at $t = \infty$ and its value is $\mathcal{E}C$. The constant CR has dimensions of time and is called *time constant* of the circuit. In one time constant $\tau (= CR)$, the charge accumulated on the capacitor is

$$q = \mathcal{E}C\left(1 - \frac{1}{e}\right) = 0{\cdot}63\,\mathcal{E}C.$$

Thus, 63% of the maximum charge is deposited in one time constant. Figure (32.30b) shows a plot of q versus t.

Discharging

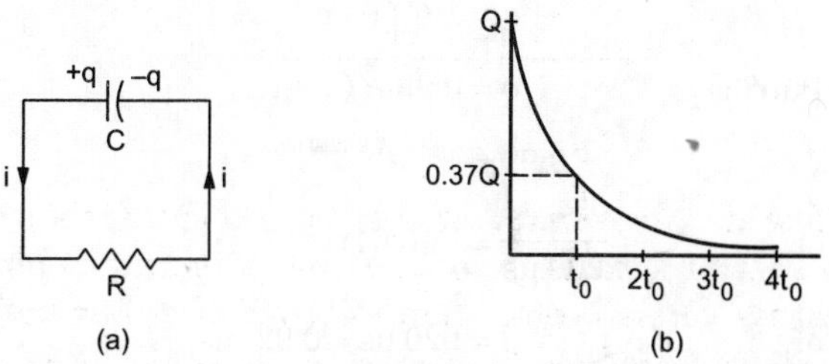

Figure 32.31

If the plates of a charged capacitor are connected through a conducting wire, the capacitor gets discharged. Again there is a flow of charge through the wires and hence there is a current. Suppose a capacitor of capacitance C has a charge Q. At $t = 0$, the plates are connected through a resistance R (figure 32.31a). Let the charge on the capacitor be q and the current in the circuit be i at time t.

Using Kirchhoff's loop law,

$$\frac{q}{C} - Ri = 0.$$

Here $i = -\frac{dq}{dt}$ because the charge q decreases as time passes.

Thus, $$R\frac{dq}{dt} = -\frac{q}{C}.$$

or, $$\frac{dq}{q} = -\frac{1}{CR}\,dt$$

or, $$\int_Q^q \frac{dq}{q} = \int_0^t -\frac{1}{CR}\,dt$$

or, $$\ln\frac{q}{Q} = -\frac{t}{CR}$$

or, $$q = Q\,e^{-t/CR}. \qquad \dots (32.17)$$

In principle, discharging is complete only at $t = \infty$. The constant CR is the time constant. At $t = CR$, the remaining charge is $q = \frac{Q}{e} = 0{\cdot}37\,Q$. Thus, 63% of the discharging is complete in one time constant. Figure (32.31b) shows the charge as a function of time.

Example 32.9

A capacitor of capacitance 100 μF *is charged by connecting it to a battery of emf* 12 V *and internal resistance* 2 Ω. *(a) Find the time constant of the circuit. (b) Find the time taken before 99% of the maximum charge is stored on the capacitor.*

Solution : The time constant is

$$\tau = CR = (100\ \mu F)\,(2\ \Omega) = 200\ \mu s.$$

The charge at time t is

$$q = \mathcal{E}C\,(1 - e^{-t/CR}).$$

Putting $$q = 0{\cdot}99\,\mathcal{E}C,$$

$$0{\cdot}99 = 1 - e^{-t/(200\ \mu s)}$$

or, $$-\frac{t}{200\ \mu s} = \ln(0{\cdot}01)$$

or, $$t = 920\ \mu s = 0{\cdot}92\ ms.$$

Example 32.10

The plates of a 50 μF *capacitor charged to* 400 μC *are connected through a resistance of* 1·0 kΩ. *Find the charge remaining on the capacitor* 1 s *after the connection is made.*

Solution : The time constant is

$$CR = (50\ \mu F)\,(1{\cdot}0\ k\Omega) = 50\ ms.$$

At $t = 1$ s, $t/CR = 1\ s/50\ ms = 20.$

The charge remaining on the capacitor is

$$q = Q\,e^{-t/CR}$$

$$= (400\ \mu C)\,e^{-20} = 8{\cdot}2\times10^{-7}\ \mu C.$$

We see that in a typical charging or discharging circuit, the time constant is of the order of a millisecond. Also, four to five time constants are sufficient for 99% of the charging or discharging. Thus, for practical purposes, we can assume that charging or discharging is complete in a fraction of a second.

32.14 ATMOSPHERIC ELECTRICITY

The earth and the atmosphere surrounding it show very interesting electric phenomena. The earth has a negative charge spread with approximately uniform density over its surface. The average surface charge density on the earth is little less than one nanocoulomb per square metre. There is a corresponding electric field of about 100 V m^{-1} in the atmosphere above the earth. This field is in the vertically downward direction. This means, if you look at a flat desert, the electric potential increases by about 100 V as you move up by 1 m. The potential keeps on increasing as one goes higher in atmosphere but the magnitude of the electric field gradually decreases. At about 50 km from the earth's surface, the field is negligible. The total potential difference between the earth's surface and the top of the atmosphere is about 400 kV.

The atmosphere contains a number of ions, both positively charged and negatively charged. The main source of these ions is *cosmic rays* which come from outside the earth, even from outside the solar system. These rays come down to the earth and ionize molecules in the air. Air contains dust particles which become charged by friction as they move through the air. This is another source of the presence of charged ions in air. Because of the electric field in the atmosphere, positive ions come down and negative ions go up. Thus, there is an electric current in the atmosphere. This current is about $3{\cdot}5\times10^{-12}$ A over a square metre area parallel to the earth's surface. When the total surface area of the earth is considered, 1800 A of current reaches the earth.

The density of ions increases with height over the earth's surface. Also, the density of air decreases and the ions can travel larger distances between collisions. Both these factors contribute to the fact that "conductivity of air" increases with altitude. At about 50 km above the earth's surface, the air becomes highly conducting. We can draw an equivalent picture by assuming that at about this height there is a perfectly conducting surface having a potential of 400 kV and current comes down from this surface to the earth.

If 1800 A of current flows towards the earth, the entire negative charge of the earth should get neutralised in about half an hour and the electric field in the atmosphere should reduce to zero. But it is not so. So, there must be some mechanism which brings negative charge back to the earth, so that the 400 kV potential difference is maintained. This situation is like that of a battery. The current provided by a battery discharges it. There is a source of emf which maintains the potential difference across the battery's terminals. So, what is the source that charges our atmospheric battery. The answer is *thunderstorms* and *lightning.*

Because of the difference in temperature and pressure between different parts of the atmosphere, air packets keep on moving in a rather systematic fashion. As the upper atmosphere is cool (temperature is around −10°C at a height of 3–4 km and −20°C at a height of 6–7 km), water vapour condenses to form small water droplets and tiny ice particles. A parcel of air with these droplets and ice particles forms a thunderstorm. A typical thunderstorm may have an average horizontal extension of about 7–8 km and a vertical extension of about 3 km. A matured thunderstorm is formed with its lower end at a height of about 3–4 km above the earth's surface and the upper end at about 6–7 km above the earth's surface.

The upper part of a thunderstorm contains excess positive charge and the lower part contains excess negative charge. The density of negative charge in the clouds in the lower part of the storm is very high. This negative charge creates a potential difference of 20 to 100 MV between these clouds and the earth. Note that this potential difference is much larger than the 400 kV between the earth and the top of atmosphere and is opposite in sign. Figure (32.32) represents a typical situation.

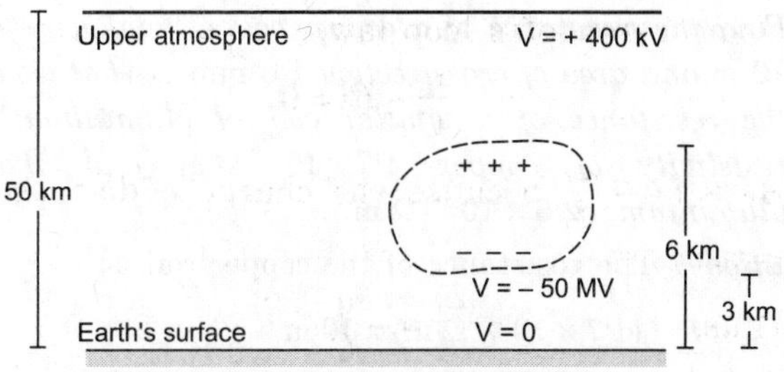

Figure 32.32

The high electric field between the lower part of the storm and the earth is often sufficient for the dielectric breakdown of air and the air becomes conducting. Negative charge thus jumps from the cloud to the earth's surface. This phenomenon is called *lightning.* The positive charge in the upper part of the storm gradually moves up to enter the high-altitude (≈ 50 km) layer of high conductivity. In one lightning stroke, about 20 C of negative charge is deposited to the earth. It takes about 5 s for the clouds to regain the charge for the next lightning stroke. There are a number of thunderstorms everyday throughout the earth. They charge the atmospheric battery by supplying negative charge to the earth and positive charge to the upper atmosphere. In the area of clear weather, the battery is discharged by the movement of positive ions towards the earth and negative ions away from it (the 1800 A current discussed earlier).

Worked Out Examples

1. *An electron moves in a circle of radius* 10 cm *with a constant speed of* $4{\cdot}0 \times 10^{6}\ \mathrm{m\,s^{-1}}$. *Find the electric current at a point on the circle.*

Solution : Consider a point A on the circle. The electron crosses this point once in every revolution. In one revolution, the electron travels $2\pi \times (10\ \mathrm{cm})$ distance. Hence, the number of revolutions made by the electron in one second is

$$\frac{4{\cdot}0\times 10^{6}\ \mathrm{m}}{20\pi\times 10^{-2}\ \mathrm{m}} = \frac{2}{\pi}\times 10^{7}.$$

The charge crossing the point A per second is

$$\frac{2}{\pi}\times 10^{7}\times 1{\cdot}6\times 10^{-19}\ \mathrm{C} = \frac{3{\cdot}2}{\pi}\times 10^{-12}\ \mathrm{C}.$$

Thus, the electric current at this point is

$$\frac{3{\cdot}2}{\pi}\times 10^{-12}\ \mathrm{A} \approx 1{\cdot}0\times 10^{-12}\ \mathrm{A}.$$

2. *A current of* $2{\cdot}0$ A *exists in a wire of cross sectional area* $1{\cdot}0\ \mathrm{mm}^{2}$. *If each cubic metre of the wire contains* $6{\cdot}0 \times 10^{28}$ *free electrons, find the drift speed.*

Solution : The current density in the wire is

$$j = \frac{i}{A} = \frac{2{\cdot}0\ \mathrm{A}}{1\ \mathrm{mm}^{2}} = 2{\cdot}0\times 10^{6}\ \mathrm{A\,m^{-2}}.$$

The drift speed is

$$v = \frac{j}{ne} = \frac{2{\cdot}0\times 10^{6}\ \mathrm{A\,m^{-2}}}{6{\cdot}0\times 10^{28}\ \mathrm{m^{-3}}\times 1{\cdot}6\times 10^{-19}\ \mathrm{C}}$$

$$= 2{\cdot}1\times 10^{-4}\ \mathrm{m\,s^{-1}}.$$

3. *Find the resistance of a copper coil of total wire-length* 10 m *and area of cross section* 1·0 mm^2. *What would be the resistance of a similar coil of aluminium? The resistivity of copper* = $1·7 \times 10^{-8}$ Ω m *and that of aluminium* = $2·6 \times 10^{-8}$ Ω m.

Solution : The resistance of the copper coil is

$$\rho \frac{l}{A} = \frac{(1·7 \times 10^{-8}\ \Omega\ \text{m}) \times 10\ \text{m}}{1·0 \times 10^{-6}\ \text{m}^2} = 0·17\ \Omega.$$

The resistance of the similar aluminium coil will be

$$\frac{(2·6 \times 10^{-8}\ \Omega\ \text{m}) \times 10\ \text{m}}{1·0 \times 10^{-6}\ \text{m}^2} = 0·26\ \Omega.$$

4. *A parallel-plate capacitor has plates of area* 10 cm^2 *separated by a distance of* 1 mm. *It is filled with the dielectric mica and connected to a battery of emf* 6 volts. *Find the leakage current through the capacitor. Resistivity of mica* = 1×10^{13} Ω m.

Solution : The resistance of the mica between the two faces is

$$\rho \frac{l}{A} = \frac{(1 \times 10^{13}\ \Omega\ \text{m}) \times 10^{-3}\ \text{m}}{10·0 \times 10^{-4}\ \text{m}^2}$$

$$= 1 \times 10^{13}\ \Omega.$$

The leakage current $= \dfrac{6\ \text{V}}{1 \times 10^{13}\ \Omega} = 6 \times 10^{-13}$ A.

5. *Find the resistance of a hollow cylindrical conductor of length* 1·0 m *and inner and outer radii* 1·0 mm *and* 2·0 mm *respectively. The resistivity of the material is* $2·0 \times 10^{-8}$ Ω m.

Solution : The area of cross section of the conductor through which the charges will flow is

$$A = \pi(2·0\ \text{mm})^2 - \pi(1·0\ \text{mm})^2$$

$$= 3·0 \times \pi\ \text{mm}^2.$$

The resistance of the wire is, therefore,

$$R = \rho \frac{l}{A} = \frac{(2·0 \times 10^{-8}\ \Omega\ \text{m}) \times 1·0\ \text{m}}{3·0 \times \pi \times 10^{-6}\ \text{m}^2} = 2·1 \times 10^{-3}\ \Omega.$$

6. *A battery of emf* 2 V *and internal resistance* 0·5 Ω *is connected across a resistance of* 9·5 Ω. *How many electrons cross through a cross section of the resistance in* 1 *second?*

Solution : The current in the circuit is

$$i = \frac{2\ \text{V}}{9·5\ \Omega + 0·5\ \Omega} = 0·2\ \text{A}.$$

Thus, a net transfer of 0·2 C per second takes place across any cross section in the circuit. The number of electrons crossing the section in 1 second is, therefore,

$$\frac{0·2\ \text{C}}{1·6 \times 10^{-19}\ \text{C}} = 0·125 \times 10^{19} = 1·25 \times 10^{18}.$$

7. *A battery of emf* 2·0 volts *and internal resistance* 0·10 Ω *is being charged with a current of* 5·0 A. *What is the potential difference between the terminals of the battery?*

Solution :

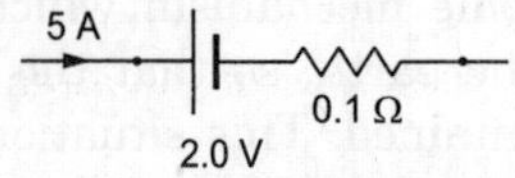

Figure 32-W1

As the battery is being charged, the current goes into the positive terminal as shown in figure (32-W1). The potential drop across the internal resistance is

$$5·0\ \text{A} \times 0·10\ \Omega = 0·50\ \text{V}.$$

Hence, the potential drop across the terminals will be

$$2·0\ \text{V} + 0·50\ \text{V} = 2·5\ \text{V}.$$

8. *Figure (32-W2) shows n batteries connected to form a circuit. The resistances denote the internal resistances of the batteries which are related to the emf's as* $r_i = k\mathcal{E}_i$ *where k is a constant. The solid dots represent the terminals of the batteries. Find (a) the current through the circuit and (b) the potential difference between the terminals of the ith battery.*

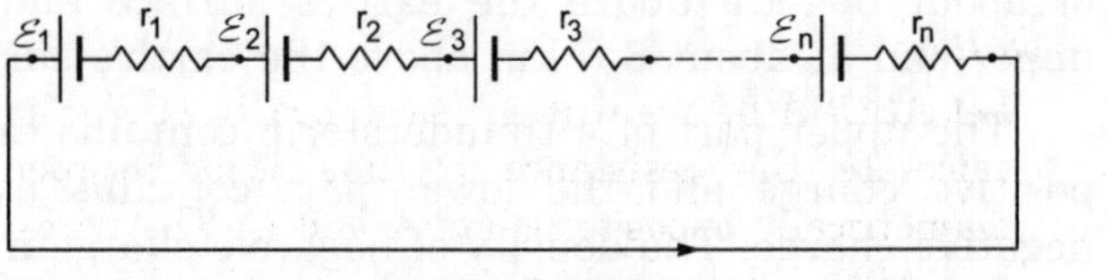

Figure 32-W2

Solution : (a) Suppose the current is i in the indicated direction. Applying Kirchoff's loop law,

$$\mathcal{E}_1 - ir_1 + \mathcal{E}_2 - ir_2 + \mathcal{E}_3 - ir_3 + \ldots + \mathcal{E}_n - ir_n = 0$$

or, $$i = \frac{\mathcal{E}_1 + \mathcal{E}_2 + \mathcal{E}_3 + \ldots + \mathcal{E}_n}{r_1 + r_2 + r_3 + \ldots + r_n}$$

$$= \frac{\mathcal{E}_1 + \mathcal{E}_2 + \mathcal{E}_3 + \ldots + \mathcal{E}_n}{k(\mathcal{E}_1 + \mathcal{E}_2 + \mathcal{E}_3 + \ldots + \mathcal{E}_n)} = \frac{1}{k}.$$

(b) The potential difference between the terminals of the ith battery is

$$\mathcal{E}_i - ir_i$$

$$= \mathcal{E}_i - \left(\frac{1}{k}\right)(k\mathcal{E}_i) = 0.$$

9. *A copper rod of length* 20 cm *and cross-sectional area* 2 mm^2 *is joined with a similar aluminium rod as shown in figure (32-W3). Find the resistance of the combination between the ends. Resistivity of copper* = $1·7 \times 10^{-8}$ Ω m *and that of aluminium* = $2·6 \times 10^{-8}$ Ω m.

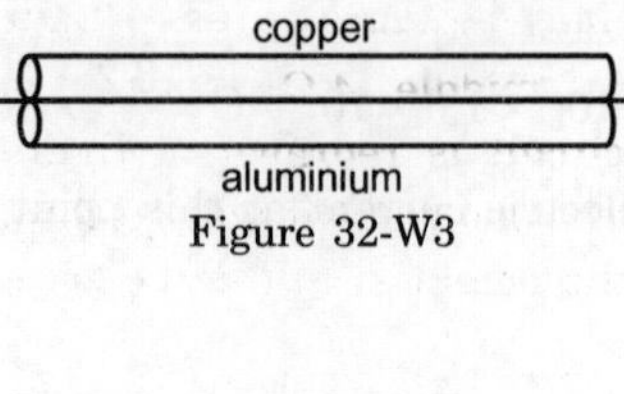

Figure 32-W3

Solution : The resistance of the copper rod

$$= \rho \frac{l}{A} = \frac{(1{\cdot}7 \times 10^{-8}\ \Omega\ \text{m}) \times (20 \times 10^{-2}\ \text{m})}{2{\cdot}0 \times 10^{-6}\ \text{m}^2}$$

$$= 1{\cdot}7 \times 10^{-3}\ \Omega.$$

Similarly, the resistance of the aluminium rod

$$= 2{\cdot}6 \times 10^{-3}\ \Omega.$$

These rods are joined in parallel so that the equivalent resistance R between the ends is given by

$$\frac{1}{R} = \frac{1}{1{\cdot}7 \times 10^{-3}\ \Omega} + \frac{1}{2{\cdot}6 \times 10^{-3}\ \Omega}$$

or, $$R = \frac{1{\cdot}7 \times 2{\cdot}6}{4{\cdot}3} \times 10^{-3}\ \Omega \approx 1{\cdot}0\ \text{m}\Omega.$$

10. *A wire of resistance 10 Ω is bent to form a complete circle. Find its resistance between two diametrically opposite points.*

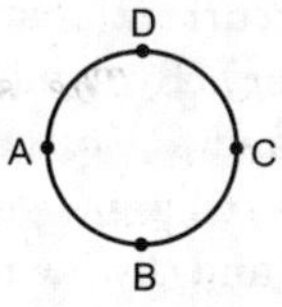

Figure 32-W4

Solution :

Let *ABCDA* be the wire of resistance 10 Ω. We have to calculate the resistance of this loop between the diametrically opposite points *A* and *C*. The wires *ADC* and *ABC* will have resistances 5 Ω each. These two are joined in parallel between *A* and *C*. The equivalent resistance *R* between *A* and *C* is, therefore, given by

$$R = \frac{5\ \Omega \times 5\ \Omega}{5\ \Omega + 5\ \Omega} = 2{\cdot}5\ \Omega.$$

11. *Find the currents in the different resistors shown in figure (32-W5).*

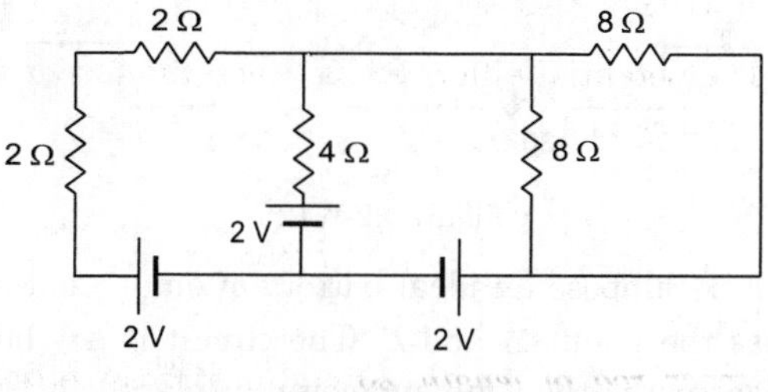

Figure 32-W5

Solution : The two 2 Ω resistors are in series so that their equivalent resistance is 4 Ω. The two 8 Ω resistors are in parallel and their equivalent resistance is also 4 Ω. The circuit may be redrawn as in figure (32-W6a). Suppose the middle 4 Ω resistor is removed. The remaining circuit is redrawn in figure (32-W6b). It is easy to see that no current will go through any resistor. If we take the potential at *b* to be zero, the potential at

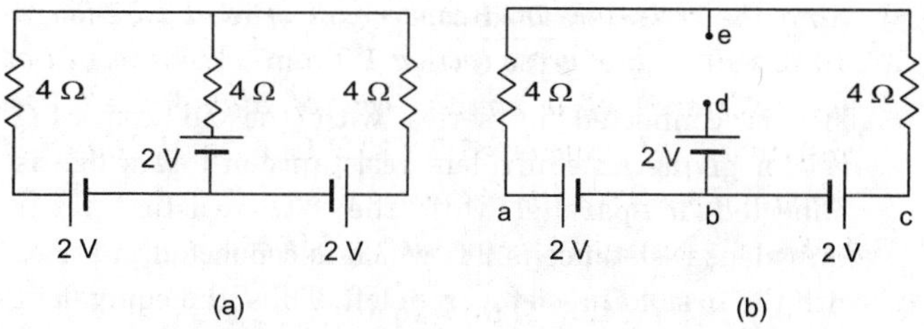

Figure 32-W6

d will be 2 V. The potential at *a* and *c* will also be 2 V. As there is no current in the 4 Ω resistors, the potential at *e* will also be 2 V. Thus, there is no potential difference between *d* and *e*. When a 4 Ω resistor is added between *d* and *e*, no current will be drawn into it and hence no change will occur in the remaining part of the circuit. This circuit is then the same as the given circuit. Thus, the current in all the resistors in the given circuit is zero.

12. *Find the current supplied by the battery in the circuit shown in figure (32-W7).*

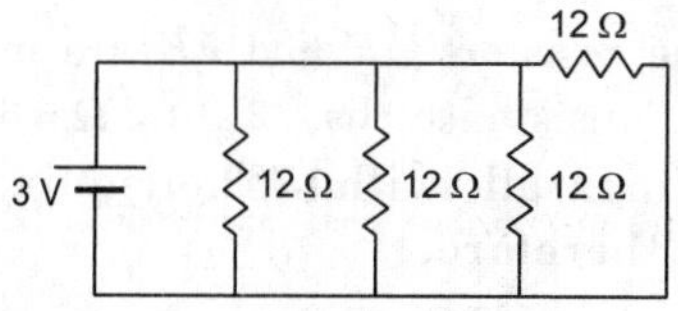

Figure 32-W7

Solution : All the resistors shown in the figure are connected in parallel between the terminals of the battery. The equivalent resistance R between the terminals is, therefore, given by

$$\frac{1}{R} = \frac{1}{12\ \Omega} + \frac{1}{12\ \Omega} + \frac{1}{12\ \Omega} + \frac{1}{12\ \Omega}$$

or, $$R = 3\ \Omega.$$

The current supplied by the battery is

$$i = \frac{V}{R} = \frac{3\ \text{V}}{3\ \Omega} = 1\ \text{A}.$$

13. *Find the equivalent resistance between the points a and b of the network shown in figure (32-W8).*

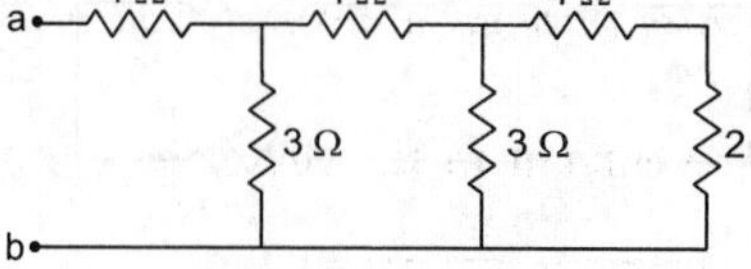

Figure 32-W8

Solution : The two resistors 4 Ω and 2 Ω at the right end are joined in series and may be replaced by a single resistor of 6 Ω. This 6 Ω is connected with the adjacent 3 Ω resistor in parallel. The equivalent resistance of these two is

$$\frac{6\,\Omega \times 3\,\Omega}{6\,\Omega + 3\,\Omega} = 2\,\Omega.$$

This is connected in series with the adjacent 4 Ω resistor giving an equivalent resistance of 6 Ω which is connected in parallel with the 3 Ω resistor. Their equivalent resistance is 2 Ω which is connected in series with the first 4 Ω resistor from left. Thus, the equivalent resistance between a and b is 6 Ω.

14. *Find the effective resistance between the points A and B in figure (32-W9).*

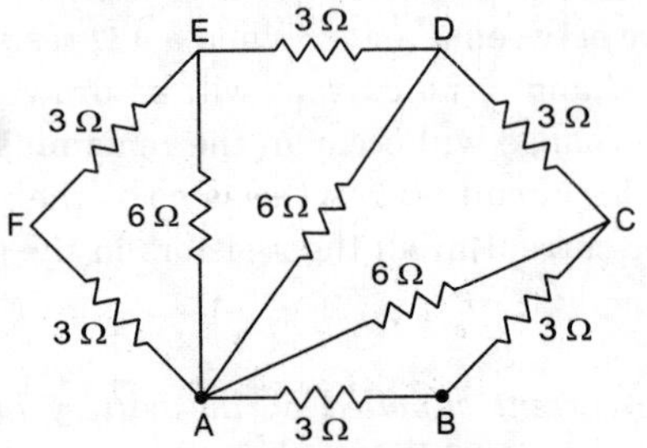

Figure 32-W9

Solution : The resistors AF and FE are in series. Their equivalent resistance is $3\,\Omega + 3\,\Omega = 6\,\Omega$. This is connectedinparallelwithAE.Theirequivalentbetween A and E is, therefore,

$$\frac{6\,\Omega \times 6\,\Omega}{6\,\Omega + 6\,\Omega} = 3\,\Omega.$$

This 3 Ω resistance between A and E is in series with ED and the combination is in parallel with AD. Their equivalent between A and D is again 3 Ω.

Similarly, the equivalent of this 3 Ω, DC and AC is 3 Ω. This 3 Ω is in series with CB and the combination is in parallel with AB. The equivalent resistance between A and B is, therefore,

$$\frac{6\,\Omega \times 3\,\Omega}{6\,\Omega + 3\,\Omega} = 2\,\Omega.$$

15. *Find the equivalent resistance of the network shown in figure (32-W10) between the points a and b when (a) the switch S is open and (b) the switch S is closed.*

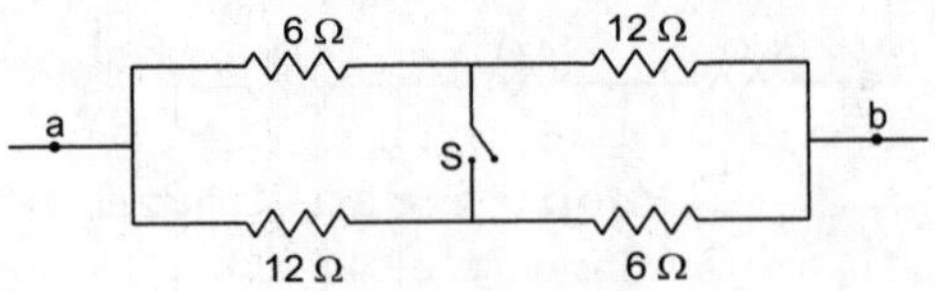

Figure 32-W10

Solution : (a) When the switch is open, 6 Ω and 12 Ω resistors on the upper line are in series giving an equivalent of 18 Ω. Similarly, the resistors on the lower line have equivalent resistance 18 Ω. These two 18 Ω resistances are connected in parallel between a and b so that the equivalent resistance is 9 Ω.

(b) When the switch is closed, the 6 Ω and 12 Ω resistors on the left are in parallel giving an equivalent resistance of 4 Ω. Similarly, the two resistors on the right half are equivalent to 4 Ω. These two are connected in series between a and b so that the equivalent resistance is 8 Ω.

16. *Each resistor shown in figure (32-W11) has a resistance of 10 Ω and the battery has an emf of 6 V. Find the current supplied by the battery.*

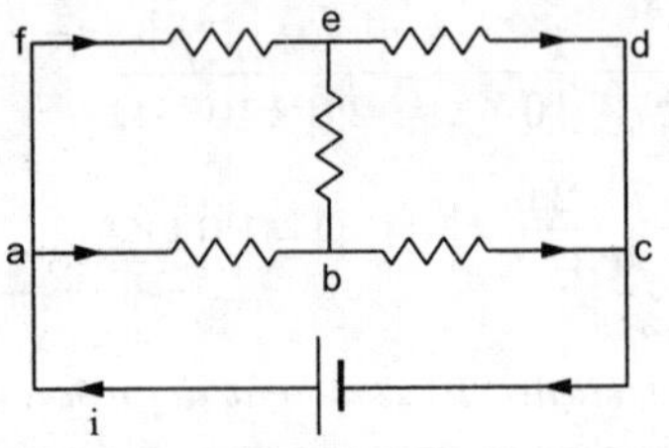

Figure 32-W11

Solution : Suppose a current i starts from the positive terminal of the battery. By symmetry, it divides equally in the resistors ab and fe, so that each of these carries a current $i/2$. The current going into the negative terminal is also i and by symmetry, equal currents should come from ed and bc. Thus, the current in ed is also $i/2$ and hence there will be no current in eb.

We have,

$$V_a - V_c = (V_a - V_b) + (V_b - V_c)$$

or, $$6\text{ V} = \frac{i}{2} \times 10\,\Omega + \frac{i}{2} \times 10\,\Omega$$

giving $$i = 0{\cdot}6\text{ A}.$$

This is a balanced Wheatstone bridge.

17. *Find the equivalent resistance of the network shown in figure (32-W12) between the points A and B.*

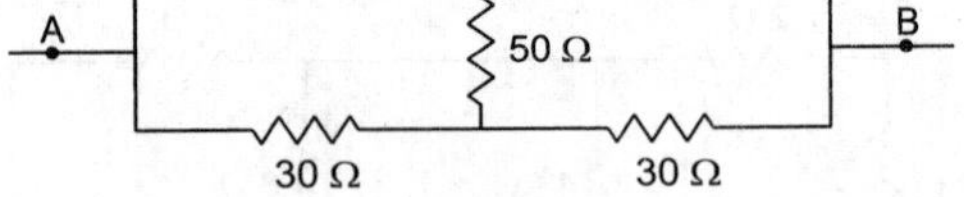

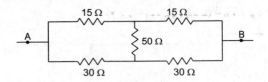

Figure 32-W12

Solution : Suppose an ideal battery of emf $\mathcal{E}$ is connected across the points A and B. The circuit is a Wheatstone bridge with the galvanometer replaced by a 50 Ω resistance. As the bridge is balanced $(R_1/R_2 = R_3/R_4)$, there will be no current through the 50 Ω resistance. We can just remove the 50 Ω resistance without changing any other current. The circuit is then equivalent to two resistances 30 Ω and 60 Ω connected in parallel. The equivalent resistance is

$$R = \frac{(30\,\Omega) \times (60\,\Omega)}{(30\,\Omega) + (60\,\Omega)} = 20\,\Omega.$$

18. *In the circuit shown in figure (32-W13a) E, F, G and H are cells of emf 2, 1, 3 and 1 V respectively. The resistances 2, 1, 3 and 1 Ω are their respective internal resistances. Calculate (a) the potential difference between B and D and (b) the potential differences across the terminals of each of the cells G and H.*

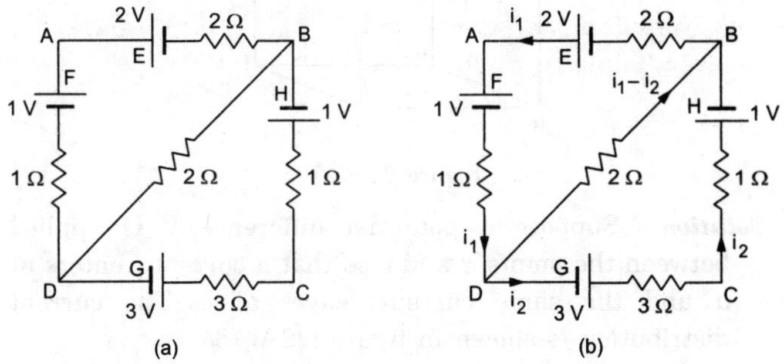

Figure 32-W13

Solution : Suppose a current i_1 goes in the branch *BAD* and a current i_2 in the branch *DCB*. The current in *DB* will be $i_1 - i_2$ from the junction law. The circuit with the currents shown is redrawn in figure (32-W13b). Applying the loop law to *BADB* we get,

$$(2\ \Omega)i_1 - 2\ \text{V} + 1\ \text{V} + (1\ \Omega)i_1 + (2\ \Omega)(i_1 - i_2) = 0$$

or, $\quad (5\ \Omega)i_1 - (2\ \Omega)i_2 = 1\ \text{V}. \quad \ldots \text{(i)}$

Applying the same law to the loop *DCBD*, we get

$$-3\ \text{V} + (3\ \Omega)i_2 + (1\ \Omega)i_2 + 1\ \text{V} - (2\ \Omega)(i_1 - i_2) = 0$$

or, $\quad -(2\ \Omega)i_1 + (6\ \Omega)i_2 = 2\ \text{V}. \quad \ldots \text{(ii)}$

From (i) and (ii),

$$i_1 = \frac{5}{13}\ \text{A},\ i_2 = \frac{6}{13}\ \text{A}$$

so that $i_1 - i_2 = -\frac{1}{13}\ \text{A}.$

The current in *BD* is from *B* to *D*.

(a) $V_B - V_D = (2\ \Omega)\left(\frac{1}{13}\ \text{A}\right) = \frac{2}{13}\ \text{V}.$

(b) The potential difference across the cell *G* is

$$V_C - V_D = -(3\ \Omega)i_2 + 3\ \text{V}$$

$$= \left(3\ \text{V} - \frac{18}{13}\ \text{V}\right) = \frac{21}{13}\ \text{V}.$$

The potential difference across the cell *H* is

$$V_C - V_B = (1\ \Omega)i_2 + 1\ \text{V} = (1\ \Omega)\left(\frac{6}{13}\ \text{A}\right) + 1\ \text{V} = \frac{19}{13}\ \text{V}.$$

19. *Find the equivalent resistance between the points a and b of the circuit shown in figure (32-W14a).*

Solution : Suppose a current *i* enters the circuit at the point *a*, a part i_1 goes through the 10 Ω resistor and the rest $i - i_1$ through the 5 Ω resistor. By symmetry, the current *i* coming out from the point *b* will be composed of a part i_1 from the 10 Ω resistor and $i - i_1$ from the 5 Ω resistor. Applying Kirchhoff's junction law, we can find the current through the middle 5 Ω resistor. The current distribution is shown in figure (32-W14b).

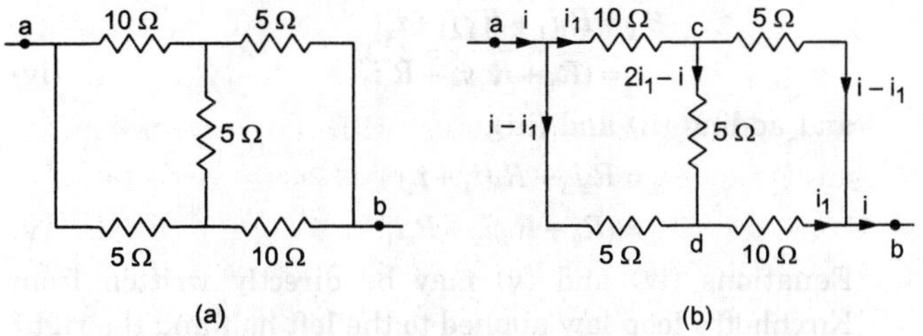

Figure 32-W14

We have

$$V_a - V_b = (V_a - V_c) + (V_c - V_b)$$

$$= (10\ \Omega)i_1 + (5\ \Omega)(i - i_1)$$

$$= (5\ \Omega)i + (5\ \Omega)i_1. \quad \ldots \text{(i)}$$

Also, $\quad V_a - V_b = (V_a - V_c) + (V_c - V_d) + (V_d - V_b)$

$$= (10\ \Omega)i_1 + (5\ \Omega)(2i_1 - i) + (10\ \Omega)i_1$$

$$= -(5\ \Omega)i + (30\ \Omega)i_1 \quad \ldots \text{(ii)}$$

Multiplying (i) by 6 and subtracting (ii) from it, we eliminate i_1 and get,

$$5(V_a - V_b) = (35\ \Omega)i$$

or, $\quad \frac{V_a - V_b}{i} = 7\ \Omega.$

Thus, the equivalent resistance between the points *a* and *b* is 7 Ω.

20. *Find the currents going through the three resistors R_1, R_2 and R_3 in the circuit of figure (32-W15a).*

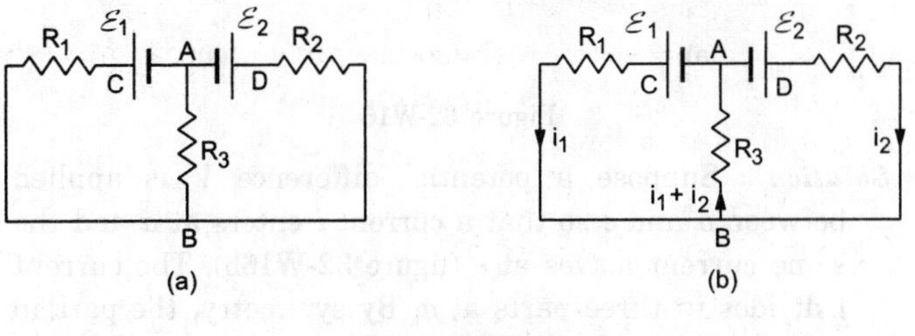

Figure 32-W15

Solution : Let us take the potential of the point *A* to be zero. The potential at *C* will be $\mathcal{E}_1$ and that at *D* will be $\mathcal{E}_2$. Let the potential at *B* be *V*. The currents through the three resistors are i_1, i_2 and $i_1 + i_2$ as shown in figure (32.15b). Note that the current directed towards *B* equals the current directed away from *B*.

Applying Ohm's law to the three resistors R_1, R_2 and R_3, we get

$$\mathcal{E}_1 - V = R_1 i_1 \quad \ldots \text{(i)}$$

$$\mathcal{E}_2 - V = R_2 i_2 \quad \ldots \text{(ii)}$$

and $\quad V - 0 = R_3(i_1 + i_2). \quad \ldots \text{(iii)}$

Adding (i) and (iii),

$$\mathcal{E}_1 = R_1 i_1 + R_3(i_1 + i_2)$$
$$= (R_1 + R_3)i_1 + R_3 i_2 \qquad \ldots \text{(iv)}$$

and adding (ii) and (iii),

$$\mathcal{E}_2 = R_2 i_2 + R_3(i_1 + i_2)$$
$$= (R_2 + R_3)i_2 + R_3 i_1. \qquad \ldots \text{(v)}$$

Equations (iv) and (v) may be directly written from Kirchhoff's loop law applied to the left half and the right half of the circuit.

Multiply (iv) by $(R_2 + R_3)$, (v) by R_3 and subtract to eliminate i_2. This gives

$$i_1 = \frac{\mathcal{E}_1(R_2 + R_3) - \mathcal{E}_2 R_3}{(R_1 + R_3)(R_2 + R_3) - R_3^2}$$
$$= \frac{\mathcal{E}_1(R_2 + R_3) - \mathcal{E}_2 R_3}{R_1 R_2 + R_2 R_3 + R_3 R_1}.$$

Similarly, eliminating i_1 from (iv) and (v) we obtain,

$$i_2 = \frac{\mathcal{E}_2(R_1 + R_3) - \mathcal{E}_1 R_3}{R_1 R_2 + R_2 R_3 + R_3 R_1}.$$

And so,

$$i_1 + i_2 = \frac{\mathcal{E}_1 R_2 + \mathcal{E}_2 R_1}{R_1 R_2 + R_2 R_3 + R_3 R_1}.$$

21. *Find the equivalent resistance between the points a and c of the network shown in figure (32-W16a). Each resistance is equal to r.*

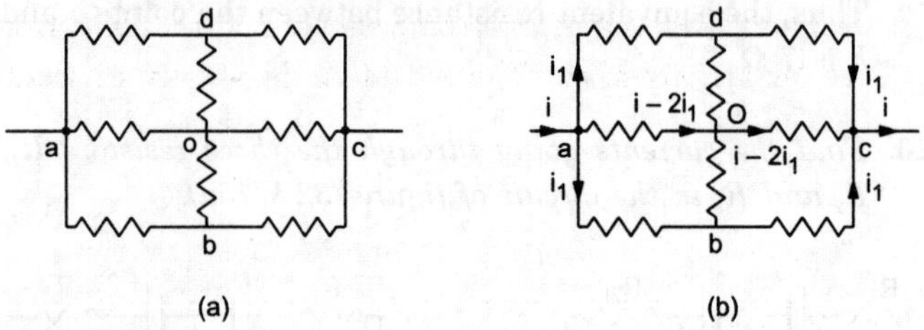

Figure 32-W16

Solution : Suppose a potential difference V is applied between a and c so that a current i enters at a and the same current leaves at c (figure 32-W16b). The current i divides in three parts at a. By symmetry, the part in ad and in ab will be equal. Let each of these currents be i_1. The current through ao is $i - 2i_1$. Similarly, currents from dc, bc and oc combine at c to give the total current i. Since the situation at c is equivalent to that at a, by symmetry, the currents in dc and bc will be i_1 and that in oc will be $i - 2i_1$.

Applying Kirchhoff's junction law at d, we see that the current in do is zero. Similarly, the current in ob is zero. We can remove do and ob for further analysis. It is then equivalent to three resistances, each of value $2r$, in parallel. The equivalent resistance is, therefore, $2r/3$.

22. *Twelve wires, each having resistance r, are joined to form a cube as shown in figure (32-W17). Find the equivalent resistance between the ends of a face diagonal such as a and c.*

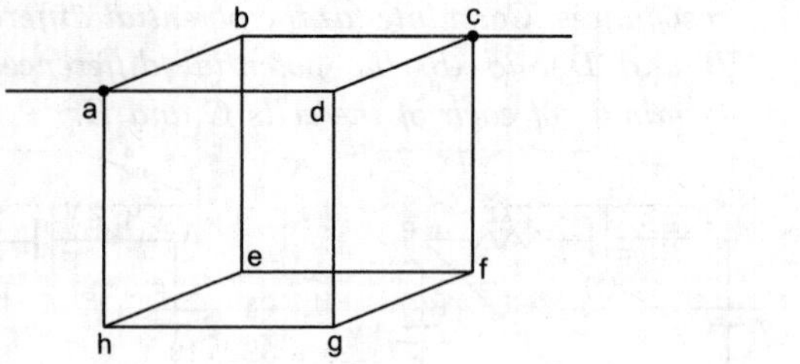

Figure 32-W17

Solution : Suppose a potential difference V is applied between the points a and c so that a current i enters at a and the same current leaves at c. The current distribution is shown in figure (32-W18a).

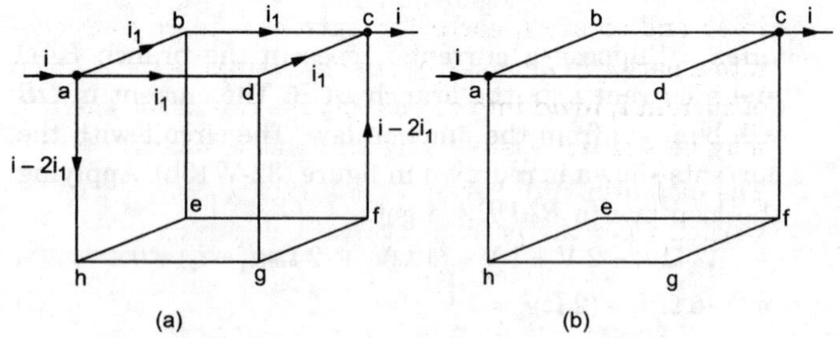

Figure 32-W18

By symmetry, the paths ad and ab are equivalent and hence will carry the same current i_1. The path ah will carry the remaining current $i - 2i_1$ (using Kirchhoff's junction law). Similarly at junction c, currents coming from dc and bc will be i_1 each and from fc will be $i - 2i_1$. Kirchhoff's junction law at b and d shows that currents through be and dg will be zero and hence may be ignored for further analysis. Omitting these two wires, the circuit is redrawn in figure (32-W18b).

The wire hef and hgf are joined in parallel and have equivalent resistance $\frac{(2r)(2r)}{(2r)+(2r)} = r$ between h and f. This is joined in series with ah and fc giving equivalent resistance $r + r + r = 3r$. This $3r$ is joined in parallel with adc $(2r)$ and abc $(2r)$ between a and c.

The equivalent resistance R between a and c is, therefore, given by

$$\frac{1}{R} = \frac{1}{3r} + \frac{1}{2r} + \frac{1}{2r},$$

giving $$R = \frac{3}{4}r.$$

23. *Find the equivalent resistance of the circuit of the previous problem between the ends of an edge such as a and b in figure (32-W19a).*

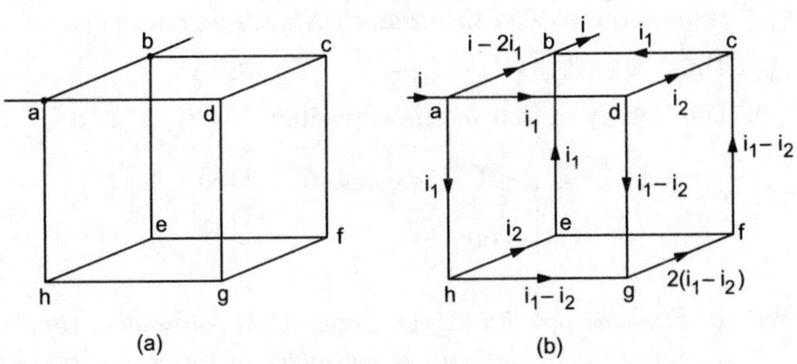

Figure 32-W19

Solution : Suppose a current i enters the circuit at the point a and the same current leaves the circuit at the point b. The current distribution is shown in figure (32-W19b). The paths through ad and ah are equivalent and carry equal current i_1. The current through ab is then $i - 2i_1$.

The same distribution holds at the junction b. Currents in eb and cb are i_1 each. The current i_1 in ah is divided into a part i_2 in he and $i_1 - i_2$ in hg. Similar is the division of current i_1 in ad into dc and dg. The rest of the currents may be written easily using Kirchhoff's junction law.

The potential difference V between a and b may be written from the paths ab, $aheb$ and $ahgfcb$ as

$$V = (i - 2i_1)r$$

$$V = (i_1 + i_2 + i_1)r$$

and $$V = [i_1 + (i_1 - i_2) + 2(i_1 - i_2) + (i_1 - i_2) + i_1]r$$

which may be written as

$$V = (i - 2i_1)r$$

$$V = (2i_1 + i_2)r$$

and $$V = (6i_1 - 4i_2)r.$$

Eliminating i_1 and i_2 from these equations,

$$\frac{V}{i} = \frac{7}{12}r$$

which is the equivalent resistance.

24. *Find the equivalent resistance between the points a and b of the infinite ladder shown in figure (32-W20a).*

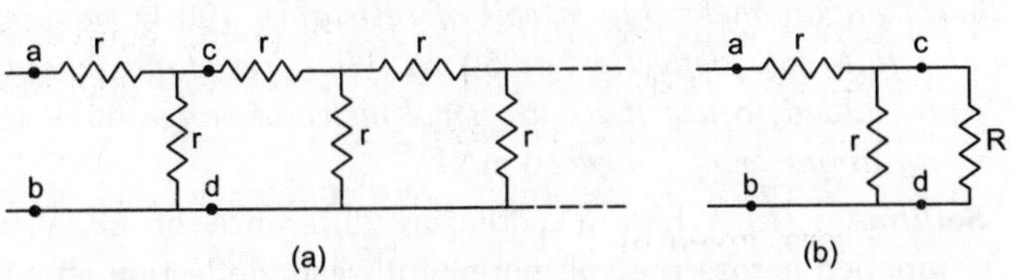

Figure 32-W20

Solution : Let the equivalent resistance between a and b be R. As the ladder is infinite, R is also the equivalent resistance of the ladder to the right of the points c and d. Thus, we can replace the part to the right of cd by a resistance R and redraw the circuit as in figure (32-W20b).

This gives

$$R = r + \frac{rR}{r + R}$$

or, $$rR + R^2 = r^2 + 2rR$$

or, $$R^2 - rR - r^2 = 0$$

or, $$R = \frac{r + \sqrt{r^2 + 4r^2}}{2} = \frac{1 + \sqrt{5}}{2}r.$$

25. *Find the equivalent resistance of the network shown in figure (32-W21) between the points a and b.*

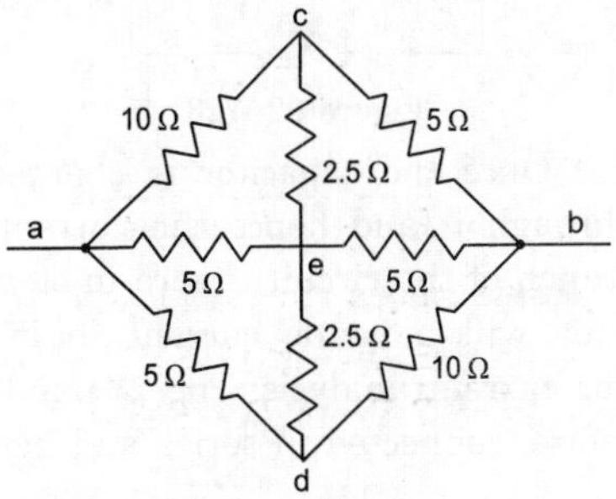

Figure 32-W21

Solution :

Suppose a current i enters the network at point a and the same current leaves it at point b. Suppose, the currents in ac, ad and ae are i_1, i_2 and i_3 respectively. Similar will be the distribution of current at b. The current i leaving at b is composed of i_1 from db, i_2 from cb and i_3 from eb. The situation is shown in figure (32-W22a).

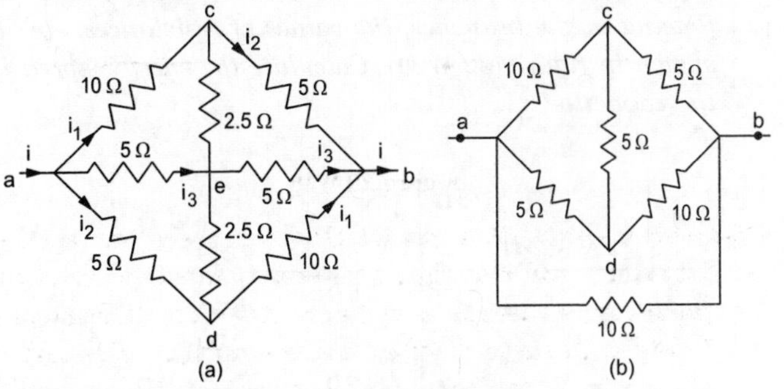

Figure 32-W22

As the current in ae is equal to that in eb, the current in ce will be equal to the current in ed from the junction law. If we assume that the branches ced and aeb do not physically touch at e, nothing will be changed in the current distribution. We can then represent the branch aeb by a single resistance of 10 Ω connected between a and b. Similarly, the branch ced may be replaced a single 5 Ω resistor between c and d. The circuit is redrawn in figure (32-W22b). This is same as the circuit in figure (32-W14a) connected in parallel with a resistance of 10 Ω. So the network is equivalent to a parallel combination of 7 Ω and 10 Ω resistor. The equivalent resistance of the whole network is, therefore,

$$R = \frac{(7\ \Omega) \times (10\ \Omega)}{7\ \Omega + 10\ \Omega} \approx 4{\cdot}1\ \Omega.$$

26. *(a) Find the current i supplied by the battery in the network shown in figure (32-W23) in steady state. (b) Find the charge on the capacitor.*

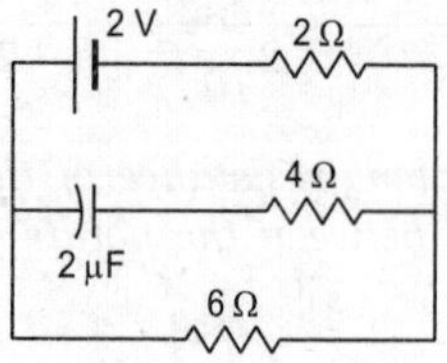

Figure 32-W23

Solution : (a) Once the capacitor is charged, no current will go through it and hence the current through the middle branch of the circuit is zero in steady state. The 4 Ω resistor will have no current in it and may be omitted for current analysis. The 2 Ω and 6 Ω resistors are, therefore, connected in series and hence

$$i = \frac{2\ \text{V}}{2\ \Omega + 6\ \Omega} = 0{\cdot}25\ \text{A}.$$

(b) The potential drop across the 6 Ω resistor is $6\ \Omega \times 0{\cdot}25\ \text{A} = 1{\cdot}5\ \text{V}$. As there is no current in the 4 Ω resistor, there is no potential drop across it. The potential difference across the capacitor is, therefore, 1·5 V. The charge on this capacitor is

$$Q = CV = 2\ \mu\text{F} \times 1{\cdot}5\ \text{V} = 3\ \mu\text{C}.$$

27. *A part of a circuit in steady state along with the currents flowing in the branches, the values of resistances, etc., is shown in figure (32-W24). Calculate the energy stored in the capacitor.*

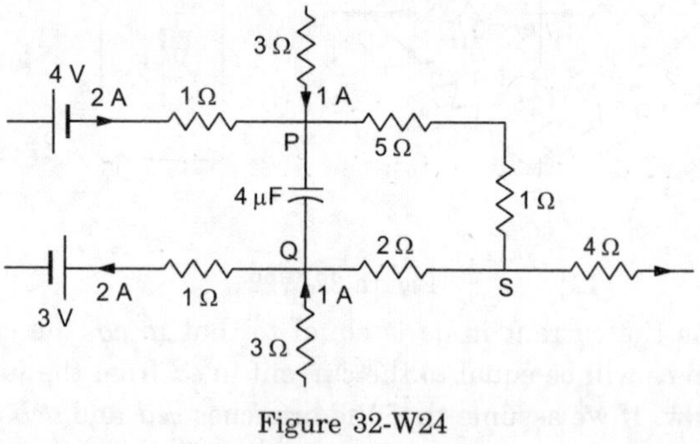

Figure 32-W24

Solution : To get the energy stored in the capacitor, we shall calculate the potential difference between the points *P* and *Q*. In steady state, there is no current in the capacitor branch. Applying Kirchhoff's junction law at *P*, the current in the 5 Ω – 1 Ω branch will be 3 A and hence

$$V_P - V_S = 6\ \Omega \times 3\ \text{A} = 18\ \text{V}.$$

Applying the same theorem at *Q*, the current in the 2 Ω resistor will be 1 A towards *Q* so that

$$V_S - V_Q = 2\ \Omega \times 1\ \text{A} = 2\ \text{V}.$$

Thus, $V_P - V_Q = (V_P - V_S) + (V_S - V_Q) = 20\ \text{V}$.

The energy stored in the capacitor

$$= \frac{1}{2} CV^2 = \frac{1}{2} \times 4\ \mu\text{F} \times 400\ \text{V}^2$$

$$= 800\ \mu\text{J}.$$

28. *(a) Find the potential drops across the two resistors shown in figure (32-W25a). (b) A voltmeter of resistance 600 Ω is used to measure the potential drop across the 300 Ω resistor. What will be the measured potential drop ?*

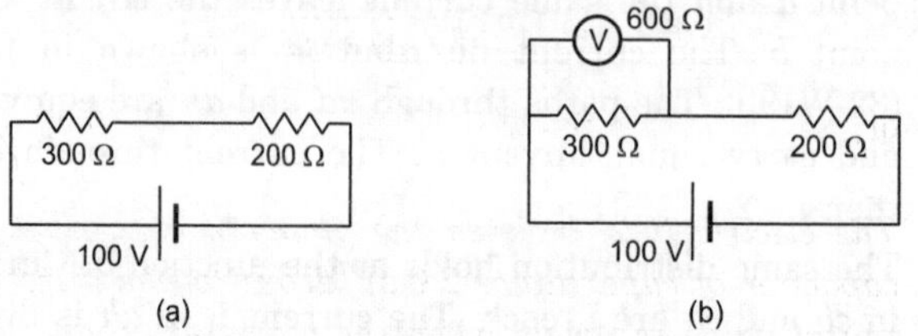

Figure 32-W25

Solution :

(a) The current in the circuit is $\dfrac{100\ \text{V}}{300\ \Omega + 200\ \Omega} = 0{\cdot}2\ \text{A}$.

The potential drop across the 300 Ω resistor is

$$300\ \Omega \times 0{\cdot}2\ \text{A} = 60\ \text{V}.$$

Similarly, the drop across the 200 Ω resistor is 40 V.

(b) The equivalent resistance, when the voltmeter is connected across 300 Ω, is (figure 32-W25b)

$$R = 200\ \Omega + \frac{600\ \Omega \times 300\ \Omega}{600\ \Omega + 300\ \Omega} = 400\ \Omega.$$

Thus, the main current from the battery is

$$i = \frac{100\ \text{V}}{400\ \Omega} = 0{\cdot}25\ \text{A}.$$

The potential drop across the 200 Ω resistor is, therefore, $200\ \Omega \times 0{\cdot}25\ \text{A} = 50\ \text{V}$ and that across 300 Ω is also 50 V. This is also the potential drop across the voltmeter and hence the reading of the voltmeter is 50 V.

29. *A galvanometer has a coil of resistance 100 Ω showing a full-scale deflection at 50 μA. What resistance should be added to use it as (a) a voltmeter of range 50 V (b) an ammeter of range 10 mA ?*

Solution : (a) When a potential difference of 50 V is applied across the voltmeter, full-scale deflection should take place. Thus, 50 μA should go through the coil. We

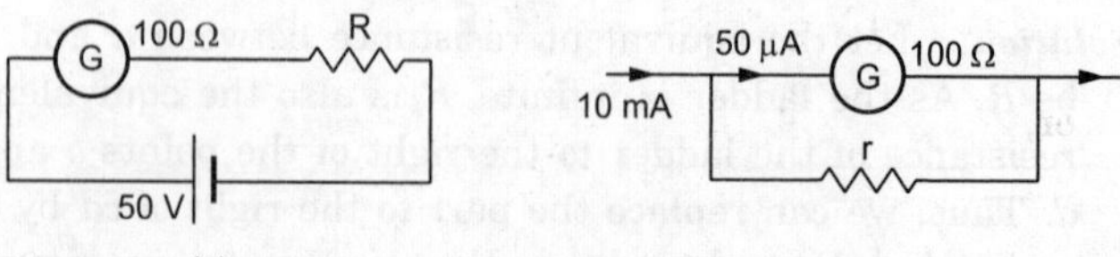

Figure 32-W26

add a resistance R in series with the given coil to achieve this (figure 32-W26a).

We have,

$$50\ \mu A = \frac{50\ V}{100\ \Omega + R}$$

or, $R = 10^6\ \Omega - 100\ \Omega \approx 10^6\ \Omega.$

(b) When a current of 10 mA is passed through the ammeter, 50 μA should go through the coil. We add a resistance r in parallel to the coil to achieve this (figure 32-W26b).

The current through the coil is

$$50\ \mu A = (10\ mA)\frac{r}{r + 100\ \Omega}$$

or, $r \approx 0{\cdot}5\ \Omega.$

30. *The electric field between the plates of a parallel-plate capacitor of capacitance 2·0 μF drops to one third of its initial value in 4·4 μs when the plates are connected by a thin wire. Find the resistance of the wire.*

Solution : The electric field between the plates is

$$E = \frac{Q}{A\varepsilon_0} = \frac{Q_0}{A\varepsilon_0} e^{-t/RC}$$

or, $E = E_0\, e^{-t/RC}.$

In the given problem, $E = \frac{1}{3}E_0$ at $t = 4{\cdot}4\ \mu s$.

Thus, $\frac{1}{3} = e^{-\frac{4{\cdot}4\ \mu s}{RC}}$

or, $\frac{4{\cdot}4\ \mu s}{RC} = \ln 3 = 1{\cdot}1$

or, $R = \frac{4{\cdot}4\ \mu s}{1{\cdot}1 \times 2{\cdot}0\ \mu F} = 2{\cdot}0\ \Omega.$

31. *A capacitor is connected to a 12 V battery through a resistance of 10 Ω. It is found that the potential difference across the capacitor rises to 4·0 V in 1 μs. Find the capacitance of the capacitor.*

Solution : The charge on the capacitor during charging is given by

$$Q = Q_0(1 - e^{-t/RC}).$$

Hence, the potential difference across the capacitor is

$$V = Q/C = Q_0/C(1 - e^{-t/RC}).$$

Here at $t = 1\ \mu s$, the potential difference is 4 V whereas the steady state potential difference is $Q_0/C = 12$ V. So,

$$4\ V = 12\ V(1 - e^{-t/RC})$$

or, $1 - e^{-t/RC} = \frac{1}{3}$

or, $e^{-t/RC} = \frac{2}{3}$

or, $\frac{t}{RC} = \ln\left(\frac{3}{2}\right) = 0{\cdot}405$

or, $RC = \frac{t}{0{\cdot}405} = \frac{1\ \mu s}{0{\cdot}405} = 2{\cdot}469\ \mu s$

or, $C = \frac{2{\cdot}469\ \mu s}{10\ \Omega} \approx 0{\cdot}25\ \mu F.$

32. *A capacitor charged to 50 V is discharged by connecting the two plates at t = 0. If the potential difference across the plates drops to 1·0 V at t = 10 ms, what will be the potential difference at t = 20 ms ?*

Solution : The potential difference at time t is given by

$$V = Q/C = (Q_0/C)\, e^{-t/RC}$$

or, $V = V_0 e^{-t/RC}$

According to the given data,

$$1\ V = (50\ V)\, e^{-10\ ms/RC}$$

or, $e^{-10\ ms/RC} = \frac{1}{50}.$

The potential difference at t = 20 ms is

$$V = V_0 e^{-t/RC}$$

$$= (50\ V)\, e^{-20\ ms/RC} = (50\ V)\left(e^{-10\ ms/RC}\right)^2$$

$$= 0{\cdot}02\ V.$$

33. *A 5·0 μF capacitor having a charge of 20 μC is discharged through a wire of resistance 5·0 Ω. Find the heat dissipated in the wire between 25 to 50 μs after the connections are made.*

Solution : The charge on the capacitor at time t after the connections are made is

$$Q = Q_0\, e^{-t/RC}$$

or, $i = \frac{dQ}{dt} = -(Q_0/RC)\, e^{-t/RC}.$

Heat dissipated during the time t_1 to t_2 is

$$U = \int_{t_1}^{t_2} i^2 R\, dt$$

$$= \int_{t_1}^{t_2} \frac{Q_0^{\ 2}}{RC^2} e^{-2t/RC}\, dt$$

$$= \frac{Q_0^2}{2\,C}\left(e^{-\frac{2t_1}{RC}} - e^{-\frac{2t_2}{RC}}\right). \quad \text{... (i)}$$

The time constant RC is $5\ \Omega \times 5{\cdot}0\ \mu F = 25\ \mu s$.

Putting $t_1 = 25\ \mu s$, $t_2 = 50\ \mu s$ and other values in (i),

$$U = \frac{(20\ \mu C)^2}{2 \times 5{\cdot}0\ \mu F}(e^{-2} - e^{-4}) = 4{\cdot}7\ \mu J.$$

□

QUESTIONS FOR SHORT ANSWER

1. Suppose you have three resistors each of value 30 Ω. List all the different resistances you can obtain using them.
2. A proton beam is going from east to west. Is there an electric current ? If yes, in what direction ?
3. In an electrolyte, the positive ions move from left to right and the negative ions from right to left. Is there a net current ? If yes, in what direction ?
4. In a TV tube, the electrons are accelerated from the rear to the front. What is the direction of the current ?
5. The drift speed is defined as $v_d = \Delta l / \Delta t$ where Δl is the distance drifted in a long time Δt. Why don't we define the drift speed as the limit of $\Delta l / \Delta t$ as $\Delta t \to 0$?
6. One of your friends argues that he has read in previous chapters that there can be no electric field inside a conductor. And hence there can be no current through it. What is the fallacy in this argument ?
7. When a current is established in a wire, the free electrons drift in the direction opposite to the current. Does the number of free electrons in the wire continuously decrease ?
8. A fan with copper winding in its motor consumes less power as compared to an otherwise similar fan having aluminium winding. Explain.
9. The thermal energy developed in a current-carrying resistor is given by $U = i^2Rt$ and also by $U = Vit$. Should we say that U is proportional to i^2 or to i ?
10. Consider a circuit containing an ideal battery connected to a resistor. Do "work done by the battery" and "the thermal energy developed" represent two names of the same physical quantity ?
11. Is work done by a battery always equal to the thermal energy developed in electrical circuits ? What happens if a capacitor is connected in the circuit ?
12. A nonideal battery is connected to a resistor. Is work done by the battery equal to the thermal energy developed in the resistor ? Does your answer change if the battery is ideal ?
13. Sometimes it is said that "heat is developed" in a resistance when there is an electric current in it. Recall that heat is defined as the energy being transferred due to the temperature difference. Is the statement under quotes technically correct ?
14. We often say "a current is going through the wire". What goes through the wire, the charge or the current ?
15. Would you prefer a voltmeter or a potentiometer to measure the emf of a battery ?
16. Does a conductor become charged when a current is passed through it ?
17. Can the potential difference across a battery be greater than its emf ?

OBJECTIVE I

1. A metallic resistor is connected across a battery. If the number of collisions of the free electrons with the lattice is somehow decreased in the resistor (for example, by cooling it), the current will
   (a) increase (b) decrease
   (c) remain constant (d) become zero.
2. Two resistors A and B have resistances R_A and R_B respectively with $R_A < R_B$. The resistivities of their materials are ρ_A and ρ_B.
   (a) $\rho_A > \rho_B$ (b) $\rho_A = \rho_B$ (c) $\rho_A < \rho_B$
   (d) The information is not sufficient to find the relation between ρ_A and ρ_B.
3. The product of resistivity and conductivity of a cylindrical conductor depends on
   (a) temperature (b) material
   (c) area of cross section (d) none of these.
4. As the temperature of a metallic resistor is increased, the product of its resistivity and conductivity
   (a) increases (b) decreases
   (c) remains constant (d) may increase or decrease.
5. In an electric circuit containing a battery, the charge (assumed positive) inside the battery
   (a) always goes from the positive terminal to the negative terminal
   (b) may go from the positive terminal to the negative terminal
   (c) always goes from the negative terminal to the positive terminal
   (d) does not move.
6. A resistor of resistance R is connected to an ideal battery. If the value of R is decreased, the power dissipated in the resistor will
   (a) increase (b) decrease (c) remain unchanged.
7. A current passes through a resistor. Let K_1 and K_2 represent the average kinetic energy of the conduction electrons and the metal ions respectively.
   (a) $K_1 < K_2$ (b) $K_1 = K_2$
   (c) $K_1 > K_2$ (d) Any of these three may occur.
8. Two resistors R and $2R$ are connected in series in an electric circuit. The thermal energy developed in R and $2R$ are in the ratio
   (a) 1 : 2 (b) 2 : 1 (c) 1 : 4 (d) 4 : 1.
9. Two resistances R and $2R$ are connected in parallel in an electric circuit. The thermal energy developed in R and $2R$ are in the ratio
   (a) 1 : 2 (b) 2 : 1 (c) 1 : 4 (d) 4 : 1.
10. A uniform wire of resistance 50 Ω is cut into 5 equal parts. These parts are now connected in parallel. The

equivalent resistance of the combination is
(a) 2 Ω (b) 10 Ω (c) 250 Ω (d) 6250 Ω.

11. Consider the following two statements:
(A) Kirchhoff's junction law follows from conservation of charge.
(B) Kirchhoff's loop law follows from conservative nature of electric field.
(a) Both A and B are correct.
(b) A is correct but B is wrong.
(c) B is correct but A is wrong.
(d) Both A and B are wrong.

12. Two nonideal batteries are connected in series. Consider the following statements:
(A) The equivalent emf is larger than either of the two emfs.
(B) The equivalent internal resistance is smaller than either of the two internal resistances.
(a) Each of A and B is correct.
(b) A is correct but B is wrong.
(c) B is correct but A is wrong.
(d) Each of A and B is wrong.

13. Two nonideal batteries are connected in parallel. Consider the following statements:
(A) The equivalent emf is smaller than either of the two emfs.
(B) The equivalent internal resistance is smaller than either of the two internal resistances.
(a) Both A and B are correct.
(b) A is correct but B is wrong.
(c) B is correct but A is wrong.
(d) Both A and B are wrong.

14. The net resistance of an ammeter should be small to ensure that
(a) it does not get overheated
(b) it does not draw excessive current
(c) it can measure large currents
(d) it does not appreciably change the current to be measured.

15. The net resistance of a voltmeter should be large to ensure that
(a) it does not get overheated
(b) the readings fall within the scale
(c) it can measure large potential differences
(d) it does not appreciably change the potential difference to be measured.

16. Consider a capacitor-charging circuit. Let Q_1 be the charge given to the capacitor in a time interval of 10 ms and Q_2 be the charge given in the next time interval of 10 ms. Let 10 μC charge be deposited in a time interval t_1 and the next 10 μC charge is deposited in the next time interval t_2.
(a) $Q_1 > Q_2, t_1 > t_2$ (b) $Q_1 > Q_2, t_1 < t_2$
(c) $Q_1 < Q_2, t_1 > t_2$ (d) $Q_1 < Q_2, t_1 < t_2$

OBJECTIVE II

1. Electrons are emitted by a hot filament and are accelerated by an electric field as shown in figure (32-Q1). The two stops at the left ensure that the electron beam has a uniform cross-section.
(a) The speed of the electron is more at B than at A.
(b) The electric current is from left to right.
(c) The magnitude of the current is larger at B than at A.
(d) The current density is more at B than at A.

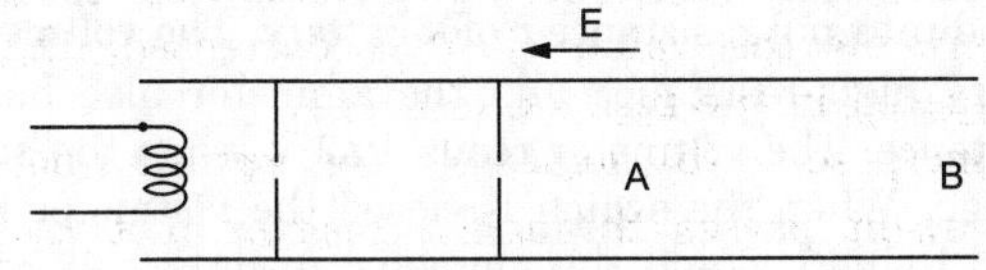

Figure 32-Q1

2. A capacitor with no dielectric is connected to a battery at $t = 0$. Consider a point A in the connecting wires and a point B in between the plates.
(a) There is no current through A.
(b) There is no current through B.
(c) There is a current through A as long as the charging is not complete.
(d) There is a current through B as long as the charging is not complete.

3. When no current is passed through a conductor,
(a) the free electrons do not move
(b) the average speed of a free electron over a large period of time is zero
(c) the average velocity of a free electron over a large period of time is zero
(d) the average of the velocities of all the free electrons at an instant is zero.

4. Which of the following quantities do not change when a resistor connected to a battery is heated due to the current ?
(a) Drift speed (b) Resistivity
(c) Resistance (d) Number of free electrons

5. As the temperature of a conductor increases, its resistivity and conductivity change. The ratio of resistivity to conductivity
(a) increases (b) decreases (c) remains constant
(d) may increase or decrease depending on the actual temperature.

6. A current passes through a wire of nonuniform cross-section. Which of the following quantities are independent of the cross section ?
(a) The charge crossing in a given time interval
(b) Drift speed
(c) Current density
(d) Free-electron density

7. Mark out the correct options.
(a) An ammeter should have small resistance.
(b) An ammeter should have large resistance.

(c) A voltmeter should have small resistance.
(d) A voltmeter should have large resistance.

8. A capacitor of capacitance 500 μF is connected to a battery through a 10 kΩ resistor. The charge stored on the capacitor in the first 5 s is larger than the charge stored in the next
(a) 5 s (b) 50 s (c) 500 s (d) 5000 s

9. A capacitor C_1 of capacitance 1 μF and a capacitor C_2 of capacitance 2 μF are separately charged by a common battery for a long time. The two capacitors are then separately discharged through equal resistors. Both the discharge circuits are connected at $t = 0$.
(a) The current in each of the two discharging circuits is zero at $t = 0$.
(b) The currents in the two discharging circuits at $t = 0$ are equal but not zero.
(c) The currents in the two discharging circuits at $t = 0$ are unequal.
(d) C_1 loses 50% of its initial charge sooner than C_2 loses 50% of its initial charge.

EXERCISES

1. The amount of charge passed in time t through a cross-section of a wire is
$$Q(t) = At^2 + Bt + C.$$
(a) Write the dimensional formulae for A, B and C.
(b) If the numerical values of A, B and C are 5, 3 and 1 respectively in SI units, find the value of the current at $t = 5$ s.

2. An electron gun emits $2{\cdot}0 \times 10^{16}$ electrons per second. What electric current does this correspond to?

3. The electric current existing in a discharge tube is 2·0 μA. How much charge is transferred across a cross-section of the tube in 5 minutes?

4. The current through a wire depends on time as
$$i = i_0 + \alpha t,$$
where $i_0 = 10$ A and $\alpha = 4 \text{ A s}^{-1}$. Find the charge crossed through a section of the wire in 10 seconds.

5. A current of 1·0 A exists in a copper wire of cross-section $1{\cdot}0 \text{ mm}^2$. Assuming one free electron per atom calculate the drift speed of the free electrons in the wire. The density of copper is 9000 kg m^{-3}.

6. A wire of length 1 m and radius 0·1 mm has a resistance of 100 Ω. Find the resistivity of the material.

7. A uniform wire of resistance 100 Ω is melted and recast in a wire of length double that of the original. What would be the resistance of the wire?

8. Consider a wire of length 4 m and cross-sectional area 1 mm^2 carrying a current of 2 A. If each cubic metre of the material contains 10^{29} free electrons, find the average time taken by an electron to cross the length of the wire.

9. What length of a copper wire of cross-sectional area $0{\cdot}01 \text{ mm}^2$ will be needed to prepare a resistance of 1 kΩ? Resistivity of copper $= 1{\cdot}7 \times 10^{-8}$ Ω m.

10. Figure (32-E1) shows a conductor of length l having a circular cross section. The radius of cross section varies linearly from a to b. The resistivity of the material is ρ. Assuming that $b - a << l$, find the resistance of the conductor.

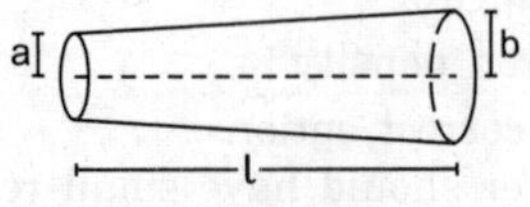

Figure 32-E1

11. A copper wire of radius 0·1 mm and resistance 1 kΩ is connected across a power supply of 20 V. (a) How many electrons are transferred per second between the supply and the wire at one end? (b) Write down the current density in the wire.

12. Calculate the electric field in a copper wire of cross-sectional area $2{\cdot}0 \text{ mm}^2$ carrying a current of 1 A. The resistivity of copper $= 1{\cdot}7 \times 10^{-8}$ Ω m.

13. A wire has a length of 2·0 m and a resistance of 5·0 Ω. Find the elecric field existing inside the wire if it carries a current of 10 A.

14. The resistances of an iron wire and a copper wire at 20°C are 3·9 Ω and 4·1 Ω respectively. At what temperature will the resistances be equal? Temperature coefficient of resistivity for iron is $5{\cdot}0 \times 10^{-3} \text{ K}^{-1}$ and for copper it is $4{\cdot}0 \times 10^{-3} \text{ K}^{-1}$. Neglect any thermal expansion.

15. The current in a conductor and the potential difference across its ends are measured by an ammeter and a voltmeter. The meters draw negligible currents. The ammeter is accurate but the voltmeter has a zero error (that is, it does not read zero when no potential difference is applied). Calculate the zero error if the readings for two different conditions are 1·75 A, 14·4 V and 2·75 A, 22·4 V.

16. Figure (32-E2) shows an arrangement to measure the emf $\mathcal{E}$ and internal resistance r of a battery. The voltmeter has a very high resistance and the ammeter also has some resistance. The voltmeter reads 1·52 V when the switch S is open. When the switch is closed the voltmeter reading drops to 1·45 V and the ammeter reads 1·0 A. Find the emf and the internal resistance of the battery.

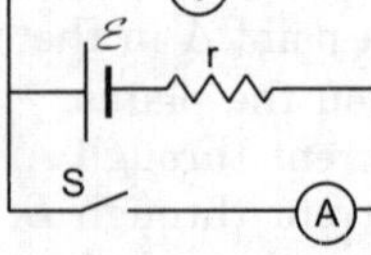

Figure 32-E2

17. The potential difference between the terminals of a battery of emf 6·0 V and internal resistance 1 Ω drops to 5·8 V when connected across an external resistor. Find the resistance of the external resistor.

18. The potential difference between the terminals of a 6·0 V battery is 7·2 V when it is being charged by a current of 2·0 A. What is the internal resistance of the battery ?

19. The internal resistance of an accumulator battery of emf 6 V is 10 Ω when it is fully discharged. As the battery gets charged up, its internal resistance decreases to 1 Ω. The battery in its completely discharged state is connected to a charger which maintains a constant potential difference of 9 V. Find the current through the battery (a) just after the connections are made and (b) after a long time when it is completely charged.

20. Find the value of i_1/i_2 in figure (32-E3) if (a) $R = 0·1\ \Omega$, (b) $R = 1\ \Omega$ (c) $R = 10\ \Omega$. Note from your answers that in order to get more current from a combination of two batteries they should be joined in parallel if the external resistance is small and in series if the external resistance is large as compared to the internal resistances.

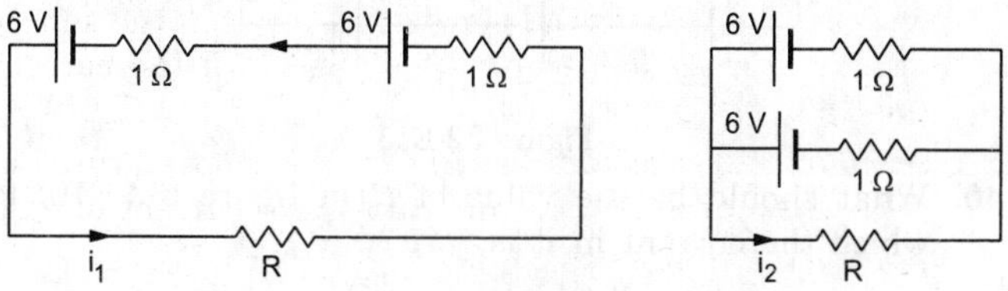

Figure 32-E3

21. Consider $N = n_1 n_2$ identical cells, each of emf $\mathcal{E}$ and internal resistance r. Suppose n_1 cells are joined in series to form a line and n_2 such lines are connected in parallel. The combination drives a current in an external resistance R. (a) Find the current in the external resistance. (b) Assuming that n_1 and n_2 can be continuously varied, find the relation between n_1, n_2, R and r for which the current in R is maximum.

22. A battery of emf 100 V and a resistor of resistance 10 kΩ are joined in series. This system is used as a source to supply current to an external resistance R. If R is not greater than 100 Ω, the current through it is constant up to two significant digits. Find its value. This is the basic principle of a *constant-current source.*

23. If the reading of ammeter A_1 in figure (32-E4) is 2·4 A, what will the ammeters A_2 and A_3 read ? Neglect the resistances of the ammeters.

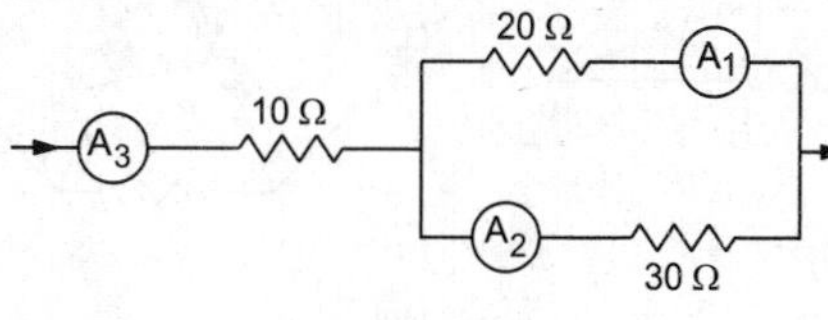

Figure 32-E4

24. The resistance of the rheostat shown in figure (32-E5) is 30 Ω. Neglecting the meter resistance, find the minimum and maximum currents through the ammeter as the rheostat is varied.

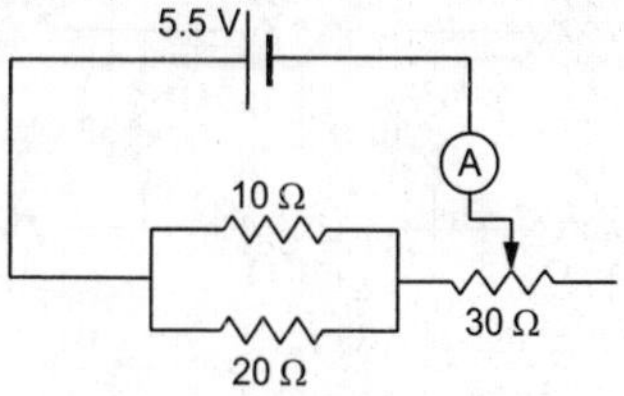

Figure 32-E5

25. Three bulbs, each having a resistance of 180 Ω, are connected in parallel to an ideal battery of emf 60 V. Find the current delivered by the battery when (a) all the bulbs are switched on, (b) two of the bulbs are switched on and (c) only one bulb is switched on.

26. Suppose you have three resistors of 20 Ω, 50 Ω and 100 Ω. What minimum and maximum resistances can you obtain from these resistors ?

27. A bulb is made using two filaments. A switch selects whether the filaments are used individually or in parallel. When used with a 15 V battery, the bulb can be operated at 5 W, 10 W or 15 W. What should be the resistances of the filaments ?

28. Figure (32-E6) shows a part of a circuit. If a current of 12 mA exists in the 5 kΩ resistor, find the currents in the other three resistors. What is the potential difference between the points A and B ?

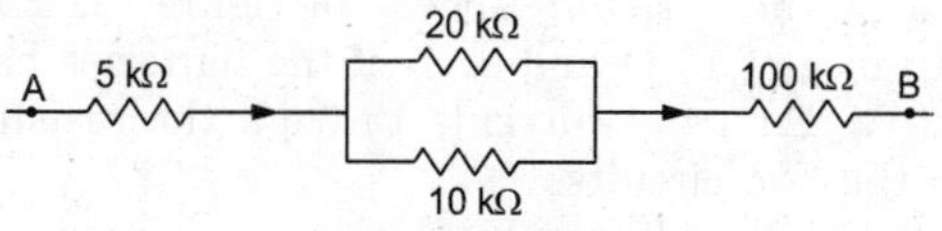

Figure 32-E6

29. An ideal battery sends a current of 5 A in a resistor. When another resistor of value 10 Ω is connected in parallel, the current through the battery is increased to 6 A. Find the resistance of the first resistor.

30. Find the equivalent resistance of the network shown in figure (32-E7) between the points a and b.

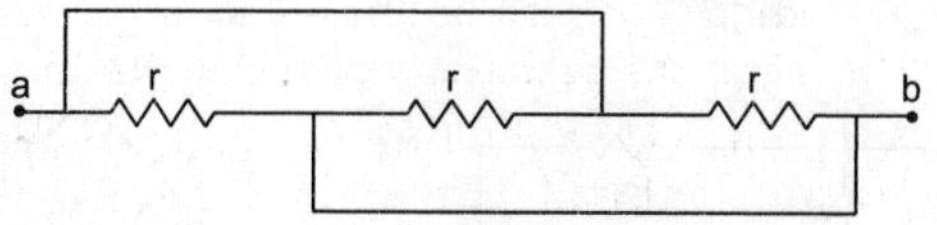

Figure 32-E7

31. A wire of resistance 15·0 Ω is bent to form a regular hexagon $ABCDEFA$. Find the equivalent resistance of the loop between the points (a) A and B, (b) A and C and (c) A and D.

32. Consider the circuit shown in figure (32-E8). Find the current through the 10 Ω resistor when the switch S is (a) open (b) closed.

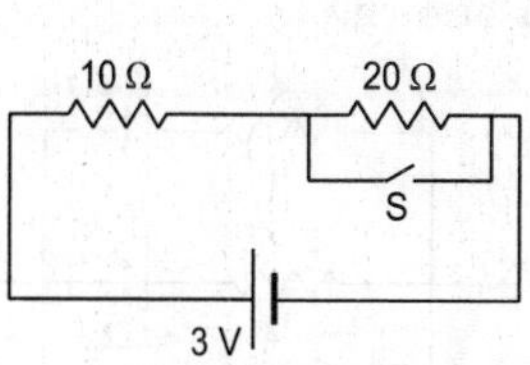

Figure 32-E8

33. Find the currents through the three resistors shown in figure (32-E9).

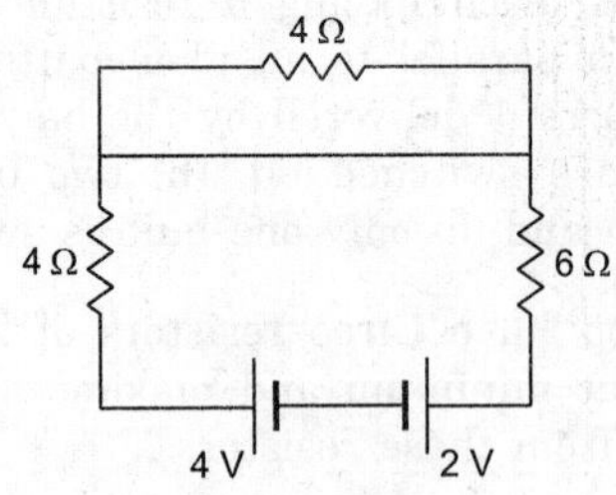

Figure 32-E9

34. Figure (32-E10) shows a part of an electric circuit. The potentials at the points a, b and c are 30 V, 12 V and 2 V respectively. Find the currents through the three resistors.

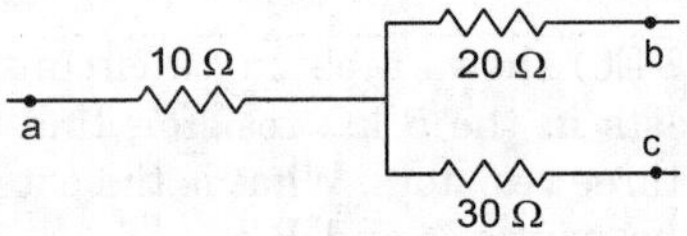

Figure 32-E10

35. Each of the resistors shown in figure (32-E11) has a resistance of 10 Ω and each of the batteries has an emf of 10 V. Find the currents through the resistors a and b in the two circuits.

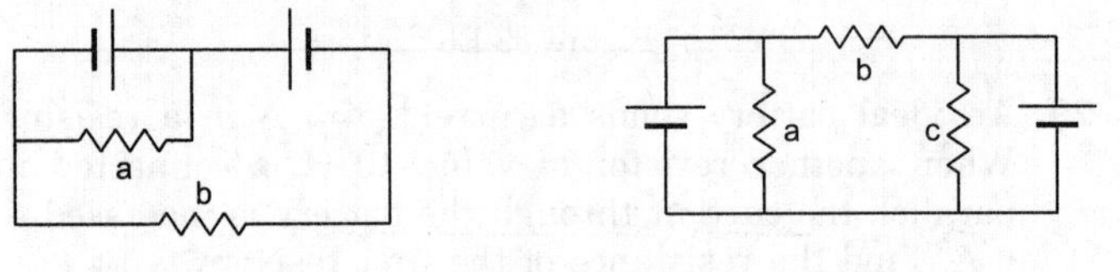

Figure 32-E11

36. Find the potential difference $V_a - V_b$ in the circuits shown in figure (32-E12).

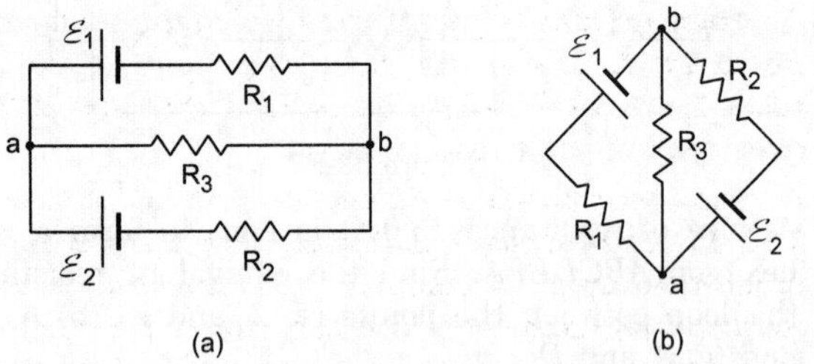

Figure 32-E12

37. In the circuit shown in figure (32-E13), $\mathcal{E}_1 = 3$ V, $\mathcal{E}_2 = 2$ V, $\mathcal{E}_3 = 1$ V and $r_1 = r_2 = r_3 = 1$ Ω. Find the potential difference between the points A and B and the current through each branch.

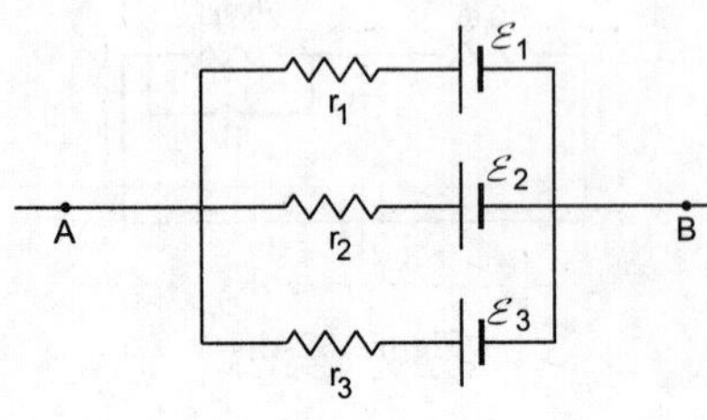

Figure 32-E13

38. Find the current through the 10 Ω resistor shown in figure (32-E14).

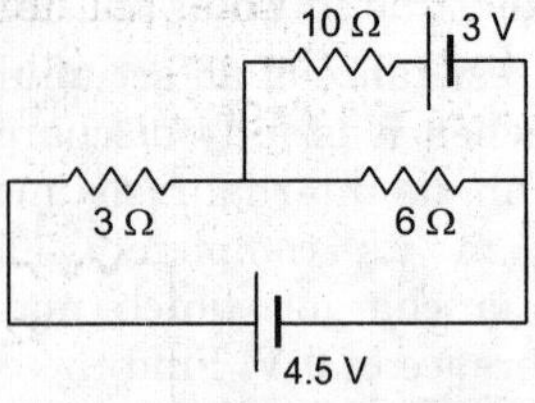

Figure 32-E14

39. Find the current in the three resistors shown in figure (32-E15).

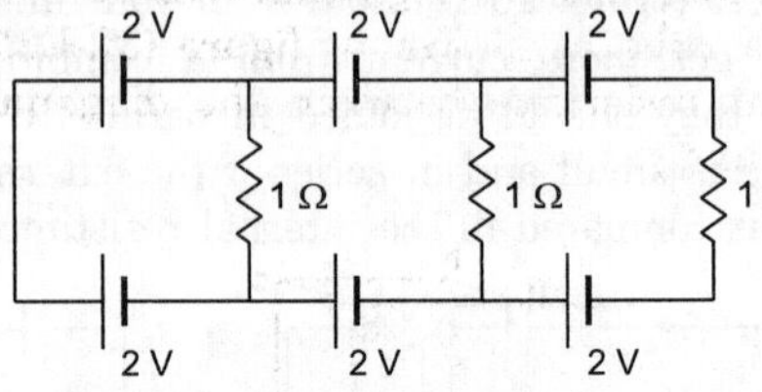

Figure 32-E15

40. What should be the value of R in figure (32-E16) for which the current in it is zero?

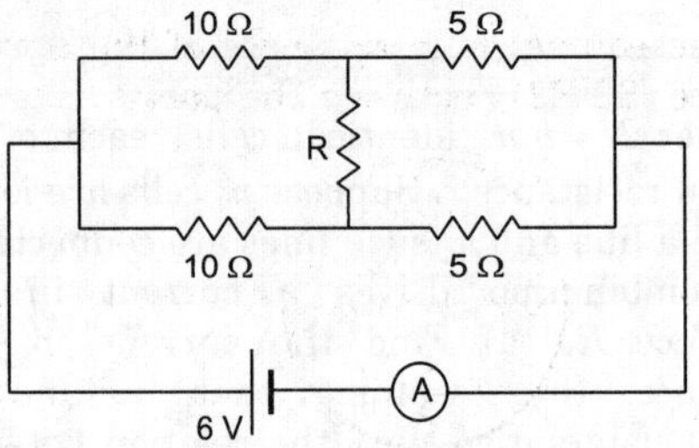

Figure 32-E16

41. Find the equivalent resistance of the circuits shown in figure (32-E17) between the points a and b. Each resistor has a resistance r.

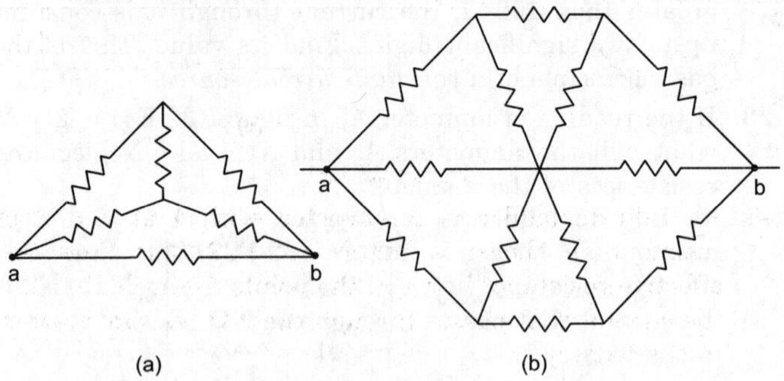

Figure 32-E17

42. Find the current measured by the ammeter in the circuit shown in figure (32-E18).

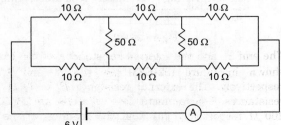

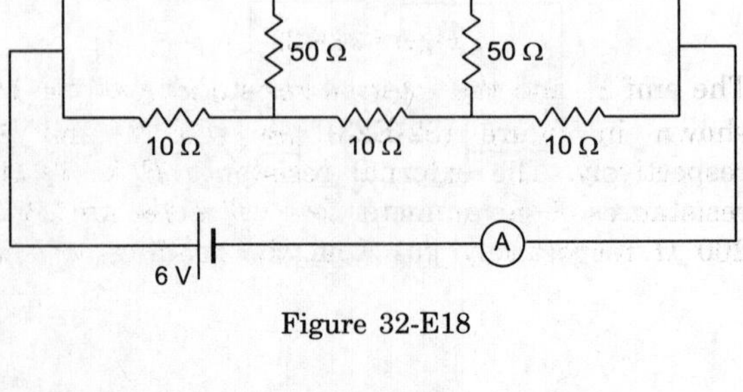

Figure 32-E18

43. Consider the circuit shown in figure (32-E19a). Find (a) the current in the circuit, (b) the potential drop across the 5 Ω resistor, (c) the potential drop across the 10 Ω resistor. (d) Answer the parts (a), (b) and (c) with reference to figure (32-E19b).

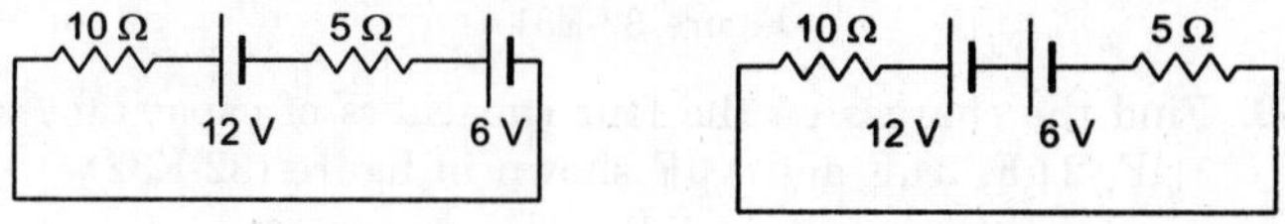

Figure 32-E19

44. Twelve wires, each having equal resistance r, are joined to form a cube as shown in figure (32-E20). Find the equivalent resistance between the diagonally opposite points a and f.

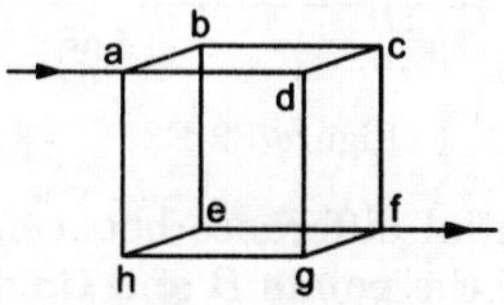

Figure 32-E20

45. Find the equivalent resistances of the networks shown in figure (32-E21) between the points a and b.

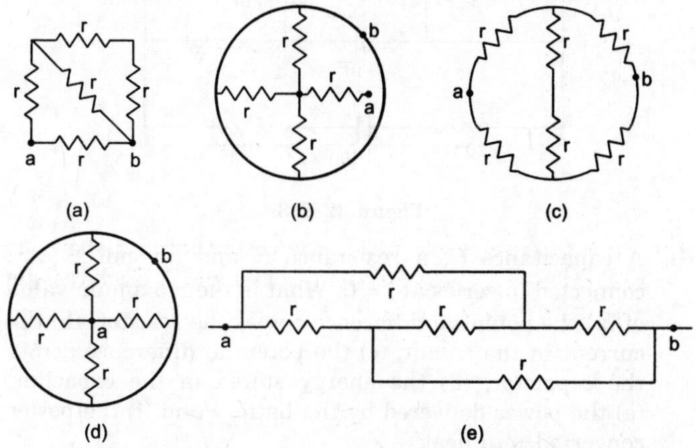

Figure 32-E21

46. An infinite ladder is constructed with 1 Ω and 2 Ω resistors as shown in figure (32-E22). (a) Find the effective resistance between the points A and B. (b) Find the current that passes through the 2 Ω resistor nearest to the battery.

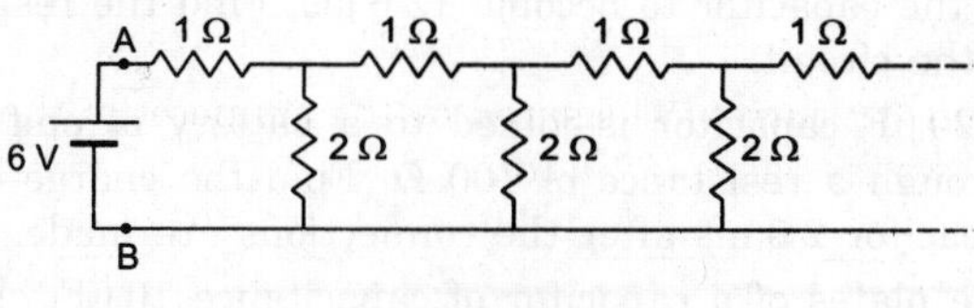

Figure 32-E22

47. The emf $\mathcal{E}$ and the internal resistance r of the battery shown in figure (32-E23) are 4·3 V and 1·0 Ω respectively. The external resistance R is 50 Ω. The resistances of the ammeter and voltmeter are 2·0 Ω and 200 Ω respectively. (a) Find the readings of the two meters. (b) The switch is thrown to the other side. What will be the readings of the two meters now ?

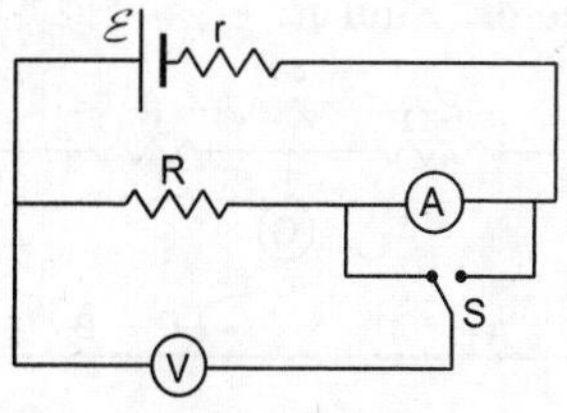

Figure 32-E23

48. A voltmeter of resistance 400 Ω is used to measure the potential difference across the 100 Ω resistor in the circuit shown in figure (32-E24). (a) What will be the reading of the voltmeter ? (b) What was the potential difference across 100 Ω before the voltmeter was connected ?

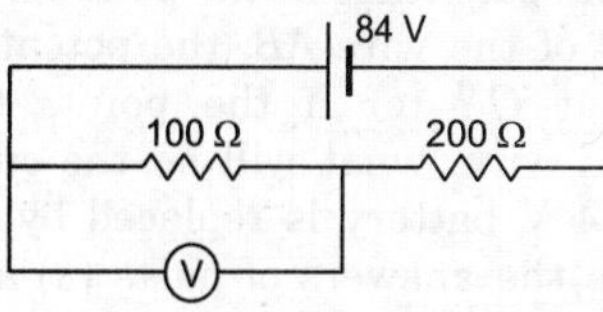

Figure 32-E24

49. The voltmeter shown in figure (32-E25) reads 18 V across the 50 Ω resistor. Find the resistance of the voltmeter.

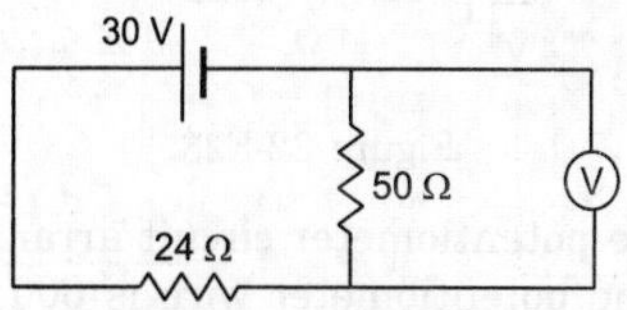

Figure 32-E25

50. A voltmeter consists of a 25 Ω coil connected in series with a 575 Ω resistor. The coil takes 10 mA for full scale deflection. What maximum potential difference can be measured on this voltmeter ?

51. An ammeter is to be constructed which can read currents up to 2·0 A. If the coil has a resistance of 25 Ω and takes 1 mA for full-scale deflection, what should be the resistance of the shunt used ?

52. A voltmeter coil has resistance 50·0 Ω and a resistor of 1·15 kΩ is connected in series. It can read potential differences upto 12 volts. If this same coil is used to construct an ammeter which can measure currents up to 2·0 A, what should be the resistance of the shunt used ?

53. The potentiometer wire AB shown in figure (32-E26) is 40 cm long. Where should the free end of the galvanometer be connected on AB so that the galvanometer may show zero deflection ?

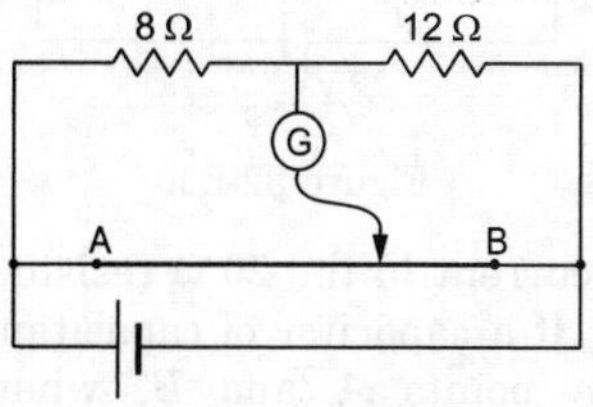

Figure 32-E26

54. The potentiometer wire AB shown in figure (32-E27) is 50 cm long. When $AD = 30$ cm, no deflection occurs in the galvanometer. Find R.

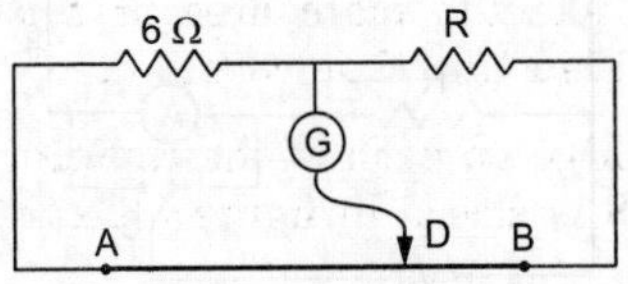

Figure 32-E27

55. A 6-volt battery of negligible internal resistance is connected across a uniform wire AB of length 100 cm. The positive terminal of another battery of emf 4 V and internal resistance 1 Ω is joined to the point A as shown in figure (32-E28). Take the potential at B to be zero. (a) What are the potentials at the points A and C ? (b) At which point D of the wire AB, the potential is equal to the potenial at C? (c) If the points C and D are connected by a wire, what will be the current through it ? (d) If the 4 V battery is replaced by 7·5 V battery, what would be the answers of parts (a) and (b) ?

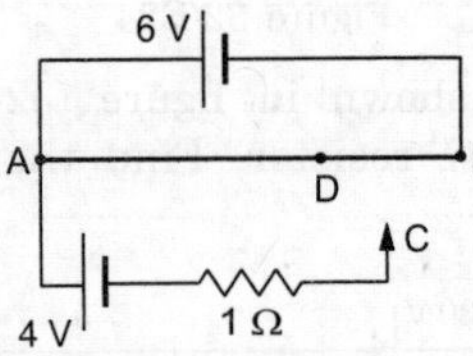

Figure 32-E28

56. Consider the potentiometer circuit arranged as in figure (32-E29). The potentiometer wire is 600 cm long. (a) At what distance from the point A should the jockey touch the wire to get zero deflection in the galvanometer? (b) If the jockey touches the wire at a distance of 560 cm from A, what will be the current in the galvanometer ?

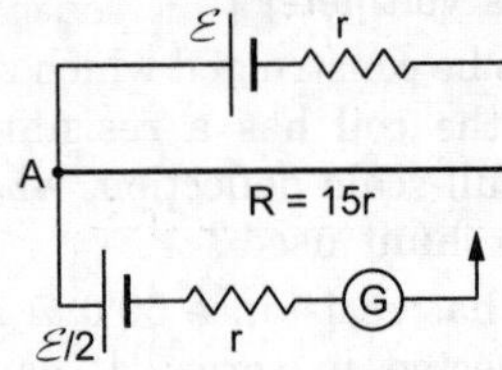

Figure 32-E29

57. Find the charge on the capacitor shown in figure (32-E30).

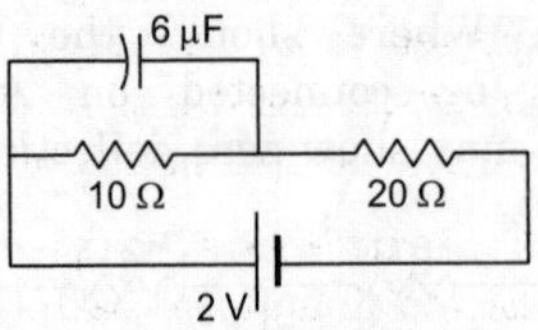

Figure 32-E30

58. (a) Find the current in the 20 Ω resistor shown in figure (32-E31). (b) If a capacitor of capacitance 4 μF is joined between the points A and B, what would be the electrostatic energy stored in it in steady state ?

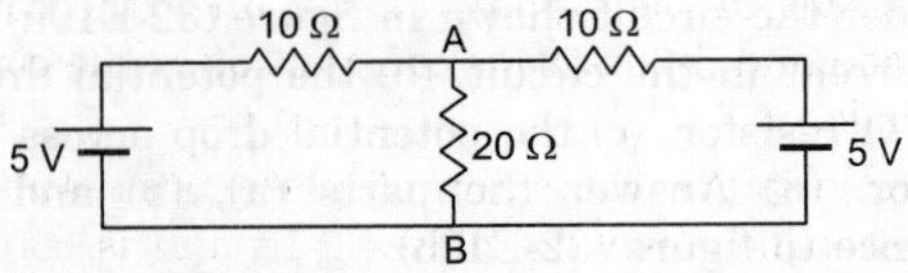

Figure 32-E31

59. Find the charges on the four capacitors of capacitances 1 μF, 2 μF, 3 μF and 4 μF shown in figure (32-E32).

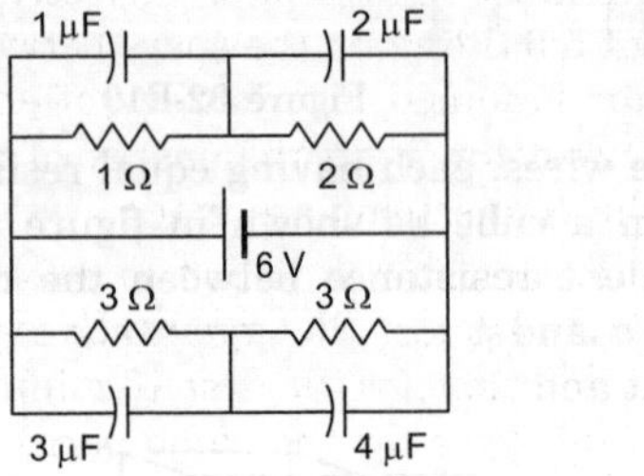

Figure 32-E32

60. Find the potential difference between the points A and B and between the points B and C of figure (32-E33) in steady state.

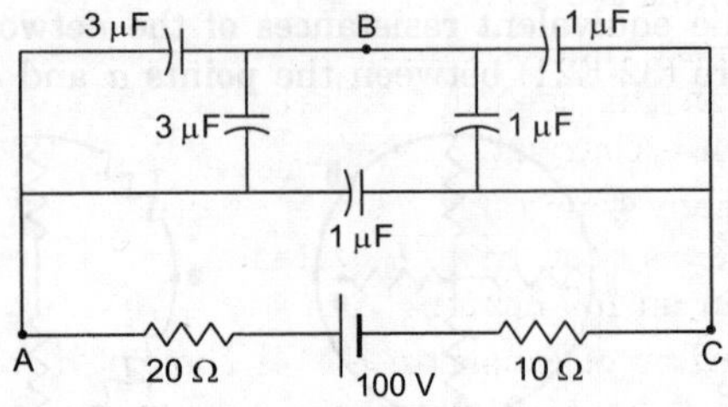

Figure 32-E33

61. A capacitance C, a resistance R and an emf $\mathcal{E}$ are connected in series at $t = 0$. What is the maximum value of (a) the potential difference across the resistor, (b) the current in the circuit, (c) the potential difference across the capacitor, (d) the energy stored in the capacitor, (e) the power delivered by the battery and (f) the power converted into heat.

62. A parallel-plate capacitor with plate area 20 cm^2 and plate separation 1·0 mm is connected to a battery. The resistance of the circuit is 10 kΩ. Find the time constant of the circuit.

63. A capacitor of capacitance 10 μF is connected to a battery of emf 2 V. It is found that it takes 50 ms for the charge on the capacitor to become 12·6 μC. Find the resistance of the circuit.

64. A 20 μF capacitor is joined to a battery of emf 6·0 V through a resistance of 100 Ω. Find the charge on the capacitor 2·0 ms after the connections are made.

65. The plates of a capacitor of capacitance 10 μF, charged to 60 μC, are joined together by a wire of resistance 10 Ω at $t = 0$. Find the charge on the capacitor in the circuit at (a) $t = 0$, (b) $t = 30$ μs, (c) $t = 120$ μs and (d) $t = 1{\cdot}0$ ms.

66. A capacitor of capacitance 8·0 μF is connected to a battery of emf 6·0 V through a resistance of 24 Ω. Find the current in the circuit (a) just after the connections are made and (b) one time constant after the connections are made.

67. A parallel-plate capacitor of plate area 40 cm^2 and separation between the plates 0·10 mm is connected to a battery of emf 2·0 V through a 16 Ω resistor. Find the electric field in the capacitor 10 ns after the connections are made.

68. A parallel-plate capacitor has plate area 20 cm^2, plate separation 1·0 mm and a dielectric slab of dielectric constant 5·0 filling up the space between the plates. This capacitor is joined to a battery of emf 6·0 V through a 100 kΩ resistor. Find the energy of the capacitor 8·9 μs after the connections are made.

69. A 100 μF capacitor is joined to a 24 V battery through a 1·0 MΩ resistor. Plot qualitative graphs (a) between current and time for the first 10 minutes and (b) between charge and time for the same period.

70. How many time constants will elapse before the current in a charging *RC* circuit drops to half of its initial value ? Answer the same question for a discharging *RC* circuit.

71. How many time constants will elapse before the charge on a capacitor falls to 0·1% of its maximum value in a discharging *RC* circuit ?

72. How many time constants will elapse before the energy stored in the capacitor reaches half of its equilibrium value in a charging *RC* circuit ?

73. How many time constants will elapse before the power delivered by the battery drops to half of its maximum value in an *RC* circuit ?

74. A capacitor of capacitance *C* is connected to a battery of emf $\mathcal{E}$ at $t = 0$ through a resistance *R*. Find the maximum rate at which energy is stored in the capacitor. When does the rate has this maximum value?

75. A capacitor of capacitance 12·0 μF is connected to a battery of emf 6·00 V and internal resistance 1·00 Ω through resistanceless leads. 12·0 μs after the connections are made, what will be (a) the current in the circuit, (b) the power delivered by the battery, (c) the power dissipated in heat and (d) the rate at which the energy stored in the capacitor is increasing.

76. A capacitance *C* charged to a potential difference *V* is discharged by connecting its plates through a resistance *R*. Find the heat dissipated in one time constant after the connections are made. Do this by calculating $\int i^2 R\, dt$ and also by finding the decrease in the energy stored in the capacitor.

77. By evaluating $\int i^2 R dt$, show that when a capacitor is charged by connecting it to a battery through a resistor, the energy dissipated as heat equals the energy stored in the capacitor.

78. A parallel-plate capacitor is filled with a dielectric material having resistivity ρ and dielectric constant *K*. The capacitor is charged and disconnected from the charging source. The capacitor is slowly discharged through the dielectric. Show that the time constant of the discharge is independent of all geometrical parameters like the plate area or separation between the plates. Find this time constant.

79. Find the charge on each of the capacitors 0·20 ms after the switch *S* is closed in figure (32-E34).

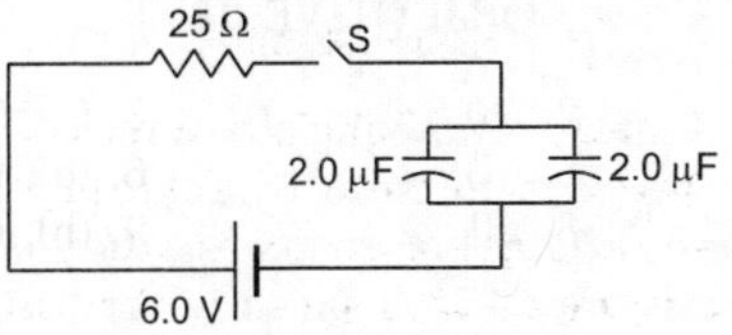

Figure 32-E34

80. The switch *S* shown in figure (32-E35) is kept closed for a long time and is then opened at $t = 0$. Find the current in the middle 10 Ω resistor at $t = 1·0$ ms.

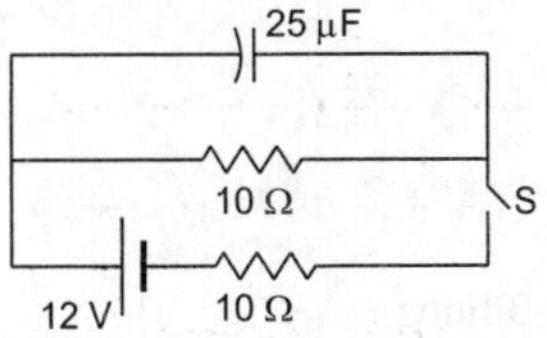

Figure 32-E35

81. A capacitor of capacitance 100 μF is connected across a battery of emf 6·0 V through a resistance of 20 kΩ for 4·0 s. The battery is then replaced by a thick wire. What will be the charge on the capacitor 4·0 s after the battery is disconnected ?

82. Consider the situation shown in figure (32-E36). The switch is closed at $t = 0$ when the capacitors are uncharged. Find the charge on the capacitor C_1 as a function of time *t*.

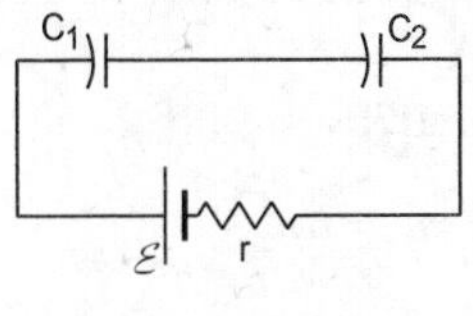

Figure 32-E36

83. A capacitor of capacitance *C* is given a charge *Q*. At $t = 0$, it is connected to an uncharged capacitor of equal capacitance through a resistance *R*. Find the charge on the second capacitor as a function of time.

84. A capacitor of capacitance *C* is given a charge *Q*. At $t = 0$, it is connected to an ideal battery of emf $\mathcal{E}$ through a resistance *R*. Find the charge on the capacitor at time *t*.

□

ANSWERS

OBJECTIVE I

1. (a) 2. (d) 3. (d) 4. (c) 5. (b) 6. (a)
7. (c) 8. (a) 9. (b) 10. (a) 11. (a) 12. (b)
13. (c) 14. (d) 15. (d) 16. (b)

OBJECTIVE II

1. (a) 2. (b), (c) 3. (c), (d)
4. (d) 5. (a) 6. (a), (d)
7. (a), (d) 8. all 9. (b), (d)

EXERCISES

1. (a) IT^{-1}, I, IT (b) 53 A
2. $3·2 \times 10^{-3}$ A
3. $6·0 \times 10^{-4}$ C
4. 300 C
5. 0·074 mm s^{-1}
6. $\pi \times 10^{-6}$ Ω m
7. 400 Ω
8. $3·2 \times 10^{4}$ s ≈ 8·9 hours
9. 0·6 km
10. $\frac{\rho l}{\pi ab}$
11. (a) $1·25 \times 10^{17}$ (b) $6·37 \times 10^{5}$ A/m^2
12. 8·5 mV m^{-1}
13. 25 V m^{-1}
14. 84·5°C
15. 0·4 V
16. 1·52 V, 0·07 Ω
17. 29 Ω
18. 0·6 Ω
19. (a) 0·3 A (b) 3 A
20. (a) 0·57 (b) 1 (c) 1·75
21. (a) $\frac{n_1\mathcal{E}}{R + \frac{n_1 r}{n_2}}$ (b) $rn_1 = Rn_2$
22. 10 mA
23. 1·6 A, 4·0 A
24. 0·15 A, 0·83 A
25. (a) 1·0 A (b) 0·67 A (c) 0·33 A
26. 12·5 Ω, 170 Ω
27. 45 Ω, 22·5 Ω
28. 4 mA in 20 kΩ resistor, 8 mA in 10 kΩ resistor and 12 mA in 100 kΩ resistor, 1340 V
29. 2 Ω
30. $r/3$
31. (a) 2·08 Ω (b) 3·33 Ω (c) 3·75 Ω
32. (a) 0·1 A (b) 0·3 A
33. zero in the upper 4 Ω resistor and 0·2 A in the rest two
34. 1 A through 10 Ω, 0·4 Ω through 20 Ω and 0·6 A through 30 Ω
35. 1 A in a and zero in b in both the circuits
36. (a) $\dfrac{\frac{\mathcal{E}_1}{R_1} + \frac{\mathcal{E}_2}{R_2}}{\frac{1}{R_1} + \frac{1}{R_2} + \frac{1}{R_3}}$ (b) same as (a)
37. 2 V, $i_1 = 1$ A, $i_2 = 0$, $i_3 = -1$ A
38. zero
39. zero
40. any value of R will do
41. (a) $r/2$ (b) $4r/5$
42. 0·4 A
43. (a) 1·2 A (b) 6 V (c) 12 V (d) same as the parts (a), (b) and (c)
44. $\frac{5}{6}r$
45. (a) $\frac{5}{8}r$ (b) $\frac{4}{3}r$ (c) r (d) $\frac{r}{4}$ (e) r
46. (a) 2 Ω (b) 1·5 A
47. (a) 0·1 A, 4·0 V (b) 0·08 A, 4·2 V
48. (a) 24 V (b) 28 V
49. 130 Ω
50. 6 V
51. $1·25 \times 10^{-2}$ Ω
52. 0·251 Ω
53. 16 cm from A
54. 4 Ω
55. (a) 6 V, 2 V (b) AD = 66·7 cm (c) zero (d) 6 V, – 1·5 V, no such point D exists.
56. (a) 320 cm (b) $\frac{3\mathcal{E}}{22r}$
57. 4 μC
58. (a) 0·2 A (b) 32 μJ
59. 2 μC, 8 μC, 9 μC and 12 μC
60. 25 V, 75 V
61. (a) $\mathcal{E}$ (b) $\frac{\mathcal{E}}{R}$ (c) $\mathcal{E}$ (d) $\frac{1}{2}C\mathcal{E}^2$ (e) $\frac{\mathcal{E}^2}{R}$ (f) $\frac{\mathcal{E}^2}{R}$
62. 0·18 μs
63. 5 kΩ
64. 76 μC
65. (a) 60 μC (b) 44 μC (c) 18 μC (d) 0·003 μC
66. (a) 0·25 A (b) 0·09 A
67. $1·7 \times 10^{4}$ V m^{-1}
68. $6·3 \times 10^{-10}$ J
70. 0·69 in both cases
71. 6·9

72. 1·23
73. 0·69
74. $\frac{\mathcal{E}^2}{4R}$, $CR \ln 2$
75. (a) 2·21 A (b) 13·2 W (c) 4·87 W (d) 8·37 W
76. $\frac{1}{2}(1-1/e^2)CV^2$
78. $\varepsilon_0 \rho K$
79. 10·37 μC
80. 11 mA
81. 70 μC
82. $q = \mathcal{E}C(1-e^{-t/rc})$, where $C = \frac{C_1C_2}{C_1+C_2}$.
83. $\frac{Q}{2}(1-e^{-2t/RC})$
84. $C\mathcal{E}(1-e^{-t/CR}) + Q e^{-t/CR}$

□

CHAPTER 33

THERMAL AND CHEMICAL EFFECTS OF ELECTRIC CURRENT

We have seen that an electric current through a resistor increases its thermal energy. Also, there are other situations in which an electric current can produce or absorb thermal energy. All these are termed as thermal effects of electric current. We shall study them in sections (33.1) to (33.6). The chemical effects, such as electrolysis, are discussed in sections (33.7) onwards.

33.1 JOULE'S LAWS OF HEATING

When there is an electric current in a resistor, the thermal energy of the resistor increases. If the potential difference between the ends of a resistor is V and a current i passes through it, the work done by the electric field on the free electrons in time t is

$$W = (\text{potential difference}) \times (\text{charge})$$
$$= V(it)$$
$$= (iR)\,(it) = i^2Rt. \qquad \ldots (33.1)$$

The work by the field is converted into thermal energy of the resistor through the collisions with the lattice. This thermal energy is generally referred to as the *heat produced in the resistor* and is denoted by H. (Strictly speaking, this energy is not heat as it does not correspond to any temperature difference. Because of the increased thermal energy, the temperature of the resistor may rise. It may then transfer "heat" to the surrounding.) It follows from equation (33.1) that

(a) the heat produced in a given resistor in a given time is proportional to the square of the current in it, i.e.,

$$H \propto i^2$$

(b) the heat produced in a given resistor by a given current is proportional to the time for which the current exists in it, i.e.,

$$H \propto t$$

(c) the heat produced in a resistor by a given current in a given time is proportional to its resistance, i.e.,

$$H \propto R.$$

The heating effects of an electric current were studied by James Prescott Joule and he arrived at the three laws stated above. These are thus known as *Joule's laws*.

Example 33.1

Find the heat developed in each of the three resistors shown in figure (33.1) in 1 minute.

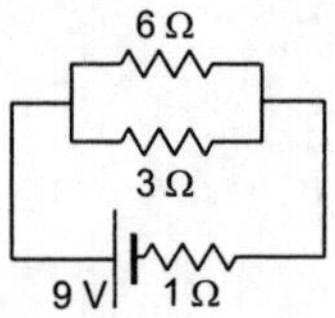

Figure 33.1

Solution : The equivalent resistance of 6 Ω and 3 Ω resistors is

$$\frac{(6\ \Omega)\times(3\ \Omega)}{6\ \Omega + 3\ \Omega} = 2\ \Omega.$$

This is connected in series with the 1 Ω resistor. The equivalent resistance of the circuit is

$$R = 2\ \Omega + 1\ \Omega = 3\ \Omega.$$

The current through the battery is

$$i = \frac{9\ \text{V}}{3\ \Omega} = 3\ \text{A}.$$

The current through the 1 Ω resistor is, therefore, 3 A. The heat developed in this resistor is

$$H = i^2Rt$$
$$= (3\ \text{A})^2 \times (1\ \Omega) \times (60\ \text{s}) = 540\ \text{J}.$$

The current through the 6 Ω resistor is

$$(3\ \text{A}) \times \frac{3\ \Omega}{6\ \Omega + 3\ \Omega} = 1\ \text{A}.$$

The heat developed in it

$$= (1\ \text{A})^2 \times (6\ \Omega) \times (60\ \text{s}) = 360\ \text{J}.$$

The current through the 3 Ω resistor is 3 A – 1 A = 2 A. The heat developed in it

$$= (2\ \mathrm{A})^2 \times (3\ \Omega) \times (60\ \mathrm{s}) = 720\ \mathrm{J}.$$

33.2 VERIFICATION OF JOULE'S LAWS

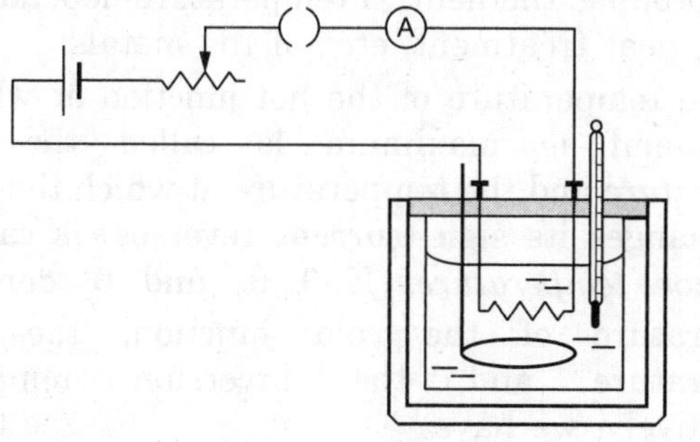

Figure 33.2

Figure (33.2) shows the apparatus and the connections. K-oil is taken in a copper calorimeter provided with a nonconducting lid and a stirrer. A resistor is dipped in the oil. It is joined to the external circuit through the leads coming out of the lid of the calorimeter. A thermometer is provided to measure the temperature of the oil. The calorimeter is called *Joule's calorimeter*.

$H \propto i^2$

The external circuit consists of a battery, a rheostat and a plug key in series with the resistor. An ammeter is also connected in the circuit to measure the current. The temperature θ_1 of the K-oil is noted. The plug key is closed to pass a constant current through the circuit for a known time t. The value of the current i_1 is measured by the ammeter. The liquid is stirred continuously and the final temperature θ_2 is noted. Thus, the rise in temperature $\Delta\theta_1 = \theta_2 - \theta_1$ is calculated.

The system is allowed to cool down to room temperature. The resistance of the rheostat is changed and the key is closed. The current i_2 is measured by the ammeter and is passed for the same time t. The rise in temperature $\Delta\theta_2$ is found as above.

The heat produced in the resistor is used to increase the temperature of the K-oil. Thus, the heat produced is proportional to the rise in temperature. It is found that

$$\frac{\Delta\theta_1}{\Delta\theta_2} = \frac{i_1^2}{i_2^2}.$$

This shows that $\Delta\theta \propto i^2$

or, $$H \propto i^2.$$

$H \propto t$

The arrangement described above can also be used to verify the second law, $H \propto t$. A current i is passed through the resistor and the temperature is noted at regular time intervals. It is found that the temperature rises uniformly, i.e., it increases by equal amounts in equal times. This shows that equal amounts of heat are produced in equal time intervals. Thus, the heat produced is proportional to the time.

$H \propto R$

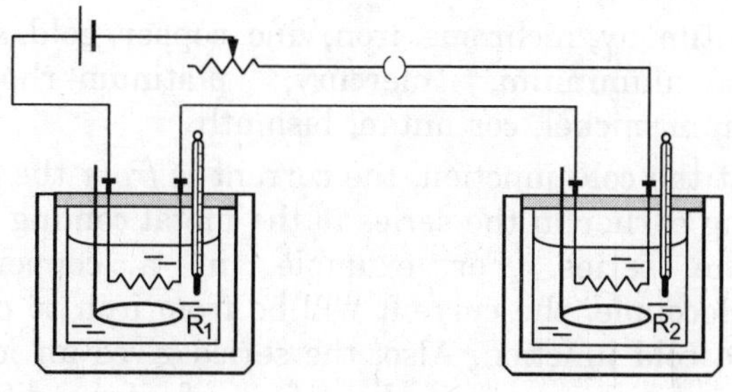

Figure 33.3

To verify this law, two Joule's calorimeters are taken (figure 33.3). Equal amounts of K-oil are taken in the two calorimeters. Different resistances R_1 and R_2 are dipped in the K-oil and the two are joined in series. The system is connected to a battery, a rheostat and a plug key. The initial temperatures of the two calorimeters are noted and a current is passed for some time. The temperatures of the two calorimeters are noted at the end. Let $\Delta\theta_1$ be the rise in the temperature of the first calorimeter and $\Delta\theta_2$ be the rise in the temperature of the second calorimeter. The heat produced in each resistor is proportional to the rise in the temperature of the corresponding calorimeter. It is found that

$$\frac{\Delta\theta_1}{\Delta\theta_2} = \frac{R_1}{R_2}$$

or, $$\Delta\theta \propto R$$

or, $$H \propto R.$$

33.3 SEEBECK EFFECT

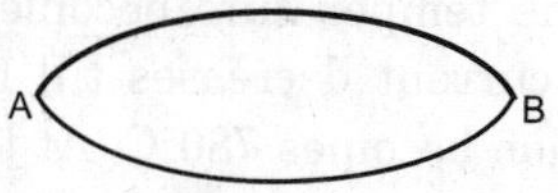

Figure 33.4

Figure (33.4) shows two metallic strips, made of different metals and joined at the ends to form a loop. If the junctions are kept at different temperatures, there is an electric current in the loop. This effect is called the *Seebeck effect* and the emf developed is called the *Seebeck emf* or *thermo-emf*.

The magnitude and the direction of the emf depend on the metals and the temperatures of the hot and cold junctions. Such a combination of two metals is called a *thermocouple.*

Thermoelectric Series

For given temperatures of hot and cold junctions, the direction of the current in a thermocouple depends on the metals chosen. Metals are arranged in a particular sequence which may be used to predict the direction of the current in the temperature range 0°C to 100°C. This sequence known as the *thermoelectric series*, is as follows:

antimony, nichrome, iron, zinc, copper, gold, silver, lead, aluminium, mercury, platinum–rhodium, platinum, nickel, costantan, bismuth.

At the cold junction, the current is *from* the metal coming earlier in the series *to* the metal coming latter in the series. For example, in a copper–iron thermocouple, the current will be from iron to copper at the cold junction. Also, the series gives an idea of the relative magnitude of emf for different thermocouples. Farther apart two metals lie in the series, larger is the emf produced.

Neutral and Inversion Temperature

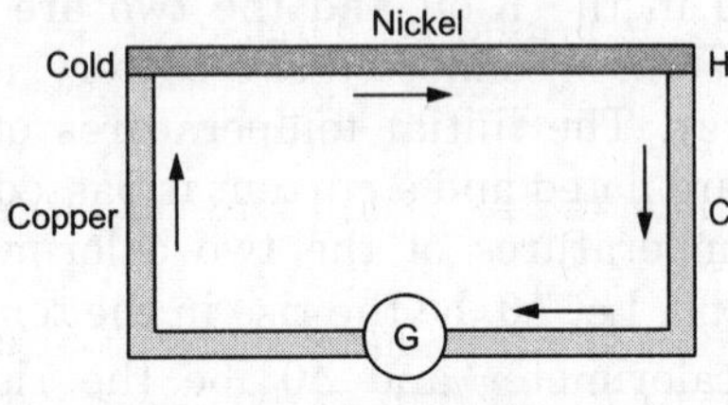

Figure 33.5

Figure (33.5) shows a copper–nickel thermocouple. A sensitive galvanometer is connected in series to measure the current. Suppose one of the junctions is kept at a fixed low temperature 0°C and the other is gradually heated. There will be a current in the circuit as shown in the figure. At the cold junction it is from copper to nickel and at the hot junction it is from nickel to copper. As the temperature of the hot junction is gradually increased, the magnitude of the current increases till the temperature becomes nearly 390°C. After this, the current decreases till the temperature of the hot junction becomes 780°C. At this temperature the current becomes zero. If the hot junction is heated further, the direction of the current is reversed and the magnitude increases.

If the cold junction of the copper–nickel thermocouple is not at 0°C but say at 10°C, the current will be again maximum when the hot junction is at 390°C. But the inversion of the direction of the current will take place at 770°C instead of 780°C. As the current is proportional to the emf developed, the above observations also indicate the behaviour of the thermo-emf.

Copper and nickel were taken above only as an example. The behaviour of any other thermocouple will be, in general, similar. The numeric values will, of course, be different. Also even for a copper–nickel thermocouple, the neutral temperature depends on the purity, heat treatment, etc., of the metals.

The temperature of the hot junction at which the thermo-emf is maximum is called the *neutral temperature* and the temperature at which the thermo-emf changes its sign (current reverses) is called the *inversion temperature.* If θ_c, θ_n and θ_i denote the temperature of the cold junction, the neutral temperature and the inversion temperature respectively, we have

$$\theta_n - \theta_c = \theta_i - \theta_n. \qquad \text{... (33.2)}$$

At this stage, let us explain the sign convention. The thermo-emf developed in a thermocouple of metals A and B is denoted by $\mathcal{E}_{AB}$ and is taken to be positive if the direction of the current is from A to B at the hot junction.

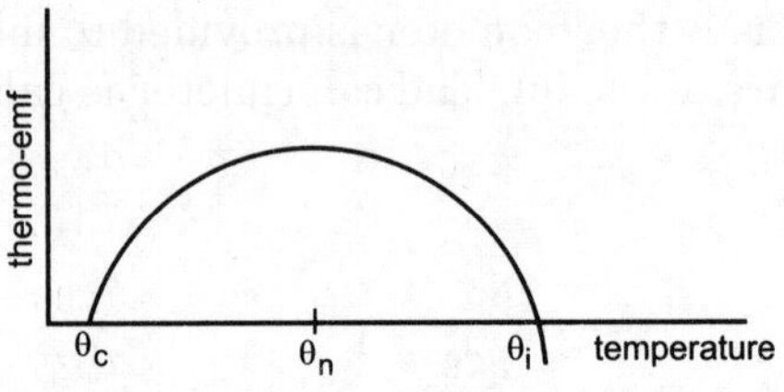

Figure 33.6

Figure (33.6) shows graphically the variation in thermo-emf as the temperature of the hot junction changes. If the cold junction is at 0°C and the hot junction at θ (in Celsius), the thermo-emf depends on the temperature as

$$\mathcal{E}_{AB} = a_{AB}\theta + \frac{1}{2} b_{AB}\theta^2 \qquad \text{... (33.3)}$$

where a_{AB} and b_{AB} are constants for the pair of metals A and B.

This gives

$$\frac{d\mathcal{E}_{AB}}{d\theta} = a_{AB} + b_{AB}\theta. \qquad \text{... (33.4)}$$

The quantity $\frac{d\mathcal{E}_{AB}}{d\theta}$ is called *thermoelectric power* at temperature θ.

The emf is maximum when $\frac{d\mathcal{E}_{AB}}{d\theta} = 0$ or, $\theta = -\frac{a_{AB}}{b_{AB}}$.

This is the neutral temperature. The emf becomes zero at $\theta = -2a_{AB}/b_{AB}$. This is the inversion temperature.

Example 33.2

The cold junction of a thermocouple is maintained at 10°C. No thermo-emf is developed when the hot junction is maintained at 530°C. Find the neutral temperature.

Solution : Clearly, 530°C is the inversion temperature θ_i of the couple. If θ_n be the neutral temperature and θ_c be the temperature of the cold junction,

$$\theta_i - \theta_n = \theta_n - \theta_c$$

or, $$\theta_n = \frac{\theta_i + \theta_c}{2} = \frac{530°C + 10°C}{2} = 270°C.$$

Table (33.1) gives the values of a and b for some of the metals with lead. Note that there is no neutral temperature or inversion temperature above 0°C for the thermocouple if a and b have the same sign.

Table 33.1 : *Coefficients a and b for thermocouples*

Metal with lead (Pb)	a $\mu V°C^{-1}$	b $\mu V°C^{-2}$
Aluminium	– 0·47	0·003
Bismuth	– 43·7	– 0·47
Copper	2·76	0·012
Gold	2·90	0·0093
Iron	16·6	– 0·030
Nickel	19·1	– 0·030
Platinum	– 1·79	– 0·035
Silver	2·50	0·012
Steel	10·8	– 0·016

Law of Intermediate Metal

Suppose $\mathcal{E}_{AB}$ = thermo-emf between metals A and B

$\mathcal{E}_{AC}$ = thermo-emf between metals A and C

and $\mathcal{E}_{BC}$ = thermo-emf between metals B and C.

Also, suppose the temperatures of the cold junctions are the same in the three cases and the temperatures of the hot junctions are also the same in the three cases.

Then, $$\mathcal{E}_{AB} = \mathcal{E}_{AC} - \mathcal{E}_{BC}. \quad \text{... (33.5)}$$

This law is known as the *law of intermediate metal.*

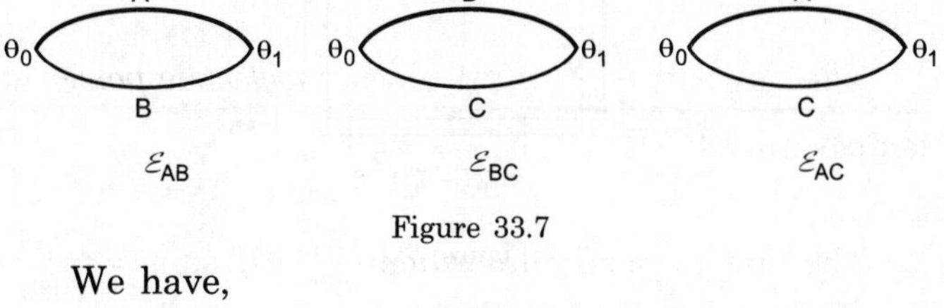

Figure 33.7

We have,

$$\mathcal{E}_{AB} = a_{AB}\theta + \frac{1}{2}b_{AB}\theta^2$$

$$\mathcal{E}_{BC} = a_{BC}\theta + \frac{1}{2}b_{BC}\theta^2$$

$$\mathcal{E}_{AC} = a_{AC}\theta + \frac{1}{2}b_{AC}\theta^2.$$

Equation (33.5) gives

$$a_{AB} = a_{AC} - a_{BC} \text{ and } b_{AB} = b_{AC} - b_{BC}.$$

Table (33.1) may, therefore, be used to find the values of a and b for any pair of metals listed.

Example 33.3

Using table (33.1), find a and b coefficients for a copper–iron thermocouple.

Solution :

$$a_{Cu,\,Fe} = a_{Cu,\,Pb} - a_{Fe,\,Pb}$$
$$= 2·76\ \mu V°C^{-1} - 16·6\ \mu V°C^{-1} = -13·8\ \mu V°C^{-1}.$$

$$b_{Cu,\,Fe} = b_{Cu,\,Pb} - b_{Fe,\,Pb}$$
$$= 0·012\ \mu V°C^{-2} + 0·030\ \mu V°C^{-2} = 0·042\ \mu V°C^{-2}.$$

Law of Intermediate Temperatures

Let $\mathcal{E}_{\theta_1,\theta_2}$ denote the thermo-emf of a given thermocouple when the temperatures of the junctions are maintained at θ_1 and θ_2. Then,

$$\mathcal{E}_{\theta_1,\theta_2} = \mathcal{E}_{\theta_1,\theta_3} + \mathcal{E}_{\theta_3,\theta_2}. \quad \text{... (33.6)}$$

This is known as the *law of intermediate temperature.*

The two laws given by equations (33.5) and (33.6) show that we can include any metal wire or a galvanometer, etc. in the thermocouple circuit without changing the emf in the circuit.

33.4 PELTIER EFFECT

Suppose the two junctions of a thermocouple are initially at the same temperature and an electric current is passed through the circuit by using an external battery. It is observed that heat is produced at one junction and is absorbed at the other. Thus, one junction is warmed up and the other is cooled down due to the currents through the junctions. It is reverse of the Seebeck effect and is called the *Peltier effect.* If the direction of the current is reversed, the cooling and warming are also reversed. This means, the junction which was originally warmed up, now cools down and vice-versa. The heat absorbed or liberated at the junction is proportional to the charge passed through the junction. If an amount ΔH of heat is produced or absorbed when a charge ΔQ is passed through the junction, we define *Peltier emf* as

$$\Pi_{AB} = \frac{\Delta H}{\Delta Q} = \frac{\text{Peltier heat}}{\text{charge transferred}}.$$

The Peltier emf Π_{AB} across a junction of two metals A and B is taken as positive if heat is absorbed by the junction when there is an electric current from A to B through the junction. When two different metals are joined at a point, this much emf is developed across the junction.

The heat developed in Peltier effect should not be confused with the Joule heat when a current is passed through a resistor. Joule heat always warms up the resistor whatever be the direction of the current. But one has both Peltier heating and Peltier cooling of the junction depending on the direction of the current.

Another difference is that the Peltier heat in a given time is proportional to the current through the junction whereas the Joule heat is proportional to the square of the current,

$$H_{Peltier} \propto i, \qquad H_{Joule} \propto i^2.$$

Also, the Peltier heating or cooling is observed only at a junction, whereas the Joule heating is throughout the resistor.

33.5 THOMSON EFFECT

If a metallic wire has a nonuniform temperature and a current is passed through it, heat may be absorbed or produced in different sections of the wire. This heat is over and above the Joule heat i^2Rt and is called the *Thomson heat*. The effect itself is called the *Thomson effect*.

Thomson heat, produced or absorbed in a small section of a given wire, is proportional to the charge passed through the section and the temperature difference between the ends of the section.

If a charge ΔQ is passed through a small section of the wire having a temperature difference ΔT between the ends, the Thomson heat is

$$\Delta H = \sigma(\Delta Q)\,(\Delta T)$$

where σ is a constant for a given metal at a given temperature. The quantity

$$\sigma \Delta T = \frac{\Delta H}{\Delta Q} = \frac{\text{Thomson heat}}{\text{charge transferred}}$$

is called the *Thomson emf.*

In fact, this much amount of emf is produced when the ends of the section of the wire are maintained at different temperatures.

The constant σ is called the *Thomson coefficient.* It is taken to be positive if heat is absorbed when a current is passed from the low-temperature end to the high-temperature end. Copper, silver, zinc, antimony, cadmium, etc., have positive σ. Iron, cobalt, nickel, bismuth, platinum, etc., have negative σ. In these metals heat is absorbed when current is passed from hotter end to the colder end. In lead, σ is almost zero.

33.6 EXPLANATION OF SEEBECK, PELTIER AND THOMSON EFFECTS

The density of free electrons is different in different metals. When two different metals are joined to form a junction, the electrons tend to diffuse from the side with higher concentration to the side with lower concentration. This produces an emf across the junction. This emf is the Peltier emf. If a current is forced through the junction, positive or negative work is done on the charge carriers depending on the direction of the current. Accordingly, thermal energy is either produced or absorbed.

If the temperature of a metal piece is not uniform everywhere, density of free electrons varies inside the metal. The electrons tend to diffuse from the higher-concentration regions to the lower-concentration regions. This gives rise to an emf between the hot and the cold parts of the metal. This emf is the Thomson emf. If a current is forced through a wire having nonuniform temperature, positive or negative work is done on the charge carriers depending on the direction of the current. Accordingly, thermal energy is either produced or absorbed.

The density of free electrons in a metal depends on the temperature. Hence, the Peltier emf developed across a junction depends on the temperature of the junction. In a thermocouple, there are two junctions. If these junctions are maintained at the same temperature, the Peltier emf's developed across the two junctions balance each other and there is no net Peltier emf in the loop. If the junctions are at different temperatures, the emf's developed across the junctions are different and there is a net Peltier emf in the loop. Also, when the junctions of a thermocouple are kept at different temperatures, each of the two metal pieces has nonuniform temperature. Thus, a Thomson emf is developed across its ends. The emf's are different for the two metals and hence there is a net Thomson emf in the loop because of this effect. The actual emf developed in a thermocouple loop is the algebraic sum of the net Peltier emf and the net Thomson emf developed in the loop.

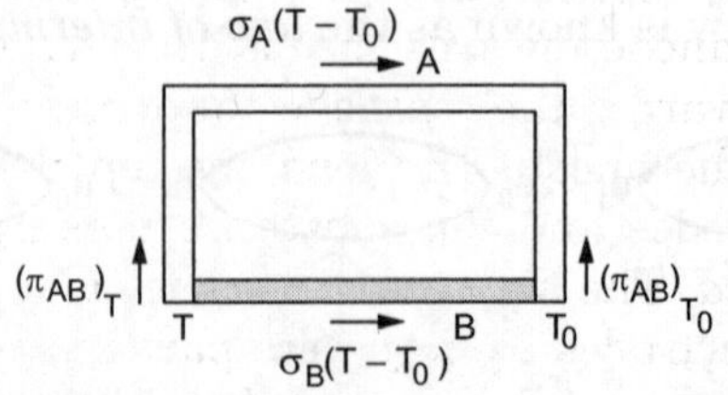

Figure 33.8

Referring to figure (33.8), we can write the thermo-emf $\mathcal{E}_{AB}$ in the loop as

$$\mathcal{E}_{AB} = (\Pi_{AB})_T - (\Pi_{AB})_{T_0} + (T - T_0)(\sigma_A - \sigma_B). \quad \ldots \ (33.6)$$

Thus, Seebeck emf is a combination of two Peltier emf's and two Thomson emf's.

33.7 ELECTROLYSIS

Several liquids are found to be good conductors of electricity. Solutions of inorganic salts in water, dilute acids and bases are examples of conducting liquids. Such a liquid is called an *electrolyte* and the vessel with the electrolyte is called an *electrolytic cell.* The mechanism of electric conduction in electrolytes is quite different from that in metals. Let us understand the process with a specific example.

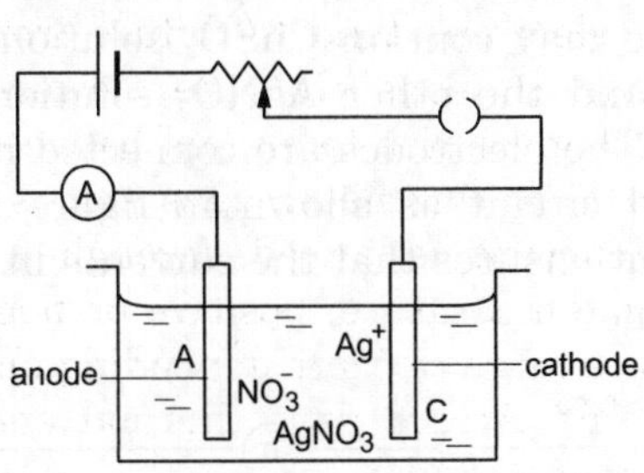

Figure 33.9

Let us take a solution of silver nitrate ($AgNO_3$) in an electrolytic cell and immerse two silver rods in it (figure 33.9). Electric current is passed through the solution by connecting the rods to an external battery. The current enters the solution through the rod A, called the *anode* and it leaves the solution through the rod C, called the *cathode.* These rods are collectively called *electrodes.* We find that as time passes, silver gets deposited on the cathode C and an equal amount of silver is removed from the anode A.

A fraction of the molecules of the dissolved $AgNO_3$ are separated in two parts, Ag^+ and NO_3^-, each of which has electric charge. These are called *ions.* An ion with positive charge is called *cation* and an ion with negative charge is called *anion.* Here Ag^+ is the cation and NO_3^- is the anion. These ions move freely in the solution. When a battery is connected to the electrodes, electric field is produced in the solution from the anode towards the cathode. Thus, the cations move towards the cathode and the anions move towards the anode. The ions give up their charges at the electrodes and the substance making up the ions is *liberated.* The liberated substance may get deposited on the electrodes or may take part in some secondary chemical reaction. In case of $AgNO_3$, the Ag^+ ions (cation) move to the cathode, the charge is given up there and the silver atoms are deposited on the cathode. In fact an Ag^+ ion receives an electron from the cathode to become neutral Ag atom,

$$Ag^+ + e = Ag.$$

The NO_3^- ion (anion) moves to the anode and gives its extra electron to it. The NO_3^- ion is converted to NO_3,

$$NO_3^- = NO_3 + e.$$

The NO_3 so formed reacts with a silver atom of the anode to form $AgNO_3$ which gets dissolved in the solution. This way, silver is continuously removed from the anode and deposited on the cathode with the concentration of the electrolyte remaining unchanged. The movement of cations (positive charge) towards the cathode and anions (negative charge) towards the anode make the current in the electrolyte.

The electron given up by an anion to the anode is passed through the battery back to the cathode which has supplied one electron to the cation. This way, the potential difference between the electrodes is maintained. Also, the number of electrons passed through the battery is equal to the number of electrons absorbed or released at each electrode. In other words, the charge passed through the circuit is equal to the charge released at each electrode.

When a current passes through an electrolyte, chemical changes occur in the electrolyte and substances are liberated at the electrodes. This process is called *electrolysis.*

33.8 FARADAY'S LAWS OF ELECTROLYSIS

After systematically studying electrolysis, Faraday discovered two laws:

(a) The mass of a substance liberated at an electrode is proportional to the charge passing through the electrolyte.

(b) The mass of a substance liberated at an electrode by a given amount of charge is proportional to the chemical equivalent of the substance.

If an electric current i is passed through an electrolyte for a time t, the amount of charge passed is $Q = it$. According to the first law, the amount of the substance liberated at an electrode is

$$m \propto Q \quad \ldots \ (i)$$

or, $$m \propto it$$

or, $$m = Zit \quad \ldots \ (33.7)$$

where Z is a constant for the substance being liberated. The constant Z is called the *electrochemical equivalent* (ECE) of the substance. The SI unit of ECE is kilogram coulomb^{-1} written as kg C^{-1}.

The chemical equivalent of a substance is equal to its relative atomic mass divided by its valency. Relative atomic mass of a substance is the ratio of the mass of its atom to the 1/12 of the mass of a ^{12}C atom. The relative atomic mass of silver is 108 and its valency is 1. Thus, the chemical equivalent of silver is 108. The relative atomic mass and valency of copper are 63·5 and 2 respectively. The chemical equivalent is, therefore, 31·75. For oxygen, the chemical equivalent is 16/2 = 8.

If E denotes the chemical equivalent of a substance being liberated at an electrode, from the second law,

$$m \propto E.$$

Combining with (i) it gives

$$m \propto EQ.$$

or,
$$m = \frac{1}{K} EQ \qquad \dots (33.8)$$

where K is a universal constant having the value $9{\cdot}6485 \times 10^{7}\ \mathrm{C\ kg^{-1}}$.

Example 33.4

Calculate the electric current required to deposit 0·972 g *of chromium in three hours. ECE of chromium is* 0·00018 g C^{-1}.

Solution : We have

$$m = Zit$$

or,
$$0{\cdot}972\ \mathrm{g} = (0{\cdot}00018\ \mathrm{g\ C^{-1}})\ i\ (3 \times 3600\ \mathrm{s})$$

or,
$$i = \frac{0{\cdot}972}{0{\cdot}00018 \times 3 \times 3600}\ \mathrm{A} = 0{\cdot}50\ \mathrm{A}.$$

Verification of Faraday's Laws

1st law

An electrolytic cell is connected to a battery, a rheostat, a key and an ammeter in series as in figure (33.9). The cathode is cleaned, dried, weighed and then inserted in the electrolytic cell. A constant current i_1 is passed for a measured time t. The current is measured by the ammeter. Slight adjustment of the rheostat may be necessary to keep the current constant. The cathode is taken out, washed without rubbing in gently-flowing water and is dried. It is weighed again and the mass m_1 of the deposit is obtained. The cathode is reinserted in the cell and the rheostat position is changed. This allows a different current i_2 when the circuit is completed. This current is passed for the same time t and the mass m_2 of the deposit is obtained. It is found that

$$\frac{m_1}{m_2} = \frac{i_1}{i_2}.$$

Thus,
$$m \propto i. \qquad \dots (i)$$

Similarly, two experiments are done with the same current but for different times t_1 and t_2. If the masses of the deposits are m_1' and m_2' respectively, it is found that

$$\frac{m_1'}{m_2'} = \frac{t_1}{t_2}$$

or,
$$m \propto t. \qquad \dots (ii)$$

From (i) and (ii),

$$m \propto it$$

or,
$$m \propto Q.$$

So, the first law is verified.

2nd law

To verify the second law, one can take two electrolytic cells containing different electroytes. To be specific, one may contain $CuSO_4$ solution with copper electrodes and the other $AgNO_3$ solution with silver electrodes. The electrodes are connected in series with an external circuit as shown in figure (33.10). This arrangement ensures that the currents in the two cells are the same.

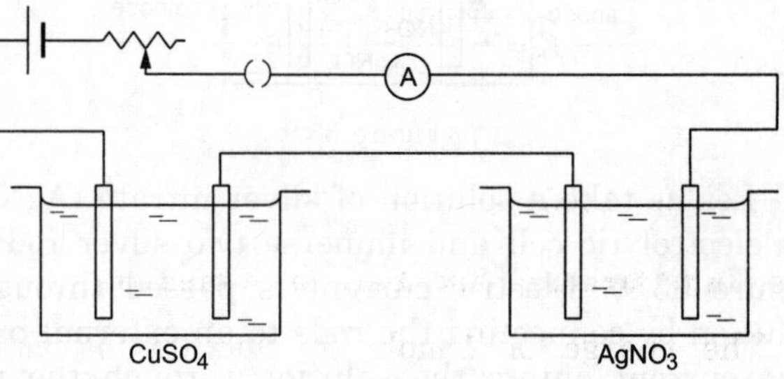

Figure 33.10

The cathodes are cleaned, dried, weighed and then inserted in the respective cells. The current is passed for some time and then the cathodes are taken out. They are washed without rubbing in gently-flowing water, dried and weighed. Thus, the masses of the deposits are obtained. If m_1 and m_2 are the masses of copper and silver deposited, it is found that

$$\frac{m_1}{m_2} = \frac{E_1}{E_2}$$

where E_1 and E_2 are the chemical equivalents of copper and silver respectively. So, the second law is verified.

Faraday's Laws and Ionic Theory

Faraday's laws of electrolysis can be easily understood in terms of the ionic character for the conduction in an electrolyte. Suppose a substance of valency v is liberated at an electrode. Its ion will carry a positive or a negative charge of magnitude ve. To neutralise this ion, the battery has to supply or take up a charge ve. If the total charge passing through the battery is Q, the number of ions neutralised is

$$N = \frac{Q}{ve}$$

Suppose, the relative atomic mass of the substance is A. Now 1/12 of the mass of a ^{12}C atom is one atomic mass unit (amu) and has the value $1{\cdot}6605 \times 10^{-27}$ kg. Let us denote this quantity as m_u. The mass of an atom of the substance is then

$$m_a = A\, m_u.$$

This can also be taken as the mass of an ion because the difference in ionic mass and atomic mass is negligible. The mass of the N ions neutralised at the electrode is

$$m = N A\, m_u$$

$$= \frac{Q}{ve} A\, m_u.$$

But $\frac{A}{v}$ is the chemical equivalent E, so that

$$m = \frac{1}{e/m_u} EQ.$$

Thus, $m \propto Q$ and $m \propto E$ which are Faraday's laws.

The constant

$$\frac{e}{m_u} = K = \frac{1{\cdot}6022 \times 10^{-19}\ \text{C}}{1{\cdot}6605 \times 10^{-27}\ \text{kg}}$$

$$= 9{\cdot}6485 \times 10^{7}\ \text{C kg}^{-1}$$

as mentioned earlier.

The Unit "faraday" and Faraday Constant

The charge of 1 mole of electrons is called 1 faraday. So faraday is a unit of charge and its relation with coulomb is

$$1\ \text{faraday} = (1{\cdot}6022 \times 10^{-19}\ \text{C}) \times (6{\cdot}022 \times 10^{23})$$

$$= 96485\ \text{C}.$$

The quantity *charge per mole of electrons* is called Faraday constant and is denoted by the symbol F. Thus,

$$F = 96485\ \text{C mol}^{-1}$$

$$= 1\ \text{faraday mol}^{-1}.$$

Suppose, 1 faraday of charge is passed through an electrolyte. The amount of electrons taken up or supplied at an electrode is 1 mole. Since each ion takes up or gives up v electrons, the amount of ions liberated is $\frac{1}{v}$ moles. The mass of 1 mole of the substance is A gram (A = relative atomic mass), so that the mass of these ions is $\frac{A}{v}$ gram = E gram. The amount E gram of a substance is called 1 gram-equivalent of this substance. So, 1 *faraday of charge liberates one gram-equivalent of any substance in electrolysis.*

33.9 VOLTAMETER OR COULOMBMETER

An electrolytic cell can be used to measure electric currents or amounts of charge. The current to be measured is passed through the electrolytic cell for a known time t. If the mass deposited in time t is m and the electrochemical equivalent of the material is Z,

$$m = Zit$$

or,

$$i = \frac{m}{Zt}.$$

The charge passed is $it = m/Z$.

When an electrolytic cell is used to measure electric current it is called a *voltameter* or a *coulombmeter*. Quite often, the word voltameter is used to mean just the electrolytic cell whatever be its use.

A copper voltameter may be used for routine laboratory measurements. The electrolyte is $CuSO_4$ solution in water in the ratio of about 1 : 4 by weight. A copper plate placed in the middle serves as the cathode and two connected copper plates on the two sides of the cathode are used as the anode. In this arrangement, shown schematically in figure (33.11), both sides of the cathode plate receive the deposit.

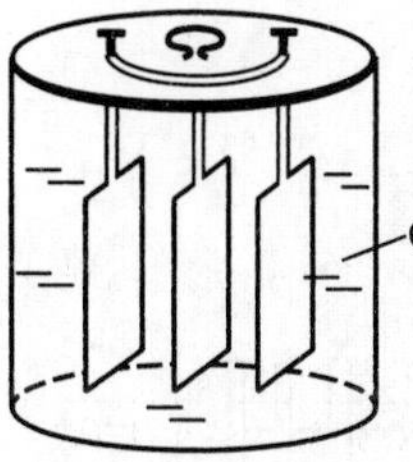

Figure 33.11

A silver voltameter (figure 33.12) is used when high accuracy is needed. The electrolyte is silver nitrate solution in water in the ratio of 1 : 5 to 1 : 6. The solution is taken in a platinum cup. The cup itself acts as the cathode. The anode is made of a silver rod placed in the middle. A porcelain cup which is porous to the electrolyte surrounds the anode. This prevents the impurities in the anode to reach the cathode.

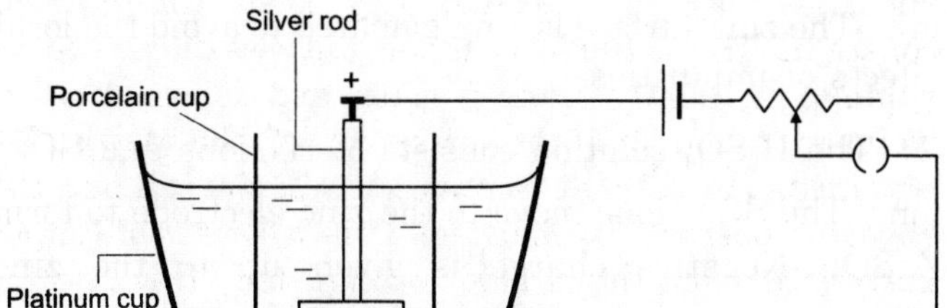

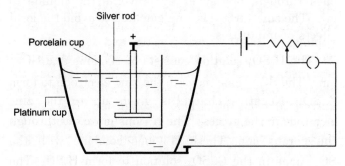

Figure 33.12

Because of the high accuracy attainable, silver voltameters are used in laboratories for standardization purposes.

33.10 PRIMARY AND SECONDARY CELLS

When a metal electrode is dipped in an electrolyte, negative or positive ions tend to go from the electrolyte to the electrode. Thus, an emf is produced between the electrolyte and the electrode. If two electrodes of different metals are dipped in an electrolyte, the emf's produced at the two electrodes are different and there is a net emf between the electrodes. This forms a *voltaic cell*, also called simply a *cell*. The electrode at higher potential is called the *positive electrode* and that at lower potential is called the *negative electrode*. Terminals connected to these electrodes are called positive and negative terminals respectively. This is the basic theory of a voltaic cell in which electrolysis is used to produce an emf between two terminals.

A cell is called *primary* if it is used only for discharge. The current leaves the cell at the positive terminal, goes through the external circuit and enters the cell at the negative terminal. A *secondary* cell on the other hand can be discharged as well as charged; the current can go both ways in the cell.

33.11 PRIMARY CELLS

Daniell Cell

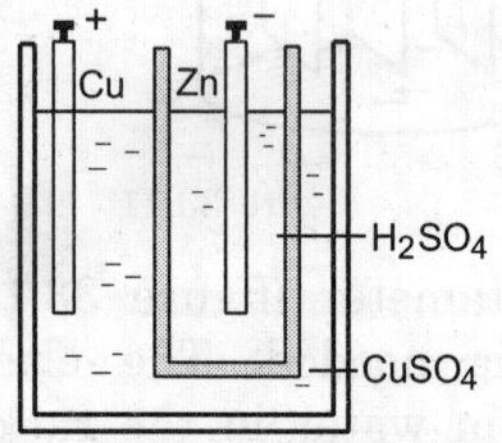

Figure 33.13

In the simplest form, a Daniell cell consists of a zinc electrode in a dilute H_2SO_4 solution and a copper electrode in $CuSO_4$ solution. The two solutions are separated by a porous cup which allows any gas to pass through, but generally prevents the liquids to mix. The zinc surface is amalgamated to avoid the local effects of impurities.

The H_2SO_4 solution consists of H^+ ions and SO_4^{--} ions. The SO_4^{--} ions move to the zinc electrode to form $ZnSO_4$. Negative charge is given up to the zinc electrode in the process. The H^+ ions move out through the porous cup. These H^+ ions combine with the SO_4^{--} ions in the $CuSO_4$ solution to form H_2SO_4. The Cu^{++} ions in the outer vessel move towards the copper electrode. Copper is deposited on the copper electrode and positive charge is given up to this electrode in the process. This arrangement prevents hydrogen from collecting near the anode. Any hydrogen collected near the anode may stop the function of the cell. This problem is called the *polarization* of the cell.

Because of the chemical actions described, the positive charge is accumulated on the copper electrode and negative charge on the zinc electrode. Thus an emf is produced. The zinc electrode works as the negative electrode and the copper electrode works as the positive electrode.

Daniel cell is used when a continuous current is needed. The emf of a Daniell cell is around 1·09 V and its internal resistance is around 1 Ω.

Leclanche Cell

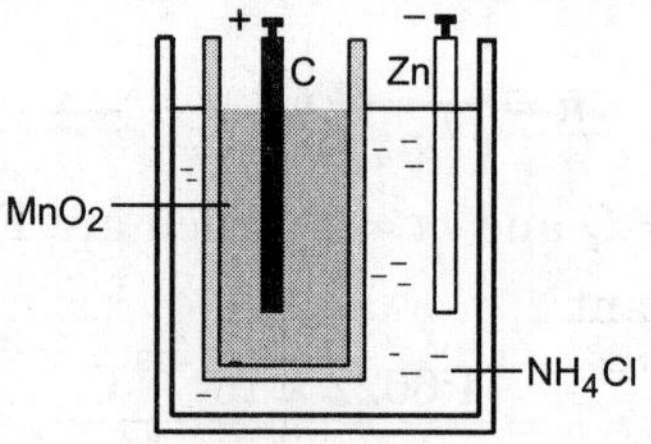

Figure 33.14

A Leclanche cell has a carbon and a zinc electrode in a solution of NH_4Cl. The carbon electrode is packed in a porous cup containing MnO_2. The zinc electrode forms the negative terminal and the carbon forms the positive terminal. When a current passes through the cell, the Cl^- ions combine with zinc and the NH_4^+ ions move towards the carbon electrode. The NH_4^+ separates into ammonia (NH_3) and hydrogen (H^{4}). The H^+ ion enters the porous cup. The positive charge is given to the carbon electrode. The hydrogen reacts with MnO_2 present there to form Mn_2O_3 and water. Thus, MnO_2 prevents hydrogen from collecting on the anode which could otherwise stop the cell's function.

The depolarizing action (absorbing hydrogen in some chemical reaction) is quite slow in Leclanche cell. Thus, if the cell is used continuously, hydrogen starts collecting at the carbon electrode and the cell is not able to supply enough current. Thus, the cell is used when intermittent currents are needed. Its emf is about 1·5 V.

Dry Cell

This is a special kind of Leclanche cell in which both NH_4Cl and MnO_2 are prepared in the form of a paste. The paste is contained in a zinc container which itself works as the negative electrode. The whole system is sealed so that the paste does not dry up. The internal resistance of a dry cell is very small, of the order of 0·1 Ω.

33.12 SECONDARY CELL : LEAD ACCUMULATOR

In a secondary cell, one can pass current in both directions. When current leaves the cell at the positive terminal and enters the cell at the negative terminal, the cell is discharged. This is the normal working of the cell. Chemical energy is converted into electrical energy in this case. If the cell is connected to some other source of larger emf, current may enter the cell at the positive terminal and leave it at the negative terminal. The electric energy is then converted into chemical energy and the cell gets charged. The most commonly used secondary cell is a lead accumulator.

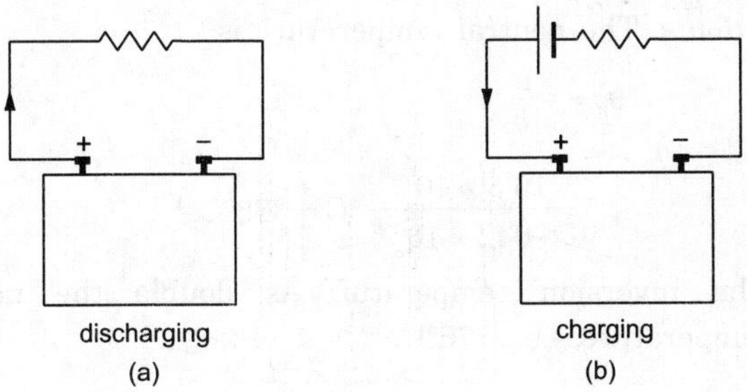

Figure 33.15

Lead Accumulator

In principle, a lead accumulator consists of electrodes made of PbO_2 and of Pb immersed in dilute sulphuric acid (H_2SO_4). The specific gravity of the solution should be between 1·20 and 1·28. PbO_2 acts as the positive electrode and Pb as the negative electrode. While discharging, the SO_4^{--} ions move towards the Pb electrode, give up the negative charge and form $PbSO_4$ there (figure 33.16a). The H^+ ions move to the PbO_2 electrode, give up the positive charge and reduce PbO_2 to PbO,

$$PbO_2 + 2\,H = PbO + H_2O.$$

The PbO so formed reacts with the H_2SO_4 to form $PbSO_4$ and water.

$$PbO + H_2SO_4 = PbSO_4 + H_2O$$

Thus, $PbSO_4$ is formed at both the electrodes. As the sulphuric acid is used up in discharging, the specific gravity of the acid decreases. When the specific gravity falls to 1·15, the cell is considered to be fully discharged and any further current drawn from it may permanently damage the electrodes.

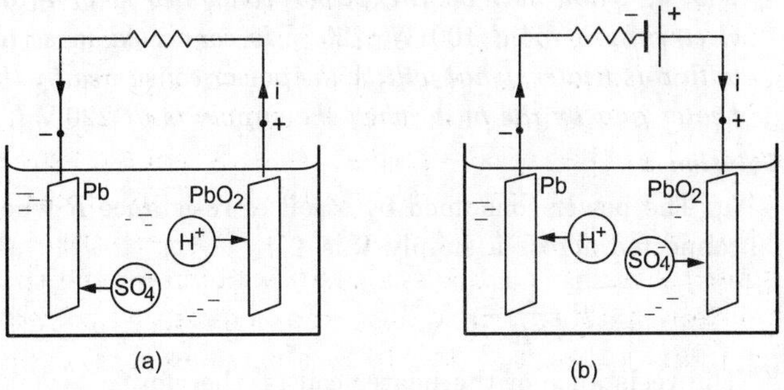

Figure 33.16

The charging process is reverse of discharging. A current is forced from the positive to the negative electrode inside the cell. The H^+ ions move towards the negative electrode and react with the $PbSO_4$ present there (which was formed during discharging).

$$PbSO_4 + 2\,H = Pb + H_2SO_4.$$

At the positive electrode, the reaction is

$$PbSO_4 + SO_4 + 2\,H_2O = PbO_2 + 2\,H_2SO_4.$$

Thus, the $PbSO_4$ deposited at the two electrodes is dissolved, Pb is deposited at the negative electrode and PbO_2 at the positive electrode. This restores the capacity of the cell to provide current. The emf of a lead accumulator is about 2·05 V when fully charged. In the discharged condition, the emf may fall to 1·8 V.

A practical lead accumulator contains several plates of lead connected together to form the negative electrode and several plates of lead peroxide connected together to form the positive electrode. This increases the capacity of the accumulator. These plates are separated from each other by insulating separators.

For commercial use, several such cells are connected in series and assembled together in one case. A six volt battery is obtained by connecting three such cells and a twelve volt battery is obtained by connecting six such cells.

The capacity of an accumulator is measured in ampere–hour. Thus, a 100 ampere–hour accumulator can supply 20 A current for 5 hours or 10 A current for 10 hours.

Worked Out Examples

1. *A current of* 30 A *is registered when the terminals of a dry cell of emf* 1·5 *volts are connected through an ammeter. Neglecting the meter resistance, find the amount of heat produced in the battery in* 10 *seconds.*

Solution : The current in the circuit will be

$$i = \frac{\mathcal{E}}{r}$$

or, $$30\text{ A} = \frac{1{\cdot}5\text{ V}}{r} \quad \text{giving } r = 0{\cdot}05\ \Omega.$$

The amount of heat produced in the battery

$$= i^2 rt = (30\text{ A})^2 \times (0{\cdot}5\ \Omega) \times 10\text{ s} = 450\text{ J}.$$

2. *A room heater is rated* 500 W, 220 V. *(a) Find the resistance of its coil. (b) If the supply voltage drops to* 200 V, *what will be the power consumed? (c) If an electric bulb rated* 100 W, 220 V *is connected in series with this heater, what will be the power consumed by the heater and by the bulb when the supply is at* 220 V?

Solution :

(a) The power consumed by a coil of resistance R when connected across a supply V is

$$P = \frac{V^2}{R}.$$

The resistance of the heater coil is, therefore,

$$R = \frac{(220\text{ V})^2}{500\text{ W}} = 96{\cdot}8\ \Omega.$$

(b) If the supply voltage drops to 200 V, the power consumed will be

$$P = \frac{V^2}{R} = \frac{(200\text{ V})^2}{96{\cdot}8\ \Omega} = 413\text{ W}.$$

(c) The resistance of the 100 W, 220 V bulb is

$$R = \frac{(220\text{ V})^2}{100\text{ W}} = 484\ \Omega.$$

If this is connected in series with the heater of $96{\cdot}8\ \Omega$, the current i will be

$$i = \frac{220\text{ V}}{484\ \Omega + 96{\cdot}8\ \Omega} = 0{\cdot}379\text{ A}.$$

Thus, the power consumed by the heater

$$= i^2 \times 96{\cdot}8\ \Omega = 0{\cdot}144 \times 96{\cdot}8\text{ W} = 13{\cdot}9\text{ W}$$

and that by the bulb

$$= i^2 \times 484\ \Omega = 69{\cdot}7\text{ W}.$$

3. *A battery of emf* $\mathcal{E}$ *and internal resistance r is used in a circuit with a variable external resistance R. Find the value of R for which the power consumed in R is maximum.*

Solution : The current in the resistance R is

$$i = \frac{\mathcal{E}}{r + R}.$$

The power consumed in R is

$$P = i^2 R = \frac{\mathcal{E}^2 R}{(r + R)^2}.$$

It is maximum when $\frac{dP}{dR} = 0$. We have

$$\frac{dP}{dR} = \mathcal{E}^2 \left[\frac{(r + R)^2 - 2R(r + R)}{(r + R)^4}\right].$$

It is zero when

$$(r + R)^2 = 2R(r + R)$$

or, $$R = r.$$

4. *The junctions of a* Ni–Cu *thermocouple are maintained at* 0°C *and* 100°C. *Calculate the Seebeck emf produced in the loop.* $a_{Ni,\,Cu} = 16{\cdot}3 \times 10^{-6}\ \text{V°C}^{-1}$ *and* $b_{Ni,\,Cu} = -0{\cdot}042 \times 10^{-6}\ \text{V°C}^{-2}$.

Solution :

$$\mathcal{E}_{Ni,\,Cu} = a_{Ni,\,Cu}\theta + \frac{1}{2} b_{Ni,\,Cu}\theta^2$$

$$= (16{\cdot}3 \times 10^{-6} \times 100)\text{V} + \frac{1}{2}(-0{\cdot}042 \times 10^{-6} \times 10^4)\text{V}$$

$$= 1{\cdot}42 \times 10^{-3}\text{ V}.$$

5. *Find the neutral and inversion temperatures for* Ni–Cu *thermocouple with the cold junction at* 0°C. *Use data from previous example.*

Solution : The neutral temperature is

$$\theta_n = -\frac{a}{b}$$

$$= \frac{16{\cdot}3 \times 10^{-6}}{0{\cdot}042 \times 10^{-6}}\ \text{°C} = 388\text{°C}.$$

The inversion temperature is double the neutral temperature, i.e., 776°C.

6. *An electric current of* 0·4 A *is passed through a silver voltameter for half an hour. Find the amount of silver deposited on the cathode. ECE of silver* = $1{\cdot}12 \times 10^{-6}$ kg C^{-1}.

Solution : Using the formula $m = Zit$, the mass of silver deposited

$$= (1{\cdot}12 \times 10^{-6}\text{ kg C}^{-1})\,(0{\cdot}4\text{ A})\,(30 \times 60\text{ s})$$

$$= 8{\cdot}06 \times 10^{-4}\text{ kg} = 0{\cdot}806\text{ g}.$$

7. *A silver and a copper voltameter are connected in series with a* 12·0 V *battery of negligible resistance. It is found that* 0·806 g *of silver is deposited in half an hour. Find (a) the mass of the copper deposited and (b) the energy supplied by the battery. ECE of silver* = $1{\cdot}12 \times 10^{-6}$ kg C^{-1} *and that of copper* = $6{\cdot}6 \times 10^{-7}$ kg C^{-1}.

Solution :

(a) For silver voltameter, the formula $m = Zit$ gives

$$0{\cdot}806\text{ g} = (1{\cdot}12 \times 10^{-6}\text{ kg C}^{-1})\, i(30 \times 60\text{ s})$$

or, $$i = 0{\cdot}4\text{ A}.$$

As the two voltameters are connected in series, the same current passes through the copper voltameter. The mass of copper deposited is

$$m = Zit$$

$$= (6{\cdot}6 \times 10^{-7}\text{ kg}^{-1}\text{C})\,(0{\cdot}4\text{ A})\,(30 \times 60\text{ s})$$

$$= 4{\cdot}75 \times 10^{-4}\text{ kg} = 0{\cdot}475\text{ g}.$$

This could also be obtained by using $\frac{m_1}{m_2} = \frac{Z_1}{Z_2}$ for series circuit.

(b) Energy supplied by the battery = Vit

$= (12 \text{ V}) (0{\cdot}4 \text{ A}) (30 \times 60 \text{ s}) = 8{\cdot}64 \text{ kJ}.$

8. *A current of* 1 A *is passed through a dilute solution of sulphuric acid for some time to liberate* 1 g *of oxygen. How much hydrogen is liberated during this period? How long was the current passed? Faraday constant* = 96500 C mol^{-1}.

Solution : The relative atomic mass of oxygen = 16 and its valency = 2 so that the chemical equivalent $E = \frac{16}{2} = 8.$ Chemical equivalent of hydrogen = 1.

$$\frac{m_{oxygen}}{m_{hydrogen}} = \frac{E_{oxygen}}{E_{hydrogen}} = \frac{8}{1}$$

or, $$m_{hydrogen} = \frac{m_{oxygen}}{8} = \frac{1 \text{ g}}{8} = 0{\cdot}125 \text{ g}.$$

We have, 1 g of oxygen $= \frac{1}{8}$ gram-equivalent.

The charge needed to liberate $\frac{1}{8}$ gram-equivalent

$$= \frac{1}{8} \text{ faraday}$$

$$= \frac{96500}{8} \text{ C} \cong 1{\cdot}12 \times 10^4 \text{ C}.$$

As the current is 1 A, the time taken is

$$t = \frac{Q}{i} = \frac{1{\cdot}2 \times 10^4 \text{ C}}{1 \text{ A}}$$

$$= 1{\cdot}2 \times 10^4 \text{ s}$$

= 3 hours 20 minutes.

□

QUESTIONS FOR SHORT ANSWER

1. If a constant potential difference is applied across a bulb, the current slightly decreases as time passes and then becomes constant. Explain.
2. Two unequal resistances R_1 and R_2 are connected across two identical batteries of emf $\mathcal{E}$ and internal resistance r (figure 33-Q1). Can the thermal energies developed in R_1 and R_2 be equal in a given time. If yes, what will be the condition?

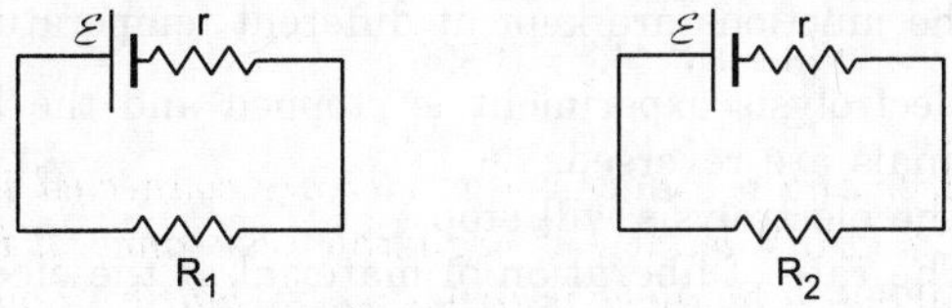

Figure 33-Q1

3. When a current passes through a resistor, its temperature increases. Is it an adiabatic process?
4. Apply the first law of thermodynamics to a resistor carrying a current i. Identify which of the quantities ΔQ, ΔU and ΔW are zero, which are positive and which are negative.
5. Do all the thermocouples have a neutral temperature?
6. Is inversion temperature always double of the neutral temperature? Does the unit of temperature have an effect in deciding this question?
7. Is neutral temperature always the arithmetic mean of the inversion temperature and the temperature of the cold junction? Does the unit of temperature have an effect in deciding this question?
8. Do the electrodes in an electrolytic cell have fixed polarity like a battery?
9. As temperature increases, the viscosity of liquids decreases considerably. Will this decrease the resistance of an electrolyte as the temperature increases?

OBJECTIVE I

1. Which of the following plots may represent the thermal energy produced in a resistor in a given time as a function of the electric current?

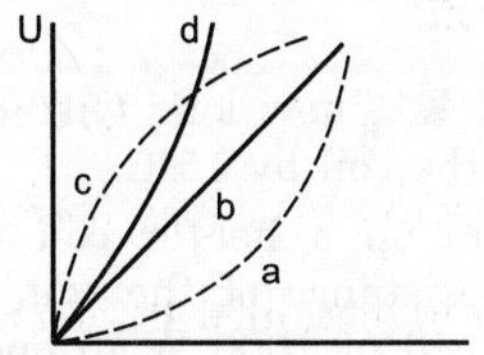

Figure 33-Q2

2. A constant current i is passed through a resistor. Taking the temperature coefficient of resistance into account, indicate which of the plots shown in figure (33-Q3) best

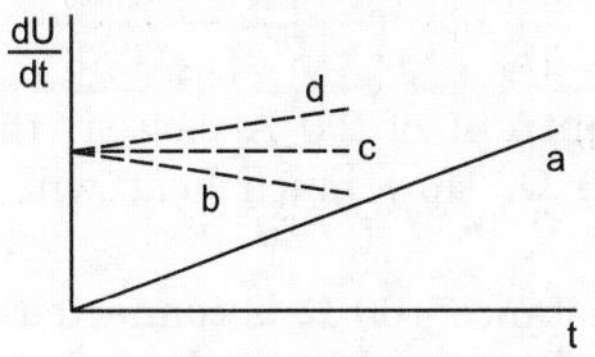

Figure 33-Q3

represents the rate of production of thermal energy in the resistor.

3. Consider the following statements regarding a thermocouple.
   (A) The neutral temperature does not depend on the temperature of the cold junction.
   (B) The inversion temperature does not depend on the temperature of the cold junction.
   (a) Both A and B are correct.
   (b) *A* is correct but B is wrong.
   (c) *B* is correct but A is wrong.
   (d) Both A and B are wrong.
4. The heat developed in a system is proportional to the current through it.
   (a) It cannot be Thomson heat.
   (b) It cannot be Peltier heat.
   (c) It cannot be Joule heat.
   (d) It can be any of the three heats mentioned above.
5. Consider the following two statements.
   (A) Free-electron density is different in different metals.
   (B) Free-electron density in a metal depends on temperature.
   Seebeck effect is caused
   (a) due to both A and B
   (b) due to A but not due to B
   (c) due to B but not due to A
   (d) neither due to A nor due to B.
6. Consider the statements A and B in the previous question. Peltier effect is caused
   (a) due to both A and B
   (b) due to A but not due to B
   (c) due to B but not due to A
   (d) neither due to A nor due to B.
7. Consider the statements A and B in question 5. Thomson effect is caused
   (a) due to both A and B
   (b) due to A but not due to B
   (c) due to B but not due to A
   (d) neither due to A nor due to B.
8. Faraday constant
   (a) depends on the amount of the electrolyte
   (b) depends on the current in the electrolyte
   (c) is a universal constant
   (d) depends on the amount of charge passed through the electrolyte.

OBJECTIVE II

1. Two resistors having equal resistances are joined in series and a current is passed through the combination. Neglect any variation in resistance as the temperature changes. In a given time interval,
   (a) equal amounts of thermal energy must be produced in the resistors
   (b) unequal amounts of thermal energy may be produced
   (c) the temperature must rise equally in the resistors
   (d) the temperature may rise equally in the resistors.
2. A copper strip *AB* and an iron strip *AC* are joined at *A*. The junction *A* is maintained at 0°C and the free ends *B* and *C* are maintained at 100°C. There is a potential difference between
   (a) the two ends of the copper strip
   (b) the copper end and the iron end at the junction
   (c) the two ends of the iron strip
   (d) the free ends *B* and *C*.
3. The constants *a* and *b* for the pair silver–lead are 2·50 μV°C^{-1} and 0·012 μV°C^{-2} respectively. For a silver–lead thermocouple with colder junction at 0°C,
   (a) there will be no neutral temperature
   (b) there will be no inversion temperature
   (c) there will not be any thermo-emf even if the junctions are kept at different temperatures
   (d) there will be no current in the thermocouple even if the junctions are kept at different temperatures.
4. An electrolysis experiment is stopped and the battery terminals are reversed.
   (a) The electrolysis will stop.
   (b) The rate of liberation of material at the electrodes will increase.
   (c) The rate of liberation of material will remain the same.
   (d) Heat will be produced at a greater rate.
5. The electrochemical equivalent of a material depends on
   (a) the nature of the material
   (b) the current through the electrolyte containing the material
   (c) the amount of charge passed through the electrolyte
   (d) the amount of this material present in the electrolyte.

EXERCISES

1. An electric current of 2·0 A passes through a wire of resistance 25 Ω. How much heat will be developed in 1 minute ?
2. A coil of resistance 100 Ω is connected across a battery of emf 6·0 V. Assume that the heat developed in the coil is used to raise its temperature. If the heat capacity of the coil is 4·0 J K^{-1}, how long will it take to raise the temperature of the coil by 15°C ?
3. The specification on a heater coil is 250 V, 500 W. Calculate the resistance of the coil. What will be the resistance of a coil of 1000 W to operate at the same voltage ?

4. A heater coil is to be constructed with a nichrome wire ($\rho = 1{\cdot}0 \times 10^{-6}$ Ωm) which can operate at 500 W when connected to a 250 V supply. (a) What would be the resistance of the coil ? (b) If the cross-sectional area of the wire is $0{\cdot}5$ mm^2, what length of the wire will be needed ? (c) If the radius of each turn is 4·0 mm, how many turns will be there in the coil ?

5. A bulb with rating 250 V, 100 W is connected to a power supply of 220 V situated 10 m away using a copper wire of area of cross section 5 mm^2. How much power will be consumed by the connecting wires ? Resistivity of copper = $1{\cdot}7 \times 10^{-8}$ Ωm.

6. An electric bulb, when connected across a power supply of 220 V, consumes a power of 60 W. If the supply drops to 180 V, what will be the power consumed ? If the supply is suddenly increased to 240 V, what will be the power consumed ?

7. A servo voltage stabiliser restricts the voltage output to 220 V ± 1%. If an electric bulb rated at 220 V, 100 W is connected to it, what will be the minimum and maximum power consumed by it ?

8. An electric bulb marked 220 V, 100 W will get fused if it is made to consume 150 W or more. What voltage fluctuation will the bulb withstand ?

9. An immersion heater rated 1000 W, 220 V is used to heat 0·01 m^3 of water. Assuming that the power is supplied at 220 V and 60% of the power supplied is used to heat the water, how long will it take to increase the temperature of the water from 15°C to 40°C ?

10. An electric kettle used to prepare tea, takes 2 minutes to boil 4 cups of water (1 cup contains 200 cc of water) if the room temperature is 25°C. (a) If the cost of power consumption is Re 1·00 per unit (1 unit = 1000 watt–hour), calculate the cost of boiling 4 cups of water. (b) What will be the corresponding cost if the room temperature drops to 5°C ?

11. The coil of an electric bulb takes 40 watts to start glowing. If more than 40 W is supplied, 60% of the extra power is converted into light and the remaining into heat. The bulb consumes 100 W at 220 V. Find the percentage drop in the light intensity at a point if the supply voltage changes from 220 V to 200 V.

12. The 2·0 Ω resistor shown in figure (33-E1) is dipped into a calorimeter containing water. The heat capacity of the calorimeter together with water is 2000 J K^{-1}. (a) If the circuit is active for 15 minutes, what would be the rise in the temperature of the water ? (b) Suppose the 6·0 Ω resistor gets burnt. What would be the rise in the temperature of the water in the next 15 minutes ?

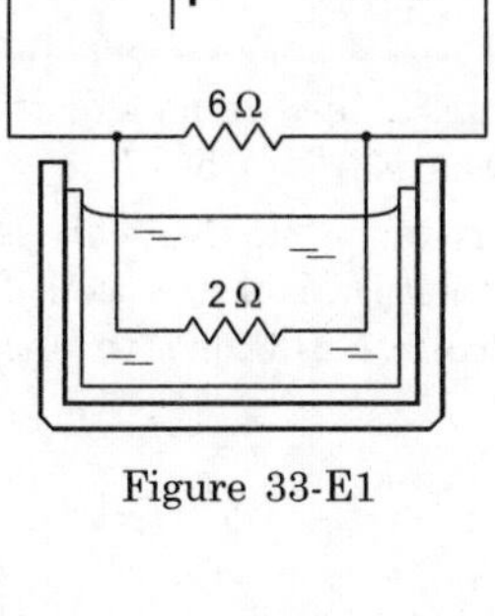

Figure 33-E1

13. The temperatures of the junctions of a bismuth–silver thermocouple are maintained at 0°C and 0·001°C. Find the thermo-emf (Seebeck emf) developed. For bismuth–silver, $a = -46 \times 10^{-6}$ V°C^{-1} and $b = -0{\cdot}48 \times 10^{-6}$ V°C^{-2}.

14. Find the thermo-emf developed in a copper–silver thermocouple when the junctions are kept at 0°C and 40°C. Use the data in table (33.1).

15. Find the neutral temperature and inversion temperature of copper–iron thermocouple if the reference junction is kept at 0°C. Use the data in table (33.1).

16. Find the charge required to flow through an electrolyte to liberate one atom of (a) a monovalent material and (b) a divalent material.

17. Find the amount of silver liberated at cathode if 0·500 A of current is passed through $AgNO_3$ electrolyte for 1 hour. Atomic weight of silver is 107·9 g mol^{-1}.

18. An electroplating unit plates 3·0 g of silver on a brass plate in 3·0 minutes. Find the current used by the unit. The electrochemical equivalent of silver is $1{\cdot}12 \times 10^{-6}$ kg C^{-1}.

19. Find the time required to liberate 1·0 litre of hydrogen at STP in an electrolytic cell by a current of 5·0 A.

20. Two voltameters, one having a solution of silver salt and the other of a trivalent-metal salt, are connected in series and a current of 2 A is maintained for 1·50 hours. It is found that 1·00 g of the trivalent metal is deposited. (a) What is the atomic weight of the trivalent metal ? (b) How much silver is deposited during this period ? Atomic weight of silver is 107·9 g mol^{-1}.

21. A brass plate having surface area 200 cm^2 on one side is electroplated with 0·10 mm thick silver layers on both sides using a 15 A current. Find the time taken to do the job. The specific gravity of silver is 10·5 and its atomic weight is 107·9 g mol^{-1}.

22. Figure (33-E2) shows an electrolyte of AgCl through which a current is passed. It is observed that 2·68 g of silver is deposited in 10 minutes on the cathode. Find the heat developed in the 20 Ω resistor during this period. Atomic weight of silver is 107·9 g mol^{-1}.

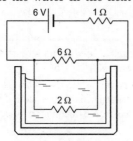

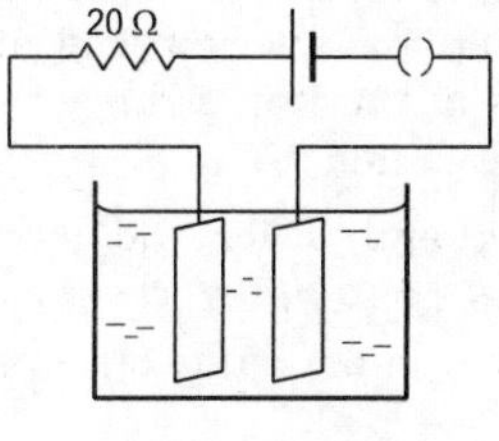

Figure 33-E2

23. The potential difference across the terminals of a battery of emf 12 V and internal resistance 2 Ω drops to 10 V when it is connected to a silver voltameter. Find the silver deposited at the cathode in half an hour. Atomic weight of silver is 107·9 g mol^{-1}.

24. A plate of area 10 cm^2 is to be electroplated with copper (density 9000 kg m^{-3}) to a thickness of 10 micrometres on both sides, using a cell of 12 V. Calculate the energy spent by the cell in the process of deposition. If this energy is used to heat 100 g of water, calculate the rise in the temperature of the water. ECE of copper $= 3 \times 10^{-7}$ kg C^{-1} and specific heat capacity of water $= 4200$ J kg^{-1} K^{-1}.

□

ANSWERS

OBJECTIVE I

1. (a) 2. (d) 3. (b) 4. (c) 5. (a) 6. (b)
7. (c) 8. (c)

OBJECTIVE II

1. (a), (d) 2. all 3. (a), (b)
4. (c) 5. (a)

EXERCISES

1. 6.0×10^{3} J
2. 2·8 min
3. 125 Ω, 62·5 Ω
4. (a) 125 Ω (b) 62·5 m (c) ≈ 2500 turns
5. 8·4 mW
6. 40 W, 71 W
7. 98 W, 102 W
8. up to 270 V
9. 29 minutes
10. (a) 7 paise (b) 9 paise
11. 29%
12. (a) 2·9°C (b) 3·6°C
13. -4.6×10^{-8} V
14. 1.04×10^{-5} V
15. 330°C, 659°C
16. (a) 1.6×10^{-19} C (b) 3.2×10^{-19} C
17. 2·01 g
18. 15 A
19. 29 minutes
20. (a) 26·8 g mol^{-1} (b) 12·1 g
21. 42 minutes
22. 190 kJ
23. 2 g
24. 7·2 kJ, 17 K

□

CHAPTER 34

MAGNETIC FIELD

34.1 INTRODUCTION

If a charge q is placed at rest at a point P near a metallic wire carrying a current i, it experiences almost no force. We conclude that there is no appreciable electric field at the point P. This is expected because in any volume of wire (which contains several thousand atoms) there are equal amounts of positive and negative charges. The wire is electrically neutral and does not produce an electric field.*

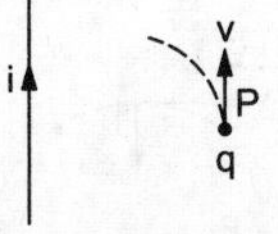

Figure 34.1

However, if the charge q is projected from the point P in the direction of the current (figure 34.1), it is deflected towards the wire (q is assumed positive). There must be a field at P which exerts a force on the charge when it is projected, but not when it is kept at rest. This field is different from the electric field which always exerts a force on a charged particle whether it is at rest or in motion. This new field is called *magnetic field* and is denoted by the symbol $\vec{B}$. The force exerted by a magnetic field is called *magnetic force*.

34.2 DEFINITION OF MAGNETIC FIELD $\vec{B}$

If a charged particle is projected in a magnetic field, in general, it experiences a magnetic force. By projecting the particle in different directions from the same point P with different speeds, we can observe the following facts about the magnetic force:

(a) There is one line through the point P, such that, if the velocity of the particle is along this line, there is no magnetic force. We define the direction of the magnetic field to be along this line (the direction is not uniquely defined yet, because there are two opposite directions along any line).

(b) If the speed of the particle is v and it makes an angle θ with the line identified in (a), i.e., with the direction of the magnetic field, the magnitude of the magnetic force is proportional to $|v \sin\theta|$.

(c) The direction of the magnetic force is perpendicular to the direction of the magnetic field as well as to the direction of the velocity.

(d) The force is proportional to the magnitude of the charge q and its direction is opposite for positive and negative charges.

All the above facts may be explained if we define the magnetic field by the equation

$$\vec{F} = q\vec{v} \times \vec{B}. \qquad \dots (34.1)$$

By measuring the magnetic force $\vec{F}$ acting on a charge q moving at velocity $\vec{v}$, we can obtain $\vec{B}$. If $\vec{v} \parallel \vec{B}$, the force is zero. By taking magnitudes in equation (34.1), we see that the force is proportional to $|v \sin\theta|$. By the rules of vector product, the force is perpendicular to both $\vec{B}$ and $\vec{v}$. Also, the observation (d) follows from equation (34.1).

Equation (34.1) uniquely determines the direction of $\vec{B}$ from the rules of vector product. The SI unit of magnetic field is newton/ampere meter. This is written as tesla and abbreviated as T. Another unit in common use is gauss (G). The relation between gauss and tesla is $1\ \text{T} = 10^{4}\ \text{G}$.

The unit weber/meter^2 is also used for magnetic field and is the same as tesla. Tesla is quite a large unit for many practical applications. We have a magnetic field of the order of 10^{-5} T near the earth's surface. Large superconducting magnets are needed to produce a field of the order of 10 T in laboratories.

---

* In fact, there is a small charge density on the surface of the wire which does produce an electric field near the wire. This field is very small and we shall neglect it.

In the older days, the term *magnetic induction* was used for this field $\vec{B}$.

Example 34.1

A proton is projected with a speed of 3×10^6 m s^{-1} horizontally from east to west. A uniform magnetic field $\vec{B}$ of strength $2{\cdot}0 \times 10^{-3}$ T exists in the vertically upward direction. (a) Find the force on the proton just after it is projected. (b) What is the acceleration produced?

Solution :

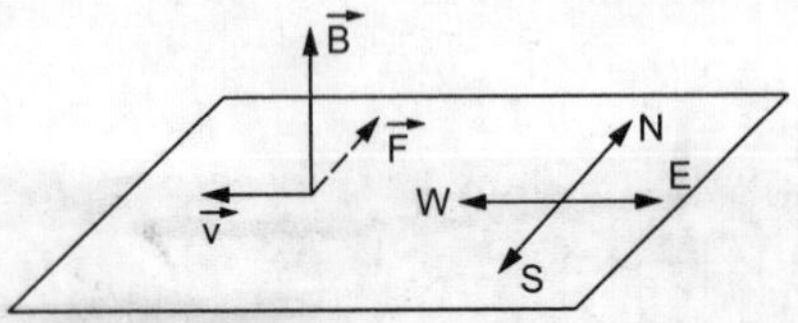

Figure 34.2

(a) The situation is shown in figure (34.2). The force is perpendicular to $\vec{B}$ hence it is in the horizontal plane through the proton. In this plane, it is perpendicular to the velocity $\vec{v}$. Thus, it is along the north-south line. The rule for vector product shows that $\vec{v} \times \vec{B}$ is towards north. As the charge on the proton is positive, the force $\vec{F} = q\vec{v} \times \vec{B}$ is also towards north. The magnitude of the force is

$$F = qvB \sin\theta$$
$$= (1{\cdot}6 \times 10^{-19}\ \text{C})(3{\cdot}0 \times 10^6\ \text{m s}^{-1})(2{\cdot}0 \times 10^{-3}\ \text{T})$$
$$= 9{\cdot}6 \times 10^{-16}\ \text{N}.$$

(b) The acceleration of the proton is

$$a = \frac{F}{m} = \frac{9{\cdot}6 \times 10^{-16}\ \text{N}}{1{\cdot}67 \times 10^{-27}\ \text{kg}}$$
$$= 5{\cdot}8 \times 10^{11}\ \text{m s}^{-2}.$$

34.3 RELATION BETWEEN ELECTRIC AND MAGNETIC FIELDS

Figure (34.3) shows a long wire carrying a current i and a charge q having a velocity v parallel to the current as seen by an observer S. There is no electric field, but there is a magnetic field which exerts a force on the charge and the charge is attracted towards the wire.

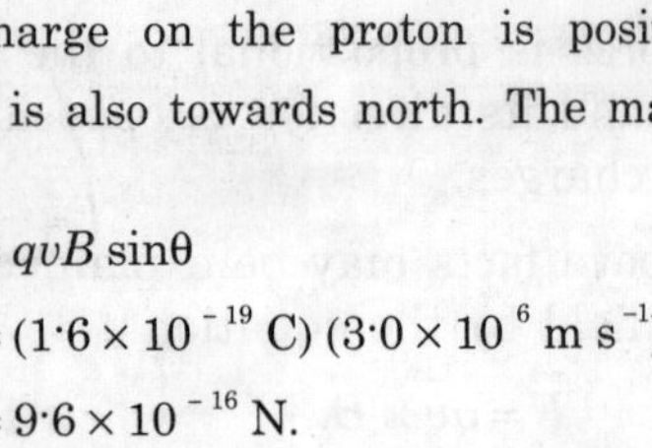

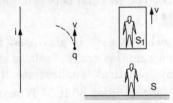

Figure 34.3

Now consider another observer S_1 who is moving at a uniform velocity v parallel to the wire. In this frame the charge is at rest and hence, the magnetic field (if any) cannot exert any force on the charge. However, the observer S_1 also sees that the charge is attracted by the wire. In fact, the acceleration of the charge is the same for both S and S_1 as they are unaccelerated with respect to each other. Hence, there must be an electric field in the frame of S_1. What was a pure magnetic field in the frame of S turns out to be a combination of electric field and magnetic field in the frame of S_1. We conclude that the electric field and the magnetic field are not basically independent. They are two aspects of the same entity which we call *electromagnetic field*. Whether the electromagnetic field will show up as an electric field or a magnetic field or a combination, depends on the frame from which we are looking at the field. If we are confined to a particular frame, we can treat the electric field and the magnetic field as separate entities.

34.4 MOTION OF A CHARGED PARTICLE IN A UNIFORM MAGNETIC FIELD

As the magnetic force on a particle is perpendicular to the velocity, it does not do any work on the particle. Hence, the kinetic energy or the speed of the particle does not change due to the magnetic force.

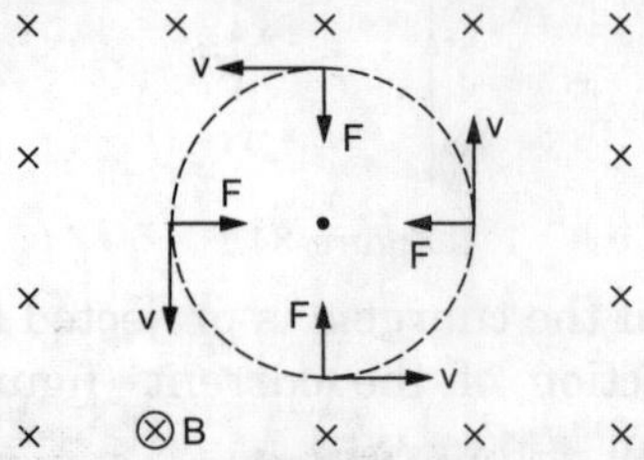

Figure 34.4

In figure (34.4), the magnetic field B is perpendicular to the paper and going into it. (This direction is, by convention, shown as ⊗. The direction coming out of the paper is, by convention, shown as ⊙. The circle around the cross or around the dot is quite often omitted.) A charge q is projected with a speed v in the plane of the paper. The velocity is perpendicular to the magnetic field. The force is $F = qvB$ in the direction perpendicular to both v and B. This force will deflect the particle without changing the speed and the particle will move along a circle perpendicular to the field. The magnetic force provides the centripetal force. If r be the radius of the circle,

$$qvB = m\frac{v^2}{r}$$

or, $$r = \frac{mv}{qB}. \quad \ldots (34.2)$$

The time taken to complete the circle (time period) is

$$T = \frac{2\pi r}{v} = \frac{2\pi m}{qB}. \quad \ldots (34.3)$$

We see that the time period is independent of the speed v. If the particle moves faster, the radius is larger, it has to move a longer distance to complete the circle so that the time taken is the same.

The frequency of revolution is

$$\nu = \frac{1}{T} = \frac{qB}{2\pi m}. \qquad \dots (34.4)$$

This frequency is called the *cyclotron frequency.*

Example 34.2

A particle having a charge of 100 μC *and a mass of* 10 mg *is projected in a uniform magnetic field of* 25 mT *with a speed of* 10 m s^{-1}. *If the velocity is perpendicular to the magnetic field, how long will it take for the particle to come back to its original position for the first time after being projected.*

Solution : The particle moves along a circle and returns to its original position after completing the circle, that is after one time period. The time period is

$$T = \frac{2\pi m}{qB}$$

$$= \frac{2\pi \times (10 \times 10^{-6}\ \text{kg})}{(100 \times 10^{-6}\ \text{C}) \times (25 \times 10^{-3}\ \text{T})} = 25\ \text{s}.$$

If the velocity of the charge is not perpendicular to the magnetic field, we can break the velocity in two components— $v_{\parallel}$, parallel to the field and $v_{\perp}$, perpendicular to the field. The component $v_{\parallel}$ remains unchanged as the force $q\vec{v} \times \vec{B}$ is perpendicular to it. In the plane perpendicular to the field, the particle traces a circle of radius $r = \frac{mv_{\perp}}{qB}$ as given by equation (34.2). The resultant path is a helix (figure 34.5).

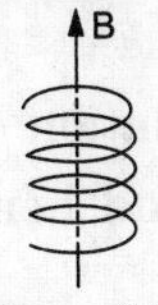

Figure 34.5

34.5 MAGNETIC FORCE ON A CURRENT-CARRYING WIRE

Suppose a conducting wire, carrying a current i, is placed in a magnetic field $\vec{B}$. Consider a small element dl of the wire (figure 34.6). The free electrons drift with a speed v_d opposite to the direction of the current. The relation between the current i and the drift speed v_d is

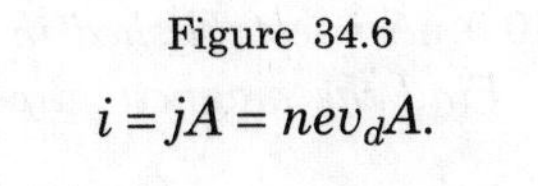

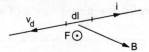

Figure 34.6

$$i = jA = nev_dA. \qquad \dots \text{(i)}$$

Here A is the area of cross-section of the wire and n is the number of free electrons per unit volume. Each electron experiences an average magnetic force

$$\vec{f} = -e\vec{v}_d \times \vec{B}.$$

The number of free electrons in the small element considered is $nAdl$. Thus, the magnetic force on the wire of length dl is

$$d\vec{F} = (nAdl)(-e\vec{v}_d \times \vec{B}).$$

If we denote the length dl along the direction of the current by $\vec{dl}$, the above equation becomes

$$d\vec{F} = nAev_d\, \vec{dl} \times \vec{B}.$$

Using (i),

$$d\vec{F} = i\, \vec{dl} \times \vec{B}. \qquad \dots (34.5)$$

The quantity $i\,\vec{dl}$ is called a *current element.*

If a straight wire of length l carrying a current i is placed in a uniform magnetic field $\vec{B}$, the force on it is

$$\vec{F} = i\,\vec{l} \times \vec{B}. \qquad \dots (34.6)$$

Example 34.3

Figure (34.7) shows a triangular loop PQR carrying a current i. The triangle is equilateral with edge-length l. A uniform magnetic field B exists in a direction parallel to PQ. Find the forces acting on the three wires PQ, QR and RP separately.

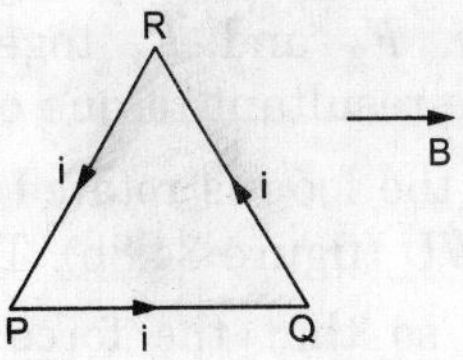

Figure 34.7

Solution : The force on the wire PQ is

$$\vec{F}_1 = i\,\vec{PQ} \times \vec{B} = 0$$

as the field $\vec{B}$ is parallel to $\vec{PQ}$.

The force on QR is

$$\vec{F}_2 = i\,\vec{QR} \times \vec{B}$$

or, $$F_2 = ilB \sin 120°$$

$$= \frac{\sqrt{3}}{2} ilB.$$

From the rule of vector product, this force is perpendicular to the plane of the diagram and is going into it.

The force on RP is

$$\vec{F}_3 = i\,\vec{RP} \times \vec{B}$$

or, $$F_3 = i\,lB \sin 120° = \frac{\sqrt{3}}{2} ilB.$$

From the rule of vector product, this force is perpendicular to the plane of the diagram and is coming out of it.

34.6 TORQUE ON A CURRENT LOOP

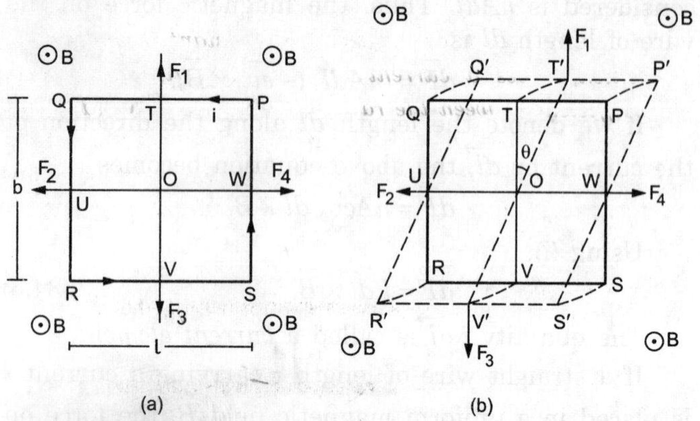

Figure 34.8

Figure (34.8a) shows a rectangular loop *PQRS* carrying a current *i* and placed in a uniform magnetic field *B*. The magnetic forces F_1, F_2, F_3 and F_4 on the wires *PQ*, *QR*, *RS* and *SP* are obtained by using the equation $\vec{F} = i\vec{l} \times \vec{B}$. These forces act from the middle points *T*, *U*, *V*, *W* of the respective sides. Clearly, $F_1 = F_3 = ilB$ and $F_2 = F_4 = ibB$ in figure (34.8a). The resultant force is, therefore, zero. Also, F_1 and F_3 have the same line of action so they together produce no torque. Similarly, F_2 and F_4 together produce no torque. Hence, the resultant torque on the loop is zero.

Now suppose the loop is rotated through an angle θ about the line *WU* (figure 34.8b). The wire *PQ* shifts parallel to itself so that the force $\vec{F}_1 = i\vec{l} \times \vec{B}$ on it remains unchanged in magnitude and direction. Its point of application *T* shifts to *T*′. Similarly, the force on *RS* remains $\vec{F}_3$ but the point of application shifts to *V*′. The line *TV* gets rotated by an angle θ to take the position *T*′*V*′. This line makes an angle θ with the force F_1 and F_3. The torque of F_1 about *O* has magnitude

$$\left| \vec{OT'} \times \vec{F}_1 \right| = \left(\frac{b}{2} \right) \times F_1 \times \sin\theta = \frac{b}{2} (ilB) \sin\theta.$$

This torque acts along the line *UW*. The torque of F_3 about *O* is also $\frac{b}{2}$ $(ilB) \sin\theta$ along the same direction.

As the wire *QR* rotates about *WU*, the plane containing the wire and the magnetic field does not change. The force on the wire is perpendicular to this plane and hence its direction remains unchanged. Also, the point of application *U* remains the same. Similar is the case for the wire *SP*. The forces on *QR* and *SP* are, therefore, equal and opposite and act along the same line. They together produce no torque.

The net torque acting on the loop is, therefore,

$$\Gamma = \frac{b}{2} (ilB) \sin\theta + \frac{b}{2} (ilB) \sin\theta = b(ilB) \sin\theta$$
$$= i\,AB \sin\theta.$$

Let us define the *area-vector* $\vec{A}$ of the loop in the following way. The magnitude of $\vec{A}$ is equal to the area enclosed by the loop and the direction of $\vec{A}$ is perpendicular to the plane of the loop and is towards the side from which the current looks anticlockwise. Thus, in figure (34.8a), the area-vector $\vec{A}$ points towards the viewer. It is drawn from the centre *O* of the loop. Another way to get the direction of $\vec{A}$ is to use the right-hand thumb rule. If you curl your fingers of the right hand along the current, the stretched thumb gives the direction of $\vec{A}$.

The definition of area-vector is valid for a closed loop of any shape, not necessarily rectangular.

In figure (34.8a), the angle between the area-vector $\vec{A}$ and the magnetic field $\vec{B}$ is zero. As the loop rotates, the area-vector also rotates by an angle θ and hence the angle between $\vec{A}$ and $\vec{B}$ becomes θ. Taking the direction of the torque (along *UW*) into consideration,

$$\vec{\Gamma} = i\vec{A} \times \vec{B} = \vec{\mu} \times \vec{B} \quad \text{... (34.7)}$$

where $\vec{\mu} = i\vec{A}$ is called the *magnetic dipole moment* or simply *magnetic moment* of the current loop.

We have already discussed an electric dipole. A pair of charges $-q$, $+q$ separated by a distance *l* forms an electric dipole of dipole moment $p = ql$. The direction is from $-q$ to $+q$. If such a dipole is placed in a uniform electric field, a torque

$$\vec{\Gamma} = \vec{p} \times \vec{E}$$

acts on the dipole. Equation (34.7) is similar to this equation in structure and hence $\vec{\mu}$ is called magnetic dipole moment.

If there are *n* turns in the loop, each turn experiences a torque. The net torque is

$$\vec{\Gamma} = ni\vec{A} \times \vec{B}.$$

We still write it as $\vec{\Gamma} = \vec{\mu} \times \vec{B}$ with the magnetic dipole moment defined as

$$\vec{\mu} = ni\vec{A}. \quad \text{... (34.8)}$$

Equations (34.7) and (34.8) are obtained by considering a rectangular loop. However, these equations are valid for plane loops of any shape.

Example 34.4

A current of 10·0 nA *is established in a circular loop of radius* 5·0 cm. *Find the magnetic dipole moment of the current loop.*

Solution : The magnetic dipole moment is

$$\vec{\mu} = i\vec{A}.$$

Thus, $\mu = i\pi r^2 = (10 \times 10^{-9}\ \text{A})\ (3{\cdot}14) \times (5 \times 10^{-2}\ \text{m})^2$

$$= 7{\cdot}85 \times 10^{-11}\ \text{A m}^2.$$

Worked Out Examples

1. *A charge of 2·0 μC moves with a speed of $2{\cdot}0 \times 10^6$ m s^{-1} along the positive x-axis. A magnetic field $\vec{B}$ of strength $(0{\cdot}20\,\vec{j} + 0{\cdot}40\,\vec{k})$T exists in space. Find the magnetic force acting on the charge.*

Solution : The force on the charge

$$= q\vec{v} \times \vec{B}$$

$$= (2{\cdot}0 \times 10^{-6}\ \text{C})\ (2{\cdot}0 \times 10^6\ \text{m s}^{-1}\ \vec{i}) \times (0{\cdot}20\,\vec{j} + 0{\cdot}40\,\vec{k})\ \text{T}$$

$$= 4{\cdot}0(0{\cdot}20\,\vec{i} \times \vec{j} + 0{\cdot}40\,\vec{i} \times \vec{k})\ \text{N}$$

$$= (0{\cdot}8\,\vec{k} - 1{\cdot}6\,\vec{j})\ \text{N}.$$

2. *A wire is bent in the form of an equilateral triangle PQR of side 10 cm and carries a current of 5·0 A. It is placed in a magnetic field B of magnitude 2·0 T directed perpendicularly to the plane of the loop. Find the forces on the three sides of the triangle.*

Solution :

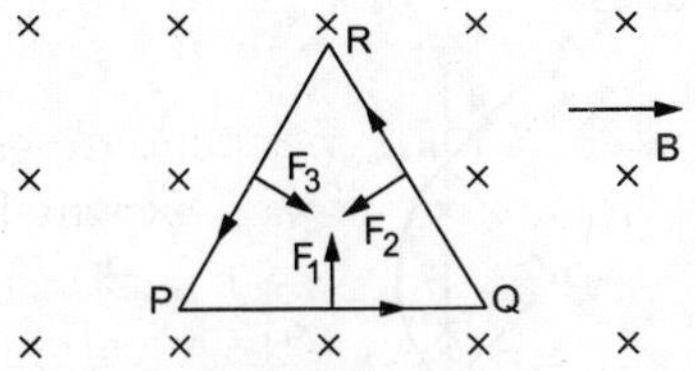

Figure 34-W1

Suppose the field and the current have directions as shown in figure (34-W1). The force on *PQ* is

$$\vec{F_1} = i\,\vec{l} \times \vec{B}$$

or, $F_1 = 5{\cdot}0\ \text{A} \times 10\ \text{cm} \times 2{\cdot}0\ \text{T} = 1{\cdot}0\ \text{N}.$

The rule of vector product shows that the force F_1 is perpendicular to *PQ* and is directed towards the inside of the triangle.

The forces $\vec{F_2}$ and $\vec{F_3}$ on *QR* and *RP* can also be obtained similarly. Both the forces are 1·0 N directed perpendicularly to the respective sides and towards the inside of the triangle.

The three forces $\vec{F_1}$, $\vec{F_2}$, and $\vec{F_3}$ will have zero resultant, so that there is no net magnetic force on the triangle. This result can be generalised. Any closed current loop, placed in a homogeneous magnetic field, does not experience a net magnetic force.

3. *Figure (34-W2) shows two long metal rails placed horizontally and parallel to each other at a separation l. A uniform magnetic field B exists in the vertically downward direction. A wire of mass m can slide on the rails. The rails are connected to a constant current source which drives a current i in the circuit. The friction coefficient between the rails and the wire is μ. (a) What should be the minimum value of μ which can prevent the wire from sliding on the rails? (b) Describe the motion of the wire if the value of μ is half the value found in the previous part.*

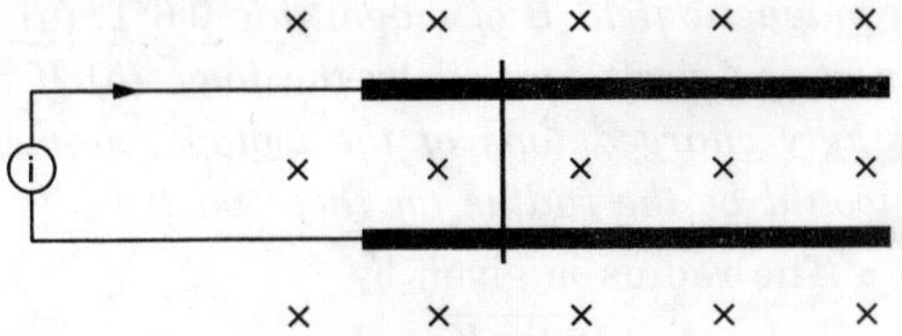

Figure 34-W2

Solution :

(a) The force on the wire due to the magnetic field is

$$\vec{F} = i\,\vec{l} \times \vec{B}$$

or, $$F = ilB.$$

It acts towards right in the given figure. If the wire does not slide on the rails, the force of friction by the rails should be equal to *F*. If μ_0 be the minimum coefficient of friction which can prevent sliding, this force is also equal to $\mu_0\, mg$. Thus,

$$\mu_0\, mg = ilB$$

or, $$\mu_0 = \frac{ilB}{mg}\cdot$$

(b) If the friction coefficient is $\mu = \frac{\mu_0}{2} = \frac{ilB}{2\,mg}$, the wire will slide towards right. The frictional force by the rails is

$$f = \mu mg = \frac{ilB}{2}\ \text{towards left.}$$

The resultant force is $ilB - \frac{ilB}{2} = \frac{ilB}{2}$ towards right. The acceleration will be $a = \frac{ilB}{2\,m}\cdot$ The wire will slide towards right with this acceleration.

4. *A proton, a deuteron and an alpha particle moving with equal kinetic energies enter perpendicularly into a magnetic field. If r_p, r_d and r_a are the respective radii of the circular paths, find the ratios r_p/r_d and r_p/r_a.*

Solution : We have $r = \frac{mv}{qB} = \frac{\sqrt{2\,mK}}{qB}$

where $K = \frac{1}{2}mv^2 =$ kinetic energy.

Thus, $r_p = \frac{\sqrt{2\, m_p K}}{q_p B}$, $r_d = \frac{\sqrt{2\, m_d K}}{q_d B}$

and $r_a = \frac{\sqrt{2\, m_a K}}{q_a B}$.

We get $\frac{r_p}{r_d} = \frac{q_d}{q_p}\sqrt{\frac{m_p}{m_d}} = \frac{q_p}{q_p}\sqrt{\frac{m_p}{2\, m_p}} = \frac{1}{\sqrt{2}}$

and $\frac{r_p}{r_a} = \frac{q_a}{q_p}\sqrt{\frac{m_p}{m_a}} = \frac{2\, q_p}{q_p}\sqrt{\frac{m_p}{4\, m_p}} = 1.$

5. *Singly charged magnesium (A = 24) ions are accelerated to kinetic energy 2 keV and are projected perpendicularly into a magnetic field B of magnitude 0·6 T. (a) Find the radius of the circle formed by the ions. (b) If there are also singly charged ions of the isotope magnesium-26, what would be the radius for these particles?*

Solution : The radius is given by

$$r = \frac{mv}{qB} = \frac{\sqrt{2\, mK}}{qB}$$

For ^{24}Mg ions, $m = 24 \times m_p$ approximately and $q = 1{\cdot}6 \times 10^{-19}$ C.

Putting the values,

$$r = \frac{\sqrt{2 \times 24 \times 1{\cdot}67 \times 10^{-27}\ \text{kg} \times 2000 \times 1{\cdot}6 \times 10^{-19}\ \text{J}}}{1{\cdot}6 \times 10^{-19}\ \text{C} \times 0{\cdot}6\ \text{T}}$$

$$= 0{\cdot}053\ \text{m} = 5{\cdot}3\ \text{cm}.$$

For ^{26}Mg, the radius r' will be given by

$$r' = \frac{\sqrt{2\, m'K}}{qB}$$

or, $r' = r\sqrt{\frac{m'}{m}} = 5{\cdot}3\ \text{cm}\sqrt{\frac{26}{24}} = 5{\cdot}5\ \text{cm}.$

6. *A particle having a charge 20 μC and mass 20 μg moves along a circle of radius 5·0 cm under the action of a magnetic field B = 1·0 T. When the particle is at a point P, a uniform electric field is switched on and it is found that the particle continues on the tangent through P with a uniform velocity. Find the electric field.*

Solution :

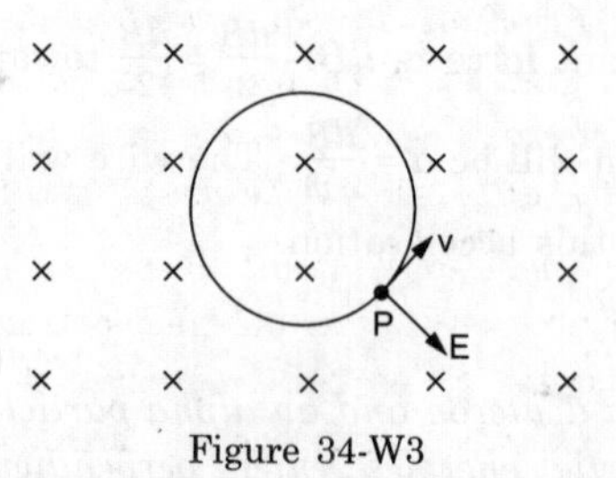

Figure 34-W3

When the particle moves along a circle in the magnetic field B, the magnetic force is radially inward. If an electric field of proper magnitude is switched on which is directed radially outwards, the particle may experience no force. It will then move along a straight line with uniform velocity. This will be the case when

$$qE = qvB \text{ or, } E = vB.$$

The radius of the circle in a magnetic field is given by

$$r = \frac{mv}{qB}$$

or, $v = \frac{rqB}{m}$

$$= \frac{(5{\cdot}0 \times 10^{-2}\ \text{m})\,(20 \times 10^{-6}\ \text{C})\,(1{\cdot}0\ \text{T})}{20 \times 10^{-9}\ \text{kg}} = 50\ \text{m s}^{-1}.$$

The required electric field is

$$E = vB = (50\ \text{m s}^{-1})\,(1.0\ \text{T})$$

$$= 50\ \text{V m}^{-1}.$$

This field will be in a direction which is radially outward at *P*.

7. *A particle of mass $m = 1{\cdot}6 \times 10^{-27}$ kg and charge $q = 1{\cdot}6 \times 10^{-19}$ C moves at a speed of $1{\cdot}0 \times 10^{7}$ m s^{-1}. It enters a region of uniform magnetic field at a point E, as shown in figure (34-W4). The field has a strength of 1·0 T. (a) The magnetic field is directed into the plane of the paper. The particle leaves the region of the field at the point F. Find the distance EF and the angle θ. (b) If the field is coming out of the paper, find the time spent by the particle in the region of the magnetic field after entering it at E.*

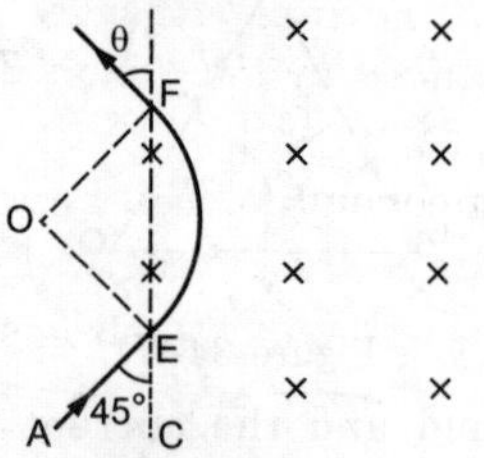

Figure 34-W4

Solution : (a) As the particle enters the magnetic field, it will travel in a circular path. The centre will be on the line perpendicular to its velocity and the radius r will be $\frac{mv}{qB}$ · The direction of the force $q\vec{v} \times \vec{B}$ shows that the centre will be outside the field as shown in figure (34-W4). As $\angle AEO = 90°$ (as AE is tangent and OE is radius) and $\angle AEC = 45°$, we have $\angle OEF = 45°$. As $OE = OF$ (they are radii of the circular arc), $\angle OFE = \angle OEF = 45°$. Also, OF is perpendicular to the velocity of the particle at F, so that $\theta = 45°$. From triangle OEF,

$$EF = 2.OE \cos \angle OEF$$

$$= 2 \cdot \frac{mv}{qB} \cdot \frac{1}{\sqrt{2}}$$

$$= \frac{\sqrt{2} \times (1{\cdot}6 \times 10^{-27}\ \text{kg}) \times (10^{7}\ \text{m s}^{-1})}{(1{\cdot}6 \times 10^{-19}\ \text{C}) \times 1{\cdot}0\ \text{T}}$$

$$= \sqrt{2} \times 10^{-1}\ \text{m} = 14\ \text{cm}.$$

(b)

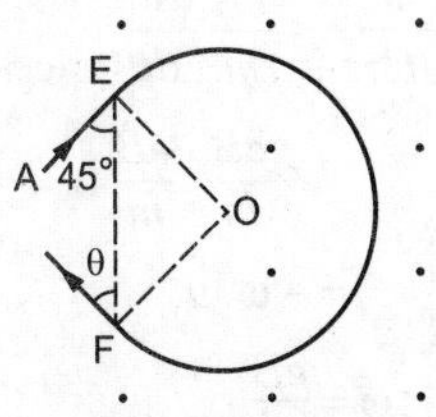

Figure 34-W5

If the magnetic field is coming out of the paper, the direction of the force $q\vec{v}\times\vec{B}$ shows that the centre O will be inside the field region as shown in figure (34-W5). Again $\angle AEO = 90°$, giving

$$\angle OEF = \angle OFE = 45°.$$

Thus, the angle $EOF = 90°$. The particle describes three fourths of the complete circle inside the field. As the speed v is uniform, the time spent in the magnetic field will be

$$\frac{3}{4}\times\frac{2\pi r}{v}=\frac{3\pi mv}{2vqB}=\frac{3\pi m}{2qB}$$

$$=\frac{3\times 3{\cdot}14\times 1{\cdot}6\times 10^{-27}\text{ kg}}{2\times 1{\cdot}6\times 10^{-19}\text{ C}\times 1{\cdot}0\text{ T}}=4{\cdot}7\times 10^{-8}\text{ s}.$$

8. *A beam of protons with a velocity of* 4×10^{5} m s^{-1} *enters a uniform magnetic field of* 0·3 T. *The velocity makes an angle of* 60° *with the magnetic field. Find the radius of the helical path taken by the proton beam and the pitch of the helix.*

Solution : The components of the proton's velocity along and perpendicular to the magnetic field are

$$v_{\|}=(4\times 10^{5}\text{ m s}^{-1})\cos 60° = 2\times 10^{5}\text{ m s}^{-1}.$$

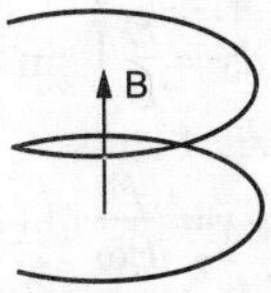

Figure 34-W6

and $\quad v_{\perp}=(4\times 10^{5}\text{ m s}^{-1})\sin 60° = 2\sqrt{3}\times 10^{5}\text{ m s}^{-1}.$

As the force $q\vec{v}\times\vec{B}$ is perpendicular to the magnetic field, the component $v_{\|}$ will remain constant. In the plane perpendicular to the field, the proton will describe a circle whose radius is obtained from the equation

$$qv_{\perp}B=\frac{mv_{\perp}^{2}}{r}$$

or, $$r=\frac{mv_{\perp}}{qB}=\frac{(1{\cdot}67\times 10^{-27}\text{ kg})\times(2\sqrt{3}\times 10^{5}\text{ m s}^{-1})}{(1{\cdot}6\times 10^{-19}\text{ C})\times(0{\cdot}3\text{ T})}$$

$$\approx 0{\cdot}012\text{ m} = 1{\cdot}2\text{ cm}.$$

The time taken in one complete revolution in the plane perpendicular to B is

$$T=\frac{2\pi r}{v_{\perp}}=\frac{2\times 3{\cdot}14\times 0{\cdot}012\text{ m}}{2\sqrt{3}\times 10^{5}\text{ m s}^{-1}}.$$

The distance moved along the field during this period, i.e., the pitch

$$=\frac{(2\times 10^{5}\text{ m s}^{-1})\times 2\times 3{\cdot}14\times 0{\cdot}012\text{ m}}{2\sqrt{3}\times 10^{5}\text{ m s}^{-1}}$$

$$=0{\cdot}044\text{ m} = 4{\cdot}4\text{ cm}.$$

The qualitative nature of the path of the protons is shown in figure (34-W6).

9. *A rectangular coil of size* 3·0 cm × 4·0 cm *and having* 100 turns, *is pivoted about the z-axis as shown in figure (34-W7). The coil carries an electric current of* 2·0 A *and a magnetic field of* 1·0 T *is present along the y-axis. Find the torque acting on the coil if the side in the x–y plane makes an angle* θ = 37° *with the x-axis.*

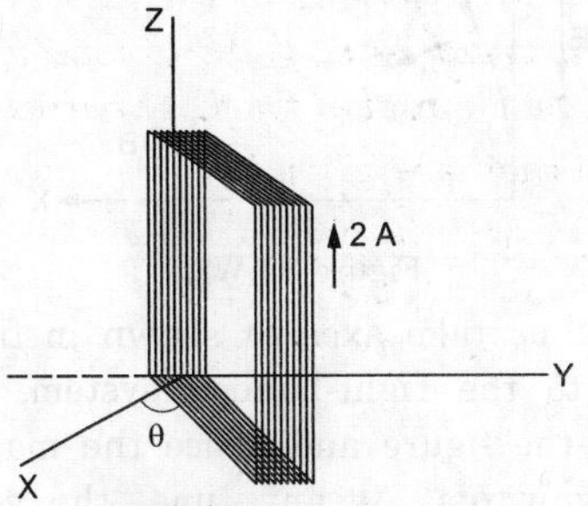

Figure 34-W7

Solution : The magnetic moment of the loop is $\vec{\mu}=ni\vec{A}$ where n is the number of turns, i is the current and $\vec{A}$ is the area-vector. The direction of $\vec{A}$ is determined by the sense of the current and in this case it lies in the fourth quadrant making an angle $\theta = 37°$ with the negative y-axis.

Torque $\vec{\Gamma}=\vec{\mu}\times\vec{B}=ni\vec{A}\times\vec{B}.$

Thus, $\quad \Gamma = 100\times(2\text{ A})\times(12\times 10^{-4}\text{ m}^{2})\times 1\text{ T}\times\sin 37°$

$$=0{\cdot}14\text{ Nm}.$$

The torque is along the positive z-axis.

10. *An electron moves with a constant speed v along a circle of radius r. (a) Find the equivalent current through a point on its path. (b) Find the magnetic moment of the circulating electron. (c) Find the ratio of the magnetic moment to the angular momentum of the electron.*

Solution : (a) Consider a point P on the path of the electron. In one revolution of the electron, a charge e crosses the point P. As the frequency of revolution is $v/(2\pi r)$, the charge crossing P in unit time, i.e., the electric current is

$$i=\frac{ev}{2\pi r}.$$

(b) The area A enclosed by this circular current is πr^{2} so that the magnetic moment of the current is

$$\mu = iA=\left(\frac{ev}{2\pi r}\right)(\pi r^{2})=\frac{evr}{2}$$

in a direction perpendicular to the loop.

(c) The angular momentum of the electron is $l = mvr$. Its direction is opposite to that of the magnetic moment. Thus,

$$\frac{\mu}{l} = \frac{-evr}{2\,mvr} = \frac{-e}{2\,m}.$$

11. *An electron is released from the origin at a place where a uniform electric field E and a uniform magnetic field B exist along the negative y-axis and the negative z-axis respectively. Find the displacement of the electron along the y-axis when its velocity becomes perpendicular to the electric field for the first time.*

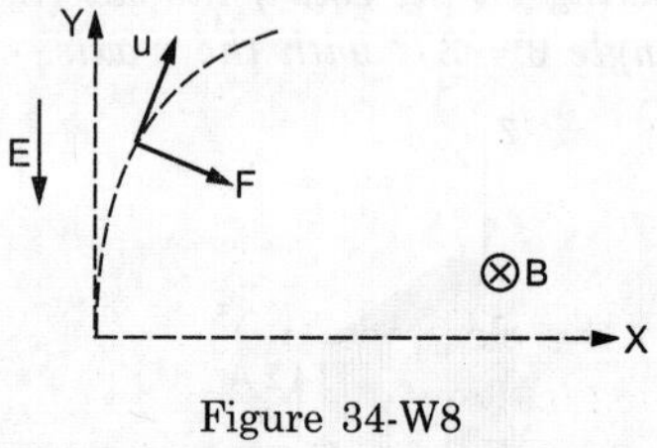

Figure 34-W8

Solution : Let us take axes as shown in figure (34-W8). According to the right-handed system, the *z*-axis is upward in the figure and hence the magnetic field is shown downwards. At any time, the velocity of the electron may be written as

$$\vec{u} = u_x\,\vec{i} + u_y\,\vec{j}.$$

The electric and magnetic fields may be written as

$$\vec{E} = -E\,\vec{j}$$

and $$\vec{B} = -B\,\vec{k}$$

respectively. The force on the electron is

$$\vec{F} = -e(\vec{E} + \vec{u} \times \vec{B})$$
$$= eE\,\vec{j} + eB(u_y\,\vec{i} - u_x\,\vec{j}).$$

Thus, $F_x = eu_y B$

and $F_y = e(E - u_x B)$.

The components of the acceleration are

$$a_x = \frac{du_x}{dt} = \frac{eB}{m}\,u_y \qquad \text{... (i)}$$

and $$a_y = \frac{du_y}{dt} = \frac{e}{m}(E - u_x B). \qquad \text{... (ii)}$$

We have,

$$\frac{d^2u_y}{dt^2} = -\frac{eB}{m}\frac{du_x}{dt}$$
$$= -\frac{eB}{m}\cdot\frac{eB}{m}\,u_y$$
$$= -\omega^2 u_y$$

where $$\omega = \frac{eB}{m}. \qquad \text{... (iii)}$$

This equation is similar to that for a simple harmonic motion. Thus,

$$u_y = A\sin(\omega t + \delta) \qquad \text{... (iv)}$$

and hence,

$$\frac{du_y}{dt} = A\,\omega\cos(\omega t + \delta). \qquad \text{... (v)}$$

At $t = 0$, $u_y = 0$ and $\frac{du_y}{dt} = \frac{F_y}{m} = \frac{eE}{m}$.

Putting in (iv) and (v),

$$\delta = 0 \text{ and } A = \frac{eE}{m\omega} = \frac{E}{B}.$$

Thus, $$u_y = \frac{E}{B}\sin\omega t.$$

The path of the electron will be perpendicular to the *y*-axis when $u_y = 0$. This will be the case for the first time at *t* where

$$\sin\omega t = 0$$

or, $$\omega t = \pi$$

or, $$t = \frac{\pi}{\omega} = \frac{\pi m}{eB}.$$

Also, $$u_y = \frac{dy}{dt} = \frac{E}{B}\sin\omega t$$

or, $$\int_0^y dy = \frac{E}{B}\int_0^t \sin\omega t\,dt$$

or, $$y = \frac{E}{B\omega}(1 - \cos\omega t).$$

At $$t = \frac{\pi}{\omega},$$

$$y = \frac{E}{B\omega}(1 - \cos\pi) = \frac{2E}{B\omega}.$$

Thus, the displacement along the *y*-axis is

$$\frac{2E}{B\omega} = \frac{2Em}{BeB} = \frac{2Em}{eB^2}.$$

□

QUESTIONS FOR SHORT ANSWER

1. Suppose a charged particle moves with a velocity *v* near a wire carrying an electric current. A magnetic force, therefore, acts on it. If the same particle is seen from a frame moving with velocity *v* in the same direction, the charge will be found at rest. Will the magnetic force become zero in this frame ? Will the magnetic field become zero in this frame ?

2. Can a charged particle be accelerated by a magnetic field ? Can its speed be increased ?
3. Will a current loop placed in a magnetic field always experience a zero force ?
4. The free electrons in a conducting wire are in constant thermal motion. If such a wire, carrying no current, is placed in a magnetic field, is there a magnetic force on each free electron? Is there a magnetic force on the wire?
5. Assume that the magnetic field is uniform in a cubical region and is zero outside. Can you project a charged particle from outside into the field so that the particle describes a complete circle in the field ?
6. An electron beam projected along the positive x-axis deflects along the positive y-axis. If this deflection is caused by a magnetic field, what is the direction of the field ? Can we conclude that the field is parallel to the z-axis ?
7. Is it possible for a current loop to stay without rotating in a uniform magnetic field ? If yes, what should be the orientation of the loop ?
8. The net charge in a current-carrying wire is zero. Then, why does a magnetic field exert a force on it ?
9. The torque on a current loop is zero if the angle between the positive normal and the magnetic field is either $\theta = 0$ or $\theta = 180°$. In which of the two orientations, the equilibrium is stable ?
10. Verify that the units weber and volt second are the same.

OBJECTIVE I

1. A positively charged particle projected towards east is deflected towards north by a magnetic field. The field may be
(a) towards west (b) towards south
(c) upward (d) downward.
2. A charged particle is whirled in a horizontal circle on a frictionless table by attaching it to a string fixed at one point. If a magnetic field is switched on in the vertical direction, the tension in the string
(a) will increase (b) will decrease
(c) will remain the same (d) may increase or decrease.
3. Which of the following particles will experience maximum magnetic force (magnitude) when projected with the same velocity perpendicular to a magnetic field ?
(a) Electron (b) Proton (c) He^{+} (d) Li^{++}
4. Which of the following particles will describe the smallest circle when projected with the same velocity perpendicular to a magnetic field ?
(a) Electron (b) Proton (c) He^{+} (d) Li^{+}
5. Which of the following particles will have minimum frequency of revolution when projected with the same velocity perpendicular to a magnetic field ?
(a) Electron (b) Proton (c) He^{+} (d) Li^{+}
6. A circular loop of area 1 cm^2, carrying a current of 10 A, is placed in a magnetic field of 0·1 T perpendicular to the plane of the loop. The torque on the loop due to the magnetic field is
(a) zero (b) 10^{-4} N m (c) 10^{-2} N m (d) 1 N m
7. A beam consisting of protons and electrons moving at the same speed goes through a thin region in which there is a magnetic field perpendicular to the beam. The protons and the electrons
(a) will go undeviated
(b) will be deviated by the same angle and will not separate
(c) will be deviated by different angles and hence separate
(d) will be deviated by the same angle but will separate.
8. A charged particle moves in a uniform magnetic field. The velocity of the particle at some instant makes an acute angle with the magnetic field. The path of the particle will be
(a) a straight line (b) a circle
(c) a helix with uniform pitch
(d) a helix with nonuniform pitch.
9. A particle moves in a region having a uniform magnetic field and a parallel, uniform electric field. At some instant, the velocity of the particle is perpendicular to the field direction. The path of the particle will be
(a) a straight line (b) a circle
(c) a helix with uniform pitch
(d) a helix with nonuniform pitch.
10. An electric current i enters and leaves a uniform circular wire of radius a through diametrically opposite points. A charged particle q moving along the axis of the circular wire passes through its centre at speed v. The magnetic force acting on the particle when it passes through the centre has a magnitude
(a) $qv\frac{\mu_0 i}{2a}$ (b) $qv\frac{\mu_0 i}{2\pi a}$ (c) $qv\frac{\mu_0 i}{a}$ (d) zero.

OBJECTIVE II

1. If a charged particle at rest experiences no electromagnetic force,
(a) the electric field must be zero
(b) the magnetic field must be zero
(c) the electric field may or may not be zero
(d) the magnetic field may or may not be zero.

2. If a charged particle kept at rest experiences an electromagnetic force,
(a) the electric field must not be zero
(b) the magnetic field must not be zero
(c) the electric field may or may not be zero
(d) the magnetic field may or may not be zero.

3. If a charged particle projected in a gravity-free room deflects,
(a) there must be an electric field
(b) there must be a magnetic field
(c) both fields cannot be zero
(d) both fields can be nonzero.

4. A charged particle moves in a gravity-free space without change in velocity. Which of the following is/are possible ?
(a) $E = 0, B = 0$ (b) $E = 0, B \neq 0$
(c) $E \neq 0, B = 0$ (d) $E \neq 0, B \neq 0$

5. A charged particle moves along a circle under the action of possible constant electric and magnetic fields. Which of the following are possible ?
(a) $E = 0, B = 0$ (b) $E = 0, B \neq 0$
(c) $E \neq 0, B = 0$ (d) $E \neq 0, B \neq 0$

6. A charged particle goes undeflected in a region containing electric and magnetic field. It is possible that
(a) $\vec{E} \parallel \vec{B}$, $\vec{v} \parallel \vec{E}$ (b) $\vec{E}$ is not parallel to $\vec{B}$
(c) $\vec{v} \parallel \vec{B}$ but $\vec{E}$ is not parallel to $\vec{B}$
(d) $\vec{E} \parallel \vec{B}$ but $\vec{v}$ is not parallel to $\vec{E}$.

7. If a charged particle goes unaccelerated in a region containing electric and magnetic fields,
(a) $\vec{E}$ must be perpendicular to $\vec{B}$
(b) $\vec{v}$ must be perpendicular to $\vec{E}$
(c) $\vec{v}$ must be perpendicular to $\vec{B}$
(d) E must be equal to vB.

8. Two ions have equal masses but one is singly-ionized and the other is doubly-ionized. They are projected from the same place in a uniform magnetic field with the same velocity perpendicular to the field.
(a) Both ions will go along circles of equal radii.
(b) The circle described by the singly-ionized charge will have a radius double that of the other circle.
(c) The two circles do not touch each other.
(d) The two circles touch each other.

9. An electron is moving along the positive x-axis. You want to apply a magnetic field for a short time so that the electron may reverse its direction and move parallel to the negative x-axis. This can be done by applying the magnetic field along
(a) y-axis (b) z-axis (c) y-axis only (d) z-axis only.

10. Let $\vec{E}$ and $\vec{B}$ denote electric and magnetic fields in a frame S and $\vec{E'}$ and $\vec{B'}$ in another frame S' moving with respect to S at a velocity $\vec{v}$. Two of the following equations are wrong. Identify them.
(a) $B_y' = B_y + \dfrac{vE_z}{c^2}$ (b) $E_y' = E_y - \dfrac{vB_z}{c^2}$
(c) $B_y' = B_y + vE_z$ (d) $E_y' = E_y + vB_z$

EXERCISES

1. An alpha particle is projected vertically upward with a speed of $3{\cdot}0 \times 10^4$ km s^{-1} in a region where a magnetic field of magnitude 1·0 T exists in the direction south to north. Find the magnetic force that acts on the α-particle.

2. An electron is projected horizontally with a kinetic energy of 10 keV. A magnetic field of strength $1{\cdot}0 \times 10^{-7}$ T exists in the vertically upward direction. (a) Will the electron deflect towards right or towards left of its motion ? (b) Calculate the sideways deflection of the electron in travelling through 1 m. Make appropriate approximations.

3. A magnetic field of $(4{\cdot}0 \times 10^{-3} \vec{k})$ T exerts a force of $(4{\cdot}0\,\vec{i} + 3{\cdot}0\,\vec{j}) \times 10^{-10}$ N on a particle having a charge of $1{\cdot}0 \times 10^{-9}$ C and going in the x–y plane. Find the velocity of the particle.

4. An experimenter's diary reads as follows: "a charged particle is projected in a magnetic field of $(7{\cdot}0\,\vec{i} - 3{\cdot}0\,\vec{j}) \times 10^{-3}$ T. The acceleration of the particle is found to be $(\square\,\vec{i} + 7{\cdot}0\,\vec{j}) \times 10^{-6}$ m s^{-2}". The number to the left of $\vec{i}$ in the last expression was not readable. What can this number be ?

5. A 10 g bullet having a charge of 4·00 μC is fired at a speed of 270 m s^{-1} in a horizontal direction. A vertical magnetic field of 500 μT exists in the space. Find the deflection of the bullet due to the magnetic field as it travels through 100 m. Make appropriate approximations.

6. When a proton is released from rest in a room, it starts with an initial acceleration a_0 towards west. When it is projected towards north with a speed v_0, it moves with an initial acceleration $3a_0$ towards west. Find the electric field and the minimum possible magnetic field in the room.

7. Consider a 10-cm long portion of a straight wire carrying a current of 10 A placed in a magnetic field of 0·1 T making an angle of 53° with the wire. What magnetic force does the wire experience ?

8. A current of 2 A enters at the corner d of a square frame $abcd$ of side 20 cm and leaves at the opposite corner b. A magnetic field $B = 0{\cdot}1$ T exists in the space in a direction perpendicular to the plane of the frame as shown in figure

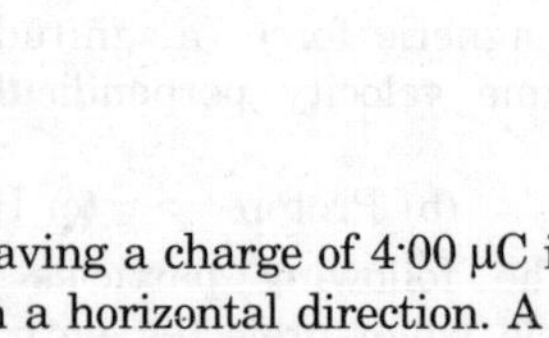

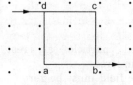

Figure 34-E1

(34-E1). Find the magnitude and direction of the magnetic forces on the four sides of the frame.

9. A magnetic field of strength 1·0 T is produced by a strong electromagnet in a cylindrical region of radius 4·0 cm as shown in figure (34-E2). A wire, carrying a current of 2·0 A, is placed perpendicular to and intersecting the axis of the cylindrical region. Find the magnitude of the force acting on the wire.

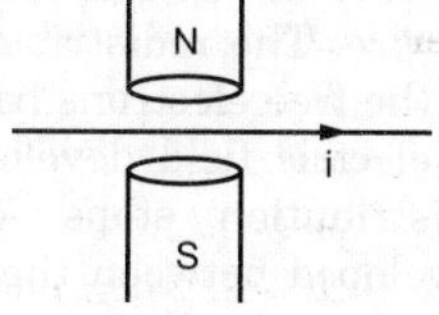

Figure 34-E2

10. A wire of length l carries a current i along the x-axis. A magnetic field exists which is given as $\vec{B} = B_0(\vec{i} + \vec{j} + \vec{k})$ T. Find the magnitude of the magnetic force acting on the wire.

11. A current of 5·0 A exists in the circuit shown in figure (34-E3). The wire PQ has a length of 50 cm and the magnetic field in which it is immersed has a magnitude of 0·20 T. Find the magnetic force acting on the wire PQ.

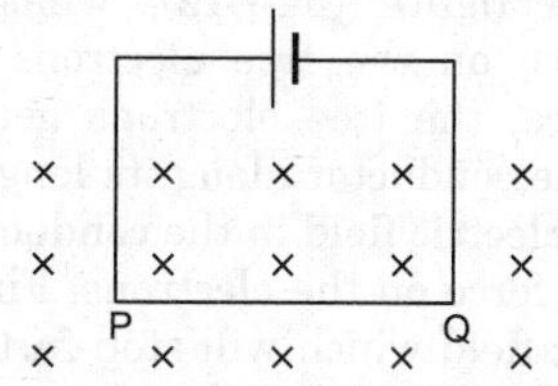

Figure 34-E3

12. A circular loop of radius a, carrying a current i, is placed in a two-dimensional magnetic field. The centre of the loop coincides with the centre of the field (figure 34-E4). The strength of the magnetic field at the periphery of the loop is B. Find the magnetic force on the wire.

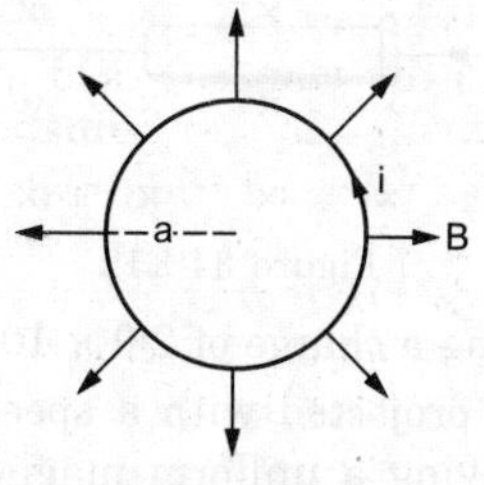

Figure 34-E4

13. A hypothetical magnetic field existing in a region is given by $\vec{B} = B_0\,\vec{e_r}$, where $\vec{e_r}$ denotes the unit vector along the radial direction. A circular loop of radius a, carrying a current i, is placed with its plane parallel to the x–y plane and the centre at (0, 0, d). Find the magnitude of the magnetic force acting on the loop.

14. A rectangular wire-loop of width a is suspended from the insulated pan of a spring balance as shown in figure (34-E5). A current i exists in the anticlockwise direction in the loop. A magnetic field B exists in the lower region. Find the change in the tension of the spring if the current in the loop is reversed.

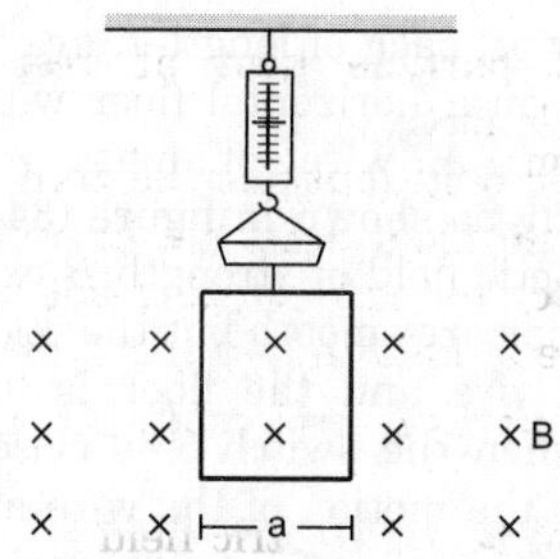

figure 34-E5

15. A current loop of arbitrary shape lies in a uniform magnetic field B. Show that the net magnetic force acting on the loop is zero.

16. Prove that the force acting on a current-carrying wire, joining two fixed points a and b in a uniform magnetic field, is independent of the shape of the wire.

17. A semicircular wire of radius 5·0 cm carries a current of 5·0 A. A magnetic field B of magnitude 0·50 T exists along the perpendicular to the plane of the wire. Find the magnitude of the magnetic force acting on the wire.

18. A wire, carrying a current i, is kept in the x–y plane along the curve $y = A\sin\left(\frac{2\pi}{\lambda}x\right)$. A magnetic field B exists in the z-direction. Find the magnitude of the magnetic force on the portion of the wire between $x = 0$ and $x = \lambda$.

19. A rigid wire consists of a semicircular portion of radius R and two straight sections (figure 34-E6). The wire is partially immersed in a perpendicular magnetic field B as shown in the figure. Find the magnetic force on the wire if it carries a current i.

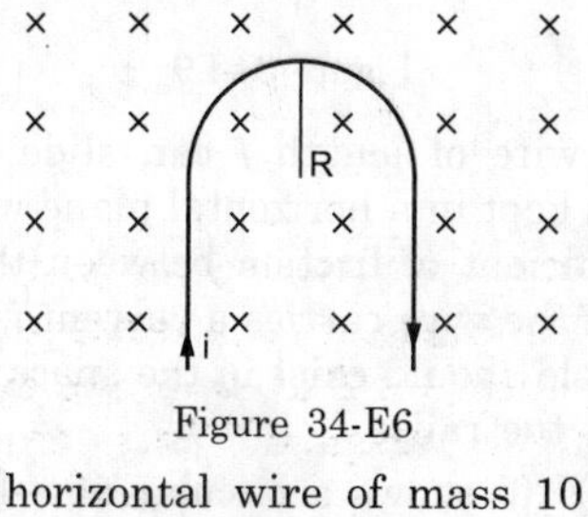

Figure 34-E6

20. A straight horizontal wire of mass 10 mg and length 1·0 m carries a current of 2·0 A. What minimum magnetic field B should be applied in the region so that the magnetic force on the wire may balance its weight ?

21. Figure (34-E7) shows a rod PQ of length 20·0 cm and mass 200 g suspended through a fixed point O by two threads of lengths 20·0 cm each. A magnetic field of strength 0·500 T exists in the vicinity of the wire PQ as shown in the figure. The wires connecting PQ with the battery are loose and exert no force on PQ. (a) Find the tension in the threads when the switch S is open. (b) A current of 2·0 A is established when the switch S is closed. Find the tension in the threads now.

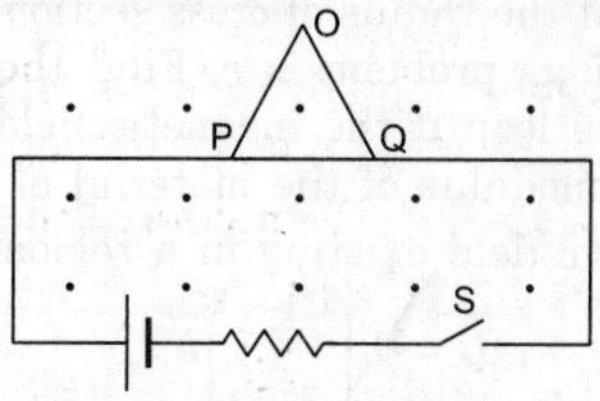

Figure 34-E7

22. Two metal strips, each of length l, are clamped parallel to each other on a horizontal floor with a separation b between them. A wire of mass m lies on them perpendicularly as shown in figure (34-E8). A vertically upward magnetic field of strength B exists in the space. The metal strips are smooth but the coefficient of friction between the wire and the floor is μ. A current i is established when the switch S is closed at the instant $t = 0$. Discuss the motion of the wire after the switch is closed. How far away from the strips will the wire reach ?

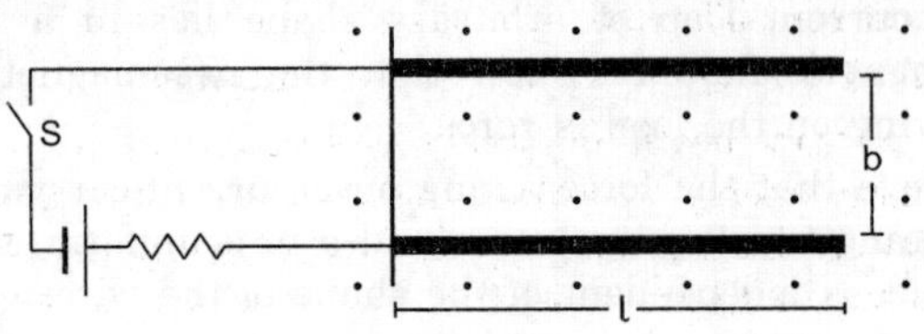

Figure 34-E8

23. A metal wire PQ of mass 10 g lies at rest on two horizontal metal rails separated by 4·90 cm (figure 34-E9). A vertically downward magnetic field of magnitude 0·800 T exists in the space. The resistance of the circuit is slowly decreased and it is found that when the resistance goes below 20·0 Ω, the wire PQ starts sliding on the rails. Find the coefficient of friction.

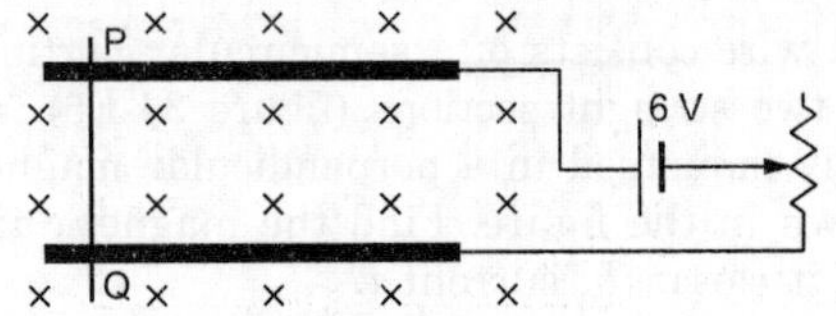

Figure 34-E9

24. A straight wire of length l can slide on two parallel plastic rails kept in a horizontal plane with a separation d. The coefficient of friction between the wire and the rails is μ. If the wire carries a current i, what minimum magnetic field should exist in the space in order to slide the wire on the rails.

25. Figure (34-E10) shows a circular wire-loop of radius a, carrying a current i, placed in a perpendicular magnetic field B. (a) Consider a small part dl of the wire. Find the force on this part of the wire exerted by the magnetic field. (b) Find the force of compression in the wire.

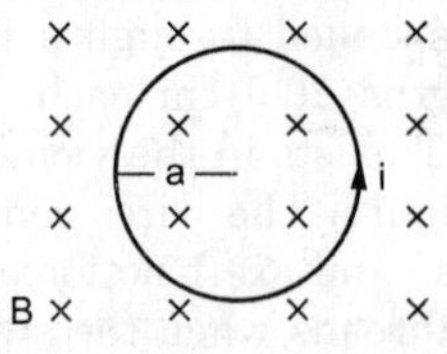

Figure 34-E10

26. Suppose that the radius of cross section of the wire used in the previous problem is r. Find the increase in the radius of the loop if the magnetic field is switched off. The Young modulus of the material of the wire is Y.

27. The magnetic field existing in a region is given by

$$\vec{B} = B_0\left(1 + \frac{x}{l}\right)\vec{k}.$$

A square loop of edge l and carrying a current i, is placed with its edges parallel to the x–y axes. Find the magnitude of the net magnetic force experienced by the loop.

28. A conducting wire of length l, lying normal to a magnetic field B, moves with a velocity v as shown in figure (34-E11). (a) Find the average magnetic force on a free electron of the wire. (b) Due to this magnetic force, electrons concentrate at one end resulting in an electric field inside the wire. The redistribution stops when the electric force on the free electrons balances the magnetic force. Find the electric field developed inside the wire when the redistribution stops. (c) What potential difference is developed between the ends of the wire ?

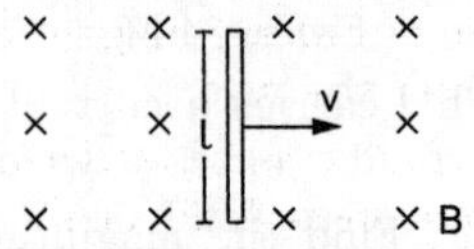

Figure 34-E11

29. A current i is passed through a silver strip of width d and area of cross section A. The number of free electrons per unit volume is n. (a) Find the drift velocity v of the electrons. (b) If a magnetic field B exists in the region as shown in figure (34-E12), what is the average magnetic force on the free electrons ? (c) Due to the magnetic force, the free electrons get accumulated on one side of the conductor along its length. This produces a transverse electric field in the conductor which opposes the magnetic force on the electrons. Find the magnitude of the electric field which will stop further accumulation of electrons. (d) What will be the potential difference developed across the width of the conductor due to the electron-accumulation ? The appearance of a transverse emf, when a current-carrying wire is placed in a magnetic field, is called *Hall effect.*

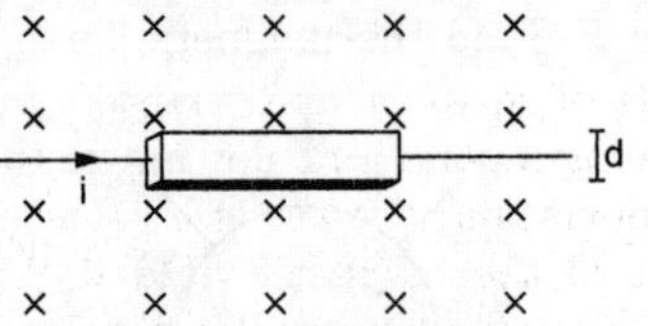

Figure 34-E12

30. A particle having a charge of $2{\cdot}0 \times 10^{-8}$ C and a mass of $2{\cdot}0 \times 10^{-10}$ g is projected with a speed of $2{\cdot}0 \times 10^{3}$ m s^{-1} in a region having a uniform magnetic field of 0·10 T. The velocity is perpendicular to the field. Find the radius of the circle formed by the particle and also the time period.

31. A proton describes a circle of radius 1 cm in a magnetic field of strength 0·10 T. What would be the radius of the circle described by an α-particle moving with the same speed in the same magnetic field ?

32. An electron having a kinetic energy of 100 eV circulates in a path of radius 10 cm in a magnetic field. Find the magnetic field and the number of revolutions per second made by the electron.

33. Protons having kinetic energy K emerge from an accelerator as a narrow beam. The beam is bent by a perpendicular magnetic field so that it just misses a plane target kept at a distance l in front of the accelerator. Find the magnetic field.

34. A charged particle is accelerated through a potential difference of 12 kV and acquires a speed of $1{\cdot}0 \times 10^{6}$ m s^{-1}. It is then injected perpendicularly into a magnetic field of strength 0·2 T. Find the radius of the circle described by it.

35. Doubly ionized helium ions are projected with a speed of 10 km s^{-1} in a direction perpendicular to a uniform magnetic field of magnitude 1·0 T. Find (a) the force acting on an ion, (b) the radius of the circle in which it circulates and (c) the time taken by an ion to complete the circle.

36. A proton is projected with a velocity of 3×10^{6} m s^{-1} perpendicular to a uniform magnetic field of 0·6 T. Find the acceleration of the proton.

37. (a) An electron moves along a circle of radius 1 m in a perpendicular magnetic field of strength 0·50 T. What would be its speed? Is it reasonable? (b) If a proton moves along a circle of the same radius in the same magnetic field, what would be its speed?

38. A particle of mass m and positive charge q, moving with a uniform velocity v, enters a magnetic field B as shown in figure (34-E13). (a) Find the radius of the circular arc it describes in the magnetic field. (b) Find the angle subtended by the arc at the centre. (c) How long does the particle stay inside the magnetic field? (d) Solve the three parts of the above problem if the charge q on the particle is negative.

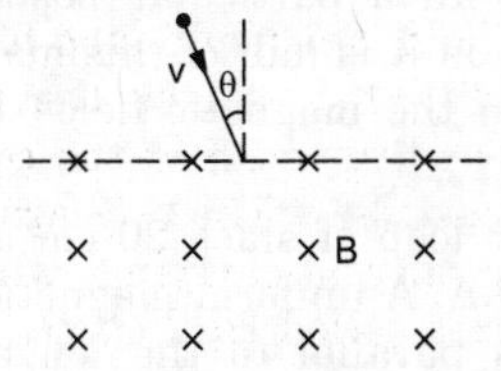

Figure 34-E13

39. A particle of mass m and charge q is projected into a region having a perpendicular magnetic field B. Find the angle of deviation (figure 34-E14) of the particle as it comes out of the magnetic field if the width d of the region is very slightly smaller than

(a) $\frac{mv}{qB}$ (b) $\frac{mv}{2qB}$ (c) $\frac{2mv}{qB}$.

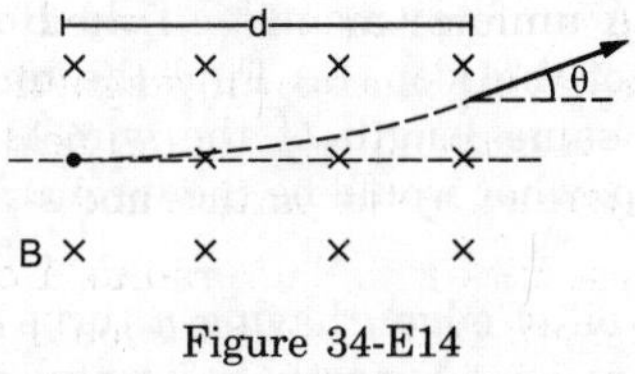

Figure 34-E14

40. A narrow beam of singly-charged carbon ions, moving at a constant velocity of $6{\cdot}0 \times 10^{4}$ m s^{-1}, is sent perpendicularly in a rectangular region having uniform magnetic field B = 0·5 T (figure 34-E15). It is found that two beams emerge from the field in the backward direction, the separations from the incident beam being 3·0 cm and 3·5 cm. Identify the isotopes present in the ion beam. Take the mass of an ion = $A(1{\cdot}6 \times 10^{-27})$ kg, where A is the mass number.

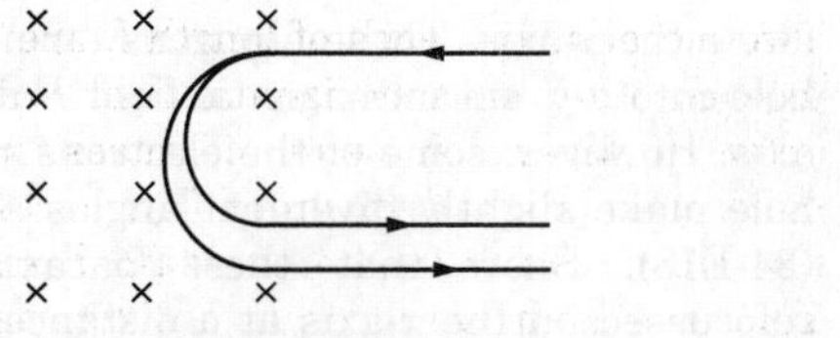

Figure 34-E15

41. Fe^{+} ions are accelerated through a potential difference of 500 V and are injected normally into a homogeneous magnetic field B of strength 20·0 mT. Find the radius of the circular paths followed by the isotopes with mass numbers 57 and 58. Take the mass of an ion = A $(1{\cdot}6 \times 10^{-27})$ kg where A is the mass number.

42. A narrow beam of singly charged potassium ions of kinetic energy 32 keV is injected into a region of width 1·00 cm having a magnetic field of strength 0·500 T as shown in figure (34-E16). The ions are collected at a screen 95·5 cm away from the field region. If the beam contains isotopes of atomic weights 39 and 41, find the separation between the points where these isotopes strike the screen. Take the mass of a potassium ion = A $(1{\cdot}6 \times 10^{-27})$ kg where A is the mass number.

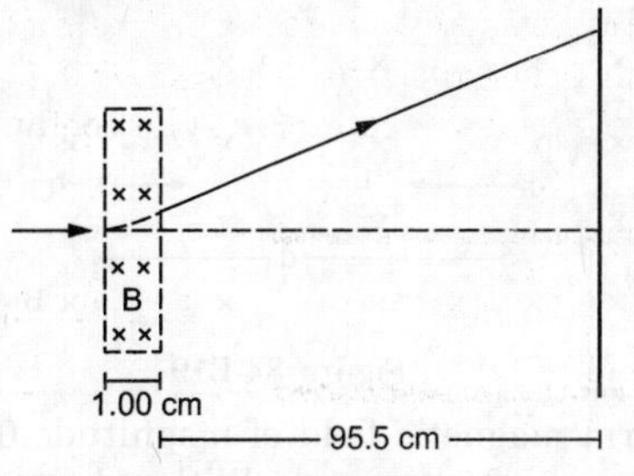

Figure 34-E16

43. Figure (34-E17) shows a convex lens of focal length 12 cm lying in a uniform magnetic field B of magnitude 1·2 T parallel to its principal axis. A particle having a charge $2{\cdot}0 \times 10^{-3}$ C and mass $2{\cdot}0 \times 10^{-5}$ kg is projected perpendicular to the plane of the diagram with a speed of 4·8 m s^{-1}. The particle moves along a circle with its centre on the principal axis at a distance of 18 cm from the lens. Show that the image of the particle goes along a circle and find the radius of that circle.

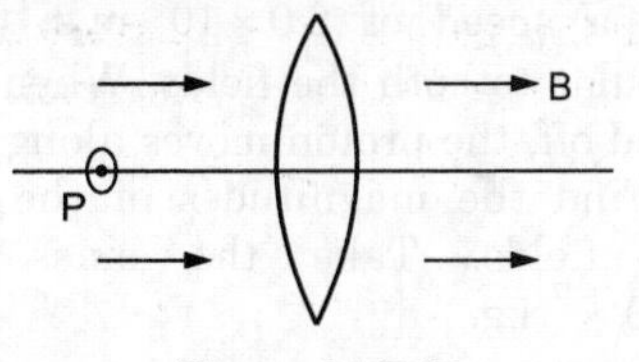

Figure 34-E17

44. Electrons emitted with negligible speed from an electron gun are accelerated through a potential difference V

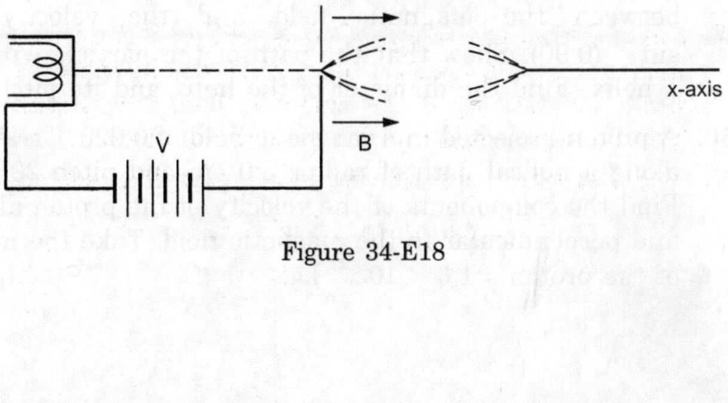

Figure 34-E18

along the x-axis. These electrons emerge from a narrow hole into a uniform magnetic field B directed along this axis. However, some of the electrons emerging from the hole make slightly divergent angles as shown in figure (34-E18). Show that these paraxial electrons are refocussed on the x-axis at a distance

$$\sqrt{\frac{8\pi^2 mV}{eB^2}}.$$

45. Two particles, each having a mass m are placed at a separation d in a uniform magnetic field B as shown in figure (34-E19). They have opposite charges of equal magnitude q. At time $t = 0$, the particles are projected towards each other, each with a speed v. Suppose the Coulomb force between the charges is switched off. (a) Find the maximum value v_m of the projection speed so that the two particles do not collide. (b) What would be the minimum and maximum separation between the particles if $v = v_m/2$? (c) At what instant will a collision occur between the particles if $v = 2v_m$? (d) Suppose $v = 2v_m$ and the collision between the particles is completely inelastic. Describe the motion after the collision.

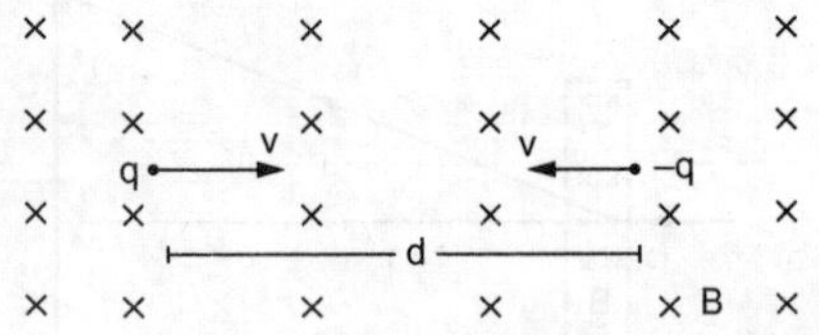

Figure 34-E19

46. A uniform magnetic field of magnitude 0·20 T exists in space from east to west. With what speed should a particle of mass 0·010 g and having a charge $1{\cdot}0 \times 10^{-5}$ C be projected from south to north so that it moves with a uniform velocity ?

47. A particle moves in a circle of diameter 1·0 cm under the action of a magnetic field of 0·40 T. An electric field of 200 V m^{-1} makes the path straight. Find the charge/mass ratio of the particle.

48. A proton goes undeflected in a crossed electric and magnetic field (the fields are perpendicular to each other) at a speed of $2{\cdot}0 \times 10^5$ m s^{-1}. The velocity is perpendicular to both the fields. When the electric field is switched off, the proton moves along a circle of radius 4·0 cm. Find the magnitudes of the electric and the magnetic fields. Take the mass of the proton $= 1{\cdot}6 \times 10^{-27}$ kg.

49. A particle having a charge of 5·0 μC and a mass of $5{\cdot}0 \times 10^{-12}$ kg is projected with a speed of 1·0 km s^{-1} in a magnetic field of magnitude 5·0 mT. The angle between the magnetic field and the velocity is $\sin^{-1}(0{\cdot}90)$. Show that the path of the particle will be a helix. Find the diameter of the helix and its pitch.

50. A proton projected in a magnetic field of 0·020 T travels along a helical path of radius 5·0 cm and pitch 20 cm. Find the components of the velocity of the proton along and perpendicular to the magnetic field. Take the mass of the proton $= 1{\cdot}6 \times 10^{-27}$ kg.

51. A particle having mass m and charge q is released from the origin in a region in which electric field and magnetic field are given by

$$\vec{B} = -B_0\,\vec{j} \text{ and } \vec{E} = E_0\,\vec{k}.$$

Find the speed of the particle as a function of its z-coordinate.

52. An electron is emitted with negligible speed from the negative plate of a parallel plate capacitor charged to a potential difference V. The separation between the plates is d and a magnetic field B exists in the space as shown in figure (34-E20). Show that the electron will fail to strike the upper plate if

$$d > \left(\frac{2m_e V}{eB_0^2}\right)^{\frac{1}{2}}.$$

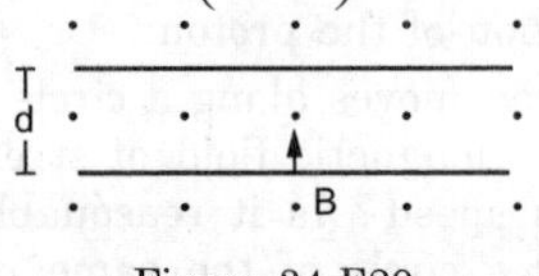

Figure 34-E20

53. A rectangular coil of 100 turns has length 5 cm and width 4 cm. It is placed with its plane parallel to a uniform magnetic field and a current of 2 A is sent through the coil. Find the magnitude of the magnetic field B, if the torque acting on the coil is 0·2 N m^{-1}.

54. A 50-turn circular coil of radius 2·0 cm carrying a current of 5·0 A is rotated in a magnetic field of strength 0·20 T. (a) What is the maximum torque that acts on the coil ? (b) In a particular position of the coil, the torque acting on it is half of this maximum. What is the angle between the magnetic field and the plane of the coil ?

55. A rectangular loop of sides 20 cm and 10 cm carries a current of 5·0 A. A uniform magnetic field of magnitude 0·20 T exists parallel to the longer side of the loop. (a) What is the force acting on the loop ? (b) What is the torque acting on the loop ?

56. A circular coil of radius 2·0 cm has 500 turns in it and carries a current of 1·0 A. Its axis makes an angle of 30° with the uniform magnetic field of magnitude 0·40 T that exists in the space. Find the torque acting on the coil.

57. A circular loop carrying a current i has wire of total length L. A uniform magnetic field B exists parallel to the plane of the loop. (a) Find the torque on the loop. (b) If the same length of the wire is used to form a square loop, what would be the torque ? Which is larger?

58. A square coil of edge l having n turns carries a current i. It is kept on a smooth horizontal plate. A uniform magnetic field B exists in a direction parallel to an edge. The total mass of the coil is M. What should be the minimum value of B for which the coil will start tipping over ?

59. Consider a nonconducting ring of radius r and mass m which has a total charge q distributed uniformly on it. The ring is rotated about its axis with an angular speed ω. (a) Find the equivalent electric current in the ring. (b) Find the magnetic moment μ of the ring. (c) Show that $\mu = \frac{q}{2m} l$ where l is the angular momentum of the ring about its axis of rotation.

60. Consider a nonconducting plate of radius r and mass m which has a charge q distributed uniformly over it. The plate is rotated about its axis with an angular speed ω. Show that the magnetic moment μ and the angular momentum l of the plate are related as $\mu = \frac{q}{2m} l$.

61. Consider a solid sphere of radius r and mass m which has a charge q distributed uniformly over its volume. The sphere is rotated about a diameter with an angular speed ω. Show that the magnetic moment μ and the angular momentum l of the sphere are related as $\mu = \frac{q}{2m} l$.

□

ANSWERS

OBJECTIVE I

1. (d)	2. (d)	3. (d)	4. (a)	5. (d)	6. (a)
7. (c)	8. (c)	9. (d)	10. (d)		

OBJECTIVE II

1. (a), (d)	2. (a), (d)	3. (c), (d)
4. (a), (b), (d)	5. (b)	6. (a), (b)
7. (a), (b)	8. (b), (d)	9. (a), (b)
10. (b), (c)		

EXERCISES

1. 9.6×10^{-12} N towards west
2. (a) left (b) ≈ 0.15 mm
3. $(-75\vec{i} + 100\vec{j})$ m s^{-1}
4. 3·0
5. 3.7×10^{-6} m
6. $\frac{ma_0}{e}$ towards west, $\frac{2ma_0}{ev_0}$ downward
7. 0·08 N perpendicular to both the wire and the field
8. 0·02 N on each wire, on da and cb towards left and on dc and ab downward
9. 0·16 N
10. $\sqrt{2} B_0 il$
11. 0·50 N towards the inside of the circuit
12. $2\pi aiB$, perpendicular to the plane of the figure going into it
13. $\frac{2\pi a^2 iB_0}{\sqrt{a^2 + d^2}}$
14. $2iBa$
17. 0·25 N
18. $i\lambda B$
19. $2iRB$, upward in the figure
20. 4.9×10^{-5} T
21. (a) 1·13 N (b) 1·25 N
22. $\frac{ilbB}{\mu mg}$
23. 0·12
24. $\frac{\mu mg}{il}$
25. (a) $idlB$ towards the centre (b) iaB
26. $\frac{ia^2B}{\pi r^2 Y}$
27. $iB_0 l$
28. (a) evB (b) vB (c) lBv
29. (a) $\frac{i}{Ane}$ (b) $\frac{iB}{An}$ upwards in the figure (c) $\frac{iB}{Ane}$ (d) $\frac{iBd}{Ane}$
30. 20 cm, 6.3×10^{-4} s
31. 2 cm
32. 3.4×10^{-4} T, 9.4×10^{6}
33. $\frac{\sqrt{2m_p K}}{el}$ where m_p = mass of a proton
34. 12 cm
35. (a) 3.2×10^{-15} N (b) 2.1×10^{-4} m (c) 1.31×10^{-7} s
36. 1.72×10^{14} m s^{-2}
37. (a) 8.8×10^{10} m s^{-1} (b) 4.8×10^{7} m s^{-1}
38. (a) $\frac{mv}{qB}$ (b) $\pi - 2\theta$ (c) $\frac{m}{qB}(\pi - 2\theta)$ (d) $\frac{mv}{qB}$, $\pi + 2\theta$, $\frac{m}{qB}(\pi + 2\theta)$
39. (a) $\pi/2$ (b) $\pi/6$ (c) π
40. ^{12}C and ^{14}C
41. 119 cm and 120 cm
42. 0·75 mm
43. 8 cm
45. (a) $\frac{qBd}{2m}$ (b) $\frac{d}{2}, \frac{3d}{2}$ (c) $\frac{\pi m}{6qB}$ (d) the particles stick together and the combined mass moves with constant speed v_m along the straight line drawn upward in the plane of figure through the point of collision

46. $49\ m\ s^{-1}$
47. $2{\cdot}5 \times 10^{5}$ C kg^{-1}
48. $1{\cdot}0 \times 10^{4}$ N C^{-1}, 0·05 T
49. 36 cm, 55 cm
50. $6{\cdot}4 \times 10^{4}$ m s^{-1}, $1{\cdot}0 \times 10^{5}$
51. $\sqrt{\dfrac{2qE_0 z}{m}}$
53. 0·5 T
54. (a) $6{\cdot}3 \times 10^{-2}$ N m (b) 60°
55. (a) zero (b) 0·02 N m parallel to the shorter side.
56. 0·13 N m
57. (a) $\dfrac{iL^2B}{4\pi}$ (b) $\dfrac{iL^2B}{16}$
58. $\dfrac{Mg}{2nil}$
59. (a) $\dfrac{q\omega}{2\pi}$ (b) $\dfrac{q\omega r^2}{2}$

□

CHAPTER 35

MAGNETIC FIELD DUE TO A CURRENT

In the previous chapter, we defined magnetic field in terms of the force it exerts on a moving charge. In this chapter, we shall discuss how a magnetic field can be produced. A magnetic field can be produced by moving charges or electric currents. The basic equation governing the magnetic field due to a current distribution is the *Biot–Savart law*.

35.1 BIOT–SAVART LAW

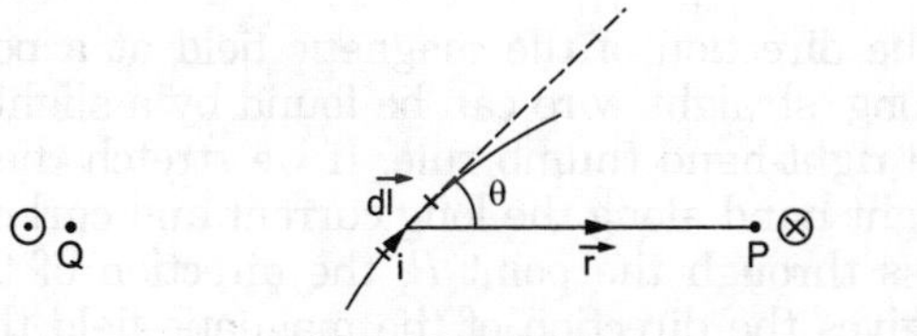

Figure 35.1

The magnetic field at a point P, due to a current element, is given by

$$d\vec{B} = \frac{1}{4\pi\varepsilon_0 c^2} i \frac{\vec{dl} \times \vec{r}}{r^3} \qquad \dots (35.1)$$

where c is the speed of light, i is the current, $\vec{dl}$ is the length-vector of the current element and $\vec{r}$ is the vector joining the current element to the point P. The quantity $\frac{1}{\varepsilon_0 c^2}$ is written as μ_0 and is called the *permeability of vacuum*. Its value is $4\pi \times 10^{-7}$ T mA^{-1}. In terms of μ_0, equation (35.1) becomes

$$d\vec{B} = \frac{\mu_0}{4\pi} i \frac{\vec{dl} \times \vec{r}}{r^3} . \qquad \dots (35.2)$$

This equation is the mathematical form of Biot–Savart Law.

The magnitude of the field is

$$dB = \frac{\mu_0}{4\pi} \frac{i dl \sin\theta}{r^2} \qquad \dots (35.3)$$

where θ is the angle between $\vec{dl}$ and $\vec{r}$. The direction of the field is perpendicular to the plane containing the current element and the point P according to the rules of cross product. If we place the stretched right-hand palm along $\vec{dl}$ in such a way that the fingers curl towards $\vec{r}$, the cross product $\vec{dl} \times \vec{r}$ is along the thumb. Usually, the plane of the diagram contains both $\vec{dl}$ and $\vec{r}$. The magnetic field $\vec{dB}$ is then perpendicular to the plane of the diagram, either going into the plane or coming out of the plane. As usual, we denote the direction going into the plane by an encircled cross and the direction coming out of the plane by an encircled dot. In figure (35.1), the magnetic field at the point P goes into the plane of the diagram and that at Q comes out of this plane.

Example 35.1

A wire placed along north–south direction carries a current of 10 A *from south to north. Find the magnetic field due to a* 1 cm *piece of wire at a point* 200 cm *north-east from the piece.*

Solution :

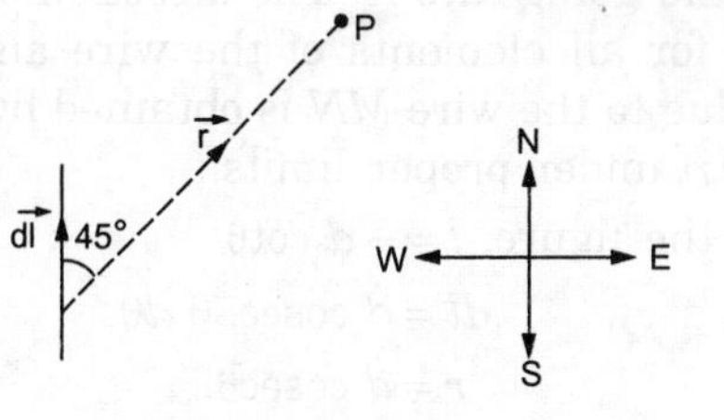

Figure 35.2

The situation is shown in figure (35.2). As the distance of P from the wire is much larger than the length of the wire, we can treat the wire as a small element. The magnetic field is given by

$$d\vec{B} = \frac{\mu_0}{4\pi} i \frac{\vec{dl} \times \vec{r}}{r^3}$$

or, $$dB = \frac{\mu_0}{4\pi} i \frac{dl \sin\theta}{r^2}$$

$$= (10^{-7}\ \text{T mA}^{-1})(10\ \text{A})\frac{(10^{-2}\ \text{m})\sin 45°}{(2\ \text{m})^2}$$

$$= 1{\cdot}8 \times 10^{-9}\ \text{T}.$$

The direction of $\vec{B}$ is the same as that of $\vec{dl} \times \vec{r}$. From the figure, it is vertically downward.

35.2 MAGNETIC FIELD DUE TO CURRENT IN A STRAIGHT WIRE

Let MN (figure 35.3) be a portion of a straight wire carrying a current i. Let P be a point at a distance $OP = d$ from it. The point O is the foot of the perpendicular from P to the wire.

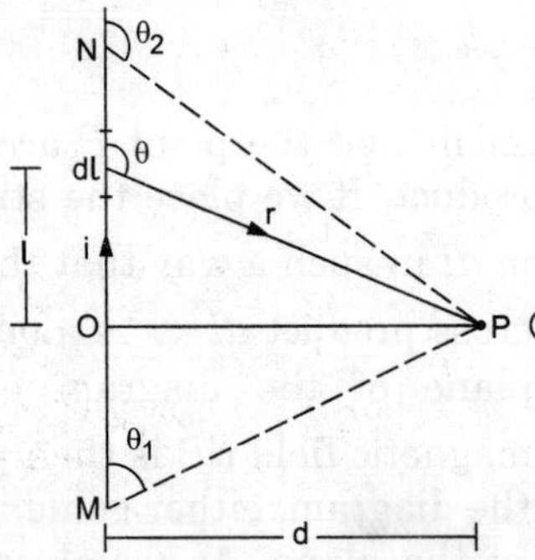

Figure 35.3

Let us consider an element dl of the wire at a distance l from the point O. The vector joining the element dl with the point P is $\vec{r}$. Let θ be the angle between $\vec{dl}$ and $\vec{r}$. The magnetic field at P due to the element is

$$dB = \frac{\mu_0}{4\pi}\, i\, \frac{dl \sin\theta}{r^2}. \qquad \text{... (i)}$$

The direction of the field is determined by the vector $\vec{dl} \times \vec{r}$. It is perpendicular to the plane of the diagram and going into it. The direction of the field is the same for all elements of the wire and hence the net field due to the wire MN is obtained by integrating equation (i) under proper limits.

From the figure, $l = -d \cot\theta$

or, $\qquad dl = d \operatorname{cosec}^2\theta\, d\theta.$

Also, $\qquad r = d \operatorname{cosec}\theta.$

Putting in (i),

$$dB = \frac{\mu_0 i}{4\pi d} \sin\theta\, d\theta$$

or,

$$B = \frac{\mu_0 i}{4\pi d}[-\cos\theta]_{\theta_1}^{\theta_2}$$

$$= \frac{\mu_0 i}{4\pi d}(\cos\theta_1 - \cos\theta_2). \qquad \text{... (35.4)}$$

Here θ_1 and θ_2 are the values of θ corresponding to the lower end and the upper end respectively.

Field on a Perpendicular Bisector

Suppose, the length $MN = a$ and the point P is on its perpendicular bisector. So,

$$OM = ON = a/2 \text{ and}$$

$$\cos\theta_1 = \frac{a/2}{\sqrt{\frac{a^2}{4} + d^2}} = \frac{a}{\sqrt{a^2 + 4d^2}}$$

and $\qquad \cos\theta_2 = -\dfrac{a}{\sqrt{a^2 + 4d^2}}.$

Equation (35.4) then becomes

$$B = \frac{\mu_0 i}{4\pi d}\frac{2a}{\sqrt{a^2 + 4d^2}}$$

$$= \frac{\mu_0 ia}{2\pi d\sqrt{a^2 + 4d^2}}. \qquad \text{... (35.5)}$$

Field due to a Long, Straight Wire

In this case $\theta_1 = 0$ and $\theta_2 = \pi$. From equation (35.4), the magnetic field is

$$B = \frac{\mu_0 i}{2\pi d}. \qquad \text{... (35.6)}$$

The direction of the magnetic field at a point P due to a long, straight wire can be found by a slight variation in the right-hand thumb rule. If we stretch the thumb of the right hand along the long current and curl our fingers to pass through the point P, the direction of the fingers at P gives the direction of the magnetic field there.

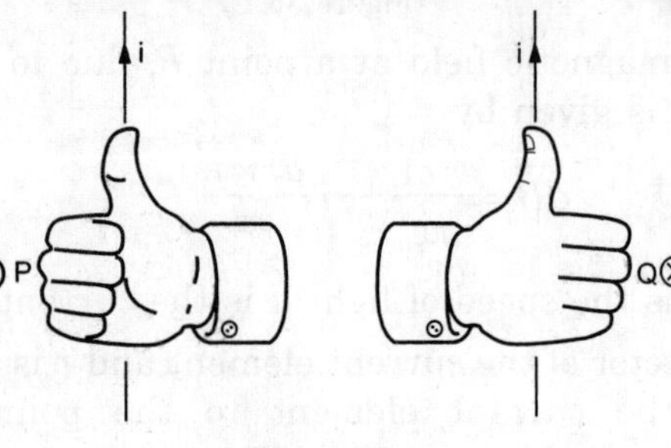

Figure 35.4

Example 35.2

Figure (35.5) shows two long, straight wires carrying electric currents in opposite directions. The separation between the wires is 5·0 cm. Find the magnetic field at a point P midway between the wires.

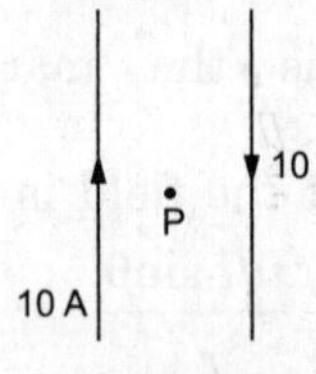

Figure 35.5

Solution : The right-hand thumb rule shows that the magnetic field at P due to each of the wires is perpendicular to the plane of the diagram and is going into it. The magnitude of the field due to each wire is

$$B = \frac{\mu_0 i}{2\pi d}$$

$$= \frac{(2 \times 10^{-7}\ \text{T mA}^{-1})\ (10\ \text{A})}{2{\cdot}5 \times 10^{-2}\ \text{m}}$$

$$= 80\ \mu\text{T}.$$

The net field due to both the wires is $2 \times 80\ \mu\text{T} = 160\ \mu\text{T}$.

We can draw magnetic field lines on the pattern of electric field lines. A tangent to a magnetic field line gives the direction of the magnetic field existing at that point. For a long straight wire, the field lines are circles with their centres on the wire (figure 35.6).

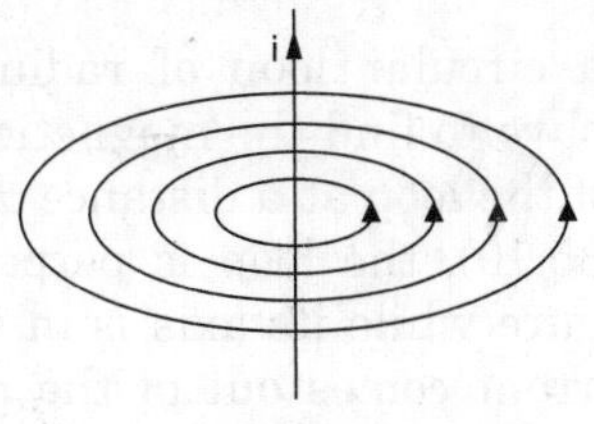

Figure 35.6

35.3 FORCE BETWEEN PARALLEL CURRENTS

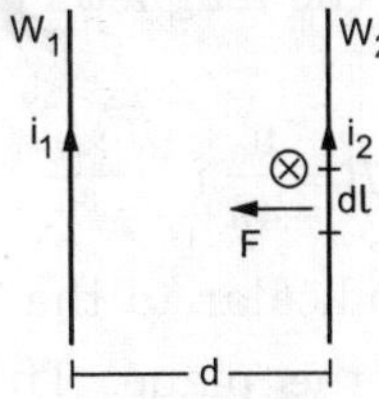

Figure 35.7

Consider two long wires W_1 and W_2 kept parallel to each other and carrying currents i_1 and i_2 respectively in the same direction (figure 35.7). The separation between the wires is d. Consider a small element dl of the wire W_2. The magnetic field at dl due to the wire W_1 is

$$B = \frac{\mu_0 i_1}{2\pi d}. \quad \ldots \text{(i)}$$

The field due to the portions of the wire W_2, above and below dl, is zero. Thus, (i) gives the net field at dl. The direction of this field is perpendicular to the plane of the diagram and going into it. The magnetic force at the element dl is

$$\vec{dF} = i_2\, \vec{dl} \times \vec{B}$$

or, $$dF = i_2\, dl \frac{\mu_0 i_1}{2\pi d}.$$

The vector product $\vec{dl} \times \vec{B}$ has a direction towards the wire W_1. Thus, the length dl of wire W_2 is attracted towards the wire W_1. The force per unit length of the wire W_2 due to the wire W_1 is

$$\frac{dF}{dl} = \frac{\mu_0 i_1 i_2}{2\pi d}. \quad \ldots (35.7)$$

If we take an element dl in the wire W_1 and calculate the magnetic force per unit length of wire W_1 due to W_2, it is again given by (35.7).

If the parallel wires carry currents in opposite directions, the wires repel each other.

Example 35.3

Two long, straight wires, each carrying an electric current of 5·0 A, *are kept parallel to each other at a separation of* 2·5 cm. *Find the magnitude of the magnetic force experienced by* 10 cm *of a wire.*

Solution : The field at the site of one wire due to the other is

$$B = \frac{\mu_0 i}{2\pi d} = \frac{(2 \times 10^{-7}\ \text{T mA}^{-1})\ (5{\cdot}0\ \text{A})}{2{\cdot}5 \times 10^{-2}\ \text{m}} = 4{\cdot}0 \times 10^{-5}\ \text{T}.$$

The force experienced by 10 cm of this wire due to the other is

$$F = i\, lB$$

$$= (5{\cdot}0\ \text{A})\ (10 \times 10^{-2}\ \text{m})\ (4{\cdot}0 \times 10^{-5}\ \text{T})$$

$$= 2{\cdot}0 \times 10^{-5}\ \text{N}.$$

Definition of Ampere

Consider two parallel wires separated by 1 m and carrying a current of 1 A each. Then $i_1 = i_2 = 1$ A and $d = 1$ m, so that from equation (35.7),

$$\frac{dF}{dl} = 2 \times 10^{-7}\ \text{N m}^{-1}.$$

This is used to formally define the unit 'ampere' of electric current. *If two parallel, long wires, kept* 1 m *apart in vacuum, carry equal currents in the same direction and there is a force of attraction of* 2×10^{-7} newton per metre *of each wire, the current in each wire is said to be* 1 ampere.

35.4 FIELD DUE TO A CIRCULAR CURRENT

Field at the Centre

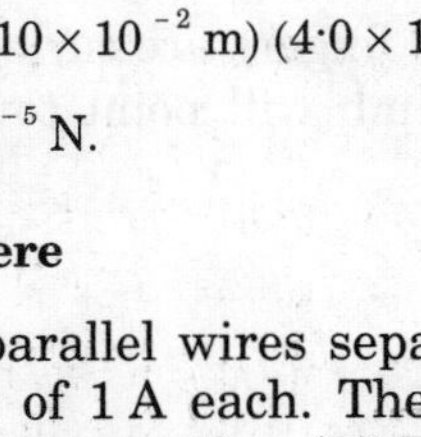

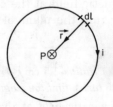

Figure 35.8

Consider a circular loop of radius a carrying a current i. We have to find the magnetic field due to this current at the centre of the loop. Consider any small element dl of the wire (figure 35.8). The magnetic field at the centre O due to the current element $i\vec{dl}$ is

$$\vec{dB} = \frac{\mu_0}{4\pi} i \frac{\vec{dl} \times \vec{r}}{r^3}$$

where $\vec{r}$ is the vector joining the element to the centre O. The direction of this field is perpendicular to the plane of the diagram and is going into it. The magnitude is

$$dB = \frac{\mu_0}{4\pi} \frac{idl}{a^2}. \quad \text{... (i)}$$

As the fields due to all such elements have the same direction, the net field is also in this direction. It can, therefore, be obtained by integrating (i) under proper limits. Thus,

$$B = \int dB = \int \frac{\mu_0 i}{4\pi a^2} dl$$

$$= \frac{\mu_0 i}{4\pi a^2} \int dl = \frac{\mu_0 i}{4\pi a^2} \times 2\pi a = \frac{\mu_0 i}{2a}.$$

The direction of the magnetic field at the centre of a circular wire can be obtained using the right-hand thumb rule. If the fingers are curled along the current, the stretched thumb will point towards the magnetic field (figure 35.9).

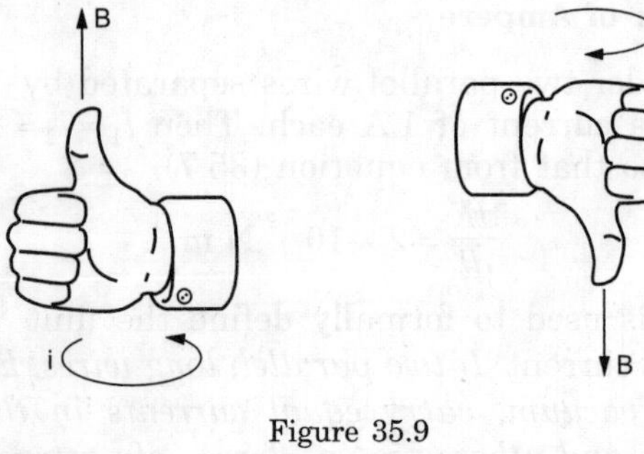

Figure 35.9

Another way to find the direction is to look into the loop along its axis. If the current is in anticlockwise direction, the magnetic field is towards the viewer. If the current is in clockwise direction, the field is away from the viewer.

In figure (35.8), the current is clockwise as seen by you. The magnetic field at the centre is away from you, i.e., is going into the plane of the diagram.

Example 35.4

A circular coil of radius 1·5 cm *carries a current of* 1·5 A. *If the coil has 25 turns, find the magnetic field at the centre.*

Solution : The magnetic field at the centre due to each turn is

$$\frac{\mu_0 i}{2a}.$$

The net field due to all 25 turns is

$$B = \frac{\mu_0 i n}{2a} = \frac{(2\pi \times 10^{-7}\ \text{T mA}^{-1})\ (1{\cdot}5\ \text{A}) \times 25}{1{\cdot}5 \times 10^{-2}\ \text{m}}$$

$$= 1{\cdot}57 \times 10^{-3}\ \text{T}.$$

Field at an Axial Point

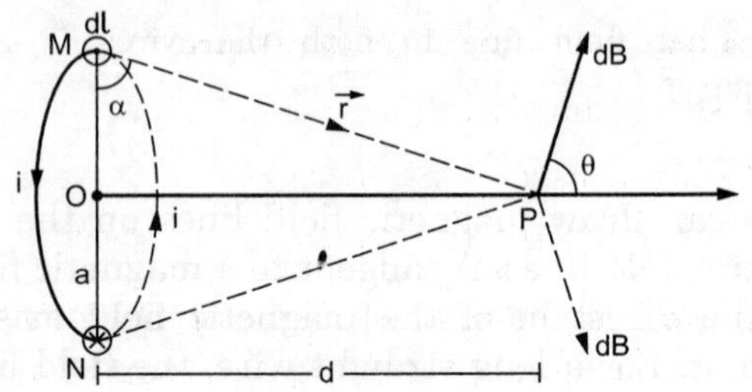

Figure 35.10

Consider a circular loop of radius a carrying a current i. We have to find the magnetic field at a point P on the axis of the loop at a distance d from its centre O. In figure (35.10), the loop is perpendicular to the plane of the figure while its axis is in the plane of the figure. The current comes out of the plane at M and goes into it at N. Consider a current element $i\vec{dl}$ of the wire at M. The vector joining the element to the point P is $\vec{r} = \vec{MP}$. The magnetic field at P due to this current element is

$$\vec{dB} = \frac{\mu_0}{4\pi} i \frac{\vec{dl} \times \vec{r}}{r^3}.$$

As $\vec{dl}$ is perpendicular to the plane of the figure, $\vec{dl} \times \vec{r}$ must be in the plane. The figure shows the direction of $\vec{dB}$ according to the rules of vector product. The magnitude of the field is

$$dB = \frac{\mu_0}{4\pi} \frac{i\ dl}{r^2} = \frac{\mu_0 i}{4\pi} \frac{dl}{a^2 + d^2}.$$

The component along the axis is

$$dB \cos\theta = \frac{\mu_0\ ia\ dl}{4\pi(a^2 + d^2)^{3/2}}. \quad \text{... (i)}$$

Now, consider the diametrically opposite current element at N. The field due to this element will have the same magnitude dB and its direction will be along the dotted arrow shown in the figure. The two fields due to the elements at M and at N have a resultant along the axis of the loop. Dividing the loop in such pairs of diametrically opposite elements, we conclude that the resultant magnetic field at P must be along the axis. The resultant field at P can, therefore, be obtained by integrating the right-hand side of (i), i.e.,

$$B = \int \frac{\mu_0\ ia}{4\pi(a^2 + d^2)^{3/2}} dl$$

$$= \frac{\mu_0 \, ia}{4\pi(a^2 + d^2)^{3/2}} \times 2\pi a$$

$$= \frac{\mu_0 \, ia^2}{2(a^2 + d^2)^{3/2}} . \qquad \ldots \text{(35.8)}$$

The right-hand thumb rule can be used to find the direction of the field.

Field at a point far away from the centre

If $d >> a$, equation (35.8) gives

$$B \approx \frac{\mu_0 \, ia^2}{2\,d^3} = \frac{2\mu_0 \, i(\pi a^2)}{4\pi\, d^3} . \qquad \ldots \text{(ii)}$$

Now, πa^2 is the area of the loop and $i(\pi a^2)$ is its magnetic dipole moment μ. Using right-hand thumb rule, we see that the direction of the area-vector $\vec{A}$ and hence of the dipole moment is along the field $\vec{B}$. The magnetic field due to this small loop at an axial point is, therefore,

$$\vec{B} = \frac{\mu_0}{4\pi} \frac{2\vec{\mu}}{d^3} . \qquad \ldots \text{(35.9)}$$

One can compare this with the expression for the electric field due to an electric dipole at a point on the dipole-axis. It is

$$\vec{E} = \frac{1}{4\pi\varepsilon_0} \frac{2\vec{p}}{d^3} ,$$

where $\vec{p}$ is the electric dipole moment.

The magnetic field at a point not on the axis is mathematically difficult to calculate. We show qualitatively in figure (35.11) the magnetic field lines due to a circular current which will give some idea of the field.

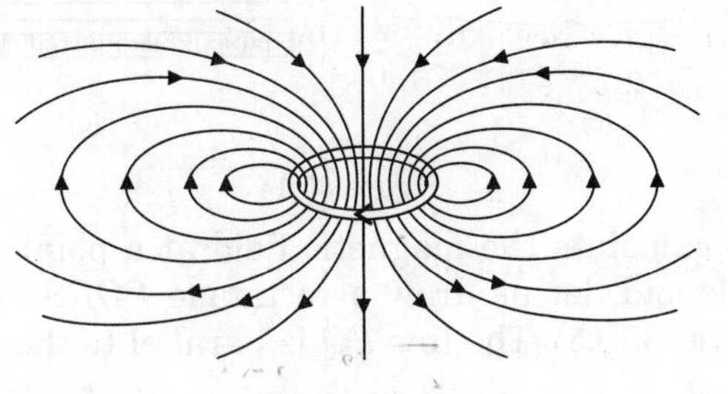

Figure 35.11

35.5 AMPERE'S LAW

Ampere's law gives another method to calculate the magnetic field due to a given current distribution. Consider any closed, plane curve (figure 35.12). Assign a sense to the curve by putting an arrow on the curve. Using the right-hand thumb rule, assign one side of the plane as positive and the other as negative. If you curl the fingers of the right hand along the arrow on the curve, the stretched thumb gives the positive side. The positive side can also be determined by looking into the loop along its axis. If the arrow on the loop is anticlockwise, the positive side is towards the viewer. If the arrow is clockwise, the positive side is away from the viewer. In figure (35.12), the positive side is going into the plane of the diagram.

Take a small length-element $\vec{dl}$ on the curve and let $\vec{B}$ be the resultant magnetic field at the position of $\vec{dl}$. Calculate the scalar product $\vec{B}\cdot\vec{dl}$ and integrate by varying $\vec{dl}$ on the closed curve. This integration is called *line integral* or *circulation* of $\vec{B}$ along the curve and is represented by the symbol

$$\oint \vec{B}\cdot\vec{dl}.$$

Now look at the currents crossing the area bounded by the curve. A current directed towards the positive side of the plane area is taken as positive and a current directed towards the negative side is taken as negative. Ampere's law then states:

The circulation $\oint \vec{B}\cdot\vec{dl}$ *of the resultant magnetic field along a closed, plane curve is equal to* μ_0 *times the total current crossing the area bounded by the closed curve provided the electric field inside the loop remains constant.* Thus,

$$\oint \vec{B}\cdot\vec{dl} = \mu_0 \, i. \qquad \ldots \text{(35.10)}$$

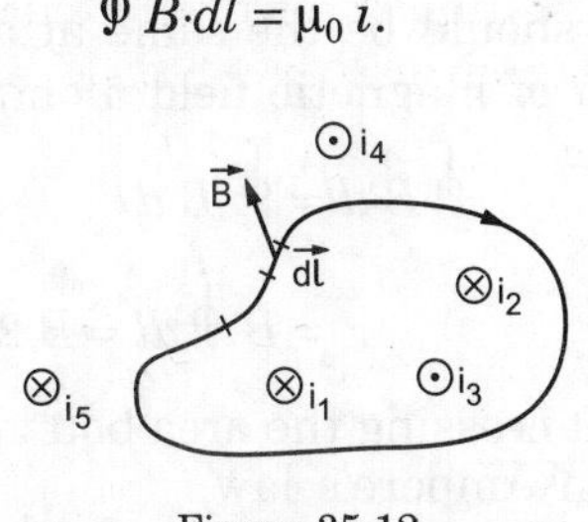

Figure 35.12

In figure (35.12), the positive side is going into the area of the diagram so that i_1 and i_2 are positive and i_3 is negative. Thus, the total current crossing the area is $i_1 + i_2 - i_3$. Any current outside the area is not included in writing the right-hand side of equation (35.10). The magnetic field $\vec{B}$ on the left-hand side is the resultant field due to all the currents existing anywhere.

Ampere's law may be derived from the Biot–Savart law and Biot–Savart law may be derived from the Ampere's law. Thus, the two are equivalent in scientific content. However, Ampere's law is more useful under certain symmetrical conditions. In such cases, the mathematics of finding the magnetic field becomes much simpler if we use the Ampere's law.

35.6 MAGNETIC FIELD AT A POINT DUE TO A LONG, STRAIGHT CURRENT

Figure (35.13a) shows a long, straight current i. We have to calculate the magnetic field at a point P

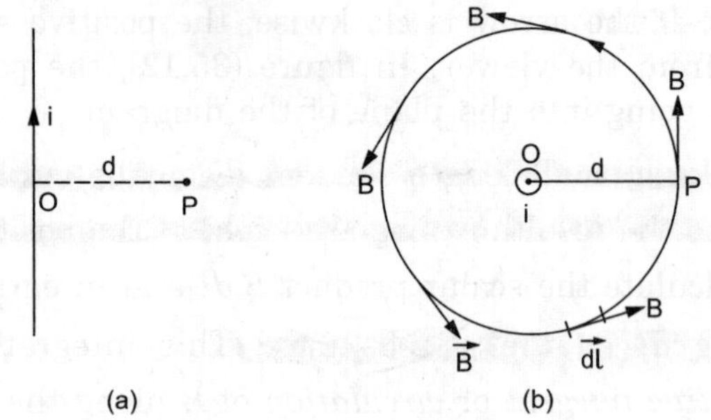

Figure 35.13

which is at a distance $OP = d$ from the wire. Figure (35.13b) shows the situation in the plane perpendicular to the wire and passing through P. The current is perpendicular to the plane of the diagram and is coming out of it.

Let us draw a circle passing through the point P and with the centre at O. We put an arrow to show the positive sense of the circle. The radius of the circle is $OP = d$. The magnetic field due to the long, straight current at any point on the circle is along the tangent as shown in the figure. Same is the direction of the length-element $\vec{dl}$ there. By symmetry, all points of the circle are equivalent and hence the magnitude of the magnetic field should be the same at all these points. The circulation of magnetic field along the circle is

$$\oint \vec{B} \cdot \vec{dl} = \oint B\, dl$$

$$= B \oint dl = B\, 2\pi d.$$

The current crossing the area bounded by the circle is i. Thus, from Ampere's law,

$$B\, 2\pi d = \mu_0\, i$$

or, $$B = \frac{\mu_0\, i}{2\pi d} \cdot$$

We have already derived this equation from Biot–Savart law (equation 35.6).

35.7 SOLENOID

A solenoid is a wire wound closely in the form of a helix. The wire is coated with an insulating material so that although the adjacent turns physically touch each other, they are electrically insulated. Generally, the length of the solenoid is large as compared to the transverse dimension. For example, if the solenoid has circular turns, the length is large as compared to its radius. If it has rectangular turns, the length should be large as compared to the edges. The magnetic field due to a current-carrying solenoid can be easily pictured by examining the field due to a circular current. The field lines due to a circular current were drawn in figure (35.11). Figure (35.14a) shows the magnetic field lines due to a circular loop A carrying a current and also due to a similar loop B placed coaxially and carrying equal current. We see that at a point P, which is quite off the axis, the magnetic fields due to the two loops are in opposite directions. On the other hand, at a point Q which is on the axis or close to the axis, the two fields are in the same direction. Figure (35.14b) shows the resultant field lines due to the two loops. A solenoid may be thought of as a stack of such circular currents placed coaxially one after the other. Figure (35.14c) represents the field due to a loosely wound solenoid. The fields at an outside point due to the neighbouring loops oppose each other, whereas at an inside point, the fields are in the same direction. These tendencies to have zero field outside and a uniform field inside become more and more effective as the solenoid is more and more tightly wound. The magnetic field inside a very tightly wound, long solenoid is uniform everywhere and is zero outside it (figure 35.14d).

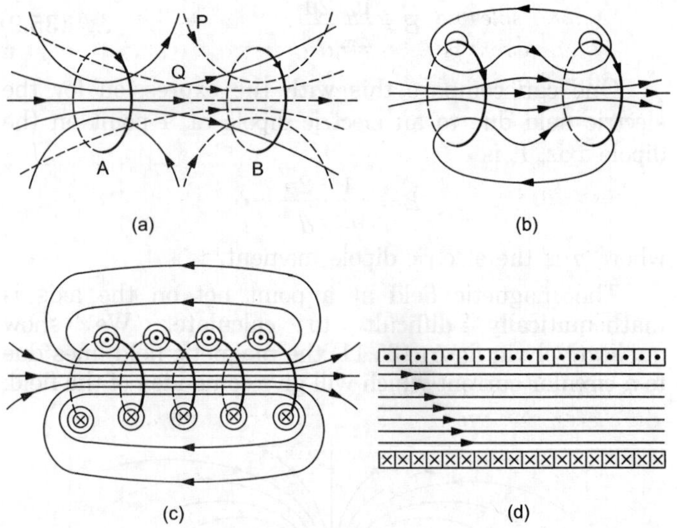

Figure 35.14

To calculate the magnetic field at a point P inside the solenoid, let us draw a rectangle $PQRS$ as shown in figure (35.15). The line PQ is parallel to the solenoid axis and hence parallel to the magnetic field $\vec{B}$ inside the solenoid. Thus,

$$\int_P^Q \vec{B} \cdot \vec{dl} = Bl.$$

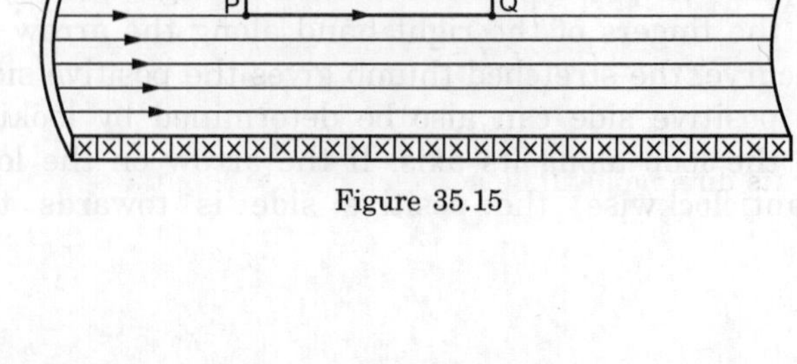

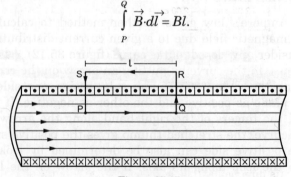

Figure 35.15

On the remaining three sides, $\vec{B}\cdot\vec{dl}$ is zero everywhere as $\vec{B}$ is either zero (outside the solenoid) or perpendicular to $\vec{dl}$ (inside the solenoid). Thus, the circulation of $\vec{B}$ along $PQRS$ is

$$\oint \vec{B}\cdot\vec{dl} = Bl.$$

Let n be the number of turns per unit length along the length of the solenoid. A total of nl turns cross the rectangle $PQRS$. Each turn carries a current i. So the net current crossing $PQRS = nli$.

Using Ampere's law,

$$\oint \vec{B}\cdot\vec{dl} = \mu_0\, nli$$

or, $$Bl = \mu_0\, nli$$

or, $$B = \mu_0\, ni. \qquad \ldots (35.11)$$

Example 35.5

A long solenoid is formed by winding 20 turns cm^{-1}. What current is necessary to produce a magnetic field of 20 mT inside the solenoid ?

Solution : The magnetic field inside the solenoid is

$$B = \mu_0\, ni$$

or, $$20 \times 10^{-3}\ \text{T} = (4\pi \times 10^{-7}\ \text{T mA}^{-1}) \times (20 \times 10^{2}\ \text{m}^{-1})i$$

or, $$i = 8{\cdot}0\ \text{A}.$$

Equation (35.11) is strictly valid only for an infinitely long solenoid. In practice, if the length of the solenoid is more than about five to six times the diameter and we are looking at the field in the middle region, we can use this equation.

35.8 TOROID

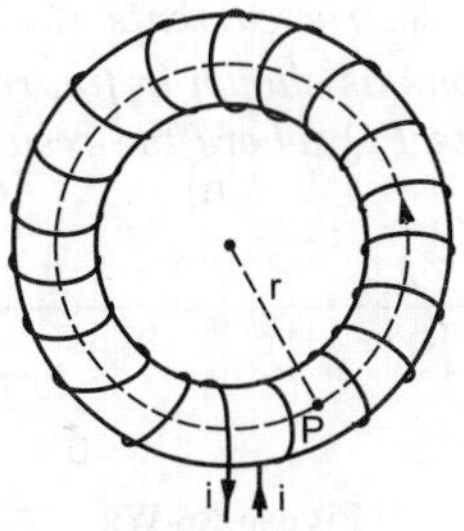

Figure 35.16

If a solenoid is bent in a circular shape and the ends are joined, we get a toroid. Alternatively, one can start with a nonconducting ring and wind a conducting wire closely on it. The magnetic field in such a toroid can be obtained by using Ampere's law.

Suppose, we have to find the field at a point P inside the toroid. Let the distance of P from the centre be r. Draw a circle through the point P and concentric with the toroid. By symmetry, the field will have equal magnitude at all points of this circle. Also, the field is everywhere tangential to the circle. Thus,

$$\oint \vec{B}\cdot\vec{dl} = \int B\, dl = B\int dl = 2\pi rB.$$

If the total number of turns is N, the current crossing the area bounded by the circle is Ni where i is the current in the toroid. Using Ampere's law on this circle,

$$\oint \vec{B}\cdot\vec{dl} = \mu_0\, Ni$$

or, $$2\pi rB = \mu_0\, Ni$$

or, $$B = \frac{\mu_0\, Ni}{2\pi r}. \qquad \ldots (35.12)$$

Worked Out Examples

1. *Two long wires a and b, carrying equal currents of* 10·0 A, *are placed parallel to each other with a separation of* 4·00 cm *between them as shown in figure (35-W1). Find the magnetic field B at each of the points P, Q and R.*

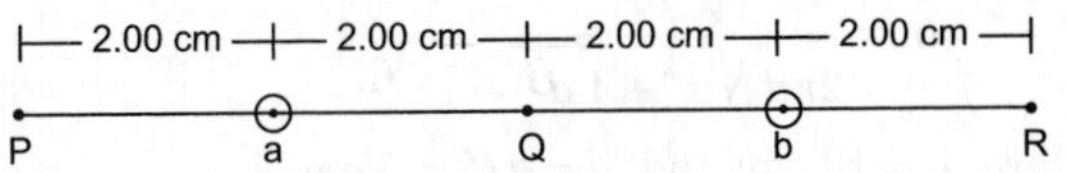

Figure 35-W1

Solution : The magnetic field at P due to the wire a has magnitude

$$B_1 = \frac{\mu_0 i}{2\pi d} = \frac{4\pi \times 10^{-7}\ \text{T mA}^{-1} \times 10\ \text{A}}{2\pi \times 2 \times 10^{-2}\ \text{m}}$$

$$= 1{\cdot}00 \times 10^{-4}\ \text{T}.$$

Its direction will be perpendicular to the line shown and will point downward in the figure.

The field at this point due to the other wire has magnitude

$$B_2 = \frac{\mu_0 i}{2\pi d} = \frac{4\pi \times 10^{-7}\ \text{T mA}^{-1} \times 10\ \text{A}}{2\pi \times 6 \times 10^{-2}\ \text{m}}$$

$$= 0{\cdot}33 \times 10^{-4}\ \text{T}.$$

Its direction will be the same as that of B_1. Thus, the resultant field will be $1{\cdot}33 \times 10^{-4}$ T also along the same direction.

Similarly, the resultant magnetic field at R will be $= 1{\cdot}33 \times 10^{-4}$ T along the direction pointing upward in the figure.

The magnetic field at point Q due to the two wires will have equal magnitudes but opposite directions and hence the resultant field will be zero.

2. *Two parallel wires P and Q placed at a separation $d = 6$ cm carry electric currents $i_1 = 5$ A and $i_2 = 2$ A in opposite directions as shown in figure (35-W2a). Find the point on the line PQ where the resultant magnetic field is zero.*

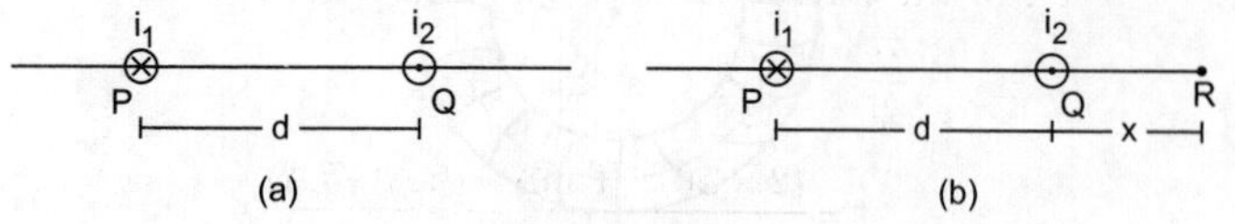

Figure 35-W2

Solution : At the desired point, the magnetic fields due to the two wires must have equal magnitude but opposite directions. The point should be either to the left of P or to the right of Q. As the wire Q has smaller current, the point should be closer to Q. Let this point R be at a distance x from Q (figure 35-W2b).

The magnetic field at R due to the current i_1 will have magnitude

$$B_1 = \frac{\mu_0 i_1}{2\pi(d+x)}$$

and will be directed downward in the plane of the figure. The field at the same point due to the current i_2 will be

$$B_2 = \frac{\mu_0 i_2}{2\pi x}$$

directed upward in the plane of the figure. If the resultant field at R is zero, we should have $B_1 = B_2$, so that

$$\frac{i_1}{d+x} = \frac{i_2}{x}$$

giving, $$x = \frac{i_2 d}{i_1 - i_2}$$

$$= \frac{(2\text{ A})\,(6\text{ cm})}{(3\text{ A})} = 4\text{ cm}.$$

3. *Two long, straight wires a and b are 2·0 m apart, perpendicular to the plane of the paper as shown in figure (35-W3). The wire a carries a current of 9·6 A directed into the plane of the figure. The magnetic field at the point p at a distance of 10/11 m from the wire b is zero. Find (a) the magnitude and direction of the current in b, (b) the magnitude of the magnetic field B at the point s and (c) the force per unit length on the wire b.*

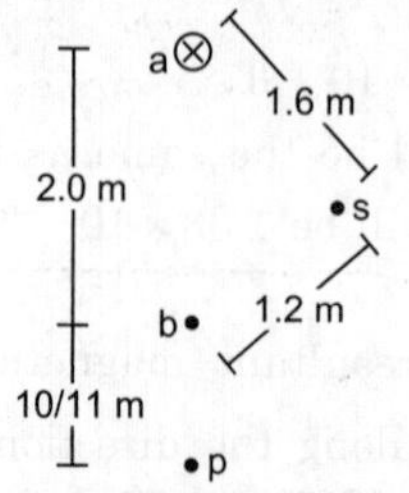

Figure 35-W3

Solution :

(a) For the magnetic field at p to be zero, the current in the wire b should be coming out of the plane of the figure so that the fields due to a and b may be opposite at p. The magnitudes of these fields should be equal, so that

$$\frac{\mu_0(9\cdot6\text{ A})}{2\pi\left(2+\frac{10}{11}\right)\text{m}} = \frac{\mu_0 i}{2\pi\left(\frac{10}{11}\right)\text{m}}$$

or, $$i = 3\cdot0\text{ A}.$$

(b) $$(ab)^2 = 4\text{ m}^2$$

$$(as)^2 = 2\cdot56\text{ m}^2$$

and $$(bs)^2 = 1\cdot44\text{ m}^2$$

so that $(ab)^2 = (as)^2 + (bs)^2$ and angle $asb = 90°$.

The field at s due to the wire a

$$= \frac{\mu_0(9\cdot6\text{ A})}{2\pi\times1\cdot6\text{ m}} = \frac{\mu_0}{2\pi}\times6\text{ Am}^{-1}$$

and that due to the wire b

$$= \frac{\mu_0}{2\pi}\frac{3\text{ A}}{1\cdot2\text{ m}} = \frac{\mu_0}{2\pi}\times2\cdot5\text{ Am}^{-1}.$$

These fields are at 90° to each other so that their resultant will have a magnitude

$$\sqrt{\left(\frac{\mu_0}{2\pi}\times6\text{ Am}^{-1}\right)^2 + \left(\frac{\mu_0}{2\pi}\times2\cdot5\text{ Am}^{-1}\right)^2}$$

$$= \frac{\mu_0}{2\pi}\sqrt{36+6\cdot25}\text{ Am}^{-1}$$

$$= 2\times10^{-7}\text{ T mA}^{-1}\times6\cdot5\text{ Am}^{-1}$$

$$= 1\cdot3\times10^{-6}\text{ T}.$$

(c) The force per unit length on the wire b

$$= \frac{\mu_0 i_1 i_2}{2\pi d} = (2\times10^{-7}\text{ T mA}^{-1})\times\frac{(9\cdot6\text{ A})\,(3\text{ A})}{2\cdot0\text{ m}}$$

$$= 2\cdot9\times10^{-6}\text{ N}.$$

4. *A current of 2·00 A exists in a square loop of edge 10·0 cm. Find the magnetic field B at the centre of the square loop.*

Solution : The magnetic fields at the centre due to the four sides will be equal in magnitude and direction. The field due to one side will be

$$B_1 = \frac{\mu_0\, ia}{2\pi d\sqrt{a^2+4d^2}}\cdot$$

Here, $a = 10$ cm and $d = a/2 = 5$ cm.

Thus,

$$B_1 = \frac{\mu_0\,(2\text{ A})}{2\pi(5\text{ cm})}\left[\frac{10\text{ cm}}{\sqrt{(10\text{ cm})^2+4(5\text{ cm})^2}}\right]$$

$$= 2\times10^{-7}\text{ T mA}^{-1}\times2\text{ A}\times\frac{1}{5\sqrt{2}\text{ cm}}$$

$$= 5\cdot66\times10^{-6}\text{ T}.$$

Hence, the net field at the centre of the loop will be

$$4 \times 5{\cdot}66 \times 10^{-6}\ \mathrm{T} = 22{\cdot}6 \times 10^{-6}\ \mathrm{T}.$$

5. *Figure (35-W4) shows a square loop made from a uniform wire. Find the magnetic field at the centre of the square if a battery is connected between the points A and C.*

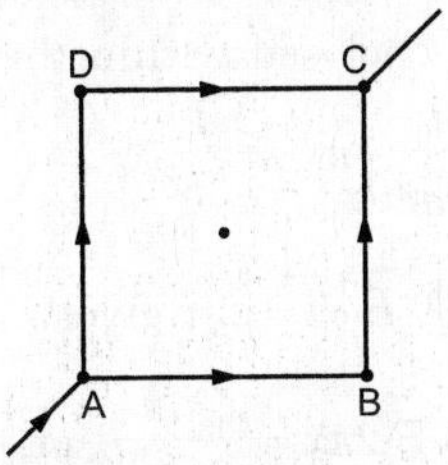

Figure 35-W4

Solution : The current will be equally divided at A. The fields at the centre due to the currents in the wires AB and DC will be equal in magnitude and opposite in direction. The resultant of these two fields will be zero. Similarly, the resultant of the fields due to the wires AD and BC will be zero. Hence, the net field at the centre will be zero.

6. *Two long wires, carrying currents i_1 and i_2, are placed perpendicular to each other in such a way that they just avoid a contact. Find the magnetic force on a small length dl of the second wire situated at a distance l from the first wire.*

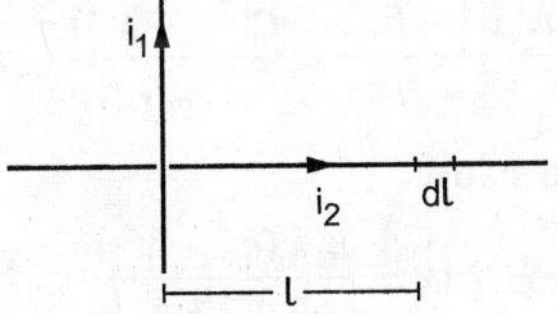

Figure 35-W5

Solution : The situation is shown in figure (35-W5). The magnetic field at the site of dl, due to the first wire is,

$$B = \frac{\mu_0 i_1}{2\pi l}.$$

This field is perpendicular to the plane of the figure going into it. The magnetic force on the length dl is,

$$dF = i_2\, dl\, B \sin 90°$$
$$= \frac{\mu_0 i_1 i_2 dl}{2\pi l}.$$

This force is parallel to the current i_1.

7. *Figure (35-W6) shows a part of an electric circuit. ABCD is a rectangular loop made of uniform wire. The length AD = BC = 1 cm. The sides AB and DC are long as compared to the other two sides. Find the magnetic force per unit length acting on the wire DC due to the wire AB if the ammeter reads 10 A.*

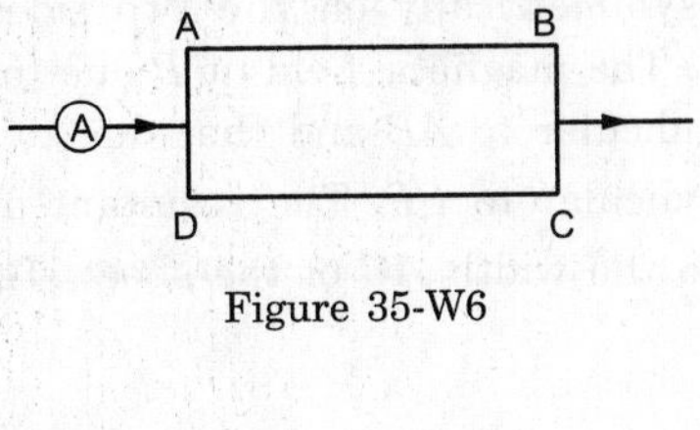

Figure 35-W6

Solution : By symmetry, each of the wires AB and DC carries a current of 5 A. As the separation between them is 1 cm, the magnetic force per unit length of DC is

$$\frac{dF}{dl} = \frac{\mu_0 i_1 i_2}{2\pi d}$$
$$= \frac{(2 \times 10^{-7}\ \mathrm{T\,m\,A^{-1}})\,(5\ \mathrm{A})\,(5\ \mathrm{A})}{1 \times 10^{-2}\ \mathrm{m}}$$
$$= 5 \times 10^{-4}\ \mathrm{TA} = 5 \times 10^{-4}\ \mathrm{N\,m^{-1}}.$$

8. *Figure (35-W7) shows a current loop having two circular arcs joined by two radial lines. Find the magnetic field B at the centre O.*

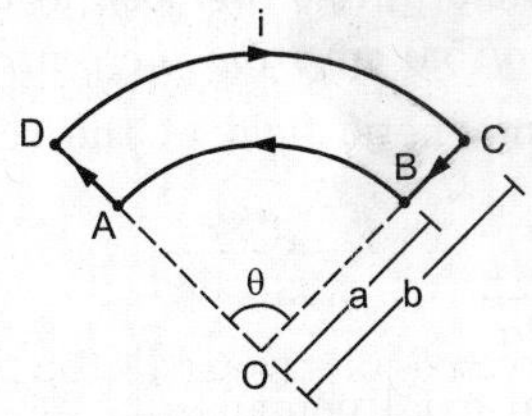

Figure 35-W7

Solution : As the point O is on the line AD, the magnetic field at O due to AD is zero. Similarly, the field at O due to BC is also zero. The field at the centre of a circular current loop is given by $B = \frac{\mu_0 i}{2a}$. The field due to the circular arc BA will be

$$B_1 = \left(\frac{\theta}{2\pi}\right)\left(\frac{\mu_0 i}{2a}\right).$$

The right-hand thumb rule shows that the field is coming out of the plane of the figure. The field due to the circular arc DC is

$$B_2 = \left(\frac{\theta}{2\pi}\right)\left(\frac{\mu_0 i}{2b}\right)$$

going into the plane of the figure. The resultant field at O is

$$B = B_1 - B_2 = \frac{\mu_0 i\theta(b-a)}{4\pi ab}$$

coming out of the plane.

9. *Find the magnetic field at the point P in figure (35-W8). The curved portion is a semicircle and the straight wires are long.*

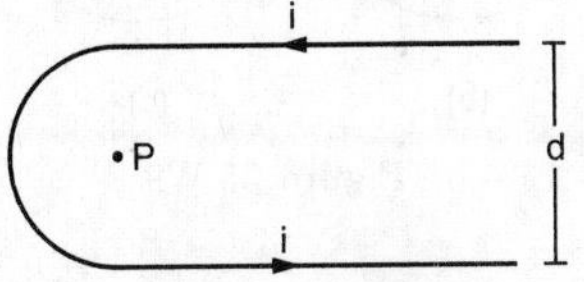

Figure 35-W8

Solution : The magnetic field at P due to any current element in the figure is perpendicular to the plane of the figure and coming out of it. The field due to the upper straight wire is

$$B_1 = \frac{1}{2} \times \frac{\mu_0 i}{2\pi\left(\frac{d}{2}\right)} = \frac{\mu_0 i}{2\pi d}.$$

Same is the field B_2 due to the lower straight wire. The field due to the semicircle of radius $(d/2)$ is

$$B_3 = \frac{1}{2} \times \frac{\mu_0 i}{2\left(\frac{d}{2}\right)} = \frac{\mu_0 i}{2d}.$$

The net field is $B = B_1 + B_2 + B_3 = \frac{\mu_0 i}{2d}\left(1 + \frac{2}{\pi}\right)$.

10. *The magnetic field B due to a current-carrying circular loop of radius* 12 cm *at its centre is* $0{\cdot}50 \times 10^{-4}$ T. *Find the magnetic field due to this loop at a point on the axis at a distance of* 5·0 cm *from the centre.*

Solution : The magnetic field at the centre of a circular loop is

$$B_0 = \frac{\mu_0 i}{2a}$$

and that at an axial point is

$$B = \frac{\mu_0 i a^2}{2(a^2 + x^2)^{3/2}}.$$

Thus, $\frac{B}{B_0} = \frac{a^3}{(a^2 + x^2)^{3/2}}$

or, $B = (0{\cdot}50 \times 10^{-4}\ \text{T}) \times \frac{(12\ \text{cm})^3}{(144\ \text{cm}^2 + 25\ \text{cm}^2)^{3/2}}$

$= 3{\cdot}9 \times 10^{-5}$ T.

11. *Consider a coaxial cable which consists of an inner wire of radius a surrounded by an outer shell of inner and outer radii b and c respectively. The inner wire carries an electric current* i_0 *and the outer shell carries an equal current in opposite direction. Find the magnetic field at a distance x from the axis where (a)* $x < a$, *(b)* $a < x < b$ *(c)* $b < x < c$ *and (d)* $x > c$. *Assume that the current density is uniform in the inner wire and also uniform in the outer shell.*

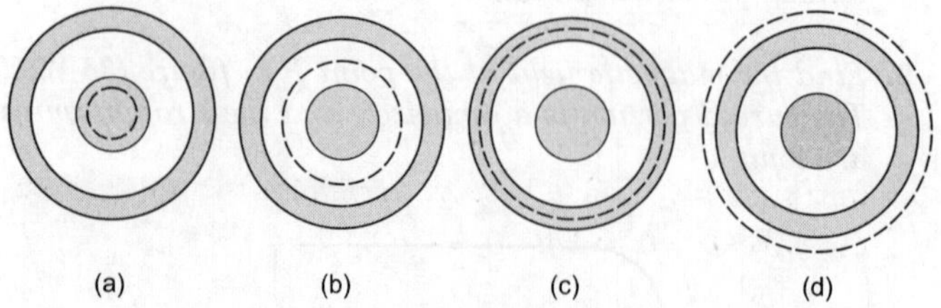

Figure 35-W9

Solution :

A cross section of the cable is shown in figure (35-W9). Draw a circle of radius x with the centre at the axis of the cable. The parts a, b, c and d of the figure correspond to the four parts of the problem. By symmetry, the magnetic field at each point of a circle will have the same magnitude and will be tangential to it. The circulation of B along this circle is, therefore,

$$\oint \vec{B} \cdot \vec{dl} = B\, 2\pi x$$

in each of the four parts of the figure.

(a) The current enclosed within the circle in part a is

$$\frac{i_0}{\pi a^2} \cdot \pi x^2 = \frac{i_0}{a^2} x^2.$$

Ampere's law $\oint \vec{B} \cdot \vec{dl} = \mu_0 i$ gives

$$B\, 2\pi x = \frac{\mu_0 i_0 x^2}{a^2} \quad \text{or,} \quad B = \frac{\mu_0 i_0 x}{2\pi a^2}.$$

The direction will be along the tangent to the circle.

(b) The current enclosed within the circle in part b is i_0 so that

$$B\, 2\pi x = \mu_0 i_0 \quad \text{or,} \quad B = \frac{\mu_0 i_0}{2\pi x}.$$

(c) The area of cross section of the outer shell is $\pi c^2 - \pi b^2$. The area of cross section of the outer shell within the circle in part c of the figure is $\pi x^2 - \pi b^2$. Thus, the current through this part is $\frac{i_0(x^2 - b^2)}{c^2 - b^2}$. This is in the opposite direction to the current i_0 in the inner wire. Thus, the net current enclosed by the circle is

$$i_0 - \frac{i_0(x^2 - b^2)}{c^2 - b^2} = \frac{i_0(c^2 - x^2)}{c^2 - b^2}.$$

From Ampere's law,

$$B\, 2\pi x = \frac{\mu_0 i_0(c^2 - x^2)}{c^2 - b^2}$$

or, $$B = \frac{\mu_0 i_0(c^2 - x^2)}{2\pi x(c^2 - b^2)}.$$

(d) The net current enclosed by the circle in part d of the figure is zero and hence

$$B\, 2\pi x = 0 \quad \text{or,} \quad B = 0.$$

12. *Figure (35-W10) shows a cross section of a large metal sheet carrying an electric current along its surface. The current in a strip of width dl is Kdl where K is a constant. Find the magnetic field at a point P at a distance x from the metal sheet.*

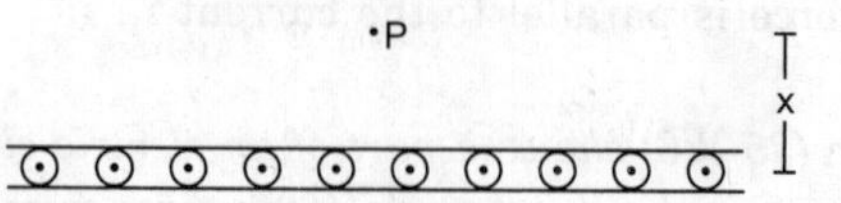

Figure 35-W10

Solution : Consider two strips A and C of the sheet situated symmetrically on the two sides of P (figure 35-W11a). The magnetic field at P due to the strip A is B_a perpendicular to AP and that due to the strip C is B_c perpendicular to CP. The resultant of these two is parallel to the width AC of the sheet. The field due to the whole sheet will also be in this direction. Suppose this field has magnitude B.

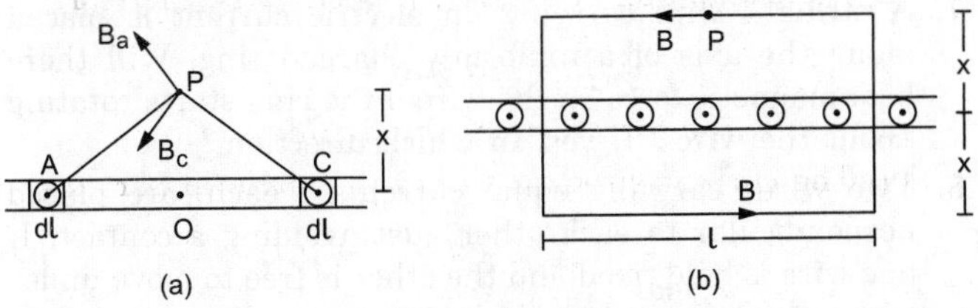

Figure 35-W11

The field on the opposite side of the sheet at the same distance will also be B but in opposite direction. Applying Ampere's law to the rectangle shown in figure (35-W11b),

$$2Bl = \mu_0 Kl$$

or, $$B = \frac{1}{2}\mu_0 K.$$

Note that it is independent of x.

13. *Consider the situation described in the previous example. A particle of mass m having a charge q is placed at a distance d from the metal sheet and is projected towards it. Find the maximum velocity of projection for which the particle does not hit the sheet.*

Solution : As the magnetic field is uniform and the particle is projected in a direction perpendicular to the field, it will describe a circular path. The particle will not hit the metal sheet if the radius of this circle is smaller than d. For the maximum velocity, the radius is just equal to d. Thus,

$$qvB = \frac{mv^2}{d}$$

or, $$qv\frac{\mu_0 K}{2} = \frac{mv^2}{d}$$

or, $$v = \frac{\mu_0 qKd}{2m}.$$

14. *Three identical long solenoids P, Q and R are connected to each other as shown in figure (35-W12). If the magnetic field at the centre of P is 2·0 T, what would be the field at the centre of Q? Assume that the field due to any solenoid is confined within the volume of that solenoid only.*

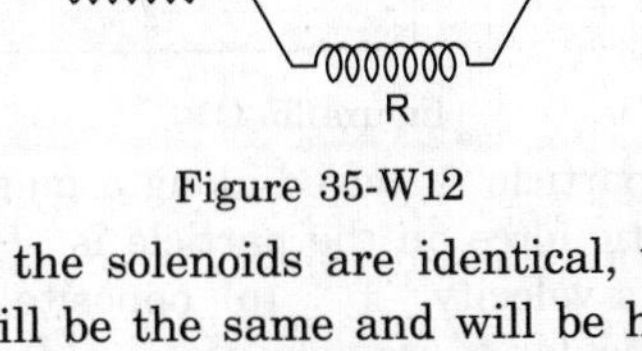

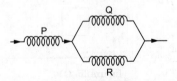

Figure 35-W12

Solution : As the solenoids are identical, the currents in Q and R will be the same and will be half the current in P. The magnetic field within a solenoid is given by $B = \mu_0 ni$. Hence the field in Q will be equal to the field in R and will be half the field in P, i.e., will be 1·0 T.

15. *A long, straight wire carries a current i. A particle having a positive charge q and mass m, kept at a distance x_0 from the wire is projected towards it with a speed v. Find the minimum separation between the wire and the particle.*

Solution :

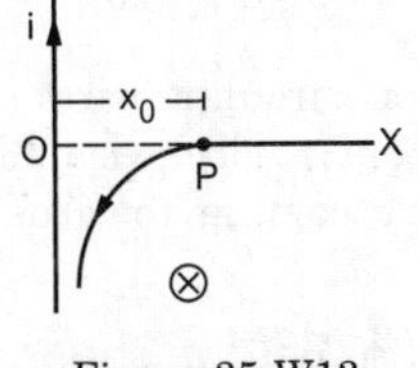

Figure 35-W13

Let the particle be initially at P (figure 35-W13). Take the wire as the y-axis and the foot of perpendicular from P to the wire as the origin. Take the line OP as the x-axis. We have, $OP = x_0$. The magnetic field B at any point to the right of the wire is along the negative z-axis. The magnetic force on the particle is, therefore, in the x–y plane. As there is no initial velocity along the z-axis, the motion will be in the x–y plane. Also, its speed remains unchanged. As the magnetic field is not uniform, the particle does not go along a circle.

The force at time t is $\vec{F} = q\vec{v} \times \vec{B}$

$$= q(\vec{i}\,v_x + \vec{j}\,v_y) \times \left(-\frac{\mu_0 i}{2\pi x}\vec{k}\right)$$

$$= \vec{j}\,qv_x\frac{\mu_0 i}{2\pi x} - \vec{i}\,qv_y\frac{\mu_0 i}{2\pi x}.$$

Thus $$a_x = \frac{F_x}{m} = -\frac{\mu_0 qi}{2\pi m}\frac{v_y}{x} = -\lambda\frac{v_y}{x} \quad \text{... (i)}$$

where $$\lambda = \frac{\mu_0 qi}{2\pi m}.$$

Also, $$a_x = \frac{dv_x}{dt} = \frac{dv_x}{dx}\frac{dx}{dt} = \frac{v_x dv_x}{dx}. \quad \text{... (ii)}$$

As $$v_x^2 + v_y^2 = v^2,$$

$$2v_x\,dv_x + 2v_y\,dv_y = 0$$

giving $$v_x\,dv_x = -v_y\,dv_y. \quad \text{... (iii)}$$

From (i), (ii) and (iii),

$$\frac{v_y\,dv_y}{dx} = \frac{\lambda v_y}{x}$$

or, $$\frac{dx}{x} = \frac{dv_y}{\lambda}.$$

Initially $x = x_0$ and $v_y = 0$. At minimum separation from the wire, $v_x = 0$ so that $v_y = -v$.

Thus $$\int_{x_0}^{x}\frac{dx}{x} = \int_0^{-v}\frac{dv_y}{\lambda}$$

or, $$\ln\frac{x}{x_0} = -\frac{v}{\lambda}$$

or, $$x = x_0 e^{-v/\lambda} = x_0 e^{-\frac{2\pi mv}{\mu_0 qi}}.$$

QUESTIONS FOR SHORT ANSWER

1. An electric current flows in a wire from north to south. What will be the direction of the magnetic field due to this wire at a point (a) east of the wire, (b) west of the wire, (c) vertically above the wire and (d) vertically below the wire?
2. The magnetic field due to a long straight wire has been derived in terms of μ_0, i and d. Express this in terms of ε_0, c, i and d.
3. You are facing a circular wire carrying an electric current. The current is clockwise as seen by you. Is the field at the centre coming towards you or going away from you ?
4. In Ampere's law $\oint \vec{B}\cdot d\vec{l} = \mu_0 i$, the current outside the curve is not included on the right hand side. Does it mean that the magnetic field B calculated by using Ampere's law, gives the contribution of only the currents crossing the area bounded by the curve ?
5. The magnetic field inside a tightly wound, long solenoid is $B = \mu_0 ni$. It suggests that the field does not depend on the total length of the solenoid, and hence if we add more loops at the ends of a solenoid the field should not increase. Explain qualitatively why the extra-added loops do not have a considerable effect on the field inside the solenoid.
6. A long, straight wire carries a current. Is Ampere's law valid for a loop that does not enclose the wire, or that encloses the wire but is not circular ?
7. A straight wire carrying an electric current is placed along the axis of a uniformly charged ring. Will there be a magnetic force on the wire if the ring starts rotating about the wire ? If yes, in which direction ?
8. Two wires carrying equal currents i each, are placed perpendicular to each other, just avoiding a contact. If one wire is held fixed and the other is free to move under magnetic forces, what kind of motion will result ?
9. Two proton beams going in the same direction repel each other whereas two wires carrying currents in the same direction attract each other. Explain.
10. In order to have a current in a long wire, it should be connected to a battery or some such device. Can we obtain the magnetic field due to a straight, long wire by using Ampere's law without mentioning this other part of the circuit ?
11. Quite often, connecting wires carrying currents in opposite directions are twisted together in using electrical appliances. Explain how it avoids unwanted magnetic fields.
12. Two current-carrying wires may attract each other. In absence of other forces, the wires will move towards each other increasing the kinetic energy. Does it contradict the fact that the magnetic force cannot do any work and hence cannot increase the kinetic energy ?

OBJECTIVE I

1. A vertical wire carries a current in upward direction. An electron beam sent horizontally towards the wire will be deflected
   (a) towards right (b) towards left
   (c) upwards (d) downwards.
2. A current-carrying, straight wire is kept along the axis of a circular loop carrying a current. The straight wire
   (a) will exert an inward force on the circular loop
   (b) will exert an outward force on the circular loop
   (c) will not exert any force on the circular loop
   (d) will exert a force on the circular loop parallel to itself.
3. A proton beam is going from north to south and an electron beam is going from south to north. Neglecting the earth's magnetic field, the electron beam will be deflected
   (a) towards the proton beam
   (b) away from the proton beam
   (c) upwards (d) downwards.
4. A circular loop is kept in that vertical plane which contains the north–south direction. It carries a current that is towards north at the topmost point. Let A be a point on the axis of the circle to the east of it and B a point on this axis to the west of it. The magnetic field due to the loop
   (a) is towards east at A and towards west at B
   (b) is towards west at A and towards east at B
   (c) is towards east at both A and B
   (d) is towards west at both A and B.
5. Consider the situation shown in figure (35-Q1). The straight wire is fixed but the loop can move under magnetic force. The loop will
   (a) remain stationary
   (b) move towards the wire
   (c) move away from the wire
   (d) rotate about the wire.

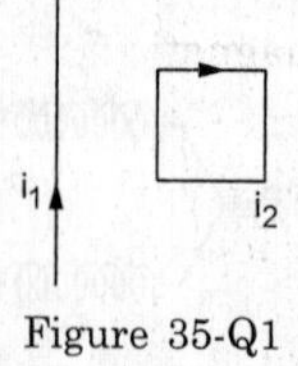

Figure 35-Q1

6. A charged particle is moved along a magnetic field line. The magnetic force on the particle is
   (a) along its velocity (b) opposite to its velocity
   (c) perpendicular to its velocity (d) zero.
7. A moving charge produces
   (a) electric field only (b) magnetic field only
   (c) both of them (d) none of them.

8. A particle is projected in a plane perpendicular to a uniform magnetic field. The area bounded by the path described by the particle is proportional to
(a) the velocity (b) the momentum
(c) the kinetic energy (d) none of these.

9. Two particles X and Y having equal charge, after being accelerated through the same potential difference enter a region of uniform magnetic field and describe circular paths of radii R_1 and R_2 respectively. The ratio of the mass of X to that of Y is
(a) $(R_1/R_2)^{1/2}$ (b) R_1/R_2 (c) $(R_1/R_2)^2$ (d) R_1R_2.

10. Two parallel wires carry currents of 20 A and 40 A in opposite directions. Another wire carrying a current antiparallel to 20 A is placed midway between the two wires. The magnetic force on it will be
(a) towards 20 A (b) towards 40 A (c) zero
(d) perpendicular to the plane of the currents.

11. Two parallel, long wires carry currents i_1 and i_2 with $i_1 > i_2$. When the currents are in the same direction, the magnetic field at a point midway between the wires is 10 μT. If the direction of i_2 is reversed, the field becomes 30 μT. The ratio i_1/i_2 is
(a) 4 (b) 3 (c) 2 (d) 1.

12. Consider a long, straight wire of cross-sectional area A carrying a current i. Let there be n free electrons per unit volume. An observer places himself on a trolley moving in the direction opposite to the current with a speed $v = \frac{i}{nAe}$ and separated from the wire by a distance r. The magnetic field seen by the observer is very nearly
(a) $\frac{\mu_0 i}{2\pi r}$ (b) zero (c) $\frac{\mu_0 i}{\pi r}$ (d) $\frac{2\mu_0 i}{\pi r}$.

OBJECTIVE II

1. The magnetic field at the origin due to a current element $i\,\vec{dl}$ placed at a position $\vec{r}$ is
(a) $\frac{\mu_0 i}{4\pi}\frac{\vec{dl}\times\vec{r}}{r^3}$ (b) $-\frac{\mu_0 i}{4\pi}\frac{\vec{r}\times\vec{dl}}{r^3}$
(c) $\frac{\mu_0 i}{4\pi}\frac{\vec{r}\times\vec{dl}}{r^3}$ (d) $-\frac{\mu_0 i}{4\pi}\frac{\vec{dl}\times\vec{r}}{r^3}$.

2. Consider three quantities $x = E/B$, $y = \sqrt{1/\mu_0\varepsilon_0}$ and $z = \frac{l}{CR}$. Here, l is the length of a wire, C is a capacitance and R is a resistance. All other symbols have standard meanings.
(a) x, y have the same dimensions.
(b) y, z have the same dimensions.
(c) z, x have the same dimensions.
(d) None of the three pairs have the same dimensions.

3. A long, straight wire carries a current along the z-axis. One can find two points in the x–y plane such that
(a) the magnetic fields are equal
(b) the directions of the magnetic fields are the same
(c) the magnitudes of the magnetic fields are equal
(d) the field at one point is opposite to that at the other point.

4. A long, straight wire of radius R carries a current distributed uniformly over its cross section. The magnitude of the magnetic field is
(a) maximum at the axis of the wire
(b) minimum at the axis of the wire
(c) maximum at the surface of the wire
(d) minimum at the surface of the wire.

5. A hollow tube is carrying an electric current along its length distributed uniformly over its surface. The magnetic field
(a) increases linearly from the axis to the surface
(b) is constant inside the tube
(c) is zero at the axis
(d) is zero just outside the tube.

6. In a coaxial, straight cable, the central conductor and the outer conductor carry equal currents in opposite directions. The magnetic field is zero
(a) outside the cable
(b) inside the inner conductor
(c) inside the outer conductor
(d) in between the two conductors.

7. A steady electric current is flowing through a cylindrical conductor.
(a) The electric field at the axis of the conductor is zero.
(b) The magnetic field at the axis of the conductor is zero.
(c) The electric field in the vicinity of the conductor is zero.
(d) The magnetic field in the vicinity of the conductor is zero.

EXERCISES

1. Using the formulae $\vec{F} = q\vec{v}\times\vec{B}$ and $B = \frac{\mu_0 i}{2\pi r}$, show that the SI units of the magnetic field B and the permeability constant μ_0 may be written as $\mathrm{N\,m^{-1}A^{-1}}$ and $\mathrm{N\,A^{-2}}$ respectively.

2. A current of 10 A is established in a long wire along the positive z-axis. Find the magnetic field $\vec{B}$ at the point (1 m, 0, 0).

3. A copper wire of diameter 1·6 mm carries a current of 20 A. Find the maximum magnitude of the magnetic field $\vec{B}$ due to this current.

4. A transmission wire carries a current of 100 A. What would be the magnetic field B at a point on the road if the wire is 8 m above the road ?

5. A long, straight wire carrying a current of 1·0 A is placed horizontally in a uniform magnetic field $B = 1{\cdot}0 \times 10^{-5}$ T pointing vertically upward (figure 35-E1). Find the magnitude of the resultant magnetic field at the points P and Q, both situated at a distance of 2·0 cm from the wire in the same horizontal plane.

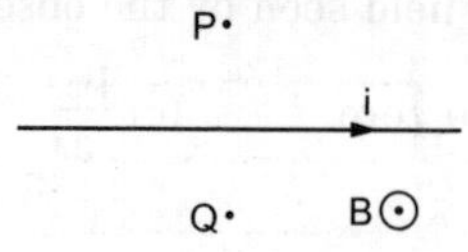

Figure 35-E1

6. A long, straight wire of radius r carries a current i and is placed horizontally in a uniform magnetic field B pointing vertically upward. The current is uniformly distributed over its cross section. (a) At what points will the resultant magnetic field have maximum magnitude ? What will be the maximum magnitude ? (b) What will be the minimum magnitude of the resultant magnetic field ?

7. A long, straight wire carrying a current of 30 A is placed in an external, uniform magnetic field of $4{\cdot}0 \times 10^{-4}$ T parallel to the current. Find the magnitude of the resultant magnetic field at a point 2·0 cm away from the wire.

8. A long, vertical wire carrying a current of 10 A in the upward direction is placed in a region where a horizontal magnetic field of magnitude $2{\cdot}0 \times 10^{-3}$ T exists from south to north. Find the point where the resultant magnetic field is zero.

9. Figure (35-E2) shows two parallel wires separated by a distance of 4·0 cm and carrying equal currents of 10 A along opposite directions. Find the magnitude of the magnetic field B at the points A_1, A_2, A_3 and A_4.

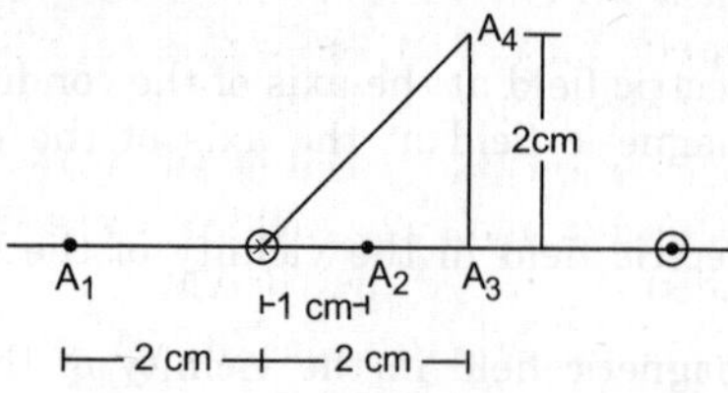

Figure 35-E2

10. Two parallel wires carry equal currents of 10 A along the same direction and are separated by a distance of 2·0 cm. Find the magnetic field at a point which is 2·0 cm away from each of these wires.

11. Two long, straight wires, each carrying a current of 5 A, are placed along the x- and y-axes respectively. The currents point along the positive directions of the axes. Find the magnetic fields at the points (a) (1 m, 1 m), (b) (– 1 m, 1 m), (c) (– 1 m, – 1 m) and (d) (1 m, – 1 m).

12. Four long, straight wires, each carrying a current of 5·0 A, are placed in a plane as shown in figure (35-E3). The points of intersection form a square of side 5·0 cm. (a) Find the magnetic field at the centre P of the square. (b) Q_1, Q_2, Q_3 and Q_4 are points situated on the diagonals of the square and at a distance from P that is equal to the length of the diagonal of the square. Find the magnetic fields at these points.

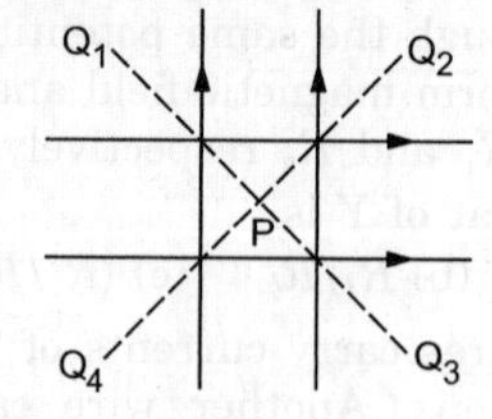

Figure 35-E3

13. Figure (35-E4) shows a long wire bent at the middle to form a right angle. Show that the magnitudes of the magnetic fields at the points P, Q, R and S are equal and find this magnitude.

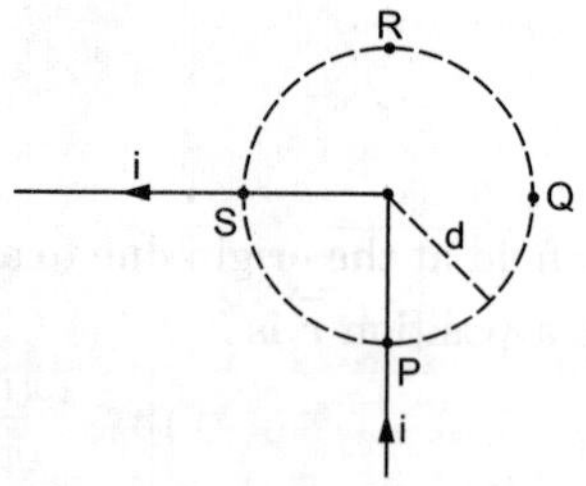

Figure 35-E4

14. Consider a straight piece of length x of a wire carrying a current i. Let P be a point on the perpendicular bisector of the piece, situated at a distance d from its middle point. Show that for $d >> x$, the magnetic field at P varies as $1/d^2$ whereas for $d << x$, it varies as $1/d$.

15. Consider a 10-cm long piece of a wire which carries a current of 10 A. Find the magnitude of the magnetic field due to the piece at a point which makes an equilateral triangle with the ends of the piece.

16. A long, straight wire carries a current i. Let B_1 be the magnetic field at a point P at a distance d from the wire. Consider a section of length l of this wire such that the point P lies on a perpendicular bisector of the section. Let B_2 be the magnetic field at this point due to this section only. Find the value of d/l so that B_2 differs from B_1 by 1%.

17. Figure (35-E5) shows a square loop $ABCD$ with edge-length a. The resistance of the wire ABC is r and that of ADC is $2r$. Find the magnetic field B at the centre of the loop assuming uniform wires.

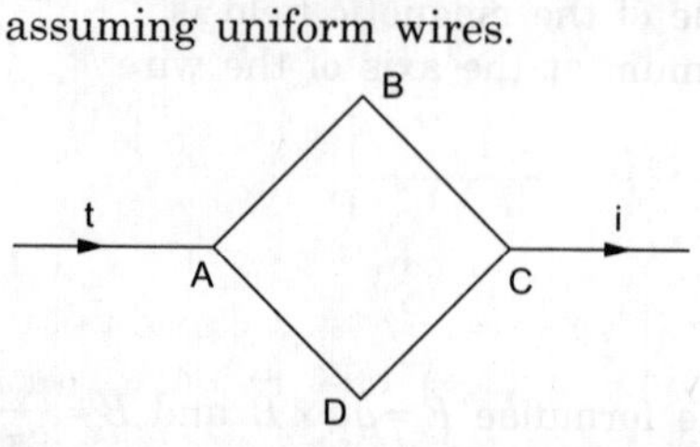

Figure 35-E5

18. Figure (35-E6) shows a square loop of edge a made of a uniform wire. A current i enters the loop at the point A and leaves it at the point C. Find the magnetic field at the point P which is on the perpendicular bisector of AB at a distance $a/4$ from it.

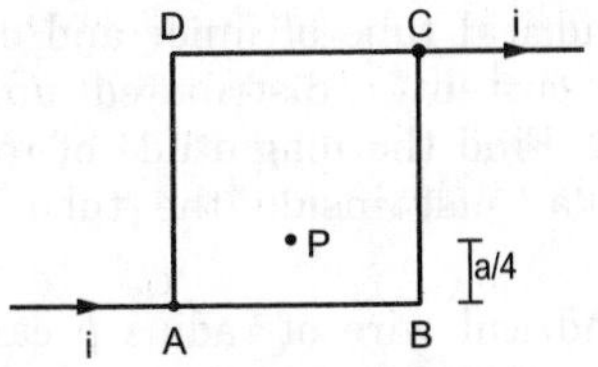

Figure 35-E6

19. Consider the situation described in the previous problem. Suppose the current i enters the loop at the point A and leaves it at the point B. Find the magnetic field at the centre of the loop.

20. The wire ABC shown in figure (35-E7) forms an equilateral triangle. Find the magnetic field B at the centre O of the triangle assuming the wire to be uniform.

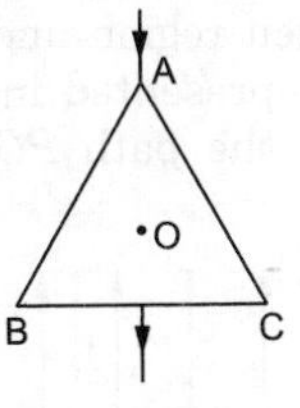

Figure 35-E7

21. A wire of length l is bent in the form of an equilateral triangle and carries an electric current i. (a) Find the magnetic field B at the centre. (b) If the wire is bent in the form of a square, what would be the value of B at the centre ?

22. A long wire carrying a current i is bent to form a plane angle α. Find the magnetic field B at a point on the bisector of this angle situated at a distance x from the vertex.

23. Find the magnetic field B at the centre of a rectangular loop of length l and width b, carrying a current i.

24. A regular polygon of n sides is formed by bending a wire of total length $2\pi r$ which carries a current i. (a) Find the magnetic field B at the centre of the polygon. (b) By letting $n \to \infty$, deduce the expression for the magnetic field at the centre of a circular current.

25. Each of the batteries shown in figure (35-E8) has an emf equal to 5 V. Show that the magnetic field B at the point P is zero for any set of values of the resistances.

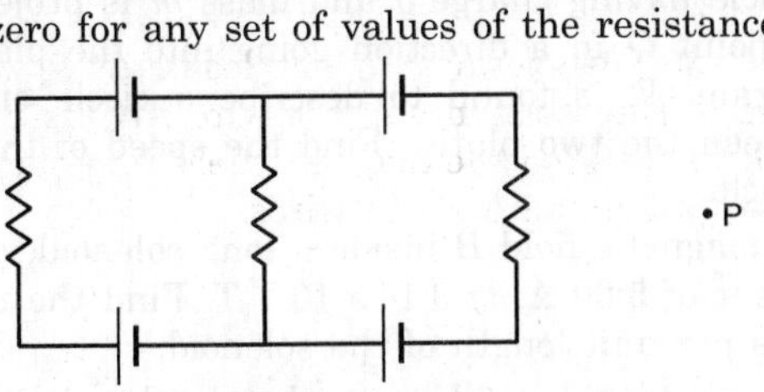

Figure 35-E8

26. A straight, long wire carries a current of 20 A. Another wire carrying equal current is placed parallel to it. If the force acting on a length of 10 cm of the second wire is $2{\cdot}0 \times 10^{-5}$ N, what is the separation between them ?

27. Three coplanar parallel wires, each carrying a current of 10 A along the same direction, are placed with a separation 5·0 cm between the consecutive ones. Find the magnitude of the magnetic force per unit length acting on the wires.

28. Two parallel wires separated by a distance of 10 cm carry currents of 10 A and 40 A along the same direction. Where should a third current be placed so that it experiences no magnetic force ?

29. Figure (35-E9) shows a part of an electric circuit. The wires AB, CD and EF are long and have identical resistances. The separation between the neighbouring wires is 1·0 cm. The wires AE and BF have negligible resistance and the ammeter reads 30 A. Calculate the magnetic force per unit length of AB and CD.

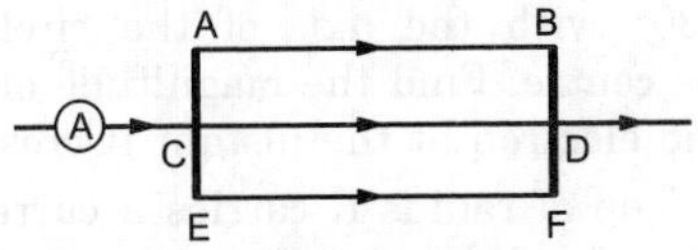

Figure 35-E9

30. A long, straight wire is fixed horizontally and carries a current of 50·0 A. A second wire having linear mass density $1{\cdot}0 \times 10^{-4}\ \text{kg m}^{-1}$ is placed parallel to and directly above this wire at a separation of 5·0 mm. What current should this second wire carry such that the magnetic repulsion can balance its weight ?

31. A square loop $PQRS$ carrying a current of 6·0 A is placed near a long wire carrying 10 A as shown in figure (35-E10). (a) Show that the magnetic force acting on the part PQ is equal and opposite to that on the part RS. (b) Find the magnetic force on the square loop.

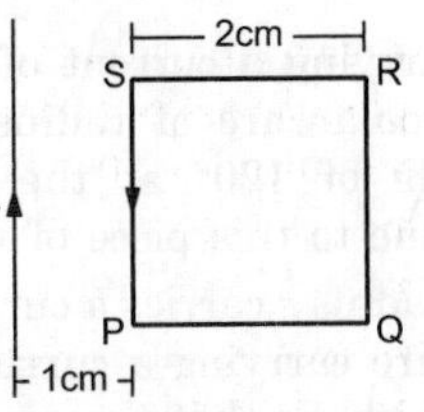

Figure 35-E10

32. A circular loop of one turn carries a current of 5·00 A. If the magnetic field B at the centre is 0·200 mT, find the radius of the loop.

33. A current-carrying circular coil of 100 turns and radius 5·0 cm produces a magnetic field of $6{\cdot}0 \times 10^{-5}$ T at its centre. Find the value of the current.

34. An electron makes 3×10^{5} revolutions per second in a circle of radius 0·5 angstrom. Find the magnetic field B at the centre of the circle.

35. A conducting circular loop of radius a is connected to two long, straight wires. The straight wires carry a current i as shown in figure (35-E11). Find the magnetic field B at the centre of the loop.

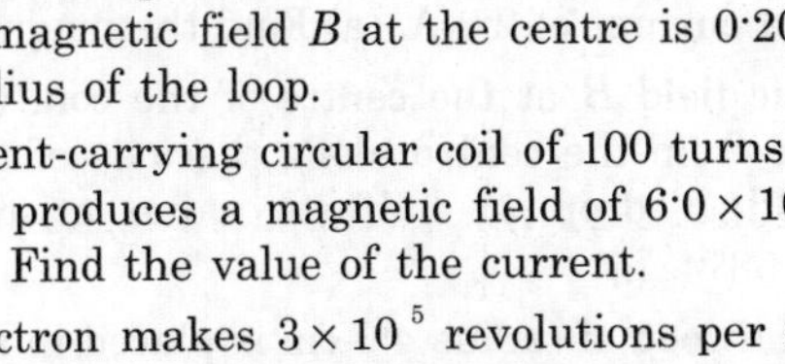

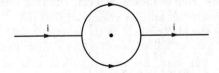

Figure 35-E11

36. Two circular coils of radii 5·0 cm and 10 cm carry equal currents of 2·0 A. The coils have 50 and 100 turns respectively and are placed in such a way that their planes as well as the centres coincide. Find the magnitude of the magnetic field B at the common centre of the coils if the currents in the coils are (a) in the same sense (b) in the opposite sense.

37. If the outer coil of the previous problem is rotated through 90° about a diameter, what would be the magnitude of the magnetic field B at the centre?

38. A circular loop of radius 20 cm carries a current of 10 A. An electron crosses the plane of the loop with a speed of $2·0 \times 10^{6}\ \mathrm{m\ s^{-1}}$. The direction of motion makes an angle of 30° with the axis of the circle and passes through its centre. Find the magnitude of the magnetic force on the electron at the instant it crosses the plane.

39. A circular loop of radius R carries a current I. Another circular loop of radius r ($<< R$) carries a current i and is placed at the centre of the larger loop. The planes of the two circles are at right angle to each other. Find the torque acting on the smaller loop.

40. A circular loop of radius r carrying a current i is held at the centre of another circular loop of radius $R (>> r)$ carrying a current I. The plane of the smaller loop makes an angle of 30° with that of the larger loop. If the smaller loop is held fixed in this position by applying a single force at a point on its periphery, what would be the minimum magnitude of this force ?

41. Find the magnetic field B due to a semicircular wire of radius 10·0 cm carrying a current of 5·0 A at its centre of curvature.

42. A piece of wire carrying a current of 6·00 A is bent in the form of a circular arc of radius 10·0 cm, and it subtends an angle of 120° at the centre. Find the magnetic field B due to this piece of wire at the centre.

43. A circular loop of radius r carries a current i. How should a long, straight wire carrying a current $4i$ be placed in the plane of the circle so that the magnetic field at the centre becomes zero ?

44. A circular coil of 200 turns has a radius of 10 cm and carries a current of 2·0 A. (a) Find the magnitude of the magnetic field $\vec{B}$ at the centre of the coil. (b) At what distance from the centre along the axis of the coil will the field B drop to half its value at the centre ? ($\sqrt[3]{4} = 1·5874 \ldots$)

45. A circular loop of radius 4·0 cm is placed in a horizontal plane and carries an electric current of 5·0 A in the clockwise direction as seen from above. Find the magnetic field (a) at a point 3·0 cm above the centre of the loop (b) at a point 3·0 cm below the centre of the loop.

46. A charge of $3·14 \times 10^{-6}$ C is distributed uniformly over a circular ring of radius 20·0 cm. The ring rotates about its axis with an angular velocity of 60.0 rad $\mathrm{s^{-1}}$. Find the ratio of the electric field to the magnetic field at a point on the axis at a distance of 5·00 cm from the centre.

47. A thin but long, hollow, cylindrical tube of radius r carries a current i along its length. Find the magnitude of the magnetic field at a distance $r/2$ from the surface (a) inside the tube (b) outside the tube.

48. A long, cylindrical tube of inner and outer radii a and b carries a current i distributed uniformly over its cross section. Find the magnitude of the magnetic field at a point (a) just inside the tube (b) just outside the tube.

49. A long, cylindrical wire of radius b carries a current i distributed uniformly over its cross section. Find the magnitude of the magnetic field at a point inside the wire at a distance a from the axis.

50. A solid wire of radius 10 cm carries a current of 5·0 A distributed uniformly over its cross section. Find the magnetic field B at a point at a distance (a) 2 cm (b) 10 cm and (c) 20 cm away from the axis. Sketch a graph of B versus x for $0 < x < 20$ cm.

51. Sometimes we show an idealised magnetic field which is uniform in a given region and falls to zero abruptly. One such field is represented in figure (35-E12). Using Ampere's law over the path $PQRS$, show that such a field is not possible.

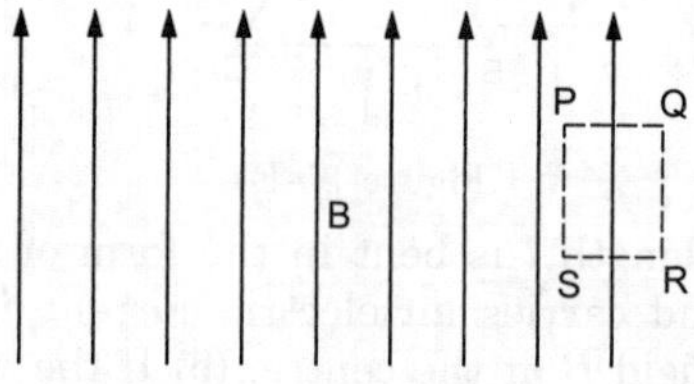

Figure 35-E12

52. Two large metal sheets carry surface currents as shown in figure (35-E13). The current through a strip of width dl is Kdl where K is a constant. Find the magnetic field at the points P, Q and R.

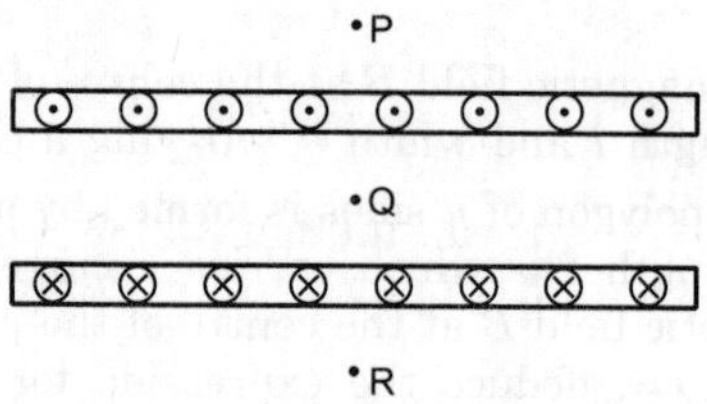

Figure 35-E13

53. Consider the situation of the previous problem. A particle having charge q and mass m is projected from the point Q in a direction going into the plane of the diagram. It is found to describe a circle of radius r between the two plates. Find the speed of the charged particle.

54. The magnetic field B inside a long solenoid, carrying a current of 5·00 A, is $3·14 \times 10^{-2}$ T. Find the number of turns per unit length of the solenoid.

55. A long solenoid is fabricated by closely winding a wire of radius 0·5 mm over a cylindrical nonmagnetic frame so that the successive turns nearly touch each other. What would be the magnetic field B at the centre of the solenoid if it carries a current of 5 A ?

56. A copper wire having resistance 0·01 ohm in each metre is used to wind a 400-turn solenoid of radius 1·0 cm and length 20 cm. Find the emf of a battery which when connected across the solenoid will cause a magnetic field of $1{\cdot}0 \times 10^{-2}$ T near the centre of the solenoid.

57. A tightly-wound solenoid of radius a and length l has n turns per unit length. It carries an electric current i. Consider a length dx of the solenoid at a distance x from one end. This contains $n\,dx$ turns and may be approximated as a circular current $i\,n\,dx$. (a) Write the magnetic field at the centre of the solenoid due to this circular current. Integrate this expression under proper limits to find the magnetic field at the centre of the solenoid. (b) Verify that if $l >> a$, the field tends to $B = \mu_0 ni$ and if $a >> l$, the field tends to $B = \frac{\mu_0 nil}{2a}$. Interpret these results.

58. A tightly-wound, long solenoid carries a current of 2·00 A. An electron is found to execute a uniform circular motion inside the solenoid with a frequency of $1{\cdot}00 \times 10^{8}$ rev s^{-1}. Find the number of turns per metre in the solenoid.

59. A tightly-wound, long solenoid has n turns per unit length, a radius r and carries a current i. A particle having charge q and mass m is projected from a point on the axis in a direction perpendicular to the axis. What can be the maximum speed for which the particle does not strike the solenoid ?

60. A tightly-wound, long solenoid is kept with its axis parallel to a large metal sheet carrying a surface current. The surface current through a width dl of the sheet is Kdl and the number of turns per unit length of the solenoid is n. The magnetic field near the centre of the solenoid is found to be zero. (a) Find the current in the solenoid. (b) If the solenoid is rotated to make its axis perpendicular to the metal sheet, what would be the magnitude of the magnetic field near its centre ?

61. A capacitor of capacitance 100 μF is connected to a battery of 20 volts for a long time and then disconnected from it. It is now connected across a long solenoid having 4000 turns per metre. It is found that the potential difference across the capacitor drops to 90% of its maximum value in 2·0 seconds. Estimate the average magnetic field produced at the centre of the solenoid during this period.

□

ANSWERS

OBJECTIVE I

1. (c)	2. (c)	3. (a)	4. (d)	5. (b)	6. (d)
7. (c)	8. (c)	9. (c)	10. (b)	11. (c)	12. (a)

OBJECTIVE II

1. (c), (d)	2. (a), (b), (c)	3. (b), (c), (d)
4. (b), (c)	5. (b), (c)	6. (a)
7. (b), (c)		

EXERCISES

2. 2 μT along the positive y-axis
3. 5·0 mT
4. 2·5 μT
5. 20 μT, zero
6. (a) looking along the current, at the leftmost points on the wire's surface, $B + \frac{\mu_0 i}{2\pi r}$

   (b) zero if $r \le \frac{\mu_0 i}{2\pi B}$, $B - \frac{\mu_0 i}{2\pi r}$ if $r > \frac{\mu_0 i}{2\pi B}$
7. 5×10^{-4} T
8. 1·0 mm west to the wire
9. (a) $0{\cdot}67 \times 10^{-4}$ T (b) $2{\cdot}7 \times 10^{-4}$ T

   (c) $2{\cdot}0 \times 10^{-4}$ T (d) $1{\cdot}0 \times 10^{-4}$ T
10. $1{\cdot}7 \times 10^{-4}$ T in a direction parallel to the plane of the wires and perpendicular to the wires
11. (a) zero (b) 2 μT along the z-axis

    (c) zero and (d) 2 μT along the negative z-axis
12. (a) zero (b) $Q_1 : 1{\cdot}1 \times 10^{-4}$ T, $\odot$, Q_2 : zero,

    $Q_3 : 1{\cdot}1 \times 10^{-4}$ T, $\otimes$, and Q_4 : zero
13. $\frac{\mu_0 i}{4\pi d}$
15. 11·5 μT
16. 0·07
17. $\frac{\sqrt{2}\,\mu_0 i}{3\pi a}$, $\otimes$
18. $\frac{2\mu_0 i}{\pi a}\left(\frac{1}{\sqrt{5}} - \frac{1}{3\sqrt{13}}\right)$
19. zero
20. zero
21. (a) $\frac{27\mu_0 i}{2\pi l}$ (b) $\frac{8\sqrt{2}\mu_0 i}{\pi l}$
22. $\frac{\mu_0 i}{2\pi x}\cot\frac{\alpha}{4}$
23. $\frac{2\mu_0 i\sqrt{l^2 + b^2}}{\pi l b}$
24. (a) $\frac{\mu_0 in^2 \sin\frac{\pi}{n}\tan\frac{\pi}{n}}{2\pi^2 r}$

26. 40 cm

27. zero on the middle wire and $6{\cdot}0 \times 10^{-4}$ N towards the middle wire on each of the rest two

28. 2 cm from the 10 A current and 8 cm from the other

29. 3×10^{-3} N m^{-1}, downward zero

30. 0·49 A in opposite directiom

31. (b) $1{\cdot}6 \times 10^{-5}$ N towards right

32. 1·57 cm

33. 48 mA

34. 6×10^{-10} T

35. zero

36. (a) $8\pi \times 10^{-4}$ T (b) zero

37. 1·8 mT

38. $16\pi \times 10^{-19}$ N

39. $\dfrac{\mu_0 \pi i l r^2}{2R}$

40. $\dfrac{\mu_0 \pi i l r}{4R}$

41. $1{\cdot}6 \times 10^{-5}$ T

42. $1{\cdot}26 \times 10^{-5}$ T

43. at a distance of $4r/\pi$ from the centre in such a way that the direction of the current in it is opposite to that in the nearest part of the circular wire

44. (a) 2·51 mT (b) 7·66 cm

45. $4{\cdot}0 \times 10^{-5}$ T, downwards in both the cases

46. $1{\cdot}88 \times 10^{15}$ m s^{-1}

47. (a) zero (b) $\dfrac{\mu_0 i}{3\pi r}$

48. (a) zero (b) $\dfrac{\mu_0 i}{2\pi b}$

49. $\dfrac{\mu_0 i a}{2\pi b^2}$

50. (a) 2·0 μT (b) 10 μT (c) 5·0 μT

52. 0, $\mu_0 K$ towards right in the figure, 0

53. $\dfrac{\mu_0 K q r}{m}$

54. 5000 turns m^{-1}

55. $2\pi \times 10^{-3}$ T

56. 1 V

57. (a) $\dfrac{\mu_0 n i}{\sqrt{1 + \left(\dfrac{2a}{l}\right)^2}}$

58. 1420 turns m^{-1}

59. $\dfrac{\mu_0 q r n i}{2m}$

60. (a) $\dfrac{K}{2n}$ (b) $\dfrac{\mu_0 K}{\sqrt{2}}$

61. $16\pi \times 10^{-8}$ T

□

CHAPTER 36

PERMANENT MAGNETS

36.1 MAGNETIC POLES AND BAR MAGNETS

We have seen that a small current loop carrying a current i, produces a magnetic field

$$\vec{B} = \frac{\mu_0}{4\pi} \frac{2\vec{\mu}}{d^3} \qquad \ldots \text{(i)}$$

at an axial point. Here $\mu = iA$ is the magnetic dipole moment of the current loop. The vector $\vec{A}$ represents the area-vector of the current loop. Also, a current loop placed in a magnetic field $\vec{B}$ experiences a torque

$$\vec{\Gamma} = \vec{\mu} \times \vec{B}. \qquad \ldots \text{(ii)}$$

We also know that an electric dipole produces an electric field

$$\vec{E} = \frac{1}{4\pi\varepsilon_0} \frac{2\vec{p}}{d^3} \qquad \ldots \text{(iii)}$$

at an axial point and it experiences a torque

$$\vec{\Gamma} = \vec{p} \times \vec{E} \qquad \ldots \text{(iv)}$$

when placed in an electric field. Equations (i) and (ii) for a current loop are similar in structure to the equations (iii) and (iv) for an electric dipole with $\vec{\mu}$ taking the role of $\vec{p}$ and $\frac{\mu_0}{4\pi}$ taking the role of $\frac{1}{4\pi\varepsilon_0}$. The similarity suggests that the behaviour of a current loop can be described by the following hypothetical model:

(a) There are two types of magnetic charges, positive magnetic charge and negative magnetic charge. A magnetic charge m placed in a magnetic field $\vec{B}$ experiences a force

$$\vec{F} = m\vec{B}. \qquad \ldots (36.1)$$

The force on a positive magnetic charge is along the field and the force on a negative magnetic charge is opposite to the field.

(b) A magnetic charge m produces a magnetic field

$$B = \frac{\mu_0}{4\pi} \frac{m}{r^2} \qquad \ldots (36.2)$$

at a distance r from it. The field is radially outward if the magnetic charge is positive and is inward if it is negative.

(c) A magnetic dipole is formed when a negative magnetic charge $-m$ and a positive magnetic charge $+m$ are placed at a small separation d. The magnetic dipole moment is $\mu = md$ and its direction is from $-m$ to $+m$. The line joining $-m$ and $+m$ is called the *axis* of the dipole.

(d) A current loop of area A carrying a current i may be replaced by a magnetic dipole of dipole moment $\mu = md = iA$ placed along the axis of the loop. The area-vector $\vec{A}$ points in the direction $-m$ to $+m$.

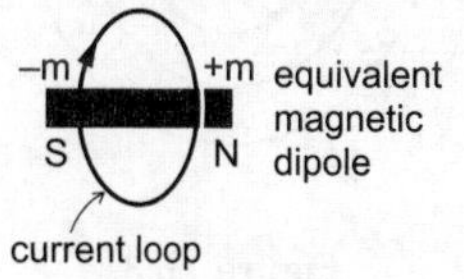

Figure 36.1

The model is very useful in studying magnetic effects and is widely used. It is customary to call a positive magnetic charge a *north pole* and a negative magnetic charge a *south pole*. They are represented by the letters N and S respectively. The quantity m is called *pole strength*. From the equation $md = iA$ or $F = mB$, we can easily see that the unit of pole strength is A–m. We can find the magnetic field due to a magnetic dipole at any point P using equation (36.2) for both the poles.

A solenoid very closely resembles a combination of circular loops placed side by side. If i be the current through it and A be the area of cross-section, the dipole moment of each turn is $\mu = iA$. In our model, each turn may be replaced by a small dipole placed at the centre of the loop along its axis. Suppose, each turn is

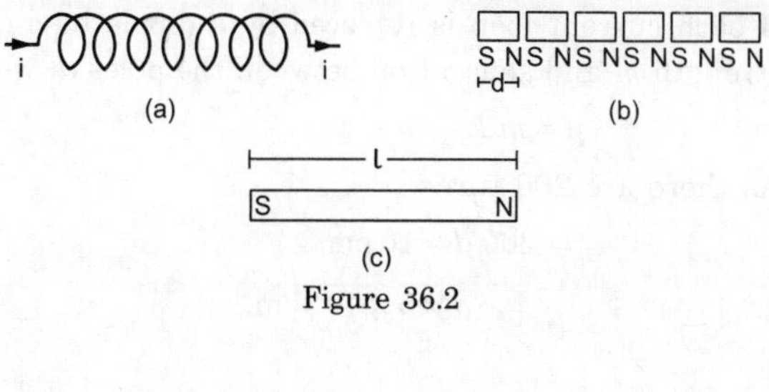

Figure 36.2

replaced by a magnetic dipole with pole strength m and separation d between the north and south poles. We have $md = iA$. Figure (36.2a) and (36.2b) show a current-carrying solenoid and its equivalent in terms of magnetic poles.

Suppose we take the value of d in such a way that the north pole of one dipole touches the south pole of the adjacent one. South poles and north poles, then, neutralise each other except at the ends. Thus, a current-carrying solenoid can be replaced by just a single south pole and a single north pole of pole strength m each, placed at a separation equal to the length of the solenoid (figure 36.2c).

We can obtain the field outside the solenoid using the above model. Each pole produces a field given by equation (36.2). The resultant field is the vector sum of the fields produced by the south pole and the north pole. Figure (36.3) shows the magnetic field lines due to a current-carrying solenoid.

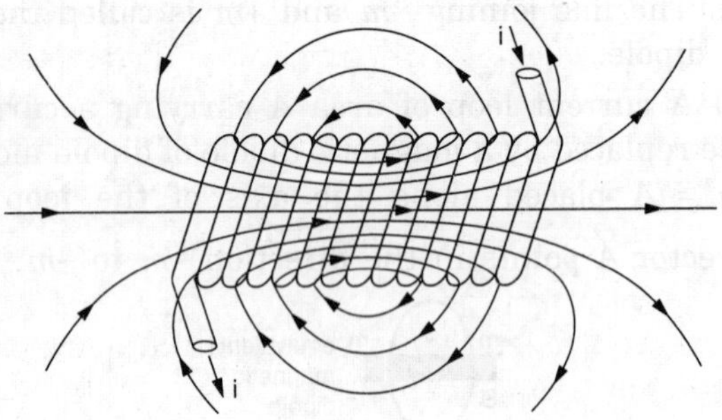

Figure 36.3

Note that the magnetic field inside the solenoid is opposite in direction from what one expects from the pole picture. The magnetic field lines are closed curves. They do not start or end at a point as is the case with electric field lines.

Example 36.1

A solenoid of length 10 cm *and radius* 1 cm *contains* 200 turns *and carries a current of* 10 A. *Find the magnetic field at a point on the axis at a distance of* 10 cm *from the centre.*

Solution : The dipole moment of each turn is

$$\mu = iA = (10\ \text{A})\ (\pi\ \text{cm}^2)$$

$$= \pi \times 10^{-3}\ \text{A m}^2.$$

If each current loop is replaced by a dipole having pole strength m and separation between the poles d, we have

$$\mu = md.$$

As there are 200 turns,

$$200\ d = 10\ \text{cm}$$

or, $$d = 5 \times 10^{-4}\ \text{m}.$$

Thus,

$$m = \frac{\mu}{d} = \frac{\pi \times 10^{-3}\ \text{A m}^2}{5 \times 10^{-4}\ \text{m}} = 2\pi\ \text{A m}.$$

We can replace the solenoid by a south pole and a north pole of equal pole strength 2π A m, separated by 10 cm. The equivalent picture is shown in figure (36.4).

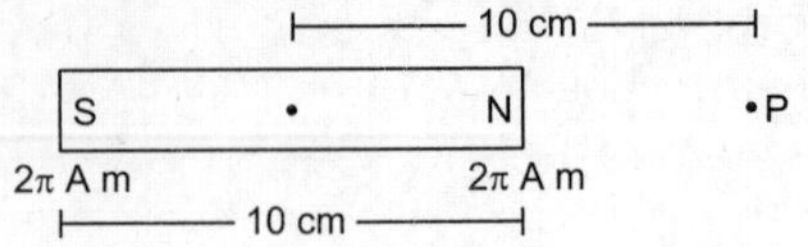

Figure 36.4

The magnetic field at P due to the north pole is

$$B_N = \frac{\mu_0}{4\pi} \frac{2\pi\ \text{A m}}{(5\ \text{cm})^2} = 2{\cdot}5 \times 10^{-4}\ \text{T}.$$

The magnetic field at P due to the south pole is

$$B_S = \frac{\mu_0}{4\pi} \frac{2\pi\ \text{A m}}{(15\ \text{cm})^2} = 0{\cdot}3 \times 10^{-4}\ \text{T}.$$

The field B_N is away from the poles and B_S is towards the poles. The resultant field at P is

$$B = B_N - B_S$$

$$= 2{\cdot}2 \times 10^{-4}\ \text{T}$$

away from the solenoid.

In nature, we find certain objects whose magnetic behaviour may be described by assuming that there is a south pole placed at a certain point in the object and a north pole placed at a different point. Such an object is called a *magnet*. A magnet in the shape of a rod or a bar is called a *bar magnet*. The poles appear at points which are slightly inside the two ends. The line joining the positions of the assumed poles is called the *magnetic axis* of the bar magnet. The magnetic field lines due to a bar magnet are similar to those shown in figure (36.3). How can a rod produce magnetic field when no electric current is passed through it ? Let us now discuss this question.

A simple model tells us that matter is made of atoms and each atom contains electrons circulating around its nucleus. These moving electrons constitute electric currents at the atomic level. The actual description of these atomic currents is quite complicated but we can assume that these atomic currents are equivalent to small, circular current loops. In magnets, these loops are arranged nearly parallel to each other and have currents in the same sense.

Figure (36.5) shows the currents in a cross section of a cylindrical bar magnet. At any point inside the

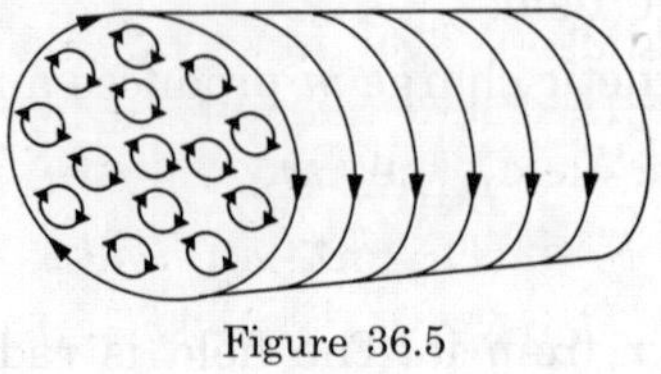

Figure 36.5

magnet, the net current is zero because the currents from the adjacent loops cancel each other. However, there is a net current along the surface as there is no cancellation of currents there. Due to such a surface current, the cylindrical magnet is equivalent to a closely-wound, current-carrying solenoid and hence produces a magnetic field similar to the solenoid. We can, therefore, treat the bar magnet as having a north pole and a south pole separated by a length l. Suppose the surface current is I per unit length of the magnet. The total current at the surface of the magnet of length l is Il. If the cross-sectional area is A, the magnetic dipole moment is

$$\mu = \text{current} \times \text{area} = IlA.$$

If the pole strength is m, the magnetic moment may also be written as $\mu = ml$.

Thus, $ml = IlA$

or, $$m = IA. \qquad \dots (36.3)$$

In the above discussion we have not considered the end effect. At the two ends of the magnet, the currents behave differently from those inside the magnet. Because of this effect, the magnetic poles appear slightly inside the bar. The distance between the locations of the assumed poles is called the *magnetic length* of the magnet. The distance between the ends is called the *geometrical length*. It is found that

$$\frac{\text{magnetic length}}{\text{geometrical length}} \approx 0{\cdot}84.$$

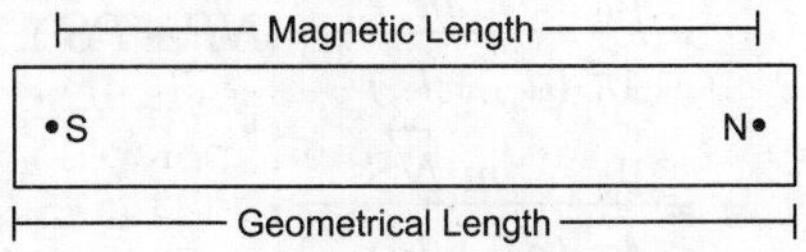

Figure 36.6

The magnetic moment of a bar magnet is conventionally denoted by M. Also, the magnetic length of a bar magnet is written as $2l$. If m be the pole strength and $2l$ the magnetic length of a bar magnet, its magnetic moment is

$$M = 2ml. \qquad \dots (36.4)$$

36.2 TORQUE ON A BAR MAGNET PLACED IN A MAGNETIC FIELD

Suppose a bar magnet of magnetic length $2l$ and pole strength m is placed in a uniform magnetic field $\vec{B}$ (figure 36.7). The angle between the magnet and the magnetic field is θ. The force on the north pole is mB along the field and that on the south pole is mB opposite to the field. The torque of these two forces is

$$\Gamma = mB\, l \sin\theta + mB\, l \sin\theta$$
$$= 2\, mB\, l \sin\theta = MB \sin\theta$$

where M is the magnetic moment of the magnet. This torque tries to rotate the magnet so as to align it with the field. We can write the torque as

$$\vec{\Gamma} = \vec{M} \times \vec{B}.$$

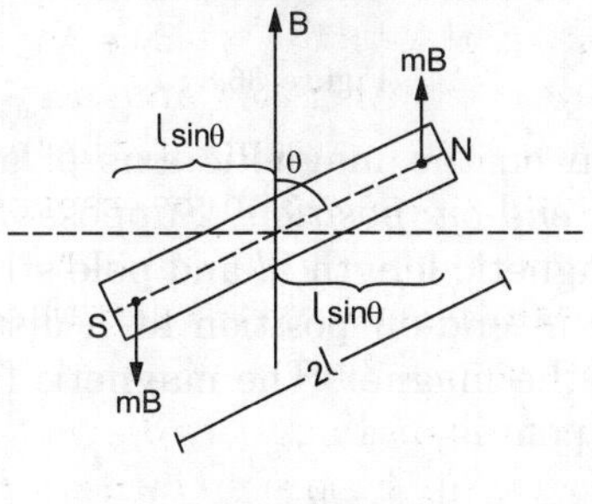

Figure 36.7

This equation is the same as that obtained earlier for a current loop. If an external agent rotates the magnet slowly, the agent has to exert a torque $MB \sin\theta$ opposite to that exerted by the field. The work done by the agent in changing the angle from θ to $\theta + d\theta$ is $dW = (MB \sin\theta) d\theta$. The work done in rotating the magnet from an angle θ_0 to θ is

$$W = \int_{\theta_0}^{\theta} MB \sin\theta\, d\theta = MB(\cos\theta_0 - \cos\theta).$$

This work is stored as the potential energy of the field–magnet system. Thus,

$$U(\theta) - U(\theta_0) = MB(\cos\theta_0 - \cos\theta).$$

If we take the potential energy at $\theta = 90°$ to be zero, the potential energy at an angle θ is

$$U(\theta) = U(\theta) - U(90°)$$
$$= -MB\cos\theta = -\vec{M}\cdot\vec{B}. \qquad \dots (36.5)$$

We see from this equation that the SI unit for the magnetic moment M may also be written as J T^{-1}.

Example 36.2

A bar magnet having a magnetic moment of $1{\cdot}0 \times 10^{4}$ J T^{-1} *is free to rotate in a horizontal plane. A horizontal magnetic field* $B = 4 \times 10^{-5}$ T *exists in the space. Find the work done in rotating the magnet slowly from a direction parallel to the field to a direction 60° from the field.*

Solution : The work done by the external agent = change in potential energy

$$= (-MB\cos\theta_2) - (-MB\cos\theta_1)$$
$$= -MB(\cos 60° - \cos 0°) = \frac{1}{2} MB$$
$$= \frac{1}{2} \times (1{\cdot}0 \times 10^{4}\ \text{J T}^{-1})\,(4 \times 10^{-5}\ \text{T}) = 0{\cdot}2\ \text{J}.$$

36.3 MAGNETIC FIELD DUE TO A BAR MAGNET

(a) End-on Position

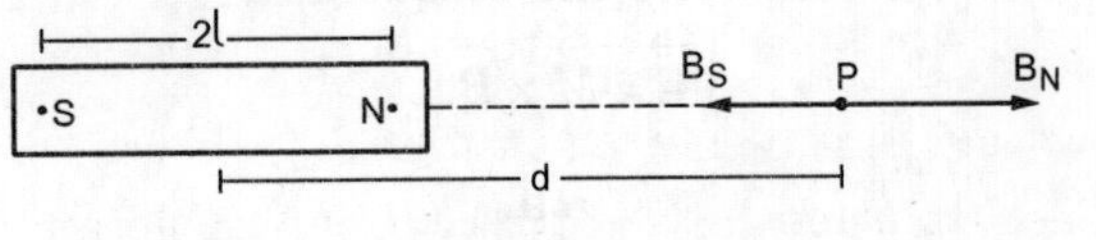

Figure 36.8

A position on the magnetic axis of a bar magnet is called an *end-on position*. Suppose SN is a bar magnet of magnetic length $2l$ and pole strength m. Let P be a point in end-on position at a distance d from the centre of the magnet. The magnetic field at P due to the north pole is

$$B_N = \frac{\mu_0}{4\pi}\frac{m}{(d-l)^2}$$

directed away from the magnet. The field due to the south pole is

$$B_S = \frac{\mu_0}{4\pi}\frac{m}{(d+l)^2}$$

directed towards the magnet. The resultant field is

$$B = B_N - B_S$$

$$= \frac{\mu_0 m}{4\pi}\left[\frac{1}{(d-l)^2} - \frac{1}{(d+l)^2}\right]$$

$$= \frac{\mu_0}{4\pi}\frac{2Md}{(d^2-l^2)^2} \quad \ldots (36.6)$$

where $M = 2ml$ is the magnetic moment of the magnet. If $d >> l$, the magnet may be called a magnetic dipole and the field at an end-on position is

$$B = \frac{\mu_0}{4\pi}\frac{2M}{d^3}. \quad \ldots (36.7)$$

Example 36.3

A magnet is 10 cm *long and its pole strength is* 120 CGS units (1 CGS unit *of pole strength* = 0·1 A m). *Find the magnitude of the magnetic field B at a point on its axis at a distance* 20 cm *from it.*

Solution :

The pole strength is m = 120 CGS units = 12 A m.

Magnetic length is $2l$ = 10 cm or l = 0·05 m.

Distance from the magnet is d = 20 cm = 0·2 m. The field B at a point in end-on position is

$$B = \frac{\mu_0}{4\pi}\frac{2Md}{(d^2-l^2)^2}$$

$$= \frac{\mu_0}{4\pi}\frac{4mld}{(d^2-l^2)^2}$$

$$= \left(10^{-7}\frac{\text{T m}}{\text{A}}\right)\frac{4 \times (12\text{ A }m) \times (0·05\text{ m}) \times (0·2\text{ m})}{[(0·2\text{ m})^2 - (0·05\text{ m})^2]^2}$$

$$= 3·4 \times 10^{-5}\text{ T}.$$

(b) Broadside-on Position

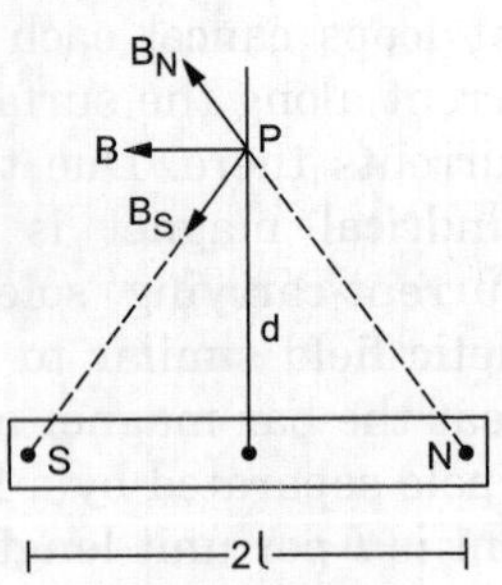

Figure 36.9

A position on a perpendicular bisector of the bar magnet is called *broadside-on position*. Let P be a point in the broadside-on position of the bar magnet at a distance d from its centre. The pole strength of the magnet is m and its magnetic length SN is $2l$. The field at P due to the north pole may be written as

$$\vec{B}_N = \frac{\mu_0}{4\pi}\frac{m\,\overrightarrow{NP}}{NP^3}.$$

This gives the magnitude as well as the direction of the field due to the north pole. The field due to the south pole is

$$\vec{B}_S = \frac{\mu_0}{4\pi}\frac{m\,\overrightarrow{PS}}{PS^3}.$$

Now, $NP = PS = (d^2 + l^2)^{1/2}$ so that the resultant field at P is

$$\vec{B} = \vec{B}_N + \vec{B}_S$$

$$= \frac{\mu_0}{4\pi}\frac{m}{(d^2+l^2)^{3/2}}(\overrightarrow{NP} + \overrightarrow{PS})$$

$$= \frac{\mu_0}{4\pi}\frac{m\,\overrightarrow{NS}}{(d^2+l^2)^{3/2}}$$

The magnitude of the field is

$$B = \frac{\mu_0}{4\pi}\frac{m\,2l}{(d^2+l^2)^{3/2}} = \frac{\mu_0}{4\pi}\frac{M}{(d^2+l^2)^{3/2}} \quad \ldots (36.8)$$

where $M = 2ml$ is the magnetic moment of the magnet. The direction of the field is parallel to the axis, from the north pole to the south pole.

If $d >> l$, the magnet may be called a magnetic dipole and the magnetic field at a point in broadside-on position is

$$B = \frac{\mu_0}{4\pi}\frac{M}{d^3}. \quad \ldots (36.9)$$

36.4 MAGNETIC SCALAR POTENTIAL

Magnetic scalar potential is defined in the same way as gravitational or electrostatic potential. We define the change in potential $V(\vec{r}_2) - V(\vec{r}_1)$ by the equation

$$V(\vec{r_2}) - V(\vec{r_1}) = -\int_{\vec{r_1}}^{\vec{r_2}} \vec{B}\cdot d\vec{r}. \quad \text{... (36.10)}$$

Generally, the potential at infinity (a point far away from all sources of magnetic field) is taken to be zero. Taking $\vec{r_1}$ equal to ∞ and $\vec{r_2} = \vec{r}$, equation (36.10) gives

$$V(\vec{r}) = -\int_{\infty}^{\vec{r}} \vec{B}\cdot d\vec{r}.$$

The component of the magnetic field in any direction is given by

$$B_l = -\frac{dV}{dl} \quad \text{... (36.11)}$$

where dl is a small distance along the given direction.

For a pole of pole strength m, the field at a distance r is

$$B = \frac{\mu_0}{4\pi}\frac{m}{r^2}$$

radially away from the pole. So the potential at a distance r is

$$V(r) = -\int_{\infty}^{r} \frac{\mu_0}{4\pi} m \frac{dr}{r^2}$$

$$= \frac{\mu_0}{4\pi}\frac{m}{r}. \quad \text{... (36.12)}$$

Magnetic Scalar Potential due to a Magnetic Dipole

Suppose, SN is a magnetic dipole of length $2l$ and pole strength m (figure 36.10). The magnetic scalar potential is needed at a point P at a distance $OP = r(>> l)$ from the centre of the dipole. The angle $PON = \theta$.

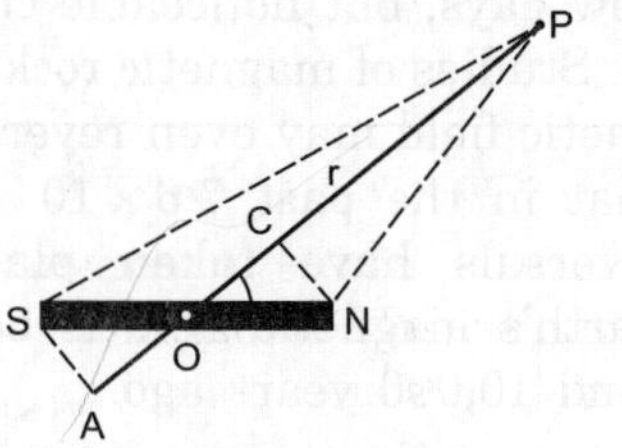

Figure 36.10

Let SA be the perpendicular from S to OP and NC be the perpendicular from N to OP. As $r >> l$,

$$PS \approx PA = PO + OA = r + l\cos\theta.$$

Similarly, $PN \approx PC = PO - OC = r - l\cos\theta.$

The magnetic scalar potential at P due to the north pole is

$$V_N = \frac{\mu_0}{4\pi}\frac{m}{NP}$$

$$= \frac{\mu_0}{4\pi}\frac{m}{r - l\cos\theta}$$

and that due to the south pole is

$$V_S = -\frac{\mu_0}{4\pi}\frac{m}{SP}$$

$$= -\frac{\mu_0}{4\pi}\frac{m}{r + l\cos\theta}.$$

The net potential at P due to the dipole is

$$V = V_N + V_S$$

$$= \frac{\mu_0 m}{4\pi}\left(\frac{1}{r - l\cos\theta} - \frac{1}{r + l\cos\theta}\right)$$

$$= \frac{\mu_0}{4\pi}\frac{m(2l\cos\theta)}{(r^2 - l^2\cos^2\theta)}$$

$$\approx \frac{\mu_0}{4\pi}\frac{M\cos\theta}{r^2}. \quad \text{... (36.13)}$$

Magnetic Field due to a Dipole

Let SN be a magnetic dipole and P be a point far away from the dipole (figure 36.11). The distance $OP = r$ and the angle $PON = \theta$. If we move a small distance PQ in the direction of OP, the value of r is changed to $r + dr$ while θ remains unchanged. Similarly, if we move a small distance PR in the direction perpendicular to OP, θ is changed from θ to $\theta + d\theta$ while r remains very nearly constant. The distance moved is $rd\theta$.

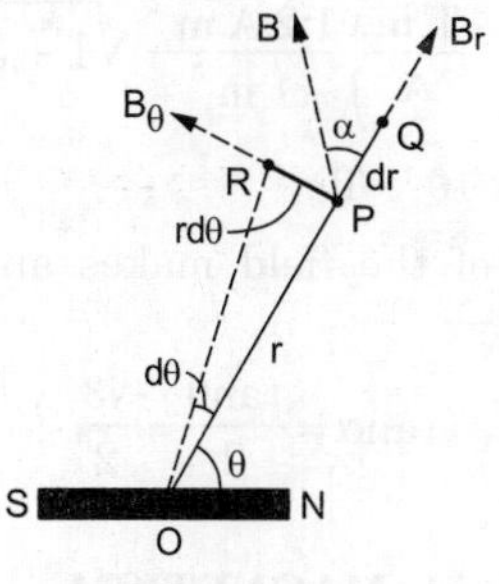

Figure 36.11

The component of magnetic field along OP is

$$B_r = -\frac{dV}{PQ} = -\left[\frac{dV}{dr}\right]_{\theta = \text{constant}}$$

$$= -\frac{\partial V}{\partial r}$$

$$= -\frac{\partial}{\partial r}\left(\frac{\mu_0}{4\pi}\frac{M\cos\theta}{r^2}\right)$$

$$= \frac{\mu_0}{4\pi}\frac{2M\cos\theta}{r^3}. \quad \text{... (i)}$$

The component perpendicular to OP is

$$B_\theta = -\frac{dV}{PR} = -\left[\frac{dV}{rd\theta}\right]_{r = \text{constant}}$$

$$= -\frac{1}{r}\frac{\partial}{\partial\theta}\left(\frac{\mu_0}{4\pi}\frac{M\cos\theta}{r^2}\right)$$

$$= \frac{\mu_0}{4\pi} \frac{M \sin\theta}{r^3}. \quad \ldots \text{(ii)}$$

The resultant magnetic field at P is

$$B = \sqrt{B_r^2 + B_\theta^2}$$

$$= \frac{\mu_0}{4\pi} \frac{M}{r^3} \sqrt{(2\cos\theta)^2 + (\sin\theta)^2}$$

$$= \frac{\mu_0}{4\pi} \frac{M}{r^3} \sqrt{1 + 3\cos^2\theta}. \quad \ldots \text{(36.14)}$$

If it makes an angle α with OP,

$$\tan\alpha = \frac{B_\theta}{B_r}.$$

From (i) and (ii),

$$\tan\alpha = \frac{\sin\theta}{2\cos\theta} = \frac{\tan\theta}{2}. \quad \ldots \text{(36.15)}$$

Example 36.4

Find the magnetic field due to a dipole of magnetic moment $1{\cdot}2\ \text{A m}^2$ *at a point* 1 m *away from it in a direction making an angle of* 60° *with the dipole-axis.*

Solution : The magnitude of the field is

$$B = \frac{\mu_0}{4\pi} \frac{M}{r^3} \sqrt{1 + 3\cos^2\theta}$$

$$= \left(10^{-7} \frac{\text{T m}}{\text{A}}\right) \frac{1{\cdot}2\ \text{A m}^2}{1\ \text{m}^3} \sqrt{1 + 3\cos^2 60°}$$

$$= 1{\cdot}6 \times 10^{-7}\ \text{T}.$$

The direction of the field makes an angle α with the radial line where

$$\tan\alpha = \frac{\tan\theta}{2} = \frac{\sqrt{3}}{2}.$$

36.5 TERRESTRIAL MAGNETISM

Earth is a natural source of magnetic field. We have magnetic field present everywhere near the earth's surface. The magnitude and direction of this field can be obtained approximately by assuming that the earth has a magnetic dipole of dipole moment about $8{\cdot}0 \times 10^{22}\ \text{J T}^{-1}$ located at its centre (figure 36.12). The axis of this dipole makes an angle of about 11·5° with the earth's axis of rotation. The dipole-axis cuts the earth's surface at two points, one near the geographical north pole and the other near the geographical south pole. The first of these points is called *geomagnetic north pole* and the other is called *geomagnetic south pole.*

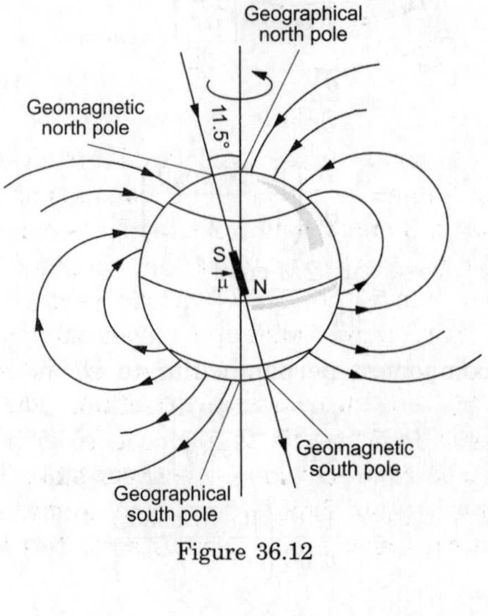

Figure 36.12

If we suspend a bar magnet freely at a point near the earth's surface, it will stay along the magnetic field there. The north pole will point towards the direction of the magnetic field. At the geomagnetic poles, the magnetic field is vertical. If we suspend the bar magnet near the geomagnetic north pole, it will become vertical with its north pole towards the earth's surface. Similarly, if we suspend a bar magnet near the geomagnetic south pole, it will become vertical with its south pole pointing towards the earth's surface. Geomagnetic poles may, therefore, be defined as "the points where a freely suspended bar magnet becomes vertical".

If we treat the assumed magnetic dipole inside the earth as a pair of north and south poles (figure 36.12), the south pole will be towards the geomagnetic north pole and the north pole will be towards the geomagnetic south pole. This may be easily remembered by using the fact that the north pole of the suspended magnet should be attracted by the south pole of the assumed dipole.

Earth's magnetic field changes both in magnitude and direction as time passes. It is fairly constant over a span of a few days, but noticeable changes occur in say, ten years. Studies of magnetic rocks have revealed that the magnetic field may even reverse its direction. It appears that in the past $7{\cdot}6 \times 10^7$ years, already 171 such reversals have taken place. The latest reversal in earth's magnetic field is believed to have occurred around 10,000 years ago.

The theory of earth's magnetic field is not yet well-understood. At present, it seems that the field results mainly due to circulating electric currents induced in the molten liquid and other conducting material inside the earth.

Elements of the Earth's Magnetic Field

The earth's magnetic field at a point on its surface is usually characterised by three quantities: (a) declination (b) inclination or dip and (c) horizontal component of the field. These are known as the *elements of the earth's magnetic field.*

Declination

A plane passing through the geographical poles (that is, through the axis of rotation of the earth) and a given point P on the earth's surface is called the *geographical meridian* at the point P. Similarly, the plane passing through the geomagnetic poles (that is, through the dipole-axis of the earth) and the point P is called the *magnetic meridian* at the point P. In other words, the magnetic meridian is a vertical plane through the point P that contains the geomagnetic poles. The magnetic field due to the earth at P must be in this plane (magnetic meridian).

The angle made by the magnetic meridian at a point with the geographical meridian is called the *declination* at that point. The knowledge of declination fixes the vertical plane in which the earth's magnetic field lies.

Navigators often use a magnetic compass needle to locate direction. A compass needle is a short and light magnetic needle, free to rotate about a vertical axis. The needle is enclosed in a small case with a glass-top. The needle stays in equilibrium when it is in magnetic meridian. Hence the north direction shown by the needle makes an angle equal to the declination with the true north and navigators have to take care of it.

Inclination or dip

The angle made by the earth's magnetic field with the horizontal direction in the magnetic meridian, is called the *inclination* or *dip* at that point.

In the magnetic nothern hemisphere, the vertical component of the earth's magnetic field points downwards. The north pole of a freely suspended magnet, therefore, *dips* (goes down).

The knowledge of declination and inclination completely specifies the direction of the earth's magnetic field.

Horizontal component of the earth's magnetic field

As the name indicates, the *horizontal component* is component of the earth's magnetic field in the horizontal direction in the magnetic meridian. This direction is towards the magnetic north.

Figure (36.13) shows the three elements. Starting from the geographical meridian we draw the magnetic meridian at an angle θ (declination). In the magnetic meridian we draw the horizontal direction specifying magnetic north. The magnetic field is at an angle δ (dip) from this direction. The horizontal component B_H and the total field B are related as

$$B_H = B\cos\delta$$

or, $$B = B_H/\cos\delta.$$

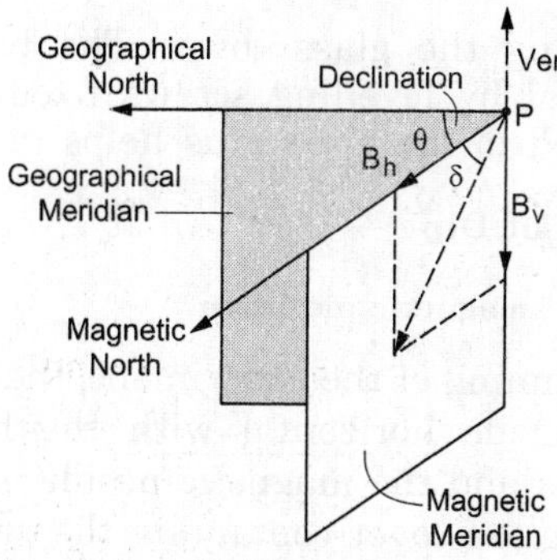

Figure 36.13

Thus, from the knowledge of the three elements, both the magnitude and direction of the earth's magnetic field can be obtained.

Example 36.5

The horizontal component of the earth's magnetic field is $3{\cdot}6 \times 10^{-5}$ T *where the dip is* 60°. *Find the magnitude of the earth's magnetic field.*

Solution : We have $B_H = B\cos\delta$

or, $$B = \frac{B_H}{\cos\delta} = \frac{3{\cdot}6\times10^{-5}\ \text{T}}{\cos 60°} = 7{\cdot}2\times10^{-5}\ \text{T}.$$

36.6 DETERMINATION OF DIP AT A PLACE

Dip Circle

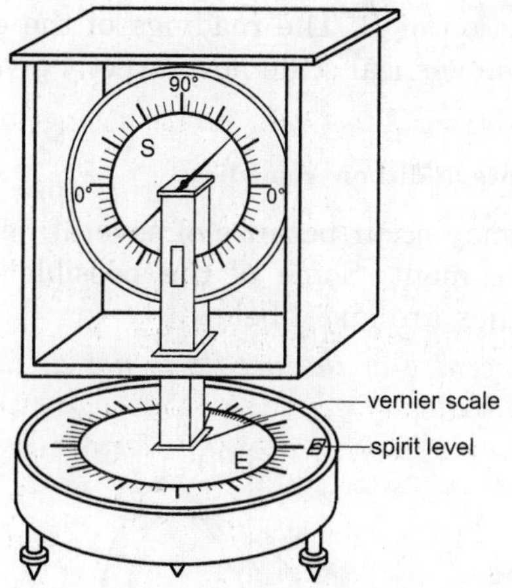

Figure 36.14

The dip at a place can be determined by an apparatus known as *dip circle*. It consists of a vertical circular scale S and a magnetic needle (a small pointed permanent magnet) pivoted at the centre of the scale. The needle can rotate freely in the vertical plane of the scale. The pointed ends move over the graduations on the scale which are marked 0°–0° in the horizontal and 90°–90° in the vertical direction. The scale S together with the needle is enclosed in a glass cover which can be rotated about a vertical axis. The angle rotated can be read from a horizontal angular scale E, fixed with the base, and a vernier scale fixed with the stand supporting the glass cover. The base can be made horizontal by levelling screws fixed with it. A spirit-level fixed to the apparatus helps in levelling.

Determination of Dip

Determination of magnetic meridian

At the beginning of the experiment, the base of the dip circle is made horizontal with the help of the levelling screws and the magnetic needle is pivoted in its place. The glass cover containing the vertical scale S and the needle is rotated about the vertical axis till the needle becomes vertical and reads 90°–90° on the vertical scale. In this condition, the plane of the circular scale S is perpendicular to the magnetic meridian. The horizontal component B_H is perpendicular to this plane and hence does not take part in rotating the needle. The needle is aligned with the vertical component B_V and hence reads 90°–90°. The reading of the vernier is noted and the glass cover is rotated exactly through 90° from this position. The plane of the circular scale S is now the same as the magnetic meridian.

Measurement of dip

When the plane of the vertical scale S is the same as the magnetic meridian, the earth's magnetic field $\vec{B}$ is in this same plane. In this case, the needle rests in the direction of $\vec{B}$. The readings of the ends of the needle on the vertical scale now directly give the value of the dip.

Possible errors and their remedies

Errors may occur because of several imperfections in the instrument. Some of the possible errors and their remedies are given below.

(a) *The centre of the needle is not at the centre of the vertical scale.*

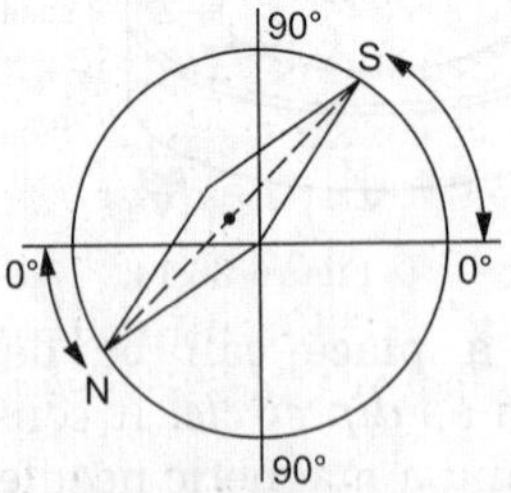

Figure 36.15

If the centre of the needle does not coincide with the centre of the scale, the readings do not represent the true dip. The reading of one end of the needle is less than the true value of the dip and the reading of the other end is greater by the same amount. Thus, both ends are read and the average is taken.

(b) 0°–0° *line is not horizontal.*

If the 0°–0° line on the scale is not horizontal, the value of dip will have some error. This error may be removed as described below.

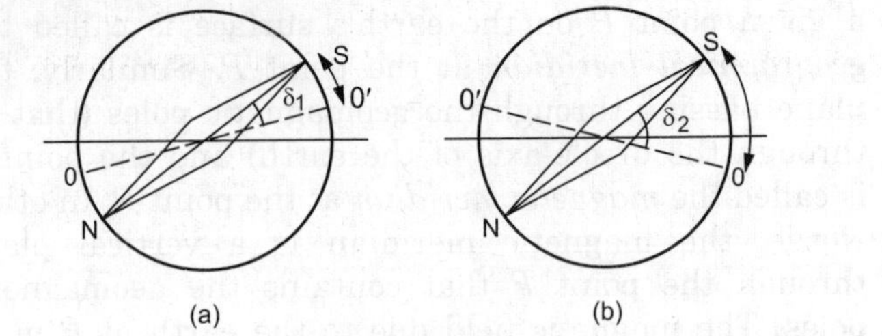

Figure 36.16

Bring the vertical scale in the magnetic meridian and note the readings of the ends of the needle (figure 36.16a). Now, rotate the circle through 180° about the vertical axis and again note the readings (figure 36.16b). The average of these readings will not have the error due to 0°–0° line.

(c) *The magnetic and the geometrical axes of the needle are different.*

In the experiment, we read the angles corresponding to the ends of the needle. If the magnetic axis is inclined at an angle with the line joining the ends, the dip obtained is in error. This error can be removed by inverting the needle on its bearing and repeating the previous readings. The average of these readings is free of this error.

(d) *Centre of mass of the needle does not coincide with the pivot.*

If the centre of mass of the needle is not at the pivot, its weight mg will have a torque and will affect the equilibrium position. To remove this error, one has to read the dip and then take out the needle. The needle should be demagnetized and then remagnetized in opposite direction. Thus, the position of the north and south poles are interchanged. The centre of mass now appears on the other side of the pivot and hence the effect of mg is also reversed. The dip is again determined with this needle and the average is taken.

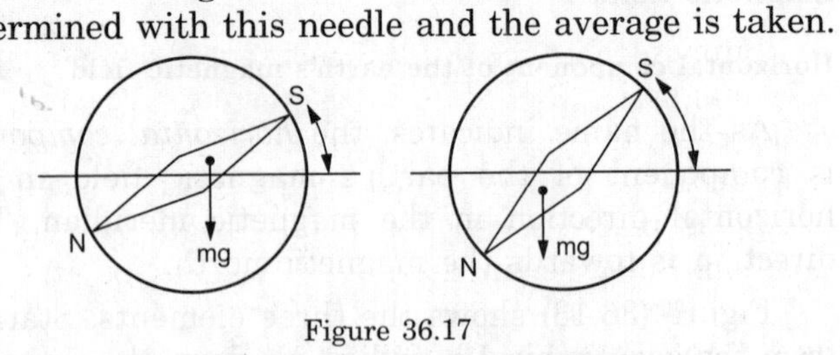

Figure 36.17

Thus, one should take 16 readings of dip and an average of all these gives the true dip.

Apparent Dip

If the dip circle is not kept in the magnetic meridian, the needle will not show the correct direction of earth's magnetic field. The angle made by the needle with the horizontal is called the *apparent dip* for this plane. If the dip circle is at an angle α to the meridian, the effective horizontal component in this plane is $B'_H = B_H \cos\alpha$. The vertical component is still B_v. If δ' is the apparent dip and δ is the true dip, we have

$$\tan\delta' = \frac{B_v}{B'_H}$$

or, $$\cot\delta' = \frac{B'_H}{B_v} = \frac{B_H \cos\alpha}{B_v}$$

or, $$\cot\delta' = \cot\delta \cos\alpha. \qquad \text{... (i)}$$

Now suppose, the dip circle is rotated through an angle of 90° from this position. It will now make an angle $(90° - \alpha)$ with the meridian. The effective horizontal component in this plane is $B''_H = B_H \sin\alpha$. If δ'' be the apparent dip, we shall have

$$\cot\delta'' = \cot\delta \sin\alpha. \qquad \text{... (ii)}$$

Squaring and adding (i) and (ii),

$$\cot^2\delta' + \cot^2\delta'' = \cot^2\delta. \qquad \text{... (36.16)}$$

Thus, one can get the true dip δ without locating the magnetic meridian.

Example 36.6

At 45° to the magnetic meridian, the apparent dip is 30°. Find the true dip.

Solution : At 45° to the magnetic meridian, the effective horizontal component of the earth's magnetic field is $B'_H = B_H \cos 45° = \frac{1}{\sqrt{2}} B_H$. The apparent dip δ' is given by

$$\tan\delta' = \frac{B_v}{B'_H} = \frac{\sqrt{2}\, B_v}{B_H} = \sqrt{2} \tan\delta$$

where δ is the true dip. Thus,

$$\tan 30° = \sqrt{2} \tan\delta$$

or, $$\delta = \tan^{-1} \sqrt{1/6}.$$

36.7 NEUTRAL POINT

Suppose at a point, the horizontal component of the magnetic field due to a magnet is equal and opposite to the earth's horizontal magnetic field. The net horizontal field is zero at such a point. If a compass needle is placed at such a point, it can stay in any position. Such a point is called a *neutral point*.

36.8 TANGENT GALVANOMETER

Tangent galvanometer is an instrument to measure an electric current. The essential parts are a vertical circular coil C of conducting wire and a small compass needle A pivoted at the centre of the coil (figure 36.18). The coil C together with its frame is fixed to a horizontal base B provided with levelling screws. Terminals T_1 and T_2 connected to the coil are

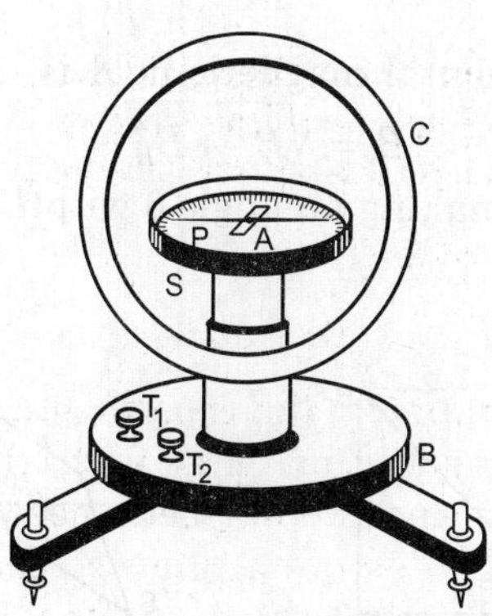

Figure 36.18

provided on this base for connecting the galvanometer to an external circuit. An aluminium pointer P is rigidly attached with the compass needle and perpendicular to it. The compass needle together with the pointer can rotate freely about the vertical axis. The ends of the pointer move over a graduated, horizontal circular scale. The graduations are marked from 0° to 90° in each quadrant. The scale, the pointer and the compass needle are enclosed in a closed cylindrical box which is placed with its centre coinciding with the centre of the coil. The box can also be rotated about the vertical axis. The upper surface of the box is made of glass so that the things inside it are visible. To avoid the errors due to parallax, a plane mirror is fixed at the lower surface of the box. While noting the reading of the pointer, the eye should be properly positioned so that the image of the pointer is just below the pointer.

When there is no current through the galvanometer, the compass needle is in magnetic north–south direction. To measure a current with the tangent galvanometer, the base is rotated in such a way that the plane of the coil is parallel to the compass needle. The plane then coincides with the magnetic meridian. The box containing the needle is rotated so that the aluminium pointer reads 0°–0° on the scale.

The current to be measured is passed through the coil. The current through the coil produces a magnetic field at the centre and the compass needle deflects under its action. The pointer deflects through the same angle and the deflection of both the ends are read from the horizontal scale. The average of these two is calculated.

Suppose the current through the coil is i. The radius of the coil is r and the number of turns in it is n. The magnetic field produced at the centre is

$$B = \frac{\mu_0\, in}{2r}. \qquad \text{... (i)}$$

This field is perpendicular to the plane of the coil. This direction is horizontal and perpendicular to the magnetic meridian and hence to the horizontal component B_H of the earth's magnetic field. The resultant horizontal magnetic field is

$$B_r = \sqrt{B^2 + B_H^2}$$

in a direction making an angle θ with B_H (figure 36.19) where

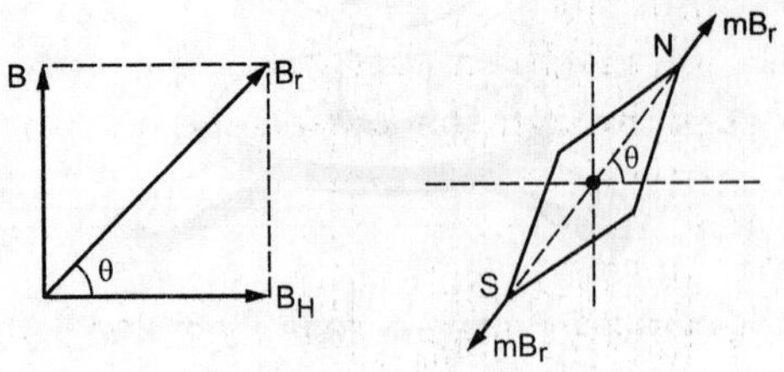

Figure 36.19

$$\tan\theta = B/B_H. \quad \text{... (ii)}$$

If m be the pole strength of the needle, the force on the north pole of the needle is mB_r along B_r and on the south pole is mB_r, opposite to B_r. The needle will stay in equilibrium when its length is parallel to B_r, because then no torque is produced by the two forces. Thus, the deflection of the needle from its original position is θ as given by (ii). Using (i) and (ii),

$$B_H \tan\theta = \frac{\mu_0 in}{2r}$$

or, $$i = \frac{2r\,B_H}{\mu_0 n}\tan\theta$$

or, $$i = K\tan\theta, \quad \text{... (36.17)}$$

where $K = \frac{2r\,B_H}{\mu_0 n}$ is a constant for the given galvanometer at a given place. This constant is called the *reduction factor* of the galvanometer. The reduction factor may be obtained by passing a known current i through the galvanometer, measuring θ and then using (36.17).

Equation (i) is strictly valid only at the centre of the coil. The poles of the needle are slightly away from the centre. Thus, the length of the needle should be small as compared to the radius of the coil.

Sensitivity

Good sensitivity means that the change in deflection is large for a given fractional change in current.

We have

$$i = K\tan\theta$$

or, $$di = K\sec^2\theta\, d\theta$$

or, $$\frac{di}{i} = \frac{K\sec^2\theta\, d\theta}{K\tan\theta} = \frac{2\,d\theta}{\sin 2\theta}$$

or, $$d\theta = \frac{1}{2}\sin 2\theta\left(\frac{di}{i}\right)$$

Thus, for good sensitivity, sin 2θ should be as large as possible. This is the case when θ = 45°. So, the tangent galvanometer is most sensitive when the deflection is around 45°.

Example 36.7

A tangent galvanometer has 66 *turns and the diameter of its coil is* 22 cm. *It gives a deflection of* 45° *for* 0·10 A *current. What is the value of the horizontal component of the earth's magnetic field ?*

Solution : For a tangent galvanometer

$$i = K\tan\theta$$

$$= \frac{2r\,B_H}{\mu_0 n}\tan\theta$$

or, $$B_H = \frac{\mu_0 ni}{2r\tan\theta}$$

$$= \frac{\left(4\pi\times 10^{-7}\,\frac{\text{T m}}{\text{A}}\right)\times 66\times(0{\cdot}1\text{ A})}{(22\times 10^{-2}\text{ m})(\tan 45°)}$$

$$= 3{\cdot}8\times 10^{-5}\text{ T}.$$

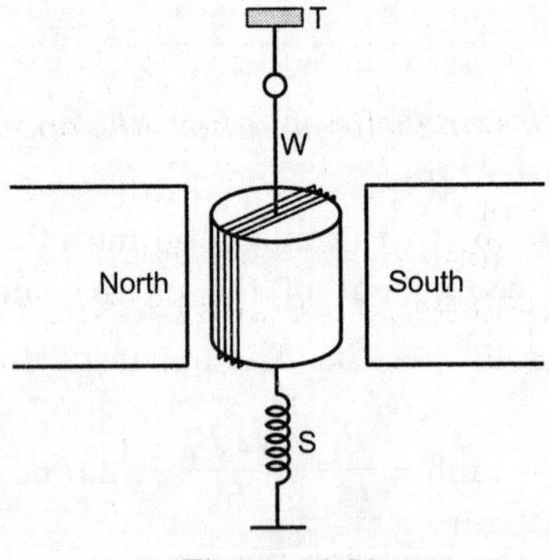

Figure 36.20

36.9 MOVING-COIL GALVANOMETER

The main parts of a moving-coil galvanometer are shown in figure (36.20). A rectangular coil of several turns is wound over a soft-iron core. The wire of the coil is coated with an insulating material so that each turn is insulated from the other and from the iron core. The coil is suspended between the two pole pieces of a strong permanent magnet. A fine strip W of phosphor bronze is used to suspend the coil. The upper end of this strip is attached to a torsion head T. The lower end of the coil is attached to a spring S also made of phosphor bronze. A small mirror is fixed on the suspension strip and is used to measure the deflection of the coil with the help of a lamp–scale arrangement. Terminals are connected to the suspension strip W and the spring S. These terminals are used to pass current through the galvanometer.

The current to be measured is passed through the galvanometer. As the coil is in the magnetic field $\vec{B}$ of the permanent magnet, a torque $\vec{\Gamma} = ni\vec{A}\times\vec{B}$ acts on the coil. Here n = number of turns, i = current in the coil, $\vec{A}$ = area-vector of the coil and $\vec{B}$ = magnetic field at the site of the coil. This torque deflects the coil from

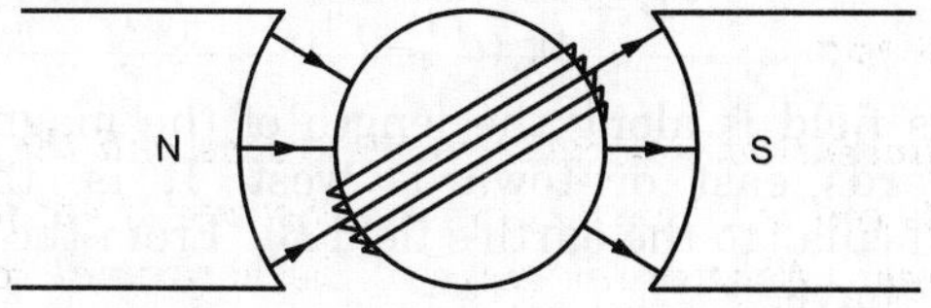

Figure 36.21

its equilibrium position.

The pole pieces are made cylindrical. As a result, the magnetic field at the arms of the coil remains parallel to the plane of the coil everywhere even as the coil rotates. The deflecting torque is then $\Gamma = niAB$. As the upper end of the suspension strip W is fixed, the strip gets twisted when the coil rotates. This produces a restoring torque acting on the coil. If the deflection of the coil is θ and the torsional constant of the suspension strip is k, the restoring torque is $k\theta$. The coil will stay at a deflection θ where

$$niAB = k\theta$$

or, $$i = \frac{k}{nAB}\theta. \quad \ldots (36.18)$$

Hence, the current is proportional to the deflection. The constant $\frac{k}{nAB}$ is called the *galvanometer constant* and may be found by passing a known current, measuring the deflection θ and putting these values in equation (36.18).

Sensitivity

The sensitivity of a moving-coil galvanometer is defined as θ/i. From equation (36.18), the sensitivity is $\frac{nAB}{k}\cdot$ For large sensitivity, the field B should be large. The presence of soft-iron core increases the magnetic field. We shall discuss in a later chapter how soft iron increases magnetic field.

36.10 SHUNT

A galvanometer is usually a delicate and sensitive instrument and only a small current is sufficient to deflect the coil to its maximum allowed value. If a current larger than this permissible value is passed through the galvanometer, it may get damaged. A small resistance R_s called *shunt*, is connected in parallel with the galvanometer to save it from such accidents. The main current i is divided in two parts,

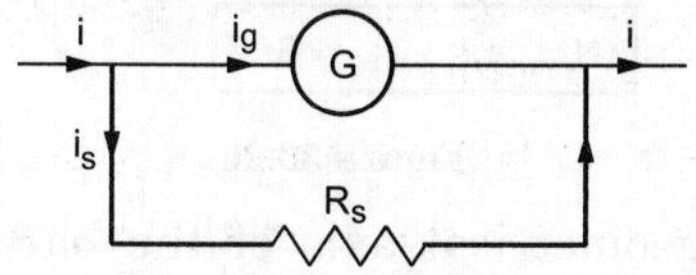

Figure 36.22

i_g through the galvanometer and remaining $i_s = i - i_g$ through the shunt. If the resistance of the galvanometer coil is R_g, we have

$$i_g = \frac{R_s}{R_s + R_g} i. \quad \ldots (36.19)$$

As R_s is much smaller than R_g, only a small fraction goes through the galvanometer.

Example 36.8

A galvanometer having a coil of resistance 20 Ω needs 20 mA *current for full-scale deflection. In order to pass a maximum current of* 2 A *through the galvanometer, what resistance should be added as a shunt?*

Solution : Out of the main current of 2 A, only 20 mA should go through the coil. The current through the coil is

$$i_g = \frac{R_s}{R_s + R_g} i$$

or, $$20\text{ mA} = \frac{R_s}{R_s + (20\ \Omega)} 2\text{ A}$$

or, $$\frac{20\text{ mA}}{2\text{ A}} = \frac{R_s}{R_s + (20\ \Omega)}$$

or, $$(10^{-2})(R_s + 20\ \Omega) = R_s$$

or, $$R_s = \frac{20}{99}\ \Omega \approx 0{\cdot}2\ \Omega.$$

36.11 TANGENT LAW OF PERPENDICULAR FIELDS

When a compass needle is placed in the earth's magnetic field, it stays along the horizontal component B_H of the field. The magnetic forces mB_H and $-mB_H$ on the poles do not produce any torque in this case. If an external horizontal magnetic field B is produced which is perpendicular to B_H, the needle deflects from its position. The situation is the same as that shown in figure (36.19). The resultant of B and B_H is

$$B_r = \sqrt{B^2 + B_H^2}$$

making an angle θ with B_H so that

$$\tan\theta = \frac{B}{B_H}\cdot \quad \ldots (i)$$

The forces on the poles are mB_r, $-mB_r$ which may produce a torque and deflect the needle. The needle can stay in a position parallel to the resultant horizontal field B_r. Thus, the deflection of the needle in equilibrium is θ. Using (i), the external magnetic field B may be written in terms of B_H and θ as

$$B = B_H \tan\theta. \quad \ldots (36.20)$$

This is known as the *tangent law of perpendicular fields*.

36.12 DEFLECTION MAGNETOMETER

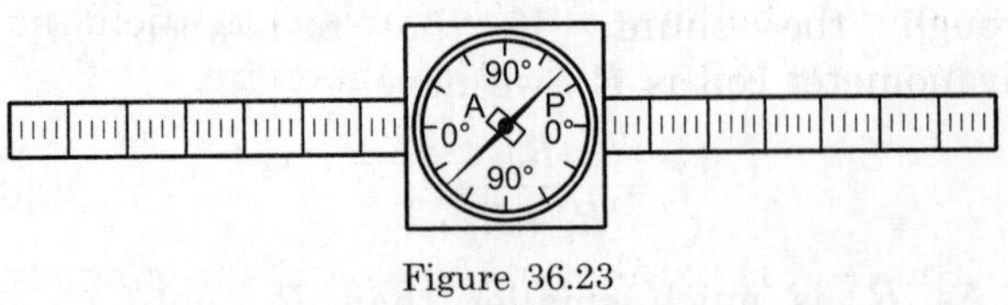

Figure 36.23

A deflection magnetometer (figure 36.23) consists of a small compass needle A pivoted at the centre of a graduated circular scale. The graduations are marked from 0° to 90° in each quadrant. An aluminium pointer P is rigidly fixed with the needle and perpendicular to it. The ends of the pointer move on the circular scale. These are enclosed in a cylindrical box known as the magnetometer box. The upper cover of the box is made of glass so that the things inside are visible. A plane mirror is fixed on the lower surface so that the pointer may be read without parallax. This arrangement is the same as that used in a tangent galvanometer.

The magnetometer box is kept in a wooden frame having two long arms. Metre scales are fitted on the two arms. The reading of a scale at any point directly gives the distance of that point from the centre of the compass needle.

The basic use of a deflection magnetometer is to determine M/B_H for a permanent bar magnet. Here M is the magnetic moment of the magnet and B_H is the horizontal component of the earth's magnetic field. This quantity M/B_H can be measured in two standard positions of the magnetometer. One is called Tan-A position of Gauss and the other is called Tan-B position of Gauss.

Tan-*A* Position

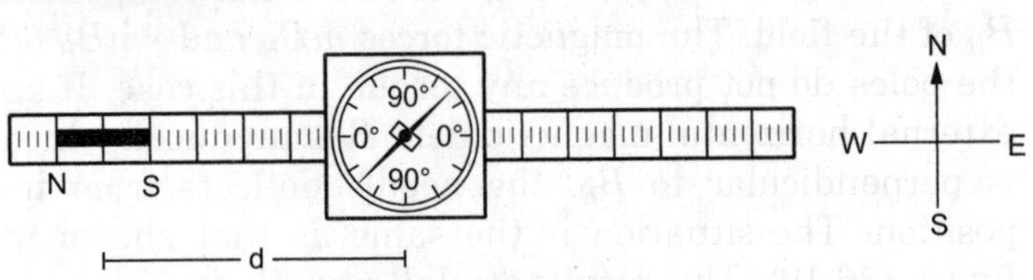

Figure 36.24

In this, the arms of the magnetometer are kept along the magnetic east–west direction. The aluminium pointer shows this direction when no extra magnets or magnetic materials are present nearby. The magnetometer box is rotated in its plane till the pointer reads 0°–0°. The magnet is now kept on one of the arms, parallel to its length (figure 36.24). The needle deflects and the deflection θ in its equilibrium position is read from the circular scale. The distance of the centre of the magnet from the centre of the compass is calculated from the linear scale on the arm.

Let d be this distance and $2l$ be the magnetic length of the magnet. In Tan-A position of the magnetometer, the compass needle is in end-on position of the bar magnet. The magnetic field due to the bar magnet at the site of the needle is, therefore,

$$B = \frac{\mu_0}{4\pi} \frac{2Md}{(d^2 - l^2)^2}.$$

This field is along the length of the magnet, that is, towards east or towards west. It is, therefore, perpendicular to the earth's field B_H. From the tangent law, we have,

$$B = B_H \tan\theta$$

or,
$$\frac{\mu_0}{4\pi} \frac{2Md}{(d^2 - l^2)^2} = B_H \tan\theta$$

or,
$$\frac{M}{B_H} = \frac{4\pi}{\mu_0} \frac{(d^2 - l^2)^2}{2d} \tan\theta. \qquad \dots (36.21)$$

Knowing all the quantities on the right-hand side, one gets M/B_H.

Possible errors and their remedies

Errors may occur due to various reasons.

(a) The pivot of the needle may not be at the centre of the circular scale (figure 36.25). To remove this error both ends of the pointer are read and the mean is taken.

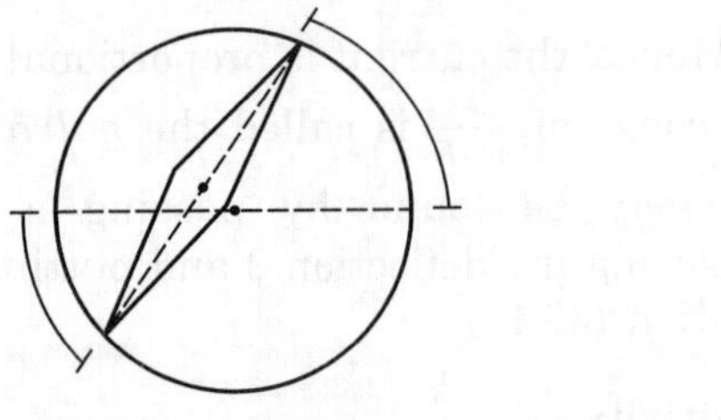

Figure 36.25

(b) The magnetic centre of the bar magnet may not coincide with its geometrical centre (figure 36.26). The measured distance d is more or less than the actual distance d_1 of the centre of the needle from the magnetic centre of the magnet. To remove the error due to this, the magnet is rotated through 180° about the vertical so that the positions of the north pole and the south pole are interchanged. The deflections are again noted with both ends of the pointer. These readings correspond to the distance d_2. The average of the sets of deflections corresponding to the distances d_1 and d_2 give the correct value approximately.

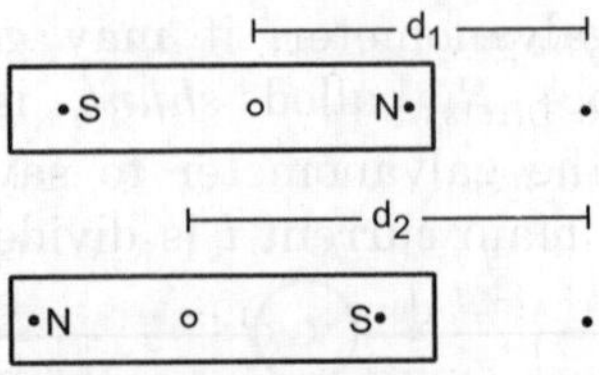

Figure 36.26

(c) The geometrical axis of the bar magnet may not coincide with the magnetic axis (figure 36.27). To

Figure 36.27

avoid error due to this, the magnet is put upside down at the same position and the readings are taken.

(d) The zero of the linear scale may not coincide with the centre of the circular scale. To remove the error due to this, the magnet is kept on the other arm of the magnetometer at the same distance from the needle and all the readings are repeated.

Thus, one gets sixteen values of θ for the same distance *d*. The mean of these sixteen values gives the correct value of θ.

Tan-*B* Position

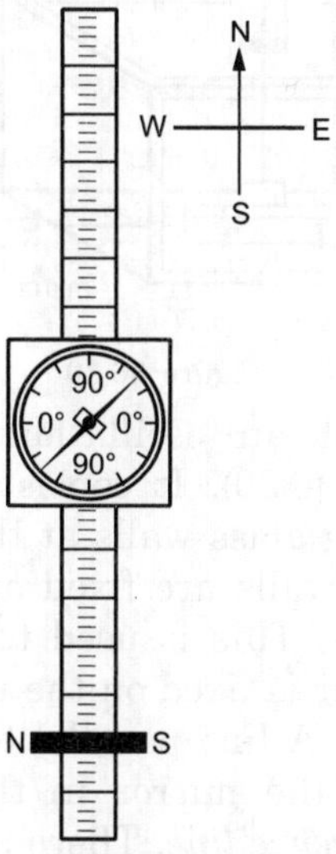

Figure 36.28

In this position, the arms of the magnetometer are kept in the magnetic north to south direction. The box is rotated so that the pointer reads 0°–0°. The bar magnet is placed on one of the arms symmetrically and at right angles to it (figure 36.28). The distance *d* of the centre of the magnet from the centre of the compass needle is calculated from the linear scale. The deflection θ of the needle is noted from the circular scale. To remove the errors due to the reasons described above, the deflections are read in various situations mentioned below. Both ends of the pointer are read. The magnet is put upside down and readings are taken. The bar magnet is rotated through 180° to interchange the positions of north and south poles and again both ends of the pointer are read. The magnet is again put upside down and readings are taken for both ends of the pointer. The magnet is kept on the other arm at the same distance and the corresponding readings are taken. The mean of these sixteen values gives correct θ for this *d*.

In tan-*B* position, the compass is in broadside-on position of the magnet. The magnetic field at the compass due to the magnet is, therefore,

$$B = \frac{\mu_0}{4\pi} \frac{M}{(d^2 + l^2)^{3/2}} .$$

The field is parallel to the axis of the magnet and hence it is towards east or towards west. The earth's magnetic field is from south to north. Using tangent law,

$$B = B_H \tan\theta$$

$$\text{or,} \quad \frac{\mu_0}{4\pi} \frac{M}{(d^2 + l^2)^{3/2}} = B_H \tan\theta$$

$$\text{or,} \quad \frac{M}{B_H} = \frac{4\pi}{\mu_0} (d^2 + l^2)^{3/2} \tan\theta. \qquad \ldots (36.22)$$

Applications of a Deflection Magnetometer

A variety of quantities may be obtained from the basic measurement of M/B_H using a deflection magnetometer. Here are some of the examples.

(a) Comparison of the magnetic moments M_1 and M_2 of two magnets

One can find M_1/B_H and M_2/B_H separately for the two magnets and then get the ratio M_1/M_2. There is another simple method known as *null method* to get M_1/M_2. The experiment can be done either in Tan-*A* position or in Tan-*B* position. The two magnets are placed on the two arms of the magnetometer. The distances of the magnets from the centre of the magnetometer are so adjusted that the deflection of the needle is zero. In this case, the magnetic field at the needle due to the first magnet is equal in magnitude to the field due to the other magnet. If the magnetometer is used in Tan-*A* position,

$$\frac{\mu_0}{4\pi} \frac{2 M_1 d_1}{(d_1^2 - l_1^2)^2} = \frac{\mu_0}{4\pi} \frac{2 M_2 d_2}{(d_2^2 - l_2^2)^2}$$

$$\text{or,} \quad \frac{M_1}{M_2} = \frac{d_2(d_1^2 - l_1^2)^2}{d_1(d_2^2 - l_2^2)^2} .$$

If the magnetometer is used in Tan-*B* position,

$$\frac{\mu_0}{4\pi} \frac{M_1}{(d_1^2 + l_1^2)^{3/2}} = \frac{\mu_0}{4\pi} \frac{M_2}{(d_2^2 + l_2^2)^{3/2}}$$

$$\text{or,} \quad \frac{M_1}{M_2} = \frac{(d_1^2 + l_1^2)^{3/2}}{(d_2^2 + l_2^2)^{3/2}} .$$

Null method is easier and better than finding M_1/B_H and M_2/B_H separately and then calculating M_1/M_2. This is because, here the deflection remains zero and the possible errors in the measurement of θ do not occur. Also, it is more sensitive, because even a small deflection from 0°–0° gives the indication that the adjustment is not perfect.

(b) Verification of inverse square law for magnetic field due to a magnetic pole

Equations (36.21) and (36.22) for M/B_H are deduced from the basic equation (36.2) giving the magnetic field due to a magnetic pole. Equation (36.2) shows that the magnetic field due to a magnetic pole is inversely proportional to the square of the distance. Thus, if we verify equation (36.21) or (36.22), inverse square law is verified.

For Tan-*A* position, from equation (36.21),

$$\cot\theta = \frac{4\pi}{\mu_0}\frac{B_H}{M}\frac{(d^2 - l^2)^2}{2d}. \qquad \text{... (i)}$$

A magnet is placed at a distance *d* in Tan-*A* position of the magnetometer and the corresponding value of deflection θ is noted. The experiment is repeated for different values of *d* and a graph between $\cot\theta$ and $\frac{(d^2 - l^2)^2}{2d}$ is plotted. The graph turns out to be a straight line passing through the origin (figure 36.29a). This is consistent with equation (i) above and hence the inverse square law is verified.

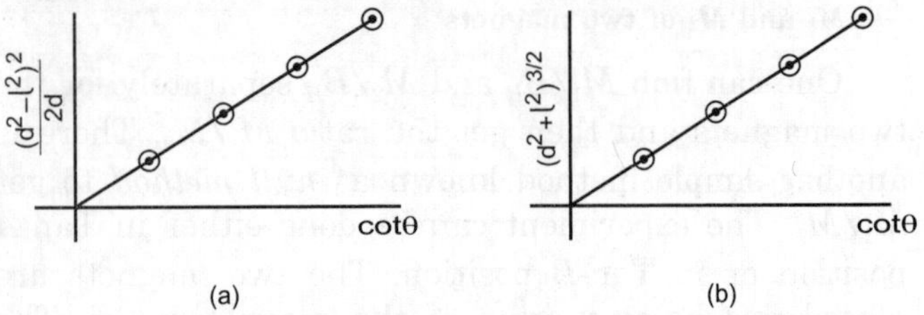

Figure 36.29

One can also do the experiment in Tan-*B* position. The deflection θ and the distance *d* are related through equation (36.22). We have,

$$\cot\theta = \frac{4\pi}{\mu_0}\frac{B_H}{M}(d^2 + l^2)^{3/2}. \qquad \text{... (ii)}$$

The values of deflection θ are noted for different values of the distance *d*. A graph is drawn between $\cot\theta$ and $(d^2 + l^2)^{3/2}$. The graph turns out to be a straight line passing through the origin (figure 36.29b). This verifies the inverse square law.

(c) Comparison of the horizontal components of the earth's magnetic field at two places

Suppose the horizontal component of the earth's magnetic field is B_{H1} at the first place and B_{H2} at the second. A deflection magnetometer is taken and a bar magnet is kept at a distance *d* in Tan-*A* position. The deflection θ_1 of the needle is noted. The magnetometer is now taken to the second place and the same magnet is kept at the same distance *d* in Tan-*A* position. The deflection θ_2 is noted. We have from equation (36.21),

$$\frac{M}{B_{H1}} = \frac{4\pi}{\mu_0}\frac{(d^2 - l^2)^2}{2d}\tan\theta_1$$

and
$$\frac{M}{B_{H2}} = \frac{4\pi}{\mu_0}\frac{(d^2 - l^2)^2}{2d}\tan\theta_2.$$

Thus,
$$\frac{B_{H1}}{B_{H2}} = \frac{\tan\theta_2}{\tan\theta_1}.$$

The experiment can also be done in Tan-*B* position. Using equation (36.22), we again get the same relation for $\frac{B_{H1}}{B_{H2}}$.

36.13 OSCILLATION MAGNETOMETER

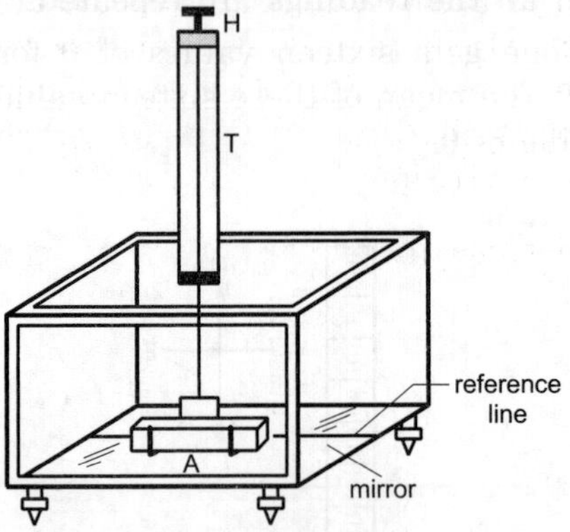

Figure 36.30

The design of an oscillation magnetometer is shown in figure (36.30). It consists of a rectangular wooden box having glass walls at the sides and at the top. Three of the walls are fixed and the fourth may be slid in and out. This is used to close or open the box. A plane mirror is fixed on the inner surface of the bottom of the box. A line parallel to the length of the box is drawn on the mirror in the middle. This is known as the *reference line*. There are levelling screws at the bottom on which the box rests. A vertical cylindrical glass tube *T*, having a torsion head *H* at its top, is fitted to the top plate of the box. A hanger *A* is suspended in the box through an unspun silk thread. The upper end of the thread is attached to the torsion head.

Measuring MB_H for a Bar Magnet

The basic use of an oscillation magnetometer is to measure MB_H for a bar magnet. To start with, the instrument is made horizontal with the help of a spirit level and the levelling screws. A compass needle is placed on the reference line and the box is rotated to make the reference line parallel to the needle. The reference line is now in the magnetic meridian. The needle is removed. A nonmagnetic heavy piece (generally made of brass) is put on the hanger. Due to the twist in the thread, the bar rotates and finally stays in equilibrium when the twist is removed. With the help of the torsion head, the bar is made parallel to the reference line in equilibrium.

The magnet is now gently placed in the hanger after removing the heavy piece. The north pole should be towards the north. The magnet is set into angular oscillation about the thread by giving it a slight angular deflection. This may be done by bringing another magnet close to the box and then removing it. The time period of oscillation is obtained by measuring the time required for, say 20 oscillations. To measure the time period accurately, one should look at the magnet through the top glass cover of the box. The eye should be positioned in such a way that the image of the magnet in the bottom mirror should be just below the magnet. Oscillations are counted as the magnet crosses the reference line. The box is kept closed at the time of oscillations, so that air currents do not disturb the oscillations.

Expression for time period

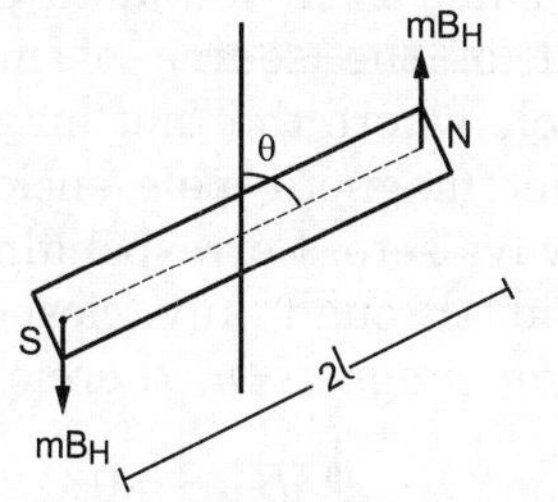

Figure 36.31

Figure (36.31) shows the position of the magnet when it is deflected through an angle θ from the mean position during its oscillation. The magnetic field in the horizontal direction is B_H from south to north. If m be the pole strength, the force on the north pole is mB_H towards north and on the south pole it is mB_H towards south. The length of the magnet is $2l$.

The torque of each of the two forces about the vertical axis is $mB_H l \sin\theta$ and it tries to bring the magnet towards the equilibrium position. The net torque about the vertical axis is

$$\Gamma = -2\, mB_H\, l \sin\theta$$

$$= -MB_H \sin\theta. \qquad \text{... (i)}$$

We neglect the torque due to the small twist produced in the thread as the magnet rotates. If the angular amplitude of oscillations is small, $\sin\theta \approx \theta$ and equation (i) becomes

$$\Gamma = -MB_H\theta.$$

Also, $\Gamma = I\alpha$

where I is the moment of inertia of the magnet about the vertical axis and α is the angular acceleration. Thus,

$$\alpha = \frac{\Gamma}{I} = -\frac{MB_H}{I}\theta$$

or, $\alpha = -\omega^2\theta$

where $\omega = \sqrt{\frac{MB_H}{I}}$. This is an equation of angular simple harmonic motion. The time period is

$$T = \frac{2\pi}{\omega} = 2\pi\sqrt{\frac{I}{MB_H}}\cdot \qquad \text{... (36.23)}$$

Calculation of MB_H

From equation (36.23), $MB_H = \frac{4\pi^2 I}{T^2}\cdot$ ... (36.24)

For a magnet of rectangular cross section, the moment of inertia about the axis of rotation is

$$I = \frac{W(a^2 + b^2)}{12}$$

where a is the geometrical length, b is the breadth and W is the mass of the magnet. Measuring these quantities and the time period, MB_H can be obtained from equation (36.24).

Example 36.9

A compass needle oscillates 20 *times per minute at a place where the dip is* 45° *and* 30 *times per minute where the dip is* 30°. *Compare the total magnetic field due to the earth at the two places.*

Solution : The time period of oscillation is given by

$$T = 2\pi\sqrt{\frac{I}{MB_H}}\cdot$$

The time period at the first place is T_1 = 1/20 minute = 3·0 s and at the second place it is T_2 = 1/30 minute = 2·0 s.

If the total magnetic field at the first place is B_1, the horizontal component of the field is

$$B_{H1} = B_1 \cos 45° = B_1/\sqrt{2}.$$

Similarly, if the total magnetic field at the second place is B_2, the horizontal component is

$$B_{H2} = B_2 \cos 30° = B_2\sqrt{3}/2.$$

We have,

$$T_1 = 2\pi\sqrt{\frac{I}{MB_{H1}}} \quad\text{and}\quad T_2 = 2\pi\sqrt{\frac{I}{MB_{H2}}}\cdot$$

Thus,

$$\frac{T_1}{T_2} = \sqrt{\frac{B_{H2}}{B_{H1}}} \quad\text{or,}\quad \frac{B_{H2}}{B_{H1}} = \frac{T_1^2}{T_2^2}$$

or,

$$\frac{B_2\sqrt{3}/2}{B_1/\sqrt{2}} = \frac{T_1^2}{T_2^2}$$

or,

$$\frac{B_2}{B_1} = \sqrt{\frac{2}{3}}\frac{T_1^2}{T_2^2} = \sqrt{\frac{2}{3}} \times \frac{9}{4} = 1\cdot 83.$$

Once we know how to measure MB_H, we can easily compare magnetic moments M_1 and M_2 by measuring

M_1B_H and M_2B_H. Similarly, we can compare the horizontal components of the earth's magnetic field at two places.

36.14 DETERMINATION OF M AND B_H

The magnetic moment of a bar magnet can be obtained by measuring M/B_H using a deflection magnetometer and MB_H using an oscillation magnetometer. If

$$M/B_H = X \text{ and } MB_H = Y,$$

we have

$$M = \sqrt{\left(\frac{M}{B_H}\right)(MB_H)} = \sqrt{XY}.$$

One can also determine the horizontal component B_H of earth's magnetic field at any place. Using any magnet one can find M/B_H and MB_H as above.

We have,

$$B_H = \sqrt{\frac{MB_H}{M/B_H}} = \sqrt{\frac{Y}{X}}.$$

If M/B_H is measured in Tan-A position,

$$X = \frac{M}{B_H} = \frac{4\pi}{\mu_0}\frac{(d^2 - l^2)^2}{2d}\tan\theta$$

and $$Y = MB_H = \frac{4\pi^2 I}{T^2}.$$

Then $$M = \sqrt{XY} = \frac{2\pi(d^2 - l^2)}{T}\sqrt{\frac{4\pi}{\mu_0}\frac{I\tan\theta}{2d}}$$

and $$B_H = \sqrt{\frac{Y}{X}} = \frac{2\pi}{T(d^2 - l^2)}\sqrt{\frac{\mu_0}{4\pi}\frac{2Id}{\tan\theta}}.$$

We can also measure M/B_H and MB_H in Tan-B position and get M and B_H as above.

36.15 GAUSS'S LAW FOR MAGNETISM

From Coulomb's law

$$E = \frac{q}{4\pi\varepsilon_0 r^2},$$

we can derive the Gauss's law for electric field, i.e.,

$$\oint \vec{E}\cdot d\vec{S} = \frac{q_{inside}}{\varepsilon_0}$$

where $\oint \vec{E}\cdot d\vec{S}$ is the electric flux and q_{inside} is the "net charge" enclosed by the closed surface.

Similarly, from the equation

$$B = \frac{\mu_0}{4\pi}\frac{m}{r^2}$$

we can derive Gauss's law for magnetism as

$$\oint \vec{B}\cdot d\vec{S} = \mu_0 m_{inside},$$

where $\oint \vec{B}\cdot d\vec{S}$ is the magnetic flux and m_{inside} is the "net pole strength" inside the closed surface. However, there is an additional feature for the magnetic case. We do not have an isolated magnetic pole in nature. At least none has been found to exist till date. The smallest unit of the source of magnetic field is a magnetic dipole where the "net magnetic pole" is zero. Hence, the net magnetic pole enclosed by any closed surface is always zero. Correspondingly, the flux of the magnetic field through any closed surface is zero. *Gauss's law for magnetism,* therefore, states that

$$\oint \vec{B}\cdot d\vec{S} = 0. \qquad \text{... (36.25)}$$

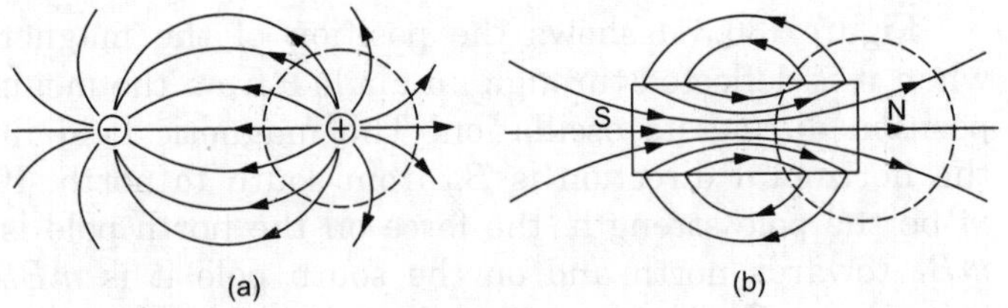

Figure 36.32

Figure (36.32a) shows the electric field lines through a closed surface which encloses one charge of an electric dipole. Figure (36.32b) shows the magnetic field lines through a closed surface which encloses one end of a bar magnet. One can see that the electric field lines only go out of the surface, giving a nonzero flux. On the other hand, the number of magnetic field lines going out of the surface is equal to the number going into it. The magnetic flux is positive at some places on the surface and is negative at others giving the total flux equal to zero.

Worked Out Examples

1. *A bar magnet has a pole strength of* 3·6 A m *and magnetic length* 8 cm. *Find the magnetic field at (a) a point on the axis at a distance of* 6 cm *from the centre towards the north pole and (b) a point on the perpendicular bisector at the same distance.*

Solution :

(a) The point in question is in end-on position, so the magnetic field is,

$$B = \frac{\mu_0}{4\pi}\frac{2Md}{(d^2 - l^2)^2}$$

$$= 10^{-7}\frac{\text{T m}}{\text{A}} \times \frac{2 \times 3{\cdot}6\text{ A m} \times 0{\cdot}08\text{ m} \times 0{\cdot}06\text{ m}}{[(0{\cdot}06\text{ m})^2 - (0{\cdot}04\text{ m})^2]^2}$$

$$= 8{\cdot}6 \times 10^{-4}\text{ T}.$$

The field will be away from the magnet.

(b) In this case the point is in broadside-on position so that the field is

$$B = \frac{\mu_0}{4\pi}\frac{M}{(d^2 + l^2)^{3/2}}$$

$$= 10^{-7}\frac{\text{T m}}{\text{A}} \times \frac{3{\cdot}6\text{ A m} \times 0{\cdot}08\text{ m}}{[(0{\cdot}06\text{ m})^2 + (0{\cdot}04\text{ m})^2]^{3/2}}$$

$$= 7{\cdot}7 \times 10^{-5}\text{ T}.$$

The field will be parallel to the magnet.

2. *A magnet is suspended by a vertical string attached to its middle point. Find the position in which the magnet can stay in equilibrium. The horizontal component of the earth's magnetic field = 25 μT and its vertical component = 40 μT. Assume that the string makes contact with the magnet only at a single point.*

Solution : The magnetic field of earth is in the north–south plane (magnetic meridian) making an angle θ with the horizontal such that

$$\tan\theta = \frac{B_V}{B_H} = \frac{40}{25}$$

or, $\theta = 58°$.

As the tension and the force of gravity act through the centre, their torque about the centre is zero. To make the net torque acting on the magnet zero, it must stay in the direction of the resultant magnetic field. Hence, it stays in the magnetic meridian making an angle of 58° with the horizontal.

3. *A magnetic needle having magnetic moment* 10 A m^2 *and length* 2·0 cm *is clamped at its centre in such a way that it can rotate in the vertical east–west plane. A horizontal force towards east is applied at the north pole to keep the needle fixed at an angle of* 30° *with the vertical. Find the magnitude of the applied force. The vertical component of the earth's magnetic field is* 40 μT.

Solution :

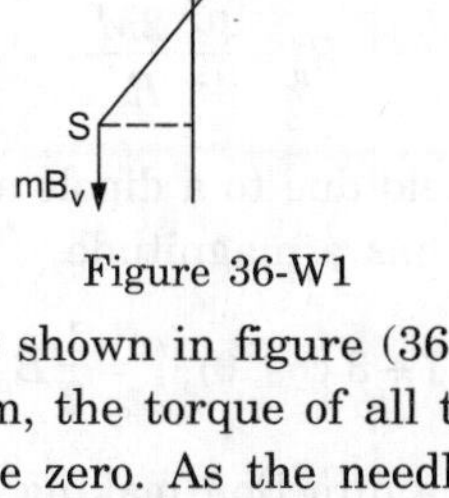

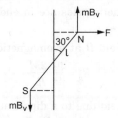

Figure 36-W1

The situation is shown in figure (36-W1). As the needle is in equilibrium, the torque of all the forces about the centre should be zero. As the needle can rotate in the vertical east–west plane, the horizontal component of earth's magnetic field is ineffective. This gives,

$$mB_V\, l \sin 30° + mB_V\, l \sin 30° = Fl\cos 30°$$

or, $$F = 2\, mB_V \tan 30°$$

$$= 2\frac{M}{2l} B_V \tan 30°$$

$$= \frac{(10\text{ A–m}^2)(40 \times 10^{-6}\text{ T})}{(1{\cdot}0 \times 10^{-2}\text{ m})\sqrt{3}}$$

$$= 2{\cdot}3 \times 10^{-2}\text{ N}.$$

4. *The magnetic scalar potential due to a magnetic dipole at a point on its axis situated at a distance of* 20 cm *from its centre is found to be* $1{\cdot}2 \times 10^{-5}$ T m. *Find the magnetic moment of the dipole.*

Solution : The magnetic potential due to a dipole is

$$V = \frac{\mu_0}{4\pi}\frac{M\cos\theta}{r^2}$$

or, $$1{\cdot}2 \times 10^{-5}\text{ T m} = \left(10^{-7}\frac{\text{T m}}{\text{A}}\right)\frac{M}{(0{\cdot}2\text{ m})^2}$$

or, $$M = 4{\cdot}8\text{ A m}^2.$$

5. *A bar magnet of magnetic moment* 2·0 A m^2 *is free to rotate about a vertical axis through its centre. The magnet is released from rest from the east–west position. Find the kinetic energy of the magnet as it takes the north–south position. The horizontal component of the earth's magnetic field is* B = 25 μT.

Solution : The magnetic potential energy of the dipole in a uniform magnetic field is given by $U = -MB\cos\theta$. As the earth's magnetic field is from south to north, the initial value of θ is π/2 and final value of θ is 0. Thus, the decrease in magnetic potential energy during the rotation is

$$U_i - U_f = -MB\cos(\pi/2) + MB\cos 0$$

$$= 2{\cdot}0\text{ A m}^2 \times 25\ \mu\text{T} = 50\ \mu\text{J}.$$

Thus, the kinetic energy in the north–south position is 50 μJ.

6. *Figure (36-W2a) shows two identical magnetic dipoles a and b of magnetic moments M each, placed at a separation d, with their axes perpendicular to each other. Find the magnetic field at the point P midway between the dipoles.*

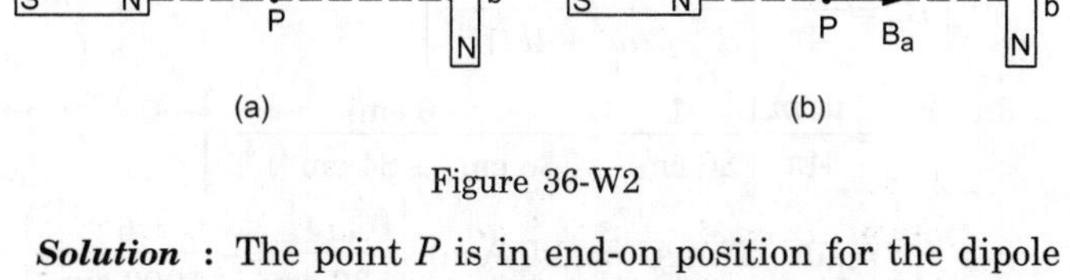

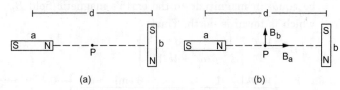

Figure 36-W2

Solution : The point P is in end-on position for the dipole a and in broadside-on position for the dipole b. The magnetic field at P due to a is $B_a = \frac{\mu_0}{4\pi}\frac{2M}{(d/2)^3}$ along the axis of a, and that due to b is $B_b = \frac{\mu_0}{4\pi} \frac{M}{(d/2)^3}$ parallel to the axis of b as shown in figure (36-W2b). The resultant field at P is, therefore,

$$B = \sqrt{B_a^2 + B_b^2}$$

$$= \frac{\mu_0 M}{4\pi (d/2)^3} \sqrt{1^2 + 2^2}$$

$$= \frac{2\sqrt{5}\, \mu_0 M}{\pi d^3}.$$

The direction of this field makes an angle α with B_a such that $\tan\alpha = B_b / B_a = 1/2$.

7. *A bar magnet of length 8 cm and having a pole strength of 1·0 A m is placed vertically on a horizontal table with its south pole on the table. A neutral point is found on the table at a distance of 6·0 cm north of the magnet. Calculate the earth's horizontal magnetic field.*

Solution :

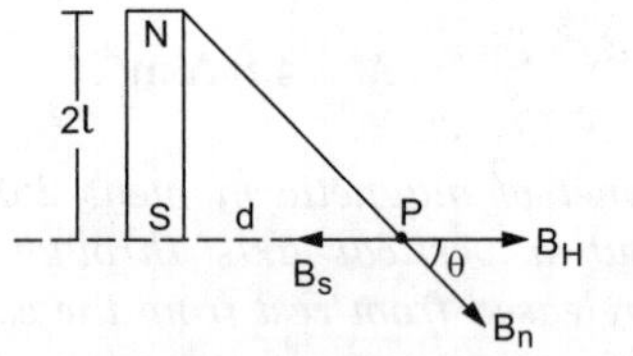

Figure 36-W3

The situation is shown in figure (36-W3). The magnetic field at P due to the south pole is

$$B_s = \frac{\mu_0}{4\pi} \frac{m}{d^2}$$

towards south and that due to the north pole is

$$B_n = \frac{\mu_0}{4\pi} \frac{m}{(d^2 + 4l^2)}$$

along NP. The horizontal component of this field will be towards north and will have the magnitude

$$= \frac{\mu_0}{4\pi} \frac{m}{(d^2 + 4l^2)} \cdot \frac{d}{(d^2 + 4l^2)^{1/2}}.$$

The resultant horizontal field due to the magnet is, therefore,

$$\frac{\mu_0}{4\pi} \frac{m}{d^2} - \frac{\mu_0}{4\pi} \frac{md}{(d^2 + 4l^2)^{3/2}}$$

towards south. As P is a neutral point, this field should be equal in magnitude to the earth's magnetic field B_H which is towards north. Thus,

$$B_H = \frac{\mu_0 m}{4\pi} \left[\frac{1}{d^2} - \frac{d}{(d^2 + 4l^2)^{3/2}} \right]$$

$$= \frac{\mu_0 m}{4\pi} \left[\frac{1}{36 \text{ cm}^2} - \frac{6 \text{ cm}}{(36 \text{ cm}^2 + 64 \text{ cm}^2)^{3/2}} \right]$$

$$= 10^{-7} \text{ T m A}^{-1} \times (1{\cdot}0 \text{ A m}) \times \left[\frac{1}{36 \text{ cm}^2} - \frac{6}{1000 \text{ cm}^2} \right]$$

$$= (10^{-7} \text{ T m}^2)\, [0{\cdot}028 - 0{\cdot}006] \times 10^4 \text{ m}^{-2}$$

$$= 22 \times 10^{-6} \text{ T} = 22\ \mu\text{T}.$$

8. *The magnetic field at a point on the magnetic equator is found to be $3{\cdot}1 \times 10^{-5}$ T. Taking the earth's radius to be 6400 km, calculate the magnetic moment of the assumed dipole at the earth's centre.*

Solution :

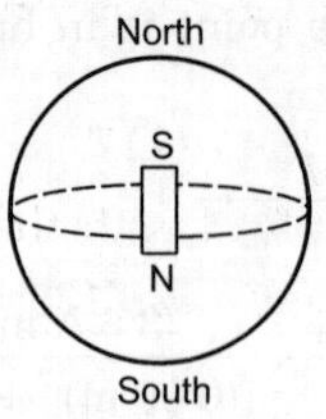

Figure 36-W4

A point on the magnetic equator is in broadside-on position of the earth's assumed dipole (figure 36-W4). The field is, therefore,

$$B = \frac{\mu_0}{4\pi} \frac{M}{R^3}$$

$$\text{or,} \quad M = \frac{4\pi}{\mu_0} BR^3$$

$$= 10^7 \text{ A m T}^{-1} \times 3{\cdot}1 \times 10^{-5} \text{ T} \times (6400 \times 10^3)^3 \text{ m}^3$$

$$= 8{\cdot}1 \times 10^{22} \text{ A m}^2.$$

9. *The earth's magnetic field at geomagnetic poles has a magnitude $6{\cdot}2 \times 10^{-5}$ T. Find the magnitude and the direction of the field at a point on the earth's surface where the radius makes an angle of 135° with the axis of the earth's assumed magnetic dipole. What is the inclination (dip) at this point?*

Solution :

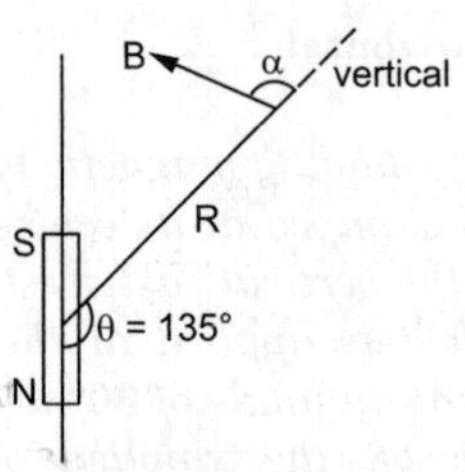

Figure 36-W5

Assuming the earth's field to be due to a dipole at the centre, geomagnetic poles are in end-on position (figure 36-W5).

The magnetic field B at geomagnetic poles is

$$B_p = \frac{\mu_0}{4\pi} \frac{2M}{R^3}.$$

The magnetic field due to a dipole at a distance R away from its centre has a magnitude

$$B = \frac{\mu_0}{4\pi} \frac{M}{R^3} (1 + 3\cos^2\theta)^{1/2} = \frac{1}{2} B_p (1 + 3\cos^2\theta)^{1/2}.$$

This field is in a direction making an angle α with the radial direction such that $\tan\alpha = (\tan\theta)/2$, as shown in the figure. At the point given, θ = 135° and thus the field B is

$$B = \frac{B_p}{2}(1 + 3\cos^2 135°)^{1/2}$$
$$= \frac{1}{2} \times 6{\cdot}2 \times 10^{-5}\ \text{T} \times 1{\cdot}58$$
$$= 4{\cdot}9 \times 10^{-5}\ \text{T}.$$

The angle α of this field with the vertical is given by

$$\tan\alpha = \frac{\tan\theta}{2} = \frac{\tan 135°}{2} = -0{\cdot}5$$

giving $\alpha = 153°$.

The inclination (dip) is the angle made by the earth's magnetic field with the horizontal plane. Here it is 153° – 90° = 63° below the horizontal.

10. *A magnetic needle free to rotate in a fixed vertical plane stays in a direction making an angle of 60° with the horizontal. If the dip at that place is 37°, find the angle of the fixed vertical plane with the meridian.*

Solution : If the vertical plane makes an angle θ with the meridian, the horizontal component of the earth's field in that plane will be $B_H\cos\theta$. Thus the apparent dip δ_1, i.e., the angle between the needle in equilibrium and the horizontal will be given by

$$\tan\delta_1 = \frac{B_V}{B_H\cos\theta} = \frac{\tan\delta}{\cos\theta}$$

or, $$\cos\theta = \frac{\tan\delta}{\tan\delta_1}$$
$$= \frac{\tan 37°}{\tan 60°} = \frac{3}{4\sqrt{3}} = \frac{\sqrt{3}}{4}$$

or, $$\theta = 64°.$$

11. *A dip circle shows an apparent dip of 60° at a place where the true dip is 45°. If the dip circle is rotated through 90°, what apparent dip will it show ?*

Solution : If δ_1 and δ_2 be the apparent dips shown by the dip circle in the two perpendicular positions, the true dip δ is given by

$$\cot^2\delta = \cot^2\delta_1 + \cot^2\delta_2$$

or, $$\cot^2 45° = \cot^2 60° + \cot^2\delta_2$$

or, $$\cot^2\delta_2 = 2/3$$

or, $$\cot\delta_2 = 0{\cdot}816 \text{ giving } \delta_2 = 51°.$$

12. *A magnetic needle of length* 10 cm, *suspended at its middle point through a thread, stays at an angle of* 45° *with the horizontal. The horizontal component of the earth's magnetic field is* 18 μT. *(a) Find the vertical component of this field. (b) If the pole strength of the needle is* 1·6 A–m, *what vertical force should be applied to an end so as to keep it in horizontal position?*

Solution :

(a)

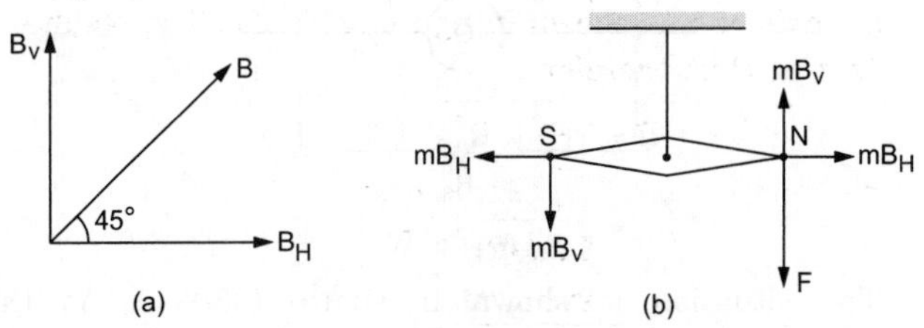

Figure 36-W6

Without the applied force, the needle will stay in the direction of the resultant magnetic field of the earth. Thus, the dip δ at the place is 45°. From figure (36-W6a),

$$\tan 45° = B_V/B_H$$

or, $$B_V = B_H = 18\ \mu\text{T}.$$

(b) When the force F is applied (figure 36-W6b), the needle stays in horizontal position. Taking torque about the centre of the magnet,

$$2mB_V \times l = F \times l$$

or, $$F = 2mB_V$$
$$= 2 \times (1{\cdot}6\ \text{A m}) \times (18 \times 10^{-6}\ \text{T})$$
$$= 5{\cdot}8 \times 10^{-5}\ \text{N}.$$

13. *A tangent galvanometer has a coil of* 50 *turns and a radius of* 20 cm. *The horizontal component of the earth's magnetic field is* $B_H = 3 \times 10^{-5}$ T. *Find the current which gives a deflection of* 45°.

Solution : We have

$$i = K\tan\theta = \frac{2rB_H}{\mu_0 n}\tan\theta$$
$$= \frac{2 \times (0{\cdot}20\ \text{m}) \times (3 \times 10^{-5}\ \text{T})}{4\pi \times 10^{-7}\ \text{T m A}^{-1} \times 50}\tan 45° = 0{\cdot}19\ \text{A}.$$

14. *A moving-coil galvanometer has* 100 *turns and each turn has an area* 2·0 cm². *The magnetic field produced by the magnet is* 0·01 T. *The deflection in the coil is* 0·05 *radian when a current of* 10 mA *is passed through it. Find the torsional constant of the suspension wire.*

Solution : We have

$$i = \frac{K}{nAB}\theta$$

or, $$K = \frac{inAB}{\theta}$$
$$= \frac{(10 \times 10^{-3}\ \text{A}) \times 100 \times (2{\cdot}0 \times 10^{-4}\ \text{m}^2) \times 0{\cdot}01\ \text{T}}{0{\cdot}05\ \text{rad}}$$
$$= 4{\cdot}0 \times 10^{-5}\ \text{N m rad}^{-1}.$$

15. *A galvanometer coil has a resistance of* 100 Ω. *When a current passes through the galvanometer,* 1% *of the current goes through the coil and the rest through the shunt. Find the resistance of the shunt.*

Solution :

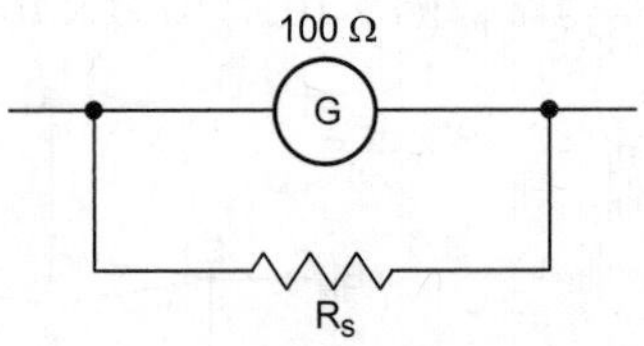

Figure 36-W7

The situation is shown in figure (36-W7). As the potential differences across the 100 Ω coil and across the shunt R_s are the same,

$$0{\cdot}01\, i \times 100\ \Omega = 0{\cdot}99\, i \times R_s$$

or, $$R_s = \frac{0{\cdot}01 \times 100}{0{\cdot}99}\ \Omega = \frac{100}{99}\ \Omega .$$

16. *The needle of a deflection magnetometer deflects through* 45° *from north to south when the instrument is used in Tan-A position with a magnet of length* 10 cm *placed at a distance of* 25 cm. *(a) Find the magnetic moment of the magnet if the earth's horizontal magnetic field is* 20 μT. *(b) If the magnetometer is used in Tan-B position with the same magnet at the same separation from the needle, what will be the deflection ?*

Solution : (a) In Tan-A position, the needle is in end-on position of the magnet so that the field at the needle due to the magnet is

$$B = \frac{\mu_0}{4\pi} \frac{2Md}{(d^2 - l^2)^2} .$$

Thus, $$\frac{\mu_0}{4\pi} \frac{2Md}{(d^2 - l^2)^2} = B_H \tan\theta$$

or, $$M = \frac{4\pi\, B_H \tan\theta (d^2 - l^2)^2}{\mu_0\, 2d}$$

$$= 10^7\ \mathrm{A\ m^{-1}\ T^{-1}} \times \frac{20 \times 10^{-6}\ \mathrm{T} \times 1 \times (625 - 25)^2 \times 10^{-8}\ \mathrm{m}^4}{2 \times 25 \times 10^{-2}\ \mathrm{m}}$$

$$= 1{\cdot}44\ \mathrm{A\ m}^2 .$$

(b) In Tan-B position, the needle is in broadside-on position of the manget, so that

$$B = \frac{\mu_0}{4\pi} \frac{M}{(d^2 + l^2)^{3/2}} = B_H \tan\theta$$

or, $$\tan\theta = \frac{10^{-7}\ \mathrm{T\ m\ A^{-1}} \times 1{\cdot}44\ \mathrm{A\ m}^2}{(625 + 25)^{3/2} \times 10^{-6}\ \mathrm{m}^3 \times 20 \times 10^{-6}\ \mathrm{T}}$$

$$= 0{\cdot}43$$

or, $$\theta = 23{\cdot}5° .$$

17. *Figure (36-W8) shows a short magnet executing small oscillations in an oscillation magnetometer in earth's magnetic field having horizontal component* 24 μT. *The time period of oscillation is* 0·10 s. *An upward electric current of* 18 A *is established in the vertical wire placed* 20 cm *east of the magnet by closing the switch S. Find the new time period.*

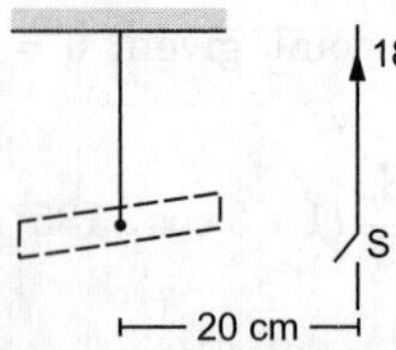

Figure 36-W8

Solution : The magnetic field at the site of the short magnet due to the vertical current is

$$B = \frac{\mu_0\, i}{2\pi d} = (2 \times 10^{-7}\ \mathrm{T\ m\ A^{-1}}) \frac{18\ \mathrm{A}}{0{\cdot}20\ \mathrm{m}}$$

$$= 18\ \mu\mathrm{T}.$$

As the wire is east of the magnet, this magnetic field will be from north to south according to the right-hand thumb rule. The earth's magnetic field has horizontal component 24 μT from south to north. Thus, the resultant field will be 6·0 μT from south to north. If T_1 and T_2 be the time periods without and with the current,

$$T_1 = \sqrt{\frac{I}{MB_H}} \text{ and } T_2 = \sqrt{\frac{I}{M(B_H - B)}}$$

or, $$\frac{T_2}{T_1} = \sqrt{\frac{B_H}{B_H - B}} = \sqrt{\frac{24\ \mu\mathrm{T}}{6\ \mu\mathrm{T}}} = 2$$

or, $$T_2 = 2T_1 = 0{\cdot}20\ \mathrm{s}.$$

18. *The frequency of oscillation of the magnet in an oscillation magnetometer in the earth's magnetic field is* 40 oscillations per minute. *A short bar magnet is placed to the north of the magnetometer, at a separation of* 20 cm *from the oscillating magnet, with its north pole pointing towards north (figure 36-W9). The frequency of oscillation is found to increase to* 60 oscillations per minute. *Calculate the magnetic moment of this short bar magnet. Horizontal component of the earth's magnetic field is* 24 μT.

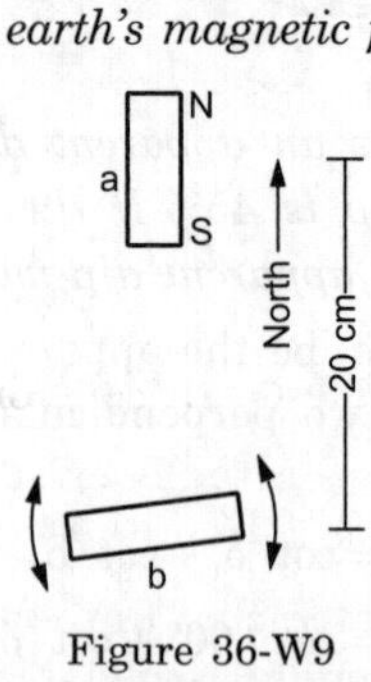

Figure 36-W9

Solution : Let the magnetic field due to the short magnet have magnitude B at the site of the oscillating magnet. From the figure, this magnetic field will be towards north and hence the resultant horizontal field will be $B_H + B$. Let M and M' denote the magnetic moments of the oscillating magnet and the other magnet respectively. If ν and ν′ be the frequencies without and with the other magnet, we have

$$\nu = \frac{1}{2\pi} \sqrt{\frac{MB_H}{I}} \text{ and}$$

$$v' = \frac{1}{2\pi}\sqrt{\frac{M(B_H + B)}{I}}$$

or, $$\frac{v'^2}{v^2} = \frac{B_H + B}{B_H}$$

or, $$\left(\frac{60}{40}\right)^2 = 1 + \frac{B}{B_H}$$

or, $$\frac{B}{B_H} = 1{\cdot}25$$

or, $$B = 1{\cdot}25 \times 24\ \mu T = 30 \times 10^{-6}\ T.$$

The oscillating magnet is in end-on position of the short magnet. Thus, the field B can be written as

$$B = \frac{\mu_0}{4\pi}\frac{2M'}{d^3}$$

or, $$M' = \frac{2\pi}{\mu_0} Bd^3$$

$$= 0{\cdot}5 \times 10^7\ A\ m^{-1}\ T^{-1} \times (30 \times 10^{-6}\ T) \times (20 \times 10^{-2}\ m)^3$$

$$= 1{\cdot}2\ A\ m^2.$$

19. *A bar magnet of mass* 100 g, *length* 7·0 cm, *width* 1·0 cm *and height* 0·50 cm *takes* π/2 seconds *to complete an oscillation in an oscillation magnetometer placed in a horizontal magnetic field of* 25 μT. *(a) Find the magnetic moment of the magnet. (b) If the magnet is put in the magnetometer with its* 0·50 cm *edge horizontal, what would be the time period?*

Solution : (a) The moment of inertia of the magnet about the axis of rotation is

$$I = \frac{m'}{12}(L^2 + b^2)$$

$$= \frac{100 \times 10^{-3}}{12}[(7 \times 10^{-2})^2 + (1 \times 10^{-2})^2]\ kg\ m^2$$

$$= \frac{25}{6} \times 10^{-5}\ kg\ m^2.$$

We have,

$$T = 2\pi\sqrt{\frac{I}{MB}} \qquad \text{... (i)}$$

or, $$M = \frac{4\pi^2 I}{BT^2} = \frac{4\pi^2 \times 25 \times 10^{-5}\ kg\ m^2}{6 \times (25 \times 10^{-6}\ T) \times \frac{\pi^2}{4}\ s^2}$$

$$\approx 27\ A\ m^2.$$

(b) In this case the moment of inertia becomes

$$I' = \frac{m'}{12}(L^2 + b'^2) \text{ where } b' = 0{\cdot}5 \text{ cm}.$$

The time period would be

$$T' = \sqrt{\frac{I'}{MB}} \qquad \text{... (ii)}$$

Dividing by equation (i),

$$\frac{T'}{T} = \sqrt{\frac{I'}{I}}$$

$$= \frac{\sqrt{\frac{m'}{12}(L^2 + b'^2)}}{\sqrt{\frac{m'}{12}(L^2 + b^2)}} = \frac{\sqrt{(7\ cm)^2 + (0{\cdot}5\ cm)^2}}{\sqrt{(7\ cm)^2 + (1{\cdot}0\ cm)^2}}$$

$$= 0{\cdot}992$$

or, $$T' = \frac{0{\cdot}992 \times \pi}{2}\ s = 0{\cdot}496\pi\ s.$$

□

QUESTIONS FOR SHORT ANSWER

1. Can we have a single north pole, or a single south pole?
2. Do two distinct poles actually exist at two nearby points in a magnetic dipole?
3. An iron needle is attracted to the ends of a bar magnet but not to the middle region of the magnet. Is the material making up the ends of a bar magnet different from that of the middle region?
4. Compare the direction of the magnetic field inside a solenoid with that of the field there if the solenoid is replaced by its equivalent combination of north pole and south pole.
5. Sketch the magnetic field lines for a current-carrying circular loop near its centre. Replace the loop by an equivalent magnetic dipole and sketch the magnetic field lines near the centre of the dipole. Identify the difference.
6. The force on a north pole, $\vec{F} = m\vec{B}$, is parallel to the field $\vec{B}$. Does it contradict our earlier knowledge that a magnetic field can exert forces only perpendicular to itself?
7. Two bar magnets are placed close to each other with their opposite poles facing each other. In absence of other forces, the magnets are pulled towards each other and their kinetic energy increases. Does it contradict our earlier knowledge that magnetic forces cannot do any work and hence cannot increase kinetic energy of a system?
8. Magnetic scalar potential is defined as

$$U(\vec{r_2}) - U(\vec{r_1}) = -\int_{\vec{r_1}}^{\vec{r_2}} \vec{B}\cdot\vec{dl}.$$

Apply this equation to a closed curve enclosing a long

straight wire. The RHS of the above equation is then $-\mu_0 i$ by Ampere's law. We see that $U(\vec{r_2}) \neq U(\vec{r_1})$ even when $\vec{r_2} = \vec{r_1}$. Can we have a magnetic scalar potential in this case ?

9. Can the earth's magnetic field be vertical at a place ? What will happen to a freely suspended magnet at such a place ? What is the value of dip here ?

10. Can the dip at a place be (a) zero (b) 90° ?

11. The reduction factor K of a tangent galvanometer is written on the instrument. The manual says that the current is obtained by multiplying this factor to tanθ. The procedure works well at Bhuwaneshwar. Will the procedure work if the instrument is taken to Nepal ? If there is some error, can it be corrected by correcting the manual or the instrument will have to be taken back to the factory ?

OBJECTIVE I

1. A circular loop carrying a current is replaced by an equivalent magnetic dipole. A point on the axis of the loop is in
(a) end-on position (b) broadside-on position
(c) both (d) none.

2. A circular loop carrying a current is replaced by an equivalent magnetic dipole. A point on the loop is in
(a) end-on position (b) broadside-on position
(c) both (d) none.

3. When a current in a circular loop is equivalently replaced by a magnetic dipole,
(a) the pole strength m of each pole is fixed
(b) the distance d between the poles is fixed
(c) the product md is fixed
(d) none of the above.

4. Let r be the distance of a point on the axis of a bar magnet from its centre. The magnetic field at such a point is proportional to
(a) $\frac{1}{r}$ (b) $\frac{1}{r^2}$ (c) $\frac{1}{r^3}$ (d) none of these.

5. Let r be the distance of a point on the axis of a magnetic dipole from its centre. The magnetic field at such a point is proportional to
(a) $\frac{1}{r}$ (b) $\frac{1}{r^2}$ (c) $\frac{1}{r^3}$ (d) none of these.

6. Two short magnets of equal dipole moments M are fastened perpendicularly at their centres (figure 36-Q1). The magnitude of the magnetic field at a distance d from the centre on the bisector of the right angle is
(a) $\frac{\mu_0}{4\pi}\frac{M}{d^3}$ (b) $\frac{\mu_0}{4\pi}\frac{\sqrt{2}M}{d^3}$ (c) $\frac{\mu_0}{4\pi}\frac{2\sqrt{2}M}{d^3}$ (d) $\frac{\mu_0}{4\pi}\frac{2M}{d^3}$.

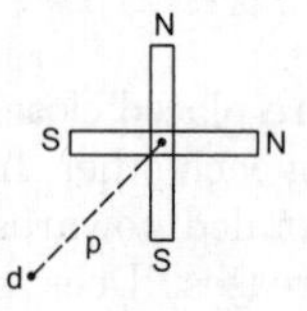

Figure 36-Q1

7. Magnetic meridian is
(a) a point (b) a line along north–south
(c) a horizontal plane (d) a vertical plane.

8. A compass needle which is allowed to move in a horizontal plane is taken to a geomagnetic pole. It
(a) will stay in north–south direction only
(b) will stay in east–west direction only
(c) will become rigid showing no movement
(d) will stay in any position.

9. A dip circle is taken to geomagnetic equator. The needle is allowed to move in a vertical plane perpendicular to the magnetic meridian. The needle will stay
(a) in horizontal direction only
(b) in vertical direction only
(c) in any direction except vertical and horizontal
(d) in any direction it is released.

10. Which of the following four graphs may best represent the current–deflection relation in a tangent galvanometer ?

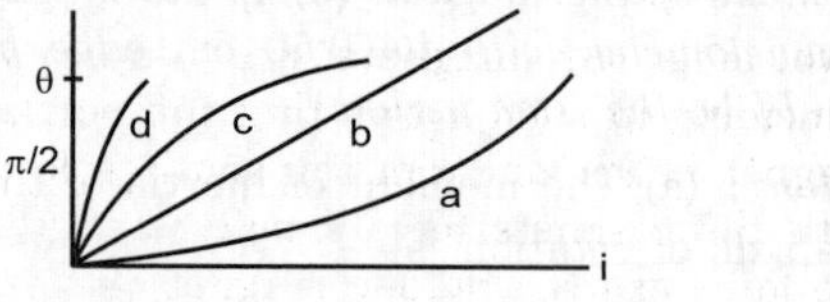

Figure 36-Q2

11. A tangent galvanometer is connected directly to an ideal battery. If the number of turns in the coil is doubled, the deflection will
(a) increase (b) decrease
(c) remain unchanged (d) either increase or decrease.

12. If the current is doubled, the deflection is also doubled in
(a) a tangent galvanometer
(b) a moving-coil galvanometer
(c) both (d) none.

13. A very long bar magnet is placed with its north pole coinciding with the centre of a circular loop carrying an electric current i. The magnetic field due to the magnet at a point on the periphery of the wire is B. The radius of the loop is a. The force on the wire is
(a) very nearly $2\pi aiB$ perpendicular to the plane of the wire
(b) $2\pi aiB$ in the plane of the wire
(c) πaiB along the magnet (d) zero.

OBJECTIVE II

1. Pick the correct options.
   (a) Magnetic field is produced by electric charges only.
   (b) Magnetic poles are only mathematical assumptions having no real existence.
   (c) A north pole is equivalent to a clockwise current and a south pole is equivalent to an anticlockwise current.
   (d) A bar magnet is equivalent to a long, straight current.

2. A horizontal circular loop carries a current that looks clockwise when viewed from above. It is replaced by an equivalent magnetic dipole consisting of a south pole S and a north pole N.
   (a) The line SN should be along a diameter of the loop.
   (b) The line SN should be perpendicular to the plane of the loop.
   (c) The south pole should be below the loop.
   (d) The north pole should be below the loop.

3. Consider a magnetic dipole kept in the north to south direction. Let P_1, P_2, Q_1, Q_2 be four points at the same distance from the dipole towards north, south, east and west of the dipole respectively. The directions of the magnetic field due to the dipole are the same at
   (a) P_1 and P_2 (b) Q_1 and Q_2
   (c) P_1 and Q_1 (d) P_2 and Q_2.

4. Consider the situation of the previous problem. The directions of the magnetic field due to the dipole are opposite at
   (a) P_1 and P_2 (b) Q_1 and Q_2
   (c) P_1 and Q_1 (d) P_2 and Q_2.

5. To measure the magnetic moment of a bar magnet, one may use
   (a) a tangent galvanometer
   (b) a deflection galvanometer if the earth's horizontal field is known
   (c) an oscillation magnetometer if the earth's horizontal field is known
   (d) both deflection and oscillation magnetometer if the earth's horizontal field is not known.

EXERCISES

1. A long bar magnet has a pole strength of 10 Am. Find the magnetic field at a point on the axis of the magnet at a distance of 5 cm from the north pole of the magnet.

2. Two long bar magnets are placed with their axes coinciding in such a way that the north pole of the first magnet is 2·0 cm from the south pole of the second. If both the magnets have a pole strength of 10 Am, find the force exerted by one magnet on the other.

3. A uniform magnetic field of $0{\cdot}20 \times 10^{-3}$ T exists in the space. Find the change in the magnetic scalar potential as one moves through 50 cm along the field.

4. Figure (36-E1) shows some of the equipotential surfaces of the magnetic scalar potential. Find the magnetic field B at a point in the region.

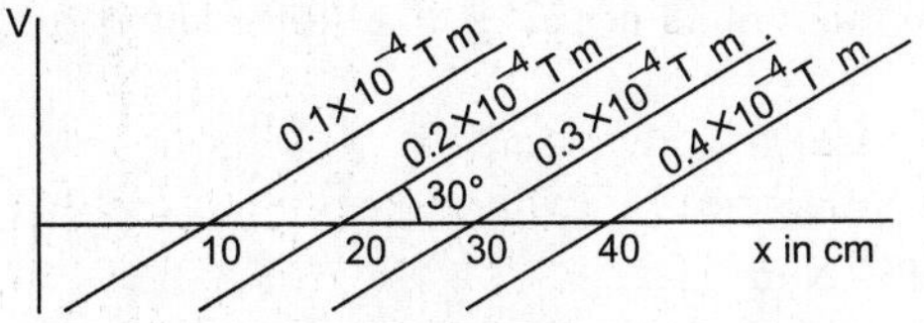

Figure 36-E1

5. The magnetic field at a point, 10 cm away from a magnetic dipole, is found to be $2{\cdot}0 \times 10^{-4}$ T. Find the magnetic moment of the dipole if the point is (a) in end-on position of the dipole and (b) in broadside-on position of the dipole.

6. Show that the magnetic field at a point due to a magnetic dipole is perpendicular to the magnetic axis if the line joining the point with the centre of the dipole makes an angle of $\tan^{-1}(\sqrt{2})$ with the magnetic axis.

7. A bar magnet has a length of 8 cm. The magnetic field at a point at a distance 3 cm from the centre in the broadside-on position is found to be 4×10^{-6} T. Find the pole strength of the magnet.

8. A magnetic dipole of magnetic moment $1{\cdot}44$ A m^2 is placed horizontally with the north pole pointing towards north. Find the position of the neutral point if the horizontal component of the earth's magnetic field is 18 μT.

9. A magnetic dipole of magnetic moment $0{\cdot}72$ A m^2 is placed horizontally with the north pole pointing towards south. Find the position of the neutral point if the horizontal component of the earth's magnetic field is 18 μT.

10. A magnetic dipole of magnetic moment $0{\cdot}72\sqrt{2}$ A m^2 is placed horizontally with the north pole pointing towards east. Find the position of the neutral point if the horizontal component of the earth's magnetic field is 18 μT.

11. The magnetic moment of the assumed dipole at the earth's centre is $8{\cdot}0 \times 10^{22}$ A m^2. Calculate the magnetic field B at the geomagnetic poles of the earth. Radius of the earth is 6400 km.

12. If the earth's magnetic field has a magnitude $3{\cdot}4 \times 10^{-5}$ T at the magnetic equator of the earth, what would be its value at the earth's geomagnetic poles ?

13. The magnetic field due to the earth has a horizontal component of 26 μT at a place where the dip is 60°. Find the vertical component and the magnitude of the field.

14. A magnetic needle is free to rotate in a vertical plane which makes an angle of 60° with the magnetic meridian. If the needle stays in a direction making an angle of $\tan^{-1}(2/\sqrt{3})$ with the horizontal, what would be the dip at that place ?

15. The needle of a dip circle shows an apparent dip of 45° in a particular position and 53° when the circle is rotated through 90°. Find the true dip.

16. A tangent galvanometer shows a deflection of 45° when 10 mA of current is passed through it. If the horizontal component of the earth's magnetic field is $B_H = 3{\cdot}6 \times 10^{-5}$ T and radius of the coil is 10 cm, find the number of turns in the coil.

17. A moving-coil galvanometer has a 50-turn coil of size 2 cm × 2 cm. It is suspended between the magnetic poles producing a magnetic field of 0·5 T. Find the torque on the coil due to the magnetic field when a current of 20 mA passes through it.

18. A short magnet produces a deflection of 37° in a deflection magnetometer in Tan-*A* position when placed at a separation of 10 cm from the needle. Find the ratio of the magnetic moment of the magnet to the earth's horizontal magnetic field.

19. The magnetometer of the previous problem is used with the same magnet in Tan-*B* position. Where should the magnet be placed to produce a 37° deflection of the needle ?

20. A deflection magnetometer is placed with its arms in north–south direction. How and where should a short magnet having $M/B_H = 40\ \text{A m}^2\ \text{T}^{-1}$ be placed so that the needle can stay in any position ?

21. A bar magnet takes $\pi/10$ second to complete one oscillation in an oscillation magnetometer. The moment of inertia of the magnet about the axis of rotation is $1{\cdot}2 \times 10^{-4}\ \text{kg m}^2$ and the earth's horizontal magnetic field is 30 μT. Find the magnetic moment of the magnet.

22. The combination of two bar magnets makes 10 oscillations per second in an oscillation magnetometer when like poles are tied together and 2 oscillations per second when unlike poles are tied together. Find the ratio of the magnetic moments of the magnets. Neglect any induced magnetism.

23. A short magnet oscillates in an oscillation magnetometer with a time period of 0·10 s where the earth's horizontal magnetic field is 24 μT. A downward current of 18 A is established in a vertical wire placed 20 cm east of the magnet. Find the new time period.

24. A bar magnet makes 40 oscillations per minute in an oscillation magnetometer. An identical magnet is demagnetized completely and is placed over the magnet in the magnetometer. Find the time taken for 40 oscillations by this combination. Neglect any induced magnetism.

25. A short magnet makes 40 oscillations per minute when used in an oscillation magnetometer at a place where the earth's horizontal magnetic field is 25 μT. Another short magnet of magnetic moment 1·6 A m² is placed 20 cm east of the oscillating magnet. Find the new frequency of oscillation if the magnet has its north pole (a) towards north and (b) towards south.

□

ANSWERS

OBJECTIVE I

1. (a)	2. (b)	3. (c)	4. (d)	5. (c)	6. (c)
7. (d)	8. (d)	9. (d)	10. (c)	11. (c)	12. (b)
13. (a)					

OBJECTIVE II

1. (a), (b)	2. (b), (d)	3. (a), (b)
4. (c), (d)	5. (b), (c), (d)	

EXERCISES

1. 4×10^{-4} T
2. $2{\cdot}5 \times 10^{-2}$ N
3. decreases by $0{\cdot}10 \times 10^{-3}$ T m
4. $2{\cdot}0 \times 10^{-4}$ T
5. (a) $1{\cdot}0\ \text{A m}^2$ and (b) $2{\cdot}0\ \text{A m}^2$
7. 6×10^{-5} A m
8. at a distance of 20 cm in the plane bisecting the dipole
9. 20 cm south of the dipole
10. 20 cm from the dipole, $\tan^{-1}\sqrt{2}$ south of east
11. 60 μT
12. $6{\cdot}8 \times 10^{-5}$ T
13. 45 μT, 52 μT
14. 30°
15. 39°
16. 570
17. 2×10^{-4} N m
18. $3{\cdot}75 \times 10^{3}\ \dfrac{\text{A m}^2}{\text{T}}$
19. 7·9 cm from the centre
20. 2·0 cm from the needle, north pole pointing towards south
21. 1600 A m²
22. 13 : 12
23. 0·076 s
24. $\sqrt{2}$ minutes
25. (a) 18 oscillations/min (b) 54 oscillations/min

□

CHAPTER 37

MAGNETIC PROPERTIES OF MATTER

37.1 MAGNETIZATION OF MATERIALS: INTENSITY OF MAGNETIZATION

Matter is made of atoms and atoms are made of nuclei and electrons. The electrons in an atom move about the nucleus in closed paths and hence constitute electric current loops. As a current loop has a magnetic dipole moment, each electron in an atom has a magnetic moment due to its orbital motion. Besides this, each electron has a permanent angular momentum which is present even if it is at rest. This permanent angular momentum is called the *spin angular momentum* of the electron and can be understood only through quantum mechanics. Corresponding to its spin, each electron has a permanent magnetic moment. This magnetic moment has a fixed magnitude $\mu_s = 9{\cdot}285 \times 10^{-24}\ \mathrm{J\,T^{-1}}$. The magnetic moment due to the motion of the electron is over and above this. The nucleus may also have a magnetic moment but it is about several thousand times smaller than the magnetic moment of an electron. The resultant magnetic moment of an atom is the vector sum of all such magnetic moments.

The magnetic moments of the electrons of an atom have a tendency to cancel in pairs. Thus, the magnetic moments of the two electrons of a helium atom cancel each other. In a number of atoms and ions, the resultant magnetic moment is zero. But in some cases, the magnetic moment of an atom is not zero. Such an atom may be represented by a magnetic dipole having a permanent magnetic moment. We shall first discuss materials made of such atoms.

Any object of finite size contains a large number of atoms. In general, the magnetic moments of these atoms are randomly oriented and there is no net magnetic moment in any volume of the material that contains more than several thousand atoms (figure 37.1a). This volume is still quite small at macroscopic scale. However, when the material is kept in an external magnetic field, torques act on the atomic dipoles and these torques try to align them parallel to the field (figure 37.1b). The alignment is only partial, because, the thermal motion of the atoms frequently changes the orientation of the atoms and hence tries to randomize the magnetic moments. The degree of alignment increases if the strength of the applied field is increased and also if the temperature is decreased. With sufficiently strong fields, the alignment is near perfect. We then say that the material is magnetically *saturated.*

When the atomic dipoles are aligned, partially or fully, there is a net magnetic moment in the direction of the field in any small volume of the material. We define the *magnetization vector* $\vec{I}$ as the magnetic moment per unit volume. It is also called the *intensity of magnetization* or simply *magnetization.* Thus,

$$\vec{I} = \frac{\text{magnetic moment}}{\text{volume}} = \frac{\vec{M}}{V} \cdot \qquad \ldots (37.1)$$

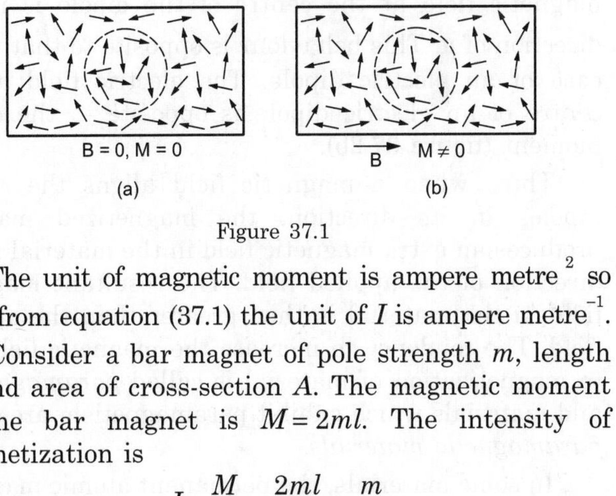

Figure 37.1

The unit of magnetic moment is ampere metre^2 so that from equation (37.1) the unit of I is ampere metre^{-1}.

Consider a bar magnet of pole strength m, length $2l$ and area of cross-section A. The magnetic moment of the bar magnet is $M = 2ml$. The intensity of magnetization is

$$I = \frac{M}{V} = \frac{2ml}{A(2l)} = \frac{m}{A} \cdot$$

Thus, for a bar magnet, the intensity of magnetization may be defined as the *pole strength per unit face area.*

Example 37.1

A bar magnet made of steel has a magnetic moment of $2{\cdot}5\ \mathrm{A\,m^2}$ *and a mass of* $6{\cdot}6 \times 10^{-3}$ kg. *If the density of steel is* $7{\cdot}9\times10^{3}$ kg m^{-3}, *find the intensity of magnetization of the magnet.*

Solution : The volume of the bar magnet is

$$V=\frac{\text{mass}}{\text{density}}=\frac{6{\cdot}6\times10^{-3}\ \text{kg}}{7{\cdot}9\times10^{3}\ \text{kg m}^{-3}}$$

$$=8{\cdot}3\times10^{-7}\ \text{m}^{3}.$$

The intensity of magnetization is

$$I=\frac{M}{V}=\frac{2{\cdot}5\ \text{A m}^{2}}{8{\cdot}3\times10^{-7}\ \text{m}^{3}}\approx3{\cdot}0\times10^{6}\ \text{A m}^{-1}.$$

37.2 PARAMAGNETISM, FERROMAGNETISM AND DIAMAGNETISM

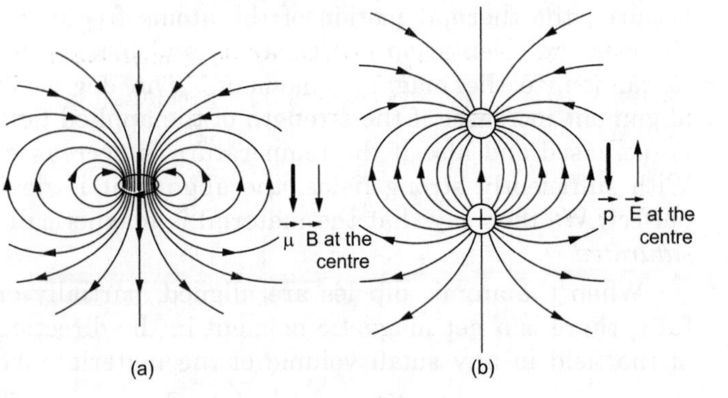

Figure 37.2

Figure (37.2a) shows a current loop and the magnetic field lines associated with it. The dipole moment $\vec{\mu}=i\vec{A}$ is also shown in the figure. The magnetic field at the centre of the dipole is in the direction of $\vec{\mu}$. This behaviour is opposite to that in the case of an electric dipole. The electric field at the centre of an electric dipole is opposite to the dipole moment (figure 37.2b).

Thus, when a magnetic field aligns the atomic dipoles in its direction, the magnetized material produces an extra magnetic field in the material in the direction of the applied field. The resultant magnetic field in the material is then greater than the applied field. The tendency to increase the magnetic field due to magnetization of material is called *paramagnetism* and materials which exhibit paramagnetism are called *paramagnetic materials.*

In some materials, the permanent atomic magnetic moments have strong tendency to align themselves even without any external field. These materials are called ferromagnetic materials and permanent magnets are made from them. The force between neighbouring atoms, responsible for their alignment, is called *exchange coupling* and it can only be explained by quantum mechanics. In normal unmagnetized state, the atoms form domains inside the material as suggested by figure (37.3). The atoms in any domain have magnetic moments in the same direction giving a net large magnetic moment to the domain. Different domains, however, have different directions of magnetic moment and hence, the material remains unmagnetized. Different domains have different sizes, the size may be as large as a millimetre in linear dimension. Remember, a volume of 1 mm^{3} contains about 10^{20} atoms !

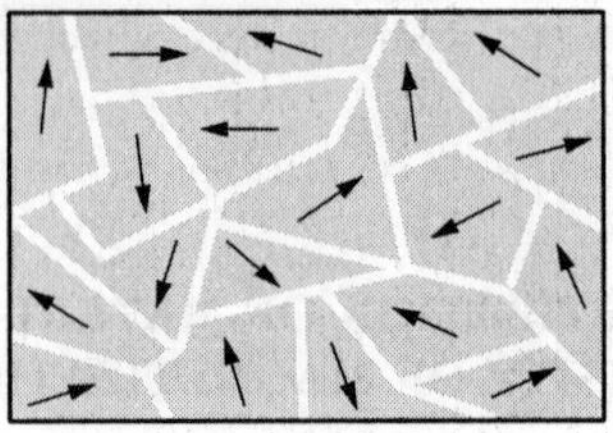

Figure 37.3

If a magnetic field is applied, the domains which are aligned along the direction of the field grow in size and those opposite to it get reduced. This happens because walls of the domains move across the sample. Also, domains may orient themselves in favour of the applied field. Figure (37.4) shows a qualitative description of the processes of domain-growing and domain-alignment.

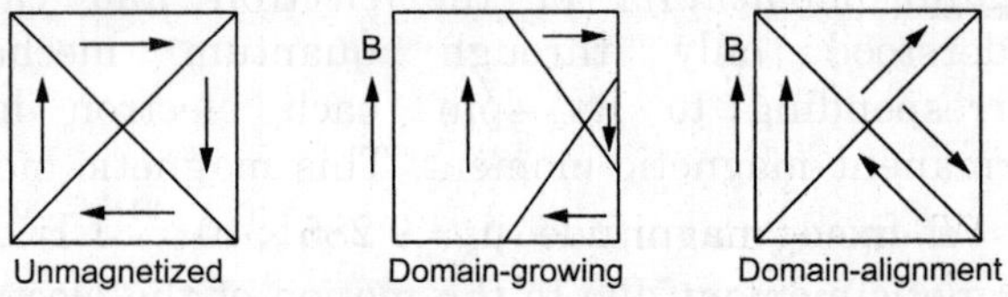

Figure 37.4

Because of the domain character of ferromagnetic materials, even if a small magnetic field is applied, it gives rise to large magnetization. The resultant field is much larger than the applied field in such a material.

Now suppose, the individual atoms of a material do not have a net magnetic dipole moment. When such a substance is placed in a magnetic field, dipole moments are induced in the atoms by the applied field. From Lenz's law, the magnetic field due to the induced magnetic moments opposes the original field. The resultant field in such materials is, therefore, smaller than the applied field. This phenomenon is called *diamagnetism* and such materials are called *diamagnetic* materials.

Magnetic moments are induced in all materials whenever a magnetic field is applied. Thus, all materials have the property of diamagnetism. However, if there is a permanent atomic magnetic moment, paramagnetism or ferromagnetism is much stronger than diamagnetism and the material does not show diamagnetic properties.

37.3 MAGNETIC INTENSITY H

When a magnetic field is applied to a material, the material gets magnetized. The actual magnetic field inside the material is the sum of the applied magnetic field and the magnetic field due to magnetization. It is convenient to define a new vector field

$$\vec{H} = \frac{\vec{B}}{\mu_0} - \vec{I} \quad \text{... (37.2)}$$

where $\vec{B}$ is the resultant magnetic field and $\vec{I}$ is the intensity of magnetization. This quantity $\vec{H}$ is called *magnetic intensity* or *magnetizing field intensity*. The unit of H is the same as that of I, that is, ampere metre $^{-1}$. If no material is present (vacuum), $\vec{I} = 0$ and we have

$$\vec{H} = \frac{\vec{B}}{\mu_0}. \quad \text{... (37.3)}$$

Thus, the magnetic intensity due to a current element $i\,\vec{dl}$ is, from Biot–Savart law,

$$d\vec{H} = \frac{1}{4\pi} \frac{i\,\vec{dl} \times \vec{r}}{r^3}. \quad \text{... (37.4)}$$

The magnetic intensity due to a magnetic pole of pole strength m at a distance r from it is

$$H = \frac{m}{4\pi r^2}. \quad \text{... (37.5)}$$

Whenever the end effects of a magnetized material can be neglected, the magnetic intensity due to magnetization is zero. This may be the case with a ring-shaped material or in the middle portion of a long rod. The magnetic intensity in a material is then determined by the external sources only, even if the material is magnetized.

Example 37.2

Find the magnetic intensity H at the centre of a long solenoid having n turns per unit length and carrying a current i (a) when no material is kept in it and (b) when a long copper rod is inserted in the solenoid.

Solution : (a) When there is no rod, the magnetic field at the centre of the solenoid is given by

$$B = \mu_0 ni.$$

The magnetic intensity is

$$H = \frac{B}{\mu_0} = ni.$$

(b) As the solenoid and the rod are long and we are interested in the magnetic intensity at the centre, the end effects may be neglected. There is no effect of the rod on the magnetic intensity at the centre. Its value in both cases are the same. Thus $H = ni$.

37.4 MAGNETIC SUSCEPTIBILITY

For paramagnetic and diamagnetic substances, the intensity of magnetization of a material is directly proportional to the magnetic intensity. Thus,

$$\vec{I} = \chi \vec{H}. \quad \text{... (37.6)}$$

The proportionality constant χ is called the *susceptibility* of the material. Table (37.1) gives susceptibility of some chosen materials. As I and H have the same dimensions, the susceptibility χ is a dimensionless constant. As there can be no magnetization in vacuum, $I = 0$ and hence $\chi = 0$. The materials with positive value of χ are paramagnetic and those with negative value of χ are diamagnetic.

Table 37.1 : *Susceptibilities of some materials*

Material	Temperature in °C	χ in 10^{-5}
Vacuum		Zero
Air	STP	0·04
Oxygen (gas)	STP	0·18
Magnesium	20	1·2
Aluminium	20	2·1
Tungsten	20	6·8
Titanium	20	7·06
Cerium	18	130
Ferric chloride	20	306
Oxygen (liquid)	– 219	490
Carbon dioxide (1 atm)	20	$-2{\cdot}3 \times 10^{-4}$
Nitrogen (1 atm)	20	$-5{\cdot}0 \times 10^{-4}$
Hydrogen (1 atm)	20	$-9{\cdot}9 \times 10^{-4}$
Sodium	20	– 0·24
Copper	18	– 0·96
Lead	18	– 1·6
Carbon (diamond)	20	– 2·2
Silver	20	– 2·6
Mercury	18	– 2·8
Gold	20	– 3·6
Carbon (graphite)	20	– 9·9
Bismuth	20	– 16·6

37.5 PERMEABILITY

The magnetic intensity is given by

$$\vec{H} = \frac{\vec{B}}{\mu_0} - \vec{I}$$

or,

$$\vec{B} = \mu_0(\vec{H} + \vec{I})$$
$$= \mu_0(\vec{H} + \chi\vec{H})$$
$$= \mu_0(1 + \chi)\vec{H}.$$

We can write,

$$\vec{B} = \mu\vec{H} \quad \text{... (37.7)}$$

where $\mu = \mu_0(1 + \chi)$ is a constant called the *permeability* of the material. The permeability of vacuum is μ_0 as $\chi = 0$ for vacuum. The constant

$$\mu_r = \frac{\mu}{\mu_0} = 1 + \chi \qquad \dots (37.8)$$

is called the *relative permeability* of the material.

The significance of relative permeability may be understood by the following simple description. Consider a long solenoid (or a toroid) having n turns per unit length and carrying a current i. The magnetic field B_0 inside the solenoid is

$$B_0 = \mu_0 ni$$

and the magnetic intensity is $H = ni$.

Now suppose, a material is inserted into the solenoid. The magnetic field now becomes

$$B = \mu H = \mu ni$$

or, $$\frac{B}{B_0} = \frac{\mu}{\mu_0} = \mu_r.$$

Thus, μ_r is the factor by which the magnetic field B is increased when a material is brought in the field.

Example 37.3

Find the per cent increase in the magnetic field B when the space within a current-carrying toroid is filled with aluminium. The susceptibility of aluminium is $2{\cdot}1 \times 10^{-5}$.

Solution : In absence of aluminium, the magnetic field is

$$B_0 = \mu_0 H.$$

As the space inside the toroid is filled with aluminium, the field becomes

$$B = \mu H = \mu_0(1 + \chi)H.$$

The increase in the field is

$$B - B_0 = \mu_0 \chi H.$$

The per cent increase is

$$\frac{B - B_0}{B_0} \times 100 = \frac{\mu_0 \chi H}{\mu_0 H} \times 100$$

$$= \chi \times 100$$

$$= 2{\cdot}1 \times 10^{-3}.$$

37.6 CURIE'S LAW

As the temperature is increased, the randomization of individual atomic magnetic moments increases, decreasing the magnetization I for a given magnetic intensity H. The resultant magnetic field B decreases, which means χ decreases as T increases. *Curie's law* states that far away from saturation, the susceptibility of a paramagnetic substance is inversely proportional to the absolute temperature:

$$\chi = \frac{c}{T} \qquad \dots (37.9)$$

where c is a constant called the *Curie constant*. When a ferromagnetic material is heated, it becomes paramagnetic at a certain temperature. This temperature is called *Curie point* or *Curie temperature*. After this, the susceptibility varies with temperature as

$$\chi = \frac{c'}{T - T_c} \qquad \dots (37.10)$$

where T_c is the Curie point and c' is a constant. The Curie point of iron is 1043 K.

Table 37.2 : *Curie temperatures for some ferromagnetic substances*

Substance	T_c (K)
Iron	1043
Cobalt	1394
Nickel	631
Gadolinium	317
Fe_2O_3	893

37.7 PROPERTIES OF DIA-, PARA- AND FERROMAGNETIC SUBSTANCES

Suppose a material is placed in an external magnetic field. If the material is paramagnetic, a small magnetization occurs in the direction of the field. If it is ferromagnetic, a large magnetization occurs in the direction of the field and if the material is diamagnetic, a small magnetization occurs opposite to the field. The lines of magnetic field $\vec{B}$, thus, become more dense in a paramagnetic or ferromagnetic material but become less dense in a diamagnetic material.

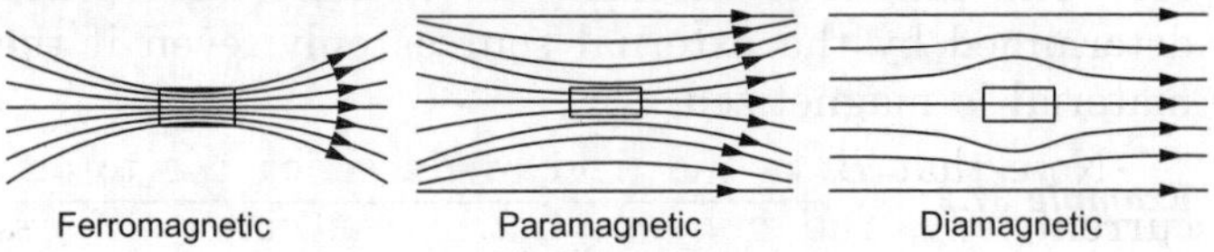

Figure 37.5

The magnetic susceptibility is a small but positive quantity ($\approx 10^{-3}$ to 10^{-5}) for paramagnetic substances; of the order of several thousands (positive) for ferromagnetic substances and small but negative for diamagnetic substances. The relative permeability $\mu_r = 1 + \chi$ is slightly more than 1 for paramagnetic, of the order of thousands for ferromagnetic and slightly less than 1 for diamagnetic substances.

Paramagnetism or diamagnetism may be found in solids, liquids or gases but ferromagnetism is normally found only in solids.

A paramagnetic substance is weakly attracted by a magnet, a ferromagnetic substance is strongly attracted by a magnet and a diamagnetic substance is weakly repelled by a magnet. Thus, when a rod is suspended in a magnetic field (figure 37.6), the rod becomes perpendicular to the field if it is diamagnetic and parallel to the field if it is paramagnetic or ferromagnetic.

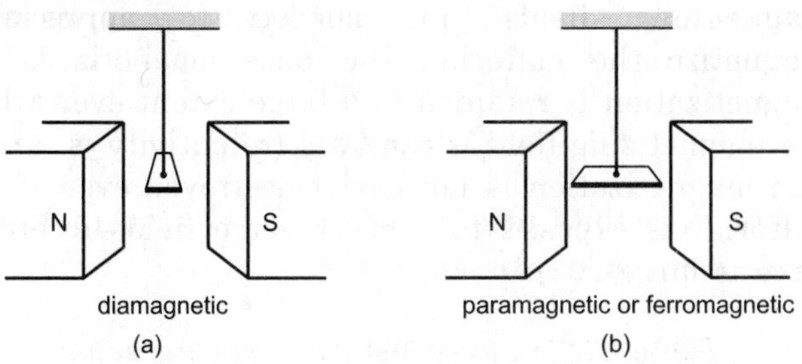

Figure 37.6

The susceptibility is inversely proportional to the absolute temperature for paramagnetic substances but it varies in a complicated way for ferromagnetic substances. For diamagnetic substances, the variation of χ with temperature is very small.

One can make permanent magnets from ferromagnetic substances only. Hysteresis (explained below) is also shown by ferromagnetic substances only.

37.8 HYSTERESIS

The magnetization in a ferromagnetic material not only depends on the magnetic intensity H but also on the previous history of the specimen. Suppose a ferromagnetic material is formed in the shape of a ring and is placed inside a toroid having n turns per unit length. A current i can be passed through the toroid to produce a magnetic intensity H in it. The magnetic field produced by the current is

$$B_0 = \mu_0 ni$$

and hence
$$H = \frac{B_0}{\mu_0} = ni. \qquad \dots \text{(i)}$$

Note that B_0 is the field produced by the toroid-current only. The ring gets magnetized and produces an extra field due to magnetization. The total field in the ring is

$$B = \mu_0(H + I)$$

or,
$$I = \frac{B}{\mu_0} - H$$

$$= \frac{B}{\mu_0} - ni. \qquad \dots \text{(ii)}$$

One can measure the total field B inside the ring by using an apparatus known as Rowland's ring. The intensity of magnetization I can then be obtained from equation (ii). Thus, from (i) and (ii) one can obtain H and I for any current.

Figure (37.7) shows a typical magnetization curve when the current is changed. In the beginning, the current is zero and the sample has no magnetization.

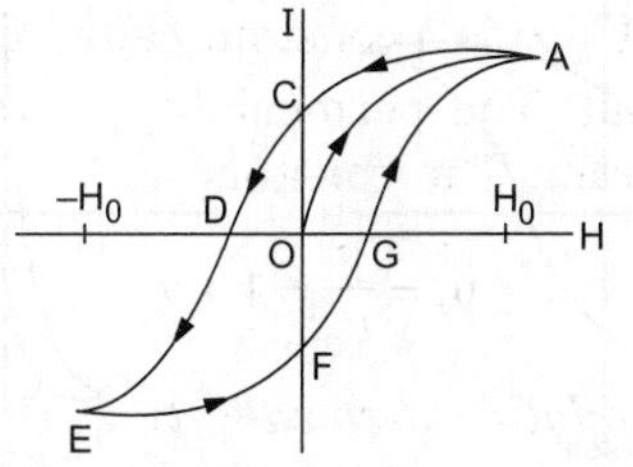

Figure 37.7

Thus, $H = 0$ and $I = 0$. This corresponds to the point O. As the current is increased, H increases and the magnetization increases. As the current is increased to a maximum, H becomes H_0 and the magnetization I becomes nearly saturated. In the whole process, the magnetization varies along the path OA. Now suppose, the current is gradually decreased. The magnetization decreases but the path OA is not retraced. As the current reduces to zero, H also becomes zero. But, there is still some magnetization left in the ring. The domains, that were aligned at the time of increasing H, are not completely randomized as the magnetic intensity H is reduced to zero. The remaining value of I at the point C is called the *retentivity* of the material. To reduce I to zero, a current must be passed in the opposite direction so as to disalign the domains forcibly. The value of H needed to make $I = 0$ is called *coercive force*. In figure (37.7), the coercive force is represented by the magnitude of H corresponding to OD. As the current is increased further in the opposite direction, the material gets magnetized in the opposite direction. The magnetization I follows the path DE as the magnetic intensity becomes $-H_0$. If the current is now reduced to zero, the magnetization I follows the path EF. Finally, if the current is increased in the original direction, the point A is reached via FGA. If we repeat the current cycle so that H changes from H_0 to $-H_0$ to H_0, the curve $ACDEFGA$ is retraced.

As H is increased and then decreased to its original value, the magnetization I, in general, does not return to its original value. This fact is called *hysteresis*. The curve $ACDEFGA$ is called the *hysteresis loop*. The area of the hysteresis loop is proportional to the thermal energy developed per unit volume of the material as it goes through the hysteresis cycle.

37.9 SOFT IRON AND STEEL

Figure (37.8) shows hysteresis loops for soft iron and steel. The retentivity and the coercive force are larger for steel than for soft iron. The area of the hysteresis loop is also larger for steel than for soft iron. Soft iron is, therefore, easily magnetized by a magnetizing field but only a small magnetization is retained when the field is removed. Also, the loss of energy, as the material is taken through periodic variations in magnetizing fields, is small. Materials

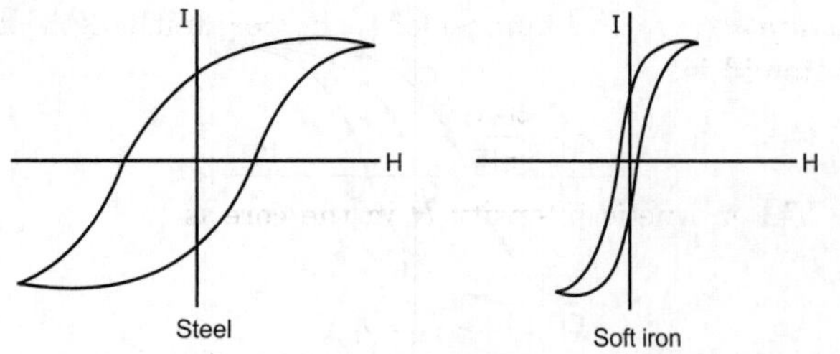

Figure 37.8

like soft iron are suitable for making electromagnets and cores inside current-carrying coils to increase the magnetic field. In transformers, moving-coil galvanometers, etc., soft-iron core is used in the coils.

On the other hand, steel and similar materials are suitable for making permanent magnets. Large magnetizing fields are needed to appreciably magnetize the material. But once magnetized, the magnetization is retained to a large extent even when the magnetizing field is removed (retentivity is large). The magnetization is not easily destroyed even if the material is exposed to stray reverse fields (coercive force is large).

Worked Out Examples

1. *A tightly-wound, long solenoid having* 50 turns cm $^{-1}$, *carries a current of* 4·00 A. *Find the magnetic intensity H and the magnetic field B at the centre of the solenoid. What will be the values of these quantities if an iron core is inserted in the solenoid and the magnetization I in the core is* $4{\cdot}00 \times 10^{6}\ \text{A m}^{-1}$?

Solution : The magnetic intensity H at the centre of a long solenoid is

$$H = ni$$

$$= 50 \times 10^{2}\ \text{m}^{-1} \times 4\ \text{A} = 2 \times 10^{4}\ \text{A m}^{-1}.$$

The magnetic field $B = \mu_0 H$

$$= 4\pi \times 10^{-7}\ \text{Tm A}^{-1} \times 2 \times 10^{4}\ \text{A m}^{-1}$$

$$= 8\pi \times 10^{-3}\ \text{T} \approx 25\ \text{mT}.$$

The value of H does not change as the iron core is inserted and remains $2 \times 10^{4}\ \text{A m}^{-1}$. The magnetic field B becomes

$$B = \mu_0 (H + I)$$

$$= (4\pi \times 10^{-7}\ \text{Tm A}^{-1})\,(2 \times 10^{4} + 4 \times 10^{6})\ \text{A m}^{-1} = 5{\cdot}05\ \text{T}.$$

It should be noted that the magnetic intensity H is very small as compared to the magnetization I in presence of the iron core.

2. *A long, cylindrical iron core of cross-sectional area* $5{\cdot}00\ \text{cm}^{2}$ *is inserted into a long solenoid having* 2000 turns m^{-1} *and carrying a current* 2·00 A. *The magnetic field inside the core is found to be* 1·57 T. *Neglecting the end effects, find the magnetization I of the core and the pole strength developed.*

Solution : The magnetic intensity H inside the solenoid is

$$H = ni = 2000\ \text{m}^{-1} \times 2\ \text{A} = 4000\ \text{A m}^{-1}.$$

Also $B = \mu_0 (H + I)$

or, $$I = \frac{B}{\mu_0} - H$$

$$= \frac{1{\cdot}57\ \text{T}}{4\pi \times 10^{-7}\ \text{Tm A}^{-1}} - 4000\ \text{A m}^{-1}$$

$$= (1{\cdot}25 \times 10^{6} - 4000)\ \text{A m}^{-1} \approx 1{\cdot}25 \times 10^{6}\ \text{A m}^{-1}.$$

Note again that the magnetization $I >> H$ for iron core. The pole strength developed at the ends is

$$m = IA$$

$$= (1{\cdot}25 \times 10^{6}\ \text{A m}^{-1}) \times (5 \times 10^{-4}\ \text{m}^{2}) = 625\ \text{A m}.$$

3. *An ideal solenoid having* 40 turns cm^{-1} *has an aluminium core and carries a current of* 2·0 A. *Calculate the magnetization I developed in the core and the magnetic field B at the centre. The susceptibility* χ *of aluminium* = $2{\cdot}3 \times 10^{-5}$.

Solution : The magnetic intensity H at the centre of the solenoid is

$$H = ni = 4000\ \text{turns m}^{-1} \times 2{\cdot}0\ \text{A}$$

$$= 8000\ \text{A m}^{-1}.$$

The magnetization is $I = \chi H$

$$= 2{\cdot}3 \times 10^{-5} \times 8000\ \text{A m}^{-1} = 0{\cdot}18\ \text{A m}^{-1}.$$

The magnetic field is $B = \mu_0 (H + I)$

$$= (4\pi \times 10^{-7}\ \text{Tm A}^{-1})\,[800 + 0{\cdot}18]\ \text{A m}^{-1} \approx 3{\cdot}2\pi \times 10^{-4}\ \text{T}.$$

Note that $H >> I$ in case of a paramagnetic core.

4. *Find (a) the magnetization I, (b) the magnetic intensity H and (c) the magnetic field B at the centre of a bar magnet having pole strength* 3·6 A m, *magnetic length* 12 cm *and cross-sectional area* $0{\cdot}90\ \text{cm}^{2}$.

Solution : (a) Magnetization $I = \dfrac{m}{A} = \dfrac{3{\cdot}6\ \text{A m}}{0{\cdot}90 \times 10^{-4}\ \text{m}^{2}}$

$$= 4 \times 10^{4}\ \text{A m}^{-1}.$$

The direction will be from the south pole to the north pole at the centre of the magnet.

(b) Magnetic intensity H_n due to the north pole is

$$H_n = \frac{1}{4\pi}\frac{m}{d^{2}} = \frac{3{\cdot}6\ \text{A m}}{4\pi \times (6 \times 10^{-2}\ \text{m})^{2}} = 79{\cdot}6\ \text{A m}^{-1}.$$

The direction will be towards the south pole. The magnetic intensity H_s at this point due to the south pole is also 79.6 A m^{-1} in the same direction. The resultant magnetic intensity is

$$H = H_n + H_s$$

$$= 159{\cdot}2 \text{ A m}^{-1} \text{ towards the south pole.}$$

(c) The magnetic field $\vec{B}$ at the centre is

$$\vec{B} = \mu_0(\vec{H} + \vec{I})$$

or, $$B = (4\pi \times 10^{-7} \text{ Tm A}^{-1})\,(4 \times 10^{4} - 159{\cdot}2) \text{ A m}^{-1}$$

$$= 5{\cdot}0 \times 10^{-2} \text{ T}.$$

The field is towards the north pole.

5. *The maximum value of the permeability of μ-metal (77% Ni, 16% Fe, 5% Cu, 2% Cr) is* $0{\cdot}126 \text{ Tm A}^{-1}$. *Find the maximum relative permeability and susceptibility.*

Solution : Relative permeability is

$$\mu_r = \frac{\mu}{\mu_0} = \frac{0{\cdot}126 \text{ Tm A}^{-1}}{4\pi \times 10^{-7} \text{ Tm A}^{-1}}$$

$$= 1{\cdot}00 \times 10^{5}.$$

Susceptibility $\chi = \mu_r - 1 \approx 1{\cdot}00 \times 10^{5}$.

6. *A toroid has a mean radius R equal to* $20/\pi$ cm, *and a total of* 400 *turns of wire carrying a current of* 2·0 A. *An aluminium ring at temperature* 280 K *inside the toroid provides the core. (a) If the magnetization I is* $4{\cdot}8 \times 10^{-2} \text{ A m}^{-1}$, *find the susceptibility of aluminium at* 280 K. *(b) If the temperature of the aluminium ring is raised to* 320 K, *what will be the magnetization ?*

Solution : (a) The number of turns per unit length of the toroid is

$$n = \frac{400}{2\pi R}.$$

The magnetic intensity H in the core is

$$H = ni$$

$$= \frac{400 \times 2{\cdot}0 \text{ A}}{2\pi \times \frac{20}{\pi} \times 10^{-2} \text{ m}} = 2000 \text{ A m}^{-1}.$$

The susceptibility is

$$\chi = I/H$$

$$= \frac{4{\cdot}8 \times 10^{-2} \text{ A m}^{-1}}{2000 \text{ A m}^{-1}} = 2{\cdot}4 \times 10^{-5}.$$

(b) The susceptibility χ of a paramagnetic substance varies with absolute temperature as $\chi = c/T$.

Thus, $\chi_2/\chi_1 = T_1/T_2$.

The susceptibility of aluminium at temperature 320 K is, therefore,

$$\chi = \frac{280}{320} \times 2{\cdot}4 \times 10^{-5} = 2{\cdot}1 \times 10^{-5}.$$

Thus, the magnetization at 320 K is

$$I = \chi H$$

$$= 2{\cdot}1 \times 10^{-5} \times 2000 \text{ A m}^{-1}.$$

$$= 4{\cdot}2 \times 10^{-2} \text{ A m}^{-1}.$$

□

QUESTIONS FOR SHORT ANSWER

1. When a dielectric is placed in an electric field, it gets polarized. The electric field in a polarized material is less than the applied field. When a paramagnetic substance is kept in a magnetic field, the field in the substance is more than the applied field. Explain the reason of this opposite behaviour.
2. The property of diamagnetism is said to be present in all materials. Then, why are some materials paramagnetic or ferromagnetic ?
3. Do permeability and relative permeability have the same dimensions ?
4. A rod when suspended in a magnetic field stays in east–west direction. Can we be sure that the field is in the east–west direction ? Can it be in the north–south direction ?
5. Why cannot we make permanent magnets from paramagnetic materials ?
6. Can we have magnetic hysteresis in paramagnetic or diamagnetic substances ?
7. When a ferromagnetic material goes through a hysteresis loop, its thermal energy is increased. Where does this energy come from ?
8. What are the advantages of using soft iron as a core, instead of steel, in the coils of galvanometers ?
9. To keep valuable instruments away from the earth's magnetic field, they are enclosed in iron boxes. Explain.

OBJECTIVE I

1. A paramagnetic material is placed in a magnetic field. Consider the following statements:

(A) If the magnetic field is increased, the magnetization is increased.

(B) If the temperature is increased, the magnetization is increased.
(a) Both A and B are true.
(b) A is true but B is false.
(c) B is true but A is false.
(d) Both A and B are false.

2. A paramagnetic material is kept in a magnetic field. The field is increased till the magnetization becomes constant. If the temperature is now decreased, the magnetization
(a) will increase (b) decrease
(c) remain constant (d) may increase or decrease.

3. A ferromagnetic material is placed in an external magnetic field. The magnetic domains
(a) increase in size (b) decrease in size
(c) may increase or decrease in size
(d) have no relation with the field.

4. A long, straight wire carries a current i. The magnetizing field intensity H is measured at a point P close to the wire. A long, cylindrical iron rod is brought close to the wire so that the point P is at the centre of the rod. The value of H at P will
(a) increase many times (b) decrease many times
(c) remain almost constant (d) become zero.

5. The magnetic susceptibility is negative for
(a) paramagnetic materials only
(b) diamagnetic materials only
(c) ferromagnetic materials only
(d) paramagnetic and ferromagnetic materials.

6. The desirable properties for making permanent magnets are
(a) high retentivity and high coercive force
(b) high retentivity and low coercive force
(c) low retentivity and high coercive force
(d) low retentivity and low coercive force.

7. Electromagnets are made of soft iron because soft iron has
(a) high retentivity and high coercive force
(b) high retentivity and low coercive force
(c) low retentivity and high coercive force
(d) low retentivity and low coercive force.

OBJECTIVE II

1. Pick the correct options.
(a) All electrons have magnetic moment.
(b) All protons have magnetic moment.
(c) All nuclei have magnetic moment.
(d) All atoms have magnetic moment.

2. The permanent magnetic moment of the atoms of a material is not zero. The material
(a) must be paramagnetic (b) must be diamagnetic
(c) must be ferromagnetic (d) may be paramagnetic.

3. The permanent magnetic moment of the atoms of a material is zero. The material
(a) must be paramagnetic (b) must be diamagnetic
(c) must be ferromagnetic (d) may be paramagnetic.

4. Which of the following pairs has quantities of the same dimensions ?
(a) Magnetic field B and magnetizing field intensity H
(b) Magnetic field B and intensity of magnetization I
(c) Magnetizing field intensity H and intensity of magnetization I
(d) Longitudinal strain and magnetic susceptibility.

5. When a ferromagnetic material goes through a hysteresis loop, the magnetic susceptibility
(a) has a fixed value (b) may be zero
(c) may be infinity (d) may be negative.

6. Mark out the correct options.
(a) Diamagnetism occurs in all materials.
(b) Diamagnetism results from the partial alignment of permanent magnetic moment.
(c) The magnetizing field intensity H is always zero in free space.
(d) The magnetic field of induced magnetic moment is opposite to the applied field.

EXERCISES

1. The magnetic intensity H at the centre of a long solenoid carrying a current of 2·0 A, is found to be 1500 A m^{-1}. Find the number of turns per centimetre of the solenoid.

2. A rod is inserted as the core in the current-carrying solenoid of the previous problem. (a) What is the magnetic intensity H at the centre ? (b) If the magnetization I of the core is found to be 0·12 A m^{-1}, find the susceptibility of the material of the rod. (c) Is the material paramagnetic, diamagnetic or ferromagnetic ?

3. The magnetic field inside a long solenoid having 50 turns cm^{-1} is increased from $2{\cdot}5 \times 10^{-3}$ T to 2·5 T when an iron core of cross-sectional area 4 cm^2 is inserted into it. Find (a) the current in the solenoid, (b) the magnetization I of the core and (c) the pole strength developed in the core.

4. A bar magnet of length 1 cm and cross-sectional area 1·0 cm^2 produces a magnetic field of $1{\cdot}5 \times 10^{-4}$ T at a point in end-on position at a distance 15 cm away from the centre. (a) Find the magnetic moment M of the magnet. (b) Find the magnetization I of the magnet. (c) Find the magnetic field B at the centre of the magnet.

5. The susceptibility of annealed iron at saturation is 5500. Find the permeability of annealed iron at saturation.

6. The magnetic field B and the magnetic intensity H in a material are found to be 1·6 T and 1000 A m^{-1}

respectively. Calculate the relative permeability μ_r and the susceptibility χ of the material.

7. The susceptibility of magnesium at 300 K is $1{\cdot}2 \times 10^{-5}$. At what temperature will the susceptibility increase to $1{\cdot}8 \times 10^{-5}$?

8. Assume that each iron atom has a permanent magnetic moment equal to 2 Bohr magnetons (1 Bohr magneton equals $9{\cdot}27 \times 10^{-24}$ A m^2). The density of atoms in iron is $8{\cdot}52 \times 10^{28}$ atoms m^{-3}. (a) Find the maximum magnetization I in a long cylinder of iron. (b) Find the maximum magnetic field B on the axis inside the cylinder.

9. The coercive force for a certain permanent magnet is $4{\cdot}0 \times 10^4$ A m^{-1}. This magnet is placed inside a long solenoid of 40 turns/cm and a current is passed in the solenoid to demagnetize it completely. Find the current.

□

ANSWERS

OBJECTIVE I

1. (b)	2. (c)	3. (c)	4. (c)	5. (b)	6. (a)
7. (d)					

OBJECTIVE II

1. (a), (b)	2. (d)	3. (b)	4. (c), (d)
5. (b), (c), (d)	6. (a), (d)		

EXERCISES

1. 7·5
2. (a) 1500 A m^{-1} (b) $8{\cdot}0 \times 10^{-5}$ (c) paramagnetic
3. (a) 0·4 A (b) $2{\cdot}0 \times 10^6$ A m^{-1} (c) 800 A m
4. (a) 2·5 A m^2 (b) $2{\cdot}5 \times 10^6$ A m^{-1} (c) 1·2 T
5. $6{\cdot}9 \times 10^{-3}$
6. $1{\cdot}3 \times 10^3$ each
7. 200 K
8. (a) $1{\cdot}58 \times 10^6$ A m^{-1} (b) 2·0 T
9. 10 A

□

CHAPTER 38

ELECTROMAGNETIC INDUCTION

38.1 FARADAY'S LAW OF ELECTROMAGNETIC INDUCTION

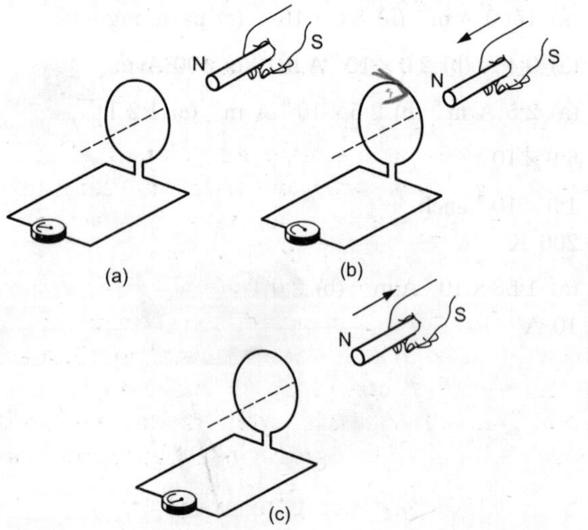

Figure 38.1

Figure (38.1a) shows a bar magnet placed along the axis of a conducting loop containing a galvanometer. There is no current in the loop and correspondingly no deflection in the galvanometer. If we move the magnet towards the loop (figure 38.1b), there is a deflection in the galvanometer showing that there is an electric current in the loop. If the magnet is moved away from the loop (figure 38.1c), again there is a current but the current is in the opposite direction. The current exists as long as the magnet is moving. Faraday studied this behaviour in detail by performing a number of experiments and discovered the following law of nature:

Whenever the flux of magnetic field through the area bounded by a closed conducting loop changes, an emf is produced in the loop. The emf is given by

$$\mathcal{E} = -\frac{d\Phi}{dt} \qquad \ldots (38.1)$$

where $\Phi = \int \vec{B} \cdot d\vec{S}$ *is the flux of the magnetic field through the area.*

We shall call the quantity Φ *magnetic flux.* The SI unit of magnetic flux is called weber which is equivalent to tesla metre^2.

The law described by equation (38.1) is called *Faraday's law of electromagnetic induction.* The flux may be changed in a number of ways. One can change the magnitude of the magnetic field $\vec{B}$ at the site of the loop, the area of the loop or the angle between the area-vector $d\vec{S}$ and the magnetic field $\vec{B}$. In any case, as long as the flux keeps changing, the emf is present. The emf so produced drives an electric current through the loop. If the resistance of the loop is R, the current is

$$i = \frac{\mathcal{E}}{R} = -\frac{1}{R}\frac{d\Phi}{dt}. \qquad \ldots (38.2)$$

The emf developed by a changing flux is called *induced emf* and the current produced by this emf is called *induced current.*

Direction of Induced Current

The direction of the induced current in a loop may be obtained using equation (38.1) or (38.2). The procedure to decide the direction is as follows:

Put an arrow on the loop to choose the positive sense of current. This choice is arbitrary. Using right-hand thumb rule find the positive direction of the normal to the area bounded by the loop. If the fingers curl along the loop in the positive sense, the thumb represents the positive direction of the normal. Calculate the flux $\Phi = \int \vec{B} \cdot d\vec{S}$ through the area bounded by the loop. If the flux increases with time, $\frac{d\Phi}{dt}$ is positive and $\mathcal{E}$ is negative from equation (38.1). Correspondingly, the current is negative. It is, therefore, in the direction opposite to the arrow put on the loop. If Φ decreases with time, $\frac{d\Phi}{dt}$ is negative, $\mathcal{E}$ is positive and the current is along the arrow.

Example 38.1

Figure (38.2) shows a conducting loop placed near a long, straight wire carrying a current i as shown. If the current increases continuously, find the direction of the induced current in the loop.

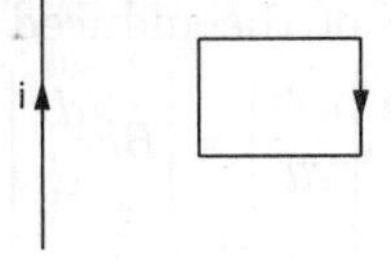

Figure 38.2

Solution : Let us put an arrow on the loop as shown in the figure. The right-hand thumb rule shows that the positive normal to the loop is going into the plane of the diagram. Also, the same rule shows that the magnetic field at the site of the loop due to the current is also going into the plane of the diagram. Thus, $\vec{B}$ and $d\vec{S}$ are along the same direction everywhere so that the flux $\Phi = \int \vec{B} \cdot d\vec{S}$ is positive. If i increases, the magnitude of Φ increases. Since Φ is positive and its magnitude increases, $\frac{d\Phi}{dt}$ is positive. Thus, $\mathscr{E}$ is negative and hence, the current is negative. The current is, therefore, induced in the direction opposite to the arrow.

38.2 LENZ'S LAW

Another way to find the direction of the induced current in a conducting loop is to use Lenz's law. The current is induced by the changing magnetic flux. The induced current itself produces a magnetic field and hence a magnetic flux. This magnetic flux may have the same sign as the original flux or it may have the opposite sign. It strengthens the original flux if it has the same sign and weakens it otherwise. Lenz's law states:

The direction of the induced current is such that it opposes the change that has induced it.

If a current is induced by an increasing flux, it will weaken the original flux. If a current is induced by a decreasing flux, it will strengthen the original flux.

Figure (38.3) shows some situations. In figure (38.3a), a magnet is brought towards a circular loop. The north pole faces the loop. As the magnet gets closer to the loop, the magnetic field increases and hence, the flux of the magnetic field through the area of the loop increases. The induced current should weaken the flux. The original field is away from the magnet, so the induced field should be towards the magnet. Using the right-hand thumb rule, we can find the direction of the current that produces a field towards the magnet.

In figure (38.3b), the wire RS slides towards left so that the area of $PQRS$ decreases. As a result, the magnetic flux through the area $PQRS$ decreases. The induced current should strengthen the original flux. The induced current should produce a magnetic field along the original field which is going into the plane of the diagram. Using the right-hand thumb rule, we find that the induced current should be clockwise as shown in the figure.

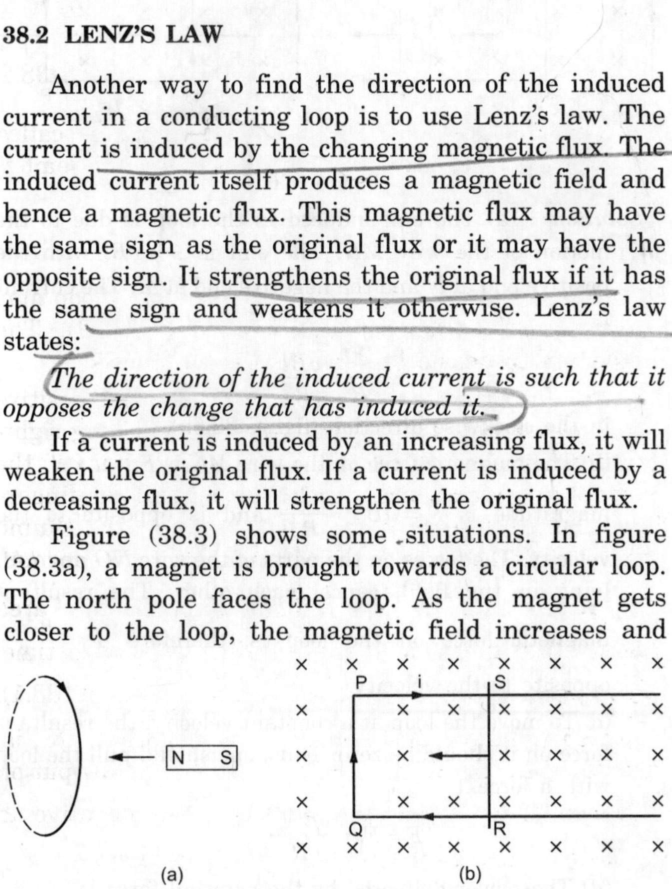

Figure 38.3

38.3 THE ORIGIN OF INDUCED EMF

An electric current is established in a conducting wire when an electric field exists in it. The flow of charges tend to destroy the field and some external mechanism is needed to maintain the electric field in the wire. It is the work done per unit charge by this external mechanism that we call emf. When the magnetic flux through a closed loop changes, an electric current results. What is the external mechanism that maintains the electric field in the loop to drive the current? In other words, what is the mechanism to produce an emf? Let us now investigate this question.

The flux $\int \vec{B} \cdot d\vec{S}$ can be changed by

(a) keeping the magnetic field constant as time passes and moving whole or part of the loop

(b) keeping the loop at rest and changing the magnetic field

(c) combination of (a) and (b), that is, by moving the loop (partly or wholely) as well as by changing the field.

The mechanism by which emf is produced is different in the two basic processes (a) and (b). We now study them under the headings *motional emf* and *induced electric field.*

Motional Emf

Figure (38.4) shows a rod PQ of length l moving in a magnetic field $\vec{B}$ with a constant velocity $\vec{v}$. The length of the rod is perpendicular to the magnetic field and the velocity is perpendicular to both the magnetic

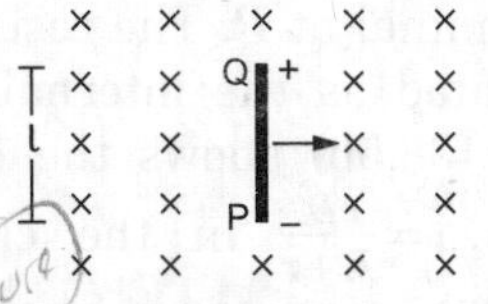

Figure 38.4

field and the rod. The free electrons of the wire also move with this velocity $\vec{v}$ together with the random velocity they have in the rod. The magnetic force due to the random velocity is zero on the average. Thus, the magnetic field exerts an average force $\vec{F}_b = q\vec{v} \times \vec{B}$ on each free electron where $q = -1.6 \times 10^{-19}$ C is the charge on the electron. This force is towards QP and hence the free electrons will move towards P. Negative charge is accumulated at P and positive charge appears at Q. An electrostatic field E is developed within the wire from Q to P. This field exerts a force $\vec{F}_e = q\vec{E}$ on each free electron. The charge keeps on accumulating until a situation comes when $F_b = F_e$

or, $\quad |q\vec{v} \times \vec{B}| = |q\vec{E}| \quad$ or, $\quad vB = E.$

After this, there is no resultant force on the free electrons of the wire PQ. The potential difference between the ends Q and P is

$$V = El = vBl.$$

Thus, it is the magnetic force on the moving free electrons that maintains the potential difference $V = vBl$ and hence produces an emf

$$\mathcal{E} = vBl. \qquad \dots (38.3)$$

As this emf is produced due to the motion of a conductor, it is called *motional emf*.

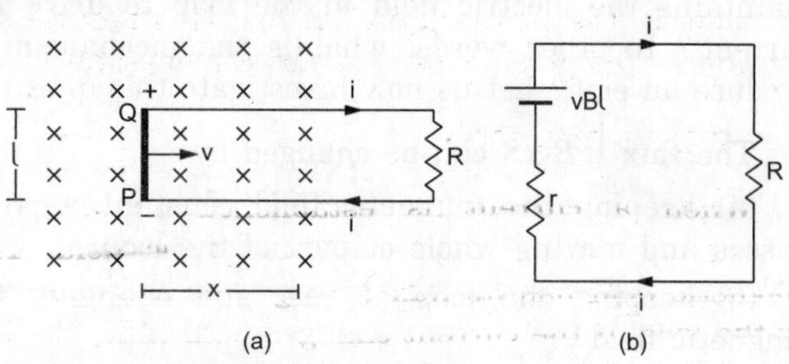

Figure 38.5

If the ends P and Q are connected by an external resistor (figure 38.5a), an electric field is produced in this resistor due to the potential difference. A current is established in the circuit. The electrons flow from P to Q via the external circuit and this tries to neutralise the charges accumulated at P and Q. The magnetic force qvB on the free electrons in the wire QP, however, drives the electrons back from Q to P to maintain the potential difference and hence the current.

Thus, we can replace the moving rod QP by a battery of emf vBl with the positive terminal at Q and the negative terminal at P. The resistance r of the rod QP may be treated as the internal resistance of the battery. Figure (38.5b) shows the equivalent circuit. The current is $i = \dfrac{vBl}{R + r}$ in the clockwise direction (induced current).

We can also find the induced emf and the induced current in the loop in figure (38.5a) from Faraday's law of electromagnetic induction. If x be the length of the circuit in the magnetic field at time t, the magnetic flux through the area bounded by the loop is

$$\Phi = Blx.$$

The magnitude of the induced emf is

$$\mathcal{E} = \left|\frac{d\Phi}{dt}\right| = \left|Bl\frac{dx}{dt}\right|$$

$$= vBl.$$

The current is $i = \dfrac{vBl}{R + r}$. The direction of the current can be worked out from Lenz's law.

Example 38.2

Figure (38.6a) shows a rectangular loop MNOP being pulled out of a magnetic field with a uniform velocity v by applying an external force F. The length MN is equal to l and the total resistance of the loop is R. Find (a) the current in the loop, (b) the magnetic force on the loop, (c) the external force F needed to maintain the velocity, (d) the power delivered by the external force and (e) the thermal power developed in the loop.

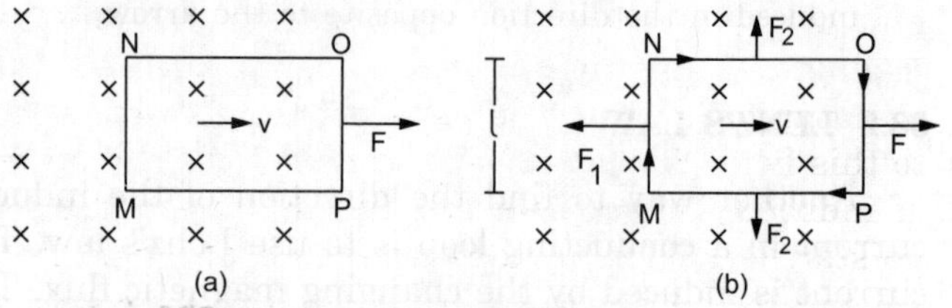

Figure 38.6

Solution : (a) The emf induced in the loop is due to the motion of the wire MN. The emf is $\mathcal{E} = vBl$ with the positive end at N and the negative end at M. The current is

$$i = \frac{\mathcal{E}}{R} = \frac{vBl}{R}$$

in the clockwise direction (figure 38.6b).

(b) The magnetic force on the wire MN is $\vec{F}_1 = i\vec{l} \times \vec{B}$. The magnitude is $F_1 = ilB = \dfrac{vB^2l^2}{R}$ and is opposite to the velocity. The forces on the parts of the wire NO and PM, lying in the field, cancel each other. The resultant magnetic force on the loop is, therefore, $F_1 = \dfrac{B^2l^2v}{R}$ opposite to the velocity.

(c) To move the loop at a constant velocity, the resultant force on it should be zero. Thus, one should pull the loop with a force

$$F = F_1 = \frac{vB^2l^2}{R}.$$

(d) The power delivered by the external force is

$$P = F v = \frac{v^2 B^2 l^2}{R}.$$

(e) The thermal power developed is

$$P = i^2 R = \left(\frac{vBl}{R}\right)^2 R = \frac{v^2 B^2 l^2}{R}.$$

We see that the power delivered by the external force is equal to the thermal power developed in the loop. This is consistent with the principle of conservation of energy.

Induced Electric Field

Consider a conducting loop placed at rest in a magnetic field $\vec{B}$. Suppose, the field is constant till $t = 0$ and then changes with time. An induced current starts in the loop at $t = 0$.

The free electrons were at rest till $t = 0$ (we are not interested in the random motion of the electrons). The magnetic field cannot exert force on electrons at rest. Thus, the magnetic force cannot start the induced current. The electrons may be forced to move only by an electric field and hence we conclude that an electric field appears at $t = 0$. This electric field is produced by the changing magnetic field and not by charged particles according to the Coulomb's law or the Gauss's law. The electric field produced by the changing magnetic field is nonelectrostatic and nonconservative in nature. We cannot define a potential corresponding to this field. We call it *induced electric field*. The lines of induced electric field are closed curves. There are no starting and terminating points of the field lines.

If $\vec{E}$ be the induced electric field, the force on a charge q placed in the field is $q\vec{E}$. The work done per unit charge as the charge moves through $\vec{dl}$ is $\vec{E}\cdot\vec{dl}$. The emf developed in the loop is, therefore,

$$\mathcal{E} = \oint \vec{E}\cdot\vec{dl}.$$

Using Faraday's law of induction,

$$\mathcal{E} = -\frac{d\Phi}{dt}$$

or, $$\oint \vec{E}\cdot\vec{dl} = -\frac{d\Phi}{dt}. \qquad \dots (38.4)$$

The presence of a conducting loop is not necessary to have an induced electric field. As long as $\vec{B}$ keeps changing, the induced electric field is present. If a loop is there, the free electrons start drifting and consequently an induced current results.

38.4 EDDY CURRENT

Consider a solid plate of metal which enters a region having a magnetic field (figure 38.7a). Consider a loop drawn on the plate, a part of which is in the

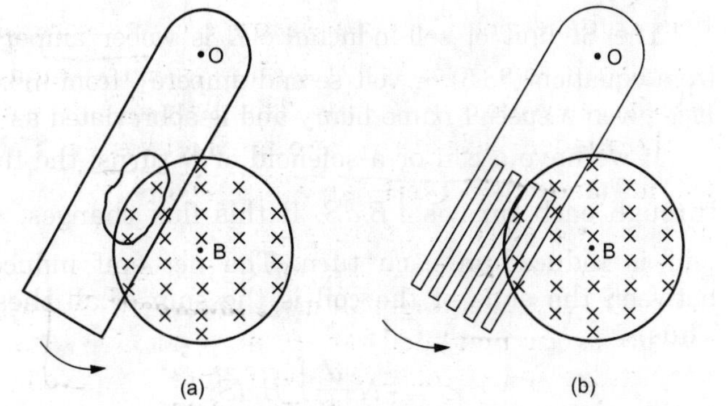

Figure 38.7

field. As the plate moves, the magnetic flux through the area bounded by the loop changes and hence a current is induced. There may be a number of such loops on the plate and hence currents are induced on the surface along a variety of paths. Such currents are called *eddy currents*. The basic idea is that we do not have a definite conducting loop to guide the induced current. The system itself looks for the loops on the surface along which eddy currents are induced. Because of the eddy currents in the metal plate, thermal energy is produced in it. This energy comes at the cost of the kinetic energy of the plate and the plate slows down. This is known as *electromagnetic damping*. To reduce electromagnetic damping, one can cut slots in the plate (figure 38.7b). This reduces the possible paths of the eddy current considerably.

38.5 SELF-INDUCTION

When a current is established in a closed conducting loop, it produces a magnetic field. This magnetic field has its flux through the area bounded by the loop. If the current changes with time, the flux through the loop changes and hence an emf is induced in the loop. This process is called *self-induction*. The name is so chosen because the emf is induced in the loop by changing the current in the same loop.

The magnetic field at any point due to a current is proportional to the current. The magnetic flux through the area bounded by a current-carrying loop is, therefore, proportional to the current. We can write

$$\Phi = Li \qquad \dots (38.5)$$

where L is a constant depending on the geometrical construction of the loop. This constant is called *self-inductance* of the loop. The induced emf $\mathcal{E}$, when the current in the coil changes, is given by

$$\mathcal{E} = -\frac{d\Phi}{dt}.$$

Using equation (38.5),

$$\mathcal{E} = -L\frac{di}{dt}. \qquad \dots (38.6)$$

The SI unit of self-inductance L is weber ampere^{-1} from equation (38.5) or volt second ampere^{-1} from (38.6). It is given a special name henry and is abbreviated as H.

If we have a coil or a solenoid of N turns, the flux through each turn is $\int \vec{B}\cdot d\vec{S}$. If this flux changes, an emf is induced in each turn. The net emf induced between the ends of the coil is the sum of all these. Thus,

$$\mathcal{E} = -N\frac{d}{dt}\int \vec{B}\cdot d\vec{S}.$$

One can compare this with equation (38.6) to get the inductance.

Example 38.3

An average induced emf of 0·20 V *appears in a coil when the current in it is changed from* 5·0 A *in one direction to* 5·0 A *in the opposite direction in* 0·20 s. *Find the self-inductance of the coil.*

Solution :

$$\text{Average } \frac{di}{dt} = \frac{(-5{\cdot}0\text{ A}) - (5{\cdot}0\text{ A})}{0{\cdot}20\text{ s}} = -50\text{ A/s}.$$

$$\text{Using } \mathcal{E} = -L\frac{di}{dt},$$

$$0{\cdot}2\text{ V} = L(50\text{ A/s})$$

$$\text{or, } L = \frac{0{\cdot}2\text{ V}}{50\text{ A/s}} = 4{\cdot}0\text{ mH}.$$

Self-inductance of a Long Solenoid

Consider a long solenoid of radius r having n turns per unit length. Suppose a current i is passed through the solenoid. The magnetic field produced inside the solenoid is $B = \mu_0 ni$. The flux through each turn of the solenoid is

$$\Phi = \int \vec{B}\cdot d\vec{S} = (\mu_0 ni)\pi r^2.$$

The emf induced in each turn is

$$-\frac{d\Phi}{dt} = -\mu_0 n\pi r^2 \frac{di}{dt}.$$

As there are nl turns in a length l of the solenoid, the net emf across a length l is

$$\mathcal{E} = -(nl)(\mu_0 n\pi r^2)\frac{di}{dt}.$$

Comparing with $\mathcal{E} = -L\frac{di}{dt}$, the self-inductance is

$$L = \mu_0 n^2 \pi r^2 l. \quad \dots (38.7)$$

We see that the self-inductance depends only on geometrical factors.

A coil or a solenoid made from thick wire has negligible resistance but a considerable self-inductance. Such an element is called an *ideal inductor* and is indicated by the symbol  .

The self-induced emf in a coil opposes the change in the current that has induced it. This is in accordance with the Lenz's law. If the current is increasing, the induced current will be opposite to the original current. If the current is decreasing, the induced current will be along the original current.

Example 38.4

Consider the circuit shown in figure (38.8). The sliding contact is being pulled towards right so that the resistance in the circuit is increasing. Its value at the instant shown is 12 Ω. *Will the current be more than* 0·50 A *or less than it at this instant ?*

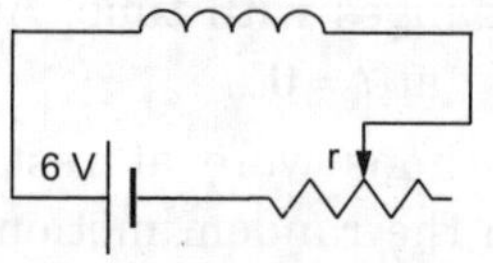

Figure 38.8

Solution : As the sliding contact is being pulled, the current in the circuit changes. An induced emf $\mathcal{E} = -L\frac{di}{dt}$ is produced across the inductor. The net emf in the circuit is $6\text{ V} - L\frac{di}{dt}$ and hence the current is

$$i = \frac{6\text{ V} - L\frac{di}{dt}}{12\ \Omega} \quad \dots \text{(i)}$$

at the instant shown. Now the resistance in the circuit is increasing, the current is decreasing and so $\frac{di}{dt}$ is negative. Thus, the numerator of (i) is more than 6 V and hence i is greater than $\frac{6\text{ V}}{12\ \Omega} = 0{\cdot}50$ A.

38.6 GROWTH AND DECAY OF CURRENT IN AN LR CIRCUIT

Growth of Current

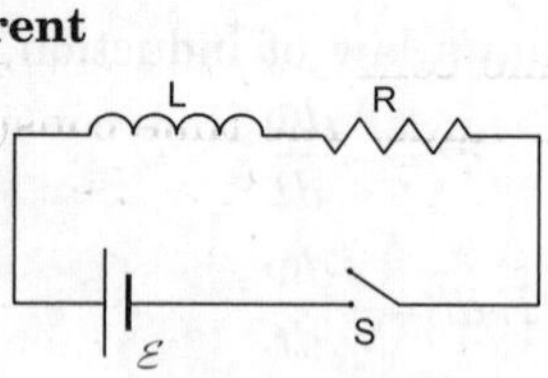

Figure 38.9

Figure (38.9) shows an inductance L, a resistance R and a source of emf $\mathcal{E}$ connected in series through a switch S. Initially, the switch is open and there is no current in the circuit. At $t = 0$, the switch is closed and the circuit is completed. As the current increases in the inductor, a self-induced emf $\left(-L\frac{di}{dt}\right)$ is produced. Using Kirchhoff's loop law,

$$\mathcal{E} - L\frac{di}{dt} = Ri$$

or, $$L\frac{di}{dt}=\mathcal{E}-Ri$$

or, $$\frac{di}{\mathcal{E}-Ri}=\frac{dt}{L}.$$

At $t=0$, $i=0$ and at time t the current is i. Thus,

$$\int_0^i \frac{di}{\mathcal{E}-Ri}=\int_0^t \frac{dt}{L}$$

or, $$-\frac{1}{R}\ln\frac{\mathcal{E}-Ri}{\mathcal{E}}=\frac{t}{L}$$

or, $$\frac{\mathcal{E}-Ri}{\mathcal{E}}=e^{-tR/L}$$

or, $$\mathcal{E}-Ri=\mathcal{E}e^{-tR/L}$$

or, $$i=\frac{\mathcal{E}}{R}(1-e^{-tR/L}). \quad \dots (38.8)$$

The constant L/R has dimensions of time and is called the *time constant* of the LR circuit. Writing $L/R=\tau$ and $\mathcal{E}/R=i_0$, equation (38.8) becomes

$$i=i_0(1-e^{-t/\tau}). \quad \dots (38.9)$$

Figure (38.10) shows the plot of the current versus time. The current gradually rises from $t=0$ and attains the maximum value i_0 after a long time. At $t=\tau$, the current is

$$i=i_0\left(1-\frac{1}{e}\right)=0.63\,i_0.$$

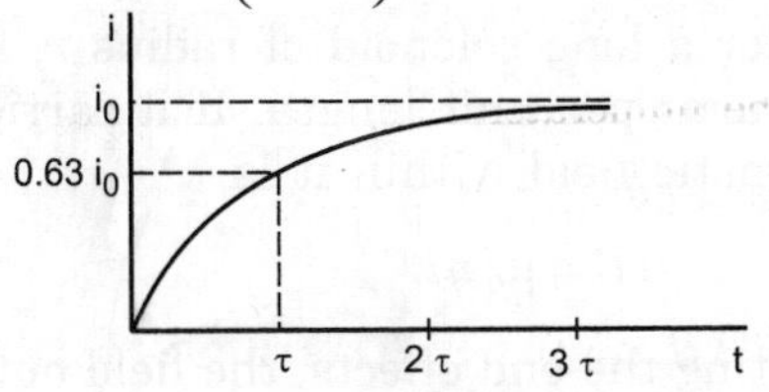

Figure 38.10

Thus, in one time constant, the current reaches 63% of the maximum value. The time constant tells us how fast will the current grow. If the time constant is small, the growth is steep. Equation (38.9) shows that $i=i_0$ at $t=\infty$. In principle, it takes infinite time for the current to attain its maximum value. In practice, however, a small number of time constants may be sufficient for the current to reach almost the maximum value.

Example 38.5

An inductor ($L=20$ mH), a resistor ($R=100\ \Omega$) and a battery ($\mathcal{E}=10$ V) are connected in series. Find (a) the time constant, (b) the maximum current and (c) the time elapsed before the current reaches 99% of the maximum value.

Solution : (a) The time constant is

$$\tau=\frac{L}{R}=\frac{20\text{ mH}}{100\ \Omega}=0.20\text{ ms}.$$

(b) The maximum current is

$$i=\mathcal{E}/R=\frac{10\text{ V}}{100\ \Omega}=0.10\text{ A}.$$

(c) Using $\quad i=i_0(1-e^{-t/\tau})$,

$$0.99\,i_0=i_0(1-e^{-t/\tau})$$

or, $$e^{-t/\tau}=0.01$$

or, $$\frac{t}{\tau}=-\ln(0.01)$$

or, $$t=(0.20\text{ ms})\ln(100)=0.92\text{ ms}.$$

Decay of Current

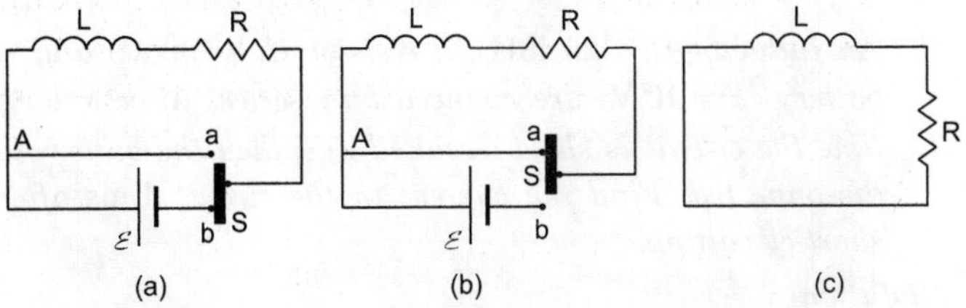

Figure 38.11

Consider the arrangement shown in figure (38.11a). The sliding switch S can be slid up and down. The circuit is complete and a steady current $i=i_0$ is maintained through the circuit. Suddenly at $t=0$, the switch S is moved to connect the point a. This completes the circuit through the wire Aa and disconnects the battery from the circuit (figure 38.11b). The special arrangement of the switch ensures that the circuit through the wire Aa is completed before the battery is disconnected. The equivalent circuit is redrawn in figure (38.11c).

As the battery is disconnected, the current decreases in the circuit. This induces an emf $\left(-L\frac{di}{dt}\right)$ in the inductor. As this is the only emf in the circuit,

$$-L\frac{di}{dt}=Ri$$

or, $$\frac{di}{i}=-\frac{R}{L}dt.$$

At $t=0$, $i=i_0$. If the current at time t be i,

$$\int_{i_0}^{i}\frac{di}{i}=\int_0^t -\frac{R}{L}dt$$

or, $$\ln\frac{i}{i_0}=-\frac{R}{L}t$$

or, $$i=i_0e^{-tR/L} \quad \dots (38.10)$$

or, $$i=i_0e^{-t/\tau} \quad \dots (38.11)$$

where $\tau=L/R$ is the time constant of the circuit.

We see that the current does not suddenly fall to zero. It gradually decreases as time passes. At $t = \tau$,

$$i = i_0 / e = 0{\cdot}37\, i_0 .$$

The current reduces to 37% of the initial value in one time constant, i.e., 63% of the decay is complete. If the time constant is small, the decay is steep. Figure (38.12) shows the plot of the current against time.

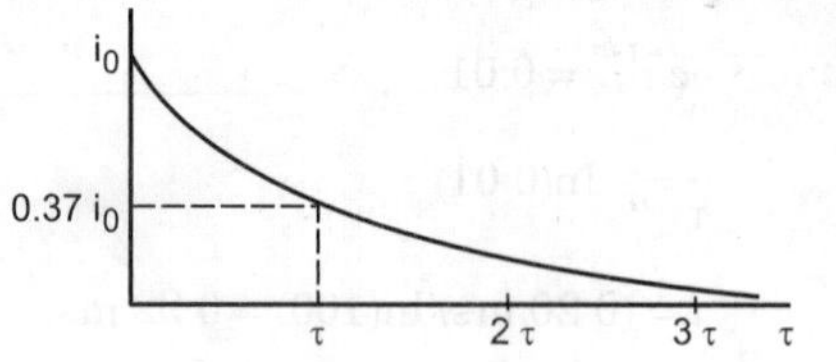

Figure 38.12

Example 38.6

An inductor ($L = 20$ mH), *a resistor* ($R = 100\ \Omega$) *and a battery* ($\mathcal{E} = 10$ V) *are connected in series. After a long time the circuit is short-circuited and then the battery is disconnected. Find the current in the circuit* 1 ms *after short-circuiting.*

Solution :

The initial current is $i = i_0 = \mathcal{E}/R = \dfrac{10\ \text{V}}{100\ \Omega} = 0{\cdot}10$ A.

The time constant is $\tau = L/R = \dfrac{20\ \text{mH}}{100\ \Omega} = 0{\cdot}20$ ms.

The current at $t = 1$ ms is

$$i = i_0\, e^{-t/\tau}$$

$$= (0{\cdot}10\ \text{A})\, e^{-(1\ \text{ms}/0{\cdot}20\ \text{ms})}$$

$$= (0{\cdot}10\ \text{A})\, e^{-5} = 6{\cdot}7 \times 10^{-4}\ \text{A}.$$

38.7 ENERGY STORED IN AN INDUCTOR

When a capacitor is charged, electric field builds up between its plates and energy is stored in it. Similarly, when an inductor carries a current, a magnetic field builds up in it and magnetic energy is stored in it.

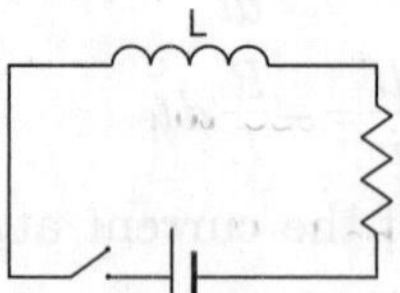

Figure 38.13

Consider the circuit shown in figure (38.13). As the connections are made, the current grows in the circuit and the magnetic field increases in the inductor. Part of the work done by the battery during the process is stored in the inductor as magnetic field energy and the rest appears as thermal energy in the resistor. After sufficient time, the current and hence the magnetic field becomes constant and further work done by the battery appears completely as thermal energy. If i be the current in the circuit at time t, we have

$$\mathcal{E} - L\frac{di}{dt} = iR$$

or, $$\mathcal{E}\, i\, dt = i^2 R\, dt + L\, i\, di$$

or, $$\int_0^t \mathcal{E}\, i\, dt = \int_0^t i^2 R\, dt + \int_0^i L\, i\, di$$

or, $$\int_0^t \mathcal{E}\, i\, dt = \int_0^t i^2 R\, dt + \frac{1}{2} L i^2. \quad \text{... (i)}$$

Now ($i\, dt$) is the charge flowing through the circuit during the time t to $t + dt$. Thus, ($\mathcal{E}\, i\, dt$) is the work done by the battery in this period. The quantity on the left-hand side of equation (i) is, therefore, the total work done by the battery in time 0 to t. Similarly, the first term on the right-hand side of equation (i) is the total thermal energy (Joule heat) developed in the resistor in time t. Thus $\frac{1}{2} Li^2$ is the energy stored in the inductor as the current in it increases from 0 to i. As the energy is zero when the current is zero, the energy stored in an inductor, carrying a current i, is

$$U = \frac{1}{2} L i^2. \quad \text{... (38.12)}$$

Energy Density in Magnetic Field

Consider a long solenoid of radius r, length l and having n turns per unit length. If it carries a current i, the magnetic field within it is

$$B = \mu_0 n i.$$

Neglecting the end effects, the field outside is zero. The self-inductance of this solenoid is, from equation (38.7),

$$L = \mu_0 n^2 \pi r^2 l.$$

The magnetic energy is, therefore,

$$U = \frac{1}{2} Li^2 = \frac{1}{2} \mu_0 n^2 \pi r^2 l\, i^2$$

$$= \frac{1}{2\,\mu_0} (\mu_0 n i)^2 V = \frac{B^2}{2\mu_0} V$$

where $V = \pi r^2 l$ is the volume enclosed by the solenoid. As the field is assumed uniform throughout the volume of the solenoid and zero outside, the energy per unit volume in the magnetic field, i.e., the energy density, is

$$u = \frac{U}{V} = \frac{B^2}{2\mu_0} \cdot \quad \text{... (38.13)}$$

In deriving this equation, we have assumed that there is no magnetic material at the site of the field.

Example 38.7

Calculate the energy stored in an inductor of inductance 50 mH *when a current of* 2·0 A *is passed through it.*

Solution : The energy stored is

$$U = \frac{1}{2} Li^2 = \frac{1}{2} (50 \times 10^{-3} \text{ H}) (2{\cdot}0 \text{ A})^2 = 0{\cdot}10 \text{ J}.$$

38.8 MUTUAL INDUCTION

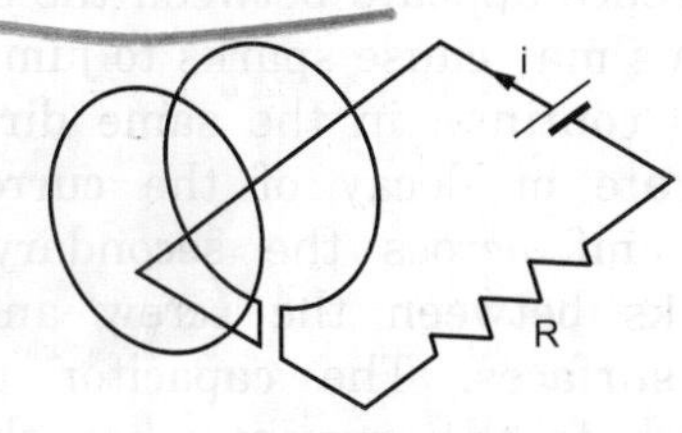

Figure 38.14

Suppose two closed circuits are placed close to each other and a current i is passed in one. It produces a magnetic field and this field has a flux Φ through the area bounded by the other circuit. As the magnetic field at a point is proportional to the current producing it, we can write

$$\Phi = Mi \quad \dots (38.14)$$

where M is a constant depending on the geometrical shapes of the two circuits and their placing. This constant is called *mutual inductance* of the given pair of circuits. If the same current i is passed in the second circuit and the flux is calculated through the area bounded by the first circuit, the same proportionality constant M appears. If there are more than one turns in a circuit, one has to add the flux through each turn before applying equation (38.14).

If the current i in one circuit changes with time, the flux through the area bounded by the second circuit also changes. Thus, an emf is induced in the second circuit. This phenomenon is called *mutual induction.* From equation (38.14), the induced emf is

$$\mathcal{E} = -\frac{d\Phi}{dt}$$

$$= -M\frac{di}{dt} \cdot \quad \dots (38.15)$$

Example 38.8

A solenoid S_1 is placed inside another solenoid S_2 as shown in figure (38.15). The radii of the inner and the outer solenoids are r_1 and r_2 respectively and the numbers of turns per unit length are n_1 and n_2 respectively. Consider a length l of each solenoid. Calculate the mutual inductance between them.

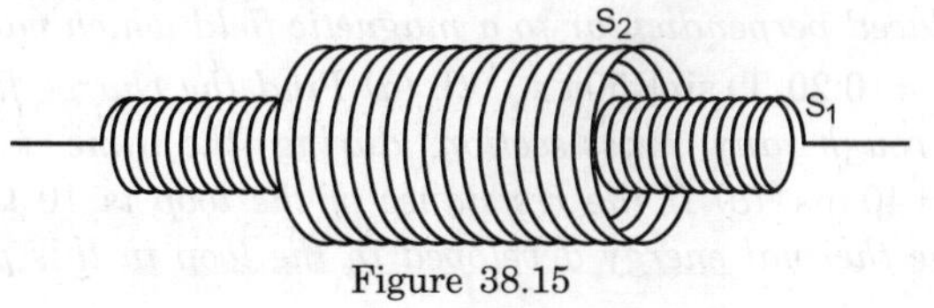

Figure 38.15

Solution : Suppose a current i is passed through the inner solenoid S_1. A magnetic field $B = \mu_0 n_1 i$ is produced inside S_1 whereas the field outside it is zero. The flux through each turn of S_2 is

$$B\pi r_1^2 = \mu_0 n_1 i \pi r_1^2.$$

The total flux through all the turns in a length l of S_2 is

$$\Phi = (\mu_0 n_1 i \pi r_1^2) n_2 l = (\mu_0 n_1 n_2 \pi r_1^2 l)\, i.$$

Thus, $$M = \mu_0 n_1 n_2 \pi r_1^2 l. \quad \dots \text{(i)}$$

38.9 INDUCTION COIL

An induction coil is used to produce a large emf from a source of low emf. The schematic design of an induction coil known as Ruhmkorff's induction coil is shown in figure (38.16). It consists of a primary coil T wound over a laminated soft-iron core and a secondary coil S wound coaxially over the primary coil. The secondary coil is connected to two rods G_1 and G_2. The separation between the rods may be adjusted.

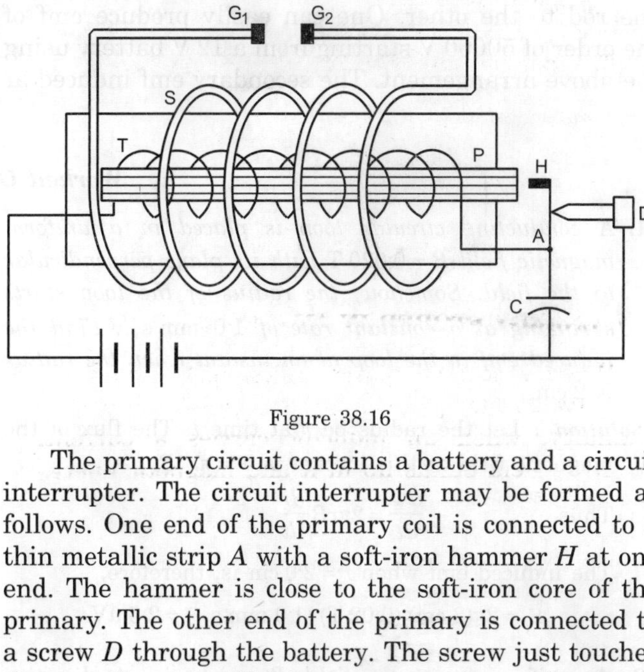

Figure 38.16

The primary circuit contains a battery and a circuit interrupter. The circuit interrupter may be formed as follows. One end of the primary coil is connected to a thin metallic strip A with a soft-iron hammer H at one end. The hammer is close to the soft-iron core of the primary. The other end of the primary is connected to a screw D through the battery. The screw just touches the metallic strip. This arrangement forms the circuit interrupter. A capacitor C is connected in parallel to the circuit interrupter as shown in the figure.

Working

(a) *Make and break*: When the screw D touches the strip A, the primary circuit is completed and a current is established in the primary circuit. Because of the current in the primary coil, the soft-iron core becomes magnetized. It attracts the iron hammer H and the contact between the screw D and the strip A is broken. The current stops in the primary circuit, the iron core is demagnetized and the strip acquires its natural position. The screw D again touches the strip and the current is established. This process of successive 'make and break' continues.

(b) *Growth and decay of current in the primary*: When the contact between the screw and the strip is made, the current grows in the primary circuit. Because of the self-inductance of the primary coil, the growth will be slow. When the contact is broken, the current suddenly decreases to zero. The rate of decay of the current when the circuit is broken is quite high as compared to the rate of growth of the current when the circuit is closed.

(c) *Induced emf in the secondary*: As the current i in the primary changes, the magnetic flux linked with the secondary also changes. This induces an emf across the ends of the secondary coil. This emf appears between the rods G_1 and G_2. When the circuit breaks, $\left|\frac{di}{dt}\right|$ is very large and hence the emf induced in the secondary is also very large. With suitable separation between the rods, one can see sparks jumping from one rod to the other. One can easily produce emf of the order of 50000 V starting from a 12 V battery using the above arrangement. The secondary emf induced at the time of break is in the opposite direction to that induced at the time of make. The high emf produced between the rods can be used to operate equipments like a discharge tube.

(d) *Role of the capacitor*: When the circuit is broken, a large emf is produced due to the self-induction in the primary which tends to drive a current in the direction of the original current. A large potential difference appears between the screw D and the strip A. This may cause sparks to jump and hence the current to continue in the same direction. This reduces the rate of decay of the current thereby reducing the emf across the secondary. Secondly, repeated sparks between the screw and the strip damage the surfaces. The capacitor provides an alternative path to the current when the circuit is broken. The current charges the capacitor. Thus, sparks do not occur across the screw–strip gap and the current drops more rapidly. This increases $\left|\frac{di}{dt}\right|$ and hence the induced emf across the secondary. Not only this, the charged capacitor soon gets discharged by sending a current through the primary in the opposite direction. Thus, the currrent changes not only from i to 0 but from i to almost $-i$. The change in flux is almost doubled and correspondingly, the induced emf across the secondary is also increased.

Worked Out Examples

1. *A conducting circular loop is placed in a uniform magnetic field $B = 0{\cdot}020$ T with its plane perpendicular to the field. Somehow, the radius of the loop starts shrinking at a constant rate of $1{\cdot}0\ \text{mm s}^{-1}$. Find the induced emf in the loop at an instant when the radius is 2 cm.*

Solution : Let the radius be r at time t. The flux of the magnetic field at this instant is $\Phi = \pi r^2 B$.

Thus, $$\frac{d\Phi}{dt} = 2\pi r B \frac{dr}{dt}.$$

The induced emf when $r = 2{\cdot}0$ cm is, therefore,

$$\mathcal{E} = 2\pi(2\ \text{cm})\,(0{\cdot}02\ \text{T})\,(1{\cdot}0\ \text{mm s}^{-1}) = 2{\cdot}5\ \mu\text{V}.$$

2. *A uniform magnetic field B exists in a direction perpendicular to the plane of a square frame made of copper wire. The wire has a diameter of 2 mm and a total length of 40 cm. The magntic field changes with time at a steady rate $dB/dt = 0{\cdot}02\ \text{T s}^{-1}$. Find the current induced in the frame. Resistivity of copper $= 1{\cdot}7 \times 10^{-8}\ \Omega$ m.*

Solution :

The area A of the loop $= \left(\frac{40\ \text{cm}}{4}\right)\left(\frac{40\ \text{cm}}{4}\right) = 0{\cdot}01\ \text{m}^2.$

If the magnetic field at an instant is B, the flux through the frame at that instant will be $\Phi = BA$. As the area remains constant, the magnitude of the emf induced will be

$$\mathcal{E} = \frac{d\Phi}{dt} = A\frac{dB}{dt}$$
$$= (0{\cdot}01\ \text{m}^2)\,(0{\cdot}02\ \text{T/s}) = 2 \times 10^{-4}\ \text{V}.$$

The resistance of the loop is $R = \rho \frac{l}{A}$

$$= \frac{(1{\cdot}7 \times 10^{-8}\ \Omega\ \text{m})\,(40\ \text{cm})}{\pi \times 1\ \text{mm}^2}$$
$$= \frac{(1{\cdot}7 \times 10^{-8}\ \Omega\ \text{m})\,(40 \times 10^{-2}\ \text{m})}{3{\cdot}14 \times 1 \times 10^{-6}\ \text{m}^2} = 2{\cdot}16 \times 10^{-3}\ \Omega.$$

Hence, the current induced in the loop will be

$$i = \frac{2 \times 10^{-4}\ \text{V}}{2{\cdot}16 \times 10^{-3}\ \Omega} = 9{\cdot}3 \times 10^{-2}\ \text{A}.$$

3. *A conducting circular loop of face area $2{\cdot}5 \times 10^{-3}\ \text{m}^2$ is placed perpendicular to a magnetic field which varies as $B = (0{\cdot}20\ \text{T}) \sin[(50\pi\ \text{s}^{-1})t]$. (a) Find the charge flowing through any cross-section during the time $t = 0$ to $t = 40$ ms. (b) If the resistance of the loop is 10 Ω, find the thermal energy developed in the loop in this period.*

Solution : The face area of the loop is $A = 2{\cdot}5 \times 10^{-3}\ \mathrm{m}^2$ and the magnetic field changes as $B = B_0 \sin \omega t$ where $B_0 = 0{\cdot}20\ \mathrm{T}$ and $\omega = 50\pi\ \mathrm{s}^{-1}$. The resistance of the loop is $R = 10\ \Omega$.

The flux through the loop at time t is

$$\Phi = B_0 A \sin \omega t.$$

The emf induced is

$$\mathcal{E} = -\frac{d\Phi}{dt} = -B_0 A\omega \cos \omega t.$$

The current is $i = \dfrac{\mathcal{E}}{R} = -\dfrac{B_0 A\omega}{R} \cos \omega t = -i_0 \cos \omega t.$

The current changes sinusoidally with the time period

$$T = \frac{2\pi}{\omega} = \frac{2\pi}{50\pi\ \mathrm{s}^{-1}} = 40\ \mathrm{ms}.$$

(a) The charge flowing through any cross-section in 40 ms is

$$Q = \int_0^T i dt = -i_0 \int_0^T \cos \omega t\, dt$$

$$= -\frac{i_0}{\omega}[\sin \omega t]_0^T = 0.$$

(b) The thermal energy produced in 40 ms is

$$H = \int_0^T i^2 R dt = i_0^2 R \int_0^T \cos^2 \omega t\, dt$$

$$= \frac{i_0^2 R}{2} \int_0^T (1 + \cos 2\omega t)\, dt$$

$$= \frac{i_0^2 R}{2}\left[t + \frac{\sin 2\omega t}{2\omega}\right]_0^T$$

$$= \frac{i_0^2 RT}{2} = \frac{B_0^2 A^2 \omega^2}{2R^2} R\left(\frac{2\pi}{\omega}\right) = \frac{\pi B_0^2 A^2 \omega}{R}$$

$$= \frac{\pi \times (0{\cdot}20\ \mathrm{T})^2 \times (2{\cdot}5 \times 10^{-3}\ \mathrm{m}^2)^2 \times (50\pi\ \mathrm{s}^{-1})}{10\ \Omega}$$

$$= 1{\cdot}25 \times 10^{-5}\ \mathrm{J}.$$

4. *A long solenoid of radius* 2 cm *has* 100 turns/cm *and is surrounded by a* 100-turn *coil of radius* 4 cm *having a total resistance of* 20 Ω. *The coil is connected to a galvanometer as shown in figure (38-W1). If the current in the solenoid is changed from* 5 A *in one direction to* 5 A *in the opposite direction, find the charge which flows through the galvanometer.*

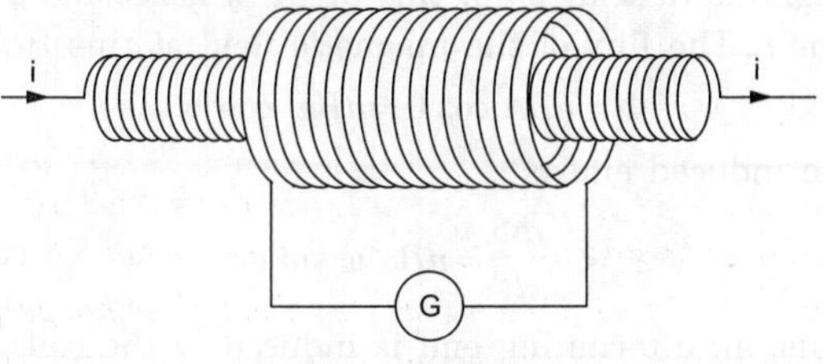

Figure 38-W1

Solution : If the current in the solenoid is i, the magnetic field inside the solenoid is $B = \mu_0 ni$ parallel to its axis. Outside the solenoid, the field will be zero. The flux of the magnetic field through the coil will be $\Phi = B\pi r^2 N$ where r is the radius of the solenoid and N is the number of turns in the coil. The induced emf will have magnitude

$$\frac{d\Phi}{dt} = N\pi r^2 \frac{dB}{dt} = \pi r^2 N\mu_0 n \frac{di}{dt}.$$

If R denotes the resistance of the coil, the current through the galvanometer is

$$I = \frac{\pi r^2 N}{R} \mu_0 n \frac{di}{dt}$$

or, $$I\, dt = \frac{\pi r^2 N}{R} \mu_0 n\, di.$$

The total charge passing through the galvanometer is

$$\Delta Q = \int I\, dt = \frac{\pi r^2 N}{R} \mu_0 n \int di$$

$$= \frac{\pi r^2 N\mu_0 n}{R} \Delta i$$

$$= \frac{\pi(2\ \mathrm{cm})^2 \times 100 \times 4\pi \times 10^{-7}\ \mathrm{TmA^{-1}} \times 100\ \mathrm{cm}^{-1} \times 10\ \mathrm{A}}{20\ \Omega}$$

$$\approx 8 \times 10^{-4}\ \mathrm{C} = 800\ \mu\mathrm{C}.$$

5. *The magnetic field B shown in figure (38-W2) is directed into the plane of the paper. ACDA is a semicircular conducting loop of radius r with the centre at O. The loop is now made to rotate clockwise with a constant angular velocity ω about an axis passing through O and perpendicular to the plane of the paper. The resistance of the loop is R. Obtain an expression for the magnitude of the induced current in the loop. Plot a graph between the induced current i and ωt, for two periods of rotation.*

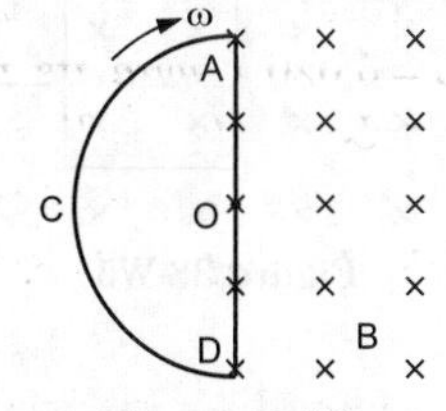

Figure 38-W2

Solution : When the loop rotates through an angle θ, which is less than π (figure 38-W3a), the area inside the field region is

$$A = \frac{\theta}{\pi}\frac{\pi r^2}{2} = \frac{\theta r^2}{2} = \frac{\omega t r^2}{2}.$$

The flux of the magnetic field at time t is

$$\Phi = BA = B\frac{\omega t r^2}{2}.$$

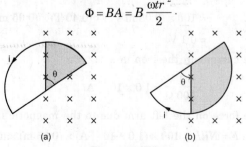

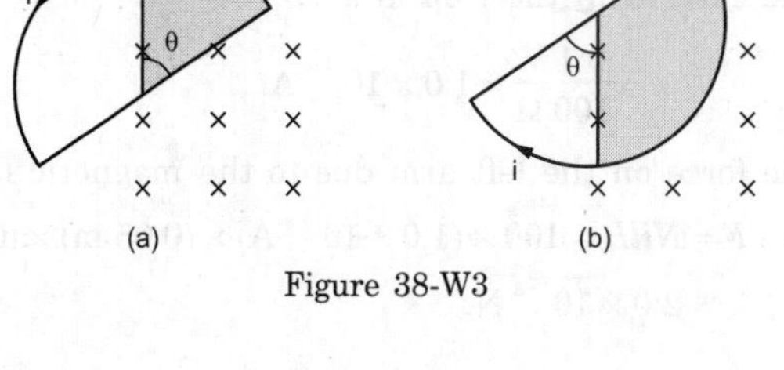

Figure 38-W3

The induced emf $= -\frac{d\Phi}{dt} = -\frac{B\omega r^2}{2}$.

The magnitude of the induced current will be

$$i = \frac{B\omega r^2}{2R}.$$

As the flux is increasing, the direction of the induced current will be anticlockwise so that the field due to the induced current is opposite to the original field.

After half a rotation, the area in the field region will start decreasing (figure 38-W3b) and will be given by

$$A(t) = \frac{\pi r^2}{2} - \frac{\omega t r^2}{2}.$$

Hence, the induced current will have the same magnitude but opposite sense. The plot for two time periods is shown in figure (38-W4).

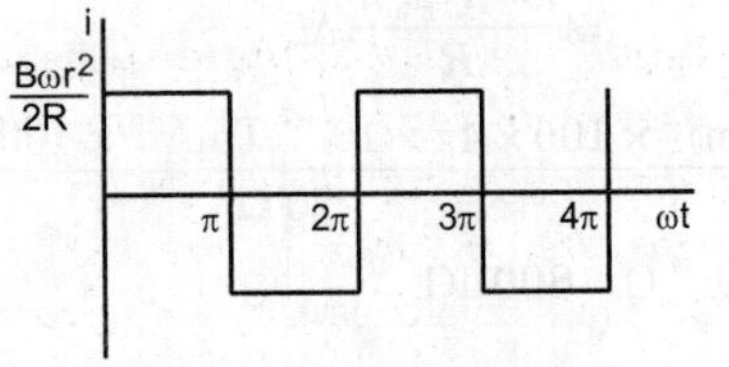

Figure 38-W4

6. *Figure (38-W5) shows a square loop having 100 turns, an area of $2{\cdot}5 \times 10^{-3}$ m^2 and a resistance of 100 Ω. The magnetic field has a magnitude $B = 0{\cdot}40$ T. Find the work done in pulling the loop out of the field, slowly and uniformly in 1·0 s.*

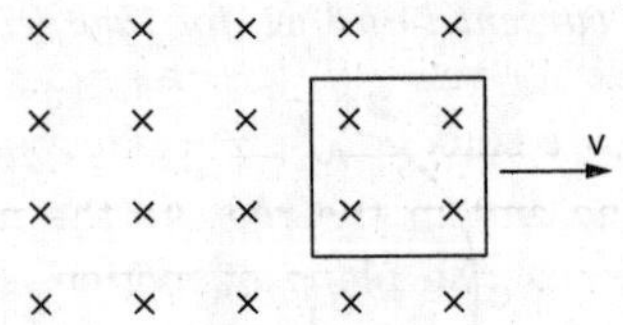

Figure 38-W5

Solution :

The side of the square is

$$l = \sqrt{2{\cdot}5 \times 10^{-3}\ \text{m}^2} = 0{\cdot}05\ \text{m}.$$

As it is uniformly pulled out in 1·0 s, the speed of the loop is

$$v = 0{\cdot}05\ \text{m s}^{-1}.$$

The emf induced in the left arm of the loop is

$$\mathcal{E} = NvBl$$
$$= 100 \times (0{\cdot}05\ \text{m s}^{-1}) \times (0{\cdot}40\ \text{T}) \times (0{\cdot}05\ \text{m})$$
$$= 0{\cdot}1\ \text{V}.$$

The current in the loop is

$$i = \frac{0{\cdot}1\ \text{V}}{100\ \Omega} = 1{\cdot}0 \times 10^{-3}\ \text{A}.$$

The force on the left arm due to the magnetic field is

$$F = NilB = 100 \times (1{\cdot}0 \times 10^{-3}\ \text{A}) \times (0{\cdot}05\ \text{m}) \times (0{\cdot}40\ \text{T})$$
$$= 2{\cdot}0 \times 10^{-3}\ \text{N}.$$

This force is towards left in the figure. To pull the loop uniformly, an external force of $2{\cdot}0 \times 10^{-3}$ N towards right must be applied. The work done by this force is

$$W = (2{\cdot}0 \times 10^{-3}\ \text{N}) \times (0{\cdot}05\ \text{m}) = 1{\cdot}0 \times 10^{-4}\ \text{J}.$$

7. *Magadh Express takes* 16 hours *to cover the distance of* 960 km *between Patna and Gaziabad. The rails are separated by* 130 cm *and the vertical component of the earth's magnetic field is* $4{\cdot}0 \times 10^{-5}$ T. *(a) Find the average emf induced across the width of the train. (b) If the leakage resistance between the rails is* 100 Ω, *find the retarding force on the train due to the magnetic field.*

Solution : As the train moves in a magnetic field, a motional emf $\mathcal{E} = vBl$ is produced across its width. Here B is the component of the magnetic field in a direction perpendicular to the plane of the motion, i.e., the vertical component.

The speed of the train is $v = \frac{960\ \text{km}}{16\ \text{h}} = 16{\cdot}67\ \text{m s}^{-1}$.

Thus, $\mathcal{E} = (16{\cdot}67\ \text{m s}^{-1})\,(4{\cdot}0 \times 10^{-5}\ \text{T})\,(1{\cdot}30\ \text{m})$

$$= 8{\cdot}6 \times 10^{-4}\ \text{V}.$$

The leakage current is $i = \mathcal{E}/R$ and the retarding force is

$$F = ilB = \frac{8{\cdot}6 \times 10^{-4}\ \text{V}}{100\ \Omega} \times 1{\cdot}3\ \text{m} \times 4{\cdot}0 \times 10^{-5}\ \text{T}$$
$$= 4{\cdot}47 \times 10^{-10}\ \text{N}.$$

8. *A square-shaped coil of edge a having n turns is rotated with a uniform angular velocity ω about one of its diagonals which is kept fixed in a horizontal position (figure 38-W6). A uniform magnetic field B exists in the vertical direction. Find the emf induced in the coil.*

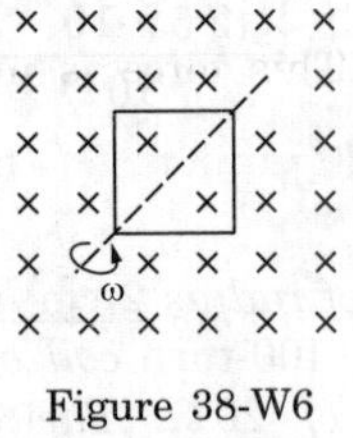

Figure 38-W6

Solution : The area of the square frame is $A = a^2$. If the normal to the frame makes an angle $\theta = 0$ with the magnetic field at $t = 0$, this angle will become $\theta = \omega t$ at time t. The flux of the magnetic field at this time is

$$\Phi = nBA\cos\theta = nBa^2\cos\omega t.$$

The induced emf is

$$\mathcal{E} = -\frac{d\Phi}{dt} = nBa^2\omega\sin\omega t.$$

Thus, an alternating emf is induced in the coil.

9. *A conducting circular loop of radius r is rotated about its diameter at a constant angular velocity ω in a*

magnetic field B perpendicular to the axis of rotation. In what position of the loop is the induced emf zero ?

Solution : Suppose, the normal to the loop is parallel to the magnetic field at $t = 0$. At time t, the normal will make an angle $\theta = \omega t$ with this position. The flux of the magnetic field through the loop is

$$\Phi = B\pi r^2 \cos \omega t$$

so that the induced emf at time t is

$$\mathcal{E} = \omega B\pi r^2 \sin \omega t.$$

This is zero when $\omega t = n\pi$, i.e., when $\theta = 0, \pi, 2\pi, \ldots$, etc. These are the positions when the plane of the loop is normal to the magnetic field. It may be noted that at these positions, the flux has the maximum magnitude.

10. *Figure (38-W7) shows a horizontal magnetic field which is uniform above the dotted line and is zero below it. A long, rectangular, conducting loop of width L, mass m and resistance R is placed partly above and partly below the dotted line with the lower edge parallel to it. With what velocity should it be pushed downwards so that it may continue to fall without any acceleration ?*

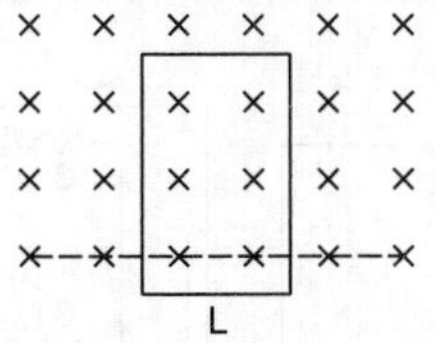

Figure 38-W7

Solution : Let the uniform velocity of fall be v. The emf is induced across the upper wire and its magnitude is $\mathcal{E} = vBl$. The current induced in the frame is

$$i = \frac{vBl}{R}$$

so that, the magnetic force on the upper arm is $F = ilB = \frac{vB^2l^2}{R}$. This force is in the upward direction. As the frame falls uniformly, this force should balance its weight. Thus,

$$mg = \frac{vB^2l^2}{R}$$

or, $$v = \frac{mgR}{B^2l^2}.$$

11. *Figure (38-W8a) shows a wire of length l which can slide on a U-shaped rail of negligible resistance. The resistance of the wire is R. The wire is pulled to the right with a constant speed v. Draw an equivalent circuit diagram representing the induced emf by a battery. Find the current in the wire using this diagram.*

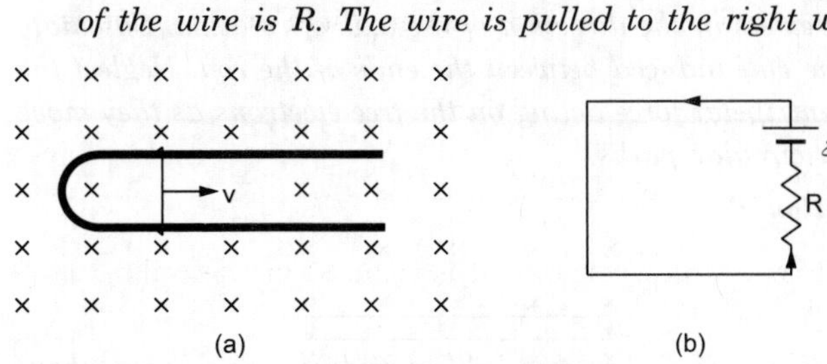

Figure 38-W8

Solution : The emf is induced due to the moving wire. The magnitude of this emf is $\mathcal{E} = vBl$. As the wire moves towards right, the force $q\vec{v} \times \vec{B}$ on a positive charge acts in the upward direction in the figure. The positive terminal of the equivalent battery appears upwards. The resistance of the wire acts as the internal resistance of the equivalent battery. The equivalent circuit is drawn in figure (38-W8b).

The current in the circuit is, from Ohm's law,

$$i = \frac{\mathcal{E}}{R} = \frac{vBl}{R}.$$

It is in the upward direction along the wire.

12. *A rod of length l is translating at a velocity v making an angle θ with its length. A uniform magnetic field B exists in a direction perpendicular to the plane of motion. Calculate the emf induced in the rod. Draw a figure representing the induced emf by an equivalent battery.*

Solution :

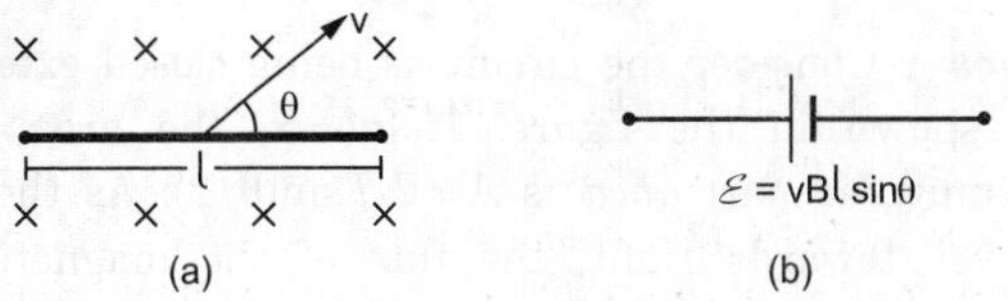

Figure 38-W9

The situation is shown in figure (38-W9a). The component of the velocity perpendicular to the length of the rod is $v_\perp = v \sin\theta$. Only this component is effective in producing the emf in the rod. As the magnetic field is perpendicular to the plane of motion, the emf induced across the ends is

$$\mathcal{E} = v_\perp Bl = vBl \sin\theta.$$

In the figure shown, the positive charges of the rod shift towards left due to the force $q\vec{v} \times \vec{B}$. Thus, the left side of the rod is electrically positive. Figure (38-W9b) shows the equivalent battery.

13. *The horizontal component of the earth's magnetic field at a place is* $3{\cdot}0 \times 10^{-4}$ T *and the dip is* 53°. *A metal rod of length* 25 cm *is placed in the north–south direction and is moved at a constant speed of* 10 cm s^{-1} *towards east. Calculate the emf induced in the rod.*

Solution : The induced emf is $\mathcal{E} = vBl$ where l is the length of the rod, v is its speed in the perpendicular direction and B is the component of the magnetic field perpendicular to both l and v. In the present case, B is the vertical component of the earth's magnetic field. The dip at a place is given by

$$\tan \delta = \frac{B_V}{B_H}$$

or, $$B_V = B_H \tan \delta$$

$$= (3{\cdot}0 \times 10^{-4}\ \text{T}) \tan 53° = 4{\cdot}0 \times 10^{-4}\ \text{T}.$$

The emf induced is $\mathcal{E} = vBl$

$$= (0{\cdot}10\ \text{m s}^{-1}) \times (4{\cdot}0 \times 10^{-4}\ \text{T}) \times (0{\cdot}25\ \text{m})$$

$$= 1{\cdot}0 \times 10^{-5}\ \text{V} = 10\ \mu\text{V}.$$

14. *An angle aob made of a conducting wire moves along its bisector through a magnetic field B as suggested by figure (38-W10a). Find the emf induced between the two free ends if the magnetic field is perpendicular to the plane of the angle.*

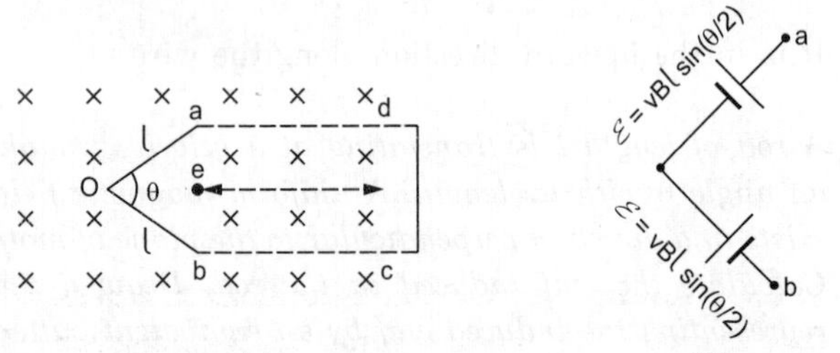

Figure 38-W10

Solution : Consider the circuit as being closed externally, as shown in the figure. If $ad = x$, the area of the rectangular part $abcd$ is $A = 2xl \sin(\theta/2)$. As the angle moves towards right, the flux of the magnetic field through this rectangular area decreases at the rate

$$\frac{d\Phi}{dt} = B\frac{dA}{dt} = 2Blv \sin(\theta/2).$$

This is also the rate of decrease of the flux through the closed circuit shown in the figure. So the induced emf is

$$\mathcal{E} = 2Blv \sin(\theta/2).$$

As the emf is induced solely because of the movement of the angle, this is the emf induced between its ends.

Alternative method

The rod oa is equivalent to a battery of emf $vBl \sin(\theta/2)$. The positive charges of oa shift towards a due to the force $q\vec{v} \times \vec{B}$. The positive terminal of the battery appears towards a. Similarly, the rod ob is equivalent to a battery of emf $vBl \sin(\theta/2)$ with the positive terminal towards o. The equivalent circuit is shown in figure (38-W10b). Clearly, the emf between the points a and b is $2\,Blv \sin(\theta/2)$.

15. *Figure (38-W11a) shows a wire ab of length l and resistance R which can slide on a smooth pair of rails. I_g is a current generator which supplies a constant current i in the circuit. If the wire ab slides at a speed v towards right, find the potential difference between a and b.*

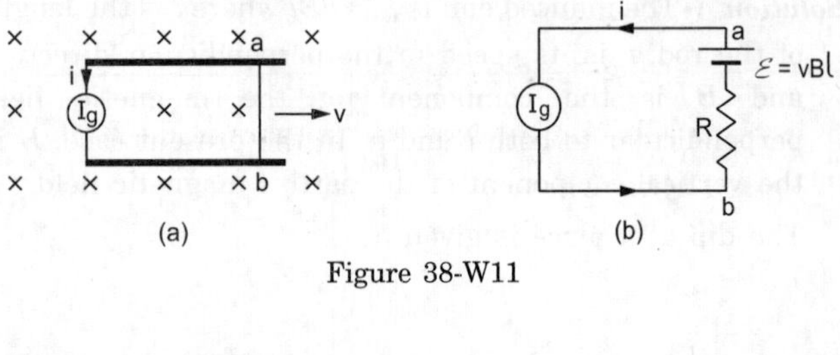

Figure 38-W11

Solution : The moving wire ab is equivalent to a battery of emf vBl having a resistance R. If it moves towards right and the magnetic field is going into the plane of the figure, the force $q\vec{v} \times \vec{B}$ will push the positive charges towards a. Thus the positive terminal of the equivalent battery is towards a. An equivalent circuit is shown in figure (38-W13b). The potential difference between a and b is

$$V_a - V_b = vBl - iR.$$

16. *A square loop of side* 10 cm *and resistance* 1 Ω *is moved towards right with a constant velocity v_0 as shown in figure (38-W12). The left arm of the loop is in a uniform magnetic field of* 2 T. *The field is perpendicular to the plane of the drawing and is going into it. The loop is connected to a network of resistors each of value* 3 Ω. *With what speed should the loop be moved so that a steady current of* 1 mA *flows in the loop.*

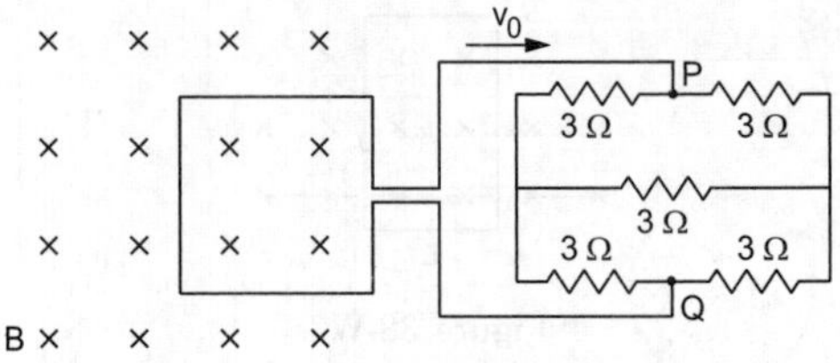

Figure 38-W12

Solution : The equivalent resistance of the network of the resistors, between P and Q will be 3 Ω. The total resistance of the circuit is 1 Ω + 3 Ω = 4 Ω.

The emf induced in the loop is

$$\mathcal{E} = vBl = v_0 (2\ \text{T})\ (10\ \text{cm}).$$

The current in the loop will be $i = \frac{\mathcal{E}}{R}$

or, $$1 \times 10^{-3}\ \text{A} = \frac{v_0 (2\ \text{T})\ (0{\cdot}1\ \text{m})}{4\ \Omega}$$

giving $$v_0 = \frac{(4\ \Omega)\ (1 \times 10^{-3}\ \text{A})}{0{\cdot}2\ \text{Tm}} = 2\ \text{cm s}^{-1}.$$

17. *A metal rod of length l rotates about an end with a uniform angular velocity ω. A uniform magnetic field $\vec{B}$ exists in the direction of the axis of rotation. Calculate the emf induced between the ends of the rod. Neglect the centripetal force acting on the free electrons as they move in circular paths.*

Solution :

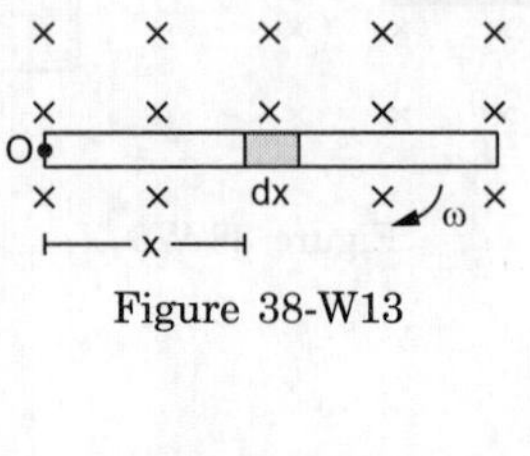

Figure 38-W13

Consider an element dx of the rod at a distance x from the axis of rotation. The linear speed of this element is ωx. The element moves in a direction perpendicular to its length as well as perpendicular to the magnetic field. The emf induced between the ends of this element is

$$d\mathcal{E} = B\,\omega x\,dx.$$

The emfs of all such elements will add to give the net emf between the ends of the rod. This emf is, therefore,

$$\mathcal{E} = \int d\mathcal{E} = \int_0^l B\,\omega x\,dx = \frac{1}{2}B\omega l^2.$$

18. *Figure (38-W14a) shows a conducting circular loop of radius a placed in a uniform, perpendicular magnetic field B. A metal rod OA is pivoted at the centre O of the loop. The other end A of the rod touches the loop. The rod OA and the loop are resistanceless but a resistor having a resistance R is connected between O and a fixed point C on the loop. The rod OA is made to rotate anticlockwise at a small but uniform angular speed ω by an external force. Find (a) the current in the resistance R and (b) the torque of the external force needed to keep the rod rotating with the constant angular velocity ω.*

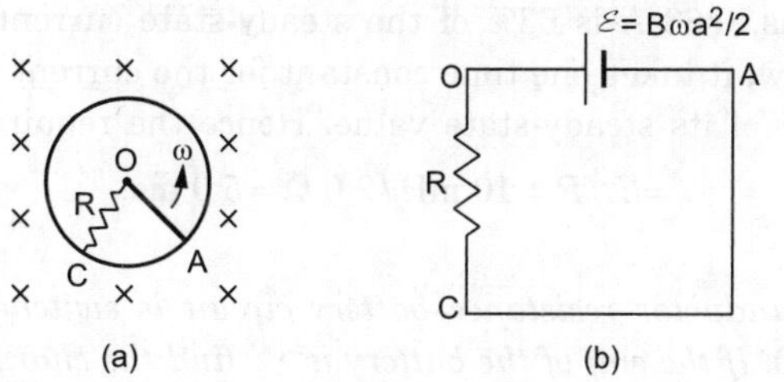

Figure 38-W14

Solution : The emf between the ends of the rotating rod is

$$\mathcal{E} = \int d\mathcal{E} = \int_0^a B\omega\,x\,dx = \frac{1}{2}B\omega\,a^2.$$

The positive charges of the rod will be pushed towards O by the magnetic field. Thus, the rod may be replaced by a battery of emf $= \frac{1}{2}B\omega\,a^2$ with the positive terminal towards O. The equivalent circuit diagram is shown in figure (38-W14b). The circular loop joins A to C by a resistanceless path.

(a) The current in the resistance R is

$$i = \frac{\mathcal{E}}{R} = \frac{B\omega\,a^2}{2R}.$$

(b) The force on the rod due to the magnetic field is $F = iaB$. As the force is uniformly distributed over OA, it may be assumed to act at the middle point of OA. The torque is, therefore,

$$\Gamma = (iaB)\,\frac{a}{2} = \frac{B^2\omega\,a^4}{4R}$$

in clockwise direction. To keep the rod rotating at uniform angular velocity, an external torque $\frac{B^2\omega\,a^4}{4R}$ in anticlockwise direction is needed.

19. *Figure (38-W15) shows a conducting loop abcdefa made of six segments ab, bc, cd, de, ef and fa, each of length l. Each segment makes a right angle with the next so that abc is in the x–z plane, cde in the x–y plane and efa is in the y–z plane. A uniform magnetic field B exists along the x-axis. If the magnetic field changes at a rate* $\frac{dB}{dt}$, *find the emf induced in the loop.*

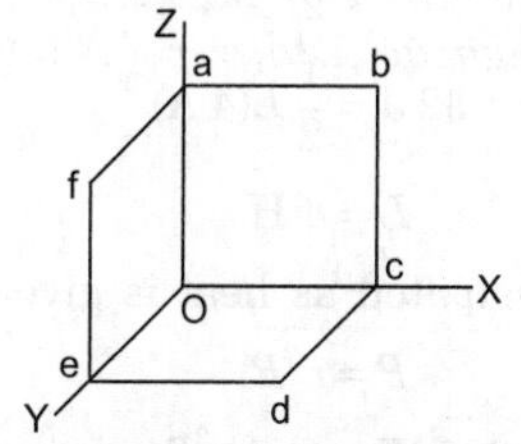

Figure 38-W15

Solution : As the magnetic field is along the x-axis, the flux through the loop is equal to the magnetic field multiplied by the area of projection of the loop on the y–z plane. This projection on the y–z plane will be $aoef$ which has an area l^2. Thus, the flux is $\Phi = Bl^2$. The induced emf is $\mathcal{E} = \frac{dB}{dt}\,l^2$.

20. *A wire of mass m and length l can freely slide on a pair of parallel, smooth, horizontal rails placed in a vertical magnetic field B (figure 38-W16). The rails are connected by a capacitor of capacitance C. The electric resistance of the rails and the wire is zero. If a constant force F acts on the wire as shown in the figure, find the acceleration of the wire.*

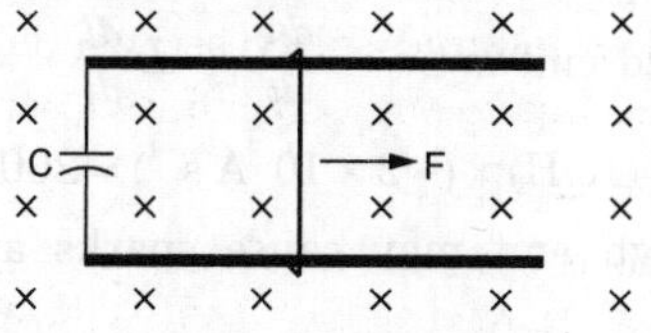

Figure 38-W16

Solution : Suppose the velocity of the wire is v at time t. The induced emf is $\mathcal{E} = vBl$. As there is no resistance anywhere, the charge on the capacitor will be

$$q = C\mathcal{E} = CvBl$$

at time t. The current in the circuit will be

$$i = \frac{dq}{dt} = CBl\,\frac{dv}{dt} = CBla.$$

Because of this current through the wire, there will be a magnetic force

$$F' = ilB = CB^2l^2a$$

towards left. The net force on the wire is $F - F'$. From Newton's law,

$$F - F' = ma$$

or, $$F - CB^2l^2a = ma$$

or, $$a = \frac{F}{m + CB^2l^2}.$$

21. *An inductor coil stores 32 J of magnetic field energy and dissipates energy as heat at the rate of 320 W when a current of 4 A is passed through it. Find the time constant of the circuit when this coil is joined across an ideal battery.*

Solution : The magnetic field energy stored in an inductor is $$U = \frac{1}{2}Li^2.$$

Thus, $$32\ \text{J} = \frac{1}{2}L(4\ \text{A})^2$$

or, $$L = 4\ \text{H}.$$

The power dissipated as heat is given by
$$P = i^2R$$

or, $$320\ \text{W} = (4\ \text{A})^2R, \text{ giving } R = 20\ \Omega.$$

The time constant of the circuit is
$$\tau = \frac{L}{R} = \frac{4\ \text{H}}{20\ \Omega} = 0{\cdot}2\ \text{s}.$$

22. A 12 V *battery connected to a* 6 Ω, 10 H *coil through a switch drives a constant current in the circuit. The switch is suddenly opened. Assuming that it took* 1 ms *to open the switch, calculate the average emf induced across the coil.*

Solution : The steady-state current is $\frac{12\ \text{V}}{6\ \Omega} = 2\ \text{A}$. The final current is zero. Thus,
$$\frac{di}{dt} = -\frac{2\ \text{A}}{1\ \text{ms}} = -2 \times 10^3\ \text{A s}^{-1}.$$

The induced emf is $\mathcal{E} = -\frac{d\Phi}{dt} = -L\frac{di}{dt}$

$$= -(10\ \text{H}) \times (-2 \times 10^3\ \text{A s}^{-1}) = 20000\text{V}.$$

Such a high emf may cause sparks across the open switch.

23. *A solenoid of inductance* 50 mH *and resistance* 10 Ω *is connected to a battery of* 6 V. *Find the time elapsed before the current acquires half of its steady-state value.*

Solution : The time constant of the circuit is
$$\tau = L/R = 50\ \text{mH}/10\ \Omega = 5\ \text{ms}.$$

The current at time t is given by
$$i = i_0(1 - e^{-t/\tau}).$$

For $$i = i_0/2,$$

$$i_0/2 = i_0(1 - e^{-t/\tau})$$

or, $$e^{-t/\tau} = \frac{1}{2}$$

or, $$\frac{t}{\tau} = \ln 2$$

giving $t = \tau \ln 2 = (5\ \text{ms})\,(0{\cdot}693) = 3{\cdot}5\ \text{ms}.$

24. *An LR circuit having* $L = 4{\cdot}0$ H, $R = 1{\cdot}0\ \Omega$ *and* $\mathcal{E} = 6{\cdot}0$ V *is switched on at* $t = 0$. *Find the power dissipated in Joule heating at* $t = 4{\cdot}0$ s.

Solution : The time constant of the circuit is
$$\tau = L/R = 4{\cdot}0\ \text{H}/1{\cdot}0\ \Omega = 4{\cdot}0\ \text{s}.$$

The current at $t = 4{\cdot}0$ s is, therefore,
$$i = \frac{\mathcal{E}}{R}(1 - e^{-t/\tau}) = (6\ \text{A})\left(1 - \frac{1}{e}\right)$$
$$= (6\ \text{A}) \times (0{\cdot}63) = 3{\cdot}8\ \text{A}.$$

The power dissipated in Joule heating $= i^2R$
$$= (3{\cdot}8\ \text{A})^2 \times 10\ \Omega \approx 140\ \Omega.$$

25. *An LR combination is connected to an ideal battery. If* $L = 10$ mH, $R = 2{\cdot}0\ \Omega$ *and* $\mathcal{E} = 2{\cdot}0$ V, *how much time will it take for the current to reach* 0·63 A ?

Solution : The steady-state current in the *LR* circuit is
$$i_0 = \mathcal{E}/R = 2{\cdot}0\ \text{V}/2{\cdot}0\ \Omega = 1\ \text{A}.$$

Thus, 0·63 A is 63% of the steady-state current. As we know, it takes one time constant for the current to reach 63% of its steady-state value. Hence the required time
$$= L/R = 10\ \text{mH}/2{\cdot}0\ \Omega = 5{\cdot}0\ \text{ms}.$$

26. *An inductor–resistance–battery circuit is switched on at* $t = 0$. *If the emf of the battery is* $\mathcal{E}$, *find the charge which passes through the battery in one time constant* τ.

Solution : The current at time t is given by
$$i = i_0(1 - e^{-t/\tau}) \text{ where } i_0 = \mathcal{E}/R.$$

The charge passed through the battery during the period t to $t + dt$ is $i\,dt$. Thus, the total charge passed during 0 to τ is
$$Q = \int_0^\tau i\,dt = i_0\int_0^\tau (1 - e^{-t/\tau})\,dt = i_0\left[t - \frac{e^{-t/\tau}}{-1/\tau}\right]_0^\tau$$
$$= i_0[\tau + \tau(e^{-1} - 1)] = i_0\,\tau/e.$$

27. *A coil of inductance* 1·0 H *and resistance* 100 Ω *is connected to a battery of emf* 12 V. *Find the energy stored in the magnetic field associated with the coil at an instant* 10 ms *after the circuit is switched on.*

Solution : The energy in the magnetic field associated with the coil is
$$U = \frac{1}{2}Li^2 = \frac{1}{2}L\left[\frac{\mathcal{E}}{R}(1 - e^{-t/\tau})\right]^2. \quad \text{... (i)}$$

The time constant of the circuit is
$$\tau = \frac{L}{R} = \frac{1{\cdot}0\ \text{H}}{100\ \Omega} = 10\ \text{ms}.$$

Putting the numerical values in (i), the energy at $t = 10$ ms is

$$\frac{1}{2} \times (1{\cdot}0 \text{ H}) \times [0{\cdot}12 \text{ A}(1 - 1/e)]^2$$

$$= 2{\cdot}8 \text{ mJ}.$$

28. *An inductance L and a resistance R are connected in series with a battery of emf $\mathcal{E}$. Find the maximum rate at which the energy is stored in the magnetic field.*

Solution :

The energy stored in the magnetic field at time t is

$$U = \frac{1}{2} Li^2 = \frac{1}{2} Li_0^2 (1 - e^{-t/\tau})^2.$$

The rate at which the energy is stored is

$$P = \frac{dU}{dt} = Li_0^2(1 - e^{-t/\tau})\,(-e^{-t/\tau})\left(-\frac{1}{\tau}\right)$$

$$= \frac{Li_0^2}{\tau}(e^{-t/\tau} - e^{-2t/\tau}). \qquad \text{... (i)}$$

This rate will be maximum when $\frac{dP}{dt} = 0$

or, $$\frac{Li_0^2}{\tau}\left(-\frac{1}{\tau} e^{-t/\tau} + \frac{2}{\tau} e^{-2t/\tau}\right) = 0$$

or, $$e^{-t/\tau} = \frac{1}{2}.$$

Putting in (i),

$$P_{max} = \frac{Li_0^2}{\tau}\left(\frac{1}{2} - \frac{1}{4}\right)$$

$$= \frac{L\mathcal{E}^2}{4R^2(L/R)} = \frac{\mathcal{E}^2}{4R}.$$

29. *Two conducting circular loops of radii R_1 and R_2 are placed in the same plane with their centres coinciding. Find the mutual inductance between them assuming $R_2 << R_1$.*

Solution : Suppose a current i is established in the outer loop. The magnetic field at the centre will be

$$B = \frac{\mu_0 i}{2R_1}.$$

As the radius R_2 of the inner coil is small compared to R_1, the flux of magnetic field through it will be approximately

$$\Phi = \frac{\mu_0 i}{2R_1} \pi R_2^2$$

so that the mutual inductance is

$$M = \frac{\Phi}{i} = \frac{\mu_0 \pi R_2^2}{2R_1}.$$

□

QUESTIONS FOR SHORT ANSWER

1. A metallic loop is placed in a nonuniform magnetic field. Will an emf be induced in the loop?
2. An inductor is connected to a battery through a switch. Explain why the emf induced in the inductor is much larger when the switch is opened as compared to the emf induced when the switch is closed.
3. The coil of a moving-coil galvanometer keeps on oscillating for a long time if it is deflected and released. If the ends of the coil are connected together, the oscillation stops at once. Explain.
4. A short magnet is moved along the axis of a conducting loop. Show that the loop repels the magnet if the magnet is approaching the loop and attracts the magnet if it is going away from the loop.
5. Two circular loops are placed coaxially but separated by a distance. A battery is suddenly connected to one of the loops establishing a current in it. Will there be a current induced in the other loop? If yes, when does the current start and when does it end? Do the loops attract each other or do they repel?
6. The battery discussed in the previous question is suddenly disconnected. Is a current induced in the other loop? If yes, when does it start and when does it end? Do the loops attract each other or repel?
7. If the magnetic field outside a copper box is suddenly changed, what happens to the magnetic field inside the box? Such low-resistivity metals are used to form enclosures which shield objects inside them against varying magnetic fields.
8. Metallic (nonferromagnetic) and nonmetallic particles in a solid waste may be separated as follows. The waste is allowed to slide down an incline over permanent magnets. The metallic particles slow down as compared to the nonmetallic ones and hence are separated. Discuss the role of eddy currents in the process.
9. A pivoted aluminium bar falls much more slowly through a small region containing a magnetic field than a similar bar of an insulating material. Explain.
10. A metallic bob A oscillates through the space between the poles of an electromagnet (figure 38-Q1). The oscillations are more quickly damped when the circuit

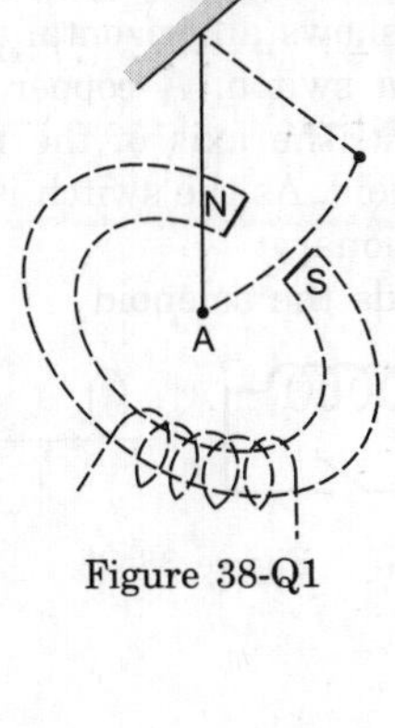

Figure 38-Q1

is on, as compared to the case when the circuit is off. Explain.

11. Two circular loops are placed with their centres separated by a fixed distance. How would you orient the loops to have (a) the largest mutual inductance (b) the smallest mutual inductance ?

12. Consider the self-inductance per unit length of a solenoid at its centre and that near its ends. Which of the two is greater ?

13. Consider the energy density in a solenoid at its centre and that near its ends. Which of the two is greater ?

OBJECTIVE I

1. A rod of length l rotates with a small but uniform angular velocity ω about its perpendicular bisector. A uniform magnetic field B exists parallel to the axis of rotation. The potential difference between the centre of the rod and an end is

(a) zero (b) $\frac{1}{8}\omega B l^2$ (c) $\frac{1}{2}\omega B l^2$ (d) $B\omega l^2$.

2. A rod of length l rotates with a uniform angular velocity ω about its perpendicular bisector. A uniform magnetic field B exists parallel to the axis of rotation. The potential difference between the two ends of the rod is

(a) zero (b) $\frac{1}{2}B\omega l^2$ (c) $B\omega l^2$ (d) $2B\omega l^2$.

3. Consider the situation shown in figure (38-Q2). If the switch is closed and after some time it is opened again, the closed loop will show

(a) an anticlockwise current-pulse
(b) a clockwise current-pulse
(c) an anticlockwise current-pulse and then a clockwise current-pulse
(d) a clockwise current-pulse and then an anticlockwise current-pulse.

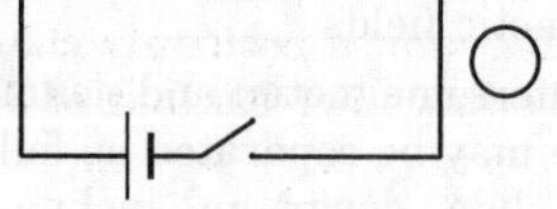

Figure 38-Q2

4. Solve the previous question if the closed loop is completely enclosed in the circuit containing the switch.

5. A bar magnet is released from rest along the axis of a very long, vertical copper tube. After some time the magnet

(a) will stop in the tube
(b) will move with almost contant speed
(c) will move with an acceleration g
(d) will oscillate.

6. Figure (38-Q3) shows a horizontal solenoid connected to a battery and a switch. A copper ring is placed on a frictionless track, the axis of the ring being along the axis of the solenoid. As the switch is closed, the ring will

(a) remain stationary
(b) move towards the solenoid
(c) move away from the solenoid
(d) move towards the solenoid or away from it depending on which terminal (positive or negative) of the battery is connected to the left end of the solenoid.

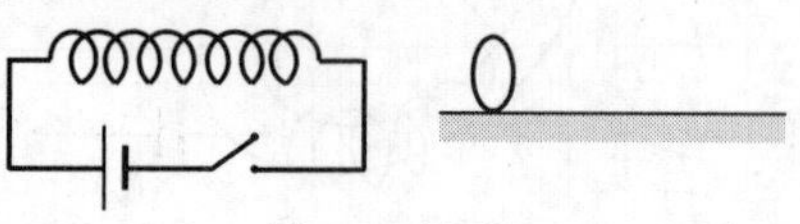

Figure 38-Q3

7. Consider the following statements:

(A) An emf can be induced by moving a conductor in a magnetic field.
(B) An emf can be induced by changing the magnetic field.

(a) Both A and B are true. (b) A is true but B is false.
(c) B is true but A is false. (d) Both A and B are false.

8. Consider the situation shown in figure (38-Q4). The wire AB is slid on the fixed rails with a constant velocity. If the wire AB is replaced by a semicircular wire, the magnitude of the induced current will

(a) increase (b) remain the same (c) decrease
(d) increase or decrease depending on whether the semicircle bulges towards the resistance or away from it.

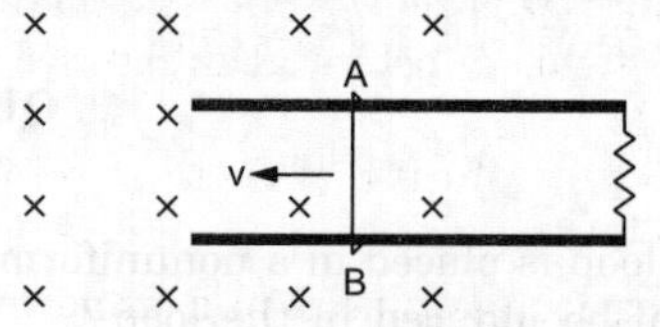

Figure 38-Q4

9. Figure (38-Q5a) shows a conducting loop being pulled out of a magnetic field with a constant speed v. Which of the four plots shown in figure (38-Q5b) may represent the power delivered by the pulling agent as a function of the speed v ?

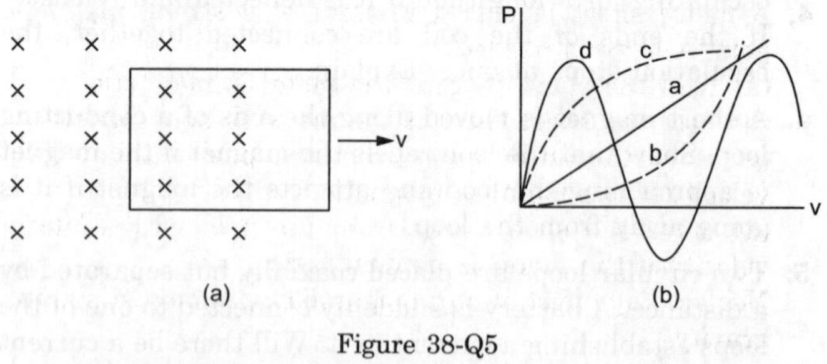

Figure 38-Q5

10. Two circular loops of equal radii are placed coaxially at some separation. The first is cut and a battery is inserted in between to drive a current in it. The current changes slightly because of the variation in resistance with temperature. During this period, the two loops

(a) attract each other (b) repel each other
(c) do not exert any force on each other
(d) attract or repel each other depending on the sense of the current.

11. A small, conducting circular loop is placed inside a long solenoid carrying a current. The plane of the loop contains the axis of the solenoid. If the current in the solenoid is varied, the current induced in the loop is
(a) clockwise (b) anticlockwise (c) zero
(d) clockwise or anticlockwise depending on whether the resistance is increased or decreased.

12. A conducting square loop of side l and resistance R moves in its plane with a uniform velocity v perpendicular to one of its sides. A uniform and constant magnetic field B exists along the perpendicular to the plane of the loop as shown in figure (38-Q6). The current induced in the loop is
(a) Blv/R clockwise (b) Blv/R anticlockwise
(c) $2Blv/R$ anticlockwise (d) zero.

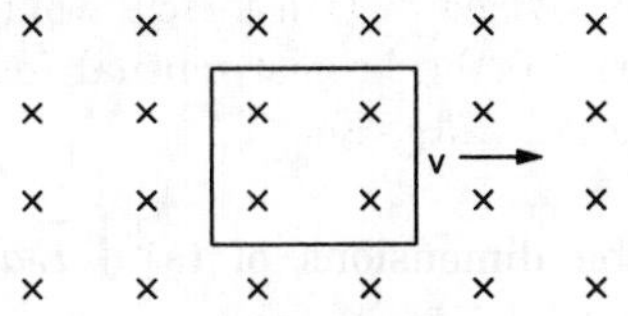

Figure 38-Q6

OBJECTIVE II

1. A bar magnet is moved along the axis of a copper ring placed far away from the magnet. Looking from the side of the magnet, an anticlockwise current is found to be induced in the ring. Which of the following may be true ?
(a) The south pole faces the ring and the magnet moves towards it.
(b) The north pole faces the ring and the magnet moves towards it.
(c) The south pole faces the ring and the magnet moves away from it.
(d) The north pole faces the ring and the magnet moves away from it.

2. A conducting rod is moved with a constant velocity v in a magnetic field. A potential difference appears across the two ends
(a) if $\vec{v} \parallel \vec{l}$ (b) if $\vec{v} \parallel \vec{B}$ (c) if $\vec{l} \parallel \vec{B}$
(d) none of these.

3. A conducting loop is placed in a uniform magnetic field with its plane perpendicular to the field. An emf is induced in the loop if
(a) it is translated
(b) it is rotated about its axis
(c) it is rotated about a diameter
(d) it is deformed.

4. A metal sheet is placed in front of a strong magnetic pole. A force is needed to
(a) hold the sheet there if the metal is magnetic
(b) hold the sheet there if the metal is nonmagnetic
(c) move the sheet away from the pole with uniform velocity if the metal is magnetic
(d) move the sheet away from the pole with uniform velocity if the metal is nonmagnetic.
Neglect any effect of paramagnetism, diamagnetism and gravity.

5. A constant current i is maintained in a solenoid. Which of the following quantities will increase if an iron rod is inserted in the solenoid along its axis ?
(a) magnetic field at the centre
(b) magnetic flux linked with the solenoid
(c) self-inductance of the solenoid
(d) rate of Joule heating.

6. Two solenoids have identical geometrical construction but one is made of thick wire and the other of thin wire. Which of the following quantities are different for the two solenoids ?
(a) self-inductance
(b) rate of Joule heating if the same current goes through them
(c) magnetic field energy if the same current goes through them
(d) time constant if one solenoid is connected to one battery and the other is connected to another battery.

7. An LR circuit with a battery is connected at $t = 0$. Which of the following quantities is not zero just after the connection ?
(a) Current in the circuit
(b) Magnetic field energy in the inductor
(c) Power delivered by the battery
(d) Emf induced in the inductor

8. A rod AB moves with a uniform velocity v in a uniform magnetic field as shown in figure (38-Q7).
(a) The rod becomes electrically charged.
(b) The end A becomes positively charged.
(c) The end B becomes positively charged.
(d) The rod becomes hot because of Joule heating.

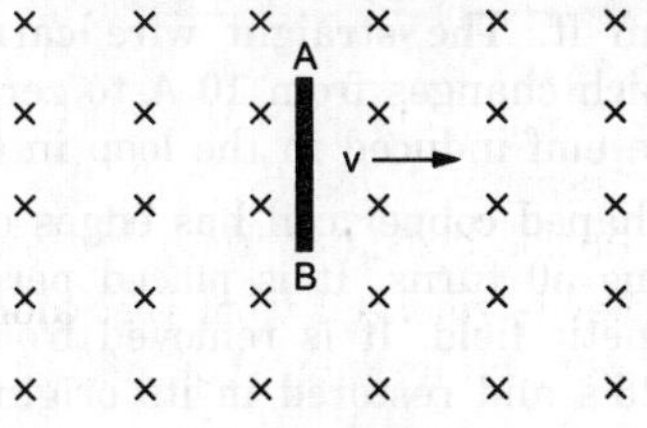

Figure 38-Q7

9. L, C and R represent the physical quantities inductance, capacitance and resistance respectively. Which of the following combinations have dimensions of frequency ?
(a) $\frac{1}{RC}$ (b) $\frac{R}{L}$ (c) $\frac{1}{\sqrt{LC}}$ (d) C/L.

10. The switches in figure (38-Q8a) and (38-8b) are closed at $t = 0$ and reopened after a long time at $t = t_0$.

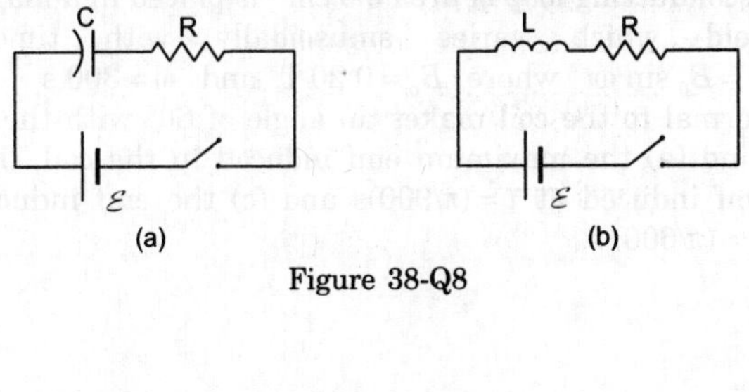

Figure 38-Q8

(a) The charge on C just after $t = 0$ is $\mathcal{E}C$.

(b) The charge on C long after $t = 0$ is $\mathcal{E}C$.

(c) The current in L just before $t = t_0$ is $\mathcal{E}/R$.

(d) The current in L long after $t = t_0$ is $\mathcal{E}/R$.

EXERCISES

1. Calculate the dimensions of (a) $\int \vec{E} \cdot d\vec{l}$, (b) vBl and (c) $\frac{d\Phi_B}{dt}$. The symbols have their usual meanings.

2. The flux of magnetic field through a closed conducting loop changes with time according to the equation, $\Phi = at^2 + bt + c$. (a) Write the SI units of a, b and c. (b) If the magnitudes of a, b and c are 0·20, 0·40 and 0·60 respectively, find the induced emf at $t = 2$ s.

3. (a) The magnetic field in a region varies as shown in figure (38-E1). Calculate the average induced emf in a conducting loop of area $2{\cdot}0 \times 10^{-3}$ m^2 placed perpendicular to the field in each of the 10 ms intervals shown. (b) In which intervals is the emf not constant? Neglect the behaviour near the ends of 10 ms intervals.

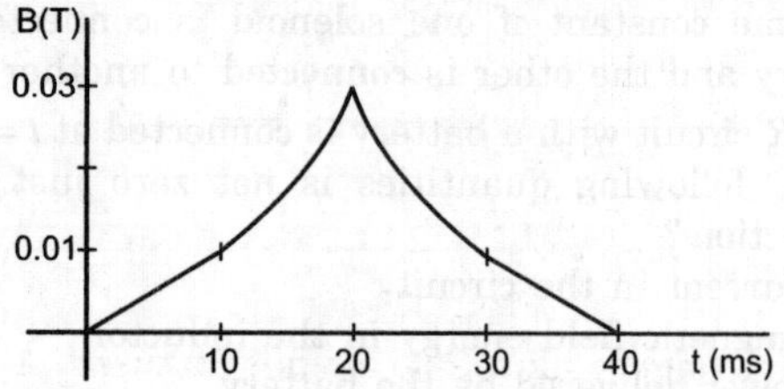

Figure 38-E1

4. A conducting circular loop having a radius of 5·0 cm, is placed perpendicular to a magnetic field of 0·50 T. It is removed from the field in 0·50 s. Find the average emf produced in the loop during this time.

5. A conducting circular loop of area 1 mm^2 is placed coplanarly with a long, straight wire at a distance of 20 cm from it. The straight wire carries an electric current which changes from 10 A to zero in 0·1 s. Find the average emf induced in the loop in 0·1 s.

6. A square-shaped copper coil has edges of length 50 cm and contains 50 turns. It is placed perpendicular to a 1·0 T magnetic field. It is removed from the magnetic field in 0·25 s and restored in its original place in the next 0·25 s. Find the magnitude of the average emf induced in the loop during (a) its removal, (b) its restoration and (c) its motion.

7. Suppose the resistance of the coil in the previous problem is 25 Ω. Assume that the coil moves with uniform velocity during its removal and restoration. Find the thermal energy developed in the coil during (a) its removal, (b) its restoration and (c) its motion.

8. A conducting loop of area 5·0 cm^2 is placed in a magnetic field which varies sinusoidally with time as $B = B_0 \sin \omega t$ where $B_0 = 0{\cdot}20$ T and $\omega = 300$ s^{-1}. The normal to the coil makes an angle of 60° with the field. Find (a) the maximum emf induced in the coil, (b) the emf induced at $\tau = (\pi/900)$s and (c) the emf induced at $t = (\pi/600)$ s.

9. Figure (38-E2) shows a conducting square loop placed parallel to the pole-faces of a ring magnet. The pole-faces have an area of 1 cm^2 each and the field between the poles is 0·10 T. The wires making the loop are all outside the magnetic field. If the magnet is removed in 1·0 s, what is the average emf induced in the loop?

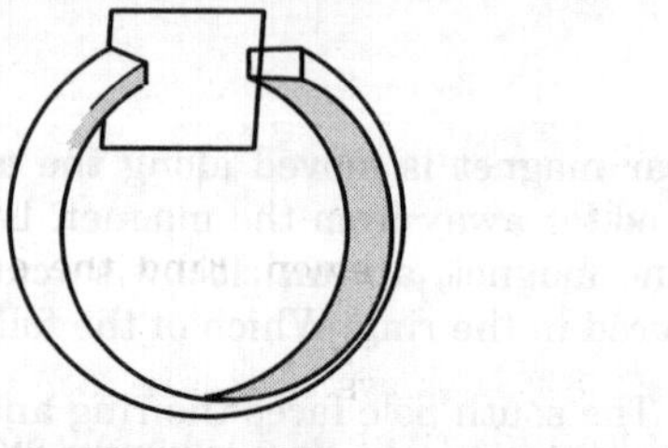

Figure 38-E2

10. A conducting square loop having edges of length 2·0 cm is rotated through 180° about a diagonal in 0·20 s. A magnetic field B exists in the region which is perpendicular to the loop in its initial position. If the average induced emf during the rotation is 20 mV, find the magnitude of the magnetic field.

11. A conducting loop of face-area A and resistance R is placed perpendicular to a magnetic field B. The loop is withdrawn completely from the field. Find the charge which flows through any cross-section of the wire in the process. Note that it is independent of the shape of the loop as well as the way it is withdrawn.

12. A long solenoid of radius 2 cm has 100 turns/cm and carries a current of 5 A. A coil of radius 1 cm having 100 turns and a total resistance of 20 Ω is placed inside the solenoid coaxially. The coil is connected to a galvanometer. If the current in the solenoid is reversed in direction, find the charge flown through the galvanometer.

13. Figure (38-E3) shows a metallic square frame of edge a in a vertical plane. A uniform magnetic field B exists in the space in a direction perpendicular to the plane of the figure. Two boys pull the opposite corners of the square to deform it into a rhombus. They start pulling the corners at $t = 0$ and displace the corners at a uniform speed u. (a) Find the induced emf in the frame at the instant when the angles at these corners reduce to 60°. (b) Find the induced current in the frame at this instant if the total resistance of the frame is R. (c) Find the total charge which flows through a side of the frame by the time the square is deformed into a straight line.

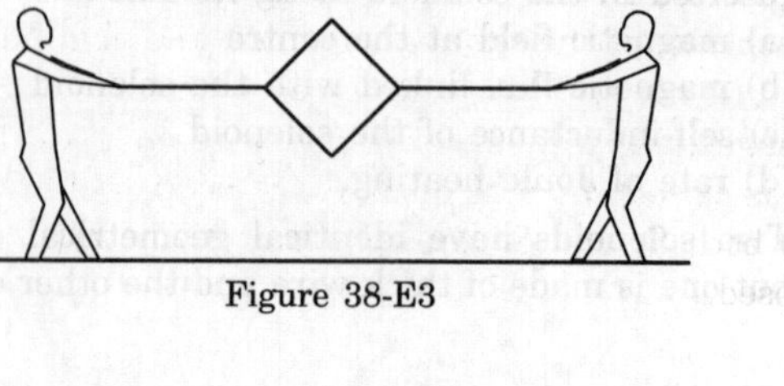

Figure 38-E3

14. The north pole of a magnet is brought down along the axis of a horizontal circular coil (figure 38-E4). As a result, the flux through the coil changes from 0·35 weber to 0·85 weber in an interval of half a second. Find the average emf induced during this period. Is the induced current clockwise or anticlockwise as you look into the coil from the side of the magnet ?

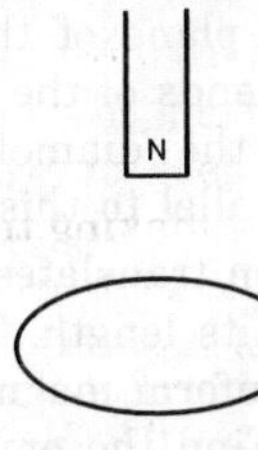

Figure 38-E4

15. A wire-loop confined in a plane is rotated in its own plane with some angular velocity. A uniform magnetic field exists in the region. Find the emf induced in the loop.

16. Figure (38-E5) shows a square loop of side 5 cm being moved towards right at a constant speed of 1 cm/s. The front edge enters the 20 cm wide magnetic field at $t = 0$. Find the emf induced in the loop at (a) $t = 2$ s, (b) $t = 10$ s, (c) $t = 22$ s and (d) $t = 30$ s.

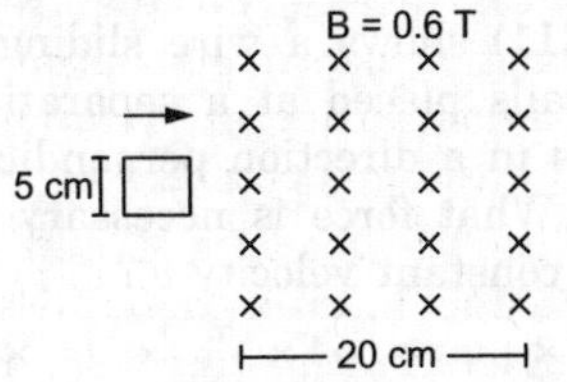

Figure 38-E5

17. Find the total heat produced in the loop of the previous problem during the interval 0 to 30 s if the resistance of the loop is 4·5 mΩ.

18. A uniform magnetic field B exists in a cylindrical region of radius 10 cm as shown in figure (38-E6). A uniform wire of length 80 cm and resistance 4·0 Ω is bent into a square frame and is placed with one side along a diameter of the cylindrical region. If the magnetic field increases at a constant rate of 0·010 T/s, find the current induced in the frame.

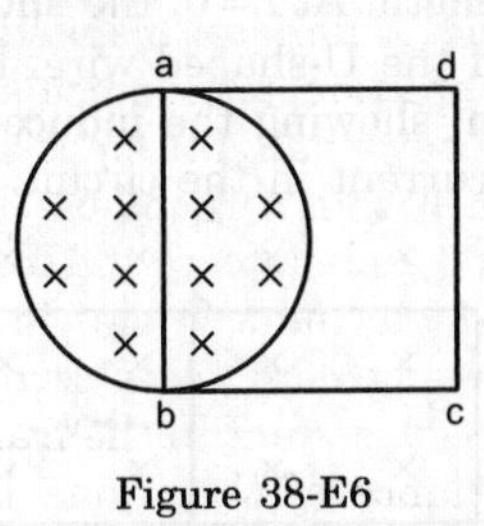

Figure 38-E6

19. The magnetic field in the cylindrical region shown in figure (38-E7) increases at a constant rate of 20·0 mT/s. Each side of the square loop *abcd* and *defa* has a length of 1·00 cm and a resistance of 4·00 Ω. Find the current (magnitude and sense) in the wire *ad* if (a) the switch S_1 is closed but S_2 is open, (b) S_1 is open but S_2 is closed, (c) both S_1 and S_2 are open and (d) both S_1 and S_2 are closed.

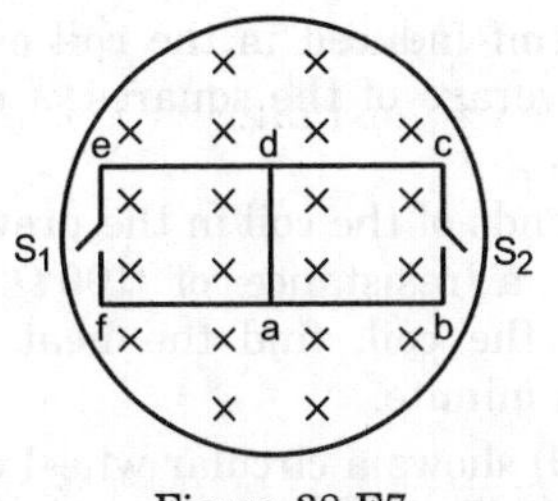

Figure 38-E7

20. Figure (38-E8) shows a circular coil of N turns and radius a, connected to a battery of emf $\mathcal{E}$ through a rheostat. The rheostat has a total length L and resistance R. The resistance of the coil is r. A small circular loop of radius a' and resistance r' is placed coaxially with the coil. The centre of the loop is at a distance x from the centre of the coil. In the beginning, the sliding contact of the rheostat is at the left end and then onwards it is moved towards right at a constant speed v. Find the emf induced in the small circular loop at the instant (a) the contact begins to slide and (b) it has slid through half the length of the rheostat.

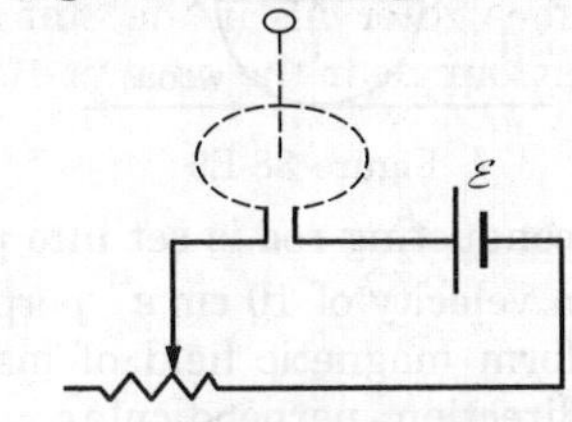

Figure 38-E8

21. A circular coil of radius 2·00 cm has 50 turns. A uniform magnetic field $B = 0·200$ T exists in the space in a direction parallel to the axis of the loop. The coil is now rotated about a diameter through an angle of 60·0°. The operation takes 0·100 s. (a) Find the average emf induced in the coil. (b) If the coil is a closed one (with the two ends joined together) and has a resistance of 4·00 Ω, calculate the net charge crossing a cross-section of the wire of the coil.

22. A closed coil having 100 turns is rotated in a uniform magnetic field $B = 4·0 \times 10^{-4}$ T about a diameter which is perpendicular to the field. The angular velocity of rotation is 300 revolutions per minute. The area of the coil is 25 cm^2 and its resistance is 4·0 Ω. Find (a) the average emf developed in half a turn from a position where the coil is perpendicular to the magnetic field, (b) the average emf in a full turn and (c) the net charge displaced in part (a).

23. A coil of radius 10 cm and resistance 40 Ω has 1000 turns. It is placed with its plane vertical and its axis parallel to the magnetic meridian. The coil is connected to a galvanometer and is rotated about the vertical diameter through an angle of 180°. Find the charge which flows through the galvanometer if the horizontal component of the earth's magnetic field is $B_H = 3·0 \times 10^{-5}$ T.

24. A circular coil of one turn of radius 5·0 cm is rotated about a diameter with a constant angular speed of 80 revolutions per minute. A uniform magnetic field $B = 0·010$ T exists in a direction perpendicular to the axis of rotation. Find (a) the maximum emf induced, (b) the average emf induced in the coil over a long period and (c) the average of the squares of emf induced over a long period.

25. Suppose the ends of the coil in the previous problem are connected to a resistance of 100 Ω. Neglecting the resistance of the coil, find the heat produced in the circuit in one minute.

26. Figure (38-E9) shows a circular wheel of radius 10·0 cm whose upper half, shown dark in the figure, is made of iron and the lower half of wood. The two junctions are joined by an iron rod. A uniform magnetic field B of magnitude $2{\cdot}00 \times 10^{-4}$ T exists in the space above the central line as suggested by the figure. The wheel is set into pure rolling on the horizontal surface. If it takes 2·00 seconds for the iron part to come down and the wooden part to go up, find the average emf induced during this period.

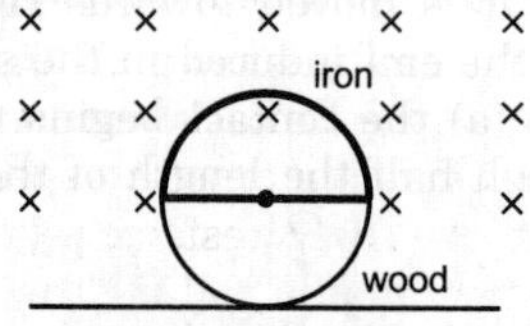

Figure 38-E9

27. A 20 cm long conducting rod is set into pure translation with a uniform velocity of 10 cm s^{-1} perpendicular to its length. A uniform magnetic field of magnitude 0·10 T exists in a direction perpendicular to the plane of motion. (a) Find the average magnetic force on the free electrons of the rod. (b) For what electric field inside the rod, the electric force on a free electron will balance the magnetic force? How is this electric field created? (c) Find the motional emf between the ends of the rod.

28. A metallic metre stick moves with a velocity of 2 m s^{-1} in a direction perpendicular to its length and perpendicular to a uniform magnetic field of magnitude 0·2 T. Find the emf induced between the ends of the stick.

29. A 10 m wide spacecraft moves through the interstellar space at a speed 3×10^{7} m s^{-1}. A magnetic field $B = 3 \times 10^{-10}$ T exists in the space in a direction perpendicular to the plane of motion. Treating the spacecraft as a conductor, calculate the emf induced across its width.

30. The two rails of a railway track, insulated from each other and from the ground, are connected to a millivoltmeter. What will be the reading of the millivoltmeter when a train travels on the track at a speed of 180 km h^{-1}? The vertical component of earth's magnetic field is $0{\cdot}2 \times 10^{-4}$ T and the rails are separated by 1 m.

31. A right-angled triangle abc, made from a metallic wire, moves at a uniform speed v in its plane as shown in figure (38-E10). A uniform magnetic field B exists in the perpendicular direction. Find the emf induced (a) in the loop abc, (b) in the segment bc, (c) in the segment ac and (d) in the segment ab.

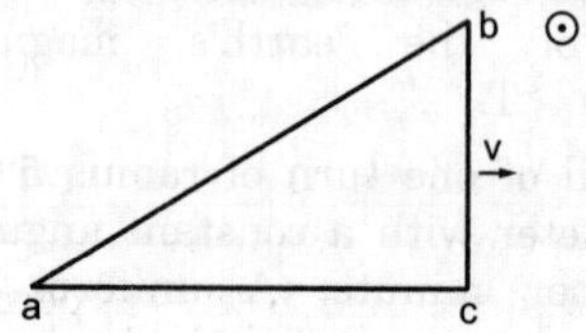

Figure 38-E10

32. A copper wire bent in the shape of a semicircle of radius r translates in its plane with a constant velocity v. A uniform magnetic field B exists in the direction perpendicular to the plane of the wire. Find the emf induced between the ends of the wire if (a) the velocity is perpendicular to the diameter joining free ends, (b) the velocity is parallel to this diameter.

33. A wire of length 10 cm translates in a direction making an angle of 60° with its length. The plane of motion is perpendicular to a uniform magnetic field of 1·0 T that exists in the space. Find the emf induced between the ends of the rod if the speed of translation is 20 cm s^{-1}.

34. A circular copper-ring of radius r translates in its plane with a constant velocity v. A uniform magnetic field B exists in the space in a direction perpendicular to the plane of the ring. Consider different pairs of diametrically opposite points on the ring. (a) Between which pair of points is the emf maximum? What is the value of this maximum emf? (b) Between which pair of points is the emf minimum? What is the value of this minimum emf?

35. Figure (38-E11) shows a wire sliding on two parallel, conducting rails placed at a separation l. A magnetic field B exists in a direction perpendicular to the plane of the rails. What force is necessary to keep the wire moving at a constant velocity v?

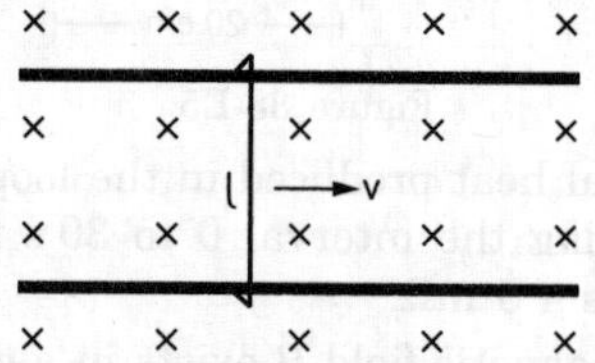

Figure 38-E11

36. Figure (38-E12) shows a long U-shaped wire of width l placed in a perpendicular magnetic field B. A wire of length l is slid on the U-shaped wire with a constant velocity v towards right. The resistance of all the wires is r per unit length. At $t = 0$, the sliding wire is close to the left edge of the U-shaped wire. Draw an equivalent circuit diagram, showing the induced emf as a battery. Calculate the current in the circuit.

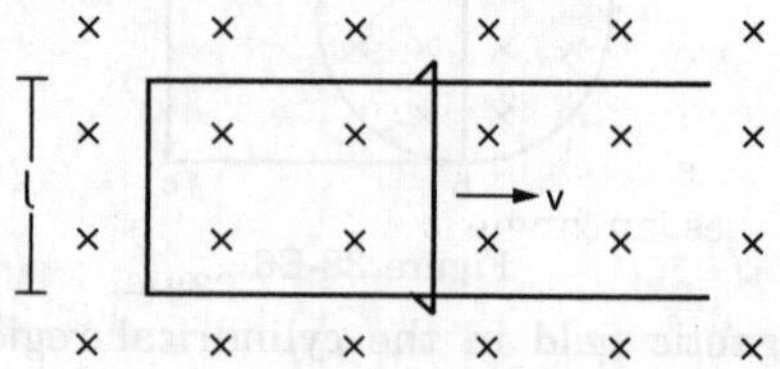

Figure 38-E12

37. Consider the situation of the previous problem. (a) Calculate the force needed to keep the sliding wire moving with a constant velocity v. (b) If the force needed just after $t = 0$ is F_0, find the time at which the force needed will be $F_0/2$.

38. Consider the situation shown in figure (38-E13). The wire PQ has mass m, resistance r and can slide on the smooth, horizontal parallel rails separated by a distance l. The resistance of the rails is negligible. A uniform magnetic field B exists in the rectangular region and a resistance R connects the rails outside the field region. At $t = 0$, the wire PQ is pushed towards right with a speed v_0. Find (a) the current in the loop at an instant when the speed of the wire PQ is v, (b) the acceleration of the wire at this instant, (c) the velocity v as a function of x and (d) the maximum distance the wire will move.

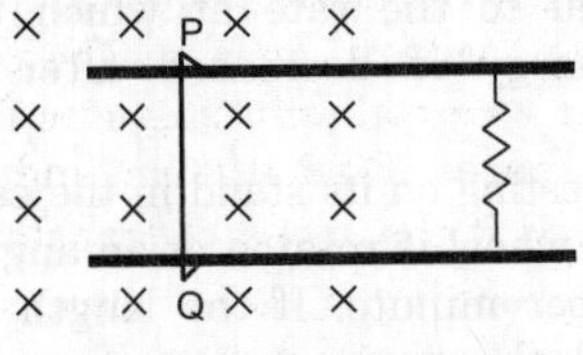

Figure 38-E13

39. A rectangular frame of wire $abcd$ has dimensions 32 cm × 8·0 cm and a total resistance of 2·0 Ω. It is pulled out of a magnetic field $B = 0·020$ T by applying a force of $3·2 \times 10^{-5}$ N (figure 38-E14). It is found that the frame moves with constant speed. Find (a) this constant speed, (b) the emf induced in the loop, (c) the potential difference between the points a and b and (d) the potential difference between the points c and d.

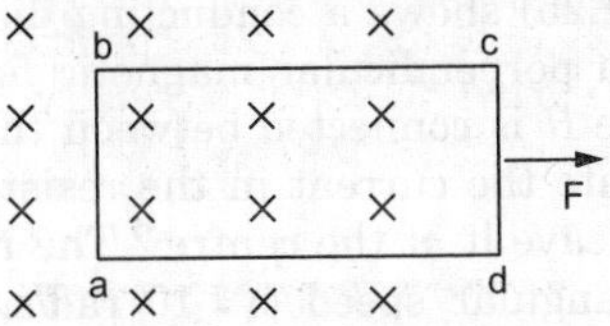

Figure 38-E14

40. Figure (38-E15) shows a metallic wire of resistance 0·20 Ω sliding on a horizontal, U-shaped metallic rail. The separation between the parallel arms is 20 cm. An electric current of 2·0 μA passes through the wire when it is slid at a rate of 20 cm s^{-1}. If the horizontal component of the earth's magnetic field is $3·0 \times 10^{-5}$ T, calculate the dip at the place.

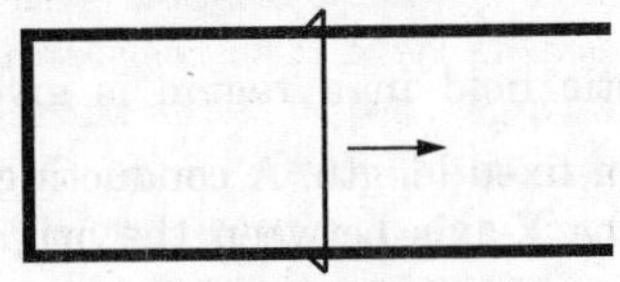

Figure 38-E15

41. A wire ab of length l, mass m and resistance R slides on a smooth, thick pair of metallic rails joined at the bottom as shown in figure (38-E16). The plane of the rails makes an angle θ with the horizontal. A vertical magnetic field B exists in the region. If the wire slides on the rails at a constant speed v, show that

$$B = \sqrt{\frac{mg R \sin\theta}{v l^2 \cos^2 \theta}}.$$

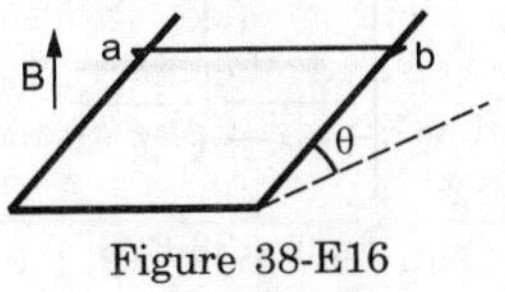

Figure 38-E16

42. Consider the situation shown in figure (38-E17). The wires P_1Q_1 and P_2Q_2 are made to slide on the rails with the same speed 5 cm s^{-1}. Find the electric current in the 19 Ω resistor if (a) both the wires move towards right and (b) if P_1Q_1 moves towards left but P_2Q_2 moves towards right.

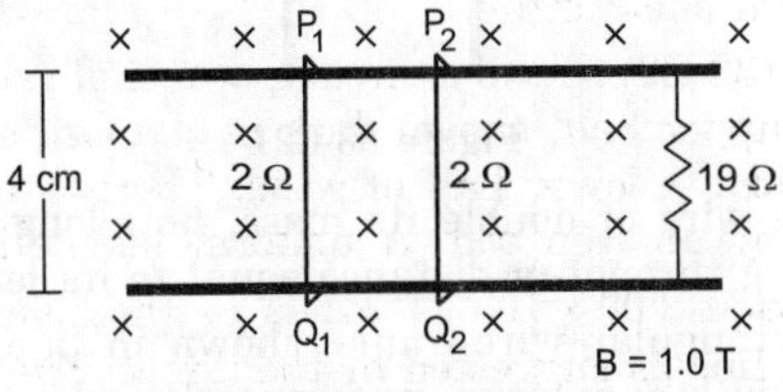

Figure 38-E17

43. Suppose the 19 Ω resistor of the previous problem is disconnected. Find the current through P_2Q_2 in the two situations (a) and (b) of that problem.

44. Consider the situation shown in figure (38-E18). The wire PQ has a negligible resistance and is made to slide on the three rails with a constant speed of 5 cm s^{-1}. Find the current in the 10 Ω resistor when the switch S is thrown to (a) the middle rail (b) the bottom rail.

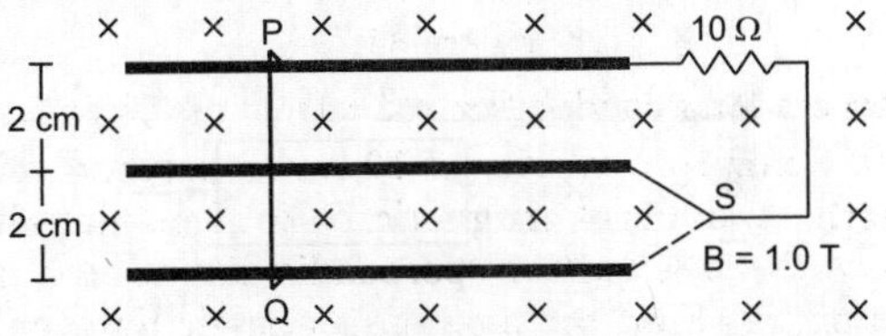

Figure 38-E18

45. The current generator I_g, shown in figure (38-E19), sends a constant current i through the circuit. The wire cd is fixed and ab is made to slide on the smooth, thick rails with a constant velocity v towards right. Each of these wires has resistance r. Find the current through the wire cd.

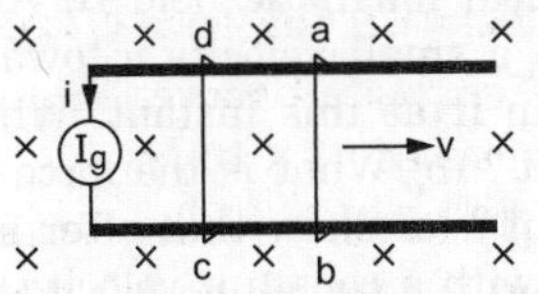

Figure 38-E19

46. The current generator I_g, shown in figure (38-E20), sends a constant current i through the circuit. The wire ab has a length l and mass m and can slide on the smooth, horizontal rails connected to I_g. The entire system lies in a vertical magnetic field B. Find the velocity of the wire as a function of time.

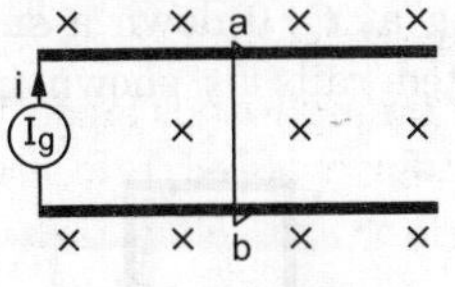

Figure 38-E20

47. The system containing the rails and the wire of the previous problem is kept vertically in a uniform horizontal magnetic field B that is perpendicular to the plane of the rails (figure 38-E21). It is found that the wire stays in equilibrium. If the wire ab is replaced by

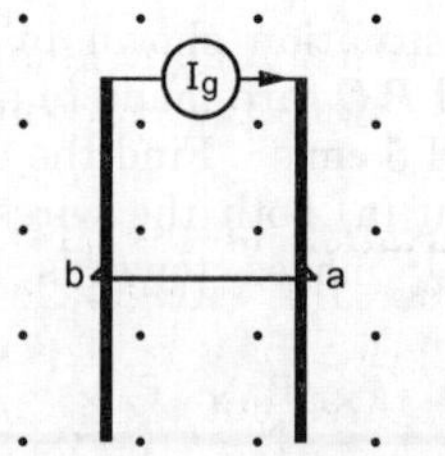

Figure 38-E21

another wire of double its mass, how long will it take in falling through a distance equal to its length ?

48. The rectangular wire-frame, shown in figure (38-E22), has a width d, mass m, resistance R and a large length. A uniform magnetic field B exists to the left of the frame. A constant force F starts pushing the frame into the magnetic field at $t = 0$. (a) Find the acceleration of the frame when its speed has increased to v. (b) Show that after some time the frame will move with a constant velocity till the whole frame enters into the magnetic field. Find this velocity v_0. (c) Show that the velocity at time t is given by

$$v = v_0(1 - e^{-Ft/mv_0}).$$

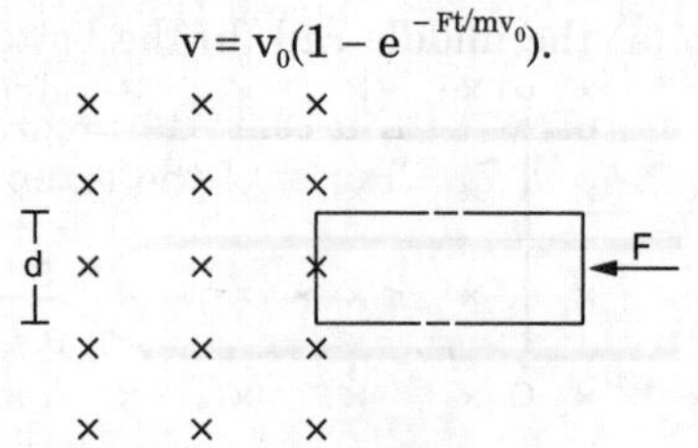

Figure 38-E22

49. Figure (38-E23) shows a smooth pair of thick metallic rails connected across a battery of emf $\mathcal{E}$ having a negligible internal resistance. A wire ab of length l and resistance r can slide smoothly on the rails. The entire system lies in a horizontal plane and is immersed in a uniform vertical magnetic field B. At an instant t, the wire is given a small velocity v towards right. (a) Find the current in it at this instant. What is the direction of the current ? (b) What is the force acting on the wire at this instant ? (c) Show that after some time the wire ab will slide with a constant velocity. Find this velocity.

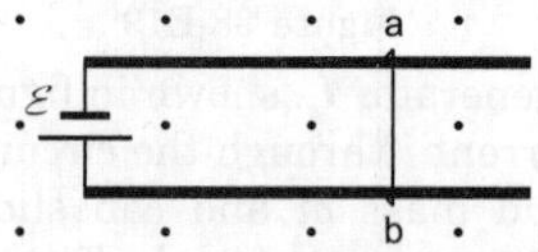

Figure 38-E23

50. A conducting wire ab of length l, resistance r and mass m starts sliding at $t = 0$ down a smooth, vertical, thick pair of connected rails as shown in figure (38-E24). A uniform magnetic field B exists in the space in a direction perpendicular to the plane of the rails. (a) Write the induced emf in the loop at an instant t when the speed of the wire is v. (b) What would be the magnitude and direction of the induced current in the wire ? (c) Find the downward acceleration of the wire at this instant. (d) After sufficient time, the wire starts moving with a constant velocity. Find this velocity v_m. (e) Find the velocity of the wire as a function of time. (f) Find the displacement of the wire as a function of time. (g) Show that the rate of heat developed in the wire is equal to the rate at which the gravitational potential energy is decreased after steady state is reached.

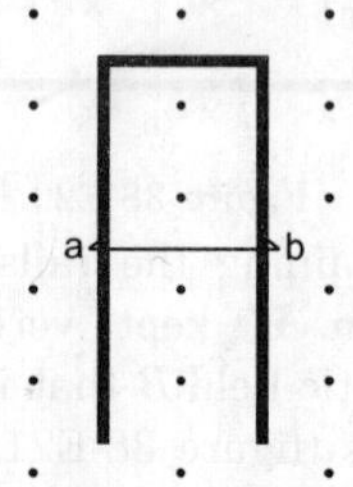

Figure 38-E24

51. A bicycle is resting on its stand in the east–west direction and the rear wheel is rotated at an angular speed of 100 revolutions per minute. If the length of each spoke is 30·0 cm and the horizontal component of the earth's magnetic field is $2{\cdot}0 \times 10^{-5}$ T, find the emf induced between the axis and the outer end of a spoke. Neglect centripetal force acting on the free electrons of the spoke.

52. A conducting disc of radius r rotates with a small but constant angular velocity ω about its axis. A uniform magnetic field B exists parallel to the axis of rotation. Find the motional emf between the centre and the periphery of the disc.

53. Figure (38-E25) shows a conducting disc rotating about its axis in a perpendicular magnetic field B. A resistor of resistance R is connected between the centre and the rim. Calculate the current in the resistor. Does it enter the disc or leave it at the centre ? The radius of the disc is 5·0 cm, angular speed $\omega = 10$ rad/s, $B = 0{\cdot}40$ T and $R = 10\ \Omega$.

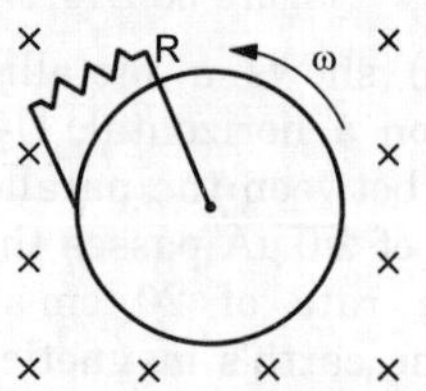

Figure 38-E25

54. The magnetic field in a region is given by $\vec{B} = \vec{k}\frac{B_0}{L}y$ where L is a fixed length. A conducting rod of length L lies along the Y-axis between the origin and the point $(0, L, 0)$. If the rod moves with a velocity $\vec{v} = v_0\,\vec{i}$, find the emf induced between the ends of the rod.

55. Figure (38-E26) shows a straight, long wire carrying a current i and a rod of length l coplanar with the wire and perpendicular to it. The rod moves with a constant velocity v in a direction parallel to the wire. The distance of the wire from the centre of the rod is x. Find the motional emf induced in the rod.

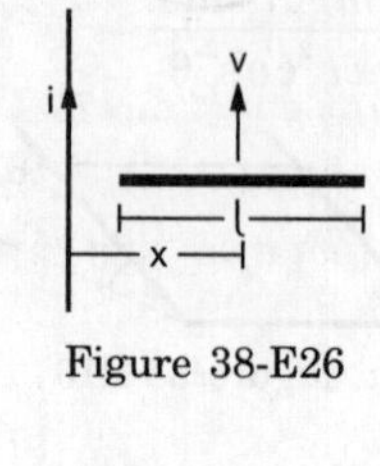

Figure 38-E26

56. Consider a situation similar to that of the previous problem except that the ends of the rod slide on a pair of thick metallic rails laid parallel to the wire. At one end the rails are connected by resistor of resistance R. (a) What force is needed to keep the rod sliding at a constant speed v? (b) In this situation what is the current in the resistance R? (c) Find the rate of heat developed in the resistor. (d) Find the power delivered by the external agent exerting the force on the rod.

57. Figure (38-E27) shows a square frame of wire having a total resistance r placed coplanarly with a long, straight wire. The wire carries a current i given by $i = i_0 \sin \omega t$. Find (a) the flux of the magnetic field through the square frame, (b) the emf induced in the frame and (c) the heat developed in the frame in the time interval 0 to $\frac{20\pi}{\omega}$.

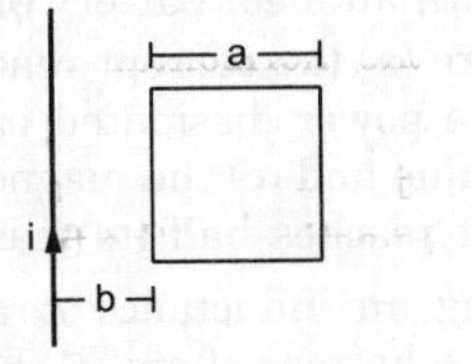

Figure 38-E27

58. A rectangular metallic loop of length l and width b is placed coplanarly with a long wire carrying a current i (figure 38-E28). The loop is moved perpendicular to the wire with a speed v in the plane containing the wire and the loop. Calculate the emf induced in the loop when the rear end of the loop is at a distance a from the wire. Solve by using Faraday's law for the flux through the loop and also by replacing different segments with equivalent batteries.

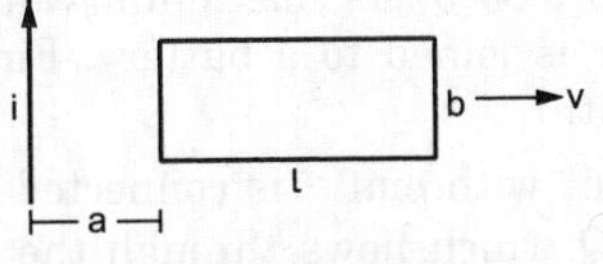

Figure 38-E28

59. Figure (38-E29) shows a conducting circular loop of radius a placed in a uniform, perpendicular magnetic field B. A thick metal rod OA is pivoted at the centre O. The other end of the rod touches the loop at A. The centre O and a fixed point C on the loop are connected by a wire OC of resistance R. A force is applied at the middle point of the rod OA perpendicularly, so that the rod rotates clockwise at a uniform angular velocity ω. Find the force.

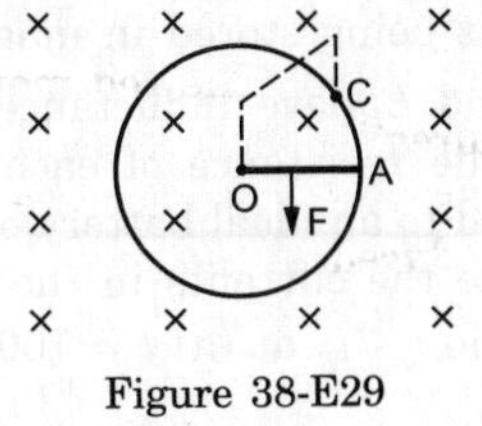

Figure 38-E29

60. Consider the situation shown in the figure of the previous problem. Suppose the wire connecting O and C has zero resistance but the circular loop has a resistance R uniformly distributed along its length. The rod OA is made to rotate with a uniform angular speed ω as shown in the figure. Find the current in the rod when $\angle AOC = 90°$.

61. Consider a variation of the previous problem (figure 38-E29). Suppose the circular loop lies in a vertical plane. The rod has a mass m. The rod and the loop have negligible resistances but the wire connecting O and C has a resistance R. The rod is made to rotate with a uniform angular velocity ω in the clockwise direction by applying a force at the midpoint of OA in a direction perpendicular to it. Find the magnitude of this force when the rod makes an angle θ with the vertical.

62. Figure (38-E30) shows a situation similar to the previous problem. All parameters are the same except that a battery of emf $\mathcal{E}$ and a variable resistance R are connected between O and C. Neglect the resistance of the connecting wires. Let θ be the angle made by the rod from the horizontal position (shown in the figure), measured in the clockwise direction. During the part of the motion $0 < \theta < \pi/4$ the only forces acting on the rod are gravity and the forces exerted by the magnetic field and the pivot. However, during the part of the motion, the resistance R is varied in such a way that the rod continues to rotate with a constant angular velocity ω. Find the value of R in terms of the given quantities.

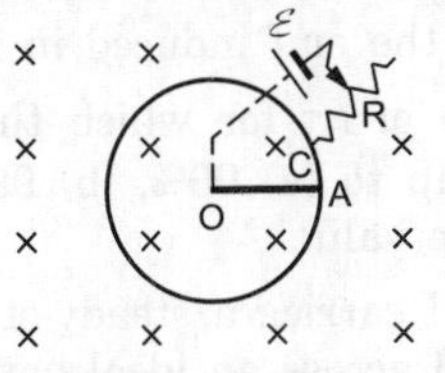

Figure 38-E30

63. A wire of mass m and length l can slide freely on a pair of smooth, vertical rails (figure 38-E31). A magnetic field B exists in the region in the direction perpendicular to the plane of the rails. The rails are connected at the top end by a capacitor of capacitance C. Find the acceleration of the wire neglecting any electric resistance.

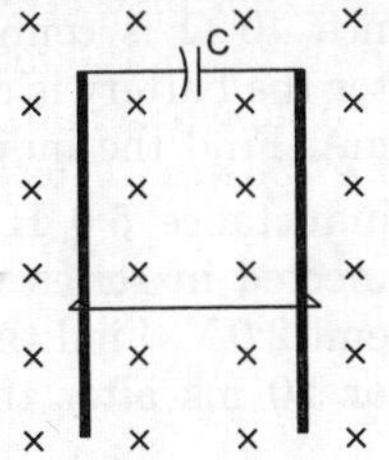

Figure 38-E31

64. A uniform magnetic field B exists in a cylindrical region, shown dotted in figure (38-E32). The magnetic field increases at a constant rate $\frac{dB}{dt}$. Consider a circle of

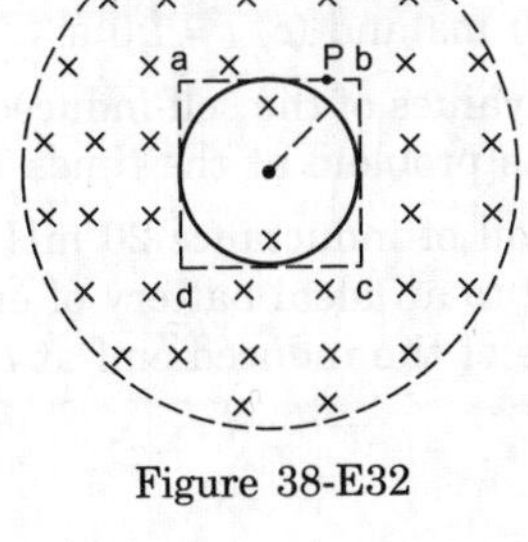

Figure 38-E32

radius r coaxial with the cylindrical region. (a) Find the magnitude of the electric field E at a point on the circumference of the circle. (b) Consider a point P on the side of the square circumscribing the circle. Show that the component of the induced electric field at P along ba is the same as the magnitude found in part (a).

65. The current in an ideal, long solenoid is varied at a uniform rate of 0·01 As^{-1}. The solenoid has 2000 turns/m and its radius is 6·0 cm. (a) Consider a circle of radius 1·0 cm inside the solenoid with its axis coinciding with the axis of the solenoid. Write the change in the magnetic flux through this circle in 2·0 seconds. (b) Find the electric field induced at a point on the circumference of the circle. (c) Find the electric field induced at a point outside the solenoid at a distance 8·0 cm from its axis.

66. An average emf of 20 V is induced in an inductor when the current in it is changed from 2·5 A in one direction to the same value in the opposite direction in 0·1 s. Find the self-inductance of the inductor.

67. A magnetic flux of 8×10^{-4} weber is linked with each turn of a 200-turn coil when there is an electric current of 4 A in it. Calculate the self-inductance of the coil.

68. The current in a solenoid of 240 turns, having a length of 12 cm and a radius of 2 cm, changes at a rate of 0·8 A s^{-1}. Find the emf induced in it.

69. Find the value of t/τ for which the current in an LR circuit builds up to (a) 90%, (b) 99% and (c) 99·9% of the steady-state value.

70. An inductor-coil carries a steady-state current of 2·0 A when connected across an ideal battery of emf 4·0 V. If its inductance is 1·0 H, find the time constant of the circuit.

71. A coil having inductance 2·0 H and resistance 20 Ω is connected to a battery of emf 4·0 V. Find (a) the current at the instant 0·20 s after the connection is made and (b) the magnetic field energy at this instant.

72. A coil of resistance 40 Ω is connected across a 4·0 V battery. 0·10 s after the battery is connected, the current in the coil is 63 mA. Find the inductance of the coil.

73. An inductor of inductance 5·0 H, having a negligible resistance, is connected in series with a 100 Ω resistor and a battery of emf 2·0 V. Find the potential difference across the resistor 20 ms after the circuit is switched on.

74. The time constant of an LR circuit is 40 ms. The circuit is connected at $t = 0$ and the steady-state current is found to be 2·0 A. Find the current at (a) $t = 10$ ms (b) $t = 20$ ms, (c) $t = 100$ ms and (d) $t = 1$ s.

75. An LR circuit has $L = 1·0$ H and $R = 20$ Ω. It is connected across an emf of 2·0 V at $t = 0$. Find di/dt at (a) $t = 100$ ms, (b) $t = 200$ ms and (c) $t = 1·0$ s.

76. What are the values of the self-induced emf in the circuit of the previous problem at the times indicated therein?

77. An inductor-coil of inductance 20 mH having resistance 10 Ω is joined to an ideal battery of emf 5·0 V. Find the rate of change of the induced emf at $t = 0$, (b) $t = 10$ ms and (c) $t = 1·0$ s.

78. An LR circuit contains an inductor of 500 mH, a resistor of 25·0 Ω and an emf of 5·00 V in series. Find the potential difference across the resistor at $t =$ (a) 20·0 ms, (b) 100 ms and (c) 1·00 s.

79. An inductor-coil of resistance 10 Ω and inductance 120 mH is connected across a battery of emf 6 V and internal resistance 2 Ω. Find the charge which flows through the inductor in (a) 10 ms, (b) 20 ms and (c) 100 ms after the connections are made.

80. An inductor-coil of inductance 17 mH is constructed from a copper wire of length 100 m and cross-sectional area 1 mm^2. Calculate the time constant of the circuit if this inductor is joined across an ideal battery. The resistivity of copper $= 1·7 \times 10^{-8}$ Ωm.

81. An LR circuit having a time constant of 50 ms is connected with an ideal battery of emf $\mathcal{E}$. Find the time elapsed before (a) the current reaches half its maximum value, (b) the power dissipated in heat reaches half its maximum value and (c) the magnetic field energy stored in the circuit reaches half its maximum value.

82. A coil having an inductance L and a resistance R is connected to a battery of emf $\mathcal{E}$. Find the time taken for the magnetic energy stored in the circuit to change from one fourth of the steady-state value to half of the steady-state value.

83. A solenoid having inductance 4·0 H and resistance 10 Ω is connected to a 4·0 V battery at $t = 0$. Find (a) the time constant, (b) the time elapsed before the current reaches 0·63 of its steady-state value, (c) the power delivered by the battery at this instant and (d) the power dissipated in Joule heating at this instant.

84. The magnetic field at a point inside a 2·0 mH inductor-coil becomes 0·80 of its maximum value in 20 μs when the inductor is joined to a battery. Find the resistance of the circuit.

85. An LR circuit with emf $\mathcal{E}$ is connected at $t = 0$. (a) Find the charge Q which flows through the battery during 0 to t. (b) Calculate the work done by the battery during this period. (c) Find the heat developed during this period. (d) Find the magnetic field energy stored in the circuit at time t. (e) Verify that the results in the three parts above are consistent with energy conservation.

86. An inductor of inductance 2·00 H is joined in series with a resistor of resistance 200 Ω and a battery of emf 2·00 V. At $t = 10$ ms, find (a) the current in the circuit, (b) the power delivered by the battery, (c) the power dissipated in heating the resistor and (d) the rate at which energy is being stored in magnetic field.

87. Two coils A and B have inductances 1·0 H and 2·0 H respectively. The resistance of each coil is 10 Ω. Each coil is connected to an ideal battery of emf 2·0 V at $t = 0$. Let i_A and i_B be the currents in the two circuit at time t. Find the ratio i_A / i_B at (a) $t = 100$ ms, (b) $t = 200$ ms and (c) $t = 1$ s.

88. The current in a discharging LR circuit without the battery drops from 2·0 A to 1·0 A in 0·10 s. (a) Find the time constant of the circuit. (b) If the inductance of the circuit is 4·0 H, what is its resistance?

89. A constant current exists in an inductor-coil connected to a battery. The coil is short-circuited and the battery is removed. Show that the charge flown through the coil after the short-circuiting is the same as that which flows in one time constant before the short-circuiting.

90. Consider the circuit shown in figure (38-E33). (a) Find the current through the battery a long time after the switch S is closed. (b) Suppose the switch is again opened at $t = 0$. What is the time constant of the discharging circuit ? (c) Find the current through the inductor after one time constant.

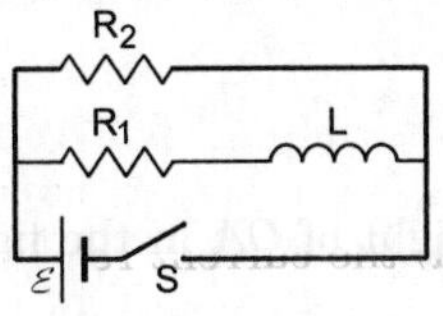

Figure 38-E33

91. A current of 1·0 A is established in a tightly wound solenoid of radius 2 cm having 1000 turns/metre. Find the magnetic energy stored in each metre of the solenoid.

92. Consider a small cube of volume 1 mm^3 at the centre of a circular loop of radius 10 cm carrying a current of 4 A. Find the magnetic energy stored inside the cube.

93. A long wire carries a current of 4·00 A. Find the energy stored in the magnetic field inside a volume of 1·00 mm^3 at a distance of 10·0 cm from the wire.

94. The mutual inductance between two coils is 2·5 H. If the current in one coil is changed at the rate of 1 As^{-1}, what will be the emf induced in the other coil ?

95. Find the mutual inductance between the straight wire and the square loop of figure (38-E27).

96. Find the mutual inductance between the circular coil and the loop shown in figure (38-E8).

97. A solenoid of length 20 cm, area of cross-section 4·0 cm^2 and having 4000 turns is placed inside another solenoid of 2000 turns having a cross-sectional area 8·0 cm^2 and length 10 cm. Find the mutual inductance between the solenoids.

98. The current in a long solenoid of radius R and having n turns per unit length is given by $i = i_0 \sin \omega t$. A coil having N turns is wound around it near the centre. Find (a) the induced emf in the coil and (b) the mutual inductance between the solenoid and the coil.

□

ANSWERS

OBJECTIVE I

1. (b)	2. (a)	3. (d)	4. (c)	5. (b)	6. (c)
7. (a)	8. (b)	9. (b)	10. (a)	11. (c)	12. (d)

OBJECTIVE II

1. (b), (c)	2. (d)	3. (c), (d)
4. (a), (c), (d)	5. (a), (b), (c)	6. (b), (d)
7. (d)	8. (b)	9. (a), (b), (c)
10. (b), (c)		

EXERCISE

1. $ML^2I^{-1}T^{-3}$ in each case
2. (a) volt/sec, volt, volt-sec (or weber) (b) 1·2 volt
3. (a) – 2·0 mV, – 4·0 mV, 4·0 mV, 2·0 mV
(b)10 ms to 20 ms and 20 ms to 30 ms
4. $7{\cdot}8 \times 10^{-3}$ V
5. 1×10^{-10} V
6. (a) 50 V (b) 50 V (c) zero
7. (a) 25 J (b) 25 J (c) 50 J
8. (a) 0·015 V (b) $7{\cdot}5 \times 10^{-3}$ V (c) zero
9. 10 μV
10. 5·0 T
11. BA/R
12. 2×10^{-4} C
13. (a) $2Bav$ (b) $2Bav/R$ (c) $a^2 B/R$
14. $\mathcal{E}$ = 1·0 V, anticlockwise
15. zero
16. (a) 3×10^{-4} V, (b) zero, (c) 3×10^{-4} V and (d) zero
17. 2×10^{-4} J
18. $3{\cdot}9 \times 10^{-5}$ A
19. (a) $1{\cdot}25 \times 10^{-7}$ A, a to d (b) $1{\cdot}25 \times 10^{-7}$ A, d to a, (c) zero (d) zero
20. $\dfrac{\pi\mu_0 N a^2 a'^2 \mathcal{E} R v}{2L(a^2+x^2)^{3/2}(R'+r)^2}$ where $R' = R$ for part (a) and $R/2$ for part (b)
21. (a) $6{\cdot}28 \times 10^{-2}$ V (b) $1{\cdot}57 \times 10^{-3}$ C
22. (a) $2{\cdot}0 \times 10^{-3}$ V (b) zero (c) $5{\cdot}0 \times 10^{-5}$ C
23. $4{\cdot}7 \times 10^{-5}$ C
24. (a) $6{\cdot}6 \times 10^{-4}$ V (b) zero (c) $2{\cdot}2 \times 10^{-7}$ V^2
25. $1{\cdot}3 \times 10^{-7}$ J

26. $1{\cdot}57 \times 10^{-6}$ V

27. (a) $1{\cdot}6 \times 10^{-21}$ N (b) $1{\cdot}0 \times 10^{-2}$ V m^{-1} (c) $2{\cdot}0 \times 10^{-3}$ V

28. 0·4 V

29. 0·09 V

30. 1 mV

31. (a) zero (b) $vB(bc)$, positive at c (c) zero (d) $vB(bc)$, positive at a

32. (a) $2rvB$ (b) zero

33. 17×10^{-3} V

34. (a) at the ends of the diameter perpendicular to the velocity, $2\,rvB$ (b) at the ends of the diameter parallel to the velocity, zero

35. zero

36. $\dfrac{Blv}{2r(l+vt)}$

37. (a) $\dfrac{B^2l^2v}{2r(l+vt)}$ (b) l/v

38. (a) $\dfrac{Blv}{R+r}$ (b) $\dfrac{B^2l^2v}{m(R+r)}$ towards left (c) $v = v_0 - \dfrac{B^2l^2x}{m(R+r)}$

(d) $\dfrac{mv_0(R+r)}{B^2l^2}$

39. (a) 25 m s^{-1} (b) $4{\cdot}0 \times 10^{-2}$ V (c) $3{\cdot}6 \times 10^{-2}$ V

(d) $4{\cdot}0 \times 10^{-3}$ V

40. $\tan^{-1}(1/3)$

42. (a) 0·1 mA (b) zero

43. (a) zero (b) 1 mA

44. (a) 0·1 mA (b) 0·2 mA

45. $\dfrac{ir - Blv}{2r}$

46. $ilBt/m$, away from the generator

47. $2\sqrt{l/g}$

48. (a) $\dfrac{RF - vl^2B^2}{mR}$ (b) $\dfrac{RF}{l^2B^2}$

49. (a) $\dfrac{1}{r}(E - vBl)$ from b to a (b) $\dfrac{lB}{r}(E - vBl)$ towards right (c) $\dfrac{E}{Bl}$

50. (a) vBl (b) $\dfrac{vBl}{r}$, b to a (c) $g - \dfrac{B^2l^2}{mr}v$ (d) $\dfrac{mgr}{B^2l^2}$

(e) $v_m(1 - e^{-gt/v_m})$ (f) $v_m t - \dfrac{v_m^2}{g}(1 - e^{-gt/v_m})$

51. $9{\cdot}4 \times 10^{-6}$ V

52. $\dfrac{1}{2}\omega r^2B$

53. 0·5 mA, leaves

54. $\dfrac{B_0 v_0 l}{2}$

55. $\dfrac{\mu_0 iv}{2\pi}\ln\left(\dfrac{2x+l}{2x-l}\right)$

56. (a) $\dfrac{v}{R}\left\{\dfrac{\mu_0 i}{2\pi}\ln\dfrac{2x+l}{2x-l}\right\}^2$ (b) $\dfrac{\mu_0 iv}{2\pi R}\ln\dfrac{2x+l}{2x-l}$

(c) $\dfrac{1}{R}\left\{\dfrac{\mu_0 iv}{2\pi}\ln\dfrac{2x+l}{2x-l}\right\}^2$ (d) same as (c)

57. (a) $\dfrac{\mu_0 ia}{2\pi}\ln\left(1+\dfrac{a}{b}\right)$ (b) $\dfrac{\mu_0 ai_0\omega\cos\omega t}{2\pi}\ln\left(1+\dfrac{a}{b}\right)$

(c) $\dfrac{5\mu_0 a^2 i_0^2\omega}{2\pi r}\ln^2\left(1+\dfrac{a}{b}\right)$

58. $\dfrac{\mu\, ilvb}{2\pi a(a+l)}$

59. $\dfrac{\omega a^3B^2}{2R}$ to the right of OA in the figure

60. $\dfrac{8}{3}\dfrac{\omega a^2B}{R}$

61. $\dfrac{\omega a^3B^2}{2R} - mg\sin\theta$

62. $\dfrac{aB(2\mathcal{E} + \omega a^2B)}{2\,mg\cos\theta}$

63. $\dfrac{mg}{m + CB^2l^2}$

64. (a) $\dfrac{r}{2}\dfrac{dB}{dt}$

65. (a) $1{\cdot}6 \times 10^{-8}$ weber (b) $1{\cdot}2 \times 10^{-7}$ V m^{-1}

(c) $5{\cdot}6 \times 10^{-7}$ V m^{-1}

66. 0·4 H

67. 4×10^{-2} H

68. 6×10^{-4} V

69. 2·3, 4·6, 6·9

70. 0·50 s

71. (a) 0·17 A (b) 0·03 J

72. 4·0 H

73. 0·66 V

74. (a) 0·44 A (b) 0·79 A (c) 1·8 A and (d) 2·0 A

75. (a) 0·27 A s^{-1} (b) 0·036 A s^{-1} and (c) $4{\cdot}1 \times 10^{-9}$ A s^{-1}

76. (a) 0·27 V (b) 0·036 V (c) $4{\cdot}1 \times 10^{-9}$ V

77. (a) $2{\cdot}5 \times 10^3$ V s^{-1} (b) 17 V s^{-1} and (c) 0·00 V s^{-1}

78. (a) 3·16 V (b) 4·97 V and (c) 5·00 V

79. (a) 1·8 mC (b) 5·7 mC and (c) 45 mC

80. 10 ms

81. (a) 35 ms (b) 61 ms (c) 61 ms

82. $\tau\ln\dfrac{1}{2-\sqrt{2}}$

83. (a) 0·40 s (b) 0·40 s (c) 1·0 W and (d) 0·64 W

84. 160 Ω

85. (a) $\frac{\mathcal{E}}{R}\{t-\frac{L}{R}(1-x)\}$

(b) $\frac{\mathcal{E}^2}{R}\{t-\frac{L}{R}(1-x)\}$

(c) $\frac{\mathcal{E}^2}{R}\{t-\frac{L}{2R}(3-4x+x^2)\}$

(d) $\frac{L\mathcal{E}^2}{2R^2}(1-x)^2$, where $x=e^{-Rt/L}$

86. (a) 6·3 mA (b) 12·6 mW (c) 8·0 mW and (d) 4·6 mW

87. (a) 1·6 (b) 1·4 (c) 1·0

88. (a) 0·14 s (b) 28 Ω

90. (a) $\frac{\mathcal{E}(R_1+R_2)}{R_1R_2}$ (b) $\frac{L}{R_1+R_2}$ (c) $\frac{\mathcal{E}}{R_1e}$

91. 7.9×10^{-4} J

92. $8\pi\times10^{-14}$ J

93. 2.55×10^{-14} J

94. 2·5 V

95. $\frac{\mu_0 a}{2\pi}\ln\left(1+\frac{a}{b}\right)$

96. $N\frac{\mu_0\pi a^2 a'^2}{2(a^2+x^2)^{3/2}}$

97. 2.0×10^{-2} H

98. (a) $\pi\mu_0 i_0 nN\omega R^2\cos\omega t$ (b) $\pi\mu_0 nNR^2$

□

CHAPTER 39

ALTERNATING CURRENT

39.1 ALTERNATING CURRENT

When a resistor is connected across the terminals of a battery, a current is established in the circuit. The current has a unique direction, it goes from the positive terminal to the negative terminal via the external resistor. The magnitude of the current also remains almost constant. If the direction of the current in a resistor or in any other element changes alternately, the current is called an *alternating current* (AC). In this chapter, we shall study the alternating current that varies sinusoidally with time. Such a current is given by

$$i = i_0 \sin(\omega t + \varphi). \quad \dots (39.1)$$

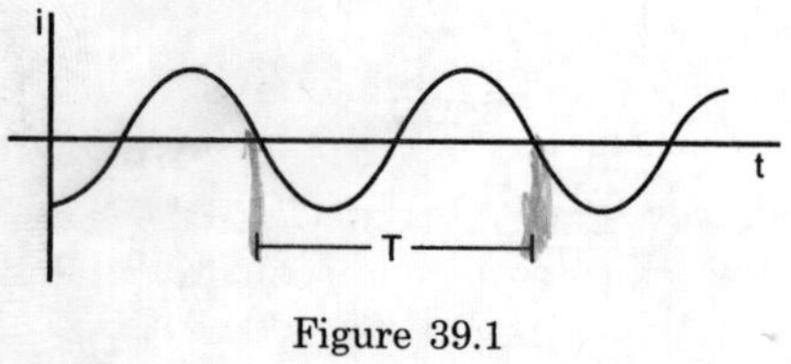

Figure 39.1

The current repeats its value after each time interval $T = 2\pi/\omega$. This time interval is called the *time period*. The current is positive for half the time period and is negative for the remaining half period. This means, its direction reverses after each half time period. The maximum value of the current is i_0 which is called the *peak current* or the *current amplitude*. To get sinusoidally varying alternating current, we need a source which can generate sinusoidally varying emf. An *AC generator,* also called an *AC dynamo*, can be used as such a source. It converts mechanical energy into electrical energy, producing an alternating emf.

39.2 AC GENERATOR, OR AC DYNAMO

Construction

A schematic design of an AC dynamo is shown in figure (39.2a). A simplified diagram of the same is shown in figure (39.2b). It consists of three main parts: a magnet, an armature with slip rings and brushes.

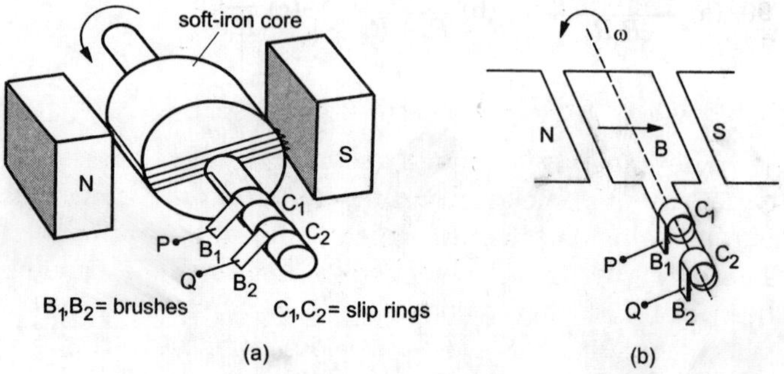

Figure 39.2

Magnet: It may be a permanent magnet or an electromagnet. The poles of the magnet face each other so that a strong uniform magnetic field $\vec{B}$ is produced between the poles.

Armature: It is a coil generally wound over a soft-iron core. The core increases the magnetic field due to its magnetization. The two ends of the coil are connected to two slip rings C_1 and C_2. The coil together with the rings can rotate in the magnetic field. The axis of rotation is in the plane of the coil but perpendicular to the magnetic field.

Brushes: Two graphite brushes B_1 and B_2 permanently touch the slip rings. As the armature rotates, the slip rings C_1 and C_2 slip against the brushes so that the contact is maintained all the time. These brushes are connected to two terminals P and Q. The external circuit is connected to these terminals.

emf Induced as the Coil Rotates

Suppose the area of the coil is A, it contains N turns and it is rotated at a constant angular velocity ω. Suppose, the plane of the coil is perpendicular to the magnetic field at $t = 0$. The total magnetic flux through each turn of the coil is BA in this position. In time t, the coil rotates through an angle $\theta = \omega t$. The flux through each turn of the coil at this time t is

$$\Phi = BA \cos \omega t.$$

Using Faraday's law, the emf induced in each turn of the coil is

$$-\frac{d\Phi}{dt} = BA\omega \sin \omega t.$$

The total emf induced in the coil is,

$$\mathcal{E} = NBA\,\omega \sin \omega t$$

$$= \mathcal{E}_0 \sin \omega t. \qquad \dots \ (39.2)$$

We see that the emf varies sinusoidally with time with an angular frequency ω and hence with a time period $T = 2\pi/\omega$. The maximum magnitude of the emf, known as *peak emf*, is $\mathcal{E}_0$.

If the terminals P and Q are connected to an external circuit, this emf drives a current in the circuit which also varies sinusoidally with time as shown in figure (39.1).

Household Power Generation

The electricity that we use in our houses is generally AC electricity and is produced in power plants using the same principle as described above. The armature is connected to a *turbine*. The turbine has a rotor with blades. Steam at high pressure, water from a height or air at high speed strikes the blades. This rotates the rotor of the turbine. As the armature is connected to the turbine, the armature also rotates and alternating emf is produced. Gensets, which are used in houses at the time of power failure, at marriage functions, at public meetings, in fields where regular electric power is not available, etc., also work on the same principle. Here a diesel or a petrol engine drives the armature.

39.3 INSTANTANEOUS AND RMS CURRENT

An alternating current is given by

$$i = i_0 \sin(\omega t + \varphi). \qquad \dots \ \text{(i)}$$

This equation gives the instantaneous current at any instant t. The current changes with time, sometimes it is positive and sometimes negative. We define the *average current* or *mean current* over a time interval 0 to t as

$$\bar{i} = \frac{\int_0^t i\,dt}{\int_0^t dt} = \frac{1}{T}\int_0^t i\,dt \cdot$$

Using (i),

$$\bar{i} = \frac{i_0}{t}\int_0^t \sin(\omega t + \varphi)\,dt = -\frac{i_0}{t}\left[\frac{\cos(\omega t + \varphi)}{\omega}\right]_0^t .$$

$$\text{or,} \quad \bar{i} = -\frac{i_0}{t}\left[\frac{\cos(\omega t + \varphi) - \cos\varphi}{\omega}\right]. \qquad \dots \ \text{(ii)}$$

For a time period, $t = T$ and $\omega T = 2\pi$ so that,

$$\bar{i} = -\frac{i_0}{T\omega}\left[\cos(2\pi + \varphi) - \cos\varphi\right] = 0.$$

If we take the average over a long time, the value of i will be the same as for one time period. This can be easily seen from equation (ii). As cosine of an angle must remain between ± 1, the numerator has a finite value. If t is large, the denominator is large and the average current $\bar{i}$ tends to zero.

The instantaneous current i could be positive or negative at a given instant but the quantity i^2 always remains positive and hence its average is also positive. The average of i^2 over a time period is

$$\overline{i^2} = \frac{\int_0^T i^2\,dt}{\int_0^T dt}$$

$$= \frac{1}{T}\int_0^T i_0^2 \sin^2(\omega t + \varphi)\,dt$$

$$= \frac{i_0^2}{2T}\int_0^T [1 - \cos 2(\omega t + \varphi)]\,dt$$

$$= \frac{i_0^2}{2T}\left[t - \frac{\sin 2(\omega t + \varphi)}{2\omega}\right]_0^T$$

$$= \frac{i_0^2}{2T}\left[T - \frac{\sin(4\pi + 2\varphi) - \sin 2\varphi}{2\omega}\right] = \frac{i_0^2}{2}.$$

This is known as the *mean square current*. The square root of mean square current is called *root-mean-square current* or rms current. This is also known as the *virtual current*. Thus, the rms current or the virtual current corresponding to the current $i = i_0 \sin(\omega t + \varphi)$ is

$$i_{rms} = \sqrt{\overline{i^2}} = \frac{i_0}{\sqrt{2}} \cdot \qquad \dots \ (39.3)$$

The equations for mean square current and root-mean-square current are derived for one time period. They are also valid if the average is calculated over a long period of time.

An alternating voltage (potential difference) may be written as

$$V = V_0 \sin(\omega t + \varphi).$$

This gives the instantaneous voltage. The mean voltage $\bar{V}$ over a complete cycle is zero, the mean square voltage over a cycle is $V_0^2/2$ and the root-mean-square voltage (rms voltage or virtual voltage) is $V_0/\sqrt{2}$. The significance of rms current and rms voltage may be shown by considering a resistor of resistance R carrying a current

$$i = i_0 \sin(\omega t + \varphi). \qquad \dots \ \text{(i)}$$

The voltage across the resistor is

$$V = Ri = (i_0 R)\sin(\omega t + \varphi). \quad \text{... (ii)}$$

The thermal energy developed in the resistor during the time t to $t + dt$ is

$$i^2 R\,dt = i_0^2 R \sin^2(\omega t + \varphi)dt.$$

The thermal energy developed in one time period is

$$U = \int_0^T i^2 R dt$$

$$= R\int_0^T i_0^2 \sin^2(\omega t + \varphi)dt$$

$$= RT\left[\frac{1}{T}\int_0^T i_0^2 \sin^2(\omega t + \varphi)dt\right]$$

$$= i_{rms}^2 RT.$$

Thus, if we pass a constant current i_{rms} through the resistor, it will produce the same thermal energy in a time period as that produced when the alternating current i passes through it. Similarly, a constant voltage V_{rms} applied across a resistor produces the same thermal energy as that produced by the voltage $V = V_0 \sin(\omega t + \varphi)$. These statements are also valid if we consider a long period of time. The alternating voltage and the alternating current are generally measured and mentioned in terms of their rms values. When we say that the household supply is 220 V AC we mean that the rms value is 220 V. The peak value would be (220 V) $\sqrt{2}$ = 311 V.

Example 39.1

The peak value of an alternating current is 5 A *and its frequency is* 60 Hz. *Find its rms value. How long will the current take to reach the peak value starting from zero?*

Solution :

The rms current is

$$i_{rms} = \frac{i_0}{\sqrt{2}} = \frac{5\text{ A}}{\sqrt{2}} = 3{\cdot}5\text{ A}.$$

The time period is

$$T = \frac{1}{\nu} = \frac{1}{60}\text{ s}.$$

The current takes one fourth of the time period to reach the peak value starting from zero. Thus, the time required is

$$t = \frac{T}{4} = \frac{1}{240}\text{ s}.$$

39.4 SIMPLE AC CIRCUITS

AC Circuit Containing only a Resistor

Figure (39.3) shows a circuit containing an AC source $\mathcal{E} = \mathcal{E}_0 \sin\omega t$ and a resistor of resistance R.

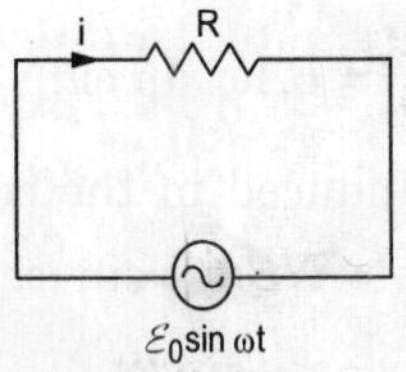

Figure 39.3

Such a circuit is also known as a *purely resistive circuit*. Notice the symbol for an AC source.

If the current at time t is i, Kirchhoff's loop law gives

$$\mathcal{E}_0 \sin\omega t = Ri$$

or, $$i = \frac{\mathcal{E}_0}{R}\sin\omega t$$

$$= i_0 \sin\omega t \quad \text{... (39.4)}$$

where $$i_0 = \frac{\mathcal{E}_0}{R}. \quad \text{... (39.5)}$$

AC Circuit Containing only a Capacitor

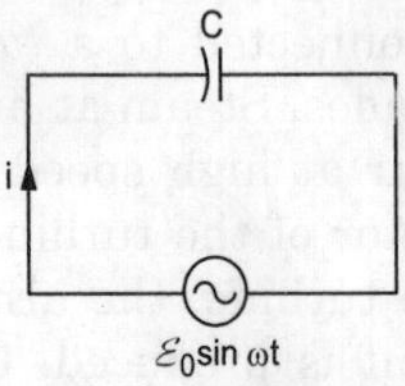

Figure 39.4

Figure (39.4) shows an AC source connected across a capacitor. The resistance of the circuit is assumed to be zero. Such a circuit is also known as a *purely capacitive circuit*. Suppose the charge on the capacitor is q and the current is i at time t. Any charge that goes through a wire accumulates on the capacitor, so that

$$idt = dq$$

or, $$i = \frac{dq}{dt}.$$

Using Kirchhoff's loop law,

$$\mathcal{E}_0 \sin\omega t = \frac{q}{C}$$

or, $$q = C\mathcal{E}_0 \sin\omega t$$

or, $$i = \frac{dq}{dt} = C\mathcal{E}_0\,\omega\cos\omega t$$

or, $$i = i_0 \cos\omega t \quad \text{... (39.6)}$$

where $$i_0 = C\mathcal{E}_0\,\omega = \frac{\mathcal{E}_0}{1/\omega C}. \quad \text{... (39.7)}$$

There are several points to be discussed. If a battery is connected across a capacitor, there is a current only for a short time in which the capacitor gets charged. After this the current becomes negligible. In case of an AC source, the current exists as along as the source is connected. We say that *a capacitor stops direct current but allows alternating current.* The physical reason behind it is obvious. The charge on a capacitor is determined by the emf of the source. In case of an AC source, the emf keeps on changing. Accordingly, the charge q keeps on changing and we get continuous current through the connecting wires and the source.

Another important point to note is the relation between the peak emf and the peak current. We have

$$i_0 = \frac{\mathcal{E}_0}{1/\omega C}$$

or, $$i_0 = \frac{\mathcal{E}_0}{X_c} \text{ where } X_c = \frac{1}{\omega C}.$$

We see that $X_c = 1/\omega C$ plays the role of effective resistance. It is called the *reactance* of the capacitor and its unit is ohm. It depends on the capacitance of the capacitor as well as on the frequency of the AC source. For a source of high frequency, the reactance $X_c = 1/\omega C$ is small and the peak current i_0 is large. For a small frequency, the reactance $1/\omega C$ is large and consequently the peak current is small.

If the frequency is zero, we get a direct-current (DC) source producing a constant emf. In this case, the reactance $1/\omega C$ is infinity and $i_0 = 0$. So the response of a capacitor to an alternating-current source depends on the frequency of the source.

The third important point concerns the phase difference between the emf and the current. We have,

$$\mathcal{E} = \mathcal{E}_0 \sin \omega t$$

and $$i = i_0 \cos \omega t = i_0 \sin(\omega t + \pi/2).$$

Thus, the current leads the emf by $\pi/2$. When the emf $\mathcal{E}$ is zero, the current has maximum magnitude. When the emf has maximum magnitude, the current is zero. Figure (39.5) shows variations in the current through the capacitor and in the emf as time passes.

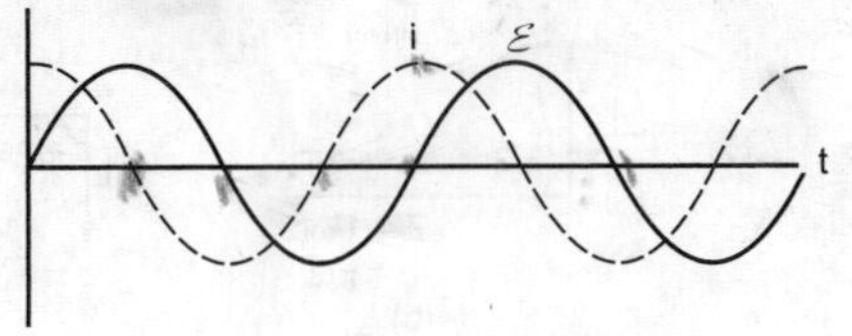

Figure 39.5

Example 39.1

Find the reactance of a capacitor ($C = 200\ \mu F$) when it is connected to (a) a 10 Hz AC source, (b) a 50 Hz AC source and (c) a 500 Hz AC source.

Solution :

The reactance is $X_c = \dfrac{1}{\omega C} = \dfrac{1}{2\pi\nu C}$.

(a) $$X_c = \frac{1}{2\pi(10\text{ Hz})(200 \times 10^{-6}\text{ F})}$$

$= 80\ \Omega$.

Similarly, the reactance is 16 Ω for 50 Hz and 1·6 Ω for 500 Hz.

AC Circuit Containing only an Inductor

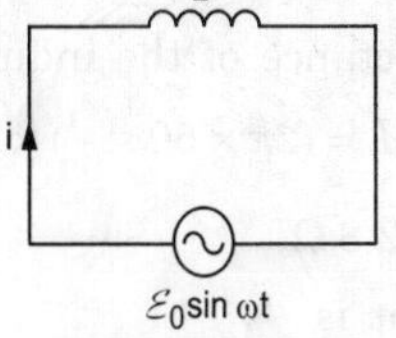

Figure 39.6

Figure (39.6) shows an inductor connected to an AC source. Such a circuit is also known as a *purely inductive circuit.*

The induced emf across the inductor is $-L\dfrac{di}{dt}$ so that from Kirchhoff's loop law,

$$\mathcal{E}_0 \sin \omega t - L\frac{di}{dt} = 0$$

or, $$\frac{di}{dt} = \frac{\mathcal{E}_0}{L} \sin \omega t$$

or, $$i = -\frac{\mathcal{E}_0}{\omega L} \cos \omega t + c \quad \text{... (i)}$$

where c is a constant. Now, average of $\cos \omega t$ over one time period is zero. Also, in the circuit we are discussing, the emf is sinusoidal and we expect the current to be sinusoidal too. Thus, average of i must be zero over one time period. Hence, from (i), $c = 0$ and

$$i = -\frac{\mathcal{E}_0}{\omega L} \cos \omega t$$

or, $$i = \frac{\mathcal{E}_0}{\omega L} \sin(\omega t - \pi/2) \quad \text{... (39.8)}$$

or, $$i = i_0 \sin(\omega t - \pi/2)$$

where $i_0 = \dfrac{\mathcal{E}_0}{\omega L}$. ... (39.9)

The constant $X_L = \omega L$ plays the role of effective resistance in this circuit. It is called the *reactance* of the inductor. It is zero for direct current ($\omega = 0$) and increases as the frequency is increased. We see from equation (39.8) that the phase of the current is $\pi/2$ less than that of the emf. The current lags behind the emf. Figure (39.7) shows plots of the current through an inductor and of the emf as time passes.

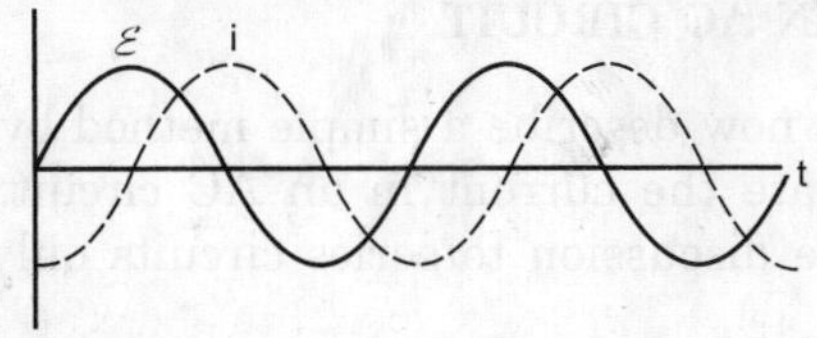

Figure 39.7

Example 39.2

An inductor (L = 200 mH) is connected to an AC source of peak emf 210 V and frequency 50 Hz. Calculate the peak current. What is the instantaneous voltage of the source when the current is at its peak value?

Solution : The reactance of the inductor is

$$X_L = \omega L = (2\pi \times 50 \text{ s}^{-1}) \times (200 \times 10^{-3} \text{ H})$$

$$= 62{\cdot}8\ \Omega.$$

The peak current is

$$i_0 = \frac{\mathcal{E}_0}{X_L} = \frac{210 \text{ V}}{62{\cdot}8\ \Omega} = 3{\cdot}3 \text{ A}.$$

As the current lags behind the voltage by $\pi/2$, the voltage is zero when the current has its peak value.

Impedance

The peak current and the peak emf in all the three circuits discussed above may be written as

$$i_0 = \frac{\mathcal{E}_0}{Z} \qquad \ldots \text{ (39.10)}$$

where $Z = R$ for a purely resistive circuit

$Z = \frac{1}{\omega C}$ for a purely capacitive circuit

and $Z = \omega L$ for a purely inductive circuit.

The peak current and the peak emf are related by equation (39.10) for any series circuit (one-loop circuit) having an AC source. The general name for Z is *impedance.* Thus, the impedance of a purely resistive circuit is R, that of a purely capacitive circuit is $1/\omega C$ and that of a purely inductive circuit is ωL.

Phase factor

We have seen that the current and the emf are, in general, not in phase in an AC circuit. If the emf is

$$\mathcal{E} = \mathcal{E}_0 \sin \omega t,$$

the current may be written as

$$i = i_0 \sin(\omega t + \varphi).$$

For a purely resistive circuit, $\varphi = 0$; for a purely capacitive circuit, $\varphi = \pi/2$ and for a purely inductive circuit, $\varphi = -\pi/2$. We shall call the constant φ the phase factor.

39.5 VECTOR METHOD TO FIND THE CURRENT IN AN AC CIRCUIT

Let us now describe a simple method by which we can calculate the current in an AC circuit. We shall confine the discussion to series circuits only. Suppose an emf

$$\mathcal{E} = \mathcal{E}_0 \sin \omega t$$

is applied in a series AC circuit which may contain a resistance, a capacitor, an inductor or any combination of these. Let us represent the resistance of a resistor by a vector of magnitude R, the reactance of a capacitance by a vector of magnitude $X_c = 1/\omega C$ and the reactance of an inductor by a vector of magnitude $X_L = \omega L$. The vector corresponding to the resistance is drawn along the X-axis, the vector for the capacitive reactance is drawn $\pi/2$ ahead of the resistance, that is, along the positive Y-axis and the vector for the inductive reactance is drawn $\pi/2$ behind the resistance, that is, along the negative Y-axis.

The impedance of the circuit, Z, and the phase factor φ are obtained by the vector sum of these three vectors. The magnitude of the vector sum gives the impedance Z, and its angle with the X-axis gives the phase factor.

Thus, if the resistance of the circuit is R and the net reactance is X, the impedance is $Z = \sqrt{R^2 + X^2}$ and $\tan\varphi = \frac{X}{R}$.

Once Z and φ are obtained, the current in the circuit can be easily written as

$$i = \frac{\mathcal{E}_0}{Z} \sin(\omega t + \varphi). \qquad \ldots \text{ (39.11)}$$

It should be clearly understood that the resistance, capacitance, inductance, etc., are not vector quantities. The above description is only a method to derive easily the equations for the current in an AC circuit. Figure (39.8) shows the construction of vector diagrams for the three circuits discussed above.

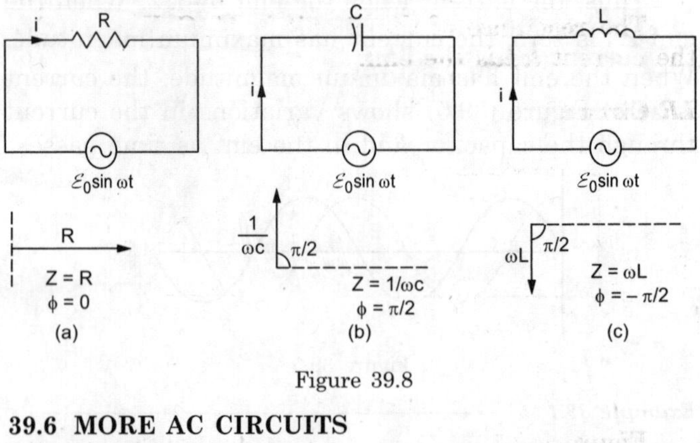

Figure 39.8

39.6 MORE AC CIRCUITS

When an AC source is connected in a circuit with a resistance and a reactance, the current varies initially in a complex way. After sufficient time, a sinusoidally varying current persists in the circuit. This steady-state current has a frequency equal to that of the source and may have a phase difference with the source. This steady-state current may be obtained by the vector method described above.

***CR* Circuit**

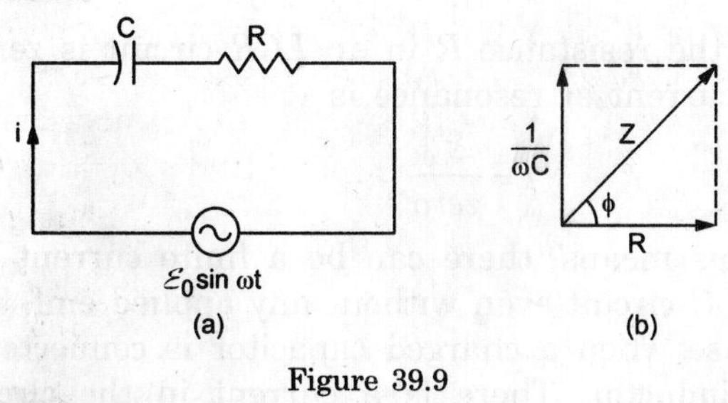

Figure 39.9

Let us find the current in a *CR* circuit using the vector method. The circuit and the corresponding vector diagram are drawn in figure (39.9). The resistance is represented by a vector of magnitude R along the x-axis and the capacitive reactance by a vector of magnitude $1/\omega C$ along the positive y-axis. The impedance of the circuit is given by the magnitude of the resultant of these two. It is

$$Z = \sqrt{R^2 + (1/\omega C)^2} \qquad \dots \text{ (i)}$$

and hence the peak current is

$$i_0 = \frac{\mathcal{E}_0}{Z} = \frac{\mathcal{E}_0}{\sqrt{R^2 + (1/\omega C)^2}}.$$

Also, the direction of the resultant makes an angle φ with the x-axis where

$$\tan\varphi = \frac{1}{\omega CR}. \qquad \dots \text{ (ii)}$$

The steady-state current in the circuit is

$$i = \frac{\mathcal{E}_0}{Z} \sin(\omega t + \varphi)$$

where Z and φ are given by equations (i) and (ii).

The reactance of the circuit is $1/\omega C$. We see that the current *leads* the emf.

***LR* Circuit**

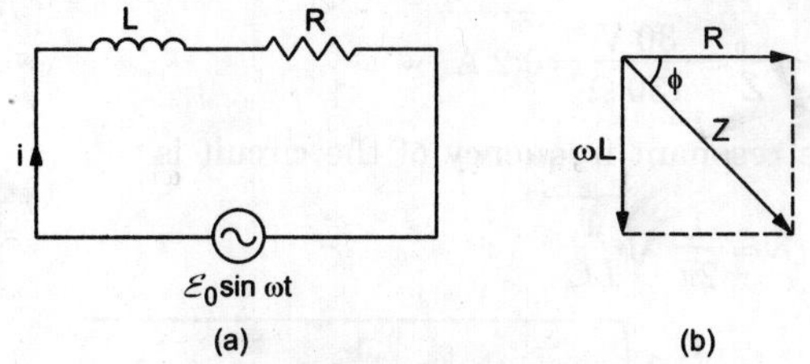

Figure 39.10

Figure (39.10) shows an inductor, a resistor and an AC source connected in series together with its vector diagram. The resistance is represented by a vector of magnitude R along the x-axis and the inductive reactance by a vector of magnitude ωL along the negative y-axis. The impedance of the circuit is equal to the magnitude of the resultant of these two. Its value is

$$Z = \sqrt{R^2 + \omega^2 L^2}. \qquad \dots \text{ (i)}$$

The resultant is at an angle φ below the x-axis where

$$\tan\varphi = \frac{\omega L}{R}. \qquad \dots \text{ (ii)}$$

The current in steady state is, therefore, given by

$$i = \frac{\mathcal{E}_0}{\sqrt{R^2 + \omega^2 L^2}} \sin(\omega t - \varphi)$$

where φ is given by equation (ii). The reactance of the circuit is ωL. We see that the current *lags* behind the emf.

***LCR* Circuit**

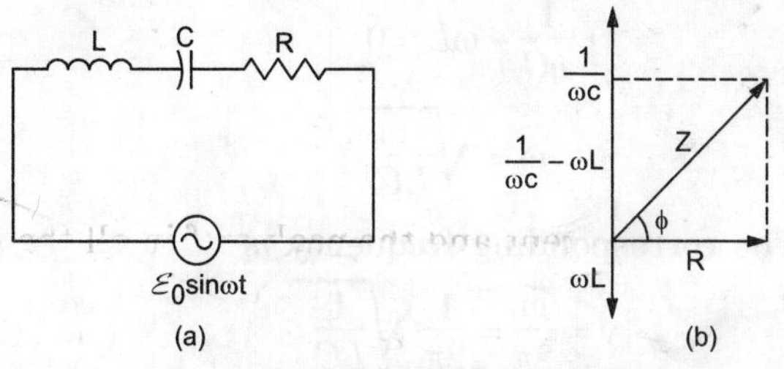

Figure 39.11

Figure (39.11) shows an inductor, a capacitor and a resistor connected in series with an AC source and the vector diagram to find the steady-state current.

The resultant of $1/\omega C$ and ωL is

$$X = X_c - X_L = \left(\frac{1}{\omega C} - \omega L\right)$$

in the direction of the positive y-axis. This is the net reactance of the circuit. The resultant of the vector for R and that for the reactance $\left(\frac{1}{C\omega} - L\omega\right)$ has a magnitude

$$Z = \sqrt{R^2 + \left(\frac{1}{\omega C} - \omega L\right)^2} \qquad \dots \text{ (39.12)}$$

which is the impedance of the circuit. This resultant makes an angle φ with the x-axis where

$$\tan\varphi = \frac{\frac{1}{\omega C} - \omega L}{R}. \qquad \dots \text{ (39.13)}$$

The steady-state current in the circuit is given by

$$i = \frac{\mathcal{E}_0}{\sqrt{R^2 + \left(\frac{1}{\omega C} - \omega L\right)^2}} \sin(\omega t + \varphi)$$

where φ is given by equation (39.13).

If $X_c = 1/\omega C$ is greater than $X_L = \omega L$, the vector for the net reactance $X_c - X_L$ is along the positive Y-axis. From equation (39.13), the phase factor φ is positive. Thus, the current *leads* the emf. If $X_c < X_L$, the vector for the net reactance is along the negative Y-axis and φ is negative. In this case, the current *lags* behind the emf. If $X_L = X_c$, the net reactance is zero. It behaves as purely resistive circuit and the vector for Z is along the X-axis. The current is in phase with the emf in this case.

If we vary the angular frequency ω of the AC source, the peak current

$$i_0 = \frac{\mathcal{E}_0}{\sqrt{R^2 + \left(\frac{1}{\omega C} - \omega L\right)^2}}$$

also varies. It is maximum when

$$\frac{1}{\omega C} - \omega L = 0$$

or,

$$\omega = \sqrt{\frac{1}{LC}}.$$

The corresponding frequency is

$$\nu = \frac{\omega}{2\pi} = \frac{1}{2\pi}\sqrt{\frac{1}{LC}}. \quad \dots (39.14)$$

This frequency is known as the *resonant frequency* of the given circuit. The peak current in this case is $i_0 = \mathcal{E}_0/R$ and the reactance is zero.

Figure (39.12) shows the variation in the peak current i_0 with the applied frequency ν of the AC source in two different circuits. The values of L as well as the values of C are the same for the two circuits. We see that if R is small, the resonance is sharp. This means, if the applied frequency is close to the resonant frequency ν_0, the current is high, otherwise it is small. An LCR circuit used at a frequency close to the resonance frequency is called *resonant circuit.*

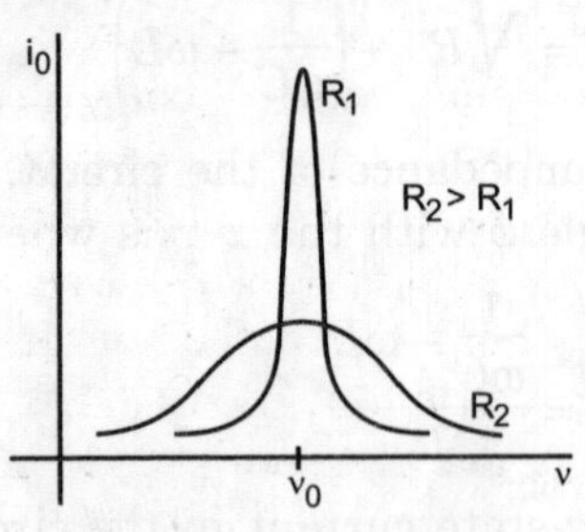

Figure 39.12

The tuning circuit of a radio or a television is an example of LCR resonant circuit. Signals are transmitted by different stations at different frequencies. The antenna receives these signals and drives a current in the tuning circuit. Only the signal corresponding to the resonant frequency is able to drive appreciable current and is further processed. When we 'tune' a radio, we change the capacitance of the tuning circuit and hence the resonant frequency changes. When this frequency matches with the frequency of the signal from the desired station, the tuning is complete.

***LC* oscillations**

If the resistance R in an LCR circuit is zero, the peak current at resonance is

$$i = \frac{\mathcal{E}_0}{zero}.$$

This means, there can be a finite current in the pure LC circuit even without any applied emf. This is the case when a charged capacitor is connected to a pure inductor. There is a current in the circuit at frequency $\nu = \frac{1}{2\pi}\sqrt{\frac{1}{LC}}$. The capacitor gets discharged sending a current in the inductor and induced emf in the inductor charges the capacitor again. Thus, the energy oscillates between electric field energy in the capacitor and magnetic field energy in the inductor. This phenomenon is called LC *oscillation*.

Example 39.3

An LCR series circuit with L = 100 mH, C = 100 μF, R = 120 Ω is connected to an AC source of emf $\mathcal{E} = (30\text{ V})\sin(100\text{ s}^{-1})t$. *Find the impedance, the peak current and the resonant frequency of the circuit.*

Solution :

The reactance of the circuit is

$$X = \frac{1}{\omega C} - \omega L$$

$$= \frac{1}{(100\text{ s}^{-1})(100 \times 10^{-6}\text{ F})} - (100\text{ s}^{-1}) \times (100 \times 10^{-3}\text{ H})$$

$$= 100\ \Omega - 10\ \Omega = 90\ \Omega.$$

The resistance is $R = 120\ \Omega$.

The impedance is

$$Z = \sqrt{R^2 + X^2}$$

$$= \sqrt{(120\ \Omega)^2 + (90\ \Omega)^2} = 150\ \Omega.$$

The peak current is

$$i_0 = \frac{\mathcal{E}_0}{Z} = \frac{30\text{ V}}{150\ \Omega} = 0{\cdot}2\text{ A}.$$

The resonant frequency of the circuit is

$$\nu = \frac{1}{2\pi}\sqrt{\frac{1}{LC}}$$

$$= \frac{1}{2\pi}\sqrt{\frac{1}{(100 \times 10^{-3}\text{ H})(100 \times 10^{-6}\text{ F})}}$$

$$\approx 50\text{ Hz}.$$

39.7 POWER IN AC CIRCUITS

Suppose an emf $\mathcal{E} = \mathcal{E}_0 \sin \omega t$ is applied in a circuit and a current $i = i_0 \sin(\omega t + \varphi)$ results. The work done by the source during the time interval t to $t + dt$ is

$$dW = \mathcal{E}\, i\, dt$$

$$= \mathcal{E}_0 \, i_0 \sin \omega t \sin(\omega t + \varphi) \, dt$$

$$= \mathcal{E}_0 \, i_0 (\sin^2 \omega t \cos \varphi + \sin \omega t \cos \omega t \sin \varphi) dt.$$

The total work done in a complete cycle is

$$W = \mathcal{E}_0 \, i_0 \cos\varphi \int_0^T \sin^2 \omega t \, dt + \mathcal{E}_0 \, i_0 \sin \varphi \int_0^T \sin \omega t \cos \omega t \, dt$$

$$= \frac{1}{2} \mathcal{E}_0 \, i_0 \cos \varphi \int_0^T (1 - \cos 2\omega t) dt + \frac{1}{2} \mathcal{E}_0 \, i_0 \sin \varphi \int_0^T \sin 2\omega t \, dt$$

$$= \frac{1}{2} \mathcal{E}_0 \, i_0 \, T \cos \varphi.$$

The average power delivered by the source is, therefore,

$$P = \frac{W}{T} = \frac{1}{2} \mathcal{E}_0 \, i_0 \cos\varphi = \left(\frac{\mathcal{E}_0}{\sqrt{2}}\right)\left(\frac{i_0}{\sqrt{2}}\right)(\cos\varphi)$$

$$= \mathcal{E}_{rms} \, i_{rms} \cos\varphi. \quad \ldots \quad (39.15)$$

This equation is derived for the average power in a complete cycle. It also represents the average power delivered in a long time.

The term $\cos\varphi$ is called the *power factor* of the circuit. For a purely resistive circuit, $\varphi = 0$ so that $\cos \varphi = 1$ and $P = \mathcal{E}_{rms} \, i_{rms}$. For purely reactive circuits (no resistance, only capacitance and/or inductance), $\varphi = \pi/2$ or $-\pi/2$. In these cases, $\cos\varphi = 0$ and hence no power is absorbed in such circuits.

39.8 CHOKE COIL

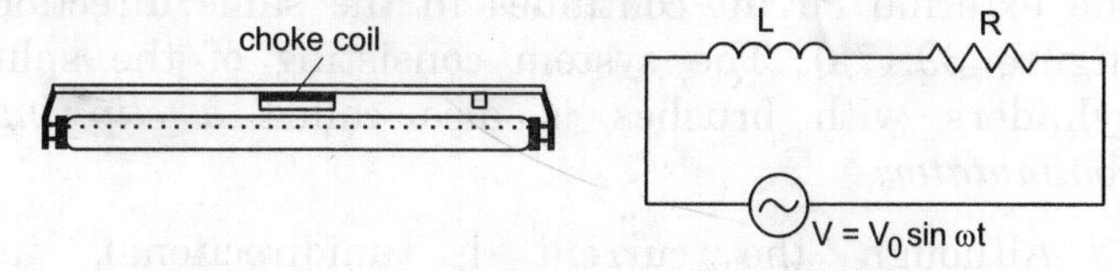

Figure 39.13

Choke coil is simply a coil having a large inductance but a small resistance. Choke coils are used with fluorescent mercury-tube fittings in houses (figure 39.13a).

At most places, the household electric power is supplied at 220 V, 50 Hz. If such a source is directly connected to a mercury tube, the tube will be damaged. To reduce the current, a choke coil is connected in series with the tube. Representing the tube by a resistor and the choke coil by an ideal inductor, the equivalent circuit is drawn in figure (39.13b). This is a simple LR circuit with impedance $Z = \sqrt{R^2 + \omega^2 L^2}$.

If the voltage applied is $V = V_0 \sin \omega t$, the peak current through the circuit is

$$i_0 = \frac{V_0}{\sqrt{R^2 + \omega^2 L^2}}.$$

The rms current is

$$i_{rms} = \frac{i_0}{\sqrt{2}} = \frac{V_0/\sqrt{2}}{\sqrt{R^2 + \omega^2 L^2}} = \frac{V_{rms}}{\sqrt{R^2 + \omega^2 L^2}}.$$

The rms voltage appearing across the resistor is

$$V_{R,\,rms} = R \, i_{rms} = \frac{R}{\sqrt{R^2 + \omega^2 L^2}} V_{rms}.$$

If the choke coil were not used, the voltage across the resistor would be the same as the applied voltage. Thus, by using the choke coil, the voltage across the resistor is reduced by a factor

$$\frac{R}{\sqrt{R^2 + \omega^2 L^2}}.$$

The advantage of using a choke coil to reduce the voltage is that an inductor does not consume power. Hence, we do not lose electric energy in the form of heat. If we connect an additional resistor in series with the tube to reduce the voltage, power will be lost in heating this additional resistor.

39.9 HOT-WIRE INSTRUMENTS

In an ordinary ammeter or voltmeter, a coil is free to rotate in the magnetic field of a fixed magnet. To measure a current or a voltage, current is passed through the coil and the coil deflects due to the torque acting on it. If an alternating current is passed through such a coil, the torque will reverse its direction each time the current changes direction and the average value of the torque will be zero. Because of friction, etc., the coil does not quickly respond to the changing torque and remains undeflected. To measure alternating currents or voltages, one would have to use a property so that the deflection of the moving part depends on i^2 and not on i. This ensures that the deflection remains independent of the direction of the current. The average of i^2 is not zero and hence a steady deflection may be obtained. Hot-wire instruments are designed to work on this principle.

Hot-wire Ammeter

The construction of a hot-wire ammeter is shown in figure (39.14). A platinum–iridium wire AB is fixed tightly between two fixed ends A and B. A spring is fixed at one end C and is permanently connected to a thin wire at the other end. The thin wire is wound several times over a cylinder D and the end is connected to the middle point of AB. The cylinder can rotate about its axis. A pointer connected to the

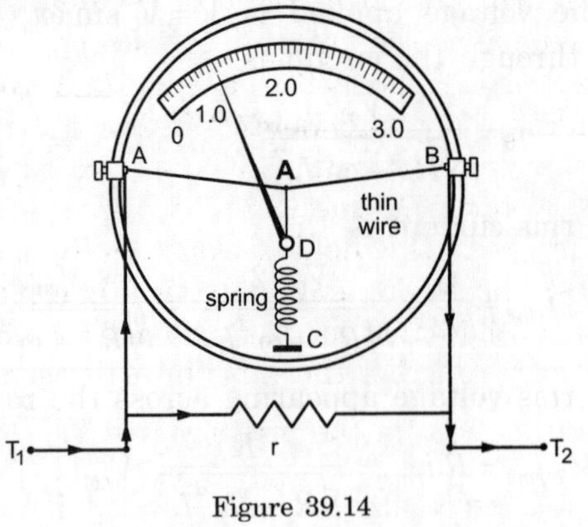

Figure 39.14

cylinder moves along a graduated scale when the cylinder rotates. A small resistance r is connected in parallel to the wire AB as a shunt. This makes the total resistance of the ammeter small so that it does not appreciably alter the current in the circuit. The points A and B are connected to the outer terminals T_1 and T_2.

The current to be measured is passed through the instrument via T_1, T_2. The wire AB gets heated due to the current, the rise in temperature being proportional to i^2_{rms}. The length of the wire increases and consequently its tension decreases. Because of the tension in the spring on the other side, the cylinder rotates a little and the pointer deflects along the scale. The deflection is proportional to i^2_{rms} but the scale is graduated in such a way that the reading gives directly the rms current.

Hot-wire Voltmeter

The construction of a hot-wire voltmeter is almost identical to a hot-wire ammeter except that a high resistance R is connected in series with the wire AB in place of the shunt r (figure 39.15). The alternating voltage to be measured is applied across T_1 and T_2. A current passes through AB and the pointer attached to the cylinder deflects. The deflection is proportional to V^2_{rms}. The scale is graduated in such a way that it reads directly the rms voltage.

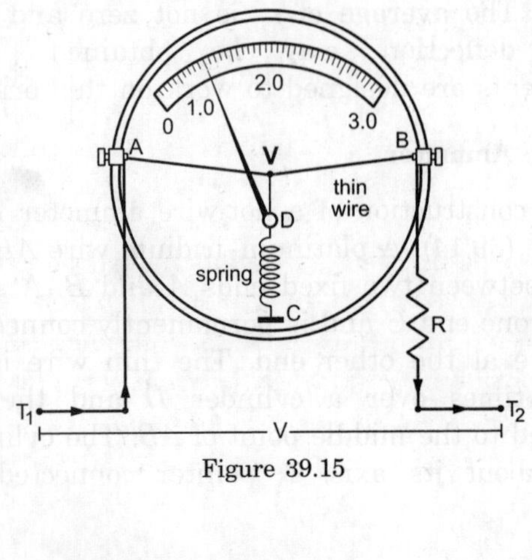

Figure 39.15

38.10 DC DYNAMO

An AC dynamo converts mechanical energy into electrical energy and it supplies alternating current in the circuit connected to it. A DC dynamo also converts mechanical energy into electrical energy but it supplies current in one direction only in the circuit connected to it.

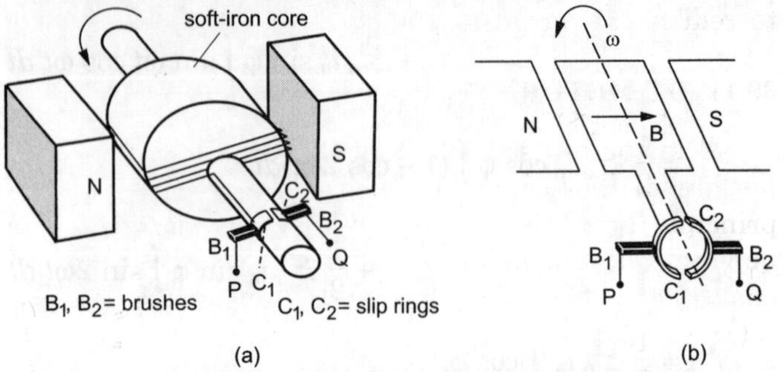

Figure 39.16

The basic design of a DC dynamo (figure 39.16a) is the same as that of an AC dynamo except for the slip rings. Figure (39.16b) shows a simplified diagram of the same. The slip rings are in the form of a split cylinder (figure 39.16). The ends of the armature (coil) are connected separately to the two halves C_1 and C_2 of the cylinders. The armature is rotated by some external agency. The split cylinder rotates with the armature. Two carbon brushes B_1 and B_2 press against the rotating halves C_1 and C_2. As the gaps pass under the brushes, the contacts to the external circuit are reversed. For half of a period of rotation, the terminal P is connected to C_1 and the terminal Q to C_2. For the other half of the period, P is connected to C_2 and Q to C_1. It is arranged in such a way that the gaps pass under the brushes at the time the emf becomes zero. Thus, although emf becomes negative, the current in the external circuit continues in the same direction (figure 39.17a). The system consisting of the split cylinders with brushes is also called a *slip-ring commutator*.

Although the current is unidirectional, its magnitude oscillates in time. To reduce the variation in the current, another coil perpendicular to the first

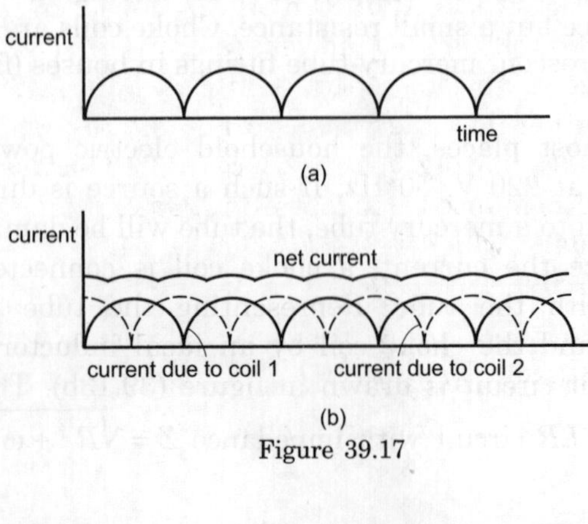

Figure 39.17

one is added in the system. The emf from this coil, again arranged properly with slip-ring commutator, is fed to the external circuit. The emf from this coil is maximum when the emf from the first coil is zero and vice versa. The sum of the two contains less oscillations and the current is more nearly constant (figure 39.17b). One can increase the number of coils to reduce the variation further.

39.11 DC MOTOR

A motor is used to convert electrical energy into mechanical energy and rotate a mechanical load. The principle of a DC motor is the same as that of a moving-coil galvanometer. The arrangement is basically the same as that of a DC dynamo. We can refer to figure (39.16) for its description. It has the field magnets, the armature, the slip rings and the brushes. A battery or the output of a DC generator is connected to the brushes through the outer terminals P and Q. The battery drives a current in the coil and because of the magnetic field, a torque acts on it. This torque rotates the coil which is on a shaft to which the mechanical load is attached. This way the load is rotated. The torque depends on the orientation of the coil besides the strength of the current in it. It is zero when the coil is perpendicular to the field and is maximum in magnitude when it is parallel to the field. As the coil rotates, an induced emf e is produced opposite to the applied emf $\mathcal{E}$. If the resistance of the circuit is R, the current at any instant is given by $i = (\mathcal{E} - e)/R$.

39.12 TRANSFORMER

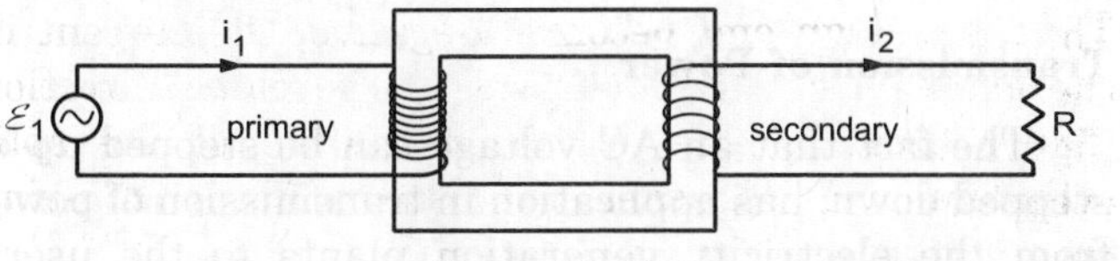

Figure 39.18

A transformer is used either to obtain a high AC voltage from a low-voltage AC source or to obtain a low AC voltage from a high-voltage AC source. The design of a simple transformer is shown in figure (39.18). Two coils are wound separately on a laminated soft-iron core. One of the coils is called the *primary* and the other is called the *secondary*. The original source of alternating voltage is connected across the primary. An induced emf appears across the ends of the secondary which is used to drive current in the desired circuit.

Suppose there are N_1 turns in the primary and N_2 turns in the secondary. An alternating emf $\mathcal{E}_1$ is applied across the primary which produces a current i_1 in the primary circuit and a current i_2 in the secondary circuit. The currents in the coils produce a magnetization in the soft-iron core and there is a corresponding magnetic field B inside the core. The field due to magnetization of the core is large as compared to the field due to the currents in the coils. We assume that the field is constant in magnitude everywhere in the core and hence its flux (BA) through each turn is the same for the primary as well as for the secondary coil. Let the flux through each turn be Φ. The emf induced in the primary is $-N_1 \frac{d\Phi}{dt}$ and that induced in the secondary is $-N_2 \frac{d\Phi}{dt} = \mathcal{E}_2$. If we neglect the resistance in the primary circuit, Kirchhoff's loop law applied to the primary circuit gives

$$\mathcal{E}_1 - N_1 \frac{d\Phi}{dt} = 0$$

or, $$\mathcal{E}_1 = N_1 \frac{d\Phi}{dt}. \qquad \text{... (i)}$$

Also, $$\mathcal{E}_2 = -N_2 \frac{d\Phi}{dt}. \qquad \text{... (ii)}$$

From (i) and (ii),

$$\mathcal{E}_2 = -\frac{N_2}{N_1}\mathcal{E}_1. \qquad \text{... (39.16)}$$

The minus sign shows that $\mathcal{E}_2$ is 180° out of phase with $\mathcal{E}_1$. Equations (i), (ii) and (39.16) are valid for all values of currents in the primary and the secondary circuits.

Power Transfer

Let us first consider the case when the terminals of the secondary are not connected to any external circuit. The secondary circuit is incomplete and the current through it is zero. Suppose, the current in the primary is i_s in this case (the subscript s stands for the source and not for the secondary). As we have neglected the resistance in the primary circuit, it is a purely inductive circuit. The current has a phase difference of 90° with the applied emf $\mathcal{E}_1$ and hence the power delivered by the AC source is zero. The power in the secondary circuit is anyway zero as there is no current in this circuit.

Now suppose, the terminals of the secondary are joined to a resistance R. There will be an alternating current i_2 through R. There will be additional emf's induced in the primary as well as in the secondary due to i_2. But the net induced emf in the primary should remain equal and opposite to the source-emf $\mathcal{E}_1$ by (i). So, there will be an additional current i_1 in the primary circuit which will cancel the emf induced due to i_2. Thus the current in the primary will be $i_s + i_1$ and in the secondary i_2. The emf in the secondary will remain $\mathcal{E}_2$ as given by (ii).

As the induced emf's due to i_1 and i_2 always cancel each other, the two alternating currents should be 180° out of phase. Also, i_2 is in phase with $\mathcal{E}_2$ (purely resistive circuit), and $\mathcal{E}_1$ is 180° out of phase with $\mathcal{E}_2$ (equation 39.16). This shows that i_1 is in phase with $\mathcal{E}_1$ (figure 39.19).

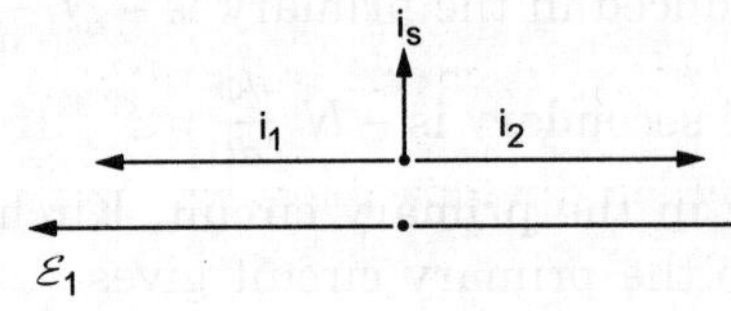

Figure 39.19

The primary current (current in the primary circuit) $i_s + i_1$, therefore, has a component i_s which is at a phase difference of 90° from the applied emf $\mathcal{E}_1$ and a component i_1 which is in phase with this emf. The power delivered by the AC source is, therefore, $\mathcal{E}_1 i_1$. The power consumed by the resistance in the secondary circuit is $\mathcal{E}_2 i_2$. Neglecting any loss of energy elsewhere,

$$\mathcal{E}_1 i_1 = \mathcal{E}_2 i_2. \quad \dots \text{(i)}$$

Using equation (39.16),

$$i_2 = -\frac{N_1}{N_2} i_1. \quad \dots (39.17)$$

The minus sign shows that i_2 is 180° out of phase with i_1.

Quite often, the additional current i_1 in the primary is much larger than the original current i_s. This can be easily shown by connecting an electric bulb in series with the primary. The bulb glows much brighter when the secondary circuit is completed than when it is open. If i_s is negligible as compared to i_1, equation (39.17) gives the relation between the net currents.

Step-up and Step-down Transformers

If $N_2 > N_1$, the secondary emf $\mathcal{E}_2$ is larger in magnitude than the primary emf $\mathcal{E}_1$. This type of transformer is called a *step-up* transformer. The secondary current is less than the primary current. The primary coil is made from a thick wire so that it can sustain the high current.

If $N_2 < N_1$, the emf in the secondary circuit is smaller in magnitude than the primary emf. This type of transformer is called a *step-down* transformer. The secondary current is more than the primary current and the wire used to make the secondary coil should be sufficiently thick to carry the high current.

Efficiency of a Transformer

In an ordinary transformer, there is some loss of energy due to primary resistance, hysteresis in the core, eddy currents in the core, etc. The efficiency of a transformer is defined as

$$\eta = \frac{\text{output power}}{\text{input power}}.$$

Efficiencies of the order of 99% can be easily achieved.

Example 39.5

A radio set operates at 6 V DC. A transformer with 18 turns in the secondary coil is used to step down the input 220 V AC emf to 6 V AC emf. This AC emf is then rectified by another circuit to give 6 V DC which is fed to the radio. Find the number of turns in the primary.

Solution :

We have,
$$\left|\frac{\mathcal{E}_2}{\mathcal{E}_1}\right| = \frac{N_2}{N_1}$$

or,
$$N_1 = \left|\frac{\mathcal{E}_1}{\mathcal{E}_2}\right| N_2 = \frac{220}{6} \times 18 = 660.$$

Transmission of Power

The fact that an AC voltage can be stepped up or stepped down, has application in transmission of power from the electricity generation plants to the users. Generally, these plants are quite far away from the actual areas where the power is used. Power is transmitted through several hundred kilometres of wires before it is used. Because of the resistance of these wires, some energy is lost in Joule heating in the form of i^2Rt. The plant can supply a fixed power depending on its capacity. If this power is supplied at a high voltage, the current is small. Correspondingly, the loss of power in transmission is small. So, the voltage at the electricity generation plant is stepped up to, say, 66 kV and fed to the transmission lines. In a town or city, the voltage is stepped down to the required value such as 220 V.

Worked Out Examples

1. *A resistance of* 20 Ω *is connected to a source of alternating current rated* 110 V, 50 Hz. *Find (a) the rms current, (b) the maximum instantaneous current in the resistor and (c) the time taken by the current to change from its maximum value to the rms value.*

Solution :

(a) The rms potential difference = 110 V and so

$$\text{the rms current} = \frac{110\ \text{V}}{20\ \Omega} = 5{\cdot}5\ \text{A}.$$

(b) The maximum instantaneous current

$$= \sqrt{2}\ (\text{rms current})$$

$$= \sqrt{2} \times 5{\cdot}5\ \text{A} = 7{\cdot}8\ \text{A}.$$

(c) Let the current be $i = i_0 \sin \omega t$.

If t_1 and t_2 be the time instants for consecutive appearances of the maximum value and the rms value of the current,

$$i_0 = i_0 \sin \omega t_1$$

and $$\frac{i_0}{\sqrt{2}} = i_0 \sin \omega t_2.$$

If $\omega t_1 = \frac{\pi}{2}$, $\omega t_2 = \frac{\pi}{2} + \frac{\pi}{4}$.

Hence, $t_2 - t_1 = \frac{\pi}{4\omega}$

$$= \frac{\pi}{4 \times 2\pi\nu} = \frac{1}{8 \times 50}\ \text{s} = 2{\cdot}5\ \text{ms}.$$

2. *The electric current in a circuit is given by* $i = i_0(t/\tau)$ *for some time. Calculate the rms current for the period* $t = 0$ *to* $t = \tau$.

Solution :

The mean square current is

$$\overline{i^2} = \frac{1}{\tau}\int_0^\tau i_0^2 (t/\tau)^2\, dt = \frac{i_0^2}{\tau^3}\int_0^\tau t^2\, dt = \frac{i_0^2}{3}.$$

Thus, the rms current is

$$i_{rms} = \sqrt{\overline{i^2}} = \frac{i_0}{\sqrt{3}}.$$

3. *A coil having a resistance of* 50·0 Ω *and an inductance of* 0·500 *henry is connected to an AC source of* 110 *volts,* 50·0 *cycle/s. Find the rms value of the current in the circuit.*

Solution :

The angular frequency $\omega = 2\pi\nu = 100\pi\ \text{s}^{-1}$.

The impedance of the coil

$$= \sqrt{R^2 + L^2\omega^2}$$

$$= \sqrt{(50\ \Omega)^2 + (0{\cdot}50\ \text{H} \times 100\pi\ \text{s}^{-1})^2}$$

$$= \sqrt{2500\ \Omega^2 + 2500\ \pi^2\Omega^2} = 164{\cdot}8\ \Omega.$$

The rms current is $\frac{\mathcal{E}_{rms}}{Z} = \frac{110\ \text{V}}{164{\cdot}8\ \Omega} \approx 0{\cdot}667\ \text{A}.$

The peak current = $\sqrt{2}$ (rms current) ≈ 0·943 A.

4. *A capacitor of capacitance* 100 μF *and a coil of resistance* 50 Ω *and inductance* 0·5 H *are connected in series with a* 110 V, 50 Hz *AC source. Find the rms value of the current.*

Solution :

The resistance of the circuit is $R = 50\ \Omega$.

The reactance of the capacitor $= \frac{1}{\omega C}$

$$= \frac{1}{(2\pi \times 50\ \text{s}^{-1})(100 \times 10^{-6}\ \text{F})} = 31{\cdot}8\ \Omega.$$

The reactance of the inductor $= \omega L$

$$= (2\pi \times 50\ \text{s}^{-1})(0{\cdot}5\ \text{henry}) = 157\ \Omega.$$

The reactance of the circuit $= X = \frac{1}{\omega C} - L\omega$

$$= 31{\cdot}8\ \Omega - 157\ \Omega = -\ 125{\cdot}2\ \Omega.$$

Hence, the impedance $Z = \sqrt{R^2 + X^2}$

$$= \sqrt{(50\ \Omega)^2 + (125{\cdot}2\ \Omega)^2} \approx 134{\cdot}6\ \Omega.$$

$$\text{The rms current} = \frac{E_{rms}}{Z} = \frac{110\ \text{V}}{134{\cdot}6\ \Omega} = 0{\cdot}82\ \text{A}.$$

5. *A capacitor of capacitance* 12·0 μF *is joined to an AC source of frequency* 200 Hz. *The rms current in the circuit is* 2·00 A. *(a) Find the rms voltage across the capacitor. (b) Find the average energy stored in the electric field between the plates of the capacitor.*

Solution :

(a) The impedance of the capacitor $= \frac{1}{\omega C}$

$$= \frac{1}{(2\pi \times 200\ \text{s}^{-1})(12\ \mu\text{F})} = 66{\cdot}3\ \Omega.$$

The rms voltage across the capacitor

$$= i_{rms} Z = 2{\cdot}0\ \text{A} \times 66{\cdot}3\ \Omega \approx 133\ \text{V}.$$

(b) The energy stored in the electric field $= \frac{1}{2} CV^2$.

Hence the average energy stored $= \frac{1}{2} C\overline{V^2}$.

But $\overline{V^2} = (V_{rms})^2$.

Thus, the average energy stored

$$= \frac{1}{2} \times (12\ \mu\text{F}) \times (133\ \text{V})^2 \approx 0{\cdot}106\ \text{J}.$$

6. *A series AC circuit contains an inductor* (20 mH), *a capacitor* (100 μF), *a resistor* (50 Ω) *and an AC source of* 12 V, 50 Hz. *Find the energy dissipated in the circuit in* 1000 s.

Solution :

The time period of the source is

$$T = 1/\nu = 20 \text{ ms}.$$

The given time 1000 s is much larger than the time period. Hence we can write the average power dissipated as

$$P_{av} = V_{rms}\, i_{rms} \cos\varphi$$

where $\cos\varphi = R/Z$ is the power factor. Thus,

$$P_{av} = V_{rms} \frac{V_{rms}}{Z}\frac{R}{Z} = \frac{R\,V_{rms}^2}{Z^2}$$

$$= \frac{(50\ \Omega)\,(12\ \text{V})^2}{Z^2}$$

$$= \frac{7200}{Z^2}\ \Omega\text{V}^2. \qquad \dots \text{(i)}$$

The capacitive reactance $\dfrac{1}{\omega C} = \dfrac{1}{2\pi \times 50 \times 100 \times 10^{-6}}\ \Omega$

$$= \frac{100}{\pi}\ \Omega.$$

The inductive reactance $= \omega L$

$$= 2\pi \times 50 \times 20 \times 10^{-3}\ \Omega = 2\pi\ \Omega.$$

The net reactance is $X = \dfrac{1}{\omega C} - \omega L$

$$= \frac{100}{\pi}\ \Omega - 2\pi\ \Omega \approx 25{\cdot}5\ \Omega.$$

Thus,

$$Z^2 = (50\ \Omega)^2 + (25{\cdot}5\ \Omega)^2 = 3150\ \Omega^2.$$

From (i), average power $P_{av} = \dfrac{7200\ \Omega\text{–V}^2}{3150\ \Omega^2} = 2{\cdot}286$ W.

The energy dissipated in 1000 s $= P_{av} \times 1000$ s

$$\approx 2{\cdot}3 \times 10^3\ \text{J}.$$

7. *An inductor of inductance* 100 mH *is connected in series with a resistance, a variable capacitance and an AC source of frequency* 2·0 kHz. *What should be the value of the capacitance so that maximum current may be drawn into the circuit ?*

Solution :

This is an *LCR* series circuit. The current will be maximum when the net reactance is zero. For this,

$$\frac{1}{\omega C} = \omega L$$

or, $$C = \frac{1}{\omega^2 L} = \frac{1}{4\pi^2 \times (2{\cdot}0 \times 10^3\ \text{s}^{-1})^2\,(0{\cdot}1\ \text{H})}$$

$$= 63\ \text{nF}.$$

8. *An inductor coil joined to a* 6 V *battery draws a steady current of* 12 A. *This coil is connected to a capacitor and an AC source of rms voltage* 6 V *in series. If the current in the circuit is in phase with the emf, find the rms current.*

Solution :

The resistance of the coil is $R = \dfrac{6\ \text{V}}{12\ \text{A}} = 0{\cdot}5\ \Omega.$

In the AC circuit, the current is in phase with the emf. This means that the net reactance of the circuit is zero. The impedance is equal to the resistance, i.e., $Z = 0{\cdot}5\ \Omega$.

The rms current $= \dfrac{\text{rms voltage}}{Z} = \dfrac{6\ \text{V}}{0{\cdot}5\ \Omega} = 12$ A.

□

QUESTIONS FOR SHORT ANSWER

1. What is the reactance of a capacitor connected to a constant DC source ?
2. The voltage and current in a series AC circuit are given by
   $$V = V_0 \cos \omega t \text{ and } i = i_0 \sin \omega t.$$
   What is the power dissipated in the circuit ?
3. Two alternating currents are given by
   $$i_1 = i_0 \sin \omega t \text{ and } i_2 = i_0 \sin\left(\omega t + \frac{\pi}{3}\right).$$
   Will the rms values of the currents be equal or different ?
4. Can the peak voltage across the inductor be greater than the peak voltage of the source in an *LCR* circuit ?
5. In a circuit containing a capacitor and an AC source, the current is zero at the instant the source voltage is maximum. Is it consistent with Ohm's law ?
6. An AC source is connected to a capacitor. Will the rms current increase, decrease or remain constant if a dielectric slab is inserted into the capacitor ?
7. When the frequency of the AC source in an *LCR* circuit equals the resonant frequency, the reactance of the circuit is zero. Does it mean that there is no current through the inductor or the capacitor ?
8. When an AC source is connected to a capacitor there is a steady-state current in the circuit. Does it mean that

the charges jump from one plate to the other to complete the circuit ?

9. A current $i_1 = i_0 \sin \omega t$ passes through a resistor of resistance R. How much thermal energy is produced in one time period ? A current $i_2 = -i_0 \sin \omega t$ passes through the resistor. How much thermal energy is produced in one time period ? If i_1 and i_2 both pass through the resistor simultaneously, how much thermal energy is produced ? Is the principle of superposition obeyed in this case ?

10. Is energy produced when a transformer steps up the voltage ?

11. A transformer is designed to convert an AC voltage of 220 V to an AC voltage of 12 V. If the input terminals are connected to a DC voltage of 220 V, the transformer usually burns. Explain.

12. Can you have an AC series circuit in which there is a phase difference of (a) 180° (b) 120° between the emf and the current ?

13. A resistance is connected to an AC source. If a capacitor is included in the series circuit, will the average power absorbed by the resistance increase or decrease ? If an inductor of small inductance is also included in the series circuit, will the average power absorbed increase or decrease further ?

14. Can a hot-wire ammeter be used to measure a direct current having a constant value ? Do we have to change the graduations ?

OBJECTIVE I

1. A capacitor acts as an infinite resistance for
(a) DC (b) AC
(c) DC as well as AC (d) neither AC nor DC.

2. An AC source producing emf

$$\mathcal{E} = \mathcal{E}_0 \left[\cos(100\,\pi\,\text{s}^{-1})t + \cos(500\,\pi\,\text{s}^{-1})t\right]$$

is connected in series with a capacitor and a resistor. The steady-state current in the circuit is found to be

$$i = i_1 \cos\left[(100\,\pi\,\text{s}^{-1})t + \varphi_1\right] + i_2 \cos\left[(500\,\pi\,\text{s}^{-1})t + \phi_2\right].$$

(a) $i_1 > i_2$ (b) $i_1 = i_2$ (c) $i_1 < i_2$
(d) The information is insufficient to find the relation between i_1 and i_2.

3. The peak voltage in a 220 V AC source is
(a) 220 V (b) about 160 V
(c) about 310 V (d) 440 V.

4. An AC source is rated 220 V, 50 Hz. The average voltage is calculated in a time interval of 0·01 s. It
(a) must be zero (b) may be zero
(c) is never zero (d) is $(220/\sqrt{2})$V.

5. The magnetic field energy in an inductor changes from maximum value to minimum value in 5·0 ms when connected to an AC source. The frequency of the source is
(a) 20 Hz (b) 50 Hz (c) 200 Hz (d) 500 Hz.

6. Which of the following plots may represent the reactance of a series LC combination ?

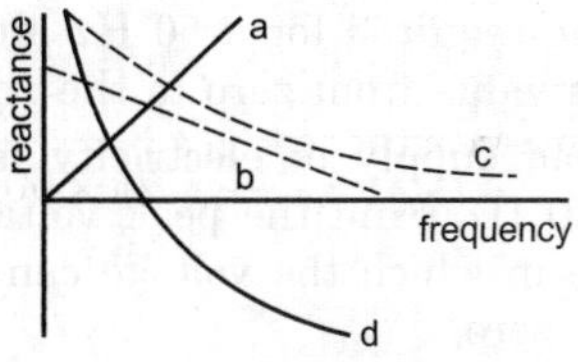

Figure 39-Q1

7. A series AC circuit has a resistance of 4 Ω and a reactance of 3 Ω. The impedance of the circuit is
(a) 5 Ω (b) 7 Ω (c) 12/7 Ω (d) 7/12 Ω.

8. Transformers are used
(a) in DC circuits only (b) in AC circuits only
(c) in both DC and AC circuits
(d) neither in DC nor in AC circuits.

9. An alternating current is given by
$i = i_1 \cos \omega t + i_2 \sin \omega t.$
The rms current is given by
(a) $\frac{i_1 + i_2}{\sqrt{2}}$ (b) $\frac{|i_1 + i_2|}{\sqrt{2}}$ (c) $\sqrt{\frac{i_1^2 + i_2^2}{2}}$ (d) $\sqrt{\frac{i_1^2 + i_2^2}{\sqrt{2}}}$.

10. An alternating current having peak value 14 A is used to heat a metal wire. To produce the same heating effect, a constant current i can be used where i is
(a) 14 A (b) about 20 A (c) 7 A (d) about 10 A.

11. A constant current of 2·8 A exists in a resistor. The rms current is
(a) 2·8 A (b) about 2 A
(c) 1·4 A (d) undefined for a direct current.

OBJECTIVE II

1. An inductor, a resistor and a capacitor are joined in series with an AC source. As the frequency of the source is slightly increased from a very low value, the reactance
(a) of the inductor increases
(b) of the resistor increases
(c) of the capacitor increases
(d) of the circuit increases.

2. The reactance of a circuit connected to an AC circuit is zero. It is possible that the circuit contains
(a) an inductor and a capacitor
(b) an inductor but no capacitor

(c) a capacitor but no inductor
(d) neither an inductor nor a capacitor.

3. In an AC series circuit, the instantaneous current is zero when the instantaneous voltage is maximum. Connected to the source may be a
(a) pure inductor (b) pure capacitor
(c) pure resistor
(d) combination of an inductor and a capacitor.

4. An inductor-coil having some resistance is connected to an AC source. Which of the following quantities have zero average value over a cycle ?
(a) Current (b) Induced emf in the inductor
(c) Joule heat
(d) Magnetic energy stored in the inductor

5. The AC voltage across a resistance can be measured using
(a) a potentiometer (b) a hot-wire voltmeter
(c) a moving-coil galvanometer
(d) a moving-magnet galvanometer.

6. To convert mechanical energy into electrical energy, one can use
(a) DC dynamo (b) AC dynamo
(c) motor (d) transformer.

7. An AC source rated 100 V (rms) supplies a current of 10 A (rms) to a circuit. The average power delivered by the source
(a) must be 1000 W (b) may be 1000 W
(c) may be greater than 1000 W
(d) may be less than 1000 W.

EXERCISES

1. Find the time required for a 50 Hz alternating current to change its value from zero to the rms value.

2. The household supply of electricity is at 220 V (rms value) and 50 Hz. Find the peak voltage and the least possible time in which the voltage can change from the rms value to zero.

3. A bulb rated 60 W at 220 V is connected across a household supply of alternating voltage of 220 V. Calculate the maximum instantaneous current through the filament.

4. An electric bulb is designed to operate at 12 volts DC. If this bulb is connected to an AC source and gives normal brightness, what would be the peak voltage of the source ?

5. The peak power consumed by a resistive coil when connected to an AC source is 80 W. Find the energy consumed by the coil in 100 seconds which is many times larger than the time period of the source.

6. The dielectric strength of air is $3{\cdot}0 \times 10^{6}$ V/m. A parallel-plate air-capacitor has area 20 cm^2 and plate separation 0·10 mm. Find the maximum rms voltage of an AC source which can be safely connected to this capacitor.

7. The current in a discharging *LR* circuit is given by $i = i_0 e^{-t/\tau}$ where τ is the time constant of the circuit. Calculate the rms current for the period $t = 0$ to $t = \tau$.

8. A capacitor of capacitance 10 μF is connected to an oscillator giving an output voltage $\mathcal{E} = (10\ \text{V})\sin \omega t$. Find the peak currents in the circuit for $\omega = 10\ s^{-1}$, $100\ s^{-1}$, $500\ s^{-1}$, $1000\ s^{-1}$.

9. A coil of inductance 5·0 mH and negligible resistance is connected to the oscillator of the previous problem. Find the peak currents in the circuit for $\omega = 100\ s^{-1}$, $500\ s^{-1}$, $1000\ s^{-1}$.

10. A coil has a resistance of 10 Ω and an inductance of 0·4 henry. It is connected to an AC source of 6·5 V, $\frac{30}{\pi}$ Hz. Find the average power consumed in the circuit.

11. A resistor of resistance 100 Ω is connected to an AC source $\mathcal{E} = (12\ \text{V}) \sin (250\ \pi\ s^{-1})t$. Find the energy dissipated as heat during $t = 0$ to $t = 1{\cdot}0$ ms.

12. In a series *RC* circuit with an AC source, $R = 300\ \Omega$, $C = 25\ \mu F$, $\mathcal{E}_0 = 50$ V and $\nu = 50/\pi$ Hz. Find the peak current and the average power dissipated in the circuit.

13. An electric bulb is designed to consume 55 W when operated at 110 volts. It is connected to a 220 V, 50 Hz line through a choke coil in series. What should be the inductance of the coil for which the bulb gets correct voltage ?

14. In a series *LCR* circuit with an AC source, $R = 300\ \Omega$, $C = 20\ \mu F$, $L = 1{\cdot}0$ henry, $\mathcal{E}_{rms} = 50$ V and $\nu = 50/\pi$ Hz. Find (a) the rms current in the circuit and (b) the rms potential differences across the capacitor, the resistor and the inductor. Note that the sum of the rms potential differences across the three elements is greater than the rms voltage of the source.

15. Consider the situation of the previous problem. Find the average electric field energy stored in the capacitor and the average magnetic field energy stored in the coil.

16. An inductance of 2·0 H, a capacitance of 18 μF and a resistance of 10 kΩ are connected to an AC source of 20 V with adjustable frequency. (a) What frequency should be chosen to maximise the current in the circuit ? (b) What is the value of this maximum current ?

17. An inductor-coil, a capacitor and an AC source of rms voltage 24 V are connected in series. When the frequency of the source is varied, a maximum rms current of 6·0 A is observed. If this inductor coil is connected to a battery of emf 12 V and internal resistance 4·0 Ω, what will be the current ?

18. Figure (39-E1) shows a typical circuit for low-pass filter. An AC input $V_i = 10$ mV is applied at the left end and

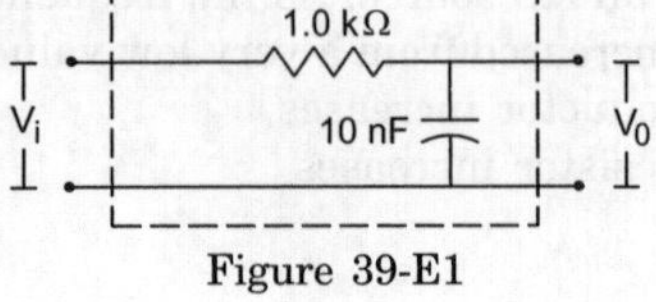

Figure 39-E1

the output V_0 is received at the right end. Find the output voltages for $\nu = 10$ kHz, 100 kHz, 1·0 MHz and 10·0 MHz. Note that as the frequency is increased the output decreases and hence the name low-pass filter.

19. A transformer has 50 turns in the primary and 100 in the secondary. If the primary is connected to a 220 V DC supply, what will be the voltage across the secondary ?

□

ANSWERS

OBJECTIVE I

1. (a)	2. (c)	3. (c)	4. (b)	5. (b)	6. (d)
7. (a)	8. (b)	9. (c)	10. (d)	11. (a)	

OBJECTIVE II

1. (a)	2. (a), (d)	3. (a), (b), (d)
4. (a), (b)	5. (b)	6. (a), (b)
7. (b), (d)		

EXERCISES

1. 2·5 ms
2. 311 V, 2·5 ms
3. 0·39 A
4. 17 volts
5. 4·0 kJ
6. 210 V
7. $\frac{i_0}{e}\sqrt{(e^2-1)/2}$
8. $1{\cdot}0 \times 10^{-3}$ A, 0·01 A, 0·05 A, 0·1 A
9. 20 A, 4·0 A, 2·0 A
10. 5/8 W
11. $2{\cdot}61 \times 10^{-4}$ J
12. 0·10 A, 1·5 W
13. 1·2 H
14. (a) 0·10 A (b) 50 V, 30 V, 10 V
15. 25 mJ, 5 mJ
16. (a) 27 Hz (b) 2 mA
17. 1·5 A
18. 8·5 mV, 1·6 mV, 0·16 mV, 16 μV
19. zero

□

CHAPTER 40

ELECTROMAGNETIC WAVES

40.1 INTRODUCTION

We have seen that in certain situations light may be described as a wave. The wave equation for light propagating in x-direction in vacuum may be written as

$$E = E_0 \sin \omega(t - x/c)$$

where E is the sinusoidally varying electric field at the position x at time t. The constant c is the speed of light in vacuum. The electric field E is in the Y–Z plane, that is, perpendicular to the direction of propagation.

There is also a sinusoidally varying magnetic field associated with the electric field when light propagates. This magnetic field is perpendicular to the direction of propagation as well as to the electric field E. It is given by

$$B = B_0 \sin \omega(t - x/c).$$

Such a combination of mutually perpendicular electric and magnetic fields is referred to as an *electromagnetic wave* in vacuum. The theory of electromagnetic wave was mainly developed by Maxwell around 1864. We give a brief discussion of this theory.

40.2 MAXWELL'S DISPLACEMENT CURRENT

We have stated Ampere's law as

$$\oint \vec{B} \cdot d\vec{l} = \mu_0 i \qquad \text{... (40.1)}$$

where i is the electric current crossing a surface bounded by a closed curve and the line integral of $\vec{B}$ (circulation) is calculated along that closed curve. This equation is valid only when the electric field at the surface does not change with time. This law tells us that an electric current produces magnetic field and gives a method to calculate the field.

Ampere's law in this form is not valid if the electric field at the surface varies with time. As an example, consider a parallel-plate capacitor with circular plates, being charged by a battery (figure 40.1). If we place a compass needle in the space between the plates, the needle, in general, deflects. This shows that there is a magnetic field in this region. Figure (40.1) also shows a closed curve γ which lies completely in the region between the plates. The plane surface S bounded by this curve is also parallel to the plates and lies completely inside the region between the plates.

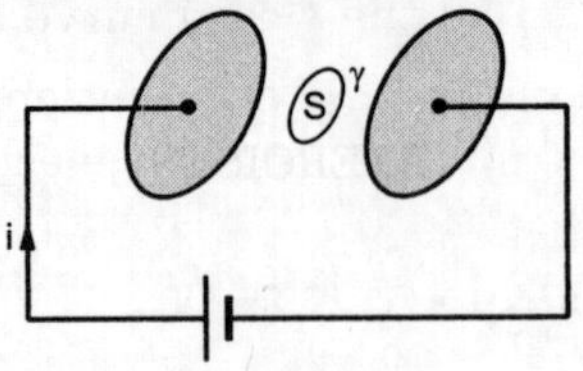

Figure 40.1

During the charging process, there is an electric current through the connecting wires. Charge is accumulated on the plates and the electric field at the points on the surface S changes. It is found that there is a magnetic field at the points on the curve γ and the circulation

$$\oint \vec{B} \cdot d\vec{l}$$

has a nonzero value. As no charge crosses the surface S, the electric current i through the surface is zero. Hence,

$$\oint \vec{B} \cdot d\vec{l} \neq \mu_0 i. \qquad \text{... (i)}$$

Now, Ampere's law (40.1) can be deduced from Biot–Savart law. We can calculate the magnetic field due to each current element from Biot–Savart law and then its circulation along the closed curve γ. The circulation of the magnetic field due to these current elements must satisfy equation (40.1). If we denote this magnetic field by $\vec{B}'$,

$$\oint \vec{B}' \cdot d\vec{l} = 0. \qquad \text{... (ii)}$$

This shows that the actual magnetic field $\vec{B}$ is different from the field $\vec{B}'$ produced by the electric currents only. So, there must be some other source of magnetic field. This other source is nothing but the changing electric field. As the capacitor gets charged, the electric field between the plates changes and this changing electric field produces magnetic field.

We know that a changing magnetic field produces an electric field. The relation between the two is given by Faraday's law

$$\oint \vec{E}\cdot\vec{dl} = -\frac{d\Phi_B}{dt}.$$

Here, $\Phi_B = \int \vec{B}\cdot\vec{dS}$ is the flux of the magnetic field through the area bounded by the closed curve along which the circulation of $\vec{E}$ is calculated. Now we find that a changing electric field produces a magnetic field. The relation between the changing electric field and the magnetic field resulting from it is given by

$$\oint \vec{B}\cdot\vec{dl} = \mu_0 \varepsilon_0 \frac{d\Phi_E}{dt}. \quad \dots (40.2)$$

Here, Φ_E is the flux of the electric field through the area bounded by the closed curve along which the circulation of $\vec{B}$ is calculated. Equation (40.1) gives the magnetic field resulting from an electric current due to flow of charges and equation (40.2) gives the magnetic field due to the changing electric field. If there exists an electric current as well as a changing electric field, the resultant magnetic field is given by

$$\oint \vec{B}\cdot\vec{dl} = \mu_0 i + \mu_0 \varepsilon_0 \left(\frac{d\Phi_E}{dt}\right)$$

or, $$\oint \vec{B}\cdot\vec{dl} = \mu_0(i + i_d) \quad \dots (40.3)$$

where $$i_d = \varepsilon_0 \frac{d\Phi_E}{dt}.$$

It was James Clerk Maxwell who generalised Ampere's law from equation (40.1) to equation (40.3). Maxwell named the term $i_d = \varepsilon_0 \frac{d\Phi_E}{dt}$ as *displacement current*. The current due to flow of charges is often called *conduction current* and is denoted by i_c.

Example 40.1

A parallel-plate capacitor is being charged. Show that the displacement current across an area in the region between the plates and parallel to it (figure 40.1) is equal to the conduction current in the connecting wires.

Solution :

The electric field between the plates is

$$E = \frac{Q}{\varepsilon_0 A}$$

where Q is the charge accumulated at the positive plate. The flux of this field through the given area is

$$\Phi_E = \frac{Q}{\varepsilon_0 A} \times A = \frac{Q}{\varepsilon_0}.$$

The displacement current is

$$i_d = \varepsilon_0 \frac{d\Phi_E}{dt} = \varepsilon_0 \frac{d}{dt}\left(\frac{Q}{\varepsilon_0}\right) = \frac{dQ}{dt}.$$

But $\frac{dQ}{dt}$ is the rate at which the charge is carried to the positive plate through the connecting wire. Thus, $i_d = i_c$.

40.3 CONTINUITY OF ELECTRIC CURRENT

Consider a closed surface enclosing a volume (figure 40.2). Suppose charges are entering into the volume and are also leaving it. If no charge is accumulated inside the volume, the total charge going into the volume in any time is equal to the total charge leaving it during the same time. The conduction current is then continuous.

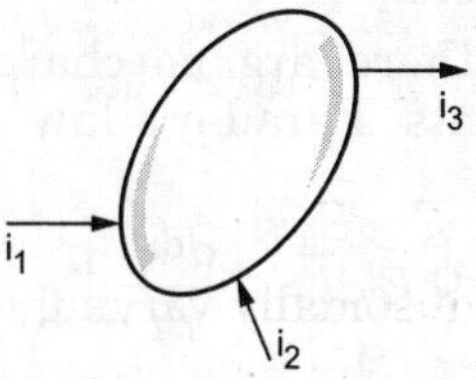

Figure 40.2

If charge is accumulated inside the volume, this continuity breaks. However, if we consider the conduction current plus the displacement current, the total current is still continuous. Any loss of conduction current i_c appears as displacement current i_d. This can be shown as follows.

Suppose a total conduction current i_1 goes into the volume and a total conduction current i_2 goes out of it. The charge going into the volume in a time dt is $i_1\,dt$ and that coming out is $i_2\,dt$. The charge accumulated inside the volume is

$$d(q_{inside}) = i_1\,dt - i_2\,dt$$

or, $$\frac{d}{dt}(q_{inside}) = i_1 - i_2. \quad \dots \text{(i)}$$

From Gauss's law,

$$\Phi_E = \oint \vec{E}\cdot\vec{dS} = \frac{q_{inside}}{\varepsilon_0}$$

or, $$\varepsilon_0 \frac{d\Phi_E}{dt} = \frac{d}{dt}(q_{inside})$$

or, $$i_d = \frac{d}{dt}(q_{inside}).$$

Comparing with (i),

$$i_1 - i_2 = i_d$$

or, $$i_1 = i_2 + i_d.$$

Thus, the total current (conduction + displacement) going into the volume is equal to the total current coming out of it.

40.4 MAXWELL'S EQUATIONS AND PLANE ELECTROMAGNETIC WAVES

The whole subject of electricity and magnetism may be described mathematically with the help of four fundamental equations:

Gauss's law for electricity $\oint \vec{E} \cdot d\vec{S} = \frac{q}{\varepsilon_0}$

Gauss's law for magnetism $\oint \vec{B} \cdot d\vec{S} = 0$

Faraday's law $\oint \vec{E} \cdot d\vec{l} = -\frac{d\Phi_B}{dt}$

Ampere's law $\oint \vec{B} \cdot d\vec{l} = \mu_0 i + \varepsilon_0 \mu_0 \frac{d\Phi_E}{dt}$.

These equations are collectively known as Maxwell's equations.

In vacuum, there are no charges and hence no conduction currents. Faraday's law and Ampere's law take the form

$$\oint \vec{E} \cdot d\vec{l} = -\frac{d\Phi_B}{dt} \quad \text{... (i)}$$

and

$$\oint \vec{B} \cdot d\vec{l} = \mu_0 \, \varepsilon_0 \frac{d\Phi_E}{dt} \quad \text{... (ii)}$$

respectively.

Let us check if these equations are satisfied by a plane electromagnetic wave given by

$$\left. \begin{aligned} E &= E_y = E_0 \sin \omega(t - x/c) \\ \text{and} \quad B &= B_z = B_0 \sin \omega(t - x/c). \end{aligned} \right] \quad \text{... (40.4)}$$

The wave described above propagates along the positive x-direction, the electric field remains along the y-direction and the magnetic field along the z-direction. The magnitudes of the fields oscillate between $\pm E_0$ and $\pm B_0$ respectively. It is a linearly polarized light, polarized along the y-axis.

Faraday's Law

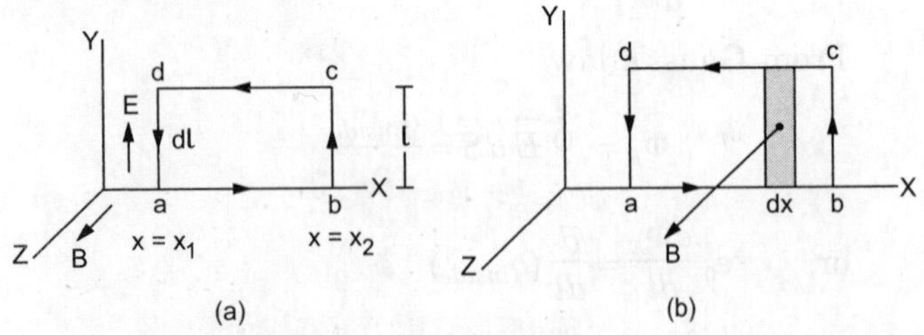

Figure 40.3

Let us consider the rectangular path $abcd$ in the x–y plane as shown in figure (40.3a). Let us evaluate the terms in the Faraday's law on this path. The electric field is parallel to the y-axis. The circulation of E is

$$\oint \vec{E} \cdot d\vec{l} = \int_a^b \vec{E} \cdot d\vec{l} + \int_b^c \vec{E} \cdot d\vec{l} + \int_c^d \vec{E} \cdot d\vec{l} + \int_d^a \vec{E} \cdot d\vec{l}$$

$$= 0 + E(x_2)\, l + 0 + E(x_1)\,(-l)$$

$$= E_0\, l\, [\sin \omega(t - x_2 / c) - \sin \omega(t - x_1/c)]. \quad \text{... (i)}$$

Next, let us calculate the flux of the magnetic field Φ_B, through the same rectangle $abcd$ (figure 40.3b). The flux through a strip of width dx at x is

$$B(x)\, l\, dx = B_0\, [\sin \omega(t - x/c)]\, l\, dx.$$

The flux through the rectangle $abcd$ is

$$\Phi_B = \int_{x_1}^{x_2} B_0\, l \sin \omega(t - x/c)\, dx$$

$$= -\frac{c}{\omega} B_0\, l[-\cos \omega(t - x_2/c) + \cos \omega(t - x_1/c)].$$

Thus,

$$\frac{d\Phi_B}{dt} = -cB_0\, l[\sin \omega(t - x_2/c) - \sin \omega(t - x_1/c)]. \quad \text{... (ii)}$$

The Faraday's law for vacuum is

$$\oint \vec{E} \cdot d\vec{l} = -\frac{d\Phi_B}{dt}.$$

Putting from (i) and (ii) in this equation, we see that Faraday's law is satisfied by the wave given by equation (40.4a) if

$$E_0 = cB_0. \quad \text{... (40.5)}$$

Ampere's Law

Let us consider the rectangular path $efgh$ in the x–z plane as shown in figure (40.4a).

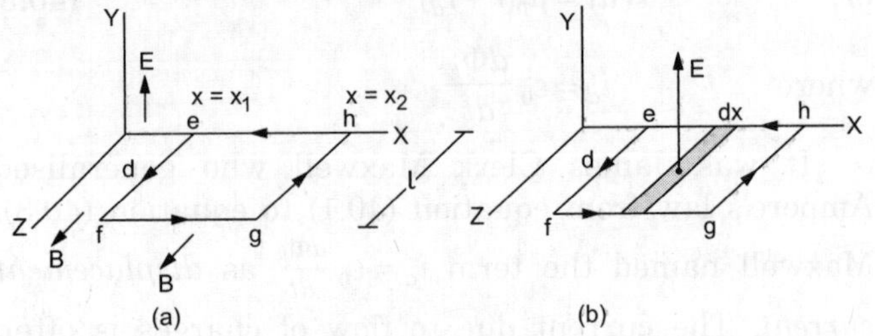

Figure 40.4

The circulation of $\vec{B}$ is

$$\oint \vec{B} \cdot d\vec{l} = \int_e^f \vec{B} \cdot d\vec{l} + \int_f^g \vec{B} \cdot d\vec{l} + \int_g^h \vec{B} \cdot d\vec{l} + \int_h^e \vec{B} \cdot d\vec{l}$$

$$= B(x_1)\, l + 0 - B(x_2)\, l + 0$$

$$= B_0\, l[\sin \omega(t - x_1/c) - \sin \omega(t - x_2/c)]. \quad \text{... (i)}$$

The flux of the electric field through the same rectangle $efgh$ (figure 40.4b) is

$$\Phi_E = \int \vec{E} \cdot d\vec{S}$$

$$= \int_{x_1}^{x_2} E(x)\, l\, dx$$

$$= E_0 l \int_{x_1}^{x_2} \sin \omega(t - x/c)\, dx$$

$$= -\frac{c}{\omega} E_0 l[-\cos \omega(t - x_2/c) + \cos \omega(t - x_1/c)]$$

or, $$\frac{d\Phi_E}{dt} = -cE_0 l[\sin \omega(t - x_2/c) - \sin \omega(t - x_1/c)]. \quad \text{... (ii)}$$

The Ampere's law for vacuum is

$$\oint \vec{B} \cdot d\vec{l} = \mu_0 \varepsilon_0 \frac{d\Phi_E}{dt}.$$

Putting from (i) and (ii) in this equation, we see that Ampere's law is satisfied if

$$B_0 = \mu_0 \varepsilon_0 c E_0$$

or, $$\mu_0 \varepsilon_0 = \frac{B_0}{E_0 c}.$$

Using equation (40.5),

$$\mu_0 \varepsilon_0 = \frac{1}{c^2}$$

or, $$c = \frac{1}{\sqrt{\mu_0 \varepsilon_0}}. \quad \text{... (40.6)}$$

Thus, Maxwell's equations have a solution giving a plane electromagnetic wave of the form (40.4) with $E_0 = cB_0$ and the speed of this wave is $\frac{1}{\sqrt{\mu_0 \varepsilon_0}}$.

In older days, μ_0 and ε_0 were defined in terms of electric and magnetic measurements. Putting these values of μ_0 and ε_0, the speed of electromagnetic waves came out to be $c = 2{\cdot}99793 \times 10^8$ m/s which was the same as the measured speed of light in vacuum. This provided a confirmatory proof that light is an electromagnetic wave.

It may be recalled that the speed of electromagnetic waves, which is the same as the speed of light, is now an exactly defined constant. Similarly, the constant $\mu_0 = 4\pi \times 10^{-7}$ T–m/A is an exactly defined constant. The quantity ε_0 is defined by the equation (40.6).

Example 40.2

The maximum electric field in a plane electromagnetic wave is 600 N C^{-1}. *The wave is going in the x-direction and the electric field is in the y-direction. Find the maximum magnetic field in the wave and its direction.*

Solution :

We have $B_0 = \frac{E_0}{c} = \frac{600 \text{ N C}^{-1}}{3 \times 10^8 \text{ m s}^{-1}} = 2 \times 10^{-6}$ T.

As $\vec{E}, \vec{B}$ and the direction of propagation are mutually perpendicular, $\vec{B}$ should be along the *z*-direction.

40.5 ENERGY DENSITY AND INTENSITY

The electric and magnetic field in a plane electromagnetic wave are given by

$$E = E_0 \sin \omega(t - x/c)$$

and $$B = B_0 \sin \omega(t - x/c).$$

In any small volume dV, the energy of the electric field is

$$U_E = \frac{1}{2} \varepsilon_0 E^2 dV$$

and the energy of the magnetic field is

$$U_B = \frac{1}{2\mu_0} B^2 dV.$$

Thus, the total energy is

$$U = \frac{1}{2} \varepsilon_0 E^2 dV + \frac{1}{2\mu_0} B^2 dV.$$

The energy density is $u = \frac{1}{2} \varepsilon_0 E^2 + \frac{1}{2\mu_0} B^2$

$$= \frac{1}{2} \varepsilon_0 E_0^2 \sin^2 \omega(t - x/c) + \frac{1}{2\mu_0} B_0^2 \sin^2 \omega(t - x/c).$$

If we take the average over a long time, the $\sin^2$ terms have an average value of 1/2. Thus,

$$u_{au} = \frac{1}{4} \varepsilon_0 E_0^2 + \frac{1}{4\mu_0} B_0^2.$$

From equations (40.5) and (40.6),

$$E_0 = cB_0 \text{ and } \mu_0 \varepsilon_0 = \frac{1}{c^2} \text{ so that,}$$

$$\frac{1}{4\mu_0} B_0^2 = \frac{\varepsilon_0 c^2}{4} \left(\frac{E_0}{c}\right)^2 = \frac{1}{4} \varepsilon_0 E_0^2.$$

Thus, the electric energy density is equal to the magnetic energy density in average.

or, $$u_{av} = \frac{1}{4} \varepsilon_0 E_0^2 + \frac{1}{4} \varepsilon_0 E_0^2 = \frac{1}{2} \varepsilon_0 E_0^2. \quad \text{... (40.7)}$$

Also, $$u_{av} = \frac{1}{4\mu_0} B_0^2 + \frac{1}{4\mu_0} B_0^2 = \frac{1}{2\mu_0} B_0^2. \quad \text{... (40.8)}$$

Example 40.3

The electric field in an electromagnetic wave is given by

$E = (50 \text{ N C}^{-1}) \sin \omega(t - x/c)$.

Find the energy contained in a cylinder of cross-section 10 cm^2 *and length* 50 cm *along the x-axis.*

Solution :

The energy density is

$$u_{av} = \frac{1}{2} \varepsilon_0 E_0^2 = \frac{1}{2} \times (8{\cdot}85 \times 10^{-12} \text{ C}^2\text{N}^{-1}\text{m}^{-2}) \times (50 \text{ N C}^{-1})^2$$

$$= 1{\cdot}1 \times 10^{-8} \text{ J m}^{-3}.$$

The volume of the cylinder is

$$V = 10 \text{ cm}^2 \times 50 \text{ cm} = 5 \times 10^{-4} \text{ m}^3.$$

The energy contained in this volume is

$$U = (1{\cdot}1 \times 10^{-8}\ \text{J m}^{-3}) \times (5 \times 10^{-4}\ \text{m}^3)$$
$$= 5{\cdot}5 \times 10^{-12}\ \text{J}.$$

Intensity

The energy crossing per unit area per unit time perpendicular to the direction of propagation is called the intensity of a wave.

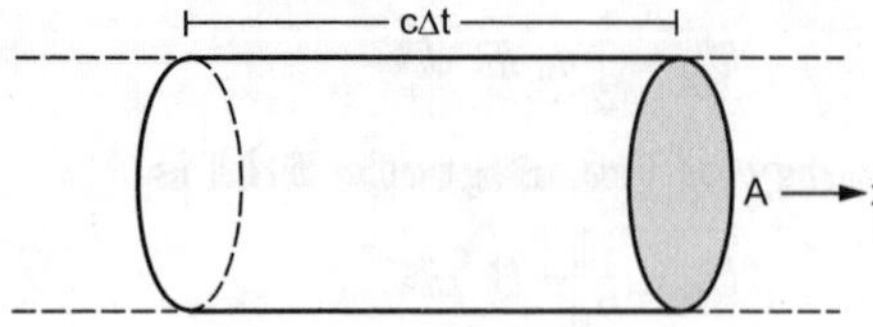

Figure 40.5

Consider a cylindrical volume with area of cross-section A and length $c\,\Delta t$ along the X-axis (figure 40.5). The energy contained in this cylinder crosses the area A in time Δt as the wave propagates at speed c. The energy contained is

$$U = u_{av}(c\,\Delta t)A.$$

The intensity is $I = \dfrac{U}{A\Delta t} = u_{av}\,c.$

In terms of maximum electric field,

$$I = \frac{1}{2}\,\varepsilon_0 E_0^2 c. \qquad \dots (40.9)$$

Example 40.4

Find the intensity of the wave discussed in example (40.3).

Solution :

The intensity is

$$I = \frac{1}{2}\varepsilon_0 E_0^2 c = (1{\cdot}1 \times 10^{-8}\ \text{J m}^{-3}) \times (3 \times 10^8\ \text{m s}^{-1})$$
$$= 3{\cdot}3\ \text{W m}^{-2}.$$

40.6 MOMENTUM

The electromagnetic wave also carries linear momentum with it. The linear momentum carried by the portion of wave having energy U is given by

$$p = \frac{U}{c} \cdot \qquad \dots (40.10)$$

Thus, if the wave incident on a material surface is completely absorbed, it delivers energy U and momentum $p = U/c$ to the surface. If the wave is totally reflected, the momentum delivered is $2U/c$ because the momentum of the wave changes from p to $-p$. It follows that electromagnetic waves incident on a surface exert a force on the surface.

40.7 ELECTROMAGNETIC SPECTRUM AND RADIATION IN ATMOSPHERE

Maxwell's equations are applicable for electromagnetic waves of all wavelengths. Visible light has wavelengths roughly in the range 380 nm to 780 nm. Today we are familiar with electromagnetic waves having wavelengths as small as 30 fm (1 fm = 10^{-15} m) to as large as 30 km. Figure (40.6) shows the electromagnetic spectrum we are familiar with. The boundaries separating different regions of spectrum are not sharply defined. The gamma ray region and the X-ray region overlap considerably. We can only say that on the average, wavelengths of gamma rays are shorter than those of X-rays.

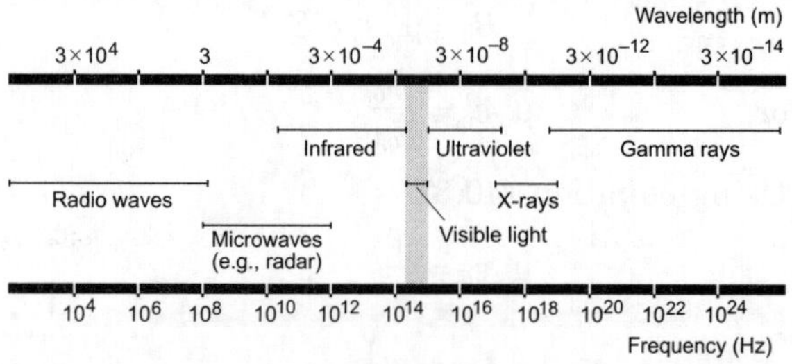

Figure 40.6

The basic source of electromagnetic waves is an accelerated charge. This produces changing electric field and changing magnetic field which constitute the wave. Radio waves may be produced by charges accelerating in AC circuits having an inductor and a capacitor. These waves are used in radio and TV communication. Microwaves are also produced by such electric circuits with oscillating current. They are used for radar systems among other applications. Microwave ovens are used for cooking. Infrared waves are emitted by the atoms and molecules of hot bodies. These waves are used in physical therapy. Among the electromagnetic waves, visible light is most familiar to us. This is emitted by atoms under suitable conditions. An atom contains electrons and the light emission is related to the acceleration of an electron inside the atom. The mechanism of emission of ultraviolet radiation is similar to that for visible light. The sun emits large amount of ultraviolet radiation. This radiation is harmful to us if absorbed in large amount. X-rays are produced most commonly when fast-moving electrons decelerate inside a metal target. X-rays are widely used in medical diagnosis. They are harmful to living tissues. Gamma rays are emitted by the nuclei and have the shortest wavelengths among the electromagnetic waves we generally deal with.

Radiation in Atmosphere

The earth is surrounded by atmosphere up to a height of about 300 km. The composition of atmosphere differs widely as one moves up. Most of the water droplets, vapour and ice particles forming clouds, are contained in a layer starting from the earth's surface up to height of about 12 km. This part is called *troposphere.* The density of air at the top of the troposphere is about one tenth of the density near the earth's surface. The atmosphere between the heights of 12 km and 50 km is called *stratosphere.* In the upper part of the stratosphere, we have a layer of ozone. The density of air at the top of the stratosphere is about 10^{-3} times the density at the surface of the earth. Then we have *mesosphere* between a height of 50 km and 80 km. The atmosphere above that is called *ionosphere.* There are no sharp boundaries between the above divisions and the numbers given are only a rough guide.

The main source of electromagnetic radiation in the atmosphere is the sun. The sun sends electromagnetic waves of different wavelengths towards the earth. A major part of it is absorbed by the atmosphere. Visible light is only weakly absorbed. Most of the infrared radiation is absorbed by the atmosphere and used to heat it. The radiation from the sun has a lot of ultraviolet radiation. The ozone layer absorbs most of this radiation and other radiations of lower wavelengths and thus protects us from their harmful effects. The ozone layer converts the ultraviolet radiation to infrared which is used to heat the atmosphere and the earth's surface. It is suspected that ozone layer is slowly being depleted and this is causing great concern to scientists and environmentalists.

Worked Out Examples

1. *A parallel-plate capacitor with plate area A and separation between the plates d, is charged by a constant current i. Consider a plane surface of area A/2 parallel to the plates and drawn symmetrically between the plates. Find the displacement current through this area.*

Solution :

Suppose the charge on the capacitor at time t is Q. The electric field between the plates of the capacitor is $E=\frac{Q}{\varepsilon_0 A}\cdot$ The flux through the area considered is

$$\Phi_E=\frac{Q}{\varepsilon_0 A}\cdot\frac{A}{2}=\frac{Q}{2\,\varepsilon_0}\cdot$$

The displacement current is

$$i_d=\varepsilon_0\frac{d\Phi_E}{dt}=\varepsilon_0\left(\frac{1}{2\,\varepsilon_0}\right)\frac{dQ}{dt}=\frac{i}{2}\cdot$$

2. *A plane electromagnetic wave propagating in the x-direction has a wavelength of* 5·0 mm. *The electric field is in the y-direction and its maximum magnitude is* 30 V m^{-1}. *Write suitable equations for the electric and magnetic fields as a function of x and t.*

Solution :

The equation for the electric and the magnetic fields in the wave may be written as

$$E=E_0\sin\omega\left(t-\frac{x}{c}\right)$$

$$B=B_0\sin\omega\left(t-\frac{x}{c}\right).$$

We have,

$$\omega=2\pi\nu=\frac{2\pi}{\lambda}c.$$

Thus, $$E=E_0\sin\left[\frac{2\pi}{\lambda}(ct-x)\right]$$

$$=(30\ \text{V m}^{-1})\sin\left[\frac{2\pi}{5{\cdot}0\ \text{mm}}(ct-x)\right].$$

The maximum magnetic field is

$$B_0=\frac{E_0}{c}=\frac{30\ \text{V m}^{-1}}{3\times10^{8}\ \text{m s}^{-1}}=10^{-7}\ \text{T}.$$

So, $$B=B_0\sin\left[\frac{2\pi}{\lambda}(ct-x)\right]$$

$$=(10^{-7}\ \text{T})\sin\left[\frac{2\pi}{5{\cdot}0\ \text{mm}}(ct-x)\right].$$

The magnetic field is along the z-axis.

3. *A light beam travelling in the x-direction is described by the electric field* $E_y=(300\ \text{V m}^{-1})\sin\omega(t-x/c)$. *An electron is constrained to move along the y-direction with a speed of* $2{\cdot}0\times10^{7}$ m s^{-1}. *Find the maximum electric force and the maximum magnetic force on the electron.*

Solution :

The maximum electric field is $E_0=300\ \text{V m}^{-1}$. The maximum magnetic field is

$$B_0=\frac{E_0}{c}=\frac{300\ \text{V m}^{-1}}{3\times10^{8}\ \text{m s}^{-1}}=10^{-6}\ \text{T}$$

along the z-direction.

The maximum electric force on the electron is

$$F_e=qE_0=(1{\cdot}6\times10^{-19}\ \text{C})\times(300\ \text{V m}^{-1})$$

$$=4{\cdot}8\times10^{-17}\ \text{N}.$$

The maximum magnetic force on the electron is

$$F_b=|q\vec{v}\times\vec{B}|_{max}=qvB_0$$

$= (1{\cdot}6 \times 10^{-19}\ \text{C}) \times (2{\cdot}0 \times 10^{7}\ \text{m s}^{-1}) \times (10^{-6}\ \text{T})$

$= 3{\cdot}2 \times 10^{-18}\ \text{N}.$

4. *Find the energy stored in a* 60 cm *length of a laser beam operating at* 4 mW.

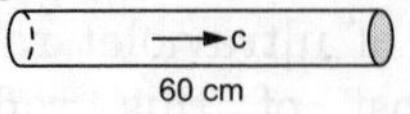

Figure 40-W1

Solution :

The time taken by the electromagnetic wave to move through a distance of 60 cm is $t = \frac{60\ \text{cm}}{c} = 2 \times 10^{-9}$ s. The energy contained in the 60 cm length passes through a cross-section of the beam in 2×10^{-9} s (figure 40-W1). But the energy passing through any cross section in 2×10^{-9} s is

$$U = (4\ \text{mW}) \times (2 \times 10^{-9}\ \text{s})$$

$$= (4 \times 10^{-3}\ \text{J s}^{-1}) \times (2 \times 10^{-9}\ \text{s})$$

$$= 8 \times 10^{-12}\ \text{J}.$$

This is the energy contained in 60 cm length.

5. *Find the amplitude of the electric field in a parallel beam of light of intensity* $2{\cdot}0\ \text{W m}^{-2}$.

Solution :

The intensity of a plane electromagnetic wave is

$$I = u_{av}\, c = \frac{1}{2}\, \varepsilon_0 E_0^2\, c$$

or, $$E_0 = \sqrt{\frac{2I}{\varepsilon_0 c}}$$

$$= \sqrt{\frac{2 \times (2{\cdot}0\ \text{W m}^{-2})}{(8{\cdot}85 \times 10^{-12}\ \text{C}^2\text{N}^{-1}\text{m}^{-2}) \times (3 \times 10^{8}\ \text{m s}^{-1})}}$$

$$= 38{\cdot}8\ \text{N C}^{-1}.$$

□

QUESTIONS FOR SHORT ANSWER

1. In a microwave oven, the food is kept in a plastic container and the microwave is directed towards the food. The food is cooked without melting or igniting the plastic container. Explain.
2. A metal rod is placed along the axis of a solenoid carrying a high-frequency alternating current. It is found that the rod gets heated. Explain why the rod gets heated.
3. Can an electromagnetic wave be deflected by an electric field ? By a magnetic field ?
4. A wire carries an alternating current $i = i_0 \sin \omega t$. Is there an electric field in the vicinity of the wire ?
5. A capacitor is connected to an alternating-current source. Is there a magnetic field between the plates ?
6. Can an electromagnetic wave be polarized ?
7. A plane electromagnetic wave is passing through a region. Consider the quantities (a) electric field, (b) magnetic field, (c) electrical energy in a small volume and (d) magnetic energy in a small volume. Construct pairs of the quantities that oscillate with equal frequencies.

OBJECTIVE I

1. A magnetic field can be produced by
   (a) a moving charge (b) a changing electric field
   (c) none of them (d) both of them.
2. A compass needle is placed in the gap of a parallel plate capacitor. The capacitor is connected to a battery through a resistance. The compass needle
   (a) does not deflect
   (b) deflects for a very short time and then comes back to the original position
   (c) deflects and remains deflected as long as the battery is connected
   (d) deflects and gradually comes to the original position in a time which is large compared to the time constant.
3. Dimensions of $1/(\mu_0 \varepsilon_0)$ is
   (a) L/T (b) T/L (c) L^2/T^2 (d) T^2/L^2.
4. Electromagnetic waves are produced by
   (a) a static charge (b) a moving charge
   (c) an accelerating charge (d) chargeless particles.
5. An electromagnetic wave going through vacuum is described by
   $$E = E_0 \sin(kx - \omega t);\ B = B_0 \sin(kx - \omega t).$$
   Then
   (a) $E_0 k = B_0 \omega$ (b) $E_0 B_0 = \omega k$
   (c) $E_0 \omega = B_0 k$ (d) none of these.

6. An electric field $\vec{E}$ and a magnetic field $\vec{B}$ exist in a region. The fields are not perpendicular to each other.
   (a) This is not possible.
   (b) No electromagnetic wave is passing through the region.
   (c) An electromagnetic wave may be passing through the region.
   (d) An electromagnetic wave is certainly passing through the region.
7. Consider the following two statements regarding a linearly polarized, plane electromagnetic wave:
   (A) The electric field and the magnetic field have equal average values.
   (B) The electric energy and the magnetic energy have equal average values.
   (a) Both A and B are true. (b) A is false but B is true.
   (c) B is false but A is true. (d) Both A and B are false.
8. A free electron is placed in the path of a plane electromagnetic wave. The electron will start moving
   (a) along the electric field
   (b) along the magnetic field
   (c) along the direction of propagation of the wave
   (d) in a plane containing the magnetic field and the direction of propagation.
9. A plane electromagnetic wave is incident on a material surface. The wave delivers momentum p and energy E.
   (a) $p = 0,\ E \neq 0$. (b) $p \neq 0,\ E = 0$.
   (c) $p \neq 0,\ E \neq 0$. (d) $p = 0,\ E = 0$.

OBJECTIVE II

1. An electromagnetic wave going through vacuum is described by
$$E = E_0 \sin(kx - \omega t).$$
   Which of the following is/are independent of the wavelength ?
   (a) k (b) ω (c) k/ω (d) $k\omega$.
2. Displacement current goes through the gap between the plates of a capacitor when the charge of the capacitor
   (a) increases (b) decreases
   (c) does not change (d) is zero.
3. Speed of electromagnetic waves is the same
   (a) for all wavelengths (b) in all media
   (c) for all intensities (d) for all frequencies.
4. Which of the following have zero average value in a plane electromagnetic wave ?
   (a) electric field (b) magnetic field
   (c) electric energy (d) magnetic energy.
5. The energy contained in a small volume through which an electromagnetic wave is passing oscillates with
   (a) zero frequency (b) the frequency of the wave
   (c) half the frequency of the wave
   (d) double the frequency of the wave.

EXERCISES

1. Show that the dimensions of the displacement current $\varepsilon_0 \frac{d\varphi_E}{dt}$ are that of an electric current.
2. A point charge is moving along a straight line with a constant velocity v. Consider a small area A perpendicular to the direction of motion of the charge (figure 40-E1). Calculate the displacement current through the area when its distance from the charge is x. The value of x is not large so that the electric field at any instant is essentially given by Coulomb's law.

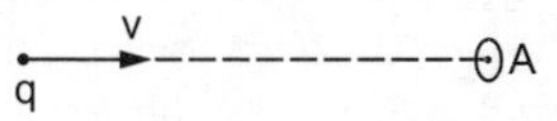

Figure 40-E1

3. A parallel-plate capacitor having plate-area A and plate separation d is joined to a battery of emf $\mathcal{E}$ and internal resistance R at $t = 0$. Consider a plane surface of area $A/2$, parallel to the plates and situated symmetrically between them. Find the displacement current through this surface as a function of time.
4. Consider the situation of the previous problem. Define displacement resistance $R_d = V/i_d$ of the space between the plates where V is the potential difference between the plates and i_d is the displacement current. Show that R_d varies with time as
$$R_d = R(e^{t/\tau} - 1).$$
5. Using $B = \mu_0 H$ find the ratio E_0/H_0 for a plane electromagnetic wave propagating through vacuum. Show that it has the dimensions of electric resistance. This ratio is a universal constant called the *impedance of free space*.
6. The sunlight reaching the earth has maximum electric field of $810\ \mathrm{V\ m^{-1}}$. What is the maximum magnetic field in this light ?
7. The magnetic field in a plane electromagnetic wave is given by
$$B = (200\ \mu\mathrm{T}) \sin[(4{\cdot}0 \times 10^{15}\ \mathrm{s^{-1}})(t - x/c)].$$
   Find the maximum electric field and the average energy density corresponding to the electric field.
8. A laser beam has intensity $2{\cdot}5 \times 10^{14}\ \mathrm{W\ m^{-2}}$. Find the amplitudes of electric and magnetic fields in the beam.
9. The intensity of the sunlight reaching the earth is $1380\ \mathrm{W\ m^{-2}}$. Assume this light to be a plane, monochromatic wave. Find the amplitudes of electric and magnetic fields in this wave.

□

ANSWERS

OBJECTIVE I

1. (d) 2. (d) 3. (c) 4. (c) 5. (a) 6. (c)
7. (a) 8. (a) 9. (c)

OBJECTIVE II

1. (c) 2. (a), (b) 3. (c), 4. (a), (b)
5. (d)

EXERCISES

2. $\frac{q\,Av}{2\pi x^3}$

3. $\frac{\mathcal{E}}{2R}\,e^{-\frac{td}{\varepsilon AR}}$

5. $377\ \Omega$

6. $2{\cdot}7\ \mu T$

7. $6\times 10^4\ N\ C^{-1}$, $0{\cdot}016\ J\ m^{-3}$

8. $4{\cdot}3\times 10^8\ N\ C^{-1}$, $1{\cdot}44\ T$

9. $1{\cdot}02\times 10^3\ N\ C^{-1}$, $3{\cdot}40\times 10^{-6}\ T$

□

CHAPTER 41

ELECTRIC CURRENT THROUGH GASES

Gases are, in general, poor conductors of electricity. This is because they do not have free charged particles in large numbers which may respond to an applied electric field. There may be some ionization due to cosmic rays and other factors, but regular recombination of ions of opposite polarity also takes place and the number of charged particles does not increase much. Electric current may be passed through a gas if we ensure that by some mechanism charged particles are continuously produced in the gas. This can be done in many ways. One such method is to apply a large potential difference across a gas column at very low pressure. Another method is to heat a metal kept in an evacuated chamber to high temperatures at which electrons are ejected from the metal. Yet another method is to pass X-rays through the gas. There are several other methods.

41.1 DISCHARGE THROUGH GASES AT LOW PRESSURE

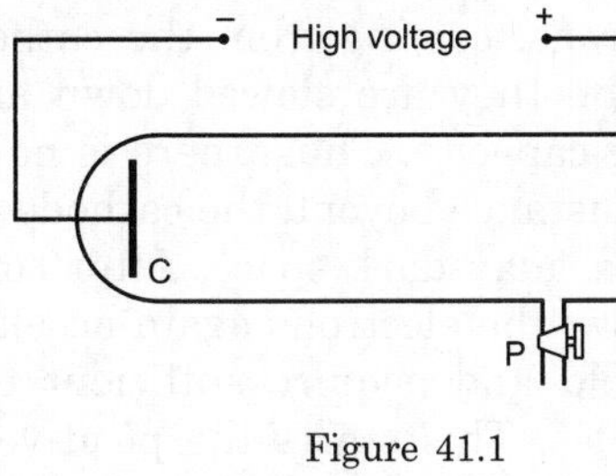

Figure 41.1

To study electric currents through gases at low pressures, one uses a glass tube known as *discharge tube*. Normally, it is a closed tube of length of about 30 cm and diameter of about 4 cm. It is fitted with two metal electrodes C and A (figure 41.1). A side tube P is used to pump out the enclosed gas so as to obtain the desired low pressure. The electrodes are connected to the secondary of an induction coil so that a high potential difference may be applied across the gas. The electrode C connected to the negative terminal is called the cathode and the electrode A connected to the positive terminal is called the anode.

Sparking Potential

If the potential difference between the electrodes is gradually increased, sparking occurs in the gas at a certain stage. The minimum potential difference which can cause sparks in a gas is called the *sparking potential*. Sparking potential depends on the pressure of the gas as well as on the separation between the electrodes. After careful studies, Paschen found that the sparking potential of a gas in a discharge tube is a function of the product of the pressure of the gas and the separation between the electrodes:

$$V = f(pd). \qquad \dots (41.1)$$

This is called the *Paschen's law*.

Low-Pressure Phenomena

In general, when a high potential difference is applied across a gas, sparking occurs in the form of irregular streaks of light. Suppose, in a typical case, the pressure of the gas is about 10 cm of mercury and sparking occurs. The sparking is accompanied by crackling noise. If the pressure of the gas is gradually decreased by pumping out the gas, a series of phenomena take place. At a pressure of about 10 mm of mercury, the irregular streaks broaden out in a luminous column extending from the anode almost up to the cathode (figure 41.2a). The crackling sound is replaced by a continuous buzzing sound. This column is known as *positive column*. The colour of the positive column depends on the nature of the enclosed gas. It

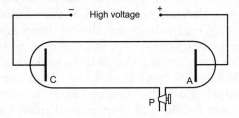

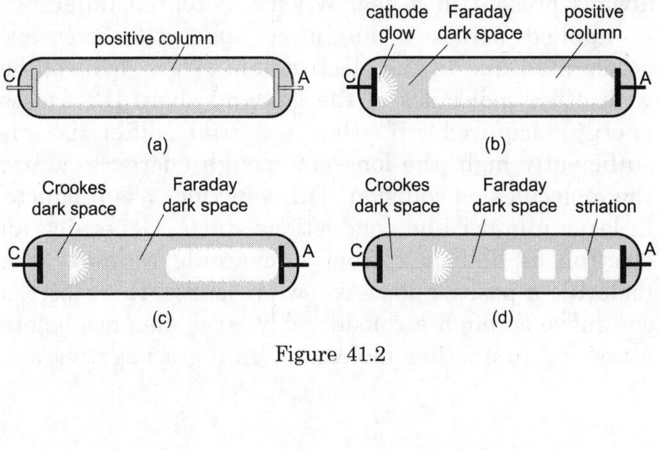

Figure 41.2

is reddish for air, bright red for neon, bluish for CO_2, etc.

As the pressure is further decreased to about 3–4 mm of mercury, the positive column decreases in length. It starts from the anode but ends well before the cathode. A bluish glow is seen around the cathode and there is a dark space between this glow and the positive column (figure 41.2b). The glow around the cathode is called *cathode glow* or *negative glow*. The dark space between the cathode glow and the positive column is called *Faraday dark space*.

When the pressure is reduced to about 1 mm of mercury, the positive column is further shortened and the length of the Faraday dark space increases. The cathode glow is detached from the cathode and a new dark space, called *Crookes dark space* (figure 41.2c), appears between the cathode and the cathode glow.

As the pressure is decreased further, the Crookes dark space and the cathode glow expand. At about 0·1 mm of mercury, the positive column is split into alternate bright and dark bands called *striations* (figure 41.2d).

With further reduction in pressure, the striations move towards the anode and finally vanish. The cathode glow also vanishes at around 0·01 mm of mercury and the Crookes dark space fills the entire tube. A new phenomenon starts at this stage. The walls of the tube begin to glow. This is called *fluorescence*. The colour of the glow depends on the nature of the glass. It is yellowish green for soda glass.

If the pressure is still decreased, the current through the gas gradually decreases and finally the tube stops conducting.

The values of pressure mentioned in the above discussion represent only typical values. The actual pressures at which these phenomena start, depend on the geometry of the discharge tube, the potential difference applied, the gas contained in the tube, etc.

Explanation of Discharge Phenomena

Due to cosmic rays and other factor, some ions are always present in a gas. When a potential difference is applied across a discharge tube, the ions are accelerated due to the electric field. They soon collide with other molecules of the gas and share the excess energy acquired. If the potential difference is sufficiently high, the ions get enough energy to ionize the molecules on collision. This way, ions are produced in large number and conductions starts. Generally, an electron is detached from a molecule to make the molecule a positive ion. At low pressures, this electron can move through a considerably large distance before attaching to another molecule forming a negative ion. These free electrons and the positive ions play important roles in discharge-tube phenomena.

Let us consider the case when the discharge tube looks the most beautiful—there is Crookes dark space, cathode glow, Faraday dark space and then alternate dark and bright bands.

The positive ions produced near the surface of the cathode are attracted towards it. Hence, the ions are accelerated as they move towards the cathode. In the process they gain kinetic energy. The ions strike the cathode with sufficient kinetic energy to liberate more electrons from its surface. These electrons are accelerated away from the cathode and they ionize the gas further by collision. Thus, ionization takes place much more rapidly near the cathode.

When a molecule gets ionized, the electron moves towards the anode and the positive ion towards the cathode. The electron being light, is swept away very fast by the electric field as compared to the slow-moving, heavy, positive ions. Thus, a positive charge density builds up near the cathode and an intense electric field is produced between the cathode and this region. The electrons emitted by the cathode acquire sufficient kinetic energy while passing through this intense electric field to ionize the neutral molecules with which they collide. These ionized molecules emit light which appears as the cathode glow. The electrons emitted from the cathode travel on the average a distance equal to the mean free path before they collide and cause cathode glow. Thus cathode glow appears some distance away from the cathode and this explains the Crookes dark space.

The slow-moving, positive ions create a positive charge density in the region of cathode glow. As the fast-moving electrons, coming from the cathode, pass through this region they are slowed down and hence lose their ionizing capacity. Thus, there is no emission of light for some distance beyond the cathode glow and this makes the Faraday dark space. After coming out of the cathode glow, the electrons again accelerate due to the electric field and acquire sufficient energy to ionize the molecules. This starts the positive column. The Faraday dark space is several times longer than the Crookes dark space because the electric field here is not as intense as it is near the cathode.

The successive process of ionizing, losing ionizing power, accelerating for some distance and again ionizing, is repeated till the electrons reach the anode. Thus, we have alternate dark and bright bands, i.e., the striations.

As the pressure is still lowered, the mean free path increases and hence the length of the Crookes dark space increases. At very low pressure, when the mean free path becomes larger than the length of the tube, the Crookes dark space fills the entire tube and no cathode glow or positive column is observed. The electrons coming out of the cathode strike the walls of the tube and this impact causes fluorescence.

41.2 CATHODE RAYS

When the pressure of the gas in a discharge tube is lowered, at a certain stage the Crookes dark space fills the whole length of the tube. The fact that the walls of the tube glows (fluorescence) shows that something is coming out from the cathode, travelling through the length of the tube and falling on the walls. As we have discussed above, this something is a stream of fast-moving electrons. This fact was recognised after a series of experiments carried out by Crookes, Thomson and others. They named these invisible streams coming from the cathode *cathode rays* and established the following main properties.

(a) *Cathode rays are emitted normally from the cathode surface. Their direction is independent of the position of the anode.*

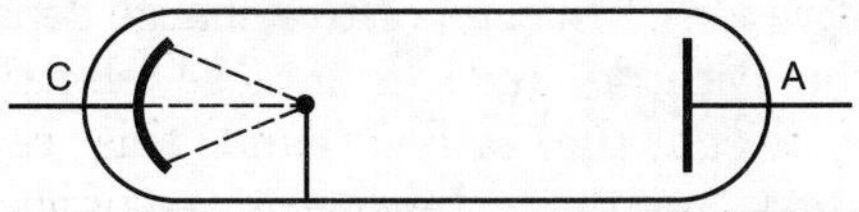

Figure 41.3

This can be shown by taking the cathode in the shape of a concave surface. If a fluorescent material is placed at the centre of curvature of the cathode surface, the material glows with maximum intensity. Any lateral shift reduces the glow.

(b) *Cathode rays travel in straight lines.*

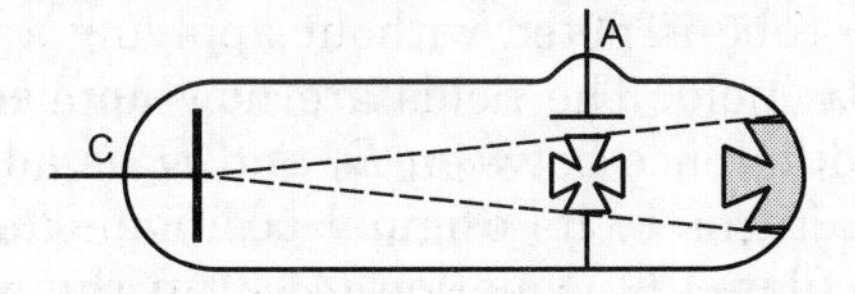

Figure 41.4

This can be shown by placing a metal cross in the path of the cathode rays. A shadow appears on the wall on the opposite side as the cathode rays do not reach there (there is no fluorescence in the shadow region). If the cross is lowered, the shadow disappears.

(c) *Cathode rays exert mechanical force on the object they strike.*

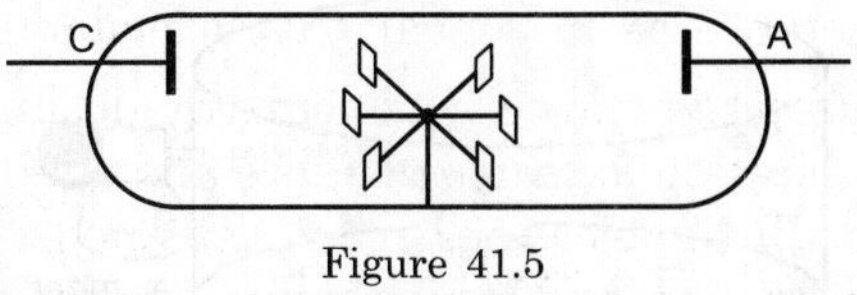

Figure 41.5

To show this, one can put a light wheel of mica in the path of the cathode rays. With proper arrangement, the wheel starts rotating as the cathode rays fall on it.

(d) *Cathode rays produce heat when they strike a material surface.*

If a blackened platinum strip is placed at the centre of curvature of a concave-shaped cathode, the strip becomes red-hot after some time.

(e) *Cathode rays produce fluorescence when they strike a number of crystals, minerals and salts.*

(f) *When cathode rays strike a solid object, specially a metal, X-rays are emitted from the object.*

(g) *Cathode rays can be deflected by an electric field and also by a magnetic field. The direction of deflection is the same as that of a stream of negatively charged particles. The deflection in such a condition is independent of the gas present, the material of the cathode, the position of the anode, etc.*

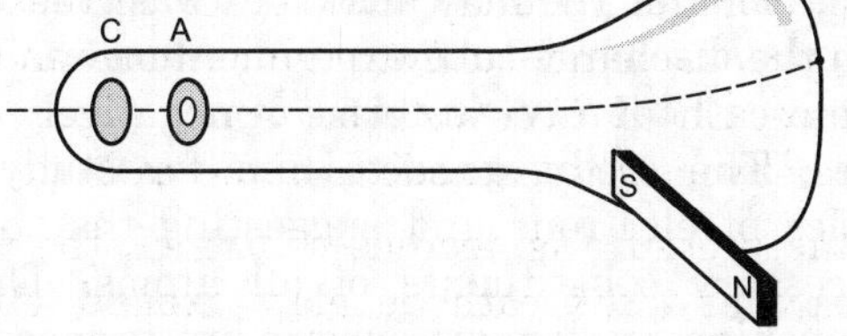

Figure 41.6

Such a deflection was studied by Thomson using an apparatus of the design similar to that shown in figure (41.6). Cathode rays start from the cathode C and pass undeflected into the larger bulb where it causes fluorescence on the opposite surface. The particular design ensures that the glow is in the shape of a small dot. If a magnet is now brought closer to the larger bulb, the dot moves on the wall showing that the rays have been deflected. The direction of the deflection confirms that cathode rays contain negatively charged particles. Similar deflection can be studied in electric field by bringing a charged rod near the larger bulb.

(h) *Cathode rays ionize the gas through which they are passed.*

(i) *Cathode rays can penetrate thin foils of metal.*

(j) *Cathode rays affect photographic plates.*

All the above properties can be easily understood once we recognise that cathode rays are nothing but a stream of fast-moving electrons.

41.3 CANAL RAYS OR POSITIVE RAYS

If the cathode of a discharge tube has holes in it and the pressure of the gas is around 1 mm of mercury, streams of faint luminous glow come out from each hole on the back side of the cathode. This shows that something is coming out of the holes. These are called *canal rays* or *positive rays.* The origin of the canal rays can be easily understood. When the molecules near the cathode are ionized, the positive ions move slowly towards the cathode. The positive ions passing through the holes constitute the positive or canal rays. The positive rays are deflected by electric and magnetic field. The direction of the deflection is the same as that of a stream of positively charged particles. They also cause fluorescence when incident on certain materials.

41.4 DISCOVERY AND PROPERTIES OF ELECTRON

The experiments on discharge tube towards the end of the nineteenth century played an important role in the discovery of electron. The fact that cathode rays are deflected in electric and magnetic field led scientists to believe that they are made of tiny negatively charged particles. These particles are the electrons as we know them today. J J Thomson (1856–1940) is often credited with the discovery of electron. This is not because he was the first to perform the discharge-tube experiment or was the first to explain cathode rays in terms of negatively charged particles. The credit goes to him for studying the properties of electrons and suggesting that electrons are necessary constituents of all atoms. The basic physics behind his famous experiment to measure the "charge by mass" (e/m) ratio of electrons is described below. This ratio is also called the *specific charge* of the electron.

Determination of e/m

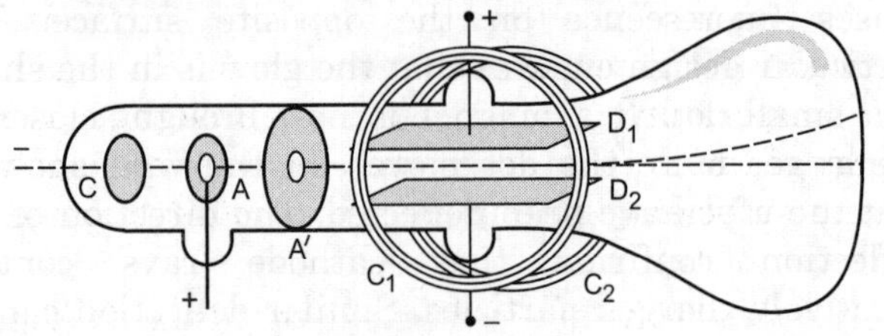

Figure 41.7

Figure (41.7) shows the basic design of Thomson's experiment to measure e/m. A large potential difference V is applied between the cathode C and the anode A sealed in a highly evacuated tube. A narrow beam of electrons, ejected from the cathode, passes through the holes in the anode A and in a parallel metal electrode A'. The beam passes through the region between the two metal plates D_1, D_2 and then strikes the end of the tube. A fluorescent material is coated on the inner surface of the tube at this end so that a visible glow is produced when electrons strike the end. The plate D_1 is connected to the positive terminal of a power supply and D_2 to the negative. Thus, a constant potential difference is maintained between them. Knowing the separation between the plates, the electric field E in the region between the plates can be computed. This field E is in the downward direction in figure (41.7) and exerts a force in the upward direction on the electrons. When the potential difference is applied, the glow at the end of the tube shifts in the upward direction.

A magnetic field B can also be applied in the region between the plates by passing electric currents in circular coils C_1, C_2. This field is perpendicular to the electric field as well as to the undeviated path of the cathode rays. If this field alone is present, the electrons move in a circular arc in the field region and hence are deflected from their straight path. The direction of the current in C_1, C_2 is so chosen that the magnetic force on the electrons is in the downward direction in the figure. Thus, the electron beam is deflected downwards due to the magnetic force.

If both the electric and the magnetic field are switched on and the values are so chosen that

$$v = E/B, \quad \text{... (i)}$$

the magnetic force evB will exactly cancel the electric force eE and the beam will pass undeflected. If the potential difference between the anode A and the cathode C is V, the speed of the electrons coming out of A is given by

$$\frac{1}{2}mv^2 = eV. \quad \text{... (ii)}$$

Putting the value of v from (i) into (ii),

$$\frac{1}{2}m\left(\frac{E}{B}\right)^2 = eV$$

or,
$$\frac{e}{m} = \frac{E^2}{2B^2V}. \quad \text{... (41.2)}$$

In an experiment, the position of the glow at the end of the tube is noted without applying any electric or magnetic field. The fields are now applied and the potential difference between D_1 and D_2 is adjusted till the glow returns to its original position. The value of e/m is calculated by equation (41.2) in this situation.

Millikan Oil-drop Experiment : Determination of e

Thomson's experiment described above, could determine the value of e/m. The value of electronic charge e was measured by Robert Andrews Millikan about fifteen years after Thomson's experiment. Millikan was awarded the Nobel Prize in physics for 1923 for this

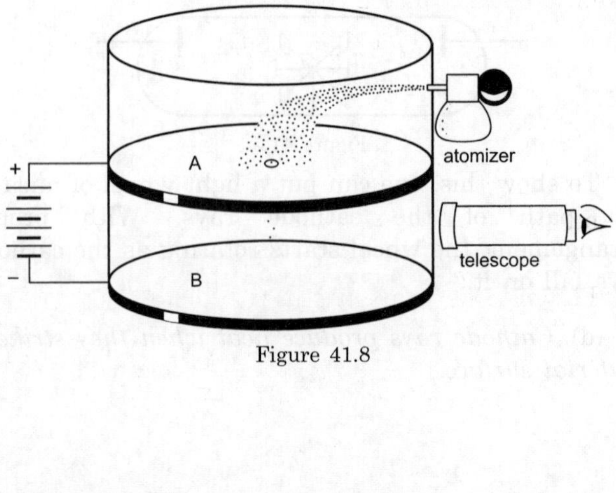

Figure 41.8

classic experiment. The basic design of the Millikan oil-drop experiment is shown in figure (41.8).

Two accurately-aligned, parallel metal plates A and B are separated by a small distance of the order of few millimetres. The plates are enclosed in a chamber with glass walls. An electric potential difference is applied between the plates to produce an electric field E in the vertically downward direction. Small droplets of oil are sprayed in the region between the plates through a hole in the upper plate A. Some of the droplets acquire electric charge due to friction with air (this process may be aided by passing X-rays through the air or by putting some radioactive material in the chamber). The chamber is illuminated by sending light horizontally through it. The drops can be seen by using a telescope placed perpendicular to the light beam. A drop looks like a bright star moving either downwards or upwards. If a droplet has a mass m and charge q, the forces on it are (a) its weight mg, (b) electric force qE, (c) buoyancy B and (d) viscous force F.

Most of the drops acquire a negative charge so that the electric force is upwards. A particular drop is chosen in the field of view of the telescope and the magnitude of the field E is adjusted to make the drop stationary. In this case, there is no force of viscosity and the other three forces add to zero. Thus,

$$qE + B = mg$$

or, $$qE = mg - B$$

$$= \frac{4}{3}\pi r^3(\rho - \sigma)g$$

or, $$q = \frac{4\pi r^3(\rho - \sigma)g}{3E}. \quad \dots \text{(i)}$$

Here r is the radius of the drop, and ρ and σ are the densities of the oil and the air respectively.

To determine the radius of the drop, the electric field is switched off. The drop accelerates downwards. After a while, the speed of the drop becomes constant. This speed v is measured by noting the time taken by the drop to fall through a predetermined distance. In this case, the viscous force $6\pi\eta rv$ and the buoyancy B taken together balance the weight mg.

$$6\pi\eta rv + \frac{4}{3}\pi r^3\sigma g = \frac{4}{3}\pi r^3\rho g$$

or, $$6\pi\eta v = \frac{4}{3}\pi r^2(\rho - \sigma)g$$

or, $$r = \left[\frac{9\eta v}{2(\rho - \sigma)g}\right]^{1/2}.$$

Putting this value of r in (i)

$$q = \frac{18\pi}{E}\sqrt{\frac{\eta^3 v^3}{2(\rho - \sigma)g}}.$$

Millikan and his coworkers repeated the experiement thousands of times and measured the charges on so many drops. It was found that each drop had a charge that was a small integral multiple of a basic value $e = 1{\cdot}6 \times 10^{-19}$ C within the accuracy of the experiment. From this observation, Millikan concluded that $e = 1{\cdot}6 \times 10^{-19}$ C is the charge on an electron. If one electron is attached to a drop, the charge on the drop is e. If two electrons are attached to a drop, the charge on the drop is $2e$ and so on.

41.5 THERMIONIC EMISSION

When a metal is heated to a high temperature, electrons escape from its surface. This phenomenon is called *thermionic emission* and the electrons coming out are called *thermions*. When an electron attempts to come out, the remaining metal, which becomes positively charged, pulls it back. The electron is thus slowed down and is able to come out only if it has got some extra kinetic energy to overcome the pull. The minimum energy that must be given to an electron to take it out of the metal is called the *work function* of the metal. Work function is denoted by the symbol φ and is different for different metals.

At ordinary temperatures, the free electrons of a metal do not have sufficient energy to come out. As the temperature is increased, the average kinetic energy of the electrons increases. Some of the electrons having sufficient kinetic energy are able to come out from the metal.

If n thermions are ejected per unit time by a metal surface, the thermionic current is $i = ne$. This current is given by the *Richardson–Dushman equation*

$$i = ne = AST^2 e^{-\varphi/kT}. \quad \dots (41.3)$$

Here S is the surface area, T is the absolute temperature of the surface, φ is the work function of the metal, k is the Boltzmann constant and A is a constant which depends only on the nature of the metal.

Example 41.1

The work function of a thermionic emitter is 4·5 eV. *By what factor does the thermionic current increase if its temperature is raised from* 1500 K *to* 2000 K?

Solution :

If i_1 and i_2 represent the thermionic currents at temperatures $T_1 = 1500$ K and $T_2 = 2000$ K respectively,

$$i_1 = AST_1^2 e^{-\varphi/kT_1}$$

and $$i_2 = AST_2^2 e^{-\varphi/kT_2}.$$

Thus, $$\frac{i_2}{i_1} = \left(\frac{T_2}{T_1}\right)^2 e^{-\frac{\varphi}{k}\left(\frac{1}{T_2} - \frac{1}{T_1}\right)}.$$

Putting the values of T_1, T_2, φ and k

$$\frac{i_2}{i_1} = 10625.$$

41.6 DIODE VALVE

A diode valve consists of a cathode which can be heated to a high temperature to emit electrons and an anode which can collect these electrons. The cathode and the anode are sealed in an evacuated glass bulb. The cathode is also called *filament* and the anode is also called *plate*. In one design, a pure tungsten wire or a thorium-coated tungsten wire is used as the cathode. This wire can be directly connected to an external circuit driving current through it and hence increasing its temperature. In another design, a hollow nickel tube coated with barium oxide is used as the cathode. The tube surrounds a heater coil. When the external circuit drives a current through the heater coil, the nickel tube gets heated by radiation. The anode is in the form of a hollow nickel cylinder which surrounds the cathode. Potential difference may be applied between the cathode and the anode by connecting a battery through the leads coming out of the sealed valve. The positive terminal of the battery is connected to the anode and the negative terminal to the cathode.

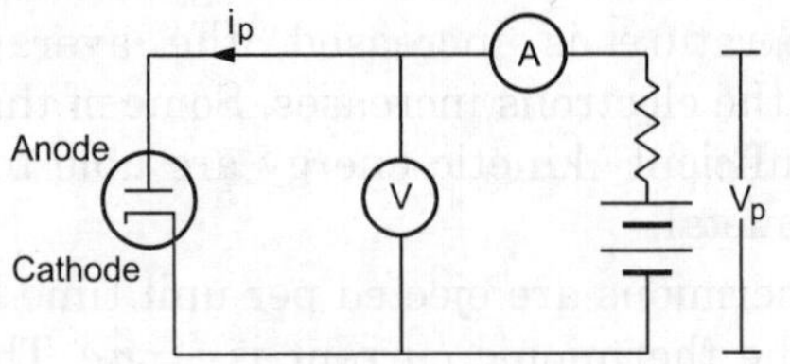

Figure 41.9

Figure (41.9) shows the symbolic representation of a diode valve and the circuit to study the current through the valve. When the cathode is heated, it emits electrons. These electrons are attracted towards the anode when a positive potential V_p (with respect to the cathode) is applied to it. This potential V_p is called the *plate voltage*. The electrons pass through the battery and then return to the cathode. Thus, an electric current i_p is established in the circuit which can be measured by the ammeter connected in the circuit. This current is called the *plate current*. If the plate voltage V_p is changed, the plate current i_p is also changed. A set of plots between the plate current and the plate voltage is called *diode characteristics*.

Diode Charactersitics

Figure (41.10) shows the nature of diode characteristics at different temperatures of the cathode. The space between the cathode and the anode contains electrons and hence, is negatively charged.

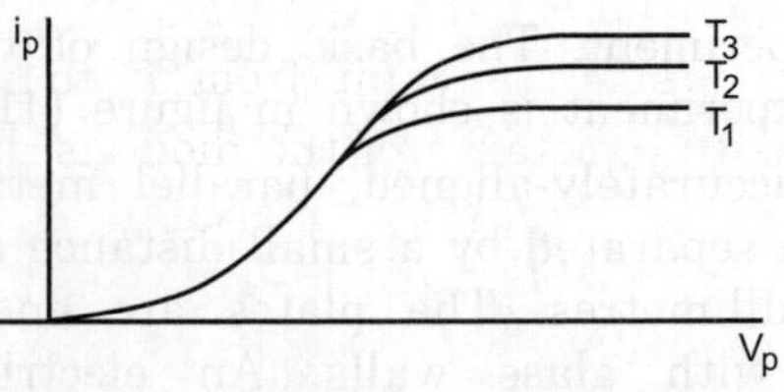

Figure 41.10

This negative charge is called the *space charge* and it repels the newly ejected electrons back to the cathode. The plate current i_p is thus reduced due to the space charge. As the plate voltage is increased, the electrons are pulled with a greater force and the effect of space charge decreases. Thus, the plate current i_p increases as the plate voltage V_p increases. When V_p is sufficiently large, all the electrons emitted by the cathode are collected by the anode and the current becomes saturated. Further increase in V_p does not increase i_p.

If the anode is given a negative potential with respect to the cathode, the electrons are pushed back towards the cathode and no current flows in the external circuit. We say that the diode *does not conduct* in this case. Thus, the diode allows current only in one direction. The electrons can leave the diode at the anode and enter into it at the cathode. Correspondingly, positive current can enter the diode at the anode and may come out at the cathode.

If the temperature of the filament is increased, greater number of electrons are ejected from the cathode and the saturation current increases.

Far from the saturation, the current is roughly proportional to $V_p^{3/2}$. Thus,

$$i_p = k\, V_p^{3/2}$$

where k is a constant for a given diode. This law is called *Langmuir–Child law*.

Dynamic Plate Resistance

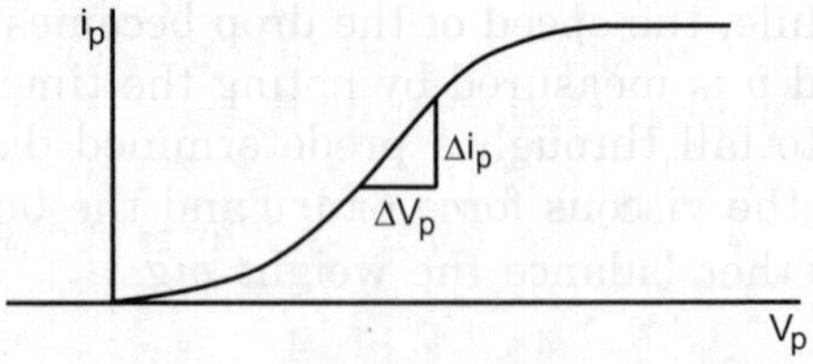

Figure 41.11

The resistance of a metallic conductor is defined as $R = V/i$. One can define the resistance of a diode using this equation. However, a more useful quantity, called the *dynamic plate resistance* of the diode, is defined as follows. Suppose the diode is operated at a plate voltage V_p and the plate current is i_p (figure 41.11). Now the plate voltage V_p is changed by a small amount to $V_p + \Delta V_p$. Consequently, the current will change by a small amount from i_p to $i_p + \Delta i_p$. The dynamic plate resistance of the diode is defined as

$$r_p = \frac{\Delta V_p}{\Delta i_p}. \quad \dots (41.4)$$

It is clear that r_p depends on the operating conditions (V_p, i_p). Referring to figure (41.11), the dynamic plate resistance is the inverse of the slope of the i_p–V_p characteristic at the operating point.

Example 41.2

When the plate voltage applied to a diode valve is changed from 40 V *to* 42 V, *the plate current increases from* 50 mA *to* 60 mA. *Calculate the dynamic plate resistance at the operating condition.*

Solution : Here $\Delta V_p = 42\text{ V} - 40\text{ V} = 2\text{ V}$

and $\Delta i_p = 60\text{ mA} - 50\text{ mA} = 10\text{ mA}$.

Thus, the dynamic plate resistance is

$$r_p = \frac{\Delta V_p}{\Delta i_p} = \frac{2\text{ V}}{10\text{ mA}} = 200\ \Omega.$$

Rectification

If a source of alternating current is conneted to a resistor, the direction of the current in the resistor changes alternately. By using a diode in the circuit, one can have current in the resistor in a fixed direction. *Obtaining a unidirectional current from an AC source is called rectification.*

Half-Wave Rectification

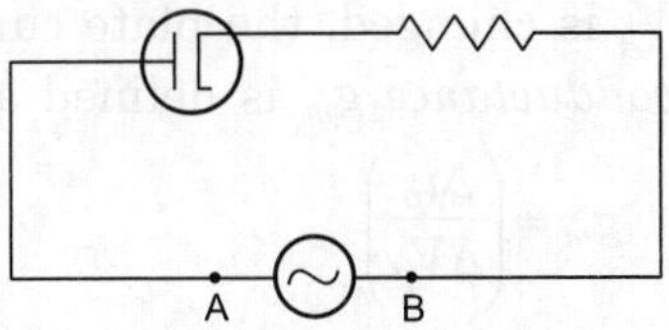

Figure 41.12

Figure (41.12) shows a circuit containing an AC source, a diode and a resistor. When the point A is at a potential higher than that of B, the anode is also at a potential higher than that of the cathode. The diode allows current to pass through. Thus, the AC source sends a current which goes through the diode, through the resistor and then back to the source. The current in the resistor is from left to right.

When the potential at A becomes less than that at B, the diode does not allow a current. There is no current in the resistance in this case.

Figure (41.13) shows the variations in the applied AC voltage (potential of A with respect to B) and the current in the resistor as time passes. The current is allowed only in the positive half-cycles and is stopped in the negative half-cycles.

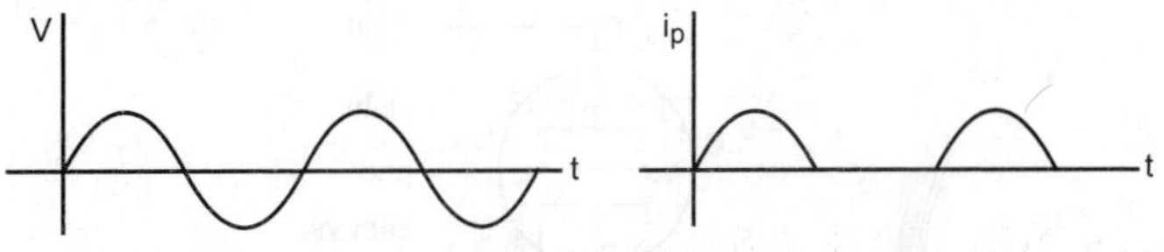

Figure 41.13

We see that the current in the resistor is always from left to right. The diode has *rectified* the AC voltage. As the current is allowed only for half the time, the rectification is called *half-wave rectificition.*

Full-Wave Rectification

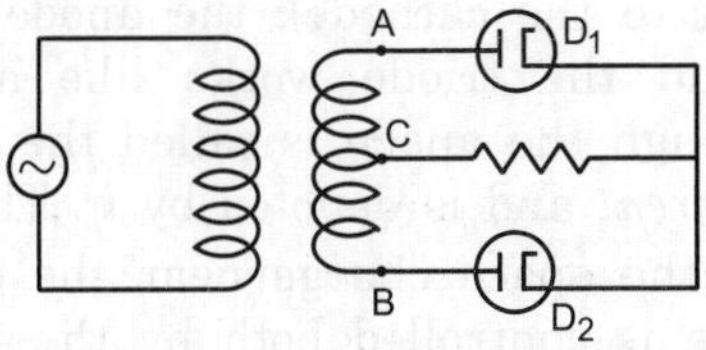

Figurre 41.14

Figure (41.14) shows the circuit for full-wave rectification. The AC source is connected to the primary of a transformer. The terminals of the secondary are connected to the anodes of two diodes D_1 and D_2. The two cathodes are connected to one end of a resistor. The other end of the resistor is connected to the centre C of the secondary of the transformer.

Let us take the potential at C to be zero. Consider a half-cycle in which the potential of A is positive and that of B is negative. The diode D_1 conducts but D_2 does not. So a current passes through D_1 and then through the resistor back to the secondary. The current in the resistor is from right to left. In the next half-cycle, the potential at B is positive and that at A is negative. The diode D_2 conducts, but D_1 does not. The current passes through D_2 and then through the resistor back to the secondary. Again, the current in the resistor is from right to left. So, the current in the resistor is from right to left in both the half-cycles. Figure (41.15) shows the variations in the applied AC voltage and the current in the resistor as time passes.

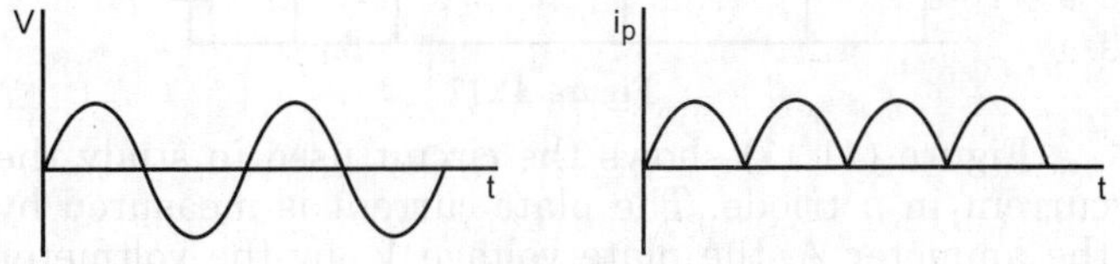

Figure 41.15

41.7 TRIODE VALVE

A triode valve is similar in construction to a diode valve except that a wire grid is inserted between the cathode and the anode. Thus, there are three external terminals in a triode which are connected to the cathode, the grid and the anode. Figure (41.16) shows the symbol of a triode valve.

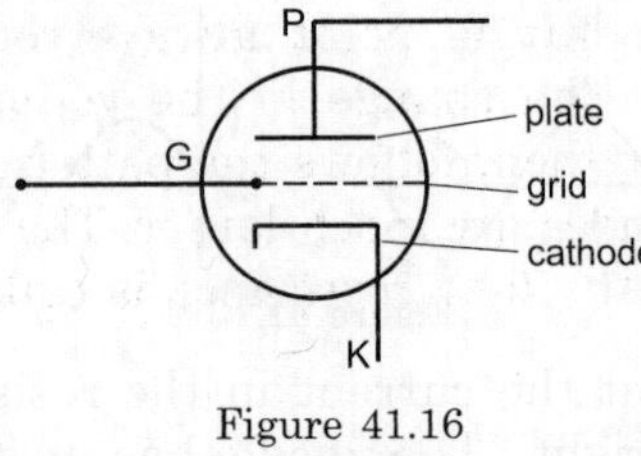

Figure 41.16

When the cathode is heated, it emits thermions. These thermions pass through the holes in the grid and reach the anode. If the anode is given a positive potential and the grid is kept at zero potential (both with respect to the cathode), the anode attracts the electrons and the triode works like a diode. The current through the anode is called the *plate current* or *anode current* and is denoted by i_p. This current is affected by the space charge near the cathode. The space charge is controlled both by the *grid voltage* V_g (with respect to the cathode) and the plate voltage V_p. If the *grid voltage* V_g is made negative, the grid repels the electrons coming from the cathode and the current decreases. If the grid voltage is made positive, it will help the electrons to go towards the anode, increasing the current. As the grid is closer to the cathode, changing grid voltage is more effective than changing plate voltage in bringing about a change in the plate current. In absence of the grid, the current is roughly given by $i_p = k\, V_p^{3/2}$. When the grid is added, the current is given by

$$i_p = k(V_p + \mu\, V_g)^{3/2}. \qquad \dots \ (41.4)$$

Thus, a grid voltage V_g has the same effect as a plate voltage μV_g. The constant μ, which may be typically of the order of 10, is called *amplification factor*.

Triode Characteristics

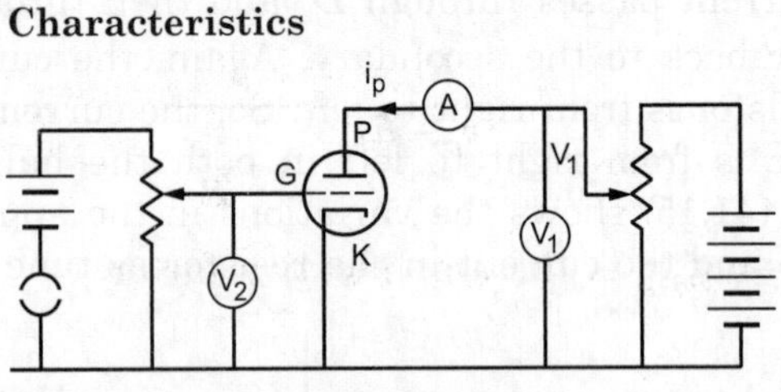

Figure 41.17

Figure (41.17) shows the circuit used to study the current in a triode. The plate current is measured by the ammeter A, the plate voltage V_p by the voltmeter V_1 and the grid voltage V_g by the voltmeter V_2. These voltages may be changed by changing the rheostat settings. The grid potential may be made positive or negative.

In a triode, there are several currents and voltages and one can draw a number of characterstic curves. More important are i_p–V_p curves at constant V_g and i_p–V_g curves at constant V_p. The curves in the first set are called the *anode characteristics* and those in the second set are called the *mutual characteristics.* Figure (41.18a) and (41.18b) show the two characteristics qualitatively.

The operating point of a triode is determined by specifying V_p, V_g and i_p. Generally, the triode is operated in the linear portions of its characteristics (figure 41.18).

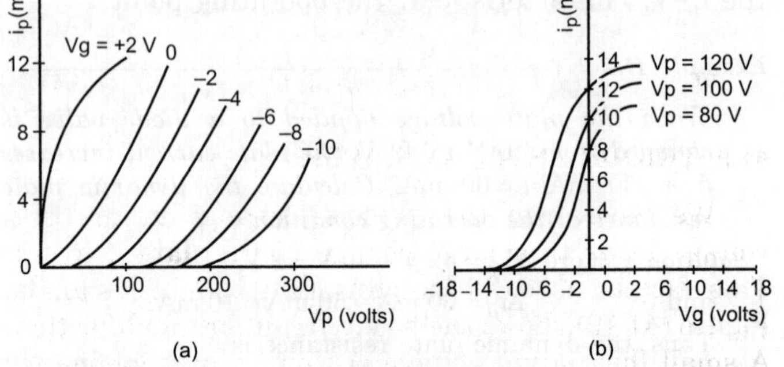

Figure 41.18

Dynamic plate resistance

If the grid voltage is kept constant and the plate voltage is changed, the plate current changes. We define the *dynamic plate resistance* r_p as

$$r_p = \left(\frac{\Delta V_p}{\Delta i_p}\right)_{\Delta V_g = 0}. \qquad \dots \ (41.5)$$

Mutual conductance

If the plate voltage V_p is kept constant and the grid voltage V_g is changed, the plate current changes. The *mutual conductance* g_m is defined as

$$g_m = \left(\frac{\Delta i_p}{\Delta V_g}\right)_{\Delta V_p = 0}. \qquad \dots \ (41.6)$$

Mutual conductance is also called *transconductance*.

If both V_g and V_p change, the plate current changes by

$$\Delta i_p = \left(\frac{\Delta i_p}{\Delta V_p}\right)_{\Delta V_g = 0} \Delta V_p + \left(\frac{\Delta i_p}{\Delta V_g}\right)_{\Delta V_p = 0} \Delta V_g$$

$$= \frac{1}{r_p}\, \Delta V_p + g_m\, \Delta V_g. \qquad \dots \ (41.7)$$

Amplification factor

If the grid voltage is increased, the plate current i_p also increases. One can bring the current back to i_p by decreasing the plate voltage V_p. The *amplification factor* μ is defined as

$$\mu = -\left(\frac{\Delta V_p}{\Delta V_g}\right)_{\Delta i_p = 0}. \qquad \dots \ (41.8)$$

The negative sign is put in the definition because if the grid voltage is increased, one should decrease the plate voltage so as to maintain the same current. Thus, ΔV_p and ΔV_g are of opposite signs so that the definition makes μ positive. This same μ is used in equation (41.4).

From equation (41.7), if $\Delta i_p = 0$,

$$-\frac{\Delta V_p}{\Delta V_g} = \frac{g_m}{1/r_p}$$

or, $$\mu = r_p \times g_m. \qquad \dots (41.9)$$

41.8 TRIODE AS AN AMPLIFIER

We have seen that a small change in the grid voltage leads to a large change in the plate current. This fact is used for amplification of small signals. Figure (41.19) shows the basic circuit for amplification. A small fluctuating voltage v_s (from a microphone for example) is included in the grid circuit. This voltage is called the *signal*. The value v_s also gives the amount by which the grid voltage changes. Thus,

$$v_s = \Delta V_g.$$

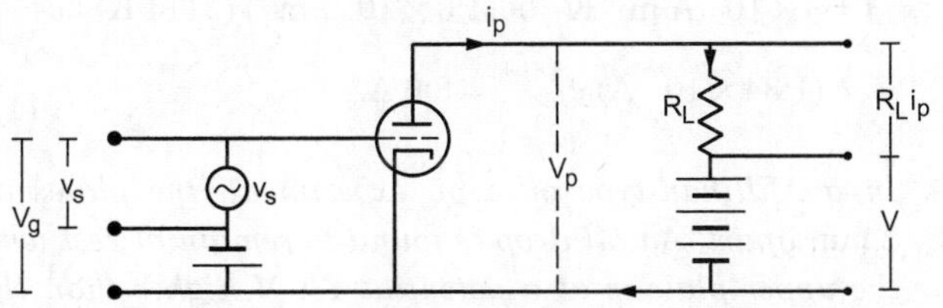

Figure 41.19

A load resistance R_L is included in the plate circuit. The value of V_g (with zero signal), and V_p are so adjusted that the operating point lies on the linear portion of the mutual characteristics (figure 41.18). As the signal v_s changes, the grid potential changes and consequently the plate current i_p changes. The voltage appearing across the load resistance also changes accordingly. Suppose that the signal is small enough so that the operating point always remains on the linear portion. The change in the voltage across the load resistance, then, follows the pattern of the signal but the amplitudes are much larger. The change in the voltage across the load resistance is called the *output voltage* v_0.

Thus,

$$v_0 = R_L \Delta i_p. \qquad \dots \text{(i)}$$

The ratio $A = \frac{v_0}{v_s}$ is called the *voltage-gain* or *gain factor*.

If V is the potential difference across the battery in the plate circuit, that across the triode is

$$V_p = V - R_L \, i_p$$

or, $$\Delta V_p = -R_L \, \Delta i_p = -v_0.$$

From equation (41.7),

$$\Delta i_p = \frac{\Delta V_p}{r_p} + g_m \, \Delta V_g$$

$$= -\frac{v_0}{r_p} + g_m \, v_s.$$

From (i), the output voltage is,

$$v_0 = R_L \, \Delta i_p$$

$$= -\frac{R_L v_0}{r_p} + R_L \, g_m \, v_s$$

or, $$v_0 \left[1 + \frac{R_L}{r_p} \right] = R_L \, g_m v_s$$

or, $$\frac{v_0}{v_s} = \frac{R_L \, g_m}{1 + \frac{R_L}{r_p}} = \frac{R_L \, g_m r_p}{r_p + R_L}$$

or, $$A = \frac{R_L \, \mu}{r_p + R_L} = \frac{\mu}{1 + \frac{r_p}{R_L}} \qquad \dots (41.10)$$

where $\mu = g_m r_p$ is the amplification factor.

Worked Out Examples

1. *The mean free path of the electrons in a discharge tube is* 20 cm. *The tube itself is* 10 cm *long. What is the length of the Crookes dark space ?*

Solution : The mean free path of the electrons is much longer than the length of the tube. Thus, the electrons, in general, do not collide in between, no ionization takes place and hence no light is emitted. The Crookes dark space fills the entire tube and hence is 10 cm long.

2. *Consider a cylindrical tube closed at one end and fitted with a conducting, movable piston at the other end. A cathode is fixed in the tube near the closed end and an anode is fixed with the piston. A gas is filled in the tube at pressure p. Using Paschen equation V = f(pd), show that the sparking potential does not change as the piston is slowly moved in or out. Assume that the temperature does not change in the process.*

Solution : As the piston is moved, the volume of the gas and hence its pressure changes. As the tube is cylindrical, the volume is proportional to the length of the tube. From Boyle's law, pd = constant and hence the sparking potential does not change as the piston is moved.

3. *The number of thermions emitted in a given time increases* 100 times *as the temperature of the emitting surface is increased from* 600 K *to* 800 K. *Find the work function of the emitter. Boltzmann constant* $k = 8{\cdot}62 \times 10^{-5}$ eV K^{-1}.

Solution : The number of thermions n, emitted by a surface, in a given time is given by (Richardson–Dushman equation)

$$n = A'ST^2 e^{-\varphi/kT}$$

where A' is a constant and other symbols have their usual meanings. Let n_1 and n_2 be the number of electrons emitted at temperatures T_1 and T_2. Then

$$\frac{n_1}{n_2} = \frac{T_1^2 \, e^{-\varphi/kT_1}}{T_2^2 \, e^{-\varphi/kT_2}}$$

or, $$\frac{n_1 T_2^2}{n_2 T_1^2} = e^{-\frac{\varphi}{k}\left(\frac{1}{T_1} - \frac{1}{T_2}\right)}$$

or, $$-\frac{\varphi}{k}\left(\frac{1}{T_1} - \frac{1}{T_2}\right) = \ln \frac{n_1 T_2^2}{n_2 T_1^2}$$

or, $$\frac{\varphi(T_2 - T_1)}{kT_1T_2} = \ln \frac{n_2 T_1^2}{n_1 T_2^2}$$

or, $$\varphi = \frac{kT_1 T_2}{T_2 - T_1} \ln \frac{n_2 T_1^2}{n_1 T_2^2}$$

$$= \frac{(8{\cdot}62 \times 10^{-5} \text{ eV K}^{-1})(600 \text{ K})(800 \text{ K})}{200 \text{ K}} \ln\left(100 \times \frac{36}{64}\right)$$

$$= 0{\cdot}83 \text{ eV}.$$

4. *The constant A in the Richardson–Dushman equation is* 60×10^4 A m^{-2}K^{-2} *for tungsten. A tungsten cathode has a total surface area of* $2{\cdot}0 \times 10^{-5}$ m^2 *and operates at* 2000 K. *The work function of tungsten is* 4·55 eV. *Calculate the electric current due to thermionic emission.*

Solution :

The Richardson–Dushman equation is

$$i = AST^2 e^{-\varphi/kT}.$$

We have, $$\frac{\varphi}{kT} = \frac{4{\cdot}55 \text{ eV}}{(8{\cdot}62 \times 10^{-5} \text{ eV K}^{-1})(2000 \text{ K})}$$

$$= 26{\cdot}4.$$

Thus, the thermionic current i is

$$= 60 \times 10^4 \text{ A m}^{-2}\text{K}^{-2} \times (2{\cdot}0 \times 10^{-5} \text{ m}^2) \times (2000 \text{ K})^2 \times e^{-26{\cdot}4}$$

$$= (4{\cdot}8 \times 10^5 \text{ A})\, e^{-26{\cdot}4} = 0{\cdot}16 \text{ mA}.$$

5. *Calculate the saturation thermionic current if* 120 W *is applied to a thoriated-tungsten filament of surface area* 1·0 cm^2. *Assume that the surface radiates like a blackbody. The required constants are*

$A = 3 \times 10^4$ A m^{-2}–K^2, $\varphi = 2{\cdot}6$ eV, $k = 8{\cdot}62 \times 10^{-5}$ eV K^{-1} *and* $\sigma = 6 \times 10^{-8}$ W m^{-2}K^{-4}.

Solution : The thermionic current is given by the Richardson–Dushman equation

$$i = AST^2 e^{-\varphi/kT}. \quad \text{... (i)}$$

When the power input to the filament equals the power radiated, the temperature becomes constant. The thermionic current then becomes saturated. The power radiated is given by the Stefan's law

$$P = S\sigma T^4$$

or, $120 \text{ W} = (1{\cdot}0 \times 10^{-4} \text{ m}^2) \times (6 \times 10^{-8} \text{ W m}^{-2}\text{K}^{-4}) \times T^4$

or, $T = 2114$ K.

Now $$\frac{\varphi}{kT} = \frac{2{\cdot}6 \text{ eV}}{(8{\cdot}62 \times 10^{-5} \text{ eV K}^{-1})(2114 \text{ K})} = 14{\cdot}26.$$

Putting in (i),

$$i = 3 \times 10^4 \text{ A m}^{-2}\text{K}^{-2} \times (1{\cdot}0 \times 10^{-4} \text{ m}^2)(2114 \text{ K})^2 e^{-14{\cdot}26}$$

$$= (1{\cdot}34 \times 10^7 \text{ A})\, e^{-14{\cdot}26} = 8{\cdot}6 \text{ A}.$$

6. *In a Millikan-type oil-drop experiment, the plates are* 8 mm *apart. An oil drop is found to remain at rest when the upper plate is at a potential* 136 V *higher than that of the lower one. When the electric field is switched off, the drop is found to fall a distance of* 2·0 mm *in* 36 seconds *with a uniform speed. Find (a) the charge on the drop and (b) the number of electrons attached to this drop. Density of oil* = 880 kg m^{-3} *and coefficient of viscosity of air* = 180 μpoise.

Solution : (a) The charge on the drop is

$$q = \frac{18\pi}{E}\sqrt{\frac{\eta^3 v^3}{2(\rho - \sigma)g}}. \quad \text{... (i)}$$

Here $$E = \frac{136 \text{ V}}{8 \times 10^{-3} \text{ m}} = 1{\cdot}7 \times 10^4 \text{ V m}^{-1}$$

$$\eta = 180 \text{ μpoise} = 1{\cdot}8 \times 10^{-5} \text{ N sm}^{-2}$$

$$v = \frac{2{\cdot}0 \text{ mm}}{36 \text{ s}} = \frac{1}{18} \times 10^{-3} \text{ m s}^{-1}$$

and $\rho = 880$ kg m^{-3}.

The density of air σ (1·29 kg m^{-3}) may be neglected in comparison to that of the oil. Putting values in (i),

$$q = 7{\cdot}93 \times 10^{-19} \text{ C}.$$

(b) The number of electrons attached to the drop is,

$$n = \frac{7.93 \times 10^{-19}\ \text{C}}{1.6 \times 10^{-19}\ \text{C}} = 4.96.$$

It is clear that 5 electrons are attached to the drop.

7. *Show that the dynamic plate resistance of a diode is* $\frac{2V}{3i}$ *where V and i are the plate voltage and the plate current respectively. Assume Langmuir–Child equation to hold.*

Solution :

The dynamic plate resistance of the diode is $R = \frac{dV}{di}$.

The Langmuir–Child equation is

$$i = cV^{3/2} \quad \ldots \text{(i)}$$

where c is a constant for a given diode. This gives

$$\frac{di}{dV} = \frac{3}{2} cV^{1/2}. \quad \ldots \text{(ii)}$$

Dividing (ii) by (i), $\frac{1}{i}\frac{di}{dV} = \frac{3}{2V}$

or, $\frac{dV}{di} = \frac{2V}{3i}$.

8. *The mutual conductance of a triode valve is* 2·5 millimho. *Find the change in the plate current if the grid voltage is changed from* –2·0 V *to* –4·5 V.

Solution :

The mutual conductance of a triode valve is

$$g_m = \left[\frac{\Delta i_p}{\Delta V_g}\right]_{\Delta V_p = 0}$$

or, $\Delta i_p = g_m \Delta V_g$

$$= (2.5 \times 10^{-3}\ \Omega^{-1}) \times (-4.5\ \text{V} + 2.0\ \text{V})$$

$$= -6.25 \times 10^{-3}\ \text{A}.$$

9. *A triode valve has amplification factor* 21 *and dynamic plate resistance* 10 kΩ. *This is used as an amplifier with a load of* 20 kΩ. *Find the gain factor of the amplifier.*

Solution :

The gain factor of a triode valve amplifier is

$$A = \frac{\mu}{1 + \frac{r_p}{R_L}}$$

where μ is the amplification factor, r_p is the plate resistance and R_L is the load resistance. Thus,

$$A = \frac{21}{1 + \frac{10\ \text{k}\Omega}{20\ \text{k}\Omega}} = 14.$$

□

QUESTIONS FOR SHORT ANSWER

1. Why is conduction easier in gases if the pressure is low ? Will the conduction continue to improve if the pressure is made as low as nearly zero ?
2. An AC source is connected to a diode and a resistor in series. Is the current through the resistor AC or DC ?
3. How will the thermionic current vary if the filament current is increased ?
4. Would you prefer a material having a high melting point or a low melting point to be used as a cathode in a diode ?
5. Would you prefer a material having a high work function or a low work function to be used as a cathode in a diode ?
6. An isolated metal sphere is heated to a high temperature. Will it become positively charged due to thermionic emission ?
7. A diode valve is connected to a battery and a load resistance. The filament is heated so that a constant current is obtained in the circuit. As the cathode continuously emits electrons, does it get more and more positively charged ?
8. Why does thermionic emission not take place in nonconductors ?
9. The cathode of a diode valve is replaced by another cathode of double the surface area. Keeping the voltage and temperature conditions the same, will the plate current decrease, increase or remain the same ?
10. Why is the linear portion of the triode characteristic chosen to operate the triode as an amplifier ?

OBJECTIVE I

1. Cathode rays constitute a stream of
   (a) electrons (b) protons
   (c) positive ions (d) negative ions.
2. Cathode rays are passing through a discharge tube. In the tube, there is
   (a) an electric field but no magnetic field

(b) a magnetic field but no electric field
(c) an electric as well as a magnetic field
(d) neither an electric nor a magnetic field.

3. Let i_0 be the thermionic current from a metal surface when the absolute temperature of the surface is T_0. The temperature is slowly increased and the thermionic current is measured as a function of temperature. Which of the following plots may represent the variation in (i/i_0) against (T/T_0)?

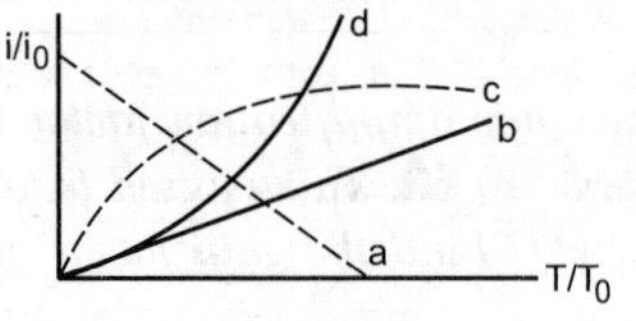

Figure 41-Q1

4. When the diode shows saturated current, dynamic plate resistance is
(a) zero (b) infinity
(c) indeterminate (d) different for different diodes.

5. The anode of a thermionic diode is connected to the negative terminal of a battery and the cathode to its positive terminal.
(a) No appreciable current will pass through the diode.
(b) A large current will pass through the diode from the anode to the cathode.
(c) A large current will pass through the diode from the cathode to the anode.
(d) The diode will be damaged.

6. A diode, a resistor and a 50 Hz AC source are connected in series. The number of current pulses per second through the resistor is
(a) 25 (b) 50 (c) 100 (d) 200.

7. A triode is operated in the linear region of its characteristics. If the plate voltage is slightly increased, the dynamic plate resistance will
(a) increase (b) decrease
(c) remain almost the same
(d) become zero.

8. The plate current in a triode valve is maximum when the potential of the grid is
(a) positive (b) zero (c) negative (d) nonpositive.

9. The amplification factor of a triode operating in the linear region depends strongly on
(a) the temperature of the cathode
(b) the plate potential (c) the grid potential
(d) the separations of the grid from the cathode and the anode.

OBJECTIVE II

1. Electric conduction takes place in a discharge tube due to the movement of
(a) positive ions (b) negative ions
(c) electrons (d) protons.

2. Which of the following are true for cathode ray?
(a) It travels along straight lines.
(b) It emits X-ray when strikes a metal.
(c) It is an electromagnetic wave.
(d) It is not deflected by magnetic field.

3. Because of the space charge in a diode valve,
(a) the plate current decreases
(b) the plate voltage increases
(c) the rate of emission of thermions increases
(d) the saturation current increases.

4. The saturation current in a triode valve can be changed by changing
(a) the grid voltage (b) the plate voltage
(c) the separation between the grid and the cathode
(d) the temperature of the cathode.

5. Mark the correct options.
(a) A diode valve can be used as a rectifier.
(b) A triode valve can be used as a rectifier.
(c) A diode valve can be used as an amplifier.
(d) A triode valve can be used as an amplifier.

6. The plate current in a diode is zero. It is possible that
(a) the plate voltage is zero
(b) the plate voltage is slightly negative
(c) the plate voltage is slightly positive
(d) the temperature of the filament is low.

7. The plate current in a triode valve is zero. The temperature of the filament is high. It is possible that
(a) $V_g > 0,\ V_p > 0$ (b) $V_g > 0,\ V_p < 0$
(c) $V_g < 0,\ V_p > 0$ (d) $V_g < 0,\ V_p < 0$.

EXERCISES

1. A discharge tube contains helium at a low pressure. A large potential difference is applied across the tube. Consider a helium atom that has just been ionized due to the detachment of an atomic electron. Find the ratio of the distance travelled by the free electron to that by the positive ion in a short time dt after the ionization.

2. A molecule of a gas, filled in a discharge tube, gets ionized when an electron is detached from it. An electric field of 5·0 kV m^{-1} exists in the vicinity of the event. (a) Find the distance travelled by the free electron in 1 μs assuming no collision. (b) If the mean free path of the electron is 1·0 mm, estimate the time of transit of the free electron between successive collisions.

3. The mean free path of electrons in the gas in a discharge tube is inversely proportional to the pressure inside it. The Crookes dark space occupies half the length of the discharge tube when the pressure is 0·02 mm of mercury. Estimate the pressure at which the dark space will fill the whole tube.

4. Two discharge tubes have identical material structure and the same gas is filled in them. The length of one tube is 10 cm and that of the other tube is 20 cm. Sparking starts in both the tubes when the potential difference between the cathode and the anode is 100 V. If the pressure in the shorter tube is 1·0 mm of mercury, what is the pressure in the longer tube ?

5. Calculate $n(T)/n(1000\text{ K})$ for tungsten emitter at T = 300 K, 2000 K and 3000 K where $n(T)$ represents the number of thermions emitted per second by the surface at temperature T. Work function of tungsten is 4·52 eV.

6. The saturation current from a thoriated-tungsten cathode at 2000 K is 100 mA. What will be the saturation current for a pure-tungsten cathode of the same surface area operating at the same temperature ? The constant A in the Richardson–Dushman equation is $60 \times 10^4 \text{ A m}^{-2}\text{K}^{-2}$ for pure tungsten and $3{\cdot}0 \times 10^4 \text{ A m}^{-2}\text{K}^{-2}$ for thoriated tungsten. The work function of pure tungsten is 4·5 eV and that of thoriated tungsten is 2·6 eV.

7. A tungsten cathode and a thoriated-tungsten cathode have the same geometrical dimensions and are operated at the same temperature. The thoriated-tungsten cathode gives 5000 times more current than the other one. Find the operating temperature. Take relevant data from the previous problem.

8. If the temperature of a tungsten filament is raised from 2000 K to 2010 K, by what factor does the emission current change ? Work function of tungsten is 4·5 eV.

9. The constant A in the Richardson–Dushman equation for tungsten is $60 \times 10^4 \text{ A m}^{-2}\text{ K}^{-2}$. The work function of tungsten is 4·5 eV. A tungsten cathode having a surface area $2{\cdot}0 \times 10^{-5}\text{ m}^2$ is heated by a 24 W electric heater. In steady state, the heat radiated by the cathode equals the energy input by the heater and the temperature becomes constant. Assuming that the cathode radiates like a blackbody, calculate the saturation current due to thermions. Take Stefan constant $= 6 \times 10^{-8}\text{ W m}^{-2}\text{ K}^{-4}$. Assume that the thermions take only a small fraction of the heat supplied.

10. A plate current of 10 mA is obtained when 60 volts are applied across a diode tube. Assuming the Langmuir–Child equation $i_p \propto V_p^{3/2}$ to hold, find the dynamic resistance r_p in this operating condition.

11. The plate current in a diode is 20 mA when the plate voltage is 50 V or 60 V. What will be the current if the plate voltage is 70 V ?

12. The power delivered in the plate circuit of a diode is 1·0 W when the plate voltage is 36 V. Find the power delivered if the plate voltage is increased to 49 V. Assume Langmuir–Child equation to hold.

13. A triode valve operates at V_p = 225 V and V_g = – 0·5 V. The plate current remains unchanged if the plate voltage is increased to 250 V and the grid voltage is decreased to – 2·5 V. Calculate the amplification factor.

14. Calculate the amplification factor of a triode valve which has plate resistance of 2 kΩ and transconductance of 2 millimho.

15. The dynamic plate resistance of a triode valve is 10 kΩ. Find the change in the plate current if the plate voltage is changed from 200 V to 220 V.

16. Find the values of r_p, μ and g_m of a triode operating at plate voltage 200 V and grid voltage –6 V. The plate characteristics are shown in figure (41-E1).

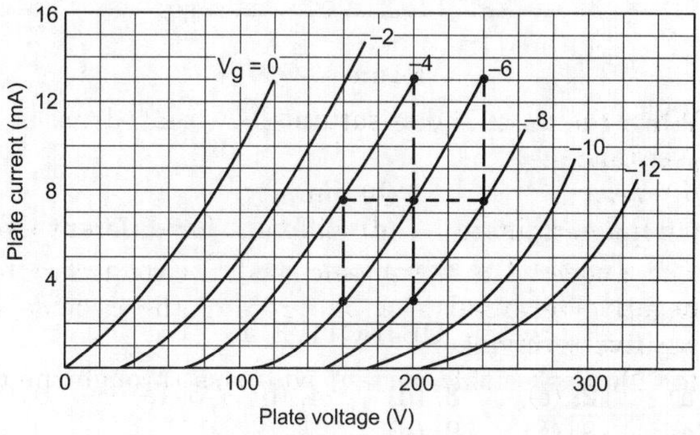

Figure 41-E1

17. The plate resistance of a triode is 8 kΩ and the transconductance is 2·5 millimho. (a) If the plate voltage is increased by 48 V, and the grid voltage is kept constant, what will be the increase in the plate current ? (b) With plate voltage kept constant at this increased value, how much should the grid voltage be decreased in order to bring the plate current back to its initial value ?

18. The plate resistance and the amplification factor of a triode are 10 kΩ and 20. The tube is operated at plate voltage 250 V and grid voltage –7·5 V. The plate current is 10 mA. (a) To what value should the grid voltage be changed so as to increase the plate current to 15 mA ? (b) To what value should the plate voltage be changed to take the plate current back to 10 mA ?

19. The plate current, plate voltage and grid voltage of a 6F6 triode tube are related as

$$i_p = 41(V_p + 7\,V_g)^{1{\cdot}41}$$

where V_p and V_g are in volts and i_p in microamperes. The tube is operated at V_p = 250 V, V_g = –20 V. Calculate (a) the tube current, (b) the plate resistance, (c) the mutual conductance and (d) the amplification factor.

20. The plate current in a triode can be written as

$$i_p = k\left(V_g + \frac{V_p}{\mu}\right)^{3/2}.$$

Show that the mutual conductance is proportional to the cube root of the plate current.

21. A triode has mutual conductance = 2·0 millimho and plate resistance = 20 kΩ. It is desired to amplify a signal by a factor of 30. What load resistance should be added in the circuit ?

22. The gain factor of an amplifier is increased from 10 to 12 as the load resistance is changed from 4 kΩ to 8 kΩ. Calculate (a) the amplification factor and (b) the plate resistance.

23. Figure (41-E2) shows two identical triode tubes connected in parallel. The anodes are connected together, the grids are connected together and the cathodes are connected together. Show that the equivalent plate resistance is half of the individual plate resistance, the equivalent mutual conductance is double the individual mutual conductance and the equivalent amplification factor is the same as the individual amplification factor.

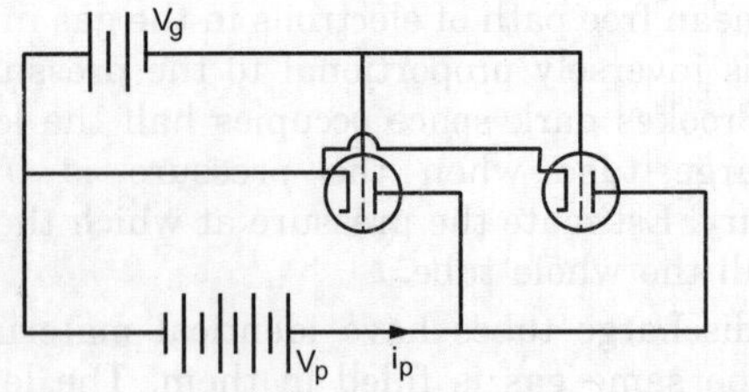

Figure 41-E2

□

ANSWERS

OBJECTIVE I

1. (a) 2. (c) 3. (d) 4. (b) 5. (a) 6. (b)
7. (c) 8. (a) 9. (d)

OBJECTIVE II

1. (a), (b), (c) 2. (a), (b) 3. (a)
4. (d) 5. (a), (b), (d) 6. all
7. (b), (c), (d)

EXERCISES

1. 7340
2. (a) 440 m (b) 1·5 ns
3. 0·01 mm of mercury
4. 0·5 mm of mercury
5. $6{\cdot}57 \times 10^{-55}$, $9{\cdot}73 \times 10^{11}$, $1{\cdot}37 \times 10^{16}$
6. 33 μA
7. 1914 K
8. 1·14
9. 1·0 mA
10. 4 kΩ
11. 20 mA
12. 2·2 W
13. 12·5
14. 4
15. 2 mA
16. 8·0 kΩ, 20 and 2·5 millimho
17. (a) 6 mA (b) 2·4 V
18. (a) –5·0 V (b) 200 V
19. (a) 30 mA (b) 2·53 kΩ (c) 2·77 millimho (d) 7
21. 60 kΩ
22. (a) 15 (b) 2 kΩ

□

CHAPTER 42

PHOTOELECTRIC EFFECT AND WAVE–PARTICLE DUALITY

42.1 PHOTON THEORY OF LIGHT

We have learnt that light has wave character as well as particle character. Depending on the situation, one of the two characters dominates. When light is passed through a double slit, it shows interference. This observation can only be understood in terms of wave theory which was discussed in detail in an earlier chapter. There are some phenomena which can only be understood in terms of the particle theory of light. When light of sufficiently low wavelength falls on a metal surface, electrons are ejected. This phenomenon is called the *photoelectric effect* and can be understood only in terms of the particle nature of light.

The particles of light have several properties in common with the material particles and several other properties which are different from the material particles. The particles of light are called *photons*. We list some of the important properties of photons.

(a) A photon always travels at a speed $c = 299,792,458 \text{ ms}^{-1} \approx 3{\cdot}0 \times 10^{8} \text{ m s}^{-1}$ in vacuum. This is true for any frame of reference used to observe the photon.

(b) The mass of a photon is not defined in the sense of Newtonian mechanics. We shall ignore this concept. We simply state that the *rest mass* of a photon is zero.

(c) Each photon has a definite energy and a definite linear momentum.

(d) Let E and p be the energy and linear momentum of a photon of light, and ν and λ be the frequency and wavelength of the same light when it behaves as a wave. Then,

$$E = h\nu = hc/\lambda$$

and

$$p = h/\lambda = E/c \quad \ldots (42.1)$$

where h is a universal constant known as the *Planck constant* and has a value $6{\cdot}626 \times 10^{-34}$ Js $= 4{\cdot}136 \times 10^{-15}$ eVs.

Thus, all photons of light of a particular wavelength λ have the same energy $E = hc/\lambda$ and the same momentum $p = h/\lambda$.

(e) A photon may collide with a material particle. The total energy and the total momentum remain conserved in such a collision. The photon may get absorbed and/or a new photon may be emitted. Thus, the number of photons may not be conserved.

(f) If the intensity of light of a given wavelength is increased, there is an increase in the number of photons crossing a given area in a given time. The energy of each photon remains the same.

Example 42.1

Consider a parallel beam of light of wavelength 600 nm and intensity 100 W m^{-2}. (a) Find the energy and linear momentum of each photon. (b) How many photons cross 1 cm^{2} area perpendicular to the beam in one second?

Solution :

(a) The energy of each photon $E = hc/\lambda$

$$= \frac{(4{\cdot}14 \times 10^{-15} \text{ eVs}) \times (3 \times 10^{8} \text{ m s}^{-1})}{600 \times 10^{-9} \text{ m}} = 2{\cdot}07 \text{ eV}.$$

The linear momentum is

$$p = \frac{E}{c} = \frac{2{\cdot}07 \text{ eV}}{3 \times 10^{8} \text{ m s}^{-1}} = 0{\cdot}69 \times 10^{-8} \text{ eVs m}^{-1}.$$

(b) The energy crossing 1 cm^{2} in one second

$$= (100 \text{ W m}^{-2}) \times (1 \text{ cm}^{2}) \times (1 \text{ s}) = 1{\cdot}0 \times 10^{-2} \text{ J}.$$

The number of photons making up this amount of energy is

$$n = \frac{1{\cdot}0 \times 10^{-2} \text{ J}}{2{\cdot}07 \text{ eV}} = \frac{1{\cdot}0 \times 10^{-2}}{2{\cdot}07 \times 1{\cdot}6 \times 10^{-19}} = 3{\cdot}0 \times 10^{16}.$$

For a given wavelength λ, the energy of light is an integer times hc/λ. Thus, the energy of light can be varied only in quantums (steps) of $\frac{hc}{\lambda}$. The photon theory is, therefore, also called the quantum theory of light.

42.2 PHOTOELECTRIC EFFECT

When light of sufficiently small wavelength is incident on a metal surface, electrons are ejected from the metal. This phenomenon is called the *photoelectric effect.* The electrons ejected from the metal are called *photoelectrons*. Let us try to understand photoelectric effect on the basis of the photon theory of light.

We know that there are large number of free electrons in a metal which wander throughout the body of the metal. However, these electrons are not free to leave the surface of the metal. As they try to come out of the metal, the metal attracts them back. A minimum energy, equal to the work function φ, must be given to an electron so as to bring it out of the metal.

When light is incident on a metal surface, the photons collide with the free electrons. In a particular collision, the photon may give all of its energy to the free electron. If this energy is more than the work function φ, the electron may come out of the metal. It is not necessary that if the energy supplied to an electron is more than φ, it will come out. The electron after receiving the energy, may lose energy to the metal in course of collisions with the atoms of the metal. Only if an electron near the surface gets the extra energy and heads towards the outside, it is able to come out. If it is given an energy E which is greater than φ, and it makes the most economical use of it, it will have a kinetic energy $(E - \varphi)$ after coming out. If it makes some collisions before coming out, the kinetic energy will be less than $(E - \varphi)$. The actual kinetic energy of such an electron will depend on the total energy lost in collisions. It is also possible that the electron makes several collisions inside the metal and loses so much energy that it fails to come out. So, the kinetic energy of the photoelectron coming out may be anything between zero and $(E - \varphi)$ where E is the energy supplied to the individual electrons. We can, therefore, write

$$K_{max} = E - \varphi.$$

Table 42.1 : *Work functions of some photosensitive metals*

Metal	Work function (eV)	Metal	Work function (eV)
Cesium	1·9	Calcium	3·2
Potassium	2·2	Copper	4·5
Sodium	2·3	Silver	4·7
Lithium	2·5	Platinum	5·6

Let monochromatic light of wavelength λ be incident on the metal surface. In the particle picture, photons of energy hc/λ fall on the surface. Suppose, a particular photon collides with a free electron and supplies all its energy to the electron. The electron gets an extra energy $E = hc/\lambda$ and may come out of metal. The maximum kinetic energy of this electron is, therefore,

$$K_{max} = \frac{hc}{\lambda} - \varphi = h\nu - \varphi. \quad \text{... (42.2)}$$

As all the photons have the same energy hc/λ, equation (42.2) gives the maximum kinetic energy of any of the ejected electrons.

Equation (42.2) is called ***Einstein's photoelectric equation.*** Einstein, after an average academic career, put forward this theory in 1905 while working as a grade III technical officer in a patent office. He was awarded the Nobel Prize in physics for 1921 for this work.

Threshold Wavelength

Equation (42.2) tells that if the wavelength λ is equal to

$$\lambda_0 = hc/\varphi,$$

the maximum kinetic energy is zero. An electron may just come out in this case. If $\lambda > \lambda_0$, the energy hc/λ supplied to the electron is smaller than the work function φ and no electron will come out. Thus, photoelectric effect takes place only if $\lambda \leq \lambda_0$. This wavelength λ_0 is called the *threshold wavelength* for the metal. The corresponding frequency

$$\nu_0 = c/\lambda_0 = \varphi/h$$

is called the *threshold frequency* for the metal. Threshold wavelength and threshold frequency depend on the metal used.

Writing $\varphi = h\nu_0$, equation (42.2) becomes

$$K_{max} = h(\nu - \nu_0). \quad \text{... (42.3)}$$

Example 42.2

Find the maximum wavelength of light that can cause photoelectric effect in lithium.

Solution : From table (42.1), the work function of lithium is 2·5 eV. The threshold wavelength is

$$\lambda = hc/\varphi.$$

$$= \frac{(4{\cdot}14 \times 10^{-15}\ \text{eVs}) \times (3 \times 10^{8}\ \text{m s}^{-1})}{2{\cdot}5\ \text{eV}}$$

$$= \frac{1242\ \text{eVnm}}{2{\cdot}5\ \text{eV}} = 497\ \text{nm}.$$

This is the required maximum wavelength.

Experimental Arrangement

A systematic study of photoelectric effect can be made in the laboratory with the apparatus shown in figure (42.1). Two metal plates C and A are sealed in a vacuum chamber. Light of reasonably short wavelength passes through a transparent window in the wall of the chamber and falls on the plate C which is called the *cathode* or the *emitter*. The electrons are emitted by C and collected by the plate A called the *anode* or the *collector*. The potential difference between the cathode and the anode can be changed with the help of the batteries, rheostat and the commutator. The anode potential can be made positive or negative with respect to the cathode. The electrons collected by the anode A flow through the ammeter, batteries, etc., and are back to the cathode C and hence an electric current is established in the circuit. Such a current is called a *photocurrent*.

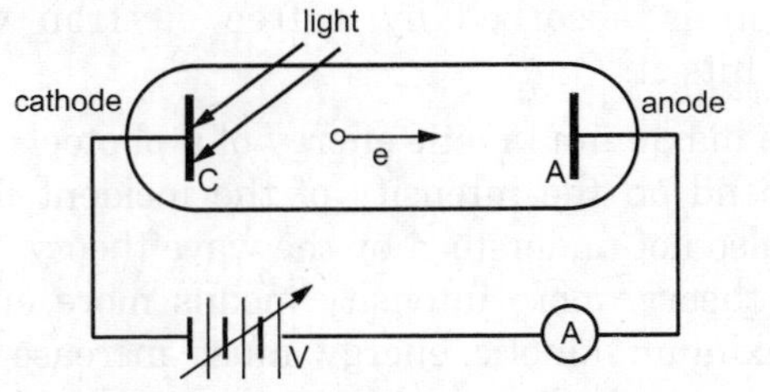

Figure 42.1

As photoelectrons are emitted from the cathode C, they move towards the anode A. At any time, the space between the cathode and the anode contains a number of electrons making up the *space charge*. This negative charge repels the fresh electrons coming from the cathode. However, some electrons are able to reach the anode and there is a photocurrent. When the anode is given a positive potential with respect to the cathode, electrons are attracted towards the anode and the photocurrent increases. The current thus depends on the potential applied to the anode. Figure (42.2) shows the variation in current with potential. If the potential

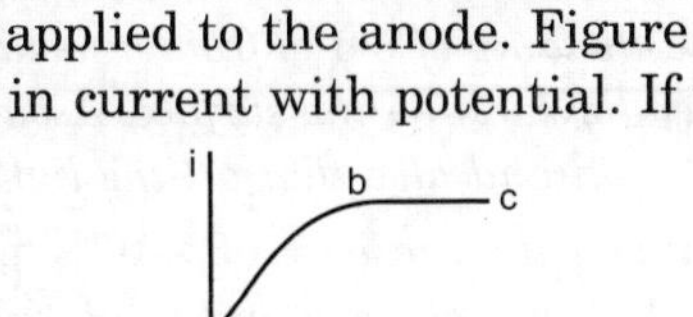

Figure 42.2

of the anode is increased gradually, a situation arrives when the effect of the space charge becomes negligible and any electron that is emitted from the cathode is able to reach the anode. The current then becomes constant and is known as the *saturation current*. This is shown by the part bc in figure (42.2). Further increase in the anode potential does not change the magnitude of the photocurrent.

If the potential of the anode is made negative with respect to the cathode, the electrons are repelled by the anode. Some electrons go back to the cathode so that the current decreases. At a certain value of this negative potential, the current is completely stopped. The smallest magnitude of the anode potential which just stops the photocurrent, is called the *stopping potential*.

The stopping potential is related to the maximum kinetic energy of the ejected electrons. To stop the current, we must ensure that even the fastest electron fails to reach the anode. Suppose, the anode is kept at a negative potential of magnitude V_0 with respect to the cathode. As a photoelectron travels from the cathode to the anode, the potential energy increases by eV_0. This is equal to the decrease in the kinetic energy of the photoelectron. The kinetic energy of the fastest photoelectron, as it reaches the anode, is $K_{max} - eV_0$. If the fastest electron just fails to reach the anode, we should have

$$eV_0 = K_{max} = \frac{hc}{\lambda} - \varphi$$

or, $$V_0 = \frac{hc}{e}\left(\frac{1}{\lambda}\right) - \frac{\varphi}{e}. \quad \dots (42.3)$$

We see that the stopping potential V_0 depends on the wavelength of the light and the work function of the metal. It does not depend on the intensity of light. Thus, if an anode potential of $-2{\cdot}0$ V stops the photocurrent from a metal when a 1 W source of light is used, the same potential of $-2{\cdot}0$ V will stop the photocurrent when a 100 W source of light of the same wavelength is used.

The saturation current increases as the intensity of light increases. This is because, a larger number of photons now fall on the metal surface and hence a larger number of electrons interact with photons. The number of electrons emitted increases and hence the current increases.

Figure (42.3a) shows plots of photocurrent versus anode potential for three different intensities of light.

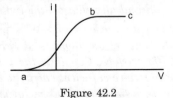

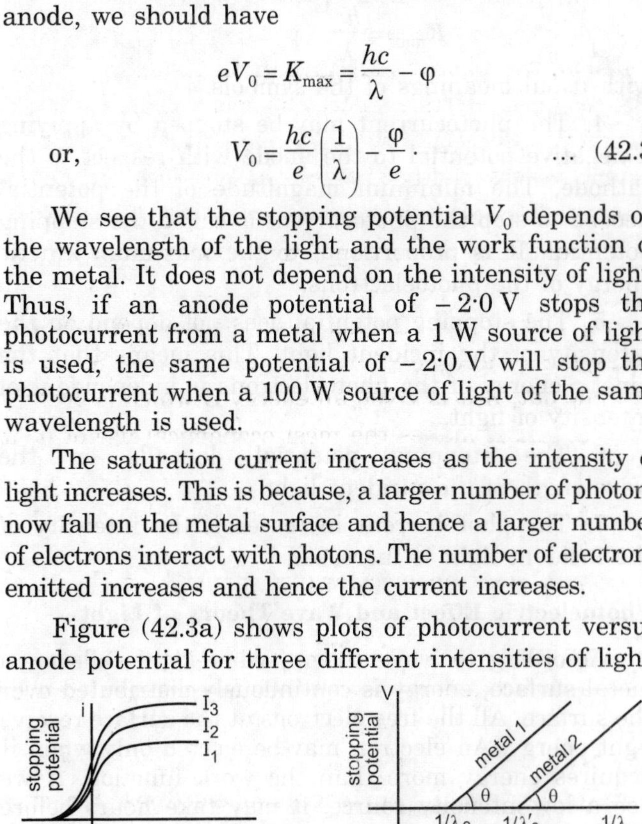

Figure 42.3

Note that the stopping potential V_0 is indepedent of the intensity of light.

The variation in stopping potential V_0 with $1/\lambda$ is shown in figure (42.3b) for cathodes of two different metals. From equation (42.3), the slope of each curve is

$$\tan\theta = \frac{hc}{e}$$

which is the same for all metals. Also, the curves intersect the $1/\lambda$ axis where V_0 is zero. Using equation (42.3), this corresponds to

$$\frac{hc}{\lambda_0} = \varphi$$

$$\text{or,} \quad \frac{1}{\lambda_0} = \frac{\varphi}{hc}$$

which is inverse of the threshold wavelength.

Let us summarise the results obtained from the experiments described above.

1. When light of sufficiently small wavelength falls on a metal surface, the metal emits electrons. The emission is almost instantaneous.

2. There is a threshold wavelength λ_0 for a given metal such that if the wavelength of light is more than λ_0, no photoelectric effect takes place.

3. The kinetic energies of the photoelectrons vary from zero to a maximum of K_{max} where

$$K_{max} = \frac{hc}{\lambda} - \varphi$$

with usual meanings of the symbols.

4. The photocurrent may be stopped by applying a negative potential to the anode with respect to the cathode. The minimum magnitude of the potential needed to stop the photocurrent is called the stopping potential. It is proportional to the maximum kinetic energy of the photoelectrons.

5. The stopping potential does not depend on the intensity of the incident light. This means that the kinetic energy of the photoelectrons is independent of intensity of light.

6. The stopping potential depends on the wavelength of the incident light.

7. The photocurrent increases if the intensity of the incident light is increased.

Photoelectric Effect and Wave Theory of Light

According to wave thoery, when light falls on a metal surface, energy is continuously distributed over the surface. All the free electrons at the surface receive light energy. An electron may be ejected only when it acquires energy more than the work function. If we use a low-intensity source, it may take hours before an electron acquires this much energy from the light. In this period, there will be many collisions and any extra energy accumulated so far will be shared with the remaining metal. This will result in no photoelectron. This is contrary to experimental observations. No matter how small is the intensity, photoelectrons are ejected and that too without any appreciable time delay. In the photon theory, low intensity means less number of photons and hence less number of electrons get a chance to absorb energy. But any fortunate electron on which a photon falls, gets the full energy of the photon and may come out immediately.

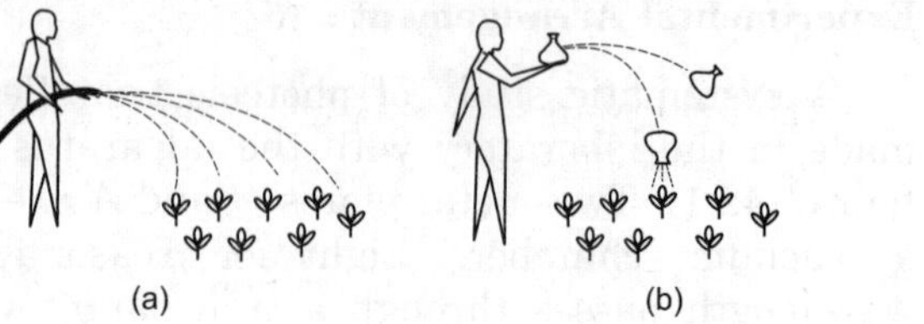

Figure 42.4

In figure (42.4), we illustrate an analogy to the wave and particle behaviour of light. In part (a), water is sprayed from a distance on an area containing several plants. Each plant receives water at nearly the same rate. It takes time for a particular plant to receive a certain amount of water. In part (b) of the figure, water is filled in identical, loosely-tied water bags and a particle physicist throws the bags randomly at the plants. When a bag collides with a plant, it sprays all its water on that plant in a very short time. In the same way, whole of the energy associated with a photon is absorbed by a free electron when the photon hits it.

The maximum kinetic energy of a photoelectron does not depend on the intensity of the incident light. This fact is also not understood by the wave theory. According to this theory, more intensity means more energy and the maximum kinetic energy must increase with the increase in intensity which is not true. The dependence of maximum kinetic energy on wavelength is also against the wave theory. There should not be any threshold wavelength according to the wave thoery. According to this theory, by using sufficiently intense light of any wavelength, an electron may be given the required amount of energy to come out. Experiments, however, show the existence of threshold wavelength.

Example 42.3

A point source of monochromatic light of 1·0 mW *is placed at a distance of* 5·0 m *from a metal surface. Light falls perpendicularly on the surface. Assume wave theory of light to hold and also that all the light falling on the circular area with radius* = $1{\cdot}0 \times 10^{-9}$ m *(which is few times the diameter of an atom) is absorbed by a single electron on the surface. Calculate the time required by the electron to receive sufficient energy to come out of the metal if the work function of the metal is* 2·0 eV.

Solution : The energy radiated by the light source per second is 1·0 mJ. This energy is spread over the total solid angle 4π. The solid angle subtended at the source by the circular area mentioned is

$$d\Omega = \frac{dA}{r^2} = \frac{\pi \times (1{\cdot}0 \times 10^{-9}\ \text{m})^2}{(5{\cdot}0\ \text{m})^2} = \frac{\pi}{25} \times 10^{-18}\ \text{sr}.$$

Hence the energy heading towards the circular area per second is

$$\frac{d\Omega}{4\pi}(1{\cdot}0\ \text{mJ}) = 10^{-20}\ \text{mJ}.$$

The time required for accumulation of 2·0 eV of energy on this circular area is

$$t = \frac{2{\cdot}0 \times 1{\cdot}6 \times 10^{-19}\ \text{J}}{10^{-20}\ \text{mJ s}^{-1}} = 3{\cdot}2 \times 10^4\ \text{s} = 8{\cdot}8\ \text{hours}.$$

The assumption of continuous absorption of energy is based on the wave theory. The above calculation shows that if this theory were correct, the first electron would be ejected not before 8·8 hours of continuous irradiation. However, in actual case, photoelectrons come out almost without any time delay after light falls on the metal.

42.3 MATTER WAVES

We have seen that light behaves in certain situations as waves and in certain other situations as particles. We know that electrons behave as particles in many of the situations. Can electrons also show wave nature in some suitable situations ? The answer is *yes*. A large number of experiments are now available in which electrons interfere like waves and produce fringes. Electron microscope is built on the basis of the wave properties of electrons. Protons, neutrons or even bigger particles have intrinsic wave properties. It is only a question of putting them under proper experimental situations to bring out their wave character.

If an electron behaves as waves, what is its wavelength ? The relation was proposed by Prince Louis Victor de Broglie in his PhD thesis for which he was awarded the Nobel Prize in physics for 1929. The wavelength is given by

$$\lambda = \frac{h}{p} \qquad \text{... (42.4)}$$

where p is the momentum of the electron and h is the Planck constant. This wavelength is known as the *de Broglie wavelength* of the electron. Same is the case with other particles such as a neutron, a proton, a molecule, etc. In fact, the equation also applies to light. When light shows its photon character, each photon has a momentum $p = h/\lambda$ (equation 42.1).

Can we apply Newton's laws to find the motion of an electron if the electron has both particle and wave characters. Indeed we should not rely upon Newton's laws to discuss the behaviour of electrons in all situations. While discussing the "scope of classical physics" it was mentioned that the classical mechanics of Newton fails for particles of very small size. A rough estimate was given that the classical mechanics works well for particles of linear size greater than 10^{-4} cm. For smaller particles, we should use *quantum mechanics* which takes into account the dual nature (wave nature and particle nature) of electrons, protons and other subatomic particles.

Worked Out Examples

Use $h = 6{\cdot}63 \times 10^{-34}\ \text{Js} = 4{\cdot}14 \times 10^{-15}\ \text{eVs}$, $c = 3 \times 10^8\ \text{m s}^{-1}$ and $m_e = 9{\cdot}1 \times 10^{-31}$ kg wherever required.

---

1. *How many photons are emitted per second by a* 5 mW *laser source operating at* 632·8 nm ?

Solution : The energy of each photon is

$$E = \frac{hc}{\lambda}$$

$$= \frac{(6{\cdot}63 \times 10^{-34}\ \text{J s}) \times (3 \times 10^8\ \text{m s}^{-1})}{(632{\cdot}8 \times 10^{-9}\ \text{m})}$$

$$= 3{\cdot}14 \times 10^{-19}\ \text{J}.$$

The energy of the laser emitted per second is 5×10^{-3} J. Thus the number of photons emitted per second

$$= \frac{5 \times 10^{-3}\ \text{J}}{3{\cdot}14 \times 10^{-19}\ \text{J}} = 1{\cdot}6 \times 10^{16}.$$

2. *A monochromatic source of light operating at* 200 W *emits* 4×10^{20} *photons per second. Find the wavelength of the light.*

Solution : The energy of each photon $= \dfrac{200\ \text{J s}^{-1}}{4 \times 10^{20}\ \text{s}^{-1}}$

$$= 5 \times 10^{-19}\ \text{J}.$$

$$\text{Wavelength} = \lambda = \frac{hc}{E}$$

$$= \frac{(6{\cdot}63 \times 10^{-34}\ \text{J s}) \times (3 \times 10^8\ \text{m s}^{-1})}{(5 \times 10^{-19}\ \text{J})}$$

$$= 4{\cdot}0 \times 10^{-7}\ \text{m} = 400\ \text{nm}.$$

3. *A hydrogen atom moving at a speed v absorbs a photon of wavelength 122 nm and stops. Find the value of v. Mass of a hydrogen atom = 1·67 × 10⁻²⁷ kg.*

Solution : The linear momentum of the photon

$$= \frac{h}{\lambda} = \frac{6{\cdot}63 \times 10^{-34}\ \text{Js}}{122 \times 10^{-9}\ \text{m}} = 5{\cdot}43 \times 10^{-27}\ \text{kg m s}^{-1}.$$

As the photon is absorbed and the atom stops, the total final momentum is zero. From conservation of linear momentum, the initial momentum must be zero. The atom should move opposite to the direction of motion of the photon and they should have the same magnitudes of linear momentum. Thus,

$$(1{\cdot}67 \times 10^{-27}\ \text{kg})\ v = 5{\cdot}43 \times 10^{-27}\ \text{kg m s}^{-1}$$

or, $$v = \frac{5{\cdot}43 \times 10^{-27}}{1{\cdot}67 \times 10^{-27}}\ \text{m s}^{-1} = 3{\cdot}25\ \text{m s}^{-1}.$$

4. *A parallel beam of monochromatic light of wavelength 500 nm is incident normally on a perfectly absorbing surface. The power through any cross-section of the beam is 10 W. Find (a) the number of photons absorbed per second by the surface and (b) the force exerted by the light beam on the surface.*

Solution :

(a) The energy of each photon is

$$E = \frac{hc}{\lambda} = \frac{(4{\cdot}14 \times 10^{-15}\ \text{eVs}) \times (3 \times 10^{8}\ \text{m s}^{-1})}{500\ \text{nm}}$$

$$= \frac{1242\ \text{eVn m}}{500\ \text{nm}} = 2{\cdot}48\ \text{eV}.$$

In one second, 10 J of energy passes through any cross section of the beam. Thus, the number of photons crossing a cross section is

$$n = \frac{10\ \text{J}}{2{\cdot}48\ \text{eV}} = 2{\cdot}52 \times 10^{19}.$$

This is also the number of photons falling on the surface per second and being absorbed.

(b) The linear momentum of each photon is

$$p = \frac{h}{\lambda} = \frac{h\nu}{c}.$$

The total momentum of all the photons falling per second on the surface is

$$= \frac{nh\nu}{c} = \frac{10\ \text{J}}{c} = \frac{10\ \text{J}}{3 \times 10^{8}\ \text{m s}^{-1}} = 3{\cdot}33 \times 10^{-8}\ \text{Ns}.$$

As the photons are completely absorbed by the surface, this much momentum is transferred to the surface per second. The rate of change of the momentum of the surface, i.e., the force on it is

$$F = \frac{dp}{dt} = \frac{3{\cdot}33 \times 10^{-8}\ \text{Ns}}{1\ \text{s}} = 3{\cdot}33 \times 10^{-8}\ \text{N}.$$

5. *Figure (42-W1) shows a small, plane strip suspended from a fixed support through a string of length l. A continuous beam of monochromatic light is incident horizontally on the strip and is completely absorbed. The energy falling on the strip per unit time is W. (a) Find the deflection of the string from the vertical if the mirror stays in equilibrium. (b) If the strip is deflected slightly from its equilibrium position in the plane of the figure, what will be the time period of the resulting oscillations ?*

Solution :

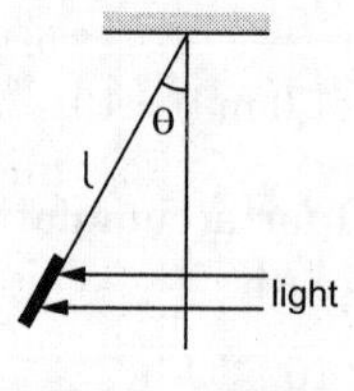

Figure 42-W1

(a) The linear momentum of the light falling per unit time on the strip is W/c. As the light is incident on the strip, its momentum is absorbed by the mirror. The change in momentum imparted to the strip per unit time is thus W/c. This is equal to the force on the strip by the light beam. In equilibrium, the force by the light beam, the weight of the strip and the force due to tension add to zero. If the string makes an angle θ with the vertical,

$$T \cos\theta = mg$$

and $$T \sin\theta = W/c.$$

Thus, $$\tan\theta = \frac{W}{mgc}.$$

(b) In equilibrium, the tension is

$$T = \left[(mg)^2 + \left(\frac{W}{c} \right)^2 \right]^{1/2}$$

or, $$\frac{T}{m} = \left[g^2 + \left(\frac{W}{mc} \right)^2 \right]^{1/2}.$$

This plays the role of effective g. The time period of small oscillations is

$$t = 2\pi \sqrt{\frac{l}{T/m}} = 2\pi \frac{\sqrt{l}}{\left[g^2 + \left(\frac{W}{mc} \right)^2 \right]^{\frac{1}{4}}}.$$

6. *A point source of light is placed at the centre of curvature of a hemispherical surface. The radius of curvature is r and the inner surface is completely reflecting. Find the force on the hemisphere due to the light falling on it if the source emits a power W.*

Solution :

The energy emitted by the source per unit time, i.e., W falls on an area $4\pi r^2$ at a distance r in unit time. Thus, the energy falling per unit area per unit time is $W/(4\pi r^2)$. Consider a small area dA at the point P of the hemisphere (figure 42-W2). The energy falling per

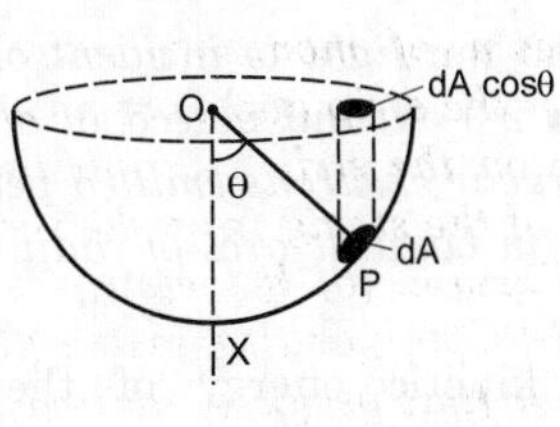

Figure 42-W2

unit time on it is $\frac{W\,dA}{4\pi r^2}\cdot$ The corresponding momentum incident on this area per unit time is $\frac{W\,dA}{4\pi r^2 c}\cdot$ As the light is reflected back, the change in momentum per unit time, i.e., the force on dA is

$$dF = \frac{2W\,dA}{4\pi r^2 c}\cdot$$

Suppose the radius OP through the area dA makes an angle θ with the symmetry axis OX. The force on dA is along this radius. By symmetry, the resultant force on the hemisphere is along OX. The component of dF along OX is

$$dF\cos\theta = \frac{2W\,dA}{4\pi r^2 c}\cos\theta.$$

If we project the area dA on the plane containing the rim, the projection is $dA\cos\theta$. Thus, the component of dF along OX is,

$$dF\cos\theta = \frac{2\,W}{4\pi r^2 c}\text{ (projection of } dA).$$

The net force along OX is

$$F = \frac{2\,W}{4\pi r^2 c}\left(\sum \text{ projection of } dA\right).$$

When all the small areas dA are projected, we get the area enclosed by the rim which is πr^2. Thus,

$$F = \frac{2\,W}{4\pi r^2 c}\times \pi r^2 = \frac{W}{2c}\cdot$$

7. *A perfectly reflecting solid sphere of radius r is kept in the path of a parallel beam of light of large aperture. If the beam carries an intensity I, find the force exerted by the beam on the sphere.*

Solution :

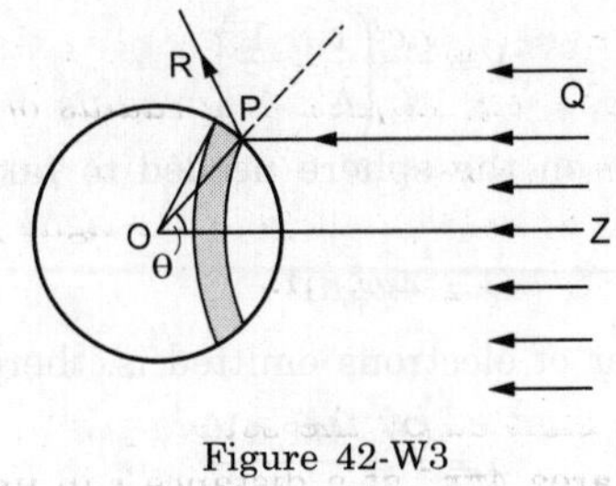

Figure 42-W3

Let O be the centre of the sphere and OZ be the line opposite to the incident beam (figure 42-W3). Consider a radius OP of the sphere making an angle θ with OZ. Rotate this radius about OZ to get a circle on the sphere. Change θ to $\theta + d\theta$ and rotate the radius about OZ to get another circle on the sphere. The part of the sphere between these circles is a ring of area $2\pi r^2 \sin\theta\, d\theta$. Consider a small part ΔA of this ring at P. Energy of the light falling on this part in time Δt is

$$\Delta U = I\Delta t(\Delta A\cos\theta).$$

The momentum of this light falling on ΔA is $\Delta U/c$ along QP. The light is reflected by the sphere along PR. The change in momentum is

$$\Delta p = 2\frac{\Delta U}{c}\cos\theta = \frac{2}{c}I\,\Delta t\,(\Delta A\cos^2\theta)$$

along the inward normal. The force on ΔA due to the light falling on it, is

$$\frac{\Delta p}{\Delta t} = \frac{2}{c}I\,\Delta A\cos^2\theta.$$

This force is along PO. The resultant force on the ring as well as on the sphere is along ZO by symmetry. The component of the force on ΔA, along ZO is

$$\frac{\Delta p}{\Delta t}\cos\theta = \frac{2}{c}I\,\Delta A\cos^3\theta.$$

The force acting on the ring is

$$dF = \frac{2}{c}I(2\pi r^2\sin\theta\, d\theta)\cos^3\theta.$$

The force on the entire sphere is

$$F = \int_0^{\pi/2}\frac{4\pi r^2 I}{c}\cos^3\theta\sin\theta\, d\theta$$

$$= -\int_{\theta=0}^{\pi/2}\frac{4\pi r^2 I}{c}\cos^3\theta\, d(\cos\theta)$$

$$= -\frac{4\pi r^2 I}{c}\left[\frac{\cos^4\theta}{4}\right]_0^{\pi/2} = \frac{\pi r^2 I}{c}\cdot$$

Note that integration is done only for the hemisphere that faces the incident beam.

8. *Find the threshold wavelengths for photoelectric effect from a copper surface, a sodium surface and a cesium surface. The work functions of these metals are* 4·5 eV, 2·3 eV *and* 1·9 eV *respectively.*

Solution : If λ_0 be the threshold wavelength and φ be the work function,

$$\lambda_0 = \frac{hc}{\varphi}$$

$$= \frac{1242\text{ eV nm}}{\varphi}\cdot$$

For copper, $\lambda_0 = \frac{1242\text{ eV nm}}{4{\cdot}5\text{ eV}} = 276\text{ nm}.$

For sodium, $\lambda_0 = \frac{1242\text{ eV nm}}{2{\cdot}3\text{ eV}} = 540\text{ nm}.$

For cesium, $\lambda_0 = \dfrac{1242 \text{ eV nm}}{1{\cdot}9 \text{ eV}} = 654 \text{ nm}.$

9. *Ultraviolet light of wavelength* 280 nm *is used in an experiment on photoelectric effect with lithium* ($\varphi = 2{\cdot}5$ eV) *cathode. Find (a) the maximum kinetic energy of the photoelectrons and (b) the stopping potential.*

Solution :

(a) The maximum kinetic energy is

$$K_{max} = \frac{hc}{\lambda} - \varphi$$

$$= \frac{1242 \text{ eV nm}}{280 \text{ nm}} - 2{\cdot}5 \text{ eV}$$

$$= 4{\cdot}4 \text{ eV} - 2{\cdot}5 \text{ eV} = 1{\cdot}9 \text{ eV}.$$

(b) Stopping potential V is given by

$$eV = K_{max}$$

or, $$V = \frac{K_{max}}{e} = \frac{1{\cdot}9 \text{ eV}}{e} = 1{\cdot}9 \text{ V}.$$

10. *In a photoelectric experiment, it was found that the stopping potential decreases from* 1·85 V *to* 0·82 V *as the wavelength of the incident light is varied from* 300 nm *to* 400 nm. *Calculate the value of the Planck constant from these data.*

Solution :

The maximum kinetic energy of a photoelectron is

$$K_{max} = \frac{hc}{\lambda} - \varphi$$

and the stopping potential is

$$V = \frac{K_{max}}{e} = \frac{hc}{\lambda e} - \frac{\varphi}{e}.$$

If V_1, V_2 are the stopping potentials at wavelengths λ_1 and λ_2 respectively,

$$V_1 = \frac{hc}{\lambda_1 e} - \frac{\varphi}{e}$$

and $$V_2 = \frac{hc}{\lambda_2 e} - \frac{\varphi}{e}.$$

This gives, $$V_1 - V_2 = \frac{hc}{e}\left(\frac{1}{\lambda_1} - \frac{1}{\lambda_2}\right)$$

or, $$h = \frac{e(V_1 - V_2)}{c\left(\dfrac{1}{\lambda_1} - \dfrac{1}{\lambda_2}\right)}$$

$$= \frac{e(1{\cdot}85 \text{ V} - 0{\cdot}82 \text{ V})}{c\left(\dfrac{1}{300 \times 10^{-9} \text{ m}} - \dfrac{1}{400 \times 10^{-9} \text{ m}}\right)}$$

$$= \frac{1{\cdot}03 \text{ eV}}{(3 \times 10^{8} \text{ m s}^{-1})\left(\dfrac{1}{12} \times 10^{7} \text{ m}^{-1}\right)}$$

$$= 4{\cdot}12 \times 10^{-15} \text{ eVs}.$$

11. *A beam of* 450 nm *light is incident on a metal having work function* 2·0 eV *and placed in a magnetic field B. The most energetic electrons emitted perpendicular to the field are bent in circular arcs of radius* 20 cm. *Find the value of B.*

Solution : The kinetic energy of the most energetic electrons is

$$K = \frac{hc}{\lambda} - \varphi$$

$$= \frac{1242 \text{ eV nm}}{450 \text{ nm}} - 2{\cdot}0 \text{ eV}$$

$$= 0{\cdot}76 \text{ eV} = 1{\cdot}2 \times 10^{-19} \text{ J}.$$

The linear momentum $= mv = \sqrt{2mK}$

$$= \sqrt{2 \times (9{\cdot}1 \times 10^{-31} \text{ kg}) \times (1{\cdot}2 \times 10^{-19} \text{ J})}$$

$$= 4{\cdot}67 \times 10^{-25} \text{ kgms}^{-1}.$$

When a charged particle is sent perpendicular to a magnetic field, it goes along a circle of radius

$$r = \frac{mv}{qB}.$$

Thus, $$0{\cdot}20 \text{ m} = \frac{4{\cdot}67 \times 10^{-25} \text{ kg m s}^{-1}}{(1{\cdot}6 \times 10^{-19} \text{ C}) \times B}$$

or, $$B = \frac{4{\cdot}67 \times 10^{-25} \text{ kg m s}^{-1}}{(1{\cdot}6 \times 10^{-19} \text{ C}) \times (0{\cdot}20 \text{ m})} = 1{\cdot}46 \times 10^{-5} \text{ T}.$$

12. *A monochromatic light of wavelength* λ *is incident on an isolated metallic sphere of radius a. The threshold wavelength is* λ_0 *which is larger than* λ. *Find the number of photoelectrons emitted before the emission of photoelectrons will stop.*

Solution : As the metallic sphere is isolated, it becomes positively charged when electrons are ejected from it. There is an extra attractive force on the photoelectrons. If the potential of the sphere is raised to V, the electron should have a minimum energy $\varphi + eV$ to be able to come out. Thus, emission of photoelectrons will stop when

$$\frac{hc}{\lambda} = \varphi + eV$$

$$= \frac{hc}{\lambda_0} + eV$$

or, $$V = \frac{hc}{e}\left(\frac{1}{\lambda} - \frac{1}{\lambda_0}\right).$$

The charge on the sphere needed to take its potential to V is

$$Q = (4\pi\varepsilon_0 a)V.$$

The number of electrons emitted is, therefore,

$$n = \frac{Q}{e} = \frac{4\pi\varepsilon_0 aV}{e}$$

$$= \frac{4\pi\varepsilon_0 ahc}{e^2}\left(\frac{1}{\lambda} - \frac{1}{\lambda_0}\right).$$

13. *Light described at a place by the equation*

$E = (100\ \mathrm{V\ m^{-1}})\ [\sin (5 \times 10^{15}\ \mathrm{s^{-1}})\ t + \sin (8 \times 10^{15}\ \mathrm{s^{-1}})t]$

falls on a metal surface having work function 2·0 eV. *Calculate the maximum kinetic energy of the photoelectrons.*

Solution : The light contains two different frequencies. The one with larger frequency will cause photoelectrons with largest kinetic energy. This larger frequency is

$$\nu = \frac{\omega}{2\pi} = \frac{8 \times 10^{15}\ \mathrm{s^{-1}}}{2\pi}.$$

The maximum kinetic energy of the photoelectrons is

$$K_{max} = h\nu - \varphi$$

$$= (4{\cdot}14 \times 10^{-15}\ \mathrm{eVs}) \times \left(\frac{8 \times 10^{15}}{2\pi}\ \mathrm{s^{-1}}\right) - 2{\cdot}0\ \mathrm{eV}$$

$$= 5{\cdot}27\ \mathrm{eV} - 2{\cdot}0\ \mathrm{eV} = 3{\cdot}27\ \mathrm{eV}.$$

□

QUESTIONS FOR SHORT ANSWER

1. Can we find the mass of a photon by the definition $p = mv$?
2. Is it always true that for two sources of equal intensity, the number of photons emitted in a given time are equal ?
3. What is the speed of a photon with respect to another photon if (a) the two photons are going in the same direction and (b) they are going in opposite directions ?
4. Can a photon be deflected by an electric field ? By a magnetic field ?
5. A hot body is placed in a closed room maintained at a lower temperature. Is the number of photons in the room increasing ?
6. Should the energy of a photon be called its kinetic energy or its internal energy ?
7. In an experiment on photoelectric effect, a photon is incident on an electron from one direction and the photoelectron is emitted almost in the opposite direction. Does this violate conservation of momentum ?
8. It is found that yellow light does not eject photoelectrons from a metal. Is it advisable to try with orange light ? With green light ?
9. It is found that photosynthesis starts in certain plants when exposed to the sunlight but it does not start if the plant is exposed only to infrared light. Explain.
10. The threshold wavelength of a metal is λ_0. Light of wavelength slightly less than λ_0 is incident on an insulated plate made of this metal. It is found that photoelectrons are emitted for sometime and after that the emission stops. Explain.
11. Is $p = E/c$ valid for electrons ?
12. Consider the de Broglie wavelength of an electron and a proton. Which wavelength is smaller if the two particles have (a) the same speed (b) the same momentum (c) the same energy ?
13. If an electron has a wavelength, does it also have a colour ?

OBJECTIVE I

1. Planck constant has the same dimensions as
   (a) force × time (b) force × distance
   (c) force × speed (d) force × distance × time.
2. Two photons having
   (a) equal wavelengths have equal linear momenta
   (b) equal energies have equal linear momenta
   (c) equal frequencies have equal linear momenta
   (d) equal linear momenta have equal wavelengths.
3. Let p and E denote the linear momentum and energy of a photon. If the wavelength is decreased,
   (a) both p and E increase
   (b) p increases and E decreases
   (c) p decreases and E increases
   (d) both p and E decrease.
4. Let n_r and n_b be respectively the number of photons emitted by a red bulb and a blue bulb of equal power in a given time.
   (a) $n_r = n_b$ (b) $n_r < n_b$ (c) $n_r > n_b$
   (d) The information is insufficient to get a relation between n_r and n_b.
5. The equation $E = pc$ is valid
   (a) for an electron as well as for a photon
   (b) for an electron but not for a photon
   (c) for a photon but not for an electron
   (d) neither for an electron nor for a photon.
6. The work function of a metal is $h\nu_0$. Light of frequency ν falls on this metal. The photoelectric effect will take place only if
   (a) $\nu \geq \nu_0$ (b) $\nu > 2\nu_0$ (c) $\nu < \nu_0$ (d) $\nu < \nu_0/2$.
7. Light of wavelength λ falls on a metal having work function hc/λ_0. Photoelectric effect will take place only if
   (a) $\lambda \geq \lambda_0$ (b) $\lambda \geq 2\lambda_0$ (c) $\lambda \leq \lambda_0$ (d) $\lambda < \lambda_0/2$.

8. When stopping potential is applied in an experiment on photoelectric effect, no photocurrent is observed. This means that
(a) the emission of photoelectrons is stopped
(b) the photoelectrons are emitted but are re-absorbed by the emitter metal
(c) the photoelectrons are accumulated near the collector plate
(d) the photoelectrons are dispersed from the sides of the apparatus.

9. If the frequency of light in a photoelectric experiment is doubled, the stopping potential will
(a) be doubled (b) be halved
(c) become more than double
(d) become less than double.

10. The frequency and intensity of a light source are both doubled. Consider the following statements.
(A) The saturation photocurrent remains almost the same.
(B) The maximum kinetic energy of the photoelectrons is doubled.
(a) Both A and B are true. (b) A is true but B is false.
(c) A is false but B is true. (d) Both A and B are false.

11. A point source of light is used in a photoelectric effect. If the source is removed farther from the emitting metal, the stopping potential
(a) will increase (b) will decrease
(c) will remain constant
(d) will either increase or decrease.

12. A point source causes photoelectric effect from a small metal plate. Which of the following curves may represent the saturation photocurrent as a function of the distance between the source and the metal ?

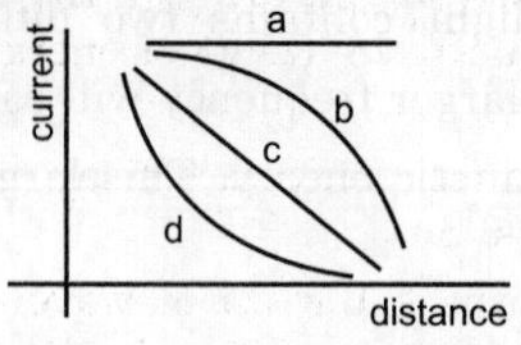

Figure 42-Q1

13. A nonmonochromatic light is used in an experiment on photoelectric effect. The stopping potential
(a) is related to the mean wavelength
(b) is related to the longest wavelength
(c) is related to the shortest wavelength
(d) is not related to the wavelength.

14. A proton and an electron are accelerated by the same potential difference. Let λ_e and λ_p denote the de Broglie wavelengths of the electron and the proton respectively.
(a) $\lambda_e = \lambda_p$ (b) $\lambda_e < \lambda_p$ (c) $\lambda_e > \lambda_p$
(d) The relation between λ_e and λ_p depends on the accelerating potential difference.

OBJECTIVE II

1. When the intensity of a light source is increased,
(a) the number of photons emitted by the source in unit time increases
(b) the total energy of the photons emitted per unit time increases
(c) more energetic photons are emitted
(d) faster photons are emitted.

2. Photoelectric effect supports quantum nature of light because
(a) there is a minimum frequency below which no photoelectrons are emitted
(b) the maximum kinetic energy of photoelectrons depends only on the frequency of light and not on its intensity
(c) even when the metal surface is faintly illuminated the photoelectrons leave the surface immediately
(d) electric charge of the photoelectrons is quantized.

3. A photon of energy $h\nu$ is absorbed by a free electron of a metal having work function $\varphi < h\nu$.
(a) The electron is sure to come out.
(b) The electron is sure to come out with a kinetic energy $h\nu - \varphi$.
(c) Either the electron does not come out or it comes out with a kinetic energy $h\nu - \varphi$.
(d) It may come out with a kinetic energy less than $h\nu - \varphi$.

4. If the wavelength of light in an experiment on photoelectric effect is doubled,
(a) the photoelectric emission will not take place
(b) the photoelectric emission may or may not take place
(c) the stopping potential will increase
(d) the stopping potential will decrease.

5. The photocurrent in an experiment on photoelectric effect increases if
(a) the intensity of the source is increased
(b) the exposure time is increased
(c) the intensity of the source is decreased
(d) the exposure time is decreased.

6. The collector plate in an experiment on photoelectric effect is kept vertically above the emitter plate. Light source is put on and a saturation photocurrent is recorded. An electric field is switched on which has a vertically downward direction.
(a) The photocurrent will increase.
(b) The kinetic energy of the electrons will increase.
(c) The stopping potential will decrease.
(d) The threshold wavelength will increase.

7. In which of the following situations the heavier of the two particles has smaller de Broglie wavelength ? The two particles
(a) move with the same speed
(b) move with the same linear momentum
(c) move with the same kinetic energy
(d) have fallen through the same height.

EXERCISES

Use $h = 6{\cdot}63 \times 10^{-34}$ J s $= 4{\cdot}14 \times 10^{-15}$ eVs, $c = 3 \times 10^{8}$ m s^{-1} and $m_e = 9{\cdot}1 \times 10^{-31}$ kg wherever needed.

1. Visible light has wavelengths in the range of 400 nm to 780 nm. Calculate the range of energy of the photons of visible light.

2. Calculate the momentum of a photon of light of wavelength 500 nm.

3. An atom absorbs a photon of wavelength 500 nm and emits another photon of wavelength 700 nm. Find the net energy absorbed by the atom in the process.

4. Calculate the number of photons emitted per second by a 10 W sodium vapour lamp. Assume that 60% of the consumed energy is converted into light. Wavelength of sodium light = 590 nm.

5. When the sun is directly overhead, the surface of the earth receives $1{\cdot}4 \times 10^{3}$ W m^{-2} of sunlight. Assume that the light is monochromatic with average wavelength 500 nm and that no light is absorbed in between the sun and the earth's surface. The distance between the sun and the earth is $1{\cdot}5 \times 10^{11}$ m. (a) Calculate the number of photons falling per second on each square metre of earth's surface directly below the sun. (b) How many photons are there in each cubic metre near the earth's surface at any instant ? (c) How many photons does the sun emit per second ?

6. A parallel beam of monochromatic light of wavelength 663 nm is incident on a totally reflecting plane mirror. The angle of incidence is 60° and the number of photons striking the mirror per second is $1{\cdot}0 \times 10^{19}$. Calculate the force exerted by the light beam on the mirror.

7. A beam of white light is incident normally on a plane surface absorbing 70% of the light and reflecting the rest. If the incident beam carries 10 W of power, find the force exerted by it on the surface.

8. A totally reflecting, small plane mirror placed horizontally faces a parallel beam of light as shown in figure (42-E1). The mass of the mirror is 20 g. Assume that there is no absorption in the lens and that 30% of the light emitted by the source goes through the lens. Find the power of the source needed to support the weight of the mirror. Take $g = 10$ m s^{-2}.

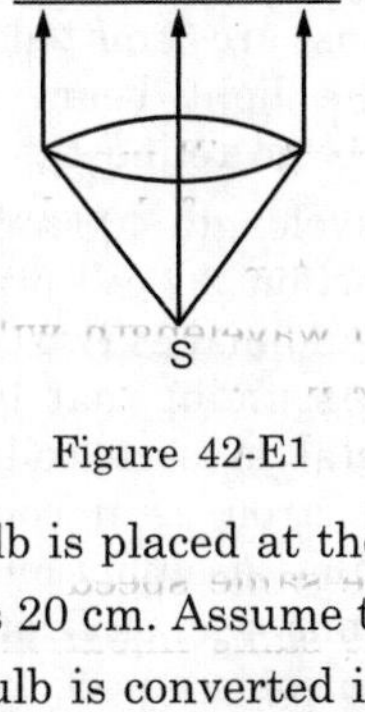

Figure 42-E1

9. A 100 W light bulb is placed at the centre of a spherical chamber of radius 20 cm. Assume that 60% of the energy supplied to the bulb is converted into light and that the surface of the chamber is perfectly absorbing. Find the pressure exerted by the light on the surface of the chamber.

10. A sphere of radius 1·00 cm is placed in the path of a parallel beam of light of large aperture. The intensity of the light is 0·50 W cm^{-2}. If the sphere completely absorbs the radiation falling on it, find the force exerted by the light beam on the sphere.

11. Consider the situation described in the previous problem. Show that the force on the sphere due to the light falling on it is the same even if the sphere is not perfectly absorbing.

12. Show that it is not possible for a photon to be completely absorbed by a free electron.

13. Two neutral particles are kept 1 m apart. Suppose by some mechanism some charge is transferred from one particle to the other and the electric potential energy lost is completely converted into a photon. Calculate the longest and the next smaller wavelength of the photon possible.

14. Find the maximum kinetic energy of the photoelectrons ejected when light of wavelength 350 nm is incident on a cesium surface. Work function of cesium = 1·9 eV.

15. The work function of a metal is $2{\cdot}5 \times 10^{-19}$ J. (a) Find the threshold frequency for photoelectric emission. (b) If the metal is exposed to a light beam of frequency $6{\cdot}0 \times 10^{14}$ Hz, what will be the stopping potential ?

16. The work function of a photoelectric material is 4·0 eV. (a) What is the threshold wavelength ? (b) Find the wavelength of light for which the stopping potential is 2·5 V.

17. Find the maximum magnitude of the linear momentum of a photoelectron emitted when light of wavelength 400 nm falls on a metal having work function 2·5 eV.

18. When a metal plate is exposed to a monochromatic beam of light of wavelength 400 nm, a negative potential of 1·1 V is needed to stop the photocurrent. Find the threshold wavelength for the metal.

19. In an experiment on photoelectric effect, the stopping potential is measured for monochromatic light beams corresponding to different wavelengths. The data collected are as follows:

wavelength (nm):	350	400	450	500	550
stopping potential(V):	1·45	1·00	0·66	0·38	0·16

Plot the stopping potential against inverse of wavelength ($1/\lambda$) on a graph paper and find (a) the Planck constant, (b) the work function of the emitter and (c) the threshold wavelength.

20. The electric field associated with a monochromatic beam becomes zero $1{\cdot}2 \times 10^{15}$ times per second. Find the maximum kinetic energy of the photoelectrons when this light falls on a metal surface whose work function is 2·0 eV.

21. The electric field associated with a light wave is given by

$$E = E_0 \sin [(1{\cdot}57 \times 10^{7}\ \text{m}^{-1})(x - ct)].$$

Find the stopping potential when this light is used in

an experiment on photoelectric effect with the emitter having work function 1·9 eV.

22. The electric field at a point associated with a light wave is $E = (100\ \mathrm{V m^{-1}}) \sin [(3{\cdot}0 \times 10^{15}\ \mathrm{s^{-1}})t] \sin [(6{\cdot}0 \times 10^{15}\ \mathrm{s^{-1}})t]$. If this light falls on a metal surface having a work function of 2·0 eV, what will be the maximum kinetic energy of the photoelectrons ?

23. A monochromatic light source of intensity 5 mW emits 8×10^{15} photons per second. This light ejects photoelectrons from a metal surface. The stopping potential for this setup is 2·0 V. Calculate the work function of the metal.

24. Figure (42-E2) is the plot of the stopping potential versus the frequency of the light used in an experiment on photoelectric effect. Find (a) the ratio h/e and (b) the work function.

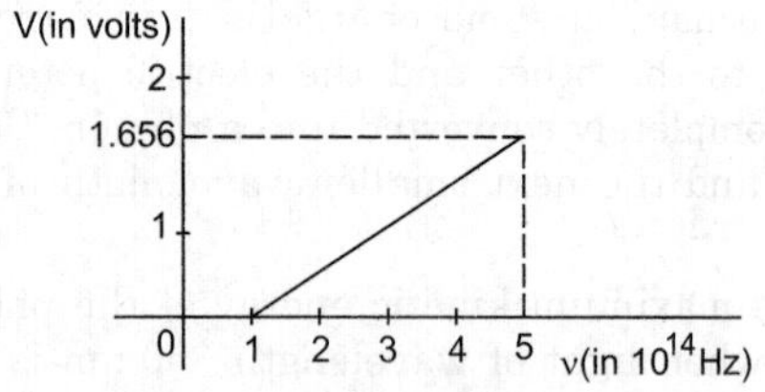

Figure 42-E2

25. A photographic film is coated with a silver bromide layer. When light falls on this film, silver bromide molecules dissociate and the film records the light there. A minimum of 0·6 eV is needed to dissociate a silver bromide molecule. Find the maximum wavelength of light that can be recorded by the film.

26. In an experiment on photoelectric effect, light of wavelength 400 nm is incident on a cesium plate at the rate of 5·0 W. The potential of the collector plate is made sufficiently positive with respect to the emitter so that the current reaches its saturation value. Assuming that on the average one out of every 10^6 photons is able to eject a photoelectron, find the photocurrent in the circuit.

27. A silver ball of radius 4·8 cm is suspended by a thread in a vacuum chamber. Ultraviolet light of wavelength 200 nm is incident on the ball for some time during which a total light energy of $1{\cdot}0 \times 10^{-7}$ J falls on the surface. Assuming that on the average one photon out of every ten thousand is able to eject a photoelectron, find the electric potential at the surface of the ball assuming zero potential at infinity. What is the potential at the centre of the ball ?

28. In an experiment on photoelectric effect, the emitter and the collector plates are placed at a separation of 10 cm and are connected through an ammeter without any cell

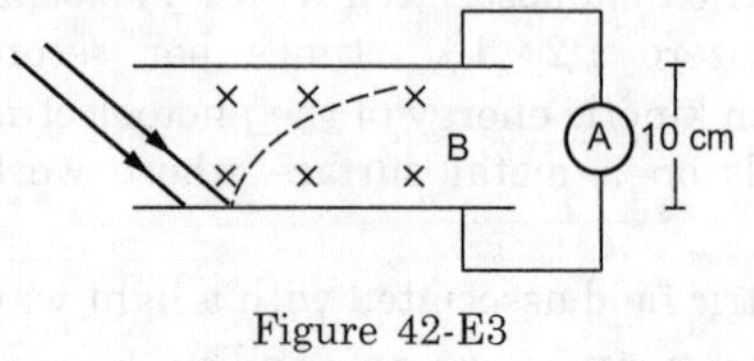

Figure 42-E3

(figure 42-E3). A magnetic field B exists parallel to the plates. The work function of the emitter is 2·39 eV and the light incident on it has wavelengths between 400 nm and 600 nm. Find the minimum value of B for which the current registered by the ammeter is zero. Neglect any effect of space charge.

29. In the arrangement shown in figure (42-E4), $y = 1{\cdot}0$ mm, $d = 0{\cdot}24$ mm and $D = 1{\cdot}2$ m. The work function of the material of the emitter is 2·2 eV. Find the stopping potential V needed to stop the photocurrent.

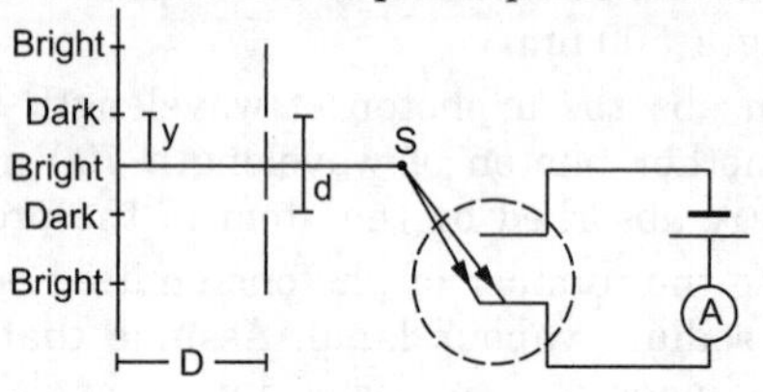

Figure 42-E4

30. In a photoelectric experiment, the collector plate is at 2·0 V with respect to the emitter plate made of copper ($\varphi = 4{\cdot}5$ eV). The emitter is illuminated by a source of monochromatic light of wavelength 200 nm. Find the minimum and maximum kinetic energy of the photoelectrons reaching the collector.

31. A small piece of cesium metal ($\varphi = 1{\cdot}9$ eV) is kept at a distance of 20 cm from a large metal plate having a charge density of $1{\cdot}0 \times 10^{-9}\ \mathrm{C\ m^{-2}}$ on the surface facing the cesium piece. A monochromatic light of wavelength 400 nm is incident on the cesium piece. Find the minimum and the maximum kinetic energy of the photoelectrons reaching the large metal plate. Neglect any change in electric field due to the small piece of cesium present.

32. Consider the situation of the previous problem. Consider the fastest electron emitted parallel to the large metal plate. Find the displacement of this electron parallel to its initial velocity before it strikes the large metal plate.

33. A horizontal cesium plate ($\varphi = 1{\cdot}9$ eV) is moved vertically downward at a constant speed v in a room full of radiation of wavelength 250 nm and above. What should be the minimum value of v so that the vertically upward component of velocity is nonpositive for each photoelectron ?

34. A small metal plate (work function φ) is kept at a distance d from a singly ionized, fixed ion. A monochromatic light beam is incident on the metal plate and photoelectrons are emitted. Find the maximum wavelength of the light beam so that some of the photoelectrons may go round the ion along a circle.

35. A light beam of wavelength 400 nm is incident on a metal plate of work function 2·2 eV. (a) A particular electron absorbs a photon and makes two collisions before coming out of the metal. Assuming that 10% of the extra energy is lost to the metal in each collision, find the kinetic energy of this electron as it comes out of the metal. (b) Under the same assumptions, find the maximum number of collisions the electron can suffer before it becomes unable to come out of the metal.

□

ANSWERS

OBJECTIVE I

1. (d)	2. (d)	3. (a)	4. (c)	5. (c)	6. (a)
7. (c)	8. (b)	9. (c)	10. (b)	11. (c)	12. (d)
13. (c)	14. (c)				

OBJECTIVE II

1. (a), (b)	2. (a), (b), (c)	3. (d)
4. (b), (d)	5. (a)	6. (b)
7. (a), (c), (d)		

EXERCISES

1. 2.56×10^{-19} J to 5.00×10^{-19} J
2. 1.33×10^{-27} kg m s^{-1}
3. 1.1×10^{-19} J
4. 1.77×10^{19}
5. (a) 3.5×10^{21} (b) 1.2×10^{13} (c) 9.9×10^{44}
6. 1.0×10^{-8} N
7. 4.3×10^{-8} N
8. 100 MW
9. 4.0×10^{-7} Pa
10. 5.2×10^{-9} N
13. 860 m, 215 m
14. 1.6 eV
15. (a) 3.8×10^{14} Hz (b) 0.91 V
16. (a) 310 nm (b) 190 nm
17. 4.2×10^{-25} kg m s^{-1}
18. 620 nm
19. (a) 4.2×10^{-15} eVs (b) 2.15 eV (c) 585 nm
20. 0.48 eV
21. 1.2 V
22. 3.93 eV
23. 1.9 eV
24. (a) 4.14×10^{-15} eVs (b) 0.414 eV
25. 2070 nm
26. 1.6 μA
27. 0.3 V in each case
28. 2.85×10^{-5} T
29. 0.9 V
30. 2.0 eV, 3.7 eV
31. 22.6 eV, 23.8 eV
32. 9.2 cm
33. 1.04×10^{6} m s^{-1}
34. $\dfrac{8\pi\varepsilon_0 dhc}{e^2 + 8\pi\varepsilon_0 \varphi d}$
35. (a) 0.31 eV (b) 4

□

CHAPTER 43

BOHR'S MODEL AND PHYSICS OF THE ATOM

43.1 EARLY ATOMIC MODELS

The idea that all matter is made of very small indivisible particles is very old. It has taken a long time, intelligent reasoning and classic experiments to cover the journey from this idea to the present day atomic models.

We can start our discussion with the mention of English scientist Robert Boyle (1627–1691) who studied the expansion and compression of air. The fact that air can be compressed or expanded, tells that air is made of tiny particles with lot of empty space between the particles. When air is compressed, these particles get closer to each other, reducing the empty space. We mention Robert Boyle here, because, with him atomism entered a new phase, from mere reasoning to experimental observations. The smallest unit of an element, which carries all the properties of the element is called an atom. Experiments on discharge tube, measurement of e/m by Thomson, etc., established the existence of negatively charged electrons in the atoms. And then started the search for the structure of the positive charge inside an atom because the matter as a whole is electrically neutral.

Thomson's Model of the Atom

Thomson suggested in 1898 that the atom is a positively charged solid sphere and electrons are embedded in it in sufficient number so as to make the atom electrically neutral. One can compare Thomson's atom to a birthday cake in which cherries are embedded. This model was quite attractive as it could explain several observations available at that time. It could explain why only negatively charged particles are emitted when a metal is heated and never the positively charged particles. It could also explain the formation of ions and ionic compounds of chemistry.

Lenard's Suggestion

Lenard had noted that cathode rays could pass through materials of small thickness almost undeviated. If the atoms were solid spheres, most of the electrons in the cathode rays would hit them and would not be able to go ahead in the forward direction. Lenard, therefore, suggested in 1903 that the atom must have a lot of empty space in it. He proposed that the atom is made of electrons and similar tiny particles carrying positive charge. But then, the question was, why on heating a metal, these tiny positively charged particles were not ejected ?

Rutherford's Model of the Atom

Thomson's model and Lenard's model, both had certain advantages and disadvantages. Thomson's model made the positive charge immovable by assuming it to be spread over the total volume of the atom. On the other hand, electrons were tiny particles and could be ejected on heating a metal. But the almost free passage of cathode rays through an atom was not consistent with Thomson's model. For that, the atom should have a lot of empty space as suggested by Lenard. So, the positive charge should be in the form of tiny particles occupying a very small volume, yet these particles should not be able to come out on heating.

It was Ernest Rutherford who solved the problem by doing a series of experiments from 1906 to 1911 on alpha particle scattering.

In these experiments, a beam of alpha particles was bombarded on a thin gold foil and their deflections were studied (figure 43.1). Most of the alpha particles passed through the gold foil either undeviated or with a small deviation. This was expected because an alpha particle is a heavy particle and will brush aside any tiny particle coming in its way. However, some of the alpha particles were deflected by large angles.

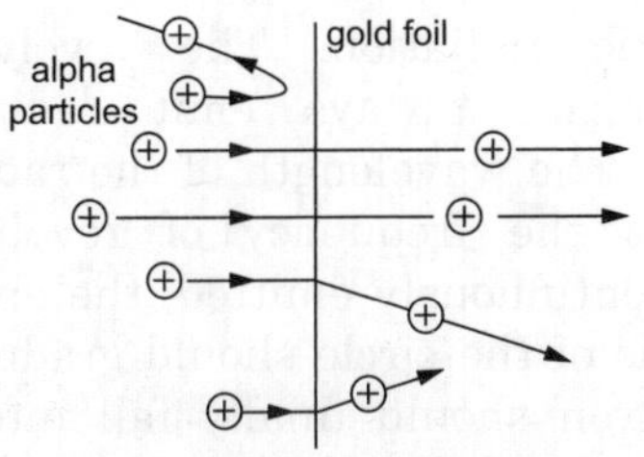

Figure 43.1

Rutherford found that some of the alpha particles, about one in 8000, were deflected by more than 90°, i.e., they were turned back by the foil.

This was interesting. When 8000 alpha particles could go through the gold atoms undeflected, why then one was forced to turn back. The alpha particle itself is about 7350 times heavier than the electron. So neither an electron, nor a similar positively charged particle could cause a large scale deflection of an alpha particle. The alpha particle must have encountered a very heavy particle in its path, a particle with mass of the order of the mass of the atom itself. Also, thousands of alpha particles go undeviated or almost undeviated. So this heavy mass in the atom should occupy a very small volume so that the atom may contain lot of empty space.

From the pattern of the scattering of alpha particles, Rutherford made quantitative analysis. He found that the heavy particle from which an alpha particle suffered large deflection, had a positive charge and virtually all the mass of the atom was concentrated in it. Its size was also estimated from the same experiment. The linear size was found to be about 10 fermi (1 fermi = 1 femtometre = 10^{-15} m) which was about 10^{-5} of the size of the linear atom. As the volume is proportional to the cube of the linear size, the volume of this positively charged particle was only about 10^{-15} of the volume of the atom.

Based on these observations, Rutherford proposed the model of *nuclear atom* which remains accepted to a large extent even today. According to this model, the atom contains a positively charged tiny particle at its centre called the *nucleus* of the atom. This nucleus contains almost all the mass of the atom. Outside this nucleus, there are electrons which move around it at some separation. The space between the nucleus and the electrons is empty and determines the size of the atom. The amount of the positive charge on the nucleus is exactly equal to the total amount of negative charges on all the electrons of the atom. Figure (43.2) shows schematic representations of an atom in Thomson's model and Rutherford's model.

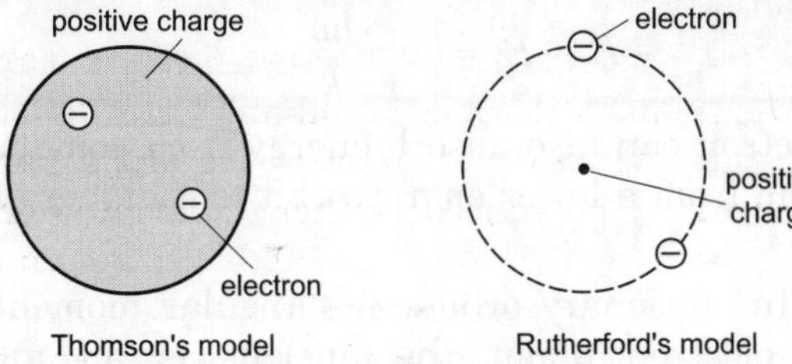

Figure 43.2

So, Rutherford's model explains the charge neutrality and the large empty space inside the atom as suggested by Lenard. It also explains why only negatively charged particles are ejected easily by an atom. It is so because the positively charged particle (nucleus) is so heavy that when an atom gets energy from heating or otherwise, this particle is hardly affected.

The movement of electrons around the nucleus was a necessary part of Rutherford's model. If the electrons were at rest, they would fall into the nucleus because of Coulomb attraction. If the electrons move in circular orbits, the Coulomb force will only change the direction of velocity providing the necessary centripetal force. This electronic motion, however, created difficulties for Rutherford's model as we shall now study.

43.2 HYDROGEN SPECTRA

When a material body is heated, it emits electromagnetic radiation. The radiation may consist of various components having different wavelengths. When the filament of an electric bulb is heated, it gives white light and all wavelengths in the visible range are present in the emitted radiation. If the emitted light is passed through a prism, components of different wavelengths deviate by different amounts and we get a continuous spectrum.

If hydrogen gas enclosed in a sealed tube is heated to high temperatures, it emits radiation. If this radiation is passed through a prism, components of different wavelengths are deviated by different amounts and thus we get the hydrogen spectrum. The most striking feature in this spectrum is that only some sharply defined, discrete wavelengths exist in the emitted radiation. For example, light of wavelength 656·3 nm is observed and then light of wavelength 486·1 nm is observed. Hydrogen atoms do not emit any radiation between 656·3 nm and 486·1 nm.

A hydrogen sample also emits radiation with wavelengths less than those in the visible range and also with wavelengths larger than those in the visible range. Figure (43.3) shows a schematic arrangement of the wavelengths present in a hydrogen spectrum. We see that the lines may be grouped in separate series. In each series, the separation between the consecutive wavelengths decreases as we go from higher wavelength to lower wavelength. In fact, the wavelengths in each series approach a limiting value known as the *series limit*. Thus, we have indicated the Lyman series (ultraviolet region), Balmer series

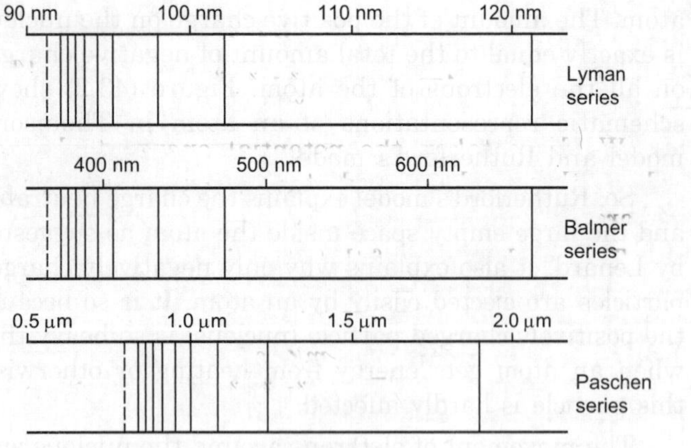

Figure 43.3

(visible region), Paschen series (infrared region), etc., in the figure.

The wavelengths nicely fit in the equation

$$\frac{1}{\lambda} = R\left(\frac{1}{n^2} - \frac{1}{m^2}\right) \qquad \ldots \text{ (43.1)}$$

where $R \approx 1{\cdot}09737 \times 10^7 \text{ m}^{-1}$ and n and m are integers with $m > n$. Lyman series can be reproduced by setting $n = 1$ and varying m from 2 onwards, Balmer series by setting $n = 2$ with $m > 2$, Paschen series by setting $n = 3$ with $m > 3$, etc.

It is said that John Jacob Balmer (1825–1898), a Swiss schoolteacher, was fond of playing with numbers. Once he complained to his physicist friend that he was getting bored as he had no numbers to play with. The friend gave him four wavelengths 656·3, 486·1, 434·1 and 420·2 nm of hydrogen spectrum and asked if Balmer could find a relation amongst them. And Balmer soon came out with his formula

$$\lambda = \frac{364{\cdot}56\, m^2}{m^2 - 4}, \text{ where } m = 3, 4, 5, 6$$

which was later put in more convenient form (equation 43.1) by Rydberg.

43.3 DIFFICULTIES WITH RUTHERFORD'S MODEL

The sharply defined, discrete wavelengths in hydrogen spectra posed a serious puzzle before physicists.

A hydrogen atom consists of an electron and a nucleus containing just a proton. The important question is why the electron does not hit the proton due to Coulomb attraction. In Rutherford's model, we assume that the electron revolves round the proton and the Coulomb force provides the necessary centripetal force to keep it moving in circular orbit. From the point of view of mechanics, a revolving electron in an atom is a satisfactory picture. But Maxwell's equations of electromagnetism show that any accelerated electron must continuously emit electromagnetic radiation. The revolving electron should, therefore, always emit radiation at all temperatures. The wavelength of the radiation should be related to the frequency of revolution. If the radiation is continuously emitted, the energy is spent and the radius of the circle should gradually decrease and the electron should finally fall into the proton. Also, the frequency of revolution changes continuously as the energy is spent, and so, the electron should emit radiation of continuously varying wavelength during the period of its motion.

The actual observations are quite different. At room temperature or below, hydrogen is very stable; it neither emits radiation nor does the electron collapse into the proton. When extra energy is supplied through heat or electric discharge, radiation is emitted, but the wavelengths are sharply defined as given by equation (43.1). These sharply defined wavelengths may be taken as the fingerprints of the element (hydrogen). Be it Calcutta, Delhi, Madras, Hyderabad, New York, London or Canberra, sun or upper atmosphere, hydrogen always emits only these fixed wavelengths. Such observations could not be explained by classical concepts and something new was about to take birth.

43.4 BOHR'S MODEL

In 1913, Niels Bohr, a great name in physics, suggested that the puzzle of hydrogen spectra may be solved if we make the following assumptions.

Bohr's Postulates

(a) The electron revolves round the nucleus in circular orbits.

(b) The orbit of the electron around the nucleus can take only some special values of radius. In these orbits of special radii, the electron does not radiate energy as expected from Maxwell's laws. These orbits are called *stationary orbits*.

(c) The energy of the atom has a definite value in a given stationary orbit. The electron can jump from one stationary orbit to other. If it jumps from an orbit of higher energy E_2 to an orbit of lower energy E_1, it emits a photon of radiation. The energy of the photon is $E_2 - E_1$. The wavelength of the emitted radiation is given by the Einstein–Planck equation

$$E_2 - E_1 = h\nu = \frac{hc}{\lambda}.$$

The electron can also absorb energy from some source and jump from a lower energy orbit to a higher energy orbit.

(d) In stationary orbits, the angular momentum l of the electron about the nucleus is an integral multiple of the Planck constant h divided by 2π,

$$l = n\frac{h}{2\pi}.$$

This last assumption is called *Bohr's quantization rule* and the assumptions (a) to (d) are known as *Bohr's postulates.*

Energy of a Hydrogen Atom

Let us now use the above postulates to find the allowed energies of the atom for different allowed orbits of the electron. The theory developed is applicable to hydrogen atoms, and ions having just one electron. Thus, it is valid for He^{+}, Li^{++}, Be^{+++}, etc. These ions are often called *hydrogen-like ions*. Let us assume that the nucleus has a positive charge Ze (i.e., there are Z protons in it) and an electron moves with a constant speed v along a circle of radius r with the centre at the nucleus. The force acting on the electron is that due to Coulomb attraction and is equal to

$$F = \frac{Ze^2}{4\pi\varepsilon_0 r^2}.$$

The acceleration of the electron is towards the centre and has a magnitude v^2/r. If m is the mass of the electron, from Newton's law,

$$\frac{Ze^2}{4\pi\varepsilon_0 r^2} = \frac{mv^2}{r}$$

or,

$$r = \frac{Ze^2}{4\pi\varepsilon_0 mv^2}. \quad \text{... (i)}$$

Also, from Bohr's quantization rule, the angular momentum is

$$mvr = n\frac{h}{2\pi} \quad \text{... (ii)}$$

where n is a positive integer.

Eliminating r from (i) and (ii), we get

$$v = \frac{Ze^2}{2\varepsilon_0 hn}. \quad \text{... (43.2)}$$

Substituting this in (ii),

$$r = \frac{\varepsilon_0 h^2 n^2}{\pi m Z e^2}. \quad \text{... (43.3)}$$

We see that the allowed radii are proportional to n^2. For each value of n, we have an allowed orbit. For $n = 1$, we have the first orbit (smallest radius), for $n = 2$, we have the second orbit and so on.

From equation (43.2), the kinetic energy of the electron in the nth orbit is

$$K = \frac{1}{2}mv^2 = \frac{mZ^2e^4}{8\varepsilon_0^2 h^2 n^2}. \quad \text{... (43.4)}$$

The potential energy of the atom is

$$V = -\frac{Ze^2}{4\pi\varepsilon_0 r} = -\frac{mZ^2e^4}{4\varepsilon_0^2 h^2 n^2}. \quad \text{... (43.5)}$$

We have taken the potential energy to be zero when the nucleus and the electron are widely separated.

The total energy of the atom is

$$E = K + V$$

$$= -\frac{mZ^2e^4}{8\varepsilon_0^2 h^2 n^2} \quad \text{... (43.6)}$$

Equations (43.2) through (43.6) give various parameters of the atom when the electron is in the nth orbit. The atom is also said to be in the *nth energy state* in this case. In deriving the expression for the total energy E, we have considered the kinetic energy of the electron and the potential energy of the electron–nucleus pair. It is assumed that the acceleration of the nucleus is negligible on account of its large mass.

Radii of different orbits

From equation (43.3), the radius of the smallest circle allowed to the electron is ($n = 1$)

$$r_1 = \frac{\varepsilon_0 h^2}{\pi m Z e^2}.$$

For hydrogen, $Z = 1$ and putting the values of other constants we get $r_1 = 53$ picometre (1 pm $= 10^{-12}$ m) or 0·053 nm. This length is called the *Bohr radius* and is a convenient unit for measuring lengths in atomic physics. It is generally denoted by the symbol a_0.

The second allowed radius is $4a_0$, third is $9a_0$ and so on. In general, the radius of the nth orbit is

$$r_n = n^2 a_0.$$

For a hydrogen-like ion with Z protons in the nucleus,

$$r_n = \frac{n^2 a_0}{Z}. \quad \text{... (43.7)}$$

Ground and excited states

From equation (43.6), the total energy of the atom in the state $n = 1$ is

$$E_1 = -\frac{mZ^2e^4}{8\varepsilon_0^2 h^2}.$$

For hydrogen atom, $Z = 1$ and putting the values of the constants, $E_1 = -13{\cdot}6$ eV. This is the energy when the electron revolves in the smallest allowed orbit $r = a_0$, i.e., the one with radius 0·053 nm. We also see from equation (43.6) that the energy of the atom in the nth energy state is proportional to $\frac{1}{n^2}$. Thus,

$$E_n = \frac{E_1}{n^2} = -\frac{13{\cdot}6\text{ eV}}{n^2} \quad \dots (43.8)$$

The energy in the state $n = 2$ is $E_2 = E_1/4 = -3{\cdot}4$ eV. In the state $n = 3$, it is $E_1/9 = -1{\cdot}5$ eV, etc. The lowest energy corresponds to the smallest circle. Note that the energy is negative and hence a larger magnitude means lower energy. The zero of energy corresponds to the state where the electron and the nucleus are widely separated. Figure (43.4) shows schematically the allowed orbits together with the energies of the atom. It also displays the allowed energies separately.

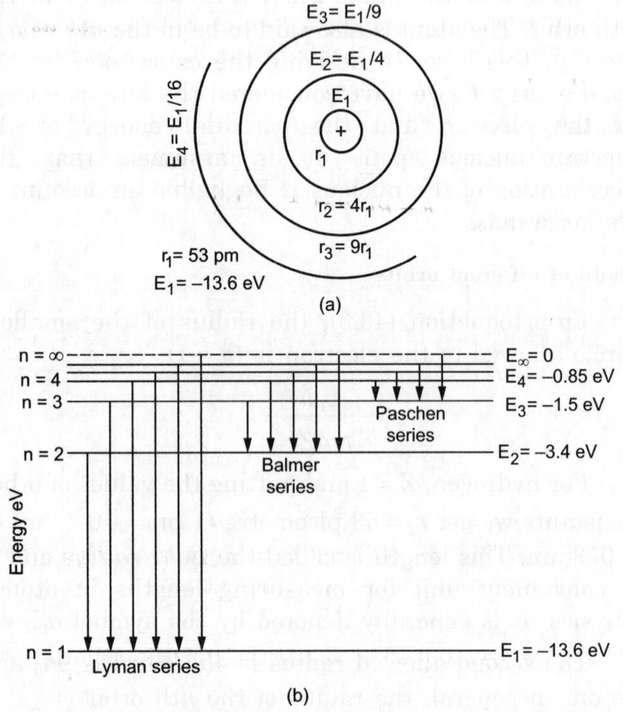

Figure 43.4

The state of an atom with the lowest energy is called its *ground state*. The states with higher energies are called *excited states*. Thus, the energy of a hydrogen atom in the ground state is $-13{\cdot}6$ eV and in the first excited state $-3{\cdot}4$ eV.

Hydrogen Spectra

We can now explain why hydrogen gas kept in a flask at room temperature does not emit radiation. This is because almost all the atoms are in the ground state and there are no orbits of lower energy to which an electron can jump. Hence, the atoms cannot emit any radiation. When energy is given in the form of heat or by electric discharge or by some other means, some of the electrons jump to the higher energy orbits $n = 2$, $n = 3$, etc. These electrons then jump back to lower energy orbits. The atoms radiate energy in the process. This explains why the atoms radiate only when they are heated or given energy in some other form.

If an electron makes a jump from the mth orbit to the nth orbit ($m > n$), the energy of the atom changes from E_m to E_n. This extra energy $E_m - E_n$ is emitted as a photon of electromagnetic radiation. The corresponding wavelength is given by

$$\frac{1}{\lambda} = \frac{E_m - E_n}{hc}$$

$$= \frac{mZ^2 e^4}{8\varepsilon_0^2 h^3 c}\left(\frac{1}{n^2} - \frac{1}{m^2}\right)$$

$$= RZ^2\left(\frac{1}{n^2} - \frac{1}{m^2}\right) \quad \dots (43.9)$$

where $R = \frac{me^4}{8\varepsilon_0^2 h^3 c}$ is called the *Rydberg constant*. Putting the values of different constants, the Rydberg constant R comes out to be $1{\cdot}0973 \times 10^7\ \text{m}^{-1}$ and equation (43.9) is in excellent agreement with the experimental formula (43.1). In terms of the Rydberg constant, the energy of the atom in the nth state is $E = \frac{-RhcZ^2}{n^2}$. Quite often, the energy of the atom is mentioned in unit of rydberg. An energy of 1 rydberg means $-13{\cdot}6$ eV. It is useful to remember that $Rhc = 13{\cdot}6$ eV.

Example 43.1

Calculate the energy of a He^+ *ion in its first excited state.*

Solution :

The energy is $E_n = \frac{-RhcZ^2}{n^2} = -\frac{(13{\cdot}6\text{ eV})Z^2}{n^2}$

For a He^+ ion, $Z = 2$ and for the first excited state, $n = 2$ so that the energy of He^+ ion in the first excited state is $-13{\cdot}6$ eV.

Example 43.2

Calculate the wavelength of radiation emitted when He^+ *makes a transition from the state* $n = 3$ *to the state* $n = 2$.

Solution :

The wavelength λ is given by

$$\frac{1}{\lambda} = RZ^2\left(\frac{1}{n^2} - \frac{1}{m^2}\right)$$

$$= 4R\left(\frac{1}{4} - \frac{1}{9}\right) = \frac{5}{9}R$$

or, $$\lambda = \frac{9}{5R} = \frac{9}{5 \times 1{\cdot}09737 \times 10^7\ \text{m}^{-1}} = 164{\cdot}0\text{ nm}.$$

Series structure

If a hydrogen atom makes transition from the state $n = 2$ to the state $n = 1$, the wavelength of the emitted radiation is given by

$$\frac{1}{\lambda} = R\left(1 - \frac{1}{4}\right) \text{ or, } \lambda = 121 \cdot 6 \text{ nm.}$$

If it makes transition from the state $n = \infty$ to the state $n = 1$, the wavelength emitted is given by

$$\frac{1}{\lambda} = R(1 - 0) \text{ or, } \lambda = 91 \cdot 2 \text{ nm.}$$

Thus, all the transitions ending at $n = 1$ correspond to wavelengths grouped between 121·6 nm and 91·2 nm. These lines constitute the *Lyman series.*

Similarly, transitions from higher states to $n = 2$ lead to emission of radiation with wavelengths between 656·3 nm and 365·0 nm. These wavelengths fall in the visible region and constitute the *Balmer series.* The transitions from higher states to $n = 3$ give rise to *Paschen series* with wavelengths between 1875 nm and 822 nm, and similarly for other series. This explains the grouping of wavelengths in different series as shown in figure (43.3).

Ionization potential

What happens if we supply more than 13·6 eV to a hydrogen atom in its ground state ? The total energy is then positive. The equations deduced above are not applicable in this case. In fact, a total energy of zero corresponds to electron and nucleus separated by an infinite distance. In this case, the electron is not bound to the nucleus and is free to move anywhere. The atom is said to be ionized, i.e., its electron has been detatched from the nucleus. Positive energy means that the atom is ionized and the electron is moving independently with some kinetic energy.

The minimum energy needed to ionize an atom is called *ionization energy.* The potential difference through which an electron should be accelerated to acquire this much energy is called *ionization potential.* Thus, ionization energy of hydrogen atom in ground state is 13·6 eV and ionization potential is 13·6 V.

Binding energy

Binding energy of a system is defined as the energy released when its constituents are brought from infinity to form the system. It may also be defined as the energy needed to separate its constituents to large distances. If an electron and a proton are initially at rest and brought from large distances to form a hydrogen atom, 13·6 eV energy will be released. The binding energy of a hydrogen atom is, therefore, 13·6 eV, same as its ionization energy.

Excitation potential

The energy needed to take the atom from its ground state to an excited state is called the *excitation energy* of that excited state. The hydrogen atom in ground state needs 10·2 eV to go into the first excited state. Thus, the excitation energy of hydrogen atom in the first excited state is 10·2 eV. The potential through which an electron should be accelerated to acquire this much of energy is called the *excitation potential.* Thus, the excitation potential of hydrogen atom in first excited state is 10·2 V.

Example 43.3

The excitation energy of a hydrogen-like ion in its first excited state is 40·8 eV. Find the energy needed to remove the electron from the ion.

Solution :

The excitation energy in the first excited state is

$$E = RhcZ^2\left(\frac{1}{1^2} - \frac{1}{2^2}\right)$$

$$= (13 \cdot 6 \text{ eV}) \times Z^2 \times \frac{3}{4}.$$

Equating this to 40·8 eV, we get $Z = 2$. So, the ion in question is He^+. The energy of the ion in the ground state is

$$E = -\frac{RhcZ^2}{1^2} = -4 \times (13 \cdot 6 \text{ eV})$$

$$= -54 \cdot 4 \text{ eV.}$$

Thus 54·4 eV is required to remove the electron from the ion.

43.5 LIMITATIONS OF BOHR'S MODEL

Bohr's model was a great success at a time when the physicists were struggling hard to understand the discrete wavelengths in hydrogen spectra. Even today the model is very popular among beginners and nonphysicists, who can 'visualise' the inside of the atom as electrons going in circles around the nucleus. However, the model did not go too far. It could not be extended for atoms or ions having more than one electron. Even helium spectrum was beyond the scope of the Bohr's model. As technology improved and the wavelengths were measured with greater accuracy, deviations were observed even in the case of hydrogen spectral lines. Thus, at least seven components having slightly different wavelengths are revealed in what was previously known as the 656·3 nm line. On the theoretical side also, the model is not quite consistent with the physics in totality. Bohr's postulates look more like a patch on Maxwell's electromagnetism. Maxwell's theory is not replaced or refuted but it is arbitrarily assumed that in certain orbits, electrons get the licence to disobey the laws of electromagnetism and are allowed not to radiate energy.

43.6 THE WAVE FUNCTION OF AN ELECTRON

Physicists now have a mathematically and logically sound theory in the name of *quantum mechanics* which describes the spectra in a much better way. A very brief introduction to this theory is given below.

We have seen in previous chapters that to understand the behaviour of light, we must use the wave picture (the electric field $\vec{E}$) as well as the particle picture (the photon). The energy of a particular 'photon' is related to the 'wavelength' of the $\vec{E}$ wave. Light going in x-direction is represented by the wave function

$$E(x, t) = E_0 \sin(kx - \omega t).$$

In general, if light can go in any direction, the wave function is

$$\vec{E}(\vec{r},t) = \vec{E}_0 \sin(\vec{k}\cdot\vec{r} - \omega t). \quad \text{... (i)}$$

If $|\vec{E}|^2$ at a certain point $\vec{r}$ is large, the intensity of light is high and we say that the 'density of photons' at that position is high. Suppose the intensity is so low that we expect only a single photon in a large volume. Even this weak light is represented by a wave given by (i) with $|\vec{E}_0|^2$ having a small value. Where is this photon at time t? We can't assign a unique position to the photon because $\vec{E}$ is spread over a large space, and wherever $\vec{E} \neq 0$ there is light. But if we put an instrument to detect the photon, we shall not detect a part of photon here and a part there. The whole photon is detected at just one point. The probability of finding the photon is more where $|\vec{E}(\vec{r}, t)|^2$ is large. To know something about the 'photon', we have to get the wave function $\vec{E}(\vec{r}, t)$ of light and correlate the wave properties with the particle properties. The wave function $\vec{E}(\vec{r}, t)$ satisfies Maxwell's equations. Similar is the case with electrons. An electron also has a wave character as well as a particle character. Its wave function is $\psi(\vec{r}, t)$ which may be obtained by solving *Schrodinger's wave equation*. The particle properties of the electron must be understood through this wave function $\psi(\vec{r}, t)$. The wave function varies continuously in space and may be extended over a large part of space at a given instant. This does not mean that the electron is spread over that large part. If we put an instrument to detect the electron at a point, we shall either detect a whole electron or none. But where will this electron be found? The answer is again hidden in $\psi(\vec{r}, t)$. Wherever $\psi \neq 0$, there is a chance to find the electron. Greater the value of $|\psi(\vec{r}, t)|^2$, greater is the probability of detecting the electron there. Not only the information about the electron's position but information about all the properties including energy is also contained in the wave function $\psi(\vec{r}, t)$.

43.7 QUANTUM MECHANICS OF THE HYDROGEN ATOM

The wave function $\psi(\vec{r}, t)$ of the electron and the possible energies E of a hydrogen atom or a hydrogen-like ion are obtained from the Schrodinger's equation

$$\frac{-h^2}{8\pi^2 m}\left[\frac{\partial^2\psi}{\partial x^2} + \frac{\partial^2\psi}{\partial y^2} + \frac{\partial^2\psi}{\partial z^2}\right] - \frac{Ze^2\psi}{4\pi\varepsilon_0 r} = E\psi. \quad \text{... (43.10)}$$

Here (x,y,z) refers to a point with the nucleus as the origin and r is the distance of this point from the nucleus. E refers to energy. The constant Z is the number of protons in the nucleus. For hydrogen, we have to put $Z = 1$. There are infinite number of functions $\psi(\vec{r})$ which satisfy equation (43.10). These functions, which are solutions of equation (43.10), may be characterised in terms of three parameters n, l and m_l. With each solution ψ_{nlm_l}, there is associated a unique value of the energy E of the atom or the ion. The energy E corresponding to the wave function ψ_{nlm_l} depends only on n and may be written as

$$E_n = -\frac{mZ^2e^4}{8\varepsilon_0^2 h^2 n^2}. \quad \text{... (43.11)}$$

These energies happen to be identical with the allowed energies calculated in Bohr's model. This explains the success of Bohr's model in quantitatively obtaining the wavelengths in a hydrogen spectrum. For each n there are n values of l, namely $l = 0, 1, 2, \ldots, n-1$ and for each l there are $2l+1$ values of m_l namely $m_l = -l, -l+1, -l+2, \ldots, l-1, l$. The parameter n is called the *principal quantum number*, l the *orbital angular momentum quantum number* and m_l the *magnetic quantum number*.

The lowest possible energy for the hydrogen atom is $-Rhc = -13{\cdot}6$ eV and the wave function of the electron in this 'ground state' is

$$\psi(\vec{r}) = \psi_{100} = \sqrt{\frac{Z^3}{\pi a_0^2}}\, e^{-r/a_0}. \quad \text{... (43.12)}$$

In Bohr's model, we say that the electron moves in a circular orbit of radius $a_0 = 0{\cdot}053$ nm in the ground state. In quantum mechanics, the very idea of orbit is invalid. In ground state, the wave function of the electron is given by equation (43.12). At any instant this wave function is spread over large distances in space, and wherever $\psi \neq 0$, the presence of electron may be felt. However, if the electron is detected by some experiment, it will be detected at one single

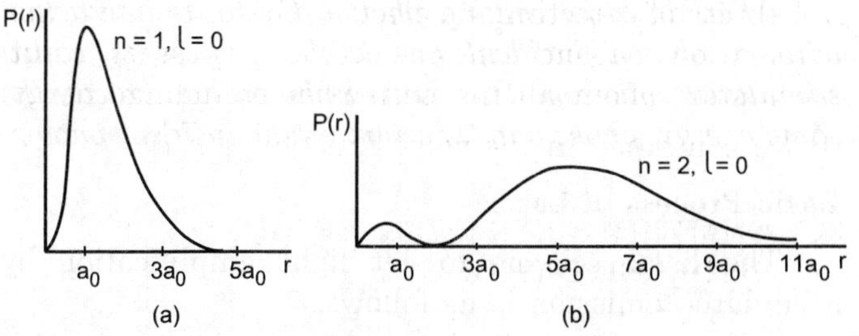

Figure 43.5

position only. The probability of finding the electron in a small volume dV is $|\psi(\vec{r})|^2 dV$. One can calculate the probability $P(r)dr$ of finding the electron at a distance between r and $r + dr$ from the nucleus. The function $P(r)$ is called linear probability density. In ground state, given by equation (43.12), $P(r)$ comes out to be

$$P(r) = \frac{4}{a_0^3} r^2 e^{-2r/a_0}.$$

A plot of $P(r)$ versus r is shown in figure (43.5a). Note that $P(r)$ is maximum at $r = a_0$. This means that the electron is more likely to be found near $r = a_0$ than at any other distance.

It may be satisfying that at least the probability of finding the electron is maximum at the same radial distance from the nucleus where the Bohr's model assigns the electron to be. However, even this cannot be stretched too far. The linear probability density $P(r)$ for $n = 2$, $l = 0$, $m = 0$ is plotted in figure (43.5b) which has two maxima, one near $r = a_0$ and the other near $r = 5{\cdot}4\ a_0$. In Bohr's model, all $n = 2$ electrons should be at $r = 4\,a_0$.

43.8 NOMENCLATURE IN ATOMIC PHYSICS

We have neglected the *spin* of the electron in the discussion so far. A very interesting property of electrons is that each electron has a permanent angular momentum whose component along any given direction is $\frac{h}{4\pi}$ or $-\frac{h}{4\pi}\cdot$ This angular momentum is different from the angular momentum resulting from the motion of the electron and is known as the *spin angular momentum* of the electron. The complete wave function of an electron also has a part depending on the state of the spin. The spin part of the wave function is characterized by a spin quantum number m_s which can take values $m_s = +1/2$ or $-1/2$. A wave function is thus characterised by n, l, m_l and m_s. A particular wave function described by particular values of n, l, m_l, m_s corresponds to a *quantum state*. For $n = 1$, we have $l = 0$ and $m_l = 0$. But m_s can be $+1/2$ or $-1/2$. So there are two quantum states corresponding to $n = 1$. For $n = 2$ there are 8 quantum states, for $n = 3$ there are 18 quantum states and so on. In general, there are $2n^2$ quantum states corresponding to a particular n. The quantum states corresponding to a particular n are together called a *major shell.* The major shell corresponding to $n = 1$ is called K shell, corresponding to $n = 2$ is called L shell, corresponding to $n = 3$ is called M shell, etc.

A very interesting and important law of nature is that *there cannot be more than one electron in any quantum state.* This is known as *Pauli exclusion principle.* Thus, a K shell can contain a maximum of 2 electrons, an L shell can contain a maximum of 8 electrons, an M shell can contain a maximum of 18 electrons and so on.

It is customary to use the symbols s, p, d, f, etc., to denote the values of the orbital angular momentum quantum number l. These symbols correspond to $l = 0$, 1, 2, 3, etc., respectively. The quantum states corresponding to a given principal quantum number n and a given orbital angular momentum quantum number l form what we call a *subshell.* Thus $n = 1$, $l = 0$ is called 1s subshell. Similarly $n = 2$, $l = 0$ is called 2s subshell, $n = 2$, $l = 1$ is called 2p subshell and so on. For atoms having more than one electron also, the concept of n, l, m_l, m_s is valid. The energy then depends on n as well as on l. Thus 1s, 2s, 2p, etc., also designate the *energy levels.* For an atom having many electrons, the quantum states are, in general, gradually filled from lower energy to higher energy to form the ground state of the atom.

We have seen that electrons obey Pauli exclusion principle. Apart from electrons, there are other particles which obey this principle. Protons and neutrons also obey this principle. Any particle that obeys Pauli exclusion principle, is called a *fermion.* Electrons, protons, neutrons are all fermions.

43.9 LASER

When an atom jumps from a higher energy state to a lower energy state, it emits a photon of light. In an ordinary source of light, atoms emit photons independently of each other. As a result, different photons have different phases and the light as a whole becomes incoherent. Also, the energy of transition differs slightly from photon to photon so that the wavelength is not uniquely defined. There is a spread $\Delta\lambda$ in the wavelength λ. The direction of light is also different for different transitions so that we do not get a strictly parallel beam of light.

LASER (Light Amplification by Stimulated Emission of Radiation) is a process by which we get a light beam which is coherent, highly monochromatic and almost perfectly parallel. The word 'laser' is also used for the light beam obtained by this process. All the photons in the light beam, emitted by different atoms at different instants, are in phase. The spread $\Delta\lambda$ in wavelength is very small, of the order of 10^{-6} nm which is about 1000 times smaller than the spread in the usual ^{86}Kr light. A beam of laser can go to the moon and return to the earth without much loss of intensity. This shows that laser may be obtained as an almost perfectly parallel beam.

To understand the process involved in laser, we have to first discuss *stimulated emission.*

Stimulated Emission

Consider an atom which has an allowed state at energy E_1 and another allowed state at a higher energy E_2. Suppose the atom is in the lower energy state E_1. If a photon of light having energy $E_2 - E_1$ is incident on this atom, the atom may absorb the photon and jump to the higher energy state E_2 (figure 43.6a). This process is called *stimulated absorption* of light photon. The incident photon has stimulated the atom to absorb the energy.

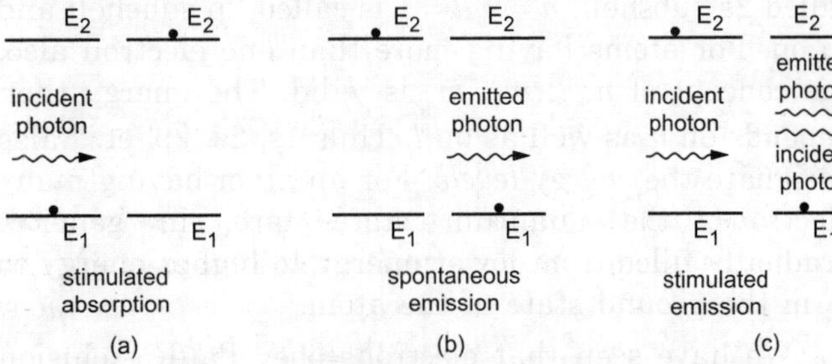

Figure 43.6

Now, suppose the atom is in the higher energy state E_2. If we just leave the atom there, it will eventually come down to the lower state by emitting a photon having energy $E_2 - E_1$ (figure 43.6b). This process is called *spontaneous emission*. Typically, an atom stays for about 10 ns in an excited state. The average time for which an atom stays in an excited state is called the *lifetime* of that state. There are atoms which have certain excited states having a lifetime of the order of a millisecond, i.e., about 10^5 times longer than the usual lifetimes. Such states are called *metastable states.*

Finally, suppose the atom is in the higher energy state E_2 and a photon having energy $(E_2 - E_1)$ is incident on it (figure 43-6c). The incident photon interacts with the atom and may cause the atom to come down to the lower energy state. A fresh photon is emitted in the process. This process is different from spontaneous emission in which the atom jumps to the lower energy state on its own. In the present case, the incident photon has 'stimulated' the atom to make the jump.

When an atom emits a photon due to its interaction with a photon incident on it, the process is called stimulated emission. The emitted photon has exactly the same energy, phase and direction as the incident photon.

Basic Process of Laser

The basic scheme to get light amplification by stimulated emission is as follows.

A system is chosen which has a metastable state having an energy E_2 (figure 43.7). There is another allowed energy E_1 which is less than E_2. The system may be a gas or a liquid in a cylindrical tube or a solid in the shape of a cylindrical rod. Suppose, by some technique, the number of atoms in the metastable state E_2 is made much larger than that in E_1. Suppose a photon of light of energy $E_2 - E_1$ is incident on one of the atoms in the metastable state. This atom drops to the state E_1 emitting a photon in the same phase, energy and direction as the first one. These two photons interact with two more atoms in the state E_2 and so on. So the number of photons keeps on increasing. All these photons have the same phase, the same energy and the same direction. So the amplification of light is achieved.

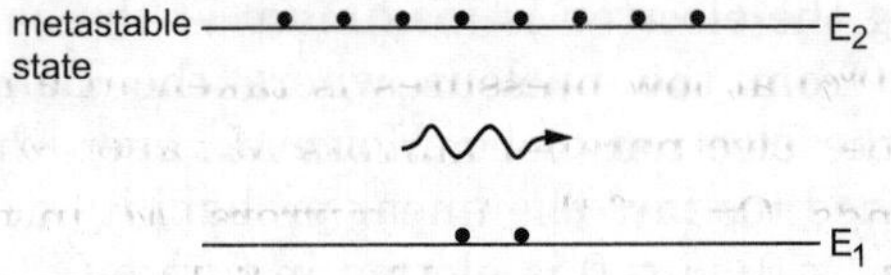

Figure 43.7

In this scheme, two arrangements are necessary. Firstly, the metastable state with energy E_2 must all the time have larger number of atoms than the number in the lower energy state. If the lower energy state has a larger number of atoms, these atoms will absorb a sizable number of photons to go up in energy. This way the stimulated emission will be weakened and the amplification will not be possible. When a higher energy state has more number of atoms than a lower energy state has, we say that *population inversion* has taken place. This is because, normally, the population in the lower energy state is higher. To sustain laser action, we need an arrangement which ensures population inversion between the states E_1 and E_2. The metastable state should continue to get atoms and the atoms should be continuously removed from the lower energy state E_1. This process is called *pumping.*

Secondly, the photons emitted due to stimulating action should stimulate other atoms to emit more photons. This means, the stimulated photons should spend enough time in the system, interacting with the atoms. To achieve this, two mirrors are fixed at the ends of the cylindrical region containing the lasing material. The mirrors reflect the photons back and forth to keep them inside the region for a long time. One of the mirrors is made slightly transmitting so that a small fraction, say 1%, of the light comes out of the region. This is the laser which becomes available to us for use.

Any photon travelling in a direction not parallel to the axis of the cylindrical region is thrown out from the sides after few reflections. The photons moving parallel to the axis remain in the region for long time and hence only the light along the axis is amplified. This explains why the laser light is highly directional.

Let us now discuss a He–Ne laser which is most widely used in classroom demonstrations.

He–Ne Laser

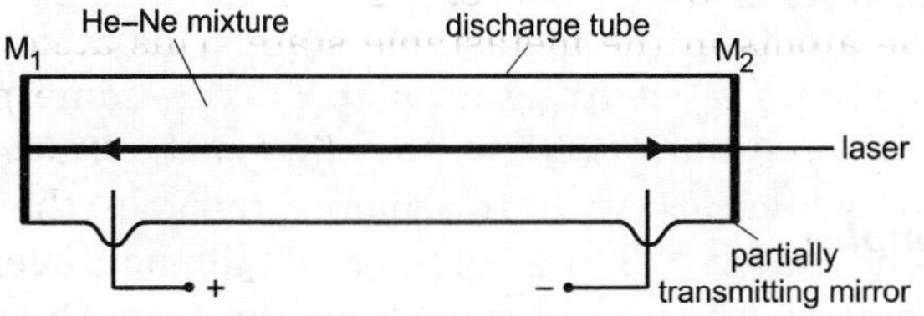

Figure 43.8

A schematic design of the system is shown in figure (43.8). A mixture of helium (about 90%) and neon (about 10%) at low pressures is taken in a cylindrical glass tube. Two parallel mirrors M_1 and M_2 are fixed at the ends. One of the two mirrors, M_2 in the figure, is slightly transmitting and laser light comes out of it. The tube contains two electrodes which are connected to a high-voltage power supply so that a large electric field is established in the tube.

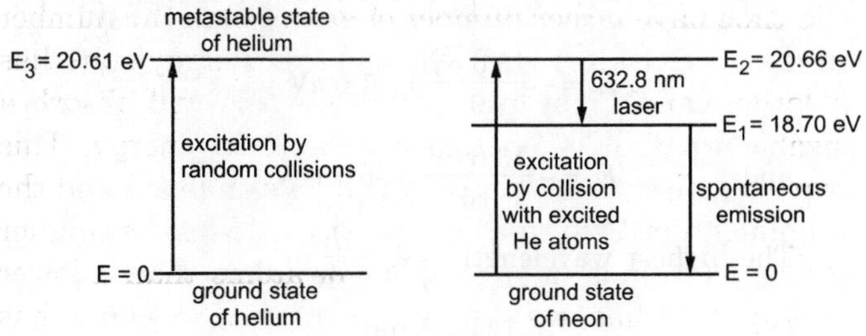

Figure 43.9

The relevant energy levels of helium and neon are shown in figure (43.9). Lasing action takes place between the state at energy $E_2 = 20{\cdot}66$ eV and the state at energy $E_1 = 18{\cdot}70$ eV of neon atoms. Helium has a metastable state at $E_3 = 20{\cdot}61$ eV which happens to be close to the level E_2 of neon. Helium is used to pump the neon atoms to the state E_2 from where they may come down to the state E_1 by stimulated emission. The energy difference is

$$E_2 - E_1 = 1{\cdot}96 \text{ eV}$$

so that the wavelength of He–Ne laser is

$$\lambda = \frac{hc}{E_2 - E_1} = 632{\cdot}8 \text{ nm}.$$

Working

When the power supply is switched on and the electric field is established, some of the atoms of the mixture get ionized. The electrons freed by these atoms are accelerated by the high electric field. These electrons collide with helium atoms to take them to the metastable state at energy E_3. Such an excited atom collides with a neon atom and transfers the extra energy to it. As a result, the helium atom comes back to its ground state and the neon atom is excited to the state at energy E_2. This process takes place continuously so that the neon atoms are continuously pumped to the state at energy E_2 to keep the population of this state large.

Stimulated emission takes place between the states at energies E_2 and E_1. As the state at energy E_1 has a small lifetime, of the order of 10 ns, these atoms readily jump to the still lower states. This way the population of the state at energy E_1 is always very small. Thus, population inversion between E_2 and E_1 is achieved and maintained.

Laser light comes out of the partially transmitting mirror.

Note that the higher energy state E_2 of neon is not itself metastable. But the metastable state of helium accumulates atoms at higher energy which take neon atoms to the level E_2 by means of collisions.

Uses of Laser

Laser was invented in 1960. Since then, laser technology has greatly advanced and now lasers have widespread use in industry, scientific research, surgery, etc.

Because of the near-perfect parallel and monochromatic character, a laser beam can be focused by a converging lens to a very small spot. This results in very high intensity over that tiny spot. It can, therefore, be used for very accurate microsurgery where a very small area is to be treated. Lasers in infrared region are used to burn away cervical tumours. These lasers are also used for cutting tissues. Lasers are used to spot-weld detached retina with great accuracy. Because of the high intensity, lasers are used to drill sharp holes in metals and diamond. In garment industry, lasers are used to cut many layers (say 50 layers at a time) of cloth without frayed edges.

Lasers are widely used to send telephone signals over long distances through optical fibres. They are also used in nuclear fusion research which is likely to be the ultimate source of energy for us.

Because of its directional properties, lasers are used in surveying. Another use of laser is to align tools and equipment in industry and scientific research. Laser light is sent to the moon from where it is reflected back to the earth without much loss of intensity. Thus, points on the moon's surface may be monitored from the earth using lasers. Laser has numerous military applications.

An interesting application of lasers is to produce holograms, which record a 3 D image of an object. When the hologram is viewed, again with a laser, the same 3 D perception is achieved as it is with the actual object.

In compact disc (CD) audio systems, a laser beam is used in place of the phonographic needle. Sound is recorded on the compact disc using digital electronic techniques. This results in great compression of the sound data and a very large number of songs, speeches etc. can be stored on a CD which is much smaller than a traditional record. Also, the playback of the music is more 'true' than traditional systems and almost without any distortion. Using lasers, video images can also be stored on discs which can be played back using a laser disc player and a TV. Since the combination of digital electronic techniques and CD allows us to store a large amount of data in a small volume, books of large volume like dictionaries and encyclopedias, are now available on CDs. This technique is now being used in computers for data retrieval and storage. Lasers are used in laser printers. The present book was also prepared with the help of a laser printer. Incredible new applications are being created everyday using lasers.

Worked Out Examples

First Bohr radius $a_0 = 53$ pm, energy of hydrogen atom in ground state = – 13·6 eV, Planck constant $h = 4{\cdot}14 \times 10^{-15}$ eVs, speed of light = 3×10^{8} m s^{-1}.

1. *Find the radius of* Li^{++} *ions in its ground state assuming Bohr's model to be valid.*

Solution : For hydrogen-like ions, the radius of the *n*th orbit is

$$a_n = \frac{n^2 a_0}{Z}.$$

For Li^{++}, $Z = 3$ and in ground state $n = 1$. The radius is

$$a_1 = \frac{53 \text{ pm}}{3} \approx 18 \text{ pm}.$$

2. *A particular hydrogen-like ion emits radiation of frequency* $2{\cdot}467 \times 10^{15}$ Hz *when it makes transition from* $n = 2$ *to* $n = 1$. *What will be the frequency of the radiation emitted in a transition from* $n = 3$ *to* $n = 1$?

Solution : The frequency of radiation emitted is given by

$$\nu = \frac{c}{\lambda} = K\left(\frac{1}{n_1^2} - \frac{1}{n_2^2}\right).$$

Thus, $2{\cdot}467 \times 10^{15} \text{ Hz} = K\left(\frac{1}{1^2} - \frac{1}{2^2}\right)$

or, $K = \frac{4}{3} \times 2{\cdot}467 \times 10^{15}$ Hz.

The frequency of the radiation emitted in the transition $n = 3$ to $n = 1$ is

$$\nu' = K\left[\frac{1}{1^2} - \frac{1}{3^2}\right]$$

$$= \frac{8}{9}K = \frac{8}{9} \times \frac{4}{3} \times 2{\cdot}467 \times 10^{15} \text{ Hz}$$

$$= 2{\cdot}92 \times 10^{15} \text{ Hz}.$$

3. *Calculate the two highest wavelengths of the radiation emitted when hydrogen atoms make transitions from higher states to* $n = 2$ *states.*

Solution : The highest wavelength corresponds to the lowest energy of transition. This will be the case for the transition $n = 3$ to $n = 2$. The second highest wavelength corresponds to the transition $n = 4$ to $n = 2$.

The energy of the state n is $E_n = \frac{E_1}{n^2}$.

Thus, $$E_2 = -\frac{13{\cdot}6 \text{ eV}}{4} = -3{\cdot}4 \text{ eV}$$

$$E_3 = -\frac{13{\cdot}6 \text{ eV}}{9} = -1{\cdot}5 \text{ eV}$$

and $$E_4 = -\frac{13{\cdot}6 \text{ eV}}{16} = -0{\cdot}85 \text{ eV}.$$

The highest wavelength is $\lambda_1 = \frac{hc}{\Delta E}$

$$= \frac{1242 \text{ eVnm}}{(3{\cdot}4 \text{ eV} - 1{\cdot}5 \text{ eV})} = 654 \text{ nm}.$$

The second highest wavelength is

$$\lambda_2 = \frac{1242 \text{ eVnm}}{(3{\cdot}4 \text{ eV} - 0{\cdot}85 \text{ eV})} = 487 \text{ nm}.$$

4. *What is the wavelength of the radiation emitted when the electron in a hydrogen atom jumps from* $n = \infty$ *to* $n = 2$?

Solution : The energy of $n = 2$ state is

$$E_2 = \frac{-13{\cdot}6 \text{ eV}}{4} = -3{\cdot}4 \text{ eV}.$$

The energy of $n = \infty$ state is zero.

The wavelength emitted in the given transition is

$$\lambda = \frac{hc}{\Delta E}$$

$$= \frac{1242 \text{ eV nm}}{3{\cdot}4 \text{ eV}} = 365 \text{ nm}.$$

5. *(a) Find the wavelength of the radiation required to excite the electron in Li^{++} from the first to the third Bohr orbit. (b) How many spectral lines are observed in the emission spectrum of the above excited system ?*

Solution : (a) The energy in the first orbit $= E_1 = Z^2 E_0$ where $E_0 = -13{\cdot}6$ eV is the energy of a hydrogen atom in ground state. Thus for Li^{++},

$$E_1 = 9E_0 = 9 \times (-13{\cdot}6 \text{ eV}).$$

The energy in the third orbit is

$$E_3 = \frac{E_1}{n^2} = \frac{E_1}{9} = -13{\cdot}6 \text{ eV}.$$

Thus, $\quad E_3 - E_1 = 8 \times 13{\cdot}6 \text{ eV} = 108{\cdot}8 \text{ eV}.$

The wavelength of radiation required to excite Li^{++} from the first orbit to the third orbit is given by

$$\frac{hc}{\lambda} = E_3 - E_1$$

or, $$\lambda = \frac{hc}{E_3 - E_1}$$

$$= \frac{1242 \text{ eV nm}}{108{\cdot}8 \text{ eV}} \approx 11{\cdot}4 \text{ nm}.$$

(b) The spectral lines emitted are due to the transitions $n = 3 \rightarrow n = 2$, $n = 3 \rightarrow n = 1$ and $n = 2 \rightarrow n = 1$. Thus, there will be three spectral lines in the spectrum.

6. *Find the wavelengths present in the radiation emitted when hydrogen atoms excited to $n = 3$ states return to their ground states.*

Solution : A hydrogen atom may return directly to the ground state or it may go to $n = 2$ and from there to the ground state. Thus, wavelengths corresponding to $n = 3 \rightarrow n = 1$, $n = 3 \rightarrow n = 2$ and $n = 2 \rightarrow n = 1$ are present in the radiation.

The energies in $n = 1$, 2 and 3 states are

$$E_1 = -13{\cdot}6 \text{ eV}$$

$$E_2 = -\frac{13{\cdot}6}{4} \text{ eV} = -3{\cdot}4 \text{ eV}$$

and $$E_3 = -\frac{13{\cdot}6}{9} \text{ eV} = -1{\cdot}5 \text{ eV}.$$

The wavelength emitted in the transition $n = 3$ to the ground state is

$$\lambda = \frac{hc}{\Delta E}$$

$$= \frac{1242 \text{ eV nm}}{13{\cdot}6 \text{ eV} - 1{\cdot}5 \text{ eV}} = 103 \text{ nm}.$$

Similarly, the wavelength emitted in the transition $n = 3$ to $n = 2$ is 654 nm and that emitted in the transition $n = 2$ to $n = 1$ is 122 nm. The wavelengths present in the radiation are, therefore, 103 nm, 122 nm and 654 nm.

7. *How many different wavelengths may be observed in the spectrum from a hydrogen sample if the atoms are excited to states with principal quantum number n ?*

Solution : From the nth state, the atom may go to $(n-1)$th state, … , 2nd state or 1st state. So there are $(n-1)$ possible transitions starting from the nth state. The atoms reaching $(n-1)$th state may make $(n-2)$ different transitions. Similarly for other lower states. The total number of possible transitions is

$$(n-1) + (n-2) + (n-3) + \ldots 2 + 1$$

$$= \frac{n(n-1)}{2}.$$

8. *Monochromatic radiation of wavelength λ is incident on a hydrogen sample in ground state. Hydrogen atoms absorb a fraction of light and subsequently emit radiation of six different wavelengths. Find the value of λ.*

Solution : As the hydrogen atoms emit radiation of six different wavelengths, some of them must have been excited to $n = 4$. The energy in $n = 4$ state is

$$E_4 = \frac{E_1}{4^2} = -\frac{13{\cdot}6 \text{ eV}}{16} = -0{\cdot}85 \text{ eV}.$$

The energy needed to take a hydrogen atom from its ground state to $n = 4$ is

$$13{\cdot}6 \text{ eV} - 0{\cdot}85 \text{ eV} = 12{\cdot}75 \text{ eV}.$$

The photons of the incident radiation should have 12·75 eV of energy. So

$$\frac{hc}{\lambda} = 12{\cdot}75 \text{ eV}$$

or, $$\lambda = \frac{hc}{12{\cdot}75 \text{ eV}}$$

$$= \frac{1242 \text{ eV nm}}{12{\cdot}75 \text{ eV}} = 97{\cdot}5 \text{ nm}.$$

9. *The energy needed to detach the electron of a hydrogen-like ion in ground state is 4 rydberg. (a) What is the wavelength of the radiation emitted when the electron jumps from the first excited state to the ground state ? (b) What is the radius of the first orbit for this atom ?*

Solution : (a) In energy units, 1 rydberg = 13·6 eV. The energy needed to detach the electron is $4 \times 13{\cdot}6$ eV. The energy in the ground state is, therefore, $E_1 = -4 \times 13{\cdot}6$ eV. The energy of the first excited state $(n = 2)$ is $E_2 = \frac{E_1}{4} = -13{\cdot}6$ eV. The energy difference is $E_2 - E_1 = 3 \times 13{\cdot}6 \text{ eV} = 40{\cdot}8$ eV. The wavelength of the radiation emitted is

$$\lambda = \frac{hc}{\Delta E}$$

$$= \frac{1242 \text{ eV nm}}{40{\cdot}8 \text{ eV}} = 30{\cdot}4 \text{ nm}.$$

(b) The energy of a hydrogen-like ion in ground state is $E = Z^2 E_0$ where Z = atomic number and $E_0 = -13{\cdot}6$ eV. Thus, $Z = 2$. The radius of the first orbit is $\frac{a_0}{Z}$ where $a_0 = 53$ pm. Thus,

$$r = \frac{53 \text{ pm}}{2} = 26{\cdot}5 \text{ pm}.$$

10. *A hydrogen sample is prepared in a particular excited state A. Photons of energy 2·55 eV get absorbed into the sample to take some of the electrons to a further excited state B. Find the quantum numbers of the states A and B.*

Solution : The allowed energies of hydrogen atoms are

$$E_1 = -13{\cdot}6 \text{ eV}$$

$$E_2 = -3{\cdot}4 \text{ eV}$$

$$E_3 = -1{\cdot}5 \text{ eV}$$

$$E_4 = -0{\cdot}85 \text{ eV}$$

$$E_5 = -0{\cdot}54 \text{ eV}.$$

We see that a difference of 2·55 eV can only be absorbed in transition $n = 2$ to $n = 4$. So the state A has quantum number 2 and the state B has quantum number 4.

11. *(a) Find the maximum wavelength λ_0 of light which can ionize a hydrogen atom in its ground state. (b) Light of wavelength λ_0 is incident on a hydrogen atom which is in its first excited state. Find the kinetic energy of the electron coming out.*

Solution : (a) To ionize a hydrogen atom in ground state, a minimum of 13·6 eV energy should be given to it. A photon of light should have this much of energy in order to ionize a hydrogen atom. Thus,

$$\frac{hc}{\lambda_0} = 13{\cdot}6 \text{ eV}$$

or,
$$\lambda_0 = \frac{1242 \text{ eV nm}}{13{\cdot}6 \text{ eV}} = 91{\cdot}3 \text{ nm}.$$

(b) The energy of the hydrogen atom in its first excited state is $-\frac{13{\cdot}6 \text{ eV}}{4} = -3{\cdot}4$ eV. Thus, 3·4 eV of energy is needed to take the electron out of the atom. The energy of a photon of the light of wavelength λ_0 is 13·6 eV. Thus, the electron coming out will have a kinetic energy 13·6 eV − 3·4 eV = 10·2 eV.

12. *Derive an expression for the magnetic field at the site of the nucleus in a hydrogen atom due to the circular motion of the electron. Assume that the atom is in its ground state and give the answer in terms of fundamental constants.*

Solution : We have

$$\frac{mv^2}{r} = \frac{e^2}{4\pi\varepsilon_0 r^2}$$

or,
$$v^2 r = \frac{e^2}{4\pi\varepsilon_0 m} \cdot \quad \text{... (i)}$$

From Bohr's quantization rule, in ground state,

$$vr = \frac{h}{2\pi m} \cdot \quad \text{... (ii)}$$

From (i) and (ii),

$$v = \frac{e^2}{2\varepsilon_0 h} \quad \text{... (iii)}$$

and
$$r = \frac{\varepsilon_0 h^2}{\pi m e^2} \cdot \quad \text{... (iv)}$$

As the electron moves along a circle, it crosses any point on the circle $\frac{v}{2\pi r}$ times per unit time. The charge crossing per unit time, that is the current, is $i = \frac{ev}{2\pi r} \cdot$ The magnetic field at the centre due to this circular current is

$$B = \frac{\mu_0 i}{2r} = \frac{\mu_0 ev}{4\pi r^2} \cdot$$

From (iii) and (iv),

$$B = \frac{\mu_0 e}{4\pi} \frac{e^2}{2\varepsilon_0 h} \times \frac{\pi^2 m^2 e^4}{\varepsilon_0^2 h^4}$$

$$= \frac{\mu_0 e^7 \pi m^2}{8\varepsilon_0^3 h^5} \cdot$$

13. *A lithium atom has three electrons. Assume the following simple picture of the atom. Two electrons move close to the nucleus making up a spherical cloud around it and the third moves outside this cloud in a circular orbit. Bohr's model can be used for the motion of this third electron but $n = 1$ states are not available to it. Calculate the ionization energy of lithium in ground state using the above picture.*

Solution : In this picture, the third electron moves in the field of a total charge $+3e - 2e = +e$. Thus, the energies are the same as that of hydrogen atoms. The lowest energy is

$$E_2 = \frac{E_1}{4} = \frac{-13{\cdot}6 \text{ eV}}{4} = -3{\cdot}4 \text{ eV}.$$

Thus, the ionization energy of the atom in this picture is 3·4 eV.

14. *A particle known as μ-meson, has a charge equal to that of an electron and mass 208 times the mass of the electron. It moves in a circular orbit around a nucleus of charge +3 e. Take the mass of the nucleus to be infinite. Assuming that the Bohr's model is applicable to this system, (a) derive an expression for the radius of the nth Bohr orbit, (b) find the value of n for which the radius of the orbit is approximately the same as that of* *the first Bohr orbit for a hydrogen atom and (c) find the wavelength of the radiation emitted when the μ-meson jumps from the third orbit to the first orbit.*

Solution : (a) We have,

$$\frac{mv^2}{r}=\frac{Ze^2}{4\pi\varepsilon_0 r^2}$$

or, $$v^2 r=\frac{Ze^2}{4\pi\varepsilon_0 m} \qquad \text{... (i)}$$

The quantization rule is $vr=\dfrac{nh}{2\pi m}$.

The radius is $$r=\frac{(vr)^2}{v^2 r}=\frac{n^2h^2}{4\pi^2m^2}\frac{4\pi\varepsilon_0 m}{Ze^2}$$

$$=\frac{n^2h^2\varepsilon_0}{Z\pi me^2}. \qquad \text{... (ii)}$$

For the given system, $Z=3$ and $m=208\ m_e$.

Thus $$r_\mu=\frac{n^2h^2\varepsilon_0}{624\pi m_e e^2}.$$

(b) From (ii), the radius of the first Bohr orbit for the hydrogen atom is

$$r_h=\frac{h^2\varepsilon_0}{\pi m_e e^2}.$$

For $r_\mu=r_h$,

$$\frac{n^2h^2\varepsilon_0}{624\pi m_e e^2}=\frac{h^2\varepsilon_0}{\pi m_e e^2}$$

or, $$n^2=624$$

or, $$n\approx 25.$$

(c) From (i), the kinetic energy of the atom is

$$\frac{mv^2}{2}=\frac{Ze^2}{8\pi\varepsilon_0 r}$$

and the potential energy is $-\dfrac{Ze^2}{4\pi\varepsilon_0 r}$.

The total energy is $E_n=-\dfrac{Ze^2}{8\pi\varepsilon_0 r}$.

Using (ii),

$$E_n=-\frac{Z^2\pi me^4}{8\pi\varepsilon_0^2 n^2h^2}=-\frac{9\times 208\ m_e e^4}{8\varepsilon_0^2 n^2h^2}$$

$$=\frac{1872}{n^2}\left(-\frac{m_e e^4}{8\varepsilon_0^2h^2}\right). \qquad \text{... (iii)}$$

But $\left(-\dfrac{m_e e^4}{8\varepsilon_0^2h^2}\right)$ is the ground state energy of hydrogen atom and hence is equal to $-13{\cdot}6$ eV.

From (iii), $E_n=-\dfrac{1872}{n^2}\times 13{\cdot}6\ \text{eV}=\dfrac{-25459{\cdot}2\ \text{eV}}{n^2}$.

Thus, $E_1=-25459{\cdot}2$ eV and $E_3=\dfrac{E_1}{9}=-2828{\cdot}8$ eV. The energy difference is $E_3-E_1=22630{\cdot}4$ eV.

The wavelength emitted is

$$\lambda=\frac{hc}{\Delta E}$$

$$=\frac{1242\ \text{eV nm}}{22630{\cdot}4\ \text{eV}}=55\ \text{pm}.$$

15. *Find the wavelengths in a hydrogen spectrum between the range* 500 nm *to* 700 nm.

Solution : The energy of a photon of wavelength 500 nm is

$$\frac{hc}{\lambda}=\frac{1242\ \text{eV nm}}{500\ \text{nm}}=2{\cdot}44\ \text{eV}.$$

The energy of a photon of wavelength 700 nm is

$$\frac{hc}{\lambda}=\frac{1242\ \text{eV nm}}{700\ \text{nm}}=1{\cdot}77\ \text{eV}.$$

The energy difference between the states involved in the transition should, therefore, be between 1·77 eV and 2·44 eV.

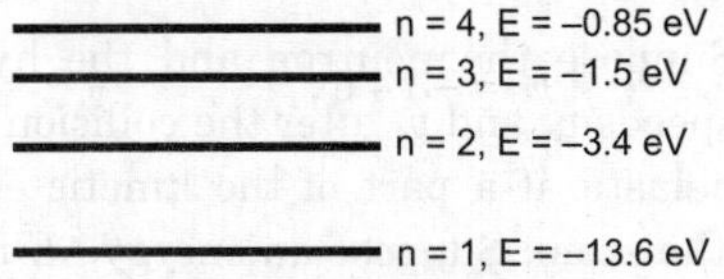

Figure 43-W1

Figure (43-W1) shows some of the energies of hydrogen states. It is clear that only those transitions which end at $n=2$ may emit photons of energy between 1·77 eV and 2·44 eV. Out of these only $n=3\rightarrow n=2$ falls in the proper range. The energy of the photon emitted in the transition $n=3$ to $n=2$ is $\Delta E=(3{\cdot}4-1{\cdot}5)$ eV $=1{\cdot}9$ eV. The wavelength is

$$\lambda=\frac{hc}{\Delta E}$$

$$=\frac{1242\ \text{eV nm}}{1{\cdot}9\ \text{eV}}=654\ \text{nm}.$$

16. *A beam of ultraviolet radiation having wavelength between* 100 nm *and* 200 nm *is incident on a sample of atomic hydrogen gas. Assuming that the atoms are in ground state, which wavelengths will have low intensity in the transmitted beam? If the energy of a photon is equal to the difference between the energies of an excited state and the ground state, it has large probability of being absorbed by an atom in the ground state.*

Solution : The energy of a photon corresponding to $\lambda=100$ nm is

$$\frac{1242\ \text{eV nm}}{100\ \text{nm}}=12{\cdot}42\ \text{eV}$$

and that corresponding to $\lambda=200$ nm is 6·21 eV.

The energy needed to take the atom from the ground state to the first excited state is

$$E_2-E_1=13{\cdot}6\ \text{eV}-3{\cdot}4\ \text{eV}=10{\cdot}2\ \text{eV},$$

to the second excited state is

$$E_3-E_1=13{\cdot}6\ \text{eV}-1{\cdot}5\ \text{eV}=12{\cdot}1\ \text{eV},$$

to the third excited state is

$$E_4 - E_1 = 13{\cdot}6\text{ eV} - 0{\cdot}85\text{ eV} = 12{\cdot}75\text{ eV, etc.}$$

Thus, 10·2 eV photons and 12·1 eV photons have large probability of being absorbed from the given range 6·21 eV to 12·42 eV. The corresponding wavelengths are

$$\lambda_1 = \frac{1242\text{ eV nm}}{10{\cdot}2\text{ eV}} = 122\text{ nm}$$

and $$\lambda_2 = \frac{1242\text{ eV nm}}{12{\cdot}1\text{ eV}} = 103\text{ nm.}$$

These wavelengths will have low intensity in the transmitted beam.

17. *A neutron moving with speed v makes a head-on collision with a hydrogen atom in ground state kept at rest. Find the minimum kinetic energy of the neutron for which inelastic (completely or partially) collision may take place. The mass of neutron ≈ mass of hydrogen = 1·67 × 10⁻²⁷ kg.*

Solution **:** Suppose the neutron and the hydrogen atom move at speeds v_1 and v_2 after the collision. The collision will be inelastic if a part of the kinetic energy is used to excite the atom. Suppose an energy ΔE is used in this way. Using conservation of linear momentum and energy,

$$mv = mv_1 + mv_2 \quad \text{... (i)}$$

and $$\frac{1}{2}mv^2 = \frac{1}{2}mv_1^2 + \frac{1}{2}mv_2^2 + \Delta E. \quad \text{... (ii)}$$

From (i), $$v^2 = v_1^2 + v_2^2 + 2\,v_1v_2.$$

From (ii), $$v^2 = v_1^2 + v_2^2 + \frac{2\Delta E}{m}.$$

Thus, $$2\,v_1v_2 = \frac{2\Delta E}{m}.$$

Hence, $$(v_1 - v_2)^2 = (v_1 + v_2)^2 - 4\,v_1v_2 = v^2 - \frac{4\Delta E}{m}.$$

As $v_1 - v_2$ must be real,

$$v^2 - \frac{4\Delta E}{m} \geq 0$$

or, $$\frac{1}{2}mv^2 > 2\Delta E.$$

The minimum energy that can be absorbed by the hydrogen atom in ground state to go in an excited state is 10·2 eV. Thus, the minimum kinetic energy of the neutron needed for an inelastic collision is

$$\frac{1}{2}mv_{min}^2 = 2 \times 10{\cdot}2\text{ eV} = 20{\cdot}4\text{ eV.}$$

18. *Light corresponding to the transition n = 4 to n = 2 in hydrogen atoms falls on cesium metal (work function = 1·9 eV). Find the maximum kinetic energy of the photoelectrons emitted.*

Solution **:** The energy of the photons emitted in transition $n = 4$ to $n = 2$ is

$$h\nu = 13{\cdot}6\text{ eV}\left[\frac{1}{2^2} - \frac{1}{4^2}\right] = 2{\cdot}55\text{ eV.}$$

The maximum kinetic energy of the photoelectrons is

$$= 2{\cdot}55\text{ eV} - 1{\cdot}9\text{ eV} = 0{\cdot}65\text{ eV.}$$

19. *A small particle of mass m moves in such a way that the potential energy $U = \frac{1}{2}m\omega^2r^2$ where ω is a constant and r is the distance of the particle from the origin. Assuming Bohr's model of quantization of angular momentum and circular orbits, show that radius of the nth allowed orbit is proportional to √n.*

Solution **:** The force at a distance r is

$$F = -\frac{dU}{dr} = -m\omega^2 r. \quad \text{... (i)}$$

Suppose the particle moves along a circle of radius r. The net force on it should be mv^2/r along the radius. Comparing with (i),

$$\frac{mv^2}{r} = m\omega^2 r$$

or, $$v = \omega r. \quad \text{... (ii)}$$

The quantization of angular momentum gives

$$mvr = \frac{nh}{2\pi}$$

or, $$v = \frac{nh}{2\pi mr}. \quad \text{... (iii)}$$

From (ii) and (iii),

$$r = \left(\frac{nh}{2\pi m\omega}\right)^{1/2}.$$

Thus, the radius of the nth orbit is proportional to $\sqrt{n}$.

□

QUESTIONS FOR SHORT ANSWER

1. How many wavelengths are emitted by atomic hydrogen in visible range (380 nm–780 nm) ? In the range 50 nm to 100 nm ?
2. The first excited energy of a He^+ ion is the same as the ground state energy of hydrogen. Is it always true that one of the energies of any hydrogen-like ion will be the same as the ground state energy of a hydrogen atom ?
3. Which wavelengths will be emitted by a sample of atomic hydrogen gas (in ground state) if electrons of energy 12·2 eV collide with the atoms of the gas ?
4. When radiation is passed through a sample of hydrogen gas at room temperature, absorption lines are observed in Lyman series only. Explain.

5. Balmer series was observed and analysed before the other series. Can you suggest a reason for such an order ?

6. What will be the energy corresponding to the first excited state of a hydrogen atom if the potential energy of the atom is taken to be 10 eV when the electron is widely separated from the proton ? Can we still write $E_n = E_1/n^2$, or $r_n = a_0 n^2$?

7. The difference in the frequencies of series limit of Lyman series and Balmer series is equal to the frequency of the first line of the Lyman series. Explain.

8. The numerical value of ionization energy in eV equals the ionization potential in volts. Does the equality hold if these quantities are measured in some other units ?

9. We have stimulated emission and spontaneous emission. Do we also have stimulated absorption and spontaneous absorption ?

10. An atom is in its excited state. Does the probability of its coming to ground state depend on whether the radiation is already present or not ? If yes, does it also depend on the wavelength of the radiation present ?

OBJECTIVE I

1. The minimum orbital angular momentum of the electron in a hydrogen atom is
(a) h (b) $h/2$ (c) $h/2\pi$ (d) h/λ.

2. Three photons coming from excited atomic-hydrogen sample are picked up. Their energies are 12·1 eV, 10·2 eV and 1·9 eV. These photons must come from
(a) a single atom (b) two atoms
(c) three atoms (d) either two atoms or three atoms.

3. Suppose, the electron in a hydrogen atom makes transition from $n = 3$ to $n = 2$ in 10^{-8} s. The order of the torque acting on the electron in this period, using the relation between torque and angular momentum as discussed in the chapter on rotational mechanics is
(a) 10^{-34} N m (b) 10^{-24} N m
(c) 10^{-42} N m (d) 10^{-8} N m.

4. In which of the following transitions will the wavelength be minimum ?
(a) $n = 5$ to $n = 4$ (b) $n = 4$ to $n = 3$
(c) $n = 3$ to $n = 2$ (d) $n = 2$ to $n = 1$.

5. In which of the following systems will the radius of the first orbit ($n = 1$) be minimum ?
(a) Hydrogen atom (b) Deuterium atom
(c) Singly ionized helium (d) Doubly ionized lithium.

6. In which of the following systems will the wavelength corresponding to $n = 2$ to $n = 1$ be minimum ?
(a) Hydrogen atom (b) Deuterium atom
(c) Singly ionized helium (d) Doubly ionized lithium.

7. Which of the following curves may represent the speed of the electron in a hydrogen atom as a function of the principal quantum number n ?

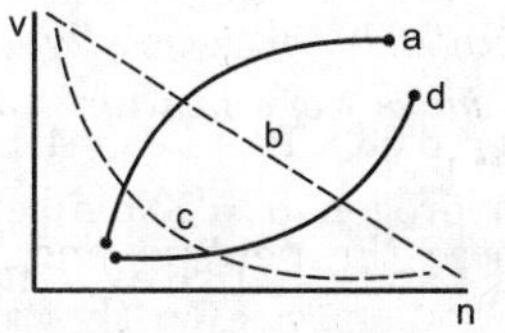

Figure 43-Q1

8. As one considers orbits with higher values of n in a hydrogen atom, the electric potential energy of the atom
(a) decreases (b) increases
(c) remains the same (d) does not increase.

9. The energy of an atom (or ion) in its ground state is –54·4 eV. It may be
(a) hydrogen (b) deuterium (c) He^+ (d) Li^{++}.

10. The radius of the shortest orbit in a one-electron system is 18 pm. It may be
(a) hydrogen (b) deuterium (c) He^+ (d) Li^{++}.

11. A hydrogen atom in ground state absorbs 10·2 eV of energy. The orbital angular momentum of the electron is increased by
(a) $1·05 \times 10^{-34}$ J s (b) $2·11 \times 10^{-34}$ J s
(c) $3·16 \times 10^{-34}$ J s (d) $4·22 \times 10^{-34}$ J s.

12. Which of the following parameters are the same for all hydrogen-like atoms and ions in their ground states ?
(a) Radius of the orbit (b) Speed of the electron
(c) Energy of the atom
(d) Orbital angular momentum of the electron

13. In a laser tube, all the photons
(a) have same wavelength (b) have same energy
(c) move in same direction (d) move with same speed.

OBJECTIVE II

1. In a laboratory experiment on emission from atomic hydrogen in a discharge tube, only a small number of lines are observed whereas a large number of lines are present in the hydrogen spectrum of a star. This is because in a laboratory
(a) the amount of hydrogen taken is much smaller than that present in the star
(b) the temperature of hydrogen is much smaller than that of the star
(c) the pressure of hydrogen is much smaller than that of the star
(d) the gravitational pull is much smaller than that in the star.

2. An electron with kinetic energy 5 eV is incident on a hydrogen atom in its ground state. The collision
(a) must be elastic (b) may be partially elastic
(c) must be completely inelastic
(d) may be completely inelastic.

3. Which of the following products in a hydrogen atom are independent of the principal quantum number n? The symbols have their usual meanings.
(a) vn (b) Er (c) En (d) vr

4. Let A_n be the area enclosed by the nth orbit in a hydrogen atom. The graph of ln (A_n/A_1) against ln(n)
(a) will pass through the origin
(b) will be a straight line with slope 4
(c) will be a monotonically increasing nonlinear curve
(d) will be a circle.

5. Ionization energy of a hydrogen-like ion A is greater than that of another hydrogen-like ion B. Let r, u, E and L represent the radius of the orbit, speed of the electron, energy of the atom and orbital angular momentum of the electron respectively. In ground state
(a) $r_A > r_B$ (b) $u_A > u_B$ (c) $E_A > E_B$ (d) $L_A > L_B$.

6. When a photon stimulates the emission of another photon, the two photons have
(a) same energy (b) same direction
(c) same phase (d) same wavelength.

EXERCISES

Planck constant $h = 6{\cdot}63 \times 10^{-34}$ Js $= 4{\cdot}14 \times 10^{-15}$ eVs, first Bohr radius of hydrogen $a_0 = 53$ pm, energy of hydrogen atom in ground state $= -13{\cdot}6$ eV, Rydberg's constant $= 1{\cdot}097 \times 10^{7}\ \text{m}^{-1}$.

1. The Bohr radius is given by $a_0 = \dfrac{\varepsilon_0 h^2}{\pi m e^2}$. Verify that the RHS has dimensions of length.

2. Find the wavelength of the radiation emitted by hydrogen in the transitions (a) $n = 3$ to $n = 2$, (b) $n = 5$ to $n = 4$ and (c) $n = 10$ to $n = 9$.

3. Calculate the smallest wavelength of radiation that may be emitted by (a) hydrogen, (b) He^+ and (c) Li^{++}.

4. Evaluate Rydberg constant by putting the values of the fundamental constants in its expression.

5. Find the binding energy of a hydrogen atom in the state $n = 2$.

6. Find the radius and energy of a He^+ ion in the states (a) $n = 1$, (b) $n = 4$ and (c) $n = 10$.

7. A hydrogen atom emits ultraviolet radiation of wavelength 102·5 nm. What are the quantum numbers of the states involved in the transition?

8. (a) Find the first excitation potential of He^+ ion. (b) Find the ionization potential of Li^{++} ion.

9. A group of hydrogen atoms are prepared in $n = 4$ states. List the wavelengths that are emitted as the atoms make transitions and return to $n = 2$ states.

10. A positive ion having just one electron ejects it if a photon of wavelength 228 Å or less is absorbed by it. Identify the ion.

11. Find the maximum Coulomb force that can act on the electron due to the nucleus in a hydrogen atom.

12. A hydrogen atom in a state having a binding energy of 0·85 eV makes transition to a state with excitation energy 10·2 eV. (a) Identify the quantum numbers n of the upper and the lower energy states involved in the transition. (b) Find the wavelength of the emitted radiation.

13. Whenever a photon is emitted by hydrogen in Balmer series, it is followed by another photon in Lyman series. What wavelength does this latter photon correspond to?

14. A hydrogen atom in state $n = 6$ makes two successive transitions and reaches the ground state. In the first transition a photon of 1·13 eV is emitted. (a) Find the energy of the photon emitted in the second transition. (b) What is the value of n in the intermediate state?

15. What is the energy of a hydrogen atom in the first excited state if the potential energy is taken to be zero in the ground state?

16. A hot gas emits radiation of wavelengths 46·0 nm, 82·8 nm and 103·5 nm only. Assume that the atoms have only two excited states and the difference between consecutive energy levels decreases as energy is increased. Taking the energy of the highest energy state to be zero, find the energies of the ground state and the first excited state.

17. A gas of hydrogen-like ions is prepared in a particular excited state A. It emits photons having wavelength equal to the wavelength of the first line of the Lyman series together with photons of five other wavelengths. Identify the gas and find the principal quantum number of the state A.

18. Find the maximum angular speed of the electron of a hydrogen atom in a stationary orbit.

19. A spectroscopic instrument can resolve two nearby wavelengths λ and $\lambda + \Delta\lambda$ if $\lambda/\Delta\lambda$ is smaller than 8000. This is used to study the spectral lines of the Balmer series of hydrogen. Approximately how many lines will be resolved by the instrument?

20. Suppose, in certain conditions only those transitions are allowed to hydrogen atoms in which the principal quantum number n changes by 2. (a) Find the smallest wavelength emitted by hydrogen. (b) List the wavelengths emitted by hydrogen in the visible range (380 nm to 780 nm).

21. According to Maxwell's theory of electrodynamics, an electron going in a circle should emit radiation of frequency equal to its frequency of revolution. What

should be the wavelength of the radiation emitted by a hydrogen atom in ground state if this rule is followed ?

22. The average kinetic energy of molecules in a gas at temperature T is 1·5 kT. Find the temperature at which the average kinetic energy of the molecules of hydrogen equals the binding energy of its atoms. Will hydrogen remain in molecular form at this temperature ? Take $k = 8{\cdot}62 \times 10^{-5}$ eV K^{-1}.

23. Find the temperature at which the average thermal kinetic energy is equal to the energy needed to take a hydrogen atom from its ground state to $n = 3$ state. Hydrogen can now emit red light of wavelength 653·1 nm. Because of Maxwellian distribution of speeds, a hydrogen sample emits red light at temperatures much lower than that obtained from this problem. Assume that hydrogen molecules dissociate into atoms.

24. Average lifetime of a hydrogen atom excited to $n = 2$ state is 10^{-8} s. Find the number of revolutions made by the electron on the average before it jumps to the ground state.

25. Calculate the magnetic dipole moment corresponding to the motion of the electron in the ground state of a hydrogen atom.

26. Show that the ratio of the magnetic dipole moment to the angular momentum ($l = mvr$) is a universal constant for hydrogen-like atoms and ions. Find its value.

27. A beam of light having wavelengths distributed uniformly between 450 nm to 550 nm passes through a sample of hydrogen gas. Which wavelength will have the least intensity in the transmitted beam ?

28. Radiation coming from transitions $n = 2$ to $n = 1$ of hydrogen atoms falls on helium ions in $n = 1$ and $n = 2$ states. What are the possible transitions of helium ions as they absorb energy from the radiation ?

29. A hydrogen atom in ground state absorbs a photon of ultraviolet radiation of wavelength 50 nm. Assuming that the entire photon energy is taken up by the electron, with what kinetic energy will the electron be ejected ?

30. A parallel beam of light of wavelength 100 nm passes through a sample of atomic hydrogen gas in ground state. (a) Assume that when a photon supplies some of its energy to a hydrogen atom, the rest of the energy appears as another photon moving in the same direction as the incident photon. Neglecting the light emitted by the excited hydrogen atoms in the direction of the incident beam, what wavelengths may be observed in the transmitted beam ? (b) A radiation detector is placed near the gas to detect radiation coming perpendicular to the incident beam. Find the wavelengths of radiation that may be detected by the detector.

31. A beam of monochromatic light of wavelength λ ejects photoelectrons from a cesium surface ($\Phi = 1{\cdot}9$ eV). These photoelectrons are made to collide with hydrogen atoms in ground state. Find the maximum value of λ for which (a) hydrogen atoms may be ionized, (b) hydrogen atoms may get excited from the ground state to the first excited state and (c) the excited hydrogen atoms may emit visible light.

32. Electrons are emitted from an electron gun at almost zero velocity and are accelerated by an electric field E through a distance of 1·0 m. The electrons are now scattered by an atomic hydrogen sample in ground state. What should be the minimum value of E so that red light of wavelength 656·3 nm may be emitted by the hydrogen ?

33. A neutron having kinetic energy 12·5 eV collides with a hydrogen atom at rest. Nelgect the difference in mass between the neutron and the hydrogen atom and assume that the neutron does not leave its line of motion. Find the possible kinetic energies of the neutron after the event.

34. A hydrogen atom moving at speed v collides with another hydrogen atom kept at rest. Find the minimum value of v for which one of the atoms may get ionized. The mass of a hydrogen atom $= 1{\cdot}67 \times 10^{-27}$ kg.

35. A neutron moving with a speed v strikes a hydrogen atom in ground state moving towards it with the same speed. Find the minimum speed of the neutron for which inelastic (completely or partially) collision may take place. The mass of neutron $\approx$ mass of hydrogen $= 1{\cdot}67 \times 10^{-27}$ kg.

36. When a photon is emitted by a hydrogen atom, the photon carries a momentum with it. (a) Calculate the momentum carried by the photon when a hydrogen atom emits light of wavelength 656·3 nm. (b) With what speed does the atom recoil during this transition ? Take the mass of the hydrogen atom $= 1{\cdot}67 \times 10^{-27}$ kg. (c) Find the kinetic energy of recoil of the atom.

37. When a photon is emitted from an atom, the atom recoils. The kinetic energy of recoil and the energy of the photon come from the difference in energies between the states involved in the transition. Suppose, a hydrogen atom changes its state from $n = 3$ to $n = 2$. Calculate the fractional change in the wavelength of light emitted, due to the recoil.

38. The light emitted in the transition $n = 3$ to $n = 2$ in hydrogen is called H_α light. Find the maximum work function a metal can have so that H_α light can emit photoelectrons from it.

39. Light from Balmer series of hydrogen is able to eject photoelectrons from a metal. What can be the maximum work function of the metal ?

40. Radiation from hydrogen discharge tube falls on a cesium plate. Find the maximum possible kinetic energy of the photoelectrons. Work function of cesium is 1·9 eV.

41. A filter transmits only the radiation of wavelength greater than 440 nm. Radiation from a hydrogen-discharge tube goes through such a filter and is incident on a metal of work function 2·0 eV. Find the stopping potential which can stop the photoelectrons.

42. The earth revolves round the sun due to gravitational attraction. Suppose that the sun and the earth are point particles with their existing masses and that Bohr's quantization rule for angular momentum is valid in the case of gravitation. (a) Calculate the minimum radius the earth can have for its orbit. (b) What is the value of the principal quantum number n for the present radius ? Mass of the earth = $6{\cdot}0 \times 10^{24}$ kg, mass of the sun = $2{\cdot}0 \times 10^{30}$ kg, earth–sun distance = $1{\cdot}5 \times 10^{11}$ m.

43. Consider a neutron and an electron bound to each other due to gravitational force. Assuming Bohr's quantization rule for angular momentum to be valid in this case, derive an expression for the energy of the neutron–electron system.

44. A uniform magnetic field B exists in a region. An electron projected perpendicular to the field goes in a circle. Assuming Bohr's quantization rule for angular momentum, calculate (a) the smallest possible radius of the electron (b) the radius of the nth orbit and (c) the minimum possible speed of the electron.

45. Suppose in an imaginary world the angular momentum is quantized to be even integral multiples of $h/2\pi$. What is the longest possible wavelength emitted by hydrogen atoms in visible range in such a world according to Bohr's model ?

46. Consider an excited hydrogen atom in state n moving with a velocity $v (v << c)$. It emits a photon in the direction of its motion and changes its state to a lower state m. Apply momentum and energy conservation principles to calculate the frequency ν of the emitted radiation. Compare this with the frequency ν_0 emitted if the atom were at rest.

□

ANSWERS

OBJECTIVE I

1. (c)	2. (d)	3. (b)	4. (d)	5. (d)	6. (d)
7. (c)	8. (b)	9. (c)	10. (d)	11. (a)	12. (d)
13. (d)					

OBJECTIVE II

1. (b)	2. (a)	3. (a), (b)	4. (a), (b)
5. (b)	6. all		

EXERCISES

2. (a) 654 nm (b) 4050 nm (c) 38860 nm
3. (a) 91 nm (b) 23 nm (c) 10 nm
4. $1{\cdot}097 \times 10^{7}\ \text{m}^{-1}$
5. 3·4 eV
6. (a) 0·265 A, –54·4 eV (b) 4·24 A, –3·4 eV
   (c) 26·5 A, –0·544 eV
7. 1 and 3
8. (a) 40·8 V (b) 122·4 V
9. 487 nm, 654 nm, 1910 nm
10. He^{+}
11. $8{\cdot}2 \times 10^{-8}$ N
12. (a) 4, 2 (b) 487 nm
13. 122 nm
14. 12·1 eV, 3
15. 23·8 eV
16. –27 eV, –12 eV
17. He^{+}, 4
18. $4{\cdot}1 \times 10^{16}\ \text{rad s}^{-1}$
19. 38
20. (a) 103 nm (b) 487 nm
21. 45·7 nm
22. $1{\cdot}05 \times 10^{5}$ K
23. $9{\cdot}4 \times 10^{4}$ K
24. $8{\cdot}2 \times 10^{6}$
25. $9{\cdot}2 \times 10^{-24}\ \text{A m}^{-2}$
26. $\dfrac{e}{2m} = 8{\cdot}8 \times 10^{10}\ \text{C kg}^{-1}$
27. 487 nm
28. $n = 2$ to $n = 3$ and $n = 2$ to $n = 4$
29. 11·24 eV
30. (a) 100 nm, 560 nm, 3880 nm
    (b) 103 nm, 121 nm, 654 nm
31. (a) 80 nm (b) 102 nm (c) 89 nm
32. $12{\cdot}1\ \text{Vm}^{-1}$
33. zero
34. $7{\cdot}2 \times 10^{4}\ \text{m s}^{-1}$
35. $3{\cdot}13 \times 10^{4}\ \text{m s}^{-1}$

36. (a) $1{\cdot}0 \times 10^{27}$ kg m s^{-1} (b) $0{\cdot}6$ m s^{-1} (c) $1{\cdot}9 \times 10^{-9}$ eV

37. 10^{-9}

38. 1·9 eV

39. 3·4 eV

40. 11·7 eV

41. 0·55 V

42. (a) $2{\cdot}3 \times 10^{-138}$ m (b) $2{\cdot}5 \times 10^{74}$

43. $-\dfrac{2\pi^2 G^2 m_n^2 m_e^3}{2h^2 n^2}$

44. (a) $\sqrt{\dfrac{h}{2\pi eB}}$ (b) $\sqrt{\dfrac{nh}{2\pi eB}}$ (c) $\sqrt{\dfrac{heB}{2\pi m^2}}$

45. 487 nm

46. $\nu = \nu_0 \left(1 + \dfrac{v}{c}\right)$

□

CHAPTER 44

X-RAYS

44.1 PRODUCTION OF X-RAYS

When highly energetic electrons are made to strike a metal target, electromagnetic radiation comes out. A large part of this radiation has wavelength of the order of 0·1 nm (≈ 1 Å) and is known as *X-ray*.

X-ray was discovered by the German physicist W C Roentgen in 1895. He found that photographic film wrapped light-tight in black paper became exposed when placed near a cathode-ray tube. He concluded that some invisible radiation was coming from the cathode-ray tube which penetrated the black paper to affect the photographic plate. He named this radiation as X-ray because its nature and properties could not be known at that time. In mathematics, we generally use the symbol x for unknown quantities. However, after some calculation we finally get the value of this unknown x. Similarly, we now know about the nature and properties of X-rays.

A device used to produce X-rays is generally called an *X-ray tube.* Figure (41.1) shows a schematic diagram of such a device. This was originally designed by Coolidge and is known as *Coolidge tube* to produce X-rays.

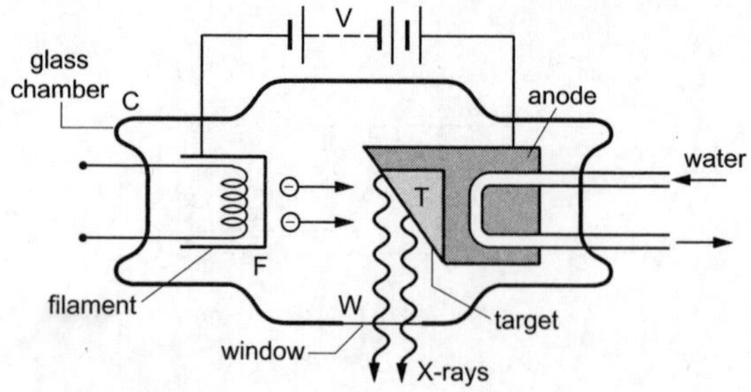

Figure 44.1

A filament F and a metallic target T are fixed in an evacuated glass chamber C. The filament is heated electrically and emits electrons by thermionic emission. A constant potential difference of several kilovolts is maintained between the filament and the target using a DC power supply so that the target is at a higher potential than the filament. The electrons emitted by the filament are, therefore, accelerated by the electric field set up between the filament and the target and hit the target with a very high speed. These electrons are stopped by the target and in the process X-rays are emitted. These X-rays are brought out of the tube through a window W made of thin mica or mylar or some such material which does not absorb X-rays appreciably.

In the process, large amount of heat is developed, and thus an arrangement is provided to cool down the tube continuously by running water.

The exact design of the X-ray tube depends on the type of use for which these X-rays are required.

44.2 CONTINUOUS AND CHARACTERISTIC X-RAYS

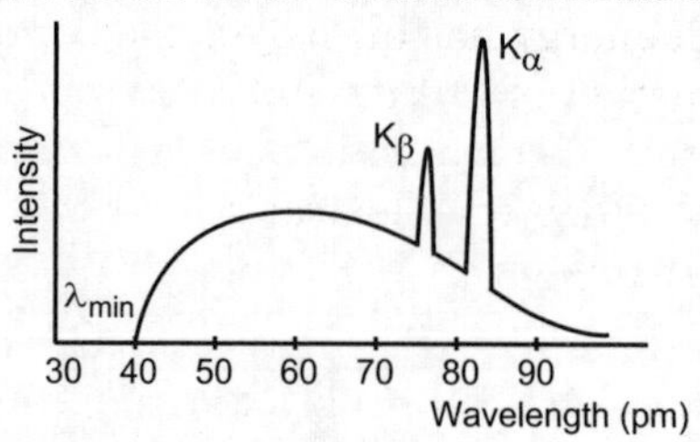

Figure 44.2

If the X-rays coming from a Coolidge tube are examined for the wavelengths present, and the intensity of different wavelength components are measured, we obtain a plot of the nature shown in figure (44.2). We see that there is a minimum wavelength below which no X-ray is emitted. This is called the *cutoff wavelength* or the *threshold wavelength.* The X-rays emitted can be clearly divided in two categories. At certain sharply defined wavelengths, the intensity of X-rays is very large as marked K_α, K_β in figure (44.2). These X-rays are known as *characteristic X-rays.* At other wavelengths the intensity varies gradually and these X-rays are called *continuous X-rays.* Let us examine the origin of these two types of X-rays.

Suppose, the potential difference applied between the target and the filament is V and electrons are emitted by the filament with negligible speed. The electrons are accelerated in their journey from the filament to the target. The kinetic energy of an electron when it hits the target is

$$K = eV. \qquad \dots (44.1)$$

As the electron enters into the target material, it readily loses its kinetic energy and is brought to rest inside the metal. The electron before finally being stopped, makes several collisions with the atoms in the target. At each collision, one of the following two processes may occur:

(a) The kinetic energy of the electron is reduced. A part of this lost kinetic energy is converted into a photon of electromagnetic radiation and the remaining part increases the kinetic energy of the colliding particle of the target. The energy received by the colliding particle goes into heating the target. The electron makes another collision with its reduced energy.

(b) The electron knocks out an inner electron of the atom with which it collides.

The fraction of kinetic energy appearing as the energy of a photon varies from collision to collision. In a certain collision, the electron may lose its entire kinetic energy to bring out a photon or it may not create a photon at all. Thus, the energy of the photon created can be anything between 0 and eV depending on how much energy has already been lost to the target and what fraction of the available energy is converted into the photon. The maximum energy of such a photon can be $E = eV$ when the electron converts all its kinetic energy into a photon in the first encounter itself.

The wavelength of the X-ray and the energy of the corresponding photon are related through the equation

$$\lambda = \frac{hc}{E}. \qquad \dots (44.2)$$

As E can take any value between zero and eV, the wavelength λ can take any value between infinity and hc/eV. This explains the origin of continuous X-rays and the cutoff wavelength. We have,

$$\lambda_{min} = \frac{hc}{eV}. \qquad \dots (44.3)$$

We see that the cutoff wavelength λ_{min} depends only on the accelerating voltage V applied between the target and the filament. It does not depend on the material of the target.

We shall now discuss what happens if the electron knocks out an inner electron from the atom with which it collides. The electrons in an atom occupy different quantum states characterized by the quantum numbers n, l, m_l, m_s. The energy primarily depends on the principal quantum number n. The two electrons corresponding to $n = 1$ are said to be in K shell, those corresponding to $n = 2$ are in L shell, etc. Suppose, the incident electron knocks out an electron from the K shell. This will create a vacancy in the K shell in the sense that now there is only one electron with $n = 1$, whereas two could be accommodated by Pauli exclusion principle. An electron from a higher energy state may make a transition to this vacant state. When such a transition takes place, the difference of energy ΔE is converted into an X-ray photon of wavelength $\lambda = hc/\Delta E$. *X-rays emitted due to electronic transition from a higher energy state to a vacancy created in the K shell are called K X-rays.*

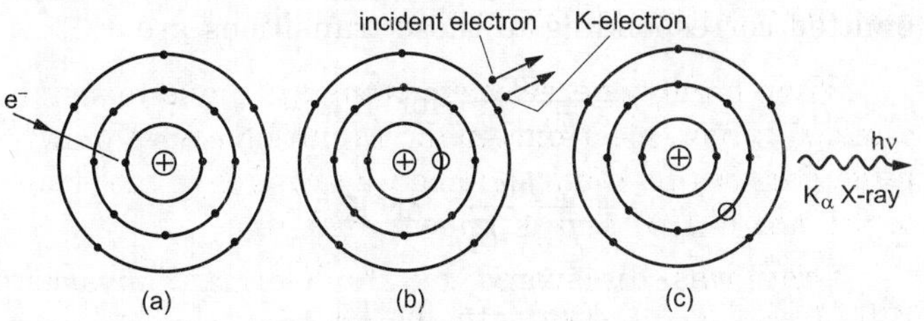

Figure 44.3

Figure (44.3) shows the process schematically. If an electron from the L shell (i.e., with $n = 2$) makes transition to the vacant state in the K shell, the X-ray emitted is called K_α *X-ray*. If an electron from the M shell makes transition to the K shell, a K_β X-ray is emitted. Similarly one defines K_γ X-ray. If a photon of K_α X-ray is emitted, the vacancy in the K shell is filled up but a vacancy is created in the L shell. This vacancy can be filled up by a transition of electron from higher shells giving L X-ray. If an electron jumps from the M shell to the vacant state in the L shell, we obtain L_α X-ray. If the vacancy in L shell is filled up by an electron of N shell ($n = 4$), L_β X-ray is emitted, and so on.

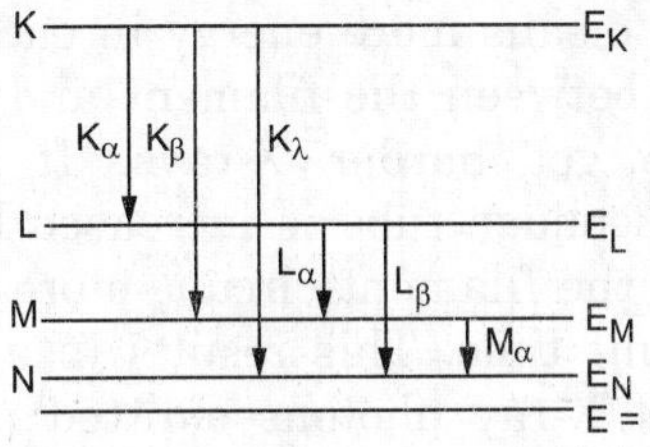

Figure 44.4

Figure (44.4) shows the energy levels of the atom when one electron is knocked out. The lowest line corresponds to the atom with all its electrons intact. This has been taken as zero energy. The energy level with label E_K is the energy of the atom when an electron from the K shell is knocked out. Similar is the interpretation for E_L, E_M, E_N, etc. Note the convention of choosing $E = 0$ in the ground state. In hydrogen atom we had chosen $E = 0$ when the electron was knocked out. The ground state of hydrogen atom then had an energy of −13·6 eV. Here the convention is opposite and the energy in the ground state is chosen to be zero. The energy in the ionized state is then positive. As the electrons in K shell are most tightly bound, maximum energy is to be given to the atom to knock out an electron from the K shell. That is why, in figure (44.4), the energy level of the atom with a vacancy in the K shell is shown highest.

The energies E_K, E_L, ..., etc., are characteristic properties of the material. For different materials, the values of these energies will be different. The values of $E_K - E_L$, $E_L - E_M$, etc., also have definite values for a given material. The wavelengths of the X-rays emitted corresponding to these transitions are

$$\lambda = \frac{hc}{E_K - E_L} \text{ for } K_\alpha,$$

$$\lambda = \frac{hc}{E_K - E_M} \text{ for } K_\beta,$$

$$\lambda = \frac{hc}{E_L - E_M} \text{ for } L_\alpha,$$

etc. These wavelengths, therefore, have definite values for a particular material. The X-rays emitted in this way are the characteristic X-rays shown in figure (44.2). They are so named because their wavelengths may be used to identify the element from which they originate.

44.3 SOFT AND HARD X-RAYS

If the accelerating voltage applied between the filament and the target is increased, the cutoff wavelength λ_{min} decreases further (equation 44.3). The X-rays of low wavelengths are called *hard X-rays* and those of large wavelength are called *soft X-rays*. Hard and soft are simply relative terms. In terms of energy, harder X-rays means more energy in each photon. So, if the voltage between the filament and the target is increased, we get harder X-rays. If the filament current in a Coolidge tube is increased by increasing the voltage in the filament circuit, more electrons are emitted per unit time. This results in an increase in the number of X-ray photons emitted per unit time and hence the intensity of X-rays is increased. The cutoff wavelength λ_{min} remains unchanged as the maximum kinetic energy of the electrons reaching the target is not affected by the filament current.

44.4 MOSELEY'S LAW

Moseley's experiments (1913–1914) on characteristic X-rays played a very important role in developing the concept of atomic number. In those days, the elements were arranged in periodic table in the increasing order of atomic weight. The periodicity in chemical properties of elements was brought out from such arrangement, though some anomalies were present. Bohr had proposed his model in the same year and there was no concept of distribution of electrons in different energy levels. During those days, Moseley measured the frequencies of characteristic X-rays from a large number of elements and plotted the square root of the frequency against its position number in the periodic table. He discovered that the plot is very close to a straight line. A portion of Moseley's plot is shown in figure (44.5) where $\sqrt{\nu}$ of K_α X-rays is plotted against the position number. From this linear relation, Moseley concluded that there must be a fundamental property of the atom which increases by regular steps as one moves from one element to the other. This quantity was later identified to be the number of protons in the nucleus and was referred to as the *atomic number*.

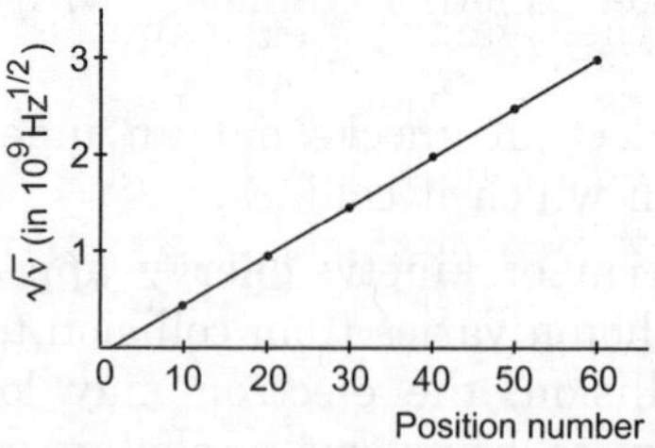

Figure 44.5

Thus, elements should be arranged in the ascending order of atomic number and not of atomic weight. This removed several discrepancies existing in the periodic table. For example, nickel has atomic weight 58·7 whereas the atomic weight of cobalt is 58·9. However, the frequency of K_α X-ray from cobalt is less than the frequency of K_α X-ray from nickel. Thus, Moseley rearranged the sequence as Co, Ni instead of Ni, Co. Similarly, several other rearrangements were made.

Moseley's observations can be mathematically expressed as

$$\sqrt{\nu} = a(Z - b) \quad \text{... (44.4)}$$

where a and b are constants. This relation is known as *Moseley's law*. We can understand Moseley's law qualitatively from Bohr's atomic model.

Consider an atom from which an electron from the K shell has been knocked out. Consider an electron from the L shell which is about to make a transition to the vacant site. It finds the nucleus of charge Ze screened by the spherical cloud of the remaining one electron in the K shell (figure 44.6). If we neglect the effect of the outer electrons and the other L electrons, the electron making the transition finds a charge $(Z - 1)e$ at the centre. One, therefore, may expect Bohr's model to give reasonable results if Z is replaced by $Z - b$ with $b \approx 1$.

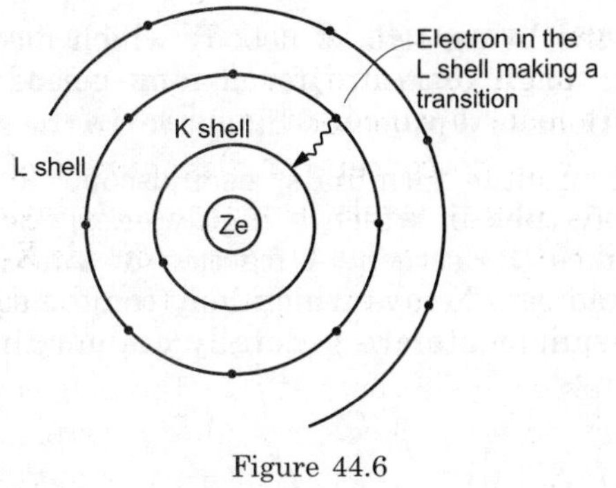

Figure 44.6

According to Bohr's model, the energy released during the transition from $n = 2$ to $n = 1$ is given by

$$\Delta E = h\nu = Rhc(Z-b)^2\left(\frac{1}{1^2}-\frac{1}{2^2}\right)$$

so that $$\sqrt{\nu} = \sqrt{\frac{3Rc}{4}}\,(Z-b)$$

which is the same as equation (44.4) with $a = \sqrt{3Rc/4}$.

Moseley was killed in the First World War at an early age of 27 years.

44.5 BRAGG'S LAW

X-rays are electromagnetic waves of short wavelengths and may be diffracted by suitable diffracting centres. However, the diffraction effects are appreciable only when the diffracting apertures are of the order of the wavelength, i.e., of the order of 0·1 nm. This is almost the size of an atom and it is difficult to construct slits with such small gaps so that X-rays can be appreciably diffracted.

In solid crystals, atoms are arranged in fairly regular pattern with interatomic gaps of the order of 0·1 nm. Common salt is an example of such a crystalline solid. Almost all the metals at ordinary temperature are crystalline. These metals may act as natural three-dimensional gratings for the diffraction of X-rays.

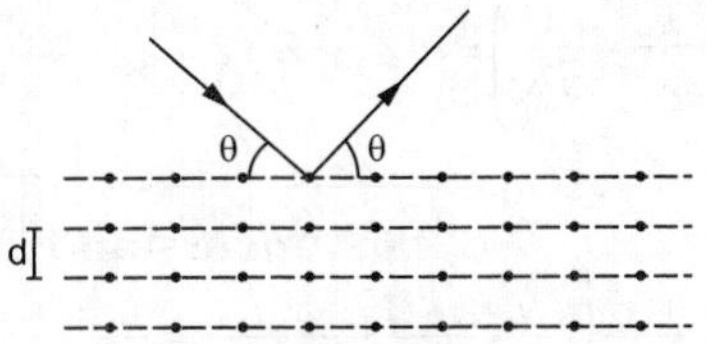

Figure 44.7

The structure of a solid can be viewed as a series of parallel planes of atoms separated by a distance d (figure 44.7). Suppose, an X-ray beam is incident on a solid, making an angle θ with the planes of the atoms. These X-rays are diffracted by different atoms and the diffracted rays interfere. In certain directions, the interference is constructive and we obtain strong reflected X-rays. The analysis shows that there will be a strong reflected X-ray beam only if

$$2d\sin\theta = n\lambda \qquad \ldots (44.5)$$

where n is an integer. For monochromatic X-rays, λ is fixed and there are some specific angles θ_1, θ_2, θ_3, ..., etc., corresponding to $n = 1, 2, 3, \ldots$, etc., in equation (44.5). Thus, if the X-rays are incident at one of these angles, they are reflected; otherwise they are absorbed. When they are reflected, the laws of reflection are obeyed, i.e., (a) the angle of incidence is equal to the angle of reflection and (b) the incident ray, the reflected ray and the normal to the reflecting plane are coplanar.

Equation (44.5) is known as *Bragg's law*.

By using a monochromatic X-ray beam and noting the angles of strong reflection, the interplanar spacing d and several informations about the structure of the solid can be obtained.

44.6 PROPERTIES AND USES OF X-RAYS

As discussed earlier, X-rays are electromagnetic waves of short wavelengths. Accordingly, it has many properties common with light. Here are some of the properties of X-rays.

(a) X-rays travel in straight lines in vacuum at a speed equal to that of light (3×10^8 m/s).

(b) X-rays are diffracted by crystals in accordance with Bragg's law.

(c) X-rays are not deflected by electric or magnetic field as it contains no charged particles.

(d) X-rays affect a photographic plate more strongly than visible light.

(e) When incident on certain materials such as barium platinocyanide, X-rays cause fluorescence (light is emitted from the material).

(f) When passed through a gas, X-rays ionize the molecules of the gas.

(g) X-rays can penetrate into several metals and other materials. Thus, they can pass through small thicknesses of aluminium, woods, plastics, human flesh etc. They are stopped by materials of high density and high atomic number.

The penetrating power of X-ray has made it popular and familiar to the general public. It is used extensively to detect diseases inside the body. It passes quite freely through the flesh but is stopped by the bones. So it can photograph the bones inside the body on a photographic film. Such a photograph is called a *radiograph*. This is used to detect and study bone fractures due to an accident. Chest radiographs are used to study diseases in lungs. Dentists also use X-ray to study teeth-decay. X-ray is also used in cancer therapy.

X-ray is used in industry and material science research. It can detect structural defects, fault of joints, welding etc. X-ray machines are used to inspect suitcases, wooden boxes etc. without opening them and can be typically found at the custom, security counters at airports etc.

X-ray can be used to detect diseases and to cure them. At the same time, random and excess exposure to X-ray may induce diseases. X-ray has a damaging effect on the living cells of a body which may lead to cell-death. High exposure for a long period (say for years) may lead to cancer or genetic defects.

TV, computer terminals, oscilloscopes etc. use a cathode-ray tube in which a highly energetic electron beam strikes the screen. A fraction of kinetic energy is converted into X-rays which may come out. Screens of these equipments are generally designed to absorb these X-rays.

Worked Out Examples

1. *Find the maximum frequency of the X-rays emitted by an X-ray tube operating at* 30 kV.

Solution : For maximum frequency, the total kinetic energy (eV) should be converted into an X-ray photon. Thus,

$$h\nu = eV$$

or, $$\nu = \frac{e}{h}V$$

$$= \frac{e \times 30 \times 10^{3}\ \mathrm{V}}{4{\cdot}14 \times 10^{-15}\ \mathrm{eV\text{–}s}}$$

$$= \frac{30}{4{\cdot}14} \times 10^{18}\ \mathrm{Hz} \approx 7{\cdot}2 \times 10^{18}\ \mathrm{Hz}.$$

2. *An X-ray tube operates at* 20 kV. *A particular electron loses* 5% *of its kinetic energy to emit an X-ray photon at the first collision. Find the wavelength corresponding to this photon.*

Solution : Kinetic energy acquired by the electron is

$$K = eV = 20 \times 10^{3}\ \mathrm{eV}.$$

The energy of the photon

$$= 0{\cdot}05 \times 20 \times 10^{3}\ \mathrm{eV} = 10^{3}\ \mathrm{eV}.$$

Thus, $$\frac{hc}{\lambda} = 10^{3}\ \mathrm{eV}$$

or, $$\lambda = \frac{hc}{10^{3}\ \mathrm{eV}}$$

$$= \frac{(4{\cdot}14 \times 10^{-15}\ \mathrm{eVs}) \times (3 \times 10^{8}\ \mathrm{m\ s^{-1}})}{10^{3}\ \mathrm{eV}}$$

$$= \frac{1242\ \mathrm{eV\ nm}}{10^{3}\ \mathrm{eV}} = 1{\cdot}24\ \mathrm{nm}.$$

3. *An X-ray tube is operated at* 20 kV *and the current through the tube is* 0·5 mA. *Find (a) the number of electrons hitting the target per second, (b) the energy falling on the target per second as the kinetic energy of the electrons and (c) the cutoff wavelength of the X-rays emitted.*

Solution : (a) $$i = ne = 0{\cdot}5 \times 10^{-3}\ \mathrm{A}$$

or, $$n = \frac{0{\cdot}5 \times 10^{-3}\ \mathrm{A}}{1{\cdot}6 \times 10^{-19}\ \mathrm{C}} = 3{\cdot}1 \times 10^{15}.$$

(b) The kinetic energy of an electron reaching the target is $K = eV$. The energy falling on the target per second

$$= n\,eV = iV = (0{\cdot}5 \times 10^{-3}\ \mathrm{A}) \times (20 \times 10^{3}\ \mathrm{V})$$

$$= 10\ \mathrm{J\ s^{-1}}.$$

(c) $$\frac{hc}{\lambda_{\min}} = eV$$

or, $$\lambda_{\min} = \frac{hc}{eV}$$

$$= \frac{1242\ \mathrm{eV\ nm}}{e(20 \times 10^{3}\ \mathrm{V})} = 0{\cdot}062\ \mathrm{nm}.$$

4. *Find the constants a and b in Moseley's equation* $\sqrt{\nu} = a(Z - b)$ *from the following data.*

Element	Z	Wavelength of K_α X-ray
Mo	42	71 pm
Co	27	178·5 pm

Solution : Moseley's equation is

$$\sqrt{\nu} = a(Z - b).$$

Thus, $$\sqrt{\frac{c}{\lambda_1}} = a(Z_1 - b) \qquad \text{... (i)}$$

and $$\sqrt{\frac{c}{\lambda_2}} = a(Z_2 - b). \qquad \text{... (ii)}$$

From (i) and (ii),

$$\sqrt{c}\left(\frac{1}{\sqrt{\lambda_1}} - \frac{1}{\sqrt{\lambda_2}}\right) = a(Z_1 - Z_2)$$

or, $$a = \frac{\sqrt{c}}{(Z_1 - Z_2)}\left(\frac{1}{\sqrt{\lambda_1}} - \frac{1}{\sqrt{\lambda_2}}\right)$$

$$= \frac{(3 \times 10^{8}\ \mathrm{m\ s^{-1}})^{1/2}}{42 - 27}\left[\frac{1}{(71 \times 10^{-12}\ \mathrm{m})^{1/2}} - \frac{1}{(178{\cdot}5 \times 10^{-12}\ \mathrm{m})^{1/2}}\right]$$

$$= 5{\cdot}0 \times 10^{7}\ (\mathrm{Hz})^{1/2}.$$

Dividing (i) by (ii),

$$\sqrt{\frac{\lambda_2}{\lambda_1}} = \frac{Z_1 - b}{Z_2 - b}$$

or, $$\sqrt{\frac{178{\cdot}5}{71}} = \frac{42 - b}{27 - b}$$

or, $$b = 1{\cdot}37.$$

5. *The* K_α *X-ray of molybdenum has wavelength* 71 pm. *If the energy of a molybdenum atom with a K electron knocked out is* 23·32 keV, *what will be the energy of this atom when an L electron is knocked out ?*

Solution : K_α X-ray results from the transition of an electron from L shell to K shell. If the energy of the atom with a vacancy in the K shell is E_K and the energy with a vacancy in the L shell is E_L, the energy of the photon emitted is $E_K - E_L$. The energy of the 71 pm photon is

$$E = \frac{hc}{\lambda}$$

$$= \frac{1242 \text{ eV nm}}{71 \times 10^{-3} \text{ nm}} = 17·5 \text{ keV}.$$

Thus, $E_K - E_L = 17·5$ keV

or, $E_L = E_K - 17·5$ keV

$= 23·32$ keV $- 17·5$ keV $= 5·82$ keV.

6. *Show that the frequency of* K_β *X-ray of a material equals the sum of the frequencies of* K_α *and* L_α *X-rays of the same material.*

Solution :

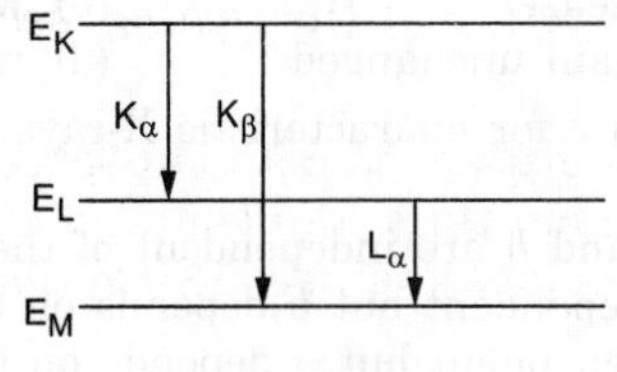

Figure 44-W1

The energy level diagram of an atom with one electron knocked out is shown in figure (44-W1).

Energy of K_α X-ray is $E_{K_\alpha} = E_K - E_L$

of K_β X-ray is $E_{K_\beta} = E_K - E_M$,

and of L_α X-ray is $E_{L_\alpha} = E_L - E_M$.

Thus, $E_{K_\beta} = E_{K_\alpha} + E_{L_\alpha}$

or, $h\nu_{K_\beta} = h\nu_{K_\alpha} + h\nu_{L_\alpha}$

or, $\nu_{K_\beta} = \nu_{K_\alpha} + \nu_{L_\alpha}$.

□

QUESTIONS FOR SHORT ANSWER

1. When a Coolidge tube is operated for some time it becomes hot. Where does the heat come from ?

2. In a Coolidge tube, electrons strike the target and stop inside it. Does the target get more and more negatively charged as time passes ?

3. Can X-rays be used for photoelectric effect ?

4. Can X-rays be polarized ?

5. X-ray and visible light travel at the same speed in vacuum. Do they travel at the same speed in glass ?

6. Characteristic X-rays may be used to identify the element from which they are coming. Can continuous X-rays be used for this purpose ?

7. Is it possible that in a Coolidge tube characterstic L_α X-rays are emitted but not K_α X-rays ?

8. Can L_α X-ray of one material have shorter wavelength than K_α X-ray of another ?

9. Can a hydrogen atom emit characteristic X-ray ?

10. Why is exposure to X-ray injurious to health but exposure to visible light is not, when both are electromagnetic waves ?

OBJECTIVE I

1. X-ray beam can be deflected
(a) by an electric field (b) by a magnetic field
(c) by an electric field as well as by a magnetic field
(d) neither by an electric field nor by a magnetic field.

2. Consider a photon of continuous X-ray coming from a Coolidge tube. Its energy comes from
(a) the kinetic energy of the striking electron
(b) the kinetic energy of the free electrons of the target
(c) the kinetic energy of the ions of the target
(d) an atomic transition in the target.

3. The energy of a photon of characteristic X-ray from a Coolidge tube comes from
(a) the kinetic energy of the striking electron
(b) the kinetic energy of the free electrons of the target
(c) the kinetic energy of the ions of the target
(d) an atomic transition in the target.

4. If the potential difference applied to the tube is doubled and the separation between the filament and the target is also doubled, the cutoff wavelength
(a) will remain unchanged (b) will be doubled

(c) will be halved
(d) will become four times the original.

5. If the current in the circuit for heating the filament is increased, the cutoff wavelength
(a) will increase (b) will decrease
(c) will remain unchanged (d) will change.

6. Moseley's law for characteristic X-rays is $\sqrt{\nu} = a(Z - b)$. In this,
(a) both a and b are independent of the material
(b) a is independent but b depends on the material
(c) b is independent but a depends on the material
(d) both a and b depend on the material.

7. Frequencies of K_α X-rays of different materials are measured. Which one of the graphs in figure (44-Q1) may represent the relation between the frequency ν and the atomic number Z.

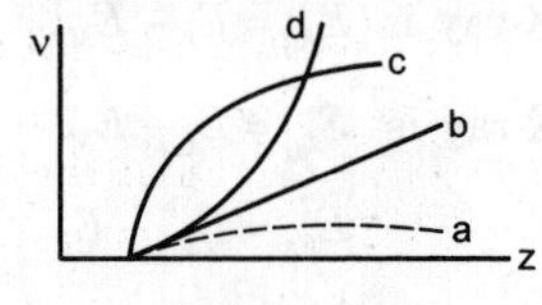

Figure 44-Q1

8. The X-ray beam coming from an X-ray tube
(a) is monochromatic
(b) has all wavelengths smaller than a certain maximum wavelength
(c) has all wavelengths greater than a certain minimum wavelength
(d) has all wavelengths lying between a minimum and a maximum wavelength.

9. One of the following wavelengths is absent and the rest are present in the X-rays coming from a Coolidge tube. Which one is the absent wavelength ?
(a) 25 pm (b) 50 pm (c) 75 pm (d) 100 pm.

10. Figure (44-Q2) shows the intensity–wavelength relations of X-rays coming from two different Coolidge tubes. The solid curve represents the relation for the tube A in which the potential difference between the target and the filament is V_A and the atomic number of the target material is Z_A. These quantities are V_B and Z_B for the other tube. Then,
(a) $V_A > V_B, Z_A > Z_B$ (b) $V_A > V_B, Z_A < Z_B$
(c) $V_A < V_B, Z_A > Z_B$ (d) $V_A < V_B, Z_A < Z_B$.

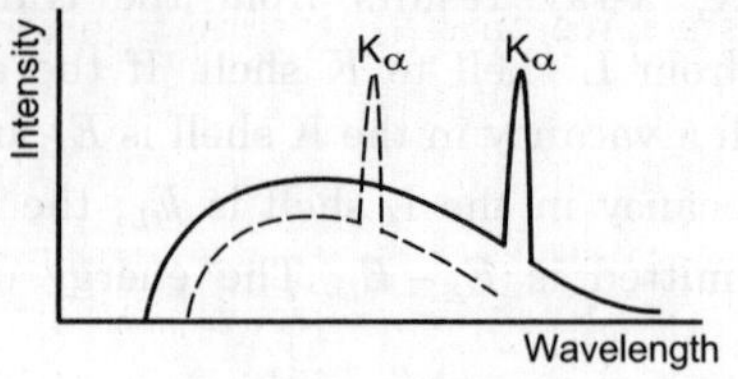

Figure 44-Q2

11. 50% of the X-ray coming from a Coolidge tube is able to pass through a 0·1 mm thick aluminium foil. If the potential difference between the target and the filament is increased, the fraction of the X-ray passing through the same foil will be
(a) 0% (b) < 50% (c) 50% (d) > 50%.

12. 50% of the X-ray coming from a Coolidge tube is able to pass through a 0·1 mm thick aluminium foil. The potential difference between the target and the filament is increased. The thickness of aluminium foil, which will allow 50% of the X-ray to pass through, will be
(a) zero (b) < 0·1 mm (c) 0·1 mm (d) > 0·1 mm.

13. X-ray from a Coolidge tube is incident on a thin aluminium foil. The intensity of the X-ray transmitted by the foil is found to be I_0. The heating current is increased so as to increase the temperature of the filament. The intensity of the X-ray transmitted by the foil will be
(a) zero (b) $< I_0$ (c) I_0 (d) $> I_0$.

14. Visible light passing through a circular hole forms a diffraction disc of radius 0·1 mm on a screen. If X-ray is passed through the same set-up, the radius of the diffraction disc will be
(a) zero (b) < 0·1 mm (c) 0·1 mm (d) > 0·1 mm.

OBJECTIVE II

1. For harder X-rays,
(a) the wavelength is higher
(b) the intensity is higher
(c) the frequency is higher
(d) the photon energy is higher.

2. Cutoff wavelength of X-rays coming from a Coolidge tube depends on the
(a) target material (b) accelerating voltage
(c) separation between the target and the filament
(d) temperature of the filament.

3. Mark the correct options.
(a) An atom with a vacancy has smaller energy than a neutral atom.
(b) K X-ray is emitted when a hole makes a jump from the K shell to some other shell.
(c) The wavelength of K X-ray is smaller than the wavelength of L X-ray of the same material.
(d) The wavelength of K_α X-ray is smaller than the wavelength of K_β X-ray of the same material.

4. For a given material, the energy and wavelength of characterstic X-rays satisfy
(a) $E(K_\alpha) > E(K_\beta) > E(K_\gamma)$ (b) $E(M_\alpha) > E(L_\alpha) > E(K_\alpha)$
(c) $\lambda(K_\alpha) > \lambda(K_\beta) > \lambda(K_\gamma)$ (d) $\lambda(M_\alpha) > \lambda(L_\alpha) > \lambda(K_\alpha)$.

5. The potential difference applied to an X-ray tube is increased. As a result, in the emitted radiation,
(a) the intensity increases
(b) the minimum wavelength increases
(c) the intensity remains unchanged
(d) the minimum wavelength decreases.

6. When an electron strikes the target in a Coolidge tube, its entire kinetic energy

(a) is converted into a photon
(b) may be converted into a photon
(c) is converted into heat
(d) may be converted into heat.

7. X-ray incident on a material
(a) exerts a force on it (b) transfers energy to it
(c) transfers momentum to it
(d) transfers impulse to it.

8. Consider a photon of continuous X-ray and a photon of characteristic X-ray of the same wavelength. Which of the following is/are different for the two photons ?
(a) Frequency (b) Energy
(c) Penetrating power (d) Method of creation

EXERCISES

Planck constant $h = 4{\cdot}14 \times 10^{-15}$ eV s^{-1}, speed of light $c = 3 \times 10^{8}$ m s^{-1}.

1. Find the energy, the frequency and the momentum of an X-ray photon of wavelength 0·10 nm.
2. Iron emits K_α X-ray of energy 6·4 keV and calcium emits K_α X-ray of energy 3·69 keV. Calculate the times taken by an iron K_α photon and a calcium K_α photon to cross through a distance of 3 km.
3. Find the cutoff wavelength for the continuous X-rays coming from an X-ray tube operating at 30 kV.
4. What potential difference should be applied across an X-ray tube to get X-ray of wavelength not less than 0·10 nm ? What is the maximum energy of a photon of this X-ray in joule ?
5. The X-ray coming from a Coolidge tube has a cutoff wavelength of 80 pm. Find the kinetic energy of the electrons hitting the target.
6. If the operating potential in an X-ray tube is increased by 1%, by what percentage does the cutoff wavelength decrease ?
7. The distance between the cathode (filament) and the target in an X-ray tube is 1·5 m. If the cutoff wavelength is 30 pm, find the electric field between the cathode and the target.
8. The short-wavelength limit shifts by 26 pm when the operating voltage in an X-ray tube is increased to 1·5 times the original value. What was the original value of the operating voltage ?
9. The electron beam in a colour TV is accelerated through 32 kV and then strikes the screen. What is the wavelength of the most energetic X-ray photon ?
10. When 40 kV is applied across an X-ray tube, X-ray is obtained with a maximum frequency of $9{\cdot}7 \times 10^{18}$ Hz. Calculate the value of Planck constant from these data.
11. An X-ray tube operates at 40 kV. Suppose the electron converts 70% of its energy into a photon at each collision. Find the lowest three wavelengths emitted from the tube. Neglect the energy imparted to the atom with which the electron collides.
12. The wavelength of K_α X-ray of tungsten is 21·3 pm. It takes 11·3 keV to knock out an electron from the L shell of a tungsten atom. What should be the minimum accelerating voltage across an X-ray tube having tungsten target which allows production of K_α X-ray ?
13. The K_β X-ray of argon has a wavelength of 0·36 nm. The minimum energy needed to ionize an argon atom is 16 eV. Find the energy needed to knock out an electron from the K shell of an argon atom.
14. The K_α X-rays of aluminium ($Z = 13$) and zinc ($Z = 30$) have wavelengths 887 pm and 146 pm respectively. Use Moseley's law $\sqrt{\nu} = a(Z - b)$ to find the wavelength of the K_α X-ray of iron ($Z = 26$).
15. A certain element emits K_α X-ray of energy 3·69 keV. Use the data from the previous problem to identify the element.
16. The K_β X-rays from certain elements are given below. Draw a Moseley-type plot of $\sqrt{\nu}$ versus Z for K_β radiation.

Element	Ne	P	Ca	Mn	Zn	Br
Energy (keV)	0·858	2·14	4·02	6·51	9·57	13·3.

17. Use Moseley's law with $b = 1$ to find the frequency of the K_α X-ray of La($Z = 57$) if the frequency of the K_α X-ray of Cu($Z = 29$) is known to be $1{\cdot}88 \times 10^{18}$ Hz.
18. The K_α and K_β X-rays of molybdenum have wavelengths 0·71 Å and 0·63 Å respectively. Find the wavelength of L_α X-ray of molybdenum.
19. The wavelengths of K_α and L_α X-rays of a material are 21·3 pm and 141 pm respectively. Find the wavelength of K_β X-ray of the material.
20. The energy of a silver atom with a vacancy in K shell is 25·31 keV, in L shell is 3·56 keV and in M shell is 0·530 keV higher than the energy of the atom with no vacancy. Find the frequency of K_α, K_β and L_α X-rays of silver.
21. Find the maximum potential difference which may be applied across an X-ray tube with tungsten target without emitting any characteristic K or L X-ray. The energy levels of the tungsten atom with an electron knocked out are as follows.

Cell containing vacancy	K	L	M
Energy in keV	69.5	11.3	2.3

22. The electric current in an X-ray tube (from the target to the filament) operating at 40 kV is 10 mA. Assume that on an average, 1% of the total kinetic energy of the electrons hitting the target are converted into X-rays. (a) What is the total power emitted as X-rays and (b) how much heat is produced in the target every second ?
23. Heat at the rate of 200 W is produced in an X-ray tube operating at 20 kV. Find the current in the circuit. Assume that only a small fraction of the kinetic energy of electrons is converted into X-rays.

24. Continuous X-rays are made to strike a tissue paper soaked with polluted water. The incoming X-rays excite the atoms of the sample by knocking out the electrons from the inner shells. Characteristic X-rays are subsequently emitted. The emitted X-rays are analysed and the intensity is plotted against the wavelength (figure 44-E1). Assuming that only K_α intensities are detected, list the elements present in the sample from the plot. Use Moseley's equation

$$\nu = (25 \times 10^{14}\ \text{Hz})\,(Z-1)^2.$$

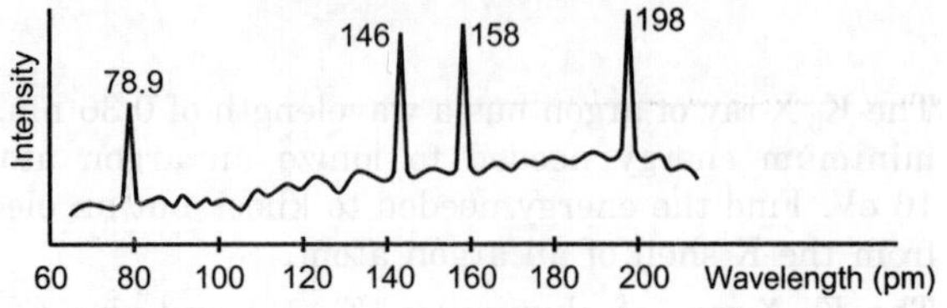

Figure 44-E1

25. A free atom of iron emits K_α X-rays of energy 6·4 keV. Calculate the recoil kinetic energy of the atom. Mass of an iron atom = $9 \cdot 3 \times 10^{-26}$ kg.

26. The stopping potential in a photoelectric experiment is linearly related to the inverse of the wavelength ($1/\lambda$) of the light falling on the cathode. The potential difference applied across an X-ray tube is linearly related to the inverse of the cutoff wavelength ($1/\lambda$) of the X-ray emitted. Show that the slopes of the lines in the two cases are equal and find its value.

27. Suppose a monochromatic X-ray beam of wavelength 100 pm is sent through a Young's double slit and the interference pattern is observed on a photographic plate placed 40 cm away from the slit. What should be the separation between the slits so that the successive maxima on the screen are separated by a distance of 0·1 mm ?

□

ANSWERS

OBJECTIVE I

1. (d)	2. (a)	3. (d)	4. (c)	5. (c)	6. (a)
7. (d)	8. (c)	9. (a)	10. (b)	11. (d)	12. (d)
13. (d)	14. (b)				

OBJECTIVE II

1. (c), (d)	2. (b)	3. (b), (c)
4. (c), (d)	5. (c), (d)	6. (b), (d)
7. all	8. (d)	

EXERCISES

1. 12·4 keV, 3×10^{18} Hz, $6{\cdot}62 \times 10^{-24}$ kg m s^{-1}
2. 10 μs by both
3. 41·4 pm
4. 12·4 kV, $2{\cdot}0 \times 10^{-15}$ J
5. 15·5 keV
6. approximately 1%
7. 27·7 kV m^{-1}
8. 15·9 kV
9. 38·8 pm
10. $4{\cdot}12 \times 10^{-15}$ eVs
11. 44·3 pm, 148 pm, 493 pm
12. 69·5 kV
13. 3·47 keV
14. 198 pm
15. calcium
17. $7{\cdot}52 \times 10^{18}$ Hz
18. 5·64 Å
19. 18·5 pm
20. $5{\cdot}25 \times 10^{18}$ Hz, $5{\cdot}98 \times 10^{18}$ Hz, $7{\cdot}32 \times 10^{17}$ Hz
21. less than 11·3 kV
22. (a) 4 W (b) 396 J
23. 10 mA
24. Zr, Zn, Cu, Fe
25. $3{\cdot}9 \times 10^{-4}$ eV
26. $\frac{hc}{e} = 1{\cdot}242 \times 10^{-6}$ Vm
27. 4×10^{-7} m

□

CHAPTER 45

SEMICONDUCTORS AND SEMICONDUCTOR DEVICES

45.1 INTRODUCTION

We have discussed some of the properties of conductors and insulators in earlier chapters. We assumed that there is a large number of almost free electrons in a conductor which wander randomly in the whole of the body, whereas, all the electrons in an insulator are tightly bound to some nucleus or the other. If an electric field $\vec{E}$ is established inside a conductor, the free electrons experience force due to the field and acquire a drift speed. This results in an electric current. The conductivity σ is defined in terms of the electric field $\vec{E}$ existing in the conductor and the resulting current density $\vec{j}$. The relation between these quantities is

$$\vec{j} = \sigma \vec{E}.$$

Larger the conductivity σ, better is the material as a conductor.

The conductivity σ of a conductor, such as copper, is fairly independent of the electric field applied and decreases as the temperature is increased. This is because as the temperature is increased, the random collisions of the free electrons with the particles in the conductor become more frequent. The electrons get less time to gain energy from the applied electric field. This results in a decrease in the drift speed and hence the conductivity decreases. The resistivity $\rho = 1/\sigma$ of a conductor increases as the temperature increases.

Almost zero electric current is obtained in insulators unless a very high electric field is applied.

We now introduce another kind of solid known as *semiconductor*. These solids do conduct electricity when an electric field is applied, but the conductivity is very small as compared to the usual metallic conductors. Silicon is an example of a semiconductor, its conductivity is about 10^{11} times smaller than that of copper and is about 10^{13} times larger than that of fused quartz. Another distinguishing feature about a semiconductor is that its conductivity increases as the temperature is increased. To understand the mechanism of conduction in solids, let us discuss qualitatively, formation of energy bands in solids.

45.2 ENERGY BANDS IN SOLIDS

The electrons of an isolated atom can have certain definite energies labelled as 1s, 2s, 2p, 3s, etc. Pauli exclusion principle determines the maximum number of electrons which can be accommodated in each energy level. An energy level consists of several quantum states and no quantum state can contain more than one electron. Consider a sodium atom in its lowest energy state. It has 11 electrons. The electronic configuration is $(1s)^2\ (2s)^2\ (2p)^6\ (3s)^1$. The levels 1s, 2s and 2p are completely filled and the level 3s contains only one electron although it has a capacity to accommodate 2. The next allowed energy level is 3p which can contain 6 electrons but is empty. All the energy levels above 3s are empty.

Now consider a group of N sodium atoms separated from each other by large distances such as in sodium vapour. There are altogether $11N$ electrons. Assuming that each atom is in its ground state, what are the energies of these $11N$ electrons ? For each atom, there are two states in energy level 1s. There are $2N$ such states which have identical energy and are filled by $2N$ electrons. Similarly, there are $2N$ states having identical energy labelled 2s, $6N$ states having identical energy labelled 2p and $2N$ states having identical energy labelled 3s. The $2N$ states of 1s, $2N$ states of 2s and $6N$ states of 2p are completely filled whereas only N of the $2N$ states of 3s are filled by the electrons and the remaining N states are empty. These ideas are shown in table (45.1) and figure (45.1).

Table 45.1 : *Quantum states in sodium vapour*

Energy level	Total states available	Total states occupied
1s	$2N$	$2N$
2s	$2N$	$2N$
2p	$6N$	$6N$
3s	$2N$	N
3p	$6N$	0

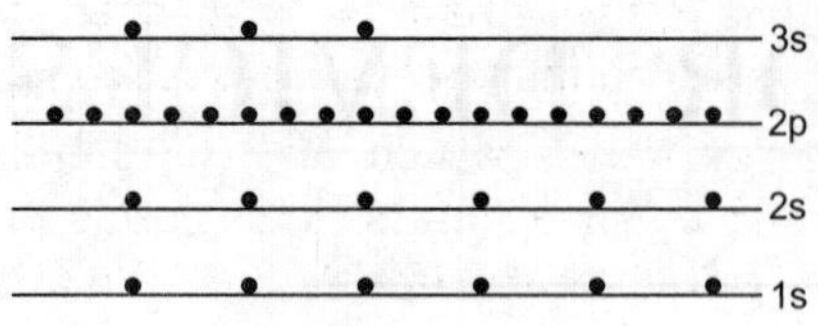

Figure 45.1

The value of energy in a particular state of an isolated sodium atom is determined by the mutual interactions among the nucleus and the 11 electrons. In the collection of the N sodium atoms that we have considered, it is assumed that the atoms are widely separated from each other and hence the electrons of one atom do not interact with those of the others to any appreciable extent. As a result, the energy of 1s states of each atom is the same as that for an isolated atom. All the 1s states, therefore, have identical energy. Similarly, all the 2s, 2p, 3s states have identical energies, respectively. Now suppose, the atoms are drawn closer to one another to the extent that the outer 3s electron of one atom starts interacting with the 3s electrons of the neighbouring atoms. Because of these interactions, the energy of the 3s states will change. It turns out that the changes in energy in all the $2N$ states of 3s level are not identical. Some of the states are shifted up in energy and some are pushed down. The magnitude of change is also different for different states of the 3s level. As a result, what was a sharply defined 3s energy, now becomes a combination of several closely spaced energies. We say that these $2N$ states have formed an *energy band*. We label this band as 3s band. The inner electrons interact weakly with each other so that this splitting of sharp energy levels into bands is less for inner electrons.

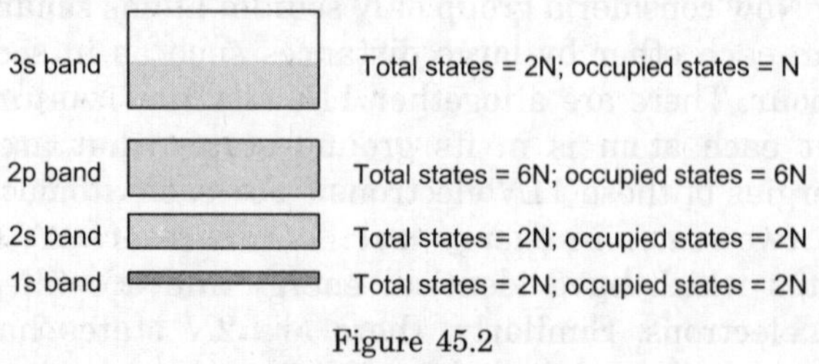

Figure 45.2

Figure (45.2) shows schematically this splitting of energy levels in bands. We have a 3s band which contains $2N$ states with slightly different energies, N of them are occupied by the N electrons of sodium atoms and the remaining N states are empty. Similarly, we talk of the 2p band which contains $6N$ states with slightly different energies and all these states are filled. Similar is the case for other inner bands. The difference between the highest energy in a band and the lowest energy in the next higher band is called the *band gap* between the two bands.

Sodium was taken only as an example. We have energy bands separated by band gaps in all solids. At 0 K, the energy is the lowest and the electrons fill the bands from the bottom according to the Pauli exclusion principle till all the electrons are accommodated. As the temperature is raised, the electrons may collide with each other and with ions to exchange energy. At an absolute temperature T, the order of energy exchanged is kT where k is the Boltzmann constant. This is known as thermal energy. At room temperature (300 K), kT is about 0·026 eV. Suppose the band gaps are much larger than kT. An electron in a completely filled band does not find an empty state with a slightly higher or a slightly lower energy. It, therefore, cannot accept or donate energy of the order of kT and hence does not take part in processes involving energy exchange. This is the case with inner bands which are, in general, completely filled. The outermost electrons which are in the highest occupied energy band, may take up this energy $\approx kT$ if empty states are available in the same band. For example, a 3s electron in sodium can take up thermal energy and go to an empty state at a slightly more energy.

Similar is the scenario when an electric field is applied by connecting the sodium metal to a battery. The electric field, in general, can supply only a small amount of energy to the electrons. Only the electrons in the highest occupied band can accept this energy. These electrons can acquire kinetic energy and move according to the electric field. This results in electric current. The electrons in the inner bands cannot accept small amounts of energy from the electric field and hence do not take part in conduction.

The energy band structure in solids may be classified in four broad types as shown in figure (45.3).

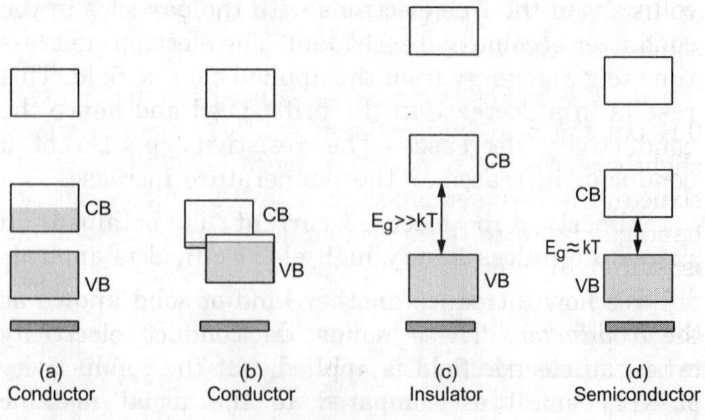

Figure 45.3

(a) The highest occupied energy band is only partially filled at 0 K (figure 45.3a). Sodium is an example of this kind. If the electronic configuration is such that the outermost subshell contains odd number of electrons, we get this type of band structure. They are good conductors of electricity because as an electric field is applied, the electrons in the partially filled band can receive energy from the field and drift accordingly.

(b) The highest occupied energy level is completely filled at 0 K and the next higher level is completely empty when the atoms are well-separated. But as the atoms come closer and these levels split into bands, the bands overlap with each other (figure 45.3b). Zinc is an example of this kind. The electronic configuration of zinc is $(1s)^2\,(2s)^2\,(2p)^6\,(3s)^2\,(3p)^6\,(3d)^{10}\,(4s)^2$. The highest energy level—that contains any electron when the zinc atoms are well-separated—is the 4s level and all the $2N$ states in it are occupied by electrons. However, in solid zinc, the 4p band overlaps with the 4*s* band. In this case also, there are empty states at energies close to the occupied states and hence these solids are also good conductors.

(c) The highest occupied energy band is completely filled and the next higher band, which is empty, is well above it (figure 45.3c). The band gap between these two bands is large. The electrons do not have empty states at an energy slightly above or below their existing energies. If an electric field is applied by connecting the two ends of such a solid to a battery, the electrons will refuse to receive energy from the field. This is because they do not find an empty state at a slightly higher energy. Diamond is an example of this kind. The gap between the lowest empty band and the highest filled band is about 6 eV. The electric field needed to supply 6 eV energy to an electron is of the order of $10^7\ \mathrm{V\,m^{-1}}$ in copper (see example 45.1). Assuming the same value for diamond; if we take a 10 cm slab of diamond, we will have to use a battery of 10^6 volts to get response from an electron. These solids are, therefore, insulators.

(d) The highest occupied band is completely filled at 0 K but the next higher band, which is empty, is only slightly above the filled band (figure 45.3d). The band structure is very similar to that of an insulator but the band gap between these two bands is small. An example is silicon in which the band gap is 1·1 eV. It is still difficult for an ordinary battery to supply an energy of the order of 1·1 eV to an electron. However, at temperatures well above 0 K, thermal collisions may push some of the electrons from the highest occupied band to the next empty band. These few electrons, in the otherwise empty band, can respond to even a weak battery because they have a large number of empty states just above their existing energy. As electrons from a filled band are pushed up in energy to land into a higher energy band, empty states are created in this filled band. These empty states allow some movement of electrons in that band and thus promote conduction. As the total number of electrons that can receive energy from the electric field is small, the conductivity is quite small as compared to common conductors. Such solids are called *semiconductors*.

The energy bands which are completely filled at 0 K are called *valence bands*. The bands with higher energies are called *conduction bands*. We are generally concerned with only the highest valence band and the lowest conduction band. So when we say valence band, it means the highest valence band. Similarly, when we say conduction band, it means the lowest conduction band. Study the labels 'conduction band (CB)' and 'valence band (VB)' in figure (45.3).

Example 45.1

The mean free path of conduction electrons in copper is about 4×10^{-8} m. *For a copper block, find the electric field which can give, on an average,* 1 eV *energy to a conduction electron.*

Solution : Let the electric field be E. The force on an electron is eE. As the electron moves through a distance d, the work done on it is eEd. This is equal to the energy transferred to the electron. As the electron travels an average distance of 4×10^{-8} m before a collision, the energy transferred is $eE(4\times10^{-8}\ \mathrm{m})$. To get 1 eV energy from the electric field,

$$eE(4\times10^{-8}\ \mathrm{m}) = 1\ \mathrm{eV}$$

or, $$E = 2{\cdot}5\times10^{7}\ \mathrm{V\,m^{-1}}.$$

Let us now consider the physical picture of conductors, insulators and semiconductors in a Bohr-type model. The inner electrons are tightly bound to the nuclei and move in their well-defined orbits. In a conductor, the outermost subshell is not completely filled and the electrons moving around one nucleus can jump to a similar orbit around some other nucleus (figure 45.4a). This is possible because there is an empty state there to accommodate the electron. For example, a 3s electron of one sodium atom can jump to the 3s orbit of some other sodium atom because out of the two 3s states only one, in general, is filled. Similar is the case with zinc-type metals. The 4p orbits in zinc atoms are, in general, empty. As the 4p band overlaps with the 4*s* band, the energy of a 4p state is not too different from a 4s state. Thus, without demanding for excessive energy, a 4s electron can jump

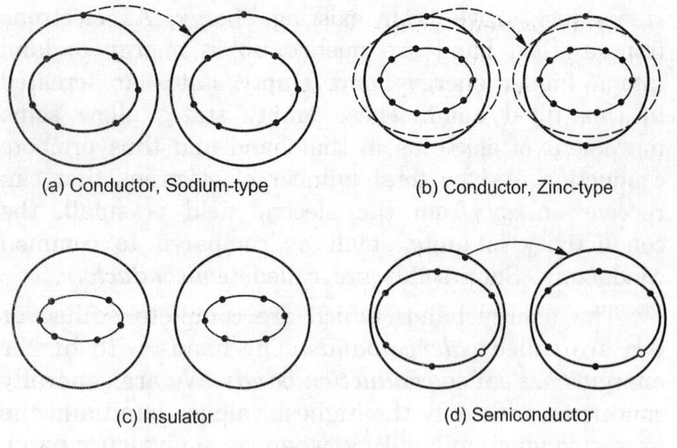

Figure 45.4

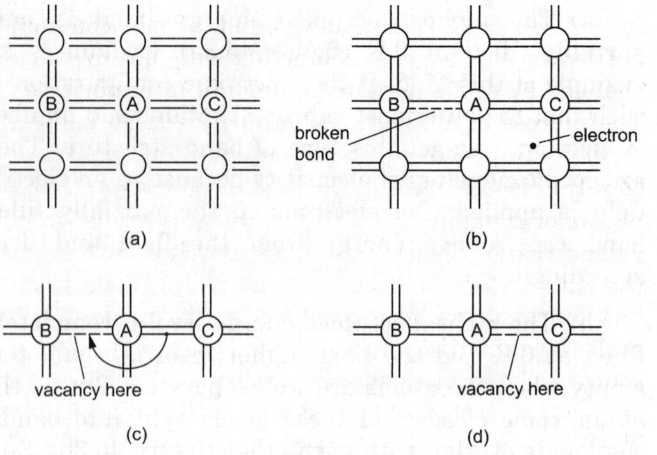

Figure 45.5

into the 4p orbit of its own atom or of some other atom (figure 45.4b).

In insulators, even the outermost electrons are tightly bound to their respective nuclei. The subshell in which they lie is completely filled and the next higher orbit is at a much higher energy. No drift is then possible (figure 45.4c).

In semiconductors at room temperature or above, some electrons move around the nuclei with a much larger radius. These large orbits are nearly empty and so the electrons in these orbits may jump from one atom to the other easily. These are the electrons in conduction band and are called *conduction electrons* (figure 45.4d).

45.3 THE SEMICONDUCTOR

As discussed above, in semiconductors the conduction band and the valence band are separated by a relatively small energy gap. For silicon, this gap is 1·1 eV. For another common semiconductor germanium, the gap is 0·68 eV.

Silicon has an atomic number of 14 and electronic configuration $(1s)^2 (2s)^2 (2p)^6 (3s)^2 (3p)^2$. The chemistry of silicon tells us that each silicon atom makes covalent bonds with the four neighbouring silicon atoms. To form a covalent bond, two silicon atoms contribute one electron each and the two electrons are shared by the two atoms. Both of these electrons are in the valence band. Due to collision, one of these valence electrons may acquire additional energy and it may start orbiting the silicon nucleus at a larger radius. Thus, the bond is broken. One electron has gone into the conduction band, it is moving in an orbit of large radius and is frequently jumping from one nucleus to another.

Figure (45.5a) represents a model of solid silicon. The four outer electrons of each atom form bonds with the four neighbouring atoms. Each bond consists of two electrons. Figure (45.5b) shows a broken bond represented by the dashed line. The electron corresponding to this bond has acquired sufficient energy and has jumped into the conduction band. So there is a vacancy for an electron at the site of the broken bond. In a semiconductor, a number of such broken bonds and conduction electrons exist. Now consider the situation shown in figure (45.5c). The bond between the atoms A and B is broken. A bonding electron between A and C can make a jump towards the left and fill the broken bond between A and B. Not much energy is needed to induce such a transfer. This is because, the electron makes transition from one bond to other only and all bond electrons have roughly the same energy.

As the broken bond AB is filled, the bond AC is broken (figure 45.5d). Thus, the vacancy has shifted towards the right. Any movement of a valence electron from one bond to a nearby broken bond may be described as the movement of vacancy in the opposite direction. It is customary in semiconductor physics to treat a vacancy in valence band as a particle having positive charge $+e$. Movement of electrons in valence band is then described in terms of movement of vacancies in the opposite directions. Such vacancies are also called *holes*.

Whenever a valence electron is shifted to conduction band, a hole is created. Thus, in a pure semiconductor, the number of conduction electrons equals the number of holes. When an electric field is applied, conduction electrons drift opposite to the field and holes drift along the field. That is why, holes are assumed to have positive charge. Conduction takes place due to the drift of conduction electrons as well as of holes. Such pure semiconductors are also called *intrinsic semiconductors*. The chemical structure of germanium is the same as that of silicon and hence the above discussion is equally applicable to it.

45.4 *p*-TYPE AND *n*-TYPE SEMICONDUCTORS

In an intrinsic semiconductor, like pure silicon, only a small fraction of the valence electrons are able to reach the conduction band. The conduction properties of a semiconductor can be drastically changed by diffusing a small amount of impurity in it. The process of diffusing an impurity is also known as *doping*. Suppose a small amount of phosphorus ($Z = 15$) is diffused into a silicon crystal. Each phosphorus atom has five outer electrons in the valence band. Some of the phosphorus atoms displace the silicon atoms and occupy their place. A silicon atom has four valence electrons locked in covalent bonds with neighbouring four silicon atoms. Phosphorus comes in with five valence electrons. Four electrons are shared with the neighbouring four silicon atoms. The fifth one moves with a large radius (≈ 30 Å) round the phosphorus ion. The energy of this extra electron is much higher than the valence electrons locked in covalent bonds. In fact, the energy levels for these extra electrons—known as impurity levels—are only slightly below the conduction band (0·045 eV for phosphorus in silicon). This small gap is easily covered by the electrons during thermal collisions and hence a large fraction of them are found in the conduction band. Figure (45.6) shows qualitatively the situation in such a doped semiconductor.

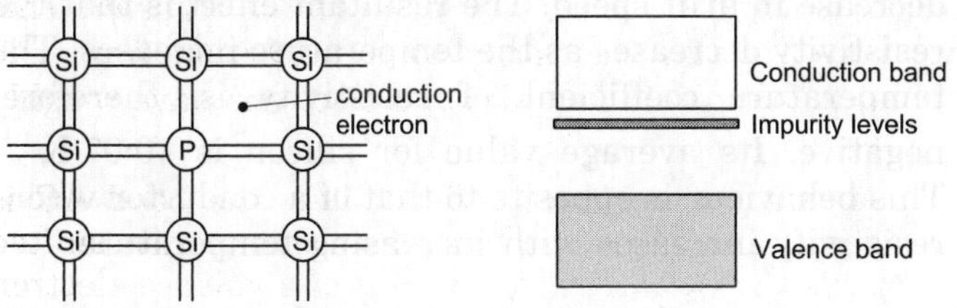

Figure 45.6

When a phosphorus atom with five outer electrons is substituted for a silicon atom, an extra electron is made available for conduction. Thus, the number of conduction electrons increases due to the introduction of a pentavalent impurity in silicon. The conduction properties are, therefore, very sensitive to the amount of the impurity. The introduction of phosphorus in the proportion of 1 in 10^6 increases the conductivity by a factor of about 10^6. Interesting desired results may be obtained by controlling the amount and distribution of impurity in a semiconductor.

Such impurities, which donate electrons for conduction, are called *donor* impurities. As the number of negative charge carriers is much larger than the number of positive charge carriers, these semiconductors are called *n-type semiconductors.* What happens if a trivalent impurity— such as aluminium— is doped into silicon ? Silicon atom with four valence electrons is substituted by an aluminium atom with three valence electrons. These three electrons are used to form covalent bonds with the neighbouring three silicon atoms but the bond with the fourth neighbour is not complete. The broken bond between the aluminium atom and its fourth neighbour can be filled by another valence electron if this electron obtains an extra energy of about 0·057 eV. A hole is then created in the valence band. We say that impurity levels are created a little above the valence band (0·057 eV for aluminium in silicon). The valence electrons can cross over to these levels leaving behind the holes, which are responsible for conduction (figure 45.7). As the energy gap ΔE between the valence band and the impurity levels is comparable to kT, large number of holes are created. The number of holes in such a doped semiconductor is much larger than the number of conduction electrons. As the majority charge carriers are holes, i.e., positive charges, these semiconductors are called *p-type semiconductors.* The impurity of this kind creates new levels which can accept valence electrons, hence these impurities are called *acceptor impurities.*

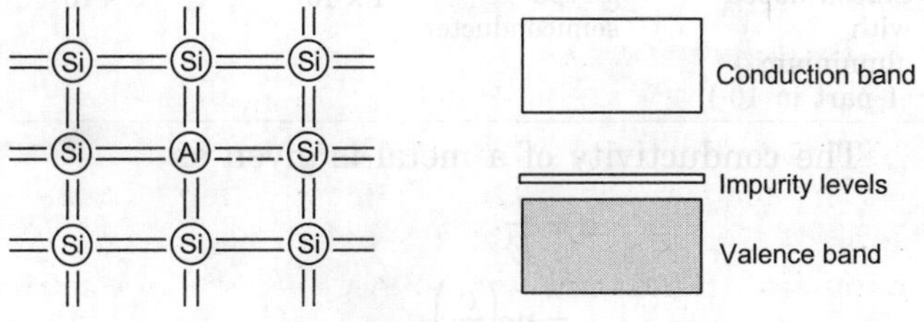

Figure 45.7

Semiconductors with an impurity doped into it are called *extrinsic semiconductor.* Figure (45.8) shows a schematic representation of intrinsic and extrinsic semiconductors.

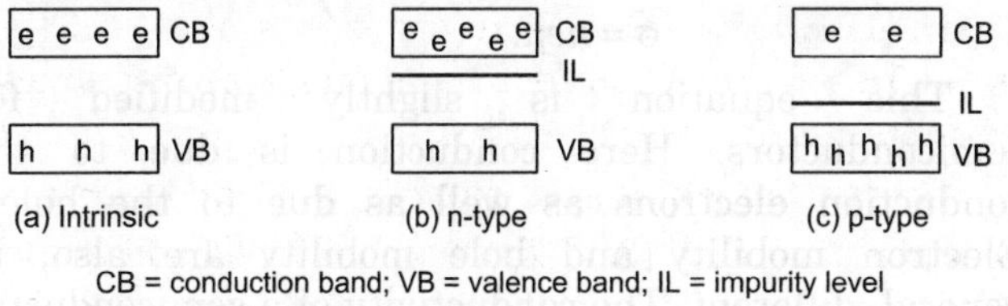

Figure 45.8

45.5 DENSITY OF CHARGE CARRIERS AND CONDUCTIVITY

Due to thermal collisions, an electron can take up or release energy. Thus, occasionally a valence electron takes up energy and the bond is broken. The electron goes to the conduction band and a hole is created. And occasionally, an electron from the conduction band loses some energy, comes to the valence band and fills up a hole. Thus, new electron–hole pairs are formed as well as old electron–hole pairs disappear. A steady-state situation is reached and the number of electron–hole pairs takes a nearly constant value. For silicon at room temperature (300 K), the number of these pairs is about $7\times10^{15}\ \mathrm{m}^{-3}$. For germanium, this number is about $6\times10^{1}\ \mathrm{m}^{-3}$.

Table (45.2) gives a rough estimate of the densities of charge carriers in a typical conductor and in some of the semiconductors. Note that the product of density of conduction electrons and density of holes is constant for a semiconductor when it is doped with impurities.

Table 45.2 : *Densities of charge carriers*

Material	Type	Density of conduction electrons (m^{-3})	Density of holes (m^{-3})
Copper	Conductor	9×10^{28}	0
Silicon	Intrinsic semiconductor	7×10^{15}	7×10^{15}
Silicon doped with phosphorus (1 part in 10^6)	*n*-type semiconductor	5×10^{22}	1×10^{9}
Silicon doped with aluminium (1 part in 10^6)	*p*-type semiconductor	1×10^{9}	5×10^{22}

The conductivity of a metal is given as

$$\sigma=\frac{j}{E}$$

$$=ne\left(\frac{v}{E}\right)$$

where n is the density of conduction electrons and v is the drift speed when an electric field E is applied. The quantity v/E is known as the *mobility* of the electrons. Writing the mobility as μ,

$$\sigma=ne\mu.$$

This equation is slightly modified for semiconductors. Here conduction is due to the conduction electrons as well as due to the holes. Electron mobility and hole mobility are also, in general, different. The conductivity of a semiconductor is, therefore, written as

$$\sigma=n_e e\,\mu_e+n_h e\,\mu_h$$

where n_e, n_h are the densities of conduction electrons and the holes respectively and μ_e, μ_h are their mobilities.

Example 45.2

Calculate the resistivity of an n-type semiconductor from the following data: density of conduction electrons $=8\times10^{13}\ \mathrm{cm}^{-3}$, density of holes $=5\times10^{12}\ \mathrm{cm}^{-3}$, mobility of conduction electron $=2\cdot3\times10^{4}\ \mathrm{cm}^2\,\mathrm{V}^{-1}\mathrm{s}^{-1}$ and mobility of holes $=100\ \mathrm{cm}^2\,\mathrm{V}^{-1}\mathrm{s}^{-1}$.

Solution : The conductivity of the semiconductor is

$$\sigma=e(n_e\,\mu_e+n_h\mu_h)$$

$$=(1\cdot6\times10^{-19}\ \mathrm{C})\,[(8\times10^{19}\ \mathrm{m}^{-3})\times(2\cdot3\ \mathrm{m}^2\,\mathrm{V}^{-1}\mathrm{s}^{-1})+(5\times10^{18}\ \mathrm{m}^{-3})\times(10^{-2}\ \mathrm{m}^{-2}\,\mathrm{V}^{-1}\mathrm{s}^{-1})]$$

$$\approx 2\cdot94\ \mathrm{Cm}^{-1}\,\mathrm{V}^{-1}\,\mathrm{s}^{-1}$$

The resistivity is $\rho=\frac{1}{\sigma}=\frac{1}{2\cdot94}\ \mathrm{m\,Vs\,C}^{-1}\approx0\cdot34\ \Omega\mathrm{m}$.

Temperature Dependence of Conductivity of a Semiconductor

If temperature is increased, the average energy exchanged in a collision increases. More valence electrons cross the gap and the number of electron–hole pairs increases. It can be shown that the number of such pairs is proportional to the factor $T^{3/2}e^{-\Delta E/2kT}$, where ΔE is the band gap. The increase in the number of electron–hole pairs results in an increase in the conductivity, i.e., a decrease in the resistivity of the material.

There is a small opposing behaviour due to the increase in thermal collisions. The drift speed and hence the mobility decreases and this contributes towards increasing the resistivity just like a conductor. However, the effect of increasing the number of charge carriers is much more prominent than the effect of the decrease in drift speed. The resultant effect is that the resistivity decreases as the temperature increases. The temperature coefficient of resistivity is, therefore, negative. Its average value for silicon is $-0\cdot07\ \mathrm{K}^{-1}$. This behaviour is opposite to that of a conductor where resistivity increases with increasing temperature.

45.6 *p-n* JUNCTION

When a semiconducting material such as silicon or germanium is doped with impurity in such a way that one side has a large number of acceptor impurities and the other side has a large number of donor impurities, we obtain a *p-n* junction. To construct a *p-n* junction, one may diffuse a donor impurity to a pure semiconductor so that the entire sample becomes *n*-type. The acceptor impurity may then be diffused in higher concentration from one side to make that side *p*-type. Figure (45.9) shows the physical structure of a typical *p-n* junction.

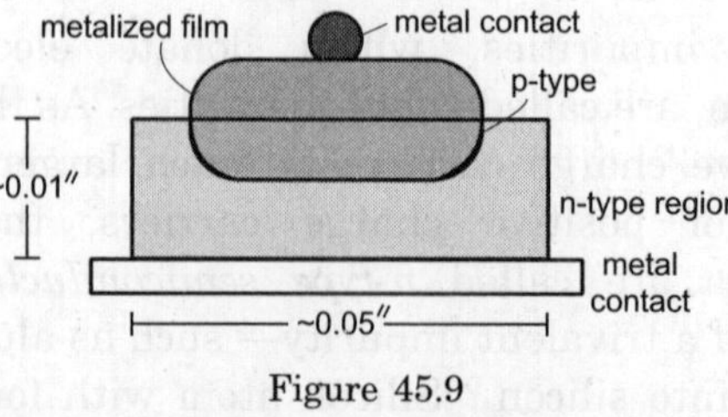

Figure 45.9

Consider the idealized situation of a *p-n* junction at the time of its formation shown in figure (45.10).

The symbol e represents a conduction electron and h represents a hole. Suppose that at the time of formation, the left-half is made p-type and the right-half n-type semiconductor. These two portions may be called p-side and n-side respectively.

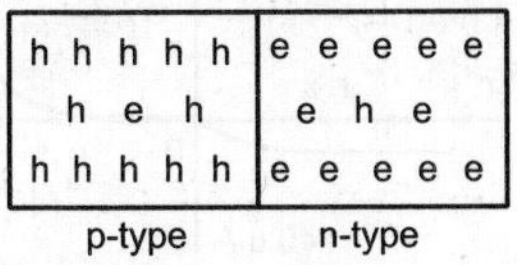

Figure 45.10

This cannot be the equilibrium situation. As there is a large concentration of holes in the left-half and only a small concentration of holes in the right-half, there will be diffusion of holes towards the right. Physically, this means that some of the valence electrons just to the right of the junction may fill up the vacancies just to the left of the junction. Similarly, because of the concentration difference, conduction electrons diffuse from the right to the left. The ions as such do not move because of their heavy masses. As the two halves (left-half and right-half) were electrically neutral in the beginning, diffusion of holes towards the right and diffusion of electrons towards the left make the right-half positively charged and the left-half negatively charged. This creates an electric field near the junction from the right to the left. Any hole near the junction is pushed by the electric field into the left-half. Similarly, any conduction electron near the junction is pushed by the electric field into the right-half. Thus, no charge carrier can remain in a small region near the junction. This region is called the *depletion layer* (figure 45.11).

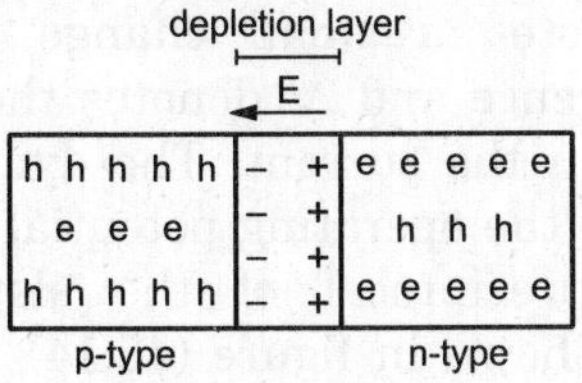

Figure 45.11

Diffusion Current

Because of the concentration difference, holes try to diffuse from the p-side to the n-side. In figure (45.11), this is from the left to the right. However, the electric field at the junction exerts a force on the holes towards the left as they come to the depletion layer. Only those holes which start moving towards the right with a high kinetic energy are able to cross the junction. Similarly, diffusion of electrons from the right to the left is opposed by the field and only those electrons which start towards the left with high kinetic energy are able to cross the junction. The electric potential of the n-side is higher than that of the p-side, the variation in potential is sketched in figure (45.12). We say that there is a *potential barrier* at the junction which allows only a small amount of diffusion. Nevertheless, there are some energetic holes and electrons which surmount the barrier and some diffusion does take place. This diffusion results in an electric current from the p-side to the n-side known as *diffusion current.*

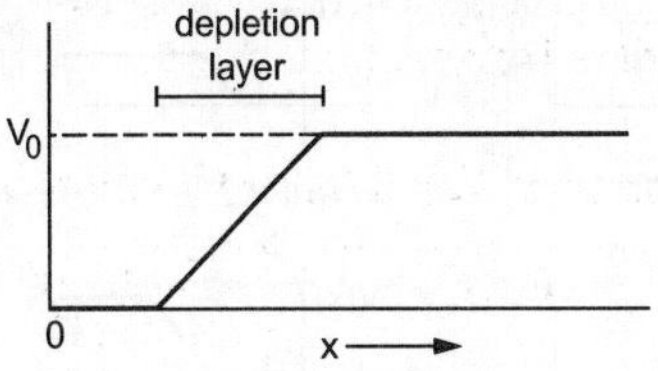

Figure 45.12

Drift Current

Because of thermal collisions, occasionally a covalent bond is broken and the electron jumps to the conduction band. An electron–hole pair is thus created. Also, occasionally a conduction electron fills up a vacant bond so that an electron–hole pair is destroyed. These processes continue in every part of the material. However, if an electron–hole pair is created in the depletion region, the electron is quickly pushed by the electric field towards the n-side and the hole towards the p-side. There is almost no chance of recombination of a hole with an electron in the depletion region. As electron–hole pairs are continuously created in the depletion region, there is a regular flow of electrons towards the n-side and of holes towards the p-side. This makes a current from the n-side to the p-side. This current is called the *drift current.*

The drift current and the diffusion current are in opposite directions. In steady state, the diffusion current equals the drift current in magnitude and there is no net transfer of charge at any cross-section. This is the case with a p-n junction kept in a cupboard.

45.7 *p-n* JUNCTION DIODE

Let us now discuss what happens if a battery is connected to the ends of a p-n junction. Figure (45.13) shows situations when (a) no battery is connected to the junction, (b) a battery is connected with its positive terminal connected to the p-side and the negative terminal connected to the n-side and (c) a battery is connected with its positive terminal connected to the n-side and the negative terminal connected to the p-side. If the positive terminal of the battery is connected to the p-side and the negative terminal to the n-side, we say that the junction is *forward-biased* (figure 45.13b). The potential of the n-side is higher than that of the p-side when no battery is connected to the junction. Due to the forward-bias connection, the potential of the p-side is raised and hence the height of the potential barrier decreases. The width of the depletion region is also reduced in forward bias (figure 45.13b).

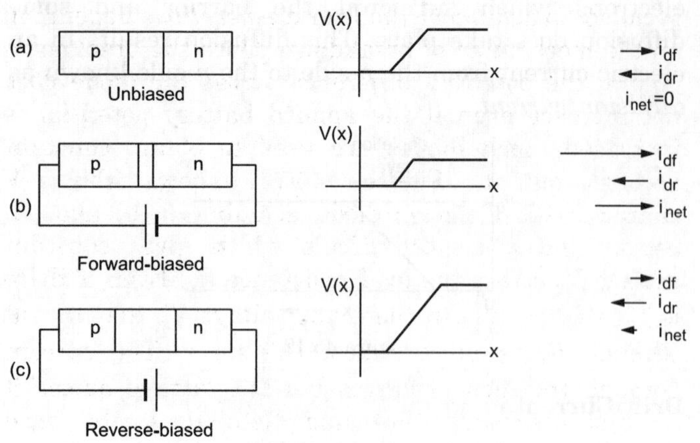

Figure 45.13

This allows more diffusion to take place. The diffusion current thus increases by connecting a battery in forward bias. The drift current remains almost unchanged because the rate of formation of new electron–hole pairs is fairly independent of the electric field unless the field is too large. Thus, the diffusion current exceeds the drift current and there is a net current from the p-side to the n-side. The diffusion increases as the applied potential difference is increased and the barrier height is decreased. When the applied potential difference is so high that the potential barrier is reduced to zero or is reversed, the diffusion increases very rapidly. The current i in the circuit thus changes nonlinearly with the applied potential difference. A p-n junction does not obey Ohm's law.

If the p-side of the junction is connected to the negative terminal and the n-side to the positive terminal of a battery, the junction is said to be *reverse-biased*. In this case, the potential barrier becomes higher as the battery further raises the potential of the n-side (figure 41.13c). The width of the depletion region is increased. Diffusion becomes more difficult and hence the diffusion current decreases. The drift current is not appreciably affected and hence it exceeds the diffusion current. So, there is a net current from the n-side to the p-side. However, this current is small as the drift current itself is small (typically in microamperes) and the net current is even smaller. Thus, during reverse bias, only a small current is allowed by the junction. We say that the junction offers a large resistance when reverse-biased.

Figure (45.14) shows a qualitative plot of current versus potential difference for a p-n junction. This is known as an *i–V characteristic* of the p-n junction. Note that the scales for the current are different for positive and negative current.

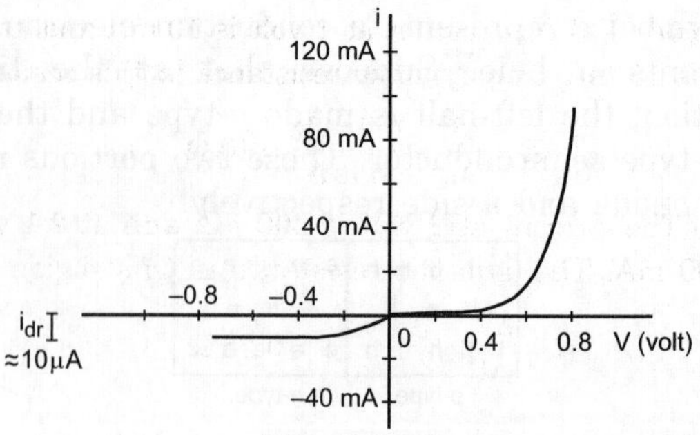

Figure 45.14

We see that the junction offers a little resistance if we try to pass an electric current from the p-side to the n-side and offers a large resistance if the current is passed from the n-side to the p-side. Any device which freely allows electric current in one direction but does not allow it in the opposite direction is called a diode. Thus, a p-n junction acts as a diode. An ideal diode should not allow any current in the reverse direction. A p-n junction diode is close to an ideal diode because the current in reverse bias is very small (few microamperes). The diode is symbolised as 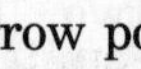 , the arrow pointing in the direction in which the current can pass freely. For a p-n junction diode, the arrow points from the p-side to the n-side. We have already studied a vacuum-tube diode based on thermionic emission in an earlier chapter.

Dynamic Resistance

The dynamic resistance of a p-n junction diode is defined as

$$R = \frac{\Delta V}{\Delta i}$$

where ΔV denotes a small change in the applied potential difference and Δi denotes the corresponding small change in the current. The dynamic resistance is a function of the operating potential difference. It is equal to the reciprocal of the slope of the i–V characteristic shown in figure (45.14).

Example 45.3

The i–V characteristic of a p-n junction diode is shown in figure (45.15). Find the approximate dynamic resistance of the p-n junction when (a) a forward bias of 1 volt is applied, (b) a forward bias of 2 volt is applied.

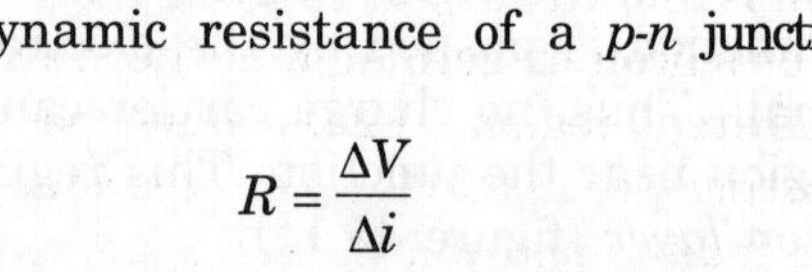

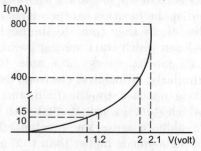

Figure 45.15

Solution : (a) The current at 1 volt is 10 mA and at 1·2 volt it is 15 mA. The dynamic resistance in this region is

$$R = \frac{\Delta V}{\Delta i} = \frac{0{\cdot}2 \text{ volt}}{5 \text{ mA}} = 40\ \Omega.$$

(b) The current at 2 volt is 400 mA and at 2·1 volt it is 800 mA. The dynamic resistance in this region is

$$R = \frac{\Delta V}{\Delta i} = \frac{0{\cdot}1 \text{ volt}}{400 \text{ mA}} = 0{\cdot}25\ \Omega.$$

Photodiode

Photodiode is a *p-n* junction whose function is controlled by the light allowed to fall on it. Suppose, the wavelength is such that the energy of a photon, hc/λ, is sufficient to break a valence bond. When such light falls on the junction, new hole–electron pairs are created. The number of charge carriers increases and hence the conductivity of the junction increases. If the junction is connected in some circuit, the current in the circuit is controlled by the intensity of the incident light.

Light-emitting Diode (LED)

When a conduction electron makes a transition to the valence band to fill up a hole in a *p-n* junction, the extra energy may be emitted as a photon. If the wavelength of this photon is in the visible range (380 nm–780 nm), one can see the emitted light. Such a *p-n* junction is known as *light-emitting diode* abbreviated as LED. For silicon or germanium, the wavelength falls in the infrared region. LEDs may be made from semiconducting compounds like gallium such as, arsenide or indium phosphide. LEDs are very commonly used in electronic gadgets as indicator lights.

Zener Diode

If the reverse-bias voltage across a *p-n* junction diode is increased, at a particular voltage the reverse current suddenly increases to a large value. This phenomenon is called *breakdown* of the diode and the voltage at which it occurs is called the *breakdown voltage*. At this voltage, the rate of creation of hole–electron pairs is increased leading to the increased current.

There are two main processes by which breakdown may occur. The holes in the *n*-side and the conduction electrons in the *p*-side are accelerated due to the reverse-bias voltage. If these minority carriers acquire sufficient kinetic energy from the electric field and collide with a valence electron, the bond will be broken and the valence electron will be taken to the conduction band. Thus a hole–electron pair will be created. Breakdown occurring in this manner is called *avalanche breakdown*. Breakdown may also be produced by direct breaking of valence bonds due to high electric field. When breakdown occurs in this manner it is called *zener breakdown*.

A diode meant to operate in the breakdown region is called an *avalanche diode* or a *zener diode* depending on the mechanism of breakdown. Once the breakdown occurs, the potential difference across the diode does not increase even if the applied battery potential is increased. Such diodes are used to obtain constant voltage output. Figure (45.16) shows the *i–V* characteristic of a zener diode including the breakdown region and a typical circuit which gives constant voltage V_0 across the load resistance R_L. Even if there is a small change in the input voltage V_i, the current through R_L remains almost the same. The current through the diode changes but the voltage across it remains essentially the same. Note the symbol used for the zener diode.

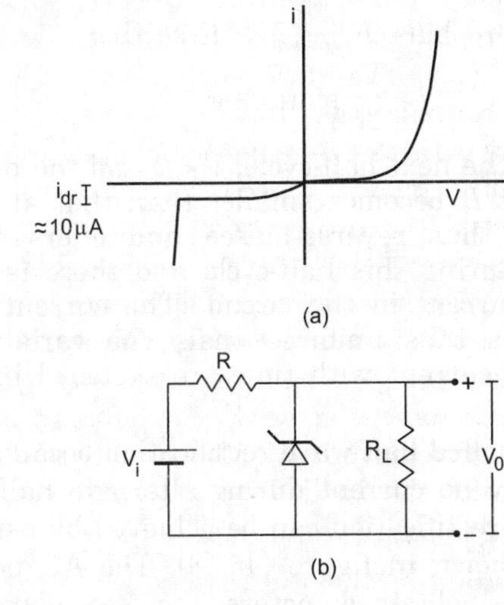

Figure 45.16

45.8 *p-n* JUNCTION AS A RECTIFIER

A rectifier is a device which converts an alternating voltage into a direct voltage. A *p-n*

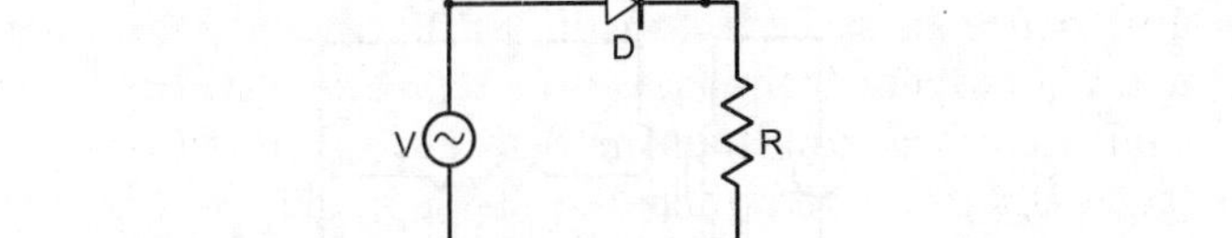

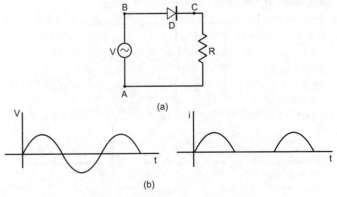

Figure 45.17

junction can be used as a rectifier because it permits current in one direction only. Figure (45.17a) shows an AC source connected to a load resistance through a *p-n* junction. The potential at the point *A* is taken to be zero. The potential at *B* varies with time as $V = V_0 \sin(\omega t + \varphi)$. During the positive half-cycle, $V > 0$ and *B* is at a higher potential than *A*. In this case, the junction is forward-biased and a current *i* is established in the resistance in the direction *C* to *A*.

The current through the resistance during this half-cycle is given by

$$i = \frac{V_0 \sin(\omega t + \varphi)}{R + R_{junction}}$$

and the potential difference across it is

$$\frac{RV_0 \sin(\omega t + \varphi)}{R + R_{junction}} .$$

Here $R_{junction}$ is the resistance offered by the *p-n* junction.

In forward bias, $R_{junction} << R$ so that

$$i \approx \frac{V_0}{R} \sin(\omega t + \varphi).$$

During the next half-cycle, $V < 0$ and the potential at the point *B* becomes smaller than that at *A*. The junction is thus reverse-biased and offers a large resistance during this half-cycle and there is only a negligible current in the circuit. The current in the resistance is thus unidirectional. The variations in voltage and current with time are sketched in figure (45.17b).

This is called half-wave rectification because there is practically no current during alternate half-cycles. A full-wave rectification can be achieved by using two diodes as shown in figure (45.18). The AC potential difference is obtained across the secondary of a transfomer and is connected in the circuit. In one half-cycle, $V_A > V_C > V_B$ so that the junction D_1 conducts but D_2 does not. The current is from *A* to D_1 to *E* to *C*. In the next half-cycle, $V_B > V_C > V_A$ so that D_2 conducts whereas D_1 does not. The current is from *B* to D_2 to *E* to *C*. In both the half-cycles, the current in the load resistance is from *E* to *C*.

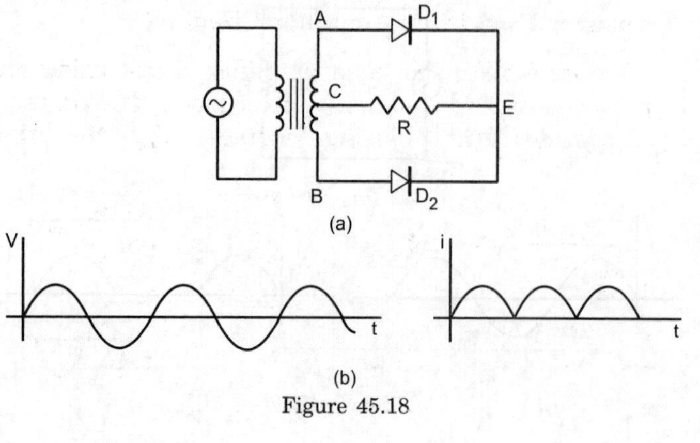

Figure 45.18

45.9 JUNCTION TRANSISTORS

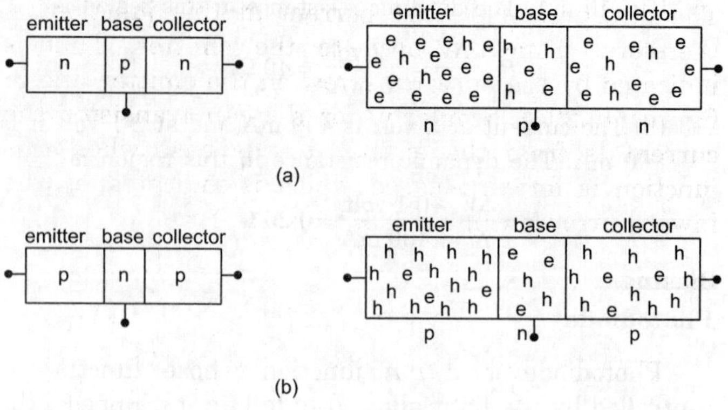

Figure 45.19

A junction transistor is formed by sandwiching a thin layer of a *p*-type semiconductor between two layers of *n*-type semiconductors or by sandwiching a thin layer of an *n*-type semiconductor between two layers of *p*-type semiconductors. In figure (45-19a), we show a transistor in which a thin layer of a *p*-type semiconductor is sandwiched between two *n*-type semiconductors. The resulting structure is called an *n-p-n* transistor. In figure (45.19b), we show a *p-n-p* transistor, where an *n*-type thin layer is sandwiched between two *p*-type layers. In actual design, the middle layer is very thin (≈ 1 μm) as compared to the widths of the two layers at the sides. The middle layer is called the *base* and is very lightly doped with impurity. One of the outer layers is heavily doped and is called *emitter*. The other outer layer is moderately doped and is called *collector*. Usually, the emitter–base contact area is smaller than the collector–base contact area. Terminals come out from the emitter, the base and the collector for external connections. Thus, a transistor is a three-terminal device.

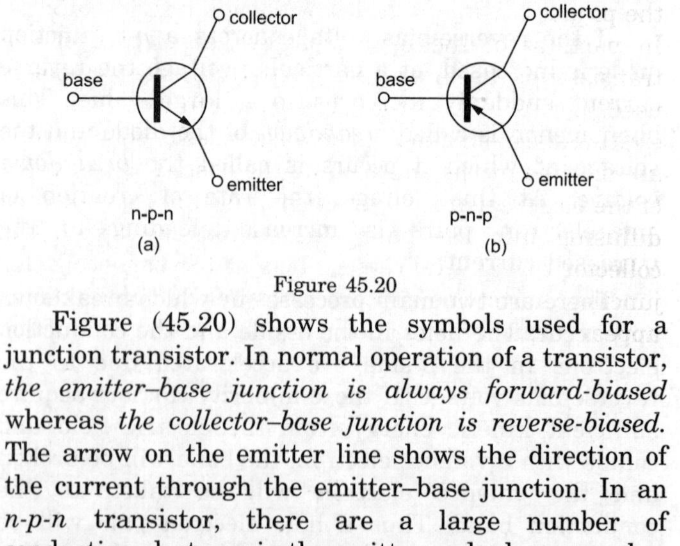

Figure 45.20

Figure (45.20) shows the symbols used for a junction transistor. In normal operation of a transistor, *the emitter–base junction is always forward-biased* whereas *the collector–base junction is reverse-biased.* The arrow on the emitter line shows the direction of the current through the emitter–base junction. In an *n-p-n* transistor, there are a large number of conduction electrons in the emitter and a large number of holes in the base. If the junction is forward-biased, the electrons will diffuse from the emitter to the base and holes will diffuse from the base to the emitter. The direction of electric current at this junction is, therefore, from the base to the emitter. This is indicated by the outward arrow on the emitter line in figure (45.20a). Similarly, for a *p-n-p* transistor the current is from the emitter to the base when this junction is forward-biased which is indicated by the inward arrow in figure (45.20b).

Biasing

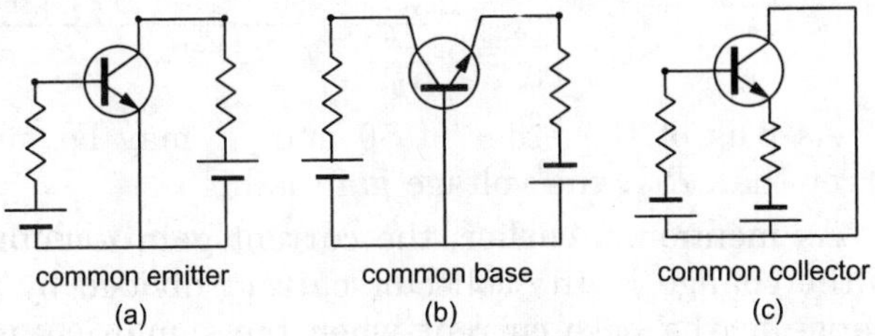

Figure 45.21

Suitable potential differences should be applied across the two junctions to operate the transitor. This is called *biasing* the transistor. A transistor can be operated in three different modes: common-emitter (or grounded-emitter), common-collector (or grounded-collector) and common-base (or grounded-base). In common-emitter mode, the emitter is kept at zero potential and the other two terminals are given appropriate potentials (figure 45.21a). Similarly, in common-base mode, the base is kept at zero potential (figure 45-21b) whereas in common-collector mode, the collector is kept at zero potential (figure 45-21c).

Working of a Transistor

Let us consider an *n-p-n* transistor connected to the proper biasing batteries as shown in figure (45.22). In part (a) of the figure, a physical picture of the transistor is used whereas in part (b), its symbol is used. Let us look at the current due to electrons. The emitter–base junction is forward-biased, so electrons are injected by the emitter into the base. The thickness of the base region is so small that most of the electrons diffusing into the base region cross over into the collector region. The reverse bias at the base–collector junction helps this process, because, as the electrons appear near this junction they are attracted by the

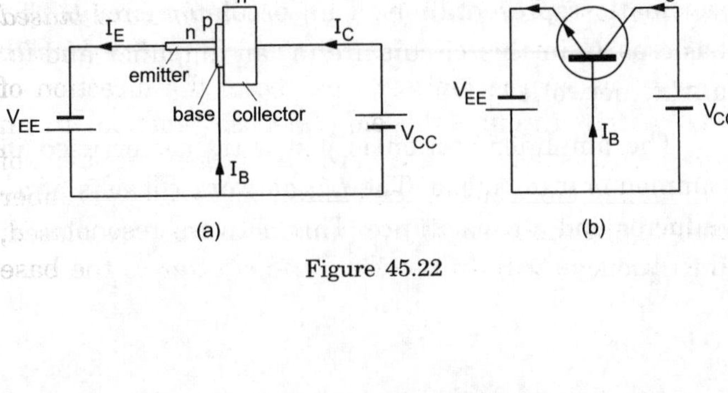

Figure 45.22

collector. These electrons go through the batteries V_{CC} and V_{EE} and are then back to the emitter.

The electrons going from the battery V_{EE} to the emitter constitute the electric current I_E in the opposite direction. This is known as *emitter current*. Similarly, the electrons going from the collector to the battery V_{CC} constitute the *collector current* I_C.

We have considered only the current due to the electrons. Similar is the story of the holes which move in the opposite direction but result in current in the same direction. Currents I_E and I_C refer to the net currents. However, since the base is only lightly doped, the hole concentration is very low and the current in an *n-p-n* transistor is mostly due to the electrons. As almost all the electrons injected into the emitter go through the collector, the collector current I_C is almost equal to the emitter current. In fact, I_C is slightly smaller than I_E because some of the electrons coming to the base from the emitter may find a path directly from the base to the battery V_{EE}. This constitutes a *base current* I_B. The physical design of the transistor ensures that such events are small and hence I_B is small. Typically, I_B may be 1% to 5% of I_E.

Using Kirchhoff's law, we can write

$$I_E = I_B + I_C. \qquad \text{... (45.1)}$$

α and β Parameters

α and β parameters of a transistor are defined as

$$\alpha = \frac{I_C}{I_E} \text{ and } \beta = \frac{I_C}{I_B}. \qquad \text{... (45.2)}$$

Using equation (45.1),

$$\frac{I_E}{I_C} = \frac{I_B}{I_C} + 1 \qquad \text{... (i)}$$

or,
$$\frac{1}{\alpha} = \frac{1}{\beta} + 1$$

or,
$$\beta = \frac{\alpha}{1 - \alpha}. \qquad \text{... (45.3)}$$

As I_B is about 1–5% of I_E, α is about 0·95 to 0·99 and β is about 20 to 100.

Transistor Used in an Amplifier Circuit

Figure (45.23) shows an amplifier circuit using an *n-p-n* transistor in common-emitter mode. The battery E_B provides the biasing voltage V_{BE} for the

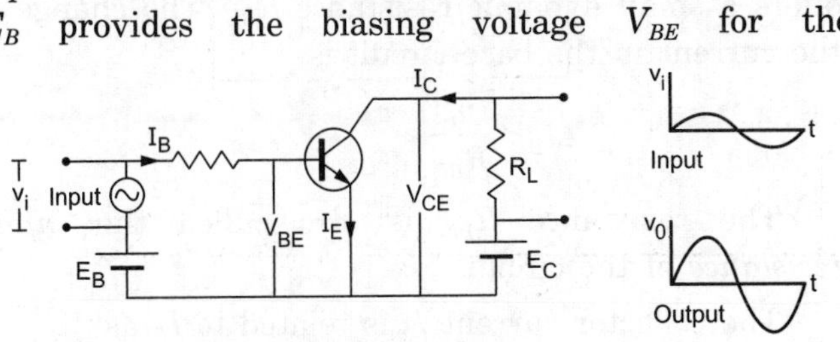

Figure 45.23

base–emitter junction. A potential difference V_{CE} is maintained between the collector and the emitter by the battery E_C. The base–emitter junction is forward-biased and so the electrons of the emitter flow towards the base. As the base region is very thin—of the order of a micrometre—and the collector is also maintained at a positive potential, most of the electrons cross the base region and move into the collector. As discussed earlier, the current I_C is about 0·95 I_E to 0·99 I_E.

The holes in the base region may diffuse into the emitter due to the forward biasing of the base–emitter junction. Also, the electrons coming from the emitter may recombine with some of the holes in the base. If the holes are lost in this way, the base will become negatively charged and will obstruct the incoming electrons from the emitter. If the base current I_B is increased by a small amount, the effect of hole-diffusion and hole–electron recombination may be neutralised and the collector current will be increased. Thus, a small change in the current I_B in the base circuit controls the larger current I_C in the collector circuit. This is the basis of amplification with the help of a transistor.

The input signal, to be amplified, is connected in series with the biasing battery E_B in the base circuit. A load resistor having a large resistance R_L is connected in the collector circuit and the output voltage is taken across this resistor. As the potential difference V_{BE} changes with time due to the input signal, the base current I_B changes. This results in a change ΔI_C in the collector current. The *current gain,* defined as $\Delta I_C / \Delta I_B$, is typically of the order of 50. The change in the voltage across R_L is, accordingly,

$$\Delta V = R_L \Delta I_C.$$

Thus, an amplified output is obtained across R_L.

Voltage gain, current gain and power gain

When a signal voltage v_i is added in the base circuit, the voltage across the load resistance changes by v_o. The ratio $\frac{v_o}{v_i}$ is called the *voltage gain* of the amplifier.

Suppose the input signal has a voltage v_i at an instant. This produces a change in the base current I_B. As the base–emitter junction is forward-biased, it offers a small dynamic resistance R_{BE}. The change in the current in the base circuit is

$$\Delta I_B = \frac{v_i}{R_{BE}} .$$

The resistance R_{BE} is also called the *input-resistance* of the circuit.

The collector current I_c is related to I_B as

$$I_c = \beta I_B.$$

Thus, the change in current I_C due to the signal voltage is,

$$\Delta I_C = \beta \Delta I_B = \beta \frac{v_i}{R_{BE}} .$$

The output voltage, i.e., the change in the voltage across the load resistance is

$$v_o = \Delta V = R_L \, \Delta I_C = \frac{\beta v_i R_L}{R_{BE}} .$$

The voltage gain is

$$\frac{v_o}{v_i} = \beta \frac{R_L}{R_{BE}} .$$

As β is of the order of 50 and R_L may be much larger than R_{BE}, the voltage gain is high.

As mentioned earlier, the current gain is defined as the change in the collector current divided by the change in the base current when the signal is added in the base circuit.

Thus, the current gain is

$$\frac{\Delta I_C}{\Delta I_B} = \beta.$$

$$\text{Power gain} = \text{voltage gain} \times \text{current gain}$$

$$= \frac{\beta^2 R_L}{R_{BE}} .$$

Transfer conductance

To have a large amplification, a small change in V_{BE} should result in a large change in the collector current I_C. This property is measured by a quantity *transfer conductance* g_m defined as

$$g_m = \frac{\Delta I_C}{\Delta V_{BE}} .$$

It is also known as *transconductance.*

Transistor Used in an Oscillator Circuit

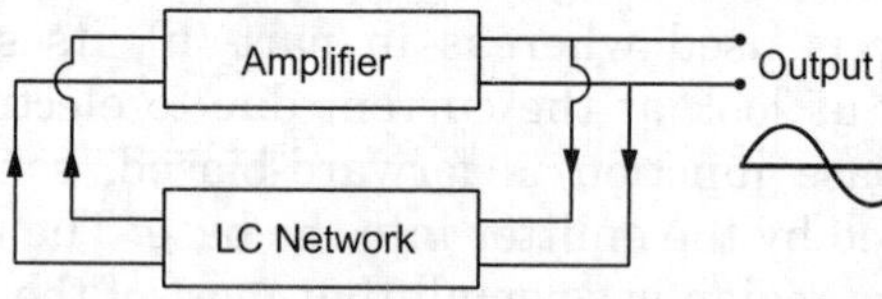

Figure 45.24

The function of an oscillator circuit is to produce an alternating voltage of desired frequency when only DC batteries are available. Figure (45.24) shows a schematic representation of an oscillator circuit. The basic parts in this circuit are (a) an amplifier and (b) an *LC* network.

The amplifier section is just a transistor used in common-emitter mode. The *LC* network consists of an inductor and a capacitance. This network resonates at a frequency

$$\nu_0 = \frac{1}{2\pi}\sqrt{\frac{1}{LC}}\,.$$

Batteries are used to bias the transistor and no external input signal is fed to the amplifying section. A part of the output signal is fed back to the input section after going through the LC network. This signal is amplified by the transistor and a part is again fed back to its input section. Thus, it is a self-sustaining device. The component with the proper frequency ν_0 gets resonantly amplified and the output acts as a source of alternating voltage of that frequency. The frequency can be varied by varying L or C.

Transistor Characteristics

Let us consider an *n-p-n* transistor in common-emitter configuration as in figure (45.23). We can view this circuit as made of an input section and an output section. The input section contains the base–emitter junction and the voltage source there whereas the output section contains the base–colletcor junction and the voltage source there. The current I_B may then be called the *input current* and the current I_C the *output current*. The voltage applied to the base–emitter junction, i.e., in the input section is V_{BE} and that applied to the base–collector junction, i.e., in the output section, is V_{CE}. When the input current I_B is plotted against the voltage V_{BE} between the base and the emitter, we get the input characteristics. Similarly, when the output current I_C is plotted against the voltage V_{CE}, we get the output characteristics.

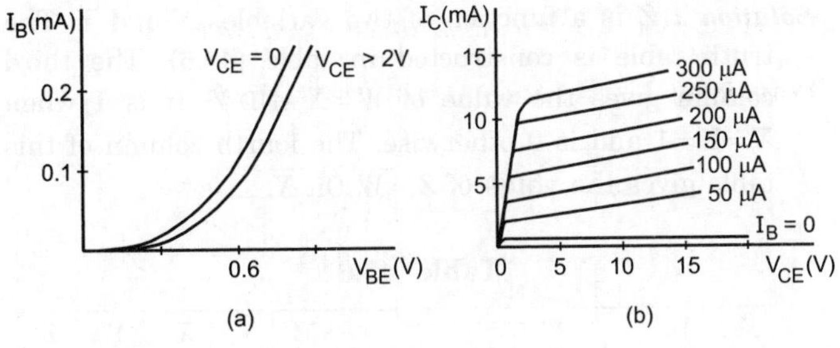

Figure 45.25

These characteristics are shown in figure (45.25). The input characteristics shown in figure (45.25a) are like those of a forward-biased *p-n* junction. If the biasing voltage is small as compared to the height of the potential barrier at the junction, the current I_B is very small. Once the voltage is more than the barrier height, the current rapidly increases. However, since most of the electrons diffused across the junction go to the collector, the net base current is very small (in microamperes) even at large values of V_{BE}.

The output characteristics are shown in figure (45.25b). For small values of the collector voltage, the collector–base junction is reverse–biased because the base is at a more positive potential. The current I_C is then small. As the electrons are forced from the emitter side, the current I_C is still quite large as compared to a single reverse-biased *p-n* junction. As the voltage V_C is increased, the current rapidly increases and becomes roughly constant once the junction is forward-biased. For higher base currents, the collector current is also high and increases more rapidly, even in forward bias.

45.10 LOGIC GATES

Logical Variables and Logical Operations

There are a number of questions which have only two answers, either YES or NO. There are a number of objects which can remain in either of two states only. An electric bulb can either be ON or OFF. A diode can either be conducting or nonconducting. A person can either be alive or dead. A statement may either be true or false. It is interesting to imagine a world in which each variable is allowed to take only two values. These values may be represented by two symbols, 0 and 1. The living state of a person is 0 if he/she is dead and is 1 if he/she is alive. The electric state of a diode is 0 if it is nonconducting and is 1 if it is conducting. Such a world may be very small because in the real world we do have quantities which assume more than two values. But let us concentrate on this small world where everything can either be answered in YES or in NO and so only two symbols 0 and 1 are needed to represent any variable.

Here is an example. A bulb, two switches and a power source are connected as shown in figure (45.26). We have three variables,

A = state of switch S_1
B = state of switch S_2
C = state of the bulb.

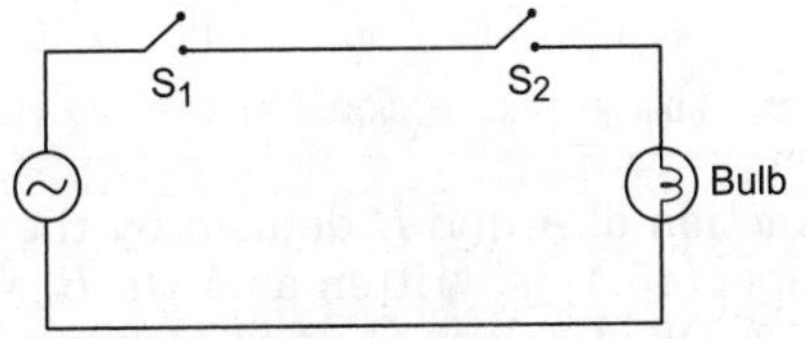

Figure 45.26

Let us assume that the variable A is 0 if the switch S_1 is open and is 1 if the switch S_1 is closed. Similar is the case for B. The variable C is 0 if the bulb is off and is 1 if it is on. Will the bulb be off or on will depend on the states of S_1 and S_2. Table (45.3) shows the dependence.

Table 45.3

Switch S_1	Switch S_2	Bulb	A	B	C
open	open	off	0	0	0
open	closed	off	0	1	0
closed	open	off	1	0	0
closed	closed	on	1	1	1

Thus, C is a *function* of A and B. If we give the value of C for all possible combinations of A and B, the function is completely specified. Thus, a function may be specified by writing a table in which the value of the function is given for all possible combinations of the values of the independent variables. Such a table is known as the *truth table* for that function.

The particular function defined by table (45.3) is written as A AND B. We say that A and B are ANDed to get C. It is also denoted by the symbol of dot. Thus $C = A{\cdot}B$ is the same as $C = A$ AND B. Quite often, the dot is omitted and we write just AB to mean A AND B. The function $C = A$ AND B is 1 if each of A and B is 1. If any of A and B is zero or both are zero, C is 0.

Let us take another example of a function of two variables. Figure (45.27) shows another circuit containing a power source, two switches S_1, S_2 and a bulb. Table (45.4) gives the state of the bulb for all possible combinations of the switches and the truth table for such a function.

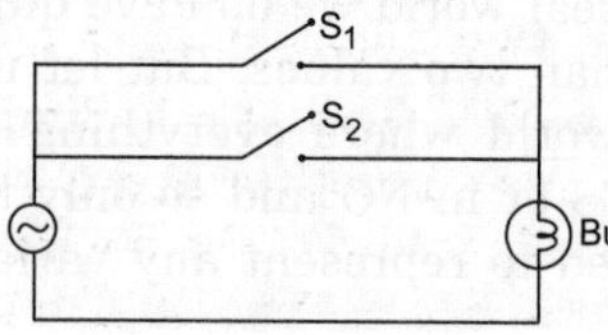

Figure 45.27

Table 45.4

Switch S_1	Switch S_2	Bulb	A	B	C
open	open	off	0	0	0
open	closed	on	0	1	1
closed	open	on	1	0	1
closed	closed	on	1	1	1

The function of A and B defined by the truth table given in table (45.4) is written as A OR B. We say that A and B are ORed to get C. It is also represented by the symbol of plus. Thus $C = A + B$ is the same as $C = A$ OR B. The function $A + B$ is 0 if each of A and B is 0. If one of the two is 1 or both of them are 1, the function is 1.

Let us now take an example of a function of a single variable. A bulb is short-circuited by a switch (figure 45.28). If the switch is open, the current goes through the bulb and it is on. If the switch is closed,

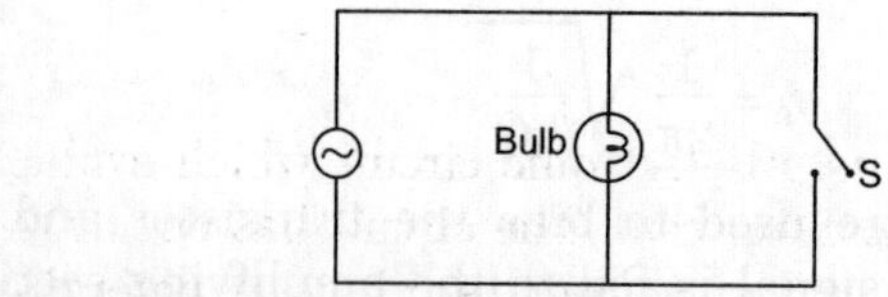

Figure 45.28

the current goes through the switch and the bulb is off (we assume ideally zero resistance in the switch). Let A be the variable showing the state of the switch and B be the variable showing the state of the bulb. Then B is a function of A. Table (45.5) describes the function and its truth table.

Table 45.5

Switch	Bulb	A	B
open	on	0	1
closed	off	1	0

The function of A described by this truth table is written as NOT A. The function NOT A is also written as $\overline{A}$. Thus, $B =$ NOT A is the same as $B = \overline{A}$.

A variable which can assume only two values is called a *logical variable.* A function of logical variables is called a *logical function.* AND, OR and NOT represent three basic operations on logical variables. The first two are operations between two logical variables. The third one is an operation on a single variable. A number of functions may be generated by using these operations.

Example 45.4

Write the truth table for the logical function $Z = (X$ AND $Y)$ OR X.

Solution : Z is a function of two variables X and Y. The truth table is constructed in table (45.6). The third column gives the value of $W = X$ AND Y. It is 1 when $X = Y = 1$ and is 0 otherwise. The fourth column of this table gives the value of $Z = W$ OR X.

Table 45.6

X	Y	W $= X$ AND Y	Z $= W$ OR X	X	Y	Z
0	0	0	0	0	0	0
0	1	0	0	0	1	0
1	0	0	1	1	0	1
1	1	1	1	1	1	1

In the first two rows, $W = 0$ and $X = 0$. Thus W OR $X = 0$. In the third row, $W = 0$ and $X = 1$. Thus W OR $X = 1$. In the fourth row, $W = X = 1$. Thus W OR $X = 1$. The last three columns of the table collect the values of X, Y and Z which is the required truth table.

This function may also be written as

$$Z = (X{\cdot}Y) + X = XY + X.$$

Logic Gates

A logic gate is an electronic circuit which evaluates a particular logical function. The circuit has one or more *input* terminals and an *output* terminal. A potential of zero (equal to the earth's potential in general) denotes the logical value 0 and a fixed positive potential V (say, + 5 V) denotes the logical value 1. Each input terminal denotes an independent variable. If zero potential is applied to an input terminal, the corresponding independent variable takes the value 0. If the positive potential V is applied to the terminal, the corresponding variable takes the value 1. The potential appearing at the output terminal denotes the value of the function. If the potential is zero, the value of the function is 0. If it is V, the value of the function is 1.

A gate may have more than one output terminals. Each output terminal then represents a separate function and the same circuit may be used to evaluate more than one functions.

Figure (45.29) shows the symbols for the logic gates to evaluate the functions AND, OR and NOT. They are known as AND gate, OR gate and NOT gate respectively. The terminals shown on the left are the input terminals and the terminal on the right is the output terminal in each case.

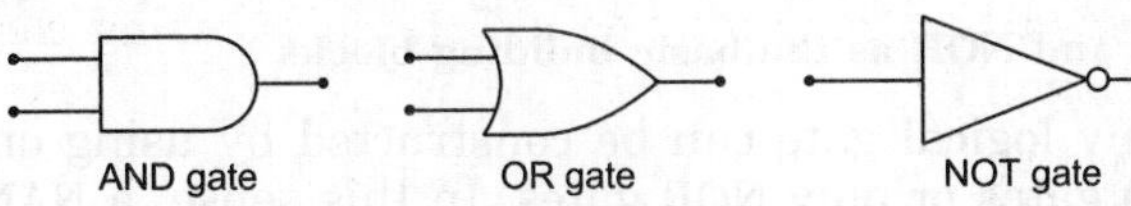

Figure 45.29

Realisation of AND and OR gates with diodes

An AND gate and an OR gate may be constructed with two *p-n* junction diodes. Figure (45.30) shows the construction for an AND gate. The circuit evaluates the function $X = A$ AND B, i.e., $X = AB$. A potential of 5 V at A denotes the logical value $A = 1$ and a potential of zero at A denotes $A = 0$, similarly for B and X.

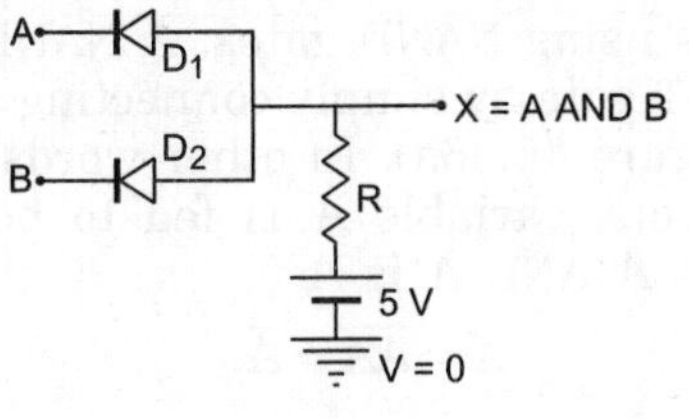

Figure 45.30

Suppose $A = 0$ and $B = 0$. The potentials at A and B are both zero so that both the diodes are forward-biased and offer no resistance. The potential at X is equal to the potential at A or B. Thus, $X = 0$. Now suppose, $A = 0$ and $B = 1$. The potential is zero at A and 5 V at B so that the diode D_1 is forward-biased. The potential at X is equal to the potential at A which is zero. Thus, if $A = 0$ and $B = 1$ then $X = 0$. Similarly, when $A = 1$ and $B = 0$ then $X = 0$. Finally, suppose $A = B = 1$. The potentials at both A and B are 5 V so that neither of the diodes is conducting. This is because if either of the diodes conducts, a current will go through the resistance R and the potential at X will become less than 5 V making the diode reverse-biased. As the diodes are not conducting, there will be no current through R and the potential at X will be equal to 5 V, i.e., $X = 1$.

Thus, the output is $X = 1$ if both the inputs A and B are 1. If any of the inputs is 0, the output is $X = 0$. Hence $X = AB$ and the circuit evaluates the AND function.

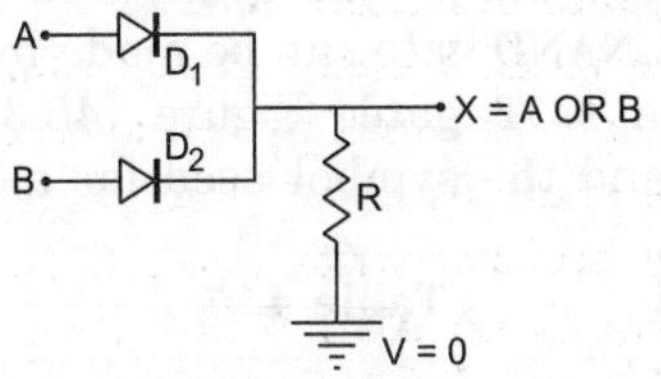

Figure 45.31

Figure (45.31) shows the construction of an OR gate using two diodes. The circuit evaluates X OR A, i.e., $X = A + B$. If $A = B = 0$, there is no potential difference anywhere in the circuit so that $X = 0$. If $A = 1$ and $B = 0$, the potential is 5 V at A and zero at B. The diode D_1 is forward-biased and offers no resistance. Thus, the potential at X is equal to the potential at A, i.e., 5 V. Thus $X = 1$. Similarly, if $A = 0$ and $B = 1$, $X = 1$. Also, if both A and B are 1, both the diodes are forward-biased and the potential at X is the same as the common potential at A and B which is 5 V. This also gives $X = 1$. Hence the circuit evaluates $X = A$ OR $B = A + B$.

Realisation of NOT gate with a transistor

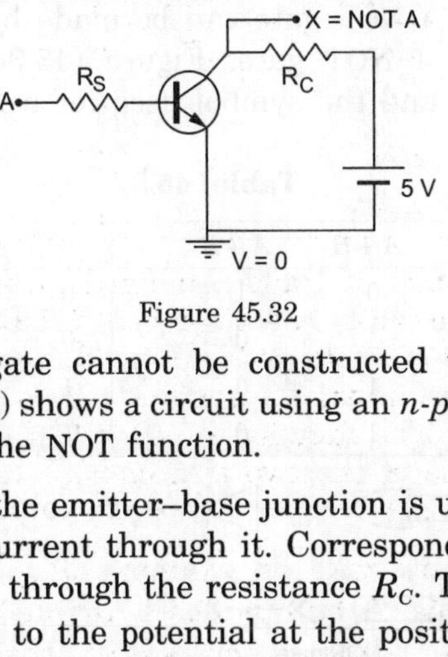

Figure 45.32

A NOT gate cannot be constructed with diodes. Figure (45.32) shows a circuit using an *n-p-n* transistor to evaluate the NOT function.

If $A = 0$, the emitter–base junction is unbiased and there is no current through it. Correspondingly, there is no current through the resistance R_C. The potential at X is equal to the potential at the positive terminal of the battery which is 5 V. Thus, if $A = 0$, $X = 1$. Note that the collector–base junction is also reverse-biased which is consistent with the fact that there is no current in the circuit.

On the other hand if the potential at A is 5 V, the base–emitter junction is forward-biased and there is a large current in the circuit. The direction of the current in the resistance R_C is from right to left in figure (45.33). The potential drops across R and its value at X becomes zero. Thus, if $A = 1, X = 0$.

NAND and NOR gates

The function $X = \text{NOT } (A \text{ AND } B)$ of two logical variables A and B is called NAND function. It is written as $X = A$ NAND B. It is also written as $X = \overline{A \cdot B}$ or simply $X = \overline{AB}$.

Tables (45.7) shows the evaluation of $\overline{AB}$ and its truth table. A NAND gate can be made by an AND gate followed by a NOT gate. Figure (45.33) shows the combination and the symbol used for a NAND gate.

Table 45.7

A	B	AB $= A$ AND B	$\overline{AB} =$ NOT(A AND B)	A	B	$\overline{AB}$
0	0	0	1	0	0	1
0	1	0	1	0	1	1
1	0	0	1	1	0	1
1	1	1	0	1	1	0

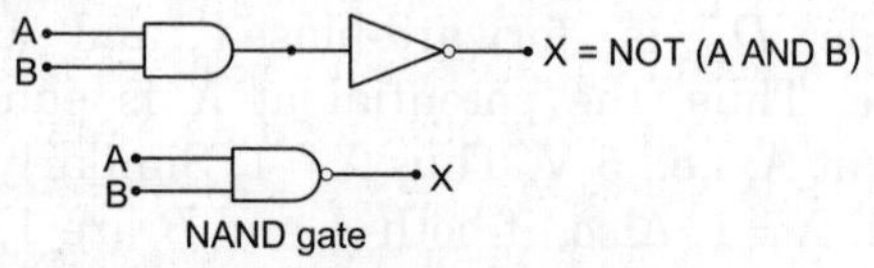

Figure 45.33

The function $X = \text{NOT } (A \text{ OR } B)$ is called a NOR function and is written as $X = A$ NOR B. It is also written as $X = \overline{A + B}$.

Table (45.8) shows the evaluation of $\overline{A + B}$ and its truth table. A NOR gate can be made by an OR gate followed by a NOT gate. Figure (45.34) shows the combination and the symbol used for a NOR gate.

Table 45.8

A	B	$A + B$	$\overline{A + B}$	A	B	$\overline{A + B}$
0	0	0	1	0	0	1
0	1	1	0	0	1	0
1	0	1	0	1	0	0
1	1	1	0	1	1	0

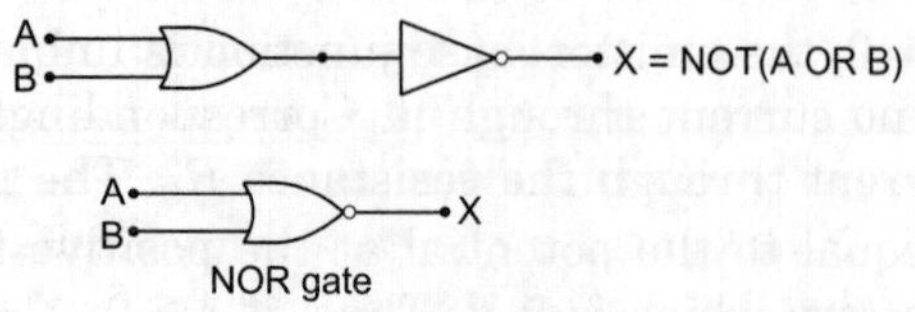

Figure 45.34

XOR gate

XOR is a function of two logical variables A and B which evaluates to 1 if one of the two variables is 0 and the other is 1. If both of the variables are 0 or both are 1, the function is zero. It is also called the *exclusive* OR function. The truth table for XOR function is given in table (45.9). Verify that

$$A \text{ XOR } B = A\overline{B} + \overline{A}B. \qquad \text{... (i)}$$

Table 45.9

A	B	A XOR B
0	0	0
0	1	1
1	0	1
1	1	0

An XOR gate can be constructed with AND, OR and NOT gates as shown in figure (45.35a). The symbol for an XOR gate is shown in figure (45.35b). We have made use of equation (i) in constructing this circuit.

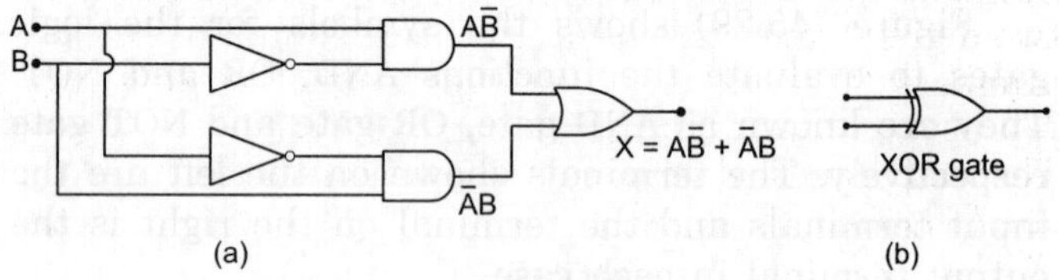

Figure 45.35

NAND and NOR as the basic building blocks

Any logical gate can be constructed by using only NAND gates or only NOR gates. In this sense, a NAND gate or a NOR gate is called a basic building block of logic circuits.

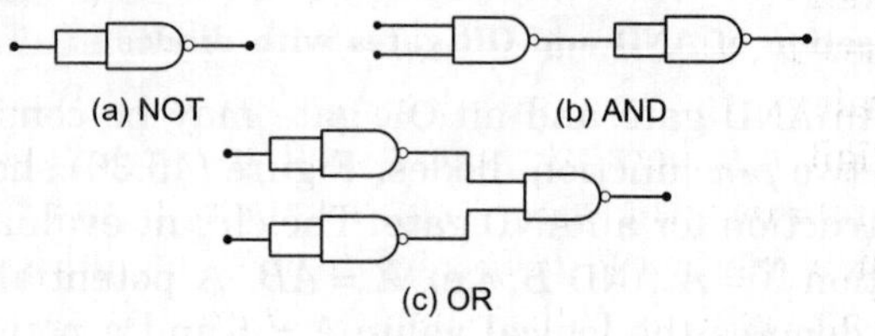

Figure 45.36

Figure (45.36) shows the construction of NOT, AND and OR gates using NAND gates. A NAND gate can be used as a NOT gate by simply connecting the two input terminals (figure 45.36a). In other words, the value of the independent variable A is fed to both the input terminals. As A AND A is A,

$$X = \overline{AA} = \overline{A}.$$

To construct an AND gate, the output of a NAND gate should be fed to a NOT gate. This is because, the output of the NAND gate is $\overline{AB}$, i.e., NOT of AB. If we pass it through a NOT gate, it is again inverted and becomes AB. Figure (45.36b) does exactly the same.

Figure (45.36c) shows the construction of an OR gate. The two input variables are first inverted by passing them through two NOT gates. The inverted signals are NANDed. Let us construct the truth table of this combination and verify that it represents an OR gate. This is done in table (45.10).

Table 45.10

A	B	$\overline{A}$	$\overline{B}$	$\overline{A}\,\overline{B}$	$\overline{\overline{A}\,\overline{B}}$
0	0	1	1	1	0
0	1	1	0	0	1
1	0	0	1	0	1
1	1	0	0	0	1

Thus, $\overline{\overline{A}\,\overline{B}}$ is 1 if either of A and B is 1 or both are 1. It is zero only if both A and B are zero. Thus, $\overline{\overline{A}\,\overline{B}} = A + B$.

Binary Mathematics : Half Adder and Full Adder

Logic gates are the basic elements in the electronic circuits used to perform mathematical calculations such as that in a computer or in a calculator. The numbers are converted into *binary system* where only two digits 0 and 1 are used. In this system, the natural numbers (1, 2, 3, 4, ... in the decimal system) are represented as 1, 10, 11, 100, 101, 110, 111, ..., etc. The mathematical operation of addition is governed by the following basic rules:

$$0 + 0 = 0$$

$$0 + 1 = 1$$

$$1 + 0 = 1$$

$$1 + 1 = 10.$$

The plus sign here represents addition of arithmetic and not the logical operation OR. When 1 is added to 1 in binary system, we get a two digit number 10. It is read as *one zero* and not as ten. It is equivalent to 'two' in decimal system. When two one-digit numbers are added and the result is a two digit number, the more significant digit (that on left) is called the *carry digit* and the less significant digit (that on right) is called the *sum digit.* The word *sum* is often used for the sum digit and *carry* for the carry digit. One should be careful about the word 'sum' because it is also used to mean the net result of addition. Table (45.11) shows the carry digit and the sum digit for the addition of one-digit binary numbers. If we treat A, B, C and S as logical variables (they can take only two values 0 and 1), each of C and S is a logical function of A and B.

Table 45.11

First number A	Second number B	Carry digit C	Sum digit S
0	0	0	0
0	1	0	1
1	0	0	1
1	1	1	0

It can be easily verified that the carry digit C is A AND B and the sum digit S is A XOR B, i.e.,

$$C = AB$$

and $$S = A\overline{B} + \overline{A}B.$$

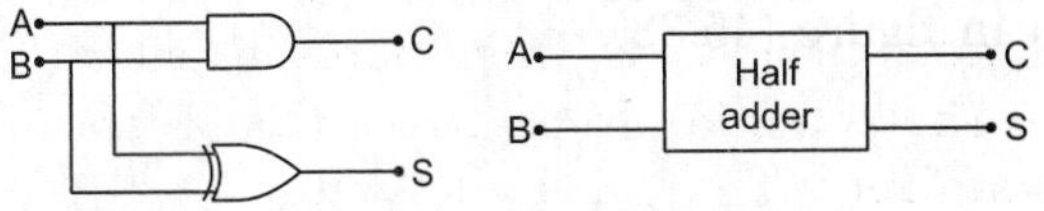

Figure 45.37

Figure (45.37) shows the circuit which takes A and B as inputs and gives C and S as outputs. Note that A and B are passed through an XOR gate to get S. The circuit described above is called a *half adder.* The symbol for a half adder is also shown in the figure.

If two numbers of more than one digit are to be added, one needs to know the addition rules for three one-digit numbers. Here are two examples, one with decimal numbers and one with binary numbers.

$$\begin{array}{r} 11 \\ \hline 768 \\ +\ 353 \\ \hline 1121 \end{array} \qquad \begin{array}{r} 111 \\ \hline 101 \\ +\ 111 \\ \hline 1100 \end{array}$$

In the first example, one has to evaluate 1 + 6 + 5 to get the sum digit as 2 and the carry digit as 1 for the second place from right. Similarly, one needs 1 + 7 + 3. In the second example, one needs the sum 1 + 0 + 1 to get the sum digit as 0 and the carry digit as 1 for the second place from right. Similarly, one needs 1 + 1 + 1 to get the sum digit as 1 and the carry digit as 1. Thus, we need a circuit which can take three inputs A_1, A_2 and A_3 and produce two outputs C and S. There are eight possible combinations of A_1, A_2 and A_3 and table (45.12) gives the values of C and S for all these combinations.

Table 45.12

A_1	A_2	A_3	C	S
0	0	0	0	0
0	0	1	0	1
0	1	0	0	1
0	1	1	1	0
1	0	0	0	1
1	0	1	1	0
1	1	0	1	0
1	1	1	1	1

One can add the digits A_1, A_2 and A_3 as follows. First add A_1 and A_2 to get the sum digit S_1 and the carry digit C_1. Now add A_3 and S_1 to get the sum digit S and the carry digit C_2. The sum digit S is the final sum digit. Now consider the two carry digits C_1 and C_2. Verify that both of C_1 and C_2 cannot be 1. If both are 0, the final carry digit is 0. If one of them is 1 and the other is 0, the final carry digit is 1. Thus, the final carry digit may be obtained as $C = C_1$ OR C_2. The circuit shown in figure (45.38) is constructed on these lines to perform the three-digit addition. Such a circuit is called a *full adder*. The symbol of full adder is also shown in figure (45.38).

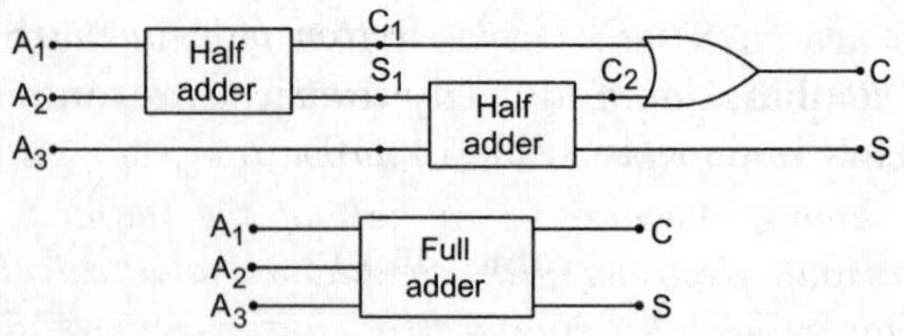

Figure 45.38

Worked Out Examples

1. *A doped semiconductor has impurity levels* 30 meV *below the conduction band. (a) Is the material n-type or p-type ? (b) In a thermal collision, an amount kT of energy is given to the extra electron loosely bound to the impurity ion and this electron is just able to jump into the conduction band. Calculate the temperature T.*

Solution : (a) The impurity provides impurity levels close to the conduction band and a number of electrons from the impurity level will populate the conduction band. Thus, the majority carriers are electrons and the material is *n*-type.

(b) According to the question, $kT = 30$ meV

or, $$T = \frac{30 \text{ meV}}{k}$$

$$= \frac{0{\cdot}03 \text{ eV}}{8{\cdot}62 \times 10^{-5} \text{ eV K}^{-1}} = 348 \text{ K}.$$

2. *The energy of a photon of sodium light* ($\lambda = 589$ nm) *equals the band gap of a semiconducting material. (a) Find the minimum energy E required to create a hole–electron pair. (b) Find the value of E/kT at a temperature of* 300 K.

Solution : (a) The energy of the photon is $E = \frac{hc}{\lambda}$

$$= \frac{1242 \text{ eV nm}}{589 \text{ nm}} = 2{\cdot}1 \text{ eV}.$$

Thus the band gap is 2·1 eV. This is also the minimum energy E required to push an electron from the valence band into the conduction band. Hence, the minimum energy required to create a hole–electron pair is 2·1 eV.

(b) At $T = 300$ K,

$$kT = (8{\cdot}62 \times 10^{-5} \text{ eV K}^{-1})(300 \text{ K})$$

$$= 25{\cdot}86 \times 10^{-3} \text{ eV}.$$

Thus, $$\frac{E}{kT} = \frac{2{\cdot}1 \text{ eV}}{25{\cdot}86 \times 10^{-3} \text{ eV}} = 81.$$

So it is difficult for the thermal energy to create the hole–electron pair but a photon of light can do it easily.

3. *A p-type semiconductor has acceptor levels* 57 meV *above the valence band. Find the maximum wavelength of light which can create a hole.*

Solution : To create a hole, an electron from the valence band should be given sufficient energy to go into one of the acceptor levels. Since the acceptor levels are 57 meV above the valence band, at least 57 meV is needed to create a hole.

If λ be the wavelength of light, its photon will have an energy hc/λ. To create a hole,

$$\frac{hc}{\lambda} \geq 57 \text{ meV}$$

or, $$\lambda \leq \frac{hc}{57 \text{ meV}}$$

$$= \frac{1242 \text{ eV nm}}{57 \times 10^{-3} \text{ eV}} = 2{\cdot}18 \times 10^{-5} \text{ m}.$$

4. *The band gap in germanium is* $\Delta E = 0{\cdot}68$ eV. *Assuming that the number of hole–electron pairs is proportional to* $e^{-\Delta E/2kT}$, *find the percentage increase in the number of charge carriers in pure germanium as the temperature is increased from* 300 K *to* 320 K.

Solution : The number of charge carriers in an intrinsic semiconductor is double the number of hole–electron pairs. If N_1 be the number of charge carriers at temperature T_1 and N_2 at T_2, we have

$$N_1 = N_0 \, e^{-\Delta E/2kT_1}$$

and $$N_2 = N_0 \, e^{-\Delta E/2kT_2}.$$

The percentage increase as the temperature is raised from T_1 to T_2 is

$$f = \frac{N_2 - N_1}{N_1} \times 100 = \left(\frac{N_2}{N_1} - 1\right) \times 100$$

$$= 100 \left[e^{\frac{\Delta E}{2k}\left(\frac{1}{T_1} - \frac{1}{T_2}\right)} - 1 \right].$$

Now $$\frac{\Delta E}{2k}\left(\frac{1}{T_1} - \frac{1}{T_2}\right)$$

$$= \frac{0{\cdot}68 \text{ eV}}{2 \times 8{\cdot}62 \times 10^{-5} \text{ eV K}^{-1}} \left(\frac{1}{300 \text{ K}} - \frac{1}{320 \text{ K}} \right)$$

$$= 0{\cdot}82.$$

Thus, $$f = 100 \times [e^{0{\cdot}82} - 1] \approx 127.$$

Thus, the number of charge carriers increases by about 127%.

5. *The concentration of hole–electron pairs in pure silicon at $T = 300$ K is 7×10^{15} per cubic metre. Antimony is doped into silicon in a proportion of 1 atom in 10^7 atoms. Assuming that half of the impurity atoms contribute electrons in the conduction band, calculate the factor by which the number of charge carriers increases due to doping. The number of silicon atoms per cubic metre is 5×10^{28}.*

Solution : The number of charge carriers before doping is equal to the number of holes plus the number of conduction electrons. Thus, the number of charge carriers per cubic metre before doping

$$= 2 \times 7 \times 10^{15} = 14 \times 10^{15}.$$

Since antimony is doped in a proportion of 1 in 10^7, the number of antimony atoms per cubic metre is $10^{-7} \times 5 \times 10^{28} = 5 \times 10^{21}$. As half of these atoms contribute electrons to the conduction band, the number of extra conduction electrons produced is $2{\cdot}5 \times 10^{21}$ per cubic metre. Thus, the number of charge carriers per cubic metre after the doping is

$$2{\cdot}5 \times 10^{21} + 14 \times 10^{15}$$

$$\approx 2{\cdot}5 \times 10^{21}.$$

The factor by which the number of charge carriers is increased

$$= \frac{2{\cdot}5 \times 10^{21}}{14 \times 10^{15}} = 1{\cdot}8 \times 10^5.$$

In fact, as the n-type impurity is doped, the number of holes will decrease. This is because the product of the concentrations of holes and conduction electrons remains almost the same. However, this does not affect our result as the number of holes is anyway too small as compared to the number of conduction electrons.

6. *A potential barrier of 0·50 V exists across a p-n junction. (a) If the depletion region is $5{\cdot}0 \times 10^{-7}$ m wide, what is the intensity of the electric field in this region ? (b) An electron with speed $5{\cdot}0 \times 10^5$ m s^{-1} approaches the p-n junction from the n-side. With what speed will it enter the p-side ?*

Solution : (a) The electric field is $E = V/d$

$$= \frac{0{\cdot}50 \text{ V}}{5{\cdot}0 \times 10^{-7} \text{ m}} = 1{\cdot}0 \times 10^6 \text{ V m}^{-1}.$$

(b)

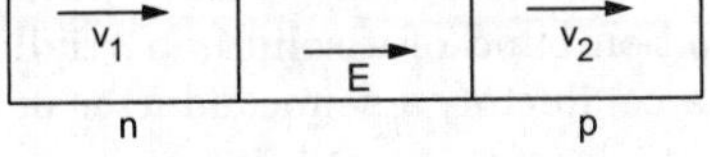

Figure 45-W1

Suppose the electron has a speed v_1 when it enters the depletion layer and v_2 when it comes out of it (figure 45-W1). As the potential energy increases by $e \times 0{\cdot}50$ V, from the principle of conservation of energy,

$$\frac{1}{2} m v_1^2 = e \times 0{\cdot}50 \text{ V} + \frac{1}{2} m v_2^2$$

or, $$\frac{1}{2} \times (9{\cdot}1 \times 10^{-31} \text{ kg}) \times (5{\cdot}0 \times 10^5 \text{ m s}^{-2})^2$$

$$= 1{\cdot}6 \times 10^{-19} \times 0{\cdot}5 \text{ J} + \frac{1}{2}(9{\cdot}1 \times 10^{-31} \text{ kg})\, v_2^2$$

or, $$1{\cdot}13 \times 10^{-19} \text{ J} = 0{\cdot}8 \times 10^{-19} \text{ J} + (4{\cdot}55 \times 10^{-31} \text{ kg})\, v_2^2.$$

Solving this, $v_2 = 2{\cdot}7 \times 10^5$ m s^{-1}.

7. *The reverse-biased current of a particular p-n junction diode increases when it is exposed to light of wavelength less than or equal to 600 nm. Assume that the increase in carrier concentration takes place due to the creation of new hole–electron pairs by the light. Find the band gap.*

Solution : The reverse-biased current is caused mainly due to the drift current. The drift current in a p-n junction is caused by the formation of new hole–electron pairs and their subsequent motions in the depletion layer. When the junction is exposed to light, it may absorb energy from the light photons. If this energy supplied by a photon is greater than (or equal to) the band gap, a hole–electron pair may be formed. Thus, the reverse-biased current will increase if the light photons have energy greater than (or equal to) the band gap. Hence the band gap is equal to the energy of a photon of 600 nm light which is

$$\frac{hc}{\lambda} = \frac{1242 \text{ eV nm}}{600 \text{ nm}} = 2{\cdot}07 \text{ eV}.$$

8. *A 2 V battery may be connected across the points A and B as shown in figure (45-W2). Assume that the resistance of each diode is zero in forward bias and infinity in reverse bias. Find the current supplied by the battery if the positive terminal of the battery is connected to (a) the point A (b) the point B.*

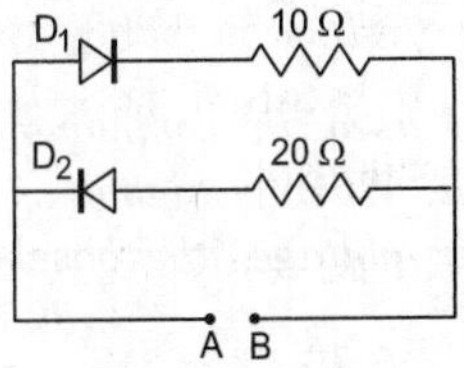

Figure 45-W2

Solution : (a) When the positive terminal of the battery is connected to the point A, the diode D_1 is forward-biased and D_2 is reverse-biased. The resistance of the diode D_1 is zero, and it can be replaced by a resistanceless wire. Similarly, the resistance of the diode D_2 is infinity, and it can be replaced by a broken wire. The equivalent circuit is shown in figure (45-W3a). The current supplied by the battery is 2 V/10 Ω = 0·2 A.

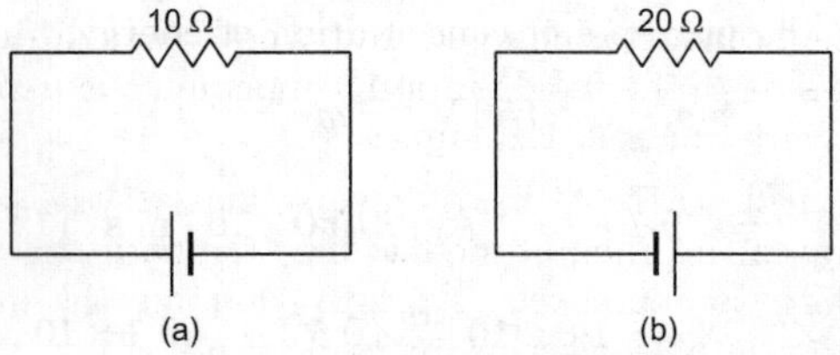

Figure 45-W3

(b) When the positive terminal of the battery is connected to the point B, the diode D_2 is forward-biased and D_1 is reverse biased. The equivalent circuit is shown in figure (45-W3b). The current through the battery is $2\ \text{V}/20\ \Omega = 0{\cdot}1\ \text{A}$.

9. *A change of* 8·0 mA *in the emitter current brings a change of* 7·9 mA *in the collector current. How much change in the base current is required to have the same change* 7·9 mA *in the collector current ? Find the values of* α *and* β.

Solution : We have,

$$I_E = I_B + I_C$$

or, $$\Delta I_E = \Delta I_B + \Delta I_C.$$

From the question, when $\Delta I_E = 8{\cdot}0\ \text{mA}$, $\Delta I_C = 7{\cdot}9\ \text{mA}$.

Thus,

$$\Delta I_B = 8{\cdot}0\ \text{mA} - 7{\cdot}9\ \text{mA} = 0{\cdot}1\ \text{mA}.$$

So a change of 0·1 mA in the base current is required to have a change of 7·9 mA in the collector current.

$$\alpha = \frac{I_C}{I_E} = \frac{\Delta I_C}{\Delta I_E}$$

$$= \frac{7{\cdot}9\ \text{mA}}{8{\cdot}0\ \text{mA}} \approx 0{\cdot}99.$$

$$\beta = \frac{I_C}{I_B} = \frac{\Delta I_C}{\Delta I_B}$$

$$= \frac{7{\cdot}9\ \text{mA}}{0{\cdot}1\ \text{mA}} = 79.$$

Check if these values of α and β satisfy the equation

$$\beta = \frac{\alpha}{1-\alpha}.$$

10. *A transistor is used in common-emitter mode in an amplifier circuit. When a signal of* 20 mV *is added to the base–emitter voltage, the base current changes by* 20 μA *and the collector current changes by* 2 mA. *The load resistance is* 5 kΩ. *Calculate (a) the factor* β, *(b) the input resistance* R_{BE}, *(c) the transconductance and (d) the voltage gain.*

Solution : (a) $\beta = \frac{\Delta I_C}{\Delta I_B} = \frac{2\ \text{mA}}{20\ \mu\text{A}} = 100.$

(b) The input resistance $R_{BE} = \frac{\Delta V_{BE}}{\Delta I_B}$

$$= \frac{20\ \text{mV}}{20\ \mu\text{A}} = 1\ \text{k}\Omega.$$

(c) Transconductance $= \frac{\Delta I_C}{\Delta V_{BE}}$

$$= \frac{2\ \text{mA}}{20\ \text{mV}} = 0{\cdot}1\ \text{mho}.$$

(d) The change in output voltage is $R_L\, \Delta I_c$

$$= (5\ \text{k}\Omega)\,(2\ \text{mA}) = 10\ \text{V}.$$

The applied signal voltage = 20 mV.

Thus, the voltage gain is,

$$\frac{10\ \text{V}}{20\ \text{mV}} = 500.$$

11. *Construct the truth table for the function X of A and B represented by figure (45-W4).*

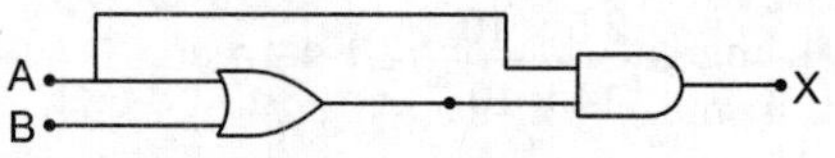

Figure 45-W4

Solution : Here an AND gate and an OR gate are used. Let the output of the OR gate be Y. Clearly, $Y = A + B$. The AND gate receives A and $A + B$ as input. The output of this gate is X. So $X = A(A + B)$. The following table evaluates X for all combinations of A and B. The last three columns give the truth table.

A	B	$Y = A + B$	$X = A(A + B)$	A	B	X
0	0	0	0	0	0	0
0	1	1	0	0	1	0
1	0	1	1	1	0	1
1	1	1	1	1	1	1

□

QUESTIONS FOR SHORT ANSWER

1. How many 1s energy states are present in one mole of sodium vapour ? Are they all filled in normal conditions ? How many 3s energy states are present in one mole of sodium vapour ? Are they all filled in normal conditions ?
2. There are energy bands in a solid. Do we have really continuous energy variation in a band or do we have very closely spaced but still discrete energy levels ?
3. The conduction band of a solid is partially filled at 0 K. Will it be a conductor, a semiconductor or an insulator ?
4. In semiconductors, thermal collisions are responsible for taking a valence electron to the conduction band. Why does the number of conduction electrons not go on increasing with time as thermal collisions continuously take place ?

5. When an electron goes from the valence band to the conduction band in silicon, its energy is increased by 1·1 eV. The average energy exchanged in a thermal collision is of the order of kT which is only 0·026 eV at room temperature. How is a thermal collision able to take some of the electrons from the valence band to the conduction band?

6. What is the resistance of an intrinsic semiconductor at 0 K?

7. We have valence electrons and conduction electrons in a semiconductor. Do we also have 'valence holes' and 'conduction holes'?

8. When a p-type impurity is doped in a semiconductor, a large number of holes are created. This does not make the semiconductor charged. But when holes diffuse from the p-side to the n-side in a p-n junction, the n-side gets positively charged. Explain.

9. The drift current in a reverse-biased p-n junction increases in magnitude if the temperature of the junction is increased. Explain this on the basis of creation of hole–electron pairs.

10. An ideal diode should pass a current freely in one direction and should stop it completely in the opposite direction. Which is closer to ideal—vacuum diode or a p-n junction diode?

11. Consider an amplifier circuit using a transistor. The output power is several times greater than the input power. Where does the extra power come from?

OBJECTIVE I

1. Electric conduction in a semiconductor takes place due to
(a) electrons only (b) holes only
(c) both electrons and holes
(d) neither electrons nor holes.

2. An electric field is applied to a semiconductor. Let the number of charge carriers be n and the average drift speed be v. If the temperature is increased,
(a) both n and v will increase
(b) n will increase but v will decrease
(c) v will increase but n will decrease
(d) both n and v will decrease.

3. Let n_p and n_e be the numbers of holes and conduction electrons in an intrinsic semiconductor.
(a) $n_p > n_e$ (b) $n_p = n_e$ (c) $n_p < n_e$ (d) $n_p \neq n_e$

4. Let n_p and n_e be the numbers of holes and conduction electrons in an extrinsic semiconductor.
(a) $n_p > n_e$ (b) $n_p = n_e$ (c) $n_p < n_e$ (d) $n_p \neq n_e$

5. A p-type semiconductor is
(a) positively charged (b) negatively charged
(c) uncharged
(d) uncharged at 0 K but charged at higher temperatures.

6. When an impurity is doped into an intrinsic semiconductor, the conductivity of the semiconductor
(a) increases (b) decreases
(c) remains the same (d) becomes zero.

7. If the two ends of a p-n junction are joined by a wire,
(a) there will not be a steady current in the circuit
(b) there will be a steady current from the n-side to the p-side
(c) there will a steady current from the p-side to the n-side
(d) there may or may not be a current depending upon the resistance of the connecting wire.

8. The drift current in a p-n junction is
(a) from the n-side to the p-side
(b) from the p-side to the n-side
(c) from the n-side to the p-side if the junction is forward-biased and in the opposite direction if it is reverse-biased
(d) from the p-side to the n-side if the junction is forward-biased and in the opposite direction if it is reverse-biased.

9. The diffusion current in a p-n junction is
(a) from the n-side to the p-side
(b) from the p-side to the n-side
(c) from the n-side to the p-side if the junction is forward-biased and in the opposite direction if it is reverse-biased
(d) from the p-side to the n-side if the junction is forward-biased and in the opposite direction if it is reverse-biased.

10. Diffusion current in a p-n junction is greater than the drift current in magnitude
(a) if the junction is forward-biased
(b) if the junction is reverse-biased
(c) if the junction is unbiased
(d) in no case.

11. Two identical p-n junctions may be connected in series with a battery in three ways (figure 45-Q1). The potential difference across the two p-n junctions are equal in
(a) circuit 1 and circuit 2 (b) circuit 2 and circuit 3
(c) circuit 3 and circuit 1 (d) circuit 1 only.

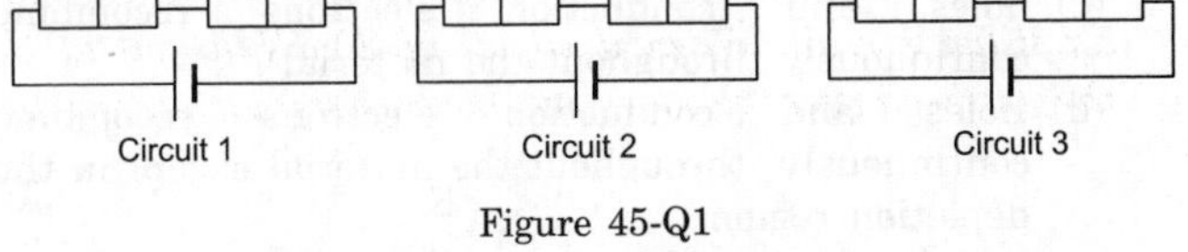

Figure 45-Q1

12. Two identical capacitors A and B are charged to the same potential V and are connected in two circuits at $t = 0$ as shown in figure (45-Q2). The charges on the

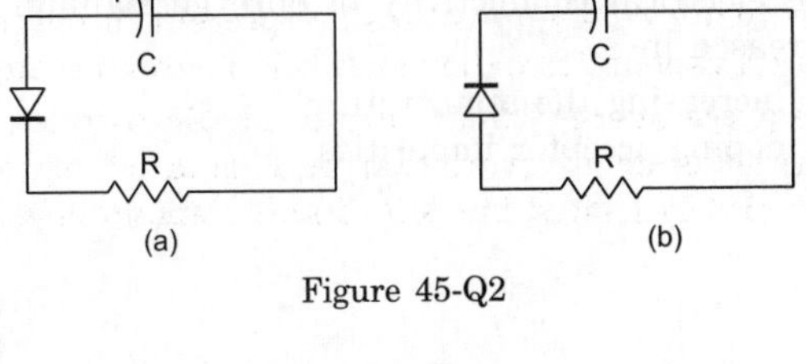

Figure 45-Q2

capacitors at a time $t = CR$ are, respectively,
(a) VC, VC (b) VC/e, VC (c) VC, VC/e (d) VC/e, VC/e.

13. A hole diffuses from the p-side to the n-side in a p-n junction. This means that
(a) a bond is broken on the n-side and the electron freed from the bond jumps to the conduction band
(b) a conduction electron on the p-side jumps to a broken bond to complete it
(c) a bond is broken on the n-side and the electron freed from the bond jumps to a broken bond on the p-side to complete it
(d) a bond is broken on the p-side and the electron freed from the bond jumps to a broken bond on the n-side to complete it.

14. In a transistor,
(a) the emitter has the least concentration of impurity
(b) the collector has the least concentration of impurity
(c) the base has the least concentration of impurity
(d) all the three regions have equal concentrations of impurity.

15. An incomplete sentence about transistors is given below: The emitter–...... junction is ___ and the collector– ...... junction is ___. The appropriate words for the dotted empty positions are, respectively,
(a) 'collector' and 'base' (b) 'base' and 'emitter'
(c) 'collector' and 'emitter' (d) 'base' and 'base'.

OBJECTIVE II

1. In a semiconductor,
(a) there are no free electrons at 0 K
(b) there are no free electrons at any temperature
(c) the number of free electrons increases with temperature
(d) the number of free electrons is less than that in a conductor.

2. In a p-n junction with open ends,
(a) there is no systematic motion of charge carriers
(b) holes and conduction electrons systematically go from the p-side to the n-side and from the n-side to the p-side respectively
(c) there is no net charge transfer between the two sides
(d) there is a constant electric field near the junction.

3. In a p-n junction,
(a) new holes and conduction electrons are produced continuously throughout the material
(b) new holes and conduction electrons are produced continuously throughout the material except in the depletion region
(c) holes and conduction electrons recombine continuously throughout the material
(d) holes and conduction electrons recombine continuously throughout the material except in the depletion region.

4. The impurity atoms with which pure silicon may be doped to make it a p-type semiconductor are those of
(a) phosphorus (b) boron (c) antimony (d) aluminium.

5. The electrical conductivity of pure germanium can be increased by
(a) increasing the temperature
(b) doping acceptor impurities
(c) doping donor impurities
(d) irradiating ultraviolet light on it.

6. A semiconducting device is connected in a series circuit with a battery and a resistance. A current is found to pass through the circuit. If the polarity of the battery is reversed, the current drops to almost zero. The device may be
(a) an intrinsic semiconductor
(b) a p-type semiconductor
(c) an n-type semiconductor
(d) a p-n junction.

7. A semiconductor is doped with a donor impurity.
(a) The hole concentration increases.
(b) The hole concentration decreases.
(c) The electron concentration increases.
(d) The electron concentration decreases.

8. Let i_E, i_C and i_B represent the emitter current, the collector current and the base current respectively in a transistor. Then
(a) i_C is slightly smaller than i_E
(b) i_C is slightly greater than i_E
(c) i_B is much smaller than i_E
(d) i_B is much greater than i_E.

9. In a normal operation of a transistor,
(a) the base–emitter junction is forward-biased
(b) the base–collector junction is forward-biased
(c) the base–emitter junction is reverse-biased
(d) the base–collector junction is reverse-biased.

10. An AND gate can be prepared by repetitive use of
(a) NOT gate (b) OR gate
(c) NAND gate (d) NOR gate.

EXERCISES

Planck constant $= 4{\cdot}14 \times 10^{-15}$ eV s,
Boltzmann constant $= 8{\cdot}62 \times 10^{-5}$ eV K^{-1}.

1. Calculate the number of states per cubic metre of sodium in 3s band. The density of sodium is 1013 kgm^{-3}. How many of them are empty ?
2. In a pure semiconductor, the number of conduction electrons is 6×10^{19} per cubic metre. How many holes are there in a sample of size 1 cm × 1 cm × 1 mm ?
3. Indium antimonide has a band gap of 0·23 eV between the valence and the conduction band. Find the temperature at which kT equals the band gap.
4. The band gap for silicon is 1·1 eV. (a) Find the ratio of the band gap to kT for silicon at room temperature 300 K. (b) At what temperature does this ratio become one tenth of the value at 300 K ? (Silicon will not retain its structure at these high temperatures.)
5. When a semiconducting material is doped with an impurity, new acceptor levels are created. In a particular thermal collision, a valence electron receives an energy equal to $2kT$ and just reaches one of the acceptor levels. Assuming that the energy of the electron was at the top edge of the valence band and that the temperature T is equal to 300 K, find the energy of the acceptor levels above the valence band.
6. The band gap between the valence and the conduction bands in zinc oxide (ZnO) is 3·2 eV. Suppose an electron in the conduction band combines with a hole in the valence band and the excess energy is released in the form of electromagnetic radiation. Find the maximum wavelength that can be emitted in this process.
7. Suppose the energy liberated in the recombination of a hole–electron pair is converted into electromagnetic radiation. If the maximum wavelength emitted is 820 nm, what is the band gap ?
8. Find the maximum wavelength of electromagnetic radiation which can create a hole–electron pair in germanium. The band gap in germanium is 0·65 eV.
9. In a photodiode, the conductivity increases when the material is exposed to light. It is found that the conductivity changes only if the wavelength is less than 620 nm. What is the band gap ?
10. Let ΔE denote the energy gap between the valence band and the conduction band. The population of conduction electrons (and of the holes) is roughly proportional to $e^{-\Delta E/2kT}$. Find the ratio of the concentration of conduction electrons in diamond to that in silicon at room temperature 300 K. ΔE for silicon is 1·1 eV and for diamond is 6·0 eV. How many conduction electrons are likely to be in one cubic metre of diamond ?
11. The conductivity of a pure semiconductor is roughly proportional to $T^{3/2} e^{-\Delta E/2kT}$ where ΔE is the band gap. The band gap for germanium is 0·74 eV at 4 K and 0·67 eV at 300 K. By what factor does the conductivity of pure germanium increase as the temperature is raised from 4 K to 300 K ?
12. Estimate the proportion of boron impurity which will increase the conductivity of a pure silicon sample by a factor of 100. Assume that each boron atom creates a hole and the concentration of holes in pure silicon at the same temperature is 7×10^{15} holes per cubic metre. Density of silicon is 5×10^{28} atoms per cubic metre.
13. The product of the hole concentration and the conduction electron concentration turns out to be independent of the amount of any impurity doped. The concentration of conduction electrons in germanium is 6×10^{19} per cubic metre. When some phosphorus impurity is doped into a germanium sample, the concentration of conduction electrons increases to 2×10^{23} per cubic metre. Find the concentration of the holes in the doped germanium.
14. The conductivity of an intrinsic semiconductor depends on temperature as $\sigma = \sigma_0 e^{-\Delta E/2kT}$, where σ_0 is a constant. Find the temperature at which the conductivity of an intrinsic germanium semiconductor will be double of its value at $T = 300$ K. Assume that the gap for germanium is 0·650 eV and remains constant as the temperature is increased.
15. A semiconducting material has a band gap of 1 eV. Acceptor impurities are doped into it which create acceptor levels 1 meV above the valence band. Assume that the transition from one energy level to the other is almost forbidden if kT is less than 1/50 of the energy gap. Also, if kT is more than twice the gap, the upper levels have maximum population. The temperature of the semiconductor is increased from 0 K. The concentration of the holes increases with temperature and after a certain temperature it becomes approximately constant. As the temperature is further increased, the hole concentration again starts increasing at a certain temperature. Find the order of the temperature range in which the hole concentration remains approximately constant.
16. In a p-n junction, the depletion region is 400 nm wide and an electric field of 5×10^{5} V m^{-1} exists in it. (a) Find the height of the potential barrier. (b) What should be the minimum kinetic energy of a conduction electron which can diffuse from the n-side to the p-side ?
17. The potential barrier existing across an unbiased p-n junction is 0·2 volt. What minimum kinetic energy a hole should have to diffuse from the p-side to the n-side if (a) the junction is unbiased, (b) the junction is forward-biased at 0·1 volt and (c) the junction is reverse-biased at 0·1 volt ?
18. In a p-n junction, a potential barrier of 250 meV exists across the junction. A hole with a kinetic energy of 300 meV approaches the junction. Find the kinetic energy of the hole when it crosses the junction if the hole approached the junction (a) from the p-side and (b) from the n-side.
19. When a p-n junction is reverse-biased, the current becomes almost constant at 25 μA. When it is forward-biased at 200 mV, a current of 75 μA is obtained. Find the magnitude of diffusion current when the diode is

(a) unbiased, (b) reverse-biased at 200 mV and (c) forward-biased at 200 mV.

20. The drift current in a *p-n* junction is 20·0 μA. Estimate the number of electrons crossing a cross section per second in the depletion region.

21. The current–voltage characteristic of an ideal *p-n* junction diode is given by

$$i = i_0\,(e^{eV/kT} - 1)$$

where the drift current i_0 equals 10 μA. Take the temperature T to be 300 K. (a) Find the voltage V_0 for which $e^{eV/kT} = 100$. One can neglect the term 1 for voltages greater than this value. (b) Find an expression for the dynamic resistance of the diode as a function of V for $V > V_0$. (c) Find the voltage for which the dynamic resistance is 0·2 Ω.

22. Consider a *p-n* junction diode having the characteristic $i = i_0(e^{eV/kT} - 1)$ where $i_0 = 20$ μA. The diode is operated at $T = 300$ K. (a) Find the current through the diode when a voltage of 300 mV is applied across it in forward bias. (b) At what voltage does the current double ?

23. Calculate the current through the circuit and the potential difference across the diode shown in figure (45-E1). The drift current for the diode is 20 μA.

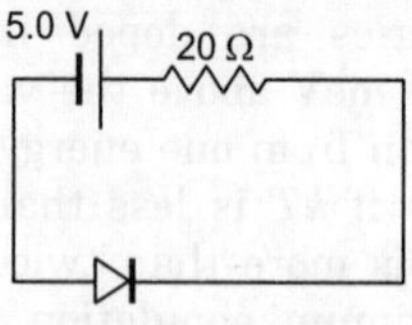

Figure 45-E1

24. Each of the resistances shown in figure (45-E2) has a value of 20 Ω. Find the equivalent resistance between A and B. Does it depend on whether the point A or B is at higher potential ?

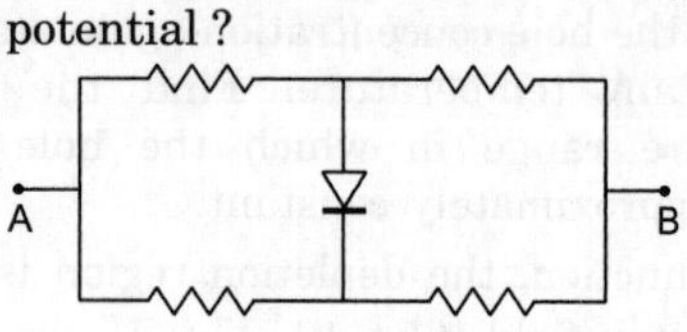

Figure 45-E2

In problems 25 to 30, assume that the resistance of each diode is zero in forward bias and is infinity in reverse bias.

25. Find the currents through the resistances in the circuits shown in figure (45-E3).

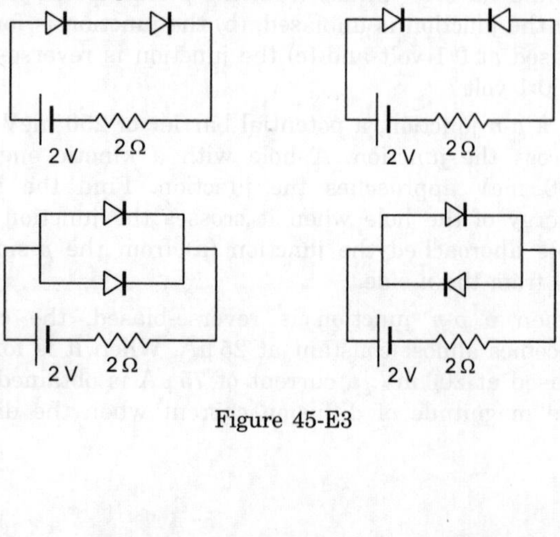

Figure 45-E3

26. What are the readings of the ammeters A_1 and A_2 shown in figure (45-E4). Neglect the resistances of the meters.

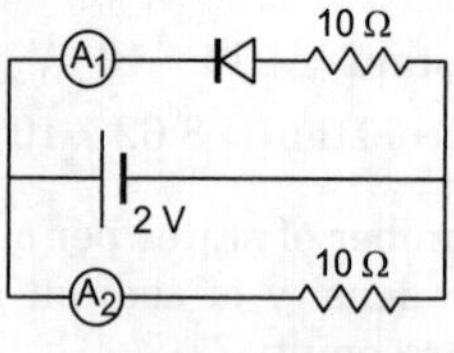

Figure 45-E4

27. Find the current through the battery in each of the circuits shown in figure (45-E5).

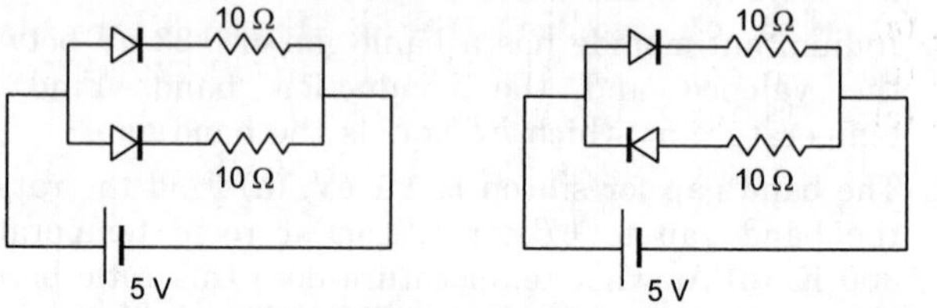

Figure 45-E5

28. Find the current through the resistance R in figure (45-E6) if (a) $R = 12$ Ω (b) $R = 48$ Ω.

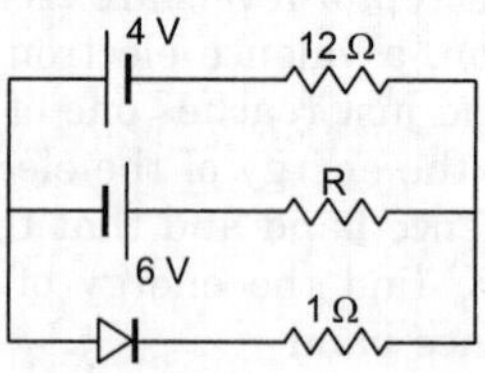

Figure 45-E6

29. Draw the current–voltage characteristics for the device shown in figure (45-E7) between the terminals A and B.

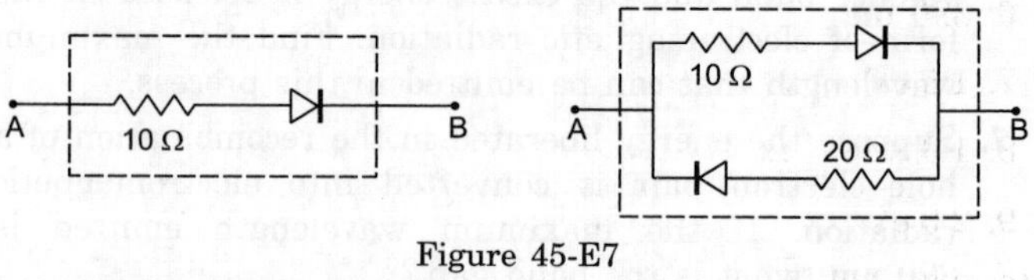

Figure 45-E7

30. Find the equivalent resistance of the network shown in figure (45-E8) between the points A and B.

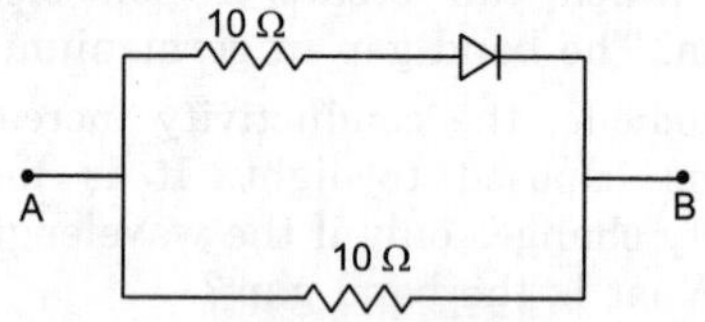

Figure 45-E8

31. When the base current in a transistor is changed from 30 μA to 80 μA, the collector current is changed from 1·0 mA to 3·5 mA. Find the current gain β.

32. A load resistor of 2 kΩ is connected in the collector branch of an amplifier circuit using a transistor in common-emitter mode. The current gain β = 50. The input resistance of the transistor is 0·50 kΩ. If the input current is changed by 50 μA, (a) by what amount does the output voltage change, (b) by what amount does the input voltage change and (c) what is the power gain ?

33. Let $X = ABC + BCA + CAB$. Evaluate X for
(a) $A = 1, B = 0, C = 1$, (b) $A = B = C = 1$, and
(c) $A = B = C = 0$.

34. Design a logical circuit using AND, OR and NOT gates to evaluate $A\overline{BC} + B\overline{CA}$.

35. Show that $AB + \overline{AB}$ is always 1.

□

ANSWERS

OBJECTIVE I

1. (c)	2. (b)	3. (b)	4. (d)	5. (c)	6. (a)
7. (a)	8. (a)	9. (b)	10. (a)	11. (b)	12. (b)
13. (c)	14. (c)	15. (d)			

OBJECTIVE II

1. (a), (c), (d)	2. (b), (c), (d)	3. (a), (d)
4. (b), (d)	5. all	6. (d)
7. (b), (c)	8. (a), (c)	9. (a), (d)
10. (c), (d)		

EXERCISES

1. $5{\cdot}3 \times 10^{28}$, $2{\cdot}65 \times 10^{28}$
2. 6×10^{12}
3. 2670 K
4. (a) 43 (b) 3000 K
5. 50 meV
6. 390 nm
7. 1·5 eV
8. $1{\cdot}9 \times 10^{-6}$ m
9. 2·0 eV
10. $2{\cdot}3 \times 10^{-33}$, almost zero
11. approximately 10^{463}
12. 1 in about $3{\cdot}5 \times 10^{10}$
13. $1{\cdot}8 \times 10^{16}$ per cubic metre
14. 318 K
15. 20 to 230 K
16. (a) 0·2 V (b) 0·2 eV
17. (a) 0·2 eV (b) 0·1 eV (c) 0·3 eV
18. (a) 50 meV (b) 550 meV
19. (a) 25 μA (b) zero (c) 100 μA
20. $3{\cdot}1 \times 10^{13}$
21. (a) 0·12 V (b) $\frac{kT}{ei_0} e^{-eV/kT}$ (c) 0·25 V
22. (a) 2 A (b) 318 mV
23. 20 μA, 4·996 V ≅ 5 V
24. 20 Ω
25. (a) 1 A (b) zero (c) 1 A (d) 1 A
26. zero, 0·2 A
27. (a) 1A (b) 0·5 A
28. (a) 0·42 A, 0·13 A
30. 5 Ω if $V_A > V_B$ and 10 Ω if $V_A < V_B$
31. 50
32. (a) 5·0 V (b) 25 mV (c) 10^4
33. (a) 1 (b) 0 (c) 0

□

CHAPTER 46

THE NUCLEUS

At the centre of an atom exists the *nucleus* which contains protons and neutrons. The electrons surround this nucleus to form the atom. As discussed earlier, this structure of atom was revealed by the experiments of Rutherford in which a beam of alpha particles was made to strike a thin gold foil. Most of the alpha particles crossed the foil without being appreciably deviated, but there were some alpha particles which suffered large deviation from their original lines of motion. The data suggested that positive charges in an atom are concentrated in a small volume which we call nucleus and this nucleus is responsible for the large deviation of alpha particles. Later on, the existence of protons and neutrons in the nucleus was established. In this chapter, we shall discuss the physics of the nucleus.

46.1 PROPERTIES OF A NUCLEUS

Nuclear Constituents

A nucleus is made of protons and neutrons. A proton has a positive charge of magnitude equal to that of an electron and has a mass of about 1840 times the mass of an electron. A neutron has a mass slightly greater than that of a proton. The masses of a proton and a neutron are

$$m_p = 1{\cdot}6726231 \times 10^{-27} \text{ kg}$$

$$\text{and} \quad m_n = 1{\cdot}6749286 \times 10^{-27} \text{ kg.}$$

It is customary in nuclear physics and high energy physics to represent mass in energy units according to the conversion formula $E = mc^2$. (Matter can be viewed as a condensed form of energy. Theory of relativity reveals that a mass m is equivalent to an energy E where $E = mc^2$.) For example, the mass of an electron is $m_e = 9{\cdot}1093897 \times 10^{-31}$ kg and the equivalent energy is

$$m_e c^2 = 510{\cdot}99 \text{ keV.}$$

Thus, the mass of an electron is $510{\cdot}99 \text{ keV c}^{-2}$. Similarly, the mass of a proton is $938{\cdot}27231 \text{ MeV c}^{-2}$ and the mass of a neutron is $939{\cdot}56563 \text{ MeV c}^{-2}$. The energy corresponding to the mass of a particle when it is at rest is called its *rest mass energy*.

Another unit which is widely used in describing mass in nuclear physics as well as in atomic physics is *unified atomic mass unit* denoted by the symbol u. It is 1/12 of the mass of a neutral carbon atom in its lowest energy state which contains six protons, six neutrons and six electrons. We have

$$1 \text{ u} = 1{\cdot}6605402 \times 10^{-27} \text{ kg} = 931{\cdot}478 \text{ MeV c}^{-2}.$$

Protons and neutrons are fermions and obey the Pauli exclusion principle like electrons. No two protons or two neutrons can have the same quantum state. But one proton and one neutron can exist in the same quantum state. Protons and neutrons are collectively called *nucleons.*

The number of protons in a nucleus is denoted by Z, the number of neutrons by N and the total number of nucleons by A. Thus, $A = Z + N$. The total number of nucleons A is also called the *mass number* of the nucleus. The number of protons Z is called the *atomic number.* A nucleus is symbolically expressed as ${}^{A}_{Z}\text{X}$ in which X is the chemical symbol of the element. Thus, ${}^{4}_{2}\text{He}$ represents helium nucleus which contains 2 protons and a total of 4 nucleons. So it contains 2 neutrons. Similarly, ${}^{238}_{92}\text{U}$ represents a uranium nucleus which contains 92 protons and 146 neutrons.

The distribution of electrons around the nucleus is determined by the number of protons Z and hence the chemical properties of an element are also determined by Z. The nuclei having the same number of protons but different number of neutrons are called *isotopes*. Nuclei with the same neutron number N but different atomic number Z are called *isotones* and the nuclei with the same mass number A are called *isobars*. All nuclei with a given Z and N are collectively called a *nuclide.* Thus, all the ${}^{56}_{26}\text{Fe}$ nuclei taken together is one nuclide and all the ${}^{32}_{16}\text{S}$ nuclei taken together is another nuclide.

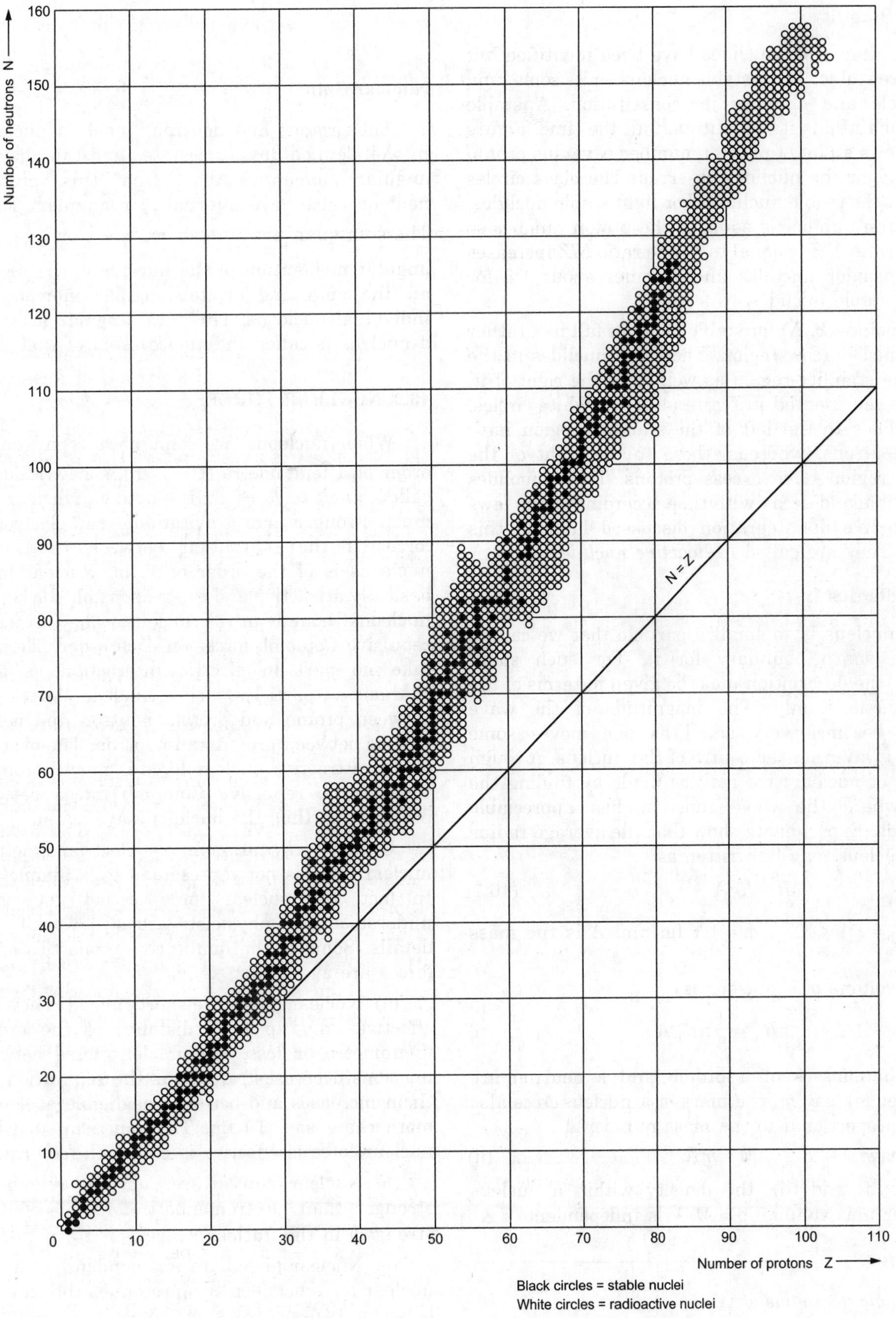
Number of neutrons N
Number of protons Z
N = Z
0
10
20
30
40
50
60
70
80
90
100
110
120
130
140
150
160
Black circles = stable nuclei
White circles = radioactive nuclei

Figure 46.1

Nuclear Stability

More than 1000 nuclides have been identified but not all are stable. An unstable nucleus emits some kind of particle and changes its constitution. A stable nucleus maintains its constitution all the time. Figure (46.1) shows a plot of neutron number N versus proton number Z for the nuclides observed. The black circles represent the stable nuclides. For light stable nuclides, the neutron number is equal to the proton number so that the ratio N/Z is equal to 1. The ratio N/Z increases for the heavier nuclides and becomes about 1·6 for heaviest stable nuclides.

The points (Z, N) for stable nuclides fall in a rather well-defined narrow region. There are nuclides to the left of the stability region as well as to the right of it. They are represented in figure (46.1) by white circles. The nuclides to the left of the stability region have excess neutrons, whereas, those to the right of the stability region have excess protons. These nuclides are unstable and decay with time according to the laws of radioactive disintegration discussed later in this chapter. They are called *radioactive nuclide.*

Nuclear Radius

The nucleus is so small a particle that we cannot define a sharp boundary for it. For such small particles, the description must be given in terms of the wave functions only. The magnitude of the wave function becomes very small as one moves some distance away from the centre of the nucleus. A rough estimate of nuclear size may be made by finding the region where the wave function has appreciable magnitude. Experiments show that the average radius R of a nucleus may be written as

$$R = R_0 A^{1/3} \quad \dots \text{(46.1)}$$

where $R_0 = 1{\cdot}1 \times 10^{-15}$ m = 1·1 fm and A is the mass number.

The volume of a nucleus is

$$V = \frac{4}{3}\pi R^3 = \frac{4}{3}\pi R_0^3 A. \quad \dots \text{(i)}$$

As the masses of a proton and a neutron are roughly equal, say m, the mass of a nucleus M is also roughly proportional to the mass number A.

We have, $$M = mA. \quad \dots \text{(ii)}$$

From (i) and (ii), the density within a nucleus (mass per unit volume) $\rho = M/V$ is independent of A.

Example 46.1

Calculate the radius of ^{70}Ge.

Solution : We have,

$$R = R_0 A^{1/3} = (1{\cdot}1 \text{ fm})\,(70)^{1/3}$$

$$= (1{\cdot}1 \text{ fm})\,(4{\cdot}12) = 4{\cdot}53 \text{ fm}.$$

Nuclear Spin

The protons and neutrons inside a nucleus move in well-defined quantum states and thus have orbital angular momenta. Apart from this, protons and neutrons also have internal spin angular momentum. The spin quantum number m_s is $+\frac{1}{2}$ or $-\frac{1}{2}\cdot$ The total angular momentum of the nucleus is the resultant of all the spin and orbital angular momenta of the individual nucleons. This total angular momentum of a nucleus is called the *nuclear spin* of that nucleus.

46.2 NUCLEAR FORCES

When nucleons are kept at a separation of the order of a femtometre (10^{-15} m), a new kind of force, called *nuclear force* starts acting. Nuclear force is much stronger than gravitational and electromagnetic forces if the separation between the interacting nucleons is of the order of 1 fm. Nuclear forces are basically attractive and are responsible for keeping the nucleons bound in a nucleus. The protons exert repulsive Coulomb forces on each other. The neutrons take no part in electric interaction as they are chargeless particles. The nuclear forces operate between proton and proton, neutron and neutron as well as between proton and neutron. The overall effect of this attractive nuclear force is much stronger than that of the repulsive Coulomb forces between the protons and thus the nucleus stays bound.

Unlike gravitational or electromagnetic force, nuclear force is not represented by a simple formula. In fact, the nuclear force is not yet completely understood and physicists are still working out the details. Some of the qualitative properties of nuclear forces are as follows:

(a) Nuclear forces are short-ranged. They are most effective only up to a distance of the order of a femtometre or less. The nuclear force between two nucleons decreases rapidly as the separation between them increases and becomes negligible at separations more than, say, 10 fm. The range up to which the nuclear force is effective is called *nuclear range.*

(b) Nuclear forces are, on an average, much stronger than electromagnetic forces (≈ 50–60 times stronger) in the nuclear range.

(c) Nuclear forces are independent of charge. The nuclear force between two protons is the same as that between two neutrons or between a proton and a neutron. Remember, the Coulomb force between two protons acts according to the well-defined Coulomb's law, over and above the nuclear force. The nuclear force itself is independent of charge.

(d) An important property of nuclear force is that it is not a central force. The force between a pair of nucleons is not solely determined by the distance between the necleons. For example, the nuclear force depends on the directions of the spins of the nucleons. The force is stronger if the spins of the nucleons are parallel (i.e., both nucleons have $m_s = +1/2$ or $-1/2$) and is weaker if the spins are antiparallel (i.e., one nucleon has $m_s = +1/2$ and the other has $m_s = -1/2$).

Many of the nuclear properties may be understood on the basis of these qualitative properties of nuclear forces.

Because of the short-range nature of nuclear force, each nucleon in a nucleus interacts only with a small number of neighbouring nucleons through the nuclear force. This explains why the density of the nucleons is roughly the same in all the nuclei.

Because of the Pauli exclusion principle, each quantum state can contain at the most two protons (with opposite spins) and two neutrons (again with opposite spins). Thus, nuclear forces favour pairing of two protons and two neutrons together. In light nuclei, the nuclear forces between the nucleons are much dominant over the Coulomb repulsion and hence the neutron number N and the proton number Z tend to be equal in light nuclei. In a heavier nucleus, the radius is large and for many nucleon-pairs, the interaction through nuclear force is not effective. On the other hand, Coulomb force is a long-range force and even the diametrically opposite protons repel each other. Thus, Coulomb repulsion becomes more effective for nuclei of larger mass number A. Stability is achieved by having more neutrons than protons because neutrons do not take part in Coulomb interaction. That is why N/Z increases with A for stable nuclides. However, one should not expect greater stability with too many neutrons because then many of these neutrons will not have pairing with protons. This will increase the energy and hence, decrease the stability. A very large nucleus cannot be stable for any value of N/Z. The heaviest stable nuclide is $^{209}_{83}Bi$.

46.3 BINDING ENERGY

We already know about the concept of binding energy of a hydrogen atom. If the constituents of a hydrogen atom (a proton and an electron) are brought from infinity to form the atom, 13·6 eV of energy is released. Thus, the binding energy of a hydrogen atom in ground state is 13·6 eV. Also, 13·6 eV energy must be supplied to the hydrogen atom in ground state to separate the constituents to large distances. Similarly, the nucleons are bound together in a nucleus and energy must be supplied to the nucleus to separate the constituent nucleons to large distances (figure 46.2a). The amount of energy needed to do this is called the *binding energy of the nucleus*. If the nucleons are initially well-separated and are brought to form the nucleus, this much energy is released (figure 46.2b).

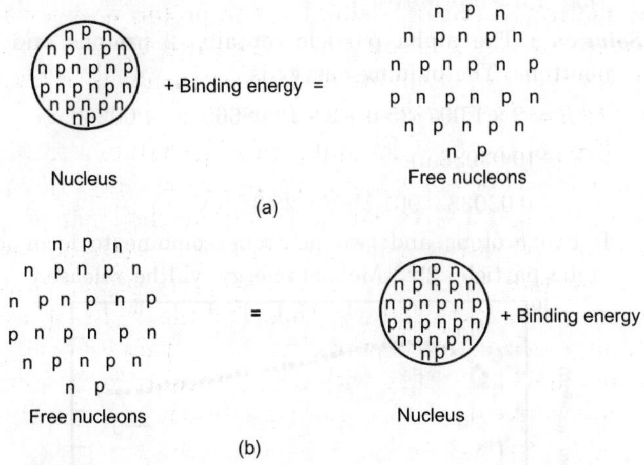

Figure 46.2

Thus, the rest mass energy of a nucleus is smaller than the rest mass energy of its constituent nucleons in free state. The difference of the two energies is the binding energy. The rest mass energy of a free proton is $m_p c^2$ and that of a free neutron is $m_n c^2$. If the nucleus has a mass M, its rest mass energy is Mc^2. If it contains Z protons and N neutrons, the rest mass energy of its nucleons in free state is $Zm_p c^2 + Nm_n c^2$. If the binding energy of the nucleus is B, we have,

$$B = (Zm_p + Nm_n - M)c^2. \quad \ldots \text{ (i)}$$

We can also use the atomic masses in place of nuclear masses. The above equation then becomes

$$B = \left[Zm\left({}^1_1\mathrm{H}\right) + N\, m_n - m\left({}^{Z+N}_{\ Z}\mathrm{X}\right)\right] c^2. \quad \ldots \text{ (46.2)}$$

Here, $m\left({}^1_1\mathrm{H}\right)$ is the mass of a hydrogen atom and $m\left({}^{Z+N}_{\ Z}\mathrm{X}\right)$ is the mass of an atom with Z protons and N neutrons. Verify that the masses of electrons cancel out in this equation. There are Z electrons in Z hydrogen atoms as well as in the atom ${}^{Z+N}_{\ Z}\mathrm{X}$. Hence, equation (46.2) is equivalent to (i) above. Such cancellations often occur and atomic masses are rather frequently used in place of nuclear masses. The small difference due to binding energy of electrons with the nucleus is neglected. As we shall see later, such cancellations do not work in the case of β-decays. Unless stated otherwise, mass of ${}^A_Z\mathrm{X}$ in this chapter will refer to the atomic mass which includes the mass of Z electrons.

Example 46.2

Calculate the binding energy of an alpha particle from the following data:

mass of $^1_1$H *atom* = 1·007825 u

mass of neutron = 1·008665 u

mass of $^4_2$He *atom* = 4·00260 u.

Take 1 u = 931 MeV c^{-2}.

Solution : The alpha particle contains 2 protons and 2 neutrons. The binding energy is

$$B = (2 \times 1{\cdot}007825\ \text{u} + 2 \times 1{\cdot}008665\ \text{u} - 4{\cdot}00260\ \text{u})c^2$$

$$= (0{\cdot}03038\ \text{u})c^2$$

$$= 0{\cdot}03038 \times 931\ \text{MeV} = 28{\cdot}3\ \text{MeV}.$$

If two protons and two neutrons combine to form an alpha particle, 28·3 MeV of energy will be released.

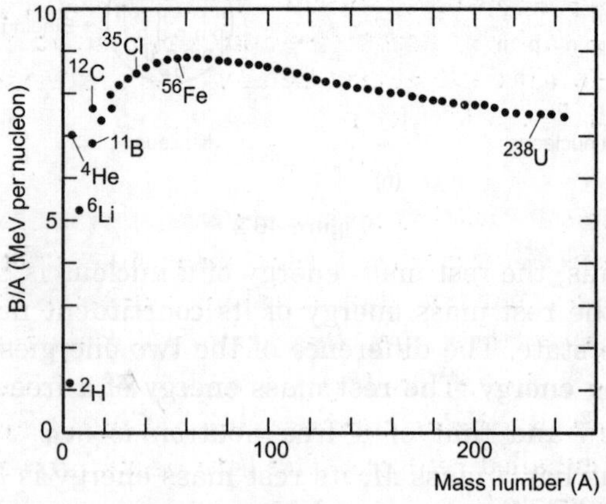

Figure 46.3

A very useful quantity in nuclear physics is binding energy per nucleon, i.e., binding energy divided by the mass number. Figure (46.3) shows a plot of binding energy per nucleon against the mass number. The binding energy of deuteron (the nucleus of heavy hydrogen containing a proton and a neutron) is 2·22 MeV so that the binding energy per nucleon is $\frac{2{\cdot}22\ \text{MeV}}{2} = 1{\cdot}11$ MeV. As we consider nuclei with increasing mass number, the binding energy per nucleon increases on an average and reaches a maximum of about 8·7 MeV for $A \approx 50$–80. For still heavier nuclei, the binding energy per nucleon slowly decreases as A increases. For uranium, one of the heaviest natural elements ($A \approx 238$), the value drops to about 7·5 MeV. It follows that the nuclei in the intermediate region, $A \approx 50$–80, are most stable as maximum energy is needed to bring out any individual nucleon from such a nucleus.

The behaviour of binding energy per nucleon versus A can be roughly understood in terms of the short-range nature of nuclear force. Because of the short range, a nucleon inside the nucleus can interact with a fixed number of nucleons surrounding it. If each nucleon is visualised as a sphere and these spheres are assumed to be closely packed, each nucelon has 12 neighbouring nucleons touching it. Thus, 12 pairs are formed with each nucleon for nuclear interaction. If all the A nucleons could be in the interior of the nucleus, there would have been $6A$ pairs. The binding energy resulting from these pairs will, therefore, be proportional to A. This energy is called *volume energy* and is written as $b_v = a_1 A$. However, all the nucleons are not in the interior. A nucleon near the surface does not interact with 12 nucleons. Thus, there is a decrease in binding energy and this decrease will be proportional to the surface area or to R^2. As $R = R_0 A^{1/3}$, this surface energy is $b_s = -a_2 A^{2/3}$. The negative sign is used because the surface effect decreases the binding energy whereas the volume effect increases it. Another factor contributing to the binding energy is the Coulomb repulsion between the protons. As Coulomb force is a long-range force, all proton-pairs participate in it. The Coulomb potential energy is, therefore, proportional to $Z(Z-1)/2$ and is inversely proportional to the nuclear radius R as the average separation between the protons will be proportional to the nuclear radius. The Coulomb contribution to the binding energy is, therefore, written as $b_c = -a_3 Z(Z-1)/A^{1/3}$. The binding energy per nucleon is, therefore,

$$\frac{B}{A} = a_1 - \frac{a_2}{A^{1/3}} - a_3 \frac{Z(Z-1)}{A^{4/3}}. \qquad \dots (46.3)$$

With suitable choices of a_1, a_2 and a_3, this equation agrees well with the general nature of the plot shown in figure (46.3). There are other effects such as that due to Pauli exclusion principle which should be included in (46.3) to make it more accurate.

Mass Excess

Consider a nucleus of mass number A. Let the mass of the neutral atom containing this nucleus be m atomic mass units. Also, let A' represent the mass A atomic mass units. Thus,

mass of the atom = m u

and $A' = A$ u.

We define *mass excess* as

$$(\text{mass of the atom} - A')\,c^2 \qquad \dots (46.4)$$

$$= (m\ \text{u} - A\ \text{u})c^2$$

$$= (m - A)\left(\frac{931\ \text{MeV}}{c^2}\right)c^2$$

$$= 931(m - A)\text{MeV}. \qquad \dots (46.5)$$

Example 46.3

The atomic mass of $^1_1$H *is* 1·00783 u. *Calculate the mass excess of hydrogen.*

Solution : The mass excess of hydrogen is $931(m - A)$MeV

$$= 931(1{\cdot}00783 - 1)\text{MeV} = 7{\cdot}29 \text{ MeV}.$$

46.4 RADIOACTIVE DECAY

Stable nuclides have definite Z, N combinations as shown by the black circles in figure (46.1). Nuclides with other Z, N combinations are also found in nature or may be prepared in laboratory. However, these nuclides are unstable and they decay into other nuclides by various processes. Two main processes by which an unstable nucleus decays are *alpha decay* and *beta decay*.

Alpha Decay

In alpha decay, the unstable nucleus emits an alpha particle reducing its proton number Z as well as its neutron number N by 2. The alpha decay process may be represented as

$$^A_Z\text{X} \rightarrow {}^{A-4}_{Z-2}\text{Y} + {}^4_2\text{He}. \qquad \dots \ (46.6)$$

As the proton number Z is changed, the element itself is changed and hence the chemical symbol of the residual nucleus is different from that of the original nucleus. The nucleus before the decay is called the *parent nucleus* and that resulting after the decay is called the *daughter nucleus.* An example of alpha decay is

$$^{212}_{83}\text{Bi} \rightarrow {}^{208}_{81}\text{Tl} + {}^4_2\text{He}.$$

The parent nucleus bismuth had 83 protons and 129 neutrons, the daughter nucleus is thallium with 81 protons and 127 neutrons.

Alpha decay occurs in all nuclei with mass number $A > 210$. We have seen that too heavy a nucleus will be unstable because of the Coulomb repulsive force. By emitting alpha particle the nucleus decreases its mass number to move towards stability.

The rest mass energy of $^{212}_{83}$Bi is larger than the sum of the rest mass energies of the products $^{208}_{81}$Tl and $^4_2$He. The difference between the rest mass energy of the initial constituents and that of the final products is called the *Q-value* of the process. Thus, if U_i is the rest mass energy of the initial constituents and U_f is that of the final products,

$$Q = U_i - U_f .$$

This definition is valid not only for alpha decay but for any nuclear process. This much energy is made available as the kinetic energy of the products. In an α-decay given by equation (46.6), the Q-value is

$$Q = \left[m\left(^A_Z\text{X}\right) - m\left(^{A-4}_{Z-2}\text{Y}\right) - m\left(^4_2\text{He}\right) \right] c^2 . \qquad \dots \ (46.7)$$

A stream of alpha particles coming from a bulk material is called *alpha ray.*

Beta Decay

Beta decay is a process in which either a neutron is converted into a proton or a proton is converted into a neutron. Thus, the ratio N/Z is altered in beta decay. If a nucleus is formed with more number of neutrons than needed for stability, a neutron will convert itself into a proton to move towards stability. Similarly, if a nucleus is formed with more number of protons than needed for stability, a proton will convert itself into a neutron. Such transformations take place because of *weak forces* operating within a neutron or a proton. When a neutron is converted into a proton, an electron and a new particle named *antineutrino* are created and emitted from the nucleus,

$$n \rightarrow p + e + \bar{\nu}. \qquad \dots \ (46.8)$$

The antineutrino is denoted by the symbol $\bar{\nu}$. It is supposed to have zero rest mass like photon, is chargeless and has spin quantum number ± 1/2. The electron emitted from the nucleus is called a *beta particle* and is denoted by the symbol β^-. A stream of such beta particles coming from a bulk of unstable nuclei is called *beta ray.* The beta decay process may be represented by

$$^A_Z\text{X} \rightarrow {}_{Z+1}^{\ \ A}\text{Y} + e + \bar{\nu}$$

$$\text{or,} \quad ^A_Z\text{X} \rightarrow {}_{Z+1}^{\ \ A}\text{Y} + \beta^- + \bar{\nu}. \qquad \dots \ (46.9)$$

It is also called *beta minus decay* as negatively charged beta particles are emitted. The rest mass energy of the initial constituents is

$$U_i = \left[m\left(^A_Z\text{X}\right) - Zm_e \right] c^2$$

and that of the final constituents is

$$U_f = \left[m\left({}_{Z+1}^{\ \ A}\text{Y}\right) - (Z+1)m_e + m_e \right] c^2 .$$

The kinetic energy available to the product particles is,

$$Q = U_i - U_f = \left[m\left(^A_Z\text{X}\right) - m\left({}_{Z+1}^{\ \ A}\text{Y}\right) \right] c^2 \qquad \dots \ (46.10)$$

where atomic masses are used. It may be noted that the rest mass energy of the electron created is not explicitly subtracted in this equation. Because of the large mass, the residual nucleus ${}_{Z+1}^{\ \ A}$Y does not share appreciable kinetic energy. Thus, the energy Q is shared by the antineutrino and the beta particle. Depending on the fraction taken away by the antineutrino, the kinetic energy of the beta particle can be anything between zero and a maximum value Q.

If the unstable nucleus has excess protons than needed for stability, a proton converts itself into a neutron. In the process, a *positron* and a *neutrino* are created and emitted from the nucleus,

$$p \rightarrow n + e^{+} + \nu. \qquad \dots (46.11)$$

The positron e^{+} has a positive electric charge equal in magnitude to the charge on an electron and has a mass equal to the mass of an electron. Positron is called the *antiparticle* of electron. When an electron and a positron collide, both the particles are destroyed and energy is made available. Similarly, neutrino and antineutrino are antiparticles of each other. When a proton in a nucleus converts itself into a neutron, the decay process is represented as

$${}^{A}_{Z}\mathrm{X} \rightarrow {}_{Z-1}^{\;\;A}\mathrm{Y} + e^{+} + \nu$$

or, $${}^{A}_{Z}\mathrm{X} \rightarrow {}_{Z-1}^{\;\;A}\mathrm{Y} + \beta^{+} + \nu. \qquad \dots (46.12)$$

This process is called *beta plus decay*. The positron so emitted is called a *beta plus* particle.

Verify that the Q-value of this decay is given by

$$Q = \left[m\left({}^{A}_{Z}\mathrm{X}\right) - m\left({}_{Z-1}^{\;\;A}\mathrm{Y}\right) - 2m_e \right] c^{2}. \qquad \dots (46.13)$$

Can an isolated proton decay to a neutron emitting a positron and a neutrino as suggested by equation (46.11) ? The mass of a neutron is larger than the mass of a proton and hence the Q-value of such a process would be negative. So, an isolated proton does not beta decay to a neutron. On the other hand, an isolated neutron decays to a proton as suggested by equation (46.8).

A similar process, known as *electron capture*, takes place in certain nuclides. In this process, the nucleus captures one of the atomic electrons (most likely an electron from the K shell). A proton in the nucleus combines with this electron and converts itself into a neutron. A neutrino is created in the process and emitted from the nucleus,

$$p + e \rightarrow n + \nu.$$

The process may be represented as

$${}^{A}_{Z}\mathrm{X} + e \rightarrow {}_{Z-1}^{\;\;A}\mathrm{Y} + \nu. \qquad \dots (46.14)$$

The Q-value of the process is

$$Q = \left[m\left({}^{A}_{Z}\mathrm{X}\right) - m\left({}_{Z-1}^{\;\;A}\mathrm{Y}\right) \right] c^{2}. \qquad \dots (46.15)$$

When an atomic electron is captured, a vacancy is created in the atomic shell and X-rays are emitted following the capture.

The daughter nucleus formed as a result of an alpha decay or a beta decay may not be stable and undergo another alpha or beta decay. Thus, a series of decays proceed till a stable nucleus is formed. An example of such a series of decays starting from ^{238}U and ending at ^{206}Pb is shown in figure (46.4).

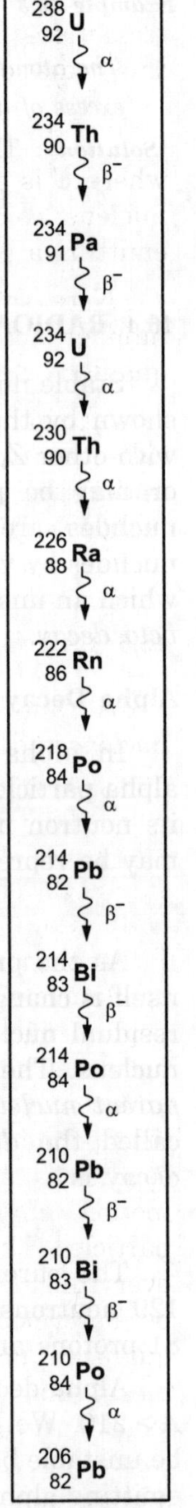

Figure 46.4

Gamma Decay

The protons and neutrons inside a nucleus move in discrete quantum states with definite energies. In the ground state, the nucleons occupy such quantum states which minimise the total energy of the nucleus. However, higher energy states are also available to the nucleons and if appropriate energy is supplied, the nucleus may be excited to higher energies. The energy differences in the allowed energy levels of a nucleus are generally large, of the order of MeVs. It is, therefore, difficult to excite the nucleus to higher energy levels by usual methods of supplying energy as heating. However, when an alpha or a beta decay takes place, the daughter nucleus is generally formed in one of its excited states. Such a nucleus in an excited state eventually comes to its ground state by emitting a photon or photons of electromagnetic radiation. The process is similar to that in a hydrogen atom when an electron jumps from a higher energy orbit to a lower energy orbit emitting a photon. A typical situation is schematically shown in figure (46.5). The parent nucleus ^{57}Co in its ground state decays to the daughter nucleus ^{57}Fe by β^{+}-decay. The nucleus ^{57}Fe is formed in its second excited state with energy 136 keV above the ground state. This nucleus in excited state may emit a photon of 136 keV and reach its ground state. Or, it may emit a photon of 122 keV and drop to its first excited state and then drop to the ground state by emitting another photon of energy 14 keV. If bulk ^{57}Co is taken, many ^{57}Fe nuclei will be formed; some will drop directly to their ground states and the rest will go via the first excited states. Thus, one will observe a stream of β^{+}-particles, 136 keV photons, 122 keV photons and 14 keV photons coming from the ^{57}Co source.

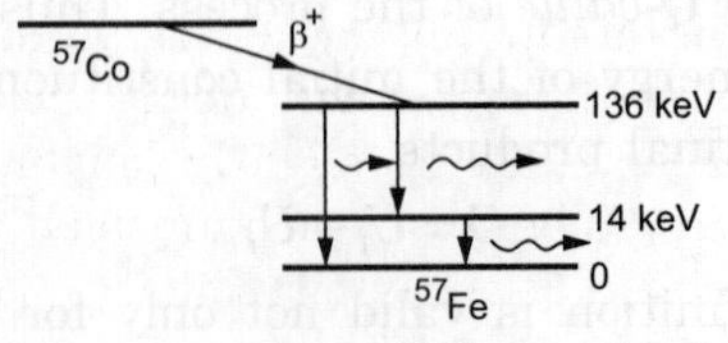

Figure 46.5

The electromagnetic radiation emitted in nuclear transitions is called *gamma ray*. The wavelength of this radiation is given by the usual relation

$$\lambda = \frac{hc}{E}$$

where E is the energy of the photon. The process of a nucleus coming down to a lower energy level by emitting a photon is called *gamma decay*.

Note that in gamma decay neither the proton number nor the neutron number changes. Only the quantum states of the nucleons change.

Alpha, beta and gamma decays are collectively called *radioactive decay* and the materials capable of undergoing radioactive decay are called *radioactive materials*. The α-, β- and γ-rays are collectively called *nuclear radiation*.

46.5 LAW OF RADIOACTIVE DECAY

A radioactive nucleus decays by emitting some nuclear radiation (α, β or γ). Suppose an alpha-active nucleus is prepared at $t = 0$. When will this nucleus emit alpha particle ? The answer to this question is that there is no fixed time at which it must decay. No rule in physics predicts the time at which it will decay. Only when it decays we know that it has done so. Putting in another way, suppose several identical active nuclei are prepared at the same instant and are kept in identical environment. They will, in general, not decay simultaneously. Some will decay quite early and some will live longer, some might live for very long periods. In classical physics of Newton, if all the conditions at present are known, the equations of motion completely determine the future course of all particles. This is called a *deterministic world* in which everything is predetermined. Radioactive decay cannot be described by classical physics. One has to use quantum mechanics to understand it. In quantum mechanics, the equations of physics do not predict the exact future of a system in terms of the present conditions. The equations only give the probability of a particular particle behaving in a particular fashion. In fact, Einstein never wholeheartedly accepted this indeterministic nature of the world.

Suppose there are N active nuclei at an instant t. How many of these nuclei will decay in the next small time interval dt ? The number will be proportional to N and to dt. Each active nucleus has a chance to decay in time interval dt. So, more the number of active nuclei at time t, more will decay in the next dt. Similarly, if you take dt slightly longer, more nuclei will decay in dt because each nucleus will have an increased chance of decaying. Thus,

$$dN = -\lambda N dt. \qquad \dots (46.16)$$

The minus sign is used because the number of active nuclei is decreasing. The constant of proportionality λ is called *decay constant* and is a constant for a given decay scheme. From equation (46.16),

$$\frac{dN}{N} = -\lambda\, dt$$

or, $$\int_{N_0}^{N} \frac{dN}{N} = -\lambda \int_0^t dt$$

or, $$\ln \frac{N}{N_0} = -\lambda t$$

or, $$N = N_0 e^{-\lambda t} \qquad \dots (46.17)$$

where N_0 is the number of active nuclei at $t = 0$. Also from (46.16), the rate of decay is

$$-\frac{dN}{dt} = \lambda N. \qquad \dots (46.18)$$

The quantity $\left(-\frac{dN}{dt}\right)$ gives the number of decays per unit time and is called the *activity* of the sample. Thus, the activity of a radioactive sample is $A = \lambda N$.

From equation (46.17), we have

$$A = A_0 e^{-\lambda t}. \qquad \dots (46.19)$$

Unit of Activity

The activity of a radioactive material is measured in terms of the disintegrations per unit time. Its SI unit is becquerel which is the same as 1 disintegration per second. It is denoted by the symbol Bq. However, the popular unit of activity is curie defined as

$$1 \text{ curie} = 3{\cdot}7 \times 10^{10} \text{ disintegrations s}^{-1}.$$

The unit 'curie' is represented by the symbol Ci.

The activity per unit mass is called *specific activity*.

Example 46.4

The decay constant for the radioactive nuclide ^{64}Cu *is* $1{\cdot}516 \times 10^{-5}\ s^{-1}$. *Find the activity of a sample containing* 1 μg *of* ^{64}Cu. *Atomic weight of copper* = 63·5 g mole^{-1}. *Neglect the mass difference between the given radioisotope and normal copper.*

Solution : 63·5 g of copper has 6×10^{23} atoms. Thus, the number of atoms in 1 μg of Cu is

$$N = \frac{6 \times 10^{23} \times 1\ \mu g}{63{\cdot}5\ g} = 9{\cdot}45 \times 10^{15}.$$

The activity = λN

$$= (1{\cdot}516 \times 10^{-5}\ s^{-1}) \times (9{\cdot}45 \times 10^{15})$$

$$= 1{\cdot}43 \times 10^{11} \text{ disintegrations s}^{-1}$$

$$= \frac{1{\cdot}43 \times 10^{11}}{3{\cdot}7 \times 10^{10}} \text{ Ci} = 3{\cdot}86 \text{ Ci}.$$

Half-life

The time elapsed before half the active nuclei decay is called *half-life* and is denoted by $t_{1/2}$. Suppose there are N_0 active nuclei at $t = 0$. The half-life $t_{1/2}$ is the time elapsed before $N_0/2$ nuclei have decayed and $N_0/2$ remain active. From equation (46.17),

$$\frac{N_0}{2} = N_0 e^{-\lambda t_{1/2}}$$

or, $e^{\lambda t_{1/2}} = 2$

or, $\lambda t_{1/2} = \ln 2$

or, $$t_{1/2} = \frac{\ln 2}{\lambda} = \frac{0{\cdot}693}{\lambda} . \qquad \ldots (46.20)$$

Equation (46.20) relates the decay constant λ and the half-life $t_{1/2}$. As the activity $\left(-\frac{dN}{dt}\right)$ is proportional to N, the activity also reduces to half its value in one half-life.

Using equation (46.20), equation (46.17) may be rewritten as

$$N = N_0 e^{-(\ln 2)\frac{t}{t_{1/2}}} = \frac{N_0}{\left(e^{\ln 2}\right)^{t/t_{1/2}}}$$

$$= \frac{N_0}{2^{t/t_{1/2}}} . \qquad \ldots (46.21)$$

Similarly, the activity at time t is

$$A = \frac{A_0}{2^{t/t_{1/2}}} . \qquad \ldots (46.22)$$

Example 46.5

The half-life of a radioactive nuclide is 20 hours. What fraction of original activity will remain after 40 hours?

Solution : We have

$$\frac{t}{t_{1/2}} = \frac{40 \text{ hours}}{20 \text{ hours}} = 2.$$

Thus,

$$A = \frac{A_0}{2^{t/t_{1/2}}} = \frac{A_0}{2^2} = \frac{A_0}{4}$$

or, $$\frac{A}{A_0} = \frac{1}{4} .$$

So one fourth of the original activity will remain after 40 hours.

Average-life

Consider a sample containing N_0 radioactive nuclei at time $t = 0$. The number of nuclei which decay between the time t and $t + dt$ is $\lambda N\, dt$. The life of these nuclei is approximately t each. The sum of the lives of these dN nuclei is $t \lambda N\, dt$. The sum of all the lives of all the N nuclei that were active at $t = 0$ will be

$$S = \int_0^\infty t \lambda N\, dt$$

$$= \lambda N_0 \int_0^\infty t e^{-\lambda t}\, dt$$

$$= \lambda N_0 \left[\left(t \frac{e^{-\lambda t}}{-\lambda} \right)_0^\infty - \int_0^\infty \frac{e^{-\lambda t}}{-\lambda}\, dt \right]$$

$$= -\lambda N_0 \left(\frac{e^{-\lambda t}}{\lambda^2} \right)_0^\infty = \frac{N_0}{\lambda} .$$

Thus, the average-life of the nuclei is

$$t_{av} = \frac{S}{N_0} = \frac{1}{\lambda} . \qquad \ldots (46.23)$$

Using equation (46.20),

$$t_{av} = \frac{t_{1/2}}{0{\cdot}693} . \qquad \ldots (46.24)$$

All the equations derived above are statistical in nature. They do not predict the exact behaviour of each radioactive nucleus, they only predict the total numbers. In one half-life, half of the active particles will decay. But which of these particles will decay in one half-life is never predicted. Suppose a traffic controller is stationed at the junction of three roads A, B and C. He counts the total number of vehicles coming towards the junction from the side A and the number turning towards B and towards C. From his observations over a long period, he can formulate a statistical law that out of the vehicles coming from the side A, 60% turn towards B and 40% turn towards C. This rule is statistical and will work well on a normal day (it will not work, say, on the Independence Day when a procession of hundreds of vehicles on road A may turn towards B). But the traffic controller will not be able to predict whether a particular vehicle coming from the side A will turn towards B or towards C. Also, the rule works only when a large number of vehicles are considered. If he considers just 5 vehicles, 4 may turn towards B, and only 1 towards C and the rule may be a total failure. Similarly, the equations developed for radioactive decay work well only when N is large.

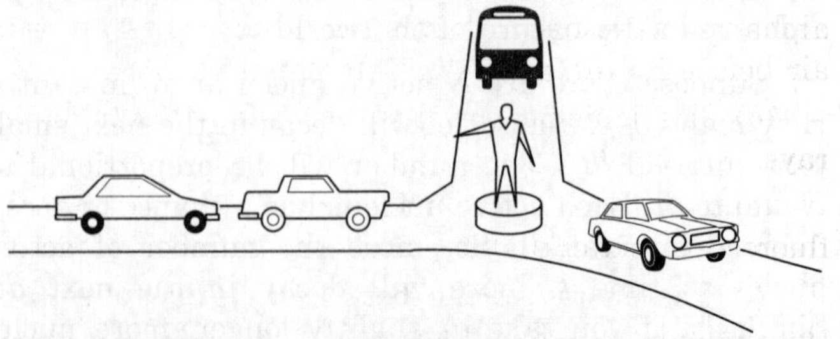

Figure 46.6

No description of radioactivity can be complete without mentioning the Curie couple. Marie Curie and her teacher-turned-husband Pierre Curie worked hard to separate the radioactive material radium chloride ($RaCl_2$) from uranium ore. They succeeded in 1902 when about 0·19 g of $RaCl_2$ was separated and its radioactivity was studied. They shared the Nobel Prize in physics for 1903 with Henri Becquerel for this work. The unit Ci is in their honour.

46.6 PROPERTIES AND USES OF NUCLEAR RADIATION

Alpha ray

(a) It is a stream of alpha particles, each particle containing two protons and two neutrons. An alpha particle is nothing but a helium nucleus.

(b) Being made of positively charged particles, alpha ray can be deflected by an electric field as well as by a magnetic field.

(c) Its penetrating power is low. Even in air, its intensity falls down to very small values within a few centimetres.

(d) Alpha rays coming from radioactive materials travel at large speeds of the order of 10^6 m s^{-1}.

(e) All the alpha particles coming from a particular decay scheme have the same energy.

(f) Alpha ray produces scintillation (flashes of light) when it strikes certain fluorescent materials, such as barium platinocyanide.

(g) It causes ionization in gases.

Beta ray

(a) It is a stream of electrons coming from the nuclei. Thus, the properties of beta ray, cathode ray, thermions, photoelectrons, etc., are all identical except for their origin. Beta particles are created at the time of nuclear transformation, whereas, in cathode ray, thermions, etc., the electrons are already present and get ejected.

(b) Being made of negatively charged particles, beta ray can be deflected by an electric field as well as by a magnetic field.

(c) Its penetrating power is greater than that of alpha ray. Typically, it can travel several metres in air before its intensity drops to small values.

(d) The ionizing power is less than that of alpha rays.

(e) Beta ray also produces scintillation in fluorescent materials, but the scintillation is weak.

(f) The energy of the beta particles coming from the same decay scheme are not equal. This is because the available energy is shared by antineutrinos. The energy of beta particles thus varies between zero and a maximum.

Beta-plus ray

Beta-plus ray has all the properties of beta ray, except that it is made of positively charged particles.

Gamma ray

(a) Gamma ray is an electromagnetic radiation of short wavelength. Its wavelength is, in general, smaller than X-rays. Many of its properties are the same as those of X-rays.

(b) Being chargeless, it is not deflected by electric or magnetic field.

(c) It has the least ionizing power and the largest penetrating power among different types of nuclear radiation.

(d) All the photons coming from a particular gamma decay scheme have the same energy.

(e) Being an electromagnetic wave, gamma ray travels in vacuum with the velocity *c*.

Nuclear radiation, specially gamma ray, is used in medicine for cancer therapy and other treatments. The ionizing power of nuclear radiation is used in factories to avoid accumulation of charge on moving parts due to friction. Presence of radioactive material ionizes the air and any charge accumulated leaks away. Carbon dating, which is based on radioactive decay of ^{14}C, is a reliable technique to estimate the 'age' of archeological samples which have carbon contents. Excess exposure to nuclear radiation is harmful for human body.

46.7 ENERGY FROM THE NUCLEUS

Energy in various forms is available around us. Matter itself is a concentrate of energy. All atoms, molecules, nuclei, etc., are in continuous motion and have large amount of kinetic energy. But the energy that we need for our daily tasks is required in specific forms. We require energy in the form of heat to cook our food. We require energy in the form of electric current for our fans and electric lamps. Cooking gas and oxygen in air contain energy but this internal energy is not in the form required to cook our food. When the two are engaged in a chemical reaction, heat is produced which is in usable form. Sources of usable energy is something not in plenty and man is now concerned about energy conservation. Traditional sources of usable energy are wood, coal, petroleum, etc., and they are only in limited amounts and might be exhausted in a few hundred years. We are getting a large amount of energy from the sun but to use an appreciable fraction of it has been a challenging task. Several centres throughout the world are working hard to develop efficient solar cells which can convert the energy from the sun to usable forms. Satellites and spaceships receive energy from the sun through such solar cells.

A solution to the energy crisis has been presented by nuclear energy. Nuclear energy may be obtained either by breaking a heavy nucleus into two nuclei of middle weight or by combining two light nuclei to form a middle-weight nucleus. The former process is called *nuclear fission* and the latter *nuclear fusion*.

The physics of fission or fusion lies in the relation between the binding energy per nucleon versus A (figure 46.3). The middle-weight nuclei are more tightly bound than heavy-weight nuclei. When the nucleons of a heavy nucleus regroup in two middle-weight nuclei, called fragments, the total binding energy increases and hence the rest mass energy decreases. The difference in energy appears as the kinetic energy of the fragments or in some other form. This is the basic principle of fission.

Similar arguments hold for fusion. Again, the light-weight nuclei are less-tightly bound than the middle-weight nuclei. Thus, if two light nuclei combine to form a middle-weight nucleus, the binding energy increases and the rest mass decreases. Energy is released in the form of kinetic energy or in some other external form.

Example 46.6

The binding energy per nucleon is 8·5 MeV *for* $A \approx 120$ *and is* 7·6 MeV *for* $A = 240$ *(see figure 46.3). Suppose a nucleus with* $A = 240$ *breaks into two nuclei of nearly equal mass numbers. Calculate the energy released in the process.*

Solution :

Suppose the heavy nucleus had Z protons and N neutrons. The rest mass energy of this nucleus would be

$$E = Mc^2 = (Zm_p + Nm_n)c^2 - B_1$$

$$= (Zm_p + Nm_n)c^2 - 7{\cdot}6 \times 240 \text{ MeV}.$$

If there are Z_1 protons and N_1 neutrons in the first fragment, its rest mass energy will be

$$E_1 = M_1c^2 = (Z_1m_p + N_1m_n)c^2 - B_2$$

$$= (Z_1m_p + N_1m_n)c^2 - (8{\cdot}5 \text{ MeV})(Z_1 + N_1).$$

Similarly, if there are Z_2 protons and N_2 neutrons in the second fragment, its rest mass energy will be

$$E_2 = (Z_2m_p + N_2m_n)c^2 - (8{\cdot}5 \text{ MeV})(Z_2 + N_2).$$

The energy released due to the breaking is

$$E - (E_1 + E_2)$$

$$= \left[(Z - Z_1 - Z_2)m_p c^2 + (N - N_1 - N_2)m_n c^2\right]$$

$$+ [(Z_1 + Z_2 + N_1 + N_2) \times 8{\cdot}5 - 240 \times 7{\cdot}6] \text{ MeV}$$

$$= 240 \times (8{\cdot}5 - 7{\cdot}6) \text{ MeV} = 216 \text{ MeV}.$$

We have used the fact that $Z_1 + Z_2 = Z$, $N_1 + N_2 = N$ and $Z_1 + Z_2 + N_1 + N_2 = Z + N = 240$. Thus, 216 MeV of energy will be released when this nucleus breaks.

46.8 NUCLEAR FISSION

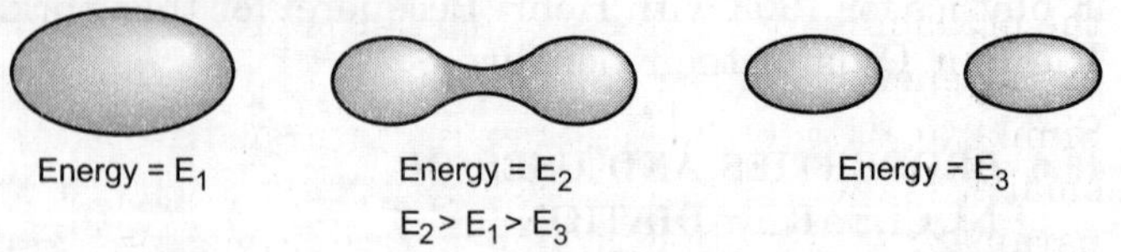

Figure 46.7

We have seen that a heavy nucleus has larger rest mass energy than that of its two middle-weight fragments. It is thus energetically favourable for the heavy nucleus to break into two middle-weight nuclei. However, before finally breaking into two parts, the heavy nucleus has to undergo a distortion which gradually increases to break the nucleus. The situation is shown in figure (46.7). The rest mass energy E_1 of the heavy nucleus is larger than the combined rest mass energy E_3 of its fragments but the energy E_2 in the intermediate state happens to be larger than E_1. Thus, it is not simple for the heavy nucleus to break spontaneously. In fact, according to classical physics, the process is impossible unless energy is supplied to the heavy nucleus to reach the intermediate state. Once it reaches the intermediate state, it can break into two parts and release energy. But the amount $E_2 - E_1$ has to be supplied to the heavy nucleus so that it may reach the intermediate state. Left to itself, the heavy nucleus will not break according to classical physics.

The world of subatomic particles is much different from that of our common day experience. According to quantum mechanics, if the final state has lesser energy than the energy in the initial state, there is a chance that the process will take place even if the intermediate state has energy greater than the initial one and no energy is supplied externally (figure 46.8).

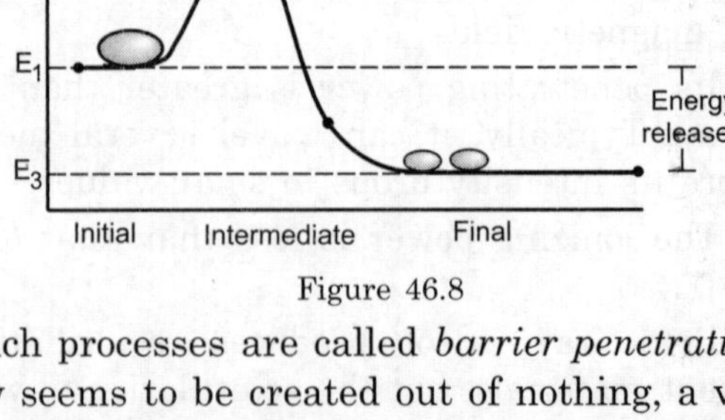

Figure 46.8

Such processes are called *barrier penetration*. The energy seems to be created out of nothing, a violation of energy conservation ! But this is a fact of the physics of small particles. The energy conservation in the usual sense may be violated for 'short times'. The amount of energy seems to be created and the time for which it is created are related through Heisenberg uncertainty relation,

$$\Delta E.\Delta t \approx h/2\pi$$

where h is the Planck constant.

Barrier penetration, though possible, is not easy. Greater the energy difference $\Delta E = E_2 - E_1$, smaller is the probability of a successful barrier penetration. This extra energy ΔE is called height of the barrier. Similarly, larger the duration of intermediate state, smaller is the probability of barrier penetration. These parameters are different for different nuclides and hence the probability that a heavy nucleus will break in a given time is different for different nuclides. Generally, this probability is extremely small except in a few nuclides. For example, the half-life of $^{238}_{92}U$ for fission reaction is about 10^{16} years. If you start with N nuclei of $^{238}_{92}U$ today, only $N/2$ will disintegrate in the next 10^{16} years. Table (46.1) shows some of the better cases where the probability of fission is appreciable.

Table 46.1 : *Fission probability*

Nuclide	Fission probability relative to ^{236}U
^{236}U	1 (arbitrarily assumed)
^{239}U	$< 1 \times 10^{-3}$
^{240}Pu	1·5
^{244}Am	$< 2 \times 10^{-4}$

46.9 URANIUM FISSION REACTOR

The most attractive bid, from a practical point of view, to achieve energy from nuclear fission is to use $^{236}_{92}U$ as the fission material. This nuclide is highly fissionable and hence is not found in nature. Natural uranium contains about 99·3% of $^{238}_{92}U$ and 0·7% of $^{235}_{92}U$. The technique is to hit a uranium sample by slow-moving neutrons (kinetic energy ≈ 0·04 eV, also called thermal neutrons). A $^{235}_{92}U$ nucleus has large probability of absorbing a slow neutron and forming $^{236}_{92}U$ nucleus. This nucleus then fissions into two parts. A variety of combinations of the middle-weight nuclei may be formed due to the fission. For example, one may have

$$^{236}_{92}U \rightarrow {}^{137}_{53}I + {}^{97}_{39}Y + 2n,$$

$$^{236}_{92}U \rightarrow {}^{140}_{56}Ba + {}^{94}_{36}Kr + 2n$$

and a number of other combinations.

During a fission event, in general, two or three neutrons are emitted. If the total number of neutrons emitted in a large number of events is divided by the number of events, the average comes out to be around 2·47. We say that on an average 2·47 neutrons (or 2·5 as a round figure) are emitted in each fission event. The two fragments generally have unequal mass numbers as is the case in the above examples. If the relative yield of different nuclei are plotted against their mass number, a plot of the type shown in figure (46.9) results. The most probable mass numbers of the fragments are around $A = 95$ and 140. The probability of having nearly equal fragments is small.

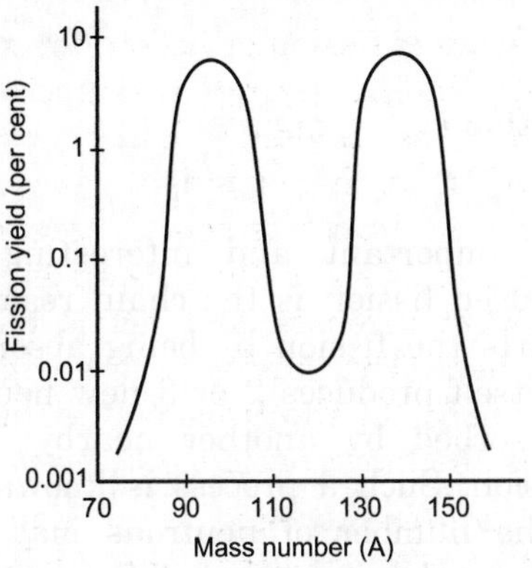

Figure 46.9

The ratio N/Z is larger in heavier nuclei than in the middle-weight nuclei (figure 46.1). Thus, the fragments will have N/Z ratio larger than that needed for stability. As a result, 2 or 3 neutrons are emitted together with the fission fragments. The fragments reduce their N/Z ratio further via beta decay in which a neutron is converted into a proton. These daughter nuclei are generally formed in excited states and consequently emit gamma rays. At some stage, a daughter nucleus can also emit another neutron. Thus, neutrons, beta particles (electrons), antineutrinos and gamma photons accompany nuclear fission. For example, in one of the reactions, ^{236}U breaks into $^{97}_{39}Y$ and $^{137}_{53}I$. These nuclei undergo the following changes:

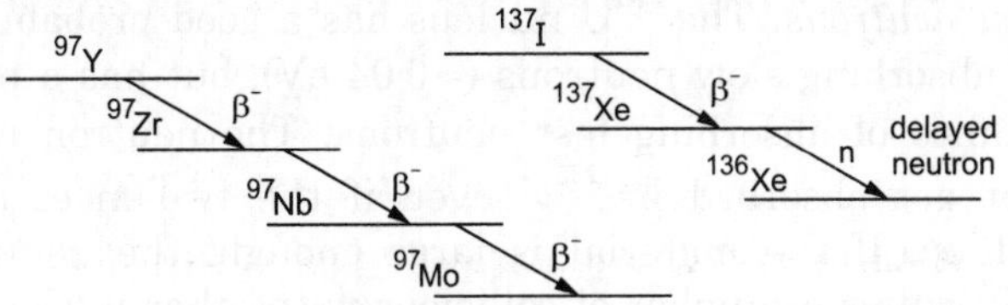

Figure 46.10

The neutron emitted by ^{137}Xe comes out an appreciable time interval after the fission as against the two neutrons emitted almost simultaneously with the fission. This is because ^{137}I decays to ^{137}Xe with its own half-life and only then ^{137}Xe emits the neutron. Such neutrons are called *delayed neutrons* and play an important role in controlling the fission rate.

In each fission event, about 200 MeV of energy is released a large part of which appears in the form of kinetic energies of the two fragments. Neutrons take away about 5 MeV. As the fragments decay, an additional energy of about 15–20 MeV is released in the form of kinetic energy of beta particles, antineutrino and photons. The fragments, formed with so much kinetic energy, are immediately stopped in the bulk uranium solid in which they are formed. This produces large amount of heat which is taken away by passing a cold liquid in pipes through the reaction area.

Chain Reaction

A very important and interesting feature of neutron-induced fission is the chain reaction. Once a neutron starts the fission by being absorbed in ^{235}U, the fission itself produces 2 or 3 new neutrons which may be absorbed by another nearby ^{235}U causing another fission. Such a process is known as a chain reaction. The number of neutrons may thus go on increasing in each generation of fission and the rate of fission may likewise increase in geometrical progression. If that happens, the whole of the material will fission out in a small time. The large amount of heat produced in such a short time will be uncontrollable and will only lead to disaster. There are ways to control the rate of chain reaction. If the fission event takes place near the surface of the bulk uranium material taken, there is a good chance that the neutrons produced will escape from the material without coming in contact with another ^{235}U. The fraction of the neutrons lost in this way will be larger if smaller pieces of uranium are taken. Controlling the size will thus control the rate of fission. Another important point is that the neutrons produced in the fission have kinetic energy ≈ 2 MeV. They are called *fast neutrons*. The ^{235}U nucleus has a good probability of absorbing slow neutrons (≈ 0·04 eV), but has a poor chance of absorbing fast neutrons. The neutron may not get absorbed in ^{235}U even if the two meet and collide. If the material is large enough, the neutron will suffer a number of collisions with other nuclei. In each collision, it will lose its kinetic energy and after some time may slow down to thermal energies ≈ 0·04 eV. It may then be absorbed by ^{235}U. But ^{238}U nuclei, which are present in large numbers (99·3%), are extremely good neutron absorbers if they get neutrons of energy 1–100 eV. These neutrons get absorbed in ^{238}U to form ^{239}U which decays generally by means other than fission. A fast neutron has to go through this 1–100 eV range before slowing down to thermal energies ≈ 0·04 eV and has a fair chance of being absorbed by ^{238}U. This neutron is, therefore, lost as far as fission is concerned.

Nuclear Reactor

Let us now consider the design and working of a typical uranium nuclear reactor (figure 46.11). Uranium is taken in the form of cylindrical rods arranged in a regular pattern in the active reactor core. The volume in the core is filled with a low-Z material such as heavy water (D_2O), graphite, beryllium, etc. This material is called *moderator*.

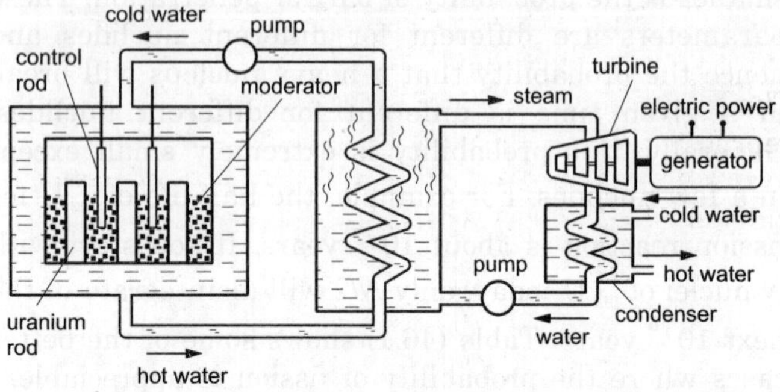

Figure 46.11

When fission takes place in a uranium rod, most of the fast neutrons produced escape from the rod and enter into the moderator. These neutrons make collisions with the particles of the moderator and thus slow down. About 25 collisions with deuteron (present in heavy water) or 100 collisions with carbon or beryllium are sufficient to slow down a neutron from 2 MeV to thermal energies. The distances between the rods are adjusted in such a way that a neutron coming from one rod is generally slowed down to thermal energies before entering the other rod. This eliminates the possibility of a neutron being absorbed by ^{238}U in 1–100 eV region. The geometry of the core is such that out of the average 2·5 neutrons produced per fission, 1 neutron is used to trigger the next fission and the remaining are lost without triggering any fission. The reaction is then sustained at a constant rate. If the rate of the loss of neutrons is decreased further, the fission rate will keep on increasing which may lead to explosion. If the rate of loss of neutrons is increased, the rate of fission will keep on decreasing and ultimately the chain reaction will stop. The finer control of fission rate is made by the *control rods* which are made of cadmium and are inserted up to a certain depth in the moderator. Cadmium is a very good neutron absorber. If the stage is set for stable chain reaction and the cadmium rods are pushed into the moderator, the reactor will be shut off. Pulling the cadmium rods out will start the reactor.

Some coolant liquid such as water at high pressure or molten sodium is passed through the reactor-core area which withdraws the heat produced in the core. The heat is used to prepare steam from water. The steam so prepared is used to run steam turbines and produce electric power. The amount of ^{235}U goes on decreasing as the uranium rod is used for fission. When ^{235}U is finished and only ^{238}U is left, the rods have to be changed.

Breeder Reactors

Although fission generates large amount of energy and the world is heavily depending on fission for its energy requirement, uranium resources are also limited. Table (46.1) shows that fission can easily take place with ^{240}Pu besides ^{236}U. But ^{239}Pu is not a naturally occurring isotope. However, ^{238}U can capture a neutron to produce ^{239}Pu which can be used as a nuclear fuel.

$$^{238}_{92}U + n \rightarrow {}^{239}_{92}U \xrightarrow{\beta^-} {}^{239}_{93}Np \xrightarrow{\beta^-} {}^{239}_{94}Pu.$$

Suppose, used uraninum rods, which contain only ^{238}U, are kept in or around a uranium-reactor core. Also suppose, the geometry is such that out of the average 2·5 neutrons produced in a fission, one neutron is absorbed by a ^{238}U nucleus in these rods resulting in ^{239}Pu. Then we produce as much nuclear fuel in the form of ^{239}Pu as we consume in the form of ^{235}U. If more than one neutron can be absorbed by these ^{238}U rods per fission then we produce more fuel than what we consume. Thus, apart from nuclear energy, these reactors give us fresh nuclear fuel which often exceeds the nuclear fuel used. Such a reactor is called a *breeder reactor.*

46.10 NUCLEAR FUSION

When two light nuclei come close to one another, within the range of attractive nuclear force ($\approx$ 1 fm), they may combine to form a bigger nucleus. The process is possible from an energy point of view because the binding energy per nucleon is small for light nuclei and increases with A until A is about 50. To bring the light nuclei within the separation of about a femtometre is, however, a difficult task. Any bulk material is composed of atoms and an atom typically has a radius of a few angstroms (1 angstrom $= 10^{-10}$ m $= 10^5$ fm). When atoms are pushed closer, their electrons cause them to repel each other. Even if all the electrons are stripped off, the nuclei themselves are positively charged and strongly repel each other. The technique thus is to heat a gas to an extremely high temperature so that the electrons are completely detached and the nuclei move within the gas with large random speeds. Two nuclei moving towards each other may come close enough to fuse into one nucleus. What must be the order of temperature which will ensure enough fusion ?

Example 46.7

Consider two deuterons moving towards each other with equal speeds in a deuteron gas. What should be their kinetic energies (when they are widely separated) so that the closest separation between them becomes 2 fm ? Assume that the nuclear force is not effective for separations greater than 2 fm. At what temperature will the deuterons have this kinetic energy on an average ?

Solution :

As the deuterons move, the Coulomb repulsion will slow them down. The loss in kinetic energy will be equal to the gain in Coulomb potential energy. At the closest separation, the kinetic energy is zero and the potential energy is $\frac{e^2}{4\pi\varepsilon_0 r}$. If the initial kinetic energy of each deuteron is K and the closest separation is 2 fm, we shall have

$$2K = \frac{e^2}{4\pi\varepsilon_0(2\text{ fm})}$$

$$= \frac{(1{\cdot}6\times10^{-19}\text{ C})^2\times(9\times10^9\text{ N m}^2\text{C}^{-2})}{2\times10^{-15}\text{ m}}$$

or, $\quad K = 5{\cdot}7\times10^{-14}$ J.

If the temperature of the gas is T, the average kinetic energy of random motion of each nucleus will be 1·5 kT. The temperature needed for the deuterons to have the average kinetic energy of $5{\cdot}7\times10^{-14}$ J will be given by

$$1{\cdot}5\,kT = 5{\cdot}7\times10^{-14}\text{ J}$$

or, $$T = \frac{5{\cdot}7\times10^{-14}\text{ J}}{1{\cdot}5\times1{\cdot}38\times10^{-23}\text{ J K}}$$

$$= 2{\cdot}8\times10^9\text{ K.}$$

One needs a temperature of the order of 10^9 K if deuterons are to be fused. The temperature inside the sun is estimated to be around $1{\cdot}5\times10^7$ K. Yet fusion is the main source of energy in the sun which it ultimately radiates to the universe including the earth. There are two main reasons why fusion can take place at a temperature even hundred times smaller than that calculated in example (46.7). One is that the energy of all the particles is not equal to the average energy. Although the average kinetic energy is 1·5 kT, there are particles which have kinetic energy much larger than 1·5 kT. Secondly, even if the kinetic energy of the two interacting nuclei is less than that needed to bring them within the nuclear range, there is a small chance of fusion through the process of *barrier penetration.*

As these reactions take place at high temperatures, they are also called *thermonuclear fusion* or *thermonuclear reactions.*

Fusion in Sun

Among the celestial bodies in which energy is produced, the sun is relatively cooler. There are stars with temperatures around 10^8 K inside. In sun and other stars, where the temperature is less than or around 10^7 K, fusion takes place dominantly by *proton–proton cycle* as follows:

$$^1H + {}^1H \rightarrow {}^2H + e^+ + \nu$$

$$^2H + {}^1H \rightarrow {}^3He + \gamma$$

$$^3He + {}^3He \rightarrow {}^4He + 2\,{}^1H$$

$$4\,{}^1H \rightarrow {}^4He + 2e^+ + 2\nu + 2\gamma$$

Note that the first two reactions should occur twice to produce two ^3He nuclei and initiate the third reaction. As a result of this cycle, effectively, four hydrogen nuclei combine to form a helium nucleus. About 26·7 MeV energy is released in the cycle. Thus, hydrogen is the fuel which 'burns' into helium to release energy. The sun is estimated to have been radiating energy for the last $4{\cdot}5 \times 10^9$ years and will continue to do so till all the hydrogen in it is used up. It is estimated that the present store of hydrogen in the sun is sufficient for the next 5×10^9 years.

In hotter stars where the temperature is $\approx 10^8$ K, another cycle known as proton–carbon cycle takes place.

$$^1H + {}^{12}C \rightarrow {}^{13}N + \gamma$$

$$^{13}N \rightarrow {}^{13}C + e^+ + \nu$$

$$^1H + {}^{13}C \rightarrow {}^{14}N + \gamma$$

$$^1H + {}^{14}N \rightarrow {}^{15}O + \gamma$$

$$^{15}O \rightarrow {}^{15}N + e^+ + \nu$$

$$^1H + {}^{15}N \rightarrow {}^{12}C + {}^4He$$

The end result of this cycle is again the fusion of four hydrogen nuclei into a helium nucleus. Carbon nucleus acts only as a catalyst.

It is clear that Coulomb repulsion becomes more and more obstructive to fusion as Z increases. Thus, it needs still higher temperatures for heavier elements to fuse. When the temperature inside a star rises, such fusions do take place to produce heavier nuclei such as

$$^4He + {}^4He + {}^4He \rightarrow {}^{12}C + \gamma.$$

The process can continue, finally producing elements in iron region ($A = 56$) where the binding energy per nucleon is maximum. Elements heavier than iron can be produced by neutron absorption and subsequent beta decay.

46.11 FUSION IN LABORATORY

In stellar objects, the material remains confined at high temperature due to gravitational pull. If we wish to make fusion as energy-producing device in laboratory, the major problem is to confine the hot plasma (when all the electrons are detached from the atoms, we get a plasma) in a small volume for extended time intervals. Producing a high temperature is obviously a major task but confinement at such high temperatures is more challenging. Solid walls can't be used as containers because no solid can sustain the high temperatures needed for fusion. The easiest thermonuclear reaction that can be handled on earth is the fusion of two deuterons (*D–D* reaction) or fusion of a deuteron with a triton (*D–T* reaction).

$$^2_1H + {}^2_1H \rightarrow {}^3_2He + n + 3{\cdot}3 \text{ MeV } (D\text{–}D)$$

$$^2_1H + {}^2_1H \rightarrow {}^3_1H + {}^1_1H + 4{\cdot}0 \text{ MeV } (D\text{–}D)$$

$$^2_1H + {}^3_1H \rightarrow {}^4_2He + n + 17{\cdot}6 \text{ MeV } (D\text{–}T)$$

One starts with deuterium gas (heavy hydrogen) or a mixture of deuterium with tritium, heat the gas to high temperatures, ensuring its confinement for reasonable period, and looks for the fusion.

Lawson criterion

J.D. Lawson showed that in order to get an energy output greater than the energy input, a fusion reactor should achieve

$$n\tau > 10^{14} \text{ s cm}^{-3}$$

where n is the density of the interacting particles and τ is the confinement time. The quantity $n\tau$ in s cm^{-3} is called *Lawson number*.

The ratio of the energy output to the energy input is known as Q of the fusion machine. For a viable fusion machine, Q should be greater than 1.

Tokamak Design

In one of the methods receiving serious attention, one uses the so-called *Tokamak* design. The deuterium plasma is contained in a toroidal region by specially designed magnetic field. The directions and magnitudes of the magnetic field are so managed in the toroidal space that whenever a charged plasma particle attempts to go out, the $q\vec{v} \times \vec{B}$ force tends to push it back into the toroidal volume. It is a difficult task to design a magnetic field which will push the particles moving in random directions with random speeds into a specified volume, but it is possible and has been done. The plasma is, therfore, confined by the magnetic field. Such confinement has been achieved for short durations (≈ few microseconds) in which some fusion occurs. Fusion thus proceeds in bursts or pulses. The heating is accomplished by passing high frequency oscillating current through the plasma gas. A schematic design is shown in figure (46.12).

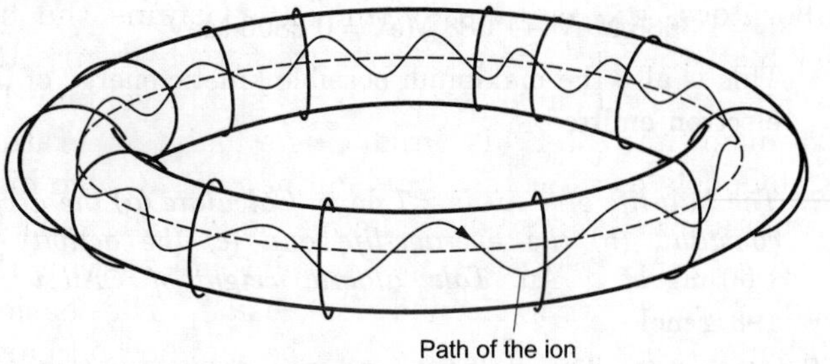

Figure 46.12

A large fusion machine known as *Joint European Torus* (JET) is designed to achieve fusion energy on this principle. A value of $Q \approx 1$ is already achieved with JET. Scientists working on this machine expect to get $Q \approx 40$ in the next 40 to 50 years.

At the Institute for Plasma Research (IPR), Ahmedabad, a small machine named *Aditya* is functioning on the Tokamak design. This machine is being used to study the properties of a plasma and a value of $n\tau \approx 10^{11}$ s cm^{-3} has been achieved for Lawson number.

Inertial Confinement

In another method known as inertial confinement, laser beams are used to confine the plasma. A small solid pellet is made which contains deuterium and tritium. Intense laser beams are directed on the pellet from many directions distributed over all sides. The lasers first vaporize the pellet converting it into plasma and then compress it from all directions because of the large pressure exerted. The density increases by 10^3 to 10^4 times the initial density and the temperature rises to high values. The fusion occurs in this period. The α-particles (He nuclei) generated by the fusion are also forced to remain inside the plasma. Their kinetic energy is lost into the plasma itself contributing further rise in temperature. Again the lasers are operated in pulses of short duration.

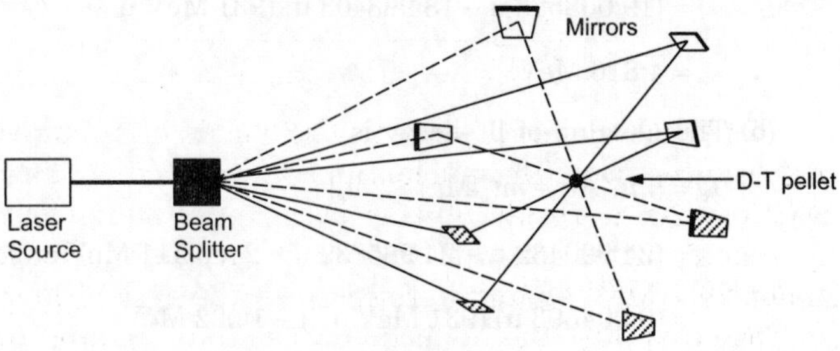

Figure 46.13

The research in fusion energy is going on. Fusion is the definite and ultimate answer to our energy problems. The 'fuel' used for fusion on earth is deuterium which is available in natural water (0·03%). And with oceans as the almost unlimited source of water, we can be sure of fuel supply for thousands of years. Secondly, fusion reactions are neat and clean. Radioactive radiation accompanying fission reactors will not be there with fusion reactors.

Worked Out Examples

1. *Calculate the electric potential energy due to the electric repulsion between two nuclei of* ^{12}C *when they 'touch' each other at the surface.*

Solution : The radius of a ^{12}C nucleus is

$$R = R_0 A^{1/3}$$

$$= (1{\cdot}1 \text{ fm})\,(12)^{1/3} = 2{\cdot}52 \text{ fm}.$$

The separation between the centres of the nuclei is $2R = 5{\cdot}04$ fm. The potential energy of the pair is

$$U = \frac{q_1 q_2}{4\pi\varepsilon_0 r}$$

$$= (9\times10^{9}\text{ N m}^2\text{C}^{-2})\,\frac{(6\times1{\cdot}6\times10^{-19}\text{ C})^2}{5{\cdot}04\times10^{-15}\text{ m}}$$

$$= 1{\cdot}64\times10^{-12}\text{ J} = 10{\cdot}2\text{ MeV}.$$

2. *Find the binding energy of* $^{56}_{26}$Fe. *Atomic mass of* ^{56}Fe *is* 55·9349 u *and that of* ^{1}H *is* 1·00783 u. *Mass of neutron* = 1·00867 u.

Solution : The number of protons in $^{56}_{26}$Fe = 26 and the number of neutrons = 56 − 26 = 30. The binding energy of $^{56}_{26}$Fe is

$$= [26\times1{\cdot}00783\text{ u} + 30\times1{\cdot}00867\text{ u} - 55{\cdot}9349\text{ u}]c^2$$

$$= (0{\cdot}52878\text{ u})c^2$$

$$= (0{\cdot}52878\text{ u})\,(931\text{ MeV u}^{-1}) = 492\text{ MeV}.$$

3. *Find the kinetic energy of the α-particle emitted in the decay* ^{238}Pu → ^{234}U + α. *The atomic masses needed are as follows:*

^{238}Pu	^{234}U	^{4}He
238·04955 u	234·04095 u	4·002603 u

Neglect any recoil of the residual nucleus.

Solution : Using energy conservation,

$$m(^{238}\text{Pu})\,c^2 = m(^{234}\text{U})c^2 + m(^{4}\text{He})c^2 + K$$

or, $$K = [m(^{238}\text{Pu}) - m(^{234}\text{U}) - m(^{4}\text{He})]c^2$$

$$= [238{\cdot}04955\text{ u} - 234{\cdot}04095\text{ u} - 4{\cdot}002603\text{ u}]\,(931\text{ MeV u}^{-1})$$

$$= 5{\cdot}58\text{ MeV}.$$

4. *Calculate the Q-value in the following decays:*

(a) $^{19}O \rightarrow {}^{19}F + e + \bar{\nu}$

(b) $^{25}Al \rightarrow {}^{25}Mg + e^{+} + \nu$.

The atomic masses needed are as follows:

^{19}O	^{19}F	^{25}Al	^{25}Mg
19·003576 u	18·998403 u	24·990432 u	24·985839 u

Solution :

(a) The Q-value of β^{-}-decay is

$$Q = [m(^{19}O) - m(^{19}F)]c^2$$
$$= [19{\cdot}003576 \text{ u} - 18{\cdot}998403 \text{ u}] (931 \text{ MeV u}^{-1})$$
$$= 4{\cdot}816 \text{ MeV}.$$

(b) The Q-value of β^{+}-decay is

$$Q = [m(^{25}Al) - m(^{25}Mg) - 2m_e]c^2$$
$$= [24{\cdot}990432 \text{ u} - 24{\cdot}985839 \text{ u} - 2 \times 0{\cdot}511 \text{ MeV c}^{-2}]c^2$$
$$= (0{\cdot}004593 \text{ u}) (931 \text{ MeV u}^{-1}) - 1{\cdot}022 \text{ MeV}$$
$$= 4{\cdot}276 \text{ MeV} - 1{\cdot}022 \text{ MeV} = 3{\cdot}254 \text{ MeV}.$$

5. *Find the maximum energy that a beta particle can have in the following decay*

$$^{176}Lu \rightarrow {}^{176}Hf + e + \bar{\nu}.$$

Atomic mass of ^{176}Lu *is* 175·942694 u *and that of* ^{176}Hf is 175·941420 u.

Solution : The kinetic energy available for the beta particle and the antineutrino is

$$Q = [m(^{176}Lu) - m(^{176}Hf)]c^2$$
$$= (175{\cdot}942694 \text{ u} - 175{\cdot}941420 \text{ u}) (931 \text{ MeVu}^{-1})$$
$$= 1{\cdot}182 \text{ MeV}.$$

This energy is shared by the beta particle and the antineutrino. The maximum kinetic energy of a beta particle in this decay is, therefore, 1·182 MeV when the antineutrino practically does not get any share.

6. *Consider the beta decay*

$$^{198}Au \rightarrow {}^{198}Hg^{*} + \beta^{-} + \bar{\nu}$$

where $^{198}Hg^{*}$ *represents a mercury nucleus in an excited state at energy* 1·088 MeV *above the ground state. What can be the maximum kinetic energy of the electron emitted ? The atomic mass of* ^{198}Au *is* 197·968233 u *and that of* ^{198}Hg *is* 197·966760 u.

Solution : If the product nucleus ^{198}Hg is formed in its ground state, the kinetic energy available to the electron and the antineutrino is

$$Q = [m(^{198}Au) - m(^{198}Hg)]c^2.$$

As $^{198}Hg^{*}$ has energy 1·088 MeV more than ^{198}Hg in ground state, the kinetic energy actually available is

$$Q = [m(^{198}Au) - m(^{198}Hg)]c^2 - 1{\cdot}088 \text{ MeV}$$
$$= (197{\cdot}968233 \text{ u} - 197{\cdot}966760 \text{ u}) (931 \text{ MeV u}^{-1}) - 1{\cdot}088 \text{ MeV}$$
$$= 1{\cdot}3686 \text{ MeV} - 1{\cdot}088 \text{ MeV} = 0{\cdot}2806 \text{ MeV}$$

This is also the maximum possible kinetic energy of the electron emitted.

7. *The half-life of* ^{198}Au *is* 2·7 days. *Calculate (a) the decay constant, (b) the average-life and (c) the activity of* 1·00 mg *of* ^{198}Au. *Take atomic weight of* ^{198}Au *to be* 198 g mol^{-1}.

Solution : (a) The half-life and the decay constant are related as

$$t_{1/2} = \frac{\ln 2}{\lambda} = \frac{0{\cdot}693}{\lambda}$$

or, $$\lambda = \frac{0{\cdot}693}{t_{1/2}} = \frac{0{\cdot}693}{2{\cdot}7 \text{ days}}$$
$$= \frac{0{\cdot}693}{2{\cdot}7 \times 24 \times 3600 \text{ s}} = 2{\cdot}9 \times 10^{-6} \text{ s}^{-1}.$$

(b) The average-life is $t_{av} = \frac{1}{\lambda} = 3{\cdot}9$ days.

(c) The activity is $A = \lambda N$. Now, 198 g of ^{198}Au has 6×10^{23} atoms. The number of atoms in 1·00 mg of ^{198}Au is

$$N = 6 \times 10^{23} \times \frac{1{\cdot}0 \text{ mg}}{198 \text{ g}} = 3{\cdot}03 \times 10^{18}.$$

Thus, $$A = \lambda N$$
$$= (2{\cdot}9 \times 10^{-6} \text{ s}^{-1}) (3{\cdot}03 \times 10^{18})$$
$$= 8{\cdot}8 \times 10^{12} \text{ disintegrations s}^{-1}$$
$$= \frac{8{\cdot}8 \times 10^{12}}{3{\cdot}7 \times 10^{10}} \text{ Ci} = 240 \text{ Ci}.$$

8. *A radioactive sample has* $6{\cdot}0 \times 10^{18}$ *active nuclei at a certain instant. How many of these nuclei will still be in the same active state after two half-lives ?*

Solution : In one half-life the number of active nuclei reduces to half the original number. Thus, in two half-lives the number is reduced to $\left(\frac{1}{2}\right)\left(\frac{1}{2}\right)$ of the original number. The number of remaining active nuclei is, therefore,

$$6{\cdot}0 \times 10^{18} \times \left(\frac{1}{2}\right) \times \left(\frac{1}{2}\right)$$
$$= 1{\cdot}5 \times 10^{18}.$$

9. *The activity of a radioactive sample falls from* 600 s^{-1} *to* 500 s^{-1} *in* 40 minutes. *Calculate its half-life.*

Solution : We have,

$$A = A_0 e^{-\lambda t}$$

or, $500\ \text{s}^{-1} = (600\ \text{s}^{-1})e^{-\lambda t}$

or, $e^{-\lambda t} = \dfrac{5}{6}$

or, $\lambda t = \ln(6/5)$

or, $\lambda = \dfrac{\ln(6/5)}{t} = \dfrac{\ln(6/5)}{40\ \text{min}}$.

The half-life is $t_{1/2} = \dfrac{\ln 2}{\lambda}$

$$= \frac{\ln 2}{\ln(6/5)} \times 40\ \text{min}$$

$$= 152\ \text{min.}$$

10. *The number of ^{238}U atoms in an ancient rock equals the number of ^{206}Pb atoms. The half-life of decay of ^{238}U is $4{\cdot}5 \times 10^{9}$ y. Estimate the age of the rock assuming that all the ^{206}Pb atoms are formed from the decay of ^{238}U.*

Solution : Since the number of ^{206}Pb atoms equals the number of ^{238}U atoms, half of the original ^{238}U atoms have decayed. It takes one half-life to decay half of the active nuclei. Thus, the sample is $4{\cdot}5 \times 10^{9}$ y old.

11. *Equal masses of two samples of charcoal A and B are burnt separately and the resulting carbon dioxide are collected in two vessels. The radioactivity of ^{14}C is measured for both the gas samples. The gas from the charcoal A gives 2100 counts per week and the gas from the charcoal B gives 1400 counts per week. Find the age difference between the two samples. Half-life of ^{14}C = 5730 y.*

Solution : The activity of sample A is 2100 counts per week. After a certain time t, its activity will be reduced to 1400 counts per week. This is because a fraction of the active ^{14}C nuclei will decay in time t. The sample B must be a time t older than the sample A.

We have,

$$A = A_0 e^{-\lambda t}$$

or, $1400\ \text{s}^{-1} = 2100\ \text{s}^{-1}\ e^{-\lambda t}$

or, $e^{-\lambda t} = \dfrac{2}{3}$

$$t = \frac{\ln(3/2)}{\lambda}$$

$$= \frac{\ln(3/2)}{0{\cdot}693}\, t_{1/2}$$

$$= \frac{0{\cdot}4055}{0{\cdot}693} \times 5730\ \text{y} = 3352\ \text{y}.$$

12. *Suppose, the daughter nucleus in a nuclear decay is itself radioactive. Let λ_p and λ_d be the decay constants of the parent and the daughter nuclei. Also, let N_p and N_d be the number of parent and daughter nuclei at time t. Find the condition for which the number of daughter nuclei becomes constant.*

Solution : The number of parent nuclei decaying in a short time interval t to $t + dt$ is $\lambda_p N_p dt$. This is also the number of daughter nuclei produced in this interval. The number of daughter nuclei decaying during the same time interval is $\lambda_d N_d dt$. The number of the daughter nuclei will be constant if

$$\lambda_p N_p dt = \lambda_d N_d dt$$

or, $\lambda_p N_p = \lambda_d N_d$.

13. *A radioactive sample decays with an average-life of 20 ms. A capacitor of capacitance 100 μF is charged to some potential and then the plates are connected through a resistance R. What should be the value of R so that the ratio of the charge on the capacitor to the activity of the radioactive sample remains constant in time?*

Solution : The activity of the sample at time t is given by

$$A = A_0 e^{-\lambda t}$$

where λ is the decay constant and A_0 is the activity at time $t = 0$ when the capacitor plates are connected. The charge on the capacitor at time t is given by

$$Q = Q_0 e^{-t/CR}$$

where Q_0 is the charge at $t = 0$ and $C = 100\ \mu\text{F}$ is the capacitance. Thus,

$$\frac{Q}{A} = \frac{Q_0}{A_0} \frac{e^{-t/CR}}{e^{-\lambda t}}.$$

It is independent of t if $\lambda = \dfrac{1}{CR}$

or, $R = \dfrac{1}{\lambda C} = \dfrac{t_{av}}{C} = \dfrac{20 \times 10^{-3}\ \text{s}}{100 \times 10^{-6}\ \text{F}} = 200\ \Omega.$

14. *A radioactive nucleus can decay by two different processes. The half-life for the first process is t_1 and that for the second process is t_2. Show that the effective half-life t of the nucleus is given by*

$$\frac{1}{t} = \frac{1}{t_1} + \frac{1}{t_2}.$$

Solution : The decay constant for the first process is $\lambda_1 = \dfrac{\ln 2}{t_1}$ and for the second process it is $\lambda_2 = \dfrac{\ln 2}{t_1}$. The probability that an active nucleus decays by the first process in a time interval dt is $\lambda_1 dt$. Similarly, the probability that it decays by the second process is $\lambda_2 dt$. The probability that it either decays by the first process or by the second process is $\lambda_1 dt + \lambda_2 dt$. If the effective decay constant is λ, this probability is also equal to λdt. Thus,

$$\lambda dt = \lambda_1 dt + \lambda_2 dt$$

or, $\lambda = \lambda_1 + \lambda_2$

or, $\frac{1}{t} = \frac{1}{t_1} + \frac{1}{t_2}$.

15. *Calculate the energy released when three alpha particles combine to form a* ^{12}C *nucleus. The atomic mass of* $^{4}_{2}He$ *is* 4·002603 u.

Solution : The mass of a ^{12}C atom is exactly 12 u. The energy released in the reaction $3\left(^{4}_{2}He\right) \rightarrow {}^{12}_{6}C$ is

$$[3\,m(^{4}_{2}He) - m(^{12}_{6}C)]c^2$$

$$= [3 \times 4{\cdot}002603\text{ u} - 12\text{ u}]\,(931\text{ MeV u}^{-1}) = 7{\cdot}27\text{ MeV}.$$

□

QUESTIONS FOR SHORT ANSWER

1. If neutrons exert only attractive force, why don't we have a nucleus containing neutrons alone ?
2. Consider two pairs of neutrons. In each pair, the separation between the neutrons is the same. Can the force between the neutrons have different magnitudes for the two pairs ?
3. A molecule of hydrogen contains two protons and two electrons. The nuclear force between these two protons is always neglected while discussing the behaviour of a hydrogen molecule. Why ?
4. Is it easier to take out a nucleon (a) from carbon or from iron (b) from iron or from lead ?
5. Suppose we have 12 protons and 12 neutrons. We can assemble them to form either a ^{24}Mg nucleus or two ^{12}C nuclei. In which of the two cases more energy will be liberated ?
6. What is the difference between cathode rays and beta rays ? When the two are travelling in space, can you make out which is the cathode ray and which is the beta ray ?
7. If the nucleons of a nucleus are separated from each other, the total mass is increased. Where does this mass come from ?
8. In beta decay, an electron (or a positron) is emitted by a nucleus. Does the remaining atom get oppositely charged ?
9. When a boron nucleus ($^{10}_{5}B$) is bombarded by a neutron, an α-particle is emitted. Which nucleus will be formed as a result ?
10. Does a nucleus lose mass when it suffers gamma decay ?
11. In a typical fission reaction, the nucleus is split into two middle-weight nuclei of unequal masses. Which of the two (heavier or lighter) has greater kinetic energy ? Which one has greater linear momentum ?
12. If three helium nuclei combine to form a carbon nucleus, energy is liberated. Why can't helium nuclei combine on their own and minimise the energy ?

OBJECTIVE I

1. The mass of a neutral carbon atom in ground state is
   (a) exact 12 u (b) less than 12 u
   (c) more than 12 u
   (d) depends on the form of carbon such as graphite or charcoal.
2. The mass number of a nucleus is equal to
   (a) the number of neutrons in the nucleus
   (b) the number of protons in the nucleus
   (c) the number of nucleons in the nucleus
   (d) none of them.
3. As compared to ^{12}C atom, ^{14}C atom has
   (a) two extra protons and two extra electrons
   (b) two extra protons but no extra electron
   (c) two extra neutrons and no extra electron
   (d) two extra neutrons and two extra electrons.
4. The mass number of a nucleus is
   (a) always less than its atomic number
   (b) always more than its atomic number
   (c) equal to its atomic number
   (d) sometimes more than and sometimes equal to its atomic number.
5. The graph of $\ln(R/R_0)$ versus $\ln A$ (R = radius of a nucleus and A = its mass number) is
   (a) a straight line (b) a parabola
   (c) an ellipse (d) none of them.
6. Let F_{pp}, F_{pn} and F_{nn} denote the magnitudes of the nuclear force by a proton on a proton, by a proton on a neutron and by a neutron on a neutron respectively. When the separation is 1 fm,
   (a) $F_{pp} > F_{pn} = F_{nn}$ (b) $F_{pp} = F_{pn} = F_{nn}$
   (c) $F_{pp} > F_{pn} > F_{nn}$ (d) $F_{pp} < F_{pn} = F_{nn}$.
7. Let F_{pp}, F_{pn} and F_{nn} denote the magnitudes of the net force by a proton on a proton, by a proton on a neutron and by a neutron on a neutron respectively. Neglect gravitational force. When the separation is 1 fm,
   (a) $F_{pp} > F_{pn} = F_{nn}$ (b) $F_{pp} = F_{pn} = F_{nn}$
   (c) $F_{pp} > F_{pn} > F_{nn}$ (d) $F_{pp} < F_{pn} = F_{nn}$.
8. Two protons are kept at a separation of 10 nm. Let F_n and F_e be the nuclear force and the electromagnetic force between them.
   (a) $F_e = F_n$ (b) $F_e >> F_n$ (c) $F_e << F_n$
   (d) F_e and F_n differ only slightly.

9. As the mass number A increases, the binding energy per nucleon in a nucleus
(a) increases (b) decreases (c) remains the same
(d) varies in a way that depends on the actual value of A.

10. Which of the following is a wrong description of binding energy of a nucleus ?
(a) It is the energy required to break a nucleus into its constituent nucleons.
(b) It is the energy made available when free nucleons combine to form a nucleus.
(c) It is the sum of the rest mass energies of its nucleons minus the rest mass energy of the nucleus.
(d) It is the sum of the kinetic energy of all the nucleons in the nucleus.

11. In one average-life,
(a) half the active nuclei decay
(b) less than half the active nuclei decay
(c) more than half the active nuclei decay
(d) all the nuclei decay.

12. In a radioactive decay, neither the atomic number nor the mass number changes. Which of the following particles is emitted in the decay ?
(a) Proton (b) Neutron (c) Electron (d) Photon

13. During a negative beta decay,
(a) an atomic electron is ejected
(b) an electron which is already present within the nucleus is ejected
(c) a neutron in the nucleus decays emitting an electron
(d) a proton in the nucleus decays emitting an electron.

14. A freshly prepared radioactive source of half-life 2 h emits radiation of intensity which is 64 times the permissible safe level. The minimum time after which it would be possible to work safely with this source is
(a) 6 h (b) 12 h (c) 24 h (d) 128 h.

15. The decay constant of a radioactive sample is λ. The half-life and the average-life of the sample are respectively
(a) $1/\lambda$ and $(\ln 2/\lambda)$ (b) $(\ln 2/\lambda)$ and $1/\lambda$
(c) $\lambda(\ln 2)$ and $1/\lambda$ (d) $\lambda/(\ln 2)$ and $1/\lambda$.

16. An α-particle is bombarded on ^{14}N. As a result, a ^{17}O nucleus is formed and a particle is emitted. This particle is a
(a) neutron (b) proton (c) electron (d) positron.

17. Ten grams of ^{57}Co kept in an open container beta-decays with a half-life of 270 days. The weight of the material inside the container after 540 days will be very nearly
(a) 10 g (b) 5 g (c) 2·5 g (d) 1·25 g.

18. Free ^{238}U nuclei kept in a train emit alpha particles. When the train is stationary and a uranium nucleus decays, a passenger measures that the separation between the alpha particle and the recoiling nucleus becomes x in time t after the decay. If a decay takes place when the train is moving at a uniform speed v, the distance between the alpha particle and the recoiling nucleus at a time t after the decay, as measured by the passenger will be
(a) $x + vt$ (b) $x - vt$ (c) x
(d) depends on the direction of the train.

19. During a nuclear fission reaction,
(a) a heavy nucleus breaks into two fragments by itself
(b) a light nucleus bombarded by thermal neutrons breaks up
(c) a heavy nucleus bombarded by thermal neutrons breaks up
(d) two light nuclei combine to give a heavier nucleus and possibly other products.

OBJECTIVE II

1. As the mass number A increases, which of the following quantities related to a nucleus do not change ?
(a) Mass (b) Volume (c) Density (d) Binding energy

2. The heavier nuclei tend to have larger N/Z ratio because
(a) a neutron is heavier than a proton
(b) a neutron is an unstable particle
(c) a neutron does not exert electric repulsion
(d) Coulomb forces have longer range compared to the nuclear forces.

3. A free neutron decays to a proton but a free proton does not decay to a neutron. This is because
(a) neutron is a composite particle made of a proton and an electron whereas proton is a fundamental particle
(b) neutron is an uncharged particle whereas proton is a charged particle
(c) neutron has larger rest mass than the proton
(d) weak forces can operate in a neutron but not in a proton.

4. Consider a sample of a pure beta-active material.
(a) All the beta particles emitted have the same energy.
(b) The beta particles originally exist inside the nucleus and are ejected at the time of beta decay.
(c) The antineutrino emitted in a beta decay has zero mass and hence zero momentum.
(d) The active nucleus changes to one of its isobars after the beta decay.

5. In which of the following decays the element does not change ?
(a) α-decay (b) β^+-decay (c) β^--decay (d) γ-decay

6. In which of the following decays the atomic number decreases ?
(a) α-decay (b) β^+-decay (c) β^--decay (d) γ-decay

7. Magnetic field does not cause deflection in
(a) α-rays (b) beta-plus rays
(c) beta-minus rays (d) gamma rays.

8. Which of the following are electromagnetic waves ?
(a) α-rays (b) Beta-plus rays
(c) Beta-minus rays (d) Gamma rays

9. Two lithium nuclei in a lithium vapour at room temperature do not combine to form a carbon nucleus because
(a) a lithium nucleus is more tightly bound than a

carbon nucleus
(b) carbon nucleus is an unstable particle
(c) it is not energetically favourable
(d) Coulomb repulsion does not allow the nuclei to come very close.

10. For nuclei with $A > 100$,
(a) the binding energy of the nucleus decreases on an average as A increases
(b) the binding energy per nucleon decreases on an average as A increases
(c) if the nucleus breaks into two roughly equal parts, energy is released
(d) if two nuclei fuse to form a bigger nucleus, energy is released.

EXERCISES

Mass of proton $m_p = 1{\cdot}007276$ u, Mass of ${}^1_1H$ atom $= 1{\cdot}007825$ u, Mass of neutron $m_n = 1{\cdot}008665$ u, Mass of electron $= 0{\cdot}0005486$ u ≈ 511 keV c^{-2}, 1 u $= 931$ MeV c^{-2}.

1. Assume that the mass of a nucleus is approximately given by $M = Am_p$ where A is the mass number. Estimate the density of matter in kgm^{-3} inside a nucleus. What is the specific gravity of nuclear matter?

2. A neutron star has a density equal to that of the nuclear matter. Assuming the star to be spherical, find the radius of a neutron star whose mass is $4{\cdot}0 \times 10^{30}$ kg (twice the mass of the sun).

3. Calculate the mass of an α-particle. Its binding energy is 28·2 MeV.

4. How much energy is released in the following reaction:

$${}^7Li + p \rightarrow \alpha + \alpha.$$

Atomic mass of ${}^7Li = 7{\cdot}0160$ u and that of ${}^4He = 4{\cdot}0026$ u.

5. Find the binding energy per nucleon of ${}^{197}_{79}Au$ if its atomic mass is 196·96 u.

6. (a) Calculate the energy released if ${}^{238}U$ emits an α-particle. (b) Calculate the energy to be supplied to ${}^{238}U$ if two protons and two neutrons are to be emitted one by one. The atomic masses of ${}^{238}U$, ${}^{234}Th$ and ${}^4He$ are 238·0508 u, 234·04363 u and 4·00260 u respectively.

7. Find the energy liberated in the reaction

$${}^{223}Ra \rightarrow {}^{209}Pb + {}^{14}C.$$

The atomic masses needed are as follows.

${}^{223}Ra$	${}^{209}Pb$	${}^{14}C$
223·018 u	208·981 u	14·003 u

8. Show that the minimum energy needed to separate a proton from a nucleus with Z protons and N neutrons is

$$\Delta E = (M_{Z-1,N} + M_H - M_{Z,N})c^2$$

where $M_{Z,N}$ = mass of an atom with Z protons and N neutrons in the nucleus and M_H = mass of a hydrogen atom. This energy is known as *proton-separation energy*.

9. Calculate the minimum energy needed to separate a neutron from a nucleus with Z protons and N neutrons in terms of the masses $M_{Z,N}$, $M_{Z,N-1}$ and the mass of the neutron.

10. ${}^{32}P$ beta-decays to ${}^{32}S$. Find the sum of the energy of the antineutrino and the kinetic energy of the β-particle. Neglect the recoil of the daughter nucleus. Atomic mass of ${}^{32}P = 31{\cdot}974$ u and that of ${}^{32}S = 31{\cdot}972$ u.

11. A free neutron beta-decays to a proton with a half-life of 14 minutes. (a) What is the decay constant? (b) Find the energy liberated in the process.

12. Complete the following decay schemes.
(a) ${}^{226}_{88}Ra \rightarrow \alpha +$
(b) ${}^{19}_{8}O \rightarrow {}^{19}_{9}F +$
(c) ${}^{25}_{13}Al \rightarrow {}^{25}_{12}Mg +$

13. In the decay ${}^{64}Cu \rightarrow {}^{64}Ni + e^+ + \nu$, the maximum kinetic energy carried by the positron is found to be 0·650 MeV. (a) What is the energy of the neutrino which was emitted together with a positron of kinetic energy 0·150 MeV? (b) What is the momentum of this neutrino in kg m s^{-1}? Use the formula applicable to a photon.

14. Potassium-40 can decay in three modes. It can decay by β^--emission, β^+-emission or electron capture. (a) Write the equations showing the end products. (b) Find the Q-values in each of the three cases. Atomic masses of ${}^{40}_{18}Ar$, ${}^{40}_{19}K$ and ${}^{40}_{20}Ca$ are 39·9624 u, 39·9640 u and 39·9626 u respectively.

15. Lithium ($Z = 3$) has two stable isotopes ${}^6Li$ and ${}^7Li$. When neutrons are bombarded on lithium sample, electrons and α-particles are ejected. Write down the nuclear processes taking place.

16. The masses of ${}^{11}C$ and ${}^{11}B$ are respectively 11·0114 u and 11·0093 u. Find the maximum energy a positron can have in the β^+-decay of ${}^{11}C$ to ${}^{11}B$.

17. ${}^{228}Th$ emits an alpha particle to reduce to ${}^{224}Ra$. Calculate the kinetic energy of the alpha particle emitted in the following decay:

$${}^{228}Th \rightarrow {}^{224}Ra^* + \alpha$$

$${}^{224}Ra^* \rightarrow {}^{224}Ra + \gamma\,(217\text{ keV}).$$

Atomic mass of ${}^{228}Th$ is 228·028726 u, that of ${}^{224}Ra$ is 224·020196 u and that of ${}^4_2He$ is 4·00260 u.

18. Calculate the maximum kinetic energy of the beta particle emitted in the following decay scheme:

$${}^{12}N \rightarrow {}^{12}C^* + e^+ + \nu$$

$${}^{12}C^* \rightarrow {}^{12}C + \gamma\,(4{\cdot}43\text{ MeV}).$$

The atomic mass of ${}^{12}N$ is 12·018613 u.

19. The decay constant of ${}^{197}_{80}Hg$ (electron capture to ${}^{197}_{79}Au$) is $1{\cdot}8 \times 10^{-4}$ s^{-1}. (a) What is the half-life? (b) What is the average-life? (c) How much time will it take to convert 25% of this isotope of mercury into gold?

20. The half-life of ^{198}Au is 2·7 days. (a) Find the activity of a sample containing 1·00 μg of ^{198}Au. (b) What will be the activity after 7 days? Take the atomic weight of ^{198}Au to be 198 g mol^{-1}.

21. Radioactive ^{131}I has a half-life of 8·0 days. A sample containing ^{131}I has activity 20 μCi at $t = 0$. (a) What is its activity at $t = 4·0$ days? (b) What is its decay constant at $t = 4·0$ days?

22. The decay constant of ^{238}U is $4·9 \times 10^{-18}$ s^{-1}. (a) What is the average-life of ^{238}U? (b) What is the half-life of ^{238}U? (c) By what factor does the activity of a ^{238}U sample decrease in 9×10^{9} years?

23. A certain sample of a radioactive material decays at the rate of 500 per second at a certain time. The count rate falls to 200 per second after 50 minutes. (a) What is the decay constant of the sample? (b) What is its half-life?

24. The count rate from a radioactive sample falls from $4·0 \times 10^{6}$ per second to $1·0 \times 10^{6}$ per second in 20 hours. What will be the count rate 100 hours after the beginning?

25. The half-life of ^{226}Ra is 1602 y. Calculate the activity of 0·1 g of $RaCl_2$ in which all the radium is in the form of ^{226}Ra. Taken atomic weight of Ra to be 226 g mol^{-1} and that of Cl to be 35·5 g mol^{-1}.

26. The half-life of a radioisotope is 10 h. Find the total number of disintegrations in the tenth hour measured from a time when the activity was 1 Ci.

27. The selling rate of a radioactive isotope is decided by its activity. What will be the second-hand rate of a one month old ^{32}P($t_{1/2}$ = 14·3 days) source if it was originally purchased for 800 rupees?

28. ^{57}Co decays to ^{57}Fe by β^{+}-emission. The resulting ^{57}Fe is in its excited state and comes to the ground state by emitting γ-rays. The half-life of β^{+}-decay is 270 days and that of the γ-emission is 10^{-8} s. A sample of ^{57}Co gives $5·0 \times 10^{9}$ gamma rays per second. How much time will elapse before the emission rate of gamma rays drops to $2·5 \times 10^{9}$ per second?

29. Carbon ($Z = 6$) with mass number 11 decays to boron ($Z = 5$). (a) Is it a β^{+}-decay or a β^{-}-decay? (b) The half-life of the decay scheme is 20·3 minutes. How much time will elapse before a mixture of 90% carbon-11 and 10% boron-11 (by the number of atoms) converts itself into a mixture of 10% carbon-11 and 90% boron-11?

30. 4×10^{23} tritium atoms are contained in a vessel. The half-life of decay of tritium nuclei is 12·3 y. Find (a) the activity of the sample, (b) the number of decays in the next 10 hours (c) the number of decays in the next 6·15 y.

31. A point source emitting alpha particles is placed at a distance of 1 m from a counter which records any alpha particle falling on its 1 cm^{2} window. If the source contains $6·0 \times 10^{16}$ active nuclei and the counter records a rate of 50000 counts/second, find the decay constant. Assume that the source emits alpha particles uniformly in all directions and the alpha particles fall nearly normally on the window.

32. ^{238}U decays to ^{206}Pb with a half-life of $4·47 \times 10^{9}$ y. This happens in a number of steps. Can you justify a single half-life for this chain of processes? A sample of rock is found to contain 2·00 mg of ^{238}U and 0·600 mg of ^{206}Pb. Assuming that all the lead has come from uranium, find the life of the rock.

33. When charcoal is prepared from a living tree, it shows a disintegration rate of 15·3 disintegrations of ^{14}C per gram per minute. A sample from an ancient piece of charcoal shows ^{14}C activity to be 12·3 disintegrations per gram per minute. How old is this sample? Half-life of ^{14}C is 5730 y.

34. Natural water contains a small amount of tritium ($^{3}_{1}H$). This isotope beta-decays with a half-life of 12·5 years. A mountaineer while climbing towards a difficult peak finds debris of some earlier unsuccessful attempt. Among other things he finds a sealed bottle of whisky. On return he analyses the whisky and finds that it contains only 1·5 per cent of the $^{3}_{1}H$ radioactivity as compared to a recently purchased bottle marked '8 years old'. Estimate the time of that unsuccessful attempt.

35. The count rate of nuclear radiation coming from a radioactive sample containing ^{128}I varies with time as follows.

Time t (minute):	0	25	50	75	100
Count rate R(10^{9} s^{-1}):	30	16	8·0	3·8	2·0

(a) Plot $\ln(R_0/R)$ against t. (b) From the slope of the best straight line through the points, find the decay constant λ. (c) Calculate the half-life $t_{1/2}$.

36. The half-life of ^{40}K is $1·30 \times 10^{9}$ y. A sample of 1·00 g of pure KCl gives 160 counts s^{-1}. Calculate the relative abundance of ^{40}K (fraction of ^{40}K present) in natural potassium.

37. $^{197}_{80}Hg$ decays to $^{197}_{79}Au$ through electron capture with a decay constant of 0·257 per day. (a) What other particle or particles are emitted in the decay? (b) Assume that the electron is captured from the K shell. Use Moseley's law $\sqrt{\nu} = a(Z - b)$ with $a = 4·95 \times 10^{7}$ s$^{-1/2}$ and $b = 1$ to find the wavelength of the K_{α} X-ray emitted following the electron capture.

38. A radioactive isotope is being produced at a constant rate $dN/dt = R$ in an experiment. The isotope has a half-life $t_{1/2}$. Show that after a time $t >> t_{1/2}$, the number of active nuclei will become constant. Find the value of this constant.

39. Consider the situation of the previous problem. Suppose the production of the radioactive isotope starts at $t = 0$. Find the number of active nuclei at time t.

40. In an agricultural experiment, a solution containing 1 mole of a radioactive material ($t_{1/2}$ = 14·3 days) was injected into the roots of a plant. The plant was allowed 70 hours to settle down and then activity was measured in its fruit. If the activity measured was 1 μCi, what per cent of activity is transmitted from the root to the fruit in steady state?

41. A vessel of volume 125 cm^{3} contains tritium (^{3}H, $t_{1/2}$ = 12·3 y) at 500 kPa and 300 K. Calculate the activity of the gas.

42. $^{212}_{83}Bi$ can disintegrate either by emitting an α-particle or by emitting a β^--particle. (a) Write the two equations showing the products of the decays. (b) The probabilities of disintegration by α- and β-decays are in the ratio 7/13. The overall half-life of ^{212}Bi is one hour. If 1 g of pure ^{212}Bi is taken at 12·00 noon, what will be the composition of this sample at 1 p.m. the same day ?

43. A sample contains a mixture of ^{110}Ag and ^{108}Ag isotopes each having an activity of $8{\cdot}0 \times 10^8$ disintegrations per second. ^{108}Ag is known to have larger half-life than ^{110}Ag. The activity A is measured as a function of time and the following data are obtained.

Time (s)	Activity (A) (10^8 disintegrations s^{-1})	Time (s)	Activity (A) (10^8 disintegrations s^{-1})
20	11·799	200	3·0828
40	9·1680	300	1·8899
60	7·4492	400	1·1671
80	6·2684	500	0·7212
100	5·4115		

(a) Plot $\ln(A/A_0)$ versus time. (b) See that for large values of time, the plot is nearly linear. Deduce the half-life of ^{108}Ag from this portion of the plot. (c) Use the half-life of ^{108}Ag to calculate the activity corresponding to ^{110}Ag in the first 50 s. (d) Plot $\ln(A/A_0)$ versus time for ^{110}Ag for the first 50 s. (e) Find the half-life of ^{110}Ag.

44. A human body excretes (removes by waste discharge, sweating, etc.) certain materials by a law similar to radioactivity. If technitium is injected in some form in a human body, the body excretes half the amount in 24 hours. A patient is given an injection containing ^{99}Tc. This isotope is radioactive with a half-life of 6 hours. The activity from the body just after the injection is 6 μCi. How much time will elapse before the activity falls to 3 μCi ?

45. A charged capacitor of capacitance C is discharged through a resistance R. A radioactive sample decays with an average-life τ. Find the value of R for which the ratio of the electrostatic field energy stored in the capacitor to the activity of the radioactive sample remains constant in time.

46. Radioactive isotopes are produced in a nuclear physics experiment at a constant rate $dN/dt = R$. An inductor of inductance 100 mH, a resistor of resistance 100 Ω and a battery are connected to form a series circuit. The circuit is switched on at the instant the production of radioactive isotope starts. It is found that i/N remains constant in time where i is the current in the circuit at time t and N is the number of active nuclei at time t. Find the half-life of the isotope.

47. Calculate the energy released by 1 g of natural uranium assuming 200 MeV is released in each fission event and that the fissionable isotope ^{235}U has an abundance of 0·7% by weight in natural uranium.

48. A uranium reactor develops thermal energy at a rate of 300 MW. Calculate the amount of ^{235}U being consumed every second. Average energy released per fission is 200 MeV.

49. A town has a population of 1 million. The average electric power needed per person is 300 W. A reactor is to be designed to supply power to this town. The efficiency with which thermal power is converted into electric power is aimed at 25%. (a) Assuming 200 MeV of thermal energy to come from each fission event on an average, find the number of events that should take place every day. (b) Assuming the fission to take place largely through ^{235}U, at what rate will the amount of ^{235}U decrease ? Express your answer in kg per day. (c) Assuming that uranium enriched to 3% in ^{235}U will be used, how much uranium is needed per month (30 days) ?

50. Calculate the Q-values of the following fusion reactions:

(a) $^2_1H + ^2_1H \rightarrow ^3_1H + ^1_1H$

(b) $^2_1H + ^2_1H \rightarrow ^3_2He + n$

(c) $^2_1H + ^3_1H \rightarrow ^4_2He + n$.

Atomic masses are $m(^2_1H) = 2{\cdot}014102$ u, $m(^3_1H) = 3{\cdot}016049$ u, $m(^3_2He) = 3{\cdot}016029$ u, $m(^4_2He) = 4{\cdot}002603$ u.

51. Consider the fusion in helium plasma. Find the temperature at which the average thermal energy 1·5 kT equals the Coulomb potential energy at 2 fm.

52. Calculate the Q-value of the fusion reaction

$$^4He + ^4He = ^8Be.$$

Is such a fusion energetically favourable ? Atomic mass of ^8Be is 8·0053 u and that of ^4He is 4·0026 u.

53. Calculate the energy that can be obtained from 1 kg of water through the fusion reaction

$$^2H + ^2H \rightarrow ^3H + p.$$

Assume that $1{\cdot}5 \times 10^{-2}$ % of natural water is heavy water D_2O (by number of molecules) and all the deuterium is used for fusion.

□

ANSWERS

OBJECTIVE I

1. (a)	2. (c)	3. (c)	4. (d)	5. (a)	6. (b)
7. (d)	8. (b)	9. (d)	10. (d)	11. (c)	12. (d)
13. (c)	14. (b)	15. (b)	16. (b)	17. (a)	18. (c)
19. (c)					

OBJECTIVE II

1. (c)	2. (c), (d)	3. (c)
4. (d)	5. (d)	6. (a), (b)
7. (d)	8. (d)	9. (d)
10. (b), (c)		

EXERCISES

1. 3×10^{17} kg m^{-3}, 3×10^{14}
2. 15 km
3. 4·0016 u
4. 17·34 MeV
5. 7·94 MeV
6. (a) 4·255 MeV (b) 24·03 MeV
7. 31·65 MeV
9. $(M_{Z,N-1} + m_n - M_{Z,N})c^2$
10. 1·86 MeV
11. (a) $8{\cdot}25 \times 10^{-4}$ s^{-1} (b) 782 keV
12. (a) $^{222}_{86}$Rn (b) $\bar{e} + \nu$ (c) $e^+ + \nu$
13. (a) 500 keV (b) $2{\cdot}67 \times 10^{-22}$ kg m s^{-1}
14. (a) $^{40}_{19}K \to\, ^{40}_{20}Ca + e^- + \bar{\nu}$, $^{40}_{19}K \to\, ^{40}_{18}Ar + e^+ + \nu$, $^{40}_{19}K + e^- \to\, ^{40}_{18}Ar + \nu$

    (b) 1·3034 MeV, 0·4676 MeV, 1·490 MeV
15. $^{6}_{3}Li + n \to\, ^{7}_{3}Li$, $^{7}_{3}Li + n \to\, ^{8}_{3}Li \to\, ^{8}_{4}Be + e^- + \bar{\nu}$, $^{8}_{4}Be \to\, ^{4}_{2}He + ^{4}_{2}He$
16. 933·6 keV
17. 5·304 MeV
18. 11·88 MeV
19. (a) 64 min (b) 92 min (c) 1600 s
20. (a) 0·244 Ci (b) 0·040 Ci
21. (a) 14 μCi (b) $1{\cdot}4 \times 10^{-6}$ s^{-1}
22. $6{\cdot}49 \times 10^{9}$ y (b) $4{\cdot}5 \times 10^{9}$ y (c) 4
23. $3{\cdot}05 \times 10^{-4}$ s (b) 38 min
24. $3{\cdot}9 \times 10^{3}$ per second
25. $2{\cdot}8 \times 10^{9}$ disintegrations s^{-1}
26. $6{\cdot}91 \times 10^{13}$
27. 187 rupees
28. 270 days
29. (a) β^+ (b) 64 min
30. (a) $7{\cdot}146 \times 10^{14}$ disintegrations s^{-1}

    (b) $2{\cdot}57 \times 10^{19}$ (c) $1{\cdot}17 \times 10^{23}$
31. $1{\cdot}05 \times 10^{-7}$ s^{-1}
32. $1{\cdot}92 \times 10^{9}$ y
33. 1800 y
34. about 83 years ago
35. (b) 0·028 min^{-1} approx. (c) 25 min approx.
36. 0·12%
37. (a) neutrino (b) 20 pm
38. $\dfrac{Rt_{1/2}}{0{\cdot}693}$
39. $\dfrac{R}{\lambda}(1 - e^{-\lambda t})$
40. $1{\cdot}26 \times 10^{-11}$ %
41. 724 Ci
42. (a) $^{212}_{83}Bi \to\, ^{208}_{81}Tl + \alpha$, $^{212}_{83}Bi \to\, ^{212}_{84}Bi \to\, ^{212}_{84}Po + e^- + \bar{\nu}$

    (b) 0·50 g Bi, 0·175 g Tl, 0·325 g Po
43. the half-life of ^{110}Ag = 24·4 s and of ^{108}Ag = 144 s
44. 4·8 hours
45. $2\tau/C$
46. $6{\cdot}93 \times 10^{-4}$ s
47. $5{\cdot}7 \times 10^{8}$ J
48. 3·7 mg
49. (a) $3{\cdot}24 \times 10^{24}$ (b) 1·264 kg per day (c) 1263 kg
50. (a) 4·05 MeV (b) 3·25 MeV (c) 17·57 MeV
51. $2{\cdot}23 \times 10^{10}$ K
52. −93·1 keV, no
53. 3200 MJ

□

CHAPTER 47

THE SPECIAL THEORY OF RELATIVITY

Special theory of relativity stems from two bold postulates put forth by Albert Einstein—regarded by many as the greatest scientific mind of all times. The ideas put forward by special theory of relativity are fascinating and to the first-time learners they seem to go against their everyday experiences—what they think is 'common sense'. However, in our brief discussion here, we shall see that the whole of special theory of relativity is *logically deduced* from Einstein's postulates. In this chapter, we shall use only the inertial frames of reference and we shall frequently use the word *frame* for *inertial frame.*

47.1 THE PRINCIPLE OF RELATIVITY

The principle of relativity is not a new concept for us. We have seen that all frames of reference that move with uniform velocities with respect to an inertial frame are themselves inertial. Newton's laws of motion are valid in the same form in all such frames. Standing on a railway platform, you can drop a stone in such a way that it hits your left foot. If you repeat the same experiment in a train moving smoothly with a uniform velocity, the stone will again strike your left foot. One cannot distinguish between two inertial frames by repeating the same experiment in the two frames. No experiment done inside the train can tell whether the train is at rest at a platform or is moving at 120 km h^{-1} with respect to the platform provided there are no jerks, the train does not speed up or speed down and it does not bend.

This is the principle of relativity. There is no preferred inertial frame. All frames are equivalent. The motion between two frames is relative—you can choose any of the frames and call it at rest and the other in motion.

We can understand this on the basis of Newton's laws of motion. These laws have the same form in all inertial frames. Whether you measure acceleration, force and mass on the platform or on the train, force always equals mass times acceleration. As the results of experiments are governed by Newton's law, identical experiments will give identical results irrespective of the frame involved. But Newton's laws govern only the experiments of mechanics ! Can we do an experiment related to electricity inside a train and tell if the train is moving or is at rest ?

47.2 ARE MAXWELL'S LAWS INDEPENDENT OF FRAME ?

Maxwell's laws tell us that electromagnetic waves propagate in vacuum with a speed $c = \sqrt{\frac{1}{\mu_0 \varepsilon_0}}$ $\approx 3 \times 10^{8}$ m s^{-1}. Light is an electromagnetic wave. If Maxwell's laws are valid in the same form in all inertial frames, light must travel with the same speed $c = 3 \times 10^{8}$ m s^{-1} in all such frames. Experiments show that this is true. Figure (47.1) shows a representative situation when two observers A and B look at a light pulse W.

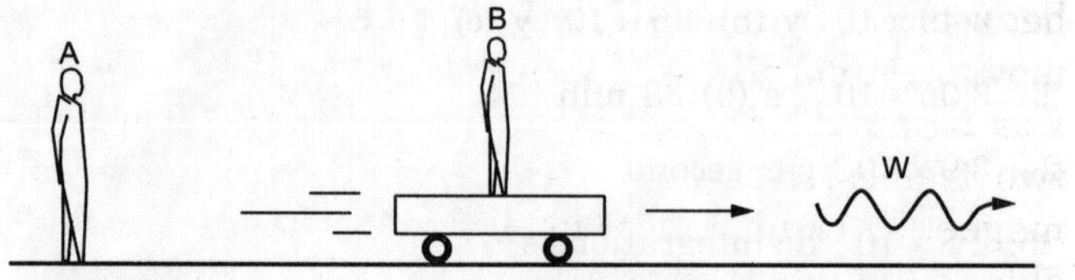

Figure 47.1

Suppose B moves away from A at a speed $u = c/2$ towards the right. The light pulse W moves away from A at a speed c towards the right, and W also moves away from B at the same speed c towards the right. Suppose at $t = 0$; A, B and W were at the same place. A notes down the distances of B and W from himself as a function of time and B notes down the distances of A and W from himself as a function of time. If you collect their diaries the next day, you will find something as given below.

Diary of A:

t	AB	AW
0	0	0
1 s	$1{\cdot}5 \times 10^{8}$ m	3×10^{8} m
2 s	3×10^{8} m	6×10^{8} m
3 s	$4{\cdot}5 \times 10^{8}$ m	9×10^{8} m

Diary of B:

t	BA	BW
0	0	0
1 s	1.5×10^{8} m	3×10^{8} m
2 s	3×10^{8} m	6×10^{8} m
3 s	4.5×10^{8} m	9×10^{8} m

It seems quite reasonable that $AB = BA$ at each t. But we also find that $AW = BW$ at each t even though $AB \neq 0$. Do we not have $AW = AB + BW$? The two diaries suggest that something is wrong somewhere. May be, $t = 1$ s of A is not the same as $t = 1$ s of B. Then AW, AB and BW are measured at different instants. Or may be, 1 m of A is not the same as 1 m of B so that AW and BW are measured in different units.

If Maxwell's equations are valid in the same form for both A and B, something is fishy here. Either the clocks of A and B do not run at the same rate or the metre sticks used by A and B are not of equal length, or both. There are two possibilities.

1. Maxwell's equations have the same form in all inertial frames. Our understanding of clocks and metre sticks, i.e., of time and length has to be revised.

2. Maxwell's equations have different forms in different inertial frames.

If the second option is correct, the experiments of electricity, magnetism and optics should behave differently in different inertial frames. The experiments of mechanics could not distinguish between a train resting at a platform and a train moving uniformly with respect to the platform. That was because Newton's laws had the same form in the two frames. But now the experiments of electricity, magnetism and optics done inside a train should be able to tell whether the train is at rest or it is moving and if it is moving, with what velocity.

Experiments show that this is not true. Even experiments of electricity, magnetism and optics done inside a train cannot tell whether it is moving or not with respect to a platform. A very sophisticated experiment of this kind was designed by Michelson and Morley which is by any standard one of the greatest experiments in physics till date. The experiment attempted to measure the earth's velocity with respect to the imagined ether frame. However, it failed and created history.

We have to accept the first option as we cannot accept the second. The speed of electromagnetic wave must be the same in all inertial frames. Einstein put these ideas in the form of two postulates known as the *postulates of special relativity*.

Postulate 1: *The laws of nature have identical form in all inertial frames.*

Postulate 2: *The speed of light in vacuum has the same value c in all inertial frames.*

47.3 KINEMATICAL CONSEQUENCES

We have seen that the postulates of special relativity require that we must revise our concepts of length and time. If we construct two identical metre sticks, put one on a railway platform and another on a moving train, they behave differently. Similarly, if we construct two identical clocks, use one in the platform frame and the other in the train frame and measure the time interval between the occurrences of two events, the results may be different. Let us investigate these phenomena in detail.

(A) A Rod Moving Perpendicular to its Length

Let us imagine a hypothetical experiment as follows. Construct two identical rods L_1 and L_2. Place them together and verify that the ends match against each other, i.e., they are of equal length. Put some red paint at the ends of L_1 and blue paint at the ends of L_2. Separate L_1 from L_2 by moving it perpendicular to its length. Now move L_1 towards L_2 with a uniform velocity v and look from the frame of reference of L_2, that is, from the L_2-frame (figure 47.2a).

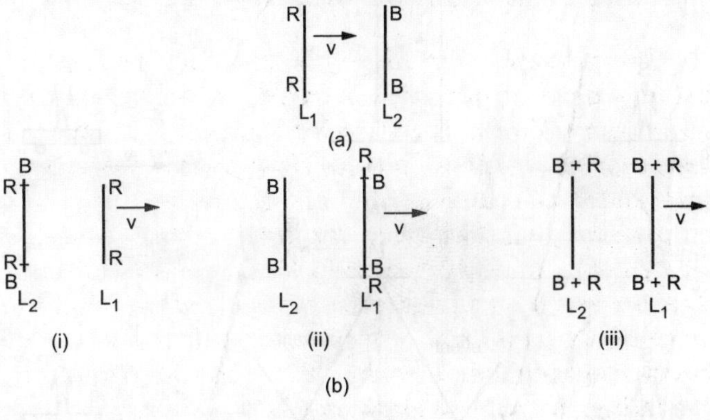

Figure 47.2

L_1 is moving, L_2 is at rest. Are the two rods still equal in length or is the moving rod shorter or is the moving rod longer? This can be checked by our experiment. As the rod L_1 passes over L_2, there are three possibilities (figure 47.2b).

(i) There are red marks on L_2 near the ends. This means that *the moving rod shrinks in its length.*

(ii) There are blue marks on L_1 near the ends. This means that *the moving rod extends in its length.*

(iii) Red and blue intermix at all the four ends. This means that *the moving rod has the same length as the stationary rod.*

Suppose option (i) is correct, i.e., L_1 leaves red marks on L_2 as it passes over L_2. This means that *the moving rod shrinks.* Now the same experiment may be observed by a person fixed with L_1, that is, from the L_1-frame. For this observer, L_1 is at rest, L_2 comes from the right and passes over L_1. Since L_2 gets red paint on it during the crossing, the observer concludes that the *moving rod extended in its length.* But by the principle of relativity you can choose any of the two rods to be at rest and the other moving. Laws of nature should have the same form in the L_1-frame and the L_2-frame. Thus, option (i) is wrong. Similarly, option (ii) is wrong. We conclude that *a rod's length remains unchanged when it is moved perpendicular to its length.*

(B) Moving Clocks (Time Dilation)

Consider another hypothetical experiment. Take a rod of length L as measured by an observer fixed with the rod and suppose that there are two mirrors fixed at the ends. Suppose a light pulse is reflected back and forth by the mirrors. Let us find the time interval between successive reflections from the mirror M_1. Let us call the first reflection 'event E_1' and the next reflection 'event E_2'. (The word 'event' also has a specialised meaning in the mathematical theory of relativity but we are using the literal meaning only.)

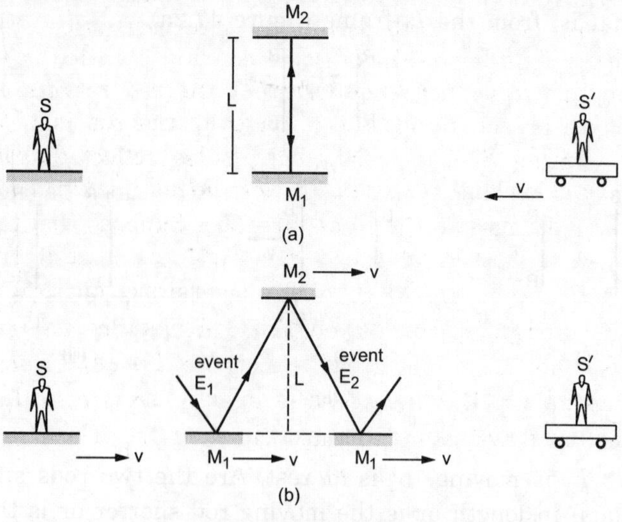

Figure 47.3

Figure (47.3a) shows the situation from a frame S in which the mirrors are at rest. The rod connecting the mirrors is not shown for clarity. The light pulse travels a distance $2L$ between successive reflections from M_1. As the speed of light is c, the time elapsed between these reflections is $\Delta t = \frac{2L}{c}$.

Now consider another frame S' moving with respect to the frame S with a speed v towards the left. From this frame, the rod and the mirrors are moving towards the right with a velocity v. The mirror M_1 at the time of the second reflection is at a place different from where it was at the time of the first reflection (figure 47.3b). If the time interval between these reflections is $\Delta t'$, the simple geometry of figure (47.3b) shows that the light pulse travels a distance

$$2\sqrt{L^2 + \left(\frac{v\Delta t'}{2}\right)^2}$$

between these reflections. Note that the length of the rod is unaltered as it moves in a direction perpendicular to its length. As the speed of light is c, the time interval between the successive reflections from M_1, is

$$\Delta t' = \frac{2}{c}\sqrt{L^2 + \left(\frac{v\Delta t'}{2}\right)^2}$$

or, $$\left(\frac{c\Delta t'}{2}\right)^2 = L^2 + \left(\frac{v\Delta t'}{2}\right)^2$$

or, $$(c^2 - v^2)\left(\frac{\Delta t'}{2}\right)^2 = L^2$$

or, $$\Delta t' = \frac{2L/c}{\sqrt{1 - v^2/c^2}}$$

or, $$\Delta t' = \frac{\Delta t}{\sqrt{1 - v^2/c^2}} = \gamma\,\Delta t \quad \ldots \quad (47.1)$$

where $\gamma = \frac{1}{\sqrt{1 - v^2/c^2}}$.

We shall use this factor again and again and hence a symbol γ is assigned to it. Note that γ is greater than 1. The time interval between the occurrences of the same two events is different as measured from different frames. In frame S, both E_1 and E_2 occur at the same place. The time interval measured from such a frame where the two events occur at the same place is called *proper time interval.* The time interval measured by a frame where the events occur at different places is called *improper time interval.* Here Δt is proper and $\Delta t'$ is improper time interval. According to equation (47.1),

The proper time interval between the occurrences of two events is smaller than the improper time interval by the factor γ.

This phenomenon is called *time dilation.*

The apparatus described above may be treated as a clock. Each reflection from the mirror M_1 can be thought of as a *tick* of the clock. We shall call it a *light-beam clock.* We see that when the clock is stationary with respect to the observer, it ticks at an interval $2L/c$ and when it moves with respect to the observer, it ticks at an interval γ $(2L/c)$. Thus,

A moving clock runs slower than a stationary clock by a factor of γ.

Remember, any of the two clocks may be taken to be stationary. Suppose A and B are two clocks moving with respect to each other. As seen from the frame of A, B runs slower and as seen from the frame of B, A runs slower.

Proper time interval

The concept of proper and improper time interval is valid for any two events and not only for two ticks of a clock.

Consider two events E_1 and E_2. Suppose, E_1 occurs at $x = 0$ at a time $t = 0$ and E_2 occurs at $x = L$ at a time t as seen from a frame S (figure 47.4).

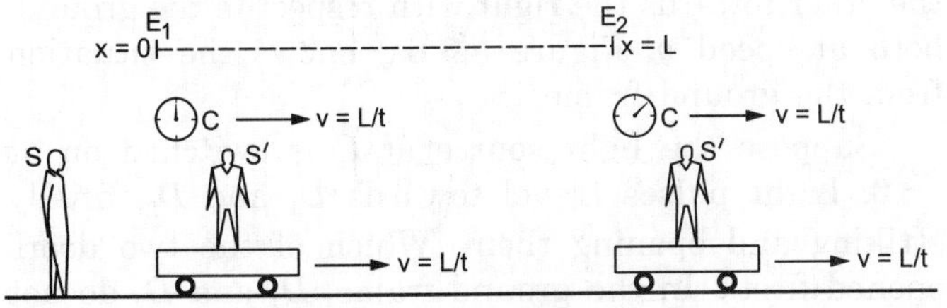

Figure 47.4

Suppose a clock C is at $x = 0$ at $t = 0$ and moves along the x-axis with a speed L/t. At time t, this clock will be at $x = L$. So this same clock is present at both the events E_1 and E_2.

Consider a frame S' moving along the x-axis at a speed L/t with respect to S. In this frame, the clock is at rest and both the events are measured on the same clock. In other words, both the events take place at the *same place in* S'.

As seen from S, the time interval between the events is t. The clock C is moving with respect to S and hence runs slower by a factor γ. The time interval between the events as measured by this clock is $t' = t/\gamma$. This is also the time interval between E_1 and E_2 in frame S' and hence is the proper time interval.

In the frame S', the events can be recorded by a single clock. All other frames where two clocks are needed to record the events, give improper time intervals. The proper time interval is smaller than an improper time interval by a factor of γ.

Example 47.1

A person in a train moving at a speed $3 \times 10^7 \text{ m s}^{-1}$ *sleeps at* 10·00 p.m. *by his watch and gets up at* 4·00 a.m. *How long did he sleep according to the clocks at the stations* ?

Solution : The time interval measured by the watch is the proper time interval because the events, 'sleeping' and 'getting up', are recorded by the single clock (the watch). The clocks at the stations represent the ground frame and in this frame he sleeps at one place and gets up at another place. Thus, the time interval measured by the station clocks is improper time interval and is more than the proper time interval.

The duration of his sleep in the ground frame is

$$\Delta t' = \gamma \Delta t = \frac{\Delta t}{\sqrt{1 - v^2/c^2}} = \frac{6 \text{ h}}{\sqrt{1 - \left(\dfrac{3 \times 10^7 \text{ m s}^{-1}}{3 \times 10^8 \text{ m s}^{-1}}\right)^2}}$$

$$= 6 \text{ h} \sqrt{\frac{100}{99}} = 6 \text{ hours } 1{\cdot}8 \text{ minutes}.$$

The speed of the train in this example is hypothetical. A typical fast train today runs at about 300 km h^{-1}. Repeat the exercise with such a train.

(C) A Rod Moving Parallel to its Length (Length Contraction)

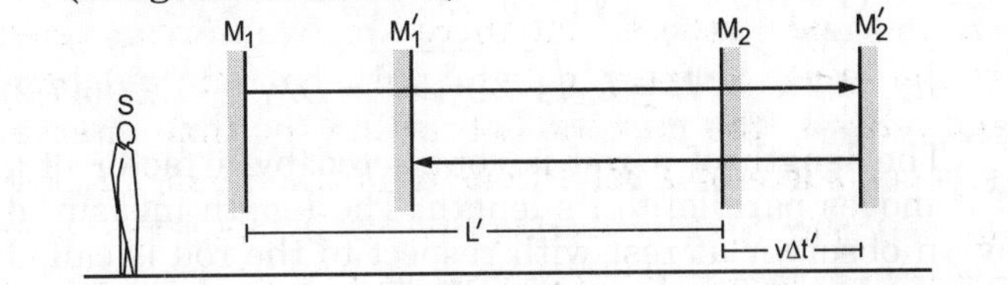

Figure 47.5

Consider the light-beam clock that we discussed. Suppose it is moved at a velocity v along its length (figure 47.5) with respect to an observer. As the rod in the light-beam clock is now moving parallel to its length, we do not know whether the rod retains its length or not. Suppose the length of the rod is L' in the frame S. Consider a light pulse reflected from M_1 and moving towards M_2. Now, M_2 is itself moving with velocity v in the same direction. Suppose that the pulse strikes M_2 at the position M_2' and that it has taken a time $\Delta t'$ to go from the position M_1 to M_2'. The mirror M_2 has moved ahead a distance $v\Delta t_1'$ so that the pulse has moved a distance $L' + v\Delta t_1'$ before striking M_2. But the speed of light pulse is c so that it must travel a distance $c\Delta t_1'$ in time $\Delta t_1'$. Thus,

$$c\Delta t_1' = L' + v\Delta t_1'$$

or,
$$\Delta t_1' = \frac{L'}{c - v}.$$

Similarly, the time taken by the pulse in its return journey from M_2 to M_1 (it strikes M_1 at the position M_1') is

$$\Delta t_2' = \frac{L'}{c + v}.$$

The total time elapsed between successive reflections from M_1 is, therefore,

$$\Delta t' = \Delta t_1' + \Delta t_2' = \frac{L'}{c - v} + \frac{L'}{c + v}$$

$$= \frac{2L'c}{c^2 - v^2}. \quad \text{... (i)}$$

But $\Delta t'$ is the improper time interval between the two reflections as they occur at different places. An observer, stationary with respect to the rod of the light-beam block, measures this interval to be $\Delta t = 2L/c$ which is the proper time interval between the same two events. Thus, from the equation (47.1),

$$\Delta t' = (\Delta t)\gamma$$

$$= \left(\frac{2L}{c}\right)\gamma. \qquad \text{... (ii)}$$

Using (i) and (ii),

$$\frac{2L'c}{c^2 - v^2} = \frac{2L}{c\sqrt{1 - v^2/c^2}}$$

$$\text{or,} \quad \frac{L'}{(1 - v^2/c^2)} = \frac{L}{\sqrt{1 - v^2/c^2}}$$

$$\text{or,} \quad L' = L\sqrt{1 - v^2/c^2} = L/\gamma. \qquad \text{... (47.2)}$$

The length of a rod is contracted by a factor of γ if it moves parallel to its length. The length measured by an observer at rest with respect to the rod is called its *rest length* or *proper length*. Thus,

The length of a rod moving parallel to itself is shorter than its rest length by the factor γ. This phenomenon is called *length contraction*.

Example 47.2

The passenger of example 47.1 slept with his head towards the engine and feet towards the guard's coach. If he measured 6 ft *in the train frame, how tall is he in the ground frame?*

Solution : In the ground frame, the passenger is moving with a velocity $c/10$. His length is thus contracted. The length measured in the train frame is the rest length of the passenger as the passenger is at rest in the train. Thus, his length in the ground frame is

$$L' = 6\text{ ft}\sqrt{1 - \left(\frac{1}{10}\right)^2} = 6\text{ ft}\sqrt{\frac{99}{100}} = 5\text{ feet } 11{\cdot}6\text{ inches.}$$

(D) Which Event Occurred Earlier ?

A very important result of special relativity that often surprises beginners is that the concept of simultaneity and ordering of events depends on frame. It is possible that an event E_1 occurs before another event E_2 in one frame but after E_2 in some other frame.

Suppose, a long box of rest length L, having two doors D_1 and D_2 at the ends, lies on the ground (figure 47.6a). At the middle point of the box, there is a light source which can be switched on or off rapidly. Suppose the mechanism is such that when a light pulse strikes a door, the door opens. There are two trains T_1 and T_2, the first moving towards the left and

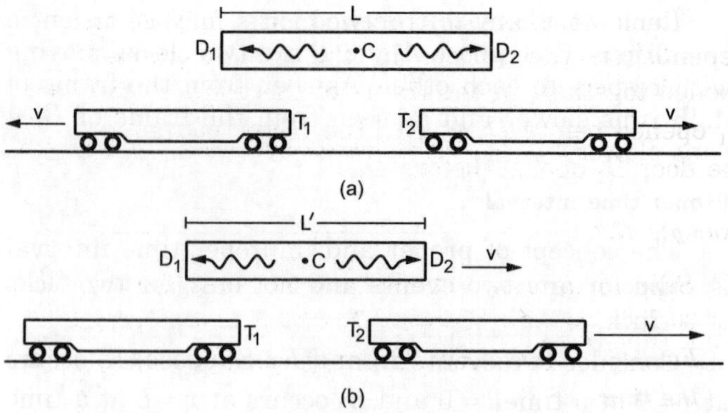

Figure 47.6

the other towards the right with respect to the ground, both at speed v. Figure (47.6a) shows the situation from the ground frame.

Suppose the light source at C is switched on at $t = 0$. Light pulses travel towards D_1 and D_2, finally striking and opening them. Which of the two doors opened first ? In the ground frame, D_1 and D_2 do not move and C is at the middle point. Both the light pulses travel with the same speed c and cover equal distances $L/2$ before striking the doors. Both the doors were opened at $t = \frac{L}{2c}$, i.e., the two events are simultaneous in the ground frame.

Now analyse the situation from the train T_1. The scene from T_1 is shown in figure (47.6b). The box is moving towards the right at a speed v. The length of the box is $L' = L\sqrt{1 - v^2/c^2}$. Consider the light pulse moving towards D_1. The door D_1 is coming towards the pulse with a velocity v. If the time taken by the pulse to reach D_1 is $\Delta t_1'$, the door has moved a distance $v\Delta t_1'$ and the pulse had to travel a distance $L'/2 - v\Delta t_1'$. Thus,

$$c\Delta t_1' = \frac{L'}{2} - v\Delta t_1'$$

$$\text{or} \quad \Delta t_1' = \frac{L'}{2(c + v)}. \qquad \text{... (47.3)}$$

Similarly, the time taken by the pulse to reach D_2 is

$$\Delta t_2' = \frac{L'}{2(c - v)}$$

$$\text{or,} \quad \Delta t_2' - \Delta t_1' = \frac{L'}{2}\left(\frac{1}{c - v} - \frac{1}{c + v}\right)$$

$$= \frac{L'v}{c^2(1 - v^2/c^2)} = \frac{Lv}{c^2\sqrt{(1 - v^2/c^2)}}$$

$$\text{or,} \quad \Delta t_2' - \Delta t_1' = \frac{Lv}{c^2}\gamma. \qquad \text{... (47.4)}$$

As $\Delta t_2' > \Delta t_1'$, the door D_2 opens after D_1 in the frame of T_1. Similar analysis from T_2 shows that D_2 opens before D_1 in the frame of T_2.

Which of the door opened first ? The answer depends on the frame. In the ground frame both opened together, in the frame of the train T_1 the door D_1 opened before D_2 and in the frame of the train T_2 the door D_2 opened before D_1.

Example 47.3

Suppose the rest length of the box in figure (47.6) is 30 light seconds. The train T_1 travels at a speed of 0·8c. Find the time elapsed between opening of D_1 and D_2 in the frame of T_1.

Solution : The box moves in the frame of T_1 with a speed of 0·8*c* so that

$$\gamma = \frac{1}{\sqrt{1-(0\cdot 8)^2}} = \frac{1}{0\cdot 6}.$$

In this frame, D_2 opens after D_1. The time elapsed between the openings of the doors is

$$\frac{Lv}{c^2}\gamma = \frac{(30 \text{ light seconds}) \times (0\cdot 8c)}{c^2 \times 0\cdot 6}$$

$$= \frac{(30 \text{ s})c \times (0\cdot 8c)}{c^2 \times 0\cdot 6} = 40 \text{ s}.$$

(E) Are the Clocks Synchronized ?

How do we synchronize two clocks separated from each other ? The readings of the two clocks must be the same at the same instant. One way of doing this is to place a light source at the middle point between the clocks and send light pulses simultaneously towards the clocks. The time $t = 0$ on a clock may be set at the arrival of the pulse at the clock. As the light pulses travel at identical speeds and the source is placed exactly midway between the clocks, this process ensures that the clocks simultaneously read $t = 0$.

Once again consider the situation of figure (47.6a) redrawn in figure (47.7). Suppose the train T_1 is very long and a series of clocks are kept on it along its length. Suppose there are clocks fixed in the box at the doors D_1 and D_2 and the hands are set at zero as the light pulses reach the doors. These clocks are synchronized in the ground frame. The doors open simultaneously in the ground frame and hence the clocks simultaneously read $t = 0$.

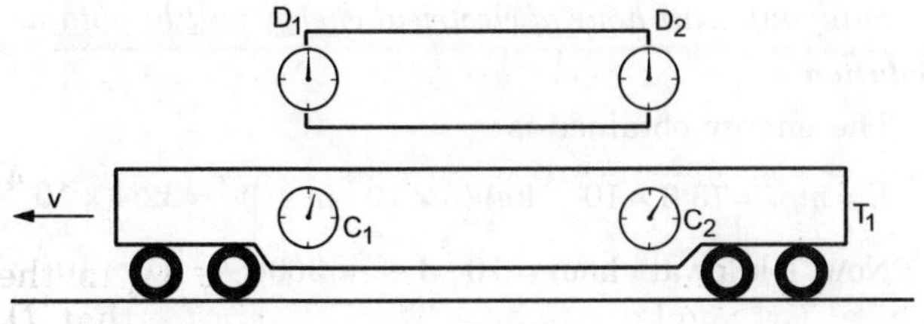

Figure 47.7

The clocks in T_1 are synchronized by the same procedure performed in the train. As the door D_1 opens, some clock C_1 on the train will be opposite to D_1 and it will have some reading, say t'_1. Similarly, as the door D_2 opens, there will be some clock C_2 on the train opposite to D_2 and it will have a reading t'_2.

We have seen that (equation 47.4) according to these clocks on T_1, door D_2 opens after D_1 and the time lag is

$$t'_2 - t'_1 = \frac{Lv}{c^2}\gamma. \quad \text{... (i)}$$

In ground frame, the doors open at the same instant $t = 0$. So the clock C_1 reads t'_1 at the same instant when C_2 reads t'_2. So in the ground frame, the train clocks are out of synchronization. The clock C_2, that is at the rear, is ahead of the clock C_1, that is at the front, by an amount

$$\Delta t = \frac{Lv}{c^2}\gamma. \quad \text{... (47.5)}$$

Here L is the separation between the doors D_1 and D_2 as measured from the ground frame. It is also the separation between C_1 and C_2 as measured from the ground frame. But the length C_1C_2 measured from the ground frame is the moving length as C_1 and C_2 are moving with respect to the ground. The distance between C_1 and C_2 in the train frame, i.e., the rest length C_1C_2, will be larger than the moving length. Thus, the rest separation of the clock C_1C_2 is $L_0 = L\gamma$ and equation (47.5) can be reframed as

$$\Delta t = \frac{L_0 v}{c^2}. \quad \text{... (47.6)}$$

The clocks of a moving frame are out of synchronization. The clock at the rear leads the one at the front by $L_0 v/c^2$, where L_0 is the rest separation between the clocks, and v is the speed of the moving frame.

Remember that the first postulate asserts that you can call any inertial frame at rest and the conclusions above are valid for all frames. In the previous example, we can very well take the train T_1 as the rest frame and then the clocks of the ground frame will be out of synchronization.

47.4 DYNAMICS AT LARGE VELOCITY

When velocities comparable to the velocity of light are involved, Newton's second law of motion, $\vec{F} = m\vec{a}$, does not adequately govern the dynamics. We shall not deduce the correct laws but state them.

The linear momentum $\vec{p}$ of a particle is defined as

$$\vec{p} = m_0 \gamma \vec{v} \quad \text{... (47.7)}$$

where m_0 is the mass of the particle as we know it in Newtonian mechanics. The quantity

$$m = m_0 \gamma = \frac{m_0}{\sqrt{1 - v^2/c^2}}$$

is called the *moving mass* of the particle when it moves at a speed v with respect to the observer. Thus, the mass of the particle is different for different observers. The mass m_0, measured by an observer at rest with respect to the particle, is called its *rest mass*.

With equation (47.7) as the definition of momentum, the law of dynamics is

$$\frac{d\vec{p}}{dt} = \vec{F}. \qquad \text{... (47.8)}$$

Equation (47.8) leads to the law of conservation of relativistic momentum. If no force acts on a particle, its momentum remains constant.

Example 47.4

A particle is kept at rest at the origin. A constant force $\vec{F}$ starts acting on it at $t = 0$. Find the speed of the particle at time t.

Solution :

The equation of motion is,

$$\frac{d\vec{p}}{dt} = \vec{F}.$$

As the particle starts from rest and the force is always in the same direction, the motion will be along this direction only. Thus, we can write

$$\frac{dp}{dt} = F$$

or, $$\int_0^p dp = \int_0^t F\,dt$$

or, $$p = Ft$$

or, $$\frac{m_0 v}{\sqrt{1 - v^2/c^2}} = Ft$$

or, $$m_0^2 v^2 = F^2 t^2 - \frac{F^2 t^2}{c^2} v^2$$

or, $$v^2 \left(m_0^2 + \frac{F^2 t^2}{c^2} \right) = F^2 t^2$$

or, $$v = \frac{Ftc}{\sqrt{m_0^2 c^2 + F^2 t^2}}$$

Note from example (47.4) that however large t may be, v can never exceed c. No matter how long you apply a force, the speed of a particle will be less than the speed c.

47.5 ENERGY AND MOMENTUM

According to relativistic dynamics, matter is a condensed form of energy. The energy E equivalent to a mass m is given by the equation

$$E = mc^2. \qquad \text{... (47.9)}$$

Thus, matter can be converted into energy and energy into matter. If work is done on a particle, energy is supplied to it. Its energy increases and hence the mass increases. Energy and mass are names for one and the same physical quantity in this viewpoint. When a particle is at rest, its mass is m_0 which is called its rest mass. The energy concentrated in it is, therefore, $E_0 = m_0 c^2$. This is called the *rest mass energy* of the particle. If the particle moves at a speed v, its mass changes to

$$m = m_0 \gamma = \frac{m_0}{\sqrt{1 - v^2/c^2}}$$

and the total energy in it becomes $E = mc^2$

$$= m_0 c^2 \left(1 - \frac{v^2}{c^2} \right)^{-1/2}$$

$$= m_0 c^2 \left(1 + \frac{v^2}{2c^2} + \frac{1}{2} \cdot \frac{3}{4} \frac{v^4}{c^4} + \dots \right)$$

$$= m_0 c^2 + \frac{1}{2} m_0 v^2 + \dots \qquad \text{... (i)}$$

The extra energy $(mc^2 - m_0 c^2)$ is called the *kinetic energy*. If $v << c$, the higher order terms in (i) are negligible and hence the kinetic energy is $K = \frac{1}{2} m_0 v^2$ as usual. Combining the equations

$$p = mv = \frac{m_0 v}{\sqrt{1 - v^2/c^2}}$$

and $$E = mc^2 = \frac{m_0 c^2}{\sqrt{1 - v^2/c^2}},$$

one can deduce that

$$E^2 = m_0^2 c^4 + p^2 c^2. \qquad \text{... (47.10)}$$

For particles having zero rest mass like photons, $m_0 = 0$ and hence from equation (47.10),

$$E = pc$$

or, $$p = E/c. \qquad \text{... (47.11)}$$

This result has already been used in previous chapters for photons.

Example 47.5

If a mass of 3·6 g is fully converted into energy, how many kilowatt hour of electrical energy will be obtained ?

Solution :

The energy obtained is

$$E = mc^2 = (3{\cdot}6 \times 10^{-3}\ \text{kg})\ (3 \times 10^8\ \text{m s}^{-1})^2 = 32{\cdot}4 \times 10^{13}\ \text{J}.$$

Now 1 kilowatt hour $= 10^3\ \text{J s}^{-1} \times 3600\ \text{s} = 3{\cdot}6 \times 10^6\ \text{J}$.

Thus, $$E = \frac{32{\cdot}4 \times 10^{13}}{3{\cdot}6 \times 10^6}\ \text{kWh} = 9 \times 10^7\ \text{kWh}.$$

47.6 THE ULTIMATE SPEED

We saw in example (47.4) that even if we continue to apply a force on a particle for a long time, its speed cannot exceed c. This is a very general result in special relativity. In fact, no information can be sent with a speed greater than c. If we assume that information can be sent with a speed greater than c, it turns out that we shall have frames in which a bullet will hit the bird before it is actually fired, a dog can die before it is born and so on. If the *effect* cannot precede its *cause* in any frame, then c is the ultimate speed for any material particle or information.

Scientists have worked out the mathematics for a world in which all the particles are moving with respect to each other with speeds greater than c. Such a world can exist without violating the postulates of relativity but these particles can never be slowed down to a speed less than c. The particles of this hypothetical world cannot interact with ours and in that world, effect will always precede its cause. Such particles are named *tachyons* and a group of physicists is working to explore the possibility of the actual existence of such particles. These large speeds and the unworldly results remind us of several stories from Indian Scriptures and no wonder the idea of tachyons was mooted by an Indian scientist E.C.G. Sudarshan.

47.7 TWIN PARADOX

As the postulates of special relativity lead to results which contradict 'common sense', a number of interesting paradoxes have been floated. We shall describe one of the most famous paradoxes of relativity—the *twin paradox*. Consider the twins Ram and Balram living happily on the earth. Ram decides to make a trip to a distant planet P, which is at rest with respect to the earth, and come back. He boards a spaceship S_1, going towards the planet with a uniform velocity. When he reaches the planet, he jumps from the spaceship S_1 to another spaceship S_2 which is going towards the earth. When he reaches the earth, he jumps out and meets his brother Balram.

As Ram returns from his trip and stands next to Balram, do they have equal age ? Or is Ram younger than Balram or is he older than Balram ?

To keep the calculations simple, let us assume the following data:

Distance between the earth and the planet = 8 light-years,

speed of S_1 with respect to earth = 0·8c, and

speed of S_2 with respect to earth = 0·8c.

When we said that the distance between the earth and the planet P is 8 light-years, was it clear to you that this length is the length as measured from the earth frame ?

First, let us analyse the events from the point of view of Balram who is on the earth. For him, both the spaceships move at a speed 0·8c. So,

$$\gamma = \frac{1}{\sqrt{1 - v^2/c^2}} = \frac{1}{0{\cdot}6}\,.$$

When Ram is on S_1, he is moving and all his clocks run slower because of time dilation. His heartbeat, pulse beat, etc., represent clocks in themselves and they all run slower. Balram calculates that Ram will take 8 light-year/0·8c = 10 years to reach the planet P. But during all these 10 years, time is passing slowly on S_1 and the clocks will read only 10 years × 0·6 = 6 years in this period. The number of breaths taken by Ram corresponds to 6 years only.

Ram jumped into S_2 for the return journey. This spaceship is also moving at 0·8c and for Balram, time passes slowly on S_2 as well. Although 10 years passed on the earth during Ram's return journey, on the spaceship the journey was clocked at 6 years. Thus, Ram has aged only 12 years whereas Balram has aged 20 years during this expedition. Ram has become younger than Balram by 8 years. This difference in aging is real in the sense that Ram shows lesser signs of aging like he has lesser white hairs than his brother.

The observation of Balram is quite consistent with the special theory of relativity. Such experiments are indeed performed in laboratories with radioactive particles. Particles are accelerated to large speeds and are kept at these speeds for quite some time by magnetic fields. These particles with large speeds have longer lives than their counterparts kept at rest in the laboratory.

The paradox arises when we analyse the events from the point of veiw of Ram. When he is in the spaceship S_1, to him the distance between the earth and the planet is not 8 light-years. The earth and the planet P are moving with respect to Ram and hence he is measuring contracted length. The separation is, therefore, 8 light-years × 0·6 = 4·8 light-years. As the planet is approaching Ram at 0·8c, the time taken by the planet to reach Ram is 4·8 light-year/0·8c = 6 years. So according to Ram's clock, he jumped from S_1 to S_2 6 years after getting into S_1. Once he is on S_2, the earth and the planet are again moving with the same speed 0·8c. Again, the earth is 4·8 light-years from the planet and is approaching at 0·8c. It takes 6 years for the earth to reach Ram. Thus, according to Ram's clock, he was out for 12 years from the earth, the same result as Balram had expected.

But how about Ram's calculation of Balram's age ? When Ram is on S_1, the earth is going away from him with a speed $0{\cdot}8c$. Ram will find that the time on the earth is passing slower by a factor of 0·6 so that Balram is aging slower than he is. The same is true when he is on S_2. During this period also, Balram is moving (towards Ram) with a speed $0{\cdot}8c$ and hence time is passing slowly for Balram. As 12 years passes on Ram's clock, he calculates that Balram's clocks have advanced only by $12 \text{ years} \times 0{\cdot}6 = 7{\cdot}2$ years in this period. According to this analysis, Ram should find that Balram is $12 - 7{\cdot}2 = 4{\cdot}8$ years younger than him.

This is the paradox. According to Ram, Balram's clocks are running slow and according to Balram, Ram's clocks are running slow. Each thinks the other is younger. Where lies the fallacy ?

The fallacy lies in the fact that Ram has changed frames whereas Balram has stayed in an inertial frame. Thus, the roles of the twins are not symmetrical. The ordering of events are different in different frames and Ram must take that into account when he changes frames. Suppose Ram gets into the spaceship S_1 when his clock reads zero. So does Balram's clock. What is the reading of the planet's clock at this instant ? According to Balram, it is zero because both the earth and the planet are at rest and the clocks are synchronized in his frame. But that is not so in S_1. As Ram gets into S_1, he may have the following conversation with the captain of the ship.

Captain: Welcome aboard S_1. I saw you on the earth, coming towards us. Your jump to board this ship was perfect. Where are you going ?

Ram: Thank you. I am going to the planet *P*. How far is it from here and how long will it take for the planet to come to us ?

Captain: Planet *P* is 4·8 light-years from us at the moment. It is coming towards us at a speed of $0{\cdot}8c$ so it will take $4{\cdot}8 \text{ light-years}/0{\cdot}8c = 6$ years for the planet *P* to reach us.

Ram: Well, the clocks on the earth and the planet are running a bit slower than ours. I have been taught that moving clocks run slow by a factor of γ. This factor is $1/0{\cdot}6$ for these clocks. So they will advance by 6 years $\times\, 0{\cdot}6 = 3{\cdot}6$ years by the time the planet reaches us.

Captain: Yes, both the clocks will advance by 3·6 years by the time you jump on the planet *P*.

Ram: The earth-clock was reading $t = 0$ as we passed the earth. This means when I jump on the planet *P* the clocks on the earth and the planet will be reading 3·6 years.

Captain: Here you are mistaken. Don't you remember that the planet's clock is not synchronized with the earth's clock ? The planet's clock is at the rear end, and hence is running 6·4 years ahead of the earth's clock. At the instant the earth's clock was reading zero, the planet's clock was reading 6·4 years. As the planet reaches us, both the clocks will advance by 3·6 years. So when you jump out of S_1, the earth's clock will be reading 3·6 years but the planet's clock will be reading 10 years.

Ram understands the logic. In the earth's frame, the two clocks read zero simultaneously. But in S_1-frame, the event "planet's clock reading zero" occurred several years before "earth's clock reading zero". Six years pass in S_1 and Ram finds that the planet *P* has reached him. He finds another spaceship S_2 which is heading towards the earth. Ram jumps onto S_2. In the process he looks at the planet's clock and finds that it is reading 10 years as calculated by him on S_1. On S_2, he starts talking to the commander of the ship.

Commander: Welcome to S_2. How long will you be with us ?

Ram: Thank you. I am going to Earth. Earth is at present 4·8 light-years from here and is coming towards us with a speed of $0{\cdot}8c$. So I will be with you for 6 years. The captain of S_1 told me that the earth's clock is reading 3·6 years at this moment whereas the planet's clock reads 10 years. There is a difference of 6·4 years in the reading because the two clocks are not synchronized. Also ....

Commander: Sorry for interrupting you, but you are mistaken. It is true that the earth's clock and the planet's clock are not synchronized as they are moving past us. Also the difference in the readings of the two clocks is 6·4 years. But the planet's clock is at the front and the earth's clock is at the rear. It is the earth's clock that is leading by 6·4 years. At the moment the planet's clock reads 10 years and hence the earth's clock must be reading 16·4 years.

Ram: Hmm... you are right. In S_1, the earth was at the front and its clock lagged behind the planet's clock. But in S_2 it is the other way round. Indeed the earth's clock reads 16·4 years whereas the planet's clock reads 10 years.

Commander: That's right. The earth's clock is reading 16·4 years at present. It will advance by another 3·6 years during the 6 years you will be with us. So it will be reading 20 years when the earth reaches you.

We see that the paradox is resolved.

Worked Out Examples

1. *A hypothetical train moving with a speed of 0·6c passes by the platform of a small station without being slowed down. The observers on the platform note that the length of the train is just equal to the length of the platform which is 200 m. (a) Find the rest length of the train. (b) Find the length of the platform as measured by the observers in the train.*

Solution : (a) The length L' of the train at a speed 0·6c is 200 m. If the rest length is L,

$$L' = L\sqrt{1 - v^2/c^2}$$

or,
$$L = \frac{L'}{\sqrt{1 - v^2/c^2}} = \frac{200 \text{ m}}{\sqrt{1 - (0·6)^2}}$$
$$= 250 \text{ m.}$$

(b) The rest length of the platform is 200 m. For the observers in the train, the platform is moving at a speed of 0·6 c. The length as measured by the observers in the train is, therefore,

$$L' = 200 \text{ m} \sqrt{1 - (0·6)^2} = 160 \text{ m.}$$

2. *Unstable pions are produced as a beam in a nuclear reaction experiment. The pions leave the target at a speed of 0·995c. The intensity of the beam reduces to half its original value as the beam travels a distance of 39 m. Find the half-life of pions (a) in the laboratory frame, (b) in their rest frame.*

Solution : (a) The intensity of the pion beam reduces to half its original value in one half-life. The half-life of the pions as measured in the laboratory is

$$t_{1/2} = \frac{39 \text{ m}}{0·995\, c} = \frac{39 \text{ m}}{0·995 \times 3 \times 10^8 \text{ m s}^{-1}}$$
$$= 1·3 \times 10^{-7} \text{ s.}$$

(b) The events—a pion leaving the target and its decaying—occur at the same place in the pion-frame. Thus, the time measured in the pion-frame is the proper time and is the smallest. It is equal to

$$t'_{1/2} = t_{1/2}\sqrt{1 - v^2/c^2} = (1·3 \times 10^{-7} \text{ s})\sqrt{1 - (0·995)^2}$$
$$= 1·3 \times 10^{-8} \text{ s.}$$

3. *Two events A and B occur at places separated by* 10^6 *km, B occurring 5 s after A. (a) Find the velocity of a frame in which these events occur at the same place. (b) What is the time interval between the events in this frame?*

Solution :

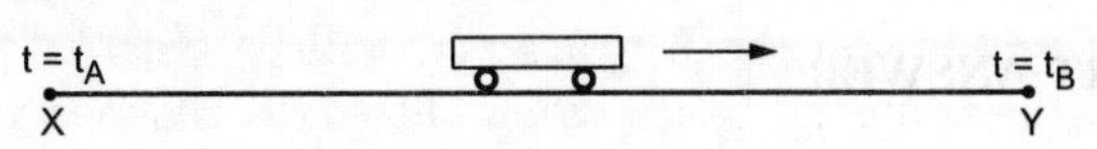

Figure 47-W1

(a) Suppose the events A and B occur at points X and Y at times t_A and t_B where $t_B = t_A + 5$ s. Consider a small train which is at the point X when the event A occurs. Suppose, this same train moves towards Y and reaches the point Y when the event B occurs. Thus, the events A and B occur at the same place in the train frame. This frame moves 10^6 km in 5 s as seen from the original frame. Thus, the velocity of the train frame is

$$v = \frac{10^6 \text{ km}}{5 \text{ s}} = 2 \times 10^8 \text{ m s}^{-1}.$$

(b) As the events A and B occur at the same place in the train frame, the time interval between the events measured in this frame is the proper interval. Thus, this time interval is

$$= (5 \text{ s})\sqrt{1 - v^2/c^2} = (5 \text{ s})\sqrt{1 - \left(\frac{2}{3}\right)^2}$$
$$= 3·7 \text{ s.}$$

4. *A satellite orbits the earth near its surface. By what amount does the satellite's clock fall behind the earth's clock in one revolution? Assume that nonrelativistic analysis can be made to compute the speed of the satellite and only the time dilation is to be taken into account for calculation of clock speeds.*

Solution : The speed of the satellite may be obtained from the equation,

$$\frac{GMm}{R^2} = \frac{mv^2}{R}$$

or,
$$v = \sqrt{\frac{GM}{R}}$$
$$= \left[\frac{(6·67 \times 10^{-11} \text{ N m}^2 \text{kg}^{-2})(6 \times 10^{24} \text{ kg})}{6400 \times 10^3 \text{ m}}\right]^{1/2}$$
$$= 7910 \text{ m s}^{-1}. \qquad \ldots \text{(i)}$$

Thus,
$$v/c = \frac{7910}{3 \times 10^8} = 2·637 \times 10^{-5}$$

or,
$$\sqrt{1 - \left(\frac{v}{c}\right)^2} = [1 - 6·95 \times 10^{-10}]^{1/2}$$
$$\approx 1 - 3·48 \times 10^{-10}.$$

The time taken by the satellite to complete one revolution is

$$T = \frac{2\pi R}{v} = \frac{6·28 \times 6400 \times 10^3 \text{ m}}{7910 \text{ m s}^{-1}} = 5080 \text{ s.}$$

The clock on the satellite will slow down as observed from the earth. If the time elapsed on the satellite's clock is t as the satellite completes one revolution (this is proper time and 5080 s is improper time),

$$t = (1 - 3·48 \times 10^{-10}) \times (5080 \text{ s})$$

or,
$$\frac{t}{5080 \text{ s}} = 1 - 3·48 \times 10^{-10}$$

or, $\dfrac{(t - 5080\text{ s})}{5080\text{ s}} = -3{\cdot}48 \times 10^{-10}$

or, $(t - 5080\text{ s}) = -1{\cdot}77 \times 10^{-6}\text{ s}.$

The satellite's clock falls behind by $1{\cdot}77 \times 10^{-6}$ s in one revolution.

5. *The radius of our galaxy is about* 3×10^{20} m. *With what speed should a person travel so that he can reach from the centre of the galaxy to its edge in* 20 *years of his lifetime ?*

Solution : Let the speed of the person be v. As seen by the person, the edge of the galaxy is coming towards him at a speed v. In 20 years (as measured by the person), the edge moves (20 y) v and reaches the person. The radius of the galaxy as measured by the person is, therefore, (20 y)v. The rest length of the radius of the galaxy is 3×10^{20} m. Thus,

$$(20\text{ y})v = (3 \times 10^{20}\text{ m})\sqrt{1 - v^2/c^2}$$

or, $(6{\cdot}312 \times 10^{8}\text{ s})^2 v^2 = (9 \times 10^{40}\text{ m}^2)(1 - v^2/c^2).$

Solving this,

$$v = 0{\cdot}9999996\ c.$$

6. *Find the speed at which the mass of an electron is double of its rest mass.*

Solution : The mass of an electron at speed v is

$$m = \frac{m_0}{\sqrt{1 - v^2/c^2}}$$

where m_0 is its rest mass. If $m = 2\, m_0$,

$$2 = \frac{1}{\sqrt{1 - v^2/c^2}}$$

or, $1 - \dfrac{v^2}{c^2} = \dfrac{1}{4}$

or, $v = \dfrac{\sqrt{3}}{2}c = 2{\cdot}598 \times 10^{8}\text{ m s}^{-1}.$

7. *Calculate the increase in mass when a body of rest mass* 1 kg *is lifted up through* 1 m *near the earth's surface.*

Solution : The increase in energy $= mgh$

$= (1\text{ kg})(9{\cdot}8\text{ m s}^{-2})(1\text{ m}) = 9{\cdot}8\text{ J}.$

The increase in mass $= \dfrac{9{\cdot}8\text{ J}}{c^2}$

$= 1{\cdot}11 \times 10^{-16}\text{ kg}.$

8. *A body of rest mass* m_0 *collides perfectly inelastically at a speed of* 0·8c *with another body of equal rest mass kept at rest. Calculate the common speed of the bodies after the collision and the rest mass of the combined body.*

Solution : The linear momentum of the first body

$$= \frac{m_0 v}{\sqrt{1 - v^2/c^2}} = \frac{m_0 \times 0{\cdot}8c}{0{\cdot}6}$$

$$= \frac{4}{3}m_0 c.$$

This should be the total linear momentum after the collision. If the rest mass of the combined body is M_0 and it moves at speed v',

$$\frac{M_0 v'}{\sqrt{1 - v'^2/c^2}} = \frac{4}{3}m_0 c. \quad \text{... (i)}$$

The energy before the collison is

$$\frac{m_0}{\sqrt{1 - v^2/c^2}}c^2 + m_0 c^2 = m_0 c^2\left(\frac{1}{0{\cdot}6} + 1\right)$$

$$= \frac{8}{3}m_0 c^2.$$

The energy after the collision is

$$\frac{M_0 c^2}{\sqrt{1 - v'^2/c^2}}$$

Thus, $$\frac{M_0 c^2}{\sqrt{1 - v'^2/c^2}} = \frac{8}{3}m_0 c^2. \quad \text{... (ii)}$$

Dividing (i) by (ii),

$$\frac{v'}{c^2} = \frac{1}{2c} \quad \text{or,} \quad v' = \frac{c}{2}.$$

Putting this value of v' in (ii),

$$M_0 = \frac{8}{3}m_0\sqrt{1 - \frac{1}{4}}$$

or, $M_0 = 2{\cdot}309\ m_0.$

The rest mass of the combined body is greater than the sum of the rest masses of the individual bodies.

□

QUESTIONS FOR SHORT ANSWER

1. The speed of light in glass is $2{\cdot}0 \times 10^{8}\text{ m s}^{-1}$. Does it violate the second postulate of special relativity ?
2. A uniformly moving train passes by a long platform. Consider the events 'engine crossing the beginning of the platform' and 'engine crossing the end of the platform'. Which frame (train frame or the platform frame) is the proper frame for the pair of events ?

3. An object may be regarded to be at rest or in motion depending on the frame of reference chosen to view the object. Because of length contraction it would mean that the same rod may have two different lengths depending on the state of the observer. Is this true ?
4. Mass of a particle depends on its speed. Does the attraction of the earth on the particle also depend on the particle's speed ?
5. A person travelling in a fast spaceship measures the distance between the earth and the moon. Is it the same, smaller or larger than the value quoted in this book ?

OBJECTIVE I

1. The magnitude of linear momentum of a particle moving at a relativistic speed v is proportional to
(a) v (b) $1 - v^2/c^2$
(c) $\sqrt{1 - v^2/c^2}$ (d) none of these.
2. As the speed of a particle increases, its rest mass
(a) increases (b) decreases
(c) remains the same (d) changes.
3. An experimenter measures the length of a rod. Initially the experimenter and the rod are at rest with respect to the lab. Consider the following statements.
(A) If the rod starts moving parallel to its length but the observer stays at rest, the measured length will be reduced.
(B) If the rod stays at rest but the observer starts moving parallel to the measured length of the rod, the length will be reduced.
(a) A is true but B is false. (b) B is true but A is false.
(c) Both A and B are true. (d) Both A and B are false.
4. An experimenter measures the length of a rod. In the cases listed, all motions are with respect to the lab and parallel to the length of the rod. In which of the cases the measured length will be minimum ?
(a) The rod and the experimenter move with the same speed v in the same direction.
(b) The rod and the experimenter move with the same speed v in opposite directions.
(c) The rod moves at speed v but the experimenter stays at rest.
(d) The rod stays at rest but the experimenter moves with the speed v.
5. If the speed of a particle moving at a relativistic speed is doubled, its linear momentum will
(a) become double (b) become more than double
(c) remain equal (d) become less than double.
6. If a constant force acts on a particle, its acceleration will
(a) remain constant (b) gradually decrease
(c) gradually increase (d) be undefined.
7. A charged particle is projected at a very high speed perpendicular to a uniform magnetic field. The particle will
(a) move along a circle
(b) move along a curve with increasing radius of curvature
(c) move along a curve with decreasing radius of curvature
(d) move along a straight line.

OBJECTIVE II

1. Mark the correct statements:
(a) Equations of special relativity are not applicable for small speeds.
(b) Equations of special relativity are applicable for all speeds.
(c) Nonrelativistic equations give exact result for small speeds.
(d) Nonrelativistic equations never give exact result.
2. If the speed of a rod moving at a relativistic speed parallel to its length is doubled,
(a) the length will become half of the original value
(b) the mass will become double of the original value
(c) the length will decrease
(d) the mass will increase.
3. Two events take place simultaneously at points A and B as seen in the lab frame. They also occur simultaneously in a frame moving with respect to the lab in a direction
(a) parallel to AB (b) perpendicular to AB
(c) making an angle of 45° with AB
(d) making an angle of 135° with AB.
4. Which of the following quantities related to an electron has a finite upper limit ?
(a) Mass (b) Momentum (c) Speed (d) Kinetic energy
5. A rod of rest length L moves at a relativistic speed. Let $L' = L/\gamma$. Its length
(a) must be equal to L' (b) may be equal to L
(c) may be more than L' but less than L
(d) may be more than L.
6. When a rod moves at a relativistic speed v, its mass
(a) must incrase by a factor of γ
(b) may remain unchanged
(c) may increase by a factor other than γ
(d) may decrease.

EXERCISES

1. The *guru* of a *yogi* lives in a Himalyan cave, 1000 km away from the house of the yogi. The yogi claims that whenever he thinks about his guru, the guru immediately knows about it. Calculate the minimum possible time interval between the yogi thinking about the guru and the guru knowing about it.

2. A suitcase kept on a shop's rack is measured 50 cm × 25 cm × 10 cm by the shop's owner. A traveller takes this suitcase in a train moving with velocity 0·6*c*. If the suitcase is placed with its length along the train's velocity, find the dimensions measured by (a) the traveller and (b) a ground observer.

3. The length of a rod is exactly 1 m when measured at rest. What will be its length when it moves at a speed of (a) 3×10^5 m s^{-1}, (b) 3×10^6 m s^{-1} and (c) 3×10^7 m s^{-1} ?

4. A person standing on a platform finds that a train moving with velocity 0·6*c* takes one second to pass by him. Find (a) the length of the train as seen by the person and (b) the rest length of the train.

5. An aeroplane travels over a rectangular field 100 m × 50 m, parallel to its length. What should be the speed of the plane so that the field becomes square in the plane frame ?

6. The rest distance between Patna and Delhi is 1000 km. A nonstop train travels at 360 km h^{-1}. (a) What is the distance between Patna and Delhi in the train frame ? (b) How much time elapses in the train frame between Patna and Delhi ?

7. A person travels by a car at a speed of 180 km h^{-1}. It takes exactly 10 hours by his wristwatch to go from the station *A* to the station *B*. (a) What is the rest distance between the two stations ? (b) How much time is taken in the road frame by the car to go from the station *A* to the station *B* ?

8. A person travels on a spaceship moving at a speed of 5*c*/13. (a) Find the time interval calculated by him between the consecutive birthday celebrations of his friend on the earth. (b) Find the time interval calculated by the friend on the earth between the consecutive birthday celebrations of the traveller.

9. According to the station clocks, two babies are born at the same instant, one in Howrah and other in Delhi. (a) Who is elder in the frame of 2301 Up Rajdhani Express going from Howrah to Delhi ? (b) Who is elder in the frame of 2302 Dn Rajdhani Express going from Delhi to Howrah.

10. Two babies are born in a moving train, one in the compartment adjacent to the engine and other in the compartment adjacent to the guard. According to the train frame, the babies are born at the same instant of time. Who is elder according to the ground frame ?

11. Suppose Swarglok (heaven) is in constant motion at a speed of 0·9999*c* with respect to the earth. According to the earth's frame, how much time passes on the earth before one day passes on Swarglok ?

12. If a person lives on the average 100 years in his rest frame, how long does he live in the earth frame if he spends all his life on a spaceship going at 60% of the speed of light.

13. An electric bulb, connected to a make and break power supply, switches off and on every second in its rest frame. What is the frequency of its switching off and on as seen from a spaceship travelling at a speed 0·8*c* ?

14. A person travelling by a car moving at 100 km h^{-1} finds that his wristwatch agrees with the clock on a tower *A*. By what amount will his wristwatch lag or lead the clock on another tower *B*, 1000 km (in the earth's frame) from the tower *A* when the car reaches there ?

15. At what speed the volume of an object shrinks to half its rest value ?

16. A particular particle created in a nuclear reactor leaves a 1 cm track before decaying. Assuming that the particle moved at 0·995*c*, calculate the life of the particle (a) in the lab frame and (b) in the frame of the particle.

17. By what fraction does the mass of a spring change when it is compressed by 1 cm ? The mass of the spring is 200 g at its natural length and the spring constant is 500 N m^{-1}.

18. Find the increase in mass when 1 kg of water is heated from 0°C to 100°C. Specific heat capacity of water = 4200 J kg^{-1}K^{-1}.

19. Find the loss in the mass of 1 mole of an ideal monatomic gas kept in a rigid container as it cools down by 10°C. The gas constant $R = 8{\cdot}3$ J K^{-1}mol^{-1}.

20. By what fraction does the mass of a boy increase when he starts running at a speed of 12 km h^{-1} ?

21. A 100 W bulb together with its power supply is suspended from a sensitive balance. Find the change in the mass recorded after the bulb remains on for 1 year.

22. The energy from the sun reaches just outside the earth's atmosphere at a rate of 1400 W m^{-2}. The distance between the sun and the earth is $1{\cdot}5 \times 10^{11}$ m. (a) Calculate the rate at which the sun is losing its mass. (b) How long will the sun last assuming a constant decay at this rate ? The present mass of the sun is 2×10^{30} kg.

23. An electron and a positron moving at small speeds collide and annihilate each other. Find the energy of the resulting gamma photon.

24. Find the mass, the kinetic energy and the momentum of an electron moving at 0·8*c*.

25. Through what potential difference should an electron be accelerated to give it a speed of (a) 0·6*c*, (b) 0·9*c* and (c) 0·99*c* ?

26. Find the speed of an electron with kinetic energy (a) 1 eV, (b) 10 keV and (c) 10 MeV.

27. What is the kinetic energy of an electron in electronvolts with mass equal to double its rest mass ?

28. Find the speed at which the kinetic energy of a particle will differ by 1% from its nonrelativistic value $\frac{1}{2} m_0 v^2$.

□

ANSWERS

OBJECTIVE I

1. (d) 2. (c) 3. (c) 4. (b) 5. (b) 6. (b)
7. (b)

OBJECTIVE II

1. (b), (d) 2. (c), (d) 3. (b)
4. (c) 5. (b), (c) 6. (a)

EXERCISES

1. 1/300 s
2. (a) 50 cm × 25 cm × 10 cm (b) 40 cm × 25 cm × 10 cm
3. (a) 0·9999995 m (b) 0·99995 m (c) 0·995 m
4. (a) $1{\cdot}8 \times 10^{8}$ m (b) $2{\cdot}25 \times 10^{8}$ m
5. 0·866*c*
6. (a) 56 nm less than 1000 km
   (b) 0·56 ns less than $\frac{500}{3}$ min
7. (a) 25 nm more than 1800 km
   (b) 0·5 ns more than 10 hours
8. $\frac{13}{12}$ y in both cases
9. (a) Delhi baby is elder (b) Howrah baby is elder
10. the baby adjacent to the guard is elder
11. 70·7 days
12. 125 y
13. $0{\cdot}6\ s^{-1}$
14. will lag by 0·154 ns
15. $\frac{\sqrt{3}c}{2}$
16. (a) 33·5 ps (b) 3·35 ps
17. $1{\cdot}4 \times 10^{-18}$
18. $4{\cdot}7 \times 10^{-12}$ kg
19. $1{\cdot}38 \times 10^{-15}$ kg
20. $6{\cdot}17 \times 10^{-17}$
21. $3{\cdot}5 \times 10^{-8}$ kg
22. (a) $4{\cdot}4 \times 10^{9}\ kg\ s^{-1}$ (b) $1{\cdot}44 \times 10^{13}$ y
23. 1·02 MeV
24. $15{\cdot}2 \times 10^{-31}$ kg, $5{\cdot}5 \times 10^{-14}$ J, $3{\cdot}65 \times 10^{-22}\ kg\ m\ s^{-1}$
25. (a) 128 kV (b) 661 kV (c) 3·1 MV
26. (a) $5{\cdot}92 \times 10^{5}\ m\ s^{-1}$ (b) $5{\cdot}85 \times 10^{7}\ m\ s^{-1}$
    (c) $2{\cdot}996 \times 10^{8}\ m\ s^{-1}$
27. 511 keV
28. $3{\cdot}46 \times 10^{7}\ m\ s^{-1}$

□

APPENDIX A

Units and Dimensions of Physical Quantities

Quantity	Common Symbol	SI Unit	Dimension
Displacement	s	METRE (m)	L
Mass	m, M	KILOGRAM (kg)	M
Time	t	SECOND (s)	T
Area	A	m^2	L^2
Volume	V	m^3	L^3
Density	ρ	$kg\ m^{-3}$	$M L^{-3}$
Velocity	v, u	$m\ s^{-1}$	$L T^{-1}$
Acceleration	a	$m\ s^{-2}$	$L T^{-2}$
Force	F	newton (N)	$ML T^{-2}$
Work	W	joule (J)(= N–m)	$ML^2 T^{-2}$
Energy	E, U, K	joule (J)	$ML^2 T^{-2}$
Power	P	watt (W)(= J s^{-1})	$ML^2 T^{-3}$
Momentum	p	kg–m s^{-1}	$ML T^{-1}$
Gravitational constant	G	N–m^2 kg^{-2}	$L^3 M^{-1} T^{-2}$
Angle	θ, φ	radian	
Angular velocity	ω	rad s^{-1}	T^{-1}
Angular acceleration	α	rad s^{-2}	T^{-2}
Angular momentum	L	kg–m^2 s^{-1}	$ML^2 T^{-1}$
Moment of inertia	I	kg–m^2	ML^2
Torque	τ	N–m	$ML^2 T^{-2}$
Angular frequency	ω	rad s^{-1}	T^{-1}
Frequency	ν	hertz (Hz)	T^{-1}
Period	T	s	T
Young's modulus	Y	N m^{-2}	$M L^{-1} T^{-2}$
Bulk modulus	B	N m^{-2}	$M L^{-1} T^{-2}$
Shear modulus	η	N m^{-2}	$M L^{-1} T^{-2}$
Surface tension	S	N m^{-1}	$M T^{-2}$
Coefficient of viscosity	η	N–s m^{-2}	$M L^{-1} T^{-1}$
Pressure	P, p	N m^{-2}, Pa	$M L^{-1} T^{-2}$
Wavelength	λ	m	L
Intensity of wave	I	W m^{-2}	$M T^{-3}$
Temperature	T	KELVIN (K)	Θ
Specific heat capacity	c	J kg^{-1}–K^{-1}	$L^2 T^{-2} K^{-1}$
Stefan's constant	σ	W m^{-2}–K^{-4}	$M T^{-3} K^{-4}$
Heat	Q	J	$ML^2 T^{-2}$
Thermal conductivity	K	W m^{-1}–K^{-1}	$ML T^{-3} K^{-1}$
Current	I	AMPERE (A)	I
Charge	q, Q	coulomb (C)	IT
Current density	j	A m^{-2}	IL^{-2}
Electrical conductivity	σ	1/Ω–m (= mho/m)	$I^2 T^3 M^{-1} L^{-3}$
Dielectric constant	k		
Electric dipole moment	p	C–m	LIT
Electric field	E	V m^{-1}(= N C^{-1})	$ML I^{-1} T^{-3}$
Potential (voltage)	V	volt (V)(= J C^{-1})	$ML^2 I^{-1} T^{-3}$
Electric flux	Φ	V–m	$ML^3 I^{-1} T^{-3}$
Capacitance	C	farad (F)	$I^2 T^4 M^{-1} L^{-2}$
Electromotive force	E	volt (V)	$ML^2 I^{-1} T^{-3}$
Resistance	R	ohm (Ω)	$ML^2 I^{-2} T^{-3}$
Permittivity of space	ε_0	C^2 N^{-1}–m^{-2} (= F m^{-1})	$I^2 T^4 M^{-1} L^{-3}$
Permeability of space	μ_0	N A^{-2}	$ML I^{-2} T^{-2}$
Magnetic field	B	tesla (T)(= Wb m^{-2})	$M I^{-1} T^{-2}$
Magnetic flux	Φ_B	weber (Wb)	$ML^2 I^{-1} T^{-2}$
Magnetic dipole moment	μ	N–m T^{-1}	IL^2
Inductance	L	henry (H)	$ML^2 I^{-2} T^{-2}$

APPENDIX B

Universal Constants (as revised in 1986)

Quantity	Symbol	Value	Unit	Uncertainty in the last two digits
Constant of gravitation	G	$6{\cdot}67259 \times 10^{-11}$	$N\text{–}m^2\,kg^{-2}$	85
Speed of light in vacuum	c	$2{\cdot}99792458 \times 10^{8}$	$m\,s^{-1}$	exact
Avogadro constant	N_A	$6{\cdot}0221367 \times 10^{23}$	mol^{-1}	36
Gas constant	R	8·314510	$J\,K^{-1}\text{–}mol^{-1}$	70
Boltzmann constant	k	$1{\cdot}380658 \times 10^{-23}$	$J\,K^{-1}$	12
		$8{\cdot}617385 \times 10^{-5}$	$eV\,K^{-1}$	73
Stefan–Boltzmann constant	σ	$5{\cdot}67051 \times 10^{-8}$	$W\,m^{-2}\text{–}K^{-4}$	19
Wien's displacement law constant	b	$2{\cdot}897756 \times 10^{-3}$	m–K	24
Charge of proton	e	$1{\cdot}60217733 \times 10^{-19}$	C	49
Mass of electron	m_e	$9{\cdot}1093897 \times 10^{-31}$	kg	54
		$5{\cdot}48579903 \times 10^{-4}$	u	13
Mass of proton	m_p	$1{\cdot}6726231 \times 10^{-27}$	kg	10
		1·007276470	u	12
Mass of neutron	m_n	$1{\cdot}6749286 \times 10^{-27}$	kg	10
		1·008664904	u	14
Permeability of vacuum	μ_0	$4\pi \times 10^{-7}$ $= 12{\cdot}566370614\ldots \times 10^{-7}$	$N\,A^{-2}$	exact
Permittivity of vacuum	ϵ_0	$\dfrac{1}{\mu_0 c^2}$ $= 8{\cdot}854187817\ldots \times 10^{-12}$	$C^2\,N^{-1}\text{–}m^{-2} = F\,m^{-1}$	exact
Faraday constant	F	96485·3029	$C\,mol^{-1}$	29
Planck constant	h	$6{\cdot}6260755 \times 10^{-34}$	J–s	40
		$4{\cdot}1356692 \times 10^{-15}$	eV–s	12
Rydberg constant	R	$1{\cdot}0973731534 \times 10^{7}$	m^{-1}	13
Ground state energy of hydrogen atom		13·605698	eV	40
Bohr radius	a_0	$5{\cdot}29177249 \times 10^{-11}$	m	24

Astronomical Constant

Quantity	Value	Unit
Mass of the sun	1.99×10^{30}	kg
Radius of the sun	6.95×10^{8}	m
Mass of the earth	5.98×10^{24}	kg
Mean radius of the earth	6.37×10^{6}	m
Mass of the moon	7.36×10^{22}	kg
Radius of the moon	1.74×10^{6}	m
Mean earth–sun distance	1.50×10^{11}	m
Mean earth–moon distance	3.84×10^{8}	m
Escape speed from the earth	11.2	$km\,s^{-1}$
Escape speed from the moon	2.38	$km\,s^{-1}$

INDEX

□